THOMSON

SOUTH-WESTERN

Bank Management, 5e
Timothy W. Koch and S. Scott MacDonald

Editor-in-Chief:
Jack W. Calhoun

Vice President, Team Director:
Michael P. Roche

Executive Editor:
Michael R. Reynolds

Developmental Editor:
Elizabeth R. Thomson

Marketing Manager:
Charlie Stutesman

Production Editor:
Starratt E. Alexander

Manufacturing Coordinator:
Sandee Milewski

Production House & Compositor:
Navta Associates, Inc.

Printer:
R.R. Donnelley & Sons Company
Willard Manufacturing Division

For permission to use material from this text or product, contact us by
Tel (800) 730-2214
Fax (800) 730-2215
http://www.thomsonrights.com

Library of Congress Control Number
2002109109

ISBN: 0-030-34297-X

5TH EDITION

BANK MANAG

TIMOTHY W. KOCH
UNIVERSITY OF SOUTH CAROLINA

S. SCOTT MACDONALD
SOUTHERN METHODIST UNIVERSITY

THOMSON

SOUTH-WESTERN

Australia · Canada · Mexico · Singapore · Spain · United Kingdom · United States

Bank managers must be increasingly aware of competitive opportunities that coincide with change. The banking industry is consolidating and diversifying simultaneously. In fact, the traditional definition of a bank has been blurred by the introduction of new products and a wave of mergers, which have dramatically expanded the scope of activities that banks engage in and where products and services are offered. Formerly, a commercial bank was defined as a firm that both accepted demand deposits and made commercial loans. Today, these two products are offered by many different types of firms, including commercial banks, savings banks, credit unions, insurance companies, investment banks, finance companies, retailers, and pension funds. Such firms are comprehensively labeled *financial services companies*. What constitutes a bank is now not as important as what products and services are offered and in what geographic markets does a financial services company compete.

The purpose of *Bank Management* is multifaceted. First, we document a shift in the landscape of the commercial banking industry by describing dramatic changes that have occurred in the past decade. These changes have forever altered the primary business model and products and services offered by competing institutions. For example, changes in the regulatory and competitive environment have essentially eliminated many of the operational differences between financial institutions. Today, the only real difference between Merrill Lynch and Bank of America is that Merrill Lynch is not regulated as a bank. Second, we apply basic finance concepts to the management of depository institutions. The text does not dwell on financial theories, but rather provides applications of theory in a decision-making framework. Third, we provide the foundation necessary to understand the unique risks faced by depository financial institutions and demonstrate how senior management effectively deals with these risks.

Senior officers are constantly evaluating their strategic options and plans. Does the bank plan to expand its scope of products and services or remain focused on lending and deposit gathering? Students of banking and managers of commercial banks, savings banks, credit unions, and other financial services firms will find *Bank Management* extremely useful in understanding how to make informed decisions about the riskiness and potential returns of different activities, products, and services. The book emphasizes analysis, decision-making and specific problem-solving techniques. The basic format introduces an issue or problem, discusses the applicable finance concepts, provides an analytical model or framework, and then applies decision-making tools using sample data. In most cases, the sample data are taken from an actual financial institution. Thus, there is considerable emphasis placed on data analysis and interpretation of real world problems and issues.

The concept of risk management serves as a unifying theme of the book. A bank's asset and liability management committee (ALCO) or risk management committee is responsible for the overall financial planning and management of the bank's profitability and risk profile. The book emphasizes how managers can develop and implement strategies to maximize stockholders' wealth by balancing the trade-offs between banking risks and returns. One of the book's primary contributions is to explain how market risk (interest rate risk, equity price risk, and foreign exchange rate risk), liquidity risk, credit risk, and operational risk are measured and how they affect a bank's capital and solvency risk. It demonstrates how risk management decisions in different areas affect each other and the overall profitability and risk of the institution.

The banking environment is constantly changing. While competition has increased the number of firms offering financial products and services, the removal of interstate branching restrictions in the U.S. has dramatically reduced the number of banks but increased the number of banking offices (primarily branches). Consolidation, in turn, has increased the proportion of banking assets controlled by the largest banks. Not surprisingly, the same trends appear globally. The United States currently has several banks that operate in all 50 states and many locales outside the U.S. The largest foreign banks have significant operations in the U.S. and throughout the world. In fact, you might not know if your bank is based outside the U.S.! Different financial institutions seem to announce acquisitions of other financial companies (not always banks) on a regular basis, and frequently these institutions are headquartered in different countries.

Increased competition also means that geography no longer limits a financial institution's trade area or the markets in which it competes. Individuals can open a checking account at a traditional depository institution, such as a local commercial bank, savings bank, or credit union, a brokerage firm, such as Charles Schwab or Merrill Lynch, or a nonbank firm, such as GE Capital, State Farm Insurance, and AT&T. You don't even have to leave your home as you can open an account via the Internet. You can deposit money electronically, transfer funds from one account to another, purchase stocks, bonds and mutual funds, or even request and receive a loan from any of these firms. Most of them will allow you to conduct this business over the phone, by mail, or over the Internet. All of these firms compete for business with each other, pay and charge market interest rates that are determined by competitive conditions, and are generally not limited in the scope of products and services they offer or the geographic regions where they offer these products.

Audience

Bank Management is designed for use in upper division undergraduate or master's level banking and financial institutions courses at universities as well as professional banking programs. As prerequisites, students should be familiar with elementary accounting, basic interest rate and bond pricing concepts, and basic macroeconomics. The book is also well suited for broad-based instructional purposes in bank training programs. For someone new to banking, the book describes the range of banking activities and demonstrates how bank managers make financial decisions. For practitioners, it explains how decisions in one area affect performance and opportunities in other areas. As such, it provides a comprehensive view of managing the entire bank with an emphasis on the trade-offs between profitability and risk.

About *Bank Management*

The book focuses on decision making and offers a unique approach to understanding bank management. Key chapters address the specific aspects of an issue or problem, how a financial model or decision framework applies, and then demonstrate the application of the model or framework using sample data. The reader not only observes how certain factors influence credit, investment, funding, and pricing decisions, but also develops an appreciation of the trade-offs between return and risk. Several Microsoft Excel templates, which include various models and applications using sample data, are available to users. A wide range of cases related to bank performance evaluation, making new loans, managing the investment portfolio, asset and liability management, and liquidity management are available via the Internet. These cases, end-of-chapter questions, and problems provide an opportunity to test the reader's understanding of important issues and data analysis.

Upon completion of reading *Bank Management,* the reader should have a solid foundation in the key issues confronting managers today, a familiarization with the basic financial models that are used to formulate decisions, and an understanding of the strengths and weaknesses of data analysis. The text and numerous applications help the reader to recognize the trade-offs involved in making financial decisions and to develop the logical thought processes needed to reach reasonable conclusions.

NEW FEATURES OF THIS EDITION

The fifth edition of the book builds on the topics and features of earlier editions, with several important changes:

- A complete regulatory update has been applied throughout the book. In particular, the impacts of nationwide interstate branching, financial modernization (Gramm-Leach-Bliley), and repeal of Glass-Steagall have reshaped the regulatory and competitive environment coverage.

- A complete discussion of the changing landscape of the financial services industry—including the impact Enron had on the industry as it changed its role from an energy company to a hedge fund.

- An updated and comprehensive evaluation of bank performance—traditional banking, investment banking, and off-balance sheet financing—and the impact this has on the analyst's job in evaluating performance. A direct comparison of PNC Bank's financial performance from 2000 - 2001 and problems associated with the use of special purpose vehicles (also used extensively by Enron) and their impact on various performance measures.

- An analysis of the most current data from the Uniform Bank Performance Report, the FDIC, and the Federal Reserve Bank, including discussion of key performance ratios, an explanation of alternative performance measures, including Economic Value Added (EVA™), return on risk adjusted capital (RAROC/RORAC), and the Balanced Scorecard.

- Comprehensive discussion of Federal Home Loan Bank advances as funding instruments and their use in liquidity management.

- Updates on hedge accounting under FAS 133 and its implications for financial services companies are fully discussed along with hedge criteria, risk exposure, and the accounting standards.

- A discussion of the current developments in credit scoring, credit reports, and applications to consumer lending.

- Extensive use of new tools and examples such as option-adjusted spread analysis are introduced to assist in the evaluation of alternative investment instruments.

- New cases in Bank Performance Analysis, Commercial Lending, Consumer Lending, and Managing a Bank's Investment Portfolio incorporate current data and issues; available on our web site http://koch.swcollege.com.

- New data and analysis on international banking and the role and size of U.S. banking abroad as well as the ownership and composition of foreign banking in the U.S. Discussion of foreign exchange risk associated with a bank having assets and liabilities denominated in different currencies.

- The book remains the only one that focuses on cash flow analysis as part of the lending decision. It introduces a comprehensive procedure to generate cash-based income statements, explains how to interpret the results, and provides an approach to forecast a potential borrower's future performance.

ORGANIZATION OF THE BOOK

The unifying theme of the book is risk management. The material is divided into six parts, each consisting of chapters that cover related issues. As a lead-in to each chapter, the text will describe a current issue or provide an example of a key topic discussed in the chapter. This introduction reinforces the risk focus by emphasizing that managers make both good and bad decisions, but consistent application of finance theory and models should lead to a better understanding of the trade-off between risk and return.

Part I, Overview of the Banking Industry and Regulation, provides background information related to bank management and current banking trends. It describes the role of competition in forcing change in banking, the move to expanded products, services, and geographic markets served, and the impact on banking industry consolidation. It also examines the organizational structure of small banks and large bank holding companies, describes the regulatory environment, and explains the impact of key banking legislation.

Part II, Evaluating Bank Performance, examines the basic risk and return features of commercial banks and how analysts evaluate performance. Chapter 3 provides key coverage because it introduces bank financial statements and presents the traditional model for evaluating bank performance using financial ratios from the Uniform Bank Performance Report (UBPR) to analyze the strengths and weaknesses of bank performance over time and versus peer institutions. It provides the foundation and building blocks for understanding how banks make a profit and the trade-offs involved in balancing credit risk, liquidity risk, market risk, operational risk, reputational risk, legal risk, and solvency risk. Chapter 4 demonstrates a variety of alternative models or frameworks to analyze performance. Each extends traditional ratio analysis by better matching peer groups, examining value added relative to a capital charge (EVA™), line of business profitability with appropriate risk capital allocation (RORAC), and measures that focus on customer satisfaction, internal processes, organizational innovation as well as financial performance (Balanced Scorecard). Chapter 5 documents recent trends in controlling noninterest expense relative to noninterest income to help meet efficiency objectives.

Part III, Managing Interest Rate Risk, demonstrates how banks measure and manage interest rate risk. It initially provides background information on the pricing of securities, total return analysis to investors, and the determinants of interest rates. It introduces funding GAP analysis and the use of earnings sensitivity analysis to assess the potential impact of interest rate and balance sheet changes on net interest income. It then describes duration gap analysis and the use of sensitivity analysis to assess the potential impact of interest rate and balance sheet changes on the market value of stockholders' equity. The discussion emphasizes the impact of embedded options and the necessity behind incorporating sensitivity analysis to assess the impact of such options on profits and risk. Later chapters describe the basic features of financial futures, forward contracts, interest rate swaps, and interest rate caps and floors and explain how banks use them to both hedge and speculate. Emphasis is directed toward understanding the models, data output, and strategies to improve performance.

Part IV, Managing the Cost of Funds, Bank Capital, and Liquidity, describes the features of bank liabilities and regulatory capital requirements. It presents a procedure for estimating the marginal cost of funds that is used in making investment decisions and pricing assets. It also explains how banks meet legal reserve requirements and manage cash assets, and it develops a model to estimate liquidity needs and plan for temporary cash deficiencies and longer-term liquidity needs. Special attention is focused on the nature of Federal Home Loan Bank advances and their use in liquidity management.

Part V, Extending Credit to Businesses and Individuals, addresses how banks manage credit risk. It initially describes basic credit analysis principles and the characteristics of different types of loans. Subsequent chapters present a procedure for estimating a business borrower's cash flow from operations and the basic credit scoring models applied to individual borrowers. Considerable emphasis is placed on interpreting financial statements and generating cash flow estimates to determine repayment prospects. A final chapter describes the basic framework of customer profitability analysis to assess whether a bank is profiting from a customer's total relationship.

Part VI, Managing the Investment Portfolio and Special Topics, describes the role of fixed-income securities in helping a bank meet profit and risk objectives. It identifies the basic objectives of a bank's investment portfolio and the nature of investment policy guidelines, and explains the basic features of taxable and tax-exempt securities that banks buy. Chapter 20 then introduces various strategies related to choosing security maturities, the composition between taxable and tax-exempt securities, and purchases or sales timed to take advantage of the business cycle. It explains the impact of embedded options on security pricing and the risk-return trade-off to investors of callable bonds and mortgage-backed securities with significant prepayment risk. The final two chapters describe recent trends in global banking activities, bank mergers and acquisitions, the management of foreign exchange risk, and the valuation of banks.

Each chapter of *Bank Management* concludes with a series of discussion questions and problems that force the student to apply the decision models introduced in the chapter. The Excel template can be used to generate and address additional problems and provides a useful tool for future work.

ANCILLARY PACKAGE

INSTRUCTOR'S MANUAL AND TEST BANK

A comprehensive Instructor's Manual and Test Bank accompanies *Bank Management*. It provides teaching objectives and outlines for each chapter. It further offers detailed answers to end-of-chapter questions and problems. Finally, multiple choice questions are provided with answers on disk.

LECTURE PRESENTATION SOFTWARE

Microsoft PowerPoint™ presentations are available to those professors who wish to incorporate multimedia in the classroom. This multimedia presentation allows the student to explore the almost unlimited number of different financial situations that banks face on a daily basis. Furthermore, it provides the instructor a method by which he or she can integrate a financial analysis spreadsheet template directly into the class presentation. Many tables and diagrams are featured in the lecture software package.

SPREADSHEET TEMPLATE

Microsoft Excel templates are available for those who wish to use microcomputers to perform and extend the data analysis presented in the book. The templates provide a generic decision model for applications related to analyzing bank performance and key financial ratios, and cash flow from operations for nonfinancial firms. Each model can be used to conduct "what if" *pro forma* sensitivity analysis beyond the period for which historical data are available. The templates also provide a full range of decision models with data for key problems and cases in the text. Students can use the templates to analyze historical balance sheet and income statement data and conduct the same "what if" analysis. This allows the user to quickly examine a range of outcomes rather than just simple, static solutions. The templates cover topics including bank performance analysis, duration analysis, risk-based capital requirements and planning, credit analysis, and customer profitability analysis.

CASES

New Cases in Bank Performance Analysis, Commercial Lending, Consumer Lending, and Managing a Bank's Investment Portfolio are available on our Web site http://koch.swcollege.com.

WEB SITE

The product support Web site, located at http://koch.swcollege.com, contains the PowerPoint slide presentation, Instructor's Manual, Spreadsheet Templates, and new Cases for instructors; and the PowerPoint slide presentation and Spreadsheet Templates for students.

ACKNOWLEDGMENTS

The fifth edition of *Bank Management* is the second edition to involve a coauthor. Throughout the writing of the book, we have relied on the assistance and expertise of many friends in the banking industry and academic community. This revision has benefited from ongoing discussions with the following individuals and former students. We especially thank Frank Adams, Linda Allen, John Barrickman, Richard Brock, Charl Butler, Steve Christensen, David Davis, Kevin Fernald, Charles Funk, Skip Hageboeck, Scott Hein, Charley Hoffman, Debra Jacobs, Jeff Judy, Ira Kawaller, Randy King, Ed Krei, Charles Moyer, Don Mullineaux, James Pappas, Ramesh Rao, Scott Reid, Joshua S. Robinson, Ron Rogers, J. T. Rose, H. Wade Schuessler, Robert Schweitzer, Ernie Swift, Tim Teske, and Buddy Wood.

We would also like to thank the reviewers who contributed invaluable comments and suggestions. These individuals are Alan E. Grunewald, Michigan State University; Rose Prasad, Central Michigan University; William H. Sackley, University of North Carolina at Wilmington; James A. Verbrugge, University of Georgia; and Alan M. Weatherford, California Polytechnic State University.

Also, we appreciate the guidance and assistance of the staff at South-Western/Thomson Learning, especially Mike Reynolds, Elizabeth Thomson, and Starratt Alexander. It was a pleasure working with them.

Finally, we want to thank our families—Susan, Michala, and Andy; and Becky, Cassy, and Erin—for their encouragement, support, and insights in seeing this project through to completion.

Timothy W. Koch, Ph.D.	S. Scott MacDonald, Ph.D.
Moore College of Business	Southwestern Graduate School of Banking
University of South Carolina	Southern Methodist University
Columbia, SC 29208	Dallas, TX 75275
June 2002	June 2002

We dedicate this book to our families, Susan, Michala, Andy, Lowell and Marilyn Koch, and Paul (posthumously), Sue, Becky, Cassy and Erin MacDonald, for their unflagging encouragement and support. It is the love and understanding of our families that allow us to pursue our dreams.

TIMOTHY W. KOCH, PH.D.

Timothy W. Koch is professor of Finance and holds the South Carolina Bankers Association chair of Banking at the University of South Carolina. He received a B.A. degree in mathematics from Wartburg College and a Ph.D. in economics from Purdue University. He has taught at Baylor University and Texas Tech University and served as director of the Texas Tech School of Banking. In addition to college teaching, Dr. Koch currently serves as President of the Graduate School of Banking at Colorado and teaches at several graduate schools for professional bankers throughout the United States. He also serves as faculty advisor to the Graduate School of Bank Investments and Financial Management offered at the University of South Carolina. He has also taught seminars on risk management to bankers in Poland, Hungary, Slovakia, and the Ukraine as part of a U.S. Treasury program to assist private banking in Eastern Europe.

Dr. Koch's research and writing focuses on bank risk management, performance analysis and improvement, the pricing of financial futures and fixed-income securities, and public finance. He has published in a wide range of academic journals, including the *Journal of Finance, Journal of Financial & Quantitative Analysis, Journal of Futures Markets, National Tax Journal, Journal of Banking and Finance, Journal of Fixed Income, Journal of Financial Research, Journal of Macroeconomics, Journal of Portfolio Management, Municipal Finance Journal*, and the *Journal of Money, Credit and Banking*. He has served as Treasurer of the Financial Management Association and President of the Eastern Finance Association. He also authored the *General Banking* curriculum materials used at many state-sponsored banking schools and is a frequent seminar leader for the banking industry.

S. SCOTT MACDONALD, PH.D.

S. Scott MacDonald is President and CEO, SW Graduate School of Banking (SWGSB) Foundation, Director of the Assemblies for Bank Directors, and Adjunct Professor of Finance, Edwin L. Cox School of Business, Southern Methodist University. He received his B.A. degree in economics from the University of Alabama and his Ph.D. from Texas A&M University. Dr. MacDonald joined the Southern Methodist University faculty as a visiting professor of Finance in 1997. He took over as director of the SWGSB Foundation in 1998. Prior to joining SMU, he was an associate professor of Finance and director of the School of Applied Banking at Texas Tech University. He also served as assistant director of Business and Financial Analysis at RRC Inc., a research consulting firm, before joining the Texas Tech faculty. He is a frequent speaker and seminar leader for the banking industry, professional programs and banking schools. Dr. MacDonald has also served as an expert resource witness before the Texas state Senate.

Dr. MacDonald is the author of many articles in journals such as the *Journal of Financial Economics, The Journal of Business, The Journal of Futures Markets, The Review of Futures Markets, Quarterly Journal of Business and Economics*, and the *Journal of Money, Credit and Banking*. He is the author of curriculum materials for the Independent Bankers Association, The Assemblies for Bank Directors, and other professional banking programs. Dr. MacDonald is the recipient of numerous teaching and research awards and is past chairman of the board of directors, Texas Tech Federal Credit Union, and an advisory board member of the Independent Bankers Association of the Texas Education Council.

To my parents, Lowell and Marilyn Koch, who have always encouraged and supported me.

Timothy W. Koch

To my parents, Paul and Sue MacDonald.

S. Scott MacDonald

TABLE OF CONTENTS

OVERVIEW OF THE BANKING INDUSTRY AND REGULATION

FUNDAMENTAL FORCES OF CHANGE IN BANKING

Deregulation, financial innovation, securitization, globalization, and advances in technology are quickly changing the nature of commercial banking. Consumers who want to open a checking account can go to a local commercial bank, savings and loan, mutual savings bank, credit union, brokerage house, such as Merrill Lynch, or deal with a discount broker like Charles Schwab. They can also contract with Intuit, a software company that provides bill payment services through the use of its Quicken software, or simply open a checking account at a virtual bank, which exists only on the Internet. Consumers who want a credit card can get one from any depository institution, gas company, department store, or national finance company. They can also get cosponsored cards from General Electric, General Motors, Ford Motor, Prudential, Merrill Lynch, Charles Schwab, IBM, and many other nonfinancial firms. Consumers simply have more choices now than ever before when purchasing financial services.

Not surprisingly, firms compete aggressively for consumers' business. Competition, in turn, puts a premium on innovation and precision in delivering service and personalizing it for individuals. In some cases, however, the opportunities are not the same for all service providers. Even though commercial banks have gained greater flexibility in diversifying their asset base across geographic boundaries and into new product lines in recent years, federal and state regulations often put them at a competitive disadvantage.

In this chapter, we examine recent competitive trends affecting the banking industry, as manifested by the greater number of suppliers of banking and financial services, as well as the greater variety of products and services offered. The banking industry is somewhat unique because it is simultaneously consolidating and diversifying. This chapter identifies five fundamental forces of change — market-driven competitive factors, product innovation and deregulation, securitization, globalization, and technological advances. It also demonstrates how these forces will lead to even more competition, greater consolidation, increased diversification, and a worldwide restructuring of financial institutions and markets. As part of the analysis, the chapter describes the structure and performance of GE Capital Services as a financial conglomerate and major bank competitor.

W hat makes a bank special? Why do we call Bank of America a 'bank,' Merrill Lynch a 'securities brokerage company,' and State Farm an 'insurance company?' The answer lies in our history with a key demarcation over 70 years ago with the implementation of the Glass-Steagall Act, the Bank Holding Company Act, and the McFadden Act, which had far-reaching consequences. Glass-Steagall created three separate industries: commercial banking, investment banking, and insurance. The Bank Holding Act determined activities closely related to banking and limited the scope of activities a company could engage in if it owned a bank. The McFadden Act limited the geographic market of banking by allowing individual states to determine the extent to which a bank could branch within or outside its home state. Under these acts, the United States developed a banking system with a large number of smaller banks that was limited in the scope of products and services that could be offered and the geographic areas where individual banks could compete. Each of these limitations was intended to reduce competition and speculation in the banking industry and thereby promote a safe, sound, and stable banking system.

Regulatory restrictions on the type of products and services and geographic scope worked quite effectively in promoting a safe banking system until the later part of the twentieth century. Until then, banks were the only firms allowed to offer checking and savings accounts and generally dominated the small business lending market. Thrift institutions (savings and loans) focused on mortgage lending. Investment banks underwrote stocks and bonds and provided brokerage services while insurance companies underwrote insurance products. Banks were further restricted to offering loan and deposit products within narrow geographic bounds. Generally, states prohibited branching entirely or limited it to surrounding counties and state borders.

Product innovations and technological advances, however, eventually allowed investment banks to circumvent regulations restricting their banking activities. In the late 1970s, Merrill Lynch effectively created an "interest-bearing checking account," something banks had not been legally allowed to offer, and money market mutual funds soon grew at a rapid rate effectively drawing funds from traditional banks. High quality corporations found that they could issue securities, such as commercial paper and corporate bonds, directly to investors and thereby circumvent bank loans. Junk bonds became an alternative financing source for small business and other companies began to encroach upon the banks' primary market. Banks were heavily regulated by state banking agencies, the FDIC, the Federal Reserve, and the Office of Comptroller of the Currency while Merrill Lynch was only regulated by the Securities and Exchange Commission (SEC). This allowed investment companies to avoid the restrictions on banks, but given Glass-Steagall and the Bank Holding Company Act, banks were restricted from moving into the investment banking companies market. It was not until the late 1980s and early 1990s that banks began to find ways around Glass-Steagall using Section 20 affiliates, which allowed them to offer a limited range and amount of investment banking products and services. During this same period, the sharp increase in prices of stocks increased the average person's awareness of higher promised returns from mutual funds and stock transactions. A greater acceptance of non-FDIC insured deposit products (mutual funds and stocks), while banks were generally restricted to offering CDs and savings accounts, further eroded banks' share of the consumer's investment wallet.

Branching restrictions were significantly responsible for the structure of the banking system. Some states allowed no branches (unit banks) such that every institution could have only one office. In some cases this meant that automatic teller machines (ATMs) were not allowed because they were viewed as branches. Not surprisingly, branch restrictions created a system of many, but smaller, independent banks as compared to the number and size of banks in other countries. Unfortunately, these same branching restrictions also prevented banks from geographically diversifying their credit risk. Thus, a unit banking state like

Texas experienced numerous failures during the late 1980s as oil prices plunged and banks collapsed as local economies crumbled. The gradual removal of branching restrictions during the 1980s and 1990s allowed banks to offer services anywhere in the country and led to creation of the first nationwide bank, Bank of America, with branches coast-to-coast. In today's environment, many firms offer coast-to-coast financial services. For example, Merrill Lynch, Edward Jones, and State Farm operate branches or offices in communities across the nation. Technological advances have also allowed banks to open electronic branches, first by using the ATM network and later by using the Internet. By the late 1990s, all branching restrictions were removed from the banking system and the number of independent banks was reduced by almost half, the number of branches increased by almost 50 percent, and the size of the largest U.S. banks increased dramatically. In fact, by size rankings, U.S. banks did not reach the largest 10 banks in the world until the 1990s and today, some of the largest banks in the world are U.S. banks.

RECENT MARKET EVENTS

To the casual observer, events of the 1990s and early 2000s involving financial institutions might seem unrelated:

- Mellon Bank buys Drexel Corp.
- Investment banks help finance hostile corporate acquisitions with junk bonds, and stock market volatility increases with dramatic intraday swings in market indexes.
- NationsBank Corp. and First Union enter investment banking by buying Montgomery Securities and Wheat First, respectively.
- NationsBank acquires Boatmen's Bancshares, Barnett Banks, and BankAmerica (the new name is Bank of America) creating the one of the largest U.S. banks and the first to have a coast-to-coast presence.
- Wells Fargo and Norwest merge, creating the second coast-to-coast bank.
- Citibank enters the insurance and domestic investment banking businesses by combining with Travelers Property and Casualty Corp., which owned Salomon Smith Barney, to form Citigroup. In 2002, Citigroup reverses track and sells part of Travelers.
- The Office of the Comptroller of the Currency (OCC) charters the first (national) virtual bank, Compubank, in Houston.
- DeutscheBank, based in Germany, buys New York-based Bankers Trust, effectively circumventing U.S. Glass-Steagall restrictions.
- Charles Schwab Corp., the king of discount brokerage, acquires U.S. Trust Corp.
- MetLife acquires Grand Bank in Kingston, N.J.
- Credit Suisse Group acquires Donaldson, Lufkin & Jenrette Inc.
- UBS AG's acquires Paine Webber Group.
- BB&T acquires over 70 regional insurance, brokerage, and real estate companies.

All of these incidents are interrelated. After decades of relative calm, financial markets and institutions are continuing to undergo structural change that will continue to permanently alter competitive relationships, business models and structures, and even the way in which we pay for goods and services. Every manager of a financial institution regularly evaluates whether the firm should and will be a buyer, seller, or remain independent, close, or continue the status quo. Every nonfinancial and financial firm, individual, and governmental unit now operates in a rapidly changing environment. The Internet has eliminated geographic borders that used to provide somewhat isolated markets. One can purchase products and services from virtually any company in the world from the privacy of their home or office.

The Glass-Steagall and Bank Holding Company Acts effectively restricted the activities of a bank to those 'closely related to banking' as defined by the Federal Reserve. The Fed, in turn, provided a list of approved activities. Over time, consumers and businesses have demanded that banks offer more products at a time when non-bank financial firms were offering banking products yet were not regulated as banks. Deregulation during the 1980s and 1990s was a natural response to these artificial restrictions on banks. Initially, Congress eliminated restrictions against interest rates that banks could pay on most of their liabilities. It followed by passing legislation that allowed banks to acquire problem institutions outside their home state, underwrite certain types of municipal bonds, and branch across state boundaries. It also permitted bank holding company acquisitions of healthy banks outside the home state. This led to the passage of the Gramm-Leach-Bliley Act in 1999, also known as the Financial Modernization Act, which made it possible for banks to create a financial holding company which could offer investment banking, insurance, and other once disallowed products and services. All of these changes coincided with Citibank's acquisition of Travelers (an insurance company) to create Citigroup, a true financial services company offering traditional banking services, investment brokerage and underwriting, as well as insurance sales and underwriting.[1]

Even though banks can now offer a wide range of services, individual firms are moving cautiously into these new areas. While the largest banks are growing in size through acquisitions of banks as well as other financial firms, many smaller banks are continuing to specialize in services catering to small business customers. The average consumer needs a checking account, ATM services, small savings account, some brokerage services, an auto loan, insurance, and a home mortgage. Almost any financial firm can offer most of these services and the competition is fierce. Banks are finding it difficult to compete in the market for these products because the intense competition is driving the price for services to the bare minimums. As a result, smaller banks have continued to specialize in serving the small business customer where personal service and customized products are essential. Larger banks, in contrast, are trying to operate as part of financial service companies, competing directly with investment banks, insurance companies, and smaller banks specializing in the product and service needs of the small business customer. The impact of Gramm-Leach-Bliley has only begun to influence the industry and so the future of the banking industry is yet to be determined!

Exhibit 1.1 lists the eleven largest financial companies in the U.S. as of March 2002. Interestingly, just 12 percent of the 5,100 registered bank holding companies had chosen this organizational structure at that time.[2] Still, these firms controlled over $6 trillion of banking assets, or almost two-thirds of total banking assets by the beginning of 2002. Note that some of these firms have a large insurance presence (Citigroup with Travelers and MetLife) while others have headquarters based outside the U.S.

Many analysts attribute much of the change in the financial services industry to deregulation. Actually, deregulation was a natural response to increased competition between depository institutions and nondepository financial firms, and between the same type of competitors across world markets rather than the catalyst of competition. Deregulation sped up the process, but did not necessarily start it. New regulations brought about the development of new products which increased competition with firms not regulated like banks, such as investment banks. Regulation also contributed to the problems of Savings and Loans in the early 1980s as S&L portfolios were restricted to long-term mortgage securities financed by short-term savings accounts. Today, we

---

[1]Some might argue that Sears, Roebuck and Co.'s combination of Allstate, Coldwell Bankers, Allstate Savings and Loan, and Dean Witter was the first true financial service company and one could not argue. Sears' combination was allowed, however, because they did not offer a full line of banking products. The Citigroup combination is unique in that it combines a full service commercial bank (rather than a savings and loan) in the group for the first time.

[2]"Financial Modernization: A New World or Status Quo?" Financial Industry Perspectives, Federal Reserve Bank of Kansas City, December 2001.

· EXHIBIT 1.1

LARGEST FINANCIAL HOLDING COMPANIES: MARCH 2002 (THOUSANDS OF DOLLARS)

Rank	Ticker	Company Name	City	State	March-02 Total Assets	Total Deposits
1	C	Citigroup, Inc.	New York	NY	1,058,000,000	NA
2	JPM	J.P. Morgan Chase & Co.	New York	NY	712,508,000	282,037,000
3	BAC	Bank of America Corporation	Charlotte	NC	619,921,000	367,200,000
4	WB	Wachovia Corporation	Charlotte	NC	319,853,000	180,033,000
5	WFC	Wells Fargo & Company	San Francisco	CA	311,509,000	189,568,000
6	WM	Washington Mutual, Inc. (not a FHC)	Seattle	WA	275,223,000	129,010,000
7	ONE	Bankone Corporation	Chicago	IL	262,947,000	158,803,000
8	MET	MetLife, Inc.* (not principally engaged in banking)	New York	NY	256,897,467	145,685
9	Private	Taunus Corporation*ª	New York	NY	227,229,000	18,976,000
10	FBF	FleetBoston Financial Corporation	Boston	MA	192,032,000	121,522,000
11	Private	ABN AMRO North America Holding Company*ᵇ	Chicago	IL	171,795,842	46,904,197

*Financial Information as of 12/31/01
ªSubsidiary of Deutsche Bank AG
ᵇSubsidiary of Stichting Prioriteit ABN AMRO Holding
SOURCE: SNL Securities, http://www.snl.com/.

consider this to be a very high interest rate risk position, enough to bring about major regulatory sanctions! Yet, in the late 1970s, this was the legally mandated balance sheet profile of S&Ls.

Five fundamental forces have transformed the structure of markets and institutions and reflect intense competition: deregulation/reregulation, financial innovation, securitization, globalization, and advances in technology. The latter factors actually represent responses to deregulation and reregulation. These combined forces have altered corporate balance sheets by inducing firms to compete in new product and geographic markets and use new financial instruments to facilitate transactions and adjust their risk profile. Although consumers have benefited from these changes, the long-term trend for financial institutions entails consolidation, realignment of corporate objectives, and diversification of products offered, as firms attempt to develop a market niche. Firms can expect regulators to closely monitor changes in risk and continually increase capital requirements, particularly against new lines of business.

The basic theme is that increased competition, brought about by continued deregulation, has encouraged banks to assume increased portfolio risks in order to earn acceptable returns. As bank regulators have tried to reduce overall risk by raising capital requirements, banks have moved assets off their balance sheets and tried to replace interest income with fee income. In these efforts, banks attempt to be more like insurance brokers, realtors, and investment bankers—competing with a broader range of firms in more product markets. As capital becomes increasingly costly or impossible to obtain, individual firms are forced to merge to continue operations.

THE FUNDAMENTAL FORCES OF CHANGE

Historically, commercial banks have been the most heavily regulated companies in the United States—and thus among the safest and most conservative businesses around. Regulations took many forms, including maximum interest rates that could be paid on deposits or charged on loans, minimum capital-to-asset ratios, minimum legal reserve requirements, limited geographic markets for full-service banking, constraints on the type of investments permitted, and restrictions on the range of products and services offered.

Although regulations limited opportunities and risks, they virtually guaranteed a profit if management did not perpetrate fraud.

Since World War II, banks and other market participants have consistently restructured their operations to circumvent regulation and meet perceived customer needs. In response, regulators or lawmakers would impose new restrictions, which market participants circumvented again. This process of regulation and market response (financial innovation) and imposition of new regulations (reregulation) is the *regulatory dialectic*.[3] One aspect of regulatory response is *financial innovation.* Securitization, globalization, and new technologies are extensions of this response in the development of new products and international competition. The fear is that the five forces have influenced financial markets and institutions so rapidly that the aggregate risk of the U.S. financial system has increased.

Rose (1993) points out that the changing nature of banking can be examined in two distinct areas: the traditional role of banks as financial intermediaries; and the evolution of banking into nontraditional roles as a result of changing regulation, technology, and financial innovation. Banks' traditional role as an intermediary has declined as new products such as cash management accounts, mutual funds, commercial paper, and junk bonds have become more prevalent. Banks have responded by accepting lower spreads, taking on more risk, and expanding their customer and product base. Banks have also expanded into nontraditional areas and products, especially investment banking activities, off-balance sheet activities, such as standby letters of credit, mortgage servicing, and credit enhancement products to generate more fee income. They are also actively pursuing the use of technology in the development and delivery of products such as business sweep accounts and Internet banking. Finally, the Gramm-Leach-Bliley Act effectively eliminates most of the remaining restrictions that have separated commercial banking, investment banking, and insurance for over 70 years. Banking organizations will continue to expand their operations by identifying specific products and services to offer and will subsequently compete against a broader array of firms.

INCREASED COMPETITION

The McFadden Act of 1927 and the Glass-Steagall Act of 1933 determined the framework within which U.S. financial institutions operated for over 70 years. The McFadden Act saw to it that banks would be sheltered from unbridled competition with other banks by extending state restrictions on geographic expansion to national banks, hence single banks with no interstate branches. The act promoted smaller banks but more banks as compared to other countries which do not restrict branching. The Glass-Steagall Act forbade banks from underwriting equities and other corporate securities as well as underwriting insurance, thereby separating banking from commerce. Commercial banking meant deposit taking and lending. Investment banks emerged to underwrite and distribute securities and insurance companies flourished to write policies and underwrite insurable risks.

Following the enactment of the Glass-Steagall Act and through the early 1980s, the commercial banking industry was quite stable. Individuals who wanted to start a new bank found it difficult to get a charter from either federal or state regulators. The Federal Reserve System (Fed), in turn, limited interest rates that banks could pay depositors, effectively subsidizing banks by mandating low-cost sources of funds. Depositors had few substitutes for saving unless they held more than $100,000.[4] As a result, bank deposits grew systematically with economic conditions. Regulations also specified maximum rates that banks could charge on certain types of loans. Such usury ceilings were intended to protect customers from

---

[3]A discussion of the regulatory dialectic can be found in Kane (1977 and 1981).

[4]In fact, the Treasury increased the minimum size of Treasury bills from $1,000 to $10,000 during this period.

price gouging and essentially passed through a portion of the value of low cost bank deposits to bank borrowers.

During this period, banks could not compete on price because the price of their inputs (deposits) was regulated (Regulation Q) and the price of their outputs (loans) was regulated (usury ceilings). For all practical purposes, all banks had the same price. Hence banks had to find other ways to compete. Banks would give away toasters, silverware sets, and wine and dine prospective customers as one means of product differentiation. Many senior bank executives spent considerable time out of the office attempting to earn business. They would take customers to lunch, dinner, golf, and so on, trying to win their business. Today, the world of banking is quite different. Banks are basically free to set the price for their services and the type of services they offer as are other companies also free to offer banking-type services at competitive prices. Bankers now compete directly on price, product offerings, and service.

COMPETITION FOR DEPOSITS

The free ride of a guaranteed spread between asset yields and liability costs abruptly ended during the late 1970s. The primary catalyst was high inflation due in part to foreign control of the oil market and the doubling of oil prices. Although ceiling rates on bank deposits limited interest to 5.25 percent on savings accounts (5.50 percent at S&Ls) and nothing on checking accounts, 8 to 12 percent inflation rates guaranteed that consumers lost purchasing power. Individuals had two choices: save less and spend more or find higher-yielding investments. In 1973, several investment banks created money market mutual funds (MMMFs), which accepted deposits from individuals and invested the proceeds in Treasury bills, large certificates of deposit (CDs), and other securities that paid market yields.[5] Not surprisingly, the attractiveness and growth of MMMFs tracked the spread between money market interest rates and Regulation Q ceilings. Without competing instruments, MMMFs increased from $10.8 billion in 1978 to $186 billion in 1981.[6] During this interval, three-month Treasury bill rates exceeded the ceiling rate on bank savings accounts by as much as 9 percent.

MMMF growth came largely at the expense of banks' and thrifts' small time deposits as depositors simply shifted to mutual fund shares. Until the passage of the Depository Institutions Deregulation and Monetary Control Act (DIDMCA) in 1980, banks were not allowed to offer interest on checking or to offer money market mutual fund accounts. Banks argued vigorously for a level playing field—equivalent regulation that would allow them to compete—such as Congress declaring MMMFs illegal or forcing them to hold reserves against shares.[7] In a practical sense, once depositors realized they could earn market rates on transactions or savings balances, Congress dared not deny them the opportunity. Instead, it passed legislation enabling banks and thrifts to offer similar accounts including money market deposit accounts (MMDAs) and Super NOWs. Both represented interest-bearing checking accounts. MMDAs limited individuals to six transfers per month (three by check and three by telephone), so were effectively savings accounts with some transactions privileges.

---

[5]Technically, money market mutual funds sell shares to individuals. The funds buy money market instruments, insured CDs or Treasury securities for example, and transfer the income to shareholders, minus a management fee. Most funds allow shareholders to write checks against their balance or transfer funds to other investments. The shares exhibit little default risk but are not directly federally insured.

[6]Money market mutual funds exceeded $2.1 trillion in the third quarter of 2001.

[7]Not only were nonbanks allowed to offer interest on accounts on which customers could write a draft (equivalent of a check), these accounts did not require the nonbank to hold reserves. A bank must hold 10 percent of all deposited funds in vault cash or as deposits at the Fed, neither of which paid interest. This effectively meant that banks could earn interest on only 90 percent of deposited money while nonbanks could earn interest on the full 100 percent of deposited money.

Super NOWs paid interest on all balances with unlimited checks. MMDAs were enormously successful after their introduction in 1982 as they grew from just over $43 billion to almost $600 billion outstanding in 1987. In subsequent years, outstanding MMDAs declined as Congress eliminated interest rate ceilings and minimum denominations for deposits. Customers could then earn market rates on all time deposits so there was less incentive to shift to MMDAs. Bank liability rate deregulation was thus complete. Banks offer interest-bearing checking accounts today under a different label than Super NOWs.

In today's environment, deposit competition takes many forms. First, institutions are virtually unconstrained in the terms they can offer. Thus, customers can negotiate any minimum denomination, market interest rate, and maturity. Firms cannot discriminate, so they make the same deposit available to all qualified customers. As such, the range of deposit products is much broader than what was previously available. Second, a wide variety of firms accept time deposits and offer checking accounts. Almost every investment company that offers mutual funds also offers a cash management account for high balance customers (some as small as $5,000) to use as part of their investment activity.[8] Individuals can have proceeds from all financial transactions automatically invested at market rates until they make new investment decisions. Until that time, they can write checks against outstanding balances. Customers can transfer money from a core money market account to over 7,000 mutual funds with many investment companies such as Fidelity Investments. Finally, the combination of advances in technology and the elimination of bank branching restrictions means that that business and consumers have substantially greater choices than before. Prior to the elimination of branching restrictions, most individuals were limited in choice to the local bank. Information about rates and prices at other institutions was difficult to obtain. The vast amount of information available on the Internet means that customers can quickly and easily obtain rate quotes from financial institutions all over the world. The elimination of branching restrictions means that just about any financial institution can open a branch in any community. Not surprisingly, the competition for deposits is fierce.

American Express, GE, Household International, and Sears similarly offer their credit card customers the opportunity to invest in small time deposits that pay competitive rates.[9] For high-balance depositors, foreign banks and branches of large U.S. banks offer Eurodollar deposits that pay higher rates than domestic certificates of deposits. Finally, deposit services are often priced to encourage customers to conduct the bulk of their banking business with one firm. Thus, as a customer's balances increase, yields increase and service charges decline. The providers often make other services, such as travel discounts and life insurance, available in a package with deposit accounts.

COMPETITION FOR LOANS

COMMERCIAL PAPER. As bank funding costs increased, competition for loans put downward pressure on loan yields and interest spreads over the cost of bank funds. High quality corporate borrowers have always had the option to issue commercial paper or long-term bonds rather than borrow from banks. The growth in MMMFs accelerated the development and growth of the commercial paper market and improved investment banks' ties with nonfinancial corporations. Investment banks continued to underwrite commercial paper

---

[8]In July 1986, Merrill Lynch announced that it would offer small- to medium-size businesses a working capital management account modeled after its cash management account for individuals. The business account would offer a $2 million credit line, check-writing capabilities, and a variety of pension, insurance, and investment services. The credit line and ancillary services were designed as substitutes for traditional working capital loans at banks.

[9]Sears sold their private label credit card to The Associates.

issues and use money market funds to purchase the paper. Because the Glass-Steagall Act prevented commercial banks from underwriting commercial paper, banks lost corporate borrowers who bypassed them by issuing commercial paper at lower cost. In 1987, commercial banks received permission from the Federal Reserve to underwrite and deal in securities using a Glass-Steagall Section 20 affiliate. In 1998, 45 banks had Section 20 powers, which included the ability to underwrite commercial paper. The Gramm-Leach-Bliley Act allows subsidiaries of a financial holding company to engage in underwriting of securities, including underwriting their securities issues.

JUNK BONDS. The development of the junk bond market extended this loan competition to medium-sized companies representing lower-quality borrowers. Junk bonds are corporate securities that are unrated or rated Ba (BB) and lower and thus are not investment grade. Historically, firms with debt ratings below Baa (BBB) were precluded from issuing significant amounts of new debt and had to rely instead on bank loans. During the early 1980s, several investment banks, particularly Drexel Burnham Lambert Inc., convinced investors that many Ba and lower rated bonds were sound investments. Historical default rates were so low that the 3.5 to 5 percent yield premium offered on the bonds more than compensated for default risk. Investment banks were soon able to help companies that could not issue prime-grade commercial paper sell junk bonds in the new issue market. These bonds had several advantages over bank loans, including access to larger amounts of funds, longer-term financing, and fewer restrictive covenants. In many cases, the interest costs were well below loan rates quoted by a bank. New issue junk bonds effectively served as substitutes for commercial loans.

In 1989, the junk bond market started a long decline as the federal government charged Drexel Burnham and its junk bond specialist, Michael Milken, with a series of securities law violations. At that time, Drexel provided much of the secondary market support for junk bonds that investors wanted to trade. With Drexel's bankruptcy filing in 1990, the secondary market shrunk and junk bond prices collapsed. Firms planning to place new junk bond issues with investors were generally unable to obtain junk financing. These customers gravitated to banks until junk bonds reclaimed their popularity. Today, the junk bond market is again quite active. Fed policymakers actually look at the interest spread between junk bond yields and yields on low default risk Treasury securities as an indicator of the appropriate monetary policy. When the spreads are extremely high, lower quality borrowers have more difficulty obtaining financing and the Federal Reserve System often provides additional liquidity to the market. This occurred in 1998 with the financial crisis in Asia and Russia.

These developments permanently altered the commercial banking industry. The growth in junk bonds reduced the pool of good-quality loans and lowered risk-adjusted yield spreads over bank borrowing costs. Banks generally responded either by increasing the riskiness of their loan portfolios or trying to move into investment banking and other service areas that generate fee income. Banks choosing the first path sacrificed long-term profitability and solvency for short-term gains. They maintained yield spreads temporarily, but increased default risk on the loans, which ultimately eroded earnings through higher loan charge-offs.

Most banks seeking greater fee income have had limited options. They would like to underwrite securities, sell new types of insurance, and offer other products without the inherent credit risk of loans. This would allow them to diversify their asset base and revenue stream and lower the risk of failure. Only recently have commercial banks been able to engage in many of these activities.

Today, different size banks pursue different strategies. Small- to medium-size banks continue to concentrate on loans but seek to strengthen customer relationships by offering personal service. They now measure their costs better and price loans and deposits to cover their costs plus meet profit targets. The best evidence is that most banks now calculate their

▪ EXHIBIT 1.2

CREDIT RISK DIVERSIFICATION: CONSUMER LOANS AND COMMERCIAL
LOANS AS A PERCENT OF TOTAL LOANS, 1991–2001

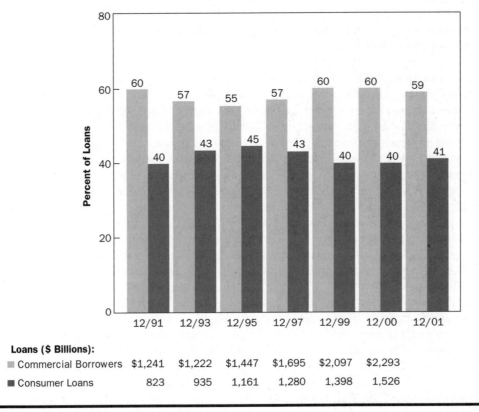

Loans ($ Billions):

	12/91	12/93	12/95	12/97	12/99	12/00
▪ Commercial Borrowers	$1,241	$1,222	$1,447	$1,695	$2,097	$2,293
▪ Consumer Loans	823	935	1,161	1,280	1,398	1,526

SOURCE: FDIC Quarterly Banking Profile, Fourth Quarter, 2001, FDIC. Available on the Internet at www.fdic.gov/databank/qbp/.

Loans to Commercial Borrowers (Credit Risk Concentrated)—These are loans that can have relatively large balances at risk to a single borrower. A single loan may represent a significant portion of an institution's capital or income. Therefore, a relatively small number of defaults could impair an institution's capital or income. These loans include commercial and industrial loans, commercial real estate, construction loans, and agricultural loans.

Consumer Loans (Credit Risk Diversified)—These are loans that typically have relatively small balances spread among a large number of borrowers. A number of defaults are likely but typically do not impair an institution's capital or income. These loans include consumer and credit card loans, 1–4 family residential mortgages, and home equity loans.

own cost of funds and price loans off this index rather than off a money center bank's prime rate. Many of these same banks have rediscovered the consumer loan. Exhibit 1.2 shows the increased concentration of consumer loans as compared to commercial loans at banks from 1991 to 1995. Consumer loans increased from 40 percent of total loans in 1991 to a high of 45 percent in 1995 while commercial loans decreased from 60 percent to 55 percent over the same period. The growth in consumer loans has slowed somewhat since 1995, due primarily to the rapid increase in default rates and personal bankruptcy rates we have seen in the late 1990s.

Rates charged on consumer loans have generally far exceeded the respective default rates and the cost of financing such that net profits have exceeded those on commercial loans. A further advantage with retail customers is that consumer deposits are much less rate sensitive than large certificates of deposit and other borrowed funds. The biggest losers are low-balance depositors who have seen service charges double to cover the bank's costs of providing transactions services.

OFF-BALANCE SHEET ACTIVITIES AND ASSETS. The largest banks move assets off the balance sheet as part of their normal business because commercial and consumer loans are risky relative to the available returns. Regulatory capital requirements raise the cost of holding loans, on balance sheet, and pricing pressures on new loans make owning loans too expensive and too risky, given the available yield spreads. Thus, some institutions consciously originate loans and securitize them, or issue securities using the loans as collateral, and effectively move the loans off the bank's balance sheet. Commercial loans on the balance sheets of the largest U.S. commercial banks have remained roughly constant at 1982 levels, while the same firms have dramatically increased off-balance sheet activity. Meanwhile, non-interest income, as a percentage of total assets, has increased to more than 2 percent at year-end 2001 from less than 1.3 percent in 1985.

This trend is not without risk. Because banks were prohibited from underwriting and distributing securities domestically, large banks emphasized international underwriting efforts and entered the financial guarantee and commitment business. Commitments and guarantees take the form of loan commitments, standby letters of credit, commitments related to interest rate swaps, currency exchange, leases, insurance on securities, and third party guarantees, all of which generate excellent fee income and do not require large capital support. However, because unfunded commitments and guarantees do not appear explicitly on published financial statements, banks continue to assume the risk that they might need to fund the commitments and make good on a defaulted obligation. This was dramatically demonstrated in late 2001 and 2002 with the bankruptcies of Enron and Kmart and problems of Tyco and other distressed firms. As these nonfinancial companies approached bankruptcy, the money and capital markets closed down to them so they drew down their credit lines at banks. Thus, just before filing for bankruptcy, Enron and Kmart increased their borrowing from banks who quickly charged off the loans and found themselves to be general creditors for a failed firm. Tyco didn't fail, but substituted bank borrowing for commercial paper issues by its CIT subsidiary when investors refused to buy CIT's commercial paper at traditional rate levels.

CAPTIVE AUTOMOBILE FINANCE COMPANIES. Much like other companies, the largest automobile manufacturers have aggressively expanded in the financial services industry as part of their long-term strategic plans. The captive finance companies of General Motors, Ford Motor, DaimlerChrysler, and Toyota Motor Credit have long provided a steady stream of financing for automobile buyers. They also provide dealer financing for inventories, capital improvements, and lease programs. Profitability of these groups also compares favorably with that of commercial banks. Part of the success is due to operations beyond automobile finance. General Motors Acceptance Corp. owns two mortgage-servicing companies and ranks as the sixth largest mortgage servicer in the United States (end of year 2001). Ford Motor Credit, the nation's largest captive auto finance company, is also the second largest diversified finance company, second only to General Electric Capital Services. The financing divisions of these companies often contribute a great deal to the parent companies' bottom line. In 2001, Ford Motor Credit contributed $1.5 billion in operating revenue, down from $2.5 billion in 2000 while the automotive division produced a loss of $9 billion, down significantly from the $5.3 billion in 2000. General Motors Acceptance Corp. and Ford Motor Credit both own a co-branded credit card: the GM Card and the Citibank Ford card. Each of these cards offers a 5 percent-of-purchase reward for the future purchase of the companies' respective automobiles.

The apparent strategy is to seek economies of scale by applying expertise in automobile financing to comparable financial enterprises. Automobiles and homes are the two most prominent consumer purchases. Banks only account for about 50 percent of auto financing while captive auto finance companies and consumer finance companies provide the rest. Most individuals make monthly payments on both types of financing, and lenders qualify borrowers using the same type of criteria. Continuous mortgage loan demand presumably helps offset the cycles in automobile sales.

OTHER FINANCE COMPANIES. General purpose finance companies cover the spectrum of lending activities. Most specialize in lending to individuals for durable goods purchases. They traditionally emphasize automobile loans, home improvement loans, and second mortgage loans, which are secured by real estate. Others specialize in lending to businesses, either directly or through factoring a firm's accounts receivable, or equipment leasing. General Electric Capital Services (GECS), a wholly owned subsidiary of General Electric, is clearly the largest diversified finance company. Besides captive automotive finance companies, the Associates First Capital, Household Finance, American Express Credit Corp., and Sears Roebuck Acceptance Corp. also finance various types of consumer and business receivables. Financing receivables (loans) for GECS were $174 billion and total assets were $425 billion in 2001, sizes that rival the largest banks in the U.S. The largest 20 finance companies are greater than $10 billion in total assets. Many of these finance companies are owned by a parent, such as GECS which is owned by General Electric. In 2001, GE's net income was $13.7 billion while GECS's net income was $5.4 billion.

Finance companies fund their investments by issuing commercial paper and long-term bonds and by borrowing directly from banks. Historically, their loans have been to relatively high credit risks. Even though their default experience exceeds that of banks, finance companies have generally earned greater returns because they price their loans at a premium, which compensates for the greater charge-offs. The returns to the largest finance companies have been as good as if not better than those of banks.

COMPETITION FOR PAYMENT SERVICES

Once the exclusive domain of banks and other depository institutions, the nation's payment system has become highly competitive. Even the Federal Reserve System's role in processing and clearing checks could be replaced by new technology. This, of course, would not come without risks. Only the Fed can prevent default by one large institution from causing the system to collapse. The real challenge for the Fed and banks in the delivery of payment processing services is emerging electronic payment systems, such as smart and stored-value cards, automatic bill payment, and bill presentment processing. Many private companies offer these products but the Fed still settles the accounts.

In *American Banker*, Diogo Teixeira commented that:

> GE Capital has almost $300 billion of financial assets. GMAC has $12 billion of financial services revenue, more than Microsoft's total corporate revenue. Microsoft has no leasing subsidiary, takes no deposits, makes no loans, and offers not a single financial product–in an age when everybody has financial products. Yet Microsoft is viewed as the threat, not GE Capital or GMAC.[10]

Why is Microsoft considered a threat to banks? Many analysts argue that the future delivery of banking services will not take place in the brick and mortar branches of a bank building but rather through smart cards, ATM networks (which the banks control), and the Internet (which banks do not control). No individual owns the Internet and any business can offer services over the Internet. Hence, more and more payments and financial services will be conducted over the Internet using smart and stored-value cards as well as private payments. The payments system is highly dynamic and constantly changing. New private digital payment methods have been created and many have failed to gain widespread acceptance.

---

[10]Teixeira, Diogo, "Comment: Banks Have Growth Opportunity in Less 'Vertical' Age," *American Banker*, July 1, 1998.

· EXHIBIT 1.3

VOLUME, DOLLAR VALUE, AND AVERAGE TRANSACTION SIZE FOR VARIOUS PAYMENT INSTRUMENTS: 1995 AND 2000

	Volume of Transactions					Value of Transactions				
	1995	2000	% Total 2000	% of Cashless Payments 2000	Growth: 1995–2000	1995	2000	% Total 2000	Growth: 1995–2000	Average Transaction Size 2000
Cash	#N/A	550,000	82.3%	#N/A		#N/A	2,200,000	0.3%		$4.00
Cheques Issued	62,963	69,000	10.3%	58.2%	1.8%	73,515,000	85,000,000	10.9%	2.9%	$1,231.88
Electronic Transactions:										
ACH	3,490	6,900	1.0%	5.8%	14.6%	12,231,500	20,300,000	2.6%	10.7%	$2,942.03
ATM	9,700	13,200	2.0%	11.1%	6.4%	656,600	800,000	0.1%	4.0%	$60.61
Credit Card	14,914	20,000	3.0%	16.9%	6.0%	879,000	1,400,000	0.2%	9.8%	$70.00
Debit Card	1,599	9,275	1.4%	7.8%	42.1%	59,100	400,000	0.1%	46.6%	$43.13
Total Retail Electronic	29,702	49,375	7.4%	41.7%	10.7%	13,826,200	22,900,000	2.9%	10.6%	$463.80
Chips	51	58	0.0%	0.0%	2.6%	310,021,200	292,147,000	37.4%	−1.2%	$5,037,017
Fed Wire	76	108	0.0%	0.1%	7.3%	222,954,100	379,756,000	48.6%	11.2%	$3,516,259
Total Wholesale Electronic	127	166	0.0%	0.1%	5.5%	532,975,300	671,903,000	85.9%	4.7%	$4,047,608
Total Electronic	29,829	49,541	7.4%	41.8%	10.7%	546,801,500	694,803,000	88.8%	4.9%	$14,025

SOURCES: Compiled from the Federal Reserve; The Nilson Report (HSN Consultants Inc., Oxnard, CA); National Automated Clearing House Association; Clearing House for Interbank Payments System; Bank Network News (Faulkner & Gray, New York, N.Y.).

Exhibit 1.3 lists total volume, value, and average size of transactions for various payment methods during the years 1995 and 2000. Although cash remains the dominant form of payment, it has the smallest payment size, averaging about $4 per transaction in 2000.[11] Large wholesale transactions, using Fed Wire and the CHIPS (Clearing House Interbank Payment System) system are fewer in number but are much larger in average transaction size. The Fed Wire, operated by the Federal Reserve System, is used to settle interbank transactions while CHIPS is a private alternative operated by the New York Clearing House Association used principally to settle foreign exchange transactions. Generally, wire transfers are "wholesale" payments made between financial institutions with an average transaction size for the Fed Wire and CHIPS of $3.5 and $5 million, respectively, in 2000.

Checks are the second most active payment method in the U.S. with just over 10 percent of transaction volume in 2000 handled by checkwriting. One of the most interesting recent developments is electronic check presentment (ECP). Several types of ECP exist but one method, point-of-sale (POS) check truncation, has been especially well received. POS check truncation occurs when a paper check does not follow the payment. For example, when someone writes a check at a store, the store electronically transmits the information from the check using an ACH (Automated Clearing House) transaction and returns the paper check to the person writing the check. According to statistics from NACHA (National Automated Clearing House Association), 32 million paper checks were converted into electronic ACH debits at retail locations in 2000, the first year that statistics for this new ACH product are available. As a result, the growth in ACH payments has been much higher than that of checks.

---

[11]It should be noted that estimating the volume and value of cash transactions is subject to much debate. The accuracy of these estimates are, therefore, questionable.

Credit cards remain the principal retail, or small value, electronic payment method. Ignoring cash, credit cards were used in almost 17 percent of the volume of transactions in 2000. Debit cards, on the other hand, are clearly the fastest growing payment method as more than 250 million debit cards are in circulation and over 80 percent of banks offer debit cards.[12] Debit cards are used for point-of-sale (POS) transactions just as one would use a credit card, but are not linked to credit. Instead, they are directly linked to the user's bank account. When used, the customer's balance is immediately reduced as if a check had cleared the account. Basically, a debit card is a check without the paper. The growth in debit cards is also a result of electronic benefits transfer (EBT) programs. EBT programs are offered by over 40 states and various governmental agencies to deliver entitlement and food assistance benefits to those with or without a bank account. In these programs, EBT cards can be used like debit or ATM cards.

Factors other than changes in electronic payments systems are also eroding banks' traditional markets. The growth and acceptance of electronic payment systems means that there is less of a need for anyone to physically go to a bank or any other financial services company. Anyone with the appropriate account can obtain cash at an ATM machine or make payment at the point-of-sale anywhere in the world, eliminating the need to go to the bank to obtain cash. Anyone can open a checking account, apply for a loan, make deposits, or receive a loan electronically. Direct deposit of paychecks, the use of credit cards, electronic bill payment, electronic check presentment, and smart cards all indicate that competition for financial services goes well beyond the traditional mechanisms we think of from the recent past.

COMPETITION FOR OTHER BANK SERVICES

Banks and their affiliates offer many products and services in addition to deposits and loans. A partial list includes trust services, brokerage, data processing, securities underwriting, real estate appraisal, credit life insurance, and personal financial consulting. Although a bank cannot directly underwrite securities domestically, there are generally two methods by which banks can enter this line of business. One is to form a financial holding company. The financial holding company owns a bank or bank holding company as well as an investment subsidiary. The investment subsidiary of a financial holding company is not restricted in the amount or type of investment underwriting engaged in. A second method is to form a subsidiary of a national bank using Glass-Steagall Section 20 subsidiaries. In 1987, commercial banks received permission from the Federal Reserve to underwrite and deal in securities through Glass-Steagall Section 20 subsidiaries and five banks established the affiliated entities.[13] Since then, the number has grown ninefold and by 1998, there were 45 Section 20 companies. Although it is possible to underwrite securities at the bank level using Section 20 subsidiaries, most experts think that banks will enter the securities business through the formation of a financial holding company due to the limitations placed on Section 20 subsidiaries. Initially, the Fed only allowed banks to earn 5 percent of their revenue in their Section 20 securities affiliates. This was raised to 10 percent in 1989 and to 25 percent in March 1997. All Section 20 affiliates have Tier 1 powers—the authority to underwrite and deal in certain municipal revenue bonds, mortgage-related securities, commercial paper, and consumer-receivable-related securities. Section 20 affiliates can also apply for Tier 2 powers, allowing them to underwrite and deal in corporate debt and equity securities. Securities powers are basically unrestricted, however, if underwriting is done through a financial holding company.

---

[12]Source: Bank Network News and the Federal Reserve.

[13]The first five Section 20s were established by Bankers Trust New York Corp., Chase Manhattan Corp., Citicorp, J.P. Morgan & Co., and PNC Financial Corp.

Another method of combining "nonbanking" companies and banking is to use exemptions in the Bank Holding Company Act, which allows a nonbank to own certain types of banks or savings banks. In particular, Merrill Lynch owns a state savings bank, Merrill Lynch Bank & Trust Co., as well as a "credit card" bank, Merrill Lynch Bank USA. These exempt 'banks' or savings banks do not force Merrill Lynch to become a bank holding company because these banks are limited; i.e., they are a savings bank and a limited bank that do not accept deposits and make commercial loans—a credit card bank. This structure allows Merrill Lynch to compete directly with banks by offering insured deposits and other banking services while avoiding regulation as a bank holding company.

Merrill Lynch began to offer its Cash Management Account (CMA) during the late 1970s in which smaller depositors (minimum deposit of $10,000) could earn 'market' rates. During this same time, banks were restricted from paying more than 5.25 percent on savings accounts and could not pay interest on checking accounts. It did not take long for Merrill Lynch's CMA account to become quite popular, especially during periods of high inflation and high interest rates. At one point, Merrill Lynch's CMA account was paying a short-term rate of almost 15 percent as compared to a bank's restricted 5.25 percent. It is no wonder the average investor began to look beyond the bank for a place to put investment dollars. It was not until the early 1980s that bank's were allowed to offer interest on checking accounts and money market deposit accounts to compete with Merrill Lynch's CMA.

The 1980s and 1990s represented a period of intense competition where nonbank competitors aggressively entered traditional banking business lines. Commercial banks competed fiercely with nonbank banks, finance companies, and high-growth thrifts for loans and deposits. Once-loyal customers moved their business for better terms. Unfortunately, the increased competition coincided with many regulatory restrictions on the type of products banks could offer as well as loan problems in energy, real estate, and agriculture, which made it even more difficult to maintain quality assets and market share. Competitors, such as investment banks, captive automobile finance companies, other finance companies, and technology firms, engaged in activities that many banks wanted, but were unable to pursue due to regulation thereby making the degree of competition even more intense.

INVESTMENT BANKING. Commercial banks consider investment banking attractive because most investment banks already offer many banking services to prime commercial customers and high net worth individuals and sell a wide range of products not available through banks. They can compete in any geographic market without the heavy regulation of the Federal Reserve, FDIC, and OCC. They earn extraordinarily high fees for certain types of transactions and can put their own capital at risk in selected investments. Of course, some risks are great such that there is the potential for highly volatile profits.

The Securities and Exchange Commission (SEC), which regulates investment banks, classifies firms in terms of their primary trading activity and head office location. Two categories of firms dominate the investment banking industry. *National full-line firms*, such as Merrill Lynch and Morgan Stanley, offer a complete set of services, including an extensive network of branch offices located throughout the United States to handle retail business. Large *investment banking firms*, such as Salomon Smith Barney and Goldman Sachs, do not have extensive branch networks and instead focus on large-scale trading, underwriting, and mergers and acquisitions. Both types of firms generate earnings from fee-based services, trading, and brokerage services. One attractive source of fees is securities underwriting in which investment banks help firms issue new equity and debt. The top investment banking houses manage the bulk of new issue investment-grade securities and thus are referred to as special bracket firms. Even though fewer than 20 firms qualify as national full-line or large investment banks, they control more than two-thirds of all assets held by investment banks. An *underwriter* typically buys the new securities from the issuer at an agreed-upon price and redistributes them to investors. As temporary owner of the securities, an underwriter acts as a *dealer* in assuming the risk that it can resell the securities at higher prices. The differential between the final sale price and the negotiated purchase price represents its profit. For this reason, an underwriter normally presells the issue by obtaining commitments from investors.[14] Underwriters may also act as agents and help issuers place new securities directly with the final investor. As such, they earn fees without taking ownership of the underlying securities. Because risk increases with issue size, investment banks frequently form *underwriting syndicates,* or groups of investment banks, to diversify the risk and increase the number of selling firms.

Investment banks also serve as brokers or dealers in secondary market transactions. Through trading departments, they make markets in previously issued securities by executing trades for selected customers or for their own account. Many trades, especially those involving retail customers, are simply *brokered,* that is, the trader matches prospective buyers and sellers. The investment bank assumes no inventory risk and earns a straight commission on the exchange. Traders may also act as *dealers,* setting bid and ask prices for every security traded. The bid indicates the price at which the firm agrees to buy securities, and the ask indicates the sales price. Dealers incur inventory risk and adjust the size of the bid-ask spread to vary the size of their inventory. If necessary, a dealer may hedge inventory risk by trading futures, swaps, and options.

Investment banks also generate substantial fees from facilitating corporate mergers and acquisitions and asset management. In the first case, an investment bank helps in the valuation and offers advice and assistance in negotiating deal terms. Corporate takeover specialists and junk bond financing spur this activity. Target companies are often those with stock market values far below the value of corporate assets. Acquiring firms issue large volumes of common stock or junk bond debt and use the proceeds to buy controlling interest in a target company's stock. After purchase, they sell some of the acquired firm's assets to refund the initial debt or to generate cash flow that covers the debt service. Companies pursuing these leveraged buyouts often earn extraordinary profits when the market values of the firms' stocks later increase. In the second case, investment banks serve as agents and manage investment funds for clients earning a management fee. This generally represents a stable, low risk source of revenue as long as the funds perform adequately.

Investment banks aggressively court merger and acquisition business. Many can raise takeover funds quickly for acquiring firms through junk bond trading relationships. However, some investment banks invest their own capital in acquired companies. Rather than rely on fee income, they pursue speculative profits that may occur if the target firm's stock increases in price after acquisitions. Merger and acquisition activity has essentially restructured corporate finance. Because it is no longer difficult to initiate a hostile takeover, many corporations have actively enhanced their balance sheets, repurchased outstanding stock, or even entrenched current management in recognition that they may be a target.

Securities trading and brokerage represent the other sources of profit. The first involves either making a market in securities or trading for the firm's own account. When making a market, a bank serves as a ready buyer and/or seller of the underlying security or commodity. For example, in foreign exchange trading, a bank may operate as a dealer by posting bid and ask quotes for which it is willing to buy and sell specific currencies. It makes a profit from the difference between the ask and bid prices. Some investment banks allow employees to trade for the bank's own account. In this situation, the trader takes speculative positions

---

[14]Original issuers let investment banks either bid competitively for the right to underwrite a new issue or negotiate directly with a single firm to handle the entire issue. Underwriters contact final investors prior to submitting a bid to assess market demand and determine a market price.

in an effort to buy the underlying asset at prices below the sale price. Obviously, speculative trading embodies greater risk. In the brokerage business, investment banks serve as customer representatives helping individuals, pension funds, and businesses buy and sell securities. As agents, the bank makes the bulk of its profit from sales commissions.

The Wall Street investment giants such as Goldman Sachs and Merrill Lynch continue to be the largest players in the merger and acquisition market, but commercial banks' share of the market has increased at a rapid pace. Acquisition of investment banking companies by banks has reshaped the banking industry during the later half of the 1990s and blurred the lines of distinction between commercial banking and investment banking. Mellon Bank owns Drexel Corp.; Bank of America owns Montgomery Securities; Citigroup owns Salomon Smith Barney; Credit Suisse owns Donaldson, Lufkin & Jenrette; UBS AG owns Paine Webber; and Regions Bank owns Morgan Keegan. Some investment firms have acquired commercial banks as well: Charles Schwab owns U.S. Trust and MetLife owns Grand Bank Kingston. Due to the restrictions of becoming a financial holding company, however, the acquisitions have generally gone the other way. It is interesting to note that Citigroup is now classified as a securities company rather than a bank.

DEREGULATION AND REREGULATION

Commercial bank regulatory agencies have always tried to control the individuals and activities associated with financial intermediation. Their fundamental purpose is to protect the public's resources and confidence in the financial system. Banking is a public trust that, if left to industry whims, might assume too much risk, ultimately leading to extensive losses and widespread lack of confidence in the soundness and integrity underlying financial intermediation. Regulations specify who is allowed to manage a bank, where banks are permitted to locate, and what products and services banks are allowed to offer, as well as specific portfolio constraints.

Deregulation is the process of eliminating existing regulations, such as the elimination of Regulation Q interest rate ceilings imposed on time and demand deposits offered by depository institutions or the repeal of sections of the Glass-Steagall Act removing restrictions on investment banking activities. Deregulation is often confused with reregulation, which is the process of implementing new restrictions or modifying existing controls on individuals and activities associated with banking. Reregulation arises in response to market participants' efforts to circumvent existing regulations.

An issue related to Federal Reserve membership arose during the 1970s and serves as an excellent example of the regulator-bank relationship. Banks that are members of the Fed are required to hold reserves in the form of nonearning cash assets equal to a percentage of qualifying liabilities. These reserves represent an implicit tax on banking operations because banks do not earn explicit interest on the assets. During the 1970s, this tax increased dramatically as short-term market interest rates increased. Banks that were not Fed members were required to hold fewer reserves and could typically hold interest-bearing securities to meet requirements. As such, their lost interest income was much smaller. To circumvent regulation, many member banks gave up Fed membership rather than absorb the loss. The FRS and Congress, concerned about losing control of the money supply, passed the Depository Institutions Monetary Control Act in 1980, which allowed interest-bearing checking accounts but forced all financial institutions that offered them to hold reserves set by the Fed. This reregulation was an attempt to reimpose regulatory control over all depository institutions.

Efforts at deregulation and reregulation generally address pricing issues, allowable geographic market penetration, or the ability to offer new products and services. Recent pricing regulations have focused on removing price controls, such as the maximum interest rates paid to depositors and the rate charged to borrowers (usury ceilings). Deregulation, addressing geographic markets, has expanded the locations where competing firms can conduct business. The Riegle-Neal Interstate Banking and Branching Efficiency Act of 1994 effectively eliminated all bank acquisition and branching restrictions as of July 1997.[15]

Finally, deregulation of the restrictions which separated commercial banking, investment banking, and insurance have allowed banks to form financial holding companies and quickly expand product choices such as insurance, brokerage services, and securities underwriting. These changes, combined with new technology, have expanded opportunities across geographic markets and produced a greater number of competitors offering banking services and intense price competition. Greater competition has, in turn, lowered aggregate returns as firms attempt to establish a permanent market presence.

FINANCIAL INNOVATION

Financial innovation is the catalyst behind the evolving financial services industry and the restructuring of financial markets. It represents the systematic process of change in instruments, institutions, and operating policies that determine the structure of our financial system. Innovations take the form of new securities and financial markets, new products and services, new organizational forms, and new delivery systems. Financial institutions change the characteristics of financial instruments traded by the public and create new financial markets, which provide liquidity. Bank managers change the composition of their banks' balance sheets by altering the mix of products or services offered and by competing in extended geographic markets. Financial institutions form holding companies and reverse holding companies, acquire subsidiaries, and merge with other entities. Finally, institutions may modify the means by which they offer products and services. Recent trends incorporate technological advances with the development of cash management accounts, including the use of automatic teller machines, home banking via computer and the Internet, and shared national and international electronic funds transfer systems.

Innovations have many causes. Firms may need to stop the loss of deposits, enter new geographic or product markets, deliver services with cheaper and better technology, increase their capital base, alter their tax position, reduce their risk profile, or cut operating costs. In virtually every case, the intent is to improve their competitive position. The external environment, evidenced by volatile economic conditions, new regulations, and technological developments, creates the opportunity for innovation.

Financial innovation related to Regulation Q evolved as depository institutions tried to slow disintermediation, in which depositors withdrew funds from fixed-rate accounts at banks and reinvested the funds in instruments paying market rates of interest. Until 1980, Regulation Q restricted banks from offering more than 5.25 percent interest on savings accounts. Regulation Q was voided in 1986 for all deposits when interest rate ceilings on savings accounts were eliminated. Until then, many banks developed new vehicles to compete with Treasury bills or other instruments, such as money market mutual funds and cash management accounts offered through brokerage houses. Citibank issued negotiable CDs and variable rate CDs. Eurodollar deposits were developed and negotiable orders of withdrawal (NOW) accounts (interest-bearing checking accounts) were permitted in Massachusetts. Federal regulators often responded to these innovations by imposing marginal reserve requirements against the new instrument, raising the interest rate ceiling, then authorizing a

---

[15]Texas and Montana opted out of interstate branching, Texas until 1999 and Montana until 2001.

- **EXHIBIT 1.4**

Date	Financial Innovation
1961	Negotiable CDs
1963	Eurodollars
1970	Government National Mortgage Association pass-through certificate created
1971	Third-party insurance as security for municipal bonds
1972	NOWs in Massachusetts
1972	Currency futures developed and traded on Chicago Mercantile Exchange
1973	Money market mutual funds
1973	Listed stock options begin trading on Chicago Board Options Exchange
1976	Treasury bill futures begin trading on Chicago Mercantile Exchange
1978	Treasury bond futures begin trading on Chicago Board of Trade
1978	Development of 1-year Treasury bill futures
1981	Interest rate swaps
1981	Floating-rate notes and Eurobonds
1983	Development of Eurodollar futures
1983	Development of options on Treasury bond futures
1983	Development of options on Eurodollar futures
1983	Collateralized mortgage obligations first issued
1984	Extensive use of junk bonds to finance leveraged buyouts
1985	Securitized car loans, leases, credit card receivables
1987	Mutual funds for bank-qualified municipal bonds
1988	Buyers' assurance plans for bank credit card purchases
1989	Insurance on credit card purchases
1990	AT&T Universal credit card
1990	Options on interest rate swaps, credit derivatives
1991	Stock index CDs popularized
1993	Credit cards with photos
1994	Prepaid debit cards
1995	Extensive use of automated bill pay and "pay-at-the pump" transactions
1996	Use of Internet banking
1997	Active use of credit derivatives
1997	Active market in securitized nonguaranteed portions of small business loans
1998	Introduction of futures contract on personal bankruptcies
2000	Electronic check presentment (ECP)
2001	Weather derivatives

new deposit instrument. Some of these restrictions remain such as the prohibition against banks paying interest on commercial demand deposits.[16]

More recent innovations with securities take the form of new futures, swaps, options, and options-on-futures contracts, or the development of markets for a wide range of securitized assets. Exhibit 1.4 lists a few of the new financial futures and options contracts which speculators and hedgers use to conduct business. Banks use financial futures to hedge interest rate and foreign exchange risk in their portfolios. They can be used to offset mismatches in maturities of assets and liabilities or different amounts of assets and liabilities denominated

---

[16]Interestingly, banks have found ways around this regulation (reg. DD) as well. Competitive pressures from investment banks and mutual fund companies have encouraged banks to offer "sweep" accounts. These accounts move a commercial customer's checking account balance to a money market account that is not a bank insured deposit account and hence can be interest bearing. The funds are then moved back as the company needs them. See Chapter 14 for a detailed discussion of sweep accounts.

in different currencies, to price fixed-rate loans or to create synthetic deposits. Several large banks also earn fee income and commissions by serving as futures merchants and advisers. The development of futures and options has led to more active trading in many of the securities that banks issue, trade, or buy for their own accounts.

Prior to the passage of the Riegle-Neal Interstate Banking and Branching Efficiency Act of 1994, which eliminated branching restrictions, financial institutions successfully circumvented restrictions against geographic expansion (Exhibit 1.5). Bank holding companies established out-of-state loan production offices, Edge Act corporations, and nonbank subsidiaries and entered into shared facility arrangements with electronic funds transfer systems. Banks established reciprocal banking pacts with other states that encouraged interstate mergers and acquisitions. Banks also used technology to circumvent geographic restrictions by offering Internet banking services — effectively incorporating a worldwide market for their services outside of their restricted markets. Of course, innovations are not restricted to banks. Major retailers such as J.C. Penney, Kroger, and Sears acquired banks, savings and loans, insurance companies, and real estate companies, enabling them to offer banking products. State Farm Insurance and related firms also now offer full commercial banking services. See the Contemporary Issues: Unitary Thrift Powers discussion. These nonbank firms operate offices nationwide without regulatory interference. Investment banks have similarly linked up with consumer banks to provide a vehicle for offering credit card and transactions services nationally.

Innovation in delivery systems normally takes the form of new technological developments to facilitate funds transfers. During the 1980s, banks popularized automatic teller machines and point-of-sale terminals in retail outlets. More recent innovations include the development of the smart cards, debit cards, home banking networks, and Internet banking. Although customer acceptance has been slow, these systems are growing at an increasing rate.

SECURITIZATION. During the early 1980s, deregulation and financial innovation increased the risk of commercial bank operations. Borrowing costs increased as depositors converted low-rate savings accounts and demand deposits into deposits bearing market rates. Deposit balances also became less stable because customers were increasingly rate sensitive, moving their balances to firms paying the highest rates. With banks, savings and loans, credit unions, and mutual funds competing for the same deposits, depositors could easily find high-rate alternatives. Because loans offer the highest gross yields, many banks tried to compensate for declining interest margins by increasing loan-to-asset ratios. Loan yields subsequently fell relative to borrowing costs as lending institutions competed for a decreasing pool of quality credits. In many cases, this eventually led to greater loan losses and long-term earnings problems.

High loan growth also raises bank capital requirements. Regulators consider most loans to be risky assets and require banks to add to their loan loss reserves and capital base the greater are their loans. Higher provisions for loan losses reduce reported net income. Because equity capital is more expensive than debt, higher capital requirements, in turn, increase the marginal cost of financing operations.

One competitive response to asset quality problems and earnings pressure has been to substitute fee income for interest income by offering more fee-based services. Banks also lower their capital requirements and reduce credit risk by selling assets and servicing the payments between borrower and lender, rather than holding the same assets to earn interest. This process of converting assets into marketable securities is called *securitization*. A bank originates assets, typically loans, combines them in pools with similar features, and sells

▪ EXHIBIT 1.5

FINANCIAL INNOVATION: GEOGRAPHIC AND PRODUCT
EXPANSION AND NEW DELIVERY SYSTEMS

A. Geographic and Product Expansion

- Commercial banks formed multibank holding companies to circumvent state restrictions against branching.
- Commercial banks formed bank holding companies to increase range of products and services, enabling diversification of operations. Nonbank subsidiaries conducted business without geographic restrictions. Independent banks formed service corporations.
- Commercial banks established loan production offices and Edge Act corporations to offer credit and international trade services nationally.
- State legislatures passed laws providing for interstate banking activities through regional pacts or nationwide activity.
- Commercial banks formed joint ventures as reverse holding companies, which offered services, such as data processing, that a single firm could not offer economically alone.
- Financial institutions other than commercial banks acquired nonbank banks, enabling them to offer a subset of banking services without being regulated under the Bank Holding Company Act. Nonbank banks can conduct business without geographic restrictions.
- Firms formed financial conglomerates to expand range of financial services. Mergers and acquisitions typically include brokerage house, insurance company, finance company, and retailer.
- Commercial banks formed subsidiaries to offer discount brokerage services and sell mutual funds.
- State legislators removed restrictions on out-of-state banks buying in-state banks.
- J.P. Morgan and Bankers Trust were allowed to underwrite corporate securities.
- Banks offer a full range of mutual funds.
- Nationwide branching
- NationsBank's acquisition of BankAmerica creates the first coast-to-coast "national" bank.
- Banks enter the investment banking area with Bankers Trust's purchase of Alex. Brown, NationsBank's purchase of Montgomery Securities, and Bank America's purchase of Robertson Stephens.
- Citicorp acquires Travelers and creates the first banking and insurance underwriting company.

B. New Delivery Systems

- Commercial banks set up automatic teller machines (ATMs) to provide convenient banking services.
- Financial institutions link ATMs into networks with shared facilities.
- Commercial banks establish point-of-sale systems in retail outlets.
- Commercial banks provide home banking services that allow customers to pay bills, transfer funds, and review statements via microcomputers.
- Financial institutions develop smart cards that contain a computer chip with customer's password or identification number, allowing instantaneous authorization.
- New York banks develop clearing system for electronic payments related to international trade, called CHIPS.
- Commercial banks develop telecommunications system, designated SWIFT, which processes electronic messages between institutions.
- Banks contract with nonbank vendors such as IBM and EDS to handle item (check) processing.
- Banks use image processing for storing and reading financial documents.
- Banks merge back office item processing operations.
- Banks use mobile and "supermarket" branches.
- Offer financial planning and investment services in branches with joint venture partners
- Market bank services through screen telephones
- Telephone bill payment
- Automated payment; e.g., "pay at the pump"
- Home banking systems, including Internet banking
- Introduction of Internet only banks
- Point-of-sale check truncation
- Smart cards, electronic money, and digital payment systems
- Consumer financial account aggregation
- Electronic bill presentment
- Financial Account Aggregation

UNITARY THRIFT POWERS

One method of entering into the banking business and avoiding most of the regulations on products and geographic boundaries was to form a Unitary Thrift Holding Company. Prior to the passage of the Gramm-Leach-Bliley Act in 1999, nonbank firms could achieve most of the benefits of owning a bank, but not being regulated as a bank, by entering the savings and loan business. They do so by applying for a unitary thrift charter that allows them to operate a single savings bank. Through this federal savings bank charter, the firm can issue deposits and make loans to any customers without altering the types of products and services the nonbank acquirer already offers. The objective is often to sell banking services to their own traditional customers, yet avoid reg-

ulation as a bank or bank holding company (see Chapter 2).

State Farm Insurance and USAA both have a unitary thrift charter and solicit their insurance members (and potentially others) for other types of financial transactions, such as deposits and consumer and residential mortgages. GE Capital, Ford, ADM (Archer Daniel Midland), and many other insurance companies and investment banks have received thrift charters. Even Hillenbrand Industries, a manufacturer of caskets, applied for a thrift charter so that it could presumably offer banking services to funeral home directors and other interested customers. Not surprisingly, commercial bankers protested loudly for a level playing field.

This inequity "loophole" was closed, but not completely eliminated, with the passing of the Financial Services Modernization Act, or Gramm-Leach-Bliley Act of 1999, which prohibits <u>new</u> unitary thrift holding company charters. Although the Gramm-Leach-Bliley Act eliminated the advantages of a unitary thrift charter for new entry into the market, it allows for all existing unitary thrift charters to continue operations. It is interesting to note that the effective date prohibiting *de novo* unitary thrift holding company applications was May 4, 1999, just one day before Walmart's application for a unitary thrift holding company application of May 5, 1999.

---

pass-through certificates, which are secured by the interest and principal payments on the original assets. Residential mortgages and mortgage-backed pass-through certificates served as the prototype. The originating bank charges fees for making the loans. If it services the loans, it collects interest and principal payments on the loans, which it passes through to certificate holders minus a servicing fee. If the bank sells the certificates without recourse, regulators permit it to take the original assets off its books.[17] The bank does not have to allocate loan-loss reserves against the assets, and its capital requirements decline proportionately. Securitization also eliminates interest rate risk associated with financing the underlying assets. In essence, the bank serves as an investment banker generating fee income from servicing the loans without assuming additional credit risk.

The objectives behind securitizing most mortgages and other loans include:

- Freeing capital for other uses
- Improving return on equity via servicing income
- Diversifying credit risk
- Obtaining new sources of liquidity
- Reducing interest rate risk

The process itself is costly because a bank must pay underwriting expenses and fees for credit enhancement guarantees. Such credit enhancements normally involve a letter of credit

---

[17]Banks that issue securities backed by their assets are legally classified as investment companies. If they are not exempted, the SEC, according to the Investment Company Act of 1940, regulates them. The SEC also requires that banks guarantee securities before it grants an exemption. This inconsistency with bank regulatory treatment effectively restricts banks to private rather than public placement for the securities. See Brenner, May 1986.

that guarantees the investor in the underlying securities that obligated payments will be made. For this guarantee, a bank will pay approximately 50 basis points.

The increased securitization of financial assets is one of the dominant financial trends of the 1980s. Banks, in particular, are eager to securitize and sell a broader base of loan receivables. This makes them loan originators as much as lenders with full credit risk. Since 1985, banks have successfully securitized commercial loans, residential mortgages, automobile loans, computer leases, Small Business Association guaranteed loans, mobile home loans, home equity loans, and credit card receivables. Most of these arrangements have been facilitated by an investment bank and involve a letter of credit guarantee from a foreign bank or insurance company, which retains some recourse with the originating bank. Bankone's credit card sale (see Contemporary Issues: Securitizing Credit Card Loans) is one example that did not involve such a guarantee. Recent Federal Reserve Board rulings have expanded banks' ability to underwrite their own securitized issues, and banks with investment banking affiliates are now major participants in this market.

Not all assets can be securitized. Loans that best qualify exhibit standard features regarding maturity, size, pricing, collateral, and use of proceeds. They typically demonstrate predictable losses over time. Residential mortgages have been the most popular because they are similar regardless of the geographic area where they originate. Commercial loans, in contrast, represent negotiated contracts and thus exhibit substantially different characteristics. Diversity increases the difficulty of pooling loans and attracting investors who do not want to investigate the features of each loan in the pool. Commercial loan losses are also highly variable. To securitize commercial loans, banks must facilitate the process by accumulating less risky credits and standardizing the loan features. Credit card receivables, automobile paper, and home equity loans dominate the non-mortgage asset-backed issues at banks.

Securitization enhances competition for the underlying assets. With standardized features, such as those on government-guaranteed mortgages, borrowers can easily compare prices and select the least costly alternative. Securitization also changes the composition of bank balance sheets because not all assets can be securitized. High-risk loans to small businesses, for example, are designed to meet the specific needs of a single firm. Because they do not have identical features, it is difficult to determine the credit quality of an entire pool of loans and to use them as collateral against security issues. Banks generally want to keep these loans in their portfolios because of their higher promised yields and the lack of a secondary market to sell or securitize the loans. This is changing, however, as several national firms are currently attempting to support the securitization of many types of small business loans. Credit card receivables and automobile loans, however, offer a sharp contrast. Terms are fairly standard and losses are predictable. The effect is that the credit quality of loans kept on the bank's books is declining.

GLOBALIZATION

Financial markets and institutions are becoming increasingly international in scope. U.S. corporations, for example, can borrow from domestic or foreign institutions. They can issue securities denominated in U.S. dollars or foreign currencies of the countries in which they do business. Foreign corporations have the same alternatives. Investors increasingly view securities issued in different countries as substitutes. Large firms thus participate in both domestic and foreign markets such that interest rates on domestic instruments closely track foreign interest rates.

Globalization is the gradual evolution of markets and institutions such that geographic boundaries do not restrict financial transactions. One country's economic policies affect the economies of other countries. Funds flow freely between countries because of efficient money and capital markets and currency exchange. The establishment of the European Community

CONTEMPORARY ISSUES

SECURITIZING CREDIT CARD LOANS

On April 10, 1986, Bankone announced that it had entered into an agreement with Salomon Brothers Inc. to sell a portion of its credit card receivables to investors via collateralized certificates. The deal was unique because investors had recourse in case of default, but Bankone retained no liability and no third-party insurance was provided. The innovation involved establishing a loss reserve fund.

Bankone created a pool of credit card receivables carrying an effective yield of 19 percent. Salomon Brothers privately placed $50 million of pass-through certificates backed by interest and principal payments on the credit card receivables. The certificates, labeled certificates for amortizing revolving debts or CARDs, carried a fixed rate of 8.35 percent and a stated maturity of five years. A portion of the difference between interest and principal payments on the receivables and payments to investors was allocated to a reserve fund. In case of defaults, proceeds were taken from the reserve to pay investors.

The reserve effectively constituted insurance and made the certificates attractive to investors. Because of the reserve, bank regulators authorized the sale and Bankone could remove the credit card loans from its books. In this instance, Bankone set the size of the reserve equal to 200 percent of its historical loss experience on credit card loans and agreed to service the loans. It retained a 30 percent interest in the pool, which essentially represented servicing income, plus kept any reserve funds in excess of actual defaults.

SOURCE: Lynn Brenner, "Credit Card Deal May Be Model for Securitization," *American Banker* (April 14, 1986), describes the basic features of the transaction.

(EC) in 1992 represents a prime example. Under the original formal agreement, 12 industrialized nations in Western Europe eliminated most trade restrictions, standardized basic product designs, reduced taxes and fees, and linked monetary control in order to facilitate trade. Today, there are now 16 countries in the EC.[18] The original intent was to have a common currency and fully integrated market that operates as one without borders. Starting in January 1999, the Euro (a European unified currency) has been usable in wholesale financial transactions in all European Union countries except for Sweden, Denmark, Greece, and the United Kingdom. Since January 2002, coins and currency Euros are the authorized and dominant transaction vehicle in the EC. Monetary policy for the single currency is set by the European Central Bank, located in Frankfurt. One presumed benefit of the Euro is that it should sharply lower inflation rates and enhance export opportunities for all member countries.

Businesses, individuals, and governments recognize that events throughout the world influence their domestic performance. They should be aware of foreign competition and foreign opportunities when developing market strategies. Chapter 21 analyzes the nature of international transactions in detail, including both the impacts of U.S. firms abroad and foreign firms in the United States.

Most large money center banks have the capability and expertise to help customers access capital in any currency in the form of either debt or equity. Many firms have offices all over the world and offer services in a wide range of product markets. Several Japanese banks, for example, serve as primary securities dealers in activities with the U.S. Federal Reserve. Some of the best known U.S. investment banks, Lehman, Goldman Sachs, PaineWebber, Blackstone, and Wasserstein, are at least partially owned by foreign investors. Borrowers look less at where the supplier of a good or service is located and more at the quality and

---

[18]The 16 countries in the EC are Austria, Belgium, Denmark, Finland, France, Germany, Greece, Ireland, Italy, Luxembourg, the Netherlands, Norway, Portugal, Spain, Sweden, and the United Kingdom.

price of the good or service. Clearly, only the largest firms can successfully compete world-wide. Globalization in financial services implies that the top layer of firms will consist of a few, very large consolidated organizations.

Although product innovation and the acquisition of domestic firms by foreign firms has led to a removable of the physical borders that separate firms internationally, technology has clearly had one of the most dramatic impacts on the globalization of markets. Technological innovations, such as the commercialization of the Internet, mean that distance is no longer a limiting factor. One can search for and purchase products and services from anywhere in the world from just about anywhere in the world. Large as well as small companies now have global markets for their products and services. Consumers and businesses now search beyond their traditional local market in pursuit of price, quality, and availability.

CAPITAL REQUIREMENTS

The regulatory agencies have long required commercial banks to operate with minimum amounts of capital. Historically, they enforced capital requirements in terms of balance sheet ratios that specified minimum amounts of capital as a fraction of total assets. Effective in 1992, banks had to meet capital standards, which tied required capital to the riskiness of bank assets.[19] The intent is to limit risk-taking.

In general, bank regulators want to increase minimum capital requirements, especially when they do not have other means to monitor or control bank risk-taking. With the widespread savings and loan failures and deficiencies in deposit insurance funds, bank stockholders were expected to assume more risk. Congress thus passed legislation that imposed formal risk-based capital requirements on all banks. Increased capital reduces risk to the insurance funds because more assets can default before a bank fails. In 1998, a large hedge fund, Long Term Capital Management, effectively failed because it assumed considerable risk. Large foreign and U.S. commercial and investment banks were heavily exposed to the firm because they had loaned substantial amounts of funds to the firm for it to use as it chose. It was clear after the firm ran into problems that the banks had not monitored their risk exposure well. Regulators responded by suggesting closer scrutiny of loans that banks make to hedge funds. This series of events was repeated with Enron's failure in late 2001. Eventually, analysts came to realize that rather than being a gas-producing energy company, Enron was in reality a large hedge fund. Banks entered into a wide array of contracts with Enron including partnerships in questionable special purpose vehicles designed to move debt off Enron's balance sheet as well as lenders and investment bankers. When Enron failed, firms like J.P. Morgan Chase and Citigroup recorded losses of approximately $3 billion and $1 billion, respectively.

The ramifications of greater capital requirements are enormous. First, equity is more expensive than debt because interest payments are deductible to the bank while dividends on stock are not. It is thus costly to issue new stock. Second, the majority of banks do not have ready access to the equity market and most banks subsequently find it extremely difficult to add capital externally. Small banks' stocks are simply not broadly traded. Banks that need capital must rely either on retaining earnings or finding a merger partner. Thus, the final impact is that increased capital requirements lead to consolidation. The largest banks, however, have found access to equity markets much quicker, easier, and cheaper. Capital-rich firms have market power to purchase capital-deficient firms relatively inexpensively.

---

[19]Chapter 13 describes bank capital requirements in detail and examines the implications for bank management.

INCREASED CONSOLIDATION

The dominant trend regarding the structure of financial institutions is that of consolidation. Consider, for example, authorization of the Resolution Trust Corporation to arrange the closings of failed thrifts and their sale to solvent institutions during the 1980s. With the asset quality problems of Texas banks, the regulators authorized acquisitions by out-of-state banks including Chemical Bank, Bankone, First Interstate, and NationsBank (formerly NCNB). Cross-industry and cross-border acquisitions have the same impact on healthy banks and nonbank financial institutions. The catalysts are obvious. Technological advances allow firms to compete for customers electronically without branch facilities on every street corner. Banks can offer the same or better quality of service, a broader list of products and services, and at lower costs by combining operations. In terms of banking capacity, there are too many banks.

Increased capital requirements further restrict growth and make it difficult to compete as a small entity. The net effect will be increasingly larger firms. The later half of the 1990s saw not only a large number of bank mergers but also several of the largest bank consolidations. As a result of lenient interstate acquisition rules and the removal of branching restrictions provided by Riegle-Neal Interstate Banking and Branching Efficiency Act of 1994, the number of banks has fallen from a high of 14,364 in 1979 to about 8,100 at the end of 2001.

Most large banks have positioned themselves to be acquirers rather than sellers. They have laid off unnecessary employees, cut other operating expenses, and sold subsidiaries to streamline operations. Many issued stock when the market was favorable. They have expanded into discount brokerage, mutual funds, derivative securities, and other fields where appropriate to generate fee income and thus diversify from a reliance on interest income. Others have tried to shrink assets and focus on specific customers, such as consumers, to improve profitability and reduce risk.

GE CAPITAL SERVICES: A FINANCIAL CONGLOMERATE

Increased competition among financial institutions has led to the development and growth of diversified financial services companies and nationwide commercial banking organizations. Community or specialty bank managers express concern that they do not possess the same resources or opportunities as financial giants and may potentially be priced out of business. Large firms that engage in predatory pricing have the power to absorb losses until small banks go under. Many analysts, however, contend that community banks have inherent advantages, ranging from a record of long-term personal service to better knowledge of customer needs because of local ownership and control. Employees of companies affiliated with financial conglomerates are often only order-takers because local officials do not make important decisions. Community banks should prosper in this environment.

Whether a community bank survives or disappears depends largely on management's ability to establish a strong market position in product areas where the bank has competitive advantages and continue to serve customer needs. In some instances, a community bank may act as a franchise of larger networks to provide services it cannot offer alone at competitive prices. Innovation in the delivery and pricing of banking services, however, has become widely accepted and expected, to the point where competition is now much more intense than during the past decade. Many customers choose an institution on the basis of the range of services offered and the potential for one-stop shopping. This has given rise to diversified financial firms with nationwide delivery systems for a broad range of financial products.

When shopping for financial services, consumers have shown a preference for institutions for their checking and savings accounts, installment loans, mortgages, retirement accounts, and general financial advice. Customers like the convenience of easy access and the ability to sit down and discuss problems when they arise for these services. They generally relied upon

GROWTH IN GECS REVENUES: 1990–2001

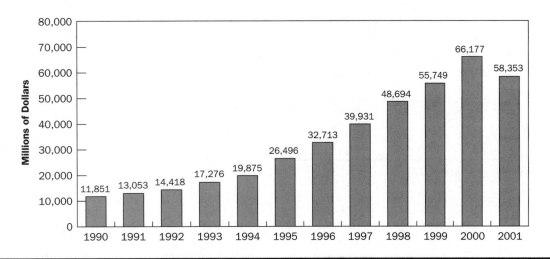

SOURCE: GE's Annual Report, 2000 (http://www.ge.com/).

larger financial conglomerates over local banks to provide stocks and bonds, life insurance, credit cards, and mutual funds due to the fact that these firms had national reputations and the local bank did not offer all of these services. Historically, banks have not been allowed to compete as aggressively in these service markets and are still developing their niche. The following discussion of GE Capital Services (GECS) documents one such large-scale financial services provider.

GE Capital Services is the financial subsidiary of General Electric, the well-known manufacturer of aircraft engines, appliances, lighting, medical systems, plastics, and power systems. GE also provides electrical distribution and control, industrial control systems, information services, and transportation systems.[20] Besides the highly profitable Capital Services company, GE also owns the National Broadcasting Company (NBC) — the most watched television network — and has a sizable investment in Paine Webber Group Inc. This financial conglomerate is one of the best managed firms in the United States and has a long record of outstanding profitability. GE Capital Services' revenues have grown by just under 19 percent a year up to 2000 but fell for the first time in over a decade in 2001. The events of September 11, 2001; the stock market meltdown; and recession of 2001 took its toll on most companies in 2001 and GE was no exception (see Exhibit 1.6). Even in 2001, GECS is still an extremely profitable division contributing approximately 40 percent of General Electric's total consolidated profits (see Exhibit 1.7)

BUSINESS GROUPS

GECS divides its operations into two segments, Financing and Specialty Insurance. The operations of GECS Financing are divided into four areas:

> *Consumer services* provides products such as private-label and bank credit card loans, personal loans, time sales and revolving credit and inventory

---

[20]For more detailed information, see the Annual Report section of GE's web site: http://www.ge.com/.

GE CAPITAL SERVICES OPERATING COMPANIES AND LINES

Segment Data (12/31/2001)	Sales (000s)	Net Earnings
General Electric Co.	74,037,000	13,684,000
GECS	58,353,000	5,417,000
Consumer Services	23,574,000	2,319,000
Equipment Management	12,542,000	1,607,000
Mid-Market Financing	8,659,000	1,280,000
Specialized Financing	2,930,000	557,000
Specialty Insurance	11,064,000	522,000
All Other	−416,000	−699,000

SOURCE: GE's Annual Report (http://www.ge.com/).

financing for retail merchants, auto leasing and inventory financing, mortgage servicing, and consumer savings and insurance services (previously included within the Specialty Insurance segment).

Equipment management provides leases, loans, sales, and asset management services for commercial and transportation equipment; for example, aircraft, trailers, auto fleets, modular space units, railroad rolling stock, data processing equipment, containers used on ocean-going vessels, and satellites.

Mid-market financing provides loans and financing and operating leases for middle-market customers for a variety of equipment; for example, data processing equipment, medical and diagnostic equipment, and equipment used in construction, manufacturing, office applications, and telecommunications activities.

Specialized financing provides loans and financing leases for major capital assets, commercial and residential real estate loans, and investments; and loans to and investments in management buyouts and corporate recapitalizations.

Specialty insurance provides U.S. and international property and casualty reinsurance, specialty insurance and life reinsurance, financial guaranty insurance (principally on municipal bonds and structured finance issues), private mortgage insurance, and creditor insurance covering international customer loan repayments.

GECS Financing is unlike some of the captive automobile finance companies in that very few of the products financed by GECS are manufactured by GECS. In 2001, GECS reported total revenues from operations of $74 billion, 11 percent more than revenue in 2000. It is actually a conglomeration of over 20 diversified businesses. Exhibit 1.8 provides a breakdown of the division's revenues in five areas: equipment management, consumer services, specialized financing, mid-market financing, and specialty insurance.

MANAGEMENT STRATEGIES

GE Capital Services' management philosophy has been to identify businesses that require a special expertise, significant capital, and where the firm can leverage its Aaa rating to its advantage. This high quality rating enables it to borrow at the cheapest rates available in both the commercial paper and bond markets. It then invests these funds in a business at

▪ EXHIBIT 1.8

GE CAPITAL SERVICES OPERATING COMPANIES AND LINES OF BUSINESS

Equipment Management
GE Americom (GE American Communications)
Aviation Services
Fleet Services
GE SeaCo and GE Capital Container Finance
It Solutions
Modular Space
Penske Truck Leasing
Rail Services
Tip (Transport International Pool)

Consumer Services
Auto Financial Services
GE Capital Australia and New Zealand
GE Capital Japan
GE Card Services
GE Financial Assurance
Global Consumer Finance
Mortgage Services

Specialized Financing
Commercial Finance
GE Equity
Real Estate
Structured Finance Group

Mid-Market Financing
Commercial Equipment Financing
European Equipment Finance
Vendor Financial Services

Specialty Insurance
Employers Reinsurance Corporation (ERC)
FGIC (Financial Guaranty Insurance Company)
GE Insurance Holdings
Mortgage Insurance

potentially high yields where it is a major player. Some of the businesses are unusual for a financial services company. For example, GE is the largest supplier of private-label credit cards and the ninth-largest credit card issuer. It operates more than 100 private-label credit card and commercial programs for retailers and manufacturers. Card Services also issues and services corporate cards, including purchasing, travel, and fleet vehicle cards for commercial customers. It currently has $18 billion in total assets and services more than 100 million cardholders to customers of Exxon, Macy's, and other retailers. These cards carry the names of the retailers, but GE earns the interest, typically at rates of 20 percent or more. When a customer complains, the retailer takes the criticism. In 1997, GECS signed an agreement to buy an equity interest in the smart card maker Gemplus. The deal will team the largest producer of chip-embedded smart cards with the financial giant GECS.

GE has the ability and financial strength to identify distressed markets where prices are temporarily low, invest in the underlying assets, then wait until the market improves before selling. For example, during the downturn in real estate following the Tax Reform Act of 1986, GECS was one of the most aggressive buyers of problem real estate. During the early 1990s alone, the Resolution Trust Corp. sold over $1 billion in distressed property from failed banks to GECS. As real estate prices rose in 1993 and thereafter, GE started to sell many of the properties, generating very handsome returns.

GE Capital Services has recently followed an aggressive growth strategy through acquisitions. In 1992, it bought two annuity companies, GNA Corp. and United Pacific Life Insurance Co., in order to enter that business on a large scale. In 1993, it bought GPA Group PLC, an Irish aircraft leasing company that was in financial distress. In 1994, it made a hostile bid for Kemper Corp., another provider of consumer and commercial financial services. This follows three years of clean-up efforts at Kemper in response to problem real estate loans. GECS sold Kemper to Paine Webber in 1994 in a stock deal. GECS added Woodchester, one of Ireland's largest financial services companies in 1997. It invested $17.2 billion in more than 75 industrial and financial services acquisitions in 1997 alone. The company made over 100 acquisitions each year from 1997 through 2000. GE, GECS's parent, acquired Honeywell, whose businesses are complementary to their Aircraft Engines, Industrial Systems and Plastics businesses.

GE Capital Services provides this full range of financial services without being a bank holding company. Although GE owns a credit card bank, these limited purpose banks are exempt from requiring GE to become a bank holding company because it does not take deposits from consumers (under $100,000 deposits) and does not make loans like a traditional commercial bank. It does, however, compete with banks in virtually all of its business lines. Because it is not a bank or bank holding company, it is not regulated like a bank and thus has significant competitive advantages. What new strategies will it pursue?

COMPETITIVE RESPONSES

Small banks view GE Capital Services as an example of unequal regulation gone bad. It operates in all 50 states, unlike independent banks that conduct business in a much smaller trade area. Through its affiliates, it offers mortgages and credit cards, which compete directly with bank products. It also provides insurance, real estate, and brokerage services not available at most banks. With its sophisticated communications and data processing network, it can process transactions at lower unit costs, a long-term competitive advantage that could force small banks to reassess their product base, customer base, and delivery system.

Although large bank holding companies and related financial services companies also recognize the competitive inequities, they are interested in forming the same types of networks. This inclination explains the extensive merger and acquisition activity across industry segments. Financial conglomerates such as Citigroup, Bank of America, ABN Amro, First Union, DeutscheBank, and American Express similarly expect to compete aggressively in most facets of consumer and commercial banking. Their preference is to continue the deregulation process along geographic and product lines.

SUMMARY

Most of the legal and regulatory differences which have historically separated various types of depository institutions are gone. Banks now compete with savings and loans, credit unions, insurance companies, and other affiliates of nationwide financial conglomerates in providing basic banking services. Most of us would not know if our depository institution was a bank, savings and loan, or credit union by the types of products and services they offer. Even though some of the same types of regulatory constraints, which separated commercial banking, investment banking, and insurance have been removed, banks do not operate on an equal footing with other nonbank firms. As a result, only the largest banks have embraced the full line of these new product powers. In fact, Citigroup is the only banking company which is a major player in all three of these areas: commercial banking, investment banking, and insurance. Many other large banking companies have, however, aggressively entered the securities business. Banks, however, are required to form a financial holding company and be regulated by the Federal Reserve System. Firms like General Electric provide all of the same basic services that Citigroup provides and GE's "banking" unit, GE Capital Services, is only 40 percent of GE's business. GE is not, however, a financial holding company.

Increased competition has arisen from financial innovation, deregulation, securitization, globalization of financial institutions and markets, and technological developments. Deregulation is the removal of regulations that limit financial institutions' activities. Financial innovation is the continual development of new products and change in market structure to circumvent regulation and meet customer needs. Securitization is the process of converting assets to marketable securities. From a bank's perspective, securitization moves assets off the balance sheet and substitutes fee income for interest income. Globalization involves the *de facto* elimination of geographic barriers to trade and financial market activity. Finally, technology has opened the door to competition from many more areas including the once sacred payments system.

Consumers and businesses benefit from lower interest rates and increased capital availability. Market participants can choose from a larger number of suppliers, which places a premium on customer service. To remain competitive, banks should identify the products with which they have a market advantage and provide personal service that distinguishes them from their competitors.

QUESTIONS

1. Many experts argue that it was not deregulation that brought about fundamental change in the banking industry — rather increases in competition from all providers of financial services. Many argue that deregulation was a response to increased competitive pressures. Outline the fundamental competitive forces of change and how this has pushed regulators and legislators to deregulate the industry.

2. What impact is securitization likely to have on the quality of assets that banks keep in their portfolios?

3. Change is always good for some participants and bad for others. Which types of banks appear best situated to gain from increased competition in the financial services arena? Which banks seem most likely to lose?

4. Describe the basic services provided by investment banks. Why are large commercial banks eager to offer investment banking services domestically?

5. Suppose that you are the president of a commercial bank in a town of 22,000 residents. There are five other banks, two savings and loans, and a credit union. Your town also has Internet access in which the residents can access services from a number of national banking organizations, and a range of discount brokerage services, insurance products, and real estate brokerage. One of the savings banks constantly pays 0.5 percent more on all deposits. Devise a strategic plan to compete against each type of institution or competitive factor. What issues will enter into the analysis?

6. What problems are likely to arise when a bank tries to securitize the following: mortgages, credit card loans, automobile loans, and small business loans?

7. Explain how the growth in commercial paper and junk bonds has affected commercial lending and yield spreads at banks.

8. Some analysts contend that the federal government plays a game of catch-up in reregulation. Bankers start the game by offering new and creative products that circumvent existing regulations. Regulators try to catch up by eliminating or rewriting old rules to reflect the new situation. Meanwhile, bankers are circumventing regulation in different areas and the process continues. Explain how offering interest on checking accounts supports this view.

9. Globalization results in more efficient financial markets. Why do some bankers fear globalization? Will globalization have a different impact on community banks than on nationwide banking organizations?

10. In what areas do captive finance companies and other finance companies compete with banks? Who has the advantage?

11. What are the basic arguments for increasing capital requirements at banks? In what ways will bank depositors, stockholders, and society in general benefit? How might each group be disadvantaged? As banks enter new lines of business such as brokerage, how much additional capital should be required? Should these new lines of business be insured by the FDIC? Why or why not?

12. Much of the intense competition in the financial services industry comes from products that are the most standardized, such as mortgages, automobile loans, money market accounts, savings accounts, and so on. These products will offer very low profit margins. If you managed a small community bank today, devise a strategy to compete in this environment.

ACTIVITIES

1. Which banks in your area seem to have best adapted to change? What criteria will you use to decide? Which nonbank financial firms compete aggressively in your area? Do they operate with any advantages or disadvantages versus banks? What about financial services available on the Internet? What portion of your financial business do you do on the Internet? How much of this business do you expect to transact on the Internet in 5, 7, 10, and 15 years?

2. How many commercial banks, savings and loans, and credit unions were there in your hometown five years ago? How many are there today? Why has the number changed? Has the range of services from the current institutions changed?

3. Do out-of-state banks have a major presence in your state and local area? Are there any foreign banks in your state? In each case, identify the strengths and weaknesses of each type of bank.

4. Many experts argue that banking has been extremely vertically integrated. Vertical integration is the degree to which a company creates all parts of its product or the degree to which it distributes and sells those products itself. It seems likely that the degree of vertical integration will fall dramatically at many banks in the future. Most banks will have to purchase Internet payment systems, mutual fund products, and investment banking products from third parties. After all, does General Motors make its own tires or purchase them? Although General Motors does produce many of the products used in the automobiles that it sells, it acts as a general contractor to produce and sell the final product. The merger between Citicorp and Travelers—Citigroup—appears to be a move toward a more vertically integrated approach to banking. Sears tried this approach once before by integrating a retail store with an investment banker (Dean Witter), a real-estate broker (Coldwell Banker), S&Ls, and insurance sales and underwriting (Allstate). This system did not appear to work as Sears has since completely divested itself of these lines of business. Do you think vertical integration will work this time? What advantages do you think the new Citigroup has that Sears did not? What about the future of smaller banks that are less vertically integrated? Do they have a future as general contractors of services? Explain.

5. Search the Internet to find web-based (virtual) banks that do not have brick and mortar branches. What products and services can a customer obtain from one of these virtual banks?

2

BANK ORGANIZATION AND REGULATION

In 1999, the U.S. Congress enacted the Financial Services Modernization Act (Gramm-Leach-Bliley Act of 1999), which dramatically altered the competitive environment for financial services firms operating in the United States. The Act generally expanded the range of services that banks could offer and lines of business that banks could enter as long as they operated with sufficient capital. Previously, domestic banks were restricted in the types of activities they could engage in within the borders of the United States. For example, banks could underwrite corporate securities outside the United States, but were not allowed to do the same domestically. Banks in other developed countries have generally been allowed to engage in these activities in their home countries as well as in the U.S. The Financial Services Modernization Act largely eliminated this differential treatment, allowed U.S. banks to enter new lines of business, and allowed other types of financial services companies to more aggressively engage in traditional banking activities.

Why were such restrictions ever imposed? More importantly, will the new regulatory environment enhance competition and benefit consumers? This chapter describes recent changes in regulation and the rationale. It also demonstrates how regulation affects the organizational structure of banking organizations and the competitive environment. The Financial Services Modernization Act was a direct result of global competitive pressures on the U.S. financial system. The great rise in the stock market during the 1990s increased the public's awareness of alternative investment vehicles. Insurance companies, investment banks, real estate firms, and other institutions could offer traditional bank services but avoid regulation as a bank. Commercial banks found themselves competing directly for funds and investments with all financial services firms, yet were at a competitive disadvantage.

———————— ■ ————————

Government agencies that regulate commercial banks have had to balance the banking system's competitiveness with general safety and soundness concerns. Historically, regulation has limited who can open, or charter, new banks and what products and services banks can offer. Imposing barriers to entry and restricting the types of activities banks can engage in clearly enhance safety and soundness, but also hinder competition. This historical approach had three drawbacks. First, it assumed that the markets for bank products, largely bank loans and deposits, could be protected and that other firms could not encroach upon these markets. Not surprisingly, investment banks, hybrid financial companies (General Electric and American Express), insurance firms, and others found ways to provide the same products as banks across different geographic markets. Second, it discriminated against U.S.-based firms versus foreign-based firms. For example, prior regulations prohibited U.S. banks from underwriting (helping businesses issue new stock or bonds) securities for firms in the U.S. In contrast, foreign banks are generally not restricted as to their domestic corporate structure and thus have long been able to circumvent U.S. restrictions on underwriting activities. Such restrictions place U.S. banks at a competitive disadvantage. Finally, historical regulation has penalized bank customers who do not have convenient access to the range of products they demand. In addition, such restrictions generally raise prices above those obtained in a purely competitive marketplace.

There are five reasons for bank regulation:

- to ensure the safety and soundness of banks and financial instruments
- to provide monetary stability
- to provide an efficient and competitive financial system
- to protect consumers from abuses by credit granting institutions, and
- to maintain the integrity of the nation's payments system.

In order to understand banks, one must understand bank regulation. Clearly, barriers that once separated banking from other activities are quickly disappearing. This creates opportunities for well-managed banks and related firms, but also puts pressure on management to perform. Managers must make decisions regarding a broad range of new issues that formerly did not affect the industry, and the decisions are increasingly complex because of changes in the economic environment, competitive pressures, and regulation. These decisions will affect the organizational structure of banks as well as the markets in which they compete with other firms.

This book focuses on commercial bank risk management. Because regulatory differences are rapidly disappearing between commercial banks, savings and loans, credit unions, and investment banks, the concepts and decision models apply generally to any of these firms and others that make loans or accept deposits. Thus, while the term *bank* serves as an abbreviation for commercial bank, the analysis encompasses the behavior of other financial institutions. The purpose of this book is to introduce and apply financial concepts to the fundamental decisions that bank managers make. It is applications-oriented, with ample reference to data and examples. Upon completing the book, the reader should understand how basic decisions are made and how decisions in one functional area of management affect decisions in other areas.

This chapter provides an overview of the banking environment by focusing on the organizational structure of the banking industry and individual banking institutions, and describing the regulatory climate in which banks operate. It initially documents how individual banks are organized to take maximum advantage of opportunities. It then summarizes what products and services banks can offer, where banks can conduct business, and what pricing restrictions apply. The final discussion introduces important regulatory issues that are currently unresolved. The material provides a useful framework for the decision analysis that follows in later chapters.

STRUCTURE OF THE BANKING INDUSTRY

The U.S. operates using a "dual banking system." Individual states as well as the federal government issue bank charters. The Office of the Comptroller of the Currency (OCC) charters *national* banks while individual state banking departments charter *state* banks and savings institutes. The Office of Thrift Supervision (OTS) charters *federal savings banks* and *savings associations*. The Federal Deposit Insurance Corporation (FDIC) insures the deposits of banks up to $100,000 per account. Bank regulation and supervision is conducted by four federal agencies (OCC, OTS, FDIC, and the Federal Reserve) as well as fifty state agencies. Although this is a complicated system, it allows for a separation of duties as well as "competition" among the various regulatory agencies to produce a safe and efficient banking system.

Credit unions represent another type of depository institution. Even though credit unions perform some of the same functions as a bank, they are cooperative nonprofit financial institutions that exist for the benefit of members. Membership in a credit union is supposedly not open to the general public. To join a credit union, one must share a "common bond" with other members. The definition of common bond, however, has expanded to incorporate a "community" and hence the differences between credit unions and banks are disappearing as well. Credit unions often operate in subsidized office space with subsidized labor and do not pay corporate or state income taxes. This tax-exempt status puts them at a competitive advantage over other banking institutions. Credit unions were first chartered at the state level in 1909. By 1934, the federal government began to charter credit unions under the Farm Credit Association, and created the National Credit Union Administration (NCUA) in 1970. A dual credit union regulatory system exists as well today as both states and the NCUA charter credit unions today.

NATIONAL VERSUS A STATE BANK CHARTER

Before issuing a new charter, the chartering agencies ensure that the (de novo) bank will have the necessary capital and management expertise to ensure soundness and allow the bank to meet the public's financial needs. The agency that charters the institution is the institution's primary regulator with primary responsibility to ensure safety and soundness of the banking system. All banks obtain FDIC deposit insurance coverage as part of the chartering process. In addition, while national banks are regulated only by federal regulatory agencies, state-chartered banks also have a primary federal regulator. The Federal Reserve is the primary federal regulator of an FDIC-insured state bank, which is a member of the Federal Reserve System, while the primary regulator of state non-Fed member banks is the FDIC. Regulatory agencies conduct periodic on-site examinations to assess a bank's condition and monitor compliance with banking laws. They issue regulations, take enforcement actions, and close banks if they fail. Exhibit 2.1 outlines the number and type of depository institutions by their charter type.

In contrast to federally regulated national banks, state-chartered banks have generally had broader powers. Many states allow securities underwriting and brokerage; real estate equity participation, development, and brokerage; and insurance underwriting and brokerage. Still, regulations for banks are more restrictive than those that apply to thrift institutions. In 1993, Wells Fargo, the seventh-largest U.S. commercial bank at the time, almost switched to a thrift charter so that it could operate under less-restrictive rules. While thrifts must maintain at least 65 percent of their assets in housing-related investments and cannot have more than 10 percent in loans to businesses, they can branch nationwide and engage in full-service

• EXHIBIT 2.1

CHARTER CLASS OF COMMERCIAL BANKS AND SAVINGS INSTITUTIONS BY THEIR PRIMARY FEDERAL REGULATOR (THOUSANDS OF DOLLARS): JUNE 2001

Charter Class	# Institutions	# Offices	Deposits*	Primary Federal Regulator
Commercial Banks	8,178	72,167	3,566,835,641	
National Charter	2,176	34,691	1,890,611,980	OCC
State Charter	6,002	37,476	1,676,223,661	
Federal Reserve Member	975	13,845	769,802,155	Fed
Federal Reserve Nonmember	5,027	23,631	906,421,506	FDIC
Savings Institutions	1,561	13,888	755,422,190	
Federal Charter Savings Associations	896	9,020	526,156,002	OTS
State Charter Savings Institutions	665	4,868	229,266,188	
FDIC-Supervised Savings Banks	520	4,325	210,542,336	FDIC
OTS-Supervised Savings Associations	145	543	18,723,852	OTS
U.S. Branches of Foreign Banks	18	18	4,069,399	
Total	9,757	86,073	4,326,327,230	

* Includes deposits in domestic offices (50 states and DC), Puerto Rico, and U.S. Territories.

underwriting and brokerage activities in insurance, real estate, and corporate instruments. Federal regulators applied pressure to convince Wells Fargo that it would not be in its best interest to switch.

UNITARY THRIFT CHARTER

A unitary thrift holding company is an institution that controls only one savings association subsidiary. Although many of the advantages of a thrift charter can be accomplished by a multithrift holding company, fewer qualifying restrictions are placed on the unitary thrift structure. With liberal branching laws, there is really no need for the multithrift charter. Non-thrift activities are essentially unrestricted when the unitary thrift meets the qualified thrift lender (QTL) test, which requires that at least 65 percent of the institution's assets be qualified thrift investments, primarily residential mortgages, and related investments.[1]

Historically there have been four advantages to a unitary thrift holding company's charter as compared to national bank charter:

- Preferential taxation
- The most liberal branching rights of all federal depository institutions
- Expanded subsidiary powers
- Virtually unlimited holding company activities

---

[1]The Economic Growth and Regulatory Paper Reduction Act of 1996 expanded the list of qualified investments to include small-business loans and increased the amount of consumer-oriented loans that can be counted as qualifying assets, effectively relaxing the QTL test. An institution that is considered a domestic building-and-loan institution under the Internal Revenue Code is also considered a qualified thrift lender under the act. See the FDIC Staff Study, "A Unified Federal Charter for Banks and Savings Associations" available on the Internet at http://www.fdic.gov/databank/bkreview/1997summ/unified.html.

The most significant disadvantage of an institution selecting a federal savings charter, rather than a national bank charter, is that there are many lending constraints. For example, nonresidential real estate may not exceed 400 percent of capital, commercial loans may not exceed 20 percent of assets with any amount in excess of 10 percent to be used for small-business loans, unsecured residential construction loans may not exceed the greater of 5 percent of assets or 100 percent of capital, and the combined total of consumer loans, commercial paper, and corporate debt securities may not exceed 35 percent of assets.

There are many non-traditional owners of thrift institutions. USAA, an AAA-rated insurance and diversified financial services institution, operates using a universal thrift charter even though it is among the nation's largest auto and home insurance companies with more than 80 subsidiaries and affiliates, including offices in Sacramento, Colorado Springs, Tampa, Seattle, Norfolk, and the Washington, D.C. area. USAA Life Insurance Company is the nation's largest direct-response provider of individual life insurance policies. USAA Investment Management Company has approximately $35 billion in assets under management and offers a family of 35 mutual funds. USAA also operates USAA Federal Savings Bank, which offers a full range of banking products including the USAA credit card, one of the top three credit card issuers in the U.S. The key point is that USAA has effectively used a thrift charter to enter lines of business historically prohibited to banks.

Two advantages of a thrift charter were recently eliminated. First, the Small Business Job Protection Act eliminated a thrift tax advantage in 1996. Prior to this Act, thrifts that met the IRS definition of a domestic building-and-loan association were allowed a tax deduction for bad debt up to 8 percent of taxable income. Today, thrifts are treated the same as banks for federal income tax purposes. The second advantage of a thrift charter was that of the most liberal branching laws of all depository institutions. Federal thrifts have long been allowed to branch interstate while state law restricted banks. This advantage was eliminated with the passage of the Riegle-Neal Interstate Banking and Branching Efficiency Act of 1994 in that banks may also now branch across state lines.

However, holders of a Federal thrift charter still have two distinct advantages. First, Federal thrifts may invest up to 3 percent of their assets in a service corporation. These service corporations may "engage in such activities reasonably related to the activities of Federal savings associations as the OTS may determine and approve." Under this liberal standard, the OTS has allowed activities not permitted national banks, such as insurance underwriting, real-estate development and real-estate management for third parties, and selling many types of insurance on an agency basis. Second, unrestricted thrift holding companies may, either directly or through their non-thrift subsidiaries, engage in all activities that do not threaten the safety and soundness of their subsidiary savings associations. There are basically no limitations on the range of activities afforded unrestricted thrift holding companies. Thus, thrift holding companies are permitted to engage in securities underwriting and dealing, real-estate investment and development, commercial and industrial enterprises, and other financial services. Some thrift holding companies have ventured into some activities not so "closely related to banking," such as the manufacture of cigarettes, containers, and furniture; owning hotels and drug stores; and providing trash collection, utilities, and advertising services.

This inequity "loophole" was closed, but not completely eliminated, with the Financial Services Modernization Act, or Gramm-Leach-Bliley Act of 1999, which prohibits *new* unitary thrift holding company charters. Although the Gramm-Leach-Bliley Act eliminated the advantages of a unitary thrift charter for new entry into the market, it allows for all existing unitary thrift charters to continue operations. It is interesting to note that the effective date prohibiting *de novo* unitary thrift holding company applications, determined retroactively, was May 4, 1999, just one day before Wal-Mart applied for a unitary thrift holding company.

COMMERCIAL BANKS, SAVINGS INSTITUTIONS, AND CREDIT UNIONS

For many years, *commercial banks* were viewed as a special type of financial organization. They were the only firms allowed to issue demand deposits and thus dominated the payments system throughout the United States. Interest-bearing checking accounts did not exist except at credit unions. Because of this status, authorities closely regulated bank operations to control deposit growth and to ensure the safety of customer deposits. Among other restrictions, government regulators required cash reserves against deposits, specified maximum interest rates banks could pay on deposits, set minimum capital requirements, and placed limits on the size of loans to borrowers. In addition to regulatory constraints, federal banking law further limited bank operations to activities closely related to banking and, in conjunction with state laws, prohibited interstate branching.

Historically, banks, savings associations, and credit unions each served a different purpose and a different market. Commercial banks mostly specialize in short-term business credit, but also make consumer loans and mortgages, and have a broad range of financial powers. Commercial banks are stock corporations whose primary purpose is to maximize shareholder wealth. Banks accept deposits in a variety of different accounts and invest these funds into loans and other financial instruments. Their corporate charters and the powers granted to them under state and federal law determines the range of their activities.

Savings institutions, savings and loan associations and savings banks, have historically specialized in real estate lending; e.g., loans for single-family homes and other residential properties. Savings associations are generally referred to as "thrifts" because they originally offered only savings or time deposits to attract funds. They have acquired a wide range of financial powers over the past two decades, and now offer checking accounts, make business and consumer loans, mortgages, and offer just virtually any other product a bank offers. Although most savings institutions are owned by shareholders ("stock" ownership), some are owned by their depositors and borrowers ("mutual" ownership). Savings institutions must maintain 65% of their assets in housing-related or other qualified assets to maintain their savings institution status. This is called the "qualified thrift lender" (QTL) test. Recent liberalization of the QTL test has allowed thrifts to use some non-housing assets to meet this requirement and in fact, many customers do not know today if their financial institution is a bank or savings institution.

The number of thrifts has declined dramatically during the last two decades. The savings and loan crisis of the 1980s forced many institutions to close or merge with others, at an extraordinary cost to the federal government. Due to liberalization of the QTL, however, there was a resurgence of interest in the thrift charter and many insurance companies, securities firms, as well as commercial firms acquired a *unitary thrift holding company* in order to own a depository institution and bypass prohibitions in the Glass Steagall Act and the Bank Holding Company Act.[2] This resurgence of interest stopped with the passage of Gramm-Leach-Bliley, which eliminated the issuance of new unitary thrift charters.

Credit unions are nonprofit institutions with an original purpose to encourage savings and provide loans within a community at low cost to their members. A "common bond" defines their members, although this common bond can be loosely defined. The members pool their funds to form the institution's deposit base and the members own and control the institution. Credit unions accept deposits in a variety of forms. All credit unions offer savings accounts or time deposits, while the larger institutions also offer checking and money market accounts. Credit unions have similarly expanded the scope of products and activities they

---

[2]Savings and loan associations and mutual savings banks are designated as thrift institutions. Non-banking firms have entered banking by obtaining a unitary thrift charter that allows them to operate a federal savings bank. Included in this group are Merrill Lynch, GE, State Farm, and many insurance companies.

offer to include almost anything a bank or savings association offers, including making home loans, issuing credit cards, and even making some commercial loans. Credit unions are exempt from federal taxation and sometimes receive subsidies, in the form of free space or supplies, from their sponsoring organizations. Although credit unions tend to be much smaller than banks or savings associations, there are several very large credit unions. Exhibit 2.2 lists the largest commercial banks, savings institutions, and credit unions as of the end of 2001.

It is fundamentally inequitable that nonbank financial institutions can offer commercial banking services, ranging from transactions accounts to commercial and consumer loans in addition to their own basic services, yet banks are precluded from offering services in the nonbank firms' primary lines of business. Full-line insurance companies and investment banks own limited service commercial banks but banks cannot own full-line insurance companies and full-service brokerage houses.[3] Commercial banks are constantly pushing the regulators to expand the list of nonbank activities allowed and the flexibility to enter the businesses with short notice.

Since 1980, all depository institutions have been able to make commercial loans, issue credit cards, establish trust departments, and enter other related lines of business. Just as significantly, the distinction between these depository institutions and other financial services firms has faded. Large brokerage houses, insurance companies, finance companies, and retailers offer transactions accounts, credit cards, and other loans that compete directly with products offered by depository institutions. Many of these firms own commercial banks and thrift institutions. Banks, on the other hand, have entered the securities business by buying brokerages or investment banks. Examples include the following acquisitions: Bankers Trust–Alex Brown, now Deutsche Bank; NationsBank–Montgomery Securities, now Bank of America; First Union–Wheat First; Bank of America–Robertson Stephens; and Regions Financial Corp — Morgan Keegan Inc. Citigroup, the largest U.S. depository institution, represents the combination of Citibank and the Travelers Insurance Company.[4]

THE ROLE OF COMMERCIAL BANKS IN THE ECONOMY

Commercial banks play an important role in facilitating economic growth. On a macroeconomic level, they represent the primary conduit of Federal Reserve monetary policy. Bank deposits represent the most liquid form of money such that the Federal Reserve System's efforts to control the nation's money supply and level of aggregate economic activity is accomplished by changing the availability of credit at banks. On a microeconomic level, commercial banks represent the primary source of credit to most small businesses and many individuals. A community's vitality typically reflects the strength of its major financial institutions and the innovative character of its business leaders.

While the economic role of commercial banks has varied little over time, the nature of commercial banks and competing financial institutions is constantly changing. Savings and loans, credit unions, brokerage firms, insurance companies, and general retail stores now offer products and services traditionally associated only with commercial banks. Commercial banks, in turn, offer a variety of insurance, real estate, and investment banking services they were once denied. The term *bank* today refers as much to the range of services traditionally offered by depository institutions as to a specific type of institution.

---

[3]For example, Prudential owns a securities firm (Prudential Investment), a bank (Prudential Bank and Trust Co., and a property firm (Prudential Real Estate). Merrill Lynch owns a bank (ML Bank and Trust).

[4]In 1998, Bank of America sold Robertson Stephens just prior to the completion of the merger with NationsBank. In 2002, Citigroup started the process to sell a portion of its ownership in its Travelers subsidiary.

· EXHIBIT 2.2

THE LARGEST COMMERCIAL BANKS, SAVINGS ASSOCIATIONS, AND CREDIT
UNIONS, 2001 (THOUSANDS OF DOLLARS)

A. Largest Federally Chartered Commercial Banks

Rank	Name	State	Total Assets	Total Loans	Total Deposits	Total Equity	Equity to Assets
1	Bank of America NA	NC	551,691,000	314,167,000	391,543,000	52,624,000	9.54%
2	Citibank NA	NY	452,343,000	284,809,000	306,923,000	37,623,000	8.32%
3	First Union NB	NC	232,785,000	123,754,000	147,749,000	16,133,000	6.93%
4	Fleet NA Bk	RI	187,949,000	126,301,000	132,464,000	19,012,000	10.12%
5	US Bk NA	OH	166,949,055	115,108,238	108,364,026	18,449,335	11.05%
6	Bank One NA	IL	161,022,572	83,639,674	107,377,268	10,990,222	6.83%
7	Wells Fargo Bk NA	CA	140,675,000	95,264,000	79,077,000	16,186,000	11.51%
8	Wachovia Bk NA	NC	71,555,121	46,996,841	46,311,053	13,670,966	19.11%
9	Keybank NA	OH	71,526,246	56,410,074	42,731,060	4,878,880	6.82%
10	PNC Bk NA	PA	62,609,780	40,452,019	46,385,132	4,887,661	7.81%

B. Largest State Chartered Commercial Banks

Rank	Name	State	Total Assets	Total Loans	Total Deposits	Total Equity	Equity to Assets
1	J.P. Morgan Chase Bk	NY	537,826,000	178,169,000	280,473,000	33,273,000	6.19%
2	Suntrust Bk	GA	102,377,306	73,515,248	67,995,077	8,687,049	8.49%
3	HSBC Bank USA	NY	84,230,380	40,801,836	58,220,243	6,898,796	8.19%
4	Bank of New York	NY	78,018,745	37,309,076	55,810,439	6,466,422	8.29%
5	Merrill Lynch Bk USA	UT	66,092,639	12,464,394	59,954,429	3,551,022	5.37%
6	State Street B&TC	MA	65,409,590	5,979,937	38,855,475	4,187,956	6.40%
7	Branch Bkg&TC	NC	54,700,008	35,731,083	32,103,069	4,742,168	8.67%
8	Southtrust Bk	AL	48,849,559	34,249,117	32,965,152	4,165,712	8.53%
9	Bankers Trust Co	NY	42,678,000	12,804,000	21,423,000	6,822,000	15.98%
10	Regions Bank	AL	42,001,585	31,508,932	31,536,453	3,242,973	7.72%

C. Largest Savings Institutions

Rank	Name		State	Total Assets	Total Loans	Total Deposits	Total Equity	Equity to Assets
1	Washington Mutual Bank, FA	S&L	CA	206,571,184	92,054,318	132,506,691	12,562,515	6.08%
2	World Svgs Bk, FSB	S&L	CA	58,443,622	34,651,936	41,505,114	4,701,922	8.05%
3	California Federal Bank	S&L	CA	56,555,539	25,906,314	42,726,581	4,124,022	7.29%
4	Charter One Bank, SSB	S&L	OH	38,165,417	25,222,939	26,104,926	2,343,285	6.14%
5	Sovereign Bank	S&L	PA	35,631,606	22,378,274	20,994,865	3,642,986	10.22%
6	Citibank, FSB	S&L	CA	31,868,249	22,679,455	21,041,103	2,707,701	8.50%
7	Washington MSB	SB	WA	31,639,000	16,806,000	19,981,000	2,044,000	6.46%
8	Dime Savings Bank of NY	S&L	NY	27,971,169	15,188,948	22,092,378	2,384,304	8.52%
9	Astoria FS&LA	S&L	NY	22,463,688	11,144,443	12,266,238	1,506,548	6.71%

D. Largest Credit Unions

Rank	Name	State	Total Assets	Total Loans	Total Deposits	Total Equity	Equity to Assets
1	U.S. Central Credit Union	KS	26,217,598	1,264,461	20,962,788	1,428,725	5.45%
2	Western Corporate	CA	12,446,130	266,338	10,108,679	820,696	6.59%
3	Navy	VA	11,188,619	8,590,064	9,075,588	1,365,675	12.21%
4	State Employees'	NC	6,301,035	5,207,140	5,645,651	488,698	7.76%
5	Boeing Employees'	WA	3,385,160	1,701,495	2,610,982	276,596	8.17%
6	Southwest Corporate	TX	3,313,673	145,774	2,594,040	313,924	9.47%
7	Pentagon	VA	3,243,137	2,406,415	2,882,056	338,609	10.44%
8	Mid-States Corporate	IL	2,987,051	159,173	2,574,479	259,016	8.67%
9	United Airlines Employees'	IL	2,852,330	1,354,201	2,498,722	341,144	11.96%
10	American Airlines	TX	2,583,594	1,269,927	2,302,387	229,820	8.90%

SOURCE: FDIC, FFIEC, Federal Reserve, and National Credit Union Administration.

Note: S&L = Savings and Loan and SB = Savings Bank

▪ EXHIBIT 2.3

NUMBER AND TOTAL ASSETS OF VARIOUS DEPOSITORY INSTITUTIONS: 1970–2001

	1970	1980	1989	1993	1997	2001*	Annual Growth Rate 1980–2001*
Commercial Banks							
Number	13,550	14,163	12,410	10,957	9,144	8,080	−1.65%
Total Assets	$517.40**	$1,484.60	$3,231.10	$3,705.90	$5,014.90	$6,569.24	8.54%
(% of Total Assets)	66.0%	63.6%	65.3%	73.9%	78.5%	78.7%	
Thrift Institutions[a]							
Number	5,669	4,594	3,011	2,327	1,779	1,533	−4.13%
Total Assets	$249.50	$783.60	$1,516.50	$1,024.50	$1,026.20	$1,299.01	5.47%
(% of Total Assets)	31.8%	33.6%	30.7%	20.4%	16.1%	15.6%	
Credit Unions*							
Number	23,819	21,930	15,205	12,720	11,238	10,145	−2.76%
Total Assets	$17.60	$67.30	$199.70	$283.50	$351.17	$477.21	11.43%
(% of Total Assets)	2.2%	2.9%	4.0%	5.7%	5.5%	5.7%	

*Credit Union data for 2001 is as of June 2001, all other data as of December 2001.

Monetary amounts are in billions of dollars.

[a]Includes savings and loan associations and mutual savings banks.

SOURCE: FDIC (http://www.fdic.gov/) and National Credit Union Administration (http://www.ncua.gov/).

Exhibit 2.3 documents changes in the number of institutions and total assets controlled by commercial banks, savings banks, and credit unions from 1970 through 2001. During the 30 years, commercial banks' share of depository institution assets varied from around 64 percent in the early 1980s, to 79 percent by 2001. This came at the expense of thrift institutions whose share dropped to 15.6 percent in 2001, while credit unions increased their share from just over 2 percent to 5.7 percent. Note the sharp drop in number of all institutions. This consolidation reflects the combined impact of failures, mergers, and acquisitions. The banking industry is now comprised of larger firms that control an increased share of loans and deposits, with the number of competitors shrinking rapidly.

These figures disguise the fact that there has been a fundamental shift in the structure of financial institutions over the past two decades. In particular, depository institutions' share of U.S. financial assets has systematically declined relative to assets held by other financial intermediaries. Exhibit 2.4 documents the shift from 1970 to 2001. During the 30 years, banks, savings and loans, and credit unions decreased their share from 61 percent to less than 31 percent. Private pension and state and local government retirement funds, mutual funds, mortgage related (mortgage assets and real estate investment trusts) and other institutions (which include securities brokers and dealers, and issuers of securitized assets) evidenced the greatest growth. This graph is dramatic evidence of the competition that depository institutions face from nonbank institutions that compete in the same general product lines, but are less regulated. The decline in banks' market share is overstated, however, because many banks strategically choose to move business off-balance sheet via securitization. When market share is measured in terms of revenues, banks have maintained their historical market share.

CONSOLIDATIONS, NEW CHARTERS AND BANK FAILURES

Structural changes within the commercial banking industry are demonstrated in Exhibit 2.5. Note the sharp increase in the number of failed banks from 1980 through 1988 with a

■ EXHIBIT 2.4

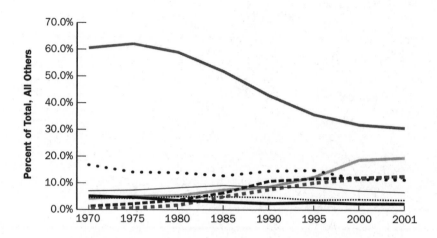

PERCENTAGE DISTRIBUTION OF U.S. FINANCIAL ASSETS HELD BY VARIOUS FINANCIAL INSTITUTIONS, 1970–2001

	Dec-70	Dec-75	Dec-80	Dec-85	Dec-90	Dec-95	Dec-00	Dec-01
▬▬ Monetary Authority	5.1%	4.6%	3.5%	2.9%	2.4%	2.8%	2.4%	2.4%
• • • • Insurance Companies	16.8%	14.1%	13.9%	12.8%	14.6%	14.9%	11.6%	11.4%
─── Pension and Retirement Funds	7.0%	7.3%	8.2%	9.1%	8.6%	8.4%	7.2%	6.7%
▪▪▪▪▪ Mutual Funds	0.6%	0.6%	1.7%	4.9%	7.6%	10.2%	11.8%	12.5%
·········· Finance Companies	4.5%	4.2%	4.9%	4.9%	4.7%	3.8%	4.0%	3.8%
▬ ▬ ▬ Mortgage Related	1.3%	2.2%	3.6%	6.3%	10.8%	11.8%	12.2%	12.8%
─── Other	4.2%	4.9%	5.3%	7.4%	8.6%	12.4%	18.8%	19.6%
▬▬▬ Depository Institutions	60.5%	62.1%	58.9%	51.8%	42.8%	35.7%	31.9%	30.7%

Year

SOURCE: Flow of Funds Accounts, Board of Governors of the Federal Reserve System. Available on the Internet at http://www.federalreserve.gov/ (http://www.federalreserve.gov/releases/).

gradual decrease to zero failures in 1996, only two in 1998 and 4 in 2001. The data for the 1980s period actually understates the true number of failures because regulators often arranged mergers during this period rather than simply close failed banks and savings and loans. The sharp increase in failures during this period coincides with economic problems throughout various sectors of the U.S. economy ranging from agriculture to energy to real estate. As regional economies faltered, problem loans grew at banks and thrifts that were overextended and subsequent losses forced closings. New charters representing the start-up of a new bank's operations declined from 1984 to 1994, increased through 1998, and then decreased through 2001.

The major force behind consolidation has been mergers and acquisitions in which existing banks combine operations in order to cut costs, improve profitability, and increase their competitive position. Bankers who either lose their jobs in a merger or choose not to work for a large banking organization often find investors to put up the capital needed to start a new bank. Both mergers and new charters slowed dramatically in late 1998 as a result of a 25 percent fall in stock values at the largest bank holding companies and in 2001 with the continuing market decline. However, the merger trend will continue, although at a slower pace, with nationwide branching and banking now allowed.

· EXHIBIT 2.5

STRUCTURAL CHANGES AMONG FDIC-INSURED COMMERCIAL BANKS, 1980–2001

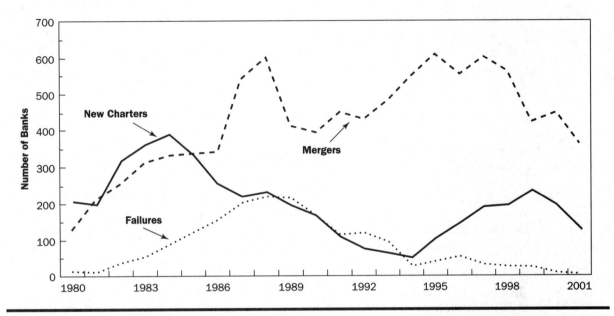

SOURCE: The FDIC Quarterly Banking Profile, FDIC, Fourth Quarter 2001. Available on the Internet at http://www.fdic.gov/ (http://www2.fdic.gov/qbp/).

THE CENTRAL BANK

Congress created the Federal Reserve System (Fed) in 1913 to serve as the central bank of the United States and to provide the nation with a safe, flexible, and more stable monetary and financial system. The Fed's role in banking and the economy has expanded over the years, but its primary focus has remained the same. The Fed's three fundamental functions are:

1. conduct the nation's monetary policy,
2. provide and maintain an effective and efficient payments system, and
3. supervise and regulate banking operations.

All three roles have a similar purpose, that of maintaining monetary and economic stability and prosperity. The Federal Reserve System is a decentralized central bank, with Reserve Banks and branches in 12 districts across the country. The Fed is coordinated by a Board of Governors in Washington, D.C., whose members are appointed by the President of the United States and confirmed by the Senate for staggered 14-year terms. The seven members of the Board of Governors are the main governing body of the Fed charged with overseeing the 12 District Reserve Banks and with helping implement national monetary policy.

MONETARY POLICY. The Fed conducts monetary policy through actions designed to influence the supply of money and credit in order to promote price stability and long-term sustainable economic growth. There are three distinct monetary policy tools: open market operations, changes in the discount rate, and changes in the required reserve ratio. *Open market operations* are conducted by the Federal Reserve Bank of New York under the direction of the Federal Open Market Committee (FOMC). The sale or purchase of U.S. government securities in the "open market" or secondary market is the Federal Reserve's most flexible means of carrying out its policy objectives. Through these transactions carried out daily, the Fed can adjust the level of reserves in the banking system and thereby influence short-term interest rates and the growth of the money supply. Fed open market purchases of securities increase liquidity, hence reserves in the banking system, by increasing bank deposit balances at the Fed. Fed open market sales of securities decrease bank reserves and liquidity by lowering deposit balances at the Fed.

Banks can borrow deposit balances, or required reserves, directly from Federal Reserve Banks with the discount rate representing the interest rate that banks pay. The Fed directly controls the discount rate, which remains fixed until the Fed formally announces a change. *Changes in the discount rate* directly affect the cost of reserve borrowing. When the Fed raises the discount rate, it discourages borrowing by making it more expensive. Fed decreases in the discount rate make borrowing less expensive. Still, the Fed changes the discount rate primarily to signal future policy toward monetary ease or tightness rather than to change bank borrowing activity. Changes in the discount rate are formally announced and trumpeted among the financial press so that market participants recognize that the Fed will likely be adding liquidity or taking liquidity out of the banking system in the future.

Changes in reserve requirements directly affect the amount of legal required reserves that banks are required to hold as an asset and thus change the amount of funds a bank can lend out. For example, a required reserve ratio of 10 percent means that a bank with $100 in demand deposit liabilities outstanding must hold $10 in legal required reserves in support of these deposits. The bank can thus lend only 90 percent of its demand deposit liabilities (DDAs). When the Fed increases (decreases) reserve requirements, it formally increases (decreases) the required reserve ratio, which directly reduces (raises) the amount of money a bank can lend per dollar of DDAs. Thus, lower reserve requirements increase bank liquidity and lending capacity while higher reserve requirements decrease bank liquidity and lending capacity.

DEPOSIT INSURANCE

The Federal Deposit Insurance Corporation (FDIC) insures the deposits of banks up to a maximum of $100,000 per account holder. Under a similar arrangement, almost all credit unions are insured by the National Credit Union Share Insurance Fund (NCUSIF), which is controlled by the NCUA. The FDIC was created by the Banking Act of 1933 in response to the large number of bank failures that followed the stock market crash of 1929. Originally the FDIC insured deposits up to $5,000. All states require newly-chartered state banks to join the FDIC and credit unions to join NCUSIF before they can accept deposits from the public. Under the 1991 Federal Deposit Insurance Corporation Improvement Act (FDICIA), both state-chartered and national banks must apply to the FDIC for deposit insurance. Previously, national banks had received insurance automatically with their new charters.

Banks find insured deposits very attractive. With FDIC insurance, depositors with less than $100,000 per qualifying account are assured that the federal government will guarantee the funds in the event that the bank fails. Deposit customers are thus willing to accept interest rates on insured deposits that are below the rates that banks would have to pay without FDIC insurance. Such deposits are generally more stable in that they don't leave the bank as quickly when the economic climate changes or when a bank's financial condition changes. Banks pay premiums for insured deposits depending on the size of the FDIC's insurance reserve and the perceived quality of the bank. As of the end of 2001, however, the FDIC insurance reserve was large enough that most banks did not pay insurance premiums.

The FDIC also acts as the primary federal regulator of state-chartered banks that do not belong to the Federal Reserve System. State banks who are members of the Federal Reserve System have that agency for their primary federal regulator. The FDIC cooperates with state banking departments to supervise and examine these banks, and has considerable authority to intervene and prevent unsafe and unsound banking practices. The FDIC also has backup examination and regulatory authority over national and Fed-member banks.

The FDIC is also the receiver of failed institutions. The FDIC declares banks and savings associations insolvent and handles failed institutions by either liquidating them or selling the institutions to redeem insured deposits.

ORGANIZATIONAL FORM OF THE BANKING INDUSTRY

The organizational structure of banking has changed significantly over the past two decades. Still, the pace of change increased dramatically in the later half of the 1990s due primarily to the impact of interstate branching, the Federal Reserve System's relaxation of securities powers restrictions using a clause in the Glass-Steagall Act, and most recently with the Gramm-Leach-Bliley Act of 1999. Banks can now branch across state lines and acquire insurance and securities firms by forming a Financial Holding Company under the provisions of Gramm-Leach-Bliley.

Legally, commercial banks are classified either as *unit banks* with all operations housed in a single office or *branch banks* with multiple offices. Prior to the enactment of the Riegle-Neal Interstate Banking and Branching Efficiency Act of 1994, which allows nationwide interstate branch banking, state law determined the extent to which commercial banks could branch.

Any organization that owns controlling interest in one or more commercial banks is a *bank holding company* (BHC). Control is defined as ownership or indirect control via the power to vote more than 25 percent of the voting shares in a bank. Prior to the enactment of interstate branching, the primary motivation behind forming a bank holding company was to circumvent restrictions regarding branching and the products and services that banks can offer. Today, the primary motive is to broaden the scope of products the bank can offer.

Unit versus Branch Banking

The current structure of the commercial banking system has been heavily influenced by historical regulations which prevented branching to one degree or another. One of the primary reasons the number of banks has declined more than 40 percent since the mid-1980s is the relaxation of branching restrictions provided by Riegle-Neal Interstate Banking and Branching Efficiency Act of 1994.[5] Exhibit 2.6 demonstrates that since the mid 1980s, the number of banks has fallen over 40 percent while the number of branches has increased over 40 percent. The true impact of the relaxation of interstate branching restrictions can be seen in Exhibit 2.7. The number of interstate branches increased dramatically after interstate branching became fully effective in 1997.

Branch banking was controlled by the McFadden Act of 1927 and later amendments which allow national banks to establish branches only to the same degree as states permit state banks to branch. States originally limited branches to help retain deposits in local communities and to provide local bank ownership and management. The fear was that large banks in metropolitan areas with branches would take deposits out of rural areas to lend in the bigger cities. Branching restrictions presumably increased credit availability in these rural areas, especially for small businesses and farmers. They also prevented a few large banks from gaining too much market power, in which case they could presumably charge higher interest rates and provide second-rate services. Most experts have analyzed the arguments against branches and concluded that they are generally unsupported.[6]

---

[5]Even though the act was passed in 1994, it did not go into effect until 1995, and was not fully effective until 1997.
[6]See Evanoff and Fortier, 1986.

· EXHIBIT 2.6

CHANGES IN THE NUMBER OF BANKS AND BANK BRANCHES, 1960–2001*

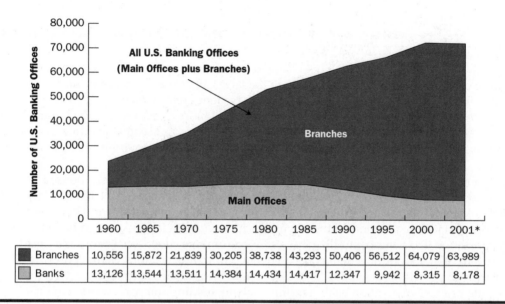

	1960	1965	1970	1975	1980	1985	1990	1995	2000	2001*
■ Branches	10,556	15,872	21,839	30,205	38,738	43,293	50,406	56,512	64,079	63,989
□ Banks	13,126	13,544	13,511	14,384	14,434	14,417	12,347	9,942	8,315	8,178

*Data for 2001 is as of June 2001.

SOURCE: FDIC / OTS Summary of Deposits (http://www.fdic.gov/).

In 1961 for example, 16 states prohibited branches, 15 states allowed them in a limited geographic area, such as the city or county where the main office was located, and 19 states permitted statewide branching. At year-end 2001, all states allowed interstate branching. As might be expected, states that limited branching had larger numbers of small banks because they operated in limited geographic markets and were less able to attract deposits. Even the largest banks suffered because they were unable to adequately grow their consumer deposit base and their operating costs were artificially high. Consider the situation in Texas, which converted from unit banking to limited branching in 1987. In 1981, there were more than 1,800 distinct commercial banks in the state. By the end of year 2001, there were just 700 independent banks.

Unit banks each have their own board of directors, a complete staff of officers, and separate documents and technology for conducting business. Clearly, operating expenses are higher for the parent company that owns and operates multiple independent banks than they would be if the parent chose to operate these banks as branches of a single "lead" bank. Obviously, the relaxation in branching restrictions and economic efficiencies is a primary motivating factor for a bank to form a bank holding company.

Risk in the banking industry is considered higher with restrictive branching because individual banks are less diversified and more prone to problems if depositors withdraw their funds en masse. Not surprisingly, states with the highest bank failure rates historically restricted branching. Branching generally reduces the number of competitors, lowers expenses, allows greater asset diversification, and expands each bank's consumer deposit base reducing the likelihood of a run on deposits. Each of these factors decreases the chances of failure, everything else being equal.

· EXHIBIT 2.7

THE NUMBER OF INTERSTATE BRANCHES OPERATED BY FDIC-INSURED COMMERCIAL BANKS AND SAVINGS INSTITUTIONS, 1994–2001.

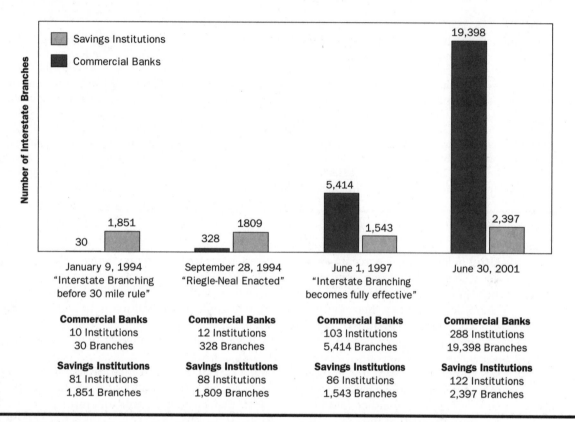

	January 9, 1994 "Interstate Branching before 30 mile rule"	September 28, 1994 "Riegle-Neal Enacted"	June 1, 1997 "Interstate Branching becomes fully effective"	June 30, 2001
Commercial Banks	10 Institutions 30 Branches	12 Institutions 328 Branches	103 Institutions 5,414 Branches	288 Institutions 19,398 Branches
Savings Institutions	81 Institutions 1,851 Branches	88 Institutions 1,809 Branches	86 Institutions 1,543 Branches	122 Institutions 2,397 Branches

SOURCE: FDIC, Summary of Deposits, June 2001, http://www.fdic.gov/ (http://www2.fdic.gov/sod/).

BANK HOLDING COMPANIES

A bank holding company is essentially a shell organization that owns and manages subsidiary firms. The holding company obtains financing from stockholders and creditors and uses the proceeds to buy stock in other companies, make loans, and purchase securities. The holding company is labeled the *parent* organization and the operating entities are the *subsidiaries*. If the parent owns at least 80 percent of a subsidiary's stock, it files a consolidated tax return.

The Bank Holding Company Act of 1956 assigned regulatory responsibility to the Federal Reserve for these companies, while leaving the supervision of banks within holding companies in the hands of their traditional regulators. The Gramm-Leach-Bliley Act also gave regulatory responsibility over *Financial Holding Companies* to the Federal Reserve. Like commercial banks, bank holding companies are heavily regulated by states and the federal government. The Bank Holding Company Act stipulates that the Board of Governors of the Federal Reserve System must approve all holding company formations and acquisitions. Approval is normally granted unless there is evidence that the acquisition will substantially lessen competition in the local banking market. The Federal Reserve examines ownership or

AT&T's UNIVERSAL CARD

In 1990, AT&T entered the bank credit card business in a big way. From scratch, it developed a bank credit card base that numbered 4.5 million accounts by the end of the year, enough to place it among the top 10 card issuers. AT&T, however, is neither a bank nor a bank holding company and thus avoids regulation by banking regulators. It can thus conduct business anywhere management chooses and bank regulators cannot restrict its business activity in nonbanking areas.

AT&T accomplished this through an ingenious arrangement with Universal Bank, a bank subsidiary of Synovus Financial Corp. AT&T advertises a Visa and MasterCard that allow customers to charge long-distance telephone calls as well as make normal credit card purchases. The cards are formally issued by Universal Bank, hence the MasterCard or Visa logo. By agreement, another subsidiary processes all transactions and bills the credit card holders. Universal bank then sells the credit card receivables to AT&T. The cards are attractive for several reasons. With the Visa and MasterCard logo, customers can use cards anywhere that other bankcards qualify. In addition, AT&T discounts telephone calls authorized with the card, offers 90-day insurance coverage of purchases, and does not charge an annual fee for use of the card, as many banks do.

control of less than 25 percent on a case-by-case basis to determine whether effective control exists. One-bank holding companies (OBHCs) control only one bank and typically arise when the owners of an existing bank exchange their shares for stock in the holding company. The holding company then acquires the original bank stock. Multibank holding companies (MBHCs) control at least two commercial banks.

Large organizations generally form OBHCs or a small number of banks in an MBHC because they want to control a bank and be able to provide traditional banking services, but more importantly want to combine the bank's capabilities with their financial activities in order to better compete nationwide. The change in interstate branching laws has meant that many MBHCs have either folded or will fold their separate banks operating across state lines into a branch of the main bank and thus eliminate the various independent banking operations. NationsBank (now Bank of America), for example, changed NationsBank Texas from being a separate bank into a branch of the North Carolina bank. Typically, however, the largest banks do not form an OBHC, but rather operate a small number of banks in an MBHC. Small organizations often form OBHCs because the owners can realize tax benefits and gain better access to funds via the capital markets. Many large organizations operate MBHCs to get the benefits from having charters in states with more relaxed corporate and usury laws and to control limited purposes banks, such as credit card banks. For example, many large MBHCs have a Delaware bank charter due to that state's corporate and usury law advantages.

Under current regulation, bank holding companies (BHCs) can acquire nonbank subsidiaries that offer products and services closely related to banking. This presumably limits speculation and thus overall risk. Many insurance companies, finance companies, and general retail firms have formed OBHCs to operate banks as part of their financial services efforts. In 1990, AT&T took the concept one step further by offering bank credit card services but avoiding regulation as an OBHC (see Contemporary Issues: AT&T's Universal Card).

The specific organizational form, permissible activities, and stream of cash flows between a holding company and its subsidiaries are described in the following sections. Subsequent sections document regulatory restrictions regarding bank products offered, geographic markets served, and pricing.

FINANCIAL HOLDING COMPANIES. The Glass-Steagall Act effectively separated commercial banking from investment banking but left open the possibility of banks engaging in investment banking activities through a Section 20 affiliate so long as the bank was not "principally engaged" in these activities. In 1987, commercial banks received permission from the Federal Reserve to underwrite and deal in securities and five banks quickly set up the necessary Section 20 subsidiaries.[7] At the beginning of 1998, there were 45 Section 20 companies. The Fed resolved the issue of "principally engaged" initially by allowing banks to earn only 5 percent of the revenue in their securities affiliates. This was raised to 10 percent in 1989 and to 25 percent in March of 1997. Pursuant to the Securities Act of 1933 and the Securities Exchange Act of 1934, these so-called Section 20 subsidiaries were required to register with the SEC as broker-dealers and are subject to all the rules applicable to broker-dealers. In addition, transactions between insured depository institutions and their Section 20 affiliates are restricted by sections 23A and 23B of the Federal Reserve Act.

The Gramm-Leach-Bliley Act of 1999 repealed the restrictions on banks affiliating with securities firms under the Glass-Steagall Act and modified portions of the Bank Holding Company Act to allow affiliations between banks and insurance underwriters. While preserving authority of states to regulate insurance, the act prohibited state actions that have the effect of preventing bank-affiliated firms from selling insurance on an equal basis with other insurance agents. The law created a new financial holding company, which was authorized to engage in: underwriting and selling insurance and securities, conducting both commercial and merchant banking, investing in and developing real estate, and other "complementary activities."

Financial holding companies (FHC) are distinct entities from bank holding companies (BHC). A company can form a BHC, an FHC, or both. The primary advantage to forming an FHC is that the entity can engage in a wide range of financial activities not permitted in the bank or in a BHC. Some of these activities include: insurance and securities underwriting and agency activities, merchant banking, and insurance company portfolio investment activities. Activities that are "complementary" to financial activities also are authorized. The primary disadvantage to forming an FHC, or converting a BHC to an FHC, is that the Fed may not permit a company to form an FHC if any one of its insured depository institution subsidiaries is not well capitalized and well managed, or did not receive at least a satisfactory rating in its most recent CRA exam. Most importantly, if any one of the insured depository institutions or affiliates of an FHC received less than a satisfactory rating in its most recent CRA exam, the appropriate Federal banking agency may not approve any additional new activities or acquisitions under the authorities granted under the act.

An FHC can own a bank or BHC or a thrift or thrift holding company. Each of these companies owns subsidiaries, while the parent financial holding company also owns other subsidiaries directly. The structure is similar to that of a bank holding company's relationship to its subsidiaries but there is one more layer of management and thus control. As commercial banks consolidate with other financial institutions, both domestically and abroad, this type of organization is expected to become more prevalent. Alternatively, we may see nonfinancial companies affiliate with banks in this type of structure. Exhibit 2.8 demonstrates a general form of an FHC in which a BHC and thrift holding company are owned by an FHC. Each of these holding companies owns subsidiaries, while the parent FHC also owns subsidiaries.

---

[7]The first five Section 20s were established by Bankers Trust New York Corp., Chase Manhattan Corp., Citicorp, J.P. Morgan & Co., and PNC Financial Corp.

ORGANIZATIONAL STRUCTURE OF FINANCIAL SERVICES COMPANY

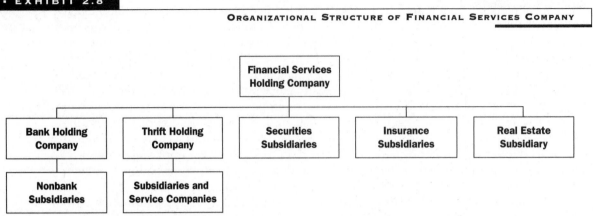

NONBANK ACTIVITIES PERMITTED BANK HOLDING COMPANIES. The Fed similarly regulates allowable nonbank activities that are "closely related to banking" in which bank holding companies may acquire subsidiaries. Restrictions came about for three reasons. First, it was feared that large financial conglomerates would control the financial system because they would have a competitive advantage. Second, there was concern that banks would require customers to buy nonbank services in order to obtain loans. Third, some critics simply did not believe that bank holding companies should engage in businesses that were not allowed banks because these businesses were less regulated and thus relatively risky.

Under amendments to the Bank Holding Company Act of 1956, the Federal Reserve allows banks to offer a wide range of services "closely related to banking" anywhere in the United States. Most of these activities relate to the extension of specific types of loans, underwriting and brokerage services, consulting services, general management services, and data processing. The largest bank holding companies must report to the Federal Reserve annually regarding the performance of their nonbank subsidiaries. They classify each subsidiary into one of several categories based on its primary activity. While the bulk of assets are concentrated in credit services, leasing, and securities brokerage, a large number of holding companies engage in insurance underwriting and operate insurance agencies. Under current law, however, national banks can underwrite only credit life insurance, provide financial guarantees on securities offerings, and sell annuities except in towns of less than 5,000. National banks can offer a wide range of insurance products in smaller towns.[8] Although the Gramm-Leach-Bliley Act specifically prohibits national banks, not currently engaged in underwriting or sale of title insurance from commencing that activity, it allows sales activities by banks in states that specifically authorize such sales for state banks, but only on the same conditions. The act also allows national bank *subsidiaries* to sell all types of insurance including title insurance and affiliates may underwrite or sell all types of insurance including title insurance.

Interestingly, the merger between Citicorp and Travelers that created Citigroup was not completely permissible at the time the merger was approved. Prior to the passage of the Gramm-Leach-Bliley Act, Citigroup would have had between two and five years to divest

---

[8]Some states permit state-chartered banks to underwrite additional types of insurance and banks in smaller communities can sell additional types of insurance.

ORGANIZATIONAL STRUCTURE OF BANK HOLDING COMPANIES

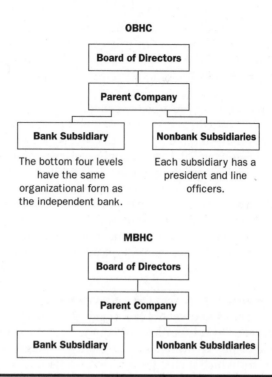

OBHC

Board of Directors

Parent Company

Bank Subsidiary	Nonbank Subsidiaries
The bottom four levels have the same organizational form as the independent bank.	Each subsidiary has a president and line officers.

MBHC

Board of Directors

Parent Company

Bank Subsidiary	Nonbank Subsidiaries

itself of Travelers' insurance underwriting. Citigroup formed a financial holding company under the provisions of the Gramm-Leach-Bliley Act and formed its integrated financial services company engaged in investment services, asset management, life insurance and property casualty insurance, and consumer lending. Its operating companies include Salomon Smith Barney, Salomon Smith Barney Asset Management, Travelers Life & Annuity, Primerica Financial Services, Travelers Property Casualty Corp., and Commercial Credit. Citigroup with all entities engaged in a wide range of businesses throughout the world.

According to federal regulation, some activities are expressly denied. Banks have long been able to underwrite federal debt securities and certain types of municipal bonds. However, from the passage of the Glass-Steagall Act in 1933 through 1987, banks could not underwrite corporate debt and equity in the U.S. In 1987, however, the Federal Reserve authorized selected "well capitalized" banks to underwrite corporate debt and corporate stock.

ORGANIZATIONAL STRUCTURE OF A BANK HOLDING COMPANY. Exhibit 2.9 outlines the simple organizational structure of both an OBHC and an MBHC. Consider first the OBHC. At the top is the board of directors for the parent organization that owns controlling interest in the subsidiaries. This board operates much like the board for an independent bank, except that its responsibilities now extend to all lines of business in which the entire organization is involved. In an OBHC the subsidiary bank normally operates like an independent bank. The only difference is that business decisions must now be reconciled with the objectives and decisions associated with the nonbank subsidiaries. Bank officers are represented on the board as are officers of the nonbank subsidiaries. In general, nonbank firms have fewer senior officers than banks.

The MBHC structure differs slightly. The substantive difference is that the parent corporation owns more than one commercial bank subsidiary. Prior to the advent of interstate banking, this enabled the banking organization to compete in different geographic markets. Even within this structure, operating styles may vary. Some MBHCs operate as closely knit units with the management of each subsidiary bank reporting daily to key personnel either at the lead bank or the parent company. In this case the subsidiaries are effectively branches. Important decisions must be approved by authorities outside the local community such that local bank officers have only limited autonomy. Local bank loan officers, for example, might have to get all loans over $100,000 approved by a regional holding company credit officer located in a different community who oversees all lending decisions. This has the advantage of guaranteeing uniformity in loan decisions. It also has disadvantages related to perceptions that local authorities have limited powers. Decisions are too often delayed and subsequently relayed to customers too late. Not surprisingly, well run community banks play on their local autonomy and "special" community focus.

Other MBHCs allow managers of subsidiary banks to retain key decision-making authority and essentially operate quasi-independently as long as performance is strong. It is more difficult for these firms to realize economies of scale — consider the inability to run a single marketing and advertising program — and thus some of the benefits of size are lost. The advantage, however, is that such banks typically retain close ties to their communities and realize the associated benefits.

HOLDING COMPANY FINANCIAL STATEMENTS AND CASH FLOWS. MBHC expansion enables banks to diversify their operations by competing in different geographic and product markets. Diversification reduces the risk of failure by stabilizing earnings. The parent company typically coordinates the operating strategies for the entire organization and provides services for which it charges fees. It assists bank subsidiaries in asset and liability management, loan review, data processing, and business development and may provide debt and equity funding. It also provides strategic planning, project analysis, and financing for nonbank subsidiaries.

While the consolidated financial statements of a holding company and its subsidiaries reflect aggregate performance, it is useful to analyze the parent company's statements alone. Exhibits 2.10 and 2.11 present the condensed balance sheet and income statement for Citigroup, a financial holding company with wholly-owned bank and nonbank subsidiaries. The parent owns four basic types of assets: balances with subsidiary and nonsubsidiary banks, securities, investments in bank and nonbank subsidiaries, and other assets. The parent company purchases loans (investments and advances) from a bank subsidiary when a credit exceeds the maximum legal loan size permitted a single member bank. These loan participations may be distributed to other banks in the holding company or kept by the parent. Finally, the parent advances funds to subsidiaries through the purchase of notes and receivables or equity. The equity investment represents the value of subsidiary stock at the time of purchase. These assets are financed by short-term debt, long-term debt, and bank holding company stockholders.

The parent's net income is derived from dividends, interest and management fees from equity in bank and nonbank subsidiaries in excess of operating expenses, interest paid on holding company debt, and other revenues including fees. The parent company also reports equity in undistributed income of subsidiaries. Subsidiary accounting requires the parent company to declare, as income, the unrealized gains in the equity of a consolidated subsidiary regardless of whether the income is actually paid (distributed) to the parent. In Exhibit 2.11, the bulk of the Citigroup's $14.1 billion in net income in 2001 came from dividends from bank holding company subsidiaries and nonbank subsidiaries.

• EXHIBIT 2.10

CITIGROUP'S MULTIBANK HOLDING COMPANY CONSOLIDATED BALANCE SHEET FOR PARENT COMPANY ONLY (MILLIONS OF DOLLARS)

Citigroup (Parent Company Only)	2001	2000
Assets		
Cash and balances due from depository institutions:		
Balances with subsidiary depository institutions.	$ 6,000	$ 78,000
Balances with unrelated depository institutions.	21,000	7,000
Securities:		
Government agencies, corporations and political subdivisions securities	48,000	0
Other debt and equity securities	1,439,000	0
Net Loans and leases	0	0
Investments in and receivables due from subsidiaries	120,622,000	87,404,000
Premises and fixed assets (including capitalized leases)	15,000	17,000
Goodwill	368,000	381,000
Other assets	368,000	491,000
Total Assets	122,887,000	88,378,000
Liabilities and Equities		
Borrowings with a remaining maturity of < one year:		
Commercial paper.	481,000	496,000
Other borrowings.	5,804,000	3,000,000
Other borrowings with a remaining maturity of > one year	25,168,000	10,947,000
Subordinated notes and debentures	4,250,000	4,250,000
Other liabilities	113,000	616,000
Balances due to subsidiaries and related institutions:		
Subsidiary banks.	100,000	28,000
Nonbank subsidiaries	5,714,000	2,835,000
Related bank holding companies	10,000	0
Equity Capital:		
Perpetual preferred stock (including related surplus)	1,525,000	1,745,000
Common stock (par value)	55,000	54,000
Surplus (exclude all surplus related to preferred stock)	23,196,000	15,635,000
Retained earnings	69,803,000	58,012,000
Accumulated other comprehensive income	−844,000	973,000
Other equity capital components	−12,488,000	−10,213,000
Total Equity	81,247,000	66,206,000
Total liabilities and Equities	122,887,000	88,378,000

Values in Millions of Dollars

The parent pays very little in income tax (Citigroup actually received a tax benefit) because 80 percent of the dividends from subsidiaries is exempt. Taxable income from the remaining 20 percent and interest income is small (or less than) relative to deductible expenses. Under IRS provisions, each subsidiary actually pays taxes quarterly on its taxable income. With a consolidated tax return, however, the parent company can use taxable income from its subsidiaries to offset its loss. Thus, the parent could report a noncash tax benefit representing the reclamation of tax overpayments by subsidiaries. The final item before net income represents the holding company's claim to $2.4 billion and $3.2 billion (in 2001) in subsidiary income from nonbank and bank holding companies (bank holding companies that the parent owns), respectively, that was not paid out as dividends.

· EXHIBIT 2.11

CITIGROUP'S MULTIBANK HOLDING COMPANY CONSOLIDATED INCOME
STATEMENT FOR PARENT COMPANY ONLY (MILLIONS OF DOLLARS)

Citigroup (Parent Company Only)	2001	2000
OPERATING INCOME:		
Income from bank subsidiaries:		
Dividends	$ 0	$ 0
Interest	0	1
Management and service fees	0	0
Other	0	0
Total	0	1
Income from nonbank subsidiaries:		
Dividends	2,586	1,535
Interest	5	50
Management and service fees	0	0
Other	1	47
Total	2,592	1,632
Income from subsidiary bank holding companies:		
Dividends	6,426	1,255
Interest	1,220	365
Management and service fees	0	0
Other	0	1
Total	7,646	1,621
Securities gains/(losses) .	0	0
All other operating income.	53	85
Total operating income	10,291	3,339
OPERATING EXPENSE:		
Salaries and employee benefits	225	145
Interest expense	1,876	762
Provision for loan and lease losses.	0	0
All other expenses.	35	110
Total operating expense	2,136	1,017
Income (loss) before taxes and undistributed income	8,155	2,322
Applicable income taxes	−322	−202
Extraordinary items, net of tax effect	−7	0
Income (loss) before undistributed income of subsidiaries and associated companies	8,470	2,524
Equity in undistributed income (losses) of subsidiaries:		
Bank	0	0
Nonbank	2,440	4,140
Subsidiary bank holding companies	3,216	6,855
Net Income (loss)	14,126	13,519

Values in Millions of Dollars

BANKING BUSINESS MODELS

When people think of banks, many think of the largest U.S. institutions, such as Bank of America, Citigroup, J.P Morgan Chase, Wells Fargo, Wachovia, Fleet National Bank, and BankOne. What many do not realize is that of the approximate 8,100 commercial banks operating in the U.S., only 80 have more than $10 billion in assets. The vast majority, approximately

5,000, have less than $100 million in assets with a legal lending limit of less than $1 million. In fact, more than 96 percent of U.S. banks have total assets less than $1 billion. Still, the largest banks (over $10 billion) hold almost 70 percent of total bank assets and follow business models far different than those of smaller banks. Banks with less than $1 billion in assets are generally called community banks, while larger banks are labeled large holding company banks, multibank holding companies, or even money center banks. Banks of the same size, however, often pursue substantially different strategies competing in different geographic markets with different products and services. Today, we separate the business model structure of banks into five categories determined by size and geographic market penetration:

- Global Banks
- Nationwide Banks
- Super Regional Banks
- Regional Banks
- Specialty Banks (Community Banks):
  - Limited Region
  - Limited Product Line

The business model of *global banks* is to have a large international presence. The United States has few global banks because restrictive banking laws and domestic economic opportunities have constrained many banks from venturing overseas in any significant way. Those that have extensive global activities include Citigroup, J.P. Morgan Chase, Bank of America, State Street Bank and Trust Company, and Bank of New York, and their activities range far beyond traditional lending and deposit gathering.

The 1998 merger between NationsBank and Bank of America, now Bank of America, created the first true *nationwide bank* with a coast-to-coast presence. The original Bank of America had operations in almost all 50 states and a dominant position in the key banking states of California, Texas, and Florida where growth is strong and the population includes a high percentage of retirees and wealthy individuals who buy fee-based banking services. Wells Fargo and Washington Mutual are also considered nationwide banks.

Super regionals banks have extensive operations in a limited geographic region of the U.S. They exist today as a direct result of interstate branching restrictions. Prior to the enactment of the Riegle-Neal Interstate Banking and Branching Efficiency Act of 1994, interstate branching was only allowed to the degree that states formed reciprocal pacts. A typical state law allowed out-of-state banks to buy banks in the home state if in-state banks were allowed to buy banks in those states. The intent was to allow in-state banks to grow and prevent large New York City and Chicago banks from entering the state. Super regional banks continue to expand their activities by entering businesses such as investment banking and insurance by acquiring regional firms. These banks include firms such as AmSouth, Wachovia, BankOne, Fleet Financial, SouthTrust, Regions Bank, and U.S. Trust, among others.

Regional banks are similar to super regional banks except that their scope is more limited geographically and in terms of products or services. BB&T is such an example. They typically operate banks in a few contiguous states. Finally, *specialty banks* are generally independent or community banks that specialize in a limited region or limited product line. Smaller specialty banks are often part of a one-bank holding company and may operate branches, but are most often linked closely with a single community in which the bank is located or they offer a limited range of products. Many bankers view community banks as synonymous with independent banks. The vast majority of banks in the United States would be considered specialty (community or independent) banks.

ORGANIZATIONAL STRUCTURE OF AN INDEPENDENT BANK

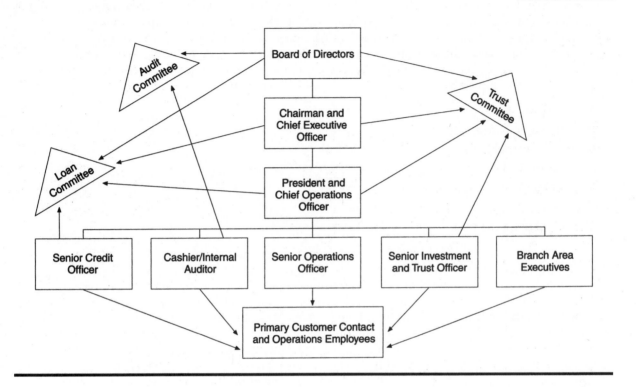

SPECIALTY BANKS (COMMUNITY BANKS)

The term *independent bank* normally refers to a bank that is not controlled by a multibank holding company or any other outside interest. A *community bank* is generally a bank that operates primarily in, or has ties to, one community. Most stock analysts designate community banks as those with less than $1 billion in assets. In the banking industry, the terms independent bank and community bank are often used interchangeably which sometimes leads to confusion. Consider a community bank that is not part of a holding company. Its general organizational form will follow the outline of Exhibit 2.12. The structure typically consists of five levels of responsibilities and reporting. At the bottom of the chart are the line personnel who have primary responsibility in customer contact and handling back room operations such as check processing and teller services. Their role is extremely important because most depositors and loan customers deal with these individuals. They largely project the bank's image and serve to market bank services.

Most independent banks separate activities into at least the four or five functional areas listed above the line personnel. A senior credit officer is responsible for implementing a bank's credit policy. The president and chief executive officer (CEO) also manage loan portfolios because they deal directly with borrowers. A bank's cashier or chief financial officer is responsible for financial management responsibilities in the areas of budgeting, accounting, and record keeping. This individual verifies that financial information conforms to regulatory guidelines and is conveyed correctly to stockholders and regulators. Each bank should also have an internal auditor who monitors financial reporting. The senior operations officer is responsible for backroom operations involving data processing, lock box services, and check processing. An independent bank may also have a senior investment officer who buys and sells securities for the investment portfolio, and also handles trust business if the bank has a trust department. Again at small banks, the president or CEO may handle these responsibilities. Finally, a bank with branches will typically designate a branch area executive. One individual may be responsible for all branches; or the branches may be segmented by city, county, or other area such that several individuals serve as branch executives and report directly to the president. If the bank is large enough, it may also separate the human resources function and designate a senior officer who reports to the president.

The next tier of management is that of the bank's chief operations officer (COO), who often carries the title of president. Senior officers in each of the functional areas normally report to this individual who then conveys the information to the CEO. At most independent banks, the CEO is in charge of the bank's entire operation. He or she often makes loans, reviews key loan and investment decisions made by others, and handles much of the bank's marketing and public relations efforts. In this case, the president is the chief operating officer only when the CEO is out of town. At the top is the bank's board of directors, which oversees the entire operation of the bank.

Outside members of the board of directors are generally key business leaders in the community and often they are significant bank customers and even bank stockholders. Inside members consist of the bank's CEO, president, and senior lending officer. The primary role of directors is to represent and serve stockholders who are the owners of the bank. A secondary role is to represent customers and employees. Directors use their expertise to oversee the broad direction of the bank, solve problems, and make decisions regarding bank policy. Their role is not to manage the bank by getting involved in day-to-day operations or the details of each specific pricing, investment, or credit decision. Because the board is ultimately responsible for the bank's performance, most banks establish directors' committees that set policy guidelines in the major functional areas and regularly monitor performance. Many banks have gotten into difficulty because directors have blindly followed the dictates of senior management instead of setting policy and monitoring performance.

The independent bank in Exhibit 2.12 has directors' committees. A loan committee oversees the lending function to ensure loan quality and verify that regulatory guidelines are met. This committee must typically approve all loans over some base amount and thus serves as a final review board. Because business leaders are familiar with the community and are experts in their own line of business, they should bring experience and keen judgment to the evaluation process. By law, any bank with a trust department must have a directors' trust committee. Trust departments handle estates, guardianships, and related services under legal trust agreements. A trust committee monitors the legal aspects of the trust business and whether trust business contributes to the bank's overall profitability. The third committee is the audit committee. Note that it is the only committee that has no inside directors. This reflects the monitoring role inherent in an audit. The committee selects the bank's auditors, reviews the audit report, and makes recommendations to management. All these activities should be independent of the bank's operating officers. Finally, the directors may have a representative on the bank's asset and liability management committee.

BANK REGULATION

Commercial banks are the most heavily regulated financial institutions in the United States. This largely reflects the historical role of banks in the payments system and providing credit to individuals and businesses, as well as the fact that banks carry FDIC insurance on their deposits. Prior to the establishment of the Federal Reserve System in 1913, private banks operated free of close government scrutiny. The frequency of abuses and large number of failed banks during the Depression forced the federal government to redesign its regulatory framework encompassing supervision and deposit insurance.

REASONS FOR REGULATION

There are five fundamental objectives of bank regulation. The first is to ensure the *safety and soundness* of banks and financial instruments. The purpose is to maintain domestic and international confidence, protect depositors and ultimately taxpayers, and maintain financial stability. With safety and soundness, a financial system provides for the efficient allocation of the nation's scarce resources because the payments system is reliable and institutions willingly extend credit that stimulates economic growth. This goal is generally accomplished by limiting risk-taking at individual institutions, by limiting entry and exit, and by the federal government's willingness to act as a lender of last resort. The difficulties with federal deposit insurance and the large number of failed institutions during the late 1980s and early 1990s demonstrate that risk-taking among depository institutions had been subsidized by U.S. taxpayers as they bore the brunt of the cost.

The second objective of bank regulation is that the Federal Reserve System uses regulation to provide *monetary stability*. This is evidenced by efforts to control the growth in the nation's money supply and maintain the efficient operation of the payments system.

The third objective is to provide an *efficient and competitive financial system.* Regulation has attempted to prevent undue concentration of banking resources that would be anticompetitive, yet allow firms to alter their product mix and delivery systems to meet economic and market needs. This goal has generally been accomplished by restricting mergers and acquisitions that reduce the number and market power of competing institutions.

The fourth objective is to *protect consumers* from abuses by credit-granting institutions. Historically, some individuals found it difficult to obtain loans for reasons not related to their financial condition. Thus, regulations now stipulate that borrowers should have equal credit opportunities such that banks cannot discriminate on the basis of race, gender, age, geographic location, etc. Lenders must also disclose why a borrower is denied a loan. The Community Reinvestment Act (CRA) will prevent a bank from acquiring another institution if the parent receives a poor CRA evaluation; that is, it is not doing enough to insure that their credit and services are available to all members of the defined community.

The final objective is to *maintain the integrity of the nation's payments system.* Thomas Hoenig, president of the Federal Reserve Bank of Kansas City, argues that the payments system revolves around banks. As long as regulators ensure that banks clear checks and settle noncash payments in a fair and predictable way, participants will have confidence that the payments media can be used to effect transactions. This is especially important given the trend toward electronic commerce and e-cash.

It is also important to recognize that regulation cannot achieve certain things. For example, regulation does not prevent bank failures. It cannot eliminate risk in the economic environment or in a bank's normal operations. It does not guarantee that bankers will make sound management decisions or act ethically. It simply serves as a guideline for sound operating policies.

Three separate federal agencies along with each state's banking department issue and enforce regulations related to a wide variety of commercial bank activities. The federal agencies are the Federal Reserve, the Federal Deposit Insurance Corporation (FDIC), and the Office of the Comptroller of the Currency (OCC). Most regulations can be classified in one of three basic categories linked to the reasons for regulation introduced earlier:

- Supervision, examination, deposit insurance, chartering activity, and product restrictions are associated with safety and soundness
- Branching, mergers and acquisitions, and pricing are related to an efficient and competitive financial system
- Consumer protection

▪ EXHIBIT 2.13

Type of Regulation	Type of Commercial Bank				
	National	State Member	Insured State Nonmember	Noninsured State Nonmember	Bank Holding Companies
Safety and Soundness					
Supervision and Examination	Comptroller	Federal Reserve and state authority	FDIC and state authority	State authority	Federal Reserve
Deposit Insurance	FDIC	FDIC	FDIC	State insurance or none	Not applicable
Chartering and Licensing	OCC	State authority	State authority	State authority	Federal Reserve and state authority
Efficiency and Competitiveness					
Branching	Comptroller	Federal Reserve and state authority	FDIC and state authority	State authority	Federal Reserve and state authority
Mergers and Acquisitions	Comptroller	Federal Reserve and state authority	FDIC and state authority	State authority	Federal Reserve and state authority
Pricing New Products	Federal Reserve and state authority	Federal Reserve and state authority	Federal Reserve and state authority	Federal Reserve and state authority	Not applicable
Consumer Protection	Federal Reserve	Federal Reserve and state authority	Federal Reserve, FDIC, and state authority	Federal Reserve and state authority	Not applicable

The different regulatory groups' responsibilities overlap, but the agencies generally coordinate policies and decisions. The Office of Thrift Supervision (OTS) has similar responsibilities for savings and loan associations. Exhibit 2.13 summarizes the division of responsibilities. A 1993 study by the Treasury Department estimated that two or more of these federal regulators supervise approximately 58 percent of commercial banks. Three or more regulators supervise 15 percent of the banks and there are even 2 percent of the banks regulated by four regulators. Not surprisingly, many bankers and legislators believe that this duplication is costly with little benefit.

SAFETY AND SOUNDNESS

NEW CHARTERS. Groups interested in starting a commercial bank have the option of requesting a new charter from the OCC or the appropriate state banking authority. The source of the charter determines how the bank is regulated. Banks chartered by the OCC are extensively regulated by three federal agencies: the OCC, Fed, and FDIC. In addition to granting charters, the OCC conducts periodic examinations of national banks, evaluates merger applications when the resulting firm is a national bank, and authorizes branches where applicable. All national banks are members of the Fed and must purchase FDIC insurance.

State-chartered banks have the option of joining the Fed and applying for FDIC insurance. It is highly unlikely, however, that a state-banking agency would approve a banking charter without the bank obtaining FDIC insurance. All state banks that choose Federal Reserve membership must obtain deposit insurance. The Fed sets reserve requirements, approves proposed mergers and new branches, and examines state member banks. It also makes loans to banks, establishes consumer regulations, authorizes the formation of bank holding companies, and approves all holding company activities and acquisitions, regardless of how a bank was chartered. Insured state banks that choose not to join the Fed are regulated predominantly by the FDIC, while noninsured nonmembers are supervised by state banking authorities.

SUPERVISION AND EXAMINATION. Regulators periodically examine individual banks and provide supervisory directives that request changes in operating policies. The purpose is to guarantee the safety and soundness of the banking system by identifying problems before a bank's financial condition deteriorates to the point where it fails and the FDIC has to pay off insured depositors. The OCC and FDIC assess the overall quality of a bank's condition according to the CAMELS system. The letters in CAMELS refer to capital adequacy, asset quality, management quality, earnings quality, liquidity, and sensitivity to market risk, respectively. The "S" is relatively new to the CAMELS system. It reflects the impact of changes in interest rates, foreign exchange rates, commodity prices, and equity prices and how they can adversely affect a financial institution's earnings or economic capital. Regulators assign ratings from 1 (best) to 5 (worst) for each category and an overall rating for all features combined.

Examiners spend most of their efforts appraising asset quality, management, and market risk.[9] The asset quality rating generally indicates the relative volume of problem loans. Examiners review the terms and documentation on loans, particularly those with past-due payments, to determine the magnitude of likely loan losses. If repayment prospects are poor, regulators may force a bank to recognize the loss and build up loan-loss reserves in support of future losses. Management quality is assessed in terms of senior officers' awareness and control of a bank's policies and performance. Examiners carefully review bank policy statements regarding loans, investments, capital, and general budgeting to determine whether the bank is well run. The lack of concern over policy statements and regulatory guidelines should have been an indicator of future problems. Capital adequacy, earnings strength, and liquidity are determined by formulas based on the composition and size of various bank balance sheet accounts. Sensitivity to market risk considers management's ability to identify, measure, monitor, and control price risk. For most banks, market risk is primarily composed of the sensitivity of their income and equity to changes in interest rates. Larger banks, however, have active trading portfolios and some exposure to equities and off-balance sheet activities, so they are more sensitive to changes in exchange rates, commodity prices, and equity prices. These facets of risk are addressed in detail in subsequent chapters.

When an examination is completed, the regulatory staff makes a series of policy recommendations that address problems it discovered. The recommendations may be informal advisories, a memorandum of understanding, or a cease and desist order. A memorandum of understanding (MOU) is a formal regulatory document that identifies specific violations and prescribes corrective action by the problem institution. A cease and desist order (C&D) is a legal document that orders a firm to stop an unfair practice under full penalty of law. Only the cease and desist order has legal standing, but each type of recommendation notifies a bank if its house is in order.

FEDERAL DEPOSIT INSURANCE. Regulators attempt to maintain public confidence in banks and the financial system through federal deposit insurance. The FDIC currently insures customer deposits up to $100,000 per account. There once were two insurance funds

---

[9]Cocheo (1986) analyzes the steps in the typical examination process of a community bank and describes the basic questions and problems that arise.

under the FDIC with the Bank Insurance Fund (BIF) for banks and the Savings Association Insurance Fund (SAIF) for savings and loans. In 1990, insured banks paid a fee equal to 19.5 cents per $100 of domestic deposits for the coverage. Insured savings associations paid 23 cents per $100 in deposits. The difference reflected the fact that when the funds were separate the savings and loan fund went bankrupt and healthy thrift institutions were required to increase their insurance payments to help replenish the fund.[10] Subsequent payments have come from higher deposit insurance assessments and general taxpayer financing directly through the Treasury. The FDIC Improvement Act of 1991 required the FDIC to assign insurance premiums based on the risk assessment of the banks and to maintain the insurance fund to a minimum level of 1.25 of insured deposits. By the late 1990s, the FDIC insurance fund was well funded (about 1.35 percent of insured deposits) and as a result, about 98 percent of all banks today pay no insurance premiums. Chapter 13 directly addresses bank capital and FDIC insurance premiums.

Deposit insurance has been especially important during times when the number of problem banks and bank failures increased. Following World War II, bank failures were negligible, given the heavy regulation of banking activities and strict policies regarding who could open and operate a bank. However, the number of bank and thrift failures rose from under 50 in 1982 to well over 200 annually in the early 1990s, only to fall to zero in 1996 and around 5 per year in 2000–2001.

When a bank or thrift fails, the government pays insured depositors the full amount of their account balance up to $100,000 per eligible account. Customers with uninsured deposits bear the risk that they will not recover the full value of their account balance. Historically, regulators have not allowed the largest institutions to fail such that uninsured depositors received *de facto* 100 percent deposit insurance. Regulators implicitly assume that large bank failures would seriously undermine public confidence in financial institutions and markets, so they generally prop up large banks with federal aid or find a merger partner. The OCC and state banking authorities officially designate banks as insolvent, but the Federal Reserve and FDIC assist in closings. Frequently, the Fed extends credit to a problem bank until an ownership transfer occurs. The FDIC's liquidation staff handles the disposition of a failed bank's assets and liabilities. These and other problems with deposit insurance are described in Chapter 13.

The Federal Reserve also serves as the federal government's lender of last resort. When a bank loses funding sources, the Fed may make a discount window loan to support operations until a solution appears. When Continental Illinois experienced difficulties in 1984, for example, the Federal Reserve loaned it more than $4 billion until it effectively nationalized the bank. The same occurred with the Bank of New England in late 1990. The Federal Reserve's crisis management, however, is not limited to direct bank assistance. In recent years, it has intervened in disputes related to the collapse of silver prices during the Hunt family's problems, junk bond financing of leveraged buyouts, the failure of securities dealers in repurchase agreements, the failures of privately insured thrift institutions in Ohio and Maryland, and the funding crisis faced by the Farm Credit System. In most cases, the injured party requests back-up financing from the Fed if a crisis worsens. In other cases, market participants simply need expert advice. As lender of last resort, the Federal Reserve has the resources and clout to advise management and prevent serious financial problems.

---

[10]Congress passed the Financial Institutions Reform, Recovery and Enforcement Act of 1989 (FIRREA) largely to address problems in the thrift industry. Specific provisions of the act are discussed later in the chapter. The two insurance funds were established to maintain the appearance that banks were distinguishable from savings and loans. In actuality, both funds were deficient at the time. Congress mandated an increase in premiums, with thrifts paying higher rates over time. Deposit insurance works because the federal government stands behind it with its full faith, credit, and taxing authority.

■ EXHIBIT 2.14

FEDERAL RESERVE BANK REGULATIONS

REGULATION	Subject	REGULATION	Subject
A	Loans to Depository Institutions	S	Reimbursement for Providing Financial Records
B	Equal Credit Opportunity	T	Margin Credit Extended by Brokers and Dealers
C	Home Mortgage Disclosure	U	Margin Credit Extended by Banks
D	Reserve Requirements	V	Guarantee of Loans for National Defense Work
E	Electronic Fund Transfers	W	Extensions of Consumer Credit (revoked)
F	Limitations on Interbank Liabilities	X	Borrowers Who Obtain Margin Credit
G	Margin Credit Extended by Parties Other	Y	Bank Holding Companies
	Than Banks, Brokers, and Dealers	Z	Truth in Lending
H	Membership Requirements for State	AA	Consumer Complaint Procedures
	Chartered Banks	BB	Community Reinvestment
I	Stock in Federal Reserve Banks	CC	Availability of Funds and Collection of Checks
J	Check Collection and Funds Transfer	DD	Truth in Savings
K	International Banking Operations	EE	Netting Eligibility for Financial Institutions
L	Interlocking Bank Relationships		
M	Consumer Leasing		
N	Relationships with Foreign Banks		
O	Loans to Executive Officers of Member Banks		
P	Member Bank Protection Standards		
Q	Interest on Demand Deposits, Advertising		
R	Interlocking Relationships Between Securities Dealers and Member Banks		

SOURCE: Web site of the Federal Reserve Bank of New York, http://www.ny.frb.org/pihome/regs.html/.

PRODUCT RESTRICTIONS. The Federal Reserve also regulates specific activities of banks, bank holding companies, and financial holding companies as indicated in Exhibit 2.14. In the area of safety and soundness, regulations take the form of restricting interlocking relationships among directors of banks and between banks and securities firms, to ensure independence, and restricting the terms of loans to insiders, such as directors, bank officers, and shareholders. A brief, and somewhat incomplete, summary of permissible activities of national banks is listed in Exhibit 2.15. Since most states have provisions that allow State banks to engage in all activities permissible for national banks, the list of permissible activities for national banks is a strong guide for the banking system. One of the provisions of the Gramm-Leach-Bliley Act was that the OCC would compile a list of permissible activities for national banks. This list is available on the OCC Internet web site: http://www.occ.treas.gov/corpapps/BankAct.pdf

EFFICIENT AND COMPETITIVE FINANCIAL SYSTEM

Regulators have spent considerable effort in recent years analyzing and modifying regulations regarding what prices they can charge and what products and services they can offer. In general, regulators approve new charters when the ownership group invests sufficient capital and hires strong management to run the bank. Branching restrictions, which used to be up to the states to determine, are no longer relevant with all states permitting interstate branching.

BRANCHING AND INTERSTATE EXPANSION. As mentioned above, individual state law has historically determined a bank's ability to branch both intrastate and interstate. The Riegle-Neal Interstate Banking and Branching Efficiency Act of 1994, however, superceded

PERMISSIBLE ACTIVITIES OF NATIONAL BANKS OR THEIR SUBSIDIARIES

General Authority

Branching: loan offices and facilities

Consulting and financial advice: financial, investment, or economic

Corporate governance

Correspondent service: hold deposits for other banks and perform services

Finder activities: serve as a finder for certain goods

Leasing: engage in personal property leasing

Lending: make, purchase, sell, service, or warehouse loans or extensions of credit

Payment services: cash management and letters of credit

Other activities and services: borrow money and support services

Fiduciary Activities: may be granted at time of charter or subsequently

General: trust activities, employee benefit accounts, and real estate brokerage

Insurance and annuities activities: insurance underwriting, reinsurance, and title insurance

Securities activities: asset securitization, broker-dealer activities, clearing and execution services, closed end mutual funds, derivatives activities, investment vehicle for bank clients, mutual find activities, on-line securities trading, options contracts, private placement services, securities brokerage (secondary and primary markets), securities exchanges, securities lending, sweeps, transfer agent, and underwriting and dealing in government and municipal securities

Technology and Electronic Activities

Digital certification: act as a certification authority

Electronic bill payments: presentment, EDI services, electronic toll collections, merchant process of credit cards via Internet, and stored value cards

Electronic commerce: commercial web site hosting, electronic marketplace, electronic storage, facilitation of electronic commerce, hyperlinks between bank and third party sites, virtual malls, and web design and development services

Electronic correspondent services

Internet access service

Internet and PC banking

Software development and production

Investments: a wide range of investments are permissible

Asset backed securities, bank stock, bankers acceptances, corporate bonds (subject to 10 percent of capital surplus), collateralized mortgage-related investments, commercial paper, foreign government loans, housing investments, insurance investments, investment in limited liability companies, money market preferred stock, mutual fund shares (limited), small business investments, stock in life insurance underwriter, trust preferred securities, and state and local bonds

SOURCE: Comptroller of the Currency, Activities Permissible for a National Bank, http://www.occ.treas.gov/ (http://www.occ.treas.gov/corpapps/BankAct.pdf/).

the McFadden Act and permits adequately capitalized and managed bank holding companies to acquire banks in any state unless the state legislature opted out. Only two states originally "opted out" of interstate banking: Texas and Montana. Texas chose to delay interstate branching until September 1999 and Montana until October 2001. Good CRA evaluations by the Federal Reserve are required before acquisitions are approved. Mergers are also subject to concentration limits (generally a merger can not mean that the bank will control more than 20 percent of deposits in the state), state laws, and CRA evaluations. The law also extended the statute of limitations to permit the FDIC and RTC (Resolution Trust Corporation) to revive lawsuits that had expired under state statutes of limitations.

Historical branching restrictions shaped the U.S. banking system of today. The U.S. has substantially more banks than any other country in the world, but it never had a bank with a coast-to-coast presence until the NationsBank and Bank of America merger. State law has historically determined the degree to which a bank could branch within the state and

INTERSTATE BRANCHES AS A PERCENTAGE OF TOTAL OFFICES FOR
FDIC-INSURED INSTITUTIONS, JUNE 2001

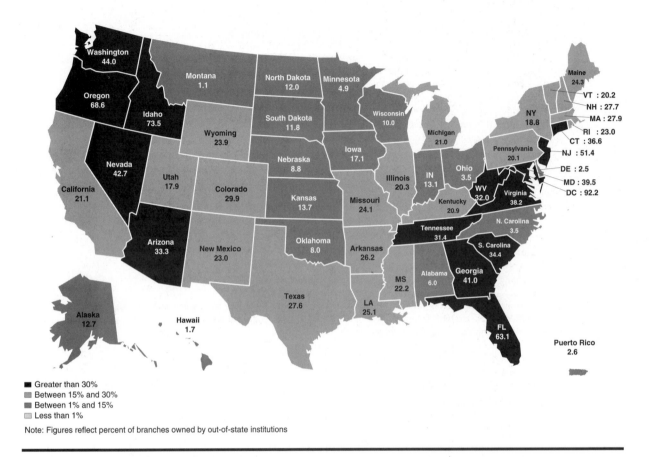

■ Greater than 30%
■ Between 15% and 30%
■ Between 1% and 15%
□ Less than 1%

Note: Figures reflect percent of branches owned by out-of-state institutions

SOURCE: FDIC/OTS Summary of Deposits, June 2001, http://www.fdic.gov/ (http://www2.fdic.gov/sod/).

whether banks can buy other banks outside their home state. Until the 1980s, these branch-ing laws were very restrictive, such that many separate smaller banks were formed. The effect of historically restrictive branching laws can be seen in Exhibits 2.16 and 2.17. Note, for example, that the percent of interstate branches in Texas is low. Texas has historically had very restrictive intrastate branching restrictions as well as having opted out of interstate branching. In June 1998, prior to Texas allowing interstate banking, only 10.6 percent of branches in Texas were owned by out-of-state banks. Bank of America (formerly NationsBank) collapsed its Texas bank into the North Carolina bank in 1999 with other banks following suit, such that the percentage of branches owned by out-of-state banks increased to 17.6 percent in 2000.

For many years most banks conducted banking business exclusively in the state where the head office was located. A few bank holding companies ventured out of state to buy banks, but these transactions were generally small. Acquisitions stopped in 1956 when the Douglas amendment to the McFadden Act restricted bank holding companies from buying controlling interest in banks located outside the home state. This presented problems dur-ing the early stages of the 1980s boom in bank and thrift failures, as there were no buyers for large problem institutions. A provision of the Garn–St Germain Act subsequently

· EXHIBIT 2.17

INTERSTATE BRANCHES OF FDIC-INSURED INSTITUTIONS, JUNE 2001

Main Office Location	Number of Institutions with Interstate Branches	Number of Interstate Branches	Deposits in Interstate Branches	Number of States/ Territories	State/Territories
Alabama	8	1,920	72,283,033	15	AR, AZ, CO, FL, GA, LA, MS, NC, NE, NM, NV, SC, TN, TX, VA
Arkansas	3	20	368,648	2	MO, OK
Arizona	1	9	78,491	1	CA
California	22	767	47,648,239	23	AZ, CO, CT, DC, FL, GU, HI, ID, IL, KS, MD, MN, MO, MP, NJ, NM, NV, NY, OR, TX, UT, VA, WA
Colorado	2	7	182,893	2	CA, UT
Connecticut	4	7	317,058	5	DC, MA, MN, NY, PA
District of Columbia	2	11	251,195	2	MD, VA
Delaware	6	24	2,096,932	6	MD, MN, NC, NJ, NY, PA
Florida	7	38	571,301	5	AL, GA, NJ, NY, PR
Georgia	10	938	48,732,900	7	AL, CA, DC, FL, MD, TN, VA
Guam	2	17	268,161	5	CA, FM, MH, MP, PW
Hawaii	2	13	849,749	6	AS, FM, GU, MH, MP, PW
Iowa	14	36	975,889	5	IL, KS, MO, NE, SD
Idaho	4	8	118,364	3	UT, WA, WY
Illinois	18	742	39,956,257	15	AZ, CA, DE, FL, IA, IN, KY, LA, MI, MO, NV, OR, PA, TX, WI
Indiana	11	153	4,540,960	8	IL, KS, KY, MI, NC, NV, OH, TN
Kansas	12	93	3,078,313	13	AZ, CA, CO, IL, KY, MO, ND, NE, NJ, NV, TX, VA, WA
Kentucky	9	34	1,010,465	8	AZ, FL, IN, MO, NV, TN, UT, WV
Louisiana	3	83	2,702,336	4	AL, FL, MS, TX
Massachusetts	12	44	1,513,424	7	CA, CT, FL, MO, NH, RI, WI
Maryland	13	170	4,529,144	5	DC, FL, PA, VA, WV
Maine	1	1	8,389	1	NH
Michigan	9	187	8,343,340	7	CA, FL, IL, IN, OH, WA, WI
Minnesota	11	1,292	42,262,781	18	CA, CO, CT, FL, IA, ID, IL, IN, MI, ND, NE, NV, OR, SD, UT, WA, WI, WY
Missouri	12	138	3,423,996	5	AR, IA, IL, KS, OK
Mississippi	5	149	4,468,444	6	AL, AR, LA, NC, TN, TX
North Carolina	11	6,966	429,131,268	28	AR, AZ, CA, CT, DC, FL, GA, IA, ID, IL, KS, KY, MD, MO, NJ, NM, NV, NY, OK, OR, PA, SC, TN, TX, UT, VA, WA, WV
North Dakota	7	188	4,708,974	11	AZ, CA, CO, IA, MN, NE, NM, SD, UT, WI, WY
Nebraska	9	202	6,012,356	9	AZ, CO, IA, KS, MN, MO, OK, SD, TX
New Hampshire	3	17	292,463	2	MA, VT
New Jersey	9	116	4,366,739	4	CT, NY, PA, TN
New Mexico	3	57	1,530,831	3	AZ, CO, TX
Nevada	2	24	2,622,023	4	CA, FL, NY, WI
New York	30	812	58,076,757	16	CA, CT, DC, DE, FL, GU, IL, MA, MD, NJ, PA, PR, TN, TX, VI, WV
Ohio	23	2,459	94,732,113	28	AK, AR, AZ, CO, FL, IA, ID, IL, IN, KY, LA, MA, ME, MI, MN, MO, NH, NY, OK, OR, PA, SC, TN, UT, VT, WA, WI, WV
Oklahoma	3	16	249,717	6	CA, DE, KS, NC, SC, TX
Oregon	4	21	522,018	2	CA, WA
Pennsylvania	18	825	38,321,359	23	AZ, CT, DE, FL, IN, KY, MA, MD, MO, MT, NC, NE, NH, NJ, NY, OH, OK, OR, RI, SC, VA, WA, WV
Puerto Rico	2	14	772,744	2	NY, VI
Rhode Island	3	1,682	104,840,658	8	CT, FL, MA, ME, NH, NJ, NY, PA
South Carolina	4	10	159,954	1	NC
South Dakota	4	14	456,993	5	MN, ND, NM, NV, TX
Tennessee	7	683	18,270,286	15	AL, AR, FL, GA, IA, IL, IN, KY, LA, MO, MS, NC, TX, VA, WV
Texas	5	87	2,932,955	8	AR, CA, GA, KS, MA, MO, NM, OK
Utah	7	399	10,396,394	5	CA, ID, NJ, OR, WA
Virginia	17	235	10,376,564	6	DC, DE, MD, NC, TN, WV
Vermont	3	33	530,095	1	NH
Washington	12	288	7,225,116	9	AZ, CA, HI, ID, MT, NV, OR, TX, UT
Wisconsin	11	57	1,924,534	5	AZ, IL, MI, MN, TX
West Virginia	12	41	730,338	4	CO, MD, OH, VA
Wyoming	1	1	31,233	1	NE

NOTE: Figures are in thousands of dollars.

SOURCE: FDIC/OTS Summary of Deposits, June 2001. Available on the Internet at http://www.fdic.gov/.

allowed interstate takeovers of failed or failing institutions, but the number of transactions was small until the late 1980s. The pace of interstate activity quickened during the mid-1980s when many states authorized some form of interstate banking. This typically resulted from some fear that in-state banks would be put at a competitive disadvantage to large out-of-state institutions. Specific provisions are described in the following sections.

GRANDFATHER CLAUSES. Prior to the passage of the Douglas amendment, 16 bank holding companies owned affiliate banks outside their home states. These banks can subsequently continue all interstate operations initiated before interstate restrictions. Seven of the groups are foreign-based, and nine have their main office in the U.S. Several of these banking organizations, such as Norwest (now part of Wells Fargo) and NCNB (now Bank of America) have aggressively expanded into other states through normal channels via the purchase of failed and healthy institutions.

TAKEOVERS OF FAILING INSTITUTIONS. Federal regulations permit financial institutions to acquire failed firms in other states. When a firm fails, regulators solicit bids from interested parties and select the best bid, determined by the type, location, and offering price of the acquiring firm. Both commercial banks and savings and loans can submit bids. Intrastate bidders of the same type, however, generally have the advantage. Once in a state, a firm can expand by buying other sound institutions in that state as permitted by law.

It was this provision, allowing a bank to acquire a failing institution, that was the backbone of some of the largest financial institutions today. In June 1983, Bank of America Corp. in California purchased Seafirst Corp. in Washington. Chase Manhattan Bank in New York purchased several privately insured savings and loans in Ohio in 1985. New York's Citicorp similarly acquired several failed savings and loans, allowing it to enter the California, Illinois, Florida, Maryland, and Nevada markets. In 1986, First Interstate entered Oklahoma by purchasing the state's second largest bank when it was ordered closed. In Texas, Chemical Bank purchased Texas Commerce, NCNB purchased First Republic Bancorp., and Bank One acquired 20 of MCorp's (Texas) largest banks.

STATE AUTHORIZATION. Through 1993, efforts to extend interstate banking focused on convincing state legislatures to permit reciprocal agreements. Before 1980, no states allowed interstate acquisitions. By the end of 1993, only Hawaii did not allow some form of interstate banking. Most allowed both out-of-state banks and thrifts to acquire in-state firms or open new banks. Some states saw an opportunity to increase capital availability in-state simply by opening their doors. These states include those that are geographically isolated, such as Alaska, as well as those that had severe economic problems, such as Oklahoma and Texas. Other states used interstate compacts as a defense mechanism to allow their in-state banks to grow large enough to compete with national money center banks. These states include those in the Northeast and Southeast that entered regional compacts that prohibited banks in certain states (especially California and New York) from entering.

MERGERS AND ACQUISITIONS. Regulators closely monitor bank expansion through mergers and acquisitions. The intent is to protect consumers from undue concentration of banking resources and to provide for the efficient delivery of services. Research generally shows that economies of scale in banking are reached at a relatively small firm size, in general, for banks with up to $1 billion in assets. Large size is thus not justified strictly on the basis of lower unit production costs. Too many resources under one firm's control, however, may adversely affect pricing and credit availability. A different regulatory agency must approve each merger, depending on the classification of the surviving bank. National banks are approved by the OCC, state member banks by the Federal Reserve, state nonmember insured banks by the FDIC, and uninsured nonmembers by the appropriate state authority. See Chapter 22 for a complete discussion of bank mergers and acquisitions.

Historically, regulators applied strict criteria when evaluating potential anti-competitive effects. They would define the geographic market in which the acquired firm operated, determine the number of direct competitors, and calculate concentration measures that indicated the degree of control by the combined firm versus all competitors. Because commercial banks were viewed as the only direct competitors, bank mergers and acquisitions were frequently denied if the acquiring firm already had a presence in the market. In the current environment, however, the criteria are much more flexible. Other depository institutions and nonbank financial institutions are included as competitors. The relevant geographic market now includes a much broader area, which typically lowers the degree of concentration and makes it easier to approve an acquisition.[11] Regulators seem to agree that expansion via merger and acquisition is necessary to improve the safety and soundness of the nation's banking system. It is also easier to regulate a smaller number of distinct firms.

NONBANK BANKS. Even before commercial banks had explicit interstate banking authority, they could conduct business nationwide through holding company subsidiaries. Most large banking organizations have established Edge Act corporations, loan production offices, and consumer banks outside their home state. Edge Act corporations provide a full range of banking services but, by law, deal only in international transactions. There are two types of Edge corporations: banks and investment companies. Banking Edges operate as commercial banks, accepting deposits and making loans to firms with international business. Investment Edges engage strictly in activities outside the United States that are permitted under federal regulation. Loan production offices (LPOs) make commercial loans but do not accept deposits. Consumer banks accept deposits but make only consumer loans. Federal Reserve approval of these firms allowed large bank holding companies to form an interstate banking network throughout the nation even prior to the enactment of nationwide interstate branching. Federal legislation restricted this activity in 1987 so that geographic expansion in this form slowed.

PRICING. Prior to 1980, legislation limited the rates that banks could pay on certain types of deposits and the rates they could charge on certain types of loans. The Fed wanted to control money growth and banks were the sole supplier of demand deposits, the primary component of the money supply. Banks were essentially guaranteed a positive spread between the yield on assets and the interest cost of most liabilities and the system of banks was safe. There was also a national policy of making housing available and affordable to as many families as possible. Thus, savings and loans were allowed to pay slightly higher regulated rates on interest-bearing deposits than banks as long as they invested a significant portion of their assets in mortgages or other housing-related investments. While these price controls did not necessarily make the financial system more efficient, they did channel resources in desired areas. Banks competed equally with other banks primarily in terms of service and the range of noncredit products.

---

[11]When evaluating anti-competitive effects during the 1980s, the Federal Reserve used the Herfindahl-Hirschmann Index (HHI) to measure market concentration. The HHI is computed by identifying the appropriate market, then summing the squares of each competitor's market share. For example, three competing firms with market shares of 50 percent, 30 percent, and 20 percent would produce an index of 3,800 (2,500+900+400). To be guaranteed approval, the HHI after a merger or acquisition must be no greater than 1,800 and/or cause the HHI to increase by 200. Since 1990, regulators have been much more lenient in approving transactions that violate this standard.

Interest rate ceilings were phased out beginning in 1980. Today, banks can compete without restriction on most interest rates they pay on deposits or charge on loans. This provides for a more efficient allocation of resources, but puts a greater burden on bank managers to assess and manage risk.

CONSUMER PROTECTION. State legislatures and the Federal Reserve have implemented numerous laws and regulations to protect the rights of individuals who try to borrow. The purposes are wide ranging, varying from restricting deceptive advertising or trade practices to prohibiting discrimination. Exhibit 2.14 lists the broad areas in which the Federal Reserve has established regulations, including those of consumer regulations. Regs. AA, B, BB, C, E, M, S, Z, and DD apply specifically to consumer regulation. Equal credit opportunity (Reg. B), for example, makes it illegal for any lender to discriminate against a borrower on the basis of race, sex, marital status, religion, age, or national origin. It establishes guidelines for structuring loan applications and specifies how information can be used in making credit decisions. Community reinvestment prohibits redlining in which lenders as a matter of policy do not lend in certain geographic markets. Chapter 17 summarizes the key federal regulations as they pertain to consumer borrowing. Reg. Z requires disclosure of effective rates of interest, total interest paid, the total of all payments, as well as full disclosure as to why a customer was denied credit.

TRENDS IN FEDERAL LEGISLATION AND REGULATION

The fundamental focus of federal banking legislation and regulation since 1970 has been to better define and expand the product and geographic markets served by depository institutions, and to increase competition. Subsequent problems with failed savings and loans and commercial banks raised concerns that only a few large organizations would survive because all financial institutions would eventually have the same powers and large firms would drive small firms out of business. Today, the banking and financial services industry is evolving into a new and more exciting industry full of challenges and opportunities. Smaller banks appear to have opportunities in providing specialized products and services. Larger banks have expanded their product mix and have blurred the distinction between a bank, securities firm, and insurance company.

Key legislative and regulatory changes have attempted to address these basic issues: What is a bank? Where can banks conduct business? What products can banks offer and what interest rates may they charge or pay? Significant regulatory developments are identified in the following section, with particular attention paid to the Depository Institutions Deregulation and Monetary Control Act of 1980 (DIDMCA), the Garn–St Germain Depository Institutions Act of 1982 (GSG), the Financial Services Modernization Act (Gramm-Leach-Bliley Act of 1999), and the U.S. Patriot Act of 2001which are credited with accelerating changes in the current banking environment, facilitating the thrift and banking crisis, and in stabilizing the deposit insurance funds.

KEY FEDERAL LEGISLATION: 1956–2001

Since the collapse of so many banks in the 1930s—almost 4,000 institutions failed in 1933—federal and state governments have closely regulated the activities of commercial banks. In addition to providing deposit insurance and periodic examinations, the regulations specify where banks can locate offices, what products they can offer, and what interest rates they can charge and pay. Only recently have they removed many restrictions. The trend appears to be toward greater competition and market determination of prices, available services, and allowing institutions to fail.

Legislation from 1956 to 1970 focused on limiting bank geographic and product expansion and restricting interest rate competition on deposits. To achieve this, regulators needed a formal designation of what constituted a bank. The operational definition through the early 1980s was that *a commercial bank both accepted demand deposits and made commercial loans.* Not surprisingly, this lead to the development of limited-service banks that offered just deposit services or just credit services, but avoided regulation as banks because they did not do both. Banks were generally restricted to operating within very narrow geographic markets, until they created limited-service banks that could locate anywhere.

Legislation of the late 1970s and early 1980s focused on the deregulation of pricing and products within the banking system. Interest rate ceilings were removed and banks and savings institutions were allowed to offer interest on checking accounts. A limited number of banks were allowed to offer discount stock brokerage and money market deposit accounts were authorized to allow banks to compete with products offered by brokerage firms, such as Merrill Lynch's Cash Management Account.

By the early 1980s, regulation was sidetracked by bills designed to assist the beleaguered S&L industry and to ensure that commercial banks did not succumb to the same fate. Regulation subsequently returned to deregulation of the banking industry, allowing new brokerage, underwriting, and insurance powers on a limited basis. With the rolling recession of the late 1980s and early 1990s, many commercial banks throughout the U.S. suffered severe asset quality problems leading to numerous failures. The early 1990s saw legislation designed to solve the leftover problems from the S&L crisis as well as address commercial bank asset quality and capital problems. By the mid-1990s, legislation again turned to deregulation of the financial services industry (note we did not use the term banking industry) and culminated with the Gramm-Leach-Bliley Act, considered the most comprehensive and far-reaching banking legislation since the enactment of Glass-Steagall. In fact, this act repealed Glass-Steagall.

BANKS VERSUS NONBANK BANKS. While many firms would like to offer banking services, some do not want to be regulated as commercial banks or bank holding companies. This is especially true of insurance companies, brokerage firms, and general retailers where banking services supplement their primary line of business. Banking regulation provides this opportunity.

In 1956, Congress passed the Bank Holding Company Act. Its fundamental intent was to enable government regulators to control the concentration of resources by large banking organizations and to ensure that banks engaged in activities closely related to banking. Under the Act and later amendments, the Fed must approve all bank holding company formations and acquisitions of banks and nonbanks. The Fed also rules on what activities bank holding companies can and cannot engage in. Many firms would like to offer banking services, but do not want to be regulated as commercial banks or bank holding companies. Because the regulations are prohibitive, they cannot own banks and still avoid these restrictions.

In 1980, Gulf & Western acquired a bank and sold its commercial loan portfolio, creating the first limited-service bank. Other nonbank institutions quickly followed suit including Prudential-Bache, Merrill Lynch, Sears, Fidelity Mutual Funds, and Beneficial Finance. Large commercial banking organizations similarly located limited-service banks outside their home states in order to expand their presence nationwide.

Small commercial banks and savings and loans protested the fact that limited-service banks were simply a means for firms in any line of business to engage in most banking activities but avoid regulation as banks. In 1983, the Fed agreed and attempted to restrict limited-service banks by redefining commercial loans to include the purchase of commercial paper, certificates of deposit, and bankers' acceptances. It also included interest-bearing checking accounts in its definition of demand deposits. Limited-service banks could no longer offer interest-bearing transactions accounts, and those that sold off their commercial loans could no longer invest in corporate securities unless they chose to register as bank holding companies. In 1986, the U.S. Supreme Court ruled that the Federal Reserve's definition exceeded its authority and thus nonbank banks were legal. Federal legislation in 1987, however, prohibited these banks from being chartered so that competition now comes only from those grandfathered firms.

Finally, even though the Glass-Steagall Act of 1933 explicitly distinguished between commerce and banking in determining what products different firms could offer, banks have historically been allowed to underwrite all types of securities, including stocks, outside the United States. Large firms, such as Citigroup, Bankers Trust (now part of Deutsche Bank), and J.P. Morgan, have generated a substantial share of their net income from these international activities. With the repeal of Glass-Steagall, banks are rapidly expanding into the investment banking area and have grown to be major players in the investment banking market. This is due to the relaxation of Glass-Steagall Section 20 affiliates powers and the repeal of Glass-Steagall.

THE DEPOSITORY INSTITUTIONS DEREGULATION AND MONETARY CONTROL ACT OF 1980

DIDMCA was the culmination of long-standing efforts to change the structure of the financial services industry. While specific reforms had been debated since 1961, the economic environment in the late 1970s magnified financial institutions' operating problems and forced legislation. Remember that rates depository institutions could pay on most deposits were fixed by Regulation Q. From 1976 through 1979, the monthly inflation rate, as measured by the consumer price index, increased from under 5 percent (annually) to over 15 percent. Money market interest rates similarly rose from around 6 percent to over 14 percent. During the same period, the prime rate changed 65 times, considerably more often than in previous years.

This period coincided with the extraordinary growth of money market mutual funds. These funds simply sell shares to individuals, usually with a fixed unit price of $1, and use the proceeds to buy money market instruments such as Treasury bills, bank certificates of deposit, and commercial paper. None of these instruments were subject to Regulation Q ceilings so shareholders effectively received money market rates less a small service charge. Money market mutual funds would even provide transactions privileges by allowing individuals to write checks as long as the minimum amount was several hundred dollars. Many individuals effectively substituted these shares for bank deposits.

Market participants subsequently altered their behavior. Savers earning fixed and relatively low interest rates on deposits subject to Regulation Q withdrew their funds and invested in alternative instruments paying market rates. Commercial banks that were required by Fed membership to hold large amounts of nonearning reserves withdrew from the system because the opportunity cost grew prohibitive. Usury ceilings limited the rates lenders could charge and many homebuyers, farmers, and small businesses could not obtain credit because lenders were less willing to extend credit. As a result, banks and savings and loans saw their cost of funds rise yet could not raise asset yields to keep pace. Savings and loans holding long-term mortgages at below-market rates experienced a severe profit and cash flow squeeze. Under this pressure, Congress approved DIDMCA and dramatically altered the long-term operating environment of financial institutions.

The stated goals of DIDMCA were to improve Federal Reserve monetary control, to allow institutions to pay market rates on deposits, and to expand the range of services offered. The intent was to gradually equalize treatment of different types of depository firms and increase competition. The most significant components of DIDMCA are summarized in Exhibit 2.18.

▪ EXHIBIT 2.18

KEY PROVISIONS OF THE DEPOSITORY INSTITUTIONS DEREGULATION AND MONETARY CONTROL ACT OF 1980

Improvement of Monetary Control
- Extends reserve requirements set by Federal Reserve to all federally insured depository institutions.
- Imposes new reserve requirements on transactions accounts and nonpersonal time deposits offered by banks and thrift institutions that are not Federal Reserve members. Over time, all firms of equal size will be subject to same percentage requirements.
- Allows all depository institutions that offer transactions accounts to borrow at Federal Reserve discount window.

Pricing of Federal Reserve Services
- Federal Reserve must explicitly price services provided to financial institutions based on cost of providing services.
- All services are available to member and nonmember institutions.

Interest Rate Ceilings and Deposit Insurance
- Phase out interest rate ceilings on deposits at financial institutions.
- Overrides state limits on deposit rates.
- Overrides state usury ceilings on loans for residential property unless reimposed by state legislatures.
- Raises ceiling rates on business and agriculture loans to 5 percent over discount rate.
- Increases federal deposit insurance to $100,000 at all federally insured institutions.

New Powers for Banks and Thrift Institutions
- Authorizes depository institutions to offer negotiable orders of withdrawal accounts.
- Authorizes credit unions to issue share drafts.
- Allows new investment for thrifts:
  Up to 20 percent of assets in consumer loans, commercial paper, corporate debt securities.
  Up to 5 percent of assets in education, community development, unsecured construction loans.
- Allows shares of open-end investment companies to satisfy liquidity requirements.
- Authorizes thrifts to issue credit cards and provide trust services.
- Allows qualifying thrifts to issue mutual capital certificates that constitute net worth.

In October 1979, the Federal Reserve announced that it would examine the monetary aggregates more closely in the future as intermediate targets of monetary policy. Implicitly, less attention would be paid to short-term interest rates. DIDMCA made control of money growth easier. Prior to 1980, nonmember commercial banks were subject to reserve requirements set by states. Savings and loans' reserves were set by thrift regulators. Only member banks had to hold reserves according to Federal Reserve guidelines. DIDMCA extended reserve requirements to all institutions offering transactions accounts and provided that the amount would be equal for similar sized firms after a phase-in period. For most institutions, reserve requirement ratios were lowered. In return, all firms gained access to the discount window and the Fed began explicitly to charge for services that it used to provide for free.

Most importantly, the act provided for the removal of interest rate ceilings. One set of regulations mandated that the Depository Institutions Deregulation Committee, made up of the chief officers of the four main regulatory agencies, phase out rate ceilings on time and savings deposits by 1986. Another set superseded state usury ceilings on loans for residential real property and business and agriculture loans over $25,000. The message was that borrowers and lenders should get accustomed to paying and charging market rates.[12] Coincidentally, FDIC insurance coverage was raised to $100,000 from $40,000 per account at all institutions. While this was done in part to adjust for inflation, it granted a significant

---

[12]Rate ceilings on all bank liabilities except demand deposits were removed in March 1986, after which the Depository Institutions Deregulation Committee was terminated.

THE LONG-TERM EFFECT OF $100,000 DEPOSIT INSURANCE

Prior to DIDMCA, federal deposit insurance amounted to $40,000 per account. Due at least in part to the efforts of the U.S. League of Savings Institutions, the savings and loan association lobbying arm, and the chairman of the House Banking Committee, Fernand St. Germain, Congress raised coverage to $100,000 with little debate. The effect, however, was monumental and immediate.

Brokerage houses quickly negotiated deals with aggressive thrifts and banks to sell certificates of deposit in $100,000 blocks to interested investors anywhere in the world. Because the principal was fully federally insured, an investor did not have to worry about the issuer defaulting—the insurance (the U.S. Treasury) would pay. To attract funds, a bank or thrift needed only to pay a rate that was slightly above the prevailing market rate. Unfortunately, there were no controls on the banks and thrifts regarding how to invest the funds.

As later performance revealed, many of these institutions speculated on real estate or simply frittered the money away. Thrift managers were essentially playing with the government's (taxpayer's) money. Thrift failures alone cost taxpayers an estimated $150 billion.

competitive advantage to banks and thrifts in attracting new deposits. Increased insurance made bank deposits safer than money market mutual funds and helped banks recoup some of their lost deposits. Contemporary Issues: The Long-Term Effect of $100,000 Deposit Insurance summarizes the analysis behind the decision to increase deposit insurance, which played a critical role in subsequent thrift failures.

Finally, DIDMCA granted new powers to depository institutions. First, all institutions could legally offer interest-bearing transactions accounts; banks and thrifts could offer negotiable orders of withdrawal (NOWs); and credit unions could offer share drafts.[13] Second, thrift institutions were authorized to invest additional assets in consumer loans and corporate securities. These assets could presumably be repriced more frequently and thus would reduce thrifts' exposure to increases in the cost of funds. The Act further authorized thrifts to offer credit card and trust services like those at commercial banks. Finally, thrifts were allowed to issue mutual capital certificates, which were acquired by federal regulators and included in thrifts' capital base. In essence, the regulators provided liquidity to capital-deficient firms with limited access to borrowed funds.

THE GARN–ST GERMAIN DEPOSITORY INSTITUTIONS ACT OF 1982

GSG continued the deregulation process. Thrifts were having difficulty competing for deposits and earning high enough yields on assets to be profitable. In many cases their cost of funds exceeded asset yields because they were paying market rates on deposits, but the bulk of assets still carried below market mortgage rates. Rising interest rates effectively raised interest expense more than interest income grew. Key provisions, listed in Exhibit 2.19, expanded deposit sources of funds, granted new asset powers, and provided for emergency takeovers of failing institutions.

---

[13]New England firms were allowed to offer these accounts in the mid-1970s. Prior to 1980, other institutions circumvented Regulation Q restrictions by creating new accounts such as automatic transfers from savings. See Chapters 12 and 14.

• EXHIBIT 2.19

KEY PROVISIONS OF THE GARN–ST GERMAIN DEPOSITORY INSTITUTIONS ACT OF 1982

New Sources of Deposit Funds

- Authorizes depository institutions to issue money market deposit account:
  Minimum balance of $2,500
  No minimum maturity
  No interest rate ceiling
  Limit of six transactions per month with three by check
  Federal insurance
- Allows governments to open NOW accounts.
- Allows federally chartered S&Ls to issue demand deposits to firms and individuals with which they have business loan relationships.

Expanded Powers

- Authorizes thrifts to make commercial loans and overdraft loans.
- Preempts state restrictions against due-on-sale clauses in mortgage contracts.
- Increases legal lending limit for any single customer as percentage of commercial bank capital and surplus.
- Permits thrifts to switch between state and federal charters, between mutual and stock form of organization, between savings and loan and savings bank charters.

Emergency Regulatory Powers

- Allows regulatory agencies to arrange mergers and acquisitions for problem institutions across geographic and institutional barriers.
- Allows regulators to make loans to problem firms or acquiring firms.
- Allows regulators to guarantee assets and liabilities of problem institutions.
- Allows regulators to issue net worth certificates to problem institutions.

GSG authorized three new sources of funds. The first, the money market deposit account (MMDA), was created to stop the flow of funds to unregulated money market mutual funds. Initially, there was no limit on the rate that banks could pay on balances in excess of $2,500. Depositors could write up to three checks per month with an additional three telephone transfers allowed, and the first $100,000 was federally insured. The Depository Institutions Deregulation Committee later authorized Super NOW accounts, which had the same basic features as MMDAs except that the number of transactions was unlimited. By 1986, all minimum balance requirements and rate ceilings on MMDAs and Super NOWs had been eliminated. The second new source was that all governmental units were permitted to hold NOW accounts. Previously, only individuals and nonprofit, nongovernment organizations could open accounts. Third, federal savings and loans could accept demand deposits from qualifying business loan customers.

Most of the expanded asset powers were designed to benefit thrifts. GSG authorized them to make commercial loans, to enforce due-on-sale clauses in mortgage contracts, and to convert to stock associations. The first two provisions enabled savings and loans to increase the interest sensitivity of asset holdings and enter new markets. Conversion to stock ownership from mutual organizations increased each firm's ability to raise capital. Commercial banks were allowed to increase loan limits for individual borrowers to 15 percent of bank capital and surplus for unsecured credits and 25 percent for secured credits.

The last set of provisions allowed mergers and acquisitions of problem financial institutions across state lines. According to GSG, federal regulators can arrange the acquisition of a failed firm by any type of insured institution, regardless of location. Qualified investors include commercial banks, bank holding companies, insured savings and loans, and other companies.

Both DIDMCA and GSG had their greatest impact on the risk-taking incentives to managers of banks and thrifts. Consider the manager of a small thrift which was locked in to a portfolio of fixed-rate mortgages that yielded less than what the firm was paying on its liabilities. Its interest expense would change with changes in market interest rates, while its interest income would remain relatively constant. As rates increased, the firm loses. Federal deposit insurance provided a strategy to offset such problems. Why not package deposits into $100,000 units that carried full deposit insurance, and sell the deposits to individuals and businesses throughout the country? Any firm could easily sell such units through brokers who simply called potential investors and offered to pay a premium over the prevailing deposit rate. Buyers of the deposits would not be at risk because the federal government would pay off the claim if the thrift failed. The thrift in turn would take the proceeds from these brokered deposits and invest in higher yielding, and riskier, assets than mortgages. If the assets paid the promised returns, the thrift could pay the new depositors and use the profits to offset losses on the old mortgages.

This is what many thrift managers did. Deposit insurance essentially allowed them to borrow at the government's (taxpayer's) risk, yet speculate with the proceeds to reap personal gains. If the thrift failed, managers lost only their jobs and any equity they might own in the thrift. The temptation was so great, however, that numerous thrift managers fraudulently used thrift resources for personal benefit and ultimately went to jail when the thrift failed and the true operating condition of the firm became known.

THE TAX REFORM ACT OF 1986

For many years the public perceived that banks did not pay their fair share of taxes. Large banks, especially those with publicly-traded stock, often used tax-sheltered investments, including municipal bonds with their tax-exempt interest and leasing and other subsidiary activities that produced accelerated depreciation allowances and foreign and investment tax credits, to reduce their reported tax liabilities close to zero. While Congress passed the Tax Reform Act of 1986 to restructure the entire federal income tax code, many provisions dramatically altered the tax treatment of commercial banks. The intent, at least in part, was to eliminate the perceived tax shelters available to banks.

Several of the act's major changes for banks are briefly summarized in Exhibit 2.20. The major benefit is that the corporate income tax rate was lowered to 34 percent. The new law also forced banks to restructure the composition of assets. The provisions generally took effect in 1987.

COMPETITIVE EQUALITY BANKING ACT OF 1987

During 1987, Congress passed the Competitive Equality Banking Act of 1987. The legislation served two main purposes. First, it formally legitimized the rights of existing nonbank banks. At the time of passage, there was concern that firms such as Sears and American Express were able to operate limited-service banks in direct competition with commercial banks, yet avoid regulation as banks or bank holding companies. The act placed restrictions on the type of products and growth of these grandfathered firms. It also prohibited new ones from being chartered. Second, it offered several provisions to assist in the handling of problem thrift institutions. Prior to the act, many savings and loans were operating at a loss and depleting their capital. The Federal Savings and Loan Insurance Corporation (FSLIC), the federal agency that insured thrifts, found that its reserves were depleted from large payouts to depositors at thrift closings, so that the fund was technically insolvent. The act authorized the issuance of $10.8 billion in securities where the proceeds were to be used to assist in thrift closings. Healthy

· EXHIBIT 2.20

KEY PROVISIONS OF THE TAX REFORM ACT OF 1986 THAT ALTERED
THE TAX TREATMENT OF COMMERCIAL BANKS

Lowered the corporate tax rate to 34 percent

Deductions for Bad Debts

- From 1969 to 1986 banks were allowed to set up loan-loss reserves as a percentage of their loan portfolio and deduct allocations to the loss reserve from income. The Tax Reform Act retains the reserve system for banks with $400 million or less in total assets.
- All other banks can deduct only what they actually charge off during a year.
- Carrying Costs of Municipal Bonds
- Banks can deduct only 80 percent of their borrowing costs associated with buying municipals issued for essential public purposes, if the municipality issues less than $10 million in securities per year.
- Banks lose the entire interest deduction on financing costs for new purchases of all other municipal securities.

Tax Credits

- Eliminated the investment tax credit that arose when depreciable assets were purchased.
- Individual Retirement Accounts became less attractive by eliminating the tax deduction for contributions to an account for high-income individuals.
- Alternative Minimum Tax. Corporations must now calculate their federal income tax in two ways: under the regular income tax method; and under the alternative minimum tax income applying a flat 20 percent tax. They must pay the greater of the two.

savings and loans were assessed an added charge to their normal deposit insurance fee to help pay interest on the bonds. In addition, the regulator of thrifts, the Federal Home Loan Bank Board (FHLBB), was required to use supervisory forbearance and not close thrifts that did not meet the minimum net worth requirements imposed by regulation. In essence, thrifts were perceived to be only temporarily unsafe and were to be given time to work out their problems. As the later crisis indicates, forbearance and how it was implemented by the FHLBB aggravated the problems by increasing the ultimate cost of the thrift bailout.

THE FINANCIAL INSTITUTIONS REFORM, RECOVERY AND ENFORCEMENT ACT OF 1989 (FIRREA)

On August 9, 1989, President Bush signed FIRREA into law. The stated purpose of the legislation was to provide for the efficient handling of problem savings and loan associations. In short, the FSLIC was insolvent and there was widespread concern that thrift institutions were fundamentally unsafe. FIRREA addressed these problems by:

- Improving the financial condition of the deposit insurance funds
- Changing the regulatory structure of the savings and loan industry
- Raising capital requirements and restricting investment activities of savings and loans
- Strengthening the enforcement powers of regulators

Specific provisions of the Act are included in Exhibit 2.21.

The act forced thrifts to divest of all junk bonds in their portfolios by July 1, 1994. Junk bonds are high yield bonds that carry a rating lower than either Baa or BBB, or are nonrated. Such bonds are perceived to exhibit substantial default risk because the borrower is likely to not repay the full amount of principal and interest owed. Prior to FIRREA, many savings and loans owned large amounts of junk bonds that were ultimately deemed to be too risky for their portfolios. The act further restricted how much savings and loans could lend to any single borrower, which in some cases was less than outstanding loans and loan commitments.

■ EXHIBIT 2.21

SPECIFIC PROVISIONS OF THE FINANCIAL INSTITUTIONS REFORM, RECOVERY
AND ENFORCEMENT ACT (FIRREA) OF 1989

Change in Regulatory Structure
- Replaced the Federal Home Loan Bank Board, which had historically regulated savings and loans, with the Office of Thrift Supervision (OTS), a division of the U.S. Treasury.
- Eliminated the Federal S&L Insurance Corporation (FSLIC) and replaced it with two deposit insurance funds operated by the Federal Deposit Insurance Corporation (FDIC):
     The Savings Associations Insurance Fund (SAIF) for savings institutions
     The Bank Insurance Fund (BIF) for commercial banks

Improving the Condition of the Insurance Funds
- Created the Resolution Trust Corp. (RTC) and the Resolution Funding Corp. (RefCorp) to assist in the closing of failed thrift institutions.
     The RTC (under the FDIC) managed firms placed into receivership and disposed of assets obtained by the closing of failed thrifts.
     The RefCorp issued bonds authorized by congress to finance the FDIC.

Increasing Capital Requirements and Restricting Investment Powers
- Mandated that the OTS set minimum capital requirements similar to national banks.
- Forced thrifts to divest of all junk bonds.
- Forced S&Ls to meet a qualified thrift lender (QTL) test: No less than 70 percent (65 percent today) of the firm's assets must be held in mortgage-related investments.

Strengthening the Enforcement Powers of Regulators
- Authorized penalties for firms that violate the law or regulations, or misstate financial information.
- Made it easier for regulators to issue "cease and desist" orders that restrict thrift activities and even remove individuals from certain management positions.

At the time, many analysts believed that FIRREA represented the death knell for thrift institutions as a separate industry due to lower expected profits and shrinkage in size associated with higher capital requirements. Surviving thrifts generally prospered with the favorable economic climate and gradual relaxation of regulations to allow them to compete more like commercial banks.

THE FEDERAL DEPOSIT INSURANCE CORPORATION IMPROVEMENT ACT OF 1991

The Federal Deposit Insurance Corporation Improvement Act of 1991 (FDICIA) was directed at recapitalizing the deposit insurance fund. In doing so, Congress authorized the FDIC to borrow to meet its payment obligations and raise deposit insurance premiums to a level necessary to build the fund's reserves to 1.25 percent of insured deposits. It also imposed specific, restrictive sanctions on banks and thrifts whose performance fell below acceptable standards. Specifically, the provisions mandate certain regulatory actions when a bank's capital is deficient such that regulatory discretion is sharply curtailed. Congress was upset that regulators let so many institutions reach the problem stage and were determined that it would not happen again.

Exhibit 2.22 describes these features and related issues addressed by FDICIA. The legislation was quite comprehensive in its coverage and precision. Specific details were provided to correct problems that were revealed in preceding years. Because of discriminatory policy in deciding which banks should fail, the act ended the policy of allowing regulators to keep big institutions from failing while letting smaller ones fail. It forced institutions to inform all depositors of applicable rates in a Truth in Savings section that provided for precise

**KEY PROVISIONS OF THE FEDERAL DEPOSIT INSURANCE
CORPORATION IMPROVEMENT ACT OF 1991**

Safety and Soundness

- Authorized additional borrowing by the FDIC of $30 billion from the Treasury to help rebuild the Bank Insurance Fund (BIF). The FDIC must pay back the loan within 15 years.
- Specified minimum size of the reserve fund as a fraction of insured deposits.
- Provided for prompt corrective action that mandated intervention by regulators when a bank's capital falls below minimum levels.
- Limited regulators' use of too-big-to-fail bailouts of large banks. The FDIC is required to close banks in a way that uses the least amount of money from the Bank Insurance Fund (BIF).
- Limits the Federal Reserve System's ability to lend money to banks that are in financial trouble.

Consumer Protection

- Required banks to disclose information on deposit products and services in a uniform, straightforward manner, including interest rates and fees.

Deposit Insurance

- Introduced risk-based deposit insurance premiums and required the FDIC set premiums based on how risky the bank is.

Foreign Bank Activities

- Required foreign banks that accepted small U.S. deposits to obtain deposit insurance.
- Provided greater authority for regulators to accept or deny new charters and order closings.

---

calculations and measures of savings rates to allow comparisons across accounts. The act allowed regulators wider latitude in closing the operations of foreign banks because of the problems associated with the Bank of Credit and Commerce International (BCCI), which lost over $20 billion largely through fraud.

MARKET VALUE ACCOUNTING AND FASB 115. In May 1993, the Financial Accounting Standards Board issued FASB No. 115, "Accounting for Certain Investments in Debt and Equity Securities." This standard addresses the issue of market value account and applies to all investments in equity securities that have readily determinable fair values, and all investments in debt securities. Investments subject to the standard are classified in three categories:

- *Held-to-maturity securities.* Debt securities that the institution has the positive intent and ability to hold to maturity are classified as held-to-maturity securities and reported at historical (amortized) cost.

- *Trading account securities.* Debt and equity securities that are bought and held primarily for the purpose of selling (or trading) them in the near term. Trading securities are reported at fair value, with unrealized gains and losses including in earnings (net income). Trading generally reflects active and frequent buying and selling, and trading securities are generally used with the objective of generating profits on short-term differences in price.

- *Available-for-sale securities.* Debt and equity securities not classified as either held-to-maturity securities or trading securities. Available-for-sale securities are reported at fair value, with unrealized gains and losses excluded from earnings but reported as a net amount in a separate component of shareholders' equity.

One potential weakness of FASB 115 is that is does not apply to loans, including mortgage loans that have not been secured.

RIEGLE-NEAL INTERSTATE BANKING AND BRANCHING EFFICIENCY ACT OF 1994. Interstate branching became a reality in 1997. Restrictive branching laws have historically shaped the banking system in the past and interstate branching will clearly reshape the banking industry in the future. Details of the new interstate branching law were presented earlier.

THE 1998 CREDIT UNION MEMBERSHIP ACCESS ACT. Competition between credit unions and banks has heated up in recent years. The major issue from the bank's perspective has been that credit unions offer bank products to an ever increasing membership, but do not pay income or franchise taxes. This obviously gives the credit unions a significant competitive advantage over financial institutions that do pay taxes. Credit unions have expanded membership qualifications far beyond their original "common bond" scope and have begun to use "community charters." A community charter basically allows a credit union to accept anyone in a broadly defined community as a member. As credit unions continue to expand their membership and products (some credit unions offer business loans), the debate on fairness remains heated. Credit unions argue that they are nonprofit cooperatives serving the needs of their membership and like any nonprofit organization should not be taxed.

The Credit Union Membership Access Act addresses four basic areas: membership limits, business lending limits and other regulations, capital requirements, and studies of the industry required.[14] Federal credit union membership falls into one of three basic categories: single common bond, multiple common bonds, and community. The act limits additional members of these groups to the immediate family or household of the member. The act grandfathers current members, and existing federal credit unions can enroll new members from the employee groups they currently serve. Single common bond usually refers to membership from a well-defined group, such as employees of IBM. The bill also allows for multiple common bond federal credit unions to serve unrelated groups provided they have fewer than 3,000 employees or members—service to larger groups requires approval from the National Credit Union Administration and is subject to needs. New credit union charters are encouraged over the absorption of new membership scope. Finally, the bill limits community credit unions to accepting members from a "well-defined local community, neighborhood, or rural district."

FINANCIAL SERVICES MODERNIZATION ACT (GRAMM-LEACH-BLILEY ACT OF 1999). The repeal of restrictions on banks affiliating with securities firms clearly tops the list of provisions of the Gramm-Leach-Bliley Act. The act, however, was more comprehensive and addressed new powers and products of banks and the financial services industry, functional regulation of the industry, insurance powers, the elimination of new charters for unitary savings and loan holding companies and even consumer privacy protection. In fact, it is the privacy section of the bill that has some of the most far reaching implications beyond banking. Specific provisions of the act are included in Exhibit 2.23.

The law creates a new *financial holding company* under the Bank Holding Company Act. Financial holding companies are authorized to engage in: underwriting and selling insurance and securities; conducting both commercial and merchant banking; investing in and developing real estate and other "complementary activities"—but there are limits on the kinds of non-financial activities these new entities may engage in. The act also modifies portions of the Bank Holding Company Act in order to allow affiliations between banks and insurance underwriters while preserving the authority of states to regulate insurance. At the same time,

---

[14]Anason, Dean, "The Major Provisions of Controversial New Law," *American Banker*, August 10, 1998.

· EXHIBIT 2.23

KEY PROVISIONS OF THE FINANCIAL SERVICES MODERNIZATION ACT (GRAMM-LEACH-BLILEY ACT OF 1999)

Title I — Facilitating Affiliation Among Banks, Securities Firms, and Insurance Companies
- Repeals the restrictions on banks affiliating with securities firms contained in sections 20 and 32 of the Glass-Steagall Act and lifts some restrictions governing nonbank banks.
- Creates a new "financial holding company" which can engage in: insurance and securities underwriting and agency activities, merchant banking, insurance company portfolio investment activities, and activities that are "complementary" to other financial activities.
- Provides for State regulation of insurance, subject to a standard that no State may discriminate against persons affiliated with a bank.
- Streamlines bank holding company supervision by clarifying the regulatory roles of the Federal Reserve as the umbrella holding company supervisor, and the State and other Federal financial regulators which 'functionally' regulate various affiliates.
- Prohibits FDIC assistance to affiliates and subsidiaries of banks and thrifts.
- Allows a national bank to engage in new financial activities in a financial subsidiary, except for insurance underwriting, merchant banking, insurance company portfolio investments, real estate development, and real estate investment, so long as the aggregate assets of all financial subsidiaries do not exceed 45% of the parent bank's assets or $50 billion, whichever is less.
- Merchant banking activities may be approved as a permissible activity beginning 5 years after the date of enactment of the Act.
- Provides for national treatment for foreign banks wanting to engage in the new financial activities authorized under the Act.

Title II — Functional Regulation
- Amends the Federal securities laws to incorporate functional regulation of bank securities activities and provides for a rulemaking and resolution process between the SEC and the Federal Reserve regarding new hybrid products.
- Provides for limited exemptions from broker-dealer registration for transactions.
- Addresses potential conflicts of interest in the mutual fund business and requires banks that advise mutual funds to register as investment advisers.

Title III — Insurance
- National bank subsidiaries are permitted to sell all types of insurance including title insurance. Affiliates may underwrite or sell all types of insurance including title insurance.
- State insurance and Federal regulators may seek an expedited judicial review of disputes with equalized deference.
- Allows multi-state insurance agency licensing.

Title IV — Unitary Savings And Loan Holding Companies
- Eliminates de novo unitary thrift holding company applications after May 4, 1999.
- Existing unitary thrift holding companies may only be sold to financial companies.

Title V — Privacy
- Requires disclosure of privacy policy regarding the sharing of non-public personal information.
- Requires an "opt-out" opportunity for the sharing of non-public personal information with nonaffiliated third parties.
- Assigns authority for enforcement to the FTC and the Federal banking agencies, the NCUA and the SEC, according to their respective jurisdictions, and provides for enforcement of the subtitle by the States.

Title VI — Federal Home Loan Bank System Modernization
- Provides access to banks with less than $500 million in assets access advances for loans to small businesses, small farms, and small agri-businesses.
- Provides for a new permanent capital structure for the Federal Home Loan Bank.

Title VII — Other Provisions
- Requires ATM to post a notice on the machine that a fee will be charged.
- Directs the Federal Reserve Board to conduct a study of the default rates, delinquency rates, and profitability of CRA loans.

SOURCE: Senate Banking Committee, Gramm-Leach-Bliley Act of 1999, Information, http://www.senate.gov/~banking/conf/.

the act prohibits states from preventing bank-affiliated firms from selling insurance on an equal basis with other insurance agents. It also amends the Community Reinvestment Act to require that the respective insured depository institution receive and maintain a satisfactory CRA rating before a financial holding company can be formed and requires public disclosure of bank-community CRA-related agreements.

The act also addresses the issue of functional regulation and makes the Federal Reserve responsible for financial holding companies. It specifically streamlines bank holding company supervision by establishing the Federal Reserve as the umbrella holding company supervisor while State and other Federal regulators 'functionally' regulate the various affiliates of the holding company. Because banks can now engage in securities, insurance, and commerce businesses, the act provides for a rulemaking and resolution process between the SEC and the Fed and allows multi-state insurance agency licensing.

The act eliminates the issuing of new unitary savings and loan holding company charters. Earlier discussions about the unitary thrift charter indicated that this was a significant loophole to the Bank Holding Company Act as well as provisions of Glass-Steagall. To avoid a "market" for existing unitary thrift charters, existing unitary thrift holding companies may only be sold to financial holding companies and affiliations and acquisitions between commercial firms and unitary thrift institutions are prohibited.

Even the growth of the Internet and the technology age clearly reached this bill as there are extensive provisions restricting the disclosure of nonpublic customer information by financial institutions. The bill requires all financial institutions to provide customers the opportunity to "opt-out" of the sharing of the customers' nonpublic information with unaffiliated third parties, and imposes criminal penalties on anyone who obtains customer information from a financial institution under false pretenses. The act assigns authority for enforcing these provisions to the Federal Trade Commission, Federal banking agencies, NCUA, and SEC, according to their respective jurisdictions, and provides for enforcement by the states.

The act provided banks with less than $500 million in assets access to long-term advances for loans to small businesses, small farms, and small agri-businesses from the Federal Home Loan Bank (FHLB). This provided smaller banks with a needed new source of funding. Other provisions included ATM fee disclosures as well as several directed studies on subordinated debt for larger banks and default and profitability of CRA loans.

USA PATRIOT ACT

On October 26, 2001, President Bush signed the USA Patriot Act (USAPA). This act gives broad new powers to both domestic law enforcement and international intelligence agencies. The bill requires changes, some significant and some small, to about 15 different statutes. There are several sections of the act pertaining to online activities and surveillance as well as money laundering, immigration, and providing for the victims of terrorism, including those of September 11, 2001. Some of the most important aspects that pertain to banking are:

- Requires additional reporting, due diligence, and "know-your-customer" standards for private banking and correspondent relationships.
- Requires special monitoring of correspondent and alien accounts opened by institutions and individuals in countries of "primary" money-laundering concern.
- Requires special reporting and monitoring of the beneficial ownership and activity of certain foreign and private banking customers.
- Requires the development of new anti-laundering programs, due diligence policies, and controls to ensure the detection and reporting of laundering.

Banks doing business with certain foreign banks or customers have a greater responsibility and heightened duty of investigation. They are required to monitor and share information more broadly than previously required. They are required to make additional efforts to document their ongoing execution of these obligations. This act increases the financial systems role in the war on terrorism.

CURRENT UNRESOLVED REGULATORY ISSUES

Bank regulation continually evolves in response to economic and competitive conditions. At any time, managers of banks express concern regarding limitations on their allowable activities and unfavorable competitive conditions, while regulators try to respond by identifying the appropriate rules to guide behavior and achieve the objectives presented earlier. During the early 2000s, many issues were under debate regarding the future structure and operating environment of financial services institutions. Key facets of the debate are identified below, with the topics discussed in greater detail throughout the book.

CAPITAL ADEQUACY

During the 1980s, bank and thrift failures soared. The U.S. economy experienced what is referred to as a rolling recession in which different geographic markets suffered significant economic problems. Consider, for example, the farm crisis in the Midwest, problems with the steel industry in the Mideast, the energy problems in the Southwest, and real estate problems throughout the country. Failures correspondingly increased reflecting both economic problems and general mismanagement.

Effective in 1992, banks and thrifts were subject to minimum capital requirements designed to reduce the overall risk of the banking industry. These requirements stipulated the minimum amount of stockholders' equity and maximum amount of debt that banks can use to finance their assets. The greater the equity, the lower the risk of the credit granting institution. The 1992 standards based the minimum equity on the general default riskiness of bank assets. The current debate focuses on how much capital is enough. As banks enter into new product areas, the concern of regulators is that the FDIC may be underwriting additional risks not covered by a bank's capital position. Regulators would like to increase the minimum requirement because it reduces the likelihood of failure. Bankers, in contrast, argue that it is expensive and difficult to obtain additional equity, and high requirements restrict their competitiveness.

Regulators have followed the "capital is king" approach during the late 1990s. Well-capitalized banks have been allowed to expand the range of products they offer including establishing affiliates that can underwrite and deal in securities. Well-capitalized banks' regulatory burdens are lessened as well. The difficulty is in identifying which firms are truly well capitalized and which firms need additional capital.

TOO BIG TO FAIL

Historically, regulators have not allowed the largest commercial banks to fail. For example, in 1991 the Bank of New England, with $22 billion in assets, failed and all depositors were fully protected. When large banks have gotten into trouble, regulators have arranged mergers or acquisitions and effectively protected depositors who held balances in excess of $100,000. Thus, federal deposit insurance was extended to all depositors regardless of their balances. In contrast, small banks are routinely allowed to fail and uninsured depositors lose a portion of their uninsured balance. One month before the Bank of New England's failure, Freedom National Bank in Harlem, with $98 million in assets, failed. Here uninsured depositors received approximately 50 cents per dollar of uninsured deposits. Isn't this discriminatory? Why are large banks not allowed to fail? FDICIA altered this effective in 1995 because regulators are not allowed to protect uninsured depositors of large banks at failure unless this is shown to be the least costly method. The Gramm-Leach-Bliley Act provides for a study of the use of subordinated debt to protect the financial system and the FDIC insurance fund from too-big-to-fail. Subordinated debt would be uninsured and hence unsafe banks would find a significant cost to issuing this debt. The hope is that requiring a large bank to issue subordinated debt would mean that market discipline, which would provide for lower costs of debt for lower risk banks, would prevail upon the larger banks to control risk.

DEPOSIT INSURANCE REFORM

The structure of deposit insurance during the 1980s clearly contributed to the high rate of failures and huge cost of the thrift bailout. The ongoing debate concerns the appropriate structure, purpose, and cost of deposit insurance. If it is truly insurance, shouldn't premiums paid by banks reflect their risk and thus probability of failure? FDICIA required the FDIC to assess insurance premiums based on a bank's risk. Each bank is assigned to one of three general capital categories: well-capitalized, adequately-capitalized, and under-capitalized. Each bank is then assigned to one of three supervisory categories within each capital category. Every three months FDIC assessment rates are adjusted to ensure that the premiums adequately reflect a bank's risk position and that the target Designated Reserve Ratio (DRR) of 1.25 percent of insured deposits is maintained.

This worked well for a short period of time but due to the exceptional profitability and lack of bank failures during the later part of the 1990s, almost all banks paid the same flat rate insurance premium of zero percent of domestic deposits from 1998 to 2001. The insurance fund is well funded in that the DDR was around 1.35 percent in 2001. Approximately 2 percent of banks (the riskiest banks) paid insurance premiums in 2001.

The second issue is the amount of deposit insurance coverage. In order to reduce the incentive for bank managers to take excessive risks caused by the insurance funds paying off depositors in the case of failure, shouldn't coverage be reduced from $100,000 per account? There is, however, just as much talk about increasing deposit insurance to $200,000 today. Finally, if the regulators will not allow the largest banks to fail, shouldn't insurance premiums be based on foreign deposits as well as domestic deposits?

HEDGE FUNDS

During 1998, Long-Term Capital Management, a U.S.-based hedge fund managed by well-known bankers, with two Nobel prize winners as part of the management team, effectively failed and was bailed out by a consortium of financial institutions. The Fed helped arrange the bailout. A hedge fund is essentially a mutual fund where there are a limited number of investors and fund managers can take virtually any positions buying or selling financial and nonfinancial assets. They accept capital from investors and borrow extensively to speculate on price moves. Banks are some of the lenders to these funds. In 1998, bank regulators became concerned that hedge funds were taking excessive risks and banks were potentially unaware of these risks. Similar issues arose when Enron, the world's largest natural gas distributor and pipeline company, filed for bankruptcy in December 2001.

Enron had effectively become a trader of oil, gas, weather futures, broadband, and other financial products rather than a holder of hard, physical assets. In essence, it was a hedge fund. While management prided itself on the firm's ability to measure and manage risk, excessive risk-taking and huge bets on certain positions ultimately forced the firm into bankruptcy when the rating agencies downgraded Enron's debt and the firm was unable to raise additional capital. The ongoing debate is whether hedge funds should disclose more information so that investors are aware of a fund's risk exposure. There is also concern that these funds should be regulated or that banks that lend to these funds should be forced to operate with additional capital.

NEW POWERS

Banks are continually pressing for additional investment powers and the opportunity to enter new lines of business. Many banks, for example, would like to offer full lines of securities and insurance products and be regulated to a lesser degree as securities firms are. It is ironic that with all the new powers granted to banks at the end of the 1990s, they were still not allowed to offer interest on business checking accounts through 2001. Investment firms, however, could offer "sweep" accounts that effectively allow them to pay interest on business accounts. Although banks can offer sweep accounts, they must sweep business accounts out of FDIC insured deposits. This effectively means that they must sweep them to investment firms, or start their own mutual fund!

SUMMARY

According to historical regulatory definition, a commercial bank is a firm that both accepts demand deposits and makes commercial loans. Although this has been the legal definition, it is not fundamentally useful today. Banks can now own and operate securities businesses, insurance companies, and other financial services firms and such firms can own and operate banks. It is now more appropriate to refer to the banking industry as a combination of traditional banks, represented by community and regional banks and savings associations, and more complex financial services firms. Managers can choose an organizational structure that allows them to offer a wide range of products and services and compete across many different geographic markets.

The Comptroller of the Currency and state banking departments approve new bank charters and, along with the Federal Reserve and FDIC, regulate and examine qualifying banks. Many banks operate as unit banks with only one office while others are part of branch banking systems. Both unit and branch banks may be part of a bank holding company, which owns controlling interest in subsidiary banks. Through holding companies, many banking organizations engage in activities closely related to banking, such as leasing, data processing, investment banking, and mortgage banking. Federal legislation now permits interstate banking, which represents a significant catalyst for change.

Commercial banks compete with other banks and depository institutions. Savings and loans, in particular, can offer identical deposit products and invest in the same assets, as well as possess additional real estate, investment, and insurance powers. Banks also compete with limited-service banks, or nonbank banks, that operate as part of nationwide financial service companies. Depending on their choice of organizational structure, banks can also compete with securities firms, real estate firms, insurance companies, finance companies, and other providers of financial services.

This chapter describes the organizational structure of the commercial banking industry and the legislation and regulation that guide operating policies. Early restrictions regarding branching encouraged the formation of holding companies and the development of nonbank banks as a means of circumventing branching restrictions. The impact of interest deregulation and increased deposit insurance was to encourage risk-taking by banks and thrifts, so that many firms failed during the 1980s and early 1990s. Congress approved legislation (FIRREA) in 1989 that substantially restructured the thrift industry by redefining acceptable business activities. The current regulatory trend is to remove differences in opportunities now available to different types of financial services companies, and thus expand the number of competitors in most product areas. The Financial Modernization Act of 1999 greatly enhanced such opportunities such that all managers must constantly assess what businesses and products their firms should offer and in what form.

QUESTIONS

1. What are the advantages of a bank having many branches in a city or state as opposed to just one main office location? What are the disadvantages?

2. What are the basic assets and liabilities of a multibank holding company? In what form does a holding company generate income?

3. What are the primary differences between a bank holding company and a financial holding company?

4. Will specialty or small community banks be able to compete successfully with larger commercial banks now that interstate banking is allowed? Will small community banks be able to compete successfully with firms such as Merrill Lynch, Charles Schwab, Bank of America, BankOne, and Household International?

5. Exhibit 2.4 documents the sharp drop in financial assets controlled by depository institutions. Explain why banks are losing market share. What must happen for them to reverse this trend? Explain why mutual funds and pension funds are increasing their market shares.

6. Explain why there are so many different bank regulatory agencies. Devise a regulatory structure that would improve the existing system.

7. What are the basic objectives of banking regulation? How do regulators attempt to achieve these objectives?

8. Federal deposit insurance used to cover a maximum of $40,000 per eligible account. It was later raised to $100,000 per account. What cost and/or risk did this present to the FDIC? What role, if any, did this play in the banking industry's problems during the 1980s?

9. What does the acronym CAMELS refer to in bank examinations? What are the most important facets of an examination?

10. Why were commercial banks prohibited from underwriting corporate securities within the United States but not abroad? How can a bank engage in underwriting corporate securities today?

11. Exhibits 2.16 and 2.17 document the share of in-state deposits held by out-of-state bank holding companies. Find the state where you live. Explain why the share listed is high, low, or in the middle. Discuss recent trends in bank mergers and acquisitions within your state.

12. Describe five levels of management typically found in an independent bank. Which level do you think is the most important? Why?

13. Why might banking regulators prohibit banks from underwriting insurance products? Why might they prohibit banks from buying real estate assets as an investment? Determine whether current banking law has changed or is expected to change to allow Citigroup (Citicorp and Travelers merger) to remain intact.

14. Is the purpose of bank regulation to prevent bank failures?

15. What are the duties of outside members of a bank's board of directors? To whom are directors responsible?

16. Outline the major provisions of the Gramm-Leach-Bliley Act of 1999. Many experts considered this bill to favor larger multibank holding companies. What are some of the advantages or disadvantages of this bill to the largest and smallest banks? Do you think this bill will hasten the reduction in the number of smaller banks?

ACTIVITIES

1. What banks headquartered out-of-state have a major presence in your state? List their competitive advantages and disadvantages versus in-state banks. What nonbank banks offer competing products in your market? Make a list of which firms will allow you to open a checking account. Which firms will allow you to borrow money as an individual? Are they all banks? If not, what type of firm are they?

2. There are many proponents of expanding the types of activities allowed banks in the United States. Do you think the United States should allow banks to provide any service? What are the primary advantages of expanded powers? What are the primary disadvantages? Choose a large multibank holding company you might be familiar with and compare the services offered with those of a smaller community bank that you or someone you know uses. Does the community bank offer all the services you demand? Does the larger multibank? Do you use these services at a bank? Why or why not?

APPENDIX

IMPORTANT BANKING LEGISLATION

- **National Bank Act of 1864** (Chapter 106, 13 STAT. 99). Established a national banking system and the chartering of national banks.

- **Federal Reserve Act of 1913** (P.L. 63-43, 38 STAT. 251, 12 USC 221). Established the Federal Reserve System as the central banking system of the U.S.

- **To Amend the National Banking Laws and the Federal Reserve Act** (P.L. 69-639, 44 STAT. 1224). Also known as the McFadden Act of 1927. Prohibited interstate banking.

- **Banking Act of 1933** (P.L. 73-66, 48 STAT. 162). Also known as the Glass-Steagall Act. Established the FDIC as a temporary agency. Separated commercial banking from investment banking, establishing them as separate lines of commerce.

- **Banking Act of 1935** (P.L. 74-305, 49 STAT. 684). Established the FDIC as a permanent agency of the government.

- **Federal Deposit Insurance Act of 1950** (P.L. 81-797, 64 STAT. 873). Revised and consolidated earlier FDIC legislation into one act. Embodied the basic authority for the operation of the FDIC.

- **Bank Holding Company Act of 1956** (P.L. 84-511, 70 STAT. 133). Required Federal Reserve Board approval for the establishment of a bank holding company. Prohibited bank holding companies headquartered in one state from acquiring a bank in another state.

- **International Banking Act of 1978** (P.L. 95-369, 92 STAT. 607). Brought foreign banks within the federal regulatory framework. Required deposit insurance for branches of foreign banks engaged in retail deposit-taking in the U.S.

- **Financial Institutions Regulatory and Interest Rate Control Act of 1978** (P.L. 95-630, 92 STAT. 3641). Also known as FIRIRCA. Created the Federal Financial Institutions Examination Council. Established limits and reporting requirements for bank insider transactions. Created major statutory provisions regarding electronic fund transfers.

- **Depository Institutions Deregulation and Monetary Control Act of 1980** (P.L. 96-221, 94 STAT. 132). Also known as DIDMCA. Established "NOW Accounts." Began the phase-out of interest rate ceilings on deposits. Established the Depository Institutions Deregulation Committee. Granted new powers to thrift institutions. Raised the deposit insurance ceiling to $100,000.

- **Depository Institutions Act of 1982** (P.L. 97-320, 96 STAT. 1469). Also known as Garn–St Germain. Expanded FDIC powers to assist troubled banks. Established the Net Worth Certificate program. Expanded the powers of thrift institutions.

- **Competitive Equality Banking Act of 1987** (P.L. 100-86, 101 STAT. 552). Also known as CEBA. Established new standards for expedited funds availability. Recapitalized the Federal Savings and Loan Insurance Corporation (FSLIC). Expanded FDIC authority for open bank assistance transactions, including bridge banks.

- **Financial Institutions Reform, Recovery and Enforcement Act of 1989** (P.L. 101-73, 103 STAT. 183). Also known as FIRREA. FIRREA's purpose was to restore the public's confidence in the savings and loan industry. FIRREA abolished the Federal Savings and Loan Insurance Corporation (FSLIC), and the FDIC was given the responsibility of insuring the deposits of thrift institutions in its place. The FDIC insurance fund created to cover thrifts was named the Savings Association Insurance Fund (SAIF), while the fund covering banks was called the Bank Insurance Fund (BIF). FIRREA also abolished the Federal Home Loan Bank Board. Two new agencies, the Federal Housing Finance Board (FHFB) and the Office of Thrift Supervision (OTS), were created to replace it. Finally, FIRREA created the Resolution Trust Corporation (RTC) as a temporary agency of the government. The RTC was given the responsibility of managing and disposing of the assets of failed institutions. An Oversight Board was created to provide supervisory authority over the policies of the RTC, and the Resolution Funding Corporation (RFC) was created to provide funding for RTC operations.

- **Crime Control Act of 1990** (P.L. 101-647, 104 STAT. 4789). Title XXV of the Crime Control Act, known as the Comprehensive Thrift and Bank Fraud Prosecution and Taxpayer Recovery Act of 1990, greatly expanded the authority of Federal regulators to combat financial fraud. This act prohibited undercapitalized banks from making golden parachute and other indemnification payments to institution-affiliated parties. It also increased penalties and prison time for those convicted of bank crimes, increased the powers and authority of the FDIC to take enforcement actions against institutions operating in an unsafe or unsound manner, and gave regulators new procedural powers to recover assets improperly diverted from financial institutions.

- **Federal Deposit Insurance Corporation Improvement Act of 1991** (P.L. 102-242, 105 STAT. 2236). Also known as FDICIA. FDICIA greatly increased the powers and authority of the FDIC. Major provisions recapitalized the Bank Insurance Fund and allowed the FDIC to strengthen the fund by borrowing from the Treasury. The act mandated a least-cost resolution method and prompt resolution approach to problem and failing banks and ordered the creation of a risk-based deposit insurance assessment scheme. Brokered deposits and the solicitation of deposits were restricted, as were the nonbank activities of insured state banks. FDICIA created new supervisory and regulatory examination standards and put forth new capital requirements for banks. It also expanded prohibitions against insider activities and created new Truth in Savings provisions.

- **Housing and Community Development Act of 1992** (P.L. 102-550, 106 STAT. 3672). Established regulatory structure for government-sponsored enterprises (GSEs), combated money laundering, and provided regulatory relief to financial institutions.

- **RTC Completion Act** (P.L. 103-204, 107 STAT. 2369). Required the RTC to adopt a series of management reforms and to implement provisions designed to improve the agency's record in providing business opportunities to minorities and women when issuing RTC contracts or selling assets. Expanded the existing affordable housing programs of the RTC and the FDIC by broadening the potential affordable housing stock of the two agencies. Increased the statute of limitations on RTC civil lawsuits from three years to five, or to the period provided in state law, whichever is longer. In cases in which the statute of limitations has expired, claims can be revived for fraud and intentional misconduct resulting in unjust enrichment or substantial loss to the thrift. Provided final funding for the RTC and established a transition plan for transfer of RTC resources to the FDIC. The RTC's sunset date was set at December 31, 1995, at which time the FDIC assumed its conservatorship and receivership functions.

- **Riegle Community Development and Regulatory Improvement Act of 1994** (P.L. 103-325, 108 STAT. 2160). Established a Community Development Financial Institutions Fund, a wholly owned government corporation that would provide financial and technical assistance to CDFIs. Contains several provisions aimed at curbing the practice of "reverse redlining" in which non-bank lenders target low and moderate income homeowners, minorities, and the elderly for home equity loans on abusive terms. Relaxes capital requirements and other regulations to encourage the private sector secondary market for small business loans. Contains more than 50 provisions to reduce bank regulatory burden and paperwork requirements. Requires the Treasury Dept. to develop ways to substantially reduce the number of currency transactions filed by financial institutions. Contains provisions aimed at shoring up the National Flood Insurance Program.

- **Riegle-Neal Interstate Banking and Branching Efficiency Act of 1994** (P.L. 103-328, 108 STAT. 2338). Permits adequately capitalized and managed bank holding companies to acquire banks in any state one year after enactment. Concentration limits apply and CRA evaluations by the Federal Reserve are required before acquisitions are approved. Beginning June 1, 1997, allows interstate mergers between adequately capitalized and managed banks, subject to concentration limits, state laws, and CRA evaluations. Extends the statute of limitations to permit the FDIC and RTC to revive lawsuits that had expired under state statutes of limitations.

- **Economic Growth and Regulatory Paperwork Reduction Act of 1996** (P.L. 104-208, 110 STAT. 3009). Modified financial institution regulations, including regulations impeding the flow of credit from lending institutions to businesses and consumers. Amended the Truth in Lending Act and the Real Estate Settlement Procedures Act of 1974 to streamline the mortgage lending process. Amended the FDIA to eliminate or revise various application, notice, and recordkeeping requirements to reduce regulatory burden and the cost of credit. Amended the Fair Credit Reporting Act to strengthen consumer protections relating to credit reporting agency practices. Established consumer protections for potential clients of consumer repair services. Clarified lender liability and federal agency liability issues under the CERCLA. Directed FDIC to impose a special assessment on depository institutions to recapitalize the SAIF, aligned SAIF assessment rates with BIF assessment rates, and merged the SAIF and BIF into a new Deposit Insurance Fund.

■ **Gramm-Leach-Bliley Act of 1999** (P.L. 106-102, 113 STAT 1338). Repeals last vestiges of the Glass-Steagall Act of 1933. Modifies portions of the Bank Holding Company Act to allow affiliations between banks and insurance underwriters. While preserving authority of states to regulate insurance, the act prohibits state actions that have the effect of preventing bank-affiliated firms from selling insurance on an equal basis with other insurance agents. Law creates a new financial holding company under section 4 of the BHCA, authorized to engage in: underwriting and selling insurance and securities, conducting both commercial and merchant banking, investing in and developing real estate and other "complimentary activities." There are limits on the kinds of non-financial activities these new entities may engage in. Allows national banks to underwrite municipal bonds. Restricts the disclosure of nonpublic customer information by financial institutions. All financial institutions must provide customers the opportunity to "opt-out" of the sharing of the customers' nonpublic information with unaffiliated third parties. The act imposes criminal penalties on anyone who obtains customer information from a financial institution under false pretenses. Amends the Community Reinvestment Act to require that financial holding companies cannot be formed before their insured depository institutions receive and maintain a satisfactory CRA rating. Also requires public disclosure of bank-community CRA-related agreements. Grants some regulatory relief to small institutions in the shape of reducing the frequency of their CRA examinations if they have received outstanding or satisfactory ratings. Prohibits affiliations and acquisitions between commercial firms and unitary thrift institutions. Makes significant changes in the operation of the Federal Home Loan Bank System, easing membership requirements and loosening restrictions on the use of FHLB funds.

II

EVALUATING BANK PERFORMANCE

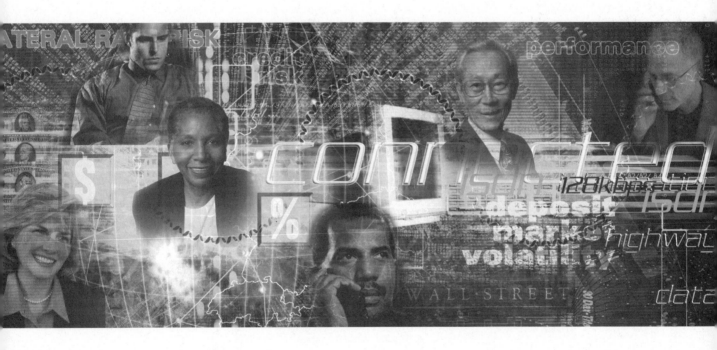

3

Analyzing Bank Performance: Using the UBPR

After more than three years of squabbling over documents, accounting procedures, loan exposure, and multiple earnings restatements, the Office of the Comptroller of the Currency closed the $1.3 billion Hamilton Bank on January 11, 2002, and appointed the Federal Deposit Insurance Corporation as receiver. The FDIC immediately started preparing for the possible sale of $1 billion in loans. On January 14, 2002, NASDAQ halted trading in the stock of the bank's parent, Hamilton Bancorp. The closure was the climax of a three-year battle between regulators and Hamilton Bank over accounting practices and the bank's loan portfolio, which was built around loans to nonfinancial firms and banks in Latin America and to importers/exporters in South Florida. In 2001, Hamilton agreed to the OCC's demands to start charging-off some of the Latin American loans. As of September 30, 2001, the bank had about $80 million in equity remaining and $75.1 million in loans that were non-performing, or about 8% of total loans. The bank's charge-offs and losses on sales of Latin American loans resulted in a net loss in excess of $28 million for 2001.

At the time the OCC closed Hamilton Bank, it still reported a 7.25 percent risk-based capital ratio, which made it "undercapitalized" for regulatory purposes. The OCC used its power in conjunction with the FDIC under "prompt corrective action" provided by the Federal Deposit Insurance Corporation Improvement Act of 1991 to close a bank when its capital falls below minimum levels in order to protect the FDIC insurance fund. At the last safety-and-soundness examination of Hamilton, shortly before its failure, the OCC indicated that the bank's condition had deteriorated from its already unsatisfactory condition reported in prior exams. The OCC also stated that management had failed to make progress in resolving the problems and that the board of directors failed to hold management accountable for the needed improvements. The OCC said that the bank's capital was rapidly being depleted and that classified loans had increased to over 150 percent of capital. Hamilton had been operating under a cease-and-desist order that imposed significant operational and financial guidelines upon reserves to cover foreign loans, the purchase and sale of loans, and required capital levels. As an example of its problems, Hamilton sold loans to Ecuadorean banks valued at $38.3 million for $22.3 million in cash during the third quarter of 2001, improving asset quality, but depleting capital.

Although banks fail for different reasons, Hamilton is unusual because it successfully battled over accounting principals with regulators for almost three years. Hamilton restated 1999 and 2000 earnings to report a $7.3 million loss and then reported a $24.7 million loss (about one-third of total equity) for the second quarter of 2001. How can a bank's loan exposure get this extreme? Did a few large bad loans surprise managers and bring about failure? Did the bank's managers disguise loan problems that were always there? The OCC apparently believed that managers hid the problem loans and the bank's profits were systematically overstated and true profits were below average—hence the requirement to restate earnings.

Many banks experience dramatic changes in profits from one period to the next or relative to what stock analysts expect. In many cases, profits are lower because of unanticipated loan losses. PNC Bank, discussed extensively in this chapter, is a prime example. In 2000, PNC reported a return on equity of almost 19 percent, but reported only a 9.3 percent return in 2001 due to loan charge-offs. In other cases, profits are higher because of extraordinary growth in noninterest income. A key point is that it is becoming increasingly difficult to evaluate performance by looking at reported balance sheet and income statement data. Net income can be managed, or manipulated, by bank managers to disguise potential problems.

This chapter presents a procedure for analyzing bank performance using periodic balance sheet and income statement data. It describes the components of financial statements, provides a framework for comparing the trade-offs between profitability and risk, and compares the performance of a small community bank with that of a large super regional banking organization. It uses data presented in a bank's Uniform Bank Performance Report (UBPR) to demonstrate the analysis.

From 1985 to 1990, 1,016 commercial banks failed throughout the United States, a rate of just over 169 bank failures each year. Many other banks avoided closing only because of arranged mergers and forbearance, or were placed on the regulators' problem bank list—indicating severe operating difficulties. The recent trend, however, has been quite favorable as only 27 banks failed from 1995 to 2001, or fewer than 4 per year. Can an objective observer identify problem institutions before they fail? Is it possible to distinguish between strong and weak banks on the basis of reported earnings and balance sheet figures? How should risk be measured? How can the trade-off between risk and profitability be evaluated? These and other questions have become increasingly important as banks face greater competition from nontraditional competitors and regulators demonstrate a willingness to close banks.

U.S. commercial banks reported record aggregate profits every year throughout the 1990s. Return on equity and return on assets set new standards for the banking industry in the late 1990s (see Exhibit 3.1) with the year 2001 representing the eleventh year of record profits. While the events of September 11, 2001 and the recession of 2001 reduced returns to shareholders, they appear to be earnings events rather than solvency events. The 1990s evidenced improved asset quality with fewer loan defaults, higher interest income on assets relative to interest expense on liabilities, and significantly greater noninterest income relative to noninterest expense. By the end of 2001, however, loan losses had begun to increase, particularly at larger banks. The primary problem areas have been personal (individual) bankruptcies, relatively high losses on credit card loans, trading account losses, commercial and industrial loan losses, and restructuring charges as a result of mergers and acquisitions at the largest banks.[1]

---

[1]A good reference for up-to-date banking statistics on the Internet is the FDIC's Web page at www.fdic.gov.

· EXHIBIT 3.1

TRENDS IN RETURN ON EQUITY AND RETURN ON ASSETS FOR COMMERCIAL BANKS, 1934–2001

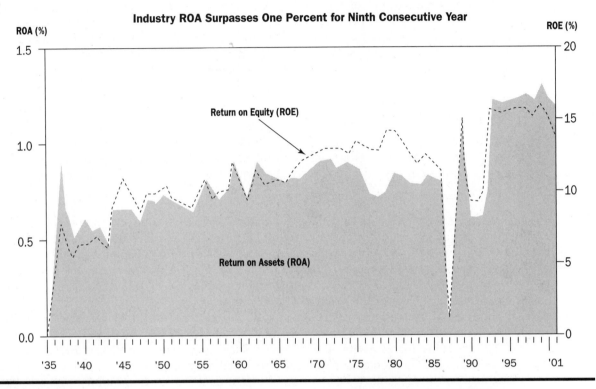

SOURCE: FDIC Quarterly Banking Profile, Fourth Quarter 2001, http://www.fdic.gov/, http://www2.fdic.gov/qbp.

This chapter explains how to evaluate commercial bank performance. The analysis begins by introducing bank financial statements. A return on equity framework is then used to describe the trade-offs between profitability and risk and provide measures that differentiate between high- and low-performance banks. The analytical framework is applied to data for PNC Bank, a large multibank company own by PNC Bank Corp., and Community National Bank, a representative specialized community bank.[2] The analysis allows us to compare the financial characteristics of different-sized banks. The chapter also introduces the CAMELS system used by federal supervisors to rate banks. Finally, because banks can disguise adverse changes in their performance from year to year, special attention is paid to financial statement manipulation.

COMMERCIAL BANK FINANCIAL STATEMENTS

Like other financial intermediaries, commercial banks facilitate the flow of funds from surplus spending units (savers) to deficit spending units (borrowers). Their financial characteristics

---

[2]PNC Bank Corp. is a large and complex banking organization. We will only deal with PNC Bank in this chapter, assuming that PNC Bank can be evaluated independently of PNC Bank Corp. As will be discussed in the following chapter, one must look at the holding company level to fully understand the bank's performance.

largely reflect government-imposed operating restrictions and peculiar features of the specific markets served. Three characteristics stand out. First, because their function is primarily financial, most banks own few fixed assets. They have few fixed costs and thus low operating leverage. Second, many bank liabilities are payable on demand or carry short-term maturities so depositors can renegotiate deposit rates as market interest rates change. As a result, interest expense changes coincidentally with short-run changes in market interest rates. This creates significant asset allocation and pricing problems. Third, banks operate with less equity capital than nonfinancial companies, which increases financial leverage and the volatility of earnings. Each characteristic presents special problems and risks to the bank manager.

THE BALANCE SHEET

A bank's balance sheet presents financial information comparing what a bank owns with what it owes and the ownership interest of stockholders. Assets indicate what the bank owns; liabilities represent what the bank owes; and equity refers to the owners' interest such that:

$$\text{Assets} = \text{Liabilities} + \text{Equity} \tag{3.1}$$

Balance sheet figures are calculated at a particular point in time and thus represent stock values. Regulators require that banks report balance sheet and income statement data quarterly, so figures are available publicly at the end of March, June, September, and December each year. Balance sheets for two banking organizations are shown in Exhibit 3.2. The first two blocks of data represent the consolidated statement for PNC Bank. PNC Bank is the principal subsidiary bank of the *financial holding company*, The PNC Financial Services Group, headquartered in Pittsburgh, Pennsylvania (www.pncbank.com).[3] At year-end 2001, PNC Bank reported assets of $62.6 billion, representing approximately 90 percent of the holding company's consolidated assets. Total assets declined significantly for PNC in 2001, compared to 2000, due to loan problems in late 2001. See Contemporary Issues: The Fall of Enron and Its Impact on PNC Bank. The final two blocks of data are for Community National Bank (CNB), which represents a typical small independent bank. This bank's main office is located in a metropolitan area with three branches and no nonbank subsidiaries. At year-end 2001, CNB had $156.3 million in assets. At year-end 2001, PNC Bank held approximately 6.6 percent of its assets in nonearning cash and due from banks, 21.2 percent in investments, and 63.6 percent in loans. CNB held 5.4 percent of its assets in nonearning cash and due from banks, 24.6 percent in investments, and 65.7 percent in net loans. PNC, which had a proportionately larger loan portfolio than CNB in 2000, fewer investments, and fewer noninterest bearing cash and due balances from banks, changed its portfolio rather dramatically in one year. At the end of 2001, as a percentage of assets, PNC held proportionately fewer loans and investments but more nonearning assets than CNB. Generally, large banks tend to have larger loan portfolios (as a percentage of total assets) and a smaller proportion of investments than do smaller banks. What a difference a year made to PNC's portfolio and performance. In short summary, significant loan losses in 2001 forced PNC to reduce its loan portfolio and its lower profitability reflects these problems.

The PNC Financial Services Group is a *financial holding company* as discussed in Chapter 2. Its corporate legal structure consists of two subsidiary banks and over 70 active nonbank subsidiaries. PNC Bank, headquartered in Pittsburgh, is the Corporation's principal bank subsidiary. The holding company operates seven major lines of business engaged in community banking, corporate banking, real estate finance, asset-based lending, wealth management, asset management, and mutual fund services:

---

[3]PNC went through a major restructuring from 2000–2001. See more details on PNC later in the chapter.

· EXHIBIT 3.2

2000–2001 BALANCE SHEET INFORMATION FOR PNC BANK AND COMMUNITY NATIONAL BANK

BALANCE SHEET	PNC BANK						COMMUNITY NATIONAL BANK					
	% Cha	12/31/00 $1,000	% of Total	% Cha	12/31/01 $1,000	% of Total	% Cha	12/31/00 $1,000	% of Total	% Cha	12/31/01 $1,000	% of Total
Assets												
LOANS:												
Real estate loans	−5.5%	23,403,724	37.0%	−26.8%	17,136,390	27.4%	16.6%	50,801	37.0%	27.1%	64,569	41.3%
Commercial loans	−5.4%	18,180,941	28.8%	−19.6%	14,616,251	23.3%	12.0%	26,621	19.4%	34.7%	35,849	22.9%
Individual loans	−10.6%	3,529,627	5.6%	−7.6%	3,261,827	5.2%	9.4%	5,933	4.3%	−48.8%	3,037	1.9%
Agricultural loans	−58.9%	1,717	0.0%	−36.2%	1,096	0.0%	0.0%	0	0.0%	0.0%	0	0.0%
Other LN&LS in domestic off.	−3.0%	4,588,422	7.3%	2.7%	4,710,235	7.5%	66.8%	6,458	4.7%	−99.6%	29	0.0%
LN&LS in foreign off.	273.9%	347,421	0.5%	123.8%	777,443	1.2%	0.0%	0	0.0%	0.0%	0	0.0%
Gross loans & leases	−5.1%	50,051,852	79.2%	−19.1%	40,503,242	64.7%	17.2%	89,813	65.4%	15.2%	103,484	66.2%
Less: unearned income	7.5%	96,913	0.2%	−47.1%	51,223	0.1%	−100.0%	0	0.0%	0.0%	0	0.0%
Loan & lease loss allowance	−0.8%	648,833	1.0%	−7.1%	602,790	1.0%	−7.3%	706	0.5%	20.3%	849	0.5%
Net Loans & Leases	−5.2%	49,306,106	78.0%	−19.2%	39,849,229	63.6%	17.5%	89,107	64.9%	15.2%	102,635	65.7%
INVESTMENTS:												
U.S. Treasury & Agency securities	−43.3%	1,887,310	3.0%	82.9%	3,451,036	5.5%	8.7%	22,369	16.3%	34.3%	30,044	19.2%
Municipal securities	37.4%	45,237	0.1%	−58.7%	18,679	0.0%	N/A	721	0.5%	−0.3%	719	0.5%
Foreign debt securities	0.8%	27,401	0.0%	−5.7%	25,835	0.0%	0.0%	0	0.0%	0.0%	0	0.0%
All other securities	−6.0%	2,971,309	4.7%	196.4%	8,805,746	14.1%	0.0%	255	0.2%	−100.0%	0	0.0%
Interest bearing bank balances	69.4%	167,916	0.3%	−6.1%	157,670	0.3%	0.0%	0	0.0%	N/A	500	0.3%
Fed funds sold & resales	−63.6%	217,241	0.3%	39.0%	301,986	0.5%	0.9%	11,790	8.6%	−39.1%	7,175	4.6%
Trading account assets	−35.8%	168,345	0.3%	189.4%	487,251	0.8%	0.0%	0	0.0%	0.0%	0	0.0%
Total Investments	−26.9%	5,484,759	8.7%	141.5%	13,248,203	21.2%	8.0%	35,135	25.6%	9.4%	38,438	24.6%
Total Earning Assets	−8.0%	54,790,865	86.7%	−3.1%	53,097,432	84.8%	14.6%	124,242	90.5%	13.5%	141,073	90.3%
Nonint cash & due from banks	26.2%	3,565,214	5.6%	16.6%	4,156,160	6.6%	13.9%	7,813	5.7%	8.0%	8,440	5.4%
Acceptances	2.5%	52,401	0.1%	−11.4%	46,417	0.1%	0.0%	0	0.0%	0.0%	0	0.0%
Premises, fixed assets, & capital leases	6.3%	800,722	1.3%	0.0%	800,451	1.3%	5.8%	3,546	2.6%	17.6%	4,171	2.7%
Other real estate owned	−26.6%	15,047	0.0%	−38.0%	9,325	0.0%	0.0%	0	0.0%	N/A	625	0.4%
Investment in unconsolidated subs.	32.8%	4,320	0.0%	48.1%	6,400	0.0%	0.0%	0	0.0%	0.0%	0	0.0%
Other assets	−20.8%	3,957,334	6.3%	13.6%	4,493,595	7.2%	14.8%	1,730	1.3%	14.0%	1,972	1.3%
Total Assets	−7.3%	63,185,903	100.0%	−0.9%	62,609,780	100.0%	14.4%	137,331	100.0%	13.8%	156,281	100.0%

continued

NOTE: Figures are in thousands of dollars; LN&LS refers to loans and leases; "% Cha" refers to percentage change from the previous year.
SOURCE: FDIC Uniform Bank Performance Reports, http://www.fdic.gov (http://www2.fdic.gov/ubpr/).

• CONTINUED

2000–2001 BALANCE SHEET INFORMATION FOR PNC BANK AND COMMUNITY NATIONAL BANK

	PNC BANK						COMMUNITY NATIONAL BANK					
BALANCE SHEET	% Cha	12/31/00 $ 1,000	% of Total	% Cha	12/31/01 $ 1,000	% of Total	% Cha	12/31/00 $ 1,000	% of Total	% Cha	12/31/01 $ 1,000	% of Total
Liabilities												
Demand deposits	0.2%	6,581,761	10.4%	21.9%	8,024,609	12.8%	25.3%	49,424	36.0%	20.1%	59,382	38.0%
All NOW & ATS accounts	6.7%	1,228,615	1.9%	16.1%	1,426,841	2.3%	3.2%	9,121	6.6%	95.8%	17,862	11.4%
Money market deposit accounts	12.9%	19,973,653	31.6%	11.0%	22,173,721	35.4%	22.3%	24,265	17.7%	-12.7%	21,185	13.6%
Other savings deposits	-11.5%	1,856,609	2.9%	1.8%	1,889,720	3.0%	-3.9%	5,486	4.0%	18.1%	6,477	4.1%
Time deposits under $100M	3.3%	10,549,034	16.7%	-21.9%	8,243,535	13.2%	1.0%	23,233	16.9%	-0.5%	23,118	14.8%
Core Deposits	6.5%	40,189,672	63.6%	3.9%	41,758,426	66.7%	15.2%	111,529	81.2%	14.8%	128,024	81.9%
Time deposits of $100M or more	7.3%	3,412,724	5.4%	-32.0%	2,320,116	3.7%	10.3%	14,391	10.5%	10.3%	15,877	10.2%
Deposits held in foreign offices	-30.6%	2,397,676	3.8%	-3.8%	2,306,590	3.7%	0.0%	0	0.0%	0.0%	0	0.0%
Total Deposits	3.7%	46,000,072	72.8%	0.8%	46,385,132	74.1%	14.6%	125,920	91.7%	14.3%	143,901	92.1%
Fed funds purchased & resale	-23.0%	1,586,709	2.5%	-63.3%	582,306	0.9%	0.0%	1,000	0.7%	0.0%	1,000	0.6%
Other borrowings inc mat < 1 yr	-66.8%	2,496,693	4.0%	-29.0%	1,773,503	2.8%	0.0%	0	0.0%	0.0%	0	0.0%
Memo: S.T. non-core funding	-41.3%	9,080,920	14.4%	-32.8%	6,099,247	9.7%	13.6%	13,726	10.0%	11.8%	15,345	9.8%
Memo: Volatile liabilities	-39.0%	9,893,802	15.7%	-29.4%	6,982,515	11.2%	9.6%	15,391	11.2%	9.7%	16,877	10.8%
Other borrowings inc mat > 1 yr	-34.1%	3,793,924	6.0%	17.4%	4,455,233	7.1%	0.0%	0	0.0%	0.0%	0	0.0%
Acceptances & other liabilities	61.5%	2,904,691	4.6%	16.1%	3,372,710	5.4%	-44.9%	382	0.3%	-3.1%	370	0.2%
Total Liabilities before Sub. Notes	-7.7%	56,782,089	89.9%	-0.4%	56,568,884	90.4%	14.1%	127,302	92.7%	14.1%	145,271	93.0%
Sub. notes & debentures	0.0%	1,152,698	1.8%	0.0%	1,153,235	1.8%	0.0%	0	0.0%	0.0%	0	0.0%
Total Liabilities	-7.5%	57,934,787	91.7%	-0.4%	57,722,119	92.2%	14.1%	127,302	92.7%	14.1%	145,271	93.0%
All Common and Preferred Capital	-5.2%	5,251,116	8.3%	-6.9%	4,887,661	7.8%	17.7%	10,029	7.3%	9.8%	11,010	7.0%
Total Liabilities & Capital	-7.3%	63,185,903	100.0%	-0.9%	62,609,780	100.0%	14.4%	137,331	100.0%	13.8%	156,281	100.0%
Memoranda:												
Officer, shareholder loans (#)	100.0%	4	0.0%	0.0%	4	0.0%	0.0%	1	0.0%	0.0%	1	0.0%
Officer, shareholder loans ($)	6.8%	19,539	0.0%	7.1%	20,933	0.0%	24.4%	1,120	0.8%	7.0%	1,198	0.8%
Non-investment ORE	-26.6%	15,047	0.0%	-38.0%	9,325	0.0%	0.0%	0	0.0%	N/A	625	0.4%
Loans held for sale	-71.5%	1,655,003	2.6%	135.7%	3,900,766	6.2%	0.0%	0	0.0%	0.0%	0	0.0%
Held-to-maturity securities	0.0%	0	0.0%	0.0%	0	0.0%	-5.2%	11,837	8.6%	-57.3%	5,056	3.2%
Available-for-sale-securities	-24.7%	4,931,257	7.8%	149.5%	12,301,296	19.6%	37.7%	11,508	8.4%	123.4%	25,707	16.4%
Total Securities	-24.7%	4,931,257	7.8%	149.5%	12,301,296	19.6%	12.0%	23,345	17.0%	31.8%	30,763	19.7%
All Brokered Deposits	56.3%	586,684	0.9%	100.3%	1,175,114	1.9%	0.0%	0	0.0%	0.0%	0	0.0%

- **PNC Bank's Regional Community Bank** offers lending, deposit, and online investment services to more than 3.3 million households and 180,000 business banking customers in Pennsylvania, New Jersey, Delaware, Ohio, Kentucky, and Indiana.

- **PNC Bank's Corporate Banking** provides a full range of financial products and services to businesses and government entities.

- **PNC Real Estate Finance** is full-service provider of credit products, capital markets, and financing and operational services to real estate customers throughout the product and market life cycles.

- **PNC Business Credit** specializes in providing secured financing to businesses nationally, and with more than $5 billion in commitments under management, and is the nation's sixth largest asset-based lender.

- **PNC Advisors** offers investment management, brokerage, personal trust, estate planning, and traditional banking services to individual clients and investment management and 401(k) products and services to institutional clients.

- **Blackrock** is a large asset manager with $164.5 billion in assets under management; Blackrock combines PNC's investment advisory and asset management capabilities under a single organization.

- **PFPC** is the largest full-service mutual fund transfer agent and the second largest fund accounting provider in the United States.

BANK ASSETS. Bank assets fall into one of four general categories: loans, investment securities, noninterest cash and due from banks, and other assets. **Loans** are the major asset in most banks' portfolios and generate the greatest amount of income before expenses and taxes. They also exhibit the highest default risk and some are relatively illiquid. **Investment securities** are held to earn interest, help meet liquidity needs, speculate on interest rate movements, meet pledging requirements, and serve as part of a bank's dealer functions. **Noninterest cash and due from banks** consists of vault cash, deposits held at Federal Reserve Banks, deposits held at other financial institutions, and cash items in the process of collection. These assets are held to meet customer withdrawal needs and legal reserve requirements, assist in check clearing and wire transfers, and affect the purchase and sale of Treasury securities. **Other assets** are residual assets of relatively small magnitudes such as bankers acceptances, premises and equipment, other real estate owned, and other smaller amounts.

Loans. A bank negotiates loan terms with each borrower that vary with the use of proceeds, source of repayment, and type of collateral. Maturities range from call loans payable on demand to residential mortgages amortized over 30 years. The interest rate may be fixed over the life of the loan or vary with changes in market interest rates. Similarly, the loan principal may be repaid periodically or as a lump sum. Exhibit 3.2 groups loans into six categories according to the use of proceeds: real estate, commercial, individuals, agricultural, other loans in domestic offices, and loans in foreign offices. **Real estate loans** are loans secured by real estate and generally consist either of property loans secured by first mortgages or interim construction loans. **Commercial loans** consist of commercial and industrial loans, loans to financial institutions, and obligations (other than securities) to states and political subdivisions. Commercial loans appear in many forms but typically finance a firm's working capital needs, equipment purchases, and plant expansions. This category also includes credit extended to other financial institutions, security brokers, and dealers. **Loans to individuals** include those negotiated directly with individuals for household, family, and other personal expenditures, and those obtained indirectly through the purchase of retail paper. Loans made for the purchase of credit card items and durable goods comprise the greatest volume of this consumer credit. **Agricultural loans** appear in many forms but typically finance agricultural production and include other loans to farmers. **Other loans in domestic offices** include all other loans and all lease-financing receivables in domestic offices. International loans, labeled **loans and leases in foreign offices,** are essentially business loans and lease receivables made to foreign enterprises or loans guaranteed by foreign governments. Many large U.S. banks substantially increased their international lending throughout the 1970s and early 1980s, eventually to find that many borrowers could not service the debt. International loans carry significant risks beyond normal default risk. Many large banks with significant international exposure experienced large losses due to the international crisis in late 1998. During the fourth quarter of 2001, FleetBoston charged-off over $700 million in loans to Argentina when local governments and businesses could not pay. PNC also took a significant $615 million after-tax charge in the fourth quarter of 2001, as it wrote down loans, venture capital, and its auto leasing business. Finally, the dollar amount of **outstanding leases** is included in gross loans because lease financing is an alternative to direct loans.

Two adjustments are made to **gross loans and leases** to obtain a **net loan** figure. First, unearned income is deducted from gross interest received. **Unearned income** is income that has accrued but not yet been paid. Second, gross loans are reduced by the dollar magnitude of a bank's **loan and lease loss allowance** (loan loss reserve), which exists in recognition that some loans will not be repaid. The reserve's maximum size is determined by tax law but increases with the growth in problem loans and decreases with net loan charge-offs. A bank is permitted a tax deduction for net additions to the loss reserve, denoted as the provision for loan losses on the income statement.[4]

Investment securities. The primary attraction to investment securities is that they earn interest, and administration and transaction costs are extremely low. Banks also concentrate their purchases on higher quality instruments so that defaults are rare. When interest rates fall, as they did during much of 1990s, most investment securities increase in value because they eventually carry above average interest rates. Banks can either earn very attractive yields relative to their borrowing costs or sell the securities at a gain. Of course, when rates rise, investment securities decrease in value as they carry below market interest rates. In terms of liquidity, banks own a large amount of *short-term securities*—those with a maturity of one year or less—that can be easily sold to obtain cash. Because of their lower risk, they generally earn less interest than what can be earned on longer-term securities. These short-term investments include interest-bearing bank balances (deposits due from other banks), federal funds sold, securities purchased under agreement to resell (repurchase agreements or RPs), Treasury bills, and municipal tax warrants. They have maturities ranging from overnight to one year and carry returns that vary quickly with changes in money market conditions. They are extremely liquid as they can be easily sold at a price close to that initially paid by the bank.

Long-term investment securities consist of notes and bonds that have a maturity of more than one year and generate taxable or tax-exempt interest. Treasury securities and obligations of federal agencies, such as the Farm Credit Association, comprise the bulk of taxable investments.[5] Banks also purchase mortgage-backed securities and small amounts of foreign and corporate bonds. Most of these carry fixed-rate interest rates with maturities up to 20 years. Until 1983, banks owned more state and municipal securities than any other investor group. These securities are classified as **general obligation** or **revenue bonds,** and typically pay interest that is

---

[4]The reported provision for loan losses is normally less than the actual tax deduction allowed by the Internal Revenue Service and claimed by the bank.

[5]The asset category "U.S. Treasury & Agency Securities" listed in the Uniform Bank Performance Report is somewhat misleading. This category is actually defined as the total of U.S. Treasury and Agency securities and corporate obligations. This, in practice, would include almost all of the securities in a bank's portfolio except for municipal, foreign, and equity securities. For more information, consult the UBPR User's Guide available from the FFIEC on the Internet at www.ffiec.gov.

exempt from federal income taxes. Recent changes in bank tax rules, however, have made most municipal securities unattractive to banks.[6] Banks cannot generally purchase corporate stock as an investment, but can own it under two conditions: if it is acquired as collateral on a loan, and as members of the Federal Reserve System or Federal Home Loan Bank system wherein they own stock in the Federal Reserve Bank and Federal Home Loan Bank.

Accounting for Securities. At purchase, a bank must designate the objective behind buying investment securities as either held-to-maturity, trading, or available-for-sale. Following FASB 115, **held-to-maturity securities** are recorded on the balance sheet at amortized cost. This treatment reflects the objective to hold the securities until they mature so that the expected income is interest income with a return of principal at maturity. A bank actively buys and sells **trading account securities** principally to speculate on interest rate movements and profit on price changes. These securities are typically held for brief periods, such as a few days, so the bank marks the securities to market (reports them at current market value) on the balance sheet and reports unrealized gains and losses on the income statement. All other investment securities are classified as **available-for-sale** because management may choose to sell them prior to final maturity. As such, they are recorded at market value on the balance sheet with a corresponding change to stockholders' equity as unrealized gains and losses on securities holdings. There is no reporting of gains or losses on the income statement with these securities.

Many large banks also operate as security dealers that maintain an inventory of securities for resale and underwrite municipal issues. Banks who form a *financial holding company* can underwrite and deal in bonds and equity securities (see Chapter 2). The inventory, which is listed as trading account securities on the balance sheet, is comprised mainly of Treasury obligations and collateralized mortgage obligations. The bank earns interest on this inventory but also tries to profit on the difference between the purchase and sale price of the securities. It subsequently bears the risk that the market value of its inventory might decrease. Large banks, in addition, earn fee income by underwriting municipal securities.

Noninterest cash and due from banks. This asset category consists of vault cash, deposits held at Federal Reserve Banks, deposits held at other financial institutions, and cash items in the process of collection. **Vault cash** is coin and currency that the bank holds to meet customer withdrawals. **Deposits held at Federal Reserve** are demand balances used to meet legal reserve requirements, assist in check clearing and wire transfers, or effect the purchase and sale of Treasury securities. The amount of required reserve deposits is set by regulation as a fraction of qualifying bank deposit liabilities and currently stands at 10 percent of transactions deposits. Banks hold balances at other financial institutions, called correspondent banks, primarily to purchase services. The amount is determined by the volume and cost of services provided such that income from investing the deposits at least covers the cost of the services provided by the correspondent bank. The largest component of cash, **cash items in the process of collection (CIPC),** represents checks written against other institutions and presented to the bank for payment for which credit has not been given. To verify that actual balances support each check, the bank delays credit until the check clears or a reasonable time elapses. The volume of net deferred credit is commonly called *float*.

Other assets. Residual assets of relatively small magnitudes, including customers' liability to the bank under acceptances (acceptances), the depreciated value of bank premises and equipment, other real estate owned (OREO), investment in unconsolidated subsidiaries, interest receivable, and prepaid expenses make up the majority of assets in this category. For many problem banks, **other real estate owned** is substantial because it normally represents property taken as collateral against a loan that was unpaid. As indicated earlier, commercial banks own relatively few fixed assets. They operate with low fixed costs relative to nonfinancial firms and exhibit low operating leverage.

---

[6]As noted in Chapter 2, the Tax Reform Act of 1986 eliminated bank deductions for borrowing costs associated with financing the purchase of most municipal bonds. The impact of this tax change is described in Chapter 20.

Bank Liabilities and Stockholders' Equity. Bank funding sources are classified according to the type of debt instrument and equity component. The characteristics of various debt instruments differ in terms of check-writing capabilities, interest paid, maturity, whether they carry FDIC insurance, and whether they can be traded in the secondary market. Historically, banks were limited in what interest rates they could pay on different types of deposits. Since 1986, all interest rate restrictions have been eliminated, except for the prohibition of interest on corporate demand deposits. Banks can now compete for deposits by offering unrestricted interest rates on virtually all of their liabilities. Larger banks also issue subordinated notes and debentures, which are basically long-term uninsured debt. The components of equity (common and preferred capital) also have different characteristics and arise under varied circumstances such as the issuance of stock, net income not paid out as dividends, and Treasury stock or related transactions.

Demand deposits are transactions accounts held by individuals, partnerships, corporations, and governments that pay no interest. Prior to the Depository Institutions Act of 1980, they served as the only legal transactions account nationally that could be offered by depository institutions. Businesses now own the bulk of existing demand deposits because they are not allowed to own interest-bearing transactions accounts at banks.

NOW, ATS accounts, and **Money Market Deposit Accounts (MMDAs)** represent interest-bearing transactions accounts.[7] **Negotiable orders of withdrawal (NOW)** and **automatic transfers from savings (ATS)** accounts pay interest set by each bank without federal restrictions. Banks often require minimum balances before a depositor earns interest, impose service charges, and may limit the number of free checks a customer can write each month, but these terms vary among institutions. NOWs are available only to noncommercial customers. MMDAs similarly pay market rates, but a customer is limited to no more than six checks or automatic transfers each month. This restriction exempts banks from holding required reserves against MMDAs as they are technically savings accounts. With no required reserves, banks can pay higher rates of interest on MMDAs versus NOWs for the same effective cost.

Savings and time deposits have, in the past, represented the bulk of interest-bearing liabilities at banks. Today, however, MMDAs and time deposits under $100,000 have become the larger source of interest-bearing liabilities. Passbook savings deposits are small-denomination accounts that have no set maturity and no check-writing capabilities. Two general time deposit categories exist with a $100,000 denomination separating the groups. **Time deposits of $100,000 or more** are labeled jumbo certificates of deposit (CDs) and are negotiable with a well-established secondary market. Anyone who buys a jumbo CD can easily sell it in the secondary market as long as the issuing bank is not suffering known problems. The most common maturities are one month, three months, and six months, with $1 million the typical size. Most CDs are sold to nonfinancial corporations, local governmental units, and other financial institutions. The features of smaller **time deposits under $100,000** are not as standardized. Banks and customers negotiate the maturity, interest rate, and dollar magnitude of each deposit. The only stipulation is that small time deposits carry early withdrawal penalties whereby banks reduce the effective interest paid if a depositor withdraws funds prior to the stated maturity date. Most banks market standardized instruments so that customers are not confused. **Brokered deposits** typically refers to jumbo CDs that a bank obtains through a brokerage house that markets the CDs to its customers. These are separated because the bank has virtually no customer contact with the holders of these CDs, and the funds will leave the bank quickly when a competitor offers a higher rate. On several occasions, bank regulators have designated other bank deposits as brokered deposits depending on the rate paid to customers. Specifically, if a bank pays an above-market rate, such as 3 percent on NOWs, when all other

---

[7]Prior to 1983, banks and savings and loans could not pay market interest rates on most deposits under $100,000. Limits were gradually removed so that, by 1986, only demand deposit rates were restricted.

competitors in the same trade area are paying 2 percent, regulators may choose to designate the NOWs as brokered deposits because the bank is viewed as "buying the funds." Banks that fund operations by marketing time deposits on the Internet suffer the same problem as they generally pay rates substantially above rates paid by local (geographic) competitors.

Most banks closely monitor changes in their core deposits, which consist of demand deposits, NOW and ATS accounts, MMDAs, savings, other savings and time deposits less than $100,000. As the name suggests, **core deposits** are stable deposits that are typically not withdrawn over short periods of time. The owners are not highly rate sensitive, such that the interest elasticity is low, and do not move their balances to another institution when it pays a higher rate. Core deposits represent a more permanent funding base than large denomination, volatile (noncore) liabilities. They are also attractive because they are relatively cheap compared to the interest cost of noncore liabilities.

Deposits held in foreign offices refer to the same types of dollar-denominated demand and time deposits discussed above except that the balances are issued by a bank subsidiary (owned by the bank holding company) located outside the United States. The average foreign deposit balance is generally quite large. Nonfinancial corporations engaged in international trade and governmental units own most of these deposits.

Large banks also rely on other rate-sensitive borrowings that can be used to acquire funds quickly. Federal funds purchased and resales are the most popular source. Federal funds are immediately available funds that holders can transfer immediately. Resales represent securities sold under agreement to repurchase (RPs) and are essentially collateralized federal funds borrowings. These funds are traded in multiples of $1 million overnight or with extended maturities. Reputable banks need only offer a small premium over the current market rate to acquire funds. Large banks also issue commercial paper through their holding companies. Commercial paper represents short-term, unsecured corporate promissory notes.

Liabilities that are highly rate-sensitive do not represent a stable source of funding, particularly when a bank gets into trouble. They are normally issued in denominations above the amount that is federally insured so the depositor bears some risk of default. Thus, if a bank reports problems or a competitor offers a higher rate, customers are quite willing to move their deposits. Jumbo CDs, deposits in foreign offices, federal funds purchased, RPs, and other borrowings with maturities of less than one year, are subsequently referred to as **volatile (noncore) liabilities,** purchased liabilities, or hot money. The UPBR defines the sum of these accounts as **short-term noncore funding.**[8]

Subordinated notes and debentures consist of notes and bonds with maturities in excess of one year. Most meet requirements as bank capital for regulatory purposes. Unlike deposits, the debt is not federally insured and claims of bondholders are subordinated to claims of depositors. Thus, when a bank fails, depositors are paid before subordinated debt holders. Other liabilities include acceptances outstanding, taxes and dividends payable, trade credit, and other miscellaneous claims.

All common and preferred capital, or stockholders' equity, is the ownership interest in the bank. Common and preferred stock are listed at their par values while the surplus account represents the amount of proceeds received by the bank in excess of par when it issued the stock. Retained earnings represent the bank's cumulative net income since the firm started operation, minus all cash dividends paid to stockholders. Other equity is small and usually reflects capital reserves. The book value of equity equals the difference between the book value of assets and aggregate liabilities. A detailed discussion of each component of stockholders' equity and associated regulatory requirements appears in Chapter 13.

---

[8]Short-term noncore funding is normally defined in the UBPR as certificates of deposit and open account time deposits of $100,000 or more, brokered deposits less than $100,000, other borrowings, and deposits in foreign offices, securities sold under agreements to repurchase, federal funds purchased with maturities less than one year, as well as cumulative foreign currency translation adjustments and demand notes issued to the United States Treasury.

■ **EXHIBIT 3.3**

NONINTEREST INCOME PROVIDES A GROWING PROPORTION
OF BANK'S TOTAL NET REVENUE, 1980–2001

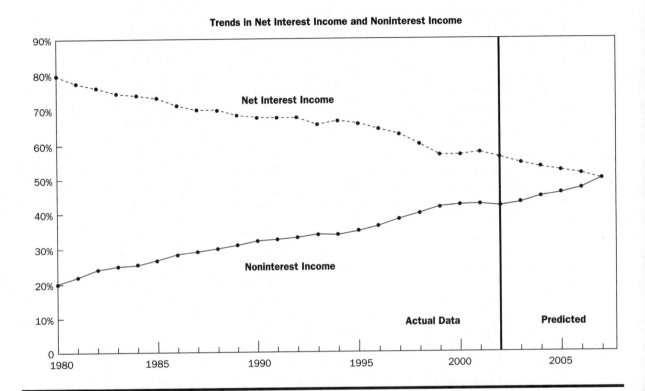

Trends in Net Interest Income and Noninterest Income

NOTE: Total net revenue equals net interest income plus noninterest income. Predicted values are based on a simple negative 3 percent growth rate in net interest income.
SOURCE: Historical data from the FDIC's Historical Statistics on Banking, http://www.fdic.gov (http://www2.fdic.gov/hsob/).

THE INCOME STATEMENT

A bank's income statement reflects the financial nature of banking, as interest on loans and investments comprises the bulk of revenue. Net interest income made up approximately 77 percent of total net revenue at a bank in 1981, but only about 58 percent of total net revenue at the end of 2001. The trend away from net interest income and toward noninterest income, as shown in Exhibit 3.3, has played a major role in changing bank management.

The income statement format starts with **interest income,** then subtracts **interest expense** to produce **net interest income.** As described below, net interest income must be large enough to cover a bank's expenses and taxes such that changes in net interest income dramatically affect aggregate profitability. The other major source of bank revenue is **noninterest income,** which is comprised primarily of deposit service charges, fee income, and trust income. After adding noninterest income, banks subtract **noninterest expense,** which represents overhead costs primarily for the expense of people, buildings, and equipment. Although banks constantly try to increase their noninterest income and reduce noninterest expense, the latter usually exceeds the former such that the difference is labeled the bank's burden. Formally, a bank's **burden** equals noninterest expense minus noninterest income. The next step is to subtract **provisions for loan and lease losses,** which represent management's estimate of potential lost incremental revenue from bad loans. The resulting figure essentially represents operating income before securities transactions and taxes. Next, **realized gains or losses** from the sale of securities are added to produce pretax net operating income. Such gains or losses arise from selling investment securities prior to final maturity when the sales price differs from the purchase (or amortized) price. Subtracting applicable income taxes, tax equivalent adjustments, and any extraordinary items yields net income.

Formally, a bank's sources of revenue are interest income (II), noninterest income (OI), and securities gains (SG). A bank's expenses include interest expense (IE), noninterest expense (OE), provisions for loan losses (PLL), securities losses (negative SG), and taxes, including accounting adjustments and extraordinary items (T). A bank's burden (Burden) and efficiency ratio (EFF) indicate how well it controls noninterest expense relative to noninterest income and relative to operating income before provisions and taxes. With these components, a bank's net interest income (NII) equals (II − IE), burden equals (OE − OI), and EFF [OE/(NII + OI)] equals a bank's efficiency ratio. Conceptually, a bank's net income (NI) can be viewed as having five contributing factors: net interest income, burden, provisions for loan losses, securities gains (losses), and taxes:

$$NII = II - IE \qquad (3.2)$$

$$Burden = OE - OI \qquad (3.3)$$

$$EFF = \frac{OE}{II + OI} \qquad (3.4)$$

$$NI = NII - Burden - PLL + SG - T \qquad (3.5)$$

Income statements for the two banking organizations are presented in Exhibit 3.4. Not surprisingly, the components of net income differ substantially reflecting their diverse portfolios. Net income for PNC Bank equaled $471.7 million in 2001, down significantly from 2000 as a result of large loan charge-offs and the resulting $0.9 billion provisions for loan loss expense. Community National Bank's net income was down as well in 2001 to $1.16 million due primarily to lower net interest income, operating expense that increased more than noninterest income, and higher provisions for loan losses. Many banks experienced lower net interest income in 2001, due to the large drop in interest rates over the year. The contribution of each of the four components is summarized below.

Components of Net Income in 2001	PNC ($000)	CNB ($000)
Net interest income (NII)	2,185,188	7,212
− Burden	(659,421)	(5,184)
− Provisions for loan losses (PLL)	(898,743)	(372)
+ Securities gains (losses) (SG)	123,985	0
− Taxes (T)	(279,277)	(501)
= Net income (NI)	471,732	1,155

Interest income is the sum of interest and fees earned on all of a bank's assets, including loans, deposits held at other institutions, municipal and taxable securities, and trading account securities. It also includes rental receipts from lease financing. All income is taxable, except for the interest on state and municipal securities and some loan and lease income, which is exempt from federal income taxes. The **estimated tax benefit** for loan and lease financing and tax-exempt securities income is the estimated dollar tax benefit from not paying taxes on these items. For comparative purposes, tax-exempt interest income can be converted to a taxable equivalent (te) amount by dividing tax-exempt interest by one minus the bank's marginal income tax rate. The estimated tax benefit on municipal securities can be approximated by:[9]

---

[9]Actually, the estimated tax benefit is calculated on the UBPR using a tax-equivalent adjustment worksheet. You can find this worksheet on the FFIEC's Web page at http://www.ffiec.gov/.

EXHIBIT 3.4

INCOME STATEMENTS OF PNC BANK AND COMMUNITY NATIONAL BANK

INCOME STATEMENT	PNC BANK						COMMUNITY NATIONAL BAN					
	% Cha	2000 $1,000	% of Total	% Cha	2001 $1,000	% of Total	% Cha	2000 $1,000	% of Total	% Cha	2001 $1,000	% of Total
Interest Income:												
Interest and fees on loans	-2.2%	3,845,374	62.1%	-22.2%	2,992,253	52.0%	16.2%	8,478	72.4%	0.8%	8,547	72.5%
Income from lease financing	29.7%	208,494	3.4%	24.1%	258,790	4.5%	0.0%	0	0.0%	0.0%	0	0.0%
Memo: Fully taxable	-0.9%	4,021,924	64.9%	-19.8%	3,224,394	56.1%	15.9%	8,450	72.1%	1.1%	8,547	72.5%
Tax-exempt	-7.2%	31,944	0.5%	-16.6%	26,649	0.5%	N/A	28	0.2%	-100.0%	0	0.0%
Estimated tax benefit	-8.2%	15,701	0.3%	-14.7%	13,394	0.2%	N/A	14	0.1%	-100.0%	0	0.0%
Income on Loans & Leases (TE)	-1.0%	4,069,569	65.7%	-19.8%	3,264,437	56.8%	16.4%	8,492	72.5%	0.6%	8,547	72.5%
Other security income	-20.6%	328,410	5.3%	-100.0%	0	0.0%	6.8%	1,407	12.0%	-100.0%	0	0.0%
U.S. Treasury & Agency securities	0.0%	0	0.0%	N/A	65,970	1.1%	0.0%	0	0.0%	N/A	620	5.3%
Mortgage-backed securities	0.0%	0	0.0%	N/A	446,662	7.8%	0.0%	17	0.1%	N/A	541	4.6%
Estimated tax benefit	-48.8%	791	0.0%	-19.8%	634	0.0%	N/A	33	0.3%	5.9%	18	0.2%
All other securities income	-48.2%	1,611	0.0%	3,257.0%	54,082	0.9%	N/A	33	0.3%	9.1%	36	0.3%
Memo: Tax-exempt securities income	-48.2%	1,611	0.0%	-21.6%	1,263	0.0%	N/A	33	0.3%	9.1%	36	0.3%
Investment Interest Income (TE)	-20.9%	330,812	5.3%	71.5%	567,348	9.9%	10.5%	1,457	12.4%	-16.6%	1,215	10.3%
Interest on due from banks	55.3%	8,137	0.1%	-33.1%	5,447	0.1%	0.0%	0	0.0%	N/A	7	0.1%
Interest on Fed funds sold & resales	30.2%	44,290	0.7%	-71.4%	12,664	0.2%	79.9%	858	7.3%	-49.0%	438	3.7%
Trading account income	-13.0%	2,374	0.0%	-38.2%	1,467	0.0%	0.0%	0	0.0%	0.0%	0	0.0%
Total Interest Income (TE)	-2.5%	4,455,182	71.9%	-13.6%	3,851,363	67.0%	18.9%	10,807	92.2%	-5.6%	10,207	86.6%
Interest Expense:												
Int on deposits held in foreign offices	63.7%	111,622	1.8%	-51.7%	53,928	0.9%	0.0%	0	0.0%	0.0%	0	0.0%
Interest on CD's over $100M	8.4%	211,127	3.4%	-28.4%	151,082	2.6%	45.1%	820	7.0%	-2.6%	799	6.8%
Interest on all other deposits:	25.7%	1,286,558	20.8%	-22.7%	993,952	17.3%	18.9%	2,320	19.8%	-7.0%	2,158	18.3%
Total Interest Expense on Deposits	25.1%	1,609,307	26.0%	-25.5%	1,198,962	20.8%	24.8%	3,140	26.8%	-5.8%	2,957	25.1%
Interest on Fed funds purchased & resale	22.5%	168,549	2.7%	-41.0%	99,507	1.7%	190.0%	58	0.5%	-34.5%	38	0.3%
Interest on trad liab & oth borrowings	-37.7%	473,858	7.7%	-38.3%	292,561	5.1%	0.0%	0	0.0%	0.0%	0	0.0%
Interest on mortgages & leases	0.0%	0	0.0%	0.0%	0	0.0%	0.0%	0	0.0%	0.0%	0	0.0%
Interest on sub. notes & debentures	14.9%	84,270	1.4%	-10.8%	75,145	1.3%	0.0%	0	0.0%	0.0%	0	0.0%
Total Interest Expense	3.5%	2,335,984	37.7%	-28.7%	1,666,175	29.0%	26.1%	3,198	27.3%	-6.3%	2,995	25.4%
Net Interest Income (TE)	-8.3%	2,119,198	34.2%	3.1%	2,185,188	38.0%	16.1%	7,609	65.0%	-5.2%	7,212	61.2%

continued

NOTE: Figures are in thousands of dollars; TE refers to tax equivalent; % Cha refers to percentage change from previous years.

SOURCE: FDIC Uniform Bank Performance Reports, http://www.fdic.gov, (http://www2.fdic.gov/ubpr/).

- CONTINUED

INCOME STATEMENTS OF PNC BANK AND COMMUNITY NATIONAL BANK

INCOME STATEMENT	PNC BANK						COMMUNITY NATIONAL BANK					
	% Cha	2000 $1,000	% of Total	% Cha	2001 $1,000	% of Total	% Cha	2000 $1,000	% of Total	% Cha	2001 $1,000	% of Total
Noninterest Income:												
Fiduciary activities	21.7%	771,456	12.5%	-52.6%	365,434	6.4%	0.0%	0	0.0%	0.0%	0	0.0%
Deposit service charges	3.9%	335,720	5.4%	6.0%	355,931	6.2%	1.2%	750	6.4%	10.7%	830	7.0%
Trading revenue	-190.8%	34,225	0.6%	132.3%	79,504	1.4%	0.0%	0	0.0%	0.0%	0	0.0%
Other foreign transactions	0.0%	0	0.0%	0.0%	0	0.0%	0.0%	0	0.0%	0.0%	0	0.0%
Other noninterest income	-47.4%	576,427	9.3%	69.3%	975,630	17.0%	-66.4%	158	1.3%	370.9%	744	6.3%
Total noninterest income	-14.7%	1,717,828	27.7%	3.4%	1,776,499	30.9%	-25.0%	908	7.8%	73.3%	1,574	13.4%
Adjusted Operating Income (TE)	-11.3%	3,837,026	62.0%	3.2%	3,961,687	68.9%	9.7%	8,517	72.7%	3.2%	8,786	74.6%
Noninterest Expenses:												
Personnel expenses	-9.9%	978,446	15.8%	7.9%	1,055,515	18.4%	7.6%	3,100	26.5%	25.5%	3,892	33.0%
Occupancy expense	-30.5%	279,144	4.5%	8.7%	303,353	5.3%	6.8%	806	6.9%	32.0%	1,064	9.0%
Other operating expense (incl. intangibles)	-0.9%	931,085	15.0%	15.7%	1,077,052	18.7%	5.8%	1,526	13.0%	18.1%	1,802	15.3%
Total Noninterest Expenses	-9.8%	2,188,675	35.3%	11.3%	2,435,920	42.4%	6.9%	5,432	46.4%	24.4%	6,758	57.4%
Provision: Loan & Lease Losses	-15.1%	133,000	2.1%	575.7%	898,743	15.6%	40.8%	200	1.7%	86.0%	372	3.2%
Pretax Operating Income (TE)	-13.1%	1,515,351	24.5%	-58.6%	627,024	10.9%	13.5%	2,885	24.6%	-42.6%	1,656	14.1%
Realized G/L hld-to-maturity sec.	0.0%	0	0.0%	0.0%	0	0.0%	0.0%	0	0.0%	0.0%	0	0.0%
Realized G/L avail-for-sale sec.	-116.6%	19,561	0.3%	533.8%	123,985	2.2%	-100.0%	0	0.0%	0.0%	0	0.0%
Pretax Net Operating Income (TE)	-5.5%	1,534,912	24.8%	-51.1%	751,009	13.1%	17.1%	2,885	24.6%	-42.6%	1,656	14.1%
Applicable income taxes	-7.0%	511,194	8.3%	-49.0%	260,608	4.5%	5.6%	974	8.3%	-50.4%	483	4.1%
Current tax equivalent adjustment	-11.6%	16,493	0.3%	-14.9%	14,029	0.2%	N/A	31	0.3%	-41.9%	18	0.2%
Other tax equivalent adjustments	0.0%	0	0.0%	0.0%	0	0.0%	0.0%	0	0.0%	0.0%	0	0.0%
Applicable Income Taxes (TE)	-7.1%	527,687	8.5%	-48.0%	274,637	4.8%	9.0%	1,005	8.6%	-50.1%	501	4.3%
Net Operating Income	-4.7%	1,007,225	16.3%	-52.7%	476,372	8.3%	22.0%	1,880	16.0%	-38.6%	1,155	9.8%
Net extraordinary items	0.0%	0	0.0%	N/A	(4,640)	-0.1%	0.0%	0	0.0%	0.0%	0	0.0%
Net income	-4.7%	1,007,225	16.3%	-53.2%	471,732	8.2%	22.0%	1,880	16.0%	-38.6%	1,155	9.8%
Cash dividends declared	-40.1%	650,000	10.5%	61.5%	1,050,000	18.3%	-6.1%	460	3.9%	-21.7%	360	3.1%
Retained earnings	-1,333.4%	357,225	5.8%	-261.9%	(578,268)	-10.1%	35.1%	1,420	12.1%	-44.0%	795	6.7%
Memo: Net international income	0.0%	0	0.0%	0.0%	0	0.0%	0.0%	0	0.0%	0.0%	0	0.0%
Memo: Total operating income	-4.2%	6,192,571	100.0%	-7.1%	5,751,847	100.0%	14.6%	11,715	100.0%	0.6%	11,781	100.0%
Memo: Net operating income	-11.3%	3,837,026	62.0%	3.2%	3,961,687	68.9%	9.7%	8,517	72.7%	3.2%	8,786	74.6%

$$\text{Estimated tax benefit} = \frac{\text{municipal interest income}}{1 - \text{bank marginal tax rate}} = \text{tax-equivalent municipal interest income}$$

Tax equivalent municipal interest for PNC equaled $1,897 million including a $0.634 million tax benefit in 2001. PNC also had tax benefits from loan and lease financing estimated at $ 13.394 million. Total tax equivalent income on loans and leases was $ 3.264 billion. CNB had an estimated $18,000 tax benefit from municipal securities and zero in estimated tax benefits from loans and leases in 2001. The 1986 change in tax laws made municipal securities less attractive to commercial banks, which has substantially lowered the municipal holdings of both PNC and CNB over time.[10]

Interest expense is the sum of interest paid on all interest-bearing liabilities, including transactions accounts (NOW, ATS, and MMDA), time and savings deposits, short-term non-core liabilities, and long-term debt. Gross interest income minus gross interest expense is labeled **net interest income.** This figure is important because its variation over time indicates how well management is controlling interest rate risk.

Noninterest income is becoming increasingly important because of pricing pressure on net interest income. It is composed largely of trust or **fiduciary income,** which reflects what a bank earns from operating a trust department, and **fees and deposit service charges,** which reflect charges on checking account activity, safe-deposit boxes, and many other transactions. These latter items typically generate the bulk of noninterest income. **Trading revenues** reflect commissions and profits or gains from operating a trading account and, thus, from making a market in securities. The entries **other foreign transactions** and **other noninterest income** reflect gains and losses on all nontrading foreign transactions and all other fee-based income, respectively.

Noninterest expense is composed primarily of **personnel expense,** which includes salaries and fringe benefits paid to bank employees, **occupancy expense** from rent and depreciation on equipment and premises, and **other operating expenses,** including technology expenditures, utilities, and deposit insurance premiums. Noninterest expense far exceeds noninterest income at most banks, hence the label burden. Reducing this burden will improve profitability. Because most banks today face great pressure to keep net interest income from shrinking, they have aggressively tried to raise fee income and cut overhead expenses to support profit growth.

Provision for loan and lease losses is a deduction from income representing a bank's periodic allocation to its loan and lease loss allowance (loan loss reserve) on the balance sheet. Conceptually, management is allocating a portion of income to a reserve to protect against potential loan losses. It is a noncash expense, but indicates management's perception of the quality of the bank's loans. It is subtracted from net interest income in recognition that some of the reported interest income overstates what will actually be received when some of the loans go into default. Although management determines the size of the provision and, thus, what is reported to stockholders, Internal Revenue Service (IRS) rules specify the maximum allowable tax deduction. As is discussed later, provisions for loan and lease losses differ from loan charge-offs, which indicate loans and leases that a bank formally recognizes as uncollectable and charges-off against the loss reserve.

Realized securities gains (or losses) arise when a bank sells securities from its investment portfolio at prices above (or below) the initial or amortized cost to the bank. All such profits are reported and taxed as ordinary income. Securities gains are generally viewed as an unpredictable and unstable source of income because it is difficult to forecast interest rates and whether the bank can sell securities for a profit or loss. Realized securities gains (or losses) are listed separately for *held-to-maturity securities* and *available-for-sale securities.* Generally, securities change in value as interest rates change, but the gains or losses are unrealized—meaning that the bank has not sold the securities to capture the change in value.

---

[10]See Chapter 18 for more details.

Pretax Net Operating Income (te) equals tax-equivalent net interest income, plus noninterest income, minus noninterest expense, minus provision for loan losses, plus realized securities gains (or losses). It represents the bank's operating profit before taxes and extraordinary items. **Net income** is the operating profit less all federal, state, and local income taxes, plus or minus any accounting adjustments and **extraordinary items.**[11] The reported income tax figure equals estimated taxes to be paid over time (applicable income taxes), not actual tax payments. Accounting adjustments generally represent a restatement of earnings resulting from a change in accounting treatment of certain transactions. In addition to applicable income taxes, two additional tax items are subtracted from pretax net operating income: **current tax equivalent adjustment** and **other tax equivalent adjustments.** The current tax equivalent adjustment simply reverses the current part of the tax benefit included in interest income on loan and lease financing, as well as the estimated tax benefit from municipal securities. Other tax equivalent adjustments reverse the remainder of the tax equivalent adjustment included in interest income on loans, leases, and municipal securities income. This is an estimate of the tax benefit that is attributable to tax loss carrybacks.

Finally, **total revenue (TR),** or **total operating income (TOI),** equals total interest income plus noninterest income and realized securities gains (losses). It is comparable to net sales for a nonfinancial firm. **Total operating expense (EXP)** equals the sum of interest expense, noninterest expense, and provisions for loan losses, and is comparable to cost of goods sold plus other operating expenses at a nonfinancial firm.

THE RELATIONSHIP BETWEEN THE BALANCE SHEET AND INCOME STATEMENT

A bank's balance sheet and income statement are interrelated. The composition of assets and liabilities and the relationships between different interest rates determine net interest income. The mix of deposits between consumer and commercial customers affects the services provided and, thus, the magnitude of noninterest income and noninterest expense. The ownership of nonbank subsidiaries increases fee income, but often raises noninterest expense. The following analysis emphasizes these interrelationships. Let:

A_i	=	dollar magnitude of the ith asset
L_j	=	dollar magnitude of the jth liability
NW	=	dollar magnitude of stockholders' equity
y_i	=	average pretax yield on the ith asset
c_j	=	average interest cost of the jth liability,

where n equals the number of assets and m equals the number of liabilities. The balance sheet identity in Equation 3.1 can be restated as:

$$\sum_{i=1}^{n} A_i = \sum_{j=1}^{m} L_j + NW \tag{3.6}$$

Interest earned on each asset equals the product of the average yield (y_i) and the average dollar investment (A_i). Thus:

$$\text{Interest income} = \sum_{i=1}^{n} y_i A_i$$

Similarly, interest paid on each liability equals the product of the average interest cost (c_j) and the average dollar funding (L_j) from that source, so that:

---

[11] Extraordinary items can include such items as revenue from the sale of real assets, the sale of a subsidiary, and other one-time transactions. It is important that analysts distinguish between these one-time gains and normal operating income and expenses. One-time transactions are nonrecurring and, thus, affect the income statement only in the period they appear. As such, reported net income may overstate true operating income.

$$\text{Interest expense} = \sum_{j=1}^{m} c_j L_j$$

Net interest income (NII) equals the difference:

$$NII = \sum_{i=1}^{n} y_i A_i - \sum_{j=1}^{m} c_j L_j \tag{3.7}$$

This restatement of NII indicates what factors can cause net interest income to change over time or differ between institutions. First, net interest income changes when the *composition* or *volume* of assets and liabilities change. In terms of Equation 3.7, as portfolio composition changes, the respective As and Ls change in magnitude. This alters net interest income because each A_i or L_j is multiplied by a different interest rate. Second, even if portfolio composition is unchanged, the average *rate* earned on assets (asset yields) and *rate* paid on liabilities (interest costs) may rise or fall due to changing interest rates and lengthening or shortening of maturities on the underlying instruments.

Analysts, for example, generally distinguish between retail and wholesale banks based on their target customers. Each type of bank has a fundamentally different balance sheet composition reflecting the preferences of its customers. Retail banks are those that focus on individual consumer banking relationships. Thus, individual demand, savings, and time deposits comprise most of the liabilities, while consumer and small business loans linked to key individuals are a higher fraction of the loan portfolio. Wholesale banks deal primarily with commercial customers such that they operate with fewer consumer deposits, more purchased (noncore) liabilities, and hold proportionately more business loans to large firms. This difference in portfolio composition, in turn, produces different yields on earning assets (y_i) and costs of liabilities (c_j).

Noninterest income, noninterest expense, and provisions for loan losses indirectly reflect the same balance sheet composition. The greater is a bank's loan portfolio, the greater is its operating overhead and provision for loan losses. Likewise, banks that emphasize consumer loans operate with more noninterest expense (overhead). They often invest in extensive branch systems and equipment to attract consumer deposits and handle small, multiple-payment consumer loans. Bank holding companies with nonbank subsidiaries, on the other hand, generate more fee income.

A bank's net income thus varies with the magnitudes of assets and liabilities and the associated cash flows:

$$NI = \sum_{i=1}^{n} y_i A_i - \sum_{j=1}^{m} c_j L_j - \text{Burden} - \text{PLL} + \text{SG} - \text{T} \tag{3.8}$$

Net income in excess of dividend payments to shareholders increases retained earnings and, thus, net worth or total equity.

THE RETURN ON EQUITY MODEL

In 1972, David Cole introduced a procedure for evaluating bank performance via ratio analysis.[12] This procedure, summarized in Exhibit 3.5, enables an analyst to evaluate the source and magnitude of bank profits relative to selected risks taken. This section employs the **return on equity model** to analyze bank profitability and identifies specific measures of credit risk, liquidity risk, interest rate risk, operational risk, and capital risk. The ratios are used to assess the performance of the two banking organizations introduced earlier.

---

[12]The following discussion is based on the Dupont system of financial analysis and adaptations by Cole (1972). A more meaningful definition of return on equity is the ratio of net income minus dividends on preferred stock to common stockholders' equity, because it indicates the potential return to common stockholders.

• EXHIBIT 3.5

DECOMPOSITION OF RETURN ON EQUITY: THE NATURE OF BANK PROFITS

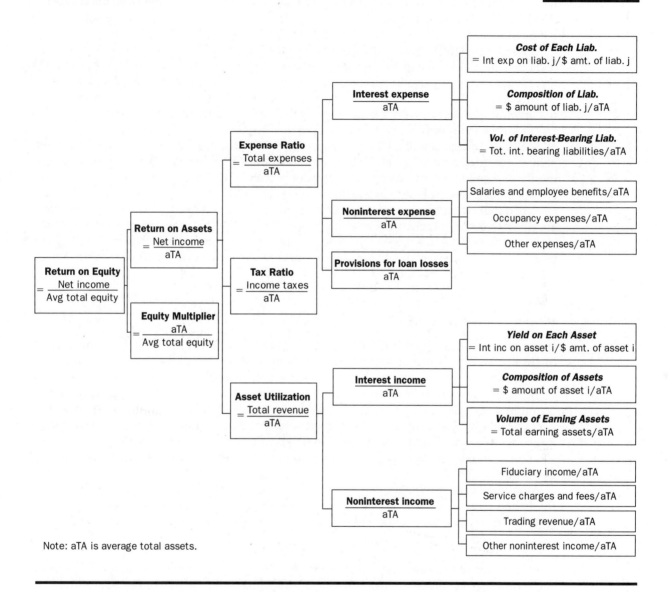

Note: aTA is average total assets.

THE UNIFORM BANK PERFORMANCE REPORT

The Uniform Bank Performance Report (UBPR) is a comprehensive analytical tool created by the FDIC from the Federal Financial Instituting Examination Council (FFIEC) quarterly Call Reports for bank supervisory purposes.[13] The UBPR contains a wealth of profitability and risk information presented in a consistent and uniformed manner. Although the 22 pages of data

---

[13]Complete UBPR reports, including peer group data can be found at the FDIC's Internet Web page at www.fdic.gov (www2.fdic.gov/ubpr) in the FDIC Uniform Bank Performance Report section. Anyone can also obtain a UBPR for any bank or FDIC-insured savings bank by calling or by writing the FDIC. The UBPR is available for banks since 1986, and for FDIC-insured savings banks since 1990. Public disclosure tapes can also be obtained. Data for thrift institutions are available via a Uniform Thrift Performance Report (UTPR).

and ratio information might appear a bit intimidating, the advantage of this report over "typical" financial statements is the uniformity in the presentation of the data. Once you learn how to use one UBPR, you can evaluate any bank's or savings bank's performance. Most of the UBPR for PNC Bank is contained in the Appendix to this chapter. All data for Community National Bank were obtained from its UBPR as well.

The year-end UBPR consists of information over a consecutive five-year period. Non-year-end reports provide data on the current quarter, one-year prior to the current quarter, and the three latest year-end periods. Although the strength of the UBPR is its consistency, there are unfortunately several different versions of the report. These versions, however, differ only by the amount of detail provided with larger banks' UBPRs providing more information. The report format is updated virtually every year.

The data contained in the UBPR consist of three basic types: bank-level ratios and dollar values, peer group averages, and bank percentile ranks. Bank-level dollar values consist primarily of detailed income statement and balance sheet data. Ratios provide data on almost all aspects of a specific bank's profitability and risk (BANK). Peer group averages (PEER) are classified into twenty-five different groups based on the size of banks, their general location, and their number of branches. Percentile ranks (PCT) allow for more comprehensive analysis and rank each bank's ratio, within the peer group, in ascending order, from 0 to 99. Each percentile rank indicates that the associated ratio is above that fraction of peer banks' ratios. A basic table of contents for the UBPR is included in the Appendix.

PROFITABILITY ANALYSIS

If you cornered a group of bank presidents and asked them to summarize performance for the past year, most would quote either their bank's return on equity or return on assets. If these measures were higher than peers, they would drop the phrase "high-performance bank" in the conversation. Of course, for a firm to report higher returns, it must either take on more risk, price assets and liabilities better, or realize cost advantages compared to peers. The following analysis starts with these aggregate profit measures, then decomposes return on assets into component ratios to determine why performance varies from peers. Chapter 4 offers a critique of this model and describes alternative methods of evaluating performance.

Aggregate bank profitability is measured and compared in terms of return on equity (ROE) and return on assets (ROA). The ROE model simply relates ROE to ROA and financial leverage, then decomposes ROA into its contributing elements. By definition:

$$\text{ROE} = \text{Net income} / \text{Average total equity}$$

ROE equals net income divided by average total equity and, thus, measures the percentage return on each dollar of stockholders' equity.[14] It is the aggregate return to stockholders before dividends. The higher the return the better, as banks can add more to retained earnings and pay more in cash dividends when profits are higher.

ROA equals net income divided by average total assets and, thus, measures net income per dollar of average assets owned during the period. ROE is linked to ROA by the equity

---

[14]Balance sheet figures should always be averaged for use with income statement figures. This reduces any distortion caused by unusual transactions around reporting dates. All balance sheet values listed in Exhibit 3.2 are for end of period (EOP). Average total assets and average total loans and leases data are included in Exhibit 3.6. Average total assets and average total loans reported in Exhibit 3.6 were used in the calculated ratios presented in Exhibits 3.6 and 3.7 when called for and when possible. All other ratios, which call for "average" balance sheet figures, calculated in Exhibits 3.6 and 3.7, use averages of annual data. See Contemporary Issues: Using Averages of Balance Sheet Data and Interpreting Financial Ratios Using the UBPR.

multiplier (EM), which equals average total assets divided by total equity, via the following accounting identity:

$$\text{ROE} = \frac{\text{Net income}}{\text{Average total assets}} \times \frac{\text{Average total assets}}{\text{Average total equity}} = \text{ROA} \times \text{EM} \qquad (3.9)$$

A bank's equity multiplier compares assets with equity such that large values indicate a large amount of debt financing relative to stockholders' equity. EM thus measures financial leverage and represents both a profit and risk measure. Consider two competing banks, each holding $100 million in assets with the identical composition. Asset quality is the same. One bank is financed with $90 million in debt and $10 million in total equity, while the other bank is financed with $95 million in debt and just $5 million in total equity. In this example, EM equals 10x for the first bank and 20x for the second bank.

EM = 10x = $100/$10 for the bank with $10 million in equity
EM = 20x = $100/$5 for the bank with $5 million in equity

EM affects a bank's profits because it has a multiplier impact on ROA to determine a bank's ROE. In the above example, if both banks earned 1 percent on assets, the first bank would report an ROE of 10 percent, while the second bank's ROE would equal 20 percent. Financial leverage works to the bank's advantage when earnings are positive, as the second bank provides shareholders a return that is twice that of its competitor. But, there are two sides to leverage, as it also accentuates the negative impact of losses. If each bank reported an ROA equal to −1 percent, the second bank's ROE would equal −20 percent, or twice the loss of the first bank. Equation 3.9 suggests that higher ROE targets can be obtained either by increasing ROA or increasing financial leverage.

EM represents a risk measure because it reflects how many assets can go into default before a bank becomes insolvent. Consider the ratio of total equity to total assets, or 1/EM. This ratio equals 10 percent for the first bank in the example, and 5 percent for the second bank. Although both banks hold identical assets, the first is in a less risky position because twice as many of its assets can default (and, thus, be reduced in value to zero on the balance sheet) compared to the second bank before it is insolvent. Thus, a high EM raises ROE when net income is positive, but also indicates high capital or solvency risk.

EXPENSE RATIO AND ASSET UTILIZATION

The Dupont Analysis has been used for many years and can be modified slightly for use in a financial institution. It represents a straightforward decomposition of ROA. The UBPR provides a wealth of data to assist in the analysis of a bank's or thrift institution's performance.[15] The basic return on total assets, ROA, is composed of two principal parts: income generation and expense control (including taxes). Recall that net income (NI) is:

$$\text{NI} = \text{Total revenue (TR)} - \text{Total operating expenses (EXP)} - \text{Taxes} \qquad (3.10)$$

Total revenue (TR) is analogous to net sales plus other income at a nonfinancial company, and equals the sum of interest income, noninterest income, and securities gains (losses).[16]

---

[15]Similar information can be obtained on credit unions from the National Credit Union Administration, www.ncua.gov.

[16]Extraordinary income and expense are included in the definitions of total revenue and total expense. Because they are one-time occurrences, they should be excluded when evaluating operating performance and comparing key ratios over time and versus peers. We assume that extraordinary income and expense are relatively small. If they are substantive, they should be excluded from the analysis. As such, net income would equal net income before extraordinary income.

Total operating expenses (EXP) equal the sum of interest expense, noninterest expense, and provisions for loan and lease losses. Dividing both sides by **average total assets (aTA)** "decomposes" ROA into its components:[17]

$$ROA = \frac{NI}{aTA} = \frac{TR}{aTA} - \frac{EXP}{aTA} - \frac{Taxes}{aTA} \qquad (3.11)$$

Hence, a bank's ROA is composed of asset utilization (AU), the expense ratio (ER), and the tax ratio (TAX).

$$ROA = AU - ER - TAX \qquad (3.12)$$

where:

AU = Total revenue/aTA
ER = Total operating expenses/aTA
TAX = Applicable income taxes/aTA

The greater is AU and the lower are ER and TAX, the higher is ROA.

Expense Decomposition: Expense Ratio Components (ER). Consider first the expense ratio (ER), which has a very intuitive interpretation. For example, an ER of 6 percent indicates that a bank's gross operating expenses equal 6 percent of total investment; that is, total assets. Thus, the lower (greater) is the ER, the more (less) efficient a bank will be in controlling expenses. Suppose that two banks have the same total assets, but one reports total expenses that are twice as large as the other's. This means that ER is twice as large. To produce this difference, the bank with the greater ER reported higher expenses.

The decomposition of ER appears at the top of Exhibit 3.5. Three additional ratios isolate the impact of specific types of operating expenses:

Interest expense ratio	=	Interest expense (IE)/aTA
Noninterest expense ratio	=	Noninterest expense (OE)/aTA
Provision for loan loss ratio	=	Provisions for loan losses (PLL)/aTA

The sum of these ratios equals the total expense ratio:[18]

$$ER = \frac{EXP}{aTA} = \frac{IE}{aTA} + \frac{OE}{aTA} + \frac{PLL}{aTA} \qquad (3.13)$$

All other factors being equal, the lower is each ratio, the more profitable is the bank. The value of each measure compared with similar ratios of peer banks reveals whether specific types of expenses contribute to significant differences in performance. When the ratios differ, an analyst should examine additional ratios that reflect the underlying reasons and causes of the differences.

Interest expense and noninterest expense should be further examined by source. Interest expense may vary between banks for three reasons: rate, composition, or volume effects. **Rate effects** suggest that the interest cost per liability, c_j from Equation 3.7, which indicates

---

[17]The standard Dupont Analysis approach decomposes ROA into the product of profit margin (PM) and asset utilization (AU) as ROA = AU × PM, where PM equals NI/TR and AU equals TR/aTA. These ratios are not directly available in the UBPR. AU can be derived in the UBPR by adding (interest income/aTA) plus (noninterest income/aTA) plus (securities gains/aTA). PM can then be obtained indirectly by dividing ROA by AU (PM = ROA/AU).

[18]This relationship is quite useful because ER is not directly reported on the UBPR. ER can be obtained from the UBPR in two ways. First, it can be calculated as the ratio of total operating expenses to average total assets. For example, ER for PNC was 7.88 percent [(1,666,175 + 2,435,920 + 898,743)/63,486,660] in 2001. Second, ER can be calculated using relationship 3.13.

ER for PNC	7.88% = 2.62% + 3.84% + 1.42%
ER for Peer Group	6.54% = 2.90% + 3.16% + 0.48%

the average cost of financing assets, may differ between banks. The gross interest cost of each liability can be calculated by dividing interest expense on the particular liability by the average total dollar amount of the liability from the balance sheet:[19]

$$\text{Cost of liability}_j = c_j = \text{Interest expense on liability}_j / \text{Average balance of liability}_j$$

Differences in interest expense arise in part because banks pay different risk premiums indicating how the market perceives their asset quality and overall risk. The greater is the risk, the higher is the cost of liabilities. Banks also time their borrowings differently relative to the interest rate cycle. If they borrow when rates are low, their interest costs will fall below banks that issue new debt when rates are higher. Finally, banks use different maturities of deposits and debt that pay different rates depending on the yield curve at the time of issue. Typically, longer-term deposits pay higher rates than short-term deposits. The c_j will differ among banks for any of these reasons.

Composition (mix) effects suggest that the mix of liabilities may differ. Banks with substantial amounts of demand deposits pay less in interest because these deposits are noninterest bearing. A bank that relies on CDs and federal funds purchased will pay higher average rates than a bank with a larger base of lower cost demand and small time deposits because these noncore liabilities are riskier than core deposits to those advancing the funds. This represents a key advantage of core deposits over volatile or noncore liabilities. These composition effects are revealed by common size ratios that measure each liability as a percentage of average total assets.

V... ...ize that a bank may pay more or less in interest expense simply ... ...ounts of interest-be...ing debt and equity a... thu... ...abiliti...

Total revenue (TR), or total operating income, can be divided into three components:

$$TR = \text{Interest Income (II)} + \text{Noninterest Income (OI)} + \text{Realized Security Gains or Losses (SG)}$$

Dividing both sides by average total assets produces: [20]

$$AU = \frac{TR}{aTA} = \frac{II}{aTA} + \frac{OI}{aTA} + \frac{SG}{aTA} \tag{3.14}$$

This indicates how much of a bank's gross yield on assets results from interest income, noninterest income, and realized securities gains (losses). Interest income may differ between banks for the same three reasons discussed with interest expense: rate, composition, and volume effects. For the **rate effect,** an examination of pretax (gross) yields per asset, y_i from Equation 3.7, allows the bank to compare realized interest yields with those of peer banks. Differences may reflect different maturities, the timing of purchases relative to the interest rate cycle, or a different composition of holdings within each asset category. For example, a bank that invests heavily in new construction loans should earn higher gross yields on loans than a bank that lends primarily to Fortune 500 companies because construction loans are riskier. Differences in investment security yields, in turn, typically reflect differences in average maturities with higher yields on longer-term securities. Gross yields on assets can be calculated similar to costs of liabilities by dividing interest income on the particular asset by the average dollar amount of the asset from the balance sheet: [21]

Yield on asset$_i$ = y_i = Interest income on asset$_i$ /Avera

and why differences might exist with peers. It also identifies whether other income might be biased by substantial nonrecurring items. When a bank reports extraordinary income, an analyst should subtract the amount from net income before calculating the performance ratios. This purges extraordinary income so that a truer picture of operating performance appears.

The last factor affecting ROA is a bank's tax payments. Generally, applicable income taxes are divided by average assets per Equation 3.11. In summary form:

$$ROE = [AU - ER - TAX] \times EM \tag{3.15}$$

Several other aggregate profitability measures are commonly cited. These include net interest margin (NIM), spread, burden, and efficiency ratios:

$$NIM = \text{Net interest income}/\text{Average earning assets}$$

$$\text{Spread (SPRD)} = \frac{\text{Interest income}}{\text{Average earning assets}} - \frac{\text{Interest expense}}{\text{Average interest-bearing liabilities}}$$

$$\text{Burden ratio} = \frac{\text{Noninterest expense} - \text{Noninterest income}}{aTA}$$

$$\text{Efficiency ratio (EFF)} = \frac{\text{Noninterest expense}}{NII + \text{Noninterest income}}$$

Ne... .ual, noncurrent, NIM) is a summary measure of the net interest return on income-... UBPR presents a series of ratios tials the average yield on earning assets min... and expected future losses. These include the ba.. me provisions for loan losses to average total assets, the loan and lease loss allowance (loan loss reserve) as a percentage of total loans, earning coverage of net losses, and loan and lease loss allowance to net losses. When management expects to charge-off large amounts of loans, it will build up the allowance for loan losses. It does this by adding to provisions for loan losses. Thus, a large allowance may indicate both good and bad performance. If asset quality is poor, a bank needs a large allowance because it will need to charge-off many loans. The allowance should be large because charge-offs will deplete it. Cash flows from loans will decline along with reported interest income. In this case, a high loss reserve signals bad performance. With high quality assets, banks charge-off fewer loans, so the allowance can be proportionately less. A bank with a large allowance for loan losses and few past due, nonaccrual, or nonperforming loans will not need all of the reserve to cover charge-offs, which will be low. Such a bank has reported provisions for loan losses that are higher than needed such that prior period net income is too low. This is good performance.

Ideally, management should relate the size of the loan loss reserve to noncurrent loans, which represent potential charge-offs. With a reserve equal to noncurrent loans (100 percent coverage), a bank should be well protected because it shouldn't expect to charge-off all nonperforming and non-accrual loans. GAAP accounting principals and Call Reporting guidelines require that a bank's loan loss reserve be adequate to cover the known and inherent risk in the loan portfolio. For tax purposes, however, the maximum allowable deduction for losses and the size of the reserve are set by IRS rules. Thus, prudent management could lead to a conflict with the IRS. Banks with under $500 million in assets can use a reserve for bad debt system for tax purposes. Using this system, the IRS requires the bank to use a 5-year historical average charge-off method for calculating provisions for loan losses. Banks with over $500 million in assets use a direct charge-off method for tax purposes. In either case, when regulators consider the current loan portfolio to be more risky, or historical charge-offs have been low, regulators and GAAP accounting require higher provisions or a greater loan loss

reserve than the IRS will allow. This leads to the unpleasant situation in which the bank must expense greater provisions than the IRS will allow them to deduct from taxable income. That is, the excess is not tax deductible!

Another ratio used to measure a bank's ability to cover current period losses is **earnings coverage of net losses.** This is a measure of net operating income before taxes, securities gains (losses), extraordinary items, and the provision for loan losses divided by net loan and lease losses. It indicates how many times current earnings can cover current net charge-offs. A higher ratio signals greater coverage and, thus, greater protection. However, for the ratio to be useful, a bank must consistently report realistic figures for earnings and net losses. It is widely known that when banks have asset quality problems, management often plays games by deferring the recognition of charge-offs, thereby understating reserves and overstating earnings. Thus, the ratio is less revealing than ratios that directly incorporate the size of the loss reserve.

Three other sources of credit risk should be identified. First, banks that lend in a narrow geographic area or concentrate their loans to a certain industry have risk that is not fully measured by balance sheet or historical charge-off data. This **lack of diversification** could dramatically affect a majority of the bank's portfolio if economic factors negatively affected the geographic or industry concentration. This type of bank could be subject to risks that the rest of the banking industry is not subject to in its operations. Second, banks with **high loan growth** often assume greater risk, as credit analysis and review procedures are less rigorous. In many instances, the loans perform for a while, but losses eventually rise. Thus, high loan growth rates, particularly when the loans are generated externally through acquisitions or entering new trade areas, often lead to future charge-offs. Third, banks that lend funds in foreign countries take country risk. **Country risk** refers to the potential loss of interest and principal on international loans due to borrowers in a country refusing to make timely payments, as per a loan agreement. In essence, foreign governments and corporate borrowers may default on their loans due to government controls over the actions of businesses and individuals, internal politics that may disrupt payments, general market disruptions, and problems that arise when governments reduce or eliminate subsidies used as a source of repayment.

Ideally, it would be useful to examine the credit files of a bank to assess the quality of specific loans. Although this information is provided to regulators, it is not available to the public. Regulators, in fact, assign each bank a rating for asset quality (A for asset quality) as part of the CAMELS rating system. There has been some discussion of publishing these ratings, a policy that analysts desire but bankers fear.

Liquidity Risk

Liquidity risk is the current and potential risk to earnings and the market value of stockholders' equity that results from a bank's inability to meet payment or clearing obligations in a timely and cost-effective manner. This risk can be the result of either funding problems or market liquidity risk. **Funding liquidity risk** is the inability to liquidate assets or obtain adequate funding from new borrowing. The inability of the bank to easily unwind or offset specific exposures without significant losses from inadequate market depth or market disturbances is called **market liquidity risk.** This risk is greatest when risky securities are trading at high premiums to low-risk Treasury securities because market participants are avoiding high-risk borrowers. Liquidity risk is greatest when a bank cannot anticipate new loan demand or deposit withdrawals, and does not have access to new sources of cash.

Liquidity is often discussed in terms of assets with reference to an owner's ability to convert the asset to cash with minimal loss from price depreciation. Most banks hold some assets that can be readily sold near par to meet liquidity needs. Still, banks can access new funds not only through the sale of liquid assets, but also by directly issuing new liabilities at reasonable cost. Thus, when banks need cash, they can either sell assets or increase borrowing.

Liquidity risk measures indicate both the bank's ability to cheaply and easily borrow funds and the quantity of liquid assets near maturity or available-for-sale at reasonable prices. The equity-to-asset ratio and volatile (net non-core) liability-to-asset ratio represent the bank's equity base and borrowing capacity in the money markets. **Volatile liabilities** or net noncore liabilities, as they are listed in the UBPR, include large CDs (over 100,000), deposits in foreign offices, federal funds purchased, repurchase agreements, and other borrowings with maturities less than one year.[25] If two banks hold similar assets, the one with the greater total equity or lower financial leverage can take on more debt with less chance of becoming insolvent. A bank that relies less on jumbo CDs, federal funds, RPs, Eurodollars, and commercial paper, can issue greater amounts of new debt in this form. In both instances, the cost of borrowing is lower than that for a bank with the opposite profile.

Core deposits are stable deposits that are not highly interest-rate sensitive. These types of deposits are less sensitive to the interest rate paid but more sensitive to the fees charged, services rendered, and location of the bank. Thus, a bank will retain most of these deposits even when interest rates paid by competitors increase relative to the bank's own rates. As such, the interest elasticity of the demand for core deposits is low. Core deposits include demand deposits, NOW accounts, MMDAs, and small time deposits that the bank expects to remain on deposit over the business cycle. The greater are core deposits, the lower are unexpected deposit withdrawals and potential new funding requirements. Volatile or purchased liquidity is also related to asset quality. The lower are high-risk assets relative to equity, the greater is the bank's borrowing capacity and the lower are its borrowing costs.

Banks purchase short-term investment securities for yield and to satisfy liquidity needs. Federal funds sold, securities purchased under agreement to resell, and unpledged available-for-sale securities are the most liquid assets. Short-term securities are generally more liquid than longer-term securities because they are less volatile in price and the bank gets its principal back earlier if it holds the securities until maturity. Banks are, however, generally more willing to sell any security that currently trades at a price above book value because, at worst, they can report a securities gain.

Pledging requirements often stipulate that banks pledge either Treasury or municipal securities as collateral against deposit liabilities such as Treasury deposits, municipal deposits, and borrowings from Federal Reserve banks. These pledged securities are often held by a third-party trustee and cannot be sold without a release. The greater is the proportion of securities pledged, the smaller is the proportion that might be available for sale.

Cash assets are held to meet customer withdrawals and legal reserve requirements or to purchase services from other financial institutions. Banks attempt to minimize cash holdings because they do not earn interest. For this reason, cash assets do not represent a source of long-term liquidity for the bank. Cash balances held at banks for clearing purposes can decline temporarily but must be replenished to meet reserves or pay for correspondent services. Cash items in the process of collection (CIPC) vary with the volume of checks handled and cannot be manipulated by the bank. Cash assets as a group are thus illiquid because a bank cannot reduce its holdings for any length of time. **Liquid assets,** therefore, consist of unpledged, marketable short-term securities that are classified as available-for-sale, plus federal funds sold and securities purchased under agreement to resell.

Although it is difficult to assess loan liquidity from general balance sheet information, loans can provide liquidity in two ways. First, cash inflows from periodic interest and principal payments can be used to meet cash outflows. Second, some loans are highly marketable and can be sold to other institutions. For example, the federal government guarantees a large portion of Small Business Administration (SBA) loans. The guaranteed portion of an SBA loan is

---

[25]The UBPR also includes brokered deposits less than $100,000 and maturing within one year in the definition of net noncore liabilities.

highly marketable because default risk is low. Finally, held-to-maturity securities are not liquid because they cannot be sold prior to maturity unless certain restrictive conditions are met.

MARKET RISK

Market risk is the current and potential risk to earnings and stockholders' equity resulting from adverse movements in market rates or prices. The three areas of market risk are: interest rate or reinvestment rate risk, equity or security price risk, and foreign exchange risk. Traditional **interest rate risk** analysis compares the sensitivity of interest income to changes in asset yields with the sensitivity of interest expense to changes in the interest costs of liabilities. This is done using **funding GAP** and **earnings sensitivity** analysis. The purpose is to determine how much net interest income will vary with movements in market interest rates. A more comprehensive portfolio analysis approach compares the duration of assets with the duration of liabilities using **duration gap** and **market value of equity sensitivity** analysis to assess the impact of rate changes on net interest income and the market value (or price) of stockholders' equity. Duration is an elasticity measure that indicates the relative price sensitivity of different securities.[26]

Both funding GAP and duration gap focus on mismatched asset and liability maturities and durations as well as potential changes in interest rates. An asset or liability is **rate sensitive** if management expects it be repriced within a certain time period. A bank's net interest sensitivity position, or funding GAP between assets and liabilities, is approximated by comparing the dollar amount of assets with liabilities that can be repriced over similar time frames. The dollar difference between rate-sensitive assets and rate-sensitive liabilities for 30 days, 30 to 90 days, and so forth, indicates whether more assets or liabilities will reprice within a given time interval. If this measure is positive, the bank will likely realize a decrease in net interest income if the level of short-term interest rates falls. If the measure is negative, the bank's net interest income will likely increase with a decline in rates, but decrease with rising rates. The larger is the absolute value of the ratio, the greater is risk. In practice, most banks conduct earnings sensitivity or market value of equity sensitivity analysis to examine volatility in net interest income and stockholders' equity to best identify interest rate risk exposures. Unfortunately, data contained in the UBPR are insufficient to evaluate a bank's interest rate risk position.

Equity and security price risk examines how changes in market prices, interest rates, and foreign exchange rates affect the market values of any equities, fixed-income securities, foreign currency holdings, and associated derivative and other off-balance sheet contracts. Large banks must conduct value-at-risk analysis to assess the risk of loss with their portfolio of these trading assets and hold specific amounts of capital in support of this market risk. Small banks identify their exposure by conducting sensitivity analysis. Value-at-risk analysis is introduced in Chapter 4 but is generally beyond the scope of this book.

Foreign exchange risk arises from changes in foreign exchange rates that affect the values of assets, liabilities, and off-balance sheet activities denominated in currencies different from the bank's domestic (home) currency. It exists because some banks hold assets and issue liabilities denominated in different currencies. When the amount of assets differs from the amount of liabilities in a currency, any change in exchange rates produces a gain or loss that affects the market value of the bank's stockholders' equity. This risk is also found in off-balance sheet loan commitments and guarantees denominated in foreign currencies. This risk is also known as *foreign currency translation risk*. Banks that do not conduct business in

---

[26]Chapter 8 presents funding GAP and Chapter 9 formally defines duration measures and demonstrates their application to risk analysis and management.

nondomestic currencies do not directly assume this risk. Most banks measure foreign exchange risk by calculating measures of net exposure by each currency. A bank's net exposure is the amount of assets minus the amount of liabilities denominated in the same currency. Thus, a bank has a net exposure for each currency for which it books assets and liabilities. The potential gain or loss from the exposure is indicated by relating each net exposure to the potential change in the exchange rate for that currency versus the domestic currency.

OPERATIONAL RISK

Operational risk refers to the possibility that operating expenses might vary significantly from what is expected, producing a decline in net income and firm value. The Basel Committee defines operational risk as "the risk of loss resulting from inadequate or failed internal processes, people, and systems, or from external events."[27] A new focus of the Basel II Accord is operational risk (see Chapter 13 for more details on capital requirements). Starting in 2005, the proposed Basel capital requirements will require a bank to make capital allocations for operational risk. The focus is on the optimum use of capital in the technology and business process operations of a financial institution. The events of September 11, 2001 tragically demonstrated the need for banks to protect themselves against operational risk to their systems and people. From a capital adequacy point of view, this covers technology risks, management- and people-related operational risks, and legal risks.

There are many causes of earnings variability in a bank's operating policies. Some banks are relatively inefficient in controlling direct costs and employee processing errors. Banks must also absorb losses due to employee and customer theft and fraud. A bank's operating risk is closely related to its operating policies and processes and whether it has adequate controls. Losses from external events, such as an electrical outage, are easy to identify but difficult to forecast because they are not tied to specific tasks or products within the bank. Operational risk is difficult to measure directly but is likely greater the higher are the numbers of divisions or subsidiaries, employees, and loans to insiders. Typical measures of operating risk are linked to expense control or productivity and include ratios such as total assets per employee and total personnel expense per employee. Recently, banks have used a matrix form of measurement whereby management identifies and quantifies potential losses by type of event and the line of business where the event has an impact.

Because operating performance depends on the technology a bank uses, success in controlling this risk depends on whether a bank's system of delivering products and services is efficient and functional. Many banks have in-house support systems that provide check-clearing and cash settlement services. Other banks contract these services out to third-party vendors such as IBM and EDS. Today, the rapid acceptance of Internet banking and online bill payment has introduced a new operating risk. Most banks are dependent on third-party software and technology professionals to provide this product. The risks to the bank can be great if the proper controls are not implemented. Today, regulators are carefully monitoring not only the bank's Internet banking activities but also the Internet banking solutions providers. Operational risk also arises from the more difficult to measure risks of unexpected losses that might occur as the result of inadequate information systems, operational problems, breaches in internal controls, fraud, or unforeseen catastrophes. There is no meaningful way to estimate the likelihood of fraud or other contingencies from published data. The key is to have strong internal audit procedures with follow-up to reduce exposures.

---

[27]See "What is Operational Risk?, " Economic Letter, Federal Reserve Bank of San Francisco, January 25, 2002, by Jose Lopez.

LEGAL AND REPUTATION RISK

Almost by definition, legal and reputation risk are quite difficult to measure. **Legal risk** is the risk that unenforceable contracts, lawsuits, or adverse judgments could disrupt or negatively effect the operations, profitability, condition, or solvency of the institution. **Reputation risk** is the risk that negative publicity, either true or untrue, adversely affects a bank's customer base or brings forth costly litigation, hence negatively affecting profitability. Because these risks are basically unforeseen, they are all but impossible to measure.

CAPITAL OR SOLVENCY RISK

Capital risk is not considered a separate risk because all of the risks mentioned previously will, in one form or another, affect a bank's capital and hence solvency. It does, however, represent the risk that a bank may become insolvent and fail. A firm is technically insolvent when it has negative net worth or stockholders' equity. The economic net worth of a firm is the difference between the market value of its assets and liabilities. Thus, **capital risk** refers to the potential decrease in the market value of assets below the market value of liabilities, indicating economic net worth is zero or less. If such a bank were to liquidate its assets, it would not be able to pay all creditors, and would be bankrupt. A bank with equity capital equal to 10 percent of assets can withstand a greater percentage decline in asset value than a bank with capital equal to only 6 percent of assets. One indicator of capital risk is a comparison of stockholders' equity with the bank's assets. The greater equity is to assets, the greater is the amount of assets that can default without the bank becoming insolvent. Chapter 13 introduces more formal risk-based capital ratios that indicate solvency risk.

A bank that assumes too much risk can become insolvent and fail. Operationally, a failed bank's cash inflows from debt service payments, new borrowings, and asset sales are insufficient to meet mandatory cash outflows due to operating expenses, deposit withdrawals, and maturing debt obligations. A cash flow deficiency is caused by the market's evaluation that the market value of bank equity is falling and potentially negative. High credit risk typically manifests itself through significant loan charge-offs. High interest rate risk manifests itself through mismatched maturities and durations between assets and liabilities. High operational risk appears with costs being out of control. Banks operating with high risk are expected to have greater capital than banks with low risk. When creditors and shareholders perceive that a bank has high risk, they demand a premium on bank debt and bid share prices lower. This creates liquidity problems by increasing the cost of borrowing and potentially creating a run on the bank. Banks ultimately fail because they cannot independently generate cash to meet deposit withdrawals and operate with insufficient capital to absorb losses if they were forced to liquidate assets. As such, the market value of liabilities exceeds the market value of assets.

Capital risk is closely tied to financial leverage, asset quality, and a bank's overall risk profile; the more risk that is taken, the greater is the amount of capital required. High amounts of fixed-rate sources of funds increase the expected volatility of a firm's income because interest payments are mandatory. If a bank was funded entirely from common equity, it would pay dividends, but these payments are discretionary. Omitting dividends does not produce default. Firms with high capital risk—evidenced by low capital-to-asset ratios—exhibit high levels of financial leverage, have a higher cost of capital, and normally experience greater periodic fluctuations in earnings.

Finally, many banks engage in activities off-balance sheet. This means that they enter into agreements that do not have a balance sheet reporting impact until a transaction is effected. An example might be a long-term loan commitment to a potential borrower. Until the customer actually borrows the funds, no loan is booked as part of the bank's assets. Banks earn fees when they engage in off-balance sheet agreements. These agreements, in turn, entail some risk as the bank must perform under the contract. As an example, Enron borrowed billions of dollars against outstanding credit lines right before it declared bankruptcy at year-end 2001. Early in 2002, PNC reclassified its treatment of a presumed asset sale and reduced net income for the prior year (2001) by $155 million due to a disagreement with the Federal Reserve Board on the method used to move some assets off its books. The $155 million was a charge that PNC took to income after adding loans it had moved off-balance sheet in the fourth quarter of 2001 back on its balance sheet. The rules about "qualified special purpose entities" and FASB 140 are considered vague and will most likely change as a result of the collapse of Enron. See the section on Financial Statement Manipulation and the Contemporary Issues Box: The Fall of Enron and Its Impact on PNC Bank.

Off-balance sheet risk refers to the volatility in income and market value of bank equity that may arise from unanticipated losses due to these off-balance sheet liabilities. To account for the potential risk of off-balance sheet activities, the risk-based capital requirements require a bank to convert off-balance sheet activities to "on-balance" sheet equivalents and hold capital against these activities. Appropriate risk measures include all the risk measures discussed earlier as well as ratios measuring the ratio of: Tier 1 capital and total risk-based capital to risk-weighted assets, equity capital to total assets, dividend payout, and the growth rate in Tier 1 capital. **Tier 1 capital** is total common equity capital plus noncumulative preferred stock, plus minority interest in unconsolidated subsidiaries, less ineligible intangibles. **Risk-weighted assets** are the total of risk-adjusted assets where the risk weights are based on four risk classes of assets. See Chapter 13 for more details on calculation of capital at banks. Importantly, a bank's dividend policy also affects its capital risk by influencing retained earnings.

MAXIMIZING THE MARKET VALUE OF BANK EQUITY

A bank manager's role is to make and implement decisions that increase the value of shareholders' wealth.[28] Firm value is, in turn, closely tied to the underlying portfolio risk and return profile. The greater is perceived risk relative to expected returns, the lower is perceived value as shareholders discount anticipated cash flows to a greater degree. The lower is perceived risk, the lower is the discount rate, but the lower are expected cash flows. Banks with actively traded common stock can look to quoted share prices and cumulative market value as measures of firm value. Share prices are determined by return prospects versus risk characteristics and capture the market's perception of historical and anticipated performance.

Given the objective of maximizing the market value of bank equity, managers pursue strategies in several policy areas including:

1. Asset management (composition and volume)
2. Liability management (composition and volume)
3. Management of off-balance sheet activities
4. Interest rate margin or spread management
5. Credit risk management
6. Liquidity management

---

[28]An extensive literature suggests that bank managers may pursue goals other than wealth maximization, such as trying to capture the greatest market share or expense preference behavior in which owners and managers extract benefits by having the bank pay expenses for individuals that might normally be paid from personal resources. Heggestad (1979) summarizes key concepts and empirical results related to these alternative objectives. See Chapter 4 for a discussion of some of these alternative objectives.

7. Management of noninterest expense

8. Tax management

Each area of strategic decisions is closely tied with a bank's profitability, as measured in Equation 3.8. The primary responsibilities are to acquire assets through appropriate financing and to control the burden while maintaining an acceptable risk profile. Bank regulators attempt to help managers keep their firm operating by regulating allowable activities.

Bank regulation is largely designed to limit risk taking by commercial banks. Regulation limits the activities of a bank, although the 1999 Gramm-Leach-Bliley Financial Services Modernization Act has dramatically expanded these permissible activities. Regulators also limit the size of a loan to any single borrower to reduce the concentration of bank resources. To assess bank risk, regulators routinely examine the quality of assets, mismatched maturities of assets and liabilities, and internal operating controls. If they determine that a bank has assumed too much risk, they require additional equity capital.

EVALUATING BANK PERFORMANCE: AN APPLICATION

The following discussion analyzes the financial data of PNC introduced in Exhibits 3.2, 3.4, and 3.6. It examines the data for 2001 relative to peer banks and summarizes trends from 1997 to 2001. Profitability is characterized according to the ROE model in terms of UBPR data, and is contrasted with the firm's risk position in the five categories noted.

PNC's PROFITABILITY AND RISK VERSUS PEERS IN 2001

Profitability Analysis. Profitability ratios are provided in Exhibit 3.7. The first column in 2001, "CALC," contains the ratios calculated using data listed in Exhibits 3.2, 3.4, and 3.6. The second column, titled "UBPR," provides profitability ratios taken directly from the UBPR. The third column, titled "PEER1," represents peer group comparative figures obtained from the UBPR for other U.S. banks with more than $10 billion in assets.[29] The equations provided in the chapter apply to data in the column labeled "CALC." Because the UBPR uses several different methods of averaging balance sheet data, the calculated ratios will not always be exactly equal to the UBPR ratios. Quarterly average balance sheet data are not published in the UBPR except for average total assets and average total loans. When other average balance sheet data are needed to calculate a ratio, the average value is obtained by using the average of 2000 and 2001 end-of-year data. The calculated values are provided as a reference in applying the formulas and equations presented earlier in the chapter. Because the use of quarterly average balance sheet data will generally provide more accurate ratios, the following analysis will use ratios obtained directly from the UBPR and compare these with the listed peer group figures.[30]

PNC's profitability fell dramatically in 2001, such that the return to shareholders, ROE, equaled 9.37 percent, well below that of peers and that for 2000.[31] This was generated by an

---

[29]There are actually twenty-four bank peer groups. Peer group 1 is for banks over $10 billion.

[30]Although the following analysis will directly compare PNC's ratio to the peer group, it is important to recognize that the peer group may or may not be the appropriate comparison. To say a bank is doing better than the peer does not always indicate that the bank is "doing well."

[31]The ROE reported in the UBPR under the column "UBPR," and listed in the second column of Exhibit 3.7, is 9.37%. ROE calculated for 2001 from data presented in Exhibits 3.2 and 3.4 is 9.31% = 471,732/(5,541,015 + 5,251,116)/2. Ratios reported in the UBPR use one of three types of averages of quarterly figures from balance sheet data. For this reason, some of the ratios calculated using data from Exhibits 3.2 and 3.4 will not equal those reported in the UBPR in the appendix. See the box on Calculating and Interpreting Financial Ratios Using the UBPR.

▪ EXHIBIT 3.7

PROFITABILITY MEASURES FOR PNC BANK AND COMMUNITY NATIONAL BANK: 2000–2001

FINANCIAL RATIOS	UPBR Pg#	PNC BANK 2000 UPBR	2000 PEER1	2001 CALC	2001 UPBR	2001 PEER1	COMMUNITY NATIONAL BANK 2000 UPBR	2000 PEER7	2001 CALC	2001 UPBR	2001 PEER7
Profitability Ratios											
ROE: Net Income/Average Total Equity	11	18.94%	13.82%	9.31%	9.37%	13.68%	20.28%	13.06%	10.98%	11.04%	11.81%
ROA: Net Income/Avg TA	1	1.50%	1.09%	0.74%	0.77%	1.12%	1.44%	1.14%	0.81%	0.82%	1.07%
AU: Total Revenue/Avg TA	1 calc	9.24%	9.19%	9.06%	9.10%	8.27%	9.00%	8.79%	8.29%	8.30%	8.24%
ER: Total Expenses (Less Taxes)/Avg TA	1 calc	6.96%	7.47%	7.88%	7.88%	6.54%	6.77%	7.08%	7.13%	7.13%	6.69%
Memo: PM: Net Income/Total Revenue	1 calc	16.23%	11.86%	8.38%	8.46%	13.54%	16.00%	12.97%	9.80%	9.88%	12.99%
EM: Avg TA/Avg Total Equity	6 calc	12.63x	12.50x	12.41x	12.12x	11.88x	14.51x	11.45x	13.96x	13.72x	11.11x
EB: Earning Assets/Avg TA	6	86.95%	89.02%	85.76%	85.13%	88.31%	90.38%	91.57%	90.36%	89.65%	91.52%
NIM: Net Interest Margin (te)	1	3.58%	3.76%	4.05%	3.95%	3.71%	6.41%	4.74%	5.44%	5.59%	4.49%
Spread (te)	3 calc	3.11%	3.14%	3.62%	3.44%	3.31%	4.99%	3.89%	4.02%	4.27%	3.75%
Efficiency Ratio	1 calc	57.17%	59.44%	61.49%	61.15%	59.51%	63.66%	63.64%	76.92%	76.90%	65.35%
Burden/Avg Total Assets	1 calc	0.71%	1.25%	1.04%	1.04%	1.22%	3.47%	2.49%	3.65%	3.65%	2.39%
Noninterest Income/Noninterest exp.	1 calc	78.29%	60.69%	72.93%	72.92%	61.39%	16.79%	25.89%	23.29%	23.32%	28.01%
Expenses											
ER*: Expense Ratio Components		6.96%	7.47%	7.88%	7.88%	6.54%	6.77%	7.08%	7.13%	7.13%	6.69%
Total Interest Expense/Avg TA	1	3.49%	3.90%	2.62%	2.62%	2.90%	2.45%	3.51%	2.11%	2.11%	3.14%
Memo: Interest Expense/Avg Earn Assets	1	3.94%	4.31%	3.09%	2.98%	3.21%	2.69%	3.78%	2.26%	2.32%	3.39%
Noninterest Expenses/Avg TA	1	3.27%	3.18%	3.84%	3.84%	3.16%	4.17%	3.36%	4.76%	4.76%	3.32%
Personnel Expenses	3	1.46%	1.35%	1.66%	1.66%	1.39%	2.38%	1.77%	2.74%	2.74%	1.77%
Occupancy Expense	3	0.42%	0.41%	0.48%	0.48%	0.39%	0.62%	0.52%	0.75%	0.75%	0.50%
Other Operating Expense (Incl. Intangibles)	3	1.39%	1.37%	1.70%	1.70%	1.31%	1.17%	1.06%	1.27%	1.27%	1.04%
Provision: Loan & Lease Losses/Avg TA	1	0.20%	0.39%	1.42%	1.42%	0.48%	0.15%	0.21%	0.26%	0.26%	0.23%
Income Taxes/Avg TA	1 calc	0.78%	0.63%	0.43%	0.45%	0.61%	0.79%	0.57%	0.35%	0.35%	0.48%
Income											
AU: Asset Utilization (Income Components):		9.24%	9.19%	9.06%	9.10%	8.27%	9.00%	8.79%	8.29%	8.30%	8.24%
Interest Income/Avg TA	1	6.65%	7.32%	6.07%	6.10%	6.27%	8.30%	7.92%	7.18%	7.19%	7.29%
Memo: Avg Yield on Earning Assets	1	7.52%	8.08%	7.14%	6.93%	6.96%	9.10%	8.52%	7.69%	7.91%	7.88%
Noninterest Income/Avg TA	1	2.56%	1.93%	2.80%	2.80%	1.94%	0.70%	0.87%	1.11%	1.11%	0.93%
Realized Security Gains (Losses)/Avg TA	1	0.03%	-0.06%	0.20%	0.20%	0.06%	0.00%	0.00%	0.00%	0.00%	0.02%

CALC indicates data must be calculated from the UPBR; Avg TA = average total assets from Exhibit 3.6; $100M = $100,000,000.

NOTE: Calculated ratios which require balance sheet averages use the average of current year and prior year balance sheet data.

continued

· CONTINUED

PROFITABILITY MEASURES FOR PNC BANK AND COMMUNITY NATIONAL BANK: 2000–2001

RATE, VOLUME, AND COMPOSITION EFFECTS	UPBR Pg#	PNC BANK 2000 UPBR	2000 PEER1	CALC	2001 UPBR	PEER1	COMMUNITY NATIONAL BANK 2000 UPBR	2000 PEER7	CALC	2001 UPBR	PEER7
Interest Expense: Composition, Rate and Volume Effects											
Rate: Avg interest cost of liabilities	3	4.41%	4.94%	3.52%	3.49%	3.65%	4.11%	4.63%	3.67%	3.64%	4.13%
Memo: Interest expense / Earning assets	1	3.94%	4.31%	3.09%	2.98%	3.21%	2.69%	3.78%	2.26%	2.32%	3.39%
Volume: All interest-bearing debt (avg)/avg TA	**1**	79.02%	79.45%	75.34%	75.29%	79.81%	59.78%	75.83%	55.52%	57.90%	76.04%
Mix and Cost of Individual Liabilities:*											
Total deposits (avg)/avg TA:	6	67.28%	66.58%	73.44%	70.93%	66.78%	91.91%	85.51%	91.90%	91.65%	85.39%
Cost (rate): Int bearing Total deposits	3	4.23%	4.41%	3.08%	3.18%	3.30%	4.08%	4.54%	3.67%	3.64%	4.09%
Core deposits (avg)/avg TA	6	58.74%	49.81%	65.14%	63.74%	51.70%	81.11%	73.32%	81.59%	80.85%	72.12%
Transaction (NOW & ATS) accounts (avg)/avg TA	6	1.77%	1.28%	2.11%	1.96%	1.36%	6.43%	9.78%	9.19%	7.16%	9.59%
Cost (rate): Transaction (NOW & ATS) Accts*	3	2.98%	2.32%	N/A	2.17%	1.96%	1.42%	2.11%	N/A	0.90%	1.65%
Money market deposit accounts (avg)/avg TA	6	28.31%	16.97%	33.50%	33.11%	20.14%	20.29%	12.44%	15.48%	18.01%	12.55%
Other savings deposits (avg)/avg TA	6	2.97%	7.07%	2.98%	2.95%	7.53%	4.26%	8.43%	4.07%	4.21%	8.07%
Cost (rate): Other savings deposits*	3	1.62%	2.06%	N/A	2.08%	2.00%	2.57%	2.54%	N/A	2.40%	2.74%
Time deposits under $100M (avg)/avg TA	6	15.69%	12.38%	14.94%	14.77%	11.46%	16.86%	25.15%	15.79%	16.27%	24.90%
Cost (rate): All other time dep. (CD < $100M)*	6	5.82%	5.79%	N/A	5.21%	5.31%	5.34%	5.63%	N/A	5.60%	5.44%
Memo: S.T. non-core funding (avg)/avg TA	6	17.48%	28.81%	12.07%	11.02%	26.65%	10.25%	13.37%	9.90%	10.30%	13.59%
Memo: Volatile liabilities (avg)/avg TA	6-calc	18.66%	30.00%	13.42%	12.27%	26.21%	11.53%	14.06%	10.99%	11.49%	14.48%
Large certificates of dep (inc. brokered) (avg)/avg TA	6	4.85%	8.38%	4.56%	4.37%	7.66%	10.79%	11.56%	10.31%	10.80%	12.62%
Cost (rate): CD's over $100M	3	6.30%	5.92%	5.27%	5.46%	4.94%	5.55%	5.81%	5.28%	5.09%	5.38%
Deposits held in foreign offices (avg)/avg TA	6	3.69%	6.39%	3.74%	2.83%	5.09%	0.00%	0.00%	0.00%	0.00%	0.00%
Cost (rate): Deposits held in foreign offices	3	6.31%	4.72%	2.29%	4.13%	2.58%	0.00%	0.00%	N/A	0.00%	0.00%
Fed funds purchased & resale (avg)/avg TA	6	2.28%	8.61%	1.72%	2.28%	8.93%	0.74%	1.47%	0.68%	0.69%	1.20%
Cost (rate): Fed funds purchased & resale	6	7.37%	6.17%	9.18%	4.19%	3.80%	5.80%	4.40%	3.80%	3.80%	2.53%
Memo: All brokered deposits (avg)/avg TA	6	0.60%	2.29%	1.40%	1.41%	2.12%	0.00%	0.13%	0.00%	0.00%	0.23%
All common and preferred capital (avg)/avg TA	6	7.92%	8.00%	8.06%	8.25%	8.42%	6.89%	8.73%	7.17%	7.29%	9.00%
Interest Income: Composition, Rate and Volume Effects											
Rate: Avg yield on Avg TA											
Memo: Avg yield on earn. assets (rate)	1	7.52%	8.08%	7.14%	6.93%	6.96%	9.10%	8.52%	7.69%	7.91%	7.88%
Volume: Earn assets (avg)/avg TA	6	86.95%	89.02%	85.76%	85.13%	88.31%	90.38%	91.57%	90.36%	89.65%	91.52%
Nonearning assets (avg)/avg TA		13.05%	10.71%	14.24%	14.88%	11.42%	9.62%	8.15%	9.64%	10.34%	8.19%
Mix and Cost of Individual Assets:*											
Total loans (gross loans less unearned inc.) (avg)/avg TA	6	76.87%	64.18%	71.87%	69.69%	63.43%	61.49%	65.48%	65.83%	65.47%	65.94%
Yield (rate): Total loans & leases (te)	3	7.90%	8.63%	7.29%	7.29%	7.44%	10.42%	9.37%	9.06%	9.06%	8.71%
Total investments (avg)/avg TA:	6-calc	11.04%	21.38%	14.89%	16.46%	21.89%	29.42%	23.93%	25.06%	24.71%	23.45%
Yield (rate): Total investment securities (TE):	3	4.98%	6.72%	6.58%	5.55%	6.28%	6.20%	6.47%	4.49%	5.13%	6.17%
Yield (rate): Total investment securities (Book):	3	4.97%	6.57%	6.58%	5.54%	6.13%	6.13%	6.12%	4.42%	5.05%	5.80%
Interest-bearing bank balances (avg)/avg TA	6	0.18%	0.84%	0.26%	0.20%	0.82%	0.00%	0.33%	0.17%	0.14%	0.58%
Yield (rate): Interest-bearing bank balances	3	7.02%	5.95%	3.35%	5.33%	4.87%	0.00%	3.99%	N/A	4.44%	2.93%
Fed funds sold & resales (avg)/avg TA	6	1.01%	2.34%	0.41%	0.58%	3.43%	12.24%	2.61%	6.46%	7.79%	3.85%
Yield (rate): Fed funds sold & resales	3	6.30%	6.33%	4.88%	3.86%	3.82%	6.22%	6.15%	4.62%	3.99%	3.50%
Trading account assets (avg)/avg TA	6	0.33%	1.09%	0.52%	0.59%	1.18%	0.00%	0.00%	0.00%	0.00%	0.00%
Held-to-maturity securities (avg)/avg TA	6	0.00%	1.12%	0.00%	0.00%	0.71%	9.22%	3.60%	5.75%	5.28%	2.71%
Available-for-sale securities (avg)/avg TA	6	9.52%	15.99%	13.70%	15.09%	15.75%	7.96%	17.39%	12.67%	11.50%	16.31%

*Following the UBPR, all "Mix" or composition values are averages of current and prior period.
For example, "Total deposits (avg)/avg TA" equals average total deposits to average total assets.

USING AVERAGES OF BALANCE SHEET DATA AND INTERPRETING FINANCIAL RATIOS USING THE UBPR

The interpretation of historical financial data typically begins with ratio analysis. To be meaningful, ratios must be calculated consistently and compared with benchmark figures. Ratios are constructed by dividing one balance sheet or income statement item by another. The value of any ratio depends on the magnitude of both the numerator and denominator and will change when either changes.

Several rules apply when constructing ratios. First, remember that balance sheet items are stock figures measuring value at a point in time, while income statement items are flow figures measuring value over time, such as one year. When constructing ratios combining balance sheet and income statement figures, average balance sheet data should be used. For example, suppose that only year-end balance sheet figures for 2000 and 2001 are available along with 2001 income statement figures. Return on equity in 2001 is calculated as the ratio of 2001 net income to one-half the sum of year-end 2000 and 2001 total equity. It would be better to use quarterly average balance sheet figures, with daily averages the best. In fact, the UBPR calculates three different types of average assets and liabilities for use on selected pages.

The first type of average used in the UBPR is a *cumulative* or year-to-date average of the one-quarter averages for assets and liabilities reported in the call report. The resulting year-to-date averages are used as the denominator in earnings ratios, yield and rate calculations found on pages 1 and 3 of the UBPR. As an example, the average assets used for page 1 earnings analysis in the September 30th UBPR would reflect an average of the quarterly average assets reported in March, June and September of the current year. The second type of average used in the UBPR is a *year-to-date* average of end-of-period balances reported in the call report from the

beginning of the year forward. To provide an accurate average, the asset or liability balance at the prior year-end is also included. Averages calculated in this manner are used to determine the percentage composition of assets and liabilities on page 6. For example, the September 30th year-to-date average total loans is composed of the spot balances for total loans from the call report for the prior December, and current March, June, and September divided by 4. The final type of average used in the UBPR is a *moving* four-quarter average using quarterly average data. These averages are used as the denominator in last-four-quarters income analysis on page 12. A four-quarter window compares four quarters of income/expense to selected assets or liabilities averaged for a similar period of time. Thus, average assets used in the September 30 UBPR analysis of net income on page 12 would include the quarterly average assets for the prior December, and current March, June, and September. That average creates a window stretching from October 1 of the prior year to September 30 of the current year.

All balance sheet values listed in Exhibit 3.2 are for end-of-period (EOP). Average total assets and average total loans and leases data are included in Exhibit 3.6. Average total assets and average total loans reported in Exhibit 3.6 were used in the calculated ratios presented in Exhibits 3.6 and 3.7 when called for and when possible. All other ratios, which call for "average" balance sheet figures, calculated in Exhibits 3.6 and 3.7 use averages of annual data. A special note, however, applies to composition of asset and liability data that compares to page 06 of the UBPR. The UBPR uses averages in the numerator as well as the denominator. For example, average total loans (gross loans less unearned income) to average total assets is calculated using end-of-period balance sheet data as:

$$71.87\% = \{[(40,503,242 - 51,223) + (50,051,852 - 96,913)]/2\} / [(62,609,780 + 63,185,903)/2]$$

The equivalent value reported in the UBPR for PNC is 69.69 percent. Recall that the UBPR uses averages of quarterly data rather than averages of end-of-year data.

The second rule that applies is that a single ratio by itself is generally meaningless. Calculate ratios over different intervals to discern notable changes. Determine whether the changes are due to factors affecting the numerator or denominator. This typically requires comparing trends in two related ratios. Third, compare ratios with similar figures from a control or representative peer group at the same point in time. The peer group represents average performance for a comparable firm. Of course, it is extremely important to identify the correct peer group. Peers should be the same approximate size, operate in the same geographic and product markets, and have the same strategies. The UBPR identifies peers by size, state, and metropolitan or nonmetropolitan along with the number of branches. This is generally too broad a group to be meaningful. Most banks create their own peer groups to compare performance.

Accounting data may not reflect accepted accounting procedures and may be manipulated. Important data, such as the volume of a bank's outstanding loan commitments and other off-balance sheet activities, may be omitted. This potentially biases traditional ratios. The UBPR now provides a section on "Off-Balance Sheet Items." Footnotes to financial statements generally provide sources and an explanation for many calculations. Additional explanations for balance sheet, income statement, and ratio calculations can be obtain from the UBPR Users Manual available from the FDIC or on the Internet at www.FFIEC.gov.

ROA of 0.77 percent and an equity multiplier of 12.12x. Profitability at the bank was much lower, while the degree of leverage was higher than peers. PNC used more debt financing (its equity multiplier was higher) such that its higher ROE reflected a significantly lower ROA with a greater degree of financial leverage. If PNC had used the same financial leverage as peers (11.88x), its ROE would have been even lower (8.32 percent) relative to peers. Thus, PNC appears to be a low performing bank in 2001. The bank's lower returns, combined with a greater degree of risk (higher leverage), is indicative of the loan problems experienced in 2001. The 2001 performance is in sharp contrast to what appeared to be a high performing bank in 2000. One of the greatest challenges in evaluating a bank, or any company, is that a higher degree of risk typically first shows up as higher reported profits. Only later, as the higher rate, higher risk loans begin to go bad, does the bank report higher charge-offs or additional provisions for loan losses. PNC is a low performance bank in 2001 because it used more financial leverage, indicating higher risk, and still reported significantly lower aggregate profits.

PNC's lower ROA is generated by an asset utilization of 9.10 percent, an expense ratio of 7.88 percent, and a tax ratio of 0.45 percent such that:

$$\text{ROA} = 0.77\% = 9.10\% - 7.88\% - 0.45\%$$

The expense ratio of 7.88 percent (versus 6.54 percent for peers) indicates that PNC was less efficient than its peers in controlling total expenses. Asset utilization, on the other hand, indicates that PNC's gross return on assets (9.10 percent) was much higher than peers (8.27 percent) and PNC's tax ratio of 0.45 percent was lower than that for peers at 0.61 percent. As we will see, PNC's lower tax position was a direct result of the large loan charge-offs and resulting large provisions for loan losses—a deductible expense. Thus, PNC's lower profitability is attributed to much higher expenses that offset the higher revenue and lower taxes relative to peers. By breaking down asset utilization into interest income and noninterest income and the expense ratio into interest and noninterest expense and provisions for loan losses, we can better determine the operational strengths and weaknesses of PNC's profitability.

PNC's higher overall expenses are attributed to noninterest expense and provisions for loan losses, not interest expense or taxes. PNC actually paid 0.28 percent less in interest expense relative to average assets than peers (2.62 percent versus peers of 2.90 percent). This difference suggests that PNC operates differently than peers in at least one of the areas of *rates* paid, liability *composition,* and *volume* of interest-bearing liabilities. The rate effect shows that PNC's average cost of interest-bearing liabilities was 16 basis points lower than peers (3.49 versus 3.65 percent). Of benefit was the 12 basis points lower average cost of total deposits (3.18 versus 3.30 percent for peers). Although the interest cost of each liability was higher than peers, with the exception of all other time deposits (CDs < $100M), a favorable mix, or composition effect, lowered overall interest expense. The favorable composition effect was evidenced by the larger volume of relatively inexpensive core deposits, which produced the overall lower interest expense. PNC relied on 63.74 percent core deposits (51.70 percent for peers). These core deposits include noninterest-bearing checking accounts, interest-bearing checking accounts and money market funds, all of which pay little or no interest. Lower interest expenses were, therefore, the result of PNC's reliance on a less expensive composition of funds offset by a higher average rate paid on these funds. Specifically, PNC held substantially more of the less expensive core deposits and significantly fewer of the more expensive volatile or purchased liabilities (12.27 percent versus 26.21 percent for peers). Finally, we know that the volume effect was positive because PNC's volume of interest-bearing liabilities was a smaller fraction of average assets than that of peers (75.29 percent versus 79.81 percent). Thus, even though PNC used a greater degree of financial leverage (that is, the bank relied proportionally more on borrowed funds), fewer of these funds were interest bearing. A greater reliance on noninterest-bearing demand deposits and acceptances meant that average interest-bearing liabilities were smaller for PNC than peers. In this case, two of the three factors—a less expensive composition of funds and a lower volume of interest-bearing liabilities—produce the lower aggregate interest expense for PNC relative to peers.

Profitability for PNC was lowered by the bank's higher noninterest expense to assets (3.84 versus 3.16 percent for peers). The major contributing factor to PNC's higher overall expenses and the significantly lower profitability was the substantial provisions for loan losses at 1.42 percent of assets compared to peers' 0.48 percent of assets. It is interesting to note that PNC's ROA would have been 1.71 percent $(9.10 - 2.62 - 3.84 - 0.48 - 0.45)$ if its provisions were comparable with peers. This, in turn, would have have generated a 20.73 percent ROE. Clearly, PNC's higher risk loan portfolio has come back to haunt the bank with substantial write-offs for 2001.

In terms of net interest margin (NIM), PNC's lower interest expense more than compensated for its lower interest income. PNC delivers banking services through an extensive branching network, including some foreign branches. The component costs of noninterest expense (overhead) reveal proportionately greater personnel expense, suggesting that PNC operates with more personnel and higher salaries and benefits than at peer banks; greater occupancy expenses, reflecting the large branch network; and greater other operating expense. This branch network allows PNC to obtain less expensive core deposits. PNC's ability to control noninterest expense relative to net operating income is summarized by its efficiency ratio, which is higher than peers, using the data relative to total assets on page 1 of the UBPR.

$$
\begin{array}{ll}
\underline{\text{PNC}} & \underline{\text{Peers}} \\
\text{EFF} = 3.84\%/(6.10\% - 2.62\%) + 2.80 & \text{EFF} = 3.16\%/(6.27\% - 2.90\%) + 1.94\% \\
\quad\;\; = 61.15\% & \qquad\;\; = 59.51\%
\end{array}
$$

These figures suggest that PNC's overhead expense control, relative to income generation, is not as good as peers. PNC pays just over 61 cents per $1 of operating revenue while peers pay about 59.5 cents for overhead. PNC's efficiency ratio dropped dramatically in 2001, a direct result of a major restructuring in late 2001. Banks use the efficiency ratio to measure the trade-offs of higher noninterest expense from a larger branch network to produce lower interest cost through more core deposits and greater noninterest income.

PNC's loan problems in 2001 forced management to restructure the business processes. PNC's provisions for loan losses were historically very low, about one-half that of the peers, but were triple the rates for peers in 2001. A careful review of credit risk is clearly necessary to determine whether the provisions are high enough relative to asset quality.

Consider next the components of asset utilization (AU). Even though PNC's AU was much greater than peers, its interest income was lower (6.10 versus 6.27 percent for peers) and noninterest income was significantly higher (2.80 versus 1.94 percent for peers). Again, lower interest income could be due to lower yields on assets, fewer loans, a smaller volume of earning assets, or a combination of these. Upon examining the rate effect, we find that PNC earned a slightly lower average gross yield on earning assets, 6.93 percent, compared with that of peers', 6.95 percent. PNC generally earned lower yields on both loans and investments. In terms of the composition effect, PNC held substantially more loans in 2001, but the favorable impact was reduced by the fact that these loans earned 15 basis points less than peers. PNC has historically operated with substantially more loans than peer banks, but loan sales in late 2001 lowered the loan portfolio from about 77 percent of assets to 70 percent of assets. If PNC did indeed "sell " its higher risk loans, this could mean improved profitability and lower risk in the future. Only time will tell.

PNC also operated with fewer investment securities that earned 73 basis points less than peers. The lower yield on loans and securities, combined with a reduced volume of loans and an increase in the volume of investments (although a higher amount than peers, investments pay a lower rate), is the primary reason for PNC's lower reported interest income. The lower yield on loans might suggest lower risk, but the higher volume of loans suggests higher risk. Loan rates were also lower in 2000, and it does not appear that this was indicative of a lower risk loan portfolio. As such, the analyst should carefully examine the bank's credit risk.

Finally, the volume effect indicates that PNC's earnings base was more than three percent less than peers, indicating that PNC invested a smaller portion of its total assets in interest-bearing assets. This factor also leads to the lower aggregate interest income.

The net effect of the interest income and interest expense differences is revealed in the net interest margin (NIM). In 2001, PNC's NIM was 24 basis points higher than that for peer banks. Thus, the lower interest expense did offset the lower interest income relative to earning assets. It is important to note, however, that NIM is calculated before provisions for loan losses and ignores actual net charge-offs and a bank's asset quality. The apparent lower quality of PNC's loan portfolio more than offset any gains in NIM.

Noninterest income, on the other hand, was much higher at PNC. PNC and other large banking organizations have generally structured their banking business to rely proportionately more on noninterest income and less on loan income. In fact, one of the primary motives to PNC's loan sales in 2001 was a restructuring of its primary business to reflect asset management and the custody business as core operations. PNC wanted to restructure its core business and operate a bank with a "low-risk " balance sheet. Following this model, management stated the objective to become more selective in the types of loans made. Many large banks generally encourage loans to businesses with more easily verifiable credit qualities, hence lower loan fees. This assists them in keeping overhead cost down and in cross-selling other products, thus producing more noninterest income in the form of product and service fees. Consistent with the sale of more products, PNC's higher noninterest income is generated from fiduciary activities, service charges, and other noninterest income sources (investment banking, advisory, brokerage, and underwriting fees and commissions) such that the bank appears to have pursued the noninterest strategy more aggressively than peers.[32]

Composition of Noninterest Income in 2001*	PNC	Banks: Assets >$10B*	All Commercial Banks
Number of institutions reporting	1	80	8,080
Total noninterest income	2.80%	2.66%	2.40%
Fiduciary activities	0.57%	0.34%	0.32%
Service charges on deposit accounts	0.56%	0.42%	0.41%
Trading account gains & fees	0.12%	0.27%	0.19%
Investment banking, advisory, brokerage, and underwriting fees and commissions	0.81%	0.18%	0.14%
Venture capital revenue	0.00%	−0.02%	−0.01%
Net servicing fees	0.06%	0.21%	0.18%
Net securitization income	0.01%	0.31%	0.25%
Insurance commission fees and income	0.01%	0.04%	0.04%
Net gains (losses) on sales of loans	0.05%	0.05%	0.07%
Net gains (losses) on sales of other real estate owned	−0.01%	0.00%	0.00%
Net gains (losses) on sales of other assets (excluding securities)	0.00%	0.05%	0.03%
Other noninterest income	0.62%	0.81%	0.78%

*Peer data for banks with assets greater than $10 billion are taken from a different source than the UBPR. These data are obtained from the FDIC's SDI system (http://www3.fdic.gov/sdi). The UBPR "trims" the upper 5% and lower 5% of data to adjust for outliers. The data presented in the above table represent all banks in the respective asset category. Obviously, as compared to the UBPR peer figure of 1.94 percent for all banks in excess of $10 billion, the largest banks do a good job of producing noninterest income.

---

[32]Other noninterest income and fee income include: investment banking, advisory, brokerage and underwriting fees and commissions, venture capital revenue, net servicing fees, net securitization income, insurance commissions and fees, net gains (losses) on sales of loans, other real estate owned, other assets, and other noninterest income.

PNC's more aggressive noninterest position is emphasized by the fact that PNC's burden was better than peers as a fraction of assets (1.04 versus 1.22 percent), indicating that the bank performed better than peers in generating noninterest income to cover its noninterest expense.

The following table summarizes the profitability differences between PNC and peers. As indicated, PNC reported a much lower ROE due to its lower return on assets with the use of more financial leverage. In addition, PNC's lower returns to the bank were a result of greater income generation which was mitigated by much higher expenses and taxes. In particular, the lower ROA was due primarily to a much higher PLL. Net interest income contributed more to net income than peers and PNC's burden was better than peers due to high noninterest income relative to noninterest expenses. PNC's much higher PLL also allowed for somewhat lower taxes, all resulting in an overall lower ROA.

PNC
December 31, 2001

	UBPR	PEER1	Diff	Results
ROE: Net Income/Average Total Equity	9.37%	13.68%	−4.31%	Lower return to shareholders
ROA: Net Income/Avg TA	0.77%	1.12%	−0.35%	From a lower return on investment
EM: Average TA/Average Total Equity	12.12x	11.88x	0.24x	And a higher degree of financial leverage
AU: Total Revenue/Avg TA	9.10%	8.27%	0.83%	Higher gross revenue
ER: Total Expenses (Less Taxes)/Avg TA	7.88%	6.54%	1.34%	Higher total expenses
TAX: Tax/Avg TA	0.45%	0.61%	−0.16%	Lower reported taxes
ROA: Net Income/Avg TA	0.77%	1.12%	−0.35%	Results in a lower net income
Income and Expense Decomposition:				
Interest Income/Average TA	6.10%	6.27%	−0.17%	Lower interest income
Total Interest Expense/Avg TA	2.62%	2.90%	−0.28%	Lower interest expense
NIM: Net Interest Margin (te)	3.95%	3.71%	0.24%	Results in a higher net interest income
Noninterest Income/Avg TA	2.80%	1.94%	0.86%	Higher noninterest income
Noninterest Expenses/Avg TA	3.84%	3.16%	0.68%	Higher noninterest expenses
Burden/Avg. TA	1.04%	1.22%	−0.18%	Results in a lower burden
Provision: Loan & Lease Losses/Avg TA	1.42%	0.48%	0.94%	Higher provisions for loan losses
Realized Security Gains (Losses)/Avg TA	0.20%	0.06%	0.14%	Higher securities gains (losses)
Income Taxes/Avg TA	0.45%	0.61%	−0.16%	Lower reported taxes
ROA: Net Income/Avg TA	0.77%	1.12%	−0.35%	Results in a lower return on assets

Risk Analysis. Higher returns are generally indicative of above average risk, while lower returns should indicate a lower risk position. As evidenced by PNC's lower relative returns, this might not always be the case. In addition, what appeared to be a high return in the past suggests that the bank took above average risk in prior periods and suffered the consequences in 2001, relative to peers. One of the problems in evaluating financial statements is that they are aggregate measures of past "reported " performance and might not be accurate in representing the current financial position of the company. As was the case with PNC, losses associated with the loan portfolio were restated twice, casting a shadow on management and lowering the confidence one might have in the reported financials. Events in late 2001 and 2002 clearly indicate that reported profits from the past were "overstated." The true risk of a company cannot always be determined by evaluating aggregate data such as balance sheets and income statements. Often, the analyst must dig deeper in the footnotes and off-balance sheet activities to discover risk not reported on these financials. With this said, the follow section will discuss the analysis of reported financial statements, with the understanding that the analysis is only as accurate as the reported data. See the following section on Financial Statement Manipulation.

Selected risk ratios for PNC and CNB appear in Exhibit 3.8. Additional data used to calculate some of the risk ratios, including loan charge-offs, past due loans, and noncurrent loans are taken from the supplemental data in Exhibit 3.6 and the UBPR for PNC included in the Appendix. Exhibit 3.8 lists selected risk measures categorized under the risk types introduced earlier.

In terms of credit risk in 2001, PNC held a higher fraction of assets in loans and its loan loss experience overall was almost 3 times higher than peers. What a difference a year made. In 2000, PNC reported very low net loan losses, at about one quarter of one percent—about half that of peers. In 2001, PNC reported net losses well over 2 percent. Gross loan losses were similar to net losses with few recoveries. Recoveries were low for both PNC and the peers. The peers' net loan losses of 0.63 percent was, historically, quite low. Banks in general reported very low loan losses due to the strong U.S. economy during the 1990s. Unfortunately, loan losses once again began to rise in 2001, and PNC's increase was substantial. The economy moved into recession by the end of 2001, and the tragic events of September 11, 2001, exacerbated the economic slowdown. The timing of PNC's charge-offs, however, may have had more to do with how they had reported their higher risk loan sales. That is, the losses most likely were present in 2000, just not reported. This would indicate that profits in 2000 were overstated and clearly demonstrates the need to examine a longer time series of data when assessing overall credit risk as management can readily manipulate figures in any one year. Many argue that lending is a "last in–first out system." That is, the last loans made during the peak of an economic expansion are most likely to default first.

With respect to potential losses, PNC's nonperforming loans (those more than "90 days past due") were a higher percentage of total loans compared with peers, but total nonaccrual loans were actually lower than peers, leading to a smaller total noncurrent loans to total loans ratio for PNC of 1.05 percent (1.31 percent for peers). This figure is only slightly above the 2000 ratio. With respect to prospective charge-offs, PNC is positioned slightly better. That is, if PNC accurately recognized its loan losses with the extraordinary 2.19 percent gross charge-off in 2001 and sold the problem loans, future losses should be less. Lower total noncurrent loans would be an indicator of a "higher" quality loan portfolio at the end of 2001. The analyst should consider the fact, however, that PNC's total noncurrent loans were below peers in 2000 as well, and this measure might not always be an accurate indicator of future loan problems! Finally, PNC's loan and lease loss allowance (reserves) relative to total loans and earnings coverage of net losses are well below peers—indicating poor coverage of current and potential losses. The low earnings coverage was a result of both higher charge-offs and low earnings from higher provisions for loan losses. Using data from pages 1 and 7 of the UBPR, the ratio of reserves to noncurrent loans can be approximated at 0.70 for PNC (1.05 /1.49) and 0.81 for peers (1.31/1.62), indicating lower reserve coverage for PNC. In summary, fewer noncurrent loans do not make up for the lower loan and lease loss allowance, lower earnings coverage, larger loan portfolio, and substantial charge-offs by PNC for 2001. If PNC had actually sold its problem loans without recourse, the portfolio might actually exhibit lower risk. The data for 2001, however, do not provide a great deal of confidence in that conclusion.

PNC's liquidity risk in 2001 appears much better than in 2000, with more core deposits and fewer volatile liabilities, fewer loans but also fewer short-term investments. PNC has substantially more core deposits and almost half as many volatile (noncore) liabilities. This indicates that PNC has more stable deposits, and greater capacity to issue new volatile liabilities because it relies proportionately less on these high cost funds. PNC's lower equity position and loan problems, however, might hinder its ability to provide liquidity through borrowing. PNC's net loans to total deposits and net loans to core deposits ratios indicate a loan portfolio financed proportionately less by volatile funds. These ratios provide a direct comparison of the bank's least liquid assets, loans, to the most stable funding source, deposits. Finally, both a smaller fraction of assets in available-for-sale securities and almost no short-term investments (0.74 versus 6.74 percent for peers) indicate that PNC operates with less asset liquidity than peers. On the positive side, fewer pledged securities indicates that more of these liquid assets could be used to satisfy liquid needs.

· EXHIBIT 3.8

RISK MEASURES FOR PNC BANK AND COMMUNITY NATIONAL BANK: 2000–2001

RISK RATIOS	UPBR Pg#	PNC BANK 2000 UPBR	2000 PEER1	CALC	2001 UPBR	2001 PEER1	COMMUNITY NATIONAL BANK 2000 UPBR	2000 PEER7	CALC	2001 UPBR	2001 PEER7
Credit Risk											
Gross Loss/Avg Tot LN&LS	7	0.35%	0.56%	2.19%	2.19%	0.76%	0.33%	0.22%	0.27%	0.27%	0.27%
Net Loss/Avg Tot LN&LS	7	0.26%	0.43%	2.11%	2.11%	0.63%	0.31%	0.16%	0.24%	0.24%	0.21%
Recoveries/Avg Tot LN&LS	7	0.09%	0.12%	0.08%	0.08%	0.12%	0.02%	0.05%	0.02%	0.02%	0.05%
Recoveries to Prior Credit Loss	7	23.51%	30.12%	19.8%	19.78%	26.90%	6.33%	31.64%	8.50%	8.52%	33.01%
90 Days Past Due/EOP LN&LS	8A	0.25%	0.19%	0.42%	0.42%	0.23%	0.32%	0.13%	2.49%	2.49%	0.16%
Total Nonaccrual LN&LS/EOP LN&LS	8A	0.71%	0.74%	0.63%	0.63%	0.97%	0.05%	0.40%	0.42%	0.42%	0.49%
Total Noncurrent EOP LN&LS	8A	0.96%	0.99%	1.05%	1.05%	1.31%	0.38%	0.59%	2.91%	2.91%	0.71%
LN&LS Allowance to Total LN&LS	7	1.30%	1.48%	1.49%	1.49%	1.62%	0.79%	1.23%	0.82%	0.82%	1.24%
LN&LS Allowance/Net Losses	7	4.90x	4.60x	0.64x	0.64x	3.13x	276.00%	15.34x	3.71x	371.00%	12.71x
Earn Coverage of Net Losses	7	12.32x	11.46x	1.60x	1.62x	6.93x	1,193.00%	33.17x	8.78x	883.00%	27.11x
Net Loan and Lease Growth Rate	1	−5.23%	26.93%	−19.18%	−19.18%	8.39%	17.48%	16.13%	15.18%	15.18%	12.18%
Liquidity Risk											
%Total (EOP) Assets (except where noted)											
Total Equity	11	8.31%	8.03%	7.81%	7.81%	8.36%	7.30%	8.86%	7.05%	7.05%	8.92%
Core Deposits	10	63.61%	49.59%	65.14%	66.70%	52.73%	81.21%	72.77%	81.59%	81.92%	72.29%
S.T. Non-core Funding	10	14.37%	28.27%	58.15%	9.74%	25.13%	9.99%	13.45%	82.85%	9.82%	13.31%
Avg Volatile Liabilities/Avg TA	6 calc*	18.66%	30.00%	13.41%	12.27%	26.21%	11.53%	14.06%	11.00%	11.49%	14.48%
Net Loans & Leases/Total Deposits	10	107.19%	96.26%	85.91%	85.91%	93.01%	70.76%	76.78%	71.32%	71.32%	77.33%
Net Loans & Leases/Core Deposits	10	122.68%	137.94%	95.43%	95.43%	123.03%	79.90%	90.91%	80.17%	80.17%	92.11%
Available-for-Sale Securities (Avg)/Avg TA	6	9.52%	15.99%	13.70%	15.09%	15.75%	7.96%	17.39%	12.67%	11.50%	16.31%
Short-Term Investments	10	0.66%	5.81%	N/A	0.74%	6.74%	12.30%	6.72%	N/A	8.50%	6.44%
Pledged Securities	10	74.50%	55.99%	N/A	45.01%	52.38%	50.66%	41.89%	N/A	34.27%	38.82%
Capital Risk											
Tier 1 Capital/Risk-weighted Assets	11A	9.34%	8.49%	8.73%	8.69%	9.20%	11.80%	12.38%	10.73%	10.73%	12.37%
Total RBC/Risk-Weighted Assets	11A	12.15%	11.21%	12.24%	12.19%	12.03%	12.64%	13.48%	11.58%	11.58%	13.48%
Tier 1 Leverage Capital/Total Assets	11A	8.77%	7.04%	7.55%	7.65%	7.12%	7.31%	8.71%	6.91%	7.02%	8.65%
Equity Capital/Total Assets	11	8.31%	8.03%	7.81%	7.81%	8.36%	7.30%	8.86%	7.05%	7.05%	8.92%
Dividend Payout	11	64.53%	64.59%	222.58%	211.54%	68.90%	24.47%	34.72%	31.17%	30.85%	33.65%
Growth Rate in Total Equity Capital	11	−5.23%	32.87%	−6.92%	−6.92%	19.03%	17.68%	15.95%	9.78%	9.78%	11.09%
Equity Growth Less Asset Growth	11	2.10%	4.78%	−6.01%	−6.01%	3.39%	3.33%	2.72%	−4.02%	−4.02%	−0.32%
Operational Risk											
Total Assets/Number of Employees	3	3,840x	4,780x	3,923x	3,920x	4,730x	2,250x	2,630x	2,404x	2,400x	2,720x
Personnel Expense Number of Employees	3	59.40x	55.47x	66.14x	66.14x	58.28x	50.82x	41.82x	59.88x	59.88x	43.83x
Efficiency Ratio	1 calc*	57.17%	59.44%	61.49%	61.15%	59.51%	63.66%	63.64%	76.92%	76.90%	65.35%

EOP refers to end-of-period.
*CALC indicates data must be calculated from the UPBR.

Still, the fact that the bank's asset quality measures are somewhat uncertain means that its ability to borrow might be limited. Large, or volatile borrowings are "asset quality sensitive." This means that the degree to which a bank can borrow to satisfy liquidity needs is sensitive to the market's perception of the bank's asset quality. A strong core-funding base is needed to make up for lower perceived asset quality and higher equity levels.

PNC's true credit risk is difficult to access due to the substantial changes that occurred in 2001, but would generally be considered to be higher than peers. The true picture of liquidity risk is mixed as well due to the uncertainty of the asset quality with some positive and some negative signals. The higher core deposit base, lower volatile liability position, and lower loans to core deposits would indicate lower liquidity risk. Poor asset quality versus peers indicates higher liquidity risk.

Higher-risk banks are expected to hold greater capital while lower-risk banks might be able to hold less capital than comparable peer banks. PNC's equity to asset ratio indicates that PNC had lower end-of-period total equity relative to end-of-period total assets than peer banks. Still, it is required by regulation to have a Tier 1 capital ratio of at least 4 percent and a total capital ratio of at least 8 percent relative to risk assets. Both of these ratios are greater than comparable peer ratios and substantially exceeded the regulatory minimums. Banks with more than 10 percent total risk-based capital to risk weighted assets are considered to be "well capitalized" and PNC's total risk-based capital was 12.19 percent (see Chapter 13 for details on risk-based capital). PNC's dividend payout was very high at 211.54 percent of earnings. The substantial reduction in total assets as a result of the sale of billions of dollars in loans meant that PNC's large dividend reflected a constant dividend payment to stockholders, even with the temporary drop in earnings. The dividends were paid to the holding company. As a result, equity fell more than assets.[33] Higher equity capital and higher risk-based capital reflect the greater amount of risk assets, such as loans, that PNC holds relative to peers. Again, given the caveat that the existing loan portfolio is sound, capital risk appears to be somewhat lower for PNC even with its greater loan portfolio.

The bank's interest rate risk position is indicated by the difference between repriceable assets and liabilities. Unfortunately, UBPR data on interest rate risk are very limited. Total interest rate risk cannot be determined without more detailed rate-sensitivity data and measures of duration that will be discussed in Chapters 8 and 9.

Operational risk is also difficult to assess because only limited information is available. PNC operates with fewer assets per employee, indicating the bank employed more people relative to its asset base. This could indicate a lower productivity level, but most likely reflects the larger branch network PNC employs to gather their inexpensive core deposit base. It appears, however, that although the cost benefit trade-offs of PNC's large branch bank system and higher noninterest expenses worked in the past, 2001 data indicate that the bank's lower cost of funds, lower interest income, higher amount of noninterest income, and higher amount of noninterest expense lead to a higher efficiency ratio of 61.15 versus peers of 59.51 percent. PNC also exhibits higher personnel expenses per employee. This indicates a higher paid labor force that could be due to the geographic region in which PNC operates.

PNC's profit performance was well below peers as it appears that the bank assumed substantially greater risk in the past in an effort to achieve higher returns. A dramatic "cleansing" of the loan portfolio produced low profits for 2001, but if the extraordinary loss provisions were removed, PNC performed well above peers. The challenge facing the analyst is to assess the remaining loan portfolio. If PNC did indeed purge all high risk loans, the company is positioned to be a high performance bank in the near future.

---

[33]Actually assets fell by 0.9 percent while equity fell by 6.9 percent.

THE FALL OF ENRON AND ITS IMPACT ON PNC BANK

When Enron announced that it would file a voluntary petition for Chapter 11 reorganization on December 2, 2001, the world was shocked as it was the largest U.S. bankruptcy in recent history. Throughout the 1990s and early 2000s, Enron had transformed itself from a pure energy company to an energy broker and giant hedge fund. Prior to its failure, many market participants viewed Enron as a 'New Economy' success story with its highly profitable (at least as reported in audited financial statements) move from hard assets (natural gas production and processing) to soft assets (trading activities). However, as it was eventually discovered, Enron engaged in many questionable activities including not reporting losses from business activities that the firm inappropriately moved off-balance sheet. Enron was thus able to hide losses on the business activities and/or use its off-balance sheet activities to artificially inflate reported earnings.

Most banks also enter into agreements that do not have a balance sheet reporting impact until a transaction is effected. An example might be a long-term loan commitment to a potential borrower. Until the customer actually borrows the funds, no loan is reported on the bank's assets. Banks earn fees on loan commitments whether or not the funds are ever actually borrowed. Other examples of off-balance sheet activities at banks include providing guarantees and positions in derivative contracts such as interest rate swaps and financial futures. Obviously, off-balance sheet positions generate noninterest income but also entail some risk as the bank must perform under the contracts.

From 1999–2001, PNC had been moving out of certain lending businesses by selling off $20 billion in loans and reducing unfunded loan commitments by $25 billion. In October 2001, PNC reported lower net income due in a large part to problems with its venture capital business. On January 3, 2002, PNC announced that it was taking a $615 million after-tax charge in the fourth quarter of 2001 as it wrote down loans on its venture capital and auto leasing business. It took a specific $424 million charge for moving loans to the "held for sale" category and indicated that it would sell about $3.1 billion in loans and $8.2 billion in letters of credit and unfunded commitments. The stock market reacted favorably as PNC's stock price increased from $56 to $58.50 a share. The positive response echoed the market's sentiment on bad loans that the sooner you recognize them and move them off the balance sheet, the better.

In late January, it was reported that the Federal Reserve and SEC were examining the special third-party structure that PNC used to shift assets off the balance sheet in late 2001. Not surprisingly, PNC's shares immediately dropped almost 10 percent in price as the use of such off-balance sheet accounting was reminiscent of the Enron fiasco. PNC reclassified its treatment of the problematic deals and subsequently lowered its reported net income for 2001 by $155 million. The earnings were restated due to new risks of special purpose vehicles. Then, just as things were beginning to get better, PNC again lowered its 2001 earnings in late February, 2002 by another $35 million because it had not properly recorded a loss from a residential mortgage banking business.

An important lesson is that reported balance sheet and income statement figures may not always be an accurate measure of a firm's profitability and risk profile. As banks engage in more and more off-balance sheet activities and begin to produce more fee income from related products and services, assets become less representative of risks and less a measure of potential profitability. Fee income is often generated from services not identifiable from listed assets. The traditional model based on assets generating income, might well not be representative of the future of the banking industry.

PNC'S PROFITABILITY VERSUS RISK: 1997–2001

PNC's 2001 performance can be better understood by examining trends in the performance ratios for the five prior years. Page 1 of the UBPR presented in the Appendix to this chapter presents key profitability and risk ratios from 1997 to 2001. During this period, assets increased approximately $4.57 billion while net income decreased $409 million. Profitability and total assets were clearly negatively affected by loan sales and the resulting write-offs taken in 2001. Assets actually fell $3.49 billion from 2000 to 2001, and income was less than half of its 2000 level. The reduction in assets was driven by a 19 percent fall in loans and the fall in income was driven almost exclusively by $898 million in provisions for loan losses, up from $133 million in 2000. The bank's ROA had consistently been above peers and often equal to or greater than

1.5 percent and would have been at this level or above again in 2001 if it had reported similar provisions as peers. This information, however, indicates that PNC's past profitability was likely overstated. Historically, PNC's interest income was similar to peers until 2000, when it fell significantly below peer averages and remained below in 2001. Interest expense was also historically above peers, fell below peers in 2000, and remained below in 2001. PNC's noninterest expense and noninterest income were generally above peers as well. Although noninterest income fell from its high in 1998, it remained well above peers whose noninterest income also fell during this time period. Noninterest expense decreased, and decreased more than noninterest income, until 2001, when it increased relative to assets. PNC's smaller asset base, combined with the existing overhead structure, produces higher overhead costs relative to the new smaller loan portfolio. PNC will likely attempt to improve its new business model in this area. PNC's net interest income to total assets fell since 1997, along with peers, indicating less profitability, but it improved in 2001, while peers ratio did not.

Net losses to average total loans were historically low since 1997, but increased substantially in 2001. Generally, PNC's loan loss allowance to total loans exceeded peers and earnings coverage was above peers, again until 2001, when both of these measures fell substantially. Clearly, PNC was aggressive in charging off loans in 2001, and this reduced their reserve position.

PNC generally operated with a mixed liquidity picture with much higher core deposits, lower volatile liabilities, fewer liquid assets, and a much greater loan portfolio. Although PNC historically had a strong core deposit base, it grew consistently as a percent of assets while peer banks' core deposits did not. PNC's net non-core deposit dependence dropped dramatically as well over this five-year period, leading to a strong liquidity position from borrowing, assuming a high quality of assets. The bank's loan-to-asset ratio grew over time, reducing liquidity, until 2001, when the bank sold billions in loans. Tier 1 capital ratios show that PNC kept its equity capital base above peers.

CAMELS RATINGS

Federal and state regulators regularly assess the financial condition of each bank and specific risks faced via on-site examinations and periodic reports. Federal regulators rate banks according to the Uniform Financial Institutions Rating system, which now encompasses six general categories of performance under the label CAMELS. Each letter refers to a specific category, including:

C = capital adequacy

A = asset quality

M = management quality

E = earnings

L = liquidity

S = sensitivity to market risk

The sixth category, sensitivity to market risk, has only been used since January 1, 1997. The **capital component (C)** signals the institution's ability to maintain capital commensurate with the nature and extent of all types of risk and the ability of management to identify, measure, monitor, and control these risks. **Asset quality (A)** reflects the amount of existing credit risk associated with the loan and investment portfolio as well as off-balance sheet activities. The **management category (M)** reflects the adequacy of the board of directors and senior management systems and procedures to identify, measure, monitor, and control risks. Regulators emphasize the existence and use of policies and processes to manage risks within targets. **Earnings (E)** reflects not only the quantity and trend in earnings, but also the factors that may affect the sustainability or quality or earnings. **Liquidity (L)** reflects the adequacy of the institution's current and prospective sources of liquidity and funds management practices. Finally, the last category, **sensitivity to market risk (S),** reflects the degree to which changes in interest rates, foreign exchange rates, commodity prices, and equity prices can adversely affect earnings or economic capital.

Regulators numerically rate each bank in each category, ranging from the highest or best rating (1) to the worst or lowest (5) rating. It also assigns a composite rating for the bank's overall operation. A composite rating of 1 or 2 indicates a fundamentally sound bank. A rating of 3 indicates that the bank shows some underlying weakness that should be corrected. A rating of 4 or 5 indicates a problem bank with some near-term potential for failure. Exhibit 3.9 shows a dramatic increase in problem commercial banks and savings banks with 4 and 5 ratings, from 1984 through 1987, then a dramatic reduction through 1996, where only 117 banks were given these lowest ratings, and the gradual reduction in the last few years with only 114 banks and savings banks receiving the lowest rating by the end-of-year 2001. The mid- to late 1980s were considered the "worst of times" while the mid- to late 1990s were considered the "best of times" for banking. Although not dramatic, bank regulators started becoming concerned about the slight rise in problem banks, charge-offs, and noncurrent loans by late 2001.

PERFORMANCE CHARACTERISTICS OF DIFFERENT-SIZED BANKS

Commercial banks of different sizes exhibit sharply different operating characteristics. Some differences reflect government regulation; others are associated with variances in the markets served. Prior to the mid-1980s, small banks generated higher ROAs, on average, and generally assumed less risk. This has changed with increased competition, expansion into new product and geographic markets, and more recent economic events. Today, according to the data in Exhibit 3.10, it appears that the most profitable banks are those with $300 million to $500 million in assets and more than $1 billion in assets generating ROEs greater than 13.4%. The lowest ROA is produced by the smallest banks, with less than $100 million in assets. This section examines differences in the risk-return performance of different-sized banks.

Consider the distinction between wholesale and retail banks. Wholesale banks focus their credit efforts on the largest commercial customers and purchase substantial funds from large corporate and government depositors. Retail banks, in contrast, obtain considerably more of their deposits from individual and small business deposits and emphasize small- to middle-sized commercial lending, consumer loans, mortgage loans, and agriculture loans. Within each category, there are significant differences in the types of loans and funding sources. For example, the largest U.S. money center and nationwide retail banks compete in more product and geographic markets than other large, regional banks. Smaller banks' performance often reflects local economic conditions, which differ dramatically across geographic regions. Recognizing these difficulties and limitations of grossly classifying banks by size, it is still useful to compare aggregate performance by size.

Summary profitability and risk measures for all U.S. banks, as of end-of-year 2001, appear in Exhibit 3.10. The banks are divided into six groups by total assets. The seventh column indicates general trends in each ratio going from the smallest banks with less than $100 million in assets to the largest banks with assets greater than $10 billion. The final two columns provide average performance ratios for all commercial banks and all depository institutions. As indicated by the

■ EXHIBIT 3.9

NUMBER OF COMMERCIAL AND SAVINGS BANKS ON THE FDIC'S "PROBLEM LIST," 1985–2001

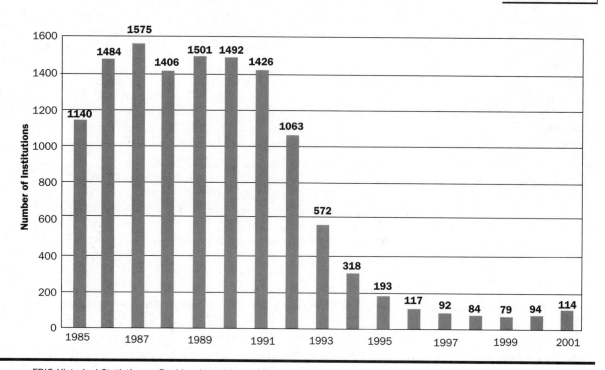

SOURCE: FDIC Historical Statistics on Banking, http://www.fdic.gov/(http://www2.fdic.gov/hsob).

trend size column, many of the ratios exhibit a consistent relationship with size. ROE, for example, generally increases with size, but banks with $1 to $10 billion in assets report the highest return to shareholders (ROE) of 13.77 percent. The largest banks' return to shareholders ranks second in the size category, but is followed closely by banks in the $300 to $500 million in assets category. Many experts would argue that this is a direct result of the dilution of earnings due to the extraordinary number of mergers that have occurred for this bank size class (see Chapter 22 on merger and acquisition activity). ROA increases with size up to the $500 million to $1 billion in assets category, with the smallest banks having the lowest return on assets and the largest banks having the second lowest. The low return to the smallest banks can be attributed to their extremely low noninterest income, while the largest banks' lower return can be attributed to their low average net interest margin and higher noninterest expense. The reduction in net interest margins is a result of lower yields on earning assets, not a higher cost of funds for the largest banks. The lower cost of funds for the largest banks is a change in position as, until 2001, the largest banks typically reported a higher cost of funds. The largest banks are generally offering very standardized loans and deposit products, hence competition is steep and margins smaller.

The largest banks generally employ fewer people per dollar of assets than smaller banks. Noninterest expense control generally increases with size, but many factors affect this ratio and, hence, the pattern is not clear. Banks in the $100–$300 million asset category do, however, have the lowest noninterest expense relative to earning assets. Banks with assets between $1–$10 billion have the lowest efficiency ratios, which indicates that these banks have the best trade-offs between net interest margin, noninterest expense, and noninterest income. This contradicts, somewhat, the primary reason given for large bank mergers, an increase in operational efficiency. Larger banks do, however, generate significantly more

· EXHIBIT 3.10

SUMMARY PROFITABILITY AND RISK MEASURES FOR DIFFERENT-SIZED BANKS, END-OF-YEAR 2001

	< $100M	$100M to $300M	$300M to $500M	$500M to $1B	$1B to $10B	> $10B	Trend with Size	All Comm Banks	All Institutions
Number of institutions reporting	4,486	2,350	509	335	320	80	↓	8,080	9,613
Total assets (in billions)	221.6	396.8	195.0	227.6	915.4	4,612.8	~	6,569.2	7,868.2
Total deposits (in billions)	187.7	331.2	158.7	178.5	625.0	2,910.5	↑	4,391.6	5,189.4
Net income (in millions)	1,912	4,364	2,351	2,607	11,518	51,559	↑	74,310	87,606
% of unprofitable institutions	11.19	3.40	1.77	2.09	3.12	1.25	~	7.54	7.65
% of institutions with earn gains	49.53	63.28	71.91	71.04	69.06	62.50	↑ then ↓	56.73	56.57
Performance ratios (%)									
Return on equity	8.07	11.62	13.41	12.38	13.77	13.43	generally ↑	13.10	13.04
Return on assets	0.91	1.16	1.28	1.20	1.31	1.13	↑ then ↓	1.16	1.14
Equity capital ratio	10.90	9.83	9.45	9.63	9.76	8.77	↓	9.09	8.99
Net interest margin	4.23	4.35	4.37	4.39	4.31	3.71	↓	3.90	3.78
Yield on earning assets	7.83	7.93	7.87	7.90	7.76	7.06	↓	7.29	7.31
Cost of funding earn assets	3.61	3.58	3.50	3.52	3.45	3.35	↓	3.40	3.53
Earning assets to total assets	91.39	91.26	90.88	91.17	89.49	83.03	↓	85.23	86.31
Efficiency ratio	69.59	63.70	62.14	62.07	55.75	56.83	↓	57.72	57.73
Noninterest inc to earn assets	1.11	1.42	1.94	2.04	2.62	3.19	↑	2.85	2.54
Noninterest exp to earn assets	3.74	3.71	3.98	4.07	4.02	4.07	↑	4.03	3.77
LN&LS loss provision to assets	0.30	0.34	0.35	0.46	0.66	0.74	↑	0.67	0.60
Asset Quality									
Net charge-offs to LN&LS	0.34	0.38	0.40	0.48	1.03	1.06	↑	0.94	0.83
Loss allow to Noncurr LN&LS	128.12	142.30	161.03	161.06	167.67	123.46	↑ then ↓	131.04	127.61
Loss allowance to LN&LS	1.41	1.39	1.40	1.55	1.79	1.97	↑	1.85	1.67
Net LN&LS to deposits	71.11	75.93	78.91	82.95	88.72	89.68	↑	87.06	90.33
Capital Ratios									
Core capital (leverage) ratio	10.63	9.40	8.93	8.98	8.74	7.23	↓	7.79	7.79
Tier 1 risk-based capital ratio	15.87	13.52	12.50	12.15	11.83	8.86	↓	9.90	10.27
Total risk-based capital ratio	16.96	14.66	13.69	13.38	13.77	12.16	↓	12.72	12.89

SOURCE: FDIC Statistics on Depository Institutions (SDI), http://www.fdic.gov/(http://www.fdic.gov/sdi/main.asp).

noninterest income (service charges and fees) but have some of the highest noninterest expenses and the lowest net interest margin of all asset classes.

Equity-to-asset ratios decrease with size (the equity multiplier increases with size) because larger banks operate with less equity and more debt. Regulation effectively mandates the equity multiplier relationship as regulators require more equity at smaller banks to compensate for less asset diversification and more limited borrowing options. Percentage equity requirements were equalized in 1985, and raised effective in 1992, but small banks strategically choose to operate with a greater equity cushion.

The risk ratios at the bottom of Exhibit 3.10 reveal several other systematic differences. In particular, larger banks invest more in loans and report higher net charge-offs. Not reported in this data, but available using peer group averages, smaller banks generally operate with greater core deposits and, thus, have a more stable funding base, especially compared with the largest banks. Noncore funding (volatile liabilities) to long-term assets is much greater at the largest banks, indicating a heavier reliance on purchased money. This reflects the larger banks' reputation advantage both nationally and internationally, which means they have far greater access to purchased funds in the money and capital markets.

FINANCIAL STATEMENT MANIPULATION

The usefulness of bank financial statements depends on the quality and consistency of the data. Ideally, banks would use the same accounting rules in each period and isolate the effects of nonrecurring events. This would make comparisons over time and between banks simple. Unfortunately, banks have wide discretion in reporting certain items and can use extraordinary transactions to disguise unfavorable events or trends. Analysts should delete the impact of any unusual changes to make valid comparisons.

Banks use numerous techniques to manage earnings or, as some would say, to manipulate their financial statements. The primary ones are the use of nonrecurring extraordinary transactions, discretionary interpretation of reporting requirements, discretionary timing of reported loan charge-offs, off-balance sheet special purpose vehicles (as in the case of Enron and PNC), and accounting changes that mask true operating performance. The net effect is to potentially distort the magnitude of period-ending balance sheet figures, net income, and related ratios, which makes comparisons difficult over time and versus peers. In most cases, banks do not violate federal regulations or generally accepted accounting principles. Often, the reporting techniques are mandated.

The recent failure of Enron is indicative of the problems associated with special purpose vehicles, the ambiguous accounting requirements associated with them, and the lack of guidance from the regulatory authorities on what is or is not acceptable. In general, parent companies create a "special-purpose vehicle" (SPV) as an independent company. The SPV acquires funds from lenders and investors. The parent company then sells assets to the SPV, such as loans or shares of stock, and in return gets the proceeds from the lenders and investors. Rather than counting the funds as debt on the books of the parent company, however, it counts them as debt to the SPV, thereby possibly understating the parent's risk. Income, on the other hand, is reported by the parent company, thereby possibly overstating its income. Everything works well unless the SPV fails and the parent is required to "make good" on the loans to the SPV. The real issue is to what degree the parent company has exposure to the debts of the SPV. If the assets of the SPV are backed by government guarantees or insurance, accounting rules (FAS 140) generally allow for these off-balance sheet activities to remain off the balance sheet. Unfortunately, there is vague guidance on when and how the activities of SPVs must be consolidated into the financial statements of the parent.

Many banks have long engaged in window dressing for size purposes, or increasing period-ending assets or deposits and SPVs are only one method. Some banks want to be the largest or fastest-growing bank in their market because customers like to associate with "bigness." One technique used to increase total assets is to encourage large business customers to borrow from the bank temporarily rather than issue commercial paper. The bank finances the loans in the federal funds market. Another involves inducing institutions to which the bank provides correspondent services to increase their deposit balances at the bank. Some large banks similarly solicit short-term deposits from overseas entities. None of these transactions materially alters earnings, but all give a false impression of true size.

In some instances, banks engage in transactions that substantially improve their perceived operating performance. Some banks eliminate borrowing from Federal Reserve Banks because of the perception that such borrowing indicates weakness, paying off Federal Reserve loans just prior to the reporting date. The biggest reporting problems arise when banks attempt to offset declines in reported net income or improve credit quality measures. Some banks smooth earnings by underreporting provisions for loan losses when profits are otherwise low, and over reporting provisions for loan losses when profits are otherwise high. This reduces the volatility in earnings and helps management meet earnings targets set by the board of directors or stock analysts. They might also sell nonconventional assets for one-time profits or understate problem loans. In many cases, banks have temporarily sold loan participations just before reporting periods to reduce loan exposures. Transactions and reporting requirements involving preferred stock, nonperforming loans, securities transactions, and nonrecurring asset sales complicate the evaluation process.

PREFERRED STOCK

Many large banking organizations have recently issued preferred stock to help meet equity capital requirements imposed by regulators. Preferred stock does not pay interest, but instead pays dividends out of earnings available for common stockholders. Banks that use preferred stock overstate their NIM and other profitability measures relative to actual fixed charges. Operating performance is best compared by netting preferred dividends from income when computing profit measures.

Consider the income statements and profitability measures for the $1.5 billion bank listed in Exhibit 3.11. The two columns of data summarize the bank's performance with alternative financing. The first column assumes that the bank finances $10 million of earning assets with long-term debt issued at 11 percent. The second column summarizes performance when the bank issues 500,000 shares of $20 par value perpetual preferred stock. A contractual annual dividend of $2.40 per share yields 12 percent to preferred stockholders. The magnitude and composition of assets is assumed to be identical in both cases.

If the bank issues debt, its net interest income is $60.9 million, with a NIM of 4.87 percent. Net income is just under $9.5 million, producing an ROA of 0.63 percent and an ROE of 12.38 percent. Earnings per share of common stock equals $3.14, with 3 million shares outstanding. The preferred stock issue substantially alters these profitability measures. First, interest expense is $1.1 million less without the debt, so that net interest income equals $62 million and NIM equals 4.96 percent. Net income and ROA similarly increase to $10 million and 0.67 percent, respectively. However, common stockholders are actually worse off with the preferred issue. ROE, net of preferred dividends, actually drops 80 basis points to 11.58 percent, while net earnings per common share decline to $2.93. Issues of preferred stock clearly distort changes in NIM and ROA over time.

NONPERFORMING LOANS

Loans are designated as nonperforming when they are placed on nonaccrual status or when the terms are substantially altered in a restructuring. Nonaccrual means that banks deduct all interest on the loans that was recorded but not actually collected. Banks have traditionally stopped accruing interest when debt payments were more than 90 days past due. However, the interpretation of when loans qualified as past due varies widely. Many banks did not place loans on nonaccrual if they were brought under 90 days past due by the end of the reporting period. This permitted borrowers to make late partial payments and the banks to report all interest as accrued, even when it was not collected. On occasion, banks would lend the borrower the funds that were used to make the late payment.

The impact of this practice on financial statements is twofold. First, nonperforming loans are understated on the balance sheet, so that credit risk is actually higher than it appears. Second, interest accrued but not collected increases net interest income, thus overstating NIM, ROA, and ROE. In response to foreign loan problems at large banks in 1983 and 1984, federal regulators formally tightened the accounting rules for nonperforming loans. On July 1, 1984, loans were put on nonaccrual as soon as any repayment went beyond 90 days past due. Interest could not be recorded until the bank received an actual payment or the loan was made current.

• EXHIBIT 3.11

IMPACT OF PREFERRED STOCK ON REPORTED EARNINGS

Data Items	Debt	Preferred Stock
Interest income	$146,000	$146,000
Interest expense	85,100	84,000
Net interest income	60,900	62,000
Noninterest income	40,000	40,000
Noninterest expenses	90,000	90,000
Income before taxes	10,900	12,000
Taxes	1,494	2,000
Net income	9,406	10,000
Cash dividends on preferred stock		1,200
Net income available for common equity	$9,406	$8,800
Total assets ($ millions)	$1,500.00	$1,500.00
Earning assets ($ millions)	$1,250.00	$1,250.00
Total equity (net of preferred stock) ($ millions)	$76.00	$76.00
Return on assets	0.63%	0.67%
Net interest margin	4.87%	4.96%
Return on equity (net of preferred dividends)	12.38%	11.58%
# shares of common stock	3,000,000	3,000,000
# shares of preferred stock		500,000
Earnings per share (net of preferred dividends)	$3.14	2.93

NOTE: Figures are in thousands of dollars except where noted.

A related factor that distorts financial reports is the bank's provisions for loan losses and the allowance (reserve) for loan losses. For tax purposes, the maximum size of the reserve and the allowable deduction for losses is set by IRS regulations. However, management uses discretion in determining how much it should report as provisions for loan losses in financial statements. During some periods, banks have minimized the provision, understating the reported reserve for losses and overstating earnings. Severe loan problems in the early 1980s forced many banks to report large provisions for losses to compensate for prior understatements.

SECURITIES GAINS AND LOSSES

Prior to 1983, banks reported gains and losses on securities transactions after net income from operations. The rationale was that securities transactions were not a normal part of bank operations and could be easily manipulated to alter net income. Traditional ROA calculations used net operating income and, thus, excluded any impact of securities sales and purchases. In 1983, the SEC required banks to include securities gains and losses in net operating income. It is now possible for a bank to offset a potential decline in other earnings with securities gains, thereby distorting historical operating performance. More recently, FASB 115 requires banks to designate the objective behind buying investment securities as either held-to-maturity, trading, or available-for-sale. Held-to-maturity securities are recorded on the balance sheet at amortized cost. Trading account securities are those securities that the bank actively buys and sells, principally to speculate on interest rate movements and profit on price changes. These securities must be marked to market (reported at current market value) on the balance sheet and unrealized gains (losses) reported on the income statement.

All other investment securities are classified as available-for-sale and, as such, recorded at market value on the balance sheet with a corresponding change to stockholders' equity as unrealized gains and losses on securities holdings. There is no reporting of gains or losses on the income statement with these securities. This account standard is designed to make the financial statements more closely match the bank's intended purpose when buying the securities. Unfortunately, regulators have often required a bank to report all securities of a certain type, such as Treasury bills, as available-for-sale if the bank ever sells as security prior to maturity. Hence, most banks report all investment securities as "available-for-sale" today due to restrictions against selling a security prior to maturity if the security is classified as "held-to-maturity."

NONRECURRING SALES OF ASSETS

Banks can often bolster earnings with one-time sales of assets. Most sales involve real estate, subsidiaries, lease assets, or hidden assets that banks have acquired through debt restructuring and foreclosures. Typically, many foreclosed assets are listed at little value on the bank's books, but may generate large gains if the problem customer's performance improves. The Lockheed Corporation's debt restructuring is a good example. In the early 1970s, Lockheed ran into financial difficulty and restructured its loan commitments from creditors. As part of the agreement, many large banks acquired Lockheed common stock. By the early 1980s, the value of the stock had soared so that banks sold their shares for substantial profits. Manufacturer's Hanover, Bankers Trust, J.P. Morgan, and Irving Bank each reported large gains in 1983 from the sale of these securities.

In 1983, Mercantile Texas Corp. reported a similar $7.2 million pretax gain from the sale of $90 million in credit card receivables to Southwest Bancshares Inc. Interestingly, the two bank holding companies had agreed to merge that same year. Although the merger was not formally approved until 1984, Mercantile effectively sold its receivables to itself and reported the profit to shareholders. Shareholders actually lost with the transaction, though, because Mercantile had to pay taxes on the gain. By 1989, the merged bank, renamed MCorp, failed and was sold to Bank One, which used MCorp as its entree into the Texas market.

The essential point is that once a bank sells the asset, it cannot do it again. Thus, the gain or loss will have a one-time impact on earnings. A careful analysis requires that these extraordinary gains or losses be excluded from any comparison of the bank's performance with other banks, and with its own performance over time as the trend behavior will be biased.

SUMMARY

This chapter introduces financial statements of commercial banks and presents a procedure for analyzing bank profitability and risks using historical data. The procedure involves decomposing aggregate profit ratios into their components to help identify key factors that influence performance. It then associates financial ratios for credit risk, liquidity risk, market risk, operational risk, reputational risk, legal risk, and capital or solvency risk to demonstrate the trade-off between risks and returns. Actual bank data are provided for PNC Bank and a smaller Community National Bank. The model developed is applied to the actual data for PNC bank to interpret performance in 2001, versus peer banks, and over the period from 1997 to 2001. The same performance ratios are then used to compare the profitability and risk profile of two different-sized banking groups. The final sections introduce the regulator CAMELS ratings, describe how banks may manipulate financial data to alter summary profit and risk measures, and draw comparisons between high performance and failed banks.

QUESTIONS

1. What are the major categories of bank assets and their approximate percentage contribution to total resources? What are the major categories of bank liabilities? What are the fundamental differences between them?

2. Banks typically differentiate between interest and noninterest income and expense. What are the primary components of each? Define net interest income and burden. What does a bank's efficiency ratio measure?

3. Using PNC in Exhibit 3.2 as a typical large bank, which balance sheet accounts would be affected by the following transactions? Indicate at least two accounts with each transaction.
   a. Arturo Rojas opens a money market deposit account with $5,000. The funds are loaned in the overnight market for one week.
   b. Just as a real estate developer pays off a strip shopping mall loan, a new resident optometrist takes out a mortgage on a home.
   c. The bank hires an investment banker to sell shares of stock to the public. It plans to use the proceeds to finance additional commercial loans.

4. Arrange the following items into an income statement. Label each item, place it in the appropriate category, and determine the bank's bottom line net income.
   Interest paid on time deposit under $100,000
   Interest paid on jumbo CDs $101,000
   Interest received on U.S. Treasury and agency securities $44,500
   Fees received on mortgage originations $23,000
   Dividends paid to stockholders of $0.50 per share for 5,000 shares
   Provisions for loan losses $18,000
   Interest and fees on loans $189,700
   Interest paid on interest checking accounts $33,500
   Interest received on municipal bonds $60,000
   Employee salaries and benefits $145,000
   Purchase of a new computer system $50,000
   Service charge receipts from customer accounts $41,000
   Occupancy expense for bank building $22,000
   Taxes of 34 percent of taxable income are paid
   Trust department income equals $15,000

5. What are the primary sources of risk facing bank managers? Describe how each potentially affects bank performance. Provide one financial ratio to measure each type of risk and explain how to interpret high versus low values.

6. Bank L operates with an equity-to-asset ratio of 5 percent, while Bank S operates with a similar ratio of 8 percent. Calculate the equity multiplier for each bank and the corresponding return on equity if each bank earns 1.5 percent on assets. Suppose, instead, that both banks report an ROA of 1.2 percent. What does this suggest about financial leverage?

7. Define each of the following components of the Return on Equity model and discuss their interrelationships:
   a. ROE
   b. ROA
   c. EM
   d. ER
   e. AU

8. Explain why profitability ratios at small banks typically differ from those at the largest money center banks.

9. Regulators use the CAMELS system to analyze bank risk. What does CAMELS stand for and what financial ratios might best capture each factor?

10. Rank the following assets from lowest to highest liquidity risk:
>   3-month Treasury bills
>   1-year construction loan
>   4-year car loan with monthly payments
>   5-year Treasury bond
>   5-year municipal bond
>   1-year individual loan to speculate in stocks
>   3-month Treasury bill pledged as collateral

11. In each pair below, indicate which asset exhibits the greatest credit risk. Describe why.
    a. Commercial loan to a Fortune 500 company or a loan to a corner grocery store
    b. Commercial loans to two businesses in the same industry; one is collateralized by accounts receivable from sales, while the other is collateralized by inventory as work-in-process
    c. 5-year Ba-rated municipal bond or a 5-year agency bond from the Federal Home Loan Mortgage Corp. (Freddie Mac)
    d. 1-year student loan (college) or a 1-year car loan

12. What ratios on common-sized financial statements would indicate a small bank versus a large, multibank holding company? Cite at least five.

13. In some instances, when a bank borrower cannot make the promised principal and interest payment on a loan, the bank will extend another loan for the customer to make the payment.
    a. Is the first loan classified as a nonperforming loan?
    b. What is the rationale for this type of lending?
    c. What are the risks in this type of lending?

14. Suppose that your bank had reported a substantial loss during the past year. You are meeting with the bank's board of directors to discuss whether the bank should make its traditional (25 years straight) dividend payment to common stockholders. Provide several arguments that the bank should authorize and make the dividend payment. Then, provide several arguments that it should not make the payment. What should decide the issue?

15. Explain how each of the following potentially affects a bank's liquidity risk:
    a. Most (95 percent) of the bank's securities holdings are classified as held-to-maturity.
    b. The bank's core deposit base is a low (35 percent) fraction of total assets.
    c. The bank's securities all mature after eight years.
    d. The bank has no pledged securities out of the $10 million in securities it owns.

PROBLEMS

1. Evaluate the performance of Community National Bank relative to peer banks using the data in Exhibits 3.2, 3.4, 3.6, 3.7, and 3.8. Did the bank perform above or below average that year? Did it operate with more or less relative risk?
    a. Conduct a return on equity decomposition analysis for the year in question, identifying where the bank's performance compared favorably and unfavorably with peer banks.

    b. Compare the bank's risk measures with those of peer banks. What are the implications of any significant differences?

    c. What recommendations would you make to adjust the bank's risk and return profile to improve its performance?

2. The summary UBPR page for Citibank, NA is shown on the following page. Average total assets for Citibank were $404,102 million as of December 31, 2001. Use the data from December 31, 2001, to explain whether this bank was a high or low performance bank. Discuss specifically (1) financial leverage, (2) expense control, and (3) the contribution of interest and noninterest income to overall bank profitability. List three areas that management should focus on to improve performance. Using the limited information provided, evaluate Citibank's credit, liquidity, and capital risk.

CERT # 7213	DIST/RSSD: 02 / 476810		CITIBANK, NATIONAL ASSOCIATION		NEW YORK CITY, NY		PAGE 01
CHARTER # 1461	COUNTY: NEW YORK		SUMMARY RATIOS		4/1/02 8:15:51 PM		

	12/31/2001			12/31/2000			12/31/1999			12/31/1998		12/31/1997	
AVERAGE ASSETS ($)	404,101,500			349,170,000			307,042,250			287,903,000		252,113,750	
NET INCOME ($)	5,270,000			4,923,000			3,079,000			1,700,000		2,634,000	
NUMBER OF BANKS IN PEER GROUP	69			70			67			64		58	
	BANK	PEER1	PCT	BANK	PEER1	PCT	BANK	PEER1	PCT	BANK	PEER1	BANK	PEER1
EARNINGS AND PROFITABILITY													
PERCENT OF AVERAGE ASSETS:													
INTEREST INCOME (TE)	6.78	6.27	64	7.51	7.32	57	7.58	6.75	86	7.90	7.04	7.81	7.17
– INTEREST EXPENSE	3.32	2.90	77	4.35	3.90	77	4.22	3.21	98	4.63	3.47	4.39	3.45
NET INTEREST INCOME (TE)	3.46	3.33	45	3.15	3.40	28	3.36	3.53	27	3.27	3.59	3.42	3.75
+ NONINTEREST INCOME	2.90	1.94	84	3.51	1.93	85	3.09	2.25	79	2.70	2.14	2.66	2.06
– NONINTEREST EXPENSE	3.79	3.16	75	4.17	3.18	81	4.35	3.36	80	4.64	3.47	4.32	3.52
= PROVISION: LOAN&LEASE LOSSES	0.59	0.48	71	0.39	0.39	69	0.53	0.26	89	0.50	0.28	0.30	0.27
= PRETAX OPERATING INCOME (TE)	1.98	1.64	67	2.11	1.78	71	1.57	2.09	14	0.84	1.94	1.46	2.04
+ REALIZED GAINS/LOSSES SEC	0.06	0.06	65	0.15	-0.06	98	0.05	0.00	88	0.12	0.04	0.23	0.03
= PRETAX NET OPERATING INC (TE)	2.04	1.72	65	2.25	1.70	77	1.62	2.08	14	0.96	1.99	1.69	2.07
NET OPERATING INCOME	1.31	1.12	64	1.41	1.09	78	1.00	1.32	14	0.59	1.27	1.04	1.33
ADJUSTED NET OPERATING INCOME	1.23	1.21	48	1.36	1.09	64	1.00	1.33	13	0.59	1.31	1.06	1.32
NET INCOME ADJUSTED SUB S		1.12			1.09			1.32			1.27		1.33
NET INCOME	1.30	1.12	64	1.41	1.09	78	1.00	1.32	14	0.59	1.27	1.04	1.33
MARGIN ANALYSIS:													
AVG EARNING ASSETS TO AVG ASSETS	85.04	90.15	12	91.47	90.80	52	92.05	90.61	60	93.87	90.70	94.30	90.73
AVG INT-BEARING FUNDS TO AVG AST	77.04	79.81	32	76.04	79.45	28	75.57	77.33	36	72.87	76.06	72.95	75.17
INT INC (TE) TO AVG EARN ASSETS	7.98	6.96	92	8.21	8.08	54	8.23	7.46	86	8.41	7.79	8.28	7.92
INT EXPENSE TO AVG EARN ASSETS	3.91	3.21	91	4.76	4.31	77	4.58	3.55	98	4.93	3.83	4.66	3.80
NET INT INC-TE TO AVG EARN ASSET	4.07	3.71	60	3.45	3.76	29	3.65	3.90	25	3.48	3.97	3.62	4.14
LOAN & LEASE ANALYSIS													
NET LOSS TO AVERAGE TOTAL LN&LS	1.05	0.63	82	0.69	0.43	78	0.85	0.42	89	0.83	0.42	0.46	0.42
EARNINGS COVERAGE OF NET LOSS(X)	3.78	6.93	32	5.54	11.46	28	3.89	11.19	5	2.63	11.02	6.12	13.98
LN&LS ALLOWANCE TO NET LOSSES(X)	2.02	3.13	31	2.95	4.60	32	2.84	4.27	29	3.30	4.92	6.00	5.94
LN&LS ALLOWANCE TO TOTAL LN&LS	1.91	1.62	72	1.86	1.48	78	2.22	1.44	91	2.58	1.52	2.77	1.65
NON-CUR LN&LS TO GROSS LN&LS	2.07	1.31	82	1.55	0.99	87	1.78	0.76	92	2.05	0.77	1.87	0.78
LIQUIDITY													
NET NON-CORE FUND DEPENDENCE	80.03	35.24	95	81.25	40.16	94	79.96	40.47	94	77.39	36.79	77.19	33.62
NET LOANS & LEASES TO ASSETS	61.76	61.01	45	63.54	64.01	40	62.39	63.77	42	59.09	62.99	56.92	61.74
CAPITALIZATION													
TIER ONE LEVERAGE CAPITAL	7.16	7.12	50	6.68	7.04	36	6.57	7.06	36	6.36	6.92	6.38	6.93
CASH DIVIDENDS TO NET INCOME	32.50	69.27	15	11.98	66.60	11	60.90	66.43	47	29.41	62.32	66.44	71.09
RETAIN EARNS TO AVG TOTAL EQUITY	11.80	3.50	90	17.62	3.34	97	5.84	5.34	51	6.64	6.03	5.23	5.20
RESTR+NONAC+RE ACQ TO EQCAP+ALLL	12.22	7.06	84										
GROWTH RATES													
ASSETS	18.38	14.33	78	16.53	26.22	63	8.97	13.97	48	14.63	30.19	8.92	509.13
TIER ONE CAPITAL	28.70	15.18	84	20.36	25.72	67	5.63	17.65	33	17.13	29.12	6.82	417.11
NET LOANS & LEASES	15.06	8.39	71	18.69	26.93	61	15.06	12.60	69	19.00	30.77	-0.79	436.60
SHORT-TERM INVESTMENTS	35.78	78.80	61	12.90	53.14	50	-11.39	26.16	42	10.64	43.67	33.98	85.86
SHORT-TERM NON-CORE FUNDING	24.60	6.17	72	23.69	22.83	66	14.15	35.58	39	27.62	39.52	11.66	1,771.78

* ONE OR MORE MERGERS, CONSOLIDATIONS, OR PURCHASES HAVE OCCURRED DURING THE PERIOD.
12/31/01

APPENDIX

TABLE OF CONTENTS FOR THE UBPR

CERT #6384
CHARTER #1316

DIST/RSSD: 04/817824
COUNTY: ALLEGHENY

PNC BANK, NATIONAL ASSOCIATION
SUMMARY RATIOS

PITTSBURGH, PA

PAGE 01
4/1/02 5:31:48 PM

	12/31/2001 BANK	PEER1	PCT	12/31/2000 BANK	PEER1	PCT	12/31/1999 BANK	PEER1	PCT	12/31/1998 BANK	PEER1	12/31/1997 BANK	PEER1
AVERAGE ASSETS ($000)	63,486,660			66,975,064			9,105,444			69,511,00		58,915,553	
NET INCOME ($000)	491,731			1,007,226			1,057,038			1,008,240		900,886	
NUMBER OF BANKS IN PEER GROUP	69			70			67			64		58	
EARNINGS AND PROFITABILITY													
PERCENT OF AVERAGE ASSETS:													
INTEREST INCOME (TE)	6.10	6.27	35	6.65	7.32	21	6.61	6.75	35	7.18	7.04	8.09	7.17
– INTEREST EXPENSE	2.62	2.90	28	3.49	3.90	22	3.27	3.21	57	3.60	3.47	3.98	3.45
NET INTEREST INCOME (TE)	3.47	3.33	47	3.16	3.40	29	3.35	3.53	26	3.57	3.59	4.12	3.75
+ NONINTEREST INCOME	2.80	1.94	81	2.56	1.93	77	2.92	2.25	76	3.04	2.14	2.33	2.06
– NONINTEREST EXPENSE	3.84	3.16	77	3.27	3.18	56	3.51	3.36	70	4.19	3.47	3.98	3.52
– PROVISION: LOAN&LEASE LOSSES	1.42	0.48	94	0.20	0.39	35	0.23	0.26	45	0.31	0.28	0.11	0.27
= PRETAX OPERATING INCOME (TE)	1.02	1.64	25	2.26	1.78	77	2.52	2.09	82	2.11	1.94	2.36	2.04
+ REALIZED GAINS/LOSSES SEC	0.20	0.06	88	0.03	−0.06	91	−20.17	0.00	5	0.17	0.04	0.07	0.03
= PRETAX NET OPERATING INC (TE)	1.21	1.72	27	2.29	1.70	81	2.35	2.08	79	2.28	1.99	2.42	2.07
NET OPERATING INCOME	0.78	1.12	27	1.50	1.09	83	1.53	1.32	80	1.45	1.27	1.53	1.33
ADJUSTED NET OPERATING INCOME	0.71	1.21	18	1.50	1.21	74	1.53	1.33	82	1.13	1.31	1.19	1.32
NET INCOME ADJUSTED SUB S													
NET INCOME	0.77	1.12	27	1.50	1.09	83	1.53	1.32	79	1.45	1.27	1.53	1.33
MARGIN ANALYSIS:													
AVG EARNING ASSETS TO AVG ASSETS	87.99	90.15	25	88.42	90.80	26	89.91	90.61	38	90.75	90.70	90.42	90.73
AVG INT-BEARING FUNDS TO AVG AST	75.29	79.81	20	79.02	79.45	42	79.38	77.33	64	79.00	76.06	78.26	75.17
INT INC (TE) TO AVG EARN ASSETS	6.93	6.96	38	7.52	8.08	21	7.36	7.46	36	7.91	7.79	8.95	7.92
INT EXPENSE TO AVG EARN ASSETS	2.98	3.21	32	3.94	4.31	28	3.63	3.55	58	3.97	3.83	4.40	3.80
NET INT INC-TE TO AVG EARN ASSET	3.95	3.71	55	3.58	3.76	35	3.72	3.90	26	3.94	3.97	4.55	4.14
LOAN & LEASE ANALYSIS													
NET LOSS TO AVERAGE TOTAL LN&LS	2.11	0.63	98	0.26	0.43	32	0.29	0.42	38	0.79	0.42	0.59	0.42
EARNINGS COVERAGE OF NET LOSS(X)	1.62	6.93	7	12.32	11.46	67	12.15	11.19	67	3.76	11.02	5.34	13.98
LN&LS ALLOWANCE TO NET LOSSES(X)	0.64	3.13	5	4.90	4.60	67	4.16	4.27	54	1.62	4.92	3.51	5.94
LN&LS ALLOWANCE TO TOTAL LN&LS	1.49	1.62	51	1.30	1.48	38	1.22	1.44	27	1.25	1.52	1.76	1.65
NON-CUR LN&LS TO GROSS LN&LS	1.05	1.31	45	0.96	0.99	54	0.83	0.76	60	0.95	0.77	1.03	0.78
LIQUIDITY													
NET NON CORE FUND DEPENDENCE	20.10	35.24	20	24.15	40.16	14	35.98	40.47	42	36.42	36.79	37.04	33.62
NET LOANS & LEASES TO ASSETS	63.65	61.01	50	78.03	64.01	90	76.30	63.77	88	79.69	62.99	75.42	61.74
CAPITALIZATION													
TIER ONE LEVERAGE CAPITAL	7.65	7.12	74	8.77	7.04	92	7.65	7.06	73	7.72	6.92	8.03	6.93
CASH DIVIDENDS TO NET INCOME	213.53	69.27	97	64.53	66.60	52	102.74	66.43	83	70.32	62.32	75.48	71.09
RETAIN EARNS TO AVG TOTAL EQUITY	−10.64	3.50	1	6.72	3.34	71	−0.50	5.34	17	4.92	6.03	4.44	5.20
RESTR+NONAC+RE ACQ TO EQCAP+ALLL	4.80	7.06	35										
GROWTH RATES													
ASSETS	−20.91	14.33	20	−7.33	26.22	8	−4.27	13.97	14	2.18	30.19	21.69	509.13
TIER ONE CAPITAL	−12.46	15.18	5	6.02	25.72	30	−6.82	17.65	8	4.23	29.12	24.98	417.11
NET LOANS & LEASES	−19.18	8.39	8	−25.23	26.93	12	−8.35	12.60	8	7.97	30.77	33.84	436.60
SHORT TERM INVESTMENTS	11.84	78.80	44	−41.42	53.14	19	8.03	26.16	52	−49.54	43.67	−42.13	85.86
SHORT TERM NON CORE FUNDING	−32.83	6.17	20	−41.28	22.83	5	8.04	35.58	29	−24.24	39.52	22.82	1,771.78

* ONE OR MORE MERGERS, CONSOLIDATIONS OR PURCHASES HAVE OCCURRED DURING THE PERIOD.
12/31/01

CERT #6384
CHARTER #1316

DIST/RSSD: 04/817824
COUNTY: ALLEGHENY

PITTSBURGH, PA

PAGE 02
4/1/02 5:31:51 PM

PNC BANK, NATIONAL ASSOCIATION
INCOME STATEMENT--REVENUE AND EXPENSES ($000)

	12/31/2001	12/31/2000	12/31/1999	12/31/1998	12/31/1997	PERCENT CHANGE 1 YEAR
INTEREST AND FEES ON LOANS	2,992,253	3,845,374	3,931,743	4,446,579	4,139,465	-22.19
INCOME FROM LEASE FINANCING	258,790	208,494	160,760	121,608	89,718	24.12
TAX-EXEMPT	26,649	31,944	34,436	39,891	35,045	-16.58
ESTIMATED TAX BENEFIT	13,394	15,701	17,111	20,197	18,038	
INCOME ON LOANS & LEASES (TE)	3,264,437	4,069,569	4,109,614	4,588,384	4,247,221	-19.78
U S TREAS & AGENCY (EXCL MBS)	65,970	NA	NA	NA	NA	
MORTGAGE BACKED SECURITIES	446,662	NA	NA	NA	NA	
ESTIMATED TAX BENEFIT	634	791	1,544	3,359	4,437	
ALL OTHER SECURITIES	54,082	NA	NA	NA	NA	
TAX EXEMPT SECURITIES INCOME	1,263	1,611	3,109	6,635	8,621	-21.60
INVESTMT INTEREST INCOME (TE)	567,348	330,812	418,364	368,652	478,233	71.50
INTEREST ON DUE FROM BANKS	5,447	8,137	5,238	5,830	11,930	-33.06
INT ON FED FUNDS SOLD & RESALES	12,664	44,290	34,006	23,585	30,884	-71.41
TRADING ACCOUNT INCOME	1,467	2,374	2,729	2,445	416	-38.21
OTHER INTEREST INCOME	19,998	NA	NA	NA	NA	
TOTAL INTEREST INCOME (TE)	3,871,362	4,455,183	4,569,952	4,988,896	4,768,684	-13.10
INT ON DEPOSITS IN FOREIGN OFF	53,928	111,622	68,205	65,672	94,506	-51.69
INT ON TIME DEP OVER $100M	151,082	211,127	194,714	238,544	238,509	-28.44
INTEREST ON ALL OTHER DEPOSITS	993,952	1,286,558	1,023,807	1,051,049	1,058,108	-22.74
INT ON FED FUNDS PURCH & REPOS	99,507	168,549	137,612	191,768	149,947	-40.96
INT TRAD LIAB & OTH BORROWINGS	292,561	473,858	760,033	897,833	756,283	-38.26
INT ON MORTGAGES & LEASES	NA	NA	NA	NA	NA	
INT ON SUB NOTES & DEBENTURES	75,145	84,270	73,313	60,659	46,190	-10.83
TOTAL INTEREST EXPENSE	1,666,175	2,335,984	2,257,684	2,505,525	2,343,543	-28.67
NET INTEREST INCOME (TE)	2,205,187	2,119,199	2,312,268	2,483,371	2,425,141	4.06
NONINTEREST INCOME	1,776,499	1,717,828	2,014,857	2,114,359	1,371,554	3.42
ADJUSTED OPERATING INCOME (TE)	3,981,686	3,837,027	4,327,125	4,597,730	3,796,695	3.77
NON-INTEREST EXPENSE	2,435,920	2,188,675	2,427,447	2,911,717	2,343,936	11.30
PROVISION: LOAN & LEASE LOSSES	898,743	133,000	156,640	217,961	65,000	575.75
PRETAX OPERATING INCOME (TE)	647,023	1,515,352	1,743,038	1,468,052	1,387,759	-57.30
REALIZED G/L HLD-TO-MATURITY SEC	0	0	0	0	0	NA
REALIZED G/L AVAIL-FOR SALE SEC	123,985	19,561	-117,962	119,057	40,817	533.84
PRETAX NET OPERATING INC (TE)	771,008	1,534,913	1,625,076	1,587,109	1,428,576	-49.77
APPLICABLE INCOME TAXES	260,608	511,194	549,382	555,313	505,215	
CURRENT TAX EQUIV ADJUSTMENT	14,029	16,493	18,656	23,556	22,475	
OTHER TAX EQUIV ADJUSTMENTS	0	0	0	0	0	
NET OPERATING INCOME	274,637	527,687	568,038	578,869	527,690	
NET OPERATING INCOME	496,371	1,007,226	1,057,038	1,008,240	900,886	-50.72
NET EXTRAORDINARY ITEMS	-4,640	0	0	0	0	
NET INCOME	491,731	1,007,226	1,057,038	1,008,240	900,886	-51.18
CASH DIVIDENDS DECLARED	1,050,000	650,000	1,086,000	709,000	680,025	61.54
RETAINED EARNINGS	-558,269	357,226	-28,962	299,240	220,861	-256.28
MEMO: NET INTERNATIONAL INCOME	0	0	0	0	0	NA

PAGE 03
4/1/02 5:31:52 PM

PITTSBURGH, PA

PNC BANK, NATIONAL ASSOCIATION
NONINTEREST INCOME AND EXPENSES ($000) AND YIELDS

CERT #6384
CHARTER #1316
DIST/RSSD: 04/817824
COUNTY: ALLEGHENY

	12/31/2001	12/31/2000	12/31/1999	12/31/1998	12/31/1997
NONINTEREST INCOME & EXPENSES	365,434	771,456	634,045	636,629	462,220
FIDUCIARY ACTIVITIES	355,931	335,720	323,231	307,642	290,552
DEPOSIT SERVICE CHARGES	19,504	34,225	-37,707	83,579	21,309
TRADING REVENUE	NA	NA	NA	NA	NA
OTHER FOREIGN TRANSACTIONS					
OTHER NONINTEREST INCOME	975,630	576,427	1,095,288	1,086,509	597,473
NONINTEREST INCOME	1,776,499	1,717,828	2,014,857	2,114,359	1,371,554
PERSONNEL EXPENSE	1,055,515	978,446	1,086,137	1,175,148	1,004,453
OCCUPANCY EXPENSE	303,353	279,144	401,473	354,378	327,197
OTHER OPER EXP(INCL INTANGIBLES)	1,077,052	931,085	939,837	1,382,191	1,012,286
TOTAL OVERHEAD EXPENSE	2,435,920	2,188,675	2,427,447	2,911,717	2,343,936
DOMESTIC BANKING OFFICES(#)	683	698	687	724	751
FOREIGN BRANCHES (#)	8	8	8	8	8
ASSETS PER DOMESTIC OFFICE	90,484	89,996	99,099	98,241	92,740
NUMBER OF EQUIVALENT EMPLOYEES	15,958	16,472	18,776	22,348	21,305

PERCENT OF AVERAGE ASSETS	2001 BANK	PEER1	PCT	2000 BANK	PEER1	PCT	1999 BANK	PEER1	PCT	1998 BANK	PEER1	1997 BANK	PEER1
PERSONNEL EXPENSE	1.66	1.39	72	1.46	1.35	61	1.57	1.47	63	1.69	1.50	1.70	1.54
OCCUPANCY EXPENSE	0.48	0.39	72	0.42	0.41	54	0.58	0.43	82	0.51	0.44	0.56	0.47
OTHER OPER EXP(INCL INTANGIBLES)	1.70	1.31	77	1.39	1.37	60	1.36	1.41	54	1.99	1.48	1.72	1.46
TOTAL OVERHEAD EXPENSE	3.84	3.16	77	3.27	3.18	56	3.51	3.36	70	4.19	3.47	3.98	3.52
OVERHEAD LESS NONINT INC	1.04	1.15	38	0.70	1.17	22	0.60	1.15	14	1.15	1.35	1.65	1.41
OTHER INCOME & EXPENSE RATIOS													
AVG PERSONNEL EXP PER EMPL($000)	66.14	58.28	67	59.40	55.47	69	57.85	52.86	69	52.58	50.75	47.15	50.66
ASSETS PER EMPLOYEE ($MILLION)	3.92	4.73	44	3.84	4.78	45	3.63	4.30	51	3.19	3.90	3.27	3.78
MARGINAL TAX RATE	35.00			35.00			35.00			35.00		35.00	

YIELD ON OR COST OF:	2001 BANK	PEER1	PCT	2000 BANK	PEER1	PCT	1999 BANK	PEER1	PCT	1998 BANK	PEER1	1997 BANK	PEER1
TOTAL LOANS & LEASES (TE)	7.29	7.44	32	7.90	8.63	14	7.66	7.97	25	8.19	8.41	9.35	8.55
LOANS IN DOMESTIC OFFICES	7.28	7.39	34	7.89	8.69	15	7.63	7.97	26	8.16	8.39	9.35	8.59
REAL ESTATE	7.41	7.55	34	7.36	8.60	7	7.34	8.12	11	7.84	8.40	9.91	8.57
COMMERCIAL & INDUSTRIAL	7.38	7.41	50	8.49	9.19	23	8.05	8.00	52	7.92	8.36	8.19	8.44
INDIVIDUAL	7.52	8.15	28	9.15	9.78	52	9.13	9.33	52	10.99	10.25	10.86	10.44
CREDIT CARD	0.00	4.93	52	NA	0.00	98	NA	0.00	98	NA	0.00	NA	0.00
AGRICULTURAL	7.10	6.41	40	8.76	8.36	38	8.60	7.54	61	8.49	7.97	22.02	8.39
LOANS IN FOREIGN OFFICES	8.69	2.24	90	8.70	2.70	87	8.37	2.51	91	10.89	3.51	7.09	3.81
TOTAL INVESTMENT SECURITIES(TE)	5.55	6.28	22	4.98	6.72	2	5.59	6.39	7	5.79	6.58	7.02	6.73
TOTAL INVESTMENT SECURITIES(BOOK)	5.54	6.13	25	4.97	6.57	2	5.57	6.22	14	5.74	6.41	6.95	6.56
U S TREAS & AGENCY (EXCL MBS)	4.54	5.48	24	NA	0.00	98	NA	0.00	98	NA	0.00	NA	0.00
MORTGAGE BACKED SECURITIES	6.17	6.42	22	NA	0.00	98	NA	0.00	98	NA	0.00	NA	0.00
ALL OTHER SECURITIES	3.54	5.84	11	NA	0.00	98	NA	0.00	98	NA	0.00	NA	0.00
INTEREST-BEARING BANK BALANCES	5.33	4.87	71	7.02	5.95	76	6.21	5.37	76	6.29	6.24	9.48	5.84
FEDERAL FUNDS SOLD & RESALES	3.86	3.82	55	6.30	6.33	39	5.06	5.25	45	5.22	5.66	3.57	5.72
TOTAL-INT BEARING DEPOSITS	3.18	3.30	37	4.23	4.41	35	3.52	3.72	32	3.86	4.23	4.55	4.28
TRANSACTION ACCOUNTS	2.17	1.96	62	2.98	2.32	67	2.59	1.96	70	2.41	2.35	2.57	2.08
OTHER SAVINGS DEPOSITS	2.08	2.00	61	1.62	2.06	36	1.51	1.98	26	1.84	2.39	2.02	2.41
TIME DEPS OVER $100M	5.46	4.94	65	6.30	5.92	70	5.27	4.98	75	6.39	5.38	8.79	5.45
ALL OTHER TIME DEPOSITS	5.21	5.31	47	5.82	5.79	61	5.00	5.01	48	5.15	5.44	5.97	5.44
FOREIGN OFFICE DEPOSITS	4.13	2.58	78	6.31	4.72	83	5.09	4.05	83	5.51	4.69	5.71	4.66
FEDERAL FUNDS PURCHASED & REPOS	4.19	3.80	80	7.37	6.17	94	4.47	4.89	13	5.15	5.17	6.31	5.34
OTHER BORROWED MONEY	4.46	5.18	34	4.14	6.24	12	5.38	5.83	54	5.89	5.96	6.01	5.47
SUBORD NOTES & DEBENTURES	6.52	4.27	72	7.31	5.55	74	6.97	4.94	75	7.18	4.99	7.97	5.69
ALL INTEREST-BEARING FUNDS	3.49	3.65	35	4.41	4.94	23	4.12	4.16	48	4.56	4.56	5.08	4.58

CERT #6384
CHARTER #1316

DIST/RSSD: 04 / 817824
COUNTY: ALLEGHENY

PITTSBURGH, PA
PAGE 04
4/1/02 5:31:55 PM

PNC BANK, NATIONAL ASSOCIATION
BALANCE SHEET - ASSETS, LIABILITIES AND CAPITAL ($000)

	12/31/2001	12/31/2000	12/31/1999	12/31/1998	12/31/1997	PERCENT CHANGE 1 QTR	PERCENT CHANGE 1 YEAR
ASSETS:							
REAL ESTATE LOANS	17,136,390	23,403,724	24,775,627	23,865,234	23,276,309	-1.63	-26.78
COMMERCIAL LOANS	14,616,251	18,180,941	19,210,571	20,020,701	16,712,125	-7.69	-19.61
INDIVIDUAL LOANS	3,261,827	3,529,627	3,949,726	7,479,982	9,411,563	-0.80	-7.59
AGRICULTURAL LOANS	1,096	1,717	4,176	3,291	7,824	6.20	-36.17
OTHER LN&LS IN DOMESTIC OFFICES	4,710,235	4,588,422	4,728,638	6,095,857	4,172,625	-5.56	2.65
LN&LS IN FOREIGN OFFICES	777,443	347,421	92,920	93,648	57,743	30.56	123.78
GROSS LOANS & LEASES	40,503,242	50,051,852	52,761,658	57,558,713	53,638,189	-3.85	-19.08
LESS: UNEARNED INCOME	51,223	96,913	90,125	74,906	124,409		
LN&LS ALLOWANCE	602,790	648,833	643,905	718,873	939,800	-12.96	-7.10
NET LOANS & LEASES	39,849,229	49,306,106	52,027,628	56,764,934	52,573,980	-3.63	-19.18
U S TREASURY & AGENCY SECURITIES	3,451,036	1,887,310	3,327,865	3,393,428	4,589,646	5.78	82.85
MUNICIPAL SECURITIES	18,679	45,237	32,932	60,406	120,640	-4.99	-58.71
FOREIGN DEBT SECURITIES	25,835	27,401	27,176	23,806	26,323	-5.49	-5.72
ALL OTHER SECURITIES	8,805,746	2,971,309	3,160,079	2,380,076	2,666,837	34.31	196.36
INTEREST-BEARING BANK BALANCES	157,670	167,916	99,152	139,128	575,024	47.80	-6.10
FEDERAL FUNDS SOLD & RESALES	301,986	217,241	596,424	503,873	672,568		
TRADING ACCOUNT ASSETS	487,251	168,345	262,316	190,921	234,086	-15.70	189.44
TOTAL INVESTMENTS	13,248,203	5,484,759	7,505,944	6,691,638	8,885,124		
TOTAL EARNING ASSETS	53,097,432	54,790,865	59,533,572	63,456,572	61,459,104		
NONINT CASH & DUE FROM BANKS	4,156,160	3,565,214	2,825,972	2,543,636	4,032,671	24.09	16.58
ACCEPTANCES	46,417	52,401	51,128	48,769	55,862		
PREMISES, FIX ASSTS, CAP LEASES	800,451	800,722	753,408	788,383	816,931	-1.22	-0.03
OTHER REAL ESTATE OWNED	9,325	15,047	20,503	33,575	47,912	45.82	-38.03
INV IN UNCONSOLIDATED SUBS	6,400	4,320	3,252	4,273	3,588		
OTHER ASSETS	4,493,595	3,957,334	4,999,476	4,355,213	3,294,333	-41.83	13.55
TOTAL ASSETS	62,609,780	63,185,903	68,187,311	71,230,421	69,710,401	-3.23	-0.91
AVERAGE ASSETS DURING QUARTER	62,838,680	62,706,833	67,699,026	72,021,559	66,237,413	1.30	0.21
LIABILITIES							
DEMAND DEPOSITS	8,024,609	6,581,761	6,566,570	7,260,300	7,941,357	20.15	21.92
ALL NOW & ATS ACCOUNTS	1,426,841	1,228,615	1,151,582	1,099,994	936,116	14.28	16.13
MONEY MARKET DEPOSIT ACCOUNTS	22,173,721	19,973,653	17,691,693	16,988,379	14,324,132	2.14	11.01
OTHER SAVINGS DEPOSITS	1,889,720	1,856,609	2,097,495	2,478,782	2,560,580	1.29	1.78
TIME DEP UNDER $100M	8,243,535	10,549,034	10,212,847	11,179,408	12,370,783	-6.06	-21.86
CORE DEPOSITS	41,758,426	40,189,672	37,720,187	39,006,863	38,132,783	3.67	3.90
TIME DEP OF $100M OR MORE	2,320,116	3,412,724	3,179,539	4,927,216	3,094,653	-12.05	-32.02
DEPOSITS IN FOREIGN OFFICES	2,306,500	2,397,676	3,454,618	399,027	3,144,711	403.29	-3.80
TOTAL DEPOSITS	46,385,132	46,000,072	44,354,344	44,333,106	44,372,147	6.94	0.84
FEDERAL FUNDS PURCH & RESALE	582,306	1,586,709	2,060,884	1,698,578	4,116,501		
OTHER BORROWINGS INCL MAT <1YR	1,773,503	2,496,693	7,520,807	7,976,219	9,919,397	43.65	-28.97
MEMO: SHT TERM N CORE FUNDING	6,099,247	9,080,247	15,463,542	14,312,251	18,890,734	6.58	-32.83
OTHER BORROWINGS WITH MAT >1YR	4,455,233	3,793,924	5,759,258	8,578,171	3,335,785	-19.51	17.43
ACCEPTANCES & OTHER LIABILITIES	3,372,710	2,904,691	1,798,842	1,459,583	1,401,556	-39.86	16.11
TOTAL LIABILITIES (INCL MORTG)	56,568,884	56,782,089	61,494,135	64,045,657	63,145,386	-2.50	-0.38
SUBORD NOTES AND DEBENTURES	1,153,235	1,152,698	1,152,161	901,452	761,088	0.01	0.05
ALL COMMON & PREFERRED CAPITAL	4,887,661	5,251,116	5,541,015	6,283,312	5,803,927	-11.55	-6.92
TOTAL LIABILITIES & CAPITAL	62,609,780	63,185,903	68,187,311	71,230,421	69,710,401	-3.23	-0.91
MEMORANDA:							
OFFICER, SHAREHOLDER LOANS (#)	4	4	2	2	7		
OFFICER, SHAREHOLDER LOANS ($)	20,933	19,539	18,298	14,820	277,049	-5.80	7.13
NON-INVESTMENT ORE	9,325	15,047	20,503	33,575	47,912	45.82	-38.03
LOANS HELD FOR SALE	3,900,766	1,655,003	5,798,088	3,233,546	2,324,102	NA	NA
HELD-TO-MATURITY SECURITIES	0	0	0	0	7	NA	NA
AVAILABLE-FOR-SALE-SECURITIES	12,301,296	4,931,257	6,548,052	5,857,716	7,403,446	24.68	149.46
ALL BROKERED DEPOSITS	1,175,114	586,684	375,282	1,233,264	465,587	-10.85	100.30

CERT #6384
CHARTER #1316
DIST/RSSD: 04/817824
COUNTY: ALLEGHENY
PNC BANK, NATIONAL ASSOCIATION
BALANCE SHEET—PERCENTAGE COMPOSITION OF ASSETS AND LIABILITIES
PITTSBURGH, PA
PAGE 06
4/1/02 5:32:04 PM

	12/31/2001			12/31/2000			12/31/1999			12/31/1998		12/31/1997	
	BANK	PEER1	PCT	BANK	PEER1	PCT	BANK	PEER1	PCT	BANK	PEER1	BANK	PEER1
ASSETS, PERCENT OF AVG ASSETS													
TOTAL LOANS	63.88	60.78	60	72.59	60.98	70	75.05	60.62	86	77.54	60.54	73.47	60.20
LEASE FINANCING RECEIVABLES	5.81	2.65	87	4.28	3.20	70	3.23	2.93	61	2.40	2.79	1.94	2.68
LESS: LN&LS ALLOWANCE	1.02	0.97	60	0.96	0.92	61	0.95	0.95	57	1.19	0.99	1.43	1.06
NET LOANS & LEASES	68.67	63.17	61	75.91	64.05	83	77.33	63.52	89	78.75	62.98	73.99	62.24
INTEREST-BEARING BANK BALANCES	0.20	0.82	54	0.18	0.84	54	0.13	1.07	47	0.27	1.25	0.36	1.87
FEDERAL FUNDS SOLD & RESALES	0.58	3.43	31	1.01	2.34	43	0.69	2.85	33	0.62	2.96	1.75	3.80
TRADING ACCOUNT ASSETS	0.59	1.18	61	0.33	1.09	56	0.39	1.05	52	0.26	1.40	0.15	1.95
HELD-TO-MATURITY SECURITIES	0.00	0.71	47	0.00	1.12	45	0.00	1.36	45	0.00	1.90	0.00	2.11
AVAILABLE-FOR-SALE SECURITIES	15.09	15.75	45	9.52	15.99	21	10.07	15.56	26	9.19	15.52	11.73	14.29
TOTAL EARNING ASSETS	85.13	88.31	17	86.95	89.02	26	88.61	88.76	38	89.09	88.71	87.98	88.55
NONINT CASH & DUE FROM BANKS	5.50	4.19	74	4.16	4.07	57	3.40	4.64	23	3.80	5.02	5.41	5.41
PREMISES, FIX ASSTS & CAP LEASES	1.27	1.05	67	1.14	1.05	57	1.08	1.14	42	1.15	1.22	1.22	1.26
OTHER REAL ESTATE OWNED	0.02	0.04	45	0.03	0.03	53	0.04	0.03	75	0.06	0.04	0.10	0.06
ACCEPTANCES & OTHER ASSETS	8.09	6.14	71	7.72	5.56	77	6.87	5.18	77	5.89	4.87	5.28	4.69
SUBTOTAL	14.87	11.69	82	13.05	10.98	73	11.39	11.24	61	10.90	11.28	12.02	11.45
TOTAL ASSETS	100.00	100.00		100.00	100.00		100.00	100.00		99.99	100.00	100.00	100.00
STANDBY LETTERS OF CREDIT	6.50	4.17	70	6.49	4.25	71	7.03	4.81	70	7.48	4.70	7.63	5.13
LIABILITIES, PERCENT OF AVG ASST													
DEMAND DEPOSITS	10.95	8.23	75	10.01	8.89	64	9.84	10.93	44	10.67	12.52	12.73	14.04
ALL NOW & ATS ACCOUNTS	1.96	1.36	77	1.77	1.28	74	1.55	1.54	58	1.37	1.75	1.21	1.96
MONEY MARKET DEPOSIT ACCOUNTS	33.11	20.14	87	28.31	16.97	90	25.41	16.24	86	21.55	14.72	19.38	14.59
OTHER SAVINGS DEPOSITS	2.95	7.53	30	2.97	7.07	25	3.36	7.93	22	3.63	7.53	4.26	7.37
TIME DEP LESS THAN $100M	14.77	11.46	65	15.69	12.38	64	15.37	12.06	67	16.91	13.70	18.19	14.42
CORE DEPOSITS	63.74	51.70	81	58.74	49.81	70	55.54	50.64	55	54.12	52.32	55.76	53.81
TIME DEP OF $100M OR MORE	4.37	7.66	22	4.85	8.38	21	5.51	7.03	38	5.21	7.09	4.54	6.59
DEPOSITS IN FOREIGN OFFICES	2.83	5.09	52	3.69	6.39	53	2.74	6.94	41	3.73	6.77	2.75	7.80
TOTAL DEPOSITS	70.93	66.78	68	67.28	66.58	54	63.79	66.42	38	63.06	67.86	63.05	69.82
FEDERAL FUNDS PURCH & REPOS	2.28	8.93	10	2.28	8.61	8	2.60	9.94	7	3.32	10.01	4.47	9.05
OTHER BORROWINGS INCL <1 YR	2.79	4.53	42	7.84	6.62	69	11.18	5.93	85	12.55	4.84	17.02	5.13
MEMO: SHT TERM CORE FUNDING	11.02	26.65	8	17.48	28.81	16	21.00	28.57	29	23.46	27.47	27.12	26.61
OTHER BORROWINGS >1 YR	7.82	5.05	77	9.55	4.52	87	9.93	4.19	85	8.91	3.97	4.05	3.29
ACCEPTANCES & OTHER LIABILITIES	6.11	3.03	92	3.41	2.52	73	2.48	2.64	52	2.24	2.56	2.10	2.65
TOTAL LIABILITIES (INCL MORTG)	89.94	89.98	38	90.36	90.41	42	89.98	90.47	32	90.08	90.59	90.70	90.92
SUBORDINATED NOTES & DEBENTURES	1.81	1.45	64	1.72	1.43	57	1.53	1.44	48	1.21	1.36	0.97	1.35
ALL COMMON & PREFERRED CAPITAL	8.25	8.42	51	7.92	8.00	50	8.49	7.85	70	8.71	7.85	8.33	7.64
TOTAL LIABILITIES & CAPITAL	99.99	100.00		100.00	100.00		100.00	100.00		100.00	100.00	99.99	100.00
MEMO: ALL BROKERED DEPOSITS	1.41	2.12	60	0.60	2.29	42	0.86	1.11	60	1.20	0.99	0.98	0.89
INSURED BROKERED DEP	0.00	1.22	35	0.00	1.22	30	0.00	0.47	36	0.00	0.51	0.00	0.47
DIRECT & INDIRECT INV IN RE	0.00	0.01	81	0.00	0.01	81	0.00	0.00	83	0.00	0.01	0.00	0.01
LOANS HELD FOR SALE	4.81	3.00	75	8.19	2.30	90	7.89	1.88	89	5.28	2.20	3.22	1.51

CERT #6384 DIST/RSSD: 04/817824
CHARTER #1316 COUNTY: ALLEGHENY

PNC BANK, NATIONAL ASSOCIATION
ANALYSIS OF CREDIT ALLOWANCE AND LOAN MIX

PITTSBURGH, PA PAGE 07 4/1/02 5:32:07 PM

	12/31/2001 BANK	PEER1	PCT	12/31/2000 BANK	PEER1	PCT	12/31/1999 BANK	PEER1	PCT	12/31/1998 BANK	PEER1	12/31/1997 BANK	PEER1
CHANGE: CREDIT ALLOWANCE ($000)													
BEGINNING BALANCE	648,833			643,905			718,873			939,800		745,426	
GROSS CREDIT LOSSES	980,672			181,385			208,026			516,340		377,722	
MEMO: LOANS HFS WRITEDOWN	637,086												
RECOVERIES	35,886			48,917			53,200			73,860		110,109	
NET CREDIT LOSSES	944,786			132,468			154,826			442,480		267,613	
PROVISION FOR CREDIT LOSS	898,743			133,000			156,640			217,961		65,000	
OTHER ADJUSTMENTS	0			4,396			−76,782			3,592		396,987	
ENDING BALANCE	602,790			648,833			643,905			718,873		939,800	
AVERAGE TOTAL LOANS & LEASES	44,804,389			51,542,871			53,675,215			56,032,063		45,425,743	
ANALYSIS RATIOS	BANK	PEER1	PCT	BANK	PEER1	PCT	BANK	PEER1	PCT	BANK	PEER1	BANK	PEER1
LOSS PROVISION TO AVERAGE ASSETS	1.42	0.48	94	0.20	0.39	35	0.23	0.26	45	0.31	0.28	0.11	0.27
RECOVERIES TO PRIOR CREDIT LOSS	19.78	26.90	37	23.51	30.12	45	10.30	31.28	7	19.55	35.95	75.25	141.36
NET LOSS TO AVERAGE TOTAL LN&LS	2.11	0.63	98	0.26	0.43	32	0.29	0.42	38	0.79	0.42	0.59	0.42
GROSS LOSS TO AVERAGE TOT LN&LS	2.19	0.76	98	0.35	0.56	30	0.39	0.56	32	0.92	0.59	0.83	0.62
RECOVERIES TO AVERAGE TOT LN&LS	0.08	0.12	41	0.09	0.12	40	0.10	0.15	33	0.13	0.16	0.24	0.19
LN&LS ALLOWANCE TO TOTAL LN&LS	1.49	1.62	51	1.30	1.48	38	1.22	1.44	27	1.25	1.52	1.76	1.65
LN&LS ALLOWANCE TO NET LOSSES (X)	0.64	3.13	5	4.90	4.60	67	4.16	4.27	54	1.62	4.92	3.51	5.94
LN&LS ALL TO NONACCRUAL LN&LS (X)	2.37	1.93		1.83	2.24		2.08	3.09		2.50	3.77	3.49	3.78
EARN COVER OF NET LN&LS LOSS (X)	1.62	6.93	7	12.32	11.46	67	12.15	11.19	67	3.76	11.02	5.34	13.98
NET LOSSES BY TYPE OF LN&LS													
REAL ESTATE LOANS	0.28	0.18	75	0.04	0.10	39	0.03	0.08	39	0.05	0.05	0.04	0.07
LOANS TO FINANCE COMML REAL EST	0.00	0.06	77	−0.01	0.01	9	0.01	−0.01	91	0.00	0.00	−0.09	−0.02
CONSTRUCTION & LAND DEV	−0.01	0.07	7	0.08	0.02	81	0.01	−0.01	70	0.12	−0.04	0.04	−0.04
SECURED BY FARMLAND	0.00	0.28	64	0.26	0.01	94	1.32	0.02	97	−0.03	0.02	0.15	0.09
SINGLE & MULTI FAMILY MORTGAGE	0.10	0.15	61	0.06	0.12	46	0.05	0.10	44	0.04	0.07	0.08	0.08
HOME EQUITY LOANS	0.07	0.18	41	0.05	0.14	40	0.06	0.13	44	−0.02	0.10	0.08	0.09
1-4 FAMILY NON-REVOLVING	0.11	0.13	67	0.06	0.11	53	0.06	0.10	54	0.05	0.06	0.08	0.08
MULTIFAMILY LOANS	−0.01	0.03	11	−0.01	0.01	15	−0.07	−0.02	13	0.00	0.01	−0.05	−0.01
NON-FARM NON-RESIDENTIAL MTG	1.49	0.13	95	−0.06	0.04	5	−0.09	0.00	19	0.10	−0.01	−0.20	−0.03
RE LOANS IN FOREIGN OFFICES	NA	0.01	90	NA	0.00	98	NA	0.00	98	NA	0.00	NA	0.00
AGRICULTURAL LOANS	2.72	0.27	91	0.16	0.18	71	1.75	0.23	94	0.31	0.13	0.15	0.27
COMMERCIAL AND INDUSTRIAL LOANS	5.14	1.30	95	0.54	0.69	49	0.20	0.50	23	0.57	0.41	0.18	0.29
LEASE FINANCING	0.32	0.43	54	0.22	0.26	56	0.35	0.25	67	0.39	0.24	0.26	0.21
LOANS TO INDIVIDUALS	0.45	1.16	27	0.36	1.26	22	1.70	1.41	69	3.58	1.70	2.66	2.03
CREDIT CARD PLANS	0.00	1.80	58	3.02	3.43	54	8.49	3.14	95	7.38	4.20	6.06	4.43
ALL OTHER LOANS & LEASES	1.29	0.30	87	0.19	0.19	67	0.44	0.34	70	0.14	0.20	−0.19	0.27
LOANS TO FOREIGN GOVERNMENTS	NA	−0.03	95	0.00	−0.31	95	0.00	0.00	92	0.00	0.02	0.00	−1.37

CERT #6384
CHARTER #1316

DIST/RSSD: 04 / 817824
COUNTY: ALLEGHENY

PNC BANK, NATIONAL ASSOCIATION
ANALYSIS OF LOAN AND LEASE ALLOWANCE AND LOAN MIX

PITTSBURGH, PA

PAGE 07A
4/1/02 5:32:09 PM

	12/31/2001			12/31/2000			12/31/1999			12/31/1998		12/31/1997	
	BANK	PEER1	PCT	BANK	PEER1	PCT	BANK	PEER1	PCT	BANK	PEER1	BANK	PEER1
LOAN MIX, % AVERAGE GROSS LN&LS													
CONSTRUCTION & DEVELOPMENT	2.74	4.75	35	2.31	3.91	38	2.14	3.23	38	2.12	2.89	2.22	2.45
1-4 FAMILY RESIDENTIAL	33.57	25.68	77	38.70	23.90	87	35.47	22.95	80	32.99	24.33	33.62	23.93
HOME EQUITY LOANS	4.93	4.33	65	3.61	3.63	54	2.91	3.07	50	2.82	3.22	3.52	3.42
OTHER REAL ESTATE LOANS	6.60	13.10	21	6.32	12.72	21	7.26	12.32	27	7.17	11.96	6.73	11.17
FARMLAND	0.05	0.26	37	0.06	0.22	38	0.06	0.20	44	0.07	0.21	0.05	0.14
MULTIFAMILY	0.90	1.29	52	0.89	1.40	45	1.23	1.29	58	1.03	1.18	0.49	1.14
NON-FARM NON-RESIDENTIAL	5.64	11.12	20	5.36	10.75	21	5.97	10.44	26	6.07	10.23	6.19	9.68
TOTAL REAL ESTATE	42.90	45.66	41	47.33	42.11	64	44.87	39.59	54	42.28	40.31	42.57	38.50
FINANCIAL INSTITUTION LOANS	0.18	1.57	50	0.25	1.44	42	1.09	0.91	67	1.15	0.95	1.88	1.18
AGRICULTURAL LOANS	0.00	0.38	15	0.01	0.36	21	0.01	0.35	20	0.01	0.34	0.01	0.32
COMMERCIAL & INDUSTRIAL LOANS	36.25	24.46	82	35.17	26.30	76	33.95	27.19	73	30.73	26.05	29.91	26.33
LOANS TO INDIVIDUALS	7.58	10.07	38	6.99	11.02	29	9.04	12.21	41	15.69	12.41	18.39	13.92
CREDIT CARD LOANS	0.06	0.96	35	0.24	1.40	21	1.34	1.76	55	6.88	2.36	6.82	3.27
MUNICIPAL LOANS	1.20	0.38	85	1.06	0.41	84	1.15	0.46	85	1.13	0.57	1.27	0.66
ACCEPTANCES OF OTHER BANKS	0.00	0.00	84	0.00	0.00	76	0.00	0.01	75	0.00	0.01	0.00	0.01
FOREIGN OFFICE LOANS & LEASES	1.07	2.14	70	0.36	2.76	69	0.17	3.38	60	0.13	4.56	0.16	6.11
ALL OTHER LOANS	3.45	2.65	81	3.46	3.17	67	5.61	3.90	77	5.89	4.31	3.24	4.20
LEASE FINANCING RECEIVABLES	7.36	4.22	75	5.38	4.98	61	4.12	4.60	55	3.00	4.37	2.57	4.22
SUPPLEMENTAL:													
LOANS TO FOREIGN GOVERNMENTS	0.00	0.04	62	0.00	0.07	61	0.00	0.11	48	0.01	0.12	0.01	0.19
LOANS TO FINANCE COMML REAL EST	2.87	0.90	91	2.88	0.84	91	3.00	1.08	88	2.42	1.10	1.16	0.99
MEMORANDUM (% OF AVG TOT LOANS):													
LOAN & LEASE COMMITMENTS	82.32	55.55	78	68.34	58.43	70	70.91	69.11	63	91.26	70.00	96.86	75.04
LOANS SOLD DURING THE QUARTER	NA	0.00	98	NA	0.00	98	NA	0.00	98	NA	0.00	NA	0.00
OFFICER, SHAREHOLDER LOANS	0.06	0.48	37	0.04	0.49	25	0.04	0.67	25	0.03	0.75	0.54	0.96
OFFICER, SHAREH LOANS TO ASSETS	0.03	0.29	35	0.03	0.30	26	0.03	0.38	26	0.02	0.43	0.40	0.56
OTHER REAL ESTATE OWNED % ASSETS													
CONSTRUCTION & LAND DEVELOPMENT	0.00	0.00	90	0.00	0.00	87	0.00	0.00	83	0.01	0.00	0.01	0.01
FARMLAND	0.00	0.00	97	0.00	0.00	97	0.00	0.01	98	0.00	0.02	0.00	0.02
1-4 FAMILY	0.01	0.02	60	0.02	0.02	74	0.03	0.01	91	0.03	0.02	0.04	0.02
MULTIFAMILY	0.00	0.00	97	0.00	0.01	95	0.00	0.00	95	0.00	0.00	0.00	0.00
NON-FARM-NON-RESID	0.01	0.01	70	0.01	0.00	71	0.01	0.01	64	0.02	0.02	0.05	0.02
FOREIGN OFFICES	0.00	0.00	91	0.00	0.00	91	0.00	0.00	92	0.00	0.00	0.00	0.00
SUBTOTAL	0.02	0.04	47	0.03	0.03	56	0.04	0.03	76	0.06	0.04	0.10	0.05
DIRECT AND INDIRECT INV	0.00	0.00	92	0.00	0.00	92	0.00	0.00	92	0.00	0.00	0.00	0.00
TOTAL	0.02	0.04	45	0.03	0.03	53	0.04	0.03	75	0.06	0.04	0.10	0.06
ASSET SERVICING % ASSETS													
MORTG SERV W RECOURSE	0.00	0.48	52	NA	0.00	98	NA	0.00	98	NA	0.00	NA	0.00
MORTG SERV WO RECOURSE	0.00	13.06	40	NA	0.00	98	NA	0.00	98	NA	0.00	NA	0.00
OTHER FINANCIAL ASSETS	111.86	1.85	98	NA	0.00	98	NA	0.00	98	NA	0.00	NA	0.00
TOTAL	111.86	18.93	92	NA	0.00	98	NA	0.00	98	NA	0.00	NA	0.00

CERT #6384
CHARTER #1316
DIST/RSSD: 04/817824
COUNTY: ALLEGHENY
PAGE 08
4/1/02 5:32:12 PM

PNC BANK, NATIONAL ASSOCIATION — PITTSBURGH, PA
ANALYSIS OF PAST DUE, NONACCRUAL & RESTRUCTURED LOANS & LEASES

NON-CURRENT LN&LS ($000)	12/31/2001	12/31/2000	12/31/1999	12/31/1998	12/31/1997
90 DAYS AND OVER PAST DUE	169,798	125,264	128,531	258,187	281,691
TOTAL NONACCRUAL LN&LS	253,945	354,651	309,309	287,304	268,973
TOTAL NON-CURRENT LN&LS	423,743	479,915	437,840	545,491	550,664
LN&LS 30-89 DAYS PAST DUE	332,103				
RESTRUCTURED LN&LS 90+ DAYS P/D	0	0	0	0	0
RESTRUCTURED LN&LS NONACCRL	0	380	0	1,114	1,735
RESTRUCTURE LN&LS 30-89 DAYS PD	0				
CURRENT RESTRUCTURED LN&LS	0	0	0	0	0
ALL OTHER REAL ESTATE OWNED	9,325	15,047	20,503	33,575	47,912

% OF NON-CURR LN&LS BY LN TYPE

	2001 BANK	2001 PEER1	2001 PCT	2000 BANK	2000 PEER1	2000 PCT	1999 BANK	1999 PEER1	1999 PCT	1998 BANK	1998 PEER1	1997 BANK	1997 PEER1
REAL ESTATE LNS-90+ DAYS P/D	0.47	0.23	78	0.25	0.17	67	0.27	0.18	76	0.47	0.23	0.54	0.22
-NONACCRUAL	0.14	0.73	11	0.11	0.57	11	0.45	0.53	45	0.57	0.60	0.68	0.75
-TOTAL	0.61	1.02	38	0.36	0.79	16	0.72	0.78	54	1.04	0.89	1.22	1.01
-30-89 DAYS P/D	0.67	1.33	25										
LNS FIN COML RE-90+ DAYS P/D	0.00	0.04	72	0.00	0.01	83	0.00	0.03	82	0.00	0.02	0.22	0.01
-NONACCRUAL	0.00	0.21	61	0.01	0.24	63	0.01	0.12	57	0.01	0.10	0.03	0.18
-TOTAL	0.00	0.27	58	0.01	0.32	60	0.01	0.20	54	0.02	0.15	0.26	0.23
-30-89 DAYS P/D	0.01	0.47	62										
CONST & LAND DEV-90+ DAYS P/D	0.35	0.10	87	0.02	0.06	61	0.27	0.07	88	1.36	0.10	0.52	0.14
-NONACCRUAL	0.15	0.72	35	0.12	0.50	35	0.18	0.56	39	0.18	0.66	0.62	1.44
-TOTAL	0.50	0.85	45	0.13	0.62	25	0.46	0.66	52	1.54	0.80	1.14	1.63
-30-89 DAYS P/D	0.35	1.29	30										
SINGLE & MULTI MTG-90+ DAYS P/D	0.53	0.30	78	0.26	0.23	60	0.29	0.25	64	0.37	0.29	0.40	0.26
-NONACCRUAL	0.08	0.44	14	0.04	0.48	11	0.31	0.35	44	0.35	0.47	0.34	0.56
-TOTAL	0.60	0.85	47	0.30	0.77	14	0.60	0.73	50	0.72	0.86	0.74	0.88
-30-89 DAYS P/D	0.76	1.46	30										
NON-FARM/RESI MTG-90+ DAYS P/D	0.22	0.10	81	0.30	0.06	92	0.17	0.06	86	0.75	0.11	1.29	0.11
-NONACCRUAL	0.51	0.76	37	0.62	0.64	57	1.39	0.78	77	1.97	0.80	2.61	1.22
-TOTAL	0.74	0.89	47	0.92	0.72	64	1.56	0.86	82	2.72	0.99	3.90	1.35
-30-89 DAYS P/D	0.36	0.93	25										
RE LNS FOR OFF-90+ DAYS P/D	NA	0.00	90	NA	0.00	98	NA	0.00	98	NA	0.00	NA	0.00
-NONACCRUAL	NA	0.07	88	NA	0.00	98	NA	0.00	98	NA	0.00	NA	0.00
-TOTAL	NA	0.13	87	NA	0.00	98	NA	0.00	98	NA	0.00	NA	0.00
-30-89 DAYS P/D	NA	0.11	87										
COML & INDUST LNS-90+ DAYS P/D	0.36	0.12	90	0.20	0.09	80	0.13	0.07	76	0.22	0.09	0.31	0.06
-NONACCRUAL	1.53	1.91	38	1.68	1.32	70	0.92	0.90	51	0.75	0.68	0.63	0.60
-TOTAL	1.88	2.06	48	1.89	1.44	71	1.04	0.99	54	0.96	0.79	0.94	0.67
-30-89 DAYS P/D	0.99	1.12	50										
LOANS TO INDIVDLS-90+ DAYS P/D	0.78	0.34	80	0.66	0.44	73	0.76	0.60	70	1.29	0.63	1.12	0.74
-NONACCRUAL	0.08	0.23	48	0.03	0.18	42	0.04	0.11	50	0.04	0.14	0.08	0.17
-TOTAL	0.86	0.66	67	0.69	0.68	54	0.80	0.79	64	1.33	0.84	1.19	0.96
-30-89 DAYS P/D	1.45	2.16	32										

CERT #6384
CHARTER #1316

DIST/RSSD: 04/817824
COUNTY: ALLEGHENY

PNC BANK, NATIONAL ASSOCIATION
ANALYSIS OF PAST DUE, NONACCRUAL & RESTRUCTURED LOANS & LEASES

PITTSBURGH, PA

PAGE 08A
4/1/02 5:32:15 PM

% OF NON-CURR LN&LS BY LN TYPE

	12/31/2001			12/31/2000			12/31/1999			12/31/1998		12/31/1997	
	BANK	PEER1	PCT	BANK	PEER1	PCT	BANK	PEER1	PCT	BANK	PEER1	BANK	PEER1
CREDIT CARD PLANS–90+ DAYS P/D	0.00	0.43	60	0.34	0.57	49	0.24	0.64	39	2.04	0.85	1.75	1.20
–NONACCRUAL	0.00	0.01	92	0.00	0.05	69	0.00	0.09	58	0.00	0.09	0.00	0.07
–TOTAL	0.00	0.50	58	0.34	0.71	42	0.24	0.86	29	2.04	1.04	1.75	1.38
–30–89 DAYS P/D	0.00	0.93	57										
FOREIGN GOVT LNS–90+ DAYS P/D	NA	0.00	98	NA	0.00	97	0.00	0.00	94	0.00	0.00	0.00	0.00
–NONACCRUAL	NA	0.02	90	NA	0.01	91	0.00	0.01	85	0.00	0.18	0.00	0.01
–TOTAL	NA	0.02	90	NA	0.01	90	0.00	0.05	82	0.00	0.19	0.00	0.01
–30–89 DAYS P/D	NA	0.14	88										
LEASE FINANCING–90+ DAYS P/D	0.03	0.05	67	0.03	0.06	64	0.05	0.06	67	0.04	0.04	0.05	0.03
–NONACCRUAL	0.24	0.37	52	0.04	0.30	46	0.05	0.17	58	0.03	0.18	0.00	0.17
–TOTAL	0.27	0.42	51	0.07	0.40	43	0.10	0.29	45	0.08	0.24	0.05	0.20
–30–89 DAYS P/D	0.48	0.62	57										
AGRICULTURAL LNS–90+ DAYS P/D	0.00	0.05	65	0.00	0.09	61	0.00	0.10	55	0.00	0.06	22.51	0.07
–NONACCRUAL	2.37	1.30	75	0.00	1.15	35	0.00	1.24	41	2.13	1.00	0.51	1.38
–TOTAL	2.37	1.39	75	0.00	1.37	28	0.00	1.43	35	2.13	1.11	23.02	1.86
–30–89 DAYS P/D	1.82	0.90	77										
OTHER LN&LS–90+ DAYS P/D	0.58	0.07	91	0.12	0.08	78	0.13	0.07	73	0.11	0.07	0.03	0.04
–NONACCRUAL	0.24	0.37	64	0.57	0.33	76	0.50	0.18	86	0.12	0.18	0.10	0.12
–TOTAL	0.81	0.54	77	0.69	0.43	78	0.63	0.26	88	0.23	0.26	0.13	0.16
–30–89 DAYS P/D	0.55	0.56	61										
GROSS LN&LS–90+ DAYS P/D	0.42	0.23	81	0.25	0.19	66	0.24	0.21	64	0.45	0.23	0.53	0.23
–NONACCRUAL	0.63	0.97	34	0.71	0.74	54	0.59	0.53	61	0.50	0.49	0.50	0.52
–TOTAL	1.05	1.31	45	0.96	0.99	54	0.83	0.76	60	0.95	0.77	1.03	0.78
–30–89 DAYS P/D	0.82	1.29	22										

OTHER PERTINENT RATIOS:

	12/31/2001			12/31/2000			12/31/1999			12/31/1998		12/31/1997	
	BANK	PEER1	PCT	BANK	PEER1	PCT	BANK	PEER1	PCT	BANK	PEER1	BANK	PEER1
NON-CUR LN&LS TO-LN&LS ALLOWANCE	70.30	82.15	38										
–EQUITY CAPITAL	8.67	9.87	51										
%TOTAL P/D LN&LS-INCL NONACCRUAL	1.87	2.66	30	0.80	0.77	71	0.67	0.67	61	0.70	0.67	0.69	0.65
IENC-LOANS TO TOTAL LOANS	NA	0.00	98										
NON CURR LNS + OREO TO LNS + OREO	1.07	1.38	41										
NON-CURR RESTRUCT DEBT/GR LN&LS	0.00	0.00	82										
CURR+NON-CURR RESTRUCT/GR LN&LS	0.00	0.00	82										
CURRENT RESTRUCT LN&LS	0.00	0.00	77										

CERT #6384
CHARTER #1316

DIST/RSSD: 04/817824
COUNTY: ALLEGHENY

PITTSBURGH, PA

PAGE 09
4/1/02 5:32:17 PM

PNC BANK, NATIONAL ASSOCIATION
INTEREST RATE RISK ANALYSIS AS A PERCENT OF ASSETS

	12/31/2001 BANK	12/31/2001 PEER1	12/31/2001 PCT	12/31/2000 BANK	12/31/2000 PEER1	12/31/2000 PCT	12/31/1999 BANK	12/31/1999 PEER1	12/31/1999 PCT	12/31/1998 BANK	12/31/1998 PEER1	12/31/1997 BANK	12/31/1997 PEER1
LONG ASSETS INSTS W/OPTIONS	20.17	16.34	67	25.14	14.94	87	24.69	15.97	77	20.66	17.48	20.30	16.18
MORTGAGE LOANS & PASS THRUS													
LOANS & SECURITIES OVER 15 YRS	2.23	5.98	37	2.49	4.60	40	1.57	4.65	32	1.73	4.83	2.58	3.85
LOANS & SECURITIES 5-15 YRS	6.81	3.91	85	12.66	3.87	94	12.25	4.55	94	8.97	4.44	6.13	3.75
OTHER LOANS AND SECURITIES	57.46	56.80	45	57.00	60.61	33	57.34	60.01	36	64.22	57.24	60.82	57.66
LOANS & SECURITIES OVER 15 YRS	2.27	1.94	67	1.79	1.70	63	1.57	1.47	63	0.91	1.38	1.87	1.22
LOANS & SECURITIES 5-15 YRS	8.51	6.69	75	9.25	7.56	70	10.80	7.34	76	11.30	6.90	7.17	5.63
TOTAL LOANS & SECURITIES OVR 15	4.50	8.26	32	4.27	6.47	43	3.14	6.28	30	2.64	6.34	4.45	5.23
CMO'S TOTAL	6.04	4.09	67	3.66	4.10	63	3.84	3.68	64	3.13	4.21	5.49	3.59
AVG LIFE OVER 3 YEARS	3.88	2.44	70	2.77	2.37	67	3.02	2.53	67	0.76	2.18	0.54	1.91
STRUCTURED NOTES	3.67	0.00	98	0.00	0.01	78	0.00	0.01	70	0.00	0.03	0.00	0.08
HIGH RISK SECURITIES	NA	0.00	98	NA	0.00	98	NA	0.00	98	0.00	0.08	0.07	0.04
MORTGAGE SERVICING	0.36	0.20	74	0.42	0.19	76	2.88	0.33	92	1.39	0.27	0.59	0.25
TOTAL	4.03	0.26	95	0.42	0.23	71	2.88	0.37	92	1.39	0.55	0.66	0.49
OVERALL RISK INDICATORS													
AVAILABLE FOR SALE	19.65	16.47	64	7.80	15.32	21	9.60	15.54	25	8.22	15.43	10.62	14.00
HELD TO MATURITY	0.00	0.58	54	0.00	1.03	46	0.00	1.30	44	0.00	1.68	0.00	1.91
OFF BALANCE SHEET	72.78	60.93	71	77.89	52.10	76	82.83	57.37	76	93.61	54.58	84.31	57.46
UNREALIZED APPN/DEPN	0.00	0.01	72	0.00	0.00	74	0.00	-0.03	89	0.00	0.02	0.00	0.02
UNREAL APP/DEP % TIER ONE CAP	0.00	0.13	64	0.00	0.04	66	0.00	-0.43	86	0.00	0.28	0.00	0.27
CONTRACTUAL MAT/REPRICE DATA													
LOANS/SECURITIES OVER 3 YEARS	31.56	31.39	48	39.58	31.59	70	37.95	32.48	64	32.75	30.61	28.44	25.81
LIABILITIES OVER 3 YEARS	4.80	3.58	68	2.91	3.22	57	5.12	2.65	80	8.82	2.74	6.03	2.22
NET 3 YEAR POSITION	26.77	27.07	45	36.67	27.75	76	32.83	29.49	60	23.93	27.72	22.40	23.34
LOANS/SECURITIES OVER 1 YEAR	41.58	43.11	42	47.92	43.77	57	45.92	43.48	48	42.61	41.67	41.50	37.57
LIABILITIES OVER 1 YEAR	12.45	8.57	74	9.55	9.22	57	13.27	7.93	76	15.93	7.80	12.06	8.06
NET OVER 1 YEAR POSITION	29.13	33.96	31	38.37	33.63	57	32.65	35.49	41	26.68	33.60	29.44	29.67
NON-MATURITY DEPOSITS	53.53	41.51	82	46.91	36.15	84	40.34	36.61	66	39.07	37.80	36.96	38.58
NON-MATURITY DEPS % LONG ASSETS	169.60	153.22	65	118.51	128.49	54	106.29	123.45	45	119.29	133.79	129.96	172.01
NET OVER 3 YEAR POSITION	-21.97	-9.87	21	-7.33	-4.27	38	-2.39	-3.92	54	-6.32	-6.90	-8.52	-12.11
AS % TIER 1 CAPITAL													
STRUCTURED NOTES	48.61	0.03	98	0.00	0.12	70	0.00	0.21	69	0.00	0.46	0.00	1.13
HIGH RISK SECURITIES	NA	0.00	98	NA	0.00	98	NA	0.00	98	0.00	1.06	0.87	0.58
MORTGAGE SERVICING (FV)	4.79	3.07	74	4.94	2.89	71	38.60	4.95	92	18.05	4.03	7.88	3.83
TOTAL	53.40	3.94	92	4.94	3.42	69	38.60	5.42	92	18.05	7.99	8.74	7.44

CERT #6384
CHARTER #1316
DIST/RSSD: 04/817824
COUNTY: ALLEGHENY

PNC BANK, NATIONAL ASSOCIATION
LIQUIDITY AND INVESTMENT PORTFOLIO

PITTSBURGH, PA
PAGE 10
4/1/02 5:32:20 PM

	12/31/2001 BANK	PEER1	PCT	12/31/2000 BANK	PEER1	PCT	12/31/1999 BANK	PEER1	PCT	12/31/1998 BANK	PEER1	12/31/1997 BANK	PEER1
SHORT TERM INVESTMENTS	463,423			414,363			707,293			654,694		1,297,356	
SHORT TERM ASSETS	9,304,052			9,320,772			12,130,113			14,057,069		12,746,506	
SHORT TERM NON CORE FUNDING	6,099,247			9,080,920			15,463,542			14,312,251		18,890,734	
NON CORE LIABILITIES	10,946,665			13,508,285			21,785,581			23,472,644		23,509,965	
DEBT SECURITIES 90+ DAYS P/D	0			0			0			0		0	
TOTAL NON-CURRENT DEBT SEC	0			0			0			0		0	
FAIR VALUE HIGH-RISK MTG SECS												37,805	
FAIR VALUE STRUCTURED NOTES	2,282,713											0	
PERCENT OF TOTAL ASSETS													
SHORT TERM INVESTMENTS	0.74	6.74	22	0.66	5.81	21	1.04	5.52	20	0.92	5.96	1.86	7.96
MARKETABLE EQUITY SEC (MES)	0.27	0.22	70	0.06	0.17	49	0.01	0.14	39	0.04	0.09	0.06	0.10
CORE DEPOSITS	66.70	52.73	81	63.61	49.59	85	55.32	49.07	57	54.76	51.44	54.70	52.96
S T NON CORE FUNDING	9.74	25.13	8	14.37	28.27	8	22.68	29.84	25	20.09	27.94	27.10	27.10
LIQUIDITY RATIO													
NET S T NONCORE FUND DEPENDENCE	10.81	21.73	20	15.98	27.57	12	25.19	29.27	38	21.80	27.45	29.33	25.03
NET NON CORE FUND DEPENDENCE	20.10	35.24	20	24.15	40.16	14	35.98	40.47	42	36.42	36.79	37.04	33.62
BROKERED DEPOSITS TO DEPOSITS	2.53	3.38	67	1.28	3.97	46	0.85	2.07	51	2.78	1.52	1.05	1.24
BROKER DEP MAT <1YR TO BKR DEPS	75.72	31.29	64	23.22	38.34	43	23.23	34.03	41	74.50	32.09	26.43	27.00
SHORT TRM INV TO S T NCORE FUND	7.60	32.00	38	4.56	20.80	35	4.57	18.43	25	4.57	21.48	6.87	29.52
SHORT TERM ASSET TO S T LIABS	81.85	83.56	54	51.86	64.30	40	52.91	66.02	36	60.38	71.69	47.18	76.78
NET S T LIAB TO ASSETS	3.30	7.35	38	13.70	13.42	52	15.83	13.42	54	12.95	11.01	20.47	9.56
NET LOANS & LEASES TO DEPOSITS	85.91	93.01	37	107.19	96.26	77	117.30	97.86	80	128.04	93.45	118.48	89.00
NET LN&LS TO CORE DEPOSITS	95.43	123.03	20	122.68	137.94	42	137.93	137.75	63	145.53	127.69	137.87	121.22
NET LN&LS & SBLC TO ASSETS	70.23	65.50	58	84.46	68.29	91	82.96	68.65	86	86.69	67.69	83.37	67.09
SECURITIES MIX													
HELD-TO-MATURITY % TOTAL SECS													
US TREAS & GOVT AGENCIES	0.00	0.11	81	0.00	0.42	71	0.00	0.40	73	0.00	0.76	0.00	1.43
MUNICIPAL SECURITIES	0.00	0.34	70	0.00	0.70	56	0.00	0.88	55	0.00	0.87	0.00	1.80
PASS-THROUGH MTG BACKED SECS	0.00	0.39	74	0.00	0.82	69	0.00	0.99	69	0.00	1.24	0.00	1.90
CMO & REMIC MTG BACKED SECS	0.00	0.11	82	0.00	0.34	74	0.00	0.36	75	0.00	0.58	0.00	1.28
ASSET BACKED SECURITIES	0.00	0.00	95	NA	0.00	98	NA	0.00	98	NA	0.00	NA	0.00
OTHER DOMESTIC DEBT SECS	0.00	0.31	77	0.00	0.81	70	0.00	0.62	69	0.00	0.88	0.00	0.80
FOREIGN DEBT SECURITIES	0.00	0.01	81	0.00	0.02	74	0.00	0.03	70	0.00	0.02	0.00	0.10
TOTAL HELD-TO-MATURITY	0.00	2.68	54	0.00	4.77	46	0.00	5.99	44	0.00	7.49	0.00	10.45
AVAILABLE-FOR-SALE % TOTAL SEC													
US TREASURY & GOVT AGENCIES	5.48	12.64	47	3.85	18.55	16	29.27	19.08	70	45.56	17.14	13.10	22.06
MUNICIPAL SECURITIES	0.15	3.40	21	0.92	4.18	35	0.50	3.75	26	1.03	4.00	1.63	3.27
PASS-THROUGH MTG BACKED SECS	20.36	30.83	37	26.19	25.45	49	13.62	27.25	33	0.08	29.67	1.39	26.34
CMO & REMIC MTG BACKED SECS	2.22	14.88	32	8.24	11.29	47	7.93	11.74	47	12.30	13.68	47.51	14.00
ASSET BACKED SECURITIES	20.33	5.56	84	NA	0.00	98	NA	0.00	98	NA	0.00	NA	0.00
OTHER DOMESTIC DEBT SECS	49.90	7.38	95	51.88	13.34	91	41.49	11.71	92	33.14	9.95	30.65	7.00
FOREIGN DEBT SECURITIES	0.21	0.68	82	0.56	0.87	80	0.42	1.65	76	0.41	1.83	0.36	2.65
INV MUT FND & OTH MKTBL	1.35	1.66	62	0.73	1.26	52	0.06	1.02	36	0.46	0.61	0.59	0.79
OTHER EQUITY SECURITIES	NA	0.00	98	7.65	3.18	88	6.71	2.92	88	7.03	2.44	4.78	2.34
TOTAL AVAILABLE-FOR-SALE	100.00	93.78	98	100.00	90.60	98	100.00	88.57	98	100.00	86.56	100.00	84.60
OTHER SECURITIES RATIOS:													
STRUC NOTE TO T1CAP	48.27	0.03	98	0.00	0.11	70	0.00	0.20	69	0.00	2.12	0.72	2.19
APP (DEP) HI RISK & STRUC/T1CAP	NA	0.00	98	NA	0.00	98	NA	0.00	98	0.00	0.01	-0.15	-0.01
APP (DEP) IN HTM SEC TO HTM SEC	NA	0.61	62	NA	0.25	64	NA	-0.68	85	NA	0.70	NA	0.89
APP (DEP) IN HTM SEC TO EQY CAP	0.00	0.11	64	0.00	0.03	66	0.00	-0.38	86	0.00	0.24	0.00	0.22
PLEDGED SECURITIES TO TOT SEC	45.01	52.38	38	74.50	55.99	73	54.38	59.04	39	69.58	60.37	54.73	58.25

PNC BANK, NATIONAL ASSOCIATION
CAPITAL ANALYSIS

CERT #6384
CHARTER #1316
DIST/RSSD: 04/817824
COUNTY: ALLEGHENY
PITTSBURGH, PA
PAGE 11
4/1/02 5:32:23 PM

	12/31/2001			12/31/2000			12/31/1999			12/31/1998		12/31/1997	
	BANK	PEER1	PCT	BANK	PEER1	PCT	BANK	PEER1	PCT	BANK	PEER1	BANK	PEER1
END OF PERIOD CAPITAL ($000)													
PERPETUAL PREFERRED	0			0			0			0		0	
+ COMMON STOCK	218,918			218,919			218,919			218,919		218,919	
+ SURPLUS	1,344,558			1,255,760			2,061,879			2,554,105		2,372,031	
+ UNDIVIDED PROFITS	3,298,500			3,845,935			3,501,465			3,532,815		3,236,981	
+ ACCUM OTHER COMP INCOME	25,685			−69,498			−241,248						
+ OTHER EQUITY CAPITAL COMP	0												
TOTAL EQUITY CAPITAL	4,887,661			5,251,116			5,541,015			6,283,312		5,803,927	
SUBORD NOTES & DEBENTURES	1,153,235			1,152,698			1,152,161			901,452		761,088	
CHANGES IN TOTAL EQUITY ($000)													
BALANCE AT BEGINNING OF PERIOD	5,251,116			5,541,015			6,283,312			5,803,927		4,629,592	
+ NET INCOME	491,731			1,007,226			1,057,038			1,008,240		900,886	
+ SALE OR PURCHASE OF CAPITAL	18,960			8,801			5,661			0		0	
+ MERGER & ABSORPTIONS	70,284			142,053			0			1,843		928,616	
+ RESTATE DUE TO ACCTG ERROR&CHG	0			0			0			0		90,197	
+ TRANS WITH PARENT	5,345			−969,849			−500,275			176,825		−95,578	
− DIVIDENDS	1,050,000			650,000			1,086,000			709,000		680,025	
+ OTHER COMPREHENSIVE INCOME	100,225			171,870			−218,721			1,477		30,239	
BALANCE AT END OF PERIOD	4,887,661			5,251,116			5,541,015			6,283,312		5,803,927	
INTANGIBLE ASSETS													
MORTGAGE SERVICING RIGHTS	199,344			155,229			1,720,128			889,181		384,608	
+ PURCH CRED CARD RELATION	0			0			0			0		320,140	
+ OTHER INTANGIBLES	4,220			18,619			9,639			17,667		25,259	
+ GOODWILL	1,016,636			1,051,192			1,109,759			1,187,223		893,040	
TOTAL INTANGIBLES	1,220,200			1,225,040			2,839,526			2,385,594		1,623,047	
MEMO: GRANDFATHERED INTANG	0			0			0			0		0	
CAPITAL RATIOS													
PERCENT OF TOTAL EQUITY:													
NET LOANS & LEASES (X)	8.15	7.35	70	9.39	7.92	76	9.39	8.22	73	9.03	7.99	9.06	8.01
SUBORD NOTES & DEBENTURES	23.59	17.56	65	21.95	18.73	54	20.79	18.91	52	14.35	18.85	13.11	19.16
LONG TERM DEBT	23.59	17.56	65	21.95	18.73	54	20.79	18.91	52	14.35	18.85	13.11	19.16
COM RE & RELATED VENTURES	101.51	137.01	35	95.98	128.97	33	102.83	127.77	36	100.24	118.73	97.65	114.83
PERCENT OF AVERAGE TOTAL EQUITY:													
NET INCOME	9.37	13.68	25	18.94	13.82	76	18.11	16.96	61	16.59	15.89	18.11	16.98
DIVIDENDS	20.01	9.51	94	12.22	9.25	67	18.61	11.10	82	11.67	9.63	13.67	11.46
RETAINED EARNINGS	−10.64	3.50	1	6.72	3.34	71	−0.50	5.34	17	4.92	6.03	4.44	5.20
OTHER CAPITAL RATIOS:													
DIVIDENDS TO NET OPER INCOME	211.54	68.90	97	64.53	64.59	52	102.74	66.54	83	70.32	62.29	75.48	71.09
EQUITY CAPITAL TO ASSETS	7.81	8.36	44	8.31	8.03	61	8.13	7.77	63	8.82	7.76	8.33	7.58
GROWTH RATES:													
TOTAL EQUITY CAPITAL	−6.92	19.03	5	−5.23	32.87	14	−11.81	12.26	7	8.26	32.31	25.37	485.28
EQUITY GROWTH LESS ASST GROWTH	−6.01	3.39	25	2.10	4.78	43	−7.54	−1.51	33	6.08	1.37	3.68	−5.91
INTANG ASSETS % TOTAL EQUITY													
MORTGAGE SERVICING RIGHTS	4.08	2.24	77	2.96	2.17	70	31.04	3.49	91	14.15	2.81	6.63	2.79
GOODWILL	20.80	11.78	72	20.02	11.41	77	20.03	10.87	77	18.89	10.30	15.39	7.73
PURCH CREDIT CARD RELATION	0.00	0.02	78	0.00	0.05	76	0.00	0.04	80	4.64	0.05	5.52	0.10
ALL OTHER INTANGIBLES	0.09	1.67	30	0.35	1.28	46	0.17	1.07	36	0.28	1.29	0.44	1.42
TOTAL INTANGIBLES	24.96	17.43	74	23.33	17.35	69	51.25	16.82	92	37.97	16.30	27.96	14.07

CERT #6384
CHARTER #1316

DIST/RSSD: 04/817824
COUNTY: ALLEGHENY

PNC BANK, NATIONAL ASSOCIATION
CAPITAL ANALYSIS

PITTSBURGH, PA

PAGE 11A
4/1/02 5:32:25 PM

RISK BASED CAPITAL ($000)	12/31/2001	12/31/2000	12/31/1999	12/31/1998	12/31/1997
TIER ONE CAPITAL					
TOTAL EQUITY CAPITAL ADJUSTED	5,750,131	6,472,461	6,215,322	6,674,497	6,177,931
-INELIGIBLE DEF TAX ASSETS	0	0	0	0	0
-INELIGIBLE INTANGIBLES	1,020,856	1,069,811	1,119,398	1,205,524	930,928
NET TIER ONE	4,729,275	5,402,650	5,095,924	5,468,972	5,247,002
TIER TWO CAPITAL					
+ QUALIF DEBT AND REDEEM PFD	873,235	977,698	1,082,161	866,452	761,088
+ CUMULATIVE PREFERRED STOCK	0	0	0	0	0
+ ALLOWABLE LN&LS LOSS ALLOW	679,876	648,833	643,905	718,873	809,545
+ UNRL GAIN MKTBL EQY SEC (45%)	0	0	0	0	0
+ OTHER TIER 2 CAPITAL COMP	350,000	NA	NA	NA	NA
NET ELIGIBLE TIER TWO	1,903,111	1,626,531	1,726,066	1,585,325	1,570,633
TOTAL RBC BEFORE DEDUCTIONS					
TIER ONE & TIER TWO	6,632,386	7,029,181	6,821,990	7,054,297	6,817,635
TIER THREE	NA	0	0	0	NA
-RECIPROCAL CAPITAL HOLDINGS	NA	NA	NA	NA	NA
-DEDUCTIONS FOR TOTAL RBC	0	NA	NA	NA	NA
TOTAL RISK-BASED CAPITAL	6,632,386	7,029,181	6,821,990	7,054,297	6,817,635
RISK-WEIGHTED ASSETS					
ON-BALANCE SHEET					
CATEGORY TWO–20%	3,194,204	1,222,745	1,254,530	1,665,912	1,866,122
CATEGORY THREE–50%	4,503,881	8,176,952	9,128,006	8,222,741	7,201,706
CATEGORY FOUR–100%	35,803,526	37,763,675	38,878,280	42,886,058	42,758,757
TOTAL ON-BALANCE SHEET	43,501,612	47,163,372	49,260,816	52,774,711	51,826,585
MEMO: CATEGORY ONE–0%	1,073,140	2,634,074	4,676,051	3,088,578	3,218,481
OFF-BALANCE SHEET					
CATEGORY TWO–20%	176,825	77,001	58,060	58,033	312,676
CATEGORY THREE–50%	672,296	227,232	833,414	635,617	191,450
CATEGORY FOUR–100%	9,943,952	10,365,854	11,574,581	12,546,305	12,432,919
TOTAL OFF-BALANCE SHEET	10,793,073	10,670,087	12,466,056	13,239,955	12,937,045
MEMO: CATEGORY ONE–0%	9,218,899	8,909,432	10,851,857	5,046,203	2,978,504
ADJUSTMENTS TO RISK-WGT ASSET					
RISK-WEIGHTED ASSET BEFORE DED	54,294,685	57,833,459	61,726,873	66,014,667	64,763,631
-INELIGIBLE DEF TAX ASSETS	NA	0	0	0	0
-INELIGIBLE INTANGIBLES	NA	0	0	0	0
-RECIPROCAL CAPITAL HOLDINGS	NA	0	0	0	0
-EXCESS ALLOWABLE LN&LS LOSS AL	0	0	0	0	0
-ALLOCATED TRANSFER RISK RESERV	0	0	0	0	0
+MARKET RISK EQUIV ASSETS	109,892	0	0	0	130,254
TOTAL RISK-WEIGHTED ASSETS	54,404,578	57,833,459	61,726,873	66,014,667	64,633,376

	12/31/2001			12/31/2000			12/31/1999			12/31/1998		12/31/1997	
RISK-BASED CAPITAL	BANK	PEER1	PCT	BANK	PEER1	PCT	BANK	PEER1	PCT	BANK	PEER1	BANK	PEER1
TIER ONE RBC TO RISK-WGT ASSETS	8.69	9.20	41	9.34	8.49	71	8.26	8.50	41	8.28	8.36	8.12	8.39
TOTAL RBC TO RISK-WEIGHT ASSETS	12.19	12.03	65	12.15	11.21	87	11.05	11.20	58	10.69	11.17	10.55	11.15
TIER ONE LEVERAGE CAPITAL	7.65	7.12	74	8.77	7.04	92	7.65	7.06	73	7.72	6.92	8.03	6.93
OTHER CAPITAL RATIO:													
DEF TAX ASSET TO T1 CAP	0.00	1.12	64	0.00	1.15	61	0.00	2.65	42	0.00	1.37	1.06	1.67

NOTE: FROM MARCH 31, 2001 FORWARD RISK BASED CAPITAL RATIOS AND DATA DO NOT INCLUDE ADJUSTMENT FOR FINANCIAL SUBSIDIARIES.
FOR BANKS WITH FINANCIAL SUBSIDIARIES PLEASE REFER TO CALL REPORT FOR INFORMATION ON THE ADJUSTMENT.

CERT # 6384
CHARTER #1316

DIST/RSSD: 04/817824
COUNTY: ALLEGHENY

PITTSBURGH, PA

PAGE 12
4/1/02 5:32:28 PM

PNC BANK, NATIONAL ASSOCIATION
ONE QUARTER ANNUALIZED INCOME ANALYSIS

	12/31/2001 BANK	PEER1	PCT	12/31/2000 BANK	PEER1	PCT	12/31/1999 BANK	PEER1	PCT	12/31/1998 BANK	PEER1	12/31/1997 BANK	PEER1
EARNINGS AND PROFITABILITY													
PERCENT OF AVERAGE ASSETS:													
INTEREST INCOME (TE)	5.36	5.68	34	6.04	7.53	8	6.68	6.94	30	7.04	7.52	10.52	7.50
−INTEREST EXPENSE	1.77	2.17	22	2.57	4.15	2	3.44	3.45	48	3.52	3.66	5.24	3.65
NET INTEREST INCOME (TE)	3.59	3.52	44	3.47	3.42	43	3.24	3.54	26	3.52	3.90	5.28	3.90
+NONINTEREST INCOME	2.57	2.07	71	1.05	1.98	19	2.99	2.48	69	3.66	2.46	2.83	2.17
−NON-INTEREST EXPENSE	4.46	3.31	82	1.77	3.20	7	3.77	3.58	69	4.50	4.07	5.01	3.72
−PROVISION: LOAN&LEASE LOSSES	4.24	0.63	98	0.27	0.52	45	0.17	0.30	36	0.63	0.32	0.15	0.33
PRETAX OPERATING INCOME (TE)	−2.54	1.58	2	2.48	1.66	83	2.29	2.14	61	2.05	1.96	2.96	2.04
+REALIZED GAINS/LOSSES SECS	−0.02	0.09	11	0.11	0.01	90	0.00	−0.02	72	0.24	0.06	0.14	0.03
PRETAX NET OPERATING INC (TE)	−2.56	1.74	2	2.59	1.68	84	2.29	2.10	63	2.29	2.03	3.10	2.10
NET OPERATING INCOME	−1.64	1.15	2	1.83	1.09	84	1.61	1.34	70	1.43	1.31	1.92	1.41
ADJUSTED NET OPERATING INCOME	−2.21	1.29	2	1.83	1.29	80	1.61	1.34	69	1.07	1.32	1.52	1.39
NET INCOME ADJUSTED SUB S		1.15			1.09			1.36			1.31		1.41
NET INCOME	−1.64	1.15	2	1.83	1.09	84	1.61	1.36	69	1.43	1.31	1.92	1.41
MARGIN ANALYSIS:													
INT INC (TE) TO AVG EARN ASSETS	6.12	6.32	37	6.80	8.33	8	7.48	7.70	33	7.75	8.34	11.57	8.30
INT EXPENSE TO AVG EARN ASSETS	2.02	2.40	22	2.89	4.57	2	3.85	3.82	52	3.88	4.04	5.76	4.02
NET INT INC-TE TO AVG EARN ASST	4.10	3.92	51	3.91	3.79	53	3.63	3.92	25	3.88	4.33	5.81	4.33
LOAN & LEASE ANALYSIS													
NET LOSS TO AVERAGE TOTAL LN&LS	7.29	0.83	98	0.34	0.58	32	0.21	0.49	16	1.22	0.50	0.69	0.52
EARNINGS COVERAGE OF NET LOSS(X)	0.35	5.51	8	10.10	8.36	70	14.89	11.08	80	2.67	10.90	5.57	9.53
LN&LS ALLOWANCE TO NET LOSSES(X)	0.20	2.17	7	3.84	3.26	69	5.81	3.70	82	1.01	4.27	2.61	4.42
CAPITALIZATION													
CASH DIVIDENDS TO NET INCOME	−97.00	61.66	7	104.71	84.86	73	135.80	76.50	76	73.54	70.45	92.44	71.99
RETAIN EARNS TO AVG TOT EQUITY	−39.00	−0.30	5	−1.05	0.92	35	−6.95	2.02	25	4.35	3.43	1.80	2.12
YIELD ON OR COST OF:													
TOTAL LOANS & LEASES (TE)	6.58	6.79	37	7.47	8.90	5	7.75	8.25	22	8.04	8.97	12.04	8.97
LOANS IN DOMESTIC OFFICES	6.53	6.68	34	7.43	8.93	5	7.72	8.29	22	8.01	8.97	12.05	8.99
REAL ESTATE	6.86	6.91	42	6.04	8.77	1	7.36	8.45	7	7.62	8.63	14.49	8.93
COMMERCIAL & INDUSTRIAL	6.56	6.40	58	8.57	9.51	14	8.73	8.66	64	7.78	9.05	9.49	8.72
INDIVIDUAL	6.44	7.81	30	11.13	10.25	66	8.22	9.65	25	11.42	11.64	12.92	11.23
CREDIT CARD PLANS	0.00	4.71	57	NA	0.00	98	NA	0.00	98	NA	0.00	NA	0.00
AGRICULTURAL	6.31	5.49	52	11.10	8.38	87	8.67	7.78	58	6.40	8.28	36.84	9.86
LOANS IN FOREIGN OFFICES	0.14	12.16	78	0.22	1.53	76	0.40	0.50	77	0.30	1.18	4.83	7.81
TOTAL INVESTMENT SECURITIES(TE)	4.87	6.06	18	0.53	6.90	2	5.88	6.53	16	5.50	7.19	9.61	6.97
TOTAL INVESTMENT SECURITIES(BOOK)	4.87	5.92	21	0.52	6.74	2	5.86	6.36	23	5.46	6.97	9.42	6.82
U S TREAS & AGENCY (EXCL MBS)	2.73	4.79	17	NA	0.00	98	NA	0.00	98	NA	0.00	NA	0.00
MORTGAGE BACKED SECURITIES	5.73	6.21	20	NA	0.00	98	NA	0.00	98	NA	0.00	NA	0.00
ALL OTHER SECURITIES	3.24	5.73	11	NA	0.00	98	NA	0.00	98	NA	0.00	NA	0.00
INTEREST-BEARING BANK BALANCES	3.01	4.14	52	6.19	7.38	43	6.29	5.79	72	5.10	6.63	11.77	6.05
FEDERAL FUNDS SOLD & RESALES	2.02	2.25	22	6.54	6.67	26	5.46	5.65	47	4.95	5.75	−4.56	5.66
TOTAL INT-BEARING DEPOSITS	2.28	2.51	37	4.85	4.71	61	3.66	3.92	30	3.76	4.53	6.40	4.49
TRANSACTION ACCOUNTS	1.64	1.43	67	3.35	2.67	67	2.42	2.09	63	2.80	2.61	4.20	2.41
OTHER SAVINGS DEPOSITS	1.37	1.46	50	1.64	2.10	39	1.54	2.09	30	1.76	2.54	2.57	2.50
TIME DEPS OVER $100M	4.68	4.21	71	7.82	6.34	92	5.33	5.32	50	4.95	5.89	13.90	5.78
ALL OTHER TIME DEPOSITS	4.29	4.50	44	6.57	6.20	76	5.12	5.22	57	5.56	6.06	8.17	5.96
DEPOSITS IN FOREIGN OFFICES	2.04	1.56	44	6.61	4.80	78	5.32	4.12	69	4.98	4.33	6.41	4.79
FEDERAL FUNDS PURCHASED & REPOS	1.94	2.26	34	14.47	6.42	97	5.02	5.41	20	4.58	5.22	8.88	5.73
OTHER BORROWED MONEY	2.64	4.52	18	−8.25	6.49	1	5.84	7.08	61	5.68	6.56	6.97	5.94
SUBORD NOTES & DEBENTURES	5.92	3.78	67	7.69	5.85	77	7.04	5.31	76	6.91	5.03	9.49	6.01
ALL INTEREST-BEARING FUNDS	2.41	2.73	28	3.27	5.22	1	4.35	4.45	48	4.41	4.83	6.71	4.84

4

ALTERNATIVE MODELS OF BANK PERFORMANCE

Which bank is larger? In 2001, Washington Mutual's year-end assets exceeded those at Fleet Boston Financial's by 17.4 percent, but Fleet Boston Financial's operating revenue (net interest income plus noninterest income) exceeded that at Washington Mutual by 33.8 percent. The answer depends on what metrics you choose to measure size. As demonstrated in Chapter 3, traditional models of bank performance emphasize return on assets (ROA) and the analysis process consists of comparing asset-based ratios over time and versus peer institutions. In this context, Washington Mutual is larger than Fleet. How then does Fleet generate more operating revenue? The answer lies in what each company does that is not measured by balance sheet accounting.

This chapter offers a critique of traditional Generally Accepted Accounting Principles (GAAP)-based performance measures used by banks. It demonstrates their limitations and describes alternative methods of analyzing performance. It introduces three different approaches to assessing performance that bank managers can use to enhance stockholder value: segment/line of business profitability analysis, economic value added (EVA), and the balanced scorecard.[1] Each offers a different perspective in measuring how well banks have done historically and in signaling where strategic efforts should be directed going forward. The chapter also describes the application of value-at-risk to the entire bank as a risk management tool.

---

[1]EVA represents economic value added and is a trademark of Stern, Stewart & Co. Other consulting firms have similar names for the equivalent concept. *The Balanced Scorecard* is the name of a book and concept introduced by Robert Kaplan and David Norton.

A CRITIQUE OF TRADITIONAL GAAP-BASED PERFORMANCE MEASURES[2]

Traditional bank performance analysis carries three basic flaws. First, it ignores the wide diversity in strategies pursued by different institutions. When Uniform Bank Performance Reports (UBPRs) were originally introduced, most banks did similar things, which were reflected in their balance sheet. They accepted deposits and made loans, and many interest rates were regulated. The primary differentiation of performance was balance sheet composition. Today, banks may pursue sharply different strategies. While some emphasize traditional deposit-gathering and lending, others offer services such as trusts, mortgage-banking, insurance, brokerage, and asset management. This is particularly true of bank holding companies that can operate subsidiaries across a wide range of businesses. At a minimum, peer comparisons should be made across firms with similar strategies. Second, a bank's total assets no longer serve as a meaningful yardstick when banks engage in off-balance sheet activities. This is the situation with Washington Mutual and Fleet Boston Financial, discussed previously. Consider the situation where two banks report the same asset size, but one also has an extensive mortgage-servicing operation that generates servicing income. If the bank with mortgage-servicing makes a profit on this activity, it will report a higher ROA, ceteris paribus. Thus, ROA should not be used to compare the two banks' performances. Finally, the analysis provides no direct information concerning how or which of the bank's activities contribute to the creation of shareholder value. It similarly ignores other performance benchmarks that customer-focused managers must consider to identify the best strategies going forward.

Although it is easy to recognize how ROA might be a biased indicator of performance, it should be noted that return on equity (ROE) doesn't suffer from the same weaknesses. When considering the entire bank, stockholders' equity must support all activities, whether on- or off-balance sheet. Thus, a comparison of net income to equity captures the returns to owners' contributions. In later sections, we describe efforts to calculate a return on allocated equity for specific lines of business within a bank or for individual products and services.

THE APPROPRIATE PEER GROUP

As long as banks have a similar strategic focus and offer similar products and services, asset size and UBPR ratios can provide meaningful comparisons. This is particularly true for smaller community banks that, even though they may be part of a one-bank holding company, limit their activities to well-defined products and services offered within a relatively small trade area. To identify the appropriate peer institutions, management should consider the following:

1. What is the bank's strategic focus?
2. What are the traditional balance sheet and off-balance sheet characteristics of firms with this focus?
3. How do the bank's activities affect its operating revenue?

Senior management must identify specific institutions that compete in similar trade areas and follow the same basic strategies. UBPR ratio comparisons will then identify important differences in performance.

---

[2]The following discussion is based partly on conversations with Mike Morrow of Morrow Consulting and David Cates of Cates Consulting.

Suppose that a community bank engages in traditional deposit-gathering and lending with little off-balance sheet activity, except for offering loan commitments. A common starting point is to determine whether the bank's strategy is more loan-driven or deposit-driven. Consider the differences. A *loan-driven bank* typically finds that asset size is determined by loan demand. Profitability is determined by loan economics, specifically by loan yields versus the cost of funds to finance loans. Because loans are relatively high risk compared with investment securities, the (before provisions) net interest margin is typically high. If loan demand determines size, banks will fund loan growth at the margin via noncore liabilities, such as federal funds, jumbo CDs, and FHLB advances. Noninterest expense will likewise be higher because the cost of making and administering loans is expensive, particularly because loan officers are among the highest paid employees of community banks. The culture at loan-driven banks often reflects the belief that "Our bank underwrites loans better than other banks." Not surprisingly, these banks are at risk that asset-quality problems will undermine performance. Earnings growth is derived from ever increasing loan volume at high margins that must cover the high noninterest cost of being in the business. Analysts who evaluate these banks assess franchise value at some multiple of core earnings.

A *deposit-driven bank* typically finds that asset size is determined by the availability and growth of core funding. The value of the bank is determined by its franchise value measured by the market share of low-cost core deposits. Profitability is determined by the bank's ability to control costs and generate noninterest income. Because deposit-driven banks own proportionately fewer loans and more securities, interest income and (before provisions) net interest margins are lower than those for loan-driven banks. Fortunately, the burden (noninterest expense minus noninterest income) is also lower. Deposit-driven banks generally experience lower volatility in provisions for loan losses. However, one large charge-off can dramatically lower profits. Earnings growth is derived from growing core deposits and the greatest risk is that management will take excessive risk in the securities portfolio to try and increase net interest margin.

When evaluating performance using GAAP-based data and UBPR ratios, a bank should compare its ratios with those from a select sample of peer institutions that are similarly loan-driven or deposit-driven. Peers should operate the same approximate number of offices in the same metropolitan or nonmetropolitan markets and have the same product and service mix. Asset-based ratios are thus directly comparable. Analysts can easily construct peer bank averages via the FDIC's web site under the Quarterly Banking Profile using specific peer institutions that they identify. (www.fdic.gov)

MEASURES BASED ON TOTAL OPERATING REVENUE

David Cates (1996) suggests that one way to circumvent the on- versus off-balance sheet comparison problem is to calculate performance measures using total operating revenue as the denominator rather than assets. Here, total operating revenue equals the sum of net interest income and noninterest income.[3] This presumably makes comparisons meaningful because both on- and off-balance sheet activities generate revenues and expenses. The **efficiency ratio,** measured as noninterest expense divided by total operating revenue, is a case in point. Analysts strongly encourage banks, regardless of size, to meet fairly specific targets in this ratio. Because operating revenue includes both interest income and noninterest (fee-based) income, it captures all activities.

---

[3]Nonrecurring revenues and expenses, such as those associated with securities gains/losses and restructuring charges, should be excluded from operating revenue.

STOCK MARKET-BASED PERFORMANCE MEASURES

Investors in bank stocks are primarily concerned with whether the bank's management is creating value for stockholders. When they compare performance over some historical period, they are less concerned with ROE, ROA, and efficiency ratios than they are with the overall total return from investing in the bank's stock. This total return equals dividends received plus stock price appreciation/depreciation relative to the initial investment. The following measure of return to stockholders indicates how well the investment in bank stock did over some period.

$$\text{Return to Stockholders} = \frac{[\text{Price}_t - \text{Price}_{t-1} + \text{Dividends}]}{\text{Price}_{t-1}} \tag{4.1}$$

where Price_t = stock price at the end of the period,

Price_{t-1} = stock price at the beginning of the period, and

Dividends = cash dividends paid plus reinvestment income during the period.

For example, suppose that you bought 100 shares of stock in PNC Financial at the beginning of 2001 for $73.06 per share. During 2001, the bank paid $1.92 per share in cash dividends that generated reinvestment income of $.09 per share. At the end of 2001, the price of a share of stock was $56.20. The return to stockholders in 2001 was thus −20.3 percent.

$$\text{Return to PNC Stockholders} = \frac{[\$56.20 - \$73.06 + \$2.01]}{\$73.06} = -0.203$$

The aggregate return for the entire bank over some period can be measured via economic value added (EVA). This measure is described in a later section.

Bank stock analysts follow a standard procedure when evaluating firm performance. They initially use GAAP-based financial information to calculate performance measures. They then adjust the data to omit the impact of nonrecurring items, such as one-time asset sales and restructuring charges. They compare these historical ratios with a carefully selected group of peer institutions, matching each bank's primary strategic focus. Based on his or her own analysis and conversations with specialists within the bank, the analyst then assesses the quality of earnings based on their sustainability, the bank's market power in specific product or service areas, and the bank's franchise value. The next step is to forecast earnings, cash flow, and market value of equity over a three- to five-year time horizon. Finally, the analyst makes a stock recommendation: accumulate (buy), neutral (hold), or below-market performance (sell). It is extremely rare, however, to see an outright sell recommendation because analysts want to remain in the good graces of the banks that they follow. Thus, they do not formally recommend selling the stock, but rather label it as likely to exhibit below-market performance. A hold recommendation thus actually means "sell the stock" for most analysts.

The consideration of stock market-based performance creates a series of additional ratios that are useful to investors and analysts. Measures that are commonly cited and included in performance evaluations are:

Earnings Per Share (EPS) =

$$\frac{\text{net income after taxes and dividends paid on preferred stock}}{\text{number of shares of common stock outstanding}}$$

$$\text{Price to Earnings (P/E Ratio)} = \frac{\text{stock price}}{\text{EPS}}$$

$$\text{Price to Book Value} = \frac{\text{stock price}}{\text{book value of equity per share}}$$

$$\text{Market Value of Equity} = \text{market value of assets} - \text{market value of liabilities; or}$$
$$\text{stock price} \times \text{number of common shares outstanding}$$

These ratios are subject to a different set of criticisms. For example, what is the appropriate measure of earnings? Should it be trailing earnings over the past 12 months, an average of earnings over the past 3 years, or projected earnings over the subsequent 12 months since we are most concerned about future earnings growth? Should earnings include extraordinary items? Furthermore, in order to estimate the number of common stock shares outstanding, each analyst must estimate how many stock options will be converted to shares, how much stock the firm will buy back, the release of new stock issues, and whether convertible bonds will be converted into stock. Estimates reflecting "fully diluted" earnings incorporate assumptions about these transactions. Thus, you will see different EPS and P/E figures for the same firm at the same point in time.

There is further concern over how the analysis process works and the impact of Internet trading in stocks and available information. The commentary in Contemporary Issues: Whisper Earnings Are Important suggests that formal analysts' earnings forecasts may not be the primary determinant of some stock price moves.

Although price to book value and market value of equity are measurable, they are typically not all that meaningful except for comparing value over time. Book value of equity may ignore the value of many off-balance sheet activities and the market value of certain on-balance sheet items. Both measures ignore a firm's franchise value, goodwill, and going concern value.

CUSTOMER-FOCUSED PERFORMANCE MEASURES

Since Kaplan and Norton (1992) introduced the concept of the balanced scorecard, many banks have recognized the importance of developing performance measures that look beyond just financial measures. The theme of the balanced scorecard is that management decisions based on financial measures must be balanced with decisions based on a firm's relationships with its customers and the effectiveness of support processes in designing and delivering products and services. The result is that line of business managers use indicators such as market share, customer retention and attrition, customer profitability, and service quality to evaluate performance. Internally, they also track productivity and employee satisfaction. Such nonfinancial indicators provide information regarding whether a bank is truly customer-focused and whether its systems are appropriate.

Cates suggests that management can start to address these concerns by dividing the bank into a Customer Bank and a House Bank. This is done by distinguishing between balance sheet and income statement items that are derived from bank customers—the Customer Bank—and items that arise when the bank is its own customer—the House Bank. Customer Bank activities include loans, core deposits, payment services, credit enhancements, asset management, and financial advisory services. Activities associated with the House Bank typically include risk management, the investment portfolio, loan participations, asset sales, servicing, large noncore liabilities, and bank-sponsored mutual funds.

In doing this, managers can assess what specific revenues and expenses are attributable to each segment. They can further allocate operating expenses to activities that support bank customers and to activities that support the bank. As such, management can obtain at least a rough estimate of segment net income. It also leads to the reporting and use of both financial and nonfinancial performance data, based on specific customers. Today, many banks attempt to measure profitability by type of loan customer (small business, middle market, consumer installment, etc.); by type of depositor; by characteristics of the relationship (account longevity, cross-sell patterns, profitability, etc.); and by delivery system (branch, ATM, telephone, home banking, etc.).

CONTEMPORARY ISSUES

WHISPER EARNINGS ARE IMPORTANT

Firms with publicly traded stock are often criticized for having too short a focus because managers are concerned about short-term earnings. The motivation is that stock analysts make recommendations based on reported and expected earnings, and a firm does not want to adversely surprise the analysts. The formal process consists of analysts "following" a specific stock or industry. Bank stock analysts might specialize in firms with global versus regional orientations. An analyst collects information on each bank that he or she follows and periodically forecasts earnings. This leads to recommendations as to whether to buy, hold, or sell the stock. The information comes from external sources, such as the periodic call and income data provided by each bank and bank holding company, periodic filings before the SEC, and from internal information obtained from bank employees. These internal sources meet either formally with analysts or informally via telephone conversations. Groups such as First Call, Zachs, and IBES collect forecasts

from the analysts who follow each bank, and report the consensus forecast (average) of earnings.

Not surprisingly, time typically elapses between when an analyst makes the original earnings forecast and when the bank formally announces its earnings. Most large firms announce quarterly earnings. Hence the concern about too short a focus on management's decision-making. The issue is "What do the analysts do with any new information they uncover after their initial forecast, but before the firm's formal announcement?" Frequently, analysts share these revised earnings forecasts only with preferred customers. On occasion they publicize them.

The term "whisper earnings" has been coined to refer to any unofficial earnings estimates, whether from an analyst or any other interested party. With the advent of the Internet and stock trading via the Internet, such whisper earnings are routinely shared among participants in online chat rooms that focus on large firms' performance. A study by Bagnoli

(1998) examined the accuracy of whisper earnings forecasts compared with published analysts' forecasts on 127 companies between 1995 and 1997. It concluded that, on average, the whisper earnings forecasts were more accurate. This is highly revealing given that many whisper earnings forecasts are quite extreme, while analysts' forecasts generally cluster around similar values because they use similar information and techniques. The implication is that an investor should try to discern the whisper earnings forecast before buying or selling stock. Summary information on whisper earnings is available on the Internet at http://www.whispernumber.com, http://www.earnings whispers.com, and http://www.investoroutlook. com for large or well-known firms one month prior to the release of actual quarterly earnings. Of course, it requires some effort to verify that the whisper earnings figures are believable.

This effort demonstrates the value of information pertaining to customer satisfaction, market share, service quality, and productivity. Certainly, banks should generate and use this information internally to help guide strategic decisions. It seems appropriate that they also provide this information to the investing public to provide a better understanding of long-term growth and earnings prospects.

LINE OF BUSINESS PROFITABILITY ANALYSIS

As the mergers between Citicorp and Travelers into Citigroup and Credit Suisse and First Boston into CSFB indicate, large banking organizations are becoming increasingly complex institutions that offer a wide range of products and services across many different lines of business. These large organizations are often organized around and managed as lines of business, which necessitates a reporting system that allows senior management to assess line of business profitability and risk. This is extremely difficult because different business units share some of the same customers and delivery systems. With regard to risk, there is no certain way to measure risk for a single line of business or bankwide, given these inter-relationships. Still, even small banks that compete in traditional loan and deposit markets can benefit from line of business profitability analysis because it helps identify where the bank's earnings come from and how risky each type of business is.

RAROC/RORAC Analysis

In order to analyze profitability and risk precisely, each line of business must have its own balance sheet and income statement. These statements are difficult to construct because many nontraditional activities, such as trust and mortgage-servicing, do not explicitly require any direct equity support. Even traditional activities, such as commercial lending and consumer banking, complicate the issue because these business units do not have equal amounts of assets and liabilities generated by customers. Furthermore, the critical issue is to determine how much equity capital to assign each unit. This is not a simple task as Kimball (1997) points out. Alternative capital allocation methods include using regulatory risk-based capital standards; assignment based on the size of assets; benchmarking each unit to "pure-play" peers that are stand-alone, publicly held firms; and measures of each line of business's riskiness.

Today, many large banks evaluate line of business profitability and risk via RAROC or RORAC systems. RAROC refers to risk-adjusted return on capital, while RORAC refers to return on risk-adjusted capital. The terms are often used interchangeably, but are formally defined as follows:

$$RAROC = \frac{\text{risk-adjusted income}}{\text{capital}} \tag{4.2}$$

$$RORAC = \frac{\text{income}}{\text{allocated risk capital}} \tag{4.3}$$

What constitutes risk-adjusted income and allocated risk capital may vary across users, but the concept is to identify some measure of return generated by a line of business and compare that return to the allocated capital. The income or return measure may be adjusted for risk (RAROC), which typically means that expected losses are subtracted from revenues along with other expenses. Alternatively, the capital measure may be adjusted for risk (RORAC), which typically means that it represents a maximum potential loss based on the probability of future returns or an amount necessary to cover loss associated with the volatility of earnings. In addition, some banks subtract a charge for capital from the return measure to estimate "economic returns."

Consider the data in Exhibit 4.1 regarding PNC's line of business profitability analysis for 2000 and 2001 that was published in the firm's 2001 annual report. PNC reported results for seven distinct lines of business. Section A of the exhibit presents summary information for each line's earnings, revenue, average assets, and return on assigned capital. Sections B and C of the exhibit list balance sheet and income statement data for two of the lines, Corporate Banking and Community Banking. The data were obtained from PNC's management accounting system based on internal assumptions about revenue and expense allocations and assignment of equity to each line of business.

Corporate Banking represents products and services provided nationally in the areas of credit, equipment leasing, treasury management, and capital markets products to large and mid-sized corporations and government entities. Given the nature of these activities, PNC identified more assets than liabilities attributable directly to the line of business. Thus, in 2001 management assigned $10.705 billion of funds and other liabilities and $1.251 billion of capital to the line so that the constructed balance sheet balanced. This capital is assigned by

· EXHIBIT 4.1

A. Financial Results for PNC by Line of Business

Year ended December 31 Dollars in millions	Earnings (Net Loss)		Revenue (a)		Return on Assigned Capital		Average Assets	
	2001	2000	2001	2000	2001	2000	2001	2000
Banking Businesses								
Regional Community Banking	$596	$590	$2,231	$2,033	22%	22%	$40,285	$38,958
Corporate Banking	(375)	241	764	844	(30)	18	16,685	17,746
PNC Real Estate Finance	38	84	213	229	10	21	5,290	5,889
PNC Business Credit	22	49	134	119	13	32	2,463	2,271
Total banking business	281	964	3,342	3,225	6	21	64,723	64,864
Asset Management and Processing								
PNC Advisors	143	173	735	792	26	32	3,330	3,500
BlackRock	107	87	533	477	25	27	684	537
PFPC	36	47	738	674	17	22	1,771	1,578
Total asset management and processing	286	307	2,006	1,943	24	28	5,785	5,615
Total business results	567	1,271	5,348	5,168	10	23	70,508	70,479
Other	(190)	(57)	(527)	(95)			(153)	(1,988)
Results from continuing operations	377	1,214	4,821	5,073	6	21	70,355	68,491
Discontinued operations	5	65					51	487
Results before cumulative effect of accounting change	382	1,279	4,821	5,073	6	22	70,406	68,978
Cumulative effect of accounting change	(5)							
Total consolidated - as reported	$377	$1,279	$4,821	$5,073	6	22	$70,406	$68,978

(a) Business revenues are presented on a taxable-equivalent basis except for BlackRock and PFPC.

benchmarking. Specifically, management assessed the riskiness and level of stockholders' equity at separate, stand-alone companies that offered similar products and services as PNC does in its Corporate Banking division, and assigned capital in the same proportion.

Data for Community Banking reveal the same process, but a different assignment to make the balance sheet balance. This line of business encompasses the bank's traditional deposit, branch-based brokerage, electronic banking and credit products to retail customers along with products to small businesses such that it is primarily a deposit-generating unit. Thus, PNC assigned $7.306 billion in assets in 2001 and $2.718 billion in capital where these

B. Corporate Banking

Year ended December 31
Taxable equivalent basis

Dollars in millions	2001	2000
Income Statement		
Credit-related revenue	$408	$411
Noncredit revenue	356	433
Total revenue	764	844
Provision for credit losses	57	79
Noninterest expense	381	394
Institutional lending repositioning	891	
Asset impairment and severance costs	16	
Pretax (loss) earnings	(581)	371
Income tax (benefit) expense	(206)	130
(Net loss) earnings	$(375)	$241
Average Balance Sheet		
Loans		
Middle market	$5,811	$6,553
Large corporate	3,103	3,193
Energy, metals, and mining	1,233	1,507
Communications	1,110	1,501
Leasing	2,322	1,844
Other	328	357
Total loans	13,907	14,955
Loans held for sale	367	800
Other assets	2,411	1,991
Total assets	$16,685	$17,746
Deposits	$4,729	$4,701
Assigned funds and other liabilities	10,705	11,714
Assigned capital	1,251	1,331
Total funds	$16,685	$17,746
Performance Ratios		
Return on assigned capital	(30)%	48%
Noncredit revenue to total revenue	64	51
Efficiency	71	46

C. Regional Community Banking

Year ended December 31
Taxable equivalent basis

Dollars in millions	2001	2000
Income Statement		
Net interest income	$1,466	$1,414
Other noninterest income	679	608
Net securities gains	86	11
Total revenue	2,231	2,033
Provision for credit losses	50	45
Noninterest expense	1,099	1,071
Vehicle leasing	135	
Asset impairment and severance costs	13	
Pretax earnings	934	917
Income taxes	338	327
Earnings	$596	$590
Average Balance Sheet		
Loans		
Consumer		
Home equity	$6,293	$5,419
Indirect automobile	814	1,215
Other consumer	835	897
Total consumer	7,942	7,531
Residential mortgage	7,912	11,619
Commercial	3,557	3,649
Vehicle leasing	1,901	1,322
Other	133	144
Total loans	21,445	24,265
Securities available for sale	10,241	5,539
Loans held for sale	1,293	1,297
Assigned assets and other assets	7,306	7,857
Total assets	$40,285	$38,958
Deposits		
Noninterest-bearing demand	$4,571	$4,548
Interest-bearing demand	5,713	5,428
Money market	12,162	10,253
Total transaction deposits	22,446	20,229
Savings	1,870	1,992
Certificates	11,906	13,745
Total deposits	36,222	35,966
Other liabilities	1,345	363
Assigned capital	2,718	2,629
Total funds	$40,285	$38,958
Performance Ratios		
Return on assigned capital	22%	22%
Noninterest income to total revenue	34	30
Efficiency	54	51

amounts were again determined by benchmarking to independent entities that offer similar services. In 2001, Community Banking contributed $596 million to PNC's earnings, the most of any line, and earned 22 percent on assigned capital. Corporate Banking reported a loss of $375 million, or −30 percent on assigned capital. These return measures are PNC's estimates of RAROC/RORAC and appear in section A of the exhibit in the fifth column of data for all lines of business. Note that PNC Advisors and BlackRock generated the highest returns in 2001, while PNC Business Credit and BlackRock reported the highest returns in 2000. PNC Business Credit deals with middle market customers, PNC Advisors deals with affluent customers, Black Rock is a publicly-traded investment management firm with over $200 billion in assets under management. This is extremely useful information in helping management decide where to allocate resources going forward. It also helps investors in PNC stock understand where the bank's earnings come from and why management pursues activities in certain lines of business. Even if the asset, liability, and capital assignments are not precisely correct, the results provide extremely useful information about trends in profitability and relative performance rankings.

FUNDS TRANSFER PRICING

When management creates a balance sheet and income statement for each line of business, it must allocate capital and either assets or liabilities to make the balance sheet balance. It must then assign a cost or yield to each of these components. The process of generating an income statement requires a comprehensive cost accounting system that allocates overhead as well as direct expenses and revenues. A particular problem, however, is to assign interest income and expense given that management assigns a pool of either assets or liabilities as a balancing item. *Internal funds transfer pricing* is generally used to make these assignments. The term *transfer price* refers to the interest rate at which a firm could buy or sell funds in the external capital markets. Although many banks initially used a pooled funds approach to assign interest rates, most now use a matched-maturity system.

Essentially, management is decomposing a bank's net interest margin so it can attribute net interest income to each line of business. When analyzing profits and risk, however, management does not want each line of business to make decisions about how much interest rate risk is appropriate and whether the bank should hedge or speculate on rate movements. A matched-maturity transfer pricing system eliminates interest rate risk issues for all but the line of business responsible for managing overall bank interest rate risk. An example will demonstrate the concept.

Consider the situation where a bank makes a $1 million 2-year fixed-rate commercial loan at 8.5 percent. It obtains the funds by issuing a $1 million 3-month time deposit at 4.5 percent. This is characterized at the top of Exhibit 4.2. Initially, the net interest margin is 4 percent. When viewed together, this bank has assumed two specific risks in this transaction. First, the position is liability sensitive because net interest income will fall if rates rise over the two years, ceteris paribus. Second, the loan has prepayment risk because the borrower, at its option, can refinance before maturity. Assume that the bank has three lines of business: a lending division, deposit-gathering division, and Treasury division. The remainder of Exhibit 4.2 demonstrates how the 4 percent net interest margin is divided among these divisions and who is responsible for interest rate risk and prepayment risk.

At the time of this transaction, rates in the external money and capital markets for 3-month and 2-year securities equal 5.2 percent and 6 percent, respectively. These rates might be those on a 3-month jumbo CD traded *on-the-run* and a 2-year CD.[4] When constructing the lending division's balance sheet, the bank wants the unit to take only business risk, not interest rate risk. Thus, management assigns a 2-year maturity funding from the Treasury division to lending at a cost of 6 percent, the rate it would have to pay if the bank bought 2-year funds in the capital market. Thus, the lending division's net interest margin is 2.5 percent. With the matched-maturity funding, lending takes no interest rate risk. The lending division, however, has sold an option to its loan customer who can prepay the loan. The internal transfer

---

[4]On-the-run issue is considered to be the most actively traded issue, typically those sold at the most recent auction.

• EXHIBIT 4.2

EXAMPLE OF INTERNAL FUNDS TRANSFER PRICING: 2-YEAR LOAN FINANCED BY A 3-MONTH DEPOSIT

Bank

Asset	Liability
Loan: 2 year $1,000,000 @8.50%	Time deposit: 3 month $1,000,000 @4.50%

Margin = 4.00%

Interest Rate Risk: Liability sensitive
Embedded Option: Prepayment risk on loan

Lending Division

Asset	Liability
Loan: 2 year $1,000,000 @8.50%	Transfer from Treasury: 2 year $1,000,000 @6.00%

Margin = 2.50%

Interest Rate Risk: None
Option: Sold prepayment option to loan customer on balance sheet; buy an option from Treasury for 0.20%.
NIM after option cost = 2.50% − 0.20% = 2.30%

Deposit-Gathering Division

Asset	Liability
Receivable from Treasury: 3-month $1,000,000 @5.20%	Time deposit: 3-month $1,000,000 @4.50%

Margin = 0.70%

Interest Rate Risk: None
Option: None

Treasury Division

Asset	Liability
Receivable from Lending: 2-year $1,000,000 @6.00%	Transfer to Deposit-Gathering: 3-month $1,000,000 @5.20%

Margin = 0.80%

Interest Rate Risk: Liability sensitive
Option: Sell option to lending division for 0.20%;
NIM after option sale = 0.80% + 0.20% = 1.00%.
Treasury has interest rate and loan prepayment risk.

pricing system should then charge the lending division the cost of buying a similar option in the external markets. Suppose this option's cost equals 20 basis points in the option's market. As noted in Exhibit 4.2, lending's net interest margin after the option cost is 2.3 percent.

Because the deposit-gathering division obtains 3-month deposits, Treasury assigns it a 3-month receivable at the prevailing money market rate of 5.2 percent, or what the unit could earn if it sold the funds externally. This matched-maturity assignment again eliminates interest rate risk for the deposit-gathering division and produces a 0.70 percent net interest margin. The Treasury's profile is summarized at the bottom of Exhibit 4.2. As described earlier, it effectively borrows from the deposit-gathering division at 5.2 percent and lends to the lending division at 6 percent, producing a net interest margin of 0.80 percent. Of course, it has mismatched the maturities of its liability and asset, so it has assumed interest rate risk. Treasury also sold a prepayment option to lending for 0.20 percent, so it has assumed the risk that the loan customer will prepay. Its net interest margin plus the option premium produce an expected return of 1 percent.

The net result of this analysis is that the initial 4 percent net interest margin has been divided among the three divisions by allocating funds on a matched-maturity basis. Lending has a pretax return of 2.3 percent, deposit-gathering 0.7 percent, and Treasury 1 percent. Only Treasury assumes interest rate risk and prepayment risk. Treasury can choose either to hedge these risks or assume the risks as part of its business strategy. Thus, interest rate changes only affect Treasury. The lending and deposit-gathering divisions can focus on other risks.[5]

RISK-ADJUSTED INCOME AND ECONOMIC INCOME

When calculating the income or return estimate in line of business profitability analysis, two adjustments are frequently made. First, the return is adjusted for risk by subtracting expected losses. This is often quite substantial for lending units. Note that with PNC's Corporate Banking in Exhibit 4.1, there was a charge for $57 million in provisions for credit losses before earnings for 2001. The line of business reported a loss for the year because it incurred non-recurring charges for institutional loan repositioning and severance costs from closing operations. Second, management is typically concerned with whether earnings exceed the firm's required return on capital. This minimum required return, or cost of equity, represents a hurdle rate, or stockholders' minimum required rate of return. The specific concern is whether RAROC is greater than the firm's cost of equity.[6] In order to evaluate whether any line of business adds value to stockholders, the return estimate must be calculated net of the required return to stockholders. In this context, the numerator in the RAROC/RORAC calculations should equal economic income (economic profit) equal to earnings after tax minus the charge for equity capital assigned to the business unit. Finally, it is important to recognize that managers find it difficult to accurately assign some revenues and costs across different lines of business. Consider overhead costs, litigation costs, or Y2K preparation expenses. Similarly, when different lines share customers, it is difficult to assess how much revenue or expense goes to each line. The key is to be consistent over time, which enables meaningful comparisons.

---

[5]Both the lending and deposit-gathering divisions potentially assume basis risk, or the risk that the spread between the transfer price and the actual loan yield and deposit cost, respectively, will vary over time. Basis risk arises when the transfer prices are based on different rates than those used to price loans or deposits to bank customers.

[6]Zaik, Walter, Kelling, and James (1996) discuss key issues related to reconciling RAROC with the capital asset pricing model and measures of the cost of equity. They note that Bank of America used the same corporatewide cost of equity to evaluate the economic profit for each line of business and not a different rate to reflect different amounts of risk. Presumably, this is appropriate because Bank of America was involved in many different lines of business and was internally diversified.

ALLOCATED RISK CAPITAL

The objective of RAROC analysis is to assist in risk management and the evaluation of line of business performance. As part of this, it is necessary to assign capital to each line of business. Having done so, the amount of assigned capital should equal the total capital for the firm. This latter requirement forces senior management to recognize the diversification aspects of each line of business.

At the beginning of this section, four procedures were mentioned to assign capital:

1. Regulatory risk-based capital standards

2. Asset size

3. Benchmarking versus "pure-play" stand-alone businesses

4. Perceived riskiness of the business unit

Kimball (1997) describes weaknesses in the first three, although many banks use each of these. The following discussion briefly explains alternative ways of measuring the riskiness of a line of business. Zaik, Walters, Kelling, and James (1996) provide the rationale for trying to measure the volatility of a business unit's market value of capital and use this to assign risk capital. Theoretically, they argue that the appropriate measure for Bank of America was the volatility in the market value of common stock. Alternatives, such as the volatility of book capital or volatility of earnings, can be criticized because book value provides no information useful to the rating agencies or capital market participants and earnings can be manipulated. Unfortunately, most lines of business do not have market value balance sheets and it is difficult to assess how much each line contributes to the overall volatility of the entire bank's market value. Practically, many banks thus focus on the volatility in economic earnings, labeled earnings-at-risk, or they estimate a value-at-risk figure.

EARNINGS-AT-RISK. Consider the case of a large bank that offers securities underwriting and letters of credit (guarantees) against customer exposures. Neither of these activities requires much capital to support day-to-day operations. Before a bank can actively engage in this business, however, it must have a strong credit and bond rating, which requires a substantial amount of risk capital. One way to measure the required risk capital is to relate it to the volatility of earnings from this line of business. This analysis is commonly referred to as *earnings-at-risk* (EAR). For example, the basic steps in the analysis applied to loans might include:

1. Using historical data for each of the past 30 months, estimate revenues obtained directly from these loans.

2. Using historical data for each of the past 30 months, estimate direct expenses from offering these services and expected losses.

3. Using the 30 observations for revenues minus expenses and losses, estimate one standard deviation of earnings. This is earnings-at-risk.

4. Estimate risk capital as one (or two or three) standard deviation(s) of earnings, divided by the risk-free interest rate.

Conceptually, this capitalizes earnings or equals the amount a business would have to invest at the risk-free rate to generate revenue that just covers a pre-determined one, two, or three standard deviations of earnings. A more risk-averse business might allocate risk capital equal to 2 or 3 standard deviations of earnings. The same entity might examine the volatility in earnings over a longer period of time to better assess the potential for adverse changes.

Suppose that the line of business related to securities underwriting and letters of credit generates the past 30 months of earnings listed in Exhibit 4.3. Over this period, the mean value

■ EXHIBIT 4.3

ALLOCATING RISK CAPITAL BASED ON EARNINGS VOLATILITY: SECURITIES
UNDERWRITING AND LETTERS OF CREDIT DIVISION

A. Monthly Revenue Less Expenses (in millions of dollars)
   1. Most Recent 30 Months Observations
      4, 3, 4.5, 5, 5.2, 4.6, 3.9, 4.3, 5, 4.7, 5.1, 5.4, 5, 4.5, 4.4,
      4.8, 5, 5.5, 5.3, 5.1, 5, 5.4, 5.7, 6.3, 6, 5.8, 5.5, 5.9, 5.5, 6.4
   2. Mean: $5.06 million
      Standard Deviation: $0.735 million
B. Allocated Risk Capital
   Assuming a risk-free rate of 5.5% (annual):

$$\left(\frac{.055}{12}\right) \times \text{Risk Capital} = \$0.735 \text{ million}$$

$$\text{Risk Capital} = \$160.364 \text{ million}$$

C. RORAC for the Most Recent Month
   1. Revenue minus expense of $6.4 million

$$\text{RORAC} = \frac{6.4}{160.364} = 0.0399 \text{ monthly, or } 47.89\% \text{ annually}$$

   2. Economic Income
      Assuming a hurdle rate of 12% annually, economic income net of the capital charge:

$$\$6.4 - (.12/12)\,\$160.364 = \$4.796 \text{ million}$$

of earnings equals $5.06 million and one standard deviation of earnings equals $0.735 million. Assuming that the appropriate risk-free interest rate is 5.5 percent, the bank would allocate $160.364 million to this line of business under an earnings-at-risk framework, if it chose to "cover" one standard deviation of earnings. Note that the last period's earnings equal $6.4 million. For this monthly period, RORAC equals 3.99 percent or 47.89 percent annually. Assuming that the hurdle rate, or minimum required return on equity, for this line of business is 12 percent annually, the economic income for this line of business is $4.8 million.

VALUE-AT-RISK. Some firms allocate risk capital on the basis of a value-at-risk (VAR) calculation. As described in the next section, U.S. bank regulation actually requires VAR analysis and capital allocation in support of large banks' trading operations. Conceptually, value-at-risk is an amount that represents the expected maximum loss on a line of business or a portfolio over a set time period, with a given probability.[7] The intent is to summarize in one figure the maximum loss faced by a firm with some reasonable confidence level. It leads to conclusions like "We estimate that there is only a 1 percent chance that this line of business will lose $25 million in value over the next month." Managers can then compare these estimates with overall firm equity to determine whether the firm is adequately protected from the risk of failure. Banks that use this framework often view the value-at-risk as their allocated risk capital for RAROC purposes.[8]

DIVERSIFICATION BENEFITS. When evaluating a firm's different lines of business, it is actually inappropriate to view each as a stand-alone operation. This is because what truly

---

[7]Jorion (1996) examines the strengths and weaknesses of VAR models and their applications.

[8]Banks also use the term *value-at-risk* to refer to the percentage change in the market value of stockholders' equity attributable to changing interest rates. This concept is discussed in Chapter 9.

matters is how much risk the line of business adds to the entire firm. For example, if a line of business generates cash flows (or has a market value) that vary inversely with the firm's other cash flows (aggregate market value), there are diversification benefits to having the line. In fact, if the cash flows are anything but perfectly positively correlated with the firm's other cash flows, there are diversification benefits. A perfectly negative correlation (-1) indicates that a line's cash flows vary exactly in the opposite direction of cash flows from another line of business. The less negative or more positive the correlation, the smaller the diversification benefits. Unfortunately, it is very difficult to accurately measure what the correlations are when different lines of business share customers and expenses. Still, many banks attempt to measure these diversification benefits.

MANAGEMENT OF MARKET RISK

In January 1998, bank regulators imposed capital requirements against the market risk associated with large banks' trading positions. The requirements apply to any U.S. bank or bank holding company that has a trading account in excess of $1 billion or accounts for 10 percent or more of bank assets. Hendricks and Hirtle (1997) reported that at year-end 1996, 17 commercial banks would have been subject to the requirements, and these 17 banks controlled almost 98 percent of all U.S. banks' trading positions.

According to regulatory definition, **market risk** is the risk of loss to earnings and capital related to changes in the market values of bank assets, liabilities, and off-balance sheet positions. Typically, market risk arises from taking positions and dealing in foreign exchange, equity, interest rate, and commodity markets, and the items affected are the securities trading account, derivatives positions, and foreign exchange positions. These new capital requirements address market risk associated with a bank's trading activities.

The benefit of this risk measurement requirement is that it forces management to think about and examine the bank's overall optimal capital structure. It provides information about how much each trading position adds to firm risk and what the likelihood is that a rogue trader or trading activities might lead to bank failure from losses in excess of firm capital. A value-at-risk estimate helps identify a maximum expected loss, which presumably should be well below the bank's actual capital. If not, more restrictive risk controls must be put in place.

Banks subject to these market risk capital requirements must show that management has a risk measurement system that is sound and integrated with the bank's overall risk management process. Specific capital requirements are based on identifying the maximum expected loss over a 10-day period with a 99th percentile confidence standard using a value-at-risk methodology. This means that management expects to lose no more than the value-at-risk amount on 99 out of 100 10-day periods. Estimates of value-at-risk have to be calculated daily, using observations of value changes over the past year. The minimum regulatory capital required in support of this potential loss equals a scaling factor times the most recent 60-day average of value-at-risk estimates.[9] See Chapter 13 for additional details of value-at-risk requirement.

VALUE-AT-RISK ESTIMATE FOR FOREIGN EXCHANGE

Exhibit 4.4 demonstrates one framework to obtain a value-at-risk estimate for a sample bank's foreign exchange trading account. The data in Exhibit 4.4 represent a histogram (frequency distribution) for 252 daily returns from the bank's trading portfolio during

---

[9]Hendricks and Hirtle (1997) note that the scaling factor used equals 3. Also, if the prior day's value-at-risk estimate exceeds the 60-day average times 3, it must be used.

▪ EXHIBIT 4.4

DAILY RETURNS ON A BANK'S FOREIGN EXCHANGE TRADING ACCOUNT

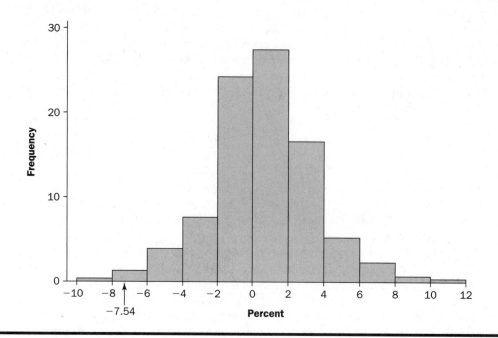

business days in 2001. The basic concept relates to identifying the maximum expected loss given the bank's recent history of daily returns on the trading portfolio. A simple empirical distribution approach to value-at-risk might involve the following. Identify the lowest 1 percent of daily price moves. With 252 trading days in 2001, this amounts to identifying the three lowest price moves (1 percent of 252). Assuming that the value of the third lowest price move is −7.54 percent, 99 percent of the daily returns exceed this figure. If the bank's exposure from its foreign exchange trading positions is $200 million, the daily value-at-risk would equal $15.08 million ($200 million × 0.0754). Conceptually, $15.08 million represents the maximum expected daily loss with a 99 percent confidence level because if past returns characterize future returns, only 1 percent of the price moves will be less than this amount.

Exhibit 4.5 presents data related to value-at-risk estimates for market risk associated with the trading portfolios at Credit Suisse First Boston (CSFB) in 1999 and 2000. Note that these reported value-at-risk estimates are for 1-day VAR values based on a 10-day holding period with a 99 percent confidence level based on data for the prior two years. CSFB continually backtests its VAR estimates by calculating actual 1-day holding period fluctuation. These values appear in the chart and demonstrate no outliers, or excess fluctuation versus the projected VAR during 2000. A separate value-at-risk figure appears for each of four risk classes: interest rate, foreign exchange, equity and commodity risk, and for the total trading portfolio. Importantly, because changes in different interest rates, foreign exchange rates, equity, and commodity prices are less than perfectly positively correlated, there is some diversification benefit from holding a portfolio of these different positions. The second row of data from the bottom characterizes an estimate of the diversification benefit from these correlations. Thus, the total value-at-risk is less than the sum of the independently calculated value-at-risk estimates.

■ EXHIBIT 4.5

MARKET RISK EXPOSURES IN TRADING PORTFOLIOS: CREDIT SUISSE GROUP

A. 99%, one-day VaR; in CHF m (Swiss francs)

Market Risk Exposure Type	Credit Suisse Group* 31 Dec. 2000	Credit Suisse Group* 31 Dec. 1999
Interest rate	235.7	284.5
Foreign exchange	22.7	70.9
Equity	98.5	102.6
Commodity	6.8	4.8
Sub-total	363.7	462.8
Diversification benefit	204.7	257.5
Total	159.0	205.3

*Credit Suisse Group does not manage its trading portfolios on a consolidated basis. The amounts provided in this column represent arithmetic sums of the respective VaR estimates of the business units plus the exposure of the Corporate Center. Management believes that this is a conservative representation of the overall risk since possible diversification benefits between business units are not considered. However, as trading portfolio-related market risks of some 85% of total VaR are concentrated at Credit Suisse First Boston, the overstatement implied by this aggregation method is limited.

B. Backtesting for Credit Suisse First Boston Daily Trading Portfolio VaR

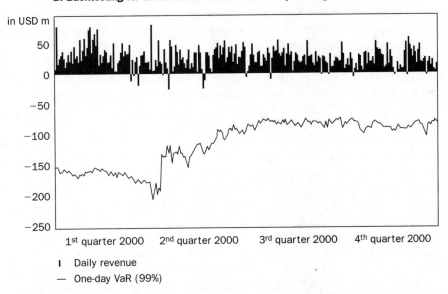

I Daily revenue
— One-day VaR (99%)

ECONOMIC VALUE ADDED

Some analysts criticize traditional earnings measures such as ROE, ROA, and EPS because they provide no information about how a bank's management is adding to shareholder value. If the objective of the firm is to maximize stockholders' wealth, such measures do not indicate whether stockholder wealth has increased over time, let alone whether it has been maximized. Stern, Stewart & Company has introduced the concepts of market value added (MVA) and its associated economic value added (EVA) in an attempt to directly link performance to shareholder wealth creation.[10] MVA follows from Miller and Modigliani's (1961) research, which measured a firm's value as the present value of all future cash flows. This, in turn, equaled the sum of invested capital and the present value of future economic profit. MVA represents the increment to market value and is determined by the present value of current and expected economic profit. Formally,

$$\text{MVA} = \text{Market Value of Capital} - \text{Historic Amount of Invested Capital} \tag{4.4}$$

MVA is difficult to measure in practice because market values can change for reasons not related to operating performance. It is also difficult or impossible to apply MVA to lines of business, which do not have readily available market values or share prices. To apply MVA, it is useful to have a measure of economic profit. Noted management consultant Peter Drucker has said, "What we generally call profits, the money left to service equity, is usually not profits at all. Until a business returns a profit that is greater than the cost of capital, it operates at a loss."[11] Thus, much like the RAROC calculation described earlier, economic profit subtracts a firm's cost of capital from some measure of profit.

Stern, Stewart & Company measures economic profit with EVA, which is equal to a firm's operating profit minus the charge for the cost of capital. Formally,

$$\text{EVA} = \text{Net Operating Profit After Tax (NOPAT)} - \text{Capital Charge} \tag{4.5}$$

where the capital charge equals the product of the firm's value of capital and the associated cost of capital. EVA serves as a better performance measure of whether a firm's operations enhance shareholder value because it recognizes that a firm must earn enough revenue to cover expenses, interest payments on debt, and the required return to stockholders. This required return to stockholders, in turn, should represent a minimum acceptable return to compensate stockholders for the risk of investing in this firm. EVA thus indicates how much value is created in a single period.

There are three basic issues when trying to measure EVA for the entire bank. First, it is often difficult to obtain an accurate measure of a firm's cost of capital. While there are many models to estimate the cost of capital, ranging from the capital asset pricing model (CAPM) to the dividend growth model, these procedures can produce substantially different estimates. Many firms subsequently use a fixed rate for the cost of capital and apply it to all lines of business.[12] The rationale is that this is appropriate if the firm is sufficiently diversified because it offers a wide range of products or services. In addition, the impact of using different costs of capital, even if they could be accurately measured, is small. Second, the amount of bank capital includes stockholders' equity, loan loss reserves, deferred (net) tax credits, nonrecurring items such as restructuring charges and unamortized securities gains. Third, NOPAT should reflect operating profit associated with the current economics of the firm. Thus, traditional GAAP-based accounting data, which distort true profits, must be modified to obtain estimates of economic profit.

When using EVA analysis for a bank, this latter requirement means that pre-tax income must be adjusted for the traditional GAAP-based treatment of loan losses, taxes, securities

---

[10]EVA is a registered trademark of Stern, Stewart & Co.

[11]See Peter Drucker, "The Information Executives Truly Need," *Harvard Business Review*, January–February 1995.

[12]According to Zaik et al. (1997), Bank of America used the same hurdle rate, or cost of capital, for all lines of business. Coca Cola also uses the same rate for all its lines of business.

gains or losses, and nonrecurring items.[13] Specifically, actual net loan charge-offs are subtracted from pre-tax income after adding back loan loss provisions. The argument is that credit risks should be recognized on a "real-time" basis and not smoothed over time with provisions for loan losses that are based on anticipated losses. Similarly, cash taxes should be subtracted to get operating earnings rather than taxes reported, which reflect deferred and other taxes payable. Securities accounting, where banks can selectively choose to take gains or losses, distort reported profits because they artificially raise or lower income by either accelerating earnings recognition or deferring it. Such gains or losses are thus netted from pre-tax income when they are taken, but amortized over the remaining maturities of the securities to obtain economic profit. Finally, nonrecurring gains or losses should be subtracted (netted) from pre-tax income when they represent transitory adjustments.

Exhibit 4.6 provides an EVA calculation for Ameribank. Balance sheet data and the associated earning asset yields and costs of liabilities appear at the top of the exhibit. Note that the bank is not well-capitalized under regulatory risk-based capital standards because its total capital ratio is less than 10 percent. According to the income statement, Ameribank reported net interest income for the year of $265.9 million and net income of $66.54 million. This produces a return on equity of 20.8 percent and return on assets of 1.33 percent.

At the bottom of the exhibit, the bank's NOPAT is shown to be $74.9 million, assuming that actual net charge-offs equal $22 million and cash tax payments equal $39 million. If the bank has risk capital of $550 million and the capital charge is 12 percent, EVA equals $8.9 million. This means that during the year, Ameribank added $8.9 million in value for stockholders in excess of the minimum required return to stockholders.

Suppose that the bank wants to reach the well-capitalized standard of total capital to risk-weighted assets of 10 percent. One approach might be to securitize, or sell without recourse, some of the bank's credit card loans. This lowers risk assets and the amount of required capital. Exhibit 4.7 documents the impact of this transaction on Ameribank's profit measures. Note that the bank is assumed to sell $1 billion of credit card loans and use the proceeds to pay off maturing CDs of $940 million and buy back $30 million in stock. With the reduction in loans, the loan loss reserve falls by $30 million, loan loss provisions decline by $30 million, and net charge-offs fall by $8 million. Noninterest income increases by $12 million, noninterest expense increases by $5 million, cash taxes fall to $31, and the amount of risk capital falls to $500 million.

According to the projected income statement and balance sheet, Ameribank would see its net income fall to $56.46 million producing an expected ROE of 19.47 percent and ROA of 1.40 percent. In this situation, ROE falls while ROA increases from the levels without the securitization. The bank's risk-based capital ratios would also increase to 8.17 percent for the Tier 1 ratio and 11.83 percent for the Total Capital ratio, both above the minimum to be well-capitalized. Note, however, that Ameribank's EVA would fall from $8.9 million to a −$15.9 million. In this framework, the credit card securitization clearly reduces the bank's contribution to shareholder value because NOPAT does not even cover the required return to shareholders. The oddity is that ROE is still quite large and ROA increases suggesting that the bank is performing better, while EVA suggests that the bank is worse off. Why is there a difference? In your thought process, you might consider the change in risk capital and the treatment of loan loss provisions and charge-offs among other factors.

---

[13]Uyemura, Kantor, and Pettit (1996) provide details in adjusting NOPAT and applying EVA analysis to measure performance for banks. As part of their analysis, they rank large U.S. banks in 1995 by MVA and MVA as a fraction of bank capital.

· EXHIBIT 4.6

EVA CALCULATION FOR AMERIBANK

A. Balance Sheet

Assets	$Millions	Rate	Liabilities & Equity	$Millions	Rate
Cash	$150	0	Demand deposits	$800	
Securities	$800	6.5%	MMDAs	$1,800	3%
Commercial loans	$2,000	9.0%	CDs	$1,300	5.5%
Credit card loans	$1,900	10.0%	Small time deposits	$680	4.5%
−Loss reserve	−$100		Deferred tax credits	$100	
Other assets	$250		Equity	$320	
Total assets	$5,000		Liabilities + equity	$5,000	

Risk-weighted assets: .50($800) + 1($2,000) + 1($1,900) + 1($250) = $4,550
Tier 1 capital = $320   Tier 1 ratio: $320/$4,550 = 7.03%
Total capital = $420   Total capital ratio: $420/$4,550 = 9.23%

B. Income Statement

Interest income: .065($800) + .090($2,000) + .10($1,900) = $422
Interest expense: .03($1,800) + .055($1,300) + .045($680) = −$156.1

Net interest income	$265.9
Provision for loan losses	−$25
Noninterest income	$60
Noninterest expense	−$190
Pre tax income	$110.90
Taxes @ 40%	$44.36
Net income	$66.54

C. Profit Measures

$$ROE = \left(\frac{66.54}{320}\right) = 20.8\% \qquad ROA = \left(\frac{66.54}{5,000}\right) = 1.33\%$$

Assuming that net charge-offs = $22, cash taxes paid = $39, and allocated risk capital = $550 with a capital charge of 12%:

NOPAT = $110.90 + $25 − $22 − $39 = $74.9
EVA = $74.9 − 0.12($550) = $8.9

THE BALANCED SCORECARD

One of the recent dramatic shifts in strategic thinking by management has recently produced a new approach to performance measurement at many firms, both financial and nonfinancial. The primary catalyst is an appreciation that financial measures alone do not provide sufficient information regarding a firm's overall performance. In addition to profit and risk measures, managers need benchmarks and targets for efforts and activities related to customer satisfaction, employee satisfaction, organizational innovation, and the development of business processes. This is particularly true if a bank is customer-focused. Doesn't it seem appropriate that management should target and measure performance along the lines of market share, service quality, customer profitability, sales performance, and customer satisfaction? Kaplan and Norton have led the thinking in this context with a series of articles and their book, *The Balanced Scorecard*, which describes the framework for integrating financial and nonfinancial performance measures and targets.

A firm's balanced scorecard represents a set of measures that gives managers an immediate, comprehensive picture of the firm's business strategy. There are at least four dimensions: financial, customer satisfaction, internal processes, and organization innovation. One

● EXHIBIT 4.7

EVA CALCULATION FOR AMERIBANK AFTER SALE OF
$1 BILLION IN CREDIT CARD LOANS

A. Change in Balance Sheet Items

Assets	Δ Amount	Liabilities	Δ Amount
Credit card loans	−$1,000	CDs	−$940
Loan loss reserve	+$30	Equity	−$30
Total assets	−$970	Total	−$970

B. Income Statement

		Change
Interest income: .065($800) + .09($2,000) + .10($900) =	$322	−$100
Interest expense: .03($1,800) + .055($460) + .045($680) =	−$109.9	−$46.2
Net interest income	$212.1	−$53.8
Provision for loan losses	+$5	+$30.0
Noninterest income	$72	+$12
Noninterest expense	−$195	−$5
Pre tax income	$94.1	−$16.8
Taxes @ 40%	$37.64	−6.72
Net income	$56.46	−10.08

C. Profit Measures: Actual net charge-offs = $14, cash taxes paid = $31, and risk capital falls to $500.

ROE = $56.46/$290 = 19.47%

ROA = $56.46/$4,030 = 1.40%

EVA = [$94.1 − $5 − $14 − $31] − $60 = −$15.9

Risk-weighted assets: .50($800) + 1($2,000) + 1($900) + 1($250) = $3,550

Tier 1 capital = $290   Tier 1 ratio: $290/$3,550 = 8.17%

Tier 2 capital = $420   Total capital ratio: $420/$3,550 = 11.83%

objective is to help managers focus on a firm's competitive agenda. A scorecard approach should help a firm be more customer-oriented, build teamwork among employees, and improve the quality of product and service delivery systems. A scorecard meets the minimal requirements as a strategic framework if someone can examine 15 to 20 of a firm's scorecard measures and be able to understand the firm's competitive strategy.

A sample balanced scorecard framework with four blocks appears in Exhibit 4.8.[14] Each addresses a different general issue for management that can be described as:

■ Financial Performance: How Do Stockholders View Our Risk and Return Profile?

■ Customer Performance: How Do Customers See Us?

■ Internal Process Management: At What Must We Excel?

■ Innovation and Learning: How Can We Continue to Improve and Create Value?

Completing a scorecard for a bank involves identifying and implementing firm objectives, performance measures, and targets, along with initiatives or action steps to achieve the objectives. Together, this scorecard represents the bank's vision for the future and management's strategy to achieve the vision.

---

[14]This list was prepared by Christopher Burgess for his thesis "Implementing the Balanced Scorecard in a Community Bank," June 1998, for the Stonier Graduate School of Banking.

· EXHIBIT 4.8

SCORECARD MEASURES

Financial Measures	Customer Measures	Internal Measures	Learning Measures
Customer profitability	Life cycle segment market share	Channel usage	Skill competency
Lifestyle segment profitability	Customer satisfaction	Product usage	Sales productivity
Product profitability	Customer retention	Percentage of revenue from new products	Employer satisfaction
Delivery channel cost	Market share	Percentage of revenue from product promotions	Employee retention
Return on investment	Customer acquisition	Product development cycle	Employee satisfaction
Revenue growth	Customer profitability	Hours with customer	Employee productivity
Deposit service cost change	Share of segment	New product revenue	Strategic job coverage ratio
Revenue mix	Depth of relationship	Cross-sale ration	Strategic information availability ratio
Sales growth and target markets	Brand name rating	Channel mix change	Personal goals alignment
Dollars past due divided by total dollar loans	Number of customer complaints	Service error rate	Revenue per employee
Fee revenue divided by total revenue	Closed accounts by reason	Request fulfillment time	Sales force average length of service
Net income	Share of wallet	Loss ratio	Turnover
Return on risk-adjusted equity	Percent of target accounts	Underwriting quality audit	Training hours divided by FTE
Net income after capital charge		Overhead ratio	Number of training programs offered
Cost of capital		Ratio of branch to on-call transactions—ATM transactions	Turnover ratio
Efficiency		Sales per sales call	Turbulence
Economic value added		Sales per referral	
Assets per employee		New sales divided by banker	
		Productivity	
		Efficiency ratio	
		New product revenue as percent of total	

SOURCE: Christopher Burgess, "Implementing the Balanced Scorecard in a Community Bank," thesis, Stonier Graduate School of Banking (American Banker's Association, June 1998).

According to Kaplan and Norton, customers are typically most concerned about time, or how long it takes to meet their needs: product/service quality represented by the level of defects; service related to whether products or services are perceived to create value; and cost. The critical issue in internal process management is to identify the firm's core competencies and structure processes to best satisfy customer needs. Today, this requires a reasonably sophisticated information system to analyze performance measures to assess the source of problems and track improvement. For innovation and learning, management should emphasize continued education and a quality work environment for employees and the research and development of new products, markets, and delivery systems. Finally, each of these three blocks should directly influence the financial performance of the firm, which is reflected in profit ratios such as ROE, ROA, efficiency ratios, EPS, and EVA, among others, as well as market share figures and risk measures.

Key performance objectives, measures, targets, and initiatives will differ across institutions. Exhibit 4.8 lists the performance measures commonly cited by banks in their scorecards. Note the comprehensive nature of the financial measures and the emphasis on customer satisfaction, market share, cross-sell ratios, customer profit ratios, product development and promotion, cost/loss ratios, and quality of service measures. Cates (1998) argues that the scorecard framework shares three themes with traditional investor analysis of banking. First, stock analysts' focus on earnings quality is analogous to the scorecard emphasis on service quality, customer satisfaction, and market share, which represent competitive factors. Second, earnings quality is also evidenced by scorecard concerns about cost and risk control. Finally, the use of targets and projections for all performance measures is comparable to what stock analysts do when they attempt to forecast firm earnings and establish a target stock price. The implication is that banks, which choose to manage across both financial and nonfinancial perspectives, will better meet competitive needs.

SUMMARY

Bank performance analysis has recently expanded beyond the simple critique of financial ratios generated from balance sheet and income statement data. At the most basic level, banks must be careful in selecting their peer group so that they obtain meaningful comparisons of key ratios with performance ratios of banks that follow the same strategies and compete in the same markets. Many community banks that compete primarily in traditional loan and deposit markets should compare their performance with other banks that pursue the same lending and deposit-gathering strategies. This often involves designating the bank as either loan-driven or deposit-driven in terms of its growth strategy and matching performance with a similarly focused group of banks. Even when banks follow similar strategies, their profit and risk ratios can vary if they conduct different types and amounts of business off-balance sheet and choose to take extraordinary gains or losses.

Recently, many financial institutions are trying to measure risk-adjusted profitability. The most popular methods are risk-adjusted return on capital (RAROC), return on risk-adjusted capital (RORAC), and economic value added (EVA). Each relates some measure of return, either risk-adjusted or not, and net of a capital charge, or not, to some measure of risk capital. As such, these measures are conceptually equivalent to ROE. The analysis is particularly useful when trying to estimate how profitable a line of business is. The particular difficulty in the analysis is in identifying risk capital. This chapter describes different approaches to the risk allocation, including benchmarking, value-at-risk, and earnings-at-risk, and provides examples of their applications to banks.

The chapter also introduces the concept of a balanced scorecard created by Kaplan and Norton (1996). This framework emphasizes that management should focus on both financial and nonfinancial performance measures and integrate them to achieve desired objectives. It describes the types of measures related to customers, internal learning and growth, and innovation.

Questions

1. List three weaknesses of basic GAAP-based financial performance measures. Explain why each represents a weakness.

2. In each of the following situations, indicate why ROE or ROA might not be comparable across Bay Bank and Cove Bank.

    a. Both banks have $5 billion in assets.

    b. Bay Bank has a large trust department and Cove Bank does not.

    c. Cove Bank lends to large, Fortune 500 companies. Bay Bank lends to small businesses.

    d. Cove Bank has a mortgage-servicing subsidiary and Bay Bank does not.

3. Suppose that you own stock in Trident Bank. Last year, the bank reported ROA = 0.95 percent, ROE = 13.47 percent, and Return to Stockholders = −5.25 percent. Did this bank perform well or poorly during the year?

4. What does the term "whisper earnings" refer to in the context of stock valuation?

5. List the steps that a bank stock analyst typically follows in making a recommendation to investors concerning a specific bank's stock.

6. When calculating a bank's earnings per share (EPS), what is the appropriate measure of earnings? Over what time period should earnings be measured?

7. Use the following information for Manor Bank (MB) at year-end to calculate the performance measures listed.

$$\text{Net income} = \$185{,}600{,}000$$

$$\text{Cash dividends paid to preferred stockholders} = \$21{,}400{,}000$$

$$\text{Number of shares of common stock outstanding} = \$30{,}191{,}000$$

$$\text{Market price of common stock} = \$84.87$$

$$\text{Book value per share of common stock} = \$63.67$$

    a. Calculate the following ratios or values:

      1. EPS

      2. P/E

      3. Price to book value

      4. Market value of equity

    b. If MB buys back 5 percent of the outstanding stock during the next year, earns the same amount of net income, and pays the same amount of dividends to preferred stockholders, calculate the impact on EPS. What will happen to MB's stock price if its P/E ratio then equals 20.5?

8. Suppose that you are an investor in bank stocks. Describe why each of the following might be important information for you to make an informed investment decision regarding whether to buy or sell a specific bank's stock.

    a. Bank's market share of core deposits

    b. Bank's market share of consumer loans

    c. Number of bank customers who are profitable under the bank's profitability analysis model

    d. Business and retail customer rating of bank's service quality

    e. Customer retention rates for trust business, private (high net worth) banking, retirement accounts, and consumer loans

    f. Productivity measures, such as assets per employee

9. Explain how the Customer Bank differs from the House Bank when analyzing a bank's performance. What types of assets, liabilities, revenues, and expenses would fall under the Customer Bank? What types would fall under the House Bank?

10. How does RAROC differ from RORAC?

11. Why is it important to conduct line of business profitability analysis?

12. What is the relevance of earnings-at-risk and value-at-risk for a specific line of business, such as commercial lending?

13. Use the data from Exhibit 4.1 for PNC to explain:
    a. Why the return on assigned capital fell from 1996 to 1997 for the National Consumer Banking division.
    b. Why the return on assigned capital for Regional Community Banking exceeded that for National Consumer Banking in 1997.
    c. Which of the seven lines of business are least profitable. To which would you allocate more resources in 1998 if you were in senior management?

14. You have collected the following financial information to estimate the profitability of leasing activities for your bank. Management has a 15 percent required return on capital for all lines of business.

$$\text{Net income} = \$42,336,000$$

$$\text{Expected losses} = \$2,975,000$$

$$\text{Risk adjusted capital} = \$253,770,000$$

    a. Did this line of business earn a sufficiently high return given the bank's requirements and internal cost allocation procedures?
    b. Suppose that this is one of the bank's riskiest lines of business. Should the bank require a higher return when analyzing the profitability of this line of business?

15. What is the specific purpose of a bank's internal funds transfer pricing system?

16. Why do U.S. bank regulations impose specific capital requirements against large banks' market risk?

17. Explain how the value-at-risk measure provides meaningful information to senior management when analyzing market risk.

18. According the the data in Exhibit 4.5 for Credit Suisse First Boston, which type of risk (risk class) represented the greatest exposure to the firm at year-end 2000? What does the term "diversification" refer to when measuring value-at-risk for the overall portfolio?

19. What does EVA measure for a bank? What would a negative value for EVA mean for a bank or for a specific line of business within a bank?

20. Describe the components of a balanced scorecard as applied to a community bank. What is the basic motivation for creating a balanced scorecard as a management tool?

PROBLEMS

You are the CEO of a $400 million community bank. You are interested in measuring your bank's profitability by line of business and have separated your operations into lending, deposit-gathering, and Treasury divisions. Only the Treasury division takes interest rate and prepayment risk. The following rates reflect yields on money and capital market instruments traded in the external (outside the bank) securities markets.

		Maturity		
3-month	6-month	1-year	2-year	3-year
6.05%	6.28%	6.87%	7.53%	8.04%

1. You recently made a 3-year, 9.75 percent fixed-rate loan to a commercial customer for $5 million. You financed the loan by issuing a 6-month time deposit at 6 percent to a local pension fund.

    a. Calculate the net interest margin for each line of business.

    b. Assume that there is a prepayment option for loans that is currently worth 35 basis points in the options market. Calculate the profit after accounting for the prepayment option for each line of business.

    c. Given your allocations, what is the Treasury division's interest rate risk?

    d. How does your analysis change if the commercial loan is priced on a floating rate basis at 6-month LIBOR (London Interbank Offer Rate) + 2 percent?

ACTIVITY

Research recently published annual reports for the largest U.S. banks and non-U.S. banks to obtain information on reported:

1. Line of business/segment profitability
2. Value-at-risk
3. Earnings-at-risk

Explain what lines of business are most profitable across firms over the same time period. Discuss the different methods of reporting value-at-risk and earnings-at-risk information and how the banks use this information.

5

MANAGING NONINTEREST INCOME AND NONINTEREST EXPENSE

A *common view among bank managers and analysts is that banks must rely less on net interest income and more on noninterest income to be more successful. The highest earning banks will be those that generate an increasing share of operating revenue from noninterest sources. A related assumption is that not all fees are created equal. Some fees are stable and predictable over time, while others are highly volatile because they derive from cyclical activities. The fundamental issue among managers is to determine the appropriate customer mix and business mix to grow profits at high rates, with a strong focus on fee-based revenues.*

This chapter examines three basic issues related to managing a bank's noninterest income and noninterest expense. First, it describes the strengths and weaknesses of commonly used financial ratios of expense control and noninterest income growth. Second, it discusses why banks should focus on customer profitability and the mix of fee-based businesses when evaluating performance. Finally, it explains how banks utilize different noninterest expense management strategies to enhance performance.

COMMON FINANCIAL RATIOS OF EXPENSE CONTROL AND NONINTEREST INCOME GROWTH

It is widely recognized that the days of record-breaking net interest margins for banks are long gone. Exhibit 5.1, for example, documents the sharp decline in NIM for different-sized FDIC-insured banks from 1990 to 2001. Note that NIM rose from 1990 to 1994, on average, and has fallen sharply thereafter for both banks under $100 million in assets and larger banks. This recent decline in NIMs reflects competitive pressures on both the cost of bank funds and yields on earning assets. Specifically, the growth in inexpensive, core deposits at banks has slowed because customers have many alternatives, such as mutual funds and cash management accounts, that offer similar transactions and savings services and pay higher

· EXHIBIT 5.1

QUARTERLY NET INTEREST MARGINS FOR FDIC-INSURED COMMERCIAL BANKS

A. Banks with < $100 Million or > $100 Million in Assets: 1990–1997*

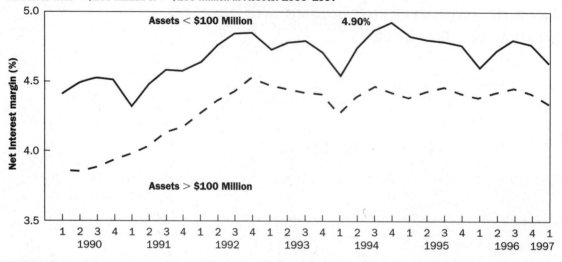

*First Quarter 1997

B. Banks with < $100 Billion or > $100 Billion in Assets: 1997–2001

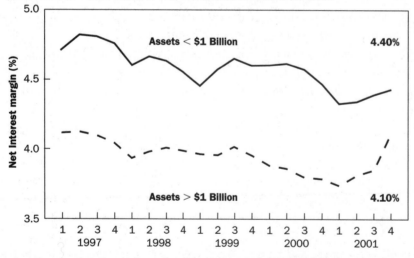

interest rates. Loan yields have similarly fallen on a relative basis because of competition from nonbank lenders, such as commercial and consumer finance companies and leasing companies, and other banks that compete for the most profitable small business loans, credit card receivables, and so on. Potential earnings difficulties are compounded by the fact that asset quality was quite strong during the late 1990s, such that loan loss provisions were low and not likely to show much improvement. The U.S. economy fell into a modest recession in March 2001, around which loan quality worsened. The impact is that banks must grow their noninterest income relative to noninterest expense if they want to see net income grow.

▪ **EXHIBIT 5.2**

NONINTEREST INCOME AS A PERCENTAGE OF NET OPERATING REVENUE, 1993–2001

Quarterly Noninterest Income, % of net Operating Revenue*

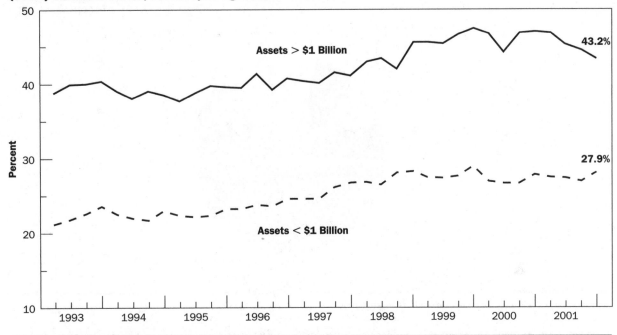

*Net operating revenue equals net interest income plus noninterest income.

SOURCE: FDIC Quarterly Banking Profile, Fourth Quarter 2001.

NONINTEREST INCOME

For years, banks have generally tried to increase noninterest income. Exhibit 5.2 documents the sustained increase in banks' noninterest income as a fraction of net operating revenue, where net operating revenue equals the sum of net interest income and noninterest income. This ratio equaled just 24.7 percent in 1984 for all FDIC-insured banks, but rose sharply in 2001 to 43.2 percent for banks with over $1 billion in assets and to 27.9 percent for smaller banks. Thus, while all banks are growing their noninterest revenues, the largest banks rely much more on this source of revenue than smaller banks that still rely more heavily on net interest income. Exhibit 5.3 documents the composition of noninterest income for all FDIC-insured banks. The biggest contributors are deposit service charges and 'other.'

The Uniform Bank Performance Report (UBPR) introduced in Chapter 3 distinguishes between service charges on a bank's deposit accounts and other sources of fee income as the components of noninterest income. Deposit service charges represent a stable source of revenue for banks, but are difficult to increase sharply over time because they are very visible and the perception is that banks "stick it to customers" when they impose the charges. For example, the October 1998 merger of Citicorp and Travelers into Citigroup focused attention on the difference between fees on transactions accounts between large and small banks. Panel A of Exhibit 5.4 summarizes the results of a 1997 Fed survey, which showed that, on average, large banks charged $18 more for noninterest checking and almost $31 more annually for interest (NOW) checking than did small banks. The average overdraft charge was more than

■ EXHIBIT 5.3

COMPOSITION OF NONINTEREST INCOME

September 30, 2001

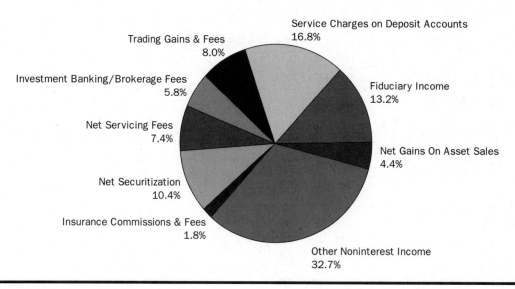

SOURCE: FDIC Quarterly Banking Profile, Fourth Quarter 2001.

$5 higher per item at large banks. Panel B documents minimum balance requirements to avoid fees and average fees charged on transactions accounts at all U.S. banks from 1994 to 1999. Accounts with a single balance and fee allow the customer to avoid a monthly fee if he or she maintains a deposit balance above the minimum. During this interval, the fees have remained fairly constant for accounts with no fees when minimum balances are maintained, and have increased slightly for accounts with mandatory fees.

Bank managers know that customers are largely price insensitive when it comes to these service charges and many fees. In terms of price elasticities, the demand for these accounts is relatively price inelastic. This means that banks can raise these charges and fees on a regular basis and their total revenues will rise. Not surprisingly, banks systematically raise fees annually but by modest amounts so as not to raise too much criticism.

Panel C of Exhibit 5.4 documents the change in fees that banks charge for special actions related to customer transaction accounts from 1994 to 1999. Special actions consist of stop-payment orders, NSF checks, overdrafts, and returned deposit items. A stop-payment order arises when a customer requests that the bank not pay a check previously written. NSF checks and overdrafts relate to checks drawn on an account when the customer has insufficient funds to cover the check. For example, a customer writes a check for $120 when he has only $80 in his account. When the check is not honored (cleared) by the bank, it is labeled an insufficient funds (NSF) item. When the check is honored, it is labeled an overdraft. A returned deposit item is a check that a customer deposits but the paying bank returns to the customer's bank because of insufficient funds in the check payer's account. As noted, the fees on all special actions consistently increased over the five years.

Other fees are typically those from loans with an increasing amount coming from fees associated with investment banking and brokerage activities. Of course, these latter fees contribute

· EXHIBIT 5.4

FEES AND MINIMUM BALANCE REQUIREMENTS AT U.S. BANKS

A. Average fees charged by U.S. banks on transactions accounts in 1997

Average Fees	Large Banks	Small Banks
Noninterest checking	$91.59	$73.56
NOW accounts	$121.44	$90.72
Overdrafts	$20.45	$15.01

B. Selected checkable accounts at banks and savings associations, average low-balance fees, and balance requirements, 1994–99
Dollars except as noted

Account	1994	1995	1996	1997	1998	1999	Percent change, 1994–99
BANKS							
Noninterest checking							
Single balance and fee[1]							
Percent offering	36.4	29.4	32.9	39.3	35.6	40.6	†
Monthly low-balance fee	6.14	6.61	6.34	6.09	6.43	6.15	.2
Minimum balance							
To avoid fee	503.62	479.22	480.26	479.41	498.61	515.62	2.4
To open	109.45	—	123.33	123.96	115.01	103.65	–5.3
Fee only[2]							
Percent offering	35.4	45.7	34.2	33.3	36.3	38.9	†
Monthly low-balance fee	4.39	4.61	5.02	4.49	4.73	5.17	17.8**
Minimum balance to open	79.88	81.62	82.15	61.43	76.34	65.20	–18.4**
NOW account							
Single balance and fee[1]							
Percent offering	40.2	43.9	44.0	56.7	50.8	54.2	†**
Monthly low-balance fee	8.02	8.49	8.11	7.81	8.07	8.39	4.6
Minimum balance							
To avoid fee	1,055.43	1,069.54	1,078.78	1,051.51	1,109.02	1,060.37	.5
To open	701.45	—	653.72	662.67	616.12	641.34	–8.6

C. Fees for selected special actions—incidence and average level at banks and savings associations, 1994–99
Dollars except as noted

Account	1994	1995	1996	1997	1998	1999	Percent change, 1994–99
BANKS							
Stop-payment orders							
Percent charging	99.8	99.0	99.4	99.2	99.7	99.9	†
Fee	13.29	13.68	13.68	13.97	14.35	15.29	15.0**
NSF Checks							
Percent charging	100.0	100.0	100.0	100.0	100.0	99.9	†
Fee	15.33	15.71	16.36	16.55	16.96	17.71	15.5**
Overdrafts							
Percent charging	99.4	98.4	100.0	97.6	98.0	99.9	†
Fee	14.92	15.67	16.28	15.73	16.65	17.45	17.0**
Deposit items returned							
Percent charging	81.7	59.0	59.3	55.7	61.7	57.1	†**
Fee	6.89	4.95	5.50	5.15	5.49	6.28	–8.9

NOTE: NSF (not sufficient funds) checks are those written without sufficient funds in the account to cover them; they are not honored by the paying bank or savings association. Overdrafts are checks written without sufficient funds but are honored by the paying institution.

[1] A monthly fee for balances below the minimum, no monthly fee for balances above the minimum, and no other charges.

[2] A monthly fee, no minimum balance to eliminate the fee, and a charge per check in some cases.

a far greater portion of noninterest income at the largest banks and explain why noninterest income is such a higher fraction of their operating revenue. As demonstrated in Exhibit 5.3, banks also generate substantial fees from trading activities, servicing, and securitization. The problem with nondeposit fees and trading revenue is that they are highly cyclical in nature because they depend on capital market activity. When mergers, acquisitions, trading, and brokerage activities are booming, banks (and investment banks) can earn enormous fees that increase with the volume of activity. When these activities decline, fee revenue shrinks accordingly. This was demonstrated late in 1998 when large banking organizations around the world reported large trading losses on activities in Russia and Asia. In 2001–2002, the same investment banks were laying off employees given the sharp drop in fee revenue.

The critical management decision is to determine the appropriate fee-based business mix. Some firms prefer mortgage banking because of the built-in hedge between loan origination and mortgage servicing. When interest rates are low or falling, firms can earn substantial origination fees from making new loans and mortgage refinancings. When interest rates are high or rising, loan originations decline but mortgage-servicing revenue increases because existing mortgages prepay slower and thus remain outstanding longer.[1] The problem with mortgage banking is that firms benefit from size because there are considerable scale economies with larger portfolios.[2] Yet, it is difficult to acquire the volume of servicing business given the extreme competitive conditions. Many large banks prefer the huge potential fee income from businesses such as leasing, subprime lending (to high default risk customers), factoring, and related activities. Not surprisingly, fees from these activities are highly volatile because the volume and quality of business changes when economic conditions change.

NONINTEREST EXPENSE

The UBPR reports three components of a bank's noninterest expense: personnel expense, which includes wages, salaries, and benefits; occupancy expense, which includes rent and depreciation on buildings and equipment; and other operating expense. The sum of these expenses is also referred to as overhead expense. For most banks, personnel expenses are the greatest reflecting the heavy dependency on people relative to capital assets.

One source of earnings growth is straightforward cost cutting. This was a primary motive for the 1991 combination of Chemical Bank and Manufacturers Hanover and many subsequent mergers, including Chase Manhattan and the "new" Chemical Bank that resulted from this earlier merger. See Contemporary Issues: The Marriage of Chemical Banking Corp. and Manufacturers Hanover. In fact, analysts and bank stock investors are constantly trying to identify likely in-market merger partners where cost savings can be substantial. With an in-market merger the two firms have significant duplication of banking offices and services such that any merger leads to the elimination of branches and personnel. Cost savings from eliminating this duplication represent an annuity to the extent that the combined firm can continue to service existing customers. Berry and McDermott (1996) reported that cost savings from in-market mergers in 1995 averaged 39 percent of the acquired bank's noninterest expense base, a substantial annuity if sustained. For mergers that were not in-market, the cost savings averaged 23 percent of the acquired bank's expenses.

---

[1] A mortgage servicer collects the actual payments from the borrower and transfers the funds, less a servicing fee, to the ultimate holder of the loan. Mortgage-servicing revenue varies directly with the amount of loans serviced. The faster that mortgages prepay, the lower are outstanding mortgage balances such that servicing revenue falls, ceteris paribus.

[2] The term *economies of scale* refers to the situation where a firm's average unit costs decrease as output increases.

The Marriage of Chemical Banking Corp. and Manufacturers Hanover

In 1990, Chemical Banking Corp. earned $291 million on $73 billion of assets; Manufacturers Hanover earned $139 million on assets of $62 billion. Combined, the firms had 45,866 employees. When the two firms merged in 1991 as Chemical Bank, analysts estimated that because both banks had significant overlapping operations in New York and other similar markets the combined firm would be able to reduce the number of employees by 25 percent without adversely affecting capacity or service quality. The bottom-line impact would potentially reach $690 million annually. What a powerful incentive for a merger!

By 1993, the combined firm had reduced the number of employees by 15 percent and net income had increased to $1.6 billion. Of course, not all of the gain in income was merger related. Eventually, Chase Manhattan and Chemical merged, leading to further cost cutting because of overlaps with Chase's activities.

Still, there are powerful costs that make such in-market mergers unattractive to many. First, many employees are laid off. Where do they find alternative work? Will outplacement services and job training be offered? The human resource costs can be enormous. Second, who

will manage the new, combined firm? Both firms typically have entrenched senior management teams that will likely fight for turf. Can the senior managers work together? Which culture will survive? Who will be CEO of the combined firm? Finally, which bank's systems and policies will be used? Many previous mergers have struggled with consolidating computer operations. Until these issues are resolved, it is difficult to effect a merger and realize potential cost savings and revenue synergies.

KEY RATIOS

Bank managers generally track a variety of financial ratios in an effort to measure and monitor a bank's ability to control expenses and generate noninterest income. The three most common types of ratios can be categorized as a bank's burden or net overhead expense, the efficiency ratio, and productivity ratios. The following discussion should be viewed in the context that any single bank's ratios will reflect the mix of businesses it represents. Some lines of business require substantial capital investments, while others are more labor intensive or may primarily be off-balance sheet in their impact.

BURDEN/NET OVERHEAD EXPENSE. As noted in Chapter 3, a bank's burden or net overhead expense equals the difference between noninterest expense and noninterest income in dollar terms or as a fraction of total assets.

$$\text{Burden} = \text{Noninterest expense} - \text{Noninterest income}$$

$$\text{Net Overhead Expense} = \frac{\text{Noninterest expense} - \text{Noninterest income}}{\text{Average assets}}$$

Because noninterest expense is higher for most banks, these measures indicate the extent to which a bank generates noninterest income to help cover its noninterest expense. The smaller its burden and net overhead, the better a bank has performed on trend and versus peers. When differences appear, managers examine the components of noninterest expense to determine whether personnel, occupancy, or other expense is greater as a fraction of assets. They will also compare service charges on deposits and other fee income as a fraction of noninterest income and assets to assess their relative performance related to asset utilization. Importantly, gains or losses on the sale of securities and other nonrecurring income and/or expense are netted or ignored when making these comparisons.

EFFICIENCY RATIO. The most popular ratio to evaluate performance is a bank's efficiency ratio. Banks frequently report this measure along with ROE, ROA, and NIM as a key driver of profitability and indicator of potential profit growth. Many banks announce their target ratio at the beginning of each year, and some banks tie employee bonuses to whether the bank meets its target. Formally, the efficiency ratio equals a bank's noninterest expense as a fraction of operating revenue, where operating revenue is the sum of net interest income and noninterest income.

$$\text{Efficiency ratio} = \frac{\text{Noninterest expense}}{\text{Net interest income} + \text{Noninterest income}}$$

The more efficient banks are presumably those with the lowest efficiency ratios. The intuition is that the ratio measures the amount of noninterest expense a bank pays per dollar of operating revenue, with a smaller number better.

Exhibit 5.5 reports average efficiency ratios from 1991 through 2001 for U.S. banks with $1 billion in assets separating the bank averages. Data for the larger banks are driven by the biggest institutions with global operations. Note the systematic decline in efficiency ratios, except for the blip in 1998 for the biggest banks indicating that banks in general have successfully lowered noninterest expense relative to operating revenue. This derives both from cost cutting and growing noninterest income. Note also the fact that larger banks have lower ratios, on average. This generally reflects a greater ability to generate noninterest income by entering businesses such as investment banking, trading, and asset management. At year-end 2001, banks with under $1 billion in assets paid an average of 64.13 cents for each dollar of revenue, while larger banks paid just 56.64 cents per dollar of revenue.

A crucial issue is whether low efficiency ratios correspond to higher profitability ratios. Osborne (1994) and Holliday (2000) argue that they do not, and banks that focus on lowering their efficiency ratio may make suboptimal decisions. Using data from 1989 to 1993 for the 50 largest U.S. banks, Osborne demonstrates that banks with the highest ROEs reported a wide range of efficiency ratios. There are two essential criticisms. First, the efficiency ratio does not take into account a bank's mix of businesses. It is perfectly logical for banks to invest in businesses where they must incur larger noninterest expense if the marginal revenue obtained from the businesses exceeds the marginal expense. Thus, while the efficiency ratio may increase or exceed peers, the investment adds value to shareholders. Second, the efficiency ratio is not directly tied to a bank's target return to shareholders. Holliday similarly argues that banks should focus on growing revenues at the lowest possible cost. If successful, banks will retain customers and increase profitability. Chapter 4 demonstrates that as long as the bank earns more than its marginal cost of capital, the investment is value enhancing. The implication is that managers who evaluate noninterest expense and revenue must carefully measure marginal cost and revenue and compare their bank's performance to similar competitors.

OPERATING RISK RATIO

Some analysts (Wilson 2001) focus on a bank's operating risk ratio in order to better differentiate performance attributable to cost controls versus fee generation. The lower is the operating risk ratio, the better is the bank's operating performance because it generates proportionately more of its revenues from fees, which are more stable and thus more valuable. The ratio subtracts fee income from noninterest expense and divides the total by NIM.

$$\text{Operating Risk Ratio} = \frac{\text{Noninterest expense} - \text{Fee income}}{\text{Net interest margin}}$$

• EXHIBIT 5.5

EFFICIENCY RATIOS OF U.S. BANKS, 1991–2001

Annual Efficiency Ratios: Banks with More or Less Than $1 Billion in Assets

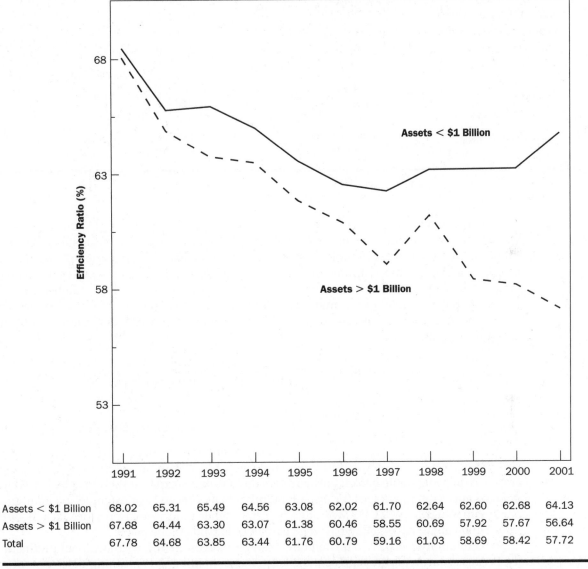

	1991	1992	1993	1994	1995	1996	1997	1998	1999	2000	2001
Assets < $1 Billion	68.02	65.31	65.49	64.56	63.08	62.02	61.70	62.64	62.60	62.68	64.13
Assets > $1 Billion	67.68	64.44	63.30	63.07	61.38	60.46	58.55	60.69	57.92	57.67	56.64
Total	67.78	64.68	63.85	63.44	61.76	60.79	59.16	61.03	58.69	58.42	57.72

NOTE: Noninterest expense less amortization of intangible assets as a percent of net interest income plus noninterest income.

SOURCE: FDIC Quarterly Banking Profile, Fourth Quarter 2001; available on the Internet at www.FDIC.gov/databank/.

Consider the data for Bay Bank and River Bank in Exhibit 5.6. Both banks report identical ROAs, overhead expense as a fraction of assets, operating revenue as a fraction of assets, and efficiency ratios, but Bay Bank reports a lower operating risk ratio. A closer review of the components of the two ratios indicates that Bay Bank generates a higher fraction of its operating revenue from fee income. Hence it reports a lower operating risk ratio.

■ EXHIBIT 5.6

OPERATING RISK RATIO SIGNALS THE BENEFIT OF FEE INCOME

Ratio	Bay Bank	River Bank
Return on Assets (ROA)	1.40%	1.40%
Net Interest Margin (NIM)	4.00%	4.50%
Fee (Noninterest) Income	1.25%	0.75%
Operating Revenue	5.25%	5.25%
Noninterest Expense	3.25%	3.25%
Efficiency Ratio:	$\dfrac{3.25\%}{4.00\% + 1.25\%} = 61.9\%$	$\dfrac{3.25\%}{4.50\% + 0.75\%} = 61.9\%$
Operating Risk Ratio:	$\dfrac{3.25\% - 1.25\%}{4.00\%} = 50.0\%$	$\dfrac{3.25\% - 0.75\%}{4.50\%} = 55.6\%$

PRODUCTIVITY RATIOS. Many managers track a variety of productivity ratios to assess whether they are getting the maximum use of employees and capital. Typical ratios, included in the UBPR, are assets per employee and average personnel expense per employee. In the first case, a higher ratio indicates that fewer employees handle business associated with a larger volume of assets. In a sense, it is an asset efficiency ratio where a high number is good. Of course, the ratio ignores the amount of off-balance sheet activity that a bank conducts. In the second case, the ratio measures the average cost of an employee when salaries and benefits are recognized.

$$\text{Assets per employee} = \frac{\text{Average assets}}{\text{Number of full-time employees}}$$

$$\text{Average personnel expense} = \frac{\text{Personnel expense}}{\text{Number of full-time employees}}$$

There is no widely recognized optimal value for either of these ratios. In fact, many high performing banks have fewer full-time employees, but pay them better than the average employee at comparable banks. Furthermore, the personnel expense ratio may be biased by large compensation packages for just a handful of bank officers. For example, a community bank with a highly paid CEO will often report a higher ratio, which provides meaningless information about how well the average employee is paid versus peers.

For community banks, two related ratios can provide useful information about productivity. Because loans typically represent the largest asset holding, it is meaningful to calculate a loans-per-employee ratio as an indicator of loan productivity. Similarly, a ratio of net income per employee generally indicates the productivity and profitability of a bank's workforce. For both of these latter ratios, a higher value indicates greater productivity.

$$\text{Loans per employee} = \frac{\text{Average loans}}{\text{Number of full-time employees}}$$

$$\text{Net income per employee} = \frac{\text{Net income}}{\text{Number of full-time employees}}$$

CUSTOMER PROFITABILITY AND BUSINESS MIX

With declining net interest margins, it is essential that bank managers identify the appropriate mix of products and lines of business because future earnings growth will likely come from fee income. Traditionally, banks have relied on deposit service charges and trust fees for those with trust departments. The key point is that not all fees are created equal and not all customers are profitable. Banks must recognize the risk associated with different sources of fee income and be able to measure whether specific customers generate more revenue than the cost of servicing their account.

WHICH CUSTOMERS ARE PROFITABLE?

The first step in identifying profitable growth is to determine which of the bank's customers and which lines of business are profitable. Chapter 4 introduced the RAROC/RORAC framework to assess the risk-adjusted return on allocated capital for a specific product or line of business. Once these returns are identified, banks should allocate resources to the businesses generating the highest expected returns over time. Data on customer profitability are similarly beneficial in helping management target niches, develop new products, and change pricing.

Chapter 18 presents a framework to assess whether a customer's total account relationship is profitable in terms of meeting the bank's target return to shareholders. Aggregate results from such analyses across different banks' customer bases reveal several interesting points. First, a small fraction of customers contribute the bulk of bank profits. In 1997, First Chicago reported that the most profitable 6 percent of its customers produced $1,600 in revenue and cost $350 to serve annually. The least profitable 14 percent of customers produced $230 in revenue and cost $700 to serve. Canadian Imperial Bank of Commerce (CIBC) similarly reported that just 20 percent of its customers were profitable.[3] In 1999, First Manhattan Consulting reported research that 70 percent of Internet banking accounts were unprofitable. This supports the widely held view that approximately 80 percent of a typical bank's customers are unprofitable, but proportionally more Internet account holders are profitable. Second, many customer profitability models show that a significant difference between profitable and unprofitable accounts is that profitable customers maintain substantial loan and investment business with the bank. Unprofitable customers go where they get the best price or do not use these products. This should encourage banks to consolidate services into packages and price the package attractively for users of multiple services. Finally, banks that want to increase revenues should identify the perceived value of services by customers and price the services accordingly. In 1995, First Chicago imposed $3 fee each time customers used a live teller in the bank's branches. Not surprisingly, this was a public relations nightmare once the media got word of it. Other Chicago banks aggressively marketed their no-fee teller services in an attempt to draw business from First Chicago. Still, First Chicago lost less than 1 percent of its customers, cut its branch employees by 30 percent, and saw ATM usage and deposits grow by 100 percent in the first three months. In 1997, First Chicago imposed a teller fee on its no-minimum-balance transactions account because customers perceived the value of low minimum balances to be far higher than the negative impact of fees. This account eventually became First Chicago's most popular one.

It is important to recognize, however, that knowing how profitable a customer is does not demonstrate how to use the information. To increase fee income, banks should attempt

---

[3]See O'Sullivan (1997) for these and other examples.

to make unprofitable customers profitable by providing them with incentives to buy more services or buy a package of services that meet their wants and needs. This often involves offering price incentives to use ATMs or other low-cost channels for delivering services. For example, Wachovia has offered a no-minimum balance, no-service charge checking account for students with the restriction that the student does not enter a branch office. Banks similarly waive fees and offer attractive interest rates to customers who are highly profitable in order to keep their relationship.

The primary difficulty with profit data is that it is descriptive, but not necessarily predictive of future customer behavior. Carroll and Tadikonda (1997) provide an example of two checking account customers who each generate a $55 profit for a bank. One maintains a high deposit balance, writes a large number of checks, and makes frequent balance inquiries. The other maintains a low balance and writes a large number of insufficient funds checks. The first customer generates investment income from the balances that exceeds the cost of check processing. The second customer generates fee income from overdrafts that covers a loss from processing checks net of any balance investment income. The point is that these two customers are quite different, even though their account profitability is the same.

A bank should treat these two customers differently in terms of how it markets other services. Specifically, management should examine customer data to assess how customers use existing services and what factors affect usage. It should then forecast likely usage and delinquencies or defaults going forward and calculate the present value of expected cash flows from selling the other services. The two customers described above will exhibit different patterns of usage and will likely generate different cash flows from any new service. It is these expected usage patterns that should be consolidated with pricing strategies.

WHAT IS THE APPROPRIATE BUSINESS MIX?

Some fee income derives from relatively stable services and lines of business, while other fees are highly volatile and reflect changing volumes and pricing. In today's environment, most banks attempt to manage fee income in a portfolio context. Fee income from deposit service charges is quite stable and will likely exhibit modest growth. Still, banks must be aware that they are at great risk from brokerage firms that continue to eat into banks' share of this business. This is particularly true of Internet brokerage firms. See Contemporary Issues: Online Brokerages Invade Banking.

Deposit charges should be balanced with fees from other lines of business or products with higher growth potential. Ed Furash argues that large banks should generate 30 percent of noninterest income from deposit activities, including ATMs, telephone banking, and home banking.[4] They should obtain another 10 to 15 percent from businesses driven by the capital markets, such as investment banking and trading. Investment banking generally refers to the combination of securities underwriting, creating markets in securities, and fees from investment or merger and acquisitions advice. Trading income derives from operating a trading desk for customers whereby the bank maintains an inventory of securities to buy and sell, and from proprietary trading of securities and derivatives for its own account. Finally, banks should generate the remaining 55 to 60 percent of noninterest income from specialty intermediation and/or fee-based operating businesses. Included in this last group of activities are specialized consumer finance, specialty leasing, factoring, insurance products, mutual fund

---

[4]A summary appears in Kantrow (1998).

ONLINE BROKERAGES INVADE BANKING

Many bankers and bank analysts view the traditional bank branch system as outdated. Long-term, it is costly and inefficient, especially when compared with alternatives such as supermarket kiosks or the Internet. Virtual banking, or the use of electronic delivery systems of banking services, is rapidly growing, both in terms of the number of firms offering services as well as the range and volume of services offered. Most analysts believe that the Internet offers great opportunity to enter this business. Still, many banks do not currently offer Internet services.

Although banks are slowly making inroads into virtual banking, many brokerage firms are aggres-sively moving into virtual banking. Consider the information below for the six largest Internet brokers. With money market checking a customer earns a market interest rate on his or her deposits and can pay bills online. Several of these brokerages own commercial banks and can offer FDIC-insured accounts. For exam-ple, Waterhouse Securities is a sub-sidiary of Toronto-Dominion bank. It owns Waterhouse National Bank, a virtual bank with no branches, that had approximately 300,000 cus-tomers in mid-2001. You can obtain a mortgage or credit card from your Internet broker and, at least with Charles Schwab, can buy insurance. Why ever enter a bank?

Once customers feel comfortable with Internet service providers and Web brokers, it will become increas-ingly difficult for banks to win them back. Look at the popularity of stock and mutual fund trading over the Internet, with fees as low as $5 per 1,000 shares traded. Once customers develop the expertise of comparing interest rates and product/service offerings over the Internet, they will be less likely to use traditional branches and other distribution channels for the same offerings. What will be the long-term impact on traditional commercial banks?

Online brokerage firms are offering more bank-type products and other financial services. Here's a sampling of what's available at six of the biggest Internet brokers:

	Money-Market Checking	FDIC-Insured Bank Accounts	Credit Card	Online Mortgage Application	Online Insurance Application
Ameritrade	✓				
E*Trade	✓		✓	✓	
Fidelity	✓		✓		
Quick & Reilly	✓	✓	✓		
Schwab	✓				✓
Waterhouse	✓	✓	✓		

SOURCE: Rebecca Buckman, "Internet Brokerage Firms Break into Banking," *The Wall Street Journal*, July 2, 1998.

sales, and investment management. In fact, this is the motivation behind banks acquiring or merging with insurance companies. It will likely lead to a number of financial services hold-ing companies that effectively offer a wide range of products ranging from credit cards, mort-gages, small business loans, consumer loans, leases, insurance, brokerage services, securities underwriting, and so on, via subsidiaries that specialize in each.

■ **EXHIBIT 5.7**

PRODUCT OFFERINGS AT COMMUNITY BANKS TO GENERATE NONINTEREST INCOME

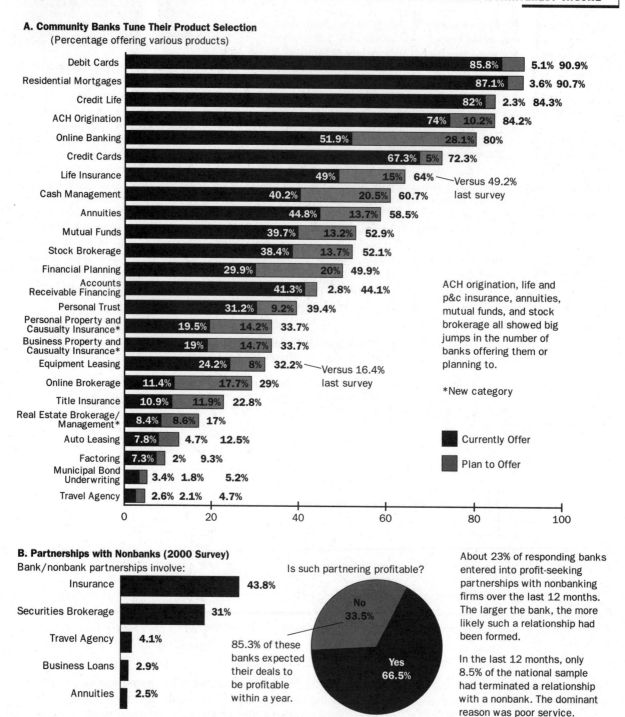

A. Community Banks Tune Their Product Selection
(Percentage offering various products)

Product	Currently Offer	Plan to Offer	Total
Debit Cards	85.8%	5.1%	90.9%
Residential Mortgages	87.1%	3.6%	90.7%
Credit Life	82%	2.3%	84.3%
ACH Origination	74%	10.2%	84.2%
Online Banking	51.9%	28.1%	80%
Credit Cards	67.3%	5%	72.3%
Life Insurance	49%	15%	64%
Cash Management	40.2%	20.5%	60.7%
Annuities	44.8%	13.7%	58.5%
Mutual Funds	39.7%	13.2%	52.9%
Stock Brokerage	38.4%	13.7%	52.1%
Financial Planning	29.9%	20%	49.9%
Accounts Receivable Financing	41.3%	2.8%	44.1%
Personal Trust	31.2%	9.2%	39.4%
Personal Property and Causalty Insurance*	19.5%	14.2%	33.7%
Business Property and Causalty Insurance*	19%	14.7%	33.7%
Equipment Leasing	24.2%	8%	32.2%
Online Brokerage	11.4%	17.7%	29%
Title Insurance	10.9%	11.9%	22.8%
Real Estate Brokerage/Management*	8.4%	8.6%	17%
Auto Leasing	7.8%	4.7%	12.5%
Factoring	7.3%	2%	9.3%
Municipal Bond Underwriting	3.4%	1.8%	5.2%
Travel Agency	2.6%	2.1%	4.7%

Life Insurance ─ Versus 49.2% last survey

Equipment Leasing ─ Versus 16.4% last survey

ACH origination, life and p&c insurance, annuities, mutual funds, and stock brokerage all showed big jumps in the number of banks offering them or planning to.

*New category

■ Currently Offer

■ Plan to Offer

(x-axis: 0, 20, 40, 60, 80, 100)

B. Partnerships with Nonbanks (2000 Survey)

Bank/nonbank partnerships involve:

Insurance	43.8%
Securities Brokerage	31%
Travel Agency	4.1%
Business Loans	2.9%
Annuities	2.5%

Is such partnering profitable?

No 33.5%

Yes 66.5%

85.3% of these banks expected their deals to be profitable within a year.

About 23% of responding banks entered into profit-seeking partnerships with nonbanking firms over the last 12 months. The larger the bank, the more likely such a relationship had been formed.

In the last 12 months, only 8.5% of the national sample had terminated a relationship with a nonbank. The dominant reason was poor service.

SOURCE: Community Bank Competitiveness Survey, 2000 and 2002.

Community banks do not have the same opportunities to enter investment banking and specialty intermediation. However, they do have other potential avenues. Many banks work with bankers' banks in the same geographic area to offer services that they could not offer independently. These bankers' banks are effectively correspondent banks that are owned by member institutions, such that community banks own the bankers' banks. Bankers' banks typically make loans to members, trade federal funds, and also offer investment trust, and data processing services. A relatively new twist finds bankers' banks offering trust services to customers of member institutions.

Alternatively, many community banks are entering new product and service areas. Exhibit 5.7 describes the results of a 1999 survey of community bankers regarding the services they offered in 2001 and the ones they planned to offer. Not surprisingly, most banks relied heavily on residential mortgages, debit cards, ACH origination, credit life insurance, and credit cards. At year-end 2001, over 78 percent of community banks expected to add online banking services, with cash management and financial planning following. As noted in Panel B, many banks were pursuing partnerships with nonbank partners, particularly in the insurance and brokerage areas, in 2000.

The logic underlying this portfolio view of fee income is that a bank is diversified when it relies on different sources of income. As economic conditions change, some businesses will generate increasing fees while others will see fees drop. This is the same rationale that applies in mortgage banking, where loan origination fees vary inversely with mortgage servicing revenue.

An obvious problem is that some managers start to view these volatile fees as permanent sources of income. In fact, they are not. This was driven home during late 1998 when the financial crisis in Russia sharply reduced the value of Russian loans and outstanding debt. Combined with the problems in Asia, the capital markets essentially shut down in terms of volume. Large banks reported sharp reductions in trading revenues and many reported large losses.

A related problem is that banks view these businesses on a transactions basis. They cut interest rates on loans so that they can book the fee income. This creates the perception that they will win the business only when they are the low price provider. Instead, banks should attempt to build the same type of customer relationships that they have successfully built with many deposit and loan customers. This can be accomplished by focusing on the customers' needs across a broad range of services, rather than on single transactions, and pricing them accordingly.

STRATEGIES TO MANAGE NONINTEREST EXPENSE

Consider the competitive environment in which commercial banks operate. The basic business of banking has always been accepting deposits and making loans. In today's world, banks are high cost producers relative to money market funds run by brokerage houses and relative to the commercial paper and bond markets used by corporate borrowers. Comparatively, noninterest expense is too high and earnings are too low. For many bank managers, this mandates austere budgets directed at controlling expenses.

Since 1985, noninterest expense at commercial banks has increased each year at a declining rate. This primarily reflects efforts to cut costs and increase profitability that are driven by a fear of being acquired and/or noncompetitive. Quite simply, senior managers of acquired banks typically find that they are looking for new positions shortly after an acquisition, a fate they most aggressively try to avoid. This begs an obvious question, however. Are there too many banks, credit unions, and other financial institutions in the United States?

Do we need three different competing institutions on every downtown street corner? If banks in the same market combined their operations, they could cut payroll and occupancy expenses, eliminate boards of directors, and use computer technology more efficiently. The cost savings would be recurring and fall right to the bottom line. In fact, potential cost savings has motivated much of the recent bank merger and acquisition activity.

When they initially consider noninterest expenses, many managers focus on reducing costs. A more comprehensive strategy, however, is to manage costs in line with strategic objectives. Doesn't it seem sensible, for example, to invest in new technologies if they will reduce operating costs long-term, even if the investment adds to noninterest expense in the near term? The basic issue is to determine whether the return on the investment exceeds the bank's weighted marginal cost of capital. If it does, the investment adds value to shareholders. Gregor and Hedges (1990) examine the relationship between the ratio of noninterest expense to assets, the relative growth rate in noninterest expense to assets, and the market-to-book value of stockholders' equity and conclude that there is no systematic link between cost management strategies and the market value of bank equity. Specifically, banks reporting the lowest expense ratios for both ratios reported the lowest market-to-book values of stockholders' equity. Banks with the highest expenses and relative expense growth actually reported the highest relative stock market values. The essential point is that there is no systematic link between reported expenses and the market value of firm equity.

COST MANAGEMENT STRATEGIES

What then is cost management? In general, it is a philosophy of allocating resources to the most profitable lines of business to achieve improved performance. There are four basic expense management strategies: expense reduction, operating efficiencies, revenue enhancement, and contribution growth.

EXPENSE REDUCTION. Many banks begin cost management efforts by identifying excessive expenses and eliminating them. Given that noninterest expenses consist primarily of personnel, occupancy, and data processing costs, these are the areas where cuts are initially made. It is not unusual to hear of banks announcing widespread employee reductions even absent any merger or acquisition. Because of the high cost of employee benefits, many banks use temporary workers who do not receive health insurance coverage and other benefits. Other common areas for cutting include the number of branch offices and employee medical benefits. Many banks have eliminated their data processing department altogether and contracted to buy data processing services from a nonbank vendor, such as IBM or EDS. In industry jargon, this is referred to as *outsourcing*. Contemporary Issues: Expense Reduction Opportunities identifies key areas in which a bank's expense structure can be improved.

OPERATING EFFICIENCIES. Another strategy is to increase operating efficiency in providing products and services. This can be achieved in one of three ways: by reducing costs but maintaining the existing level of products and services, by increasing the level of output but maintaining the level of current expenses, or by improving workflow. All of these approaches fall under the label of increasing productivity because they involve delivering products at lower unit costs. The first typically involves cutting staff and increasing work requirements to maintain output. Fewer people do the same amount or more work. The second addresses economies of scale and economies of scope in banking. *Economies of scale* are said to exist when a bank's average costs decrease as output increases. Diseconomies exist when average costs increase with greater output. *Economies of scope* focus on how the joint

CONTEMPORARY ISSUES

EXPENSE REDUCTION OPPORTUNITIES

Earnings Performance Group has identified several areas in which expense reduction opportunities typically arise. The following list introduces the broad areas and presents key questions that managers should address when evaluating their existing expense structure.

1. Identify ways to more effectively utilize automated systems.
   - Is data being keyed from a computer report into another personal computer system?
2. Eliminate redundant tasks/ functions.
3. Complete a review of all reports to determine whether they are actually used.
   - Are multiple copies produced when only one is needed?

- Would microfiche be just as adequate?
- Are there online screens that provide the same information as reports?
- Can reports be eliminated or combined?
- What happens to paper? Is it recycled?

4. Can we decrease the number of statements and/or notices mailed to a customer?
5. Reevaluate telephone expense, particularly long-distance charges.
6. If outside couriers/messengers are used, when was the last time the routes were rebid? Have the number of stops and/or routes been reviewed in relation to work available?

7. Are ZIP-sorts used to reduce postage expenses?
8. Are PC purchases and related peripherals centrally controlled?
9. What are the opportunities regarding reducing cost of copiers and/or fax machines by handling them centrally?
10. Review all contracts with outside vendors to determine the last time they were put out to bid. How are maintenance contracts handled?

costs of providing several products change as new products are added or existing product output is enhanced. The argument is that joint costs will grow by much less than the costs associated with producing products or providing services independently. For example, if a bank adds a new product line and can provide it and existing products at a lower unit cost than previously, economies of scope exist. Finally, improving workflow involves increasing productivity by accelerating the rate at which a task or function is performed. The intent is to eliminate redundant reviews or tasks and thereby shorten the time to finish a task.

The results of a Booz-Allen study, summarized by Sanford Rose (1989), identified three myths in bank managers' perceptions about noninterest expense. The first is that banks operate with high fixed costs. Fixed costs create problems because they cannot be reduced (that is, controlled) by managers. If banks eliminate some products or services, existing fixed costs must then be allocated to any remaining products. According to the study, however, only 10 percent of costs are shared among products and thus are truly fixed. The implication is that banks can eliminate products that are unprofitable or marginally profitable and the average costs of remaining products will be largely unchanged. The second myth is that banks produce many products at the point of minimum unit costs. In their study, just three out of 15 large banks were scale producers. The remaining 12 banks would be better off either merging with other banks or outsourcing products. The third myth is that most reductions in expenses are permanent and have a significant impact on overall profitability.

REVENUE ENHANCEMENT. Revenue enhancement involves changing the pricing of specific products and services but maintaining a sufficiently high volume of business so that total revenues increase. It is closely linked to the concept of price elasticity. Here, management wants to identify products or services that exhibit price inelastic demand. As such, an increase in price will lower the quantity demanded of the underlying product, but the proportionate decrease in demand is less than the proportionate increase in price. Revenues thus increase. Alternatively, management can attempt to expand volume while keeping price constant. This can often be achieved by target marketing to enlarge the base of consumers. It also is a by-product of improving product quality. If customers perceive an improvement in quality they will consume more and/or willingly pay a higher price.

CONTRIBUTION GROWTH. With the strategy of contribution growth, management allocates resources to best improve overall long-term profitability. Increases in expenses are acceptable and expected, but must coincide with greater anticipated increases in associated revenues. An example might be investing in new computer systems and technology to provide better customer service at reduced unit costs once volume is sufficiently large. In essence, expenses are cut in the long run but not in the near future.

Obviously, different banks follow different cost management strategies. This follows from differences in individual bank operating environments as determined by business mix, overall corporate strategic objectives, the geographic markets served, and history of cost management behavior. Each strategy can be successfully implemented if pursued with long-term objectives. Rather than use traditional measures of expense control to monitor performance, managers should examine noninterest expense relative to operating revenue compared with peers that offer the same business mix. Remember that cost management does not necessarily mean than expenses decline in absolute terms.

The net result of cost management is that banks will operate as leaner competitors. This should enhance long-term profitability and survival prospects in the consolidating banking industry. The negative aspects include the painful effects of replacing people with machines, requiring greater on-the-job work effort that potentially increases employee stress, and in many cases reduced support of community activities.

SUMMARY

This chapter examines three issues related to managing a bank's noninterest income and noninterest expense. First, it describes the strengths and weaknesses of commonly used financial ratios that presumably measure a bank's ability to control noninterest expense and grow noninterest income. Second, it discusses why banks should focus on customer profitability and the mix of fee-based businesses to improve operating performance. Third, it describes different cost management strategies intended to enhance performance.

The most commonly cited ratio today is the efficiency ratio, which is equal to noninterest expense divided by the sum of net interest income and noninterest income. The lower the ratio, the better a bank's performance—ceteris paribus—because it indicates how much a bank must pay in noninterest expense to generate one dollar of operating revenue. Many banks cite this ratio along with return on equity, return on assets, and net interest margin when describing performance for the whole bank. Stock analysts, in turn, cite this ratio when recommending bank stocks. Other key ratios describe a bank's productivity in terms of assets, expense, and net income relative to the number of full-time employees.

A crucial facet of managing noninterest income and expense is knowledge about the profitability of different customer relationships. This information allows management to target products and services and alter pricing strategies to ensure that customers get what they want and that the packages of services or products are profitable. Finally, it is appropriate for banks to follow many different cost management strategies as long as the objective is to enhance shareholder value.

QUESTIONS

1. When confronted with runaway noninterest expense, management's first impulse is to cut costs. What are the advantages and disadvantages of this approach? What other approaches are possible?

2. What are the primary sources of noninterest income for both a small community bank and a large bank with many subsidiaries and global operations?

3. What are the components of noninterest expense?

4. Describe why the efficiency ratio is a meaningful measure of cost control. Describe why it may not accurately measure cost control.

5. Which of the following banks evidences the better productivity? Both banks have $700 million in assets and conduct the same volume and type of business off-balance sheet.

	Tri-Cities Bank	Pacific Rail Bank
Assets per employee	$1,530,000	$1,880,000
Personnel expense per employee	$ 33,750	$ 42,600

6. Canadian Imperial Bank of Commerce (CIBC) reports that just 20 percent of its customers were profitable. Assuming that this applies to individuals' account relationships, make three recommendations to increase the profitability of these accounts.

7. Suppose that your bank imposes the following fees and/or service charges. Explain the bank's rationale and describe how you would respond as a customer.
   a. $3 per item for use of an ATM run by an entity other than your own bank
   b. $5 per transaction for using a live teller rather than an ATM or telephone transaction
   c. Increase in the charge for insufficient funds (where a customer writes a check for an amount greater than the balance available in the account) from $25 per item to $30 per item
   d. A 1 percent origination fee for refinancing a mortgage

8. What impact will online brokerages have on traditional commercial banks? Why?

9. Describe the strengths and weaknesses of expense reduction, revenue enhancement, and contribution growth strategies.

10. Your bank has just calculated the profitability of two small business customers. In both instances the bank earned a monthly profit of $375 from both Detail Labs and The Right Stuff. Detail Labs had a large loan with the bank and small balances. Its principals bought no other services from the bank. The Right Stuff had only a small loan, but used the bank for payroll processing and the firm's checking account transactions. The principals also had checking and CD accounts with the bank.
   a. What additional services or products would you suggest that the bank market to each of these customers?
   b. Discuss how the source of profitability will influence the choice of services and products that you recommend.

PROBLEM

Suppose that you operate a large bank, the performance of which is closely followed by a large number of stock analysts. You have just received a summary of five different analysts' reviews of your bank's performance. The essence of each report is that the bank must lower its efficiency ratio from the current 59 percent to less than 52 percent before the analysts will put a strong buy recommendation on the stock. Otherwise, the bank is viewed as a takeover target.

Describe several strategies that you might pursue in response to these reports. Discuss the strengths and weaknesses of each. Generally, do stock analysts have a reasonable influence on bank managers, or is their influence too great? Discuss whether management should focus on the operating risk ratio and what the likely impact of efforts to reduce this ratio will be.

MANAGING INTEREST RATE RISK

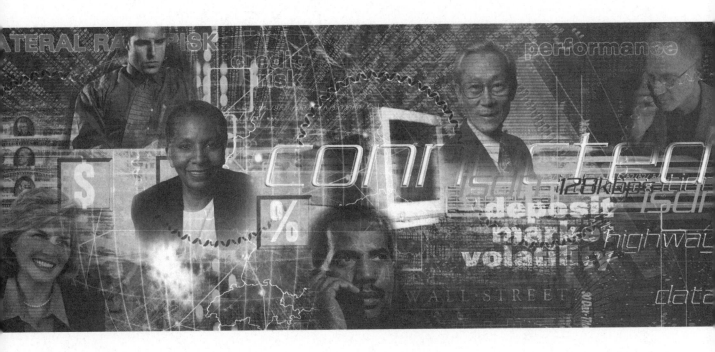

PRICING FIXED-INCOME SECURITIES

Suppose that you have $1 million to invest for one year. The interest rate quoted on every 1-year fixed-income security you consider is 8 percent. If the security pays simple interest, interest income for the year will equal $80,000. If the security pays interest compounded continuously, interest income will total $83,287, or $3,287 more. If the rate is quoted on a money market basis assuming a 360-day year, interest income will equal $81,111. The point is, interest rates are not necessarily equal. The same percentage quote may produce a different return depending on the frequency of compounding and whether the quote assumes a 360-day or 365-day year.

Of course, interest rates are important to both borrowers and investors. Regulations assist consumer borrowers by requiring banks to quote financing charges at an annual percentage rate that adjusts for these computational differences, thus enabling a direct comparison of alternative borrowing costs. Truth in Savings regulations similarly enable depositors to compare rates across various deposits. However, security investors must fend for themselves and decipher how alternative rate quotes affect the true yield.

This chapter examines four basic issues. First, it introduces the mathematics of interest rates for fixed-income securities and demonstrates the impact of compounding. Second, it describes the relationship between the interest rate on a security and the security's market price. The concepts of duration and convexity are used to measure relative price sensitivity to interest rate changes, which can then be compared between securities. Third, it explains how specific interest rates on different money market and capital market instruments are quoted. Particular attention is paid to differences between money market, bond equivalent, and effective interest rate calculations. Finally, it describes recent innovations in how securities are valued when related to viewing any fixed income security as a package of zero coupon cash flows. It introduces the concept of total return, used by investors to compare expected realized yields over some predetermined holding period. Subsequent chapters will refer to these concepts and calculations and incorporate them in various applications.

THE MATHEMATICS OF INTEREST RATES

Just as there are many different types of securities, interest rates are calculated and reported differently. Depending on the characteristics of the security and pricing conventions of securities traders, interest may be simple or compound interest, interest rates may be quoted on a discount basis or interest-bearing basis, and the assumed number of days in a year for reporting purposes may be 360 or 365. It is virtually impossible to compare quoted rates without a precise understanding of the differences in calculations.

FUTURE VALUE AND PRESENT VALUE: SINGLE PAYMENT

The mathematics of interest rates is based on the simple recognition that cash in your possession today is worth more than the same amount of cash to be received at some time in the future. For example, are you better off with $50,000 today or a contract to receive $50,000 in six months? Obviously, if you had the cash today, you could invest it for six months and it would grow in value. The difference in value depends on the relevant interest rate that characterizes your opportunity cost or investment opportunities. This concept, or more precisely that of future value and present value, provides the framework for interest rate calculations.

Suppose that at the beginning of a year, an individual purchases a security for $1,000. The seller of the security, in turn, promises to pay the individual $1,080 exactly one year later. In this scenario, $1,000 represents the present value (PV) of the security, $1,080 represents the future value after one year (FV1), and $80 is interest. Expressing the $80 relative to the initial investment as a rate of interest (i),

$$i = \$80/\$1,000 = 0.08$$

Alternatively,

$$\$1,000(1 + i) = \$1,080$$

or

$$i = \$1,080/\$1,000 - 1$$

$$= 0.08 = 8\%$$

In general, with a single payment after one year (FV1) that includes interest and the initial investment, the following relationship applies:

$$PV(1 + i) = FV1 \tag{6.1}$$

Suppose that the same individual decides to buy another 1-year security at the end of the first year and that the seller agrees to pay 8 percent on the entire $1,080 invested. Note that the individual is effectively earning interest on the initial $1,000 plus the first year's $80 in interest, so $1,080 represents the present value at the beginning of the second year. Substituting $1,080 for PV and .08 for i in Equation 6.1 reveals that the future value after the second year (FV2) equals $1,166.40.[1]

$$\$1,080(1 + 0.08) = \$1,166.40 = FV2$$

Combining this with Equation 6.1 produces

$$\$1,000(1 + .08)(1 + 0.08) = \$1,166.40 = FV2$$

---

[1]The number in the notation FV1 and FV2 refers to the number of periods from the present until the cash flow arises. This example assumes that interest is earned on interest (compounding) and that interest is compounded annually.

or

$$PV(1 + i)^2 = FV2 \qquad (6.2)$$

Alternatively, if the future value and present value are known, we can calculate the fixed annual interest rate from Equation 6.2 as:

$$i = [FV2/PV]^{1/2} - 1 \qquad (6.3)$$

Using data from the previous example,

$$i = [\$1,166.40/\$1,000]^{1/2} - 1 = 0.08$$

When an amount is invested for several periods and interest is earned on both the initial investment plus periodic interest (compound interest), the following general relationship holds:

$$PV(1 + i)^n = FVn \qquad (6.4)$$

where n represents the number of periods until the future value is determined. Equation 6.4 can be viewed from several vantage points. There are four variables. As long as three are known, we can solve for the fourth. Thus, if we know the initial present value, the periodic interest rate, and the number of years that interest applies, we can solve for the future value as in Equation 6.4. If we know everything except the interest rate, we can use Equation 6.5 to solve for i.

$$i = [FVn/PV]^{1/n} - 1 \qquad (6.5)$$

For example, the future value of $1,000 invested for six years at 8 percent per year with annual compounding (FV6) is $1,586.87.

$$\$1,000(1.08)^6 = \$1,586.87$$

Suppose, instead, that we know that with $1,000 invested today for six years, the initial investment plus accumulated interest will be worth $1,700 in six years. What is the annual interest rate? Clearly, the rate must exceed 8 percent because the future value is greater than the $1,586.87 realized above. Using Equation 6.5, we know that

$$i = [\$1,700/\$1,000]^{1/6} - 1$$

$$= 0.0925$$

Note that in both examples the interest rate used (annual rate) is matched with the frequency of compounding (annual).

In many instances, investors and borrowers want to determine the present value of some future cash payment or receipt. Investors often forecast future cash flows from an asset and want to know the value in today's dollars; that is, how much to pay. Equation 6.4 provides the calculation for the present value of a single future cash flow when we solve for PV and is restated as Equation 6.6.

$$PV = \frac{FVn}{(1 + i)^n} \qquad (6.6)$$

In this case, the future value is said to be discounted back to a present value equivalent. Suppose that you have a choice between receiving an immediate $30,000 cash payment, or $37,500 in two years. Which would you choose? Assuming you aren't in desperate need of cash today, compare the present value of $37,500 to $30,000. If your opportunity cost of money is 8 percent annually; i.e., your investment alternatives yield 8 percent per year, the present value of the $37,500 future cash flow is $32,150.

$$PV = \frac{\$37,500}{(1.08)^2} = \$32,150$$

Intuitively, you would need to invest $32,150 today at 8 percent to accumulate $37,500 in two years. Alternatively, the future cash flow is worth $2,150 more today than the immediate cash payment, so you would prefer the $37,500.

FUTURE VALUE AND PRESENT VALUE: MULTIPLE PAYMENTS

Future value and present value analysis are only slightly more complicated when more than one cash flow is involved. The only difference is that the future or present value of each cash flow is computed separately, with the cumulative value determined as the sum of the computations for each cash flow (CF).

Suppose that an individual makes a $1,000 deposit in a bank earning 8 percent annually at the beginning of each of the next two years. What is the cumulative future value of both deposits after the second year? The first deposit earns two years of interest, while the second deposit earns just one year of interest. The future value of both deposits after two years is:

$$\text{FV of first deposit} = \$1,000(1.08)^2 = \$1,166.40$$
$$\text{FV of second deposit} = \$1,000(1.08) = \underline{\$1,080.00}$$
$$\text{Cumulative future value} \quad \$2,246.40$$

In general, setting CF_n equal to the periodic cash flow in period n and assuming that all cash flows are invested at the beginning of each year at the fixed rate i, the cumulative future value of a series of cash flows (CFV_n) after n periods can be expressed as:

$$CFV_n = CF_1(1 + i)^n + CF_2(1 + i)^{n-1} + CF_3(1 + i)^{n-2} + \ldots + CF_n(1 + i) \tag{6.7}$$

This type of calculation is often used when trying to determine how much needs to be invested periodically to fund a future expenditure, such as payments for a child's college education.

The present value concept is more typically applied to a series of future cash flows. Investors may know the promised payments on a bond, or they may forecast the expected cash flows from buying a business. The present value of a series of cash flows equals the sum of the present values of the individual cash flows. Using the above notation and assumptions, the present value of a series of n cash flows can be expressed as:

$$PV = \frac{CF_1}{(1 + i)} + \frac{CF_2}{(1 + i)^2} + \frac{CF_3}{(1 + i)^3} + \ldots + \frac{CF_n}{(1 + i)^n} \tag{6.8}$$

or, using summation notation

$$PV = \sum_{t=1}^{n} \frac{CF_t}{(1 + i)^t}$$

Each future cash flow is discounted back to its present value equivalent, and the respective present values are added. Note that Equation 6.8 assumes that the same discount rate (i) applies to each cash flow. We will modify this later when we discuss the valuation of fixed income securities.

In this context, determine how much you would pay for a security that pays $90 at the end of each of the next three years plus another $1,000 at the end of the third year if the relevant interest rate is 10 percent. Using Equation 6.8,

$$PV = \frac{\$90}{(1.1)} + \frac{\$90}{(1.1)^2} + \frac{\$1,090}{(1.1)^3} = \$975.13$$

Again, if the present value, future values, and number of periods are known, we can solve Equation 6.8 for i to determine the relevant discount rate. For fixed income securities, this discount rate is the market rate of interest typically labeled the yield to maturity.[2]

SIMPLE VERSUS COMPOUND INTEREST

In practice, the amount of interest paid on a security is determined in many different ways. One difference is that interest may be computed as **simple interest** or **compound interest.** Simple interest is interest that is paid only on the initial principal invested. Bank commercial loans, for example, normally quote simple interest payments. In contrast, compound interest is interest paid on outstanding principal plus any interest that has been earned but not paid out. Most bank deposits pay compound interest.

Simple interest equals the outstanding principal amount times the periodic interest rate times the number of periods. With the previous notation, simple interest equals

$$\text{simple interest} = PV(i)n \qquad \qquad \textbf{(6.9)}$$

In this case, the interest rate i is the periodic rate while n refers to the number of periods. Thus, if n equals one year and i equals 12 percent per year, simple interest on $1,000 equals

$$\text{simple interest} = \$1{,}000(0.12)1 = \$120$$

Suppose that interest on the above contract is paid monthly. What is the monthly simple interest payment?

$$\text{monthly simple interest} = \$1{,}000(0.12)(1/12) = \$10$$

The example following Equation 6.5 showed that $1,000 invested for six years at 8 percent with annual interest compounding produced a future value of $1,586.87. This assumed that interest was earned annually on the previous years' cumulative interest. Suppose, instead, that interest is 8 percent simple interest. What will the future value of principal plus interest equal?

$$\text{simple interest} = \$1{,}000(0.08)6 = \$480$$
$$\text{original principal} = \$1{,}000$$
$$\text{future value} = \$1{,}480$$

Obviously, the actual interest varies dramatically depending on whether simple or compound interest applies.

As indicated, compound interest assumes that interest is paid on principal and interest. Each of the equations 6.1 through 6.8 uses annual interest rates and assumes annual compounding.

COMPOUNDING FREQUENCY

Interest may be compounded over a variety of intervals. In many cases, it is compounded over periods much less than one year, such as daily or monthly. Fortunately, the same formulas apply, with a small adjustment that consists of converting the annual interest rate to a periodic interest rate that coincides with the compounding interval, and letting the number of periods equal n times the number of compounding periods in a year (m):

---

[2]Another way to view the above calculation is to note that if you deposited $975.13 in an account that earns 10 percent interest per year, you could withdraw $90 at the end of each of the next two years and $1,090 at the end of the third year, which would leave a zero balance.

■ EXHIBIT 6.1

THE EFFECT OF COMPOUNDING ON FUTURE VALUE AND PRESENT VALUE

A. What is the future value after 1 year of $1,000 invested at an 8% annual nominal rate?

Compounding Interval	Number of Compounding Intervals in 1 Year (m)	Future Value (FV1)*	Effective Interest Rate*
Year	1	$1,080.00	8.00%
Semiannual	2	1,081.60	8.16
Quarter	4	1,082.43	8.24
Month	12	1,083.00	8.30
Day	365	1,083.28	8.33
Continuous	†	1,083.29	8.33

B. What is the present value of $1,000 received at the end of 1 year with compounding at 8%?

Compounding Interval	Number of Compounding Intervals in 1 Year (m)	Present Value (PV)*	Effective Interest Rate*
Year	1	$925.93	8.00%
Semiannual	2	924.56	8.16
Quarter	4	923.85	8.24
Month	12	923.36	8.30
Day	365	923.12	8.33
Continuous	†	923.12	8.33

*Most financial calculators can easily generate the required calculations.
†Continuous compounding assumes that compounding occurs over such short intervals that it is instantaneous, or that m in Equations 6.10 and 6.11 approaches infinity. Mathematically, continuous compounding is based on Euler's e such that
$\lim\limits_{m = \infty} \left(1+\dfrac{1}{m}\right)^m = e^i$, where e = 2.71828. Thus, equations 6.10 and 6.11 produce $FVn = PVe^{in}$, and $PV = \dfrac{FVn}{e^{in}}$.

$$PV(1 + i/m)^{nm} = FVn \tag{6.10}$$

and

$$PV = \frac{FVn}{(1 + i/m)^{nm}} \tag{6.11}$$

If compounding occurs daily, m equals 365 and the periodic rate equals the annual rate divided by 365. If compounding occurs monthly, m equals 12 and the periodic rate equals i divided by 12. The product of n times m (nm) is the total number of compounding periods. Exhibit 6.1 demonstrates the impact of different intra-year compounding intervals on future value and present value in line with Equations 6.10 and 6.11. As indicated, the future value after one year is greatest when compounding frequency is the highest because more frequent compounding means that interest is applied to previous interest more frequently. In a similar vein, the present value of a fixed amount is lowest when compounding frequency is highest as the more interest that can be earned, the lower is the initial value required to invest and return the same future value.

Exhibit 6.1 also demonstrates the impact of different effective interest rates. An effective interest rate, in contrast to a nominal or contract rate, incorporates the effect of compounding and thus allows a comparison of yields. Assuming compounding frequency of at least once a year, the effective annual interest rate, i*, can be calculated from Equation 6.12.[3]

$$i* = (1 + i/m)^m - 1 \tag{6.12}$$

---

[3]With continuous compounding i* = e^i − 1.

• EXHIBIT 6.2

PRICE AND YIELD RELATIONSHIPS FOR OPTION-FREE BONDS THAT ARE EQUIVALENT EXCEPT FOR THE FEATURE ANALYZED

Relationship	Impact
1. Market interest rates and bond prices vary inversely.	1. Bond prices fall as interest rates rise and rise as interest rates fall.
2. For a specific absolute change in interest rates, the proportionate increase in bond prices when rates fall exceeds the proportionate decrease in bond prices when rates rise. The proportionate difference increases with maturity and is larger the lower a bond's periodic interest payment.	2. For the identical absolute change in interest rates, a bondholder will realize a greater capital gain when rates decline than capital loss when rates increase.
3. Long-term bonds change proportionately more in price than short-term bonds for a given change in interest rates from the same base level.	3. Investors can realize greater capital gains and capital losses on long-term securities than on short-term securities when interest rates change by the same amount.
4. Low-coupon bonds change proportionately more in price than high-coupon bonds for a given change in interest rates from the same base level.	4. Low-coupon bonds exhibit greater relative price volatility than do high-coupon bonds.

THE RELATIONSHIP BETWEEN INTEREST RATES AND OPTION-FREE BOND PRICES

As indicated earlier, present value and future value are linked via precise mathematical relationships in Equations 6.4 and 6.8. This suggests that there are systematic relationships between PV, future cash flows, i, and n. In fact, much research has attempted to characterize the exact influence of each variable on the pricing relationships. The following analysis focuses on the relationship between bond prices and their associated market interest rates, and how this relationship changes as the magnitude and timing of future cash flows vary. This discussion can be characterized as the traditional analysis of bond pricing for bonds that do not have options. Exhibit 6.2 summarizes the features of four systematic price relationships. These apply to option-free securities in the traditional framework.

BOND PRICES AND INTEREST RATES VARY INVERSELY

The typical fixed-rate coupon bond, without options, has the following features: a par or face value that represents the return of principal at maturity, a final maturity in years, and a coupon payment that is fixed (hence fixed income) over the life of the bond. The other two components are the market price (PV in Equation 6.8) and the market interest rate (i in Equation 6.8). Most fixed-income bonds are initially sold in the primary market at prices close to par or face value. The fixed coupon rate, defined as the coupon payment divided by the face value, determines the amount of coupon interest that is paid periodically (typically semiannually) until final maturity. After issue, bonds trade in the secondary market, at which time their prices reflect current market conditions. Thus, current market prices reflect the size of the fixed coupon payment (coupon rate) versus the coupon interest paid (determined by the market rate) on a newly issued bond with otherwise similar features.

Market interest rates and prices on fixed-income securities vary coincidentally and are inversely related.[4] As such, prices decline when interest rates rise and prices rise when interest rates decline. The sensitivity of the price move relative to the change in interest rates is determined by the size and timing of the cash flows on the underlying security. For coupon bonds, the periodic cash flows consist of interest payments and par value at maturity. The appropriate pricing relationship is characterized by Equation 6.8 where i represents the market yield to maturity.

Consider a bond with a $10,000 face value that makes fixed semiannual interest payments of $470 and matures in exactly three years, at which time the investor receives $10,000 in principal. Note that the semiannual coupon rate is 4.7 percent ($470/$10,000). If the current market interest rate equals 4.7 percent semiannually (9.4 percent per annum), the prevailing price of the bond equals $10,000 as determined below. There are six semiannual compounding periods.

$$\text{Price} = \sum_{t=1}^{6} \frac{\$470}{(1.047)^t} + \frac{\$10,000}{(1.047)^6} = \$10,000$$

At 9.4 percent, this bond sells at a price equal to par or face value.

Now suppose that the corporate issuer of the bonds announces unexpectedly poor earnings and forecasts a declining capacity to service its debt in the future. Owners of the bonds subsequently rush to sell their holdings. What should happen to the market interest rate and price of the bond? If the announcement was truly unexpected, then the perceived riskiness of the security has increased. Holders recognize that there is a greater probability that the promised cash flows may not materialize, so they discount the expected cash flows at a higher rate. This essentially means that investors now need a larger default risk premium, reflected by a higher market interest rate, to entice them to buy the bond. If the annual yield to maturity immediately increased to 10 percent (5 percent semiannually), the price of the bond would fall to $9,847.73. With a price below par, this bond becomes a discount bond.

$$\text{Price} = \sum_{t=1}^{6} \frac{\$470}{(1.05)^t} + \frac{\$10,000}{(1.05)^6} = \$9,847.73$$

Thus, a bond's price and market interest rate vary inversely when market rates rise. If, instead, the annual market interest rate immediately fell to 8.8 percent (4.4 percent semiannually), the bond's price would rise to $10,155.24. In this scenario, the bond becomes a premium bond because its price exceeds par.

$$\text{Price} = \sum_{t=1}^{6} \frac{\$470}{(1.044)^t} + \frac{\$10,000}{(1.044)^6} = \$10,155.24$$

Exhibit 6.3 plots the relationship between the price and market interest rate on this bond. As indicated, higher bond prices are associated with lower market interest rates, and vice versa.

Again, the ratio of the annualized periodic interest payment to a bond's par value is labeled the coupon rate. In the previous example, the coupon rate equaled 9.4 percent (2 × $470/ $10,000). In bond trading circles, if this bond was issued in 2002, it would be labeled the 9.4s of 2004. The following schedule describes the general relationship among yield to maturity, coupon rate, and bond price.

---

[4]Securities that carry floating rates or variable rates pay interest that changes as market rates change. Such instruments subsequently trade close to par. The price/yield relationships in Exhibit 6.2 apply only to fixed-income securities.

• EXHIBIT 6.3

RELATIONSHIP BETWEEN PRICE AND INTEREST RATE ON A 3-YEAR, $10,000
OPTION-FREE PAR BOND THAT PAYS $470 IN SEMIANNUAL INTEREST

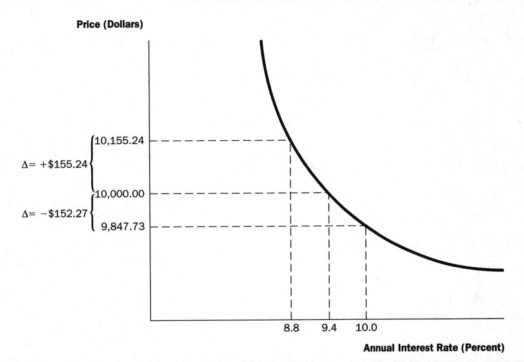

Type of Bond	Yield to Maturity vs. Coupon Rate
Par Bond	Yield to maturity = coupon rate
Discount Bond	Yield to maturity > coupon rate
Premium Bond	Yield to maturity < coupon rate

BOND PRICES CHANGE ASYMMETRICALLY TO RISING AND FALLING RATES

For a given absolute change in interest rates, the percentage increase in a bond's price will exceed the percentage decrease. Consider the price-to-yield relationship in Exhibit 6.3. When the bond is priced at par, the market rate equals 9.4 percent. If the market yield suddenly increases by 60 basis points to 10 percent, the price falls by $152.28 or 1.52 percent. If the market yield suddenly decreases by the same 60 basis points to 8.8 percent, the price rises by $155.24, or 1.55 percent. While the proportionate difference may seem small, it increases with maturity and is larger for bonds with lower periodic interest payments. The dollar difference will also increase with greater par value.

This asymmetric price relationship is due to the convex shape of the curve in Exhibit 6.3, which reflects a difference in bond duration at different interest rate levels. The duration concept and applications are discussed later in this chapter. The primary implication is that for the same change in interest rates, bondholders will realize a greater capital gain when rates fall than capital loss when rates rise for all option-free bonds.

THE EFFECT OF MATURITY ON THE RELATIONSHIP BETWEEN PRICE AND
INTEREST RATE ON FIXED-INCOME, OPTION-FREE BONDS

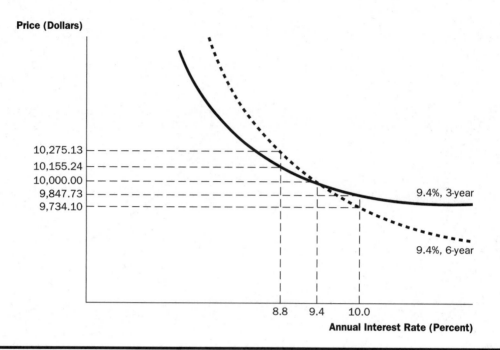

MATURITY INFLUENCES BOND PRICE SENSITIVITY

Short-term and long-term bonds exhibit different price volatility. For bonds that pay the same coupon interest rate, long-term bonds change proportionately more in price than do short-term bonds for a given rate change. Exhibit 6.4 contrasts the price-yield relationship for a 9.4 percent coupon bond with six years to maturity to that of the 3-year bond with the same 9.4 percent coupon discussed earlier. Note that the only difference between the two bonds is final maturity and thus the number of interim cash flows. When both market rates equal 9.4 percent, both bonds are priced at par. The following calculations indicate the price of the 6-year bond when the market rate rises to 10 percent and falls to 8.8 percent, respectively.

$$\text{Price} = \sum_{t=1}^{12} \frac{\$470}{(1.05)^t} + \frac{\$10{,}000}{(1.05)^{12}} = \$9{,}734.10$$

$$\text{Price} = \sum_{t=1}^{12} \frac{\$470}{(1.044)^t} + \frac{\$10{,}000}{(1.044)^{12}} = \$10{,}275.13$$

As indicated in Exhibit 6.4, when rates on both bonds increase by 60 basis points, the price of the 6-year bond falls lower than the price of the 3-year bond. The proportionate price declines are 2.66 percent and 1.52 percent, respectively. When rates decline by 60 basis points, the 6-year bond's price increases 2.75 percent while the 3-year bond's price increases by 1.55 percent.

The rationale for the different price sensitivity has to do with the basic present value in Equation 6.8. The buyer of a 6-year bond contracts to receive fixed interest payments for twice as many periods as the buyer of a 3-year bond. When priced at par, the coupon and market rate are 9.4 percent. If market rates increase, buyers of newly issued par bonds will receive periodic interest at a higher market (and coupon) rate. Holders of "old" discount bonds now receive below-market interest payments. With the 6-year bond, these below-market payments will persist for twice as long as with the 3-year bond. Thus, the price of the 6-year bond declines more than does the price of the 3-year bond. The opposite holds when interest rates fall. The holder of a 6-year bond receives above-market interest payments, which are locked in for twice as long as for the 3-year bond. Thus, the price of a 6-year bond will rise above the price of a 3-year bond.

Suppose that an investor owns a 9.4 percent coupon bond with nine years to maturity. If the market rate changes from 9.4 percent to 10 percent, its price drops from $10,000 to $9,649.31.

$$\text{Price} = \sum_{t=1}^{18} \frac{\$470}{(1.05)^t} + \frac{\$10,000}{(1.05)^{18}} = \$9,649.31$$

Not surprisingly, this is well below the price of the 6-year bond at 10 percent. The following schedule compares the percentage price changes for the 3-, 6-, and 9-year bonds when interest rates rise from 9.4 percent to 10 percent.

| | Price Change | | |
	3-Year	6-Year	9-Year
Percentage Change	−1.52%	−2.66%	−3.51%
Difference		−1.14%	−0.85%

Note that the rate of change in the percentage price decline falls from 1.14 percent to 0.85 percent as maturity lengthens. This general relationship holds: As maturity lengthens, the rate of change in the percentage price change declines. You should verify this for the 9-year bond in the case where its rate falls to 8.8 percent.

THE SIZE OF COUPON INFLUENCES BOND PRICE SENSITIVITY

High-coupon and low-coupon bonds exhibit different price volatility. Suppose that two bonds are priced to yield the same yield to maturity. For a given change in market rate, the bond with the lower coupon will change more in price than the bond with the higher coupon. This is demonstrated in Exhibit 6.5, which plots the price and yield relationship for two otherwise identical 3-year maturity instruments: a zero coupon bond with three years to maturity, and one cash flow of $10,000 paid at maturity, and the 9.4 percent coupon bond introduced earlier. As the market rate falls below 9.4 percent, the price of the zero coupon bond rises by proportionately more than the price of the coupon bond. At 8.8 percent, the price of the zero rises by 1.74 percent while the price of the 9.4 percent coupon bond rises by just 1.55 percent. The same relationship appears when the market rate rises to 10 percent. Again, this difference increases with maturity and may be quite substantial with large denomination securities.

DURATION AND PRICE VOLATILITY

The previous discussion of bond price volatility focuses on the relationship between a security's market rate of interest, periodic interest payment, and maturity. In fact, the price rules indicate that volatility changes systematically as each of these factors changes. Most financial economists look to **duration** as a comprehensive measure of these relationships. Simply focusing on interest rate changes ignores the size of interest payment and length of time until each payment is received. Because maturity simply identifies how much time elapses until

· EXHIBIT 6.5

THE EFFECTS OF COUPON ON THE RELATIONSHIP BETWEEN PRICE
AND INTEREST RATE ON FIXED-INCOME, OPTION-FREE BONDS

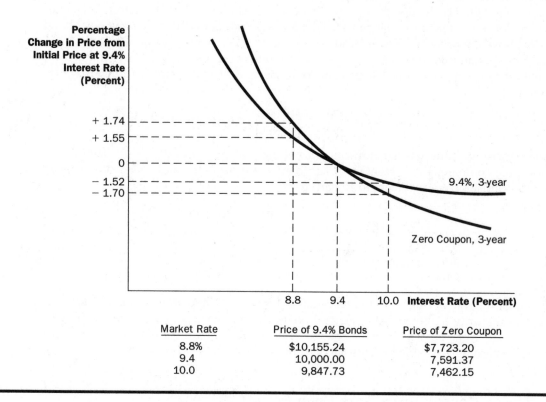

Market Rate	Price of 9.4% Bonds	Price of Zero Coupon
8.8%	$10,155.24	$7,723.20
9.4	10,000.00	7,591.37
10.0	9,847.73	7,462.15

final payment, it ignores all information about the timing and magnitude of interim payments. The size of coupon, in turn, provides no information about the rate at which interim cash flows can be reinvested or even how many cash flows are promised.

DURATION AS AN ELASTICITY MEASURE

Duration is a measure of effective maturity that incorporates the timing and size of a security's cash flows. It captures the combined impact of market rate, the size of interim payments, and maturity on a security's price volatility. Conceptually, duration is most easily understood as a measure of interest elasticity in determining a security's market value. Thus, if a security's duration is known, an investor can readily estimate the size of a change in value (or price) for different interest rate changes.[5]

There are two important interpretations of duration analysis that apply to valuing most option-free securities and portfolios without embedded options.

1. Duration is a measure of how price sensitive a security (or portfolio) is to a change in interest rates.

2. The greater (shorter) is duration, the greater (lesser) is price sensitivity.

---

[5]The following discussion uses Macaulay's measure of duration, which is introduced formally later in the chapter.

Remember when you were first introduced to the concept of price elasticity? If you knew the price elasticity of demand for a good or service, you could estimate how much quantity demanded would change when the price changed. In general,

$$\text{price elasticity of demand} = -\frac{\%\text{ change in quantity demanded}}{\%\text{ change in price}}$$

Because quantity demanded varies inversely with price changes, the minus sign converts the relative percentage changes to a positive measure. Thus, if a bank raises its charge for usage of an automatic teller machine (ATM) from 50 cents to 75 cents per transaction, and the number of monthly ATM transactions drops from 100,000 to 70,000, the price elasticity of demand is estimated at 0.6.

$$\text{price elasticity of demand} = -\frac{-30{,}000/100{,}000}{\$0.25/\$0.50} = \frac{0.3}{0.5} = 0.6$$

This elasticity measure indicates that a proportionate change in price coincides with a smaller proportionate change in quantity demanded. If the elasticity remained constant at higher prices, the bank could estimate that a further price increase to $1 per item (+33 percent) would lower usage to approximately 56,000 (-20 percent $= -0.33 \times 0.6$) items monthly.

A security's duration can similarly be interpreted as an elasticity measure. But instead of the relationship between quantity demanded and price, duration provides information about the change in market value as a result of interest rate changes. Letting P equal the price of a security and i equal the security's prevailing market interest rate, duration can be approximated by the following expression:

$$\text{Duration} \cong -\left[\frac{\dfrac{\Delta P}{P}}{\dfrac{\Delta i}{(1+i)}}\right] \tag{6.13}$$

The numerator represents the percentage change in price, while the denominator represents the approximate percentage change in interest rates.

Consider the 3-year zero coupon bond from Exhibit 6.5 that pays $10,000 at maturity. At an annual market rate of 9.4 percent, this bond's price equals $7,591.37 assuming semiannual compounding. As demonstrated later, this bond has a duration of exactly three years, or six semiannual periods. An analyst can use Equation 6.13 to estimate the change in price of this bond when its market rate changes. Restating the expression,

$$\Delta P \cong -\text{Duration}\,[\Delta i/(1+i)]P \tag{6.14}$$

Suppose the market rate rises immediately from 4.7 percent to 5 percent semiannually. Using semiannual data, the estimated change in price equals $-$130.51$, or 1.72 percent of the price.

$$\Delta P = -6[.003/1.047]\$7{,}591.37$$
$$= -\$130.51$$

This overstates the true price decline as Exhibit 6.5 demonstrates that the actual price change equals $-$129.21$.

MEASURING DURATION

Duration is measured in units of time and represents a security's effective maturity. More precisely, it is a weighted average of the time until expected cash flows from a security will be received, relative to the current price of the security. The weights are the present values of each cash flow divided by the current price. Early cash flows thus carry a greater weight than later cash flows, and the greater the size of the cash flow the greater is the weight and contribution to the duration estimate.

The following examples use Macaulay's duration, which was first introduced in 1938. While this duration measure has been modified to improve its applicability, it serves as a useful first approximation. Chapter 8, which addresses interest rate risk management issues, summarizes criticisms of Macaulay's duration and offers extensions.

Using general notation, Macaulay's duration (D) appears as:

$$D = \frac{\sum_{t=1}^{k} \dfrac{CF_t(t)}{(1+i)^t}}{\sum_{t=1}^{k} \dfrac{CF_t}{(1+i)^t}} \tag{6.15}$$

where

CF_t = dollar value of the cash flow at time t,
  t = the number of periods of time until the cash flow payment,
  i = the periodic yield to maturity of the security generating the cash flow, and
  k = the number of cash flows.

Duration is thus a weighted average of the time until the cash flows arise. As described earlier, the numerator equals the present value of each cash flow times the number of periods until the cash flow arises. The denominator is simply the price of the instrument. The weight for each cash flow equals the present value from the numerator divided by the current price (the entire denominator). The weighted average is therefore measured in some unit of time, such as days, months, etc., but is usually discussed in terms of years.

Consider the 9.4 percent, 3-year coupon bond with a face value of $10,000. The duration of this security, assuming that it is currently priced at par, is noncallable and nonputable prior to maturity, and all interest and principal payments are made as scheduled, is 5.37 semiannual periods. The calculation is demonstrated in Exhibit 6.6. Note that each cash flow is converted to its present value by discounting at the prevailing market rate of 4.7 percent. Each present value is then divided by the prevailing price ($10,000) and multiplied by the units of time until the cash flow arises. Because the largest cash flow is the principal payment received at maturity, its weight in the duration calculation is greatest at 79 percent, and the duration of 5.37 semiannual periods is close to final maturity.

Contrast duration of the coupon bond with duration of the zero coupon bond described in Exhibit 6.5. With the zero coupon security there are no interim cash flows. The only payment is $10,000 after three years. Using Equation 6.15, its estimated duration is six semiannual periods. There is only one cash flow such that an investor receives 100 percent (weight is one) of the expected cash flows back at maturity.

$$\text{Duration of 3-year zero} = \frac{[\$10,000/(1.047)^6](6)}{\$10,000/(1.047)^6} = 6$$

The 3-year coupon bond's duration is shorter at 5.37 semiannual periods because there are interim cash flows and an investor receives some of the cash payments prior to final maturity. In general, Macaulay's duration of a zero coupon security equals its final maturity. The duration of any security with interim cash flows will be less than duration.

A basic contribution of duration is that it accounts for differences in time until interim cash flows are received between securities. Large, near-term cash flows receive the greatest weight and thus shorten estimated duration. Large cash flows arising near maturity lengthen duration. In both of these examples, the bulk of cash flows was received near maturity, so duration was relatively long.

• EXHIBIT 6.6

A SAMPLE DURATION CALCULATION

A. Time Line Characterizing Cash Flows

0	1	2	3	4	5	6
	470	470	470	470	470	470
						10,000

B. Estimated Macaulay's Duration

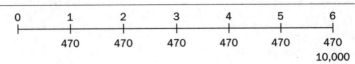

$$\text{Duration} = \frac{\dfrac{470[1]}{(1.047)^1} + \dfrac{470[2]}{(1.047)^2} + \dfrac{470[3]}{(1.047)^3} + \dfrac{470[4]}{(1.047)^4} + \dfrac{470[5]}{(1.047)^5} + \dfrac{10,470[6]}{(1.047)^6}}{10,000}$$

$$= \frac{448.9[1] + 428.8[2] + 409.5[3] + 391.1[4] + 373.6[5] + 7,948.2[6]}{10,000}$$

$$= .0449[1] + .0429[2] + .0409[3] + .0391[4] + .0374[5] + .7948[6]$$

$$= 5.37 \text{ semiannual periods (or 2.68 years)}$$

COMPARATIVE PRICE SENSITIVITY

The duration concept is useful because it enables market participants to estimate the relative price volatility of different securities. Remember the second rule for interpreting duration: the greater is duration, the greater is price sensitivity. This is reflected in Equation 6.14 and the following extension.

$$\frac{\Delta P}{P} \cong -\left[\frac{\text{Duration}}{(1 + i)}\right]\Delta i \qquad\qquad (6.16)$$

Equation 6.16 characterizes the formal elasticity relationship between interest rates and bond prices and is the same as Equation 6.14 except that the percentage change in price is on the left-hand side of the equality and Macaulay's duration is divided by one plus the market interest rate. This latter ratio is labeled **modified duration** and is widely used by bond market participants,

$$\text{modified duration} = \frac{\text{Macaulay's duration}}{(1 + i)}$$

such that the percentage price change of a security or portfolio approximately equals modified duration times the change in market rate.

These relationships are quite intuitive because they demonstrate that the greater is duration or modified duration, the greater is the percentage change and/or actual change in price for a given change in interest rates. For example, consider the two par bonds from Exhibit 6.4 that are priced at par when market rates equal 9.4 percent. According to the above formulas, the bond with the longest duration will exhibit the greatest price volatility.

This relationship is demonstrated in Exhibit 6.7 for these two coupon bonds and two zero coupon bonds. All of the bonds are assumed to carry an annual yield of 9.4 percent, but they have different prices and durations, depending on maturity and whether interim interest payments are made. Thus, the two zero coupon bonds have Macaulay durations of 6 and 12 semiannual periods equal to maturity and trade at discount prices well below their $10,000 face value. As implied above, the Macaulay durations of the coupon bonds are slightly less than maturity and the modified durations for all bonds are slightly less than the corresponding Macaulay durations.

■ **EXHIBIT 6.7**

	Type of Bond			
	3-Yr. Zero	**6-Yr. Zero**	**3-Yr. Coupon**	**6-Yr. Coupon**
Initial market rate (annual)	9.40%	9.40%	9.40%	9.40%
Initial market rate (semiannual)	4.70%	4.70%	4.70%	4.70%
Maturity value	$10,000	$10,000	$10,000	$10,000
Initial price	$7,591.37	$5,762.88	$10,000	$10,000
Duration: semiannual periods	6.00	12.00	5.37	9.44
Modified duration	5.73	11.46	5.12	9.02
Rate Increases to 10% (5% Semiannually)				
Estimated ΔP	−$130.51	−$198.15	−$153.74	−$270.45
Estimated $\dfrac{\Delta P}{P}$	−1.72%	−3.44%	−1.54%	−2.70%
Initial elasticity	0.2693	0.5387	0.2406	0.4242

Formulas

$\Delta P \cong -\text{Duration} [\Delta i/1 + i)]P$

$\dfrac{\Delta P}{P} \cong -[\text{Duration}/(1 + i)]\Delta i$

    where Duration equals Macaulay's duration.

The bottom part of the exhibit demonstrates how to interpret duration data. Suppose that market yields on all four bonds suddenly increase to 10 percent, or 5 percent semiannually. The comparative absolute change in price, percentage change in price, and initial elasticities are provided at the bottom of the exhibit. Consider the 3-year and 6-year zero coupon bonds. Using Equation 6.14, the estimated change in price is −$131 and −$198, respectively. Using Equation 6.16, the estimated percentage change in price is −1.72 percent and −3.44 percent, respectively. Thus, with the same absolute and percentage change in market rates, the longer duration 6-year bond exhibits the greater price decline both in absolute and percentage terms. This is consistent with its greater duration and interest rate elasticity of 0.5387 versus 0.2693. Consider now the two coupon bonds. Not surprisingly, the same relative price sensitivity appears. With the rate increase, the price of the bond with a duration of 9.44 semiannual periods falls by almost $271 from the same $10,000 base compared with the $154 price decline with the shorter duration bond. This is again consistent with its higher duration and interest rate elasticity.

The key implication of Exhibit 6.7 is the direct relationship between duration and relative price sensitivity. The greater is duration, the greater is a security's percentage change in price and interest rate elasticity when securities carry the same initial yields. When securities carry different yields, they can similarly be ranked by relative interest rate elasticities.

RECENT INNOVATIONS IN THE VALUATION OF FIXED-INCOME SECURITIES AND TOTAL RETURN ANALYSIS

The traditional way of valuing fixed-income securities and analyzing yields is too simplistic given the complexities of today's marketplace. There are many reasons for this. First, many investors do not hold securities until maturity so that yield to maturity is of limited interest. Second, the present value calculation in Equation 6.8 that applies to bonds assumes that all coupon payments are reinvested at the calculated yield to maturity, which is generally not the case. Many investors want to know how changes in reinvestment rates affect the actual realized yield. Third, many securities carry embedded options, such as a call or put option, which complicates valuation because it is difficult to know whether the option will be exercised and thus what cash flows an investor will actually receive. As an example, consider a bond that has a 3-year maturity and carries a fixed coupon rate but can be called anytime after one year. This means that the issuer of the security (the borrower) can repay the outstanding principal on the bond at its discretion after one year. How long will an investor receive interest payments before the bond is repaid? It may be called after one year—or not at all. To know how to value a security with options, the investor must estimate when the options will be exercised and what value they will have. Finally, it is relatively easy for anyone who owns a security to separate, or strip, the coupon payments from each other and from the principal payment on a traditional bond. The holder can buy a security, strip the promised cash flows, and sell them as distinct zero coupon securities. Alternatively, someone can buy zero coupon securities and construct a traditional coupon bond. The implication is that any fixed-income security should be priced as a package of cash flows with each cash flow discounted at the appropriate zero coupon rate.

TOTAL RETURN ANALYSIS

Many market participants attempt to estimate the actual realized yield on a bond by calculating an estimated total return.[6] This yield measure allows the investor to vary assumptions about how long he or she will hold the bond (the holding period), the rate at which interim cash flows will be reinvested (the reinvestment rate), and the value of the bond at the end of the holding period (sale value, or maturity value). The calculated total return can then be compared across securities to assess whether the return sufficiently compensates for the risks assumed.

Total return analysis applied to option-free bonds recognizes that there are three different sources of return from owning a bond: coupon interest, reinvestment income—labeled interest-on-interest—and any capital gain or loss realized at maturity or sale if the bond is sold before maturity.[7] The mathematics require that one specify a holding period, reinvestment rate or rates, and the market price of the bond at maturity or sale. Having done this, the analysis involves estimating the total future value of coupon interest, interest-on-interest, and sale/maturity value, comparing this to the initial purchase price and calculating a zero coupon yield.

Consider the 3-year, 9.4 percent coupon bond trading at par of $10,000 from Exhibit 6.3. You buy the bond expecting to hold it until it matures. Coupon interest of $470 is paid every six months so that total interest will be $2,820 (6 × $470). You believe that you can invest each of the coupon payments at a 3 percent semiannual rate through maturity. Equation 6.17 provides the formula for calculating the future value of coupon interest plus interest-on-interest with a constant reinvestment rate (r).

$$\text{future value of coupon interest + interest-on-interest} = \left[C \frac{(1 + r)^n - 1}{r} \right] \quad \text{(6.17)}$$

where C is the periodic coupon interest payment and n is the number of periods until the end of the holding period. In this case, the total future value is

$$\$470[(1.03)^6 - 1]/0.03 = \$3,040.15$$

---

[6]This discussion follows that from *Fixed Income Mathematics* by Frank Fabozzi.

[7]This analysis assumes that bonds have no options. Total return analysis for securities with options is discussed in Chapter 20.

With $2,820 in coupon interest ($C \times n$), interest-on-interest equals $220.15. Finally, if held to maturity, you will receive $10,000 return of principal after three years. The total future value of the three components of return is thus:

$$\text{Coupon interest} = \$2,820.00$$
$$\text{Interest-on-interest} = \$220.15$$
$$\text{Principal at maturity} = \$10,000.00$$
$$\text{Total} = \$13,040.15$$

The total return as a yield measure is obtained by comparing this total future value with the initial investment of $10,000 and calculating the equivalent zero coupon yield. In general,

$$\text{Total Return} = [\text{Total Future Value}/\text{Purchase Price}]^{1/n} - 1 \tag{6.18}$$

For this investment, the total return is

$$[\$13,040.15/\$10,000]^{1/6} - 1 = 1.04523 - 1 = 0.04523$$

or 9.05 annually.

Note that this is less than the 9.4 percent yield to maturity of the bond because you assumed a 3 percent semiannual reinvestment rate. Remember that the yield to maturity calculation assumes that all interim cash flows can be reinvested at the yield to maturity. If we use a 4.7 percent reinvestment rate assumption in this example, the interest-on-interest component increases to $352.86. As expected, the total return increases to 4.7 percent semiannually:

$$[(\$13,172.86/\$10,000)^{1/6} - 1] = 0.047$$

Exhibit 6.8 provides a similar application for a 9-year bond that pays a 7.30 percent coupon and currently sells for $99.62 per $100 par value. In this example, the holding period is exactly five years and the investor assumes a reinvestment rate of 6 percent annually. After five years, it is believed that a comparable bond with four years remaining until maturity will be priced to yield 7 percent to maturity. Thus, the calculation assumes a holding period far shorter than maturity and requires an estimate of the bond's sale price. Note that in this example, the bond is assumed to sell at a premium after five years, which raises the total return to 7.34 percent.

Total return is especially applicable when securities have embedded options, such as a call option or put option, or with mortgages and mortgage-backed securities where the principal can be prepaid. It allows an investor to identify how much of the yield can be attributed to reinvestment income and potential capital gains and losses. It also is important when the investor's holding period differs from maturity.

VALUING BONDS AS A PACKAGE OF CASH FLOWS

Consider the same 3-year maturity, 9.4 percent coupon bond from Exhibit 6.3, which has six remaining coupon payments of $470 and one remaining principal payment of $10,000 at maturity. This bond should be viewed as a package of seven separate cash flows. Formally, if stripped and sold separately, each of the coupon payments is labeled an interest-only security while the principal payment is a principal-only security. Because the payments can be stripped, an arbitrageur who believes the bond is currently undervalued can buy the entire bond, strip the coupons and principal payment, and sell each as a distinct zero coupon (single cash flow) bond for a profit.[8]

---

[8]If the bond is overpriced, an arbitrageur will short sell the bond and buy each of the coupons and principal payment as zero coupon instruments to reconstruct the bond and profit on the difference.

· EXHIBIT 6.8

CALCULATION OF TOTAL RETURN FOR A 9-YEAR BOND PURCHASED AT $99.62 PER $100 PAR VALUE THAT PAYS A 7.3 PERCENT (3.65 PERCENT SEMIANNUAL) COUPON AND IS HELD FOR FIVE YEARS

Assume: semiannual reinvestment rate = 3% after five years; a comparable 4-year maturity bond will be priced to yield 7% (3.5% semiannually) to maturity

Coupon interest:	$10 \times \$3.65 = \$36.50$
Interest-on-interest:	$\$3.65 [(1.03)^{10} - 1] / 0.03 - \$36.50 = \$5.34$
Sale price after five years:	$\sum_{t=1}^{8} \dfrac{\$3.65}{(1.035)^t} + \dfrac{\$100}{(1.035)^8} = \$101.03$
Total future value:	$\$36.50 + \$5.34 + \$101.03 = \$142.87$
Total return:	$[\$142.87/\$99.62]^{1/10} - 1 = 0.0367$ semiannually
	or 7.34% annually

The implication is that the bond will be priced as a package of zero coupon instruments. Thus, a different discount rate will apply to each periodic interest payment and the principal payment. The first coupon will be discounted at the 6-month zero coupon rate, the second coupon at the 1-year zero coupon rate, and so forth.

Suppose that at the time you are considering buying this bond, the following zero coupon rates apply to comparable risk securities.

Maturity	Zero coupon rate (semiannual)
6 months	3.90%
1 year	4.00%
18 months	4.20%
2 years	4.40%
30 months	4.60%
3 years	4.70%

The bond could be bought, stripped, and sold for $10,021.48.

Value of package of cash flows:

$$\frac{\$470}{(1.039)^1} + \frac{\$470}{(1.04)^2} + \frac{\$470}{(1.042)^3} + \frac{\$470}{(1.044)^4} + \frac{\$470}{(1.046)^5} + \frac{\$470}{(1.047)^6} + \frac{\$10,000}{(1.047)^6} = \$10,021.48$$

Thus, an arbitrageur could make a riskless profit of $21.48 per $10,000 of par bonds if the whole bond could be bought for $10,000.

The implication is that bond valuation is more complex than that described under the traditional analysis. It requires the use of zero coupon rates as discount rates and different discount rates at each maturity.

MONEY MARKET YIELDS

Unfortunately, while the general pricing relationships introduced above are straightforward, practical applications are complicated by the fact that interest rates on different securities are measured and quoted in different terms. This is particularly true of yields on money market instruments such as Treasury bills, federal funds, CDs, repurchase agreements, Eurodollars, bankers acceptances, and commercial paper, which have initial maturities under one year.

Some of these instruments trade on a discount basis, while others bear interest. Some yields are quoted assuming a 360-day year, while others assume a 365-day year. The following discussion extends the analysis of interest rate mathematics to money market instruments and provides procedures that allow a comparison of effective annual yields.

INTEREST-BEARING LOANS WITH MATURITIES OF ONE YEAR OR LESS

Many short-term consumer and commercial loans have maturities less than one year. The borrower makes periodic interest payments and repays the principal at maturity. The effective annual rate of interest depends on the term of the loan and the compounding frequency. If the loan has exactly one year to maturity, Equation 6.12 characterizes the effective annual yield. Thus, a 1-year loan that requires monthly interest payments at 12 percent annually (1 percent monthly) carries an effective yield to the investor of 12.68 percent.

$$i^* = (1.01)^{12} - 1 = 0.1268$$

Suppose that the same loan was made for just 90 days at an annualized stated rate of 12 percent. There is now more than one compounding period in one year. The modified form of Equation 6.12 assumes a 365-day year and calculates the number of compounding periods as 365 divided by the number of days in the contract holding period (h), which is 90 in this example. In general,

$$i^* = \left[1 + \frac{i}{(365/h)}\right]^{(365/h)} - 1 \tag{6.19}$$

This 90-day loan thus has 365/90 compounding periods in a year, and the effective annual yield is 12.55 percent.

$$i^* = \left[1 + \frac{0.12}{(365/90)}\right]^{(365/90)} - 1 = 0.1255$$

360-DAY VERSUS 365-DAY YIELDS

A security's effective annual yield must reflect the true yield to an investor who holds the underlying instrument for a full year (365 days in all but leap years). Some money market rates are, in fact, reported on the basis of an assumed 360-day year. While interest is actually earned for all 365 days in a year, the full amount of interest implied by the reported rate is earned in just 360 days. Thus, $1,000 invested for one year at 8 percent under the 360-day method pays $80 in interest after 360 days, not $80 after 365 days. Because the investor gets the same interest five days earlier, the principal and interest can be invested for five additional days, and the investor earns a higher effective rate of interest.

It is easy to convert a 360-day rate to a 365-day rate, and vice versa. This is done according to the following formula:

$$i_{365} = i_{360} (365/360)$$

where i_{365} = 365-day rate, and
i_{360} = 360-day rate

The 360-day rate is simply multiplied by a factor of 365/360. In turn, the effective annual yields must reflect both 365 days of interest and compounding frequency. Converting a 360-day yield to an effective annual yield involves two steps. First, the yield is converted to a 365-day yield. Second, the 365-day yield is used for i in Equations 6.12 and 6.19.

For example, a 1-year investment that carries an 8 percent nominal rate quoted on a 360-day basis generates a 365-day yield of 8.11 percent.

$$i_{365} = 0.08(365/360)$$
$$= 0.0811$$

This rate would be used in all formulas to compute effective yields.

DISCOUNT YIELDS

Some money market instruments, such as Treasury bills, repurchase agreements, commercial paper, and bankers acceptances, are pure discount instruments. This means that the purchase price is always less than the par value at maturity. The difference between the purchase price and par value equals the periodic interest. Yields on discount instruments are calculated and quoted on a discount basis assuming a 360-day year and thus are not directly comparable to yields on interest-bearing instruments.

The pricing equation for discount instruments used by professional traders is:

$$i_{dr} = \left[\frac{Pf - Po}{Pf}\right]\left[\frac{(360)}{h}\right] \quad (6.20)$$

where

i_{dr} = discount rate,

Po = initial price of the instrument,

Pf = final price of the instrument at maturity or sale, and

h = number of days in holding period

The discount rate has several peculiar features. First, the amount of interest earned is divided by the final price or maturity value, not by the initial amount invested, to obtain a percentage return. Second, as noted above, it assumes a 360-day year. The discount rate thus understates the effective annual rate. In order to obtain an effective yield, the formula must be modified to reflect a 365-day year and to account for the fact that returns are normally computed by dividing interest received by the amount invested. These problems can be addressed by calculating a **bond equivalent rate** (i_{be}) according to Equation 6.21.

$$i_{be} = \left[\frac{Pf - Po}{Po}\right]\left[\frac{(365)}{h}\right] \quad (6.21)$$

Consider, for example, a $1 million par value Treasury bill with exactly 182 days to maturity, priced at $964,500. The discount rate on the bill is 7.02 percent.

$$i_{dr} = \left[\frac{\$1,000,000 - \$964,500}{\$1,000,000}\right]\left[\frac{(360)}{182}\right]$$
$$= 0.0702$$

The bond equivalent rate equals 7.38 percent.

$$i_{be} = \left[\frac{\$1,000,000 - \$964,500}{\$964,500}\right]\left[\frac{(365)}{182}\right]$$
$$= 0.0738$$

To obtain an effective annual rate, incorporate compounding by applying Equation 6.19. Implicitly, an investor is assumed to reinvest the proceeds at the same periodic rate for the remainder of the 365 days in a year. Here the effective annual rate equals 7.52 percent.

SUMMARY OF MONEY MARKET YIELD QUOTATIONS AND CALCULATIONS

A. Simple Interest Rate i_s:

$$i_s = \frac{Pf - Po}{Po}$$

B. Discount Rate i_{dr}:

$$i_{dr} = \left[\frac{Pf - Po}{Pf}\right]\left[\frac{360}{h}\right]$$

C. Money Market 360-Day Rate i_{360}:

$$i_{360} = \left[\frac{Pf - Po}{Po}\right]\left[\frac{360}{h}\right]$$

D. Bond Equivalent 365-Day Rate i_{365} or i_{be}:

$$i_{365} = \left[\frac{Pf - Po}{Po}\right]\left[\frac{365}{h}\right]$$

E. Effective Annual Interest Rate $i*$:

$$i* = \left[1 + \frac{i}{(365/h)}\right]^{365/h} - 1$$

Definitions

Pf = Final value
Po = Initial value
h = Number of days in holding period

Discount Yield Quotes: Treasury bills
Repurchase agreements
Commercial paper
Bankers acceptances

Interest-Bearing, Single Payment: Negotiable CDs
Federal funds

$$i* = \left[1 + \frac{0.0738}{(365/182)}\right]^{365/182} - 1 = 0.0752$$

Yields on repurchase agreements, commercial paper, and bankers acceptances are also quoted on a discount basis. For comparative purposes with nondiscount instruments, their yields must be converted in the same manner as Treasury bills, in a two-step process. The 360-day yield is converted to a 365-day bond equivalent yield; then compounding is taken into account via Equation 6.19.

YIELDS ON SINGLE-PAYMENT, INTEREST-BEARING SECURITIES

Some money market instruments, such as large, negotiable certificates of deposit (CDs), Eurodollars, and federal funds, pay interest calculated against the par value of the security and make a single payment of both interest and principal at maturity. The nominal interest rate is quoted as a percent of par and assumes a 360-day year. The nominal rate again understates the effective annual rate.

Consider a 182-day CD with a par value of $1,000,000 and quoted yield of 7.02 percent, the same quote as the Treasury bill. The actual amount of interest paid after 182 days equals

$$(0.0702)(182/360)\$1,000,000 \text{ or } \$35,490$$

The 365-day yield is

$$i_{365} = 0.0702(365/360) = 0.0712$$

Finally, the effective annual rate is

$$i* = \left[1 + \frac{0.0712}{(365/182)}\right]^{365/182} - 1 = 0.0724$$

A careful reader will note that both the 365-day yield and effective annual rate on the CD are below the corresponding bond equivalent yield and effective annual rate on the aforementioned

Treasury bill. This demonstrates the difference between discount and interest-bearing instruments. In particular, the discount rate is calculated as a return on par value, not initial investment, as with interest-bearing instruments. Thus, a discount rate understates both the 365-day rate and effective rate by a greater percentage.

Exhibit 6.9 summarizes the conventions for interest rate quotations in the money market and identifies specific instruments priced under each convention. Market participants must be aware of how yields are quoted and calculated before they compare percentages.

SUMMARY

Interest rates play an important role in facilitating the flow of funds between lenders and borrowers. Borrowers prefer low rates that lower interest expense while lenders prefer high rates that increase interest income. This chapter provides an overview of the mathematics of interest rates to assist in comparing quoted rates between securities, and presents concepts that are useful in valuing fixed-income securities and evaluating their price sensitivity.

There are several key conclusions. First, fixed-income securities are priced according to the mathematics of present value and future value. The effective price and yield depend on the frequency of compounding. The greater is the compounding frequency, the greater is the amount of interest. Second, prices and yields on fixed-income securities without options exhibit well-defined relationships. When interest rates change, prices move inversely. The proportionate price move is relatively greater when rates fall compared to when rates rise. Similarly, the proportionate magnitude of the price move increases with maturity and decreases with the size of the coupon payment. This is largely revealed by a security's duration because the greater is duration, the greater is the proportionate price change for a given change in interest rates. Thus, longer-duration securities exhibit greater price volatility. Third, many investors use total return analysis when deciding which securities to buy. Total return analysis allows an investor to vary the assumed holding period, select different reinvestment rates, and incorporate the expected impact of selling the security prior to final maturity. All of these considerations are not permitted by the yield to maturity calculation. Finally, rates on specific money market securities differ because some are quoted on a 360-day versus 365-day basis and some are discount rates versus bond-equivalent rates. The primary point is that borrowers and lenders must carefully examine the contract terms of specific securities to understand the effective cost or yield.

QUESTIONS

1. If you invest $1,000 today in a security paying 8 percent compounded quarterly, how much will the investment be worth seven years from today?

2. If you invest $20,000 in a security today, how much will it be worth in six years? The security pays 6 percent compounded monthly.

3. What is the effective interest rate of 10 percent compounded quarterly, versus 10 percent compounded monthly?

4. Consider a $15,000 loan with interest at 12 percent compounded monthly and 24 monthly payments. How much will the loan payment be? Set up an amortization schedule for the first four months, indicating the amount and timing of principal and interest payments.

5. How much would you be willing to pay today for an investment that will return $6,800 to you eight years from today if your required rate of return is 12 percent?

6. Six years ago you placed $250 in a savings account which is now worth $1,040.28. When you put the funds into the account, you were told it would pay 24 percent interest. You expected to find the account worth $908.80. What compounding did you think this account used, and what did it actually use?

7. If you invest $9,000 today at 8 percent compounded annually, but after three years the interest rate increases to 10 percent compounded semiannually, what is the investment worth seven years from today?

8. Suppose a customer's house increased in value over five years from $150,000 to $250,000. What was the annual growth rate of the property value during this five-year interval?

9. Three local banks pay different interest rates on time deposits with 1-year maturities. Rank the three banks from highest to lowest in terms of the depositor's return.

   Bank 1—4.5 percent per year compounded annually

   Bank 2—4.3 percent per year compounded quarterly

   Bank 3—4.1 percent per year compounded daily

10. You want to buy a new car, but you know that the most you can afford for payments is $375 per month. You want 48-month financing, and you can arrange such a loan at 12 percent compounded monthly. You have nothing to trade and no down payment. The most expensive car you can purchase is: (1) an old junker for $4,000, (2) an Isuzu Rodeo for $6,000, (3) a Ford Escort for $10,000, (4) a Toyota Camry for $12,000, or (5) a Jeep for $16,000.

11. Consider a 7 percent coupon U.S. Treasury note that has a $10,000 face value and matures 10 years from today. This note pays interest semiannually. The current market interest rate on this bond is 6 percent. Would you expect the bond to be a discount, premium, or par bond? Calculate the actual price of the bond using the present value formula.

12. A Treasury security carries a fixed 6 percent annual coupon rate and matures in exactly two years. The Treasury is currently priced at $10,000 par value to yield 6 percent to maturity. Assume that you can buy the bond and strip the coupons and final principal payment and sell each of them as a zero coupon security. Given the following zero coupon rates, what price would you get for this purchase and subsequent sales?

Maturity	6-month	1-year	18-month	2-year
Zero coupon yield	5.4%	5.8%	6.2%	6.8%

13. Lamar Briggs purchased a 7 percent coupon corporate bond that matured in 10 years and paid interest semiannually. He paid $2,800 and six months later, immediately following an interest payment, he sold the bond. At the time of sale, the market interest rate on bonds of this type was 6 percent. What was Lamar's selling price? What was Lamar's rate of return for the six months? What is this return on an annual basis?

14. What is the duration of a bond with a par value of $10,000 that has a coupon rate of 6.5 percent annually and a final maturity of two years? Assume that the required rate of return is 6 percent compounded semiannually. What is the duration of a 2-year zero coupon bond that pays $10,000 at maturity and is priced to yield 6 percent with semiannual compounding? Why do the durations differ?

15. Guess the duration of the following investment. Is it less than two years, two to three years, three to four years, or greater than four years? After your guess, use a discount rate of 6 percent and calculate the present value of the cash flows and then duration.

Years from now	1	2	3	4
Cash flow	$0	$1,000	$5,000	$2,000

16. In each of the following financial situations, fill in the blank with the terms *high duration, low duration,* or *zero duration,* as appropriate.
    a. If you were considering buying a bond and you expected interest rates to increase, you would prefer a bond with a _____.
    b. Relative to a bond with a high coupon rate, a bond with a low coupon rate would have a _____.
    c. A bond with a short maturity generally has a _____ compared to a bond with a long maturity.
    d. A 1-year corporate bond with a 5 percent coupon rate has a _____ relative to a 1-year T-bill.

17. One author says that duration is the weighted average life of a financial instrument. A different one says that duration is a measure of elasticity. Which of the authors is correct? Or, are they both correct?

18. Suppose that a zero coupon bond selling at $1,000 par has a duration of four years. If interest rates increase from 6 percent to 7 percent annually, the value of the bond will fall by what amount using Equation 6.14? Use semiannual compounding. Then, use the present value formula to determine the actual price of the bond at 7 percent. What is the difference? Why is there a difference?

19. If interest rates fall from 6 percent to 5 percent, the price of the bond in the above problem will increase. Will the change in price (regardless of sign) be smaller or larger than in the above problem? Show how much by using the present value formula and Equation 6.14. How does this conclusion relate to the interpretation of duration as an approximate elasticity measure?

20. Which money market instruments are typically quoted on a discount basis?

21. What is the bond equivalent yield of a 180-day, $1 million face value Treasury bill with a discount rate of 4.5 percent?

22. For which money market instruments are rates calculated based on par value rather than purchase price?

23. You would like to purchase a T-bill that has a $10,000 face value and 270 days to maturity. The current price of the T-bill is $9,620. What is the discount rate on this security? What is its bond equivalent yield?

24. You have just purchased a 5-year maturity bond for $10,000 par value that pays $610 in coupon interest annually ($305 every six months). You expect to hold the bond until maturity. Calculate your expected total return if you can reinvest all coupon payments at 5 percent (2.5 percent semiannually). Suppose, instead, that you plan to sell the bond after two years when you expect that a similar risk 3-year bond will be priced to yield 5.2 percent to maturity. Calculate the expected sale price of the bond and your expected total return using the same reinvestment rates. Explain why the two calculated total returns differ.

25. You are planning to buy a corporate bond with a 7-year maturity that pays 7 percent coupon interest. The bond is priced at $108,500 per $100,000 par value. You expect to sell the bond in two years when a similar risk 5-year bond is priced to yield 7.2 percent annually to maturity. Assuming that you can reinvest all cash flows at an 8 percent annual rate (4 percent semiannually), calculate your expected total return over the two-year holding period.

26. You buy 100 shares in Bondex Corp. for $25 a share. Each share pays $1 in dividends every three months. You have a 5-year holding period and expect to invest all dividends received in the first two years at 6 percent, and all dividends received the next three years at 9 percent. Calculate your expected total return (as a percentage yield) if you can sell the shares at $30 each after five years.

ACTIVITY PROJECTS

1. Rates for the most popular financial instruments can be found in the *Wall Street Journal*. Collect the rates for the following securities. This information can be found on the front of the "Money and Investing" section as well as in the "Credit Markets" column.

3-month T-bill	3-month Eurodollar deposit (LIBOR)
federal funds	3-month CD
DJ 20 Bond Index	10-year municipals
1- to 10-year Treasury	10+ year Treasury

   Rank the rates from highest to lowest. Why do the rates differ?

2. Locate the first General Electric (GE) corporate bond maturing after the year 2004 as reported in the Wall Street Journal. What is its coupon rate, maturity, and stream of coupon and principal payments? At the rate of return earned most recently on the DJ 20 Bond Index, what price would you be willing to pay for this bond? Comparing this price with its closing price, is the bond earning more or less in coupon interest than the DJ Bond Index? If you were going to buy a bond, would you choose this one? What factors would you consider in selecting a bond for your portfolio?

7

THE DETERMINANTS OF INTEREST RATES

Many individuals and businesses pay close attention to movements in interest rates. Retirees living off their investments in interest-bearing securities prefer high rates because they increase their spendable income. Borrowers, such as first-time homebuyers and small businesses financing inventories, prefer low rates because this lowers their periodic interest payments. Others may look to changes in interest rates as a signal about where the economy is headed, either in terms of aggregate growth or its impact on their specific business and investment interests. Indeed in the last few years, the chairman of the Federal Reserve has increased or decreased interest rates in anticipation of future inflation based on the Federal Reserve Board's estimates of the strength of the economy. The financial markets have reacted to the unexpected portion of these announced movements in interest rates.

The financial press and television networks offer regular analyses as to whether interest rates will likely increase or decrease, and how any changes will affect consumers and businesses. Today's financial markets are even more complex. Investors anticipate information and incorporate these expectations into the pricing of securities. For example, even if IBM announced significantly higher earnings this quarter, its stock price could actually fall. The stock price would fall if investors were expecting even higher earnings. Hence, good news may not actually be good news when it is not as good as investors expect! Unfortunately, different experts arrive at fundamentally different interpretations, and thus the information is often contradictory. There is a well-known saying that if all economists were lined up end-to-end, they still wouldn't reach a conclusion. But that is the beauty of financial markets and financial analysis. If everyone knew what was going to happen, there would be no risk. There would be no need for specialized investment strategies and the volume of market activity would likely drop sharply.

This chapter addresses two fundamental issues: What determines the level of interest rates and hence the movements in those rates, and what determines the structure of interest rates or interest rate *differentials between securities? To see the importance of the first issue, consider two commonly cited views regarding the level of interest rates. One view states that the chairman of the U.S. Federal Reserve System can no longer influence interest rates as in prior periods because activity in foreign financial markets now drives U.S. interest rates. To know whether rates will increase or decrease we need only examine what the Japanese and German governments are doing with their domestic rates, whether foreign investors are more or less likely to invest in U.S. securities, and whether the global economy is contracting or expanding. Another view states that the best predictor of economic conditions is the relationship between short-term and long-term interest rates, which characterizes economic conditions.[1] In particular, within 12 to 15 months after short-term rates increase above long-term rates, the U.S. economy will likely slide into a recession. When short-term rates are below long-term rates, the economy is positioned for expansion.*

The importance of the second issue is demonstrated by the volatility in quality spreads and the near collapse of Long-Term Capital Management in late 1998.[2] Long-Term Capital Management (LTCM) is a hedge fund that had $4.8 billion in capital early in 1998 and controlled more than $160 billion in stocks and bonds through the use of leverage. It was also actively involved in using derivatives to speculate. As part of its trading strategies, LTCM placed "nondirectional" bets. This meant that the fund was betting that the relationship between interest rates would change, not that the level of interest rates would change. For example, it gambled that the yield spread between 30-year and 29-year Treasury securities would increase, in particular, that the 30-year yield would rise relative to the 29-year yield. When the spread actually fell and went negative with an inverted yield curve, LTCM lost big. It also bet that the yield differentials between government bonds of countries joining the European Union (G-7 countries) would shrink toward zero as these countries moved to a common currency. Instead, the spreads widened. The use of leverage and derivatives magnified the bets such that LTCM lost all but an estimated $200 million of its capital by the end of October 1998, and a group of 14 of the best-known financial institutions bailed the fund out before it ran out of capital.

This chapter introduces the basic determinants of interest rates and the various factors that influence the pricing of securities. It specifically addresses the impact of inflation and inflation expectations, the business cycle, and foreign financial market activity on the level of interest rates. In addition, the structure of rates and the impact of a security's maturity, default risk, marketability and liquidity, tax treatment, special features such as call and put provisions, whether it is convertible into common stock, and differences in yields are explained.

---

[1]The relationship between yields on securities that differ only in terms of maturity can be characterized by a diagram labeled a yield curve. Whether short-term rates are above or below long-term rates determines the shape of the yield curve. Yield curves are discussed in detail later in the chapter.

[2]Quality spreads refer to the differential between the yield on a risky bond and the yield on a default risk-free Treasury bond. Bonds that are rated in the four highest categories by the major rating agencies are labeled investment grade instruments. Bonds that are either nonrated or carry a rating below investment grade are labeled junk bonds. The difference between the yield on any of these risky bonds and the yield on a matched-maturity (or duration) Treasury bond is the quality spread.

DETERMINANTS OF INTEREST RATE LEVELS

Economists have expended much effort trying to identify factors that determine the level of interest rates. The explanations, or models, can be categorized under the general labels of liquidity preference theory or loanable funds theory. *Liquidity preference theory* focuses on the supply of, and demand for, liquid assets, particularly money. The model explains movements in a single interest rate, which is viewed as an average or the aggregate level of the rates on short-term securities. The *loanable funds theory* focuses on the supply of, and demand for, aggregate loanable funds throughout the economy. As such, the model analyzes factors that affect borrowers and lenders in all financial markets. It is concerned with the flow of funds between borrowers and lenders and explains movements in rates on both short-term and long-term securities. Although both theories explain interest rate movements, the loanable funds framework emphasizes the role and activity of different institutions in different markets, and thus is examined below.

LOANABLE FUNDS THEORY

The loanable funds framework divides market participants into four categories: consumers, businesses, governments, and foreign participants.[3] Within each category there are units representing both borrowers and lenders. The phrase "loanable funds" refers to the credit needs of all borrowers and the associated sources of financing provided by all lenders. Borrowing takes the form of issuing debt securities, while lending takes the form of saving, creation of new money by the government, and the dishoarding of money. When all debt markets are aggregated, the theory posits that the risk-free rate of interest is determined by the interaction of the demand for and supply of all loanable funds.

SUPPLY OF, AND DEMAND FOR, LOANABLE FUNDS

The generalized loanable funds framework is readily characterized by supply and demand analysis. The demand for loanable funds represents the behavior of borrowers and thus evidences the supply of all debt instruments. It is determined by the credit needs of individuals, businesses, government units, and foreign participants relative to various rates of interest. The supply of loanable funds represents the behavior of lenders and thus the demand for owning debt instruments. It, in turn, is derived from saving, money creation through the banking system, and the dishoarding of money.

Exhibit 7.1 illustrates this general loanable funds framework. The risk-free rate appears on the vertical axis, while the dollar volume of loanable funds appears on the horizontal axis. The demand for loanable funds (DF) slopes downward to the right, indicating that borrowers demand greater amounts of loanable funds at lower interest rates. The supply of loanable funds (SF) slopes upward to the right, indicating that the higher the rate of interest, the greater are funds provided by lenders. The intersection of the two curves determines the equilibrium interest rate, i_f, and volume of loans, Q_L.

FACTORS AFFECTING THE SUPPLY OF LOANABLE FUNDS. Lenders want to own interest-bearing securities for a variety of reasons. Individuals might have excess

---

[3]The Federal Reserve defines six categories of economic units: Households, Nonfinancial Business, Government, Banking System, Nonbank Finance, Foreign/Rest of the World.

LOANABLE FUNDS FRAMEWORK

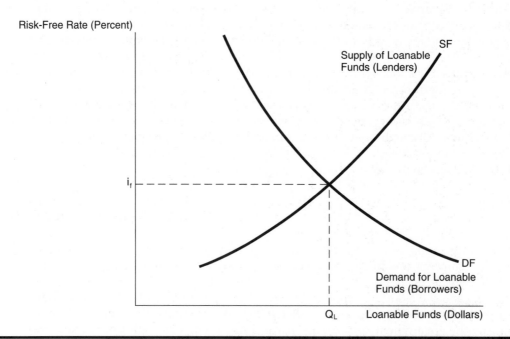

income relative to what they spend on consumption goods, or they may simply need to reinvest their stock of wealth. In addition, they may simply choose to reduce their holdings of money and substitute earning assets. The primary catalyst is the expected rate of return on loanable funds relative to expected returns on alternative investments. Equally important, however, is the relative degree of risk associated with different investments. It is not enough for a security to offer a higher yield if the likelihood of receiving the interest is extremely low. Finally, individuals buy securities as part of financial plans for future expenditures, including anticipated education, health, and retirement outlays. The supply of loanable funds by individuals thus varies with expected returns, the variability in expected returns (as a measure of risk), future spending needs, and their total wealth.

Nonfinancial businesses often have excess cash that is invested temporarily before the proceeds are used for operating or capital expenses. This cash arises due to a mismatch in the timing of cash flows and planned operating and real expenditures. The primary determinant of this supply of funds is the expected risk-adjusted return on loanable funds relative to that for real assets.

Government units affect the supply of loanable funds in two ways. First, some units, particularly state and local governments, invest excess cash in securities to provide additional revenue until the funds are needed elsewhere. Second, the federal government, through the Federal Reserve System, expands and contracts the growth rate of the banking system's reserves, thereby influencing the availability of credit and growth in the money supply. A growing money supply, and the resulting increased credit made available, increases national income and the amount of funds available for consumption and saving.

Finally, foreign investors view U.S. securities as alternatives to their own domestic securities, and purchase those with the most attractive risk/return features. This emphasizes the important fact that market participants evaluate alternative investments from a global perspective. If expected risk-adjusted yields are higher in the U.S. than in other countries, capital will flow into the United States as investors throughout the world seek out the highest net returns. During the 1980s and the 1990s, the foreign sector supplied a significant and increasing amount of loanable funds to U.S. money and capital markets.

FACTORS AFFECTING THE DEMAND FOR LOANABLE FUNDS. Many factors induce borrowers to issue interest-bearing securities. These factors primarily reflect the specific needs of the borrower, and the availability and terms associated with alternative sources of funds. Individuals borrow largely to finance the purchase of housing and durable goods, such as furniture, appliances, automobiles, and recreational vehicles. They take on more debt when economic conditions are good and are perceived to be improving. They also borrow more when the cost of borrowing is perceived to be low relative to the utility of the asset being financed or its rate of appreciation. Nonprice terms are also important, particularly when the underlying asset is an automobile. Here consumers tend to focus on the size of a down payment and the monthly payment rather than on the interest rate alone.

Businesses borrow to finance working capital needs and capital expenditures. Working capital needs consist of accounts receivable or inventory financing and typically arise because a firm is growing and does not have alternative sources of short-term credit. Similarly, when firms have profitable capital investments in new physical plants or equipment, they typically use the bond markets to obtain financing. The magnitude of their funds' needs reflects, in part, their internally generated cash flow from operations. If internal cash flow is strong, they will need to borrow less than if cash flow is weak.

Governments are always significant borrowers. State and local governmental units regularly issue debt to finance temporary imbalances in operating revenues versus expenses, and they have regular capital needs for schools, roads, water treatment facilities, and so forth. While many of these units run surpluses, most regularly issue long-term bonds for necessary capital improvements. The federal government, in contrast, has occasionally operated at a substantial budget deficit during the past two decades as revenues have fallen as much as $250 billion below outlays in a single year. The U.S. Treasury must continually finance a deficit by issuing additional securities to cover the deficiency. In recent years, federal budget surpluses have reduced government borrowing needs. Still, the budget reflects only part of the government's demand for loanable funds, as off-budget expenditures require substantial borrowing as well. Federal expenditures are not sensitive to interest rates, as the funds will be spent regardless of the interest cost. With a surplus, the government reduces outstanding debt by buying it back before it matures.

Foreign participants are also important borrowers in U.S. markets. In our global financial economy, investors view all securities as potential substitutes. Borrowers look for the cheapest sources of funds globally. U.S. corporations can issue securities denominated in yen, sterling, and deutschemarks, just as foreign borrowers can issue securities denominated in U.S. dollars. Most foreign borrowing in the United States, using dollar-denominated instruments, arises from the needs of foreign businesses.

CHANGES IN THE SUPPLY AND DEMAND FOR LOANABLE FUNDS

According to the loanable funds theory, the level of interest rates is determined as the market clearing rate, i_f, shown in Exhibit 7.1. The level of rates will increase when the demand for loanable funds increases relative to the supply of loanable funds at the prevailing rate. The level of rates will fall when the demand for loanable funds decreases relative to the supply of loanable funds. Both outcomes may result from changes in either the supply of, or demand for, loanable funds, or both.

The key issue is to determine what can cause a change in supply and demand. A quick review of supply and demand analysis reveals the answer. Examine the curves DF and SF in

Exhibit 7.1. Any change in the risk-free rate represents a movement along DF and SF. Thus, changes in i_f coincide with changes in the quantity demanded or quantity supplied (read off the horizontal axis), and do not cause the curves to shift. The diagram assumes that all other factors that potentially influence DF and SF are held constant as i_f changes. Factors that cause a change in supply and demand of loanable funds were described previously. Any factor that affects the supply of loanable funds will induce a diagrammatic shift in SF. Any factor that affects the demand for loanable funds will induce a shift in DF.

Consider the situation where state and local governments must increase their capital expenditures on roads and utilities to help remedy the decaying infrastructure of U.S. cities. Assume that growth in these outlays is financed by issuing long-term municipal bonds independent of the prevailing interest rate. The impact of issuing additional debt on the level of interest rates in a loanable funds framework can be characterized by a shift outward and to the right of the demand for loanable funds, DF_1 to DF_2, as shown in Exhibit 7.2. In other words, at the current market rate of interest, i_f municipalities want to borrow more, q_d. At the current market rate of interest (i_f), however, there will be an excess demand for loanable funds ($q_d - q_1$). This will bid up the rate of interest on loanable funds and the quantity supplied (movement up along the supply curve) and reduce the quantity demand (movement up along the demand curve). Holding all other factors constant, this increase in borrowing will increase the equilibrium municipal interest rate from i_f' to i_f'' and increase the quantity of loanable funds from q_1 to q_2. The impact on rates and the quantity of loanable funds is represented by a shift from DF_1 to DF_2 in panel A of Exhibit 7.2.

Suppose, instead, that Japanese investors refrain from buying U.S. interest-bearing securities. The catalyst may be an increase in expected risk-adjusted yields on Japanese securities, a need for funds due to a decline in the Tokyo stock market, or even a change in tax treatment of foreign derived income. Given their substantial investment in prior periods, this represents a decrease in the supply of loanable funds from SF_1 to SF_2 in section B of Exhibit 7.2. With fewer investors, the existing securities can only be sold at higher interest rates unless borrowers withdraw from the market or other investors replace the Japanese.

These examples demonstrate the application of loanable funds analysis. The framework can be used to forecast or explain broad trends in interest rates by documenting the change in the demand for loanable funds relative to the supply of loanable funds. This requires a careful review of the financial and real activities of all market participants and financial markets. The analysis is often refined to examine the behavior of specific governments or financial institutions and the supply and demand activity for specific instruments. Such historical data are provided via the **Flow of Funds Accounts** by the Board of Governors of the Federal Reserve System.[4]

INFLATION AND THE LEVEL OF INTEREST RATES

Analysts routinely attribute changes in interest rates to changes in actual or expected inflation.[5] Higher interest rates are associated with greater levels of inflation and with increases in *expected* inflation. Rates decline with lower inflationary expectations. This is intuitively

---

[4]The Appendix presents sample data from the Flow of Funds Accounts for commercial bank financial activity. You can find flow of funds data at the Federal Reserve Board of Governors World Wide Web page at: http://www.bog.frb.fed.us/releases/Z1/data.htm.

[5]In theory, inflation is defined as a continuous increase in prices. In practice, however, the U.S. government measures inflation by a variety of price indexes that track the average price change of different representative market baskets of goods and services from month to month. The Consumer Price Index (CPI), Producer Price Index (PPI), and Gross Domestic Product (GDP) deflator are commonly cited and signify average prices for goods and services sold at retail, at all stages of production, and all final goods and services, respectively. You can find CPI and PPI data from a variety of sources on the Internet, including the Bureau of Labor Statistics at: http://stats.bls.gov/datahome.htm.

CHANGES IN INTEREST RATE LEVELS

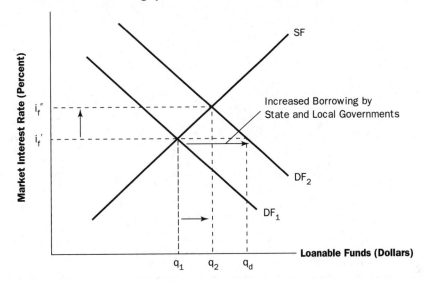

A. Increased Borrowing by State and Local Governments

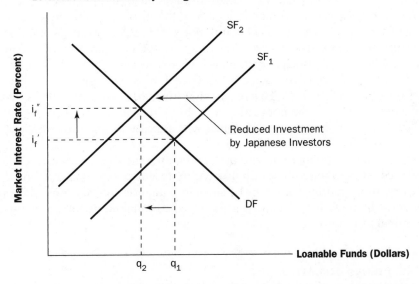

B. Reduced Investment by Foreign Investors

appealing. If it costs more to buy goods, an investor who buys a financial asset rather than real goods and services should earn a higher interest rate to compensate for the greater opportunity cost of forgone consumption. If you were to lend your car to someone for a year, you would expect to be compensated for the fact that you would be unable to use it over the course of the next year, its forgone consumption. You would also want compensation for the fact that the real value of the car would be less after one year. That is, the car would be one

· EXHIBIT 7.3

IMPACT OF INFLATION ON NOMINAL INTEREST RATES

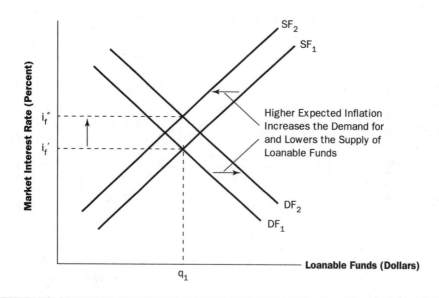

year older and would have more miles on it. This concept can be demonstrated in a loanable funds framework as well. If expected inflation increases, lenders will lend less at prevailing interest rates because the money repaid in the future will buy fewer goods, hence is worth less. That is, expected yields net of inflation will fall. Borrowers, in contrast, will borrow more to purchase goods today, when they are cheaper, and pay back the loan later expecting to make interest and principal payments with depreciated dollars. As shown in Exhibit 7.3, the demand for loanable funds increases from DF_1 to DF_2 and the supply of loanable funds decreases from SF_1 to SF_2. This means that the market clearing rate increases from i_f' to i_f''.

How much does the nominal risk-free rate increase? One theory, offered by Fisher, suggests that the nominal rate of interest will increase by the same amount as the increase in expected inflation. A second theory, proposed by Mundell and Tobin, suggests that the increase in the nominal rate will be less than the increase in expected inflation due to a real balance effect wherein individuals save more when expected inflation increases. The final theory, proposed by Darby and Feldstein, suggests that the nominal rate of interest will increase by more than the increase in expected inflation due to an increase in taxes paid on nominal income.

THE FISHER RELATION

In 1896, Irving Fisher published an article that presented an equilibrium interest rate relationship incorporating expected inflation. In the absence of taxes, the equilibrium condition decomposed the **nominal market interest rate** (i) into an **expected real interest rate** component (r), an **expected inflation premium** (p^e), and the cross-product between the real rate and expected inflation premium.

$$(1 + i) = (1 + r)(1 + p^e)$$

· EXHIBIT 7.4

RELATIONSHIP BETWEEN CHANGES IN EXPECTED INFLATION AND REAL RATE, EXPECTED INFLATION, AND NOMINAL INTEREST RATES (PERCENTAGES)

A. Fisher Relation: $i = r + p^e$

Period	Δp^e	Nominal Market Rate		Ex ante Real Rate		Expected Inflation Rate		Δi	Relationship between Δp^e and Δi
1		2	=	3	+	−1			
2	1	3	=	3	+	0	→	1	$\Delta i = \Delta p^e$
3	2	5	=	3	+	2	→	2	$\Delta i = \Delta p^e$
4	3	8	=	3	+	5	→	3	$\Delta i = \Delta p^e$
5	2	10	=	3	+	7	→	2	$\Delta i = \Delta p^e$

B. Mundell-Tobin: r varies inversely with p^e: $i = r + pe$

Period	Δp^e								
1		2.60	=	3.60	+	−1			
2	1	3.25	=	3.25	+	0	→	0.65	$\Delta i < \Delta p^e$
3	2	5.00	=	3.00	+	2	→	1.75	$\Delta i < \Delta p^e$
4	3	7.60	=	2.60	+	5	→	2.60	$\Delta i < \Delta p^e$
5	2	9.50	=	2.50	+	7	→	1.90	$\Delta i < \Delta p^e$

C. Fisher Relation with Taxes: $i = r_{at}/(1 − t) + p^e/(1 − t)$; $t = 20\%$

Period	Δp^e	Ex ante After-Tax Real Rate, r_{at}	Expected Inflation Rate, p^e	Nominal Market Rate, i		$ra/(1 − t)$		$p^e/(1 − t)$		Δi	Relationship between Δp^e and Δi
1		3	−1	2.50	=	3.75	+	−1.25	→		
2	1	3	0	3.75	=	3.75	+	0	→	1.25	$\Delta i > \Delta p^e$
3	2	3	2	6.25	=	3.75	+	2.50	→	2.50	$\Delta i > \Delta p^e$
4	3	3	5	10.00	=	3.75	+	6.25	→	3.75	$\Delta i > \Delta p^e$
5	2	3	7	12.50	=	3.75	+	8.75	→	2.50	$\Delta i > \Delta p^e$

or

$$i = r + p^e + r \times p^e \tag{7.1}$$

Equation 7.1, or its modified form (7.2), are commonly labeled the Fisher Relation.[6]

$$i = r + p^e \tag{7.2}$$

Conceptually, the expected real rate represents the required return to investors to compensate them at the margin for postponing consumption. This rate is determined before the fact (*ex ante*), which means before the actual inflation rate is known. The inflation premium represents the return required to compensate investors for their loss of purchasing power due to prices increasing during the interval that the security is outstanding.

It is important to recognize that the Fisher Relation is theoretical and thus actual data may not support it. Rational investors will demand a positive real return for postponing consumption

---

[6]The cross-product term is often dropped because it is small in magnitude relative to r and p^e. For example, if r = 5 percent and p^e = 5 percent, then $r \times p^e$ = 0.0025. If r = 5 percent and p^e = 2 percent, then $r \times p^e$ = 0.0010.

such that r is greater than zero. Consider the case where the *ex ante* real rate is constant. In this case, changes in expected inflation determine changes in the level of nominal (market quoted) rates. Panel A of Exhibit 7.4 demonstrates a 1-to-1 relationship. In this panel, the real rate is constant at 3 percent and the nominal market rate increases (decreases) by the same amount as the change in expected inflation. For example, as expected inflation changes from 2 to 5 percent, the market rate changes from 5 to 8 percent. With a constant real rate, the Fisher Relation implies that market interest rates will change in the same direction, and by the same amount, as expected inflation. This is noted in the last two columns of data.

MUNDELL-TOBIN. The Fisher Relation has evoked debate among economists. Two of the earliest criticisms were offered by Robert Mundell and James Tobin, who argued that changes in expected inflation alter the *ex ante* real rate in the opposite direction.[7] If expected inflation increases (decreases), r decreases (increases). The rationale underlying this inverse relationship is what has been referred to as a real balance or real wealth effect. An increase in inflation lowers the value of an individual's money balances because the money will buy fewer goods and services. Because money balances are a part of real wealth, real wealth declines. In order to increase real wealth to its previous level, individuals must save more of their income. This increased saving means there is an increase in the supply of loanable funds, such that the *ex ante* real rate declines. Lowered inflation expectations produce the opposite result—real wealth increases and saving falls. Hence, an increase in expected inflation lowers the real rate of interest.

If r varies inversely with p^e, any change in nominal market rates will be less than 1-to-1 with changes in expected inflation. To see this, examine panel B of Exhibit 7.4. As expected inflation increases from 2 to 5 percent, the *ex ante* real rate declines from 3 to 2.6 percent. Thus, although expected inflation increases by 3 percent, the nominal market rate increases by just 2.6 percent, from 5 percent to 7.6 percent. The Mundell and Tobin arguments suggest that the *ex ante* real rate is not constant, and market rates subsequently change in the same direction as expected inflation, but the change is less than 1-to-1. This is again revealed in the last two columns of data.

DARBY-FELDSTEIN. Michael Darby and Martin Feldstein extended the debate over the Fisher Relation by incorporating income tax effects.[8] Both authors argued that lenders are concerned primarily with expected **after-tax real rates,** and not before-tax nominal rates, i, or real rates, r, in Equation 7.2. For example, if expected inflation increases by 5 percent and nominal market rates increase by 5 percent, as suggested by the Fisher Relation, then investors would actually fare worse after taxes. To understand this, recall that the investor will be taxed on nominal market returns, i. So when nominal market rates of interest increase by the amount of expected inflation, more taxes will be paid than before. Hence, the real return after taxes will be lower!

The *ex ante* after-tax real rate of interest is defined as the nominal market rate less taxes on the nominal rate and less expected inflation:

$$r_{at} = i - it - p^e$$

or

$$r_{at} = i(1 - t) - p^e \qquad \textbf{(7.3)}$$

where r_{at} is the *ex ante* after-tax real rate and t is the marginal tax rate of the marginal lender.

---

[7]See Mundell (1963) and Tobin (1965).
[8]See Darby (1975) and Feldstein (1976).

Solving equation 7.3 for i yields

$$i = r_{at}/(1 - t) + p^e/(1 - t). \tag{7.4}$$

Equation 7.4 is the after-tax version of the Fisher Relation.

Let the *ex ante* real return be 3 percent and the expected inflation rate 2 percent, so that the nominal market rate of interest is 5 percent (3% + 2%). If the marginal tax rate is 20 percent, the after-tax real return (following equation 7.3) is 2.0 percent [5%(1 − 0.20) − 2%]. If the Fisher Relation is *correct* and expected inflation increases to 5 percent, the nominal rate will increase to 8 percent (3% + 5%). But the after-tax real rate of interest would actually fall to 1.4 percent [8%(1 − .20) − 5%]! If investors are to be made as well off as they were before the increase in expected inflation, the nominal market rate would have to increase by more than the expected increase in inflation to make up for the additional taxes that must be paid. The nominal market rate would have to increase to 10.0 percent [3%/(1 − 0.20) + 5%/(1 − 0.20) following Equation 7.4].

The primary difference between Equations 7.2 and 7.4 has to do with the tax factor multiplying the expected inflation premium. That is, investors are not just taxed on the real return but on the expected inflation portion as well. If the marginal tax rate is positive and less than 1, this tax factor [1/(1 − t)] will be greater than 1. The implication is that nominal market interest rates change by more than the change in expected inflation. Panel C of Exhibit 7.4, for example, uses a 20 percent marginal tax rate so that the tax factor equals 1.25 and assumes a constant *ex ante* real rate of 3 percent. As expected inflation changes, market interest rates change in the same direction, but the relationship is greater than 1-to-1. Thus, the increase in expected inflation from 2 percent to 5 percent coincides with an increase in market rates from 6.25 percent to 10 percent.

The belief that interest rates should change by more than expected inflation is highly intuitive given the U.S. tax system. Most loans are specified in current dollars. With inflation, taxes are imposed on nominal interest income and thus will also rise with price increases. For investors to remain at least as well off as before inflation, interest rates must increase more than inflation to provide the additional receipts necessary to pay the incremental income taxes and keep the *ex ante* real rate constant.

ACTUAL INFLATION AND MARKET INTEREST RATES

The three theories introduced above propose three different relationships between market interest rates and expected inflation, but ignore actual inflation. Unfortunately, it is difficult to test the theories empirically because it is difficult to accurately measure expected inflation and the *ex ante* real rate is not known. In addition, actual inflation may not accurately track expected inflation.

EX POST REAL RATES. The *ex post* or "realized real rate" (r*) is determined after the actual inflation rate is known. It is calculated by subtracting the actual inflation rate (p) from the observed market rate over the same time period.[9]

$$r^* = i - p \tag{7.5}$$

Because actual inflation may be above or below market interest rates, the *ex post* real rate can be either positive or negative. Exhibit 7.5 demonstrates this by plotting the market rate on

---

[9]For example, the realized real rate on the 1-year Treasury bill rate quoted December 31, 2000, would subtract the actual inflation rate over the period December 31, 2000, through December 31, 2001.

TREASURY INFLATION PROTECTED SECURITIES (TIPS)

On January 29, 1997, the U.S. Treasury auctioned a new inflation-indexed security, Treasury Inflation Protected Securities (TIPS). The auction was considered by some to be the biggest news in Treasury debt management since the introduction 20 years ago of the 30-year Treasury security. Investor interest in the new securities was stronger than expected, with demand exceeding supply by a margin of 5-to-1. Quarterly auctions were planned and additional maturities are to follow. These inflation-indexed securities were generally structured after the Real Return Bonds issued by the Government of Canada.

Inflation-indexed securities provide a degree of inflation protection for investors and potentially represent cost savings for the U.S. Treasury because it will not have to pay a premium for inflation uncertainty. The interest rate paid on these securities (known as the "real rate") provides investors with a guaranteed semiannual return above inflation. As such, investing in TIPS involves interest rate price risk, but not the inflation uncertainty risk. In comparison, we know that nominal Treasury yields are comprised of three components: a real return, an expected inflation component, and a risk premium for the uncertainty of future inflation. Inflation-indexed securities should exclude the risk premium for the

uncertainty of future inflation. Some argue, however, that not all of the inflation uncertainty has been removed because of the inflation index that the Treasury plans to use. The index for measuring the inflation rate will be the *Nonseasonally Adjusted U.S. City Average All Items Consumer Price Index for All Urban Consumers (CPI-U)*, published monthly by the Bureau of Labor Statistics (BLS). This index may not, according to some economists, represent "actual" inflation.

The interest rate, set at auction, remains fixed throughout the term of the security but the principal amount of the security is adjusted for inflation. Hence, the semiannual coupon payment, based on the principal at the time the coupon payment is made, increases over time with inflation.

How does it work? The 10-year inflation-indexed note (CUSIP No. 9128272M3) auctioned on January 29, 1997, issued on February 6, 1997, and set to mature January 15, 2007, pays a semiannual real coupon payment of 3 3/8 percent. The 6-month inflation rate, ending July 15, 1997, was 1.085 percent. This generates an index ratio of 1.01085: Assuming a $1,000.00 par value bond, the principal of the security would be 1.085 percent higher at mid-year, or $1,010.85. The first semiannual coupon payment would be based on the new inflation-adjusted princi-

pal: $17.0581 = $1,010.85 × (0.03375/2). At maturity, the security will be redeemed at the *greater* inflation-adjusted principal ($1,010.85 after six months in this example), or the par amount at original issue, $1,000.00.

Tax treatment of these securities is generally considered a negative. On the positive side, inflation-indexed securities are exempt from state and local taxes, as are other Treasury securities, but are subject to federal income tax. On the negative side, the unrealized inflation-adjusted principal component ($10.85 in the above example) is taxable even though it is not received until maturity!

The final investor concern is that the market for these types of securities is small. Liquidity is not as great as with other Treasury securities. Because these are specialized securities and designed for certain types of investors, the size of the secondary market is small and the resale value of the security is not as certain.

Eventually, many pension plans that use guaranteed income contracts (GICs) as a conservative way of assuring beneficiaries a certain rate of return may prefer TIPS for their ability to maintain current purchasing power, and the market for the securities is expected to grow.

SOURCE: Lehman Brothers, Salomon Brothers, CSFB, J.P. Morgan, U.S. Treasury.

1-year Treasury bills versus the actual *ex post* annual inflation rate measured by the Consumer Price Index (CPI), and the corresponding *ex post* real rate. Note that Equation 7.5 does not recognize the impact of taxes. If taxes were taken into account, the after-tax *ex post* real rate would equal the after-tax market rate less the inflation rate, and would be well below the values of r* shown in Exhibit 7.5.[10]

---

[10]In terms of the above notation, the after-tax *ex post* real rate equals i(1 − t) − p.

• EXHIBIT 7.5

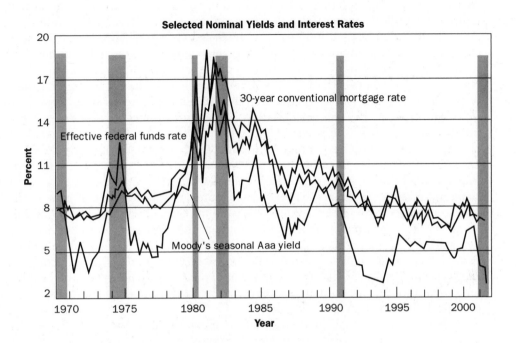

Selected Nominal Yields and Interest Rates

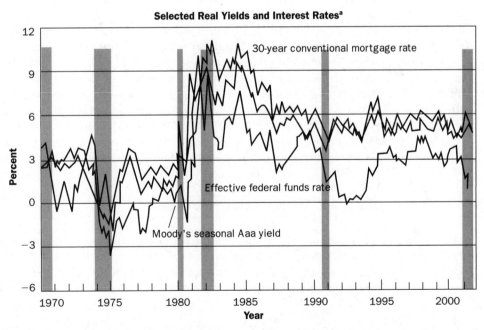

Selected Real Yields and Interest Rates[a]

NOTE: Shaded ares mark NBER-defined recessions.

[a]Nominal rates and yields minus the 12-month percent change in the Personal Consumption Expenditure Chain-type Price Index.

SOURCES: U.S. Department of Commerce, Bureau of Economic Analysis; Board of Governors of the Federal Reserve System, *Federal Reserve Statistical Releases,* "Selected Interest Rates," H.15; and the National Bureau of Economic Research, Inc. Economic Trends, Federal Reserve Bank of Cleveland, December 2001.

As indicated in Exhibit 7.5, the relationship between nominal interest rates and actual inflation has not been stable. During the 1970s, inflation regularly exceeded most interest rates so that the *ex post* real rate was negative. In late 1973 and early 1974, as well as much of 1979, r* fell as low as −5.4 percent. After inflation dropped during the 1980s, r* increased sharply because the level of interest rates did not drop coincidentally. As indicated, rates on long-term corporate bonds and mortgages and the overnight fed funds rate systematically exceeded the inflation rate, at times by as much as 10 percent. During the 1970s, investors lost considerable purchasing power while borrowers were able to repay their debts with cheaper funds. During the 1980s, this situation was reversed, with borrowers paying extremely high real rates to lenders even though interest rate levels fell. During the early 1990s, real rates were relatively high, 3 to 4 percent, even though nominal interest rates were relatively low, signifying the low rates of actual inflation. Then nominal rates fell and the *ex post* real rate of interest was as low as 0.26 percent by late 1993. Real rates subsequently increased as nominal rates increased and have remained around 2 to 3 percent through early 2001.

In terms of the three theories, these results may be due to a variety of phenomena. If actual inflation has been correctly anticipated, the data suggest that *ex ante* real rates are not constant and may, in fact, be negative. It seems more likely, however, that actual inflation does not closely track expected inflation. If this were the case, *ex post* real rates would be negative when market participants underestimate actual inflation and positive when participants overstate actual inflation. Implicitly, from 1973 through 1980, actual inflation exceeded expected inflation, while expected inflation exceeded actual inflation from 1982 through 2000. The implication of this argument is that participants do not revise their expectations for long periods of time. It does not explain why investors or borrowers do not take advantage of the persistent high or low real rates.

Although there is some evidence that price expectations are formed over long periods and thus change only with lengthy lags, it also seems plausible that there was a structural shift in the Fisher Relation during the past two decades. Specifically, some economists have argued that changes in Federal Reserve monetary policy and U.S. federal budget policy have altered the relationship between inflation and interest rates. Monetary policy has presumably accentuated the volatility of interest rates. Federal budget deficits have similarly altered long-term inflation forecasts and the volatility of rates because large deficits increase the anticipated borrowing requirements of the Treasury. Market interest rates presumably incorporate a volatility premium to capture this uncertainty.

Inspection of panel A of Exhibit 7.5 reveals that there is still a broad-based direct relationship between the level of interest rates and actual inflation. Interest rates generally rise and fall together with inflation, even though the rates of change now may vary substantially.

INTEREST RATES AND THE BUSINESS CYCLE

Most analysts agree that the level of interest rates and economic growth vary coincidentally over time. Interest rates tend to increase when total spending increases and fall when total spending falls. Trends in aggregate economic activity are typically evaluated in terms of the percentage change in real gross domestic product (GDP).[11] Real GDP rises when consumers

---

[11]This section presents a very simplified version of the macroeconomy. In actuality, the relationships are much more complex, given the nature of government intervention and international relationships. The purpose here is to provide a general flavor of interest rate relationships and spending behavior. GDP equals the dollar sum of consumption expenditures, government spending, investment expenditures, and net exports. Real GDP equals gross domestic product in current dollars divided by the GDP deflator.

▪ EXHIBIT 7.6

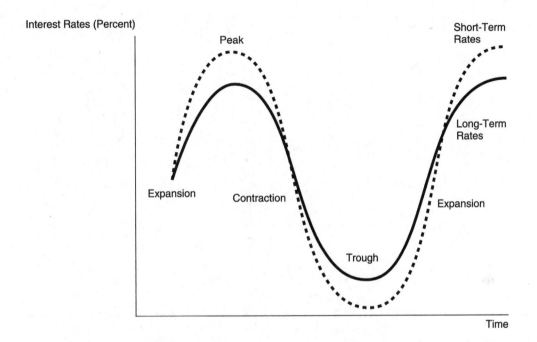

Expansion: Increasing Consumer Spending, Inventory Accumulation, and Rising Loan Demand; Federal Reserve Begins to Slow Money Growth.

Peak: Monetary Restraint, High Loan Demand, Little Liquidity.

Contraction: Falling Consumer Spending, Inventory Contraction, Falling Loan Demand; Federal Reserve Accelerates Money Growth.

Trough: Monetary Ease, Limited Loan Demand, Excess Liquidity.

increase spending, housing starts increase, businesses accumulate inventory and increase capital expenditures, and net exports increase. In general, interest rates also rise as borrowers compete for loans to finance this spending. Real GDP declines when the economy contracts. As consumers and businesses reduce spending, investment in housing slows, net exports decline, and total spending similarly declines. Interest rates typically follow and fall.

Historically, the real economy, measured by the percentage change in real GDP, has evidenced a cyclical pattern, as indicated in Exhibit 7.6. The vertical axis represents the market interest rate, the horizontal axis, time. Concentrate for the moment only on the solid line. It begins at the middle of the expansion phase of the cycle. During the expansion, consumers are spending more and businesses are borrowing to accumulate inventory and finance capital expenditures. This puts upward pressure on prices because the production of goods and services often lags behind the demand for goods and services. Interest rates increase because the demand for loanable funds increases more than the supply of loanable funds.

At peak growth in real GDP, loan demand is still high because spending is high. Consumers, however, stabilize or slow their spending and business investment follows. In an

REAL GDP AND THE TREASURY YIELD SPREAD*

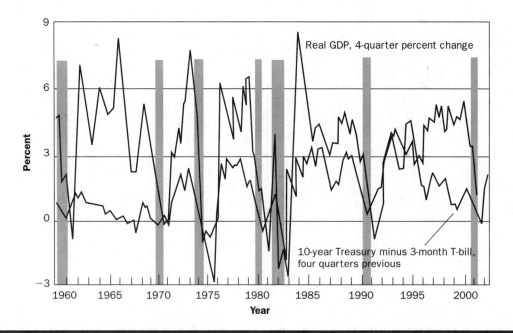

Shaded areas mark NBER-defined recessions; the yield spread equals the 10-year constant maturity Treasury yield minus the 3-month secondary market T-bill yield.
SOURCES: U.S. Department of Commerce, Bureau of Economic Analysis; Board of Governors of the Federal Reserve System, *Federal Reserve Statistical Releases*, "Selected Interest Rates," H.15; and the National Bureau of Economic Research, Inc.; Economic Trends, Federal Reserve Bank of Cleveland, January 2002.

effort to slow inflation, the Federal Reserve typically restricts credit availability by slowing the growth in the banking system's reserves. This puts upward pressure on interest rates because the supply of loanable funds shrinks while the demand for loanable funds remains relatively strong, and it leads to a contractionary phase. During the contraction, consumer spending declines, businesses reduce their inventories and postpone capital expenditures, and hence, loan demand drops. Inflation typically slows. During the latter stage of the contraction, the Federal Reserve accelerates the growth in monetary reserves in an effort to stimulate spending and reduce unemployment, and interest rates then decline. Finally, the percentage change in real GDP bottoms out at the trough, along with the level of interest rates. The cycle then repeats itself.

Obviously, the pattern represented by Exhibit 7.6 is a simplistic representation of reality. It appears, for example, that the length of an expansion equals the length of a contraction. As we can see from actual GDP data in Exhibit 7.7, expansionary periods are much longer than contractionary periods. The most recent U.S. recessions that began in late 1990 and early 2001 lasted just six months, with most of the recent earlier recessions lasting around 12 months. In contrast, expansions run longer. From 1982 to mid-1990, for example, the United States experienced the longest continuous expansionary period since World War II. During most of this period, however, interest rates fell—unlike the indications in Exhibit 7.6. Most analysts attribute this to a sharp reduction in inflation and inflation expectations, which is unusual for an expansion. The decline in rates was reversed in 1989 just prior to the 1990 recession, after which rates fell through 1993 before they moved higher. In general, interest rates have varied directly with rates of economic growth over long periods of U.S. economic activity and the spread between long-term and short-term yields narrows steeply just before recessions.

• **EXHIBIT 7.8**

YIELDS ON MONEY MARKET AND CAPITAL MARKET INSTRUMENTS

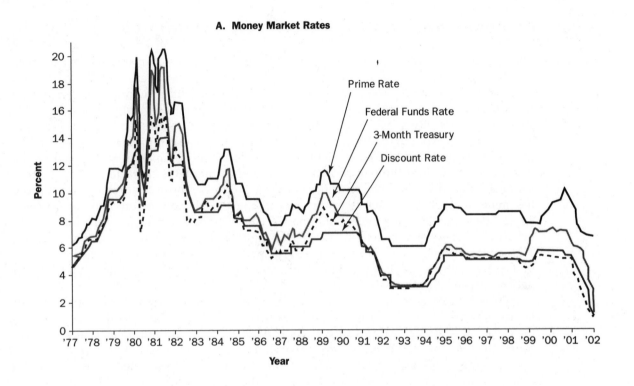

A. Money Market Rates

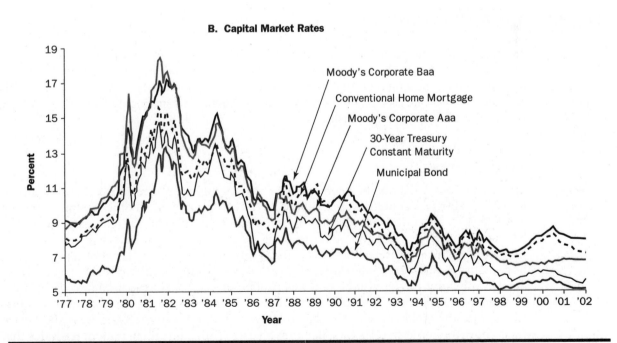

B. Capital Market Rates

SOURCE: Federal Reserve Statistical Release H15, http://www.federalreserve.gov/releases/H15/data.htm.

The expansion continued from 1991 through early 2001, representing a new record for the longest expansionary phase in U.S. history. Economic growth following the 2001 recession was slow through mid-2002.

WHY DO INTEREST RATES DIFFER BETWEEN SECURITIES?

The loanable funds framework focuses on a single, risk-free rate of interest. Obviously, there are many different securities with different features and varying degrees of risk. The difference in yields between various debt instruments is termed the **structure of interest rates.** Various debt instruments mature at different intervals, pay interest that may or may not be subject to income taxes, have call or put option features, and may even be convertible into common stock. Not surprisingly, securities with different features carry different market rates of interest. Exhibit 7.8 plots yields on a variety of money market and capital market instruments from 1977 through early 2002. The **money market** is characterized by the trading of short-term funds, with maturities of one year or less. One of the principal functions of the money market is to finance the working capital needs of corporations and governments. Typical denominations are large, more than $1,000,000. The instruments of the money market are characterized as being low risk, highly liquid and issued by highly visible "players." The **capital market,** in contrast, is designed to finance long-term funding needs. Instruments in the capital market have original maturities of more than one year and minimum denominations can be large or small.

Exhibit 7.8 clearly indicates that all interest rates are not the same. Yields on the instruments presented could differ because of maturity, default risk, marketability and liquidity, the existence of special features such as convertibility or call and put options, and tax treatment. The fundamental premise is that these characteristics have value to investors and borrowers and thus are explicitly priced in the marketplace. A market determined interest rate reflects this valuation in equilibrium along with the general level of the risk-free rate.

TERM TO FINAL MATURITY

Final maturity is important because it determines how long an investor must wait before the security issuer makes the last promised interest and principal payment. All other factors being the same, the length of time to final maturity affects a security's liquidity risk, default risk, and interest rate risk, and thus significantly influences its pricing. In general, the longer is maturity, the greater are the risks.

YIELD CURVES

A **yield curve** is a diagram that compares the market yields on securities that differ only in terms of maturity. Default risk, marketability, tax treatment, and all other features must be identical across securities in order to isolate the effects of maturity. The general relationship between a security's yield and maturity, other factors being the same, is also referred to as the **term structure of interest rates.** The visual representation provides a concise picture of how maturity influences interest rates. Examples of yield curves for Treasury securities appear in Exhibit 7.9. Notice the very steep slope of the yield curve in May 2002 in Panel A. In 2001 and 2002, the Treasury yield curve exhibited its steepest slope in recent history. In contrast, the yield curve in October 2000 was invested out to 5 years with short-term rates above longer-term rates then flat after 5 years. The figure at the bottom indicates that

ALTERNATIVE SHAPES OF THE TREASURY YIELD CURVE

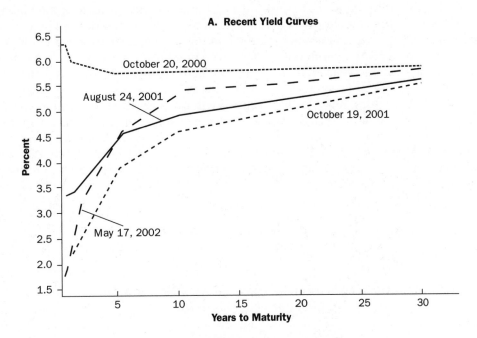

A. Recent Yield Curves

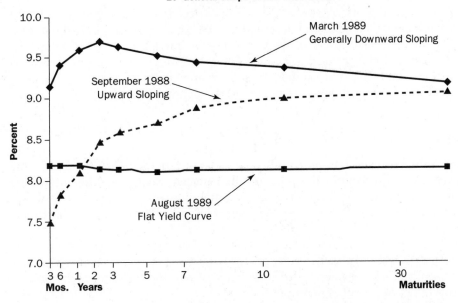

B. General Shape of the Yield Curve

the yield curve took three dramatically different shapes in less than one year. Why the different shapes? The following analysis explains the shape of the yield curve in terms of three theories: the **expectations theory,** the **liquidity premium theory,** and the **market segmentation theory.**

Although much of the literature focuses on rate expectations and constraints to borrowing and lending, these three theories differ primarily by the assumptions made about the substitutability of maturities. Specifically, the pure expectations theory assumes that various maturities are perfect substitutes and that investors will seek the highest return over their desired holding period regardless of maturity. If their desired holding period is two years, they are indifferent between holding a 2-year security; purchasing a 1-year security and rolling it over in one year; or even purchasing a 5-year security and selling it in two years. At the other extreme is the pure market segmentation theory in which various maturities are not substitutable at all. That is, if the investor has a 2-year investment horizon then nothing but a 2-year security will do; something like baking an apple pie using peaches. Both are fruit and most people will settle for either, but an apple pie with peaches is not an apple pie! Somewhere in the middle is the liquidity premium theory, which states that investors do have specific maturity preferences. In this theory, the type of preferences are very particular—lenders prefer to lend short term and borrowers prefer to borrow long term.

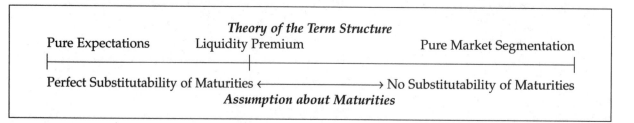

The following discussion focuses on maturity effects for Treasury securities because all Treasuries exhibit no default risk, are highly liquid, and are subject to the same tax treatment. There are problems, however, even with this comparison. To obtain a "pure" term structure, one must compare option-free, zero-coupon securities. The Treasury securities used to construct the yield curves in Exhibit 7.9 carry different coupon rates and some are callable prior to maturity such that yields are not strictly comparable.

UNBIASED EXPECTATIONS THEORY

The **unbiased expectations theory,** or pure expectations theory, focuses on the behavior of investors and attributes the relationship between yields on different maturity securities entirely to differences in expectations regarding future interest rates. Investors are indifferent to the maturity of the security they invest in and will seek the highest return over their desired holding or investment period.

Suppose you have $100,000 to invest for a 2-year period. In order to minimize default risk, you have decided to restrict your purchase to Treasury securities. With your two-year time horizon, you are considering the following options and will choose the one that maximizes expected yield over that period of time.

Option I: Invest in a 1-year Treasury. At maturity, invest in another 1-year Treasury at the prevailing rate.

Option II: Invest in a 2-year Treasury.

A call to your broker reveals that a 1-year Treasury currently yields 6.4 percent, while a 2-year Treasury yields 7.0 percent. At first glance, it might appear that option II is better because the 2-year security pays 60 basis points (0.60 percent) more than the 1-year security.

The appropriate comparison, however, is not that simple because it ignores the second year of the holding period. The key factor is that you do not know what a 1-year Treasury will yield one year from today. If the yield is high enough, two consecutive 1-year securities might yield cumulatively more in total interest than the 2-year security.

The following information, ignoring compounding, summarizes your decision. The only uncertain factor is the unknown yield one year from today.

	Expected Interest Income (Coupon Rate × $100,000)	
	Option I	Option II
Year 1	$6,400	$7,000
Year 2	?	$7,000
Total		$14,000

If the only objective is to maximize interest income, you will be indifferent between the two investment alternatives if the total interest income from option I equals the same $14,000 available from option II. In this case, interest on a 1-year Treasury purchased exactly one year from the present would have to equal $7,600 (rate = $7,600/$100,000 or 7.6%). Your decision is a straightforward rate comparison. If the rate on a 1-year Treasury acquired one year from today:

1. equals 7.6 percent, you will be indifferent between option I and option II,

2. exceeds 7.6 percent, you will buy two consecutive 1-year securities (option I),

3. is less than 7.6 percent, you will buy the 2-year security (option II).

The unbiased expectations theory attaches considerable importance to the implied interest rate or forward rate where investors are indifferent between securities with different maturities. According to this theory, the interest rate that equates the return on a series of short-term securities with the return on a long-term security for the same final maturity, reflects the market's consensus forecast of what the future interest rate will equal. In the previous example, the consensus forecast of what a 1-year Treasury will yield one year from the present is 7.6 percent, ignoring compounding. Whenever market participants change their consensus expectations, yields on different maturity securities change to reflect the new expectation. Formally,

Unbiased Expectations Theory: Long-term interest rates are an average of current and expected short-term interest rates. The expected short-term interest rate is the market's unbiased forecast of future interest rates.

Applying this to the previous data, the 2-year yield (7.0 percent) is a simple average of the current 1-year yield (6.4 percent) plus the expected 1-year yield, one year from the present (7.6 percent). The 7.6 percent implied rate represents the consensus forecast of the 1-year Treasury rate in one year.

$$7.0\% = (6.4\% + 7.6\%)/2$$

The theory applies to securities of all maturities. It implicitly assumes that investors are willing to substitute across maturities on the basis of yield differentials. Thus, if 15-year yields increase above that consistent with expectations, investors will substitute 15-year bonds for whatever bonds they hold in their portfolios. Obviously, it is assumed that these trades can be done costlessly.

The unbiased expectations theory is normally formulated in terms of compound interest rates. As such, long-term interest rates are a geometric average of current and expected short-term interest rates. Using the above data, the implied rate (f) that would make investors indifferent between options I and II can be computed as:

$$\$100{,}000 \times (1.07)^2 = \$100{,}000 \times (1.064) \times (1 + f)$$

$$f = \frac{(1.07)^2}{(1.064)} - 1$$

$$= 7.6034\%$$

With compounding, this rate slightly exceeds the 7.6 percent computed earlier.

Expected Interest Income with Compounding

	Option I	Option II
Year 1	$6,400 = 100,000 × (0.06400)	$7,000 = 100,000 × (0.07)
Year 2	$8,090 = 106,400 × (0.07603)	$7,490 = 107,000 × (0.07)
Total	$14,490	$14,490

Note that with compounding, the amount to be invested in year two is greater than the original $100,000 investment. Principal plus interest equals $106,400 under option I and $107,000 under option II.

FORWARD RATES

Conceptually, a forward rate is a rate quoted today on a forward loan that originates at some future period. The 1-year Treasury security to be issued one year from today, in the above example, is such a forward loan. As in the example, forward rates can be extracted or derived from actual yields on securities traded in the cash market. Mathematically, one need only solve a relationship that characterizes equal compound returns on two alternative investment options. Equation 7.6 expresses the current yield (at time t) on a 2-period security $(_t i_2)$ in terms of the current yield on a 1-period security $(_t i_1)$ and a 1-period forward rate, one period from the present $(_{t+1} f_1)$.

$$(1 + {_t i_2})^2 = (1 + {_t i_1})(1 + {_{t+1} f_1}) \tag{7.6}$$

Because $_t i_1$ and $_t i_2$ are readily available from the current yield curve, it is easy to solve for the one period forward rate one period from today:

$$_{t+1} f_1 = \frac{(1 + {_t i_2})^2}{(1 + {_t i_1})} - 1 \tag{7.7}$$

In general, any long-term interest rate can be expressed in terms of Equation 7.8.

$$(1 + {_t i_n})^n = (1 + {_t i_1})(1 + {_{t+1} f_1})(1 + {_{t+2} f_1}) \ldots (1 + {_{t+n-1} f_1}) \tag{7.8}$$

where

$_t i_n$ = market rate on an n-period security at time t,
$_t i_1$ = market rate on a 1-period security at time t,
$_{t+1} f_1$ = 1-period forward rate on a security to be delivered one year from the present (t+1),
$_{t+2} f_1$ = 1-period forward rate on a security to be delivered two years from the present (t+2),
$_{t+n-1} f_1$ = 1-period forward rate on a security to be delivered one period before maturity (t+n−1).

With this notation, all market interest rates are represented by the letter **i**. The *prefix* refers to the time at which the yield is quoted, with **t** representing the present. The letter **n** refers to the number of periods remaining until final maturity. All interest rates denoted by the letter **f** are forward rates. The *suffix* refers to the maturity of the underlying security.

Suppose a 3-year Treasury is currently priced to yield 7.5 percent. Combining this with the 1-year and 2-year yields discussed earlier, we can use Equation 7.8 to obtain a series of 1-year forward rates implied by the yield data. Specifically, if $_ti_3$ equals 0.075 and $_ti_2$ equals 0.070, then applying Equation 7.6 produces $_{t+2}f_1 = 0.08507$. Applying Equation 7.8 yields

$$(1.075)^3 = (1.070)^2(1 + {}_{t+2}f_1)$$

$$_{t+2}f_1 = \frac{(1.075)^3}{(1.070)^2} - 1$$

$$= 8.507\%$$

The unbiased expectations theory states that forward rates obtained from observed market interest rates equal the unbiased forecast for a security of that maturity at each respective future period. Alternatively, expectations determine why otherwise comparable securities with different maturities carry different rates. Why, for example, do the three Treasury yields presented above increase as maturity lengthens? According to the unbiased expectations theory, the answer lies in the consensus forecast—that short-term interest rates will increase in the near future. The 2-year Treasury rate exceeds the 1-year Treasury rate because the 1-year forward rate, one year from today ($_{t+1}f_1$, the market's forecast of the 1-year rate one year from today) exceeds the current 1-year Treasury rate. The same holds for the 2- and 3-year Treasury yields.

UNBIASED EXPECTATIONS, MARKET EFFICIENCY, AND ARBITRAGE

According to the unbiased or pure expectations theory, the market's consensus expectation of the future short-term interest rate equals the calculated forward rate. Assume that the current 2-year Treasury rate equals 7.0 percent and the current 1-year Treasury rate is 6.4 percent, as in our previous example. According to the unbiased expectations theory, the market consensus forecast of the 1-year Treasury rate one year from today is 7.6034 percent. Assume, for the moment, that this was not the case and that investors *expected* the 1-year Treasury rate to be 8 percent in one year. In this case, they would take option I above and invest in the 1-year Treasury security and wait until next year when they expect to earn 8 percent. Note that the 2-year investment is offering 6.4 percent the first year and only 7.6034 percent in the second year for an average two-year rate of 7.0 percent. If all market participants expect the 1-year Treasury rate to be 8 percent next year, then investors will begin to "sell the forward-rate security." That is, they would buy the 1-year Treasury security (option I) and sell the 2-year Treasury security. This would increase the price of the 1-year Treasury security and lower its yield while simultaneously lowering the price of the 2-year Treasury security and increasing its yield until the implied forward rate equaled investors' expectations. So, if investors expectations about the 1-year rate exceeded the forward rate calculated from the 1- and 2-year cash rates, the forward rate would increase:

sell the forward rate: $\dfrac{\text{sell the 2-year Treasury} \rightarrow \text{price} \downarrow \rightarrow \text{yield} \uparrow}{\text{buy the 1-year Treasury} \rightarrow \text{price} \uparrow \rightarrow \text{yield} \downarrow}$

which implies forward rate ↑

If investors expect the 1-year rate, one year from today, to be less than 7.6034 percent, they would "buy the forward rate." They would buy the 2-year security, option II, and sell the 1-year security. This would increase the price of 2-year securities, lower the rate, lower the price of the 1-year security, increase the rate, thereby lowering the forward rate.

· **EXHIBIT 7.10**

SHAPE OF THE YIELD CURVE WITH LIQUIDITY PREMIUM

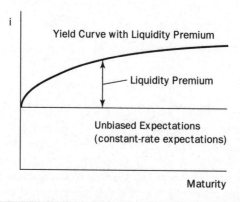

The shapes of the yield curves in Exhibit 7.9 similarly reflect different expectations regarding interest rates and thus reveal different forward rates. In March 1989, the consensus forecast was that rates would increase somewhat through two years, then decline. Thus, the yield curve increased somewhat through the shorter maturities, then systematically fell. In January 1993 and 1994, the yield curve increased sharply through the shorter maturities up to about seven years, then increased at a more modest pace. In February 1994, the Federal Reserve began to increase interest rates to quiet fears of expected inflation. The Federal Reserve increased interest rates seven times until August 1995, when it then lowered rates by 25 basis points. In January 2001, the Federal Reserve appeared to have reduced expectations about future inflation and future interest rates as long-term rates were below short-term rates.

In general, yield curves can take any shape. When long-term rates are continuously above short-term rates, the yield curve is said to be normal or upward sloping. Section B of Exhibit 7.9 indicates that the yield curve took this shape in September 1988. Note that the difference between the 30-year yield and 1-year yield was approximately 100 basis points. In January 1993, the yield curve also exhibited a normal slope, but the difference between the 30-year and 1-year yields exceeded 3.84 percent. Thus, even when the yield curve is upward sloping, it can exhibit dramatically different slopes. When long-term rates are below short-term rates, the yield curve is said to be inverted or downward sloping. This is demonstrated by the yield curve for March 1989 and January 2001.[12] Normal yield curves can generally be characterized as consistent with expectations of rising interest rates, while inverted yield curves are consistent with expectations of declining interest rates. Occasionally, the yield curve is flat as rates are approximately equal at all maturities. Section B of Exhibit 7.9 demonstrates that this was the case in August 1989. Here rates are expected to remain constant over time.

LIQUIDITY PREMIUM THEORY

The unbiased expectations theory assumes that securities that differ only in terms of maturity are perfect substitutes. Investors presumably shift between maturities on the basis of

---

[12]Actually, one would argue that the yield curve for March 1989 is a "humped" yield curve. It is quite rare to find the 30-year rate lower than the 3-month or 1-year rate. The March 1989 yield curve does, however, slope downward beyond two years.

promised yields. There is a built-in preference for short-term securities by investors because there is less price risk and less uncertainty about the future; that is, future inflation, changes in default risk, and changes in economic conditions. If the expected return on a series of short-term securities equals the expected return on a long-term security, investors will prefer the short-term securities. The **liquidity premium theory** extends the unbiased expectations theory by incorporating investor expectations of price risk in establishing market rates. Expectations, however, still dominate the fundamental shape of the yield curve. When expected returns are the same on long-term versus a series of short-term securities, for example, borrowers must pay investors a risk premium to induce them to buy the long-term securities. This premium is in addition to the nominal rate expected to prevail in the future. Because price risk increases with maturity, the risk premium increases as maturity lengthens.

Liquidity Premium Theory: Long-term rates are an average of current and expected short-term rates and liquidity premiums. The forward rate equals the expected rate plus a liquidity premium.

This theory suggests that the *forward rate* can be decomposed into two parts: the expected future short-term rate and the liquidity premium:

$$_{t+1}f_1 = {}_{t+1}e_1 + {}_{t+1}r_1 \tag{7.9}$$

where

$_{t+1}e_1$ = expected interest rate on a 1-period security, one period from the present, and
$_{t+1}r_1$ = liquidity premium component of a 1-period forward rate, one period from the present.

Unfortunately, neither the expected short-term rate nor the liquidity premium is directly observable from market information. We can only draw inferences from observed yields and calculated forward rates. If we assume that market interest rates reflect the tenets of the liquidity premium theory, several implications are apparent. First, as can be seen by Exhibit 7.10, even if the consensus forecast (expectations) is for short-term rates to remain constant, the yield curve will be continuously upward sloping. This results from the notion that liquidity premiums are positive and increase with maturity. The difference between the line representing unbiased expectations and the yield curve with a liquidity premium in Exhibit 7.10 represents the size of the liquidity premium. Longer-term rates will subsequently remain above short-term rates. Second, the normal shape of the yield curve is upward sloping because liquidity premiums impart an upward bias to long-term rates compared with short-term rates. Third, liquidity differences between very long-term securities should disappear. This explains, in part, why yield curves tend to flatten out because, at longer maturities, there is little differential price risk. Finally, when the yield curve is inverted, short-term rates are expected to decline sharply because the rate decrease must offset increasing liquidity premiums.

THE IMPACT OF CHANGING EXPECTATIONS. The Treasury yield curve has taken a variety of shapes at different times. It is often upward sloping, occasionally flat, and periodically inverts for short periods. Because it shows the relationship between interest rates and maturity at a given point in time, the yield curve will shift or change shape whenever expectations change. Consider the original example with the 1-, 2-, and 3-year Treasury securities yielding 6.4 percent, 7.0 percent, and 7.5 percent, respectively. Suppose, also, that all investors fearing a recession suddenly lower their expectations regarding future interest rates. Believing that a 1-year rate, one year from the present, will be less than 7.6034 percent, investors will purchase 2-year securities to maximize their return. This increased demand for 2-year securities relative to the available supply lowers the 2-year yield, while the reduced demand for 1-year securities raises the 1-year yield. As a result of this change in demand, short-term rates rise, long-term rates decline, and the yield curve flattens out. Depending on

CONTEMPORARY ISSUES

CAN THE TREASURY FORECAST INTEREST RATES BETTER THAN THE MARKET?

From 1991 through 1993, the yield curve for U.S. Treasury securities exhibited the steepest slope in recent history. Long-term rates exceeded short-term rates by more than 5 percent, even as interest rates fell.

The U.S. Treasury, under both the Bush and Clinton administrations, announced a policy of substituting short-term borrowing for long-term borrowing at its regular auctions of newly issued bonds. Specifically, the Treasury issued the same amount of bonds as previously planned, but reduced the amount of 10-year and 20-year bonds while increasing the amount of 1-year bonds. The stated intent was to take advantage of the lower short-term Treasury yields, which reduced the government's interest

expense and thus improved (reduced) the federal deficit.

This policy embodied an interesting philosophy regarding interest rates and their determinants. For the policy to be successful, that is, for it to to have lowered Treasury borrowing costs over time, the Treasury had to be able to replace the additional short-term debt with new debt at a lower average cost than that of the original long-term debt. According to the unbiased expectations theory, the Treasury implicitly believed that forward rates were too high and that they overstated the true levels of future interest rates. The Treasury could presumably refinance the short-term debt at a lower average cost. This might have been correct, for example, if long-term

rates had incorporated expected inflation premiums that were too large.

Of course, many analysts do not believe that any market participant, particularly government officials, can forecast interest rates better than the market. The Treasury yield curve was steep because the consensus was that short-term rates would eventually rise sharply from the low levels of the early 1990s. It is curious to note that at the same time that the Treasury was borrowing more in the short-term, individual borrowers were shifting their preferences to fixed-rate mortgages that locked-in borrowing costs for 15 or 30 years, rather than adjustable rate mortgages.

---

the degree of the change in expected rates, the yield curve could remain upward sloping, go flat, or become inverted.

Suppose, instead, that all investors suddenly expect rates to be much higher than 7.6034 percent in one year. The relative demand for 1-year Treasury securities increases while the demand for 2-year Treasuries decreases. Short-term rates would thereby fall while long-term rates would rise and the yield curve would increase in slope. The essential point is that if the basic shape of the yield curve is determined by expectations, long-term rates will change immediately relative to short-term rates to reflect changing expectations.

MARKET SEGMENTATION THEORY

Market segmentation theory is based on the premise that investors and borrowers do not view securities with different maturities as perfect substitutes. Market participants tend to concentrate their transactions within specific maturity ranges, regardless of interest rates on securities outside the preferred maturities. Interest rates are thus determined by distinct supply and demand conditions within each maturity group, and changes in interest rates do not induce substitution between different maturity securities. Hence the term *market segmentation*. That is to say, the market for short-term securities is separate from or segmented from the market for long-term securities. In the extreme case of pure or perfect market segmentation, short-term and long-term securities are not substitutable at all. As we mentioned earlier, it's like trying to make an apple pie with peaches. They may both taste good—but an apple pie made with peaches is not an apple pie.[13]

---

[13]It can be argued that most investors would not subscribe to either end of the spectrum of these theories—that is, that short-term and long-term securities are either perfect substitutes or not substitutable at all. It is useful, however, to understand the extreme cases.

There are many reasons why borrowers and lenders may restrict transactions to a specific maturity. First, they may be required to use certain maturity instruments because of government regulation. Examples are state governments which, by law, must operate with balanced operating budgets. They issue short-term debt to finance temporary imbalances between operating revenues and expenses, and long-term debt to finance capital expenditures. They cannot issue long-term debt to finance operating expenses. Second, participants may limit maturities as part of a general policy to reduce risk in their business. Commercial banks, for example, normally concentrate their investments in securities with maturities under 10 years because most of their liabilities are relatively short-term. This allows them to approximately match the maturities of their assets with the maturities of their liabilities in order to reduce the risk of losses when interest rates change. Life insurance companies similarly buy long-term securities because they can actuarially predict claim payments over long periods of time. Long-term securities offer attractive yields and can be timed to mature at intervals that coincide, on average, with expected claims. Third, participants may lack the expertise to switch maturities with any frequency, or may simply be unwilling to take advantage of opportunities because they are not profit maximizers. The U.S. Treasury falls into this last group as it generally refuses, as a matter of policy, to adjust the maturity of outstanding Treasury debt to take advantage of the prevailing yield curve.

Maturity restrictions resulting from government regulation create what can be referred to as strong-form market segmentation. Borrowers and lenders have rigid, legal restrictions that prohibit maturity substitution. Limitations resulting from other motives produce weak-form market segmentation. Implicitly, participants can be induced to shift between maturities if interest premiums are sufficiently large.

> **Market Segmentation Theory:** Interest rates on securities with different maturities are determined by distinct supply and demand conditions within each maturity. Borrowers and lenders concentrate their transactions within preferred maturities and cannot be induced to substitute between maturities by small yield changes.

Exhibit 7.11 demonstrates the impact of market segmentation on the yield curve. The analysis assumes that the maturity spectrum is divided into one market representing the supply and demand for short-term loanable funds and one market representing the supply and demand for long-term loanable funds. The diagrams display aggregate borrower and lender activity within each maturity group and are drawn to equivalent scale. The example presented outlines conditions that produce a normal, or upward sloping, yield curve. At each interest rate, the amount of funds that lenders are willing to lend relative to the amount borrowers want to borrow is greater for short-term securities than long-term securities. Thus, at a market rate of 10 percent, the short-term market is in equilibrium while lenders in the long-term market are not willing to lend all the funds that long-term borrowers want. The smaller relative demand pressure for short-term loanable funds pushes short-term rates below long-term rates and the "implied" yield curve is upward sloping.

Similar conditions could exist for an inverted or downward sloping yield curve. The borrower and lender relationships presented in Exhibit 7.11 would essentially be reversed. At each interest rate, the amount of funds that borrowers request relative to the amount that lenders are willing to commit is far greater for short-term securities than long-term securities. Thus, short-term rates exceed long-term rates and the yield curve slopes downward.

THE YIELD CURVE AND THE BUSINESS CYCLE

Many analysts track changes in the Treasury yield curve for information about where the economy is headed with regard to the business cycle. Changes in the shape of the yield curve presumably reflect changing expectations concerning where interest rates are headed, and certain patterns are associated with different stages of the business cycle. Exhibit 7.6 indicates

· EXHIBIT 7.11

MARKET SEGMENTATION AND IMPLIED SLOPE OF THE YIELD CURVE

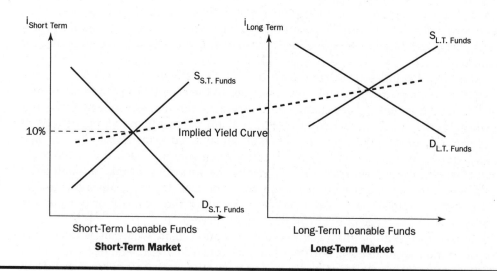

Short-Term Market   Long-Term Market

the normal relationship between the shape of the yield curve and economic conditions. Note that the dashed line characterizes the movement in short-term rates while the solid line characterizes the pattern in long-term rates. During the early stages of the expansion, unemployment and inflation are relatively low and businesses operate with some excess capacity. The Federal Reserve typically provides lenders with sufficient reserves to make new loans in order to stimulate growth. This keeps short-term rates low relative to long-term rates and the yield curve slopes upward. As consumers spend and businesses expand production, aggregate income increases. This increases borrowing requirements and interest rates move higher. Eventually, inflation starts to accelerate so that long-term rates increase, reflecting greater inflation expectations. At the peak, loan demand is high, inflation is high and rising, and the Federal Reserve acts to reduce the growth in loanable funds. This policy puts upward pressure on short-term rates and stabilizes or decreases inflation expectations, thereby moving long-term rates lower. The yield curve thus inverts. Eventually, high rates deter consumer and business spending so that real GDP declines, unemployment increases, and inflation eases. The level of interest rates moves lower with short-term rates falling farther than long-term rates, and the yield curve is again upward sloping.

The implication of Exhibit 7.6 is that the shape of the Treasury yield curve indicates where the U.S. economy is in terms of the business cycle. In particular, after the yield curve inverts, an economic slowdown typically follows. Exhibit 7.12 compares the relationship between short-term and long-term interest rates and economic growth. The solid line measures the ratio of short-term to long-term rates. When it exceeds 1.0, the yield curve is inverted. The shaded areas signify periods in which the U.S. economy was in recession. In all but two instances after World War II, the shift to an inverted yield curve preceded a recession, typically by 12 to 18 months. The relationship has been remarkably robust, except that during 1999, the yield curve inverted with no subsequent recession. Most analysts attribute this to a shift in Treasury policy. With the federal budget surpluses, the Treasury first announced that it was going to buy back long-term government bonds, then actually bought back the bonds. Not surprisingly, traders bought long-term bonds on the announcement in anticipation of future government purchases. The yield curve shift thus did not reflect any change in economic conditions.

RELATIONSHIP BETWEEN THE YIELD CURVE AND RECESSIONS

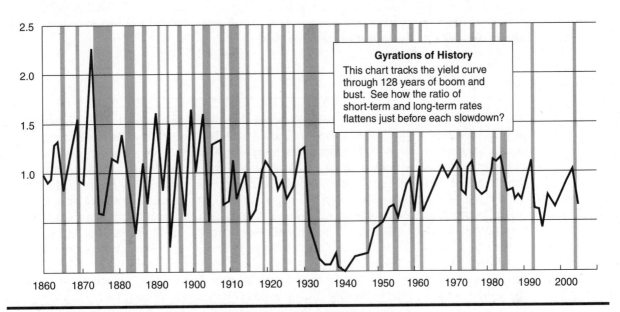

Gyrations of History
This chart tracks the yield curve through 128 years of boom and bust. See how the ratio of short-term and long-term rates flattens just before each slowdown?

SOURCE: Jack Willoughby, "Dangerous Shapes," *Forbes*, January 23, 1989; updated.

TERM TO REPRICING VARIABLE RATE AND FLOATING RATE SECURITIES

Some loan contracts call for the repayment of principal to be deferred, but loan interest rates to be adjusted at periodic intervals prior to final maturity or principal payment. Suppose, for instance, that a depositor wants to deposit $1 million in a bank for one year, but expects interest rates to increase during the coming year. A bank would like the certainty of funds remaining on deposit for the year to provide greater investment flexibility. The two parties might agree to structure the deposit as a CD with a 1-year maturity, but with the interest rate set every three months at the prevailing 3-month CD rate. The depositor is protected against rate increases because the earning rate will increase when CD rates increase, while the bank has use of the funds for the full year.

A security is classified as **variable rate** if the applicable market interest rate is changed or adjusted at predetermined intervals. The CD in the previous example is a variable rate CD. A security is classified as **floating rate** if the applicable market interest rate is tied to some index and changes whenever the index changes. A prime-based loan priced at the bank's current prime rate plus 1 percent represents such a contract. The prime rate is the base index. Whenever the bank changes its prime rate, which normally occurs at varied intervals, the contract rate on the loans changes coincidentally. A popular floating rate index used today is LIBOR. **LIBOR** is the London Interbank Offer Rate and is somewhat similar to the federal funds rate in the United States, except that the maturity is usually one to six months rather than overnight, as are federal funds. LIBOR is the rate at which large financial institutions trade dollar-denominated deposits in institutions located outside the U.S.

Variable rate securities are priced in terms of the time remaining until repricing and not final maturity. Conceptually, a lender locks in a yield only for the time until repricing, so the term to repricing reflects the effective maturity. Thus, based on the market rate, the 1-year CD in the above example is priced off of other 3-month securities and not 1-year securities. Floating rate securities are priced to reflect a premium over the base rate. This premium typically covers default risk and the cost of handling the underlying loan. Final maturity does, however, affect the market rate because it may influence default risk or other costs to the lender that potentially appear prior to maturity.

DEFAULT RISK

The pricing of fixed-income securities assumes that the size and exact timing of each cash flow in the present value calculation are known with certainty. A bond's price subsequently equals the sum of the present values of each cash flow. More precisely, a security represents nothing more than a promise to pay the contractual interest and principal at a prespecified time. Clearly, such a promise may not be kept. Default risk on debt instruments is the probability or likelihood that a borrower will not make the contractual interest and principal payments as promised. When this occurs, an investor either receives a lower payment than that promised or receives full or partial payment at a later date. In either case, the realized value of the actual cash flows will be less than those promised, so the investor fares poorly.

When there is a real possibility that the borrower will not make the scheduled payments, investors will demand a higher promised interest rate. The greater the actual or perceived likelihood of default, the higher will be the market interest rate. A basic issue in pricing securities involves setting rates that compensate investors for expected default losses.

DEFAULT RISK PREMIUMS

Not all bonds exhibit the same default risk. The U.S. Treasury, for example, can readily issue new debt to pay existing security holders because of the government's commitment and power to raise taxes or print money to raise funds. Treasury securities are, therefore, very nearly free of default risk because payment is backed by the full faith, credit, and taxing power of the federal government. Other borrowers, such as corporations in cyclical industries or those close to bankruptcy, have less predictable cash flows and investors recognize a real possibility that the firms might default. In fact, all borrowers other than the Treasury exhibit default risk that is greater than that for Treasury securities because no guarantee is as strong as the federal government's.

Analysts subsequently compare interest rates between securities by means of default risk premiums. **Default risk premiums** are calculated as the promised yield on a taxable security with default risk minus the market interest rate on a risk-free security, such as a Treasury security, of the same maturity or duration.[14] Formally,

Default risk premium = promised yield on a risky security −comparable Treasury yield **(7.10)**

The risk premium will always be positive because risky securities offer higher yields than comparable maturity Treasury securities. Because both the promised yield on a risky security and the Treasury rate are market-determined, the default risk premium represents the *expected default loss* measured as the incremental yield required on a risky security to compensate for expected losses. Exhibit 7.13 compares default risk premiums for different-rated corporate securities from 1996–2002, and for commercial paper in 2001–2002. Two conclusions stand out.

---

[14]Some securities pay interest that is not subject to federal income taxes. Yields on these securities cannot be directly compared with yields on taxable securities. Tax effects and default premiums on tax-exempt securities are addressed later in the chapter.

YIELD SPREADS AS AN APPROXIMATION OF DEFAULT RISK PREMIUMS

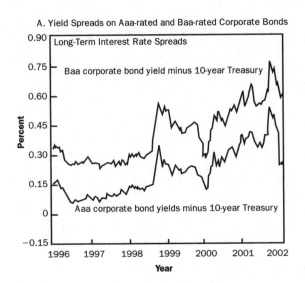

A. Yield Spreads on Aaa-rated and Baa-rated Corporate Bonds

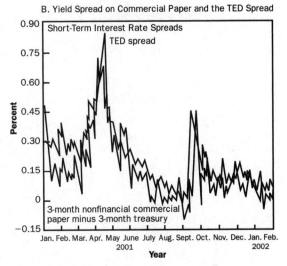

B. Yield Spread on Commercial Paper and the TED Spread

First, corporate bonds with the same 10-year maturity display different default risk premiums. For example, the *default* risk premiums on Baa-rated bonds typically exceeded those on Aaa-rated corporates by 50 to 140 basis points. Second, default risk premiums increase with maturity. Generally speaking, the farther into the future investors must wait for a return of principal, the greater is the likelihood of loss. Investors also have less confidence in their forecasts of future payments the farther into the future the payments occur. Panel B demonstrates that the yield spread on commercial paper ranged from −10 basis points to 70 basis points in 2001. Note that this spread also captures differences in liquidity. Panel B also repeats the TED spread, which is the yield differential on 3-month Eurodollars versus 3-month T-bills and is a popular indicator of default risk and short maturities.

The introduction to this chapter cited the problems faced by Long-Term Capital Management, a hedge fund that speculated in fixed-income securities. In 1998, much of the firm's capital was supporting speculative bets that default risk premiums, or quality spreads, would converge to historical norms versus their prevailing values. Because the firm leveraged its bets, it lost much of its capital when the risk premiums actually widened over the short run. The original investors lost almost all of their initial $4.8 billion in capital as the fund had to be bailed out by other financial institutions. One lesson was that default risk premiums, or quality spreads, are not predictable in the short run. Another is that excessive leverage can lead to failure.

BOND RATINGS

To accurately assess default risk, investors must analyze an issuer's ability to service debt under adverse economic conditions. This involves a careful review of the issuer's financial condition as well as specific features of each security. This analysis can be quite costly and time-consuming. Several private firms provide this service by evaluating a security's default risk and assigning a credit rating. The rating agencies charge borrowers a one-time fee prior

RATING CLASSIFICATIONS

Standard & Poor's	Moody's	Description
Investment Grade		
AAA	Aaa	Highest quality
AA	Aa	High quality, slightly more risk than top rating
A	A-1, A	Upper-medium grade, possible future impairment
BBB	Baa	Medium grade, lacks outstanding investment characteristics
Noninvestment Grade (Junk)		
BB	Ba	Some speculative characteristics
B	B	Highly speculative, small assurance of interest and principal payments
CCC	Caa	Low quality, probable default
CC	Ca	Low quality, poor prospect of attaining investment standing
C, D	C	Lowest quality, in default

Municipal Notes and Commercial Paper

Standard & Poor's Commercial Paper	Moody's Commercial Paper	Notes	Description
A-1+	P-1	MIG 1	Highest quality
A-1	P-1	MIG 2	High quality
A-2	P-2	MIG 3	Strong degree of safety
A-3	P-3	MIG 4	Satisfactory degree of safety

to the release of the rating. The borrower's objective is to obtain a rating that enhances investor interest and thereby lowers the interest rate by enough to cover the fee paid the rating agencies. Investors review these ratings and require higher promised returns from lower quality (higher default probability) securities.

Exhibit 7.14 summarizes the various ratings provided by Moody's and Standard & Poor's for bonds, short-term municipal notes, and commercial paper, ranked from highest to lowest quality. Bonds that receive ratings from Aaa (AAA) to Baa (BBB) are labeled investment grade bonds. Bonds rated Ba (BB) and lower or nonrated bonds are labeled *junk bonds*. The rating agencies periodically review an issuer's financial condition and may assign a new rating that is either higher or lower. When a rating is upgraded, market participants react favorably and bid the market rate lower. If a security is downgraded, the market rate increases to reflect a higher default risk premium.

Exhibit 7.13 further demonstrates that market participants view the rating agencies' assessment of risk as meaningful. Thus, lower-rated corporate and municipal bonds carry higher yields than Aaa-rated identical maturity bonds of the same type. Default risk premiums are greater on lower-rated instruments and increase with maturity.

MARKETABILITY AND LIQUIDITY

All assets can be converted to cash if the holder has enough time to find a buyer and negotiate terms. In many cases, it is easy to sell an asset at a predictable price because there are many buyers who know the asset's characteristics and the cost of effecting the sale is low.

Treasury bills and bonds meet this description. In other cases, it is difficult to sell an asset because buyers know little about it. A 2-acre parcel of mountain property located near a ski resort might qualify here. A buyer must determine where the land is located, if it is accessible, whether utilities are available, what similar property has sold for, and what the broker's fee is before knowing what a fair market price might be. Arriving at this price may be time consuming and costly.

LIQUIDITY EFFECTS

Liquidity refers to the speed and ease with which an asset can be converted to cash and to the certainty of the price received. Both aspects of liquidity are important. The ski resort property *can* be converted to cash very quickly if we are asking only $5. But to realize its full market value may take a significant amount of time because the parcel is not extremely marketable. **Marketability** refers to the speed and ease with which an asset can be sold. Treasury securities, on the other hand, can be sold quickly and for a fair market price just about any time of the day, and are therefore quite liquid. Highly marketable and liquid assets, such as Treasury securities, trade frequently in well-established secondary markets so that buyers and sellers can readily estimate the precise sales price. Liquidity extends the marketability concept to encompass the fact that the sale should occur with minimal unanticipated loss to the owner. In general, an asset's liquidity is closely tied to its maturity or duration.

For interest-bearing securities, liquidity depends on the issuer's reputation, the size of issue, trading volume, the source of cash flow to service the debt, whether payments are government guaranteed, and whether there are any complicated covenants that lenders have difficulty understanding. The most marketable securities are generally large issues from well-known borrowers with standardized features and no unusual covenants. It also helps if the securities carry a government guarantee and provide for debt service from a predictable cash source. Liquidity is also linked to the maturity and duration of a security that determines an asset's relative price-sensitivity to changes in interest rates. Longer maturity and duration bonds vary more in price than shorter-term and duration bonds for a given change in interest rates. Thus, when other factors are held constant, investors prefer shorter-term instruments because they take less price risk.

LIQUIDITY PREMIUMS

Investors generally prefer liquid assets over illiquid assets because they can readily sell them at predictable prices with low transactions costs. The market interest rate on a security reflects its relative liquidity, with highly liquid assets carrying the lowest rates. In general, Treasury securities are the most liquid, followed by U.S. government agency securities and highly rated corporate and municipal securities. Bond issuers can enhance the liquidity of an issue in several ways. First, if issuers obtain an investment grade rating (above BB), more participants are willing, and able, to trade their securities—hence the market is larger. Second, borrowers can purchase bond insurance that automatically enhances the rating to the highest grade by reducing default risk. Third, issuers can improve liquidity by creating a secondary market in the specific type of debt. In the early 1960s, for example, Citigroup (then City Bank) originated the jumbo CD market by agreeing to buy outstanding issues prior to maturity. Throughout the 1980s, Drexel Burnham Lambert captured the bulk of the junk bond business by making a secondary market for outstanding issues that holders needed to liquidate. Investors were more willing to buy junk securities because Drexel provided an implied guarantee that it would buy securities back or find another buyer at market prices. During much of the 1980s, this system worked well and the junk bond market flourished as volume grew from $18 billion in outstandings to more than $160 billion in 1989. At the end of 1989, however, Drexel pleaded guilty to a variety of securities violations and the firm ultimately went bankrupt. The firm's principal investment banker, Michael Milken, similarly pleaded guilty to securities fraud in early 1990. With Drexel's failure, the secondary market collapsed and junk bond owners saw their inventories quickly decline in value by 20 to 25 percent, on average, and more for the securities of bankrupt firms. As the market matured and other firms held significant inventories and quoted secondary market prices, the liquidity premium in junk bond yields declined.

SPECIAL FEATURES ON SECURITIES

Many securities contain special features or options. Some bonds have call or put options. The issuer, prior to maturity, can repurchase a bond with a call option. Because the issuer of the bond can call it back when interest rates fall, the original issue yield on these bonds is greater. Bonds with put options give the right to the lender, or investor, to require the issuer to buy back the bond at a predetermined price. If interest rates increase, or the risk of the firm increases, the investor can put the bond back to the issuer. Because this is advantageous to the investor, original promised yields will be lower on these types of bonds. Still, other bonds are issued that can be converted into the common stock of the company. This option gives the investor the right to convert the bond's fixed payments into common stock and hence reap the benefits of exceptional performance of the company. These types of bonds are generally issued at lower original promised rates than nonconvertible bonds. Obviously, if a security carries a special feature, its promised yield could be affected.

CALL AND PUT PROVISIONS

Call and put provisions alter the effective maturity of a security. A **call provision** enables the issuer of a security to call an outstanding bond for repayment at a predetermined price prior to final maturity. The call feature has value because it protects the borrower in the event that interest rates decline after the securities are originally issued. A significant decrease in rates enables a borrower to issue new debt at lower rates and use the proceeds to prepay old debt that carries higher rates. Investors are hurt because they must forgo high rates on the old debt as prepayment forces them to reinvest the proceeds at lower rates.

A call option has value to a borrower and is priced accordingly. In order to induce investors to purchase callable securities, borrowers typically stipulate that the securities must be called at a premium over par value. Often this premium is one coupon payment. Thus, a bond with a $1,000 par value might be callable at 107 percent of par. This means that the issuer would have to pay an investor $1,070 to buy back the bond regardless of whether its actual price was lower, or more likely, higher. In many cases, issuers defer for several years the initial date at which a security might be callable. A bond with a 20-year maturity might not be callable for the first five years. The premium that must be paid at call usually decreases the farther out a bond is called. The justification for a call premium is that if interest rates fall enough to make calling a bond attractive to the issuer, the market price will be well above the call price and the premium represents a sharing of the increase in value. In practice, the market price will not rise substantially above the call price because such a bond would be called eventually and any new investor would suffer a capital loss.

Investors demand higher interest rates on callable bonds compared with noncallable bonds. This compensates investors for the risk that they might lose the above-market interest if rates drop, and thus the incremental yield serves as the price of the call option. The longer the deferment period, the lower the yield that an issuer must pay. Market participants

PUT BONDS AND CORPORATE BUYOUTS

The corporate merger and acquisition craze that swept U.S. firms and financial markets throughout the 1980s created a market for another type of put bond, the intent of which was to protect bondholders from adverse price moves resulting from a buyout. In the typical buyout, one firm purchases the stock of another firm and finances the transaction primarily with new debt. The combined firm's financial leverage (debt divided by equity) increases sharply and thus the credit risk of outstanding debt tends to deteriorate. The rating agencies often respond by lowering quality ratings and bond-

holders find their claims subordinated even more. In many instances, bondholders have seen the value of their holding drop by 10 to 20 percent in a matter of days after an announced buyout. The acquisition of R.J. Reynolds by Krohlberg, Kravis & Roberts in 1988, for example, saw bondholders lose 22 percent of the value of their securities in two days. Marriott Corp. similarly announced a restructuring in which the company would divide itself into divisions, and allocated the bulk of the firm's total debt to the division with real estate interests. Not surprisingly, the value of Marriott's outstanding

bonds fell by more than 20 percent, while Marriott's stock price jumped.

Bond investors reacted to these events by filing lawsuits claiming a violation of fiduciary responsibilities, and generally refusing to purchase additional debt from buyout candidates without some form of protection. A popular option is now to attach a put feature to a bond which specifies that a bond is putable back to the issuer at par if certain adverse conditions appear as a result of a buyout proposal.

---

generally assume that a callable bond will be called, and price the security to the first call date rather than final maturity. The market rate is termed the yield to first call.

Another type of option that is becoming increasingly common is the put option. A **put option** gives the lender the right to put, or sell, a security back to the issuer at a predetermined price prior to final maturity. This option has value to the investor because the predetermined price is typically at least par, and the investor can sell the security without a loss if interest rates increase. Recall that when interest rates increase on a security without a put option, the value of the security falls; hence, the investor would have to sell the security at a loss or hold it to maturity to receive the full face value. If interest rates fall, an investor can simply hold on to the security that now pays a higher than market rate, or the security could be sold at a premium in the secondary market.

A put option can potentially reduce borrowing cost because the security is issued at a lower rate. On the other hand, a put option can prove to be costly to an issuer because it eliminates the potential for interest rate savings that could be achieved by locking in low rates, and could require the issuer to refinance the original debt at a higher rate. Whether a put option increases or decreases the company's actual borrowing costs depends on what happens to interest rates and the company's risk after original issue.

A put option can also be used to ensure the investor that the issuing company does not substantially increase their risk. Because bondholders do not have voting rights, once a bond is issued there is little they can do to control additional risk that the company may assume. If a company issues a bond with a put option and the company becomes more risky, the investor can put the bond back to the issuer. Hence, even if the general level of interest rates does not increase but the risk of the company does, the value of the bonds will still decrease. Bonds with put options provide the investor protection against increases in risk because they can be sold back at par value. On the positive side, companies with highly volatile earnings could find it easier to issue bonds with a put feature.

As with any option, a put feature is priced accordingly. Conceptually, a put option is priced much like a variable rate loan because the put decision is effective at predetermined intervals. A 20-year bond, for example, might be putable at each 1-year anniversary of the issue date for the first 10 years, after which the put option lapses. If, at the anniversary date, rates are above the rate on the security, an investor will put the bond back to the issuer who then agrees to pay a market rate rather than return principal to the investor. If the investor demands a return of principal, the issuer will find another investor to buy the security. Thus, a put bond effectively changes yield at each put period according to prevailing rates when rates rise. Put yields remain constant at each put period when rates fall.

Again, the importance of final maturity is reduced when a put feature is attached to a security. The interest rate on a put instrument is normally linked to the rate on a similar security without a put option. The link is that the length of time between put anniversary dates coincides with the maturity of the related security. Thus, a bond that is putable at one year intervals is priced at a slight premium over the prevailing 1-year rate.

CONVERTIBILITY

Some corporations issue securities that are hybrids of debt and common stock. Such securities, labeled **convertible bonds,** make fixed coupon payments like straight bonds but carry the additional provision that holders may convert the bonds to common stock at a predetermined price. The convertible owner essentially has an option that changes in value with the market's perception of the underlying corporation's financial condition. Once a bond is converted to stock, however, the transaction cannot be reversed.

Because the conversion feature has value, investors are willing to accept a yield below that offered on straight debt. The yield exceeds the dividend yield on the firm's common stock and the prespecified conversion price exceeds the prevailing value of a share of stock. For example, in 1986, Wherehouse Entertainment, Inc., issued $50 million in convertible bonds paying 6.25 percent annual interest, with the option to convert each $1,000 face value bond into 36 shares of the firm's stock. At that time, Wherehouse paid 11 percent coupon interest on its straight bonds. The conversion value of each bond in terms of stock equaled $27.50, which represented a 26 percent premium over the $22 stock price at the time of issue. This meant that an investor could convert the bond to stock if Wherehouse's stock price increased above $27.50. With convertibles, an investor earns a relatively low corporate bond yield, but might gain if the stock price rises high enough.

Convertibles are, however, riskier than straight bonds because the claims of owners are subordinated to the claims of straight debt holders. In case of default, bondholders are paid before holders of convertibles. Part of the lower interest yield thus represents a higher default risk premium. At the same time, convertibles are not as risky as common stock because their claims on the assets of the company, in the event of default, are above those of common stockholders.

INCOME TAX EFFECTS

To this point, we have discussed interest rates in terms of pretax yields. Clearly, the realized return from buying a security depends on whether an investor pays taxes on any of the proceeds. Tax payments reduce spendable cash receipts so that after-tax yields are less than promised pretax yields.

The impact of federal income taxes is readily demonstrated with the present value analysis of Chapter 6.[15] Suppose you purchased a 3-year Aaa-rated corporate bond for $10,000 that

---

[15]Some states and local governments also levy income taxes, which increases the effective marginal tax rate on income. State and local taxes are ignored in the following analysis.

pays $850 in interest at the end of each year and returns $10,000 at maturity. Your marginal tax rate is 28 percent. Because you bought the bond at par, taxes apply only against the periodic interest. Your after-tax interest income thus equals $612 annually for an effective after-tax yield (i^*) of 6.12 percent.

$$10,000 = \frac{850(1 - 0.28)}{(1 + i^*)} + \frac{850(1 - 0.28)}{(1 + i^*)^2} + \frac{850(1 - 0.28)}{(1 + i^*)^3} + \frac{10,000}{(1 + i^*)^3}$$

$$10,000 = \sum_{t=1}^{3} \frac{612}{(1 + i^*)^t} + \frac{10,000}{(1 + i^*)^3}$$

Solving for i^* produces $i^* = 0.0612$.

In general, the after-tax yield for a bond purchased at par and held to maturity equals the pretax yield, **i**, times 1 minus the investor's applicable marginal tax rate, **t**.

$$i^* = i\,(1 - t) \tag{7.11}$$

In the previous example, i^* equals $0.085(1 - 0.28)$ or 6.12 percent.

The tax treatment of bonds, purchased at a discount or premium, is slightly more complex. When an investor buys a bond for less than par value (a discount bond), a portion of the return consists of price appreciation or capital gains. Capital gains are often taxed at a lower rate than regular coupon income. As time elapses, the bond's price approaches par value even with no change in the level of interest rates. When pricing the bond, the difference between par value and the discount price is amortized over the remaining life of the bond. This represents income, and investors must pay taxes on the realized price appreciation at maturity or sale. With premium bonds, the price decreases to par value so that amortization represents a loss and thus serves to reduce taxable income.[16]

MUNICIPAL SECURITIES

Municipal securities are debt obligations issued by state and local governments and their political subdivisions, such as school districts or water treatment facilities. Most municipals pay interest that is exempt from federal income taxes, so investors are willing to accept pretax yields that are lower than those on comparable maturity and risk-taxable securities.[17] Consider a 3-year Aaa-rated municipal that is priced at $10,000 par and is otherwise comparable to the 3-year corporate yielding 8.5 percent, except that interest is tax-exempt. Suppose that the municipal pays $700 a year in interest. Its pretax yield, i_m, equals 7 percent, which is the same as its after-tax yield.

Using Equation 7.11, we know that the after-tax yield of the taxable corporate bond is 6.12 percent [$0.085 (1 - 0.28)$]. An investor who pays taxes at the 28 percent rate will prefer the municipal over the previous corporate bond because the after-tax yield is 0.88 percent higher. Municipal rates, as shown in Exhibit 7.13, are less than the pretax yields on all taxable securities of the same maturity because of this tax advantage. Municipal rates are already computed on an after-tax basis.

The tax treatment of tax-exempt discount and premium municipal bonds parallels that of taxable bonds. Specifically, any price appreciation is taxable, while premium bonds generate tax losses if they are sold or mature at prices below cost. Interest income is still tax-exempt, however.

---

[16]This discussion applies to bonds that trade at prices other than par due to interest rate changes. In the case where bonds are originally issued at a discount, taxes apply annually to amortized income regardless of whether the bondholder receives any cash.

[17]Municipals issued for private purposes, where the proceeds are effectively used by corporations, pay interest that is taxable and thus are labeled taxable municipals.

STATE AND LOCAL TAXES

Many state and local governments impose taxes that apply to income from securities, much like the federal income tax. There are subtle differences, however. First, states and localities that have an income tax specifically exempt interest on Treasury securities. Second, states and localities selectively exempt municipal interest from taxes. Most states exempt interest for all bonds issued within their home state, but tax interest on bonds issued outside their home state. The purpose is to increase the demand for in-state municipals and thereby lower in-state borrowing costs relative to other municipals. Investors must be aware of both federal and state/local income taxes before buying any security. Brokerage houses recognize the impact of state taxes by structuring municipal bond funds that buy securities from a single state and thus cater to investors from those states.

MUNICIPAL DEFAULT RISK

Due to the federal income tax exemption, pretax yields on municipals are not directly comparable with pretax yields on taxable securities. This alters the definition of a municipal default risk premium. A review of Exhibit 7.13, for example, reveals that the risky municipal yield minus the risk-free Treasury yield in each maturity group is always negative. This contradicts the intuitive notion that municipals are riskier than Treasuries.

One alternative might be to compare tax-equivalent yields on municipals with market-quoted taxable yields. A tax-equivalent municipal yield is defined as the pretax equivalent yield that a municipal would offer to provide an investor the same after-tax yield available on the municipal. It is calculated by dividing the municipal rate (i_m) by 1 minus the investor's marginal tax rate (t).

$$\text{tax-equivalent municipal yield} = i_m/(1 - t) \tag{7.12}$$

An investor in the 35 percent tax bracket would thus find that the 5-year municipal paying 4.03 percent in Exhibit 7.13 yields 6.2 percent on a tax-equivalent basis. The effective default risk premium equivalent to Equation 7.10 equals 0.74 percent (0.062 − 0.0546). The obvious problem is that this risk premium varies with the investor's tax rate. An investor in the 15 percent tax bracket, for example, would compare a 4.74 percent tax-equivalent yield to a higher Treasury yield, and the imputed risk premium would be negative.

Another alternative is to redefine the municipal default risk premium solely in terms of municipal rates. In contrast to Equation 7.10, define the municipal default risk premium as

municipal default risk premium
$$= \text{interest rate on risky municipal} - \text{interest rate on an Aaa-rated municipal} \tag{7.13}$$

Using the data from Exhibit 7.13, risk premiums on the Baa-rated municipals equal 0.38 percent, 0.41 percent, and 0.36 percent for 1-year, 5-year, and 10-year securities, respectively. Because Aaa-rated municipals are risky, the municipal default risk premium measures the incremental expected default loss on a lower-rated municipal relative to the highest grade municipal.

SUMMARY

Many factors influence interest rates. This chapter introduces a loanable funds framework that uses supply and demand analysis to characterize movements in the level of interest rates. Rates fall when the supply of loanable funds increases relative to the demand for loanable funds and rise when the opposite occurs. The level of interest rates also varies directly with changes in inflation expectations and exhibits a pattern over the business cycle—rising during expansionary periods and falling in contractionary periods.

This chapter similarly examines specific factors that affect the pricing of individual interest-bearing securities. It describes the impact of maturity, default risk, liquidity, tax treatment, and the existence of special features such as call, put, and convertibility options, and it explains differences in security yields in terms of these factors. Interest rates are generally higher the greater the default risk is, the less liquid the security is, and when call provisions exist. Interest rates are lower when default risk is low, a security is highly liquid, interest is tax-exempt, the security is convertible into common stock, and the security contains a put option. The fundamental point is that the market prices specific features of each security in terms of its value to either borrowers or lenders.

QUESTIONS

LOANABLE FUNDS THEORY

1. Use the Loanable Funds Theory to explain what would happen to the supply or demand for loanable funds if a majority of people decided they no longer need to carry cash and instead deposited all of their pocket cash into checking accounts and just used debit cards. Graphically plot what would happen to the supply and demand for loanable funds and interest rates. What is plotted on the vertical axis and what on the horizontal? Can you think of any other factors in this example that might cause the supply curve or the demand curve to shift?

2. Indicate which of the following would be a portion of the supply of loanable funds (SF) and which would be a portion of the demand for loanable funds (DF).
   a. You put $500 of your paycheck into your savings account.
   b. The local McDonald's makes a regular deposit into its demand deposit account overnight.
   c. The same McDonald's borrows enough money to expand its drive-through lane.
   d. You take out a mortgage to finance your first home.
   e. Your university deposits the tuition payments for the semester into an interest-bearing account.
   f. A major corporation issues bonds to finance a new factory.
   g. You take a cash advance on your credit card.
   h. You make a deposit into your money market mutual fund.
   i. A new sports arena in town has been financed with revenue bonds.
   j. Toyota takes excess cash from its Tennessee plant and buys Treasury bills.

3. Indicate whether the following changes in the interest rate are caused by a shift in the loanable funds demand curve (DF) or a shift in the supply curve (SF). Draw a graph to show each effect. Indicate whether interest rates will rise or fall.
   a. There is a major business expansion in the economy.
   b. A reduction in global tensions reduces spending by the military.
   c. Yuppies save substantially more money.
   d. Massive numbers of foreign investors bid for Treasury bills in large volume at the last auction.
   e. Falling world lumber prices make homes more affordable, and consumers rush to take advantage of the situation.
   f. Businesses accumulate excess inventory and no longer need to borrow money for expansion.

g. State and local governments borrow heavily to finance the decaying roads and bridges throughout the United States.

INTEREST RATES AND INFLATION

4. According to the Fisher Relation, what causes nominal market interest rates to be volatile? How long does it take before participants change inflation expectations?

5. Assume the Fisher Relation is correct and you believe that the real rate of interest is a constant 2.5 percent. If you think that inflation will be 3 percent in the upcoming year and 4 percent in the following year, what minimal rate of interest would entice you to lend money for a year? Would you accept a higher rate? What minimal rate would you demand to lend money for two years? Why? Are taxes important?

6. The major argument surrounding the Fisher Relation deals with the relationship between the real rate and expected inflation. What would Fisher, Mundell-Tobin, and Darby-Feldstein each claim that relationship to be and what is the implication of each position? What is the difference between the *ex ante* and *ex post* real-rate relationship?

7. Assume that the Fisher Relation is correct such that a 2 percent increase in expected inflation would mean that the nominal rate of interest increased by exactly 2 percent. Darby-Feldstein would argue that the nominal rate of interest would have to increase by more than 2 percent. If the nominal rate of interest only increased by 2 percent, what would the Darby-Feldstein argument say would happen to the *after-tax real-rate of interest*? Would it go up, go down, or stay the same? Explain and use a numeric example.

8. The Fisher Relation is based upon expectations of inflation and not actual inflation. Why? How often do the two differ? Can *ex ante* real rates be negative? Can *ex post* real rates be negative?

RATES AND THE BUSINESS CYCLE

9. At what point in the business cycle is the yield curve expected to be the steepest? When is it expected to be flat and at what point in the business cycle would you expect the yield curve to slope downward? Explain. What relationship between the yield curve and the business cycle can explain this expected relationship?

10. Discuss how the loanable funds theory would explain rising interest rates during the expansion phase, then falling rates during the contractionary phase, of the business cycle. Would the supply and/or the demand curve be shifting?

RATES AND SECURITIES FEATURES

11. Which one from each of the following pairs is likely to have higher default risk? Explain your reasoning.
   a. A 6-month loan or a 5-year loan to the same company
   b. A loan requiring periodic payments or a loan with all principal and interest due at the end (balloon loan)
   c. A loan to a company rated BBB by S&P or one rated A-1 by Moody's
   d. A loan to a student to buy a car or a loan to the same student to pay tuition

12. Your city government has decided to issue tax-exempt revenue bonds to finance the building of a new sports stadium. What interest rate will it have to pay if taxable bonds of comparable risk are paying 7 percent and the marginal tax rate of marginal investors in the bonds is 31 percent?

13. If the highest marginal individual tax rate is 39 percent, and the highest corporate rate is 34 percent, which group will get the greatest benefit from holding municipal securities as investments?

14. One of the biggest advantages to a firm from issuing convertible bonds rather than stock is that bondholders are paid a fixed rate of return. If the firm does well, existing shareholders do not have to pay bondholders more than the fixed return they agreed to pay. If the firm does poorly, they still have to pay bondholders the required fixed coupon payments unless the bonds are converted to common stock. Why would a firm issue convertible bonds rather than regular bonds? Under what economic conditions would convertibles be most advantageous?

YIELD CURVES AND MATURITY

You note the following yield curve in the *Wall Street Journal*.

Maturity	Yield
6 months	4.2%
1 year	4.4%
2 years	4.8%
3 years	5.1%
4 years	5.2%

15. What is the 1-year forward rate for the period beginning one year from today? If you believe the unbiased expectations theory, what does this mean? How does this interpretation change if you believe the liquidity premium theory? The market segmentation theory?

16. What is the 1-year forward rate for the period beginning two years from today? Three years from today? What is the 2-year forward rate for the period beginning two years from today?

17. Assume that you expect the real rate of interest to remain constant at 2.5 percent over the next several years. Using the data above, what do investors expect to happen to inflation in one year, two years, and three years under the Fisher equation?

18. Downward sloping yield curves are somewhat unusual. What theory of the term structure generally supports a bias toward a downward-sloping yield curve? Explain. Use this same theory to explain a downward-sloping yield curve.

19. What would be considered the repricing maturity of the following investments:
    a. A 10-year corporate bond with a 5 percent coupon rate
    b. A variable rate mortgage with the rate reset quarterly to the cost of funds of the S&L
    c. A floating rate small business loan tied to prime
    d. A 5-year callable bond with an 8 percent coupon rate, call deferred for one year
    e. A bond that is putable at 1-year intervals

20. Although it has a considerably longer maturity, an individual's mortgage usually carries a lower interest rate than his or her car loan. Why?

PROBLEMS

1. Using Treasury bond and note rates from a recent issue of the *Wall Street Journal*, fill in the following table to generate a yield curve. Interpolate (estimate) the 1-year yield.

Maturity	Yield
6 months	
1 year	
2 years	
3 years	
5 years	
10 years	

    a. Based on this data, what will be the 1-year, risk-free rate starting one year from today if you believe the unbiased expectations theory?

    b. If you believe the liquidity premium theory, do you expect the risk-free rate one year from today to be higher or lower than the number computed above?

2. When was the last time the yield curve was inverted? Did a recession follow in the time interval suggested by Exhibit 7.12? What is the current Treasury yield curve suggesting with regard to a. where the economy currently is in terms of the business cycle? and b. in what direction are interest rates headed?

3. Read your local and state tax rules on Treasury securities and in-state municipal bond interest. Explain how these taxes should affect municipal bond rates in your state. Should they be higher or lower than rates on comparable municipals issued in other states?

APPENDIX

Flow-of-Funds
U.S.-Chartered Commercial Banks
Billions of dollars; quarterly figures are seasonally adjusted annual rates

		1997	1998	1999	2000	2001
1	Gross saving	−7.5	−11.1	−10.3	−5.3	−8.4
2	Fixed nonresidential investment	19.5	23.0	22.2	24.7	23.8
3	Net acquisition of financial assets	290.8	328.1	344.1	329.2	226.5
4	Vault cash and reserves at Federal Reserve	4.8	−5.7	21.6	−25.2	0.7
5	Total bank credit	280.7	329.3	313.7	350.5	204.7
6	U.S. government securities	54.3	39.6	27.4	−16.7	42.0
7	Treasury	−6.1	−42.1	−1.9	−35.0	−31.4
8	Agency	60.4	81.6	29.3	18.2	73.4
9	Mortgage pool securities	31.1	53.7	−17.8	14.2	52.7
10	Agency-issued CMOs	17.5	8.9	4.9	−9.8	56.9
11	Other agency securities	11.8	19.1	42.2	13.8	−36.2
12	Municipal securities	2.4	8.2	5.8	3.2	6.1
13	Corporate and foreign bonds	19.6	32.4	43.3	52.4	64.6
14	Private mortgage pool securities	−1.2	0.9	0.9	−0.7	21.2
15	Privately issued CMOs	0.7	20.3	5.7	8.0	2.8
16	Other bonds	20.2	11.1	36.7	45.2	40.5
17	Total loans	203.0	248.2	234.9	308.7	84.3
18	Open market paper	−0.6	−0.1	−0.1	0.2	0.0
19	Bank loans n.e.c.	108.1	144.3	92.2	98.2	−64.5
20	Mortgages	105.5	95.8	160.6	161.5	125.9
21	Consumer credit	−14.2	−3.6	−9.2	41.7	15.6
22	Security credit	4.2	11.9	−8.7	7.1	7.2
23	Corporate equities	0.6	1.3	1.2	0.3	0.1
24	Mutual fund shares	0.8	−0.4	1.2	2.5	7.8
25	Customers' liab. on acceptances (1)	−0.2	−4.6	−2.5	−0.7	−2.3
26	Miscellaneous assets	5.5	9.1	11.3	4.7	23.3
27	Net increase in liabilities	359.0	385.2	331.2	468.9	288.4
28	Net interbank liabilities	4.2	20.4	36.0	74.6	22.9
29	Federal Reserve float	−3.6	0.9	−1.9	1.1	−0.9
30	Borrowing from Federal Reserve banks	2.0	−2.0	0.2	−0.1	−0.1
31	To domestic banking	−6.7	−2.6	−12.1	26.8	16.3
32	To foreign banks	12.6	24.0	49.7	46.8	7.6
33	Checkable deposits	−21.1	−34.4	2.8	−84.8	82.0
34	Federal government	−0.9	−14.6	36.4	−33.2	29.3
35	Rest of the world	4.4	−1.2	12.8	−9.2	2.8
36	Private domestic	−24.6	−18.6	−46.4	−42.4	49.9
37	Small time and savings deposits	143.9	186.3	72.4	210.4	238.5
38	Large time deposits	63.2	34.8	61.5	87.9	−25.6
39	Federal funds and security RPs (net)	63.4	66.8	128.7	12.8	−11.6
40	Acceptance liabilities	−0.3	−4.6	−2.5	−0.6	−2.3
41	Corporate bonds	10.7	10.5	3.7	10.6	8.3
42	Other loans and advances	19.1	46.9	40.6	26.8	25.3
43	Corporate equity issues	3.2	3.8	3.2	4.0	7.2
44	Taxes payable	1.4	1.7	1.9	2.1	2.4

continued

U.S.-Chartered Commercial Banks *(Continued)*

Billions of dollars; quarterly figures are seasonally adjusted annual rates

		1997	1998	1999	2000	2001
45	Miscellaneous liabilities	71.2	53.0	−17.1	125.0	−58.6
46	Investment by bank holding companies	40.7	55.3	2.9	53.6	59.9
47	Other	30.5	−2.4	−20.0	71.4	−118.5
48	Discrepancy	41.1	22.9	−45.5	109.6	29.8
	Memo:					
49	Credit market funds advanced (2)	274.9	312.0	317.6	399.8	187.4

(1) Included in other loans and advances.
(2) Total bank credit (line 5) less security credit (line 22) less corporate equities (line 23) less mutual fund shares (line 24) plus customers' liability on acceptances (line 25).

Foreign Banking Offices in the United States (1)

Billions of dollars; quarterly figures are seasonally adjusted annual rates

		1997	1998	1999	2000	2001
1	Gross saving	5.7	6.6	7.8	9.2	10.1
2	Fixed nonresidential investment	4.3	5.5	5.9	7.1	6.9
3	Net acquisition of financial assets	96.5	−4.8	−59.5	37.2	67.4
4	Reserves at Federal Reserve	1.8	−1.9	0.4	−1.0	0.2
5	Total bank credit	60.2	1.4	−28.9	67.3	−1.9
6	U.S. government securities	26.8	−5.5	11.8	0.0	−4.2
7	Treasury	14.4	−10.3	7.5	−0.6	13.0
8	Agency	12.5	4.8	4.3	0.6	−17.2
9	Municipal securities	0.0	0.0	0.0	0.0	0.0
10	Corporate and foreign bonds	3.1	5.8	−5.2	7.6	27.8
11	Total loans	30.3	1.1	−35.5	59.7	−25.6
12	Open market paper	−0.2	−0.1	0.4	−0.1	0.0
13	Bank loans n.e.c.	19.2	−1.9	−22.3	15.8	−20.1
14	Mortgages	−6.1	−5.5	−4.2	0.7	0.8
15	Security credit	17.5	8.6	−9.4	43.2	−6.4
16	Corporate equities	0.0	−0.0	0.0	0.0	0.0
17	Customers' liab. on acceptances (2)	−2.5	−4.7	−0.6	−0.0	−0.6
18	Miscellaneous assets	37.0	0.4	−30.4	−29.1	69.7
19	Net increase in liabilities	98.9	−2.0	−56.4	40.7	71.3
20	Net interbank liabilities	−30.4	−55.4	−43.9	−40.1	−0.8
21	To foreign banks	−17.6	−51.7	−51.2	−57.1	−20.9
22	To domestic banks	−12.7	−3.7	7.4	17.0	20.2
23	Checkable deposits	0.8	−0.2	0.4	−0.3	0.3
24	Small time and savings deposits	4.4	−3.6	−1.9	1.4	2.7
25	Large time deposits	44.7	36.5	56.7	5.6	52.3
26	Federal funds and security RPs (net)	25.6	19.7	−18.3	52.4	−12.6
27	Acceptance liabilities	−2.4	−4.8	−0.4	−0.0	−0.9

Foreign Banking Offices in the United States (1) *(Continued)*

Billions of dollars; quarterly figures are seasonally adjusted annual rates

		1997	1998	1999	2000	2001
28	Miscellaneous liabilities	56.2	5.7	−49.0	21.7	30.3
29	Foreign direct investment in U.S.	7.7	5.5	19.1	9.6	10.3
30	Due to affiliates	14.3	11.8	2.5	45.6	−30.8
31	Other	34.2	−11.5	−70.5	−33.5	50.7
32	Discrepancy	3.8	3.9	5.1	5,6	7.2
	Memo:					
33	Credit market funds advanced (3)	40.2	−11.9	−20.1	24.0	3.9

(1) Branches and agencies of foreign banks, Edge Act and Agreement corporations, New York investment companies (through 1996:Q2), and American Express Bank.
(2) Included in other loans and advances.
(3) Total bank credit (line 5) less security credit (line 15) less corporate equities (line 16) plus customers' liability on acceptances (line 17).

SOURCE: *Flow of Funds Accounts of the United States,* Board of Governors of the Federal Reserve System, Fourth Quarter, 2001.

8

Managing Interest Rate Risk: GAP and Earnings Sensitivity

Periodically, managers of financial institutions speculate on interest rate movements with the intent of increasing net interest margin. One procedure is to lengthen the maturity of assets by buying long-term option-free securities in anticipation of declining interest rates. If rates do fall, the bank can either sell the securities at a gain or benefit from locking in above-market yields. Of course, if rates rise, the bank can only sell the securities at a loss and may even end up funding the securities at a negative spread with liabilities that pay higher rates. Another procedure is to adjust deposit maturities in anticipation of future rate moves to try and lock in low funding costs. If managers expect rates to rise sufficiently, they will aggressively market long-term deposits such that the bank can lock in the funding for a long time at below-market rates.

Occasionally, these interest rate bets backfire. For example, late in 1987, First Bank System Inc. of Minneapolis reported an unrealized loss of $640 million on $8 billion in bonds that it owned. In January of 1987, the bond portfolio had an $81 million gain. Clearly, the sharp increase in interest rates during the year eroded the value of the bonds. This loss reflected aggressive risk-taking by the bank's senior management. During 1986, when rates fell, First Bank System realized almost $400 million in securities gains by selling bonds prior to maturity after their prices increased. These gains not only covered the bank's $385 million in loan losses but allowed the bank to report record profits. Anticipating a further decline in rates, the bank lengthened security maturities to an average 14 years, plus increased the overall size of the bond portfolio. At the margin, securities were financed with shorter-term liabilities.

As rates increased in 1987, the bank hedged its position so that future unanticipated rate increases would not drive the bond values lower. Unfortunately, the annual cost of hedging the bonds reached $35 million, or more than 50 percent of the bank's expected profits. Management subsequently decided to sell almost $5 billion of its bonds and reported a quarterly loss exceeding $400 million.

Why did First Bank System's management gamble on interest rates? The gamble eventually cost the president and CEO their jobs, as both resigned under pressure. The bank's stock had traded at $37 per *share early in 1987, but fell below $18 by the end of 1989, so long-term investors also lost. Should banks speculate on future interest rate movements? Should they consciously mismatch asset and liability maturities or durations? Should they hedge against the risk of loss when interest rates move adversely?*

———————————————■———————————————

This chapter examines the management of a bank's interest rate risk position in terms of GAP and earnings sensitivity analysis. In this context, interest rate risk refers to the volatility in net interest income attributable to changes in the level of interest rates and shifts in the composition and volume of bank assets and liabilities. A bank that takes substantial risk will see its net interest margin vary widely when rates increase or decrease. A bank that assumes little interest rate risk will observe little change in its performance due to rate changes. Chapter 9 extends this analysis by focusing on interest rate risk related to the volatility in a bank's market value of stockholders' equity and risk measures associated with the difference in durations of a bank's assets and liabilities.

The analysis initially introduces traditional measures of interest rate risk associated with static GAP models. These models focus on GAP as a static measure of risk and net interest income as the target measure of bank performance. It then modifies GAP analysis to focus on the sensitivity of bank earnings across different interest rate environments. This net interest income simulation, or "What if?" forecasting, provides information regarding how much net interest income changes when rates are alternatively assumed to rise and fall by various amounts. It takes into account embedded options in a bank's assets and liabilities and off-balance sheet activity, and provides a better understanding of potential changes in earnings. As such, it is labeled **earnings sensitivity analysis.** Throughout, we provide numerous examples that clarify how changes in interest rates and other factors affect potential earnings.

During the 1970s, banks viewed credit and liquidity risks as the major constraints on profitability. Subsequent events, however, focused attention on interest rate risk. In October 1979, the Federal Reserve announced that monetary policy would focus more on controlling monetary aggregates and less on stabilizing interest rates. Regulatory directives in the early 1980s largely eliminated restrictions against the interest rates paid on bank liabilities and charged on most assets. The effect was to increase interest rate volatility in general and make it more difficult for banks to manage net interest margin. Exhibit 8.1 documents the movement of the federal funds rate and 10-year Treasury rate from 1980 to 2001. Rate volatility for both of these instruments was quite high from 1980 to 1982, then largely stabilized at pre-1979 levels. Note the stability of and eventual decline in interest rates, particularly the 10-year Treasury rate, from 1984 through 1998 and again in 2001. This stability induced many bankers to increase their banks' speculative positions regarding anticipated interest rates. Subsequent rate increases in 1999–2000 led to losses.

With interest rate deregulation, banks are no longer guaranteed a profitable spread between asset yields and funding costs. Interest rate fluctuations alter bank earnings and the value of stockholders' claims unless management implements strategies to reduce their impact. Interest rate risk management is extremely important because no one can consistently forecast interest rates accurately. A bank's asset and liability management committee (ALCO), or alternatively its risk management committee, is responsible for measuring and monitoring interest rate risk. It also recommends pricing, investment, funding, and marketing strategies to achieve the desired trade-off between risk and expected return.

At the end of 1998, bank regulators were concerned that many banks had assumed too much interest rate risk. In the preceding years, many banks had sharply increased the maturities of their securities holdings and entered into off-balance sheet contracts that exposed

• EXHIBIT 8.1

INTEREST RATES, 1980–2001

Interest Rate (Percent)

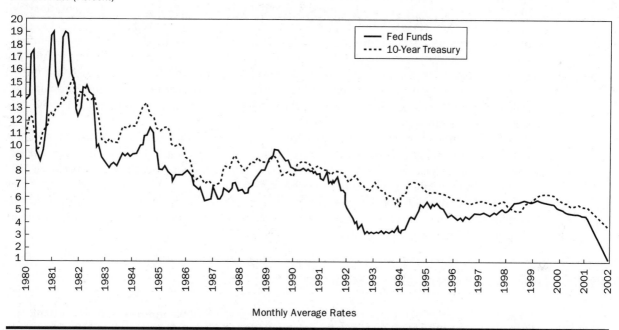

Monthly Average Rates

SOURCE: Data from the Federal Reserve Bank of ST. Louis.

them to losses in the event that interest rates increased. Similarly, they bought securities different from Treasuries including federal agency and mortgage-backed securities with little or no default risk, but with potentially long maturities. With the decline in interest rates evidenced in Exhibit 8.1, banks saw their net interest margins rise sharply. Bank profits reached record highs due primarily to increased net interest margins associated with larger loan portfolios, greater interest rate risk, increased noninterest income relative to noninterest expense, and reduced loan losses associated with improved asset quality. During 2001, many banks saw their interest income drop with declining rates as mortgage-backed securities pre-paid at high spreads and issuers called the bonds banks bought when rates were higher. The fundamental issue is whether bank managers understand the magnitude of interest rate risk that they assume and whether earnings will fall sharply when interest rates change adversely.

MEASURING INTEREST RATE RISK WITH GAP

Unexpected changes in interest rates can significantly alter a bank's profitability. One defini-tion of a bank's interest rate risk encompasses the volatility in net interest income associated with changing interest rates. Depending on the cash flow characteristics of a bank's assets and liabilities and the existence of embedded options, interest rate changes may raise or lower net interest income. Many banks and thrifts, for example, suffered serious cash flow problems when rates rose sharply from 1980 to 1982, which reduced net interest margins (NIMs). They were consequently short of funds even though they experienced few loan losses. Not surpris-ingly, the market values of the firms' equity fell to where many were economically insolvent.

Consider a traditional commercial or savings bank that makes 30-year, fixed-rate mortgage loans financed primarily with 3-month to 1-year deposits. The bank receives interest and principal payments on the mortgages monthly and pays monthly interest on deposits. The initial spread between the yields on the mortgages and cost of deposits should be large enough to cover the cost of doing business, cover the expected change in rates over the investment horizon, and provide for a reasonable profit. If all interest rates increase above expectations, however, interest expense on deposits will increase more than interest income on the mortgages because the mortgage rates are fixed while the deposit rates are variable over a shorter time. As such, the bank's net interest income will decline. If interest rates fall below expectations, the difference between interest income and interest expense will widen and net interest income will increase. Still, with falling rates, some mortgage borrowers will refinance and the bank will give up some interest income because it must reinvest the proceeds at lower rates.

Efforts at managing interest rate risk force a bank's ALCO to establish specific targets for net interest income, measure overall risk exposure, and formulate strategies to attain the targets. Specific targets and strategies presumably reflect management's view of actions that will lead to maximizing the value of the bank.

The following sections describe the traditional static GAP model and explain its shortcomings, then describe how earnings sensitivity analysis provides a meaningful extension. Important terminology is summarized in Exhibit 8.2.

TRADITIONAL STATIC GAP ANALYSIS

Traditional static GAP models attempt to measure how much interest rate risk a bank evidences at a fixed point in time by comparing the rate sensitivity of assets with the rate sensitivity of liabilities. Static GAP focuses on managing net interest income in the short run. The objective is typically to measure expected net interest income and then identify strategies to stabilize or improve it. Interest rate risk is measured by calculating GAPs over different time intervals based on aggregate balance sheet data at a fixed point in time—hence, the term static GAP. These GAP values are then examined to infer how much net interest income will change if rates change.

There are several basic steps to static GAP analysis.

1. Management develops an interest rate forecast.

2. Management selects a series of sequential time intervals for determining what amount of assets and liabilities are rate sensitive within each time interval.

3. Assets and liabilities are grouped into these time intervals, or "buckets," according to the time until the first repricing. The principal portion of the asset or liability that management expects to reprice is classified as rate sensitive. The effects of any off-balance sheet positions, such as those associated with interest rate swaps, futures, and so on, are also added to the balance sheet position according to whether the item effectively represents a rate-sensitive asset or rate-sensitive liability. A bank's static GAP then equals the dollar amount of rate-sensitive assets (RSAs) minus the dollar amount of rate-sensitive liabilities (RSLs) for each time interval.

4. Management forecasts net interest income given the interest rate environment and assumed repricing characteristics of the underlying instruments.

Note that GAP measures balance sheet values. Formally,

$$GAP = RSAs - RSLs$$

• EXHIBIT 8.2

IMPORTANT TERMINOLOGY

ALCO: Acronym for asset and liability management committee.

ALM: Acronym for asset and liability management.

Base rate: Any interest rate used as an index to price loans or deposits; quoted interest rates are typically set at some mark-up, such as 0.25% or 1%, over the base rate and thus change whenever the base rate changes.

Cost of funds: Interest expense divided by the dollar volume of interest-bearing liabilities.

Duration: A measure of the approximate price sensitivity of an asset or portfolio to a change in interest rates.

Earnings change ratio: A percentage measure that indicates how much of each type of a bank's assets or liabilities will reprice when some index rate changes. An earnings change ratio of one indicates that the underlying asset or liability changes in yield or cost one-to-one with changes in the index rate.

Earning ratio: The dollar volume of a bank's earning assets divided by the dollar volume of total assets.

Earnings sensitivity analysis: Conducting "what if" analysis by varying factors that affect interest income and expense to determine how changes in key factors affect a bank's net interest income and net interest margin. The output indicates how much net interest income will change under different interest rate scenarios in dollars and in percentage terms.

Effective GAP: The "true" measure of GAP that takes into account a specific interest rate forecast and when embedded options will either be exercised or will affect the actual repricing of an asset or liability.

Embedded option: A specific feature of a bank's asset, liability, or off-balance sheet contract that potentially changes the cash flows of the item when interest rates vary. Examples include early prepayment of principal on loans, issuers calling outstanding bonds, and depositors withdrawing funds prior to maturity.

Floating rate: Assets or liabilities that carry rates tied to the prime rate or other base rates. The instrument is repriced whenever the base rate changes.

GAP: The dollar volume of rate-sensitive assets minus the dollar volume of rate-sensitive liabilities.

GAP ratio: The dollar volume of rate-sensitive assets divided by the dollar volume of rate-sensitive liabilities.

Hedging: Taking a position or implementing a transaction to reduce overall risk associated with an existing position.

Net interest margin (NIM): Tax-equivalent net interest income divided by earning assets.

Net overhead: Noninterest income minus noninterest expense.

Nonrate GAP: Noninterest-bearing liabilities plus equity minus nonearning assets as a ratio of earning assets.

Rate-sensitive assets (RSAs): The dollar value of assets that either mature or can be repriced within a selected time period, such as 90 days.

Rate-sensitive liabilities (RSLs): The dollar value of liabilities that either mature or can be repriced within a selected time period, such as 90 days.

Simulation: An analysis of possible outcomes for net interest margin resulting from selecting hypothetical values for key variables that influence the repricing of assets, liabilities, and off-balance sheet items, and conducting forecasts to determine the effects of changes in these variables on a bank's net interest income.

Speculation: Taking a position or implementing a transaction that increases risk in hopes of earning above average returns.

Spread: The interest yield on earning assets minus the interest cost of interest-bearing funds.

Variable rate: Assets or liabilities that are automatically repriced at regular intervals.

---

where rate-sensitive assets and liabilities are those identified within each time bucket. As such, there is a periodic GAP and a cumulative GAP for each time bucket. The periodic GAP compares RSAs with RSLs across a single time bucket. The cumulative GAP compares rate-sensitive assets with rate-sensitive liabilities over all time buckets from the present through the last day in each successive time bucket. For example, the cumulative GAP through 90 days (0–90 days) equals the sum of the periodic GAPs for the two time buckets, 0–30 days and 31–90 days.

This information is used to identify the bank's interest rate risk and to develop strategies to manage this risk. Management can alter the size of the GAP to either hedge net interest income against changing interest rates or speculatively try to increase net interest income. Hedging involves reducing the volatility of net interest income either by directly adjusting the dollar amounts of rate-sensitive assets and liabilities, or by taking an off-balance sheet position such as with forwards, futures, option contracts, and interest rate swaps.[1] Changing the size of GAP to take advantage of perceived rate changes is speculative because it assumes that management can forecast interest rates better than the market.

WHAT DETERMINES RATE SENSITIVITY?

The first three steps in GAP analysis require the classification of the principal portions of specific assets and liabilities that are rate sensitive within specific time intervals. Other balance sheet items either carry fixed rates or do not earn or pay interest. Interest payments are not included directly because GAP is a balance sheet (plus off-balance sheet) measure of risk. Management typically selects a variety of time buckets that provide useful information, as outlined later. The initial issue is to determine what features make an asset or liability rate sensitive.

Consider a 0–90 day time interval. The key issue is to identify what assets and liabilities listed on a bank's balance sheet will be repriced within 90 days given the specific interest rate forecast. Note that the GAP definition requires that the person determining rate sensitivity forecast when something will be repriced. Instead, some uses of GAP analysis focus on when an asset or liability can contractually be repriced, which may not be relevant. The purpose is to ensure that the comparison of RSAs with RSLs is meaningful. Obviously, any asset or liability that matures will be repriced because the bank must reinvest the proceeds from the asset and/or must reset the deposit rate or replace the maturing liability at prevailing rates.[2] Thus, any investment security, loan, deposit, or longer-term liability that matures within 90 days—federal funds purchased, 1-month T-bills, a time deposit that matures in one month, and a working capital loan that matures in two months—is rate sensitive.

More generally, any principal payment on a loan is rate sensitive if management expects to receive it within the time interval. This includes final principal payments as well as interim principal payments, such as the principal component of the regular monthly payment on a mortgage or car loan. In addition, some assets and deposit liabilities earn or pay rates that vary contractually with some index. These instruments are repriced whenever the index changes. In this example, if management knows that the index will contractually change within 90 days, the underlying asset or liability is rate sensitive. Such is the case with a variable rate commercial loan that reprices every three months based on changes in the 3-month CD rate.

In contrast, some loans and deposits carry rates tied to indexes where the bank has no control or definite knowledge of when the index will change. For example, a commercial loan priced at 1 percent over some other bank's prime rate carries a floating rate, but may or may not be repriced with any known frequency. The loan is rate sensitive in the sense that its yield can change at any time, even daily, but its effective rate sensitivity depends on how frequently the index actually changes. For the GAP figures to be most meaningful, management must forecast when the index will change and examine the GAP and effect on net interest income accordingly. This is why the first step, having an interest rate forecast, is important.

Many asset and liability management models used by banks classify prime-based loans and other floating rate instruments as immediately repriceable. Although this is true, assuming that the indexes and base rates can contractually change at any time, the resulting GAP figure is not very meaningful because such rates do not change simultaneously or in many

---

[1]The use of interest rate swaps, caps, floors, collars, forwards, futures, and options is explained and demonstrated in Chapters 10–11.

[2]In this context, an instrument will still be repriced if rates do not change because new contract terms will be determined. As discussed later, this is important because not all rates change by the same amount at the same time.

cases all that frequently. For example, although Wall Street prime changed more than 50 times in 1980, there are years when it never changed. How a bank classifies these base rate loans and other accounts, such as NOWs and MMDAs, can dramatically alter the GAP measures reported and the effective (or actual) GAP measures if the underlying indexes do not change as assumed.

GAP analysis is essentially a balance sheet concept. The GAP measure from Step 3 indicates the principal amounts from a bank's balance sheet that management expects to reprice within a specified time interval. Expected interest income and interest expense components of cash flows are ignored in the GAP measure. In general, an asset or liability is normally classified as rate sensitive within a time interval if:

1. It matures.
2. It represents an interim, or partial, principal payment.
3. The interest rate applied to outstanding principal changes contractually during the interval.
4. The outstanding principal can be repriced when some base rate or index changes and management expects the base rate/index to change during the interval.

FACTORS AFFECTING NET INTEREST INCOME

Although GAP presumably provides information about a bank's interest rate risk exposure, many factors affect net interest income. In addition to changes in the *level* of interest rates, these include changes in the *composition* of assets and liabilities, changes in the *volume* of assets and liabilities outstanding, and changes in the *relationship* between the yields on earning assets and rates paid on interest-bearing liabilities. Some factors are at least partially controllable, while others are not. Asset and liability management examines the impact of all factors on net interest income. The following analysis documents circumstances when net interest income increases and decreases by comparing it at a hypothetical bank before and after each influence.

Consider a bank with the general balance sheet accounts listed in Exhibit 8.3. For ease of example, the RSAs and RSLs represent balance sheet amounts that are expected to be repriced within a 1-year time interval when interest rates are assumed to remain constant at current levels. Thus, the RSAs and RSLs either mature within one year, represent partial principal payments made during the next year, are variable-rate contracts that are automatically repriced within one year, or carry floating-rate yields that management forecasts will change during the year. The RSAs include short-term securities, federal funds sold, expected principal payments on loans, and the outstanding principal on all repriced variable-rate and floating rate loans. The RSLs include small time deposits and jumbo CDs maturing within one year, federal funds purchased, some interest-bearing transactions accounts, and money market deposit accounts. The crucial feature is that cash flows associated with rate-sensitive contracts vary with changes in interest rates. Fixed-rate assets and liabilities carry rates that are constant throughout the one-year time interval. Cash flows do not change unless there is a default, early withdrawal, or prepayment that is not forecasted accurately. Nonearning assets generate no explicit income, and nonpaying liabilities pay no interest. Both of these are classified as fixed-rate (at zero) in this static analysis.

Expected average earning asset yield rates and interest costs for the year appear beside each account. If these balance sheet and interest rate figures reflect average performance during the year, the bank's tax-equivalent net interest income is expected to equal $41.30 per $850 in earning assets for a net interest margin (NIM) of 4.86 percent. These figures represent

■ **EXHIBIT 8.3**

EXPECTED BALANCE SHEET COMPOSITION AND AVERAGE
INTEREST RATES FOR A HYPOTHETICAL BANK

	Assets	Average Yield Rates	Liabilities	Interest Costs
Rate-sensitive	$ 500	8%	$ 600	4%
Fixed-rate	350	11	220	6
Nonearning/Nonpaying	150		100	
Total			$ 920	
			Equity	
			$ 80	
Total	$1,000		$1,000	

Net interest income = 0.08($500) + 0.11($350) − 0.04($600) − 0.06($220)

= $78.50 − $37.20

= $41.30

Net interest margin = $41.30/$850 = 4.86%

GAP = RSAs − RSLs = $500 − $600 = −$100

NOTE: RSAs are rate-sensitive assets; RSLs are rate-sensitive liabilities. The assumed time frame for classifying RSAs and RSLs is 1 year. Yield rates are computed on a tax-equivalent basis. All rates are expected to remain constant at current levels.

benchmark estimates. During the year, the level of interest rates normally changes from that initially projected, as do the composition and volume of assets and liabilities. This bank's one-year cumulative GAP equals −$100. The sign and magnitude of GAP presumably provide information regarding interest rate risk.

CHANGES IN THE LEVEL OF INTEREST RATES

Fluctuating interest rates can increase, decrease, or not affect a bank's net interest income, depending on the portfolio mix, rate sensitivity, and GAP value. The GAP measure compares the dollar value of a bank's assets that reprice within an interval to the dollar value of liabilities that reprice within the same time frame. The sign of a bank's GAP further indicates whether interest income or interest expense will likely change more when interest rates change. A negative GAP, such as that shown in Exhibit 8.3, indicates that the bank has more RSLs than RSAs. When interest rates rise during the time interval, the bank pays higher rates on all repriceable liabilities and earns higher yields on all repriceable assets. If all rates rise by equal amounts at the same time, both interest income and interest expense rise, but interest expense rises more because more liabilities are repriced. Net interest income thus declines, as does the bank's net interest margin. When interest rates fall during the interval, more liabilities than assets are repriced at the lower rates such that interest expense falls more than interest income falls. In this case, both net interest income and net interest margin increase. Such a bank is said to be *liability sensitive.*

A positive GAP indicates that a bank has more RSAs than RSLs across some time interval. When rates rise, interest income increases more than interest expense because more assets are repriced such that net interest income similarly increases. Rate decreases have the opposite effect. Because interest income falls more than interest expense, net interest income falls. Such a bank is said to be *asset sensitive.* If the bank has a zero GAP, RSAs equal RSLs and equal interest rate changes do not alter net interest income because changes in interest income equal changes in interest expense. These relationships are summarized as follows:

GAP Summary

GAP	Change in Interest Rates	Change in Interest Income		Change in Interest Expense	Change in Net Interest Income
Positive	Increase	Increase	>	Increase	Increase
Positive	Decrease	Decrease	>	Decrease	Decrease
Negative	Increase	Increase	<	Increase	Decrease
Negative	Decrease	Decrease	<	Decrease	Increase
Zero	Increase	Increase	=	Increase	None
Zero	Decrease	Decrease	=	Decrease	None

Section A of Exhibit 8.4 shows the relationship between an increase in the level of rates and a negative GAP for the hypothetical bank. All rates are assumed to increase by an average of 1 percent during the year, with the bank's portfolio composition and size unchanged.[3] This is characterized as assuming a parallel shift in the yield curve by +1 percent. With these assumptions, the only changes are the rates on rate-sensitive assets and liabilities. Interest income increases by $5 to $83.50, but interest expense increases by $6 to $43.20, such that net interest income declines by $1 relative to that initially projected in Exhibit 8.3. NIM subsequently falls by 12 basis points to 4.74 percent.

Suppose instead that rates decrease by 1 percent relative to the base case. The average yield earned on rate-sensitive assets declines to 7 percent while the interest cost of rate-sensitive liabilities declines to 3 percent. By assumption, fixed rates do not change. Interest income falls by $5 while interest expense falls by $6 such that net interest income increases by $1. This occurs because the bank now pays lower rates on a greater amount of liabilities ($600) than assets ($500) that are now earning lower yields. NIM subsequently widens.

The change in net interest income arises because the amount of rate-sensitive assets differs from the amount of rate-sensitive liabilities and all rates are assumed to change by the same amount in the same direction. The larger the GAP difference, the greater the impact. If RSAs equaled RSLs, the change in interest income would be matched by the change in interest expense regardless of whether rates rise or fall, so that net interest income would be unchanged. In this framework, whether net interest income rises or falls depends on whether the GAP is positive or negative and how the level of interest rates changes. The following relationship summarizes this framework.

$$\Delta NII_{exp} = GAP \times \Delta i_{exp} \qquad (8.1)$$

where

ΔNII_{exp} = the expected change in net interest income over a period of time from some base amount,

GAP = cumulative GAP over the interval through the end of the period of time, and

Δi_{exp} = the expected permanent change in the level of interest rates.

Again, this applies only in the case of a parallel shift in the yield curve, which rarely occurs. Specifically, if the 1-year GAP is any positive value, net interest income increases when rates are assumed to rise and decreases when rates fall. Suppose, for example, that the above bank's initial position consists of $650 in rate-sensitive assets and $200 in fixed-rate

---

[3]Earnings sensitivity analysis recognizes that the amount of rate-sensitive assets and rate-sensitive liabilities changes when interest rates change, and that various rates change by different amounts at different times. This discussion ignores this possibility, which is why static GAP is not very meaningful as a risk measure.

■ EXHIBIT 8.4

A. 1% Increase in Level of All Short-Term Rates

	Assets	Yield Rates	Liabilities	Interest Costs
Rate-sensitive	$ 500	9%	$ 600	5%
Fixed-rate	350	11	220	6
Nonearning/Nonpaying	150		100	
			Equity	
			80	
Total	$1,000		$1,000	

Net interest income = 0.09($500) + 0.11($350) − 0.05($600) − 0.06($220)
$$= \$83.50 - \$43.20$$
$$= \$40.30$$

Net interest margin = $40.30/$850 = 4.74%
GAP = $500 − $600 = −$100

B. 1% Decrease in Spread between Asset Yields and Interest Costs

	Assets	Yield Rates	Liabilities	Interest Costs
Rate-sensitive	$ 500	8.5%	$ 600	5.5%
Fixed-rate	350	11	220	6
Nonearning/Nonpaying	150		100	
			Equity	
			80	
Total	$1,000		$1,000	

Net interest income = 0.085($500) + 0.11($350) − 0.055($600) − 0.06($220)
$$= \$81.00 - \$46.20$$
$$= \$34.80$$

Net interest margin = $34.80/$850 = 4.09%
GAP = $500 − $600 = −$100

NOTE: RSAs are rate-sensitive assets; RSLs are rate-sensitive liabilities.

assets with all other factors the same. The 1-year GAP equals $50. At the rates listed, interest income is expected to equal $74 while interest expense is still $37.20, producing $36.80 in net interest income. If rates rise by 1 percent, interest income rises by $6.50 while interest expense rises by just $6. With this smaller positive GAP, net interest income now increases by $0.50. It declines when rates fall.[4]

In this context, the sign and size of GAP provide information regarding a bank's interest rate risk position. The sign indicates the bank's interest rate bet. If GAP is positive, the bank wins (net interest income should rise) when rates rise and loses when rates fall. If GAP is negative, the bank wins when rates fall and loses when rates rise. The size of GAP indicates how much risk a bank assumes. Specifically, the farther GAP is from zero (lowest risk), the greater the potential variation in net interest income and thus, the greater the assumed risk.

---

[4]The reader should verify that interest income changes by the same amount as interest expense in these examples when the GAP equals zero.

C. Proportionate Doubling in Size

	Assets	Yield Rates	Liabilities	Interest Costs
Rate-sensitive	$1,000	8%	$1,200	4%
Fixed-rate	700	11	440	6
Nonearning/Nonpaying	300		200	
			Equity	
			160	
Total	$2,000		$2,000	

Net interest income = 0.08($1,000) + 0.11($700) − 0.04($1,200) − 0.06($440)

= $82.60

Net interest margin = $82.60/$1,700 = 4.86%

GAP = $1,000 − $1,200 = −$200

D. Increase in RSAs and Decrease in RSLs

	Assets	Yield Rates	Liabilities	Interest Costs
Rate-sensitive	$ 540	8%	$ 560	4%
Fixed-rate	310	11	260	6
Nonearning/Nonpaying	150		100	
			Equity	
			80	
Total	$1,000		$1,000	

Net interest income = 0.08($540) + 0.11($310) − 0.04($560) − 0.06($260)

= $77.30 − $38.00

= $39.30

Net interest margin = $39.30/$850 = 4.62%

GAP = $540 − $560 = −$20

CHANGES IN THE RELATIONSHIP BETWEEN SHORT-TERM ASSET YIELDS AND LIABILITY COSTS

Net interest income may similarly differ from that expected if the spread between earning asset yields and the interest cost of interest-bearing liabilities changes. Asset yields may vary relative to interest costs because of an unexpected shift in the yield curve (unequal changes in the level of different maturity interest rates are labeled a nonparallel shift in the yield curve), an increase or decrease in risk premiums, and nonsynchronous changes in indexes on floating-rate assets or liabilities. If, for instance, liabilities are short-term and assets are long-term, the spread will narrow when the yield curve inverts and will widen when the yield curve increases in slope. Similarly, asset yields may be tied to base rates that change monthly while liability costs change weekly with money market rates. Section B of Exhibit 8.4 examines the impact of a 1 percent decrease in the spread (from 4 percent to 3 percent) on rate-sensitive assets and liabilities for the year. With the portfolio composition unchanged, net interest income declines to $34.80. Of course, net interest income increases whenever the spread increases. Changes in net interest income associated with changes in the difference between different interest rates, say prime minus 3-month LIBOR are a reflection of *basis risk*.

CHANGES IN VOLUME

Net interest income varies directly with changes in the volume of earning assets and interest-bearing liabilities, regardless of the level of interest rates. Consider Section C in Exhibit 8.4 where the bank doubles in size. The portfolio composition and interest rates are unchanged. Net interest income doubles because the bank earns the same interest spread on twice the volume of earning assets such that NIM is unchanged. GAP now doubles to −$200 but is the same fraction of total assets. The net effect is that growth, by itself, leads to an increase in the dollar amount of earnings but does not alter profitability measures or the relative size of GAP to assets. A bank that alternatively contracts in size experiences a decrease in net interest income with no change in profitability measures or the relative size of GAP to assets.

CHANGES IN PORTFOLIO COMPOSITION

Any variation in portfolio mix potentially alters net interest income. A manager who wants to reduce risk for the sample bank in Exhibit 8.4 might attempt to increase asset rate sensitivity by pricing more loans on a floating-rate basis or shortening maturities of investment securities. Alternatively, the manager might decrease liability rate sensitivity by substituting longer-term CDs for overnight federal funds purchased. These transactions change both the GAP and the bank's interest rate risk position. They also change net interest income from that initially expected. Section D of Exhibit 8.4 summarizes the impact of a $40 shift of fixed-rate assets to RSAs and a corresponding $40 shift from RSLs to fixed-rate liabilities. In this case, the level of rates is unchanged and net interest income falls by $2 from the initial estimate of $41.30. This decline is caused by a decline in the average yield on earning assets which produces a $1.20 drop in interest income, and an increase in the average interest cost of liabilities that produces a $0.80 increase in interest expense. In addition to changing expected net interest income, this change in composition alters the GAP to −$20 and thus reduces the bank's interest rate risk profile.

There is no fixed relationship between changes in portfolio mix and net interest income. The impact varies with the relationships between interest rates on rate-sensitive and fixed-rate instruments and with the magnitude of funds shifts. If, for example, the change in mix was reversed in the above case, net interest income would increase. Net interest income would drop if the $40 shift in liabilities was the only change in portfolio composition. In many cases, banks change mix as part of initiatives to offset anticipated adverse changes in net interest margin. Generally, any shift to loans from securities will increase net interest income near-term because loan yields exceed most security yields on a pretax and prerisk (default loss) basis. Similarly, any shift from core deposits to noncore liabilities reduces net interest income because noncore liabilities generally carry higher interest rates.

Changes in the magnitudes of nonearning assets and nonpaying liabilities also influence net interest income and NIM. If a bank can reduce its nonearning assets, net interest income increases automatically, with the magnitude determined by how the funds are invested. For example, net interest income rises by $4 [.08($50) − 0] with a $50 shift to RSAs. A $50 shift to fixed-rate assets increases net interest income by $5.50 [.11($50) − 0]. In both cases, NIM rises because the bank's funding costs are unchanged with higher interest income.

RATE, VOLUME, AND MIX ANALYSIS

Many banks publish a summary in their annual report of how net interest income has changed over time. They separate changes attributable to shifts in asset and liability composition and volume from changes associated with movements in interest rates. Exhibit 8.5 represents such a report for Synovus, headquartered in Columbus, Ga., for 2001 versus 2000, and 2000 versus

RATE/VOLUME ANALYSIS FOR SYNOVUS BANK

	2001 Compared to 2000			2000 Compared to 1999		
	Change Due to *			Change Due to *		
	Volume	Yield/ Rate	Net Change	Volume	Yield/ Rate	Net Change
Interest earned on:						
Taxable loans, net	$149,423	(117,147)	32,276	161,222	36,390	197,612
Tax-exempt loans, net†	1,373	(586)	787	1,108	(450)	658
Taxable investment securities	(5,313)	(916)	(6,229)	4,507	2,570	7,077
Tax-exempt investment securities†	2,548	74	2,622	2,026	(206)	1,820
Interest earning deposits with banks	223	(176)	47	28	48	76
Federal funds sold and securities purchased						
under resale agreements	406	(1,745)	(1,339)	1,447	1,410	2,857
Mortgage loans held for sale	7,801	(1,680)	6,121	(113)	549	436
Total interest income	156,461	(122,176)	34,285	170,225	40,311	210,536
Interest paid on:						
Interest bearing demand deposits	6,074	(12,517)	(6,443)	1,537	5,433	6,970
Money market accounts	21,380	(36,244)	(14,864)	4,654	13,888	18,542
Savings deposits	(369)	(3,307)	(3,676)	(660)	(67)	(727)
Time deposits	32,015	(22,545)	9,470	38,824	32,812	71,636
Federal funds purchased and securities						
sold under repurchase agreements	(6,165)	(29,744)	(35,909)	23,148	15,870	39,018
Other borrowed funds	21,318	(4,272)	17,046	21,960	3,361	25,321
Total interest expense	74,253	(108,629)	(34,376)	89,463	71,297	160,760
Net interest income	$82,208	(13,547)	68,661	$80,762	(30,986)	49,776

NOTE: Figures are in thousands of dollars.

*The change in interest due to both rate and volume has been allocated to the rate component.

†Reflects taxable-equivalent adjustments using the statutory federal income tax rate of 35 percent in adjusting interest on tax-exempt loans and investment securities to a taxable-equivalent basis.

SOURCE: Synovus 2001 Annual Report.

1999. Consider the data for 2001 compared to 2000. The figures refer to the change in either interest income, interest expense, or net interest income attributable to changes in the volume of earning assets and interest-bearing liabilities—under the volume heading—or that attributable to changes in earning asset yields or rates paid on liabilities—under the yield/rate heading. The net change column represents the sum of these two figures.

The purpose is to assess what factors influence shifts in net interest income over time. For Synovus in 2001, volume effects swamped interest rate effects for interest income, with rate effects greater than volume for interest expense. From 2000 to 2001, net interest income increased by $68,661,000, of which $82,208,000 was attributed to the growth in earning assets versus interest-bearing liabilities with all interest rates held constant at 2000 levels. With volumes of the balance sheet items held constant, changes in earning asset yields and liability costs (rates) actually reduced net interest income by $13,547,000. This resulted from interest rates falling in 2001 with interest income falling more than interest expense due to rate changes alone. In 2000 versus 1999, rising rates increased interest expense more than interest income, but the larger growth in volume of earning assets versus interest-bearing liabilities offset the rate effect so that net interest income rose by almost $50 million.

This view of GAP and net interest income is simplistic. Obviously, asset yields and interest costs do not change coincidentally or by equal amounts. Even within distinct time intervals, assets and liabilities are repriced at varied intervals, producing cash flows that may differ substantially from those implied by the GAP. For example, if all RSAs from Exhibit 8.3 matured in one month while all RSLs matured in six months, projected cash flows would reflect interest rate and portfolio changes occurring five months apart such that the forecast change in net interest income could be substantially wrong.

For more meaningful comparisons, managers should calculate the GAP over relatively short periods and allow for a wide range of interest rates and repricings. The next section introduces a rate-sensitivity report, a framework that is commonly used to evaluate a bank's interest rate risk position. It essentially calculates GAPs across different time buckets. Data for Security Bank, a $100 million organization, are used to demonstrate the framework.

RATE-SENSITIVITY REPORTS

Many managers monitor their bank's risk position and potential changes in net interest income using a framework like that in Exhibit 8.6. This report classifies Security Bank's assets and liabilities as rate sensitive in selected time buckets through one year. Underlying each report should be an assumed interest rate environment. The last column lists the totals for all balance sheet items as of year-end. Each earlier column of data reflects the dollar volume of repriceable items within a distinct but sequential time period. For example, of the $9.5 million in Treasury and agency securities owned, $700,000 will be repriced in 8 to 30 days, $3.6 million is repriceable in 31 to 90 days, and so forth. All floating-rate commercial loans tied to a base rate are designated as rate sensitive from 8 to 30 days out. This classification reflects Security Bank's experience in changing base rates monthly on average during the past year. The column labeled Non Rate-Sensitive indicates amounts that do not earn or pay interest.

Figures for rate-sensitive liabilities similarly indicate when the items are expected to be repriced. Thus, NOW accounts will presumably be repriced within 91 to 180 days while a portion of money market deposit accounts will be repriced in 8 to 30 days and the bulk in 31 to 90 days. Note that savings accounts are assumed not to reprice for at least one year even though the rates can be changed more frequently. This classification differentiates between when an asset or liability can be repriced and when management believes it will be repriced. Prime-based loans can reprice daily if prime changes daily. It typically changes much less frequently. Banks can change MMDA rates daily, but unless they actually do, these deposits will only be as rate sensitive as their actual repricing schedule. A comparison of RSAs and RSLs that can change immediately would indicate differences in **contractual** repricing, but is likely not meaningful unless rates are highly volatile and these items are actually repriced as frequently as contracts allow.

Two types of GAP measures are reported at the bottom of the report. The **periodic GAP** compares RSAs with RSLs across each of the different time buckets. RSAs exceed RSLs in each interval through 30 days and for 181 days through one year, while RSLs exceed RSAs in the 31 to 90 day and 91 to 180 day intervals. The **cumulative GAP,** in contrast, measures the sum of the periodic GAPs through the longest time frame considered. Thus, the cumulative GAP at 31 to 90 days of −$15 million equals the sum of the periodic GAPs for 1 to 7 days ($1.3 million), 8 to 30 days ($4 million), and 31 to 90 days (−$20.3 million).

Each periodic GAP figure simply indicates whether more assets or liabilities can be repriced within a specific time interval. Because it ignores whether assets and liabilities in other periods can be repriced, it is not all that meaningful. Cumulative GAP figures are the most important because they directly measure a bank's net interest sensitivity through the last day of the time bucket by comparing how many assets and liabilities reprice through that last day. Thus, the cumulative GAP of −$15 million indicates that Security Bank can reprice

RATE SENSITIVITY ANALYSIS FOR SECURITY BANK, DECEMBER 31, 2001

	1–7 Days	8–30 Days	31–90 Days	91–180 Days	181–365 Days	Over 1 Year	Non Rate-Sensitive	Total
Time Frame for Rate Sensitivity								
Assets								
U.S. Treasury and agency securities		$ 0.7	$ 3.6	$ 1.2	$ 0.3	$ 3.7		$ 9.5
Money market investments			1.2	1.8				3.0
Municipal securities			0.7	1.0	2.2	7.6		11.5
Federal funds sold and repurchase agreements	$ 5.0							5.0
Commercial loans*	1.0	13.8	2.9	4.7	4.6	15.5		42.5
Installment loans	0.3	0.5	1.6	1.3	1.9	8.2		13.8
Earning assets								$ 85.3
Cash and due from banks							$ 9.0	9.0
Other assets							5.7	5.7
Nonearning assets								$ 14.7
Total assets	$ 6.3	$15.0	$10.0	$10.0	$ 9.0	$35.0	$14.7	$100.0
Liabilities and Equity								
Money market deposit accounts		$ 5.0	$12.3					$ 17.3
Time deposits < $100,000	$ 0.9	2.0	5.1	$ 6.9	$ 1.8	$ 2.9		19.6
CDs ≥ $100,000	4.1	4.0	12.9	7.9	1.2			30.1
Federal funds purchased and repurchase agreements								
NOW accounts				9.6				9.6
Savings accounts						1.9		1.9
Market-rate liabilities								$ 78.5
Demand deposits							$13.5	13.5
Other liabilities							1.0	1.0
Equity							7.0	7.0
Nonpaying liabilities and equity							21.5	$ 21.5
Total liabilities and equity	$ 5.0	$11.0	$30.3	$24.4	$3.0	$ 4.8	$21.5	$100.0
Periodic GAP	$ 1.3	$ 4.0	−$20.3	−$14.4	$6.0	$30.2		
Cumulative GAP	$ 1.3	$ 5.3	−$15.0	−$29.4	−$23.4	$ 6.8		

NOTE: Figures are in millions of dollars.

*Floating-rate loans total $10 million and are classified as repriceable in 8 to 30 days. There is no guarantee that base rates will change in this time period.

$15 million more of rate-sensitive liabilities than rate-sensitive assets during the next 90 days. The 1-year cumulative GAP indicates that $23.4 million more in liabilities can be repriced over this longer period. It is important to note that GAP figures for the interval over one year provide no new information about a bank's interest rate risk position. The periodic GAP of $30.2 simply reflects the fact that the bank has $35 million in earning assets that reprice beyond one year, while it pays interest on $4.8 million in similar long-term liabilities. The subsequent $6.8 million cumulative GAP simply measures the difference between $85.3 million in earning assets and $78.5 million in interest-bearing liabilities.

Note that the cumulative GAPs are positive for the first two periods with the remainder negative through one year. According to the previous discussion, Security Bank has positioned itself to gain if rates fall over the next year. Specifically, if rates decrease uniformly during the year, the bank's net interest income would increase unless offset by changes in portfolio mix or bank size because interest income should fall less than interest expense. If rates increase, net interest income should decline. Furthermore, the size of the GAP indicates that the bank's performance may vary substantially as the cumulative GAP through one year is almost 25 percent of total assets. Many community banks have policy statements that presumably limit interest rate risk by specifying that selected GAPs, as a fraction of earning assets, cannot fall outside of plus or minus 15 percent.

The rate sensitivity report provides a view of a bank's interest rate risk profile at a single point in time. It reflects a point estimate of risk implied by the basic concept of a static GAP. Most banks employ earnings sensitivity analysis to address weaknesses in the static GAP concept. They also evaluate interest rate risk using duration-based measures of relative asset and liability price sensitivity.

STRENGTHS AND WEAKNESSES: STATIC GAP ANALYSIS

The principal attraction of static GAP analysis is that it is easy to understand. Periodic GAPs indicate the relevant amount and timing of interest rate risk over distinct maturities and clearly suggest magnitudes of portfolio changes to alter risk. They indicate the specific balance sheet items that are responsible for the risk. GAP measures can also be easily calculated once the cash flow characteristics of each instrument are identified.

Unfortunately, the static GAP procedure also contains numerous weaknesses. First, there are serious *ex post* measurement errors. Consider, for example, loans whose rates are tied to base rates or indexes. The frequency of changes in base rates or indexes cannot be accurately forecast because management does not know when market interest rates will change. In 1980, the prime rate listed in the *Wall Street Journal*, a popular base rate for commercial loans, changed 52 times. In 1983, it changed only three times and, in 2000, it changed twice. Prime-based loans were considerably more rate sensitive in 1980, and in 2001 when it changed 11 times. GAP figures do not directly reflect this historical frequency of base rate changes. When there is uncertainty over the frequency of base rate changes because the bank cannot control rate changes, GAP measures reflect any errors in allocating loans differently than actual rate changes would require. To overcome this problem, a bank should evaluate the statistical rate sensitivity of all base rates to selected market indexes. To avoid mismeasuring risk, funds should be allocated to time buckets according to their effective (expected) rate sensitivity, which is often linked to the historical frequency of rate changes. With GAP analysis, rate sensitivity for these loans is not known.

Second, GAP analysis ignores the time value of money. The construction of maturity buckets does not differentiate between cash flows that arise at the beginning of the period versus those at the end. If a bank buys a 1-month T-bill financed by overnight borrowing in the federal funds market, the 1-month GAP is zero. This suggests no interest rate risk when, in fact, this transaction exposes the bank to losses when the federal funds rate rises. Whether a bank gains with rising or falling interest rates depends on the actual timing of repricings within each interval. Thus, a bank with a zero GAP will still see net interest income change when rates change. Similarly, GAP ignores interest flows. One attraction of duration-based measures of interest rate risk is that they incorporate the present value of all cash flows.

Third, the procedure essentially ignores the cumulative impact of interest rate changes on a bank's risk position. GAP measures should be calculated over the entire range of repricings, yet they often focus only on near-term changes in net interest income. As such, many banks evaluate GAP measures and variation in net interest income only through the upcoming year. Interest rate changes also affect the value of fixed-rate assets and liabilities and total risk beyond one year. These changes are ignored.

Fourth, liabilities that pay no interest are often ignored in rate-sensitivity comparisons because many banks allocate demand deposits as non-rate-sensitive liabilities. As such, GAP analysis does not recognize any rate risk associated with demand deposit flows, even though a bank typically loses deposits when interest rates rise. This occurs because the opportunity cost of demand deposits increases for the owners and the benefits of better cash management rise. Many compensating balance agreements, in turn, allow the owners of demand deposits to reduce the dollar amount of compensating balances when rates rise because the bank can earn a higher yield from investing these funds. To be useful, GAP analysis must allocate the rate-sensitive portion of demand deposits to the appropriate time buckets depending on their actual rate sensitivity. When rates are expected to increase, more demand deposits will be rate sensitive. It is extremely difficult, however, to know the exact rate sensitivity of these deposits.

Finally, static GAP does not capture risk associated with options embedded in the loans, securities, and deposits that banks deal with. Examples include the prepayment option that mortgage borrowers have and often exercise when interest rates fall, and the early withdrawal option that depositors have and often exercise when interest rates rise. These options have different values and a different probability of being exercised when interest rates are at different levels and rate volatility changes. The impact of these options is to alter the effective size of GAP over different time intervals when interest rates are rising versus falling and when rates are at high levels versus low levels. Earnings sensitivity analysis addresses these concerns.

LINK BETWEEN GAP AND NET INTEREST MARGIN

Some ALM programs focus on the GAP or GAP ratio when evaluating interest rate risk. When the GAP is positive, the GAP ratio is greater than one. A negative GAP, in turn, is consistent with a GAP ratio less than one.

$$\text{GAP Ratio} = \text{RSAs}/\text{RSLs}$$

Neither the GAP nor GAP ratio provide direct information on the potential variability in earnings when rates change. The GAP ratio is further deficient because it ignores size. Consider two banks that have $500 million in total assets. The first bank has $3 million in RSAs and $2 million in RSLs so that its GAP equals $1 million and its GAP ratio equals 1.5. The second bank has $300 million in RSAs and $200 million in RSLs. Its GAP equals $100 million, yet it reports the same 1.5 GAP ratio. Clearly, the second bank assumes greater interest rate risk because its net interest income will change more when interest rates change.

A better risk measure relates the absolute value of a bank's GAP to earning assets. The greater is this ratio, the greater the interest rate risk.[5] The ratio of GAP to earning assets has the additional advantage in that it can be directly linked to variations in NIM. In particular, management can determine a target value for GAP in light of specific risk objectives stated in terms of a bank's target NIM.[6]

Consider a bank with $50 million in earning assets that expects to generate a 5 percent NIM. As part of its management strategy, the bank has decided it will risk changes in NIM equal to plus or minus 20 percent during the year. Thus, NIM should fall between 4 and 6 percent. This

---

[5]Remember that risk in this context is associated with the volatility in net interest income. The use of absolute value demonstrates that the sign of GAP does not influence the volatility of net interest income, only whether net interest income rises or falls when rates change in a specific direction.

[6]Binder and Lindquist (1982) elaborate on this and provide a matrix that outlines potential GAP variances for different levels of NIM risk.

risk assessment, in conjunction with expected interest rates, imposes policy limits on an acceptable GAP. The general relationship is:

$$\frac{\text{Target GAP}}{\text{Earning assets}} = \frac{(\text{Allowable \% change in NIM})(\text{Expected NIM})}{\text{Expected \% change in interest rates}} \qquad (8.2)$$

For example, suppose that management expects interest rates to vary up to 4 percent during the upcoming year. According to Equation 8.2, the bank's ratio of its 1-year cumulative GAP (absolute value) to earning assets should not exceed 25 percent.

$$\text{Target GAP/Earning assets} = (.20)(.05)/.04 = .25$$

Equation 8.2 and management's willingness to allow only a 20 percent variation in NIM sets limits on the GAP which would be allowed to vary from −$12.5 million to $12.5 million, based on $50 million in earning assets.

Using the data from Exhibit 8.6, suppose that Security Bank's management establishes the same 20 percent variance in NIM as a risk objective but expects its NIM to equal 4.5 percent over the next year. If it expects interest rates to rise by 2 percent, it would target the GAP to earning asset ratio at no more than 45 percent. Exhibit 8.6 indicates that the bank's 1-year cumulative GAP is −$23.4 million, or 27.5 percent of earning assets. Thus, management could increase its negative GAP to as much as −$38 million and remain within its target risk profile.

The important point is that a bank's effective GAP and net interest margin are closely linked. Ideally, banks should identify the amount of net interest income at risk if interest rates change. Rather than do this directly via earnings sensitivity analysis, many banks limit the size of GAP as a fraction of assets, which indirectly limits the variation in net interest income.

EARNINGS SENSITIVITY ANALYSIS

In recent years, many bank managers have used an earnings sensitivity framework to measure and monitor interest rate risk. This framework extends static GAP analysis by making it dynamic. It does this by model simulation or "what if" analysis of all the factors that affect net interest income across a wide range of potential interest rate environments. The analysis essentially repeats static GAP analysis assuming different interest rate environments and compares expected net interest income between the different environments. The steps include:

1. Forecast interest rates.
2. Identify changes in asset and liability volume and composition under various interest rate environments.
3. Forecast when embedded options in assets and liabilities will be in the money and, hence, exercised such that prepayments change, securities are called or put, deposits are withdrawn early, or rate caps are exceeded under the assumed interest rate environments.
4. Identify which assets and liabilities will reprice over different time horizons, and by how much, under the assumed interest rate environment. Identify off-balance sheet items that have cash flow implications under the assumed rate environments.
5. Calculate (estimated) net interest income under the different assumed rate environments.
6. Compare the forecasts of net interest income across different rate environments.

The primary value of this framework is that it allows managers to assess how volatile net interest income could be across a wide range of interest rates. The typical comparison looks at seven different interest rate environments beginning with a base case, or most likely, scenario. This may be based on current rates, forward rates implied by the yield curve, or management's specific forecast of rates. Each of the other scenarios then assumes that rates move systematically higher by +1 percent, +2 percent, and +3 percent or systematically lower by −1 percent, −2 percent, and −3 percent. An important part of these forecast environments is the recognition that different customer options go "in the money" such that they are exercised at different times. In addition, management can specify different interest rate changes for different instruments such that the spread between asset yields and liability costs varies. Thus, if a bank's prime rate is assumed to increase by 1 percent, retail time deposit rates might be assumed to increase by just 0.50 percent. In each environment, management determines different amounts of assets, liabilities, and off-balance sheet positions that are effectively rate sensitive, and implicitly calculates a different effective GAP for each scenario. The output then is the change in net interest income or change in NIM from the base case. Policy or risk limits are commonly set relative to allowable changes in net interest income and NIM from the base case. A more extensive framework has managers forecast the change in noninterest income and noninterest expense across different rate environments with the final output being the change in net income versus the base case. Finally, the assumed rate may be immediate (shocks) or incurred over time (gradual).

EXERCISE OF EMBEDDED OPTIONS IN ASSETS AND LIABILITIES

To fully understand the risk inherent in a bank's operations, it is necessary to understand the different types of options that bank customers have. The most obvious options include a customer's option to refinance a loan. Although the option is not generally explicit in a loan contract, any borrower can repay a loan early. A more obvious option is the call option on a federal agency bond that a bank might own. For example, the Federal Home Loan Bank (FHLB) might issue a bond with a 3-year maturity that is callable at face value after 30 days. This means that the FHLB, at its option, can pay the bank the principal anytime after 30 days. Thus, the bank might expect to own the bond for three years, but end up owning it just 30 days or a fraction of the time until maturity. An option embedded in bank liabilities is a depositor's option to withdraw funds prior to final maturity. Such an early withdrawal might also surprise a bank by forcing it to pay the depositor back far in advance of final maturity.

Whenever options are embedded in bank assets and liabilities, managers should address three issues. The first is whether the bank is the buyer or seller of the option. This is the same as asking "Does the bank or its customer determine when the option is exercised?" The buyer is the party that controls when the option is exercised while the seller presumably receives some compensation for selling (or writing) the option. In each of the above examples, the bank is the seller of the option and the customer is the buyer. Borrowers decide when to refinance, the FHLB decides when to call (repay) the bond, and the depositor decides when to withdraw the deposit. The second issue is how, and by what amount, is the bank being compensated for selling the option, or how much it must pay if it buys the option. In the three previous cases, there may be explicit prepayment penalties on a loan and deposit (for early withdrawal) that represent fees (if they are not waived), and the bank receives a higher promised yield on a callable bond compared to the yield on an otherwise similar noncallable bond. Finally, the bank should forecast when the option will be exercised. In the above examples, this involves forecasting when a loan will be prepaid, when the agency bond will be called, and when the depositor will withdraw funds early. These forecasts, in turn, will depend on the assumed rate environment. Loan refinancing (prepayments) typically rise sharply when interest rates fall. Bonds are called when interest rates fall. Deposits are withdrawn early when deposit rates rise sufficiently.

Market participants cannot generally forecast interest rates accurately for long periods of time. The focus on embedded options is important, however, because it forces management to recognize the risks inherent in their portfolios. These risks exist even if rates do not change because there is always the possibility that rates might change. It also allows management to identify a worst case scenario and have a better sense of maximum loss potential.

When doing earnings sensitivity analysis, it is important to recognize that banks often enter into off-balance sheet contracts with explicit options that also affect interest flows. Chapter 11 introduces caps and floors on interest rates and puts and calls on interest rate futures that are used to manage interest rate risk. Each type of contract may have different cash flow effects in different rate environments that potentially alter a bank's interest income and/or interest expense. The effects of these must also be included in any forecast of net interest income volatility.

DIFFERENT INTEREST RATES CHANGE BY DIFFERENT AMOUNTS AT DIFFERENT TIMES

Earnings sensitivity analysis allows management to incorporate the impact of different competitive markets for various balance sheet accounts with alternative pricing strategies. This enables managers to forecast different spreads between asset yields and liability interest costs when rates change by different amounts. It is widely recognized, for example, that banks are quick to increase base loan rates, such as their prime rate, when interest rates increase in general, but are slow to lower base loan rates when interest rates fall. The implication is that floating rate loans are more rate sensitive in rising rate environments versus falling rate environments. In like manner, banks typically increase loan rates more than they increase deposit rates in a rising rate environment such that the spread widens. During a falling rate environment, the opposite often occurs as deposit rates lag in being lowered relative to other money market rates and certain loan rates such that the spread narrows. The implication is that although the rate sensitivity of different instruments might be nominally the same, the impact is different due to different timing of rate changes and different magnitudes of rate changes.

This impact is even more apparent when examining callable bonds that banks own as part of their investment portfolio. Consider the 3-year FHLB bond that is callable after 30 days, described earlier. If rates fall enough, the entire bond will likely be called because the FHLB can refinance at lower rates and save on interest expense. In a falling rate environment, this bond is very rate sensitive and might be classified as such in the 31 to 90 day time interval. In a rising rate environment, the bank might end up owning the bond for three years because it will not be called. As such, it is not rate sensitive because it will not be repriced for three years. It is clear that the bank's effective (actual) GAP will be different in a rising versus falling rate environment because the bond is only rate sensitive when rates fall.

The net effect is that when conducting the "what if" analysis, managers can examine the impact of these nonparallel shifts in interest rates and the differing degrees or effective rate sensitivity. Not surprisingly, the impact of interest rate changes is not as straightforward as that suggested by Equation 8.1 or simple GAP.

EARNINGS SENSITIVITY ANALYSIS: AN EXAMPLE

Consider the Rate Sensitivity Report for ABC Bank as of year-end 2001 presented in Exhibit 8.7. This report is based on the most likely interest rate scenario summarized in Charts A and B of Exhibit 8.8. ABC is a $1 billion bank that bases its analysis on forecasts of the federal funds rate (Chart A) and ties other rates to this overnight rate. Chart A also presents implied forward rates from the market for federal funds futures contracts (market implied rates), which provide a consensus forecast of expected rates. ABC conducts earnings sensitivity analysis across seven different rate environments (rate ramps) with the specific forecasts for federal funds in three rising (+1 percent, +2 percent, +3 percent), rate environments and three falling (−1 percent, −2 percent, −3 percent), as noted in Chart B. Importantly, rates are assumed to change gradually in each case. A 200 basis point (2 percent) rate change is calculated by

• EXHIBIT 8.7

ABC Rate-Sensitivity Report for Most Likely (Base Case)
Interest Rate Scenario: December 31, 2001

	Total	3 Months or Less	>3–6 Months	>6–12 Months	>1–3 Years	>3–5 Years	>5–10 Years	>10–20 Years	>20 Years
Loans									
Prime Based	100,000	100,000							
Equity Credit Lines	25,000	25,000							
Fixed Rate >1 Yr	170,000	18,000	18,000	36,000	96,000	2,000			
Var Rate Mtg 1 Yr	55,000	13,750	13,750	27,500					
30-Yr Fix Mortgage	250,000	5,127	5,129	9,329	32,792	28,916	116,789	51,918	
Consumer	100,000	6,000	6,000	12,000	48,000	28,000			
Credit Card	25,000	3,000	3,000	6,000	13,000				
Investments									
Eurodollars	80,000	80,000							
CMOs FixRate	35,000	2,871	2,872	5,224	13,790	5,284	4,959		
U.S. Treasury	75,000		5,000	5,000	25,000	40,000			
Fed Funds Sold	25,000	25,000							
Cash & Due From Banks	15,000								15,000
Loan Loss Reserve	(15,000)								(15,000)
Non-Earning Assets	60,000								60,000
Total Assets	1,000,000	278,748	53,751	101,053	228,582	104,200	121,748	51,918	60,000
Deposits									
MMDAs	240,000	240,000							
Retail CDs	400,000	60,000	60,000	90,000	160,000	30,000			
Savings	35,000								35,000
NOW	40,000								40,000
DDA Personal	55,000								55,000
Comm'l DDA	60,000	24,000							36,000
Borrowings									
Treasury Tax & Loan	25,000	25,000							
L-T Notes Fixed Rate	50,000						50,000		
Fed Funds Purchased									
Non-Int. Bearing Liabilities	30,000								30,000
Capital	65,000								65,000
Tot Liab & Equity	1,000,000	349,000	60,000	90,000	160,000	30,000	50,000		261,000
Swap: Pay Fixed/ Receive Float	50,000	50,000			(25,000)	(25,000)			
Periodic GAP		(20,252)	(6,249)	11,053	43,582	49,200	71,748	51,918	(201,000)
Cumulative GAP		(20,252)	(26,501)	(15,448)	28,134	77,334	149,082	201,000	0

MOST LIKELY INTEREST RATE SCENARIO AND RATE RAMPS

Chart A
Fed Funds Forecast vs. Implied Forward Rates

Chart B
Most Likely Forecast and Rate Ramps Dec. 2001

cumulatively adding or subtracting approximately 17 basis points per month for one year from the most likely scenario and maintaining these levels during a second year of forecasts.

Ignore for now the explanation of the data for interest rate swaps (third row of data from the bottom of Exhibit 8.7) except that the swaps effectively represent a rate-sensitive asset in the three months or less time bucket.[7] Exhibit 8.7 reports data for eight different time buckets from three months or less to over 20 years. The majority of assets are in 30-year fixed-rate mortgages, fixed-rate loans with maturities over one year, prime-based loans, and consumer loans. The majority of deposits are in the form of retail CDs and MMDAs. According to this static GAP report, ABC's 1-year cumulative GAP equals −$15,448,000, or −1.54 percent of total assets. Under static GAP analysis, the bank has little rate risk, but is positioned to lose modestly if interest rates increase through one year.

Exhibit 8.9 presents the results of earnings sensitivity analysis. The top figure is for the year 2002—one year out, while the bottom figure is for the year 2003—two years out. The seven different interest rate environments are noted on the horizontal axis with the most

---

[7]Note that the $50,000 reported for swaps in under three months effectively increases the periodic GAP without swaps of −$70,252 to a periodic GAP after swaps of −$20,252.

• EXHIBIT 8.9

EARNINGS SENSITIVITY OVER ONE YEAR AND TWO YEARS
VERSUS MOST LIKELY RATE SCENARIO

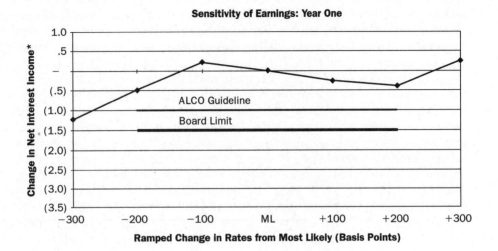

Sensitivity of Earnings: Year One

Change in Net Interest Income*

ALCO Guideline

Board Limit

Ramped Change in Rates from Most Likely (Basis Points)

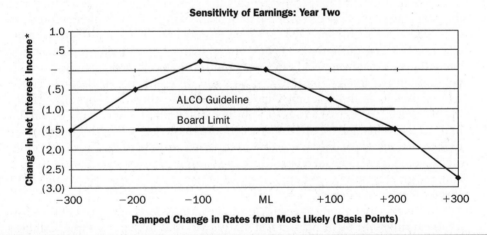

Sensitivity of Earnings: Year Two

Change in Net Interest Income*

ALCO Guideline

Board Limit

Ramped Change in Rates from Most Likely (Basis Points)

*Millions of Dollars

likely (ML) scenario in the middle. The +100, +200, and +300 listings refer to the environments where the federal funds rate is assumed to be 1 percent, 2 percent, and 3 percent higher, respectively, than the most likely scenario. The three assumed lower rate environments are identified to the left of the most likely case. The vertical axis lists the change in net interest income (NII) from the most likely scenario under each interest rate scenario. Note the zero value for the most likely case because it is the reference point for comparing forecasts from the other rate environments. Each forecast of net interest income incorporates assumed shifts in volume and composition of assets and liabilities, changes in spreads recognizing that asset yields and liability interest costs do not change coincidentally by the same amount, and different exercises of embedded customer options.

As indicated in Exhibit 8.9, net interest income will fall slightly if rates increase by 1 to 2 percent during the first year relative to the most likely scenario. If rates increase by 3 percent, net interest income will actually increase, contrary to that suggested by a negative GAP. If rates fall by 1 percent relative to the most likely case, net interest income increases slightly, but if rates fall 2 or 3 percent, net interest income also falls. This again contradicts the implications of the negative GAP from Exhibit 8.7. This is possible because the data in Exhibit 8.7 apply only to the most likely case. In each of the other rate scenarios, different amounts of assets and liabilities are rate sensitive based on the exercise of embedded options and rates on each balance sheet item are assumed to change by different amounts. When rates increase, asset yields are assumed to increase more and sooner such that spreads widen. The opposite occurs when rates fall. Thus, there is a different effective GAP for each rate scenario. If rates fall sharply by 2 or 3 percent, net interest income will fall because the effective GAP is positive. This is intuitive given that a substantial portion of ABC's assets are long term with fixed rates. When rates fall, fixed-rate loans are refinanced and more assets become rate sensitive. When rates rise, these loans are not nearly as rate sensitive. Thus, mortgage prepayments and other loan refinancings drop sharply and there are fewer overall rate-sensitive assets. Similarly, deposits are more rate sensitive when rates rise with more early withdrawals (RSLs increase), which is at least partially offset because spreads widen. These same deposits are less rate sensitive (RSLs decrease) when rates fall, but the spread between earning asset yields and the cost of interest-bearing liabilities falls. Net interest income rises in the +300 case because the increase in spread offsets the impact of a small GAP. These factors explain why net interest income might fall when rates fall and not change significantly when rates rise.

The bottom part of Exhibit 8.9 reveals the comparative forecasts under each scenario in the year 2003, or two years from the date of the report. Over this time frame, the bank loses in both sharply rising and falling rate environments. This again reflects the fact that ABC's effective GAP becomes more negative in an increasing rate environment and positive in a declining rate environment. The key point is that this analysis clearly reveals potential volatility in net interest income over sharply different rate environments. Also, ABC sets ALCO guidelines and risk policy limits according to allowable earnings sensitivity as noted in Exhibit 8.9. The bank has a board of directors' limit of a maximum $1.5 million reduction in net interest income for any two percent rate move up or down over two years. The bank violates its risk guidelines according to forecasts of year two in a +3 percent environment. Steps would have to be taken to reduce the bank's risk exposure to meet these limits. In general, the greater is the variation in forecast net interest income across rate environments, the greater is interest rate risk.

Some banks and bank analysts refer to the summary results of a bank's earnings sensitivity as **earnings-at-risk** or **net interest margin simulation.** For example, Exhibit 8.10 provides summary information for PNC and Washington Mutual regarding the potential variation in net interest income and net income across different interest rate environments. PNC's management established guidelines for acceptable amounts of interest rate risk during 2002 as "net interest income should not decrease by more than 3% if interest rates gradually increase or decrease from current rates by 100 basis points over a twelve-month period." Exhibit 8.10 indicates that PNC's simulation produced an expected 2.8 percent reduction in net interest income if rates decreased by one percent, while net interest income would fall by 0.3 percent with a one percent increase in rates. While PNC loses the most in a falling rate environment (asset sensitive), Washington Mutual is positioned to gain if rates fall and lose when rates rise versus the base case (liability sensitive). Interestingly, Washington Mutual must have additional sources of non-interest income that arise when other rates increase as the percentage reduction in net income is much less than that for net interest income.

· EXHIBIT 8.10

EARNINGS-AT-RISK FOR PNC AND WASHINGTON MUTUAL FOR A GRADUAL CHANGE IN INTEREST RATES, DECEMBER 31, 2001

	Gradual Change in Interest Rates*			
	−2%	**−1%**	**+1%**	**+2%**
PNC				
Net interest income change for next 1 year (2002)		−2.8%	−0.3%	
Washington Mutual				
Net interest income change for next 1 year (2002)		+1.47%		−5.18%
Net income change for next 1 year (2002)		+2.19%		−2.76%

*Current market rates serve as the base case for comparison for both PNC and Washington Mutual. Washington Mutual's results reflect an assumed parallel shift in the yield curve, while PNC's results reflect differential rate moves.

INCOME STATEMENT GAP

Many managers of community banks interpret their bank's interest rate risk using a simplified framework compared to comprehensive earnings sensitivity analysis. They feel comfortable with this because the complexity and size of assets and liabilities does not change dramatically over short periods of time. They similarly do not have significant risk exposure with off-balance sheet transactions that significantly affects the bank's net interest income. The models do, however, recognize the existence of embedded options and the different speeds and amounts of repricing specific assets and liabilities when rates change.

One common practice is to calculate an **income statement GAP,** or Beta GAP, that takes some of these factors into account. Consider the rate-sensitivity report presented in Exhibit 8.11 for a bank with just under $30 million in total assets. This particular report uses the prime rate as the benchmark rate and contains two forecasts of the change in net interest income: one for an environment where the bank's prime rate is assumed to fall by 100 basis points and another when prime is assumed to increase by 100 basis points over the next year. The first three columns of data relate to the case where the prime rate falls. The **balance sheet GAP** is a 1-year cumulative GAP that reflects contractual repricing and indicates that the bank is liability sensitive in the amount of −$7,466,000, or almost 25 percent of assets. The second column of data provides information about each asset's or liability's **earnings change ratio** (ECR). As the footnote suggests, this figure indicates how the yield on each asset, and rate paid on each liability, is assumed to change relative to a 1 percent drop in the prime rate. Thus, the effective yield on federal agency securities is assumed to fall by 71 basis points (0.71 percent), while the effective yield on federal funds sold will fall by 96 basis points (0.96 percent) if prime falls by 1 percent. Not surprisingly, deposit rates lag such that they generally fall by smaller amounts relative to the 1 percent drop in prime. Note that MMDA rates are assumed to fall by 60 basis points. The third column of data reports the amount of each balance sheet item that will effectively be repriced at a 1 percent lower rate and equals the ECR times the balance sheet amount. These figures represent how much of the balance sheet amount will be effectively repriced 1 percent lower.

The bank's income statement GAP is listed at −$2,077,000, as the difference between $14,343,000 in effective RSAs and $16,420,000 in effective RSLs. This is an effective GAP estimate.

· EXHIBIT 8.11

INCOME STATEMENT GAP AND EARNINGS VARIABILITY

Amounts in Thousands Report Data as of September 30, 2002	Prime Down 100bp			Prime Up 100bp		
	Balance Sheet GAP[a]	ECR[b]	Income Statement GAP	Balance Sheet GAP*	ECR[b]	Income Statement GAP
Rate-Sensitive Assets	A	B	A × B	C	D	C × D
Loans						
Fixed Rate	$ 5,661	100%	$5,661	$5,661	100%	$5,661
Floating Rate	3,678	100%	3,678	3,678	100%	3,678
Securities						
Principal Cash Flows						
Agencies	200	71%	142	200	71%	142
Agy Callables	2,940	71%	2,087	300	60%	180
CMO Fixed	315	58%	183	41	51%	20
Fed Funds Sold	2,700	96%	2,592	2,700	96%	2,592
Floating Rate						
Total Rate-Sensitive Assets	$15,494		$14,343	$12,580		$12,273
Rate-Sensitive Liabilities						
Savings	$ 1,925	75%	$1,444	$ 1,925	5%	$ 96
Money Mkt Accts	11,001	60%	6,600	11,001	40%	4,400
NOW	2,196	80%	1,757	2,196	20%	439
Fed Funds Purch/Repo	0	96%	0	0	96%	0
CDs ≥ 100M	3,468	85%	2,948	3,468	85%	2,948
CDs < 100M	4,370	84%	3,671	4,370	84%	3,671
Total Rate-Sensitive Liabilities	$22,960		$16,420	$22,960		$11,554
Rate Sensitivity Gap (Assets-Liab)	($7,466)		$2,077	($10,380)		$719
Total Assets	$29,909		$29,909	$29,909		$29,909
GAP as a Percent of Total Assets	−24.96%		−6.94%	−34.71%		2.40%
Change in Net Interest Income			$20.8			$7.2
Change in Net Interest Margin			0.07%			0.02%
Net Interest Margin			5.20%			5.20%
Percentage Change in Net Interest Margin			1.34%			0.46%

[a]One year balance sheet GAP includes all balances that may change in rate in the next 12 months.

[b]The Earnings Change Ratio (ECR) is an estimate of the change in rate of a rate-sensitive instrument per 100 basis point move in prime.

As such, we can apply Equation 8.1 to interpret the impact on net interest income. Here, a 1 percent reduction in the prime rate will lead to an estimated $20,770 increase in net interest income and a corresponding 7 basis point increase in net interest margin.

$$\Delta \text{Net interest income} = -\$2,077,000(.01) = +\$20,770$$

The three columns of data at the right of Exhibit 8.11 refer to the estimated impact of a one percent increase in the prime rate over the next year. Note that in a rising rate environment, a smaller amount of callable agency securities is assumed to be rate sensitive because fewer securities will likely be called. Also, the ECRs for some of the assets and core deposit liabilities are different, reflecting the fact that effective reinvestment rates on agency callables and CMOs will not rise as much with slower prepayments, and the bank will not increase its deposit rates in line with increases in prime or by the same amount as they would be lowered in a falling rate environment. The net impact is that the bank's effective income statement GAP is smaller at $719,000. A 1 percent increase in prime will increase net interest income by an estimated $7,190. Importantly, different assumed changes in prime will produce different estimated changes in net interest income depending on the same factors that alter a bank's effective rate sensitivity of assets and liabilities.

MANAGING THE GAP AND EARNINGS SENSITIVITY RISK

Effective GAP measures and the potential variation in net interest income indicate the general interest rate risk faced by a bank. Equation 8.1 applies in the income statement GAP framework but not the general earnings sensitivity framework. It generally suggests that if interest rates are expected to increase during the GAP period, a positive cumulative GAP will lead to an increase in net interest income. If rates are expected to fall, a negative GAP will lead to an increase in net interest income. The actual change in net interest income will meet expectations only if interest rates change in the direction and amount anticipated and if RSAs and RSLs are accurately forecast. Importantly, the size of the effective GAP or the range of variation in net interest income signify how much risk a bank is taking. The larger is the absolute value of GAP, the greater is the change in net interest income for a given change in rates. The greater is the potential variation in net interest income from the base case, the greater is the risk.

The GAP model suggests that a bank that chooses not to speculate on future interest rates can reduce interest rate risk by obtaining a zero effective GAP or no variability in net interest income. The bank is fully hedged because its interest rate risk is negligible. Of course, this zero-risk position is rarely achieved and is rarely desired. Alternatively, a bank may choose to speculate on future interest rates and actively manage the GAP. Equation 8.1 suggests that a bank can systematically increase net interest income if it can accurately forecast rates and vary its effective GAP accordingly. If management expects rates to increase, it should become more asset sensitive. If it expects rates to decrease, it should become more liability sensitive. The Contemporary Issues box, Wells Fargo: Intentionally Mismatched Maturities, discusses why management has historically tried to position itself as liability sensitive.

Listed below are steps that banks can take to reduce risk in the context of effective GAP management.

1. Calculate periodic GAPs over short time intervals.
2. Match fund repriceable assets with similar repriceable liabilities so that periodic GAPs approach zero.
3. Match fund long-term assets with non-interest-bearing liabilities.
4. Use off-balance sheet transactions, such as interest rate swaps and financial futures, to hedge.

Management may alternatively choose to alter the rate sensitivity of assets and liabilities to take greater risk. Chapter 9 discusses the specific bets that management makes

WELLS FARGO: INTENTIONALLY MISMATCHED MATURITIES

What GAP value is best? Some banks pursue a strategy of matching asset and liability maturities as closely as possible to reduce the GAP to zero and reduce the volatility of net interest income. Other banks aggressively vary the GAP in line with their interest rate forecast. If they expect rates to increase, they attempt to increase the GAP by repricing assets more frequently than liabilities. An expected decrease in rates coincides with efforts to lower the GAP and possibly make it negative by repricing relatively more liabilities sooner. Which strategy is better depends on whether management can accurately forecast rates and adjust the GAP accordingly.

Wells Fargo Bank historically pursued a strategy that was independent of short-term interest rate forecasts. The bank targeted a negative funding GAP through at least 180 days. This action followed from a belief that liquidity premiums impart a consistent upward bias to the slope of the yield curve. Even when rates were expected to remain constant, long-term rates typically exceeded short-term rates because investors, on average, preferred to own more liquid short-term securities. Rates on 6-month securities typically exceeded rates on overnight loans by 30 to 75 basis points as a premium for investors. A negative GAP associated with a short-funding strategy, where short-term deposits financed longer-term assets, allowed the bank to earn the liquidity premium as part of its spread.

Wells Fargo's managers essentially recognized that they could not forecast interest rates better than the market. The strategy will work in the long run, regardless of the near-term shape of the yield curve, because of the 30- to 75-basis-point spread on mismatched assets and liabilities with less than six months to maturity. The mismatch was generally restricted to the six-month horizon because liquidity premiums were greatest over this interval, then leveled off. Mismatches constructed with longer-term assets involved more risk but offered the same effective spread.

---

when it speculatively adjusts its effective GAP or earnings sensitivity profile. Listed below are various ways to adjust the effective rate sensitivity of a bank's assets and liabilities on-balance sheet.

Objective	Approaches
Reduce asset sensitivity	Buy longer-term securities. Lengthen the maturities of loans. Move from floating-rate loans to term loans.
Increase asset sensitivity	Buy short-term securities. Shorten loan maturities. Make more loans on a floating-rate basis.
Reduce liability sensitivity	Pay premiums to attract longer-term deposit instruments. Issue long-term subordinated debt.
Increase liability sensitivity	Pay premiums to attract short-term deposit instruments. Borrow more via non-core purchased liabilities.

The benefits and costs of these approaches are discussed at the end of Chapter 9.

SUMMARY

A bank's asset and liability management committee is responsible for monitoring and managing a bank's interest rate risk profile. This chapter initially introduces the traditional static GAP model as a means of measuring interest rate risk. It then extends the discussion to focus on earnings sensitivity analysis, which essentially represents net income simulation under different assumed interest rate environments. It allows management to assess the sensitivity of net interest income to changes in balance sheet volume and composition, shifts in the relationship between asset yields and the costs of interest-bearing liabilities, and general shifts in the level of interest rates. It is also helpful in measuring the earnings impact when options embedded in bank loans, securities, and deposits are exercised. The net result is an understanding of the relationship between how much net interest income might rise or fall over the next one to two years relative to potential interest rate changes and, thus, how much risk is assumed. It provides information regarding how management might position itself to gain if it wants to take on additional risk or how it might hedge if it wants to reduce overall risk.

QUESTIONS

1. List the basic steps in static GAP analysis. What is the objective of each?

2. Are the following assets rate sensitive within a six-month time frame? Explain.
   a. 3-month T-bill
   b. federal funds sold (daily repricing)
   c. 2-year Treasury bond with semiannual coupon payments
   d. 4-year fully amortized car loan with $450 monthly payments including both principal and interest
   e. commercial loan priced at the bank's prime rate plus 2 percent

3. Consider the following bank balance sheet and associated average interest rates. The time frame for rate sensitivity is one year.

Assets	Amount	Rate	Liabilities & Equity	Amount	Rate
Rate Sensitive	$3,300	7.3%	Rate Sensitive	$2,900	3.8%
Fixed-rate	1,400	8.7%	Fixed-rate	1,650	6.1%
Nonearning	500		Nonpaying Liabilities	650	
Total	$5,200		Total	$5,200	

   a. Calculate the bank's GAP, expected net interest income, and net interest margin if interest rates and portfolio composition remain constant during the year. This bank is positioned to profit if interest rates move in which direction?
   b. Calculate the change in expected net interest income and NIM if the entire yield curve shifts 2 percent higher during the year. Is this consistent with the bank's static GAP?
   c. Suppose that, instead of the parallel shift in the yield curve in part b, interest rates increase unevenly. Specifically, suppose that asset yields rise by 1 percent while liability rates rise by 1.75 percent. Calculate the change in net interest income and NIM. Is this uneven shift in rates more or less likely than a parallel shift?
   d. Suppose the bank converts $300 of rate-sensitive liabilities to fixed-rate liabilities during the year and interest rates remain constant. What would the bank's net interest income equal compared with the amount initially expected? Explain why there is a difference.

4. Suppose that your bank buys a T-bill that matures in six months and finances the purchase with a 3-month time deposit.
   a. Calculate the 6-month GAP associated with this transaction. What does this GAP measure indicate about interest rate risk in this transaction?
   b. Calculate the 3-month GAP associated with this transaction. Is this a better GAP measure of the bank's risk? Why or why not?

5. What is the fundamental weakness of the GAP ratio compared with GAP as a measure of interest rate risk?

6. Discuss the problems that loans tied to a bank's base rate present in measuring interest rate risk where the base rate is not tied directly to a specific market interest rate that changes on a systematic basis.

7. Consider the following asset and liability structures:

County Bank

Asset: $10 million in a 1-year, fixed-rate commercial loan
Liability: $10 million in a 3-month CD

City Bank

Asset: $10 million in a 3-year, fixed-rate commercial loan
Liability: $10 million in a 6-month CD

   a. Calculate each bank's 3-month, 6-month, and 1-year cumulative GAP.
   b. Which bank has the greatest interest rate risk exposure as suggested by each GAP measure? Consider the risk position over the different intervals.

8. Consider the Rate Sensitivity Report in Exhibit 8.6.
   a. Is Security Bank positioned to profit or lose if interest rates rise over the next 90 days?
   b. Suppose that management has misstated the rate sensitivity of the bank's money market deposit accounts because the bank has not changed the rate it pays on these liabilities for six months and doesn't plan to change them in the near future. Will the bank profit if rates rise over the next 90 days?

9. Assume that you manage the interest rate risk position for your bank. Your bank currently has a positive cumulative GAP for all time intervals through one year. You expect that interest rates will fall sharply during the year and want to reduce your bank's risk position. The current yield curve is inverted with long-term rates below short-term rates.
   a. To reduce risk, would you recommend issuing a 3-month time deposit and investing the proceeds in 1-year T-bills? Will you profit if rates fall during the year?
   b. To reduce risk, would you recommend issuing a 3-month time deposit and making a 2-year commercial loan priced at prime plus 1 percent? Why?

10. Management at Bay Bank expects its net interest margin to equal 4.8 percent during the next year. It will allow variation in NIM of just 10 percent during the year and expects interest rates to either rise or fall by 2 percent. If management expects the bank to have $400 million in earning assets, determine how large its 1-year cumulative GAP can be to not exceed the allowable variation in NIM.

11. Each of the following potentially alters the rate sensitivity of the underlying instrument. Presumably there is an embedded option associated with each. Indicate when the option is typically exercised and how it affects rate sensitivity.
   a. Fixed-rate mortgage loan with a yield of 8 percent and 30-year final maturity.
   b. Time deposit with five years remaining to maturity; carries a fixed rate of 5 percent.
   c. Commercial loan with a 2-year maturity and a floating rate set at prime plus 2.5 percent. There is a cap of 9 percent representing the maximum rate that the bank can charge on the loan.

12. What information is available from earnings sensitivity analysis that is not provided by static GAP analysis?

13. Exhibit 8.9 demonstrates that ABC Bank loses in year two if rates either rise or fall sharply from the most likely scenario. Explain why in terms of when embedded options are expected to be exercised and what happens to spreads.

14. Interpret the following earnings-at-risk data. What does it suggest regarding the bank's risk exposure?

Interest Rate Change (%)	Earnings-at-Risk	
	1 Year	2 Years
+1% shock	+2.4%	+4.9%
−1% shock	−1.7%	−5.5%
−1% yield curve inversion	+1.1%	−2.6%

15. Given the following information for E-Bank, calculate its Income Statement (Effective) GAP. How much will net interest income change if the 1-year Treasury rate falls 1 percent?

Rate-Sensitive Assets	1-Year Balance Sheet GAP	ECR
Loans	$55,120,000	82%
Securities	$28,615,000	67%
Rate-Sensitive Liabilities		
MMDAs	$41,640,000	34%
NOWs	$37,260,000	90%
CDs ≥ 100,000	$20,975,000	85%

PROBLEM

The following data are taken from the 2001 annual report for Southtrust Corporation, which reported $1.53 billion in net interest income before provisions and almost $49 billion in assets for the year. Review the information and determine the bank's risk exposure at the end of the year. Specifically, the information for interest rate swaps represents the effect of off-balance sheet transactions used to hedge interest rate risk.

1. Interpret the periodic interest rate gap and cumulative gap information. Was the bank positioned to profit or lose if interest rates fell in 2002? Explain.

2. Interpret the GAP impact of interest rate swaps. Was the bank's net interest rate risk exposure greater or lower as a result of swap activity through 1 year? Explain. Did the bank use swaps to hedge or speculate when viewed in this context?

3. Examine GAP as a fraction of earning assets. Did the bank assume much risk at year-end 2001? Explain.

Interest Rate Sensitivity Analysis
December 31, 2001

	0–30 Days	31–90 Days	91–180 Days	181–365 Days	1–5 Years	Over 5 Years	Non-interest Sensitive	Total
				(In Millions)				
Variable-rate commercial and real estate loans	$15,126.6	$ 1,143.7	$ 247.3	$ 332.7	$ 755.3	$ 88.7	$ 0.0	$17,694.3
Fixed-rate commercial and real estate loans	261.0	390.9	611.8	1,068.2	6,286.3	2,171.8	0.0	10,790.0
Other loans	2,266.7	499.2	248.7	398.2	1,367.5	158.0	0.0	4,938.3
Total loans	17,654.3	2,033.8	1,107.8	1,799.1	8,409.1	2,418.5	0.0	33,422.6
Securities	846.3	368.9	537.2	966.1	4,078.6	3,702.4	0.0	10,499.5
Other interest-earning assets	332.4	596.6	0.0	0.0	0.0	0.0	0.0	929.0
Total Interest-earning assets	18,833.0	2,999.3	1,645.0	2,765.2	12,487.7	6,120.9	0.0	44,851.1
Allowance for loan losses	0.0	0.0	0.0	0.0	0.0	0.0	(483.1)	(483.1)
Other assets	0.0	0.0	0.0	0.0	0.0	0.0	4,386.4	4,386.5
Total assets	$18,833.0	$ 2,999.3	$ 1,645.0	$ 2,765.2	$12,487.7	$ 6,120.9	3,903.4	$48,754.5
Non-interest-bearing demand deposits	$ 0.0	$ 0.0	$ 0.0	$ 0.0	$ 0.0	$ 0.0	$4,392.3	$4,392.3
Interest-bearing demand deposits ...	571.0	1,595.6	0.0	0.0	1,770.2	0.0	0.0	3,936.8
Money market deposits	753.0	2,259.0	0.0	0.0	2,008.0	0.0	0.0	5,020.0
Savings deposits	226.9	0.0	0.0	0.0	2,041.9	0.0	0.0	2,268.8
Time deposits under $100,000 ...	941.4	1,762.3	1,562.3	1,631.8	12,147.3	7.2	0.0	8,052.3
Other time deposits	4,043.2	1,728.1	1,742.8	937.4	493.4	19.0	0.0	8,963.9
Total deposits	6,535.5	7,345.0	3,305.1	2,569.2	8,460.8	26.2	4392.3	32,634.1
Short-term borrowings	4,591.5	492.8	439.6	401.4	0.0	0.0	0.0	5,925.3
FHLB advances	1,650.0	700.1	0.0	0.0	40.0	1,831.0	0.0	4,221.1
Long-term debt	200.0	25.0	0.0	0.0	301.1	737.3	0.0	1,263.4
Other liabilities	0.0	0.0	0.0	0.0	0.0	0.0	748.2	748.2
Stockholders' equity	0.0	0.0	0.0	0.0	0.0	0.0	3,962.4	3,962.4
Total liabilities and stockholders' equity	$12,977.0	$ 8,562.9	$ 3,744.7	$ 2,970.6	$8,801.9	$2,594.5	$ 9,102.9	$48,754.5
Interest rate gap	$ 5,856.0	$(5,563.6)	$(2,099.7)	$ (205.4)	$3,685.8	$3,526.4	(5,199.5)	
Effect on interest rate swaps	110.0	(844.5)	(227.5)	(395.0)	792.0	565.0		
Cumulative interest rate gap	$ 5,966.0	$ (442.1)	$(2,769.3)	$(3,369.7)	$1,108.1	$5,199.5		
Cumulative gap as a percentage of interest-earing assets—								
December 31, 2001	13.30%	(0.99)%	(6.17)%	(7.51)%	2.47%	11.59%		
December 31, 2000	3.25	(15.06)	(19.50)	(20.86)	(8.91)	10.95		

SIGNIFICANT ASSUMPTIONS:

1. Allocations to specific interest sensitivity periods are based on the earlier of the repricing or maturity dates. These allocations have been adjusted for any estimated early principle payoffs, including callable bonds, mortgage-backed securities, 1–4 family mortgages, trading securities, loans held for sale.

2. Interest-bearing demand, money market, and savings deposit account repricing volumes are based on management assumptions of the sensitivity of these accounts in relation to changes in short-term market rates.

Change in Interest Rates	Southtrust Change in Net Interest Income	
2001	$	%
	(Dollars in Thousands)	
+100 basis points	$ 3,657	0.20%
−100 basis points	(1,877)	(0.10)
2000		
+100 basis points	$(68,061)	(4.62)%
−100 basis points	32,503	2.21

4. Was Southtrust asset sensitive or liability sensitive at year-end 2001?

5. Did Southtrust exhibit greater of lesser risk in 2001 versus 2000? Explain.

9

Managing Interest Rate Risk: Duration Gap and Market Value of Equity

A *fundamental criticism of funding GAP and earnings sensitivity analysis is that they emphasize a bank's risk profile over the short run and largely ignore cash flows beyond one or two years. Yet, a bank's assets and liabilities may be substantially mismatched beyond two years and thus exhibit considerable risk, which goes undetected. Duration gap and market value of equity sensitivity analysis represent alternative methods of analyzing interest rate risk. They emphasize the price sensitivity of assets and liabilities to changes in interest rates and the corresponding impact on stockholders' equity. As the labels suggest, they incorporate estimates of the duration of assets and duration of liabilities, which reflect the value of promised cash flows through final maturity. As such, they provide a comprehensive measure of the interest rate risk embodied in the entire balance sheet of a bank. In most cases, the* implications concerning when banks win and lose are comparable to those of GAP and earnings sensitivity analysis, but the magnitude of the estimated effects may differ sharply.

This chapter examines the management of a bank's interest rate risk position in terms of duration gap and the sensitivity of the market value of stockholders' equity to changes in interest rates. In this framework, interest rate risk refers to the volatility in the market value of stockholders' equity attributable to changes in the level of interest rates. A bank that assumes substantial risk will see its value of equity rise or fall sharply when interest rates change unexpectedly.

Duration gap analysis represents an application of duration concepts to a bank's entire balance sheet. As such, the model builds on the discussion of Macaulay's duration applied to single securities that was introduced in Chapter 6. It parallels static GAP and earnings sensitivity analysis in the sense that both duration gap and the potential variation in market value of stockholders' equity are viewed as measures of risk, with more sophisticated users focusing on the latter. Some banks set targets for allowable risk in terms of how much equity values are allowed to change for specific 2 percent or 3 percent rate shocks. The analysis is dynamic in the sense that it incorporates the impact of potential rate increases and decreases and it recognizes that customers' exercise of embedded options will affect a bank's true risk exposure depending on how interest rates change. As such, the analytical procedure is similar to that for earnings sensitivity analysis. This analysis appears under such labels as market value of equity (MVE), economic value of equity (EVE), and net present value (NPV) analysis.

MEASURING INTEREST RATE RISK WITH DURATION GAP

As Chapter 6 demonstrates, duration is most easily understood as an elasticity measure. As such, it provides information regarding how much a security's price will change when market interest rates change. Recall that the longer is duration, the greater is price sensitivity. Thus, the price of a 5-year duration bond will change more than the price of a 1-year duration bond for a similar change in interest rates. **Duration gap analysis** compares the price sensitivity of a bank's total assets with the price sensitivity of its total liabilities to assess whether the market value of assets or liabilities changes more when rates change. Any differential impact will indicate how the bank's market value of equity will change. Before introducing the model, we provide a brief review of duration concepts.

DURATION, MODIFIED DURATION, AND EFFECTIVE DURATION

Market participants often use three different duration measures—Macaulay's duration, modified duration, and effective duration—as if they were the same. In fact, while the interpretations are similar, they differ in terms of how they are calculated and how they should be used.[1]

Macaulay's duration (D) is computed as a weighted average of the time until cash flows are received. The weights equal the present value of each cash flow as a fraction of the security's current price, and time refers to the length of time in the future until payment or receipt. It is measured and quoted in units of time. Conceptually, duration measures the average life of an instrument. In the context of immunization, an investor knows that by matching duration with the preferred holding period, interest rate risk can be minimized because price risk is balanced with reinvestment risk. For example, a bond with four years until final maturity with a duration of 3.5 years indicates that an investor with a 3.5-year holding period could lock in a rate of return by buying a 3.5-year duration instrument. If interest rates increase, the decrease in market value of the bond will be just offset by higher reinvestment income from the periodic coupon interest payments, so that the promised return is realized after 3.5 years. If interest rates decrease, the price appreciation will offset the lost reinvestment income. Thus, value and total return are fixed.[2]

Following is the duration formula for a security with n cash flows discounted at the market interest rate i, with an initial price P*, and t equal to the time until the cash payment is made.

$$D = \sum_{t}^{n} \frac{[\text{cash flow}_t / (1 + i)^t] \times t}{P^*} \tag{9.1}$$

---

[1]There are many other definitions of duration, using different discount rates and cash flow assumptions, that are ignored here. For a useful discussion, see Bierwag (1987), Ho (1992), and Phoa (1997).

[2]This ignores the fact that duration will change as time passes and immunization would require a rebalancing of the security or portfolio's duration. To be useful, the user must specify *ex ante* what rebalancing is appropriate.

We use this measure of price sensitivity in the approximate price elasticity relationship:

$$\frac{\Delta P}{P} \cong -\frac{D}{(1 + i)} \times \Delta i \tag{9.2}$$

with

$$\text{modified duration} = D/(1 + i) \tag{9.3}$$

Modified duration equals Macaulay's duration divided by $(1 + i)$. It has the useful feature of indicating how much the price of a security will change in percentage terms for a given change in interest rates. A 5-year zero coupon bond will have a Macaulay's duration of 10 semiannual periods or five years. Assume that its current price is $7,441 and market rate of interest is 6 percent (3 percent semiannual compounding). The bond's modified duration equals 9.71 semiannual periods (10/1.03) or 4.85 years. If the market interest rate rises to 7 percent ($\Delta i = 0.01$), the bond's price will fall by 4.85 percent, or by $361 (0.01 × 4.85 × $7,441). Securities can be easily ranked by modified duration to determine which ones are most price volatile.

Both of these measures calculate duration assuming that all promised cash flows will be realized. While this is true for option-free securities, it does not hold for securities with options. When a loan is prepaid or a bond is called, the exercise of the underlying option changes the instrument's duration. For example, a 3-year bond may be callable in one year. If market rates fall and the bond is called, its duration changes compared to when rates are higher and the bond is not called. The concept of **effective duration** is used to estimate how price sensitive a security is when the security contains embedded options. It compares a security's estimated price in a falling rate environment with an estimated price in a rising rate environment relative to the initial price times the assumed rate differential. Formally, effective duration (Eff Dur) equals:

$$\text{Eff Dur} = \frac{P_{i-} - P_{i+}}{P_0(i+ - i-)} \tag{9.4}$$

where

P_{i-} = price if rates fall,

P_{i+} = price if rates rise,

P_0 = initial (current) price,

i^+ = initial market rate plus the increase in rate, and

i^- = initial market rate minus the decrease in rate.

Consider a 3-year, 9.4 percent coupon bond selling for $10,000 par to yield 9.4 percent to maturity. This bond is callable at par and will presumably be called if rates fall 50 basis points or more. The Macaulay's duration for the option-free version of this bond with semiannual coupons and compounding was calculated in Chapter 6 to be 5.36 semiannual periods, or 2.68 years at the market rate of 4.7 percent semiannually. The modified duration was 5.12 semiannual periods or 2.56 years. If this bond is callable at par, its price will never increase much more than $10,000. When the call option is in the money—that is, when market rates fall by 0.50 percent (25 basis points semiannually) or more and the bond will likely be called—the bond's price will equal its call price of $10,000. If rates rise, the bond will not be called and its price will fall as it would without any embedded option. As noted in Chapter 6, a 30 basis point increase in rate to 5 percent semiannually will lower the price to $9,847.72. Thus, the callable bond's effective duration for a 30 basis point (0.30 percent) semiannual movement in rates either up or down is 2.54.

$$\text{Eff Dur} = \frac{\$10,000 - \$9,847.72}{\$10,000(0.05 - 0.044)} = 2.54$$

As expected, the chance that the bond will be called shortens duration from what it would be if all cash flows materialized as originally scheduled.

The use of effective duration allows the cash flows of the underlying instrument to change when interest rates change. An analyst must have rate forecasts and a model to explain the pricing of the security in different interest rate environments to calculate effective duration. It is just an approximation, but is useful because it recognizes that an embedded option may be exercised and thus dramatically alter the expected cash flows and value of a security. Effective duration also demonstrates how some securities can exhibit negative duration. Negative duration actually refers to an effective duration calculation that is negative. For this to happen, the price of a security in a declining rate environment must fall below the price in a rising rate environment, such that the numerator of Equation 9.4 is negative. This can occur when some types of mortgage-backed securities prepay so rapidly that the promised cash flow stream collapses.[3]

DURATION GAP MODEL

Duration gap (DGAP) models focus on managing net interest income or the market value of stockholders' equity, recognizing the timing of all cash flows for every security on a bank's balance sheet.[4] The following analysis emphasizes duration's use as an elasticity measure. Unlike static GAP analysis, which focuses on rate sensitivity or the frequency of repricing, duration gap analysis focuses on price sensitivity. The Contemporary Issues box, Rate Sensitivity versus Price Sensitivity clarifies the difference. Duration is an attractive measure because it is additive across securities in a portfolio. A bank's interest rate risk is indicated by comparing the weighted average duration of assets with the weighted average duration of liabilities. As with GAP analysis, the sign and magnitude of DGAP provide information about when a bank potentially wins and loses, and the magnitude of the interest rate bet. Management can adjust DGAP to hedge or accept interest rate risk by speculating on future interest rate changes.

Duration gap analysis compares the duration of bank assets with the duration of bank liabilities and examines how the market value of stockholders' equity will change when interest rates change. As with GAP and earnings sensitivity analysis, the analysis produces different outcomes in different interest rate environments. After introducing the framework of the analysis and defining duration gap, the following discussion extends this to incorporate embedded options and sensitivity analysis for potential variation in the market value of stockholders' equity.

There are four steps in duration gap analysis:

1. Management develops an interest rate forecast.
2. Management estimates the market value of bank assets, liabilities, and stockholders' equity. The market value of equity (MVE) equals the amount that makes the market value of assets equal to the market value of liabilities plus MVE.

---

[3]The standard example is a high coupon, interest only (IO) mortgage-backed security that currently prepays at a high speed. The holder of this IO receives only the interest payments on the principal outstanding for a pool of mortgages. If rates fall, the pool prepays even faster so that expected interest payments fall—perhaps to zero. With fewer payments made, the price drops. If rates increase, the pool prepays slower so that expected interest payments increase and will appear over a longer period of time. Thus, the IO's price might increase. This security will have a negative effective duration.

[4]The following discussion focuses on the market value of stockholders' equity as a target variable and follows the discussion in Kaufman (1984). Toevs (1983) addresses the use of net interest income as a target measure of performance.

CONTEMPORARY ISSUES

RATE SENSITIVITY VERSUS PRICE SENSITIVITY

GAP and duration gap represent two ways of viewing interest rate risk. To best understand the differences, you should understand how rate sensitivity differs from price sensitivity. Rate sensitivity refers to the ability to reprice the principal on an asset or liability. Price sensitivity refers to how much the price of an asset or liability will change when interest rates change. If an instrument is very rate sensitive, it is typically not very price sensitive, and vice versa.

GAP and earnings sensitivity analysis focus on how frequently the principal amount of an asset or liability will reprice. For example, if a bank's federal funds sold mature daily, this asset is extremely rate sensitive because the bank can reinvest the principal amount at the prevailing rate every 24 hours. The same federal funds sold loan is not price sensitive. Because the rate changes daily when the principal matures, the loan will be priced at par or face value daily. The changing interest will reflect the change in rates. In contrast, a 10-year zero coupon bond is not very rate sensitive because the owner cannot reinvest the principal for 10 years without selling the bond. This same bond is very price sensitive, however, because its value will rise or fall sharply in percentage terms as rates either fall or rise. Thus, rate sensitivity and price sensitivity are two alternate, but consistent, ways of interpreting a security's features.

---

3. Management estimates the weighted average duration of assets and weighted average duration of liabilities. The effects of both on- and off-balance sheet items are incorporated. These estimates are used to calculate duration gap.

4. Management forecasts changes in the market value of stockholders' equity across different interest rate environments.

The weighted average duration of bank assets (DA) is calculated as:

$$DA = \sum_{i}^{n} w_i Da_i \qquad (9.5)$$

where
A_i = market value of asset i (i equals 1, 2, . . . n),
$w_i = A_i$ divided by the market value of all bank assets (MVA) (MVA = $A_1 + A_2 + \ldots + A_n$),
Da_i = Macaulay's duration of asset i, and
n = number of different bank assets.

The weighted duration of bank liabilities (DL) is calculated similarly as:

$$DL = \sum_{j}^{m} z_j Dl_j \qquad (9.6)$$

where
L_j = market value of liability j (j equals 1, 2, . . . m),
$z_j = L_j$ divided by the market value of all bank liabilities (MVL)(MVL = $L_1 + L_2 + \ldots + L^m$),
Dl_j = Macaulay's duration of liability j, and
m = number of different bank liabilities.

With the focus on the market value of stockholders' equity (MVE) and the general level of interest rates (characterized by y):

$$\Delta MVE = \Delta MVA - \Delta MVL \qquad (9.7)$$

Using Equation 9.2 we know that $\Delta A_i = -Da_i[\Delta y/(1 + y)]A_i$; and $\Delta L_j = -Dl_j[\Delta y/(1 + y)]$, such that:

$$\Delta MVE = -[DA - (MVL/MVA) DL][\Delta y/(1 + y)]MVA \qquad (9.8)$$

If we define a bank's duration gap (DGAP) = DA − (MVL/MVA)DL, then

$$\Delta MVE \cong -DGAP[\Delta y/(1 + y)]MVA \tag{9.9}$$

Note that both DA and DL take into account the present value of all promised or expected cash flows. There is no need for time buckets or classifying assets and liabilities. Thus, duration gap indicates the difference between the weighted average duration of assets and the leverage-adjusted weighted average duration of liabilities. Hence it is an approximate estimate of the sensitivity of the MVE to changes in the level of interest rates. The leverage adjustment takes into account the existence of equity as a means of financing assets. The interest factor (y) is typically measured as some average earning asset yield across all interest-earning assets. According to Equation 9.9, the greater is DGAP, the greater is the potential variation in MVE for a given change in interest rates. As such, DGAP provides information about when a bank wins and loses and the amount of risk assumed. If DGAP is positive, an increase in rates will lower MVE, while a decrease in rates will increase MVE. If DGAP is negative, an increase in rates will increase MVE, while a decrease in rates will lower MVE. The closer DGAP is to zero, the smaller is the potential change in MVE for any change in rates.

A DURATION APPLICATION FOR BANKS

Most bank managers are concerned with the bank's total risk exposure from all assets and liabilities. When it receives cash inflows from assets prior to making its obligated payments on liabilities, it bears the risk that it may have to reinvest the proceeds at reduced rates. When it makes debt payments before it receives cash inflows, it bears the risk that borrowing costs will rise. Any differential in the timing of asset and liability cash flows is reflected in average durations.

Duration gap analysis requires that a bank specify a performance target, such as the market value of equity, and strategically manage the difference between the average duration of total assets and the average duration of total liabilities. Consider the balance sheet of the hypothetical bank in Exhibit 9.1. The bank just opened for business and all dollar amounts are market values. It owns $1,000 worth of three assets: cash, a 3-year final maturity commercial loan earning 12 percent, and a 6-year Treasury bond earning 8 percent. It pays interest on 1-year time deposits (TDs) at 5 percent and on 3-year CDs at 7 percent. The market value of equity represents the residual (plug figure) between asset and liability values and equals $80, or 8 percent of assets. The analysis assumes that there will be no defaults, prepayments, or early withdrawals. All securities make equal annual interest payments with annual compounding. Macaulay's duration for each item is listed beside the current market rate. The duration of cash is zero because cash doesn't change in value when interest rates change. Duration measures for the commercial loan, the 3-year CD, and the weighted average total asset and liability durations are computed at the bottom of the exhibit. Initially, the average duration of assets equals 2.88 years and exceeds the 1.61 year average duration of liabilities by over one year. Expected net interest income, assuming no change in interest rates, is $48 per $1,000 of assets.[5]

Interest rate risk is evidenced by the mismatch in average durations of assets and liabilities and the DGAP of 1.42 years. When interest rates change, the market values of assets and liabilities will change by different amounts, and future interest income will change relative to future interest expense. The fact that the average duration of assets exceeds the average duration of liabilities (adjusted for leverage) indicates that the market value of assets will change

---

[5]This analysis uses economic income instead of accounting income. Economic interest is calculated as the product of the market value of each asset or liability and its market interest rate. Economic income varies directly with accounting income in these examples, although the relationship is not linear. Note that the use of Macaulay's duration ignores the impact of embedded options.

- **EXHIBIT 9.1**

MVE ANALYSIS: HYPOTHETICAL BANK BALANCE SHEET

Assets	Market Value	Rate	Duration	Liabilities and Equity	Market Value	Rate	Duration
Cash	$ 100			1-yr. Time deposit	$ 620	5%	1.00 yr.
3-yr. Commercial loan	700	12%	2.69 yrs.	3-yr. Certificate of deposit	300	7%	2.81
6-yr. Treasury bond	200	8	4.99	Total liabilities	920		1.59 yrs.
			2.88 yrs.	Equity (MVE)	$ 80		
Total	$1,000				$1,000		

Weighted avg. duration of assets (DA) = ($700/$1,000)(2.69) + ($200/$1,000)(4.99) = 2.88 yrs.
Weighted avg. duration of liabilities (DL) = ($620/$920)(1) + ($300/$920)(2.81) = 1.59 yrs.
Expected economic net interest income = 0.12($700) + 0.08($200) − 0.05($620) − 0.07($300) = $48.00
DGAP = 2.88 − ($920/$1,000)(1.59) = 1.42 yrs.

Sample Duration Calculations Using Equation 9.1

$$\text{Commercial loan} = \frac{\dfrac{84}{(1.12)^1} + \dfrac{84(2)}{(1.12)^2} + \dfrac{784(3)}{(1.12)^3}}{\$700} = .107(1) + .096(2) + .797(3) = 2.69 \text{ years}$$

$$\text{Certificate of deposit} = \frac{\dfrac{21}{(1.07)^1} + \dfrac{21(2)}{(1.07)^2} + \dfrac{321(3)}{(1.07)^3}}{\$300} = .065(1) + .061(2) + .874(3) = 2.81 \text{ yrs.}$$

more than the market value of liabilities if all rates change by comparable amounts. For example, suppose that all interest rates increase by 1 percent immediately after the bank contracts for its assets and liabilities. An adjusted balance sheet at market values appears in Exhibit 9.2. It shows that with the increase in rates, the market value of assets declines by $26, the market value of liabilities decreases by $14 and the market value of equity falls by $12 to $68.

This result reflects the positive duration gap. The new value of each instrument can be obtained using Equation 9.2. The value of assets falls more than the value of liabilities because the weighted duration of assets (2.86 years) exceeds the weighted duration of liabilities (1.58 years) by a substantial amount. The equity to asset ratio declines from 8 percent to 7.1 percent. Expected net interest income similarly decreases because the bank will pay higher rates on liabilities relative to the higher yields it receives on reinvested cash inflows over the combined lifetime of the securities. Clearly, this bank's operating position has worsened with the increase in rates.

A decrease in rates produces the opposite result. Because of the duration mismatch, the market value of assets will increase more than the market value of liabilities so that the market value of equity will increase. Net interest income also rises, and the bank is better off. The general relationship between the sign of a bank's duration gap and the impact of changing rates on MVE is summarized below:

DGAP Summary

DGAP	Change in Interest Rates	Change in Market Value					
		Assets		Liabilities		Equity	
Positive	Increase	Decrease	>	Decrease	→	Decrease	
Positive	Decrease	Increase	>	Increase	→	Increase	
Negative	Increase	Decrease	<	Decrease	→	Increase	
Negative	Decrease	Increase	<	Increase	→	Decrease	
Zero	Increase	Decrease	=	Decrease	→	None	
Zero	Decrease	Increase	=	Increase	→	None	

· EXHIBIT 9.2

MVE Analysis: Hypothetical Bank Balance Sheet after an Immediate 1 Percent Increase in All Interest Rates

Assets	Market Value	Rate	Duration	Liabilities and Equity	Market Value	Rate	Duration
Cash	$100			1-yr. Time deposit	$614	6%	1.00 yr.
3-yr. Commercial loan	683	13%	2.68 yrs.	3-yr. Certificate of deposit	292	8	2.80
6-yr. Treasury bond	191	9	4.97	Total liabilities	$906		1.58 yrs.
Total	$974		2.86 yrs.	Equity (MVE)	$ 68		
					$974		

Duration of assets = .702(2.68) + .196(4.97) = 2.86 yrs.
Duration of liabilities = .68(1) + .32(2.80) = 1.58 yrs.
Expected economic net interest income = $45.81
DGAP = 2.86 − ($906/$974)(1.58) = 1.36
Change in market value of: assets = −$26
liabilities = −$14
equity = −$12

Sample Duration Calculations of Market Value Using Equation 9.2
Commercial loan: $\Delta P = (.01/1.12)(-2.69)(\$700) = -\$16.8$
Certificate of deposit: $\Delta P = (.01/1.07)(-2.81)(\$300) = -\$7.9$

Bank management can use duration measures to evaluate interest rate risk. It is, however, a static measure. The greater the absolute value of DGAP, the greater is interest rate risk. A bank that is perfectly hedged will have a DGAP of zero and thus operate with its average asset duration slightly below its average liability duration.

DGAP measures can be used to approximate the expected change in market value of equity for a given change in interest rates. In particular, Equation 9.9 can be used to estimate the change in market value of equity.[6]

Applying this to the hypothetical bank in Exhibit 9.1, the 1 percent increase in interest rates lowered the market value of equity by approximately 1.27 percent of assets, or $12.70.

$$\Delta MVE = -DGAP[\Delta y/(1 + y)]MVA$$
$$\Delta MVE = -1.42[.01/1.10]\$1,000$$
$$= -.0127[\$1,000]$$
$$= -\$12.70$$

The actual decrease was $12. This bank's assets will change in value by approximately 90 percent more than the value of its liabilities for any interest rate change, as measured by the leverage-adjusted relative average durations, and MVE will vary accordingly.

An Immunized Portfolio

To insulate, or immunize, the market value of equity from rate changes, the hypothetical bank would need to either shorten its asset duration by 1.42 years, increase its liability duration by 1.54 years (.92 × 1.54 = 1.42), or use some combination of these adjustments. For example,

---

[6]As an approximation, it is acceptable to use the average yield on total assets as the market interest rate, y. In the case of the hypothetical bank of Exhibit 9.1, y equals 10 percent [(700/1,000) .12 + (200/1,000) .08 = 0.10].

■ EXHIBIT 9.3

Bank Balance Sheet: DGAP = 0

Assets	Market Value	Rate	Duration	Liabilities and Equity	Market Value	Rate	Duration
Cash	$ 100			1-yr. Time deposit	$ 340	5%	1.00 yr.
3-yr. Commercial loan	700	12%	2.69 yrs.	3-yr.certificate of deposit	300	7	2.81
6-yr. Treasury bond	200	8	4.99	6-yr. zero-coupon CD*	280	8	6.00
			2.88 yrs.	Total liabilities	$ 920		3.11 yrs.
				Equity	$ 80		
Total	$1,000				$1,000		

DGAP = 2.88 − .92(3.11) ≅ 0

1% Increase in All Rates

Cash	$100			1-yr. Time deposits	$ 337	6%	1.00 yr.
3-yr. Commercial loan	683	13%	2.68 yrs.	3-yr. certificate of deposit	292	8	2.80
6-yr. Treasury bond	191	9	4.97	6-yr. certificate of deposit	265	9	6.00
			2.86 yrs.	Total liabilities	$ 894		3.07 yrs.
				Equity	$ 80		
Total	$974				$ 974		

*Par (maturity) value = $444.33

immunization as measured by obtaining a DGAP equal to zero, could be accomplished by reducing time deposits to $340 and issuing $280 in new 6-year zero coupon CDs (Exhibit 9.3). With this profile, DGAP approximately equals zero and any immediate rate change leaves MVE unchanged. This is demonstrated in the bottom part of the exhibit, where all interest rates are assumed to increase by 1 percent. The market value of every price sensitive account declines. Equity value remains constant at $80 because the $26 decrease in market value of assets just equals the $26 decrease in market value of liabilities. There are, of course, many other alternatives to adjust the size of DGAP to zero, but each would produce the desired hedge.

Banks may choose to target variables other than the market value of equity in managing interest rate risk. Many banks, for example, are interested in stabilizing the book value of net interest income. This can be done for a 1-year time horizon, with the appropriate duration gap measure shown below:[7]

$$DGAP^* = MVRSA(1 - DRSA) - MVRSL(1 - DRSL) \qquad (9.10)$$

where

MVRSA = cumulative market value of RSAs,

MVRSL = cumulative market value of RSLs,

DRSA = composite duration of RSAs for the given time horizon; equal to the sum of the products of each asset's duration with the relative share of its total asset market value, and

---

[7]Toevs (1983) introduces this formula and discusses its implications in detail. Alternatives include targeting the market value of net interest income by setting the duration of a bank's equity equal to the length of the time horizon that the bank wishes to use in hedging net interest income. Duration of equity (DUR EQ) can be approximated as follows, where MV refers to market value:

$$DUR\ EQ = \frac{MV\ of\ assets \times duration\ of\ assets - MV\ of\ liabilities \times duration\ of\ liabilities}{market\ value\ of\ equity}$$

DRSL = composite duration of RSLs for the given time horizon; equal to the sum of the products of each liability's duration with the relative share of its total liability market value.

If DGAP* is positive, the bank's net interest income will decrease when interest rates decrease, and increase when rates increase. If DGAP* is negative, the relationship is reversed. Only when DGAP* equals zero is interest rate risk eliminated. The important point is that banks can use duration analysis to stabilize a number of different variables reflecting bank performance.

MARKET VALUE OF EQUITY SENSITIVITY ANALYSIS

Many bank managers use a MVE sensitivity analysis framework like that for earnings sensitivity to better assess interest rate risk. The framework extends the static duration gap analysis by making it dynamic. This can be accomplished by model simulation. As with earnings sensitivity analysis, the procedure consists of conducting "what if" analysis of all the factors that affect MVE across a wide range of interest rate environments. The analysis repeats static DGAP analysis under different assumed interest rates. It is often labeled net present value (NPV) or economic value of equity (EVE) analysis.

The basic output of this analysis is a comparison of changes in MVE across different interest rate environments. It signals how volatile MVE might be compared to some base case or most likely rate scenario. Again, the typical comparison looks at seven rate environments beginning with the base case, and other scenarios that alternatively consider rates 1 percent, 2 percent, and 3 percent higher and lower, respectively. An important component of this sensitivity analysis is the projection of when embedded customer options will be exercised and what their values will be. Management also varies assumptions about rate spreads and shifts or twists in the yield curve. The same embedded options that affect earnings sensitivity, such as loan prepayments, callable and putable bonds, and early deposit withdrawals, sharply influence the estimated volatility in MVE. The greater is the potential volatility in MVE, the greater is risk.

Generally,

1. Prepayments that exceed (fall short of) that expected will shorten (lengthen) duration.
2. A bond being called will shorten duration.
3. A deposit that is withdrawn early will shorten duration. A deposit that is not withdrawn as expected will lengthen duration.

Unanticipated changes in interest rates typically cause durations to vary over time. The effective duration calculation supposedly accounts for some of this variation, and should be used in MVE analysis. Alternatively, an analyst may use an estimated price consistent with call price, expected prepayment impact, etc., for each asset or liability with an embedded opton.

MVE SENSITIVITY ANALYSIS: AN EXAMPLE

Consider ABC bank with the rate sensitivity report introduced in Exhibit 8.7 of Chapter 8. This bank had a portfolio of relatively long-term, fixed-rate mortgages and other loans financed largely by liabilities that were more rate sensitive. Charts 1 and 2 of Exhibit 8.8 summarize the most likely rate environment and six alternative rate environments. Exhibit 9.4 provides a summary of the same balance sheet data in both book value and market value terms. The final two columns of data list the book yield and estimated duration under the most likely rate scenario. Under the most likely scenario, the market value of assets exceeds

• EXHIBIT 9.4

ABC's MARKET VALUE OF STOCKHOLDERS' EQUITY

Market Value/Duration Report as of 12/31/2001
Most Likely Rate Scenario—Base Strategy

	Book Value	Market Value	Book Yield	Duration*	
Loans					
Prime Based Ln	100,000	102,000	9.00%	—	
Equity Credit Lines	25,000	25,500	8.75%	—	
Fixed Rate > 1 yr.	170,000	170,850	7.50%	1.1	
Var Rate Mtg 1 Yr.	55,000	54,725	6.90%	0.5	
30-Year Mortgage	250,000	245,000	7.60%	6.0	
Consumer Ln	100,000	100,500	8.00%	1.9	
Credit Card	25,000	25,000	14.00%	1.0	
Total Loans	725,000	723,575	8.03%	2.6	
Loan Loss Reserve	(15,000)	(11,250)	0.00%	8.0	
Net Loans	710,000	712,325	8.03%	2.5	
Investments					
Eurodollars	80,000	80,000	5.50%	0.1	
CMO Fix Rate	35,000	34,825	6.25%	2.0	
US Treasury	75,000	74,813	5.80%	1.8	
Total Investments	190,000	189,638	5.76%	1.1	
Fed Funds Sold	25,000	25,000	5.25%	—	
Cash & Due From	15,000	15,000	0.00%	6.5	
Non-Int Rel Assets	60,000	60,000	0.00%	8.0	
Total Assets	1,000,000	1,001,963	6.93%	2.6	
Deposits					
MMDA	240,000	232,800	2.25%	—	
Retail CDs	400,000	400,000	5.40%	1.1	
Savings	35,000	33,600	4.00%	1.9	
NOW	40,000	38,800	2.00%	1.9	
DDA Personal	55,000	52,250		8.0	
Comm'l DDA	60,000	58,200		4.8	
Total Deposits	830,000	815,650		1.6	
TT&L	25,000	25,000	5.00%	—	
L-T Notes Fixed	50,000	50,250	8.00%	5.9	
Fed Funds Purch	—	—	5.25%	—	
NIR Liabilities	30,000	28,500		8.0	
Total Liabilities	935,000	919,400		2.0	
Equity	65,000	82,563		9.9	
Total Liab & Equity	1,000,000	1,001,963		2.6	
					Notional
Off-Balance Sheet					
Int Rate Swaps	—	1,250	6.00%	2.8	50,000
Adjusted Equity	65,000	83,813		7.9	

NOTE: Values are in thousands of dollars.

*Duration is reported in years.

■ **EXHIBIT 9.5**

SENSITIVITY OF MARKET VALUE OF EQUITY (MVE) VERSUS MOST
LIKELY (ZERO SHOCK) INTEREST RATE SCENARIO

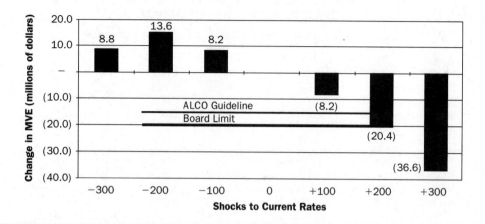

NOTE: *Sensitivity of Market Value of Equity* measures the change in the economic value of the corporation's equity under various changes in interest rates. Rate changes are instantaneous changes from current rates. The change in market value of equity is derived from the difference between changes in the market value of assets and changes in the market value of liabilities.

the book value by $1,963,000 and the market value of equity equals $82,563,000 or $17,563,000 more than book value. Note that the average duration of assets equals 2.6 years while the average duration of liabilities equals two years. For this discussion, ignore how the duration estimates for demand deposit accounts (DDAs) are obtained.[8]

Using these duration estimates and the market values listed, ABC's duration gap is 0.765 years [2.6 − (919,400/1,001,963) 2.0]. In light of the previous DGAP discussion and assuming no change in duration when rates change, a 1 percent increase in rates would be expected to reduce ABC's market value of equity by approximately $7.2 million (0.765)(0.01/1.0693) (1,001,963,000).

This estimate ignores the impact of interest rates on embedded options and the effective duration of assets and liabilities. It also ignores the impact of swaps that are noted at the bottom of the exhibit.[9] MVE sensitivity analysis incorporates these influences. Exhibit 9.5 presents a summary of the changes in MVE for six interest rate environments compared with the most likely (zero shock) rate scenario. Three of the scenarios are for higher rates (+100, +200, and +300 basis points) and three are for lower rates (−100, −200, and −300 basis points). The vertical axis lists the estimated change in MVE from the most likely case for each scenario. In contrast with earnings sensitivity analysis, which projected earnings one year forward and two years forward, there is only one comparative exhibit because duration analysis incorporates the present value of all cash flows.

Note that higher rates are associated with a decline in MVE while lower rates are associated with an increase in MVE. This is consistent with ABC having a positive duration gap in all rate environments. It is also expected given ABC's huge portfolio of long-term, fixed-rate mortgages. If rates rise unexpectedly, market values will drop substantially. If rates fall sharply, prepayments will temper the potential gains in market value because borrowers will

---

[8]Remember that demand deposits do not pay interest. A crucial part of duration analysis involves determining the effective duration of these liabilities, which typically comprise a substantial portion of most banks' liabilities.

[9]The nature and influence of interest rate swaps are described in Chapter 10.

refinance such that the bank will replace high-rate loans with lower rate ones. Thus, the benefit of selling the prepayment option to borrowers effectively places a cap on potential portfolio gains. According to Exhibit 9.5, ABC's MVE will change by $8.2 million either up or down if rates are 1 percent lower or higher than the base case. By definition, duration measures the percentage change in market value for a given change in interest rates, hence a bank's *duration of equity* measures the *percent* change in MVE that will occur with a 1 percent change in rates. Thus, ABC's duration of equity is 9.9 ($8,200/$82,563).

MVE sensitivity analysis clearly provides a different type of information to ABC's management. In contrast to the earnings sensitivity results, the bank is exposed to substantive losses in market value of equity if rates increase sharply above that expected. This is further evidenced by the fact that ABC will see its MVE decline more than the ALCO guideline if rates increase 2 percent or more from the base case. The MVE decline will exceed the limit set by the bank's Board of Directors in a +3 percent rate environment. ABC's management must address these violations of policy.

EARNINGS SENSITIVITY ANALYSIS VERSUS MVE SENSITIVITY ANALYSIS: WHICH MODEL IS BETTER?

Bankers use both static GAP and duration gap models as well as earnings sensitivity and MVE sensitivity analysis when assessing interest rate risk. Each has slightly different objectives and implications. GAP and earnings sensitivity analysis focus on the potential volatility of net interest income over distinct time intervals. Net interest income is calculated in book value terms, not market values. A bank manages the effects of volatile interest rates within each time period separately. In contrast, the duration and MVE sensitivity approach focuses on the potential variability of a bank's market value of equity. Duration gap is a single measure that summarizes the cumulative impact of interest rate changes on a bank's total portfolio. Thus, the bank continuously manages total firm rate risk according to this one number. Because the models have different objectives, they address different issues.

STRENGTHS AND WEAKNESSES: DGAP AND MVE SENSITIVITY ANALYSIS

The principal attraction of duration analysis is that it provides a comprehensive measure of interest rate risk for the total portfolio. The smaller the absolute value of DGAP, the less sensitive the market value of equity is to interest rate changes. Unlike GAP, DGAP recognizes the time value of each cash flow, avoiding the difficulty with time buckets. Cash flows that arise after one year are included in duration calculations, but often ignored in GAP calculations. Duration measures are also additive so the bank can match total assets with total liabilities rather than match individual accounts. Finally, duration analysis takes a longer-term viewpoint and provides managers with greater flexibility in adjusting rate sensitivity because they can use a wide range of instruments to balance value sensitivity.

Duration and MVE sensitivity analysis have weaknesses as well. First, it is difficult to compute duration accurately. Duration measurement requires numerous subjective assumptions. Data needs are complex, requiring information on each account's interest rate, repricing schedule, possibility of principal prepayment, call and put options, early withdrawal potential, and default probability. A bank must routinely assess the probability that contracted cash flows will be received on a timely basis, forecast the timing of base rate changes and the level of rates at the time of future cash flows, and constantly monitor whether actual cash flows conform to expectations. To be meaningful, DGAP and sensitivity analysis further require accurate forecasts of when embedded options will be exercised and what their value is. Of course, this is the same information necessary to conduct earnings sensitivity analysis.

Second, to be correct duration analysis requires that each future cash flow be discounted by a distinct discount rate reflecting the expected future rate at the time the cash flow arises. Most analysts use forward rates from the Treasury spot yield curve for this purpose. To eliminate coupon bias, they first estimate a zero coupon–equivalent yield curve, then compute forward rates. It is well known, however, that these forward rates do not accurately predict future interest rates. The complexity of calculating duration then, increases further when nonparallel shifts in the yield curve are considered.

Third, a bank must continuously monitor and adjust the duration of its portfolio. As Macaulay's duration measure indicates, duration changes with changes in interest rates. Thus, a bank should recalculate duration and MVE sensitivity and potentially restructure its balance sheet whenever rates change substantially, which could be daily or weekly. As discussed in Chapter 6, the duration calculation is only accurate for small changes in interest rates. Furthermore, even when rates are constant, duration changes with the passage of time as the time factor decreases over time. The duration of assets and liabilities may "drift" at different rates and require constant rebalancing. These problems are compounded by difficulties in estimating price effects and effective durations when there are embedded options.

Finally, it is difficult to estimate the duration on assets and liabilities that do not earn or pay interest. To get an accurate assessment of cash flows and market value changes, a bank must estimate the true rate sensitivity of demand deposits and estimate their duration. There is little agreement as to how this should be done. As noted in Exhibit 9.4, the management of ABC estimated the duration of personal DDAs at 8 years and the duration of commercial DDAs at 4.8 years. The difference presumably reflects the greater propensity of businesses to move DDAs in rising rate environments. Still, what are the estimated cash flows when DDAs have no stated fixed maturity or periodic cash payments? Many models attempt to estimate a core amount of DDAs that remain on deposit and classify these funds as having a long duration. Other, noncore DDAs are more volatile and have a shorter duration. The key point is that these are imprecise estimates. Given the size of most banks' DDA balances, any misestimate, in turn, can produce wide swings in a bank's DGAP value and wide variations in MVE sensitivity.

In summary, duration measures are highly subjective. Active management requires constant tinkering with the bank portfolio to adjust the duration gap. For many firms with simple balance sheets without significant amounts of customer options that are commonly exercised, the costs may exceed the benefits.

A CRITIQUE OF STRATEGIES TO MANAGE EARNINGS AND MARKET VALUE OF EQUITY SENSITIVITY

The business of banking involves taking risks. Most bankers feel comfortable making loans to individuals and businesses because they spend a considerable amount of time nurturing customer relationships and measuring and monitoring credit risk. In general, bankers are less comfortable taking interest rate risk. This may reflect a lack of familiarity with the relationship between risk and return or a belief that the returns have not historically warranted the risks taken. Because most banks depend on net interest margin to generate earnings growth, it is imperative that managers develop strategies to maintain or grow their net interest income over time and to maintain and grow the market value of stockholders' equity. The following discussion emphasizes the type of risks assumed in managing GAP, DGAP, and the sensitivity of net interest income and MVE to changes in interest rates. The important implication can be summarized as "know your bets."

GAP AND DGAP MANAGEMENT STRATEGIES: WHAT ARE YOUR BETS?

Chapter 8 introduced a variety of objectives and strategic approaches to manage a bank's GAP and earnings sensitivity. The discussion was incomplete because it did not address how to implement the approaches to changing asset and liability sensitivity and did not identify their risk and return trade-offs. Generally, it is widely accepted that banks do and should assume some interest rate risk. The issue is to determine how much risk is acceptable and how to best achieve the desired risk profile.

Unfortunately, it is difficult to actively vary GAP or DGAP and consistently win. First, interest rate forecasts are frequently wrong. To change an asset or liability's rate or price sensitivity accurately and increase earnings and MVE, management must predict future interest rates better than consensus market forecasts embedded in current rates and act accordingly. Second, even when rate changes are predicted correctly, banks have limited flexibility in varying GAP and DGAP and must often sacrifice yield to do so. Loan customers and depositors select terms from a range of alternatives provided by the bank such that banks have only partial control over pricing and maturities. To entice a customer to select the bank's preferred alternative, management must often offer favorable yields or prices as an inducement. This has a cost because profits are below what they otherwise would be without the inducement.

These difficulties can be demonstrated by an example. Suppose a bank is liability sensitive and operates with a negative GAP through one year and a positive DGAP. Management believes that interest rates will rise and decides to hedge by taking steps that move the GAP closer to zero through one year. At this time, the yield curve is upsloping because the consensus forecast is that interest rates will increase over time. Active GAP management strategies typically focus on increasing RSAs and lowering RSLs. If a stable MVE was desired, DGAP strategies would emphasize shortening average asset durations and lengthening average liability durations.

Consider the effect of the following strategies: the bank (1) shortens the maturities of its bond portfolio, and (2) reprices its CDs to attract long-term deposits relative to short-term deposits. With an upsloping yield curve, long-term interest rates exceed short-term interest rates. The bank will accept a lower yield initially when it buys short-term securities, and can only attract long-term deposits by paying a premium rate over short-term deposit rates. The first strategy lowers interest income near-term while the second increases interest expense. Both tend to reduce a bank's initial net interest margin, which is a cost of hedging. More importantly, management should know the explicit bets that it has made regarding future interest rates by implementing these strategies. Specifically, the bank gains in the sense that its net interest income and MVE rise only when interest rates move and remain above current forward rates. The investment in short-term rather than long-term securities is advantageous only if interest rates rise above forward rates; that is, only if rates increase above the "breakeven" yield contained in the yield curve. Long-term deposits are better than short-term deposits only in the same instance when market rates ultimately rise above forward rates. The bank loses if rates remain below forward rates because it would earn less interest income on the short-term securities versus long-term securities and could have borrowed at lower cost by issuing a series of short-term deposits rather than a long-term deposit. By adjusting GAP or DGAP management is speculating that its interest rate forecast is better than the consensus.

AN EXAMPLE

Consider the case where a liability sensitive bank loses when rates rise and management decides to reduce risk by marketing 2-year time deposits paying 6 percent to retail customers rather than 1-year time deposits paying 5.5 percent. As described in Chapter 7, these two spot rates embody a 1-year forward rate, one year from the present. The following time line and analysis indicate that this forward rate equals 6.5 percent ignoring compounding and assuming annual interest payments. This represents the deposit holder's break-even rate when comparing the two alternatives.

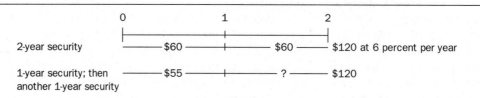

Cash flows from investing $1,000 either in a 2-year security yielding 6 percent or two consecutive 1-year securities, with the current 1-year yield equal to 5.5 percent.

Of course, it is not known today what a 1-year security will yield in one year. For the two consecutive 1-year securities to generate the same $120 in interest, ignoring compounding, the 1-year security must yield 6.5 percent one year from the present. This break-even rate is a 1-year forward rate, one year from the present.

$$6\% + 6\% = 5.5\% + ? \text{ with } ? = 6.5 \text{ percent}$$

The depositor is effectively speculating on future interest rates unless he or she has another position that this transaction offsets. Ignoring that, a depositor who acquires a 1-year time deposit today rather than the 2-year deposit is positioned to benefit relatively if a 1-year rate exceeds 6.5 percent one year from today. The depositor will lose (give up potential income) if the 1-year rate is anything less than 6.5 percent. In contrast, a depositor who buys the 2-year time deposit will benefit (lose) if the 1-year rate, one year from the present is anything below (above) 6.5 percent. By choosing one or the other, the depositor has "placed a bet" that the actual rate in one year will differ from the forward rate of 6.5 percent.

Importantly, a bank that markets the 2-year deposit has placed a similar bet. Specifically, the bank will benefit (as a borrower) by lowering its borrowing cost only if the 1-year rate exceeds 6.5 percent in one year. If this occurs, the bank will have locked in a customer with a below-market rate (6 percent versus an average of more than 6 percent). Of course, the depositor will lose, which may create a different set of problems. The implication is that even though management tries to reduce risk by reducing the bank's liability sensitivity, it could see its interest expense rise and NIM fall because of the bet against the forward rate.

The second cost follows in similar fashion. Suppose, for example, that a retail bank desires to increase RSAs because it expects interest rates to increase. While the bank plans to make only variable-rate or floating-rate loans, its customers seek fixed-rate loans because they also expect rates to rise. The bank must offer a substantial inducement, such as a significantly lower interest rate, to increase asset sensitivity and position itself for earnings growth in a rising rate environment. This would lower the interest spread and offset part of the benefit from increasing the GAP. If the bank refused to make fixed-rate loans, it would not be competitive and might lose considerable goodwill. When adjusting asset and liability maturities and durations and making pricing decisions, a bank may have to make yield concessions or assume additional interest rate risk. Active strategies to adjust earnings or MVE in light of rate forecasts may be highly speculative.

YIELD CURVE STRATEGIES

Many portfolio managers are aware of general macroeconomic and business cycle impacts on the U.S. Treasury yield curve and try to take advantage of long-term trends in rates. Exhibit 9.6 characterizes movements in the level of rates over time and shifts in the shape of the yield

· EXHIBIT 9.6

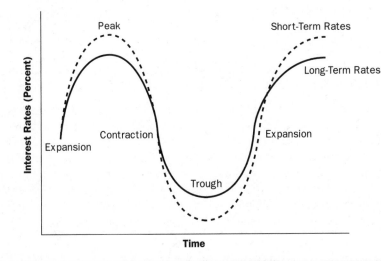

The inverted yield curve has predicted the last five recessions

DATE WHEN 1-YEAR RATE FIRST EXCEEDS 10-YEAR RATE	LENGTH OF TIME UNTIL START OF NEXT RECESSION
Apr. '68	20 months (Dec. '69)
Mar. '73	8 months (Nov. '73)
Sept. '78	16 months (Jan. '80)
Sept. '80	10 months (July '81)
Feb. '89	17 months (July '90)
Dec. '00	15 months (March '01)

Expansion: Increasing consumer spending, inventory accumulation, rising loan demand, Federal Reserve begins to slow money growth.
Peak: Monetary restraint, high loan demand, little liquidity.
Contraction: Falling consumer spending, inventory contraction, falling loan demand, Federal Reserve accelerates money growth.
Trough: Monetary ease, limited loan demand, excess liquidity.
SOURCE: Federal Reserve.

curve. Typically, analysts view business cycle effects in terms of how the 10-year (long-term) Treasury yield varies relative to the 1-year (short-term) Treasury yield.[10] Starting at the left of the diagram, the yield curve is inverted (1-year rate above the 10-year rate) during the latter stages of an expansionary period and during the peak. Both of these are characterized by strong consumer spending, strong and growing loan demand, and limited liquidity at banks because the Federal Reserve has slowed money growth out of fear that inflation expectations will get out of control. The peak is followed by a contractionary period as consumer and business spending decline along with loan demand. At some point, the Federal Reserve gets concerned that growth has slowed too much and starts to increase money growth. At the trough or recession, the Fed is providing ample liquidity to banks, but loan demand is low due to high unemployment and slow spending. Eventually, low interest rates stimulate retail spending and business investment and the economy starts to grow again.

Many analysts believe that this pattern repeats itself over time. If so, it has interesting implications for interest rate risk management. For example, when the U.S. economy hits its peak the yield curve inverts. After the yield curve inversion, the economy falls into recession. Note the data at the bottom right corner of the exhibit. This documents the last five times that the 1-year Treasury rate has exceeded the 10-year Treasury rate and the length of time until the U.S. economy was in recession. In every instance a recession followed the yield curve inversion. Since World War II, only twice has the yield curve inverted and a recession not followed. This occurred in 1965 during the Vietnam War and in 1999 when the U.S. Treasury instituted a program to buy back outstanding long-term Treasury bonds. The average lag

---

[10]In February 2001 the Treasury stopped issuing 1-year T-bills, so the comparison will involve a different short-term rate, perhaps the 6-month T-bill rate.

since 1968 is just over 14 months. The implication is that when the yield curve inverts, a recession will follow in a fairly short period of time.

Portfolio managers who want to take advantage of this trend will do the following when the yield curve inverts:

1. Buy long-term non-callable securities
2. Make fixed-rate noncallable loans
3. Price deposits on a floating rate basis
4. Follow strategies to become more liability sensitive and/or lengthen the duration of assets versus the duration of liabilities

Note that during the deepest part of the recession, the yield curve is typically at its steepest. Portfolio managers often attempt to do the opposite of that above to best position the bank. Of course, this analysis is very simplistic. Interest rates do not follow the straightforward pattern of Exhibit 9.6. Interest rates alternatively rise and fall even within general rate moves upward and downward. Managers, in turn, have internal pressures to meet loan demand at the peak, after which asset quality will deteriorate, and find higher yields at the trough, which can largely be attained by taking added credit risk or interest rate risk (buying long-term, fixed-rate assets). Still, managers should be aware of these general trends and the impact on forward rates.

SUMMARY

A bank's ALCO is responsible for monitoring the bank's risk and return profile. Traditional asset and liability management focuses on measuring interest rate risk and monitoring performance, setting policies to stabilize or increase net interest income. This chapter introduces an alternative duration gap model and market value of equity sensitivity analysis to analyze interest rate risk. Duration gap analysis considers a bank's entire balance sheet and calculates measures of the weighted average durations of all assets and all liabilities. The difference in these weighted durations adjusted for financial leverage is labeled duration gap, which provides a measure of how the market value of stockholders' equity will change when interest rates change. With duration gap analysis the target measure of performance is typically the market value of bank equity. Risk is measured by the sign and size of duration gap and the potential variation in market value of equity. A bank's ALCO again conducts sensitivity analysis across different assumed interest rate environments to assess this potential variation in market value of stockholders' equity. Greater risk is evidenced by greater potential variation.

Duration measures have their limitations including the fact that the effective price sensitivity and duration of individual assets and liabilities change with changes in interest rates. It is also difficult to accurately forecast rate changes and the price impact on customer options embedded in bank assets and liabilities. Still, duration-based sensitivity analysis represents a useful alternative to GAP and earnings sensitivity analysis because it focuses on the present value of all cash flows over the entire range of maturities.

The chapter also examines the specific assumptions managers make when they try to actively manage a bank's interest rate risk exposure. By pursuing strategies to change asset or liability rate sensitivities or durations in line with rate forecasts, managers are explicitly speculating that forward rates implied by current interest rates will not be realized in the future. Whether the bank gains or loses is determined by whether actual rates vary favorably relative to forward rates.

QUESTIONS

1. List the basic steps in duration gap analysis. What is the importance of different interest rate forecasts?

2. Which has a longer Macaulay's duration: a zero coupon bond with a 2-year maturity, or a 2-year maturity coupon bond that pays 6 percent coupon interest if they both carry a 6 percent market yield? Explain your reasoning.

3. You own a corporate bond that carries a 5.8 percent coupon rate and pays $10,000 at maturity in exactly two years. The current market yield on the bond is 6.1 percent. Coupon interest is paid semiannually and the market price is $9,944.32.
   a. Calculate the bond's Macaulay's duration and modified duration.
   b. If the market rate falls by 1 percent, what is the estimated impact on the bond's price?

4. Assume that you own a $1 million par value corporate bond that pays 7 percent in coupon interest (3.5 percent semiannually), has four years remaining to maturity, and is immediately callable at par. Its current market yield is 7 percent and it is priced at par. If rates on comparable securities fall by more than 40 basis points (0.20 percent semiannually), the bond will be called.
   a. Calculate the bond's price if the market rate increases by 50 basis points (0.25 percent semiannually) using the present value formula from Chapter 6.
   b. Calculate the bond's effective duration assuming a 50 basis point increase or decrease in market rates.

5. A 5-year zero coupon bond and 15-year zero coupon bond both carry a price of $7,500 and a market rate of 8 percent. Assuming that the market rates on both bonds fall to 7 percent, calculate the percentage change in each bond's price using equation 9.2.

6. Use duration gap analysis to determine if there is interest rate risk in the following transaction. A bank obtains $25,000 in funds from a customer who makes a deposit with a 5-year maturity that pays 5 percent annual interest compounded daily. All interest and principal are paid at the end of five years. Simultaneously, the bank makes a $25,000 loan to an individual to buy a car. The loan is at a fixed rate of 12 percent annual interest but is fully amortized with 60 monthly payments, such that the borrower pays the same dollar amount (principal plus interest) each month.

7. Compare the strengths and weaknesses of GAP and earnings sensitivity analysis with DGAP and MVE sensitivity analysis.

8. Is the following statement generally true or false? Provide your reasoning.
   "A bank with a negative GAP through three years will have a positive duration gap."

9. Conduct duration gap analysis using the following information:

Assets	Amount	Rate	Macaulay's Duration
Cash	$23,000	0%	0
Bonds	$102,000	7.2%	1.8 years
Commercial loans	$375,000	11.0%	1.5 years
Liabilities & Equity			
Small time deposits	$130,000	3.6%	4.0 years
Large CDs	$70,000	6.3%	1.0 year
Transactions accounts	$250,000	2.8%	3.3 years
Equity	$50,000		

a. Calculate the bank's duration gap if the ALCO targets the market value of stockholders' equity. Is this bank positioned to gain or lose if interest rates rise?

b. Estimate the change in market value of equity if all market interest rates fall by an average of 1.5 percent. Compare the results by applying Equation 9.2 to each balance sheet item and adding versus using Equation 9.10.

c. Provide a specific transaction that the bank could implement to immunize its interest rate risk. The transaction may be a new asset funded by a new liability or an asset sale and the simultaneous purchase of another asset.

10. Suppose that your bank currently operates with a duration gap of 2.2 years. Which of the following will serve to reduce the bank's interest rate risk?

a. Issue a 1-year zero coupon CD to a customer and use the proceeds to buy a 3-year zero coupon Treasury bond.

b. Sell $5 million in 1-year bullet (single payment) loans and buy 3-month Treasury bills.

c. Obtain 2-year funding from the Federal Home Loan Bank and lend the proceeds overnight in the federal funds market.

11. ALCO members are considering the following MVE sensitivity estimates. The figures refer to the percentage change in market value of equity compared to the base rate forecast scenario. What does the information say about the bank's overall interest rate risk?

Rate Change from Base Case

	−3%	−2%	−1%	+1%	+2%	+3%
% change in MVE	+38%	+47%	+19%	−5%	−14%	−18%

12. Discuss what impact each of the following will have, in general, on MVE sensitivity to a change in interest rates. Consider two cases where rates rise sharply and fall sharply.

a. Bank owns a high percentage of assets in bonds that are callable anytime after three months.

b. Bank pays below market rates on time deposits and market interest rates move sharply higher.

c. A large percentage of the bank's assets are in 30-year fixed-rate mortgages.

PROBLEM

Review the most recent annual reports of the largest banks throughout the world. Collect information on their summary analysis of interest rate risk. Interpret whatever data are provided for earnings-at-risk and market value of equity at risk. Note that in some instances MVE sensitivity is labeled as value-at-risk for the bank's equity.

10

FINANCIAL FUTURES, FORWARD RATE AGREEMENTS, AND INTEREST RATE SWAPS

One of the most important trends in finance over the past 25 years is the growth in derivatives and their increased use by financial institutions. Market participants can use these contracts to hedge other positions that expose them to risk or speculate on anticipated price moves. In many cases, banks can replicate on-balance sheet transactions entirely with off-balance sheet contracts so they can serve as substitute positions.

The term 'derivative' in financial markets refers to any instrument or contract that derives its value from another underlying asset, instrument, or contract. The fastest growing derivatives are interest rate swaps, caps, floors, financial futures, and options on financial futures. On several recent occasions derivatives have been in the spotlight because of their assumed role when global stock markets fell sharply in 1987 and 1989 and when Enron and other firms reported substantive losses in 2001 from derivatives positions. In these instances, regulators, politicians, and the media expressed concern over their use and growth. When used prudently, however, derivatives represent a cost-effective means to manage risk.

This chapter explains the features of financial futures, forward rate agreements (FRAs), and basic interest rate swaps and how they are used by financial institutions. It describes several applications, which show each tool's strengths and weaknesses. The applications focus on Eurodollar futures and LIBOR-based FRAs and swaps because they are the fastest growing contracts used by financial institutions. The concepts, however, apply to all related contracts. Chapter 11 extends the analysis to interest rate caps, floors, collars, and options on financial futures and introduces interest rate swaps with options along with swaptions.

———————————————■———————————————

Banking professionals constantly search for new products and opportunities to improve bank operating performance. Financial futures, forward rate agreements, and interest rate swaps are three types of derivatives that commercial banks actively use to help manage interest rate risk. Most users either hedge asset yields or the interest cost of liabilities, adjust maturities by creating synthetic liabilities, protect the value of assets from changing rates, and adjust the overall sensitivity of earnings or market value of stockholders' equity.

Interest rate deregulation and the growth in deposit products that pay market interest rates have increased financial institutions' awareness of interest rate risk. When interest rates change unexpectedly, these firms may find that their net interest income and market value of equity decline, threatening growth opportunities and financial soundness. Chapters 8 and 9 introduced GAP and earnings sensitivity analysis and duration gap and market value of equity (MVE) sensitivity analysis as measures of interest rate risk. This chapter extends the earlier discussion by describing three general tools that banks can use to manage interest rate risk. The first, financial futures contracts, have been available since 1975 but have only recently gained acceptability for their own use among banks. The second, forward rate agreements (FRAs), were introduced in 1983 to provide an explicit forward market for interest rates. The third, interest rate swaps, were introduced in 1980 and are now used actively by large and small banking organizations. Volume has increased to such levels that bank regulators are concerned that industry usage has grown beyond regulators' ability to understand and monitor the risks banks assume. Each tool can be used to complement existing strategies involving matching or consciously mismatching rate-sensitive assets and liabilities and corresponding durations, thereby altering the sensitivity of earnings and MVE. The responsibility of bank managers is to manage, not totally eliminate, risk. Entering into futures, FRAs or swap contracts that reduce risk also eliminates potential extraordinary returns from risk-taking.

CHARACTERISTICS OF FINANCIAL FUTURES

Financial futures contracts represent a commitment between two parties—a buyer and a seller—on the price and quantity of a standardized financial asset or index. The contracts are transferable because they are traded on organized exchanges called **futures markets,** and all contracts are subject to a daily settlement procedure. Buyers of futures contracts, referred to as *long* futures, agree to pay the underlying futures price, while sellers of futures contracts, referred to as *short* futures, agree to receive the futures price or deliver the underlying asset as stipulated in the contract. Thus, buyers and sellers can eliminate their commitments by taking the opposite position prior to contract expiration by selling and buying the futures contract, or by making or taking delivery of the underlying asset.

Because futures prices fluctuate daily, buyers and sellers find that their initial position changes in value daily. When futures prices increase, buyers gain at the expense of sellers, while sellers gain at the expense of buyers when futures prices fall. At the end of each day participants must pay any decrease in value or, alternatively, they receive any increase in value as part of the daily settlement procedure. When the contract expires, they pay or receive the final change in value (cash settlement) or exchange the actual underlying asset (physical delivery) for cash at the initial negotiated price. The process essentially fixes the underlying instrument's price at the time of the trade for the future date designated by the contract. The underlying financial asset may be a short-term money market instrument, a long-term bond, units of a foreign currency, precious metals, or even common stock indexes. When the underlying asset is an interest-bearing security, the contracts are labeled **interest rate futures.** Futures contracts are traded daily prior to the formal expiration/delivery date, with the price changing as market conditions dictate. These unique features stand out when compared with cash market transactions and forward contracts.

Cash or **spot** market transactions represent the exchange of any asset between two parties who agree on the asset's characteristics and price, where the buyer tenders payment and takes possession of the asset when the price is set. Most transactions take this form. A

forward contract involves two parties agreeing on an asset's characteristics, quantity, and price but defers the actual exchange until a specified future date. Forward contracts do not necessarily involve standardized assets. Both parties to the transaction must simply agree on the asset's quality and price. Because the underlying asset is not standardized, the parties deal directly with each other and there is little opportunity to walk away from the commitment prior to delivery. Finally, once the terms of a forward contract are set, the parties do not make any payments or deliveries until the specified forward transactions date. However, forward contracts often do require collateral or a letter of credit to guarantee performance.

TYPES OF FUTURES TRADERS

Futures contracts are traded on exchanges, the most prominent of which in the United States are the Chicago Board of Trade (CBT) and the Chicago Mercantile Exchange (CME). Many of the contracts traded on U.S. exchanges are also traded outside the United States such that participants have the opportunity to trade 24 hours a day. This is important, given that many trades are implemented to reduce risk and participants need immediate access to hedge instruments.

Futures traders have many different motivations and thus follow different strategies. Traders operating on the floor of an exchange are classified as either **commission brokers,** who execute trades for other parties, or **locals,** who trade for their own account. As the name suggests, commission brokers generate income by charging commissions for each trade and thus take no price risk. Locals are individuals who try to profit by buying contracts at prices less than what they sell the contracts for. As such, locals assume considerable price risk in their transactions but add liquidity to the markets.

Traders are further classified by the strategies they pursue. At one extreme is the **speculator** who takes a position with the objective of making a profit. Speculators try to guess the direction that prices will move and time their trades to sell at higher prices than the purchase price. Locals are thus speculators. Speculators are often distinguished by the time they hold their positions. A **scalper** tries to time price movements over very short time intervals and takes positions that remain outstanding for just minutes. A **day trader** similarly tries to profit from short-term price movements during trading hours in any day, but offsets the initial position before market closing so that no position remains outstanding overnight. Finally, a **position trader** is a speculator who holds a position for a longer period in anticipation of a more significant, longer-term market move.

At the other extreme is the hedger. A **hedger** has an existing or anticipated position in the cash market and trades futures contracts (or some other contract) to reduce the risk associated with uncertain changes in value of the cash position. The cash position might involve owning or buying an asset, borrowing by issuing an interest-bearing liability, or a bank's overall earnings and MVE sensitivity profile. With hedging, the trader takes a position in the futures market whose value varies in the opposite direction as the value of the cash market position. Risk is reduced because gains or losses on the futures position at least partially offset gains or losses on the cash position. The essential difference between a speculator and hedger is the objective of the trader. A speculator wants to profit on trades while a hedger wants to reduce risk.

Traders may also be classified as **spreaders** or **arbitrageurs**. Both spreaders and arbitrageurs are speculators who take relatively low risk positions. For example, a **futures spreader** may simultaneously buy a futures contract and sell a related futures contract trying to profit on anticipated movements in the price difference between the contracts. The position is generally low risk because the prices of both contracts typically move in the same direction. Losses on one contract are thus at least partially offset by gains on the other. An **arbitrageur** tries to profit by identifying the same asset that is being traded at two different prices in different markets at the same time. The arbitrageur buys the asset at the lower price and simultaneously sells it at the higher price, profiting on the difference. Arbitrage transactions are thus low risk and serve to bring prices back in line in the sense that the same asset should trade at the same price in all markets.

THE MECHANICS OF FUTURES TRADING

Futures contracts are traded on formal, organized exchanges that serve as clearinghouses. Trading occurs in an *open outcry* auction market. Each party to a futures transaction effectively trades with exchange members who, in turn, guarantee the performance of all participants. In practice, a buyer and seller are found for each transaction, but the exchange assumes all obligations at the end of each trading day, forcing members to settle their net positions. This procedure enables any trader to offset an initial position by taking the opposite position any time prior to the futures contract's delivery date. For example, a buyer of a Treasury-bill futures contract with delivery in 60 days can offset the position by selling the same contract one week later when 53 days remain to delivery. This liquidity is not found with forward contracts. It results from trading standardized assets through an exchange where each party does not have to renegotiate with the same party who initiated the contract.

Futures contracts entail cash flow obligations for buyers and sellers during the entire time the position is outstanding. At initiation of a futures position, traders must post a cash deposit or U.S. government securities as **initial margin** with the exchange member simply for initiating a transaction. In most cases, the amount is small, involving less than 5 percent of the underlying asset's value. Initial margin represents a good faith deposit that serves to cover losses if prices move against the trader. Exchange members also require traders to meet **maintenance margin** requirements that specify the minimum deposit allowable at the end of each day. Unlike margin accounts for stocks, futures margin deposits represent a form of performance bond by which a trader guarantees that mandatory payment obligations will be met. When the margin deposit falls below this minimum, the customer must deposit more funds or the exchange member can close out the account.

As futures prices vary prior to expiration of the contract, each trader must either increase the cash deposit or can withdraw any excess deposit, depending on whether prices move unfavorably or favorably. For example, a trader who buys a futures contract agrees to pay the negotiated price at delivery.[1] If the futures price increases in the interim, the market value of the initial position also rises and the buyer can withdraw this increase in contract value. If, instead, the futures price falls, the value of the initial position declines and the buyer must cover this decrease in value. Formally, exchange members identify the change in value of each trader's account at the end of every day, then credit the margin accounts of those with gains and debit the margin accounts of those with losses. The market labels this daily settlement process **marking-to-market** and the daily change in value as **variation margin.**

Every futures contract has a formal expiration date. At expiration, trading stops and participants settle their final positions. Contracts may provide for either physical delivery of the underlying asset or cash settlement. With physical delivery, the buyer of futures will make cash payment to a seller, while the seller supplies the physical asset. Because financial futures contracts involve securities, delivery is handled via the wire transfer of funds and securities. With cash settlement, there is no physical delivery as participants simply exchange the final

---

[1]Futures contracts with cash settlement at delivery differ from contracts with physical delivery in that traders settle their positions by paying or receiving the change in value of the contract between the trade date and expiration date.

change in position value after the last trading day. Less than 1 percent of financial futures contracts require physical delivery at expiration because most participants offset their futures positions in advance.

AN EXAMPLE: 90-DAY EURODOLLAR TIME DEPOSIT FUTURES

One of the fastest-growing interest rate futures contracts is the 90-day Eurodollar time deposit future. Its popularity is due to the breadth of participants who use Eurodollars, the allowance for cash settlement at delivery, and the growth of interest rate swap and option contracts based on the London Interbank Offer Rate (LIBOR). Chapter 3 briefly introduced cash market Eurodollars as comparable to jumbo CDs in the domestic market. Chapter 12 describes cash market Eurodollar time deposits in detail. Later examples with futures and options on futures build on this discussion.

Eurodollar futures contracts are traded on the International Monetary Market (IMM), a division of the Chicago Mercantile Exchange.[2] The underlying asset is a Eurodollar time deposit with a 3-month maturity. Conceptually, Eurodollars are U.S. dollar-denominated deposits in banks located outside the United States. The holder cannot write checks against the account but earns interest at a rate slightly above that on domestic CDs issued by the largest U.S. banks. Eurodollar rates are quoted on an interest-bearing basis assuming a 360-day year. Each Eurodollar futures contract represents $1 million of initial face value of Eurodollar deposits maturing 3 months after contract expiration. More than 40 separate contracts are traded at any point in time as contracts expire in March, June, September, and December, more than 10 years out from the current date.[3] Settlement or delivery is in the form of cash, with the price established from a survey of current Eurodollar rates.

Eurodollar futures contracts trade according to an index that equals 100 percent minus the futures interest rate expressed in percentage terms. An index of 91.50, for example, indicates a futures rate of 8.5 percent. Each basis point change in the futures rate equals a $25 change in value of the contract ($0.0001 \times \$1$ million $\times 90/360$). If futures rates increase, the value of the contract decreases and vice versa.

Buyers of Eurodollar futures are classified as "long" because they own a commitment regarding the final price that can be realized at expiration. Sellers are said to be "short" because they may ultimately be forced to come up with cash they may not currently have. With cash settlement, buyers and sellers of Eurodollar futures have simply agreed on the price at expiration. What the buyer owns is a commitment from the seller to pay cash if the price of the underlying asset rises in the interim. The seller owns a commitment from the buyer to pay cash if the asset price falls. Buyers make a futures profit when futures rates fall (prices rise), while sellers gain when futures rates rise (prices fall). Conceptually, profits arise because buyers can offset their initial position by selling the same futures contract after prices have increased. Sellers can similarly profit if they can buy the futures back at a lower price after rates rise. As indicated earlier with daily settlement, the Eurodollar futures contract changes in value daily when prices change, and participants can withdraw profits from their margin accounts prior to expiration.

Exhibit 10.1 indicates how *The Wall Street Journal* reports price quotes for these 3-month Eurodollar futures contracts, 3-month T-bill futures contracts, 1-month LIBOR contracts, and the Treasury yield curve for the close of business on April 2, 2002. Examine the 3-month

---

[2] Equivalent Eurodollar futures contracts are traded on the Singapore International Monetary Exchange.

[3] During the upcoming year, contracts are added for intervening months. Subsequent exhibits do not reveal price quotes for all Eurodollar futures contracts. The last day of trading (expiration day) is the second London business day prior to the third Wednesday in each delivery month.

▪ EXHIBIT 10.1

DATA FOR 3-MONTH EURODOLLAR AND T-BILL FUTURES, 1-MONTH LIBOR FUTURES, AND THE TREASURY YIELD CURVE ON APRIL 2, 2002

	OPEN	HIGH	LOW	SETTLE	CHANGE		YIELD	CHANGE	OPEN INT.
Treasury Bills (CME)-$1 mil.; pts of 100%									
June	97.81	97.84	97.81	97.84	+	.03	2.16	−.03	283
Est vol 20; vol Mon 3; open int 283, +3.									
LIBOR-1 Mo. (CME)-$3,000,000; pts of 100%									
Apr	98.09	98.09	98.08	98.09		.....	1.91	.....	15,413
May	97.96	97.99	97.95	97.98	+	.01	2.02	−.01	11.400
June	97.73	97.78	97.72	97.78	+	.05	2.22	−.05	6,442
July	97.52	97.59	97.52	97.59	+	.05	2.41	−.05	5,407
Nov	96.57	96.67	96.57	96.67	+	.08	3.33	−.08	100
Dec	96.26	96.28	96.26	96.29	+	.13	3.71	−.13	35
Est vol 2,678; vol Mon 2,033; open int 40,267, +582.									
Eurodollar (CME)-$1 Million; pts of 100%									
Apr	97.89	97.92	97.88	97.92	+	.03	2.08	−.03	61,750
May	97.68	97.73	97.68	97.73	+	.04	2.27	−.04	28,573
June	97.46	97.53	97.45	97.52	+	.05	2.48	−.05	761,291
Aug	96.97	97.04	96.97	97.04	+	.06	2.96	−.06	751
Sept	96.73	96.84	96.72	96.83	+	.10	3.17	−.10	658,902
Dec	96.08	96.22	96.07	96.21	+	.13	3.79	−.13	771,418
Mr03	95.48	95.64	95.47	95.63	+	.14	4.37	−.14	415,167
June	95.01	95.14	94.98	95.14	+	.14	4.86	−.14	316,425
Sept	94.66	94.79	94.63	94.79	+	.14	5.21	−.14	230,760
Dec	94.40	94.55	94.39	94.54	+	.13	5.46	−.13	184,073
Mr04	94.24	94.39	94.23	94.38	+	.13	5.62	−.13	130,198
June	94.07	94.23	94.06	94.21	+	.13	5.79	−.13	119,015
Sept	93.93	94.08	93.91	94.06	+	.12	5.94	−.12	112,298
Dec	93.76	93.89	93.74	93.89	+	.12	6.11	−.12	89,480
Mr05	93.70	93.82	93.68	93.83	+	.12	6.17	−.12	83,501
June	93.59	93.71	93.57	93.73	+	.11	6.27	−.11	56,616
Sept	93.49	93.62	93.48	93.63	+	.11	6.37	−.11	74,956
Dec	93.35	93.49	93.35	93.50	+	.11	6.50	−.11	44,054
Mr06	93.33	93.47	93.33	93.48	+	.10	6.52	−.10	48,562
June	93.27	93.40	93.25	93.40	+	.10	6.60	−.10	37,801
Sept	93.23	93.33	93.19	93.34	+	.10	6.66	−.10	45,223
Dec	93.08	93.21	93.07	93.22	+	.10	6.78	−.10	30,973
Mr07	93.11	93.21	93.07	93.22	+	.10	6.78	−.10	19,267
Dec	92.87	93.01	92.87	93.02	+	.10	6.98	−.10	10,986
Dc08	92.73	92.86	92.72	92.86	+	.10	7.14	−.10	4,144
Dc09	92.69	92.74	92.62	92.75	+	.09	7.25	−.09	2,219
Est vol 607,572; vol Mon 457,488; open int 4,417,394, +31,950.									

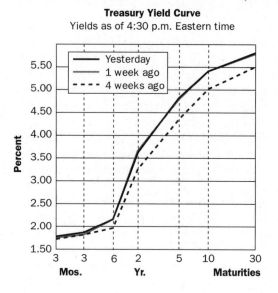

Treasury Yield Curve
Yields as of 4:30 p.m. Eastern time

— Yesterday
— 1 week ago
- - - - 4 weeks ago

SOURCE: *The Wall Street Journal*, April 2, 2002.

Eurodollar futures data. The first column of futures information indicates the settlement month and year. Except for the upcoming year, these contracts expire sequentially at 3-month intervals near the middle of each month. Each row lists price and yield data for a distinct futures contract. The next four columns report the index price quotes for each contract during the day including the opening price, high and low price, and closing settlement price. The next column headed "Change" indicates the change in settlement price from the previous day. The data under "Yield" convert the settlement price to a Eurodollar futures rate as:

$$100 - \text{settlement price} = \text{futures rate,}$$

and the second "Change" indicate the yield change from the previous day. The final column reports **open interest** equal to the total number of futures contracts outstanding at the end of the day.

For example, the Eurodollar futures contract expiring in March 2003, in a little less than 11 months, had a settlement price of 95.63 for a futures rate of 4.37 percent. The contract opened trading at 95.48, rose as high as 95.64, and fell as low as 95.47 during the day, before trading stopped. The closing price was 14 basis points above the close the prior day indicating that the futures rate fell 14 basis points. At the close of business 415,167 contracts were outstanding. Each successive row of data provides similar information. Note the column for the settlement yield, which is also labeled the futures rate. The data generally indicate that the farther out is contract expiration, the higher is the futures rate. Thus, the 3-month Eurodollar futures rate of 4.86 percent for the contract expiring in June 2003 is 49 basis points higher than that for the March 2003 contract, but is less than the 7.25 percent futures rate for the December 2009 contract. The market exhibited some volatility on this day as all of these futures rates increased relative to their values the previous day by three to 14 basis points. Finally, the open interest demonstrates that the amount of contracts outstanding declines the farther out is expiration, consistent with the fact that liquidity is greatest for the nearby futures contract and generally decreases with time until expiration.

Data for the 3-month Treasury bill futures contracts and 1-month LIBOR contracts indicate that far fewer of these futures are actively traded. In fact, the open interest on T-bill futures is quite modest given the depth of the spot T-bill market. Note also the slope of the Treasury yield curve. In April 2002, the yield curve was sharply upsloping through 10 years, then relatively flat. The difference between the 6-month and 30-year Treasury rates was 350 basis points. According to the unbiased expectations theory, an upsloping yield curve indicates a consensus forecast that short-term interest rates are expected to rise. A flat yield curve suggests that rates will remain relatively constant. One interpretation of futures rates is that they provide information about consensus expectations of future cash rates. Futures rates that increase the farther out is futures contract expiration presumably indicate an expected increase in rates. In this context a futures rate should provide similar information as a forward rate derived from cash rates representing the prevailing yield curve. Data for 3-month Eurodollar futures rates reveal a similar pattern as that for the Treasury yield curve. If these futures rates are viewed as forecasts of 3-month Eurodollar cash rates at expiration of each futures contract, the sharp increase suggests a rising Eurodollar yield curve as well.

DAILY MARKING-TO-MARKET. The cash flows associated with daily settlement of futures trading can be demonstrated by an example. Consider a trader who at the close of trading on April 2, 2002, buys one December 2002 3-month Eurodollar futures contract at 96.21, or 3.79 percent, posting $1,100 in cash as initial margin. Maintenance margin is set at $700 per contract. The futures contract expires on December 17, almost 8 months after the initial purchase, during which time the futures price and rate fluctuate daily. Because our trader is long futures, the contract increases in value when the futures price rises, or the futures rate declines. Suppose that on April 3 the futures rate falls to 3.65 percent. The trader could withdraw $350 (14 basis points × $25) from the margin account representing the increase in value of the position. For this example, assume that the funds are left in the margin account. Now suppose that the futures rate increases to 3.85 percent the next day so that the trader's long position decreases in value. The 20 basis point increase represents a $500 drop in margin such that the ending account balance would equal $950. If at market close on April 11 the December futures rate increases further to 4.05 percent, the trader must make a variation margin payment sufficient to bring the account up to $700. In this case, the account balance would have fallen by $650 to $450 and the margin contribution would equal $250 (10 basis points × $25). The exchange member may close the account if the trader does not meet the variation margin requirement.

Exhibit 10.2 reveals one possible pattern in the movement of the 3-month cash Eurodollar rate and the December 2002 futures rate after April 2. Initially, the cash rate equals 2.04 percent and the futures rate is 3.79 percent. While the cash rate declines initially then increases systematically until expiration, the futures rate immediately increases. When the contract expires on December 17, 2002, both the futures and cash rate equal 4.50 percent, and the long futures position is worth $1,775 (71 × $25) less than its value on April 2, 2002, because the Eurodollar futures rate increased 71 basis points. If the trader held the contract to expiration, the position would have immediately decreased in value as the futures rate rose and would have remained at a loss through expiration because the futures rate never went below 3.79 percent. The trader would have lost $1,775 at the close or some lesser amount if he got out of his position earlier.

· EXHIBIT 10.2

THE RELATIONSHIP BETWEEN FUTURES RATES AND
CASH RATES—ONE POSSIBLE PATTERN

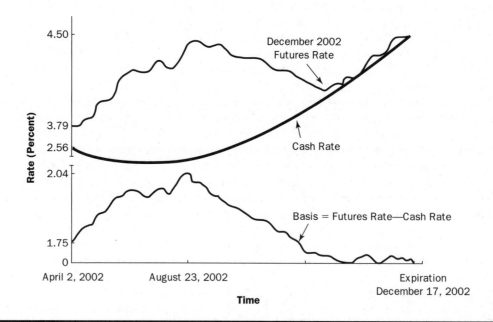

THE BASIS. The term **basis** refers to the cash price of an asset minus the corresponding futures price for the same asset at a point in time. Typically, it applies to the cash price of a security that is being hedged. For Eurodollar futures, the basis can be calculated as the futures rate minus the cash rate. Consider the previous example with 3-month December 2002 Eurodollar futures. On April 2, 2002, the cash 3-month Eurodollar time deposit rate equaled 2.04 percent. Thus, the December 2002 futures rate exceeded the prevailing cash rate by 175 basis points, which represents the basis. The bottom part of Exhibit 10.2 shows the movement in the basis associated with the cash and futures rates presented at the top of the exhibit. It initially increases to almost 256 basis points on August 23, then systematically declines as expiration approaches. Note that the basis equals zero at expiration and is close to zero prior to expiration. This is a typical pattern. Later discussions will indicate that the basis is important in determining the effectiveness of hedging interest rate risk.

The basis may not behave as nicely as it does in Exhibit 10.2. It may be positive or negative, depending on whether futures rates are above or below cash rates and may swing widely in value far in advance of contract expiration. The basis rises and falls daily as economic conditions and market sentiment change. While the basis can take any value, there are two general price relationships between futures and cash instruments. First, the basis must equal zero at expiration. This is so no trader can earn a riskless arbitrage profit. For example, suppose that the basis equals some nonzero value just prior to expiration. Any trader could buy the cheaper cash instrument or futures contract and sell the more expensive one making a riskless profit. Such arbitrage drives the two prices together. Second, because futures and cash rates must be equal at expiration, the basis normally narrows as expiration approaches. If it is positive, it declines to zero. If it is negative, it increases to zero. Both phenomena are demonstrated in Exhibit 10.2.

SPECULATION VERSUS HEDGING

Participants use futures for a variety of purposes. According to the previous discussion, futures prices may represent the consensus forecast of the underlying asset's future price at contract expiration. A trader who expects the actual price to differ from that expected and represented by the futures price can either buy or sell the future, depending on whether the contract is perceived to be undervalued or overvalued. Such a participant is a speculator who takes on additional risk to earn speculative profits. For example, a speculator who on April 2, 2002, believed that December 2002 Eurodollar futures at 3.79 percent were undervalued (futures price [rate] was too low [high]) would buy the contract, anticipating a decline in futures rates and an increase in price prior to expiration. Speculators who felt the contract was overvalued (futures price [rate] was too high [low]) would alternatively sell futures, expecting to make a profit after futures rates increased and prices fell.

The top part of Exhibit 10.3 characterizes speculation in terms of two profit diagrams for the December 2002 Eurodollar futures data from Exhibit 10.1. The first summarizes the profits and losses from buying the futures contract at the settlement price relative to possible futures prices after the contract is purchased. Specifically, on April 2, 2001, the settlement price equals 96.21. If a speculator later sells the futures contract at any higher price, he or she earns a profit equal to $25 times the difference in the sales price and 96.21. If the futures price declines and the speculator sells at less than 96.21, he or she suffers a loss. The second diagram summarizes profits and losses for the seller of the same futures contract on April 2. Not surprisingly, the seller profits when the futures price declines and loses when the price rises.

Speculation is extremely risky. For the most part, futures rates and prices on nearby contracts are determined by arbitrage activity. Even when a speculator views a contract as overvalued or undervalued, any position taken can backfire in that a major market move can overwhelm the initial mispricing. Exhibit 10.3 demonstrates that the loss potential is virtually unlimited. Pure speculative activity with single contracts is thus relatively rare.

Hedging differs from speculation in terms of the participants' risk position prior to executing a trade and overall trade objectives. Speculators take a position that increases their risk profile. Hedgers focus on avoiding or reducing risk. They enter futures transactions because their normal business operations involve certain risks that they are trying to reduce. This pre-existing risk can be at least partially offset because futures prices tend to move directly with cash prices, so futures rates closely track cash interest rates. Hedgers take the opposite position in a futures contract relative to their cash market risk so that losses in one market are reduced by gains in the other market.

For example, a trader who loses when cash market interest rates decrease will normally gain in the futures market with a long position as futures rates (prices) also decrease (increase) and the contract increases in value. This is characterized at the bottom of Exhibit 10.3. The lower left diagram adds to the long futures position a dashed line that indicates the profit and loss from an unhedged cash position. In this case the hedger loses in the cash market when prices increase (rates decrease) and gains when prices decrease (rates increase). In a *perfect hedge* the net profit, denoted by adding the profits and losses on both the futures and cash position, equals zero at each price. This is characterized by the bold horizontal line at the zero profit level. The diagram on the lower right demonstrates the identical result when a short futures position is used to offset losses from a cash position that loses when prices fall (interest rates rise).

Participants also use futures because transactions costs are lower with futures than cash assets. Subsequent hedges are really transactions whereby participants can essentially replicate cash market positions but lower their cost of taking a position. For example, an investor who has funds to invest for eight months in the Treasury market on April 2 could simply buy an 8-month Treasury bill. Alternatively, he or she could buy a 2-month Treasury

· EXHIBIT 10.3

PROFIT DIAGRAMS FOR THE DECEMBER 2002 EURODOLLAR
FUTURES CONTRACT FROM EXHIBIT 10.1

A. Speculation

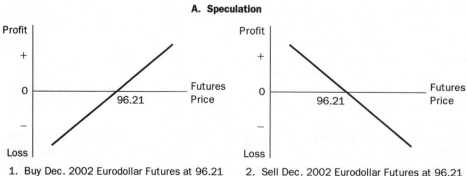

1. Buy Dec. 2002 Eurodollar Futures at 96.21   2. Sell Dec. 2002 Eurodollar Futures at 96.21

B. Hedging

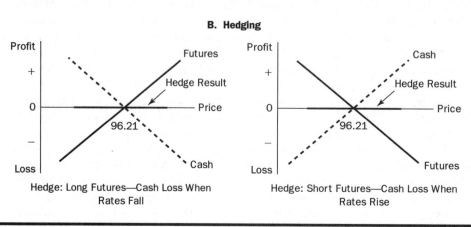

Hedge: Long Futures—Cash Loss When   Hedge: Short Futures—Cash Loss When
Rates Fall   Rates Rise

bill and two 3-month Treasury bill futures contracts that expire in June and September, respectively, and take delivery of the underlying T-bill at each expiration. The latter might be attractive if the combined yield exceeds that for the 8-month T-bill net of transactions costs.

Steps in Hedging. In general, there are seven basic steps in implementing futures hedges for financial institutions.

1. Identify the cash market risk exposure that management wants to reduce.
2. Based on the cash market risk, determine whether a long or short futures position is appropriate to reduce risk.
3. Select the best futures contract.
4. Determine the appropriate number of futures contracts to trade.
5. Implement the hedge by buying or selling futures contracts.
6. Determine when to get out of the hedge position, either by reversing the trades in Step 5, letting contracts expire, or making or taking delivery.
7. Verify that futures trading meets regulatory requirements and conforms to the bank's internal risk management policies.

The first step indicates that hedging requires each futures position to be associated with a cash position and that the objective is to reduce risk. The second step follows from Exhibit 10.3

and the fact that cash and futures rates on similar underlying instruments generally move in the same direction. If losses arise in the cash market when cash rates fall, a hedger will buy futures contracts because the futures should gain when futures rates fall. Similarly, if losses arise when cash rates rise, a hedger will sell futures contracts. The third step suggests that there is a "correct" futures contract for each cash position. In fact, the best contract is only known after the fact. What is known at the time of trading is that a hedger wants a futures contract whose rate will change in the same direction and by the same magnitude as the cash rate. Thus, a hedger chooses a "correct" futures contract where the correlation between the cash rate and futures rate is high. The other question is what contract expiration is best? Generally, a hedge will remain in place for a predetermined time interval. For reasons discussed later related to minimizing basis risk, a hedger will also generally trade the futures contract that expires immediately after the date at which the cash market risk disappears.

The fourth step addresses the determination of the appropriate *hedge ratio*, or number of futures contracts relative to the cash market exposure. There are several procedures for this, depending on whether the hedger's objective is to minimize the expected return variance or the change in total portfolio value. An example is provided later, but a detailed analysis of hedge ratios is left to other texts. The fifth step refers to the actual execution of the futures contracts trading based on the analysis of steps 1–4. Along with the decision to hedge, a hedger decides how long the hedge should be in place. In most cases, the cash market risk exposure exists for a predetermined period of time. Once cash market risk is eliminated, a hedger will get out of the hedge position. To continue to hold a long or short futures position with no linked cash position would be speculating, because changes in the futures contract would not offset any associated change in the cash position. Thus, the sixth step involves identifying when cash market risk either disappears or reaches an acceptable level. A futures trade that serves as a hedge will be kept in place as long as the cash risk exposure exists, and will be offset once the exposure is gone. There are two important extensions. First, if the cash market risk is unchanged over a period of time, it is inappropriate to trade futures contracts in and out in an attempt to time market movements. For example, a bank that trades futures in order to reduce the risk of price volatility with a portfolio of bonds should take an initial position and hold it until the bonds are sold, mature, or management decides to alter its risk preference. The bank should not sell futures initially, then buy them back only to sell futures again prior to the above ending points. Such day trading or position trading is speculative and simply increases commission costs. Second, management should determine *a priori* what its desired risk exposure is. It is appropriate for management to change its preference for risk and time whether it is hedged or unhedged accordingly. These risk preferences should not, however, change frequently over short periods such that management is constantly buying and selling futures against an unchanged cash market position. To do so is speculative because the implicit unstated intent is to time interest rate movements and trade futures to profit, rather than to reduce risk.

Finally, banks must meet strict regulatory guidelines and management must have internal policies in place that authorize hedge trades. Specifically, only certain types of positions are allowed for futures trading to constitute a hedge. Among other requirements, banks must maintain a contemporaneous hedge log that associates futures trades with the cash position in terms of the objective and nature of the trade, and they must meet strict accounting requirements for hedge gains and losses.

A LONG HEDGE

As indicated in Exhibit 10.3, a long hedge is applicable for a participant who wants to reduce cash market risk associated with a decline in interest rates. The applicable strategy is to buy futures contracts on securities similar to those evidencing the cash market risk. If cash rates decline, futures rates will typically also decline so that the value of the futures position will likely increase. Any loss in the cash market is at least partially offset by a gain in futures. Of course, if cash market rates increase, futures rates will also increase and the futures position will show a loss. Using futures essentially fixes a rate or price. This latter instance reveals an important aspect of hedging. If cash rates rise, the investor will profit more from not hedging because cash rates move favorably. A hedger thus forgoes gains associated with favorable cash market price moves. The hedge objective, however, is assumed to be risk reduction. With hedging risk is lower because the volatility of returns is lower.

The following example applies the key steps in hedging to a bank that implements a Eurodollar futures hedge. Consider the following time line.

Suppose that on April 2, 2002, your bank expects to receive a $1 million payment on November 8, 2002, and anticipates investing the funds in 3-month Eurodollar time deposits. If the bank had the funds in hand in April, it would immediately buy Eurodollar deposits. The cash market risk exposure is that the bank would like to invest the funds at today's rates, but will not have access to the funds for seven months. If cash rates move lower between April and November, the bank will realize an opportunity loss because it will have to invest the $1 million at rates below those available today. In April 2002, the market expected Eurodollar rates to increase sharply as evidenced by rising futures rates. In order to hedge, the bank should buy futures contracts such that if cash rates fall, futures rates will also likely fall and the long futures position will increase in value as an offset to the cash losses. Also, if futures rates overstate the likely increase in Eurodollar rates, a long position may capture any benefit. The best futures contract will generally be the December 2002, 3-month Eurodollar futures contract, which is the first to expire after November 2002. The contract that expires immediately after the known cash transactions date is generally best because its futures price will show the highest correlation with the cash price.

Using the data in Exhibit 10.1, the December 2002 futures rate equals 3.79 percent while the current cash market rate equals 2.04 percent. This produces a basis of 1.75 percent. Exhibit 10.4 summarizes hedge results, assuming the bank buys a December futures contract on April 2 and sells it on November 8, when the bank actually buys Eurodollars in the cash market. The 3-month Eurodollar futures contract has a $1 million par value, so each one basis point change in futures rates is worth the same $25 as a one basis point change in cash Eurodollar rates. The assumed hedge ratio is 1 to 1. Note that once the bank buys the futures contract, it is fully hedged. It implements the trade at the time it identifies the cash market risk and decides to reduce the risk. Because it plans to invest the funds in November, its cash risk will no longer exist after that time and the bank will need to get out of its initial long futures position, or it will be speculating. It is assumed that the bank has a hedge policy in place that authorizes futures trading to reduce risk associated with the planned investment of funds and that Eurodollar futures are an acceptable vehicle. It is also assumed that management has the accounting and hedge performance monitoring systems in place. The transactions are summarized at each date under the cash and futures market headings with the basis values in the final column of Exhibit 10.4.

CHANGE IN THE BASIS. The basis at the time of hedge initiation and change in basis at the time the hedge is offset determine the risk and net performance of the overall hedged position. Suppose that cash rates rise by 113 basis points through November 8 such that the bank actually invests the $1 million at 3.17 percent. This investment produces an opportunity gain of $2,825 in interest for the 3-month period as indicated by the net effect reported in the column under the cash market heading. On November 8, the December 2002 futures rate falls

▪ EXHIBIT 10.4

LONG HEDGE USING EURODOLLAR FUTURES

Date	Cash Market	Futures Market	Basis
4/2/02 (Initial futures position)	Bank anticipates investing $1 million in Eurodollars in 7 months; current cash rate = 2.04%	Bank buys one December 2002 Eurodollar futures contract at 3.79%; price = 96.21	3.79% − 2.04% = 1.75%
11/8/02 (Close futures position)	Bank invests $1 million in 3-month Eurodollars at 3.17%	Bank sells one December 2002 Eurodollar futures contract at 3.53%; price = 96.47%	3.53% − 3.17% = 0.36%
Net effect	Opportunity gain: 3.17% − 2.04% = 1.13%; 113 basis points worth $25 each = $2,825	Futures gain: 3.79% − 3.53% = 0.26%; 26 basis points worth $25 each = $650	Basis change: 0.36% − 1.75% = −1.39%

Cumulative investment income:

Interest at 3.17% = $1,000,000(.0317)(90/360) = $7,925

Profit from futures trades = $\underline{\$\ \ 650}$

Total = $8,575

$$\text{Effective return} = \$\frac{8,575}{\$1,000,000}\frac{(360)}{(90)} = 3.43\%$$

by just 26 basis points to 3.53 percent. At that time the bank sells its contract at a higher price (96.47), earning a direct profit of $650. In this case the bank gains in both the cash and futures markets. The basis on November 8 is 0.36 percent, or 139 basis points lower than on April 2.

The bank's effective percentage return is calculated at the bottom of the exhibit. The combined income equals investment income from the cash Eurodollar plus the gain on the futures trade. In this case, income consists of $7,925 in interest and $650 in futures profits for a 3.43 percent return relative to the $1 million investment. This net percentage return is 103 basis points above the initial cash Eurodollar rate on April 2. As demonstrated below, the 139 basis point differential also represents the change in basis between April and November (0.36 percent − 1.75 percent). The hedge worked because the volatility of the return from the combined futures and cash position was below the volatility of return with the unhedged cash position. With no hedge, the bank would have earned 3.17 percent.

A SHORT HEDGE

A short hedge applies to any participant who wants to reduce the risk of an increase in cash market interest rates (or reduction in cash market prices). The applicable strategy is to sell futures contracts on securities similar to those evidencing the cash market risk. If cash rates increase, futures rates will generally increase so the loss in the cash position will be at least partially offset by a gain in value of futures. Again, if cash rates actually decrease, the gain in the cash market will be offset by a loss from futures and a hedger gives up potential gains from an unhedged position. A hedger essentially fixes the rate to be realized.

The following example examines a short hedge associated with a bank that wants to protect the value of its existing securities portfolio from potential losses at future sale. Suppose that on April 2, 2002, a bank anticipates it will need to sell a 6-month Eurodollar deposit from its investment portfolio on August 17. The Eurodollar yields 4.4 percent and management, expecting a sharp increase in interest rates, would like to hedge against a decline in value of the Eurodollar at the time of sale. The cash market risk of loss is that Eurodollar time deposit rates will be higher in August. To hedge, the bank will want to immediately sell Eurodollar futures. The example assumes that the bank immediately sells one September 2002 Eurodollar futures contract and expects to buy it back in August when it sells its cash Eurodollar investment.[4]

Exhibit 10.5 summarizes the hedge results assuming the bank sells one September 2002 Eurodollar futures contract on April 2 at 3.17 percent. With a cash rate of 2.04 percent, the initial basis is 1.13 percent. On August 17, the bank buys the futures back when it liquidates its Eurodollar investment. It is assumed in the example that cash rates rise through August such that the deposit rate equals 3.00 percent at sale and the September futures rate equals 3.10 percent. In this situation, the bank has an (approximate) opportunity loss of $2,400 on its cash position and a futures loss of $175 for a net loss of $2,575.[5] Note that the 96 basis point increase in the cash rate and 7 basis point decline in the futures rate coincide with a 103 basis point decrease in the basis. Unlike the long hedge example, in this case the bank loses in the cash market and loses with futures. The hedge again works in the sense that the volatility of return (or cost) is less than with an unhedged position. If unhedged, the bank would have not realized the $175 futures loss and its total return at sale of the deposit would have been greater than with the hedge. Of course, the bank would have been in a riskier position without the futures hedge. The important point is that a hedger does not base a futures trade on expected futures profits, but rather on reducing overall risk.

CHANGE IN THE BASIS

Both the long and short hedges worked in the previous examples in the sense that the futures rate moved in line with the cash rate. With the long hedge, the futures rate fell by 26 basis points as Eurodollar rates did not increase as much as expected. Had the cash rate decreased instead of increased, the bank would have invested its funds at a yield below 2.04 percent but would have realized a greater profit on its futures position as the contract price increased even more. With the short hedge, the futures rate decreased by 7 basis points, while the cash rate rose by 96 basis points. The net effect was that the futures loss and cash loss totaled 103 basis points.

The actual risk assumed by a trader in both hedges is not that the level of interest rates will move against the cash position, but that the basis might change adversely between the time the hedge is initiated and closed. The effective return from Exhibit 10.4 equaled total income from the combined cash and futures positions relative to the investment amount. It can also be expressed as:

$$\text{Effective return} = \text{Initial cash rate} - \text{Change in basis} \tag{10.1}$$

or 3.43 percent [2.04 percent − (−1.39) percent].[6] The change in the basis ($B_2 - B_1$) equals the basis when the hedge is closed (B_2) minus the basis when the hedge is initiated (B_1). At the time a trade is initiated, the only unknown in Equation 10.1 is the basis value at closing and therefore the size of change in basis. Thus, a hedger still faces the risk that futures rates and

---

[4]Note that a $1 million 6-month Eurodollar deposit is priced differently than a $1 million 3-month Eurodollar deposit. Specifically, each basis point change is now worth $50 (.0001 × $1,000,000 × 180/360). As time elapses, the 6-month Eurodollar will approach maturity such that in August it will have less than two months to maturity.

[5]The calculation assumes that the deposit has exactly 90 days remaining maturity such that a basis point is worth $25. On August 17, however, the deposit would have less than 90 days to maturity and each basis point would be worth less than $25.

[6]Whenever a participant profits in futures, the effective return is actually higher because it could withdraw variation margin funds and invest the proceeds after futures prices moved favorably.

- **EXHIBIT 10.5**

SHORT HEDGE USING EURODOLLAR FUTURES

Date	Cash Market	Futures Market	Basis
4/2/02	Bank anticipates selling $1 million Eurodollar deposit in 127 days; current cash rate = 2.04%	Bank sells one Sept. 2002 Eurodollar futures contract at 3.17%; price = 96.83	3.17% − 2.04% = 1.13%
8/17/02	Bank sells $1 million Eurodollar deposit at 3.00%	Bank buys one Sept. 2002 Eurodollar futures contract at 3.10%; price = 96.90	3.10% − 3.00% = 0.10%
Net result:	Opportunity loss. 3.00% − 2.04% = .96%; 96 basis points worth $25 each = $2,400	Futures loss: 3.17% − 3.10% = 0.07%; 7 basis points worth $25 each = $175	Basis change: 0.10% − 1.13% = −1.03%

Effective loss = $2,400 + $175 = $2,575
Plus the value of the Eurodollar deposit at sale.

cash rates will not change coincidentally. In this long hedge example, the basis decreased from 175 to 36 basis points thereby raising the return by 139 basis points to 3.43 percent. Had the basis increased, the effective return would have decreased. The result holds true regardless of whether the level of rates increased or decreased after April 2.

The effective cost of a short hedge is also determined by Equation 10.1. The risk assumed by a hedger is again that the basis might change between the time a hedge is initiated and the time it is offset. However, the short hedger benefits when the basis increases and loses when the basis decreases. This is the opposite of a hedger who takes a long position. Using the data from the example in Exhibit 10.5, the effective cost of the Eurodollar deposit sale was 2.04 percent − (−1.03) percent, or 3.07 percent. This indicates that the bank effectively sold the Eurodollar time deposit at a 103 basis point higher yield than the rate available in April. Thus, the bank realized a lesser net value by $2,575.

Generally, directional movements in the basis are more predictable than movements in the level of cash market rates and the volatility of cash rates exceeds the volatility of the basis. The risk of hedging is thus normally less than the risk of not hedging. While basis changes can be substantial, most factors that influence cash rates influence futures rates simultaneously. Futures rates are further tied to cash rates by arbitrage activity so that the two rates move together. If the cash instrument to be hedged is the same as the instrument underlying the futures contract, arbitrageurs will trade the two instruments until the basis equals zero at futures contract expiration. This is what induces the basis to narrow toward zero as expiration approaches, per the diagram in Exhibit 10.2, and helps the hedger to estimate the *ex post* effective cost or return from a hedged position.

BASIS RISK AND CROSS HEDGING

In a perfect hedge, the profit or loss in the cash position is exactly offset by the profit or loss from the futures position. This would occur if the basis change always equaled zero. In practice, it is extremely difficult to obtain a perfect hedge and there are numerous instances when basis risk can be substantial. One such instance involves **cross hedges.** A cross hedge is one in which a participant uses a futures contract based on one security that differs from the security being hedged in the cash market. An example would be using Eurodollar futures to

HEDGING AND OPPORTUNITY LOSSES

During the summer of 1982, senior management at Berkeley Federal Savings in Milburn, New Jersey, decided to use financial futures to hedge the firm's cost of funds. Berkeley had approximately $400 million of its deposits in 6-month savings certificates paying rates that floated with current Treasury bill rates.

Berkeley decided to hedge borrowing costs on one-half of its certificates by selling $400 million in 3-month Treasury bill futures contracts. The expectation was that if cash Treasury bill rates increased and Berkeley's actual borrowing costs rose, Treasury bill futures rates would also increase so that the firm would profit by buying the futures

back at lower prices. In actuality, the opposite occurred.

In August, the bank president left for a short vacation. At that time, losses on the association's futures position totaled $200,000. During the next few days, Treasury bill cash and futures rates dropped sharply. By the time the president returned one week later, losses had reached $1.5 million after the association closed out its futures position.

The hedge worked in the sense that the firm's funding cost was stabilized as cash market gains in the form of lower interest costs on the savings certificates were offset by futures contract losses. Management was dissatisfied, however, because it paid out $1.5 million in futures

losses immediately and could have borrowed at lower rates if it had not hedged at all. The president even suggested that he would have liquidated the futures position earlier to cut futures losses had he not been on vacation. Of course, it is not a hedge if a firm liquidates its position when futures rates move adversely. The fundamental point is that hedging reduces risk but also eliminates the potential to realize gains from unhedged positions. These opportunity losses represent the cost of hedging.

hedge price movements for commercial paper transactions. The risk is potentially greater for cross hedges because futures and cash interest rates may not move closely together as they are based on different underlying securities. If the basis is volatile and unpredictable, Equation 10.1 suggests that the effective return or cost from a hedge might also be volatile and unpredictable.

Basis risk can also be substantial because futures and cash rates for the same underlying security may move in opposite directions prior to expiration. In fact, the basis change is known with certainty only when the planned cash transactions being hedged coincide with futures expirations. In this case, participants know that the basis will equal zero and thus the basis change will equal the negative of the basis at the time the hedge is initiated. Typically, however, most transactions do not coincide with futures expirations and changes in futures rates may differ sharply from changes in cash rates. It is generally the case, however, that basis volatility is lowest for the contract that expires immediately after the cash risk expiration. Finally, as Contemporary Issues: Hedging and Opportunity Losses suggests, futures trades are not riskless and often produce opportunity losses.

MICROHEDGING APPLICATIONS

One of the basic decisions that risk managers make is whether to hedge specific individual transactions or the aggregate risk exposure of the bank. The previous examples of a long hedge and short hedge involved individual transactions. Alternatively, management could choose to hedge aggregate risk exposure evidenced by a nonzero GAP or nonzero duration gap and earnings and MVE sensitivity that are nonzero. **Microhedges** refer to the hedging of a transaction associated with a specific asset, liability, or commitment. **Macrohedges** involve taking futures positions to reduce aggregate portfolio interest rate risk, typically measured by the sensitivity of earnings or MVE.

▪ EXHIBIT 10.6

CREATING A SYNTHETIC 6-MONTH EURODOLLAR LIABILITY

Summary of Relevant Eurodollar Rates and Transactions

April 2, 2002

3-month cash rate = 2.04%; bank issues a $1 million, 91-day Eurodollar deposit
6-month cash rate = 2.60%
Bank sells one September 2002 Eurodollar futures; futures rate = 3.17%

July 3, 2002

3-month cash rate = 2.88%; bank issues a $1 million, 91-day Eurodollar deposit
Buy: One September 2002 Eurodollar futures; futures rate = 3.85%

Date	Cash Market	Futures Market	Basis
4/2/02	Bank issues $1 million, 91-day Eurodollar time deposit at 2.04%; 3-mo. interest expense = $5,157.	Bank sells one September 2002 Eurodollar futures contract at 3.17%	1.13%
7/3/02	Bank issues $1 million, 91-day Eurodollar time deposit at 2.88%; 3-mo. interest expense = $7,280 (increase in interest expense over previous period = $2,123).	Bank buys one September 2002 Eurodollar futures contract at 3.23%; profit = $150.	0.35%
Net effect:	6-mo. interest expense = $12,437	Futures profit = $150; Net = $12,287	

$$\text{Effective 6-mo. borrowing cost} = \frac{\$12,437 - \$150}{\$1,000,000}\frac{(360)}{(182)} = 2.43\%$$

Interest on 6-month Eurodollar deposit issued April 2 = $13,144 at 2.60%; vs. $12,287 at 2.43%

Banks are generally restricted to using financial futures for hedging purposes under current regulations. In their accounting, they must recognize futures on a micro basis by linking each futures transaction with a specific cash instrument or commitment in a contemporaneous log of hedge transactions. Yet many analysts feel that such linkages force microhedges that may potentially increase a firm's total risk because these hedges ignore all other portfolio components. Thus, accounting requirements may focus attention on inappropriate risk measures. Macrohedging, in turn, is difficult to implement because of problems in accurately measuring a firm's overall interest rate risk and in monitoring hedging effectiveness. This section analyzes various microhedges, followed by a section on macrohedging.

CREATING A SYNTHETIC LIABILITY WITH A SHORT HEDGE

Suppose that on April 2, 2002, a large money center bank agreed to finance a $1 million 6-month working capital loan to a corporate customer. Management wanted to match fund the loan by issuing a $1 million, 6-month Eurodollar time deposit. On April 2, the 6-month cash Eurodollar rate was 2.60 percent, while the corresponding 3-month rate was 2.04 percent. The 3-month Eurodollar futures rate for September 2002 delivery equaled 3.17 percent. Rather than issue a direct 6-month Eurodollar liability at 2.60 percent, the bank created a synthetic 6-month liability by shorting futures. The objective was to use the futures market to borrow at a lower rate than the 6-month cash Eurodollar rate. It was to be achieved by initially issuing a 3-month Eurodollar, then issuing another when the first matured. A short futures position would reduce the risk of rising interest rates for the second cash Eurodollar borrowing. The following time line indicates the rate comparison. Exhibit 10.6 presents the steps.

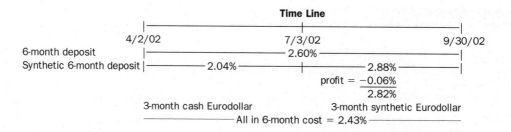

On April 2, the bank issued a $1 million, 91-day Eurodollar time deposit at 2.04 percent and simultaneously sold one September 2002 Eurodollar futures contract at 3.17 percent. Management expects to roll over its 91-day Eurodollar deposit by issuing another 3-month deposit on July 3 for an effective 6-month maturity. At that time, it will offset its futures position by buying a September 2002 futures contract. The short hedge reduces the risk of loss if cash Eurodollar rates have increased (between April 2 and July 3) when the bank reissues its deposit.

When the first 3-month deposit matured on July 3, rates had increased substantially, and the bank issued another 3-month Eurodollar deposit at 2.88 percent. It simultaneously closed out its position by buying one September 2002 futures contract at 3.23 percent. In this example, both cash and futures rates increased with the basis decreasing from 113 basis points to 35 basis points (increased cost by 78 basis points to 2.82 percent). The $150 (6 basis points) profit on the future lowered the effective increased interest expense on the cash Eurodollar deposit such that the effective cost of the second 3-month Eurodollar equaled 2.82 percent (2.88 percent − 0.06 percent). The effective borrowing cost of the synthetic 6-month Eurodollar deposit equaled 2.43 percent which was below the 2.60 percent 6-month cash rate available on April 2.

In this example, the bank "saved" $857 in interest expense ($13,144 − $12,287) which represents the difference between interest expense on a 6-month Eurodollar and the effective 6-month interest on the synthetic Eurodollar. The actual benefit, of course, depends on how cash rates change relative to futures rates. In essence, the bank has substituted basis risk for the risk that cash rates will change adversely. In this example, the bank could lose if cash rates increased substantially more than futures rates increased. Briefly, the true borrowing cost increases as the basis decreases, while the cost falls as the basis increases.

THE MECHANICS OF APPLYING A MICROHEDGE

A bank should carefully analyze the opportunities and risks associated with hedging. The following discussion demonstrates the type of information required and procedural steps underlying successful hedging programs.[7]

DETERMINE THE BANK'S INTEREST RATE RISK POSITION. To formulate the correct hedge, management must determine the bank's interest rate risk position. With a microhedge this involves examining the bank's actual and anticipated cash market position and how specific interest rate changes will affect interest income or interest expense, or the value of an underlying asset or liability. The objective is to know in what rate environment the bank loses. Frequently, banks then compare their rate forecast and their potential losses if these rates materialize. Selectively hedging when losses will arise if the forecast is realized is a form of speculation. The key hedging decision involves determining how much risk the bank will accept.

---

[7]This analysis is based on steps outlined by Kawaller, 1983.

FORECAST THE DOLLAR FLOWS OR VALUE EXPECTED IN CASH MARKET TRANSACTIONS. To determine how many futures contracts are necessary, management should estimate the dollar magnitude of anticipated cash flows with cash market transactions. This may equal the amount of investable funds, the size of a loan commitment, or the amount of liabilities to be issued or rolled over.

CHOOSE THE APPROPRIATE FUTURES CONTRACT. A bank should select a hedging vehicle that reduces interest rate risk. Because changes in the basis determine hedging risk, the appropriate futures contract is usually one whose rates most highly correlate with those of the cash asset or liability being hedged. Typically, the correlation is highest for like instruments, such as Eurodollar futures relative to cash Eurodollar deposits. If a like futures instrument is unavailable, a bank can examine historical correlations for different futures contracts and choose the contract with the highest correlation coefficient. As described earlier, the use of a futures contract that is not identical to the cash instrument being hedged is referred to as a cross hedge. It is also important to assess the liquidity of different contracts. Only when trading volume is large can a bank easily buy or sell futures at relatively stable basis levels.

DETERMINE THE CORRECT NUMBER OF FUTURES CONTRACTS. Five factors, listed below, determine the correct number of futures contracts. This calculation, or hedge ratio, is expressed numerically as:

$$NF = \frac{[A \times Mc]}{F \times Mf} b \qquad\qquad (10.2)$$

where

NF = number of futures contracts

  A = dollar value of cash flow to be hedged

  F = face value of futures contract

Mc = maturity or duration of anticipated cash asset or liability

Mf = maturity or duration of futures contract

$$b = \frac{\text{expected rate movement on cash instrument}}{\text{expected rate movement on futures contract}}$$

If futures rates are expected to move coincidentally with cash rates, b equals 1. If futures rates are expected to exhibit larger moves relative to cash rates, b is less than 1, and vice versa.[8] Using the information from Exhibit 10.6 and assuming b equals 1 with Eurodollar cash and futures rates, the bank needed one futures contract:

$$NF = \frac{\$1,000,000 \times 91 \text{ days}}{\$1,000,000 \times 90 \text{ days}} \times 1 = 1$$

DETERMINE THE APPROPRIATE TIME FRAME FOR THE HEDGE. Typically, a bank matches the length of a hedge with the timing of cash flows for the underlying asset or liability. For example, a bank that knows it will have funds to invest in 6 months will use a futures contract that expires in 6 or more months. If consecutive cash flows are expected, such as principal payments on a term loan, a bank will hedge by spreading different futures

---

[8]In practice, the appropriate factor is determined as the slope of the regression line from running a regression of cash price changes on futures price changes using historical data.

contracts over the term of the cash flows. This process, labeled **stripping futures,** consists of buying or selling equal amounts of successive futures contracts.[9]

MONITOR HEDGE PERFORMANCE. Once a hedge is in place, management should monitor interest rate changes and the bank's cash position to verify the hedge performance. One concern is that the anticipated cash position might vary. Another is that the basis might move against the cash rate, whereby the bank loses in both the cash and futures market. If the bank's risk profile changes, it may want to lift a hedge. In practice, many participants adjust their hedge when the basis moves against them, implicitly extrapolating that the movement is permanent. In doing so, they are speculating.

MACROHEDGING APPLICATIONS

Macrohedging focuses on reducing interest rate risk associated with a bank's entire portfolio rather than with individual components or transactions. As suggested in Chapters 8 and 9, macrohedging assumes that interest rate risk is best evidenced by GAP or duration gap measures and by the sensitivity of bank earnings and MVE. Banks can subsequently use futures contracts to hedge this net portfolio rate sensitivity.

HEDGING: GAP OR EARNINGS SENSITIVITY

When establishing a macrohedge, a bank should initially examine its aggregate interest rate risk position. Banks using GAP and earnings sensitivity analysis focus on the volatility in net interest income. GAP represents the dollar magnitude of rate-sensitive assets minus the dollar magnitude of rate-sensitive liabilities over different time intervals. If GAP is positive, the bank is said to be asset-sensitive because its net interest income rises when interest rates rise, and falls when interest rates fall. If GAP is negative, the bank is liability-sensitive because net interest income falls when rates increase, and rises when rates decrease. The magnitude of the potential change in net interest income indicates the sensitivity of earnings to rate changes and the aggregate amount of interest rate risk assumed.

Hedging strategies focus on whether a bank is asset- or liability-sensitive and the extent to which rate changes might alter net interest income. To balance asset sensitivity, a bank will institute a long hedge, whereby declining interest rates should generate futures profits that offset the decline in net interest income. To balance liability sensitivity, a bank would institute a short hedge. If rates subsequently increase and the bank's net interest income falls, the sale of futures should produce a profit that at least partially offsets the lost net interest income.

Consider the summary rate sensitivity data for ABC bank from Exhibit 8.7 in Chapter 8. This bank has a negative cumulative GAP through one year of over $15,448,000 under management's most likely rate scenario. Exhibit 8.9 demonstrates that if rates increase by one percent, net interest income will likely fall modestly the next year, but by almost $750,000 two years out. Suppose that the bank chooses to hedge $10 million of its −$15.4 million GAP exposure over 180 days. This partial hedge would call for the sale of 20 Eurodollar futures contracts determined by

$$NF = \frac{\$10,000,000}{\$1,000,000} \times \frac{180 \text{ days}}{90 \text{ days}} \times 1.0 = 20$$

---

[9]If the term of the cash flows exceeds the time frame for which futures contracts are available, hedgers can "stack" contracts by loading up on the last available contract and systematically switching into new futures contracts as they become available. This involves additional risk and increases transactions costs.

This assumes that the bank uses Eurodollar futures and that the expected movement between the effective interest rate on the rate-sensitive liabilities relative to the Eurodollar futures rate equals 1. The bank would likely sell 10 September 2002 and 10 December 2002 contracts that expire more than six months from year-end 2001, liquidating the hedge by periodically buying back futures at selected intervals. The hedge should work because any decline in net interest income due to rising rates should be offset by a gain on the short futures position. Also, any gain in net interest income from falling rates should be offset by a loss on the short futures position.

This type of hedge is clearly a cross hedge as the cash rate is actually a combination of several rates, all different from the Eurodollar futures rate. The bank is negatively gapped with the magnitude of change in net interest income associated with changes in short-term liability rates. The bank might alternatively choose Treasury bill futures for the hedge instrument if the correlation was higher with liability rates because money market deposit accounts paid interest tied to cash Treasury bill rates. Because the hedge matches gains in either the cash or futures market with losses in the other, the transaction essentially fixes a rate or outcome before basis changes. In effect, the short hedge moves both the GAP and earnings sensitivity closer to zero.

HEDGING: DURATION GAP AND MVE SENSITIVITY

One of the presumed advantages of duration gap analysis is that it lends itself to hedging applications. Duration gap is a single-valued measure of total interest rate risk in which a bank targets its market value of equity (MVE). Duration gap equals the weighted duration of bank assets minus the product of the weighted duration of bank liabilities and the bank's debt-to-asset ratio. A positive DGAP measure indicates that aggregate assets will vary more in value relative to aggregate liabilities when interest rates change equally. If rates increase, the market value of assets falls more than the market value of liabilities, so that MVE declines. A bank with a negative duration gap will see its equity increase in value when rates rise.

To eliminate this risk, a bank could structure its portfolio so that the duration gap equals zero. Alternatively, it can use futures to balance the value sensitivity of the portfolio. Equation 10.3 is listed below:

$$\frac{\Delta MVE}{\text{Market value of assets}} = -\frac{DGAP \times \Delta y}{(1 + y)} \tag{10.3}$$

where DGAP equals the duration gap and y equals the average interest rate for a bank's portfolio. If management wants to immunize MVE, it could set the bank's DGAP at zero. This can be done by using futures to create a synthetic DGAP that approximately equals zero. The appropriate size of a futures position can be determined by solving Equation 10.4 for the market value of futures contracts (MVF), where DF is the duration of the futures contract used, DA is the weighted duration of assets, and DL is the weighted duration of liabilities:[10]

$$\frac{DA(MVRSA)}{(1 + i_a)} - \frac{DL(MVRSL)}{(1 + i_l)} + \frac{DF \times (MVF)}{(1 + i_f)} = 0 \tag{10.4}$$

The subscripts on the interest rate measures refer to assets (a), liabilities (l), and futures (f), and all rates are assumed to change by the same amount. MVRSA and MVRSL refer to the market value of rate-sensitive assets and rate-sensitive liabilities, respectively.

---

[10]Because futures contracts have no fixed price or cash flow, they have no duration. Under certain assumptions, however, it can be shown that the duration of a futures contract equals the duration of the underlying deliverable instrument. See Kolb and Gay, 1982.

As an illustration, consider the bank balance sheet data provided for the sample bank in Exhibit 9.1 of Chapter 9. Because the bank has a positive duration gap of 1.4 years, it will see its market value of equity decline if interest rates rise. It thus needs to sell interest rate futures contracts in order to hedge its risk position. The short position indicates that the bank will make a profit if futures rates increase. This should at least partially offset any decline in the market value of equity caused by corresponding increases in cash rates. Assuming the bank uses a Eurodollar futures contract currently trading at 4.9 percent with a duration of 0.25 years, the target market value of futures contracts (MVF) can be obtained from applying Equation 10.4:

$$\frac{2.88(\$900)}{(1.10)} - \frac{1.61(\$920)}{(1.06)} + \frac{0.25(\text{MVF})}{(1.049)} = 0$$

or MVF $= -\$4,024.36$. This suggests that the bank should sell four Eurodollar futures contracts. If all interest rates increased by 1 percent, the profit on the four futures contracts would total $10,000 (4 × 100 × $25), or $2,000 less than the decrease in market value of equity associated with the increase in cash rates (see Exhibit 9.2). The discrepancy derives from using interest rate averages and a discrete number of futures contracts. The concept, however, is clear. Duration gap mismatches can be hedged through the use of futures without dramatic changes in the portfolio.

ACCOUNTING REQUIREMENTS AND TAX IMPLICATIONS

Regulators generally limit banks to using futures for hedging purposes. However, if a bank has a dealer operation, it can use futures as part of its trading activities. Regardless of how futures contracts are used, recently imposed accounting standards require that gains and losses on futures and other off-balance sheet positions be marked to market as they accrue, thereby affecting current income. Such current recognition of gains or losses clearly increases the volatility of reported earnings over short intervals. For hedging applications, futures contracts must be recognized on a micro basis by linking each contract to a specific cash instrument.

To qualify as a hedge, the use of futures must meet several criteria. A bank must show that a cash transaction exposes it to interest rate risk, a futures contract must lower the bank's risk exposure, and the bank must designate the contract as a hedge. The primary difficulty involves determining whether futures reduce bank risk. Financial Accounting Standards Board statement number 80 states that this condition is met if the correlation between price changes in futures and the hedged instrument is high. Unfortunately, there are no well-defined rules for establishing what time period should be used to calculate the correlation or even what amount of correlation is high enough. If a high correlation does not prevail, a bank must immediately stop deferring futures gains and losses and account for the proceeds as current income. As described in Contemporary Issues: Hedge Accounting and the Failure of Franklin Savings, how regulators calculate correlation can have a profound impact on the financial statements and thus regulatory viability of a futures user. In this instance, Franklin Savings failed, in part because it recorded losses differently than the regulators and courts eventually felt appropriate.

The tax treatment of futures contracts has undergone a broad transition. Prior to 1981, futures profits were taxed as ordinary income or capital gains depending on the length of the trader's holding period. Tax payments were due in the year the futures position was offset. This enabled futures traders to spread contracts by taking opposite positions in different contracts, where one produced a loss and the other a gain for similar interest rate movements. At the end of the tax year, they would take the loss to reduce taxes and defer gains. In 1981,

HEDGE ACCOUNTING AND THE FAILURE OF FRANKLIN SAVINGS

On February 16, 1990, the Office of Thrift Supervision (OTS) put Franklin Savings of Ottawa, Kansas in receivership. Ernest Fleischer, Franklin's CEO, challenged the seizure in court claiming that the action was arbitrary and capricious. The fundamental issue was whether Franklin Savings was insolvent. The determination evolved around the appropriate procedure in accounting for hedge losses.

Franklin Savings was an unorthodox thrift institution that used Federal Home Loan Bank advances and jumbo CDs obtained via brokers to fund much of the firm's assets. Franklin, in turn, used a variety of financial futures, options on financial futures, and interest rate swaps to hedge against

loss from adverse changes in interest rates. Franklin Savings used an absolute value method for computing the correlation coefficient between futures price changes and cash price changes. The OTS used a net offset method. In February 1990, the absolute value method produced a sufficiently high correlation coefficient for Franklin to qualify for hedge accounting and thus the deferral of losses. The net offset method, in contrast, produced a low correlation coefficient to where the OTS required Franklin to immediately recognize $119 million in losses that had been previously deferred. With the losses, the OTS determined that Franklin's net worth (capital) was deficient and forced the firm into receivership.

Franklin originally used the net offset method but changed to the absolute value method, which it developed, when the volatility of interest rates increased. The argument was that the net offset procedure distorted the impact of rapidly changing interest rates on actual performance. FASB 80, in fact, does not stipulate any acceptable method for estimating correlation. The curious result is that the OTS ruled Franklin Savings to be a failed institution over ambiguous accounting when there were no specific guidelines as to what is appropriate.

speculative traders were required to mark contract values to market at the end of the tax year and pay the obligated taxes in that year. Finally, the Tax Reform Act of 1986 eliminated the lower tax rate on long-term capital gains. Thus, all futures profits are taxed as ordinary income.

USING FORWARD RATE AGREEMENTS TO MANAGE RATE RISK

The previous discussion briefly introduced forward contracts and compared their features with financial futures. While there are similarities, forward contracts differ because they are negotiated between counterparties, there is no daily settlement or marking to market, and no exchange guarantees performance. In general, the buyer of a forward contract agrees to pay a specific amount at a set date in the future (settlement date) for an agreed-upon asset, currency, etc. from the counterparty representing the seller. The specified price or rate is labeled the exercise price (rate). The seller of a forward contract agrees to deliver the agreed-upon asset, currency, etc. for the specific amount at a set date when there is physical delivery. When a forward contract is cash-settled, the buyer and seller agree to exchange the difference between the exercise price and cash price at the future settlement date.

A forward rate agreement (FRA) is a type of forward contract based on interest rates. The two counterparties to an FRA agree to a **notional principal** amount that serves as a reference figure in determining cash flows. The term "notional" refers to the condition that the principal does not change hands, but is only used to calculate the value of interest payments. The buyer of the FRA agrees to pay a fixed-rate coupon payment and receive a floating-rate payment against the notional principal at some specified future date, while the seller of the FRA agrees to pay a floating-rate payment and receive the fixed-rate payment against the same notional principal. In most cases, the exercise rate is set equal to the forward rate from the prevailing yield curve reflecting the expected future interest rate. Thus, a buyer or seller of the FRA will receive cash or make cash payment only if the actual interest rate at settlement differs from that initially expected.

FRAs can be used to manage interest rate risk in the same manner as financial futures. The buyer of the FRA will receive (pay) cash when the actual interest rate at contract settlement is greater (less) than the exercise rate set at origination of the contract. The seller of the FRA will receive (pay) cash when the actual interest rate at settlement is less (greater) than the exercise rate. Note that FRAs are cash-settled at the settlement date with no interim cash flows. They are not marked-to-market and there are no margin requirements.

FORWARD RATE AGREEMENTS: AN EXAMPLE

Suppose that Metro Bank as seller enters into a receive fixed-rate/pay floating-rate FRA agreement with County Bank as buyer with a 6-month maturity based on a $1 million notional principal amount. The floating rate is 3-month LIBOR and the fixed (exercise) rate is 7 percent. Metro Bank would refer to this as a "3 vs. 6" FRA at 7 percent on a $1 million notional amount from County Bank. The phrase "3 vs. 6" refers to a 3-month interest rate observed three months from the present, for a security with a maturity date six months from the present. The only cash flow will be determined in six months at contract maturity by comparing the prevailing 3-month LIBOR with 7 percent.

Assume, for example, that in three months 3-month LIBOR equals 8 percent. In this case, County Bank would receive from Metro Bank $2,451. The interest settlement amount is $2,500 determined as:

$$\text{interest} = (.08 - .07)(90/360)\$1,000,000 = \$2,500$$

Because this represents interest that would be paid three months later at maturity of the instrument, the actual payment is discounted at the prevailing 3-month LIBOR.

$$\text{actual interest} = \$2,500/[1 + (90/360).08] = \$2,451$$

Suppose, instead, that LIBOR equals 5 percent in three months. Here, County Bank would pay Metro Bank:

$$\text{interest} = (.07 - .05)(90/360)\$1,000,000 = \$5,000$$

or

$$\$5,000/[1 + (90/360).05] = \$4,938$$

In this example, County Bank would pay fixed-rate/receive floating-rate as a hedge if it was exposed to loss in a rising rate environment. This is analogous to a short futures position. Metro Bank would take its position as a hedge if it was exposed to loss in a falling (relative to forward rate) rate environment. This is analogous to a long futures position.

POTENTIAL PROBLEMS WITH FRAS

While FRAs have some attractive features, there are several problems with using them in practice. First, like all forward contracts, FRAs are essentially credit instruments. This arises from the possibility that you might not be paid when the counterparty owes you cash. There is no clearinghouse to guarantee performance and no daily marking to market or collateral that is posted. In the past, some counterparties have reneged on forward contracts, so each participant must gauge carefully the reputation and soundness of its counterparties. Second, it is sometimes difficult to find a specific counterparty that wants to take exactly the opposite position. Because every FRA is negotiated, the parties might want different notional principal amounts or have a different settlement date. Thus, transactions costs can be large. Finally, FRAs are not as liquid as many alternatives. If a party to an FRA wants to exit the position prior to settlement, it might assign the contract to another party. But this requires that some compensation be paid. If the counterparty agrees, it might directly cancel the agreement for a fee. Alternatively, it might take exactly the opposite position with the counterparty if available, and lose only the change in price between origination of the FRA and the exit date.

BASIC INTEREST RATE SWAPS AS A RISK MANAGEMENT TOOL

Interest rate swaps originated in the Eurobond market in 1980, but have recently been one of the fastest growing off-balance sheet contracts in the world. Basic interest rate swaps are now widely used by financial institutions as hedging tools and as a means of creating synthetic balance sheet positions. This section documents the nature of swap transactions and demonstrates how financial institutions use them as a risk management tool.

CHARACTERISTICS

A **basic,** or **plain vanilla,** interest rate swap is an agreement between two parties to exchange a series of cash flows based on a specified notional principal amount. One party makes payments based on a fixed-interest rate and receives floating-rate payments, while the other party makes the floating-rate payments and receives the fixed-rate payments. The fixed rate is typically set off of prevailing Treasury note and bond rates and is quoted on a semiannual bond equivalent basis assuming a 365-day year. The floating rate is typically quoted on a money market basis assuming a 360-day year. These rates are applied against the notional principal amount that is constant over the life of the swap.[11] Maturities range from 6 months to 30 years, with most swaps in the 1- to 10-year range. In most swap transactions, a swap dealer makes a market in basic swaps and thus serves as an intermediary. As such, any party that wants to take a position can sign a master agreement with a swap dealer, which indicates the nature of the payment calculations, collateral requirements, and so on. The dealer takes the other side of the position. Thus, all transactions are effected through the dealer and any risks are manifested via the dealer's operations.

Exhibit 10.7 demonstrates how swap rates are quoted by a swap dealer. These data apply to basic interest rate swaps with 3-month LIBOR as the floating rate for all contracts. This means that all swap parties either pay or receive 3-month LIBOR versus a fixed rate that differs based on maturity. The first column indicates the term or maturity of the basic swap contract. The second column lists the prevailing U.S. Treasury spot rate with the same maturity as that for the swap. The third block of data represents the dealer's bid-offer spread relative to the prevailing Treasury rate. The final block of data provides the fixed rates for the different maturity swaps. The "bid" rates indicate the fixed rate that a swap party will receive if it pays 3-month LIBOR. The "offer" rates indicate the fixed rate that a swap party will pay if it receives 3-month LIBOR. The difference between the two represents the dealer's spread or profit potential.

This example emphasizes the role of an intermediary in processing swaps. This intermediary may simply serve as an agent with no credit risk exposure or as a dealer, where it is a

---

[11]Amortizing and accreting swaps are available where the notional principal amount decreases and increases, respectively, over time.

INTEREST RATE SWAP DEALER QUOTES FOR BASIC SWAPS: FIXED-RATE VERSUS 3-MONTH LIBOR, APRIL 2, 2002

Term	U.S. Treasuries (%)	Swap Spreads (%) (Mid-Point)	Swap Rates (%)	
			Bid	Offer
2 years	3.53	42.5	3.95	3.96
3 years	3.91	64.5	4.55	4.56
4 years	4.28	66.5	4.93	4.96
5 years	4.66	57.5	5.22	5.25
7 years	4.91	69.5	5.68	5.73
10 years	5.28	64	5.90	5.94
20 years	5.50	76.5	6.24	6.29
30 years	5.73	56.5	6.27	6.32

counterparty to each side of the transaction. As a dealer, the intermediary may enter into contracts without negotiating the other side of the swap and thus accept the risk of adverse rate changes. If it lays off the exposure to another counterparty, it hopes to earn the bid-offer spread. The intermediary's continuing role is to collect the interest payments and pay the difference to either party, depending on the contractual terms and the applicable interest rates. Today, many large commercial banks, investment banks, and Federal Home Loan Banks serve as intermediaries.

Conceptually, a basic interest rate swap is a package of FRAs. As with FRAs, swap payments are netted and the notional principal never changes hands. Consider the following example using data for a 2-year swap from Exhibit 10.7 based on 3-month LIBOR as the floating rate. This swap involves eight quarterly payments. Party FIX agrees to pay a fixed rate and Party FLT agrees to receive a fixed rate with cash flows calculated against a $10 million notional principal amount. The following rates apply.

| Party FIX: | Pay: 3.96% | Receive: 3-month LIBOR |
| Party FLT | Pay: 3-month LIBOR | Receive: 3.95% |

Exhibit 10.8 presents a time line with the expected cash flows from these two positions. Note that there are 8 valuation dates representing the 8 successive 3-month periods. Suppose that 3-month LIBOR for the first pricing interval equals 2.04 percent and there are 91 days in the 3-month period. The fixed payment for Party FIX is $98,729 and the floating rate receipt is $51,567 as calculated at the bottom of the exhibit. With netting and the swap dealer as the counterparty, Party FIX will have to pay the dealer the difference of $47,162. Assuming that Party FLT took the other side of this swap through the dealer, its floating rate payment is $51,567 while its fixed rate receipt is $98,479. Thus, Party FLT will receive the difference of $46,912 from the swap dealer. Of course, the dealer will net $250 from the spread, which will be constant across all floating rate changes as long as the two parties meet the swap terms. At the second and subsequent pricing intervals, only the applicable LIBOR is not known. As LIBOR changes, the amount that both Party FIX and Party FLT either pay or receive will change. We will discuss more about swap pricing later, but note for now that Party FIX will only receive cash at any pricing interval if 3-month LIBOR exceeds 3.96 percent. Party FLT will similarly receive cash as long as 3-month LIBOR is less than 4.95 percent. This emphasizes that the swap is a series of FRAs with each valuation date representing a distinct FRA with a different maturity.

• EXHIBIT 10.8

CASH FLOWS ASSOCIATED WITH BASIC INTEREST RATE SWAP POSITIONS

**Two-Year Maturity, $10 Million Notional Principal
with Eight Quarterly Swap Payments**

**FIX: Pay 3.96 Percent, Receive LIBOR
FLT: Pay LIBOR, Receive 3.95 Percent**

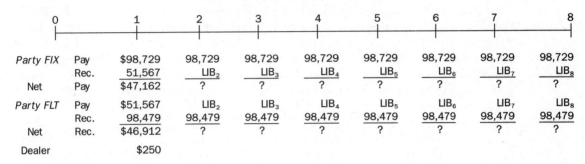

		0	1	2	3	4	5	6	7	8
Party FIX	Pay	$98,729	98,729	98,729	98,729	98,729	98,729	98,729	98,729
	Rec.	51,567	LIB_2	LIB_3	LIB_4	LIB_5	LIB_6	LIB_7	LIB_8
Net	Pay	$47,162	?	?	?	?	?	?	?
Party FLT	Pay	$51,567	LIB_2	LIB_3	LIB_4	LIB_5	LIB_6	LIB_7	LIB_8
	Rec.	98,479	98,479	98,479	98,479	98,479	98,479	98,479	98,479
Net	Rec.	$46,912	?	?	?	?	?	?	?
Dealer		$250							

Party FIX: Period 1

    Pay: 0.0396 (91/365) $10,000,000 = $98,729
    Rec: 0.0204 (91/360) $10,000,000 = $51,567

Party FLT: Period 1

    Pay: 0.0204 (91/360) $10,000,000 = $51,567
    Rec: 0.0395 (91/365) $10,000,000 = $98,479

NOTE: The notation LIB refers to 3-month LIBOR, with the subscript denoting the period for which the applicable floating LIBOR applies.

SWAP APPLICATIONS

Swaps represent another means for firms facing mismatched assets and liabilities to micro-hedge or macrohedge, or for firms that want to increase risk to adjust their earnings sensitivity in the desired way. Initially, only firms involved in the international money and capital markets used swaps, and virtually all transactions were priced in terms of LIBOR. More recently, medium-sized firms with only domestic operations have begun using swaps with many different rates, including Wall Street prime, the federal funds rate, commercial paper rate and T-bill rate, used to determine the underlying floating-rate payment obligations.

In its classic form, a plain vanilla swap arose when two firms faced substantially different interest rate risk over the same period. One firm was a high quality borrower while the other exhibited greater perceived default risk. An interest rate swap was structured to take advantage of the perceived credit quality differences by using the high quality borrower's reputation to lower each firm's borrowing cost and provide the preferred type of fixed-rate or floating-rate financing. In today's environment, these quality spread differentials have largely disappeared with the enormous growth in swap usage.

ADJUST THE RATE SENSITIVITY OF AN ASSET OR LIABILITY. The most common use of basic swaps is to adjust the rate sensitivity of a specific asset or liability. This may involve making a fixed-rate loan a floating-rate loan, converting a floating-rate liability to a fixed-rate liability, and so forth. Consider a bank that makes a $1 million, 3-year fixed-rate loan with quarterly interest at 9 percent. It finances the loan by issuing a 3-month Eurodollar deposit priced at 3-month LIBOR. The following T-account demonstrates the transaction.

Asset	Liability
Loan: $1 million, 3-year maturity	3-month Eurodollar deposit: $1 million
Rate: 9% fixed	Rate: 3-month LIBOR floating

By itself, this transaction exhibits considerable interest rate risk because the bank will see its net interest income shrink if it continues to roll-over the 3-month deposit at each maturity date and LIBOR increases. The bank is liability-sensitive and loses (gains) if LIBOR rises (falls). The bank can, however, use a basic swap to microhedge this transaction. Using the data from Exhibit 10.7 for a 3-year basic swap, the bank could agree to pay 4.56 percent and receive 3-month LIBOR against $1 million for the three years. By matching this with its continuous issuance of 3-month Eurodollars after earlier ones mature, it locks in a borrowing cost of 4.56 percent because it will both receive and pay LIBOR every quarter.[12]

Net Effect of Balance Sheet Transaction + Swap

Receive:	9% from loan + 3-month LIBOR from swap
Pay:	3-month LIBOR from Eurodollar deposit + 4.56% from swap
Net spread:	4.44%

The use of the swap enables the bank to reduce risk and lock in a spread of 4.44 percent (9 percent − 4.56 percent) on this transaction. The swap effectively fixed the borrowing cost at 4.56 percent for three years.

Consider another example where a bank has a commercial customer who demands a fixed-rate loan. The bank has a policy of making only floating-rate loans because it is liability-sensitive and does not want to take on additional interest rate risk. Ideally, the bank wants to price the loan off of prime. Suppose that the bank makes the same $1 million, 3-year fixed-rate loan as in the above case. It could enter into a 3-year basic swap involving prime as the floating-rate and a fixed-rate based off of prevailing Treasuries. Assume that it enters into such a swap with a $1 million notional principal amount, agreeing to pay a 4.56 percent fixed rate and receive prime minus 2.82 percent with quarterly payments. As indicated below, the effective interest rate received is now a floating rate equal to prime plus 162 basis points:

	Loan		Basic Swap
Receive:	9.00%		Prime − 2.82%
Pay:			4.56%
Net receipt:	Prime + (9.00% − 2.82% − 4.56%) or Prime + 1.62%		

This swap effectively converts a fixed-rate loan into a loan with a rate that floats with the prime rate.

CREATE A SYNTHETIC SECURITY. Some financial institutions view basic interest rate swaps as synthetic securities. As such, they enter into a swap contract that essentially replicates the net cash flows from a balance sheet transaction. For example, suppose that a bank buys a 3-year Treasury yielding 3.91 percent (from Exhibit 10.7) which it finances by issuing a 3-month deposit. This bank is liability-sensitive in that it will see its net interest income from this combined trade fall if the cost of the 3-month deposit rises over time. Many banks effectively finance securities with such deposits.

---

[12]The bank is accepting credit risk in the sense that if the market perceives that it is riskier over time and demands a risk premium on its future Eurodollar borrowings, it may pay more than 3-month LIBOR for the subsequent deposits.

Consider, as an alternative, simply entering into a 3-month swap agreeing to pay 3-month LIBOR and receive a fixed rate. Per the data in Exhibit 10.7, the fixed swap rate is 4.55 percent or 64 basis points above the 3-year Treasury rate. Interestingly, the swap produces a larger spread than the balance sheet transaction, yet has essentially the same interest rate risk profile. Why would management consider the balance sheet transaction as lower risk than the off-balance sheet swap? It does have to hold capital against the swap, albeit at a low percentage, and does not have to hold capital against the balance sheet position because it owns a zero-risk class asset.[13] If it no longer wanted to assume the risk, it also has the flexibility to alter its debt financing on-balance sheet at any time, and could reduce risk by issuing a longer-term deposit that matched the remaining maturity of the Treasury. Of course, the spread it earned afterward could be far different from that initially available. In contrast, it would have to exit the swap by selling its position, which might involve taking a loss. Management must determine whether the yield advantage of the swap outweighs these risks and costs.

MACROHEDGE. Banks can also use interest rate swaps to hedge their aggregate risk exposure measured by earnings and MVE sensitivity. The analysis is analogous to that with financial futures. Specifically, a bank that is liability-sensitive or has a positive duration gap will take a basic swap position that potentially produces profits when rates increase. With a basic swap, this means paying a fixed rate and receiving a floating rate. Any profits can be used to offset losses from lost net interest income or declining MVE. This would have a comparable impact as shorting financial futures. In terms of GAP analysis, a liability-sensitive bank has more rate-sensitive liabilities than rate-sensitive assets (GAP < 0 indicates RSAs < RSLs). To hedge, the bank needs the equivalent of more RSAs. A swap that pays fixed and receives floating is comparable to increasing RSAs relative to RSLs because the receipt floats (reprices) with rate changes.

Similarly, any bank that is asset-sensitive or has a negative duration gap and wants to hedge will take a swap position that potentially produces profits when rates fall. With a basic swap, this means paying a floating rate and receiving a fixed rate. If rates fall, net interest income and MVE would fall, but the swap would likely produce a gain to offset at least part of the loss. This would have the same impact as going long financial futures. In terms of GAP analysis, an asset-sensitive bank has more rate-sensitive assets than rate-sensitive liabilities (RSAs > RSLs). To hedge, the bank needs the equivalent of more RSLs. A swap that pays a floating rate and receives a fixed rate is comparable in impact to increasing RSLs relative to RSAs.

Many banks report their aggregate use of interest rate swaps in their rate sensitivity reports, and thus the aggregate impact on the banks' overall interest rate sensitivity. Such treatment allows the analyst to assess, in general, whether management uses swaps to increase or decrease overall risk. Consider the data for ABC bank from Exhibit 8.7 in Chapter 8, which presents the rate sensitivity report for year-end 2001. Note the data in the third row from the bottom of the exhibit titled "Swaps: Pay Fixed/Receive Floating." These data are summary figures that indicate the aggregate impact of ABC Bank's use of swaps across different time intervals. Under the column of rate-sensitive assets and liabilities for 3 months or less, the figure is 50,000. To determine what this figure represents, note that the bank's periodic GAP for this interval prior to the swaps' impact would have equaled −$70,252 ($278,748 − $349,000). After the swaps, the periodic GAP was −$20,252. Thus, the swaps had the equivalent effect of adding $50,000 in rate-sensitive assets within this time interval. Conceptually, ABC paid a fixed rate and received a floating rate on a $50,000 notional principal to move the periodic GAP over this interval closer to zero so that the use of swaps represented a macrohedge. The corresponding impact from 1 to 3 years and 3 to 5 years also represented a hedge.

---

[13]Risk-based capital requirements for banks are introduced in Chapter 13. Generally, banks are not required to hold capital against cash and Treasury securities that have no default risk.

At the end of the chapter there is a problem in which you are expected to analyze the rate sensitivity report of South Trust at year-end 2001. For this bank, the effect of interest rate swaps is negative through each time interval: 31–90 days, 91–180 days, and 181–365 days. In each interval, swaps make the bank's periodic GAP more negative. In the aggregate, swaps make a liability-sensitive bank more liability sensitive, such that its interest rate risk increases as measured by GAP, after the use of swaps.

PRICING BASIC SWAPS

The pricing of basic interest rate swaps is straightforward. Consider the time line in Exhibit 10.8. The floating rate, such as 3-month LIBOR in the example, is based on some predetermined money market rate or index. The payment frequency is coincidentally set at every six months, three months, or one month and is generally matched with the money market rate. The fixed rate is set at a spread above the comparable maturity Treasury note rate. For swap maturities out to five years, the swap or dealer spread is priced off of the implied yields on a strip of Eurodollar futures contracts for the same maturities. Beyond five years, the swap or dealer spread is priced off of risk premiums associated with matched maturity/duration corporate notes and bonds. These conventions are widely recognized which makes the valuation of swaps straightforward.

For example, the earlier discussion assumed that the applicable LIBOR for the first pricing date three months from the present in Exhibit 10.8 was 2.04 percent, which equals the current 3-month LIBOR rate. The implied 3-month LIBOR yield for the second pricing date, six months from the present (LIB_2), would be the futures rate on a 3-month Eurodollar futures contract that expires three months from the present. The other implied 3-month LIBOR rates (LIB_3, LIB_4, etc.) are similarly assumed to be the subsequent 3-month Eurodollar futures rates that represent successive futures expiration dates. In terms of Exhibit 10.8, Party FIX and Party FLT presumably did not know what LIBOR would be on these valuation dates. Neither would enter into the contract if it expected, *a priori*, to lose on the transaction. The implication is that a basic swap is priced as a zero net present value transaction. This means that after substituting in an expected value for LIBOR at each of the eight valuation dates, the present value of the net cash flows (netted payments and receipts) must equal zero. In essence, the fixed rate that is quoted to each party (actually, the midpoint of the two fixed rates), represents the rate that produces a zero net present value for the assumed net cash flows. Given the expected values for LIBOR read off the matched maturity Eurodollar futures contracts, the spreads over Treasury rates are determined as the mark-ups necessary to make a swap's net present value equal zero.

COMPARING FINANCIAL FUTURES, FRAS, AND BASIC SWAPS

There are many similarities between interest rate swaps, financial futures, and FRAs. Each different contract enables a party to enter an agreement, which provides for cash receipts or cash payments depending on how interest rates move. Each allows managers to alter a bank's interest rate risk exposure. None requires much of an initial cash commitment to take a position. The following table compares the positions with specific objectives.

| | Position | |
Objective	Financial Futures	FRAs & Basic Swaps
Profit if rates rise	Sell futures	Pay fixed, receive floating
Profit if rates fall	Buy futures	Pay floating, receive fixed

There are also several key differences. First, financial futures are standardized contracts based on fixed principal amounts. Parties negotiate the notional principal amount with FRAs and interest rate swaps. Financial futures require daily marking-to-market, which is not required with FRAs and swaps. This exposes futures participants to some risk and liquidity requirements that FRAs and swaps avoid. Many futures contracts cannot be traded out more than three to four years, while interest rate swaps often extend 10 to 30 years. The market for FRAs is not that liquid and most contracts are short-term. Historically, trading activity was much deeper with futures such that liquidity, especially for the nearby contracts, was far greater. Swap activity has recently grown to where participants can readily buy and sell swaps in a secondary market and thus exit a position when needed. This is especially true because of the consensus on how to value basic swaps using Eurodollar futures rates. Finally, swap documentation is quite standardized and participating firms can negotiate master agreements with partners that enhance the development of long-term business relationships.

THE RISK WITH SWAPS

While interest swaps are an alternative to futures and FRAs, they also entail risks. The recent experience of savings and loans is an example. When interest rates increased sharply during the early 1980s, many thrifts took advantage of interest rate swaps to obtain fixed-rate financing. When mortgage rates averaged 13 to 14 percent, it seemed reasonable to fix borrowing costs at 11 percent. Unfortunately for these swap players, the level of interest rates moved dramatically lower in the mid-1980s. Had thrifts waited, they could have paid much lower rates on both fixed-rate and floating-rate debt. Thus, they locked in much higher fixed interest expense for the benefit of risk reduction. The problems were compounded as homeowners took advantage of the lower rates to refinance their mortgages. In many instances, thrifts lost their high yielding, fixed-rate assets via prepayments but kept their fixed-rate interest obligations. Selling the swap obligations to a third party prior to expiration would have produced a direct income statement loss.

Similar problems arose with Long-Term Capital Management's use of swaps in 1998. This hedge fund made speculative bets that different interest rates would converge (equal the same value) over time. Because they were confident in their bet, management used swaps to increase the leverage of their position. When interest rates subsequently moved in different directions, losses on the swaps and other positions virtually depleted the firm's capital and it had to be bailed out by a consortium of financial institutions.

Market participants have developed a secondary market for swaps to reduce a firm's exposure to swap positions that it might want to exit. Straightforward plain vanilla swaps follow a standardized format stipulated by terms of the International Swap Dealers Agreement such that positions can be quickly entered and exited. The standardized features have made it easy to trade these swaps in the secondary market. Unfortunately, the more complicated is a swap, such as those introduced in Chapter 11, the more difficult it is to trade the swap in the secondary market. Each swap is a negotiated contract between two parties. When the terms are unusual, the attractiveness decreases in the secondary market because the buyer must carefully analyze and price the unusual features of the underlying swap. Without guarantees or easily identifiable default risk, the liquidity of swaps diminishes. Such swaps, particularly those with options and other nonstandardized terms, are not as readily marketable.

There is some credit risk with swaps as well, but this is not as great for a single contract as it originally seems. Remember that swap parties exchange only net interest payments. The notional principal amount never changes hands, such that a party will not lose that amount. Credit risk exists because the counterparty to a swap contract may default. This is a problem when interest rates have moved against the counterparty and you are owed money. Suppose that you have agreed to pay LIBOR and receive 7 percent with semiannual payments for 3 years. If LIBOR is above 7 percent, you must pay the counterparty such that the counterparty owes you nothing. The counterparty is concerned with your ability to pay. You accept counterparty risk when LIBOR is below 7 percent. This risk is generally associated with the swap dealer's credit standing. When either counterparty perceives that there is a meaningful probability that the other counterparty may not perform under a swap, it will require collateral in support of the swap position. The existence and value of the collateral, in turn, affect the prices that intermediaries charge for making a market in swaps. These collateral arrangements are commonly part of bilateral collateral agreements that counterparties sign when they enter the swap market. The value of the required collateral, in turn, often rises and falls with changes in the ongoing (mark-to-market) value of the swap position.

Counterparty risk is extremely important to swap participants. Firms that are actively engaged in swap transactions often limit the amount of swap business they will do with any single counterparty to limit their risk exposure. Banks should have such policy limits approved by the board of directors before entering into swap contracts.

SUMMARY

Bank managers are paid to manage risk. In many cases, it is appropriate to reduce a bank's exposure to potentially adverse changes in interest rates. Hedging with financial futures contracts, forward rate agreements (FRAs), and basic interest rate swap agreements are three methods banks can use to reduce interest rate risk. The concept underlying hedging with futures is that a bank trades financial futures such that losses or gains on its actual cash transactions due to interest rate changes are at least partially offset by gains or losses on its futures position. Risk reduction occurs because the net loss or gain is typically less with a hedge than if no futures position is taken. The same applies with forward rate agreements and interest rate swaps. A basic interest rate swap is, in fact, a package of forward rate agreements. A bank exposed to loss on balance sheet when rates rise or fall can trade fixed interest payments or receipts for floating interest payments or receipts that similarly offset the change in net interest income from balance sheet positions. Thus, when net interest income declines, the FRA and swap produce a net cash receipt. When net interest income increases, the FRA and swap require a net cash payment.

Managers must determine whether they want to hedge or, alternatively, use these derivatives to speculatively increase their risk exposure. For example, some banks view swaps as synthetic securities complete with interest rate risk. When hedging, managers must decide whether to microhedge individual transactions or macrohedge a bank's aggregate interest rate risk measured by GAP and earnings sensitivity or duration gap and MVE sensitivity. The fundamental conclusion is that managers have alternatives to alter a bank's interest rate risk position other than traditional cash transactions.

Questions

1. How does a futures contract differ from a forward contract?
2. It is said that a microhedge does not totally eliminate risk. Assume that a bank uses financial futures contracts to reduce the risk of rising rates on new borrowings. Identify what type of position the bank should take to hedge. Once a hedge is in place, what risks remain?

3. Some analysts compare the initial margin on a futures contract to a down payment. Some label it a performance bond. What is the difference between these interpretations?

4. Suppose that you are a speculator who trades 3-month Eurodollar futures. On November 5, you sell two December 3-month Eurodollar futures contracts at 94.81. The subsequent weekly quotes for the closing December Eurodollar futures price are as follows:

Date:	11/12	11/19	11/26	12/3
Price:	94.92	95.08	94.77	94.63

Calculate the weekly values in your margin account. The initial margin is $650 per contract and the maintenance margin is $400. Calculate your realized return for the entire period. Assume that you offset your futures position on December 3 at the price indicated.

5. Suppose that you are a speculator who tries to time interest rate movements on 3-month T-bill futures contracts. Use the data in Exhibit 10.1 and assume that it is April 2, 2002, to answer the following questions.
   a. What is the 3-month T-bill rate in the cash market? (Approximate it from the yield curve.) How does it differ from the June futures rate?
   b. Use the data from the Treasury yield curve for 3-month and 6-month maturities to calculate the 3-month forward rate, three months after April 2, 2002.
   c. Compare the forward rate you calculated from part b with the June 2002 T-bill futures rate. Do they provide similar information? Should they provide similar information?
   d. As a speculator, you expect cash T-bill rates to rise through December 2002.
      1. Explain precisely what expectations are consistent with selling the June 2002 T-bill futures contract to make a profit.
      2. Explain precisely what rate expectations are consistent with buying the June 2002 T-bill futures contract to make a profit.

6. Explain why cross hedges generally exhibit greater risk than hedges using a futures contract based on the underlying cash instrument hedged.

7. In each of the following cases, conduct the analysis for Step 1 and Step 2 in evaluating a hedge. Specifically assess cash market risk and determine whether the bank should buy or sell financial futures as a hedge. Explain how the hedge should work.
   a. The bank expects to receive a large, past-due principal payment on a loan in 45 days.
   b. A deposit customer notifies the bank that she will be withdrawing $5 million in 60 days. The bank will sell a Treasury security from its investment portfolio at that time to cover the withdrawal.
   c. The bank has agreed to make a 1-year fixed-rate loan at 9.5 percent. It will fund the loan by issuing four consecutive 3-month Eurodollar time deposits. It would like to lock-in its borrowing costs on the Eurodollar time deposits.
   d. The bank just won a $10 million court settlement against a supplier and will receive the payment in three months.
   e. In order to improve the bank's capital position, management decides to issue 15-year subordinated debentures (bonds). Unfortunately, this debt offering cannot be ready for another five months.

8. A bank plans to hedge using 3-month Eurodollar futures contracts based on $1 million in principal. Determine how many contracts the bank should trade (its hedge ratio) in the following situations.

    a. The bank will roll over $125 million in 6-month CDs in four months. The Eurodollar futures rate moves 1.5 times as much as the CD rate.

    b. In three months the bank will roll over $50 million in 1-month loans. The loan rates move 1-to-1 with Eurodollar futures rates.

    c. In six months the bank will extend $5 million in floating-rate loans tied to the Eurodollar cash rate. The futures and cash rates move 1-to-1.

9. A bank that hedges with financial futures cannot completely eliminate interest rate risk. Explain what basis risk is and why it exists. Is it ever possible to eliminate basis risk?

10. Explain how macrohedging differs from microhedging.

11. A bank has assets of $10 million earning an average return of 9 percent and with a weighted duration of 1.5 years. It has liabilities of $9 million paying an average rate of 6.5 percent with a weighted duration of 3.5 years. The bank wants to construct a macrohedge to reduce interest rate risk as much as possible, and plans to trade 3-month Eurodollar futures currently trading at 8 percent.

    a. Should the bank buy or sell Eurodollar futures?

    b. How many futures contracts should the bank trade?

    c. If cash interest rates rise an average of 1 percent and the Eurodollar futures rate rises by 1.10 percent, calculate how much the bank's market value of equity will change and how much the bank would earn or lose on its futures position. Was this a successful hedge?

12. What are the risks in a forward rate agreement if you are the buyer?

13. Assume that you want to speculate on how 6-month cash market LIBOR will move over the next year. You believe that consensus forecasts of future rates are too high. You can enter into an FRA and agree either to pay 7.25 percent and receive 6-month LIBOR, or pay 6-month LIBOR and receive 7.25 percent for delivery in one year. Explain which position you would take and why you expect to profit.

14. It is January 1. Your firm expects to issue (borrow) 3-month Eurodollar time deposits at the beginning of February, May, August, and November in the next year. Explain what position(s) you would take today with FRAs based on 3-month LIBOR if you wanted to fully hedge your future borrowings. Why should the hedge work? What risks do you take?

15. Discuss the role of a third-party intermediary in an interest rate swap agreement. Describe the risks assumed by the intermediary. How does the intermediary potentially profit from this activity?

16. What features of interest rate swaps make them more or less attractive than financial futures as a risk management tool?

17. Is there credit risk in an interest rate swap with an intermediary bank serving as the swap dealer. Describe when default losses might arise and which party is at risk. How can credit risk be reduced?

18. A basic interest rate swap is supposedly priced as a zero net present value transaction. Explain what this means. Use the 2-year swap data from Exhibit 10.7 to demonstrate your arguments.

19. Your firm just made a 3-year fixed-rate loan at 8.25 percent. You would like to convert this to a floating-rate loan that is priced off of 3-month LIBOR as the base rate. Explain how you could use a basic interest rate swap to accomplish this. Using the data from Exhibit 10.7, choose swap terms that convert this fixed-rate loan to a floating-rate and demonstrate the resulting rate you would earn on the loan from adding the swap to the loan position.

20. Your bank is looking for the lowest cost 2-year, fixed-rate financing. It has decided to issue four consecutive 3-month Eurodollar time deposits on-balance sheet and hedge the future borrowing costs by taking positions in the market for basic interest rate swaps. What positions are appropriate? Use the data from Exhibit 10.7 to demonstrate how swaps might be used to fix the bank's borrowing cost over two years.

PROBLEMS

I. HEDGING BORROWING COSTS

Your bank is a regular borrower in the Eurodollar market. On August 9, 2002, the head of the funds management division decides to hedge the bank's interest cost on a $10 million 3-month Eurodollar issue scheduled for November 2002. On August 9, the bank could issue $10 million in 3-month Eurodollars at 4.61 percent. The corresponding futures rates for 3-month Eurodollar futures contracts were 4.83 percent (December 2002), 5.01 percent (March 2003), and 5.38 percent (June 2003).

1. What is the bank's specific cash market risk on August 9, 2002? Should the bank buy or sell Eurodollar futures to hedge its borrowing costs? Explain how the hedge should work.

2. Which Eurodollar futures contract should the bank use? Explain why it is best. Assume that the bank takes the futures position that you recommend in questions 1 and 2 at the rate available on August 9, 2002. On November 6, 2002, the bank issues $10 million in Eurodollars at 6.25 percent. Coincidentally, it closes out (reverses) its futures position when the futures rate on the contract you chose equals 6.33 percent. Calculate the profit or loss on the futures trades, the opportunity gain or loss in the cash market, and the effective return or cost to the bank on its Eurodollar issue.

3. Suppose instead that interest rates declined after August 9 and the bank actually issued Eurodollars at 4.47 percent. Assuming it closed out its futures position at 4.59 percent, calculate the same profit/loss and return/cost components as above.

4. It is important to note that the prevailing futures rate at the time a hedge is initiated reflects consensus information regarding the future level of cash market rates. Explain conceptually why the effectiveness of hedging is influenced by the accuracy of the futures rate.

II. THE BASIS

1. Assume that your bank expects to receive $5 million in funds that it will invest in Eurodollars in four months. It plans to buy five Eurodollar futures contracts as a hedge. The current 3-month Eurodollar rate equals 5.05 percent in the cash market, and the Eurodollar futures rate for the contract purchased equals 5.39 percent. The futures contract expires one week after the bank expects to receive and invest the $5 million. Given that a hedge still encompasses basis risk, compare the basis today with what the basis will likely equal when the bank offsets its futures position as part of closing the hedge. Provide a specific forecast of the basis in 4 months and explain why you chose this basis. The bank should incorporate this expected basis change when estimating the effective return from the hedge. What is this expected effective return in your analysis? When will the actual return differ from what you expect?

2. Suppose that one minute before expiration, the 3-month March T-bill futures rate equals 6.04 percent, while the T-bill in the cash market that is deliverable against the futures contract carries a rate of 6.00 percent. As noted in Chapter 6, 3-month T-bills are discount instruments priced on a discount basis using a 360-day year. The 3-month

T-bill futures contract is based on $1 million principal such that each basis point is worth $25. Use this information and the price difference between the futures and cash instruments to explain how you can trade these instruments to earn a riskless profit. What does this indicate regarding the basis at expiration of a futures contract?

III. BASIC INTEREST RATE SWAPS

1. Management at your firm is considering one of the following:
   a. Balance Sheet Transaction: Issue a 6-month CD at 5.50 percent and use the proceeds to buy a 3-year Treasury security that carries a 7.20 percent fixed rate. It will roll over (issue new 6-month CDs) when the old one matures until funding the Treasury is no longer needed.
   b. Interest Rate Swap Transaction: Enter into a three-year basic interest rate swap where it agrees to pay 6-month LIBOR and receive a fixed 7.58 percent rate.
      1. List the advantages and disadvantages of the two alternatives versus each other.
      2. Identify the specific risks associated with each alternative.
      3. Are they both speculative?

2. Two institutions plan to issue $10 million in debt and are negotiating an interest rate swap that will help them lower their borrowing costs and obtain the preferred type (fixed-rate or floating-rate) of financing. Both are comparing their balance sheet alternatives with combined balance sheet and swap opportunities. Internet Bank has a negative GAP through three years, is liability sensitive, and would like to use the debt proceeds to invest in short-term assets to reduce its interest rate risk. Brick & Mortar Bank has a positive GAP through three years, is asset sensitive, and would like to use its debt proceeds to invest in fixed-rate assets to reduce its interest rate risk. Internet Bank can borrow at an 8.7 percent fixed rate for three years or pay the prevailing 6-month LIBOR plus 0.50 percent on floating-rate debt. Brick & Mortar Bank can borrow at an 8.15 percent fixed rate for three years or the prevailing 6-month LIBOR rate plus 0.25 percent.
   a. Explain whether and why Internet Bank needs fixed-rate or floating-rate funding to meet its objectives. Do the same for Brick & Mortar Bank.
   b. Assume that both banks issue either 3-year fixed-rate debt or 6-month floating-rate debt on-balance sheet. They want to combine this with a basic swap to obtain the cheapest form of funding that helps reduce interest rate risk. Using the following basic swap terms, indicate what position each bank should take. Explain how and why it should meet the bank's objectives. Calculate the effective cost of borrowing that each bank ends up with.

Basic Swap Terms

A. Pay 8.1%	Receive 6-month LIBOR
B. Pay 6-month LIBOR	Receive 8.03%

3. A regional bank holding company recently bought a $100 million package of mortgages that carry an average 8.5 percent yield. The holding company has established a subsidiary to manage this package. The subsidiary will finance the mortgages by selling 90-day commercial paper for which the current rate is 5.25 percent. The interest rate risk assumed by the subsidiary is evidenced by the difference in duration of the mortgages at six years and the duration of the commercial paper at 72 days. The holding company thus decides to arrange an interest rate swap through an intermediary bank to hedge the subsidiary's interest rate risk.

a. Should the subsidiary make floating-rate or fixed-rate payments in the swap market? Specifically, should the subsidiary pay fixed and receive floating, or pay floating and receive fixed? Use the following data to select specific swap terms. Explain why this swap should reduce the subsidiary's interest rate risk.

> Pay 7.37 percent and receive floating at 3-month LIBOR
> Pay 3-month LIBOR and receive 7.24 percent

b. At the first pricing of the swap when the subsidiary exchanges payments with the intermediary, LIBOR equals 6.95 percent. The notional principal amount is $100 million. Calculate the subsidiary's net cash payment or receipt with the intermediary. At the second pricing, LIBOR equals 7.66 percent. Calculate the subsidiary's net cash payment or receipt with the intermediary here.

c. What specific credit risk does the subsidiary assume in the swap you arranged? What specific credit risk does the intermediary assume? Explain by discussing when each party is at risk that it will lose if the counterparty defaults.

IV. SOUTH TRUST RATE SENSITIVITY ANALYSIS: 2001

Data for South Trust's rate sensitivity at year-end 2001 provided on the following page. Use the information to answer the following questions.

1. Toward the bottom of the table, a row of data indicate the effect of interest rate swaps. Did the bank's swap activity increase or decrease the bank's risk exposure through one year?

2. What type of basis swaps (what pay, receive position) did the bank appear to take to produce the GAP effect needed?

SOUTH TRUST INTEREST RATE SENSITIVITY ANALYSIS
December 31, 2001

	0–30 Days	31–90 Days	91–180 Days	181–365 Days	1–5 Years	Over 5 Years	Non-interest sensitive	Total
Variable-rate commercial and real estate loans	$15,126.6	$ 1,143.7	$ 247.3	$ 332.7	$ 755.3	$ 88.7	$ 0.0	$17,694.3
Fixed-rate commercial and real estate loans	261.0	390.9	611.8	1,068.2	6,286.3	2,171.8	0.0	10,790.0
Other loans	2,266.7	499.2	248.7	398.2	1,367.5	158.0	0.0	4,938.3
Total Loans	17,654.3	2,033.8	1,107.8	1,799.1	8,409.1	2,418.5	0.0	33,422.6
Securities	846.3	368.9	537.2	966.1	4,078.6	3,702.4	0.0	10,499.5
Other interest-earning assets	332.4	596.6	0.0	0.0	0.0	0.0	0.0	929.0
Total Interest-earning assets	18,833.0	2,999.3	1,645.0	2,765.2	12,487.7	6,120.9	0.0	44,851.1
Allowance for loan losses	0.0	0.0	0.0	0.0	0.0	0.0	(483.1)	(483.1)
Other assets	0.0	0.0	0.0	0.0	0.0	0.0	4,386.4	4,386.5
Total Assets	$18,833.0	$ 2,999.3	$ 1,645.0	$ 2,765.2	$12,487.7	$ 6,120.9	$ 3,903.4	$48,754.5
Non-interest-bearing demand deposits	$ 0.0	$ 0.0	$ 0.0	$ 0.0	$ 0.0	$ 0.0	$4,392.3	$4,392.3
Interest-bearing demand deposits	571.0	1,595.6	0.0	0.0	1,770.2	0.0	0.0	3,936.8
Money market deposits	753.0	2,259.0	0.0	0.0	2,008.0	0.0	0.0	5,020.0
Savings deposits	226.9	0.0	0.0	0.0	2,041.9	0.0	0.0	2,268.8
Time deposits under $100,000	941.4	1,762.3	1,562.3	1,631.8	12,147.3	7.2	0.0	8,052.3
Other time deposits	4,043.2	1,728.1	1,742.8	937.4	493.4	19.0	0.0	8,963.9
Total deposits	6,535.5	7,345.0	3,305.1	2,569.2	8,460.8	26.2	4,392.3	32,634.1
Short-term borrowings	4,591.5	492.8	439.6	401.4	0.0	0.0	0.0	5,925.3
FHLB advances	1,650.0	700.1	0.0	0.0	40.0	1,831.0	0.0	4,221.1
Long-term debt	200.0	25.0	0.0	0.0	301.1	737.3	0.0	1,263.4
Other liabilities	0.0	0.0	0.0	0.0	0.0	0.0	748.2	748.2
Stockholders' equity	0.0	0.0	0.0	0.0	0.0	0.0	3,962.4	3,962.4
Total liabilities and stockholders' equity	$12,977.0	$ 8,562.9	$ 3,744.7	$ 2,970.6	$ 8,801.9	$ 2,594.5	$ 9,102.9	$48,754.5
Interest rate gap	$ 5,856.0	$ (5,563.6)	$(2,099.7)	$ (205.4)	$ 3,685.8	$ 3,526.4	$(5,199.5)	
Effect on interest rate swaps	110.0	(844.5)	(227.5)	(395.0)	792.0	565.0		
Cumulative interest rate gap	$ 5,966.0	$ (442.1)	$ (2,769.3)	$ (3,369.7)	$ 1,108.1	$ 5,199.5		
Cumulative gap as a percentage of interest-earning assets—								
December 31, 2001	13.30%	(0.99)%	(6.17)%	(7.51)%	2.47%	11.59%		
December 31, 2000	3.25	(15.06)	(19.50)	(20.86)	(8.91)	10.95		

11

OPTIONS, CAPS, FLOORS, AND MORE COMPLEX SWAPS

Imagine a situation where your bank only makes floating rate loans. One of your best business customers approaches you and wants to borrow, but only on a fixed-rate basis. Do you try to change the customer's mind, convincing the firm to borrow at prime plus a spread? Or can you make a fixed-rate loan and effectively convert it to a floating rate loan? One alternative is to make a fixed-rate loan and simultaneously buy an interest rate cap. Everyone wins, especially the bank, if you can get the customer to pay for the cap.

In addition to futures and basic interest rate swaps, banks can use a wide range of off-balance sheet option contracts to manage interest rate risk. The interest rate cap noted above is an option on future interest rates. Banks may use options to hedge interest rate risk exposure or speculatively try to profit from future rate moves. The primary advantage of options is that a buyer can limit losses from the option position, but retain the opportunity to profit if prices (rates) move favorably. Their primary disadvantage is that price changes must be substantial before they improve on hedging with futures or swap positions because there is an up-front cost of entering the position.

Options on financial instruments represent one of the most important innovations in financial markets over the past 30 years. To participate in the options market, buyers must put up only a small fraction of the underlying asset's total value and this up-front cost is fixed. Conceptually, options are comparable to insurance. There is a cost to buying insurance represented by the cost of the option. If the underlying asset changes in value, the option holder may sell the contract and be compensated for the value adjustment. In the context of interest rate risk, you can buy insurance to protect against rising rates (buy a cap) or protect against falling rates (buy a floor). In recent years, interest rate swaps with options have also been traded via swap dealers. These contracts convey some advantages over other vehicles to manage interest rate risk.

T his chapter focuses on the use of options to manage interest rate risk at banks. The objective is to demonstrate how the features of options on financial futures, caps, floors, and interest rate swaps with options compare to those of financial futures and plain vanilla swaps in bank hedging programs. Each of these instruments has its own risk and return profile. Options, however, are unique because they limit downside risk to the buyer, equal to the up-front premium payment, but retain the benefits from favorable rate moves.

THE NATURE OF OPTIONS ON FINANCIAL FUTURES

An option contract is an agreement between two parties in which one gives the other the right, but not the obligation, to buy or sell a specific asset at a set price for a specified period of time. The buyer of an option pays a premium for the opportunity to decide whether to effect the transaction (exercise the option) when it is beneficial. The option seller (option writer) receives the initial option premium. This discussion examines options in which the underlying asset is a Eurodollar futures contract.

There are two types of options, with a buyer and seller for each transaction. A **call option** gives the buyer the right to buy a fixed amount of the underlying asset at a specific strike price for a set period of time. The seller of the call option, in turn, is obligated to deliver the underlying asset to the buyer when the buyer exercises the option. A **put option** gives the buyer the right to sell a fixed amount of the underlying asset at a specific strike price for a set period of time. The seller of a put option is obligated to buy the underlying asset when the put option buyer exercises the option. In both cases the buyer of the option determines the timing of exercise. The objective of the option seller is to profit from the premium. The objective of the buyer may be to hedge a position in the cash market, or to speculatively profit from a favorable price or rate move that increases the value of the option above the premium paid.

For example, suppose that you paid $100 for the right to buy an asset at a $750,000 exercise (strike) price at any time over the next two months. You are the buyer of a call option. Suppose that the underlying asset is currently priced at $750,000. You can profit if the asset's market value rises above $750,000, perhaps to $760,000, because you can exercise the option by immediately paying $750,000 to gain title to the asset and then sell it for $760,000 for a $10,000 gain (minus the $100 premium). Alternatively, the value of the option will increase with the price move to $760,000 and you can gain by selling the option at the higher price. If the underlying asset's price falls, you will not exercise the option and you may potentially lose your $100 premium. You may, of course, sell the option before the two months elapse and reclaim some value if the premium has not fallen to zero. If you bought a put option on the same asset with an exercise price of $750,000, you would gain if the underlying asset price fell below $750,000 because you own the right to sell the asset at this higher price.

At any point in time, the market price of the underlying asset may be above, below, or equal to the option strike price. This price comparison determines the option's value. The buyer of a call option with a strike price below the current market price can exercise the option and immediately sell the underlying asset for more than the strike price. Such an option is said to be *in the money*. In the above example, the call option is in the money if the underlying asset price is anything over $750,000. The greater the price differential, the greater the value of the position and the option premium. Similarly, a put option is in the money if the underlying asset's market price is below the strike price because the buyer can acquire the asset for sale at a price below the contracted sale price. The buyer of a put option in the above example would find the option in the money if the asset price was below $750,000. When an option holder cannot exercise the option at the same or a favorable price compared with the strike price, the option is *out of the money.* For example, a call option is out of the money when the market price of the underlying asset is below the strike price (less than $750,000 in the above example). A put option is out of the money when the market price exceeds the strike price (more than $750,000 in the above example). If the exercise and actual prices are equal, the option is *at the money.* These relationships are summarized below. Key terms are defined in Exhibit 11.1.

	Call Option	Put Option
In the Money	Market price > Strike price	Market price < Strike price
Out of the Money	Market price < Strike price	Market price > Strike price
At the Money	Market price = Strike price	Market price = Strike price

EXAMPLES USING EURODOLLAR FUTURES

Consider the data in Exhibit 11.2 for options on 90-day Eurodollar futures introduced in Chapter 10. The data represent settlement (closing) quotes for April 2, 2002. Eurodollar futures and options prices are quoted by subtracting the appropriate Eurodollar rate, measured in percentage points to two decimal places, from 100. Because the futures carry a face value of $1 million and have a 3-month maturity, each basis point change in price or interest rate has a $25 value.

The first column of options data lists various strike prices, from lowest to highest. The futures rates associated with these prices range from 3.00 percent (97.00) to 2.00 percent (98.00). The remaining columns of data list the premiums or prices of the various options. The exhibit identifies two call options that expire in June 2002 and September 2002, and two put options that expire in the same months. These option expiration dates coincide with the expiration dates on the underlying futures. Note at the bottom of the exhibit that the corresponding futures prices equal 97.52 and 96.83, respectively, for futures rates of 2.48 percent and 3.17 percent.

Consider first the call options. The Eurodollar call option with a 97.00 strike price gives the buyer the right to purchase a June 2002 Eurodollar futures contract at 97.00, or a 3.00 percent futures rate. The seller of this call option will, in turn, be required to sell a June 2002 Eurodollar futures contract when the buyer exercises the option. The buyer of the call option immediately pays the option premium of 53 basis points, or $1,325. The seller of this option immediately receives the $1,325 premium payment.[1] The option expires on June 19, 2002, when the underlying Eurodollar futures contract expires. The buyer of a call option can get out of the position in one of three ways. First, the option can expire without being exercised. Second, the buyer of the call option can exercise it prior to expiration. Third, the buyer can offset the initial transaction by reversing the trade or, in this case, by selling a June 2002 Eurodollar futures call option prior to the expiration date. The seller of the call option can get out at option expiration if the option is never exercised, by taking the short position of a June 2002 Eurodollar futures if the option is exercised, or by buying a June 2002 Eurodollar futures call option prior to expiration.

On April 2, 2002, the June 2002 Eurodollar futures price (rate) was 97.52 (2.48 percent). The June call option is in the money because the market price exceeds the strike price. A buyer

[1]The buyer of the option is not required to post any margin because the maximum loss equals the option premium and the buyer pays the premium up front. There is no cash flow obligation until the option is exercised or sold. The seller of the option must post a margin deposit with the exchange to collateralize the position because the loss potential is unlimited. If prices move against the seller, additional margin may be required.

· EXHIBIT 11.1

KEY TERMINOLOGY

At the money. An option in which the market price of the underlying asset equals the strike price.

Call option. An option in which the buyer has the right to buy an underlying asset at a predetermined strike price for a set period of time.

Cash settlement. The option buyer receives cash from the seller at option expiration equal to the difference between the value of the option and the strike price.

Collar. The combination of buying an interest rate cap and selling an interest rate floor.

Delta. Ratio of the change in option premium to the change in price of the underlying asset or contract.

Exercise an option. The buyer of an option liquidates the position by enforcing terms of the option.

Exercise price. The predetermined price at which a call option allows the buyer to buy the underlying asset; the predetermined price at which a put option allows the buyer to sell the underlying asset. Also referred to as the strike price.

Expiration date. The date on which option trading ceases. After this date, the option has no value.

Futures option. An option on a futures contract.

In the money. A call option in which the market price of the underlying asset exceeds the strike price; a put option in which the strike price exceeds the market price of the underlying asset.

Index option. An option on a stock index.

Interest rate cap. An agreement between two counterparties that limits the buyer's interest rate risk to a maximum rate. If the reference interest rate exceeds the cap rate, the buyer receives a cash payment.

Interest rate floor. An agreement between two counterparties that limits the buyer's interest rate risk to a minimum rate. If the reference interest rate is below the floor rate, the buyer receives a cash payment.

Interest rate collar. The combination of buying an interest rate cap and selling an interest rate floor to create a band within which the buyer's interest rate fluctuates. The buyer will receive cash whenever the reference interest rate exceeds the cap rate and will pay cash whenever the reference rate falls below the floor rate.

Intrinsic value. For a call option, the greater of the market price on the underlying asset or contract minus the strike price, and zero; for a put option, the greater of the strike price minus the market price of the underlying asset or contract, or zero.

Out of the money. A call option in which the strike price exceeds the market price of the underlying asset; a put option in which the market price of the underlying asset exceeds the strike price.

Premium. The price of an option.

Put option. An option in which the buyer has the right to sell the underlying asset or contract at a predetermined strike price for a set period of time.

Reverse collar. The combination of buying an interest rate floor and selling an interest rate cap to create a band within which the interest rate will fluctuate.

Strike price. The predetermined price at which a call option allows the buyer to buy the underlying asset; the predetermined price at which a put option allows the buyer to sell the underlying asset. Also referred to as the exercise price.

Time value. The difference between the option premium and the intrinsic value.

Writer. The seller of an option.

Zero cost collar. The combination of buying an interest rate cap and selling an interest rate floor on the same index for the same maturity so that the net premium on both transactions is zero. As such, the price of the cap equals the price of the floor.

could exercise the option (buy a June Eurodollar futures contract) at 97.00 and immediately sell a June Eurodollar futures at 97.52 for a gain of $1,300 (52 × $25). Note that any trader could buy a June or September call option at the same 97.00 strike price, or a call option at any of the four higher strike prices.

Each option's price, labeled the premium, reflects the consensus view of the value of the position. All options have some positive value because prices could move favorably prior to expiration until the option is in the money. Analysts frequently distinguish between an option's intrinsic value and time value. For a call option, **intrinsic value** equals the dollar value of the difference between the current market price of the underlying Eurodollar future and the strike price or zero, whichever is greater. For example, the June call option at 97.00 has an intrinsic value of $1,300. When the strike price is above the market price, a call option's intrinsic value is zero because the option cannot be exercised at a net gain. The June 2002 call option with a 97.75 strike price has such a zero intrinsic value. The **time value** of an option equals the difference between the option price and the intrinsic value. In the case of the June

▪ EXHIBIT 11.2

DATA FOR OPTIONS ON 90-DAY EURODOLLAR FUTURES, APRIL 2, 2002

	Option Premiums*			
	Calls		Puts	
Strike Price	**June**	**Sept.**	**June**	**Sept.**
9700	0.53	0.25	0.02	0.41
9725	0.30	0.14	0.08	0.56
9750	0.18	0.09	0.19	0.73
9775	0.09	0.05	0.28	0.93
9800	0.02	0.01	0.49	1.17

Monday volume: 31,051 calls; 40,271 puts
Open interest: Monday, 4,259,529 calls; 3,413,424 puts

90-Day Eurodollar Futures Prices (Rates), April 2, 2002
    June 2002:   97.52 (2.48%)
    September 2002: 96.83 (3.17%)

*Face value of futures contract is $1,000,000. Premium is stated as a percent, where 0.01 equals 1 basis point. Each basis point is worth $25 per contract.

call at 97.00, the premium equals $1,325, so the time value of the option is $25 (one basis point). This reflects the market perception that the option will be deep in the money at expiration or that rates will fall or rise little from April to June. Remember that on April 2, 3-month cash LIBOR was 2.04 percent. By definition, the premium equals the intrinsic value of the option plus the time value.

$$\text{option premium} = \text{intrinsic value} + \text{time value}$$

The intrinsic value and premium for call options with the same expiration but different strike prices decrease as the strike price increases. The reason is straightforward. The higher the strike price, the greater the price the call option buyer must pay for the underlying futures contract at exercise. Given the current fixed price of the underlying asset, the lower the price that a call option buyer can obtain the asset, the greater the option value. Data for the June call options reveal this pattern. Remember that the intrinsic value at the 97.00 strike price was $1,300. At the strike prices of 97.25 and 97.50, the intrinsic values are lower, $675 (27 basis points) and $50 (two basis points), respectively. The intrinsic value is zero at all higher strike prices. The underlying 97.52 June 2002 futures price is being compared to a successively higher strike price so the value of the call option declines.

Consider now the time values of the June 2002 call options at various strike prices. From 97.25 to 98.00 strike prices, the time values are $75, $400, $225, and $50, respectively, or 3, 16, 9, and 2 basis points. The time value of an at the money option is normally greater than the time value of other options for the same underlying asset. Options with a strike price at 97.50 are closest to at the money with the June futures price equal to 97.52. This reflects the relatively high probability that the price of the underlying asset may move favorably such that the option goes farther in the money. Buyers pay more for this opportunity. The time value of an option also normally increases with the length of time until option expiration, because the market price has a longer time to reach a profitable level and then continue to move favorably. For April 2002, there was widespread agreement that the economy was growing and rates would increase after June 2002.

Data for the put options reveal somewhat different relationships. Consider, for example, the June 2002 put option at a 97.50 strike price. The buyer of the put has the right to sell a June 2002 Eurodollar futures contract at 97.50. The seller of the put must buy a June 2002 Eurodollar futures contract if the put option buyer exercises the option. The buyer of the put immediately pays the $475 option premium while the seller receives the option premium. Again, the seller must post margin to guarantee performance, but no margin is required of the option buyer. Each can exit the position in the same manner as with the call. A put option buyer can, for example, let the option expire, exercise the option, or offset the position by selling a June put prior to expiration.

The intrinsic value of a put option is the greater of the strike price minus the underlying asset's market price, and zero. The time value again equals the option premium minus the intrinsic value. The June put option at 97.50 was slightly out of the money because the current June futures price of 97.52 was above the strike price. The entire 19 basis point premium represented time value.

Not surprisingly, for put options with the same expiration, premiums increase with higher strike prices because the option holder can sell the same underlying futures contract at a higher predetermined price. For example, the buyer of a June put option at 98.00 has the right to sell June 2002 Eurodollar futures at a price $1,200 (48 × $25) over the current price. This option is in the money with an intrinsic value of $1,200 and a time value of $25 (one basis point). For the September put options, the premiums rise as high as 117 basis points for a deep in the money option. Again, the time value is greatest for at the money put options, and time values increase the farther away an option's expiration. With a September 2002 futures price of 96.83, these puts are in the money with the consensus view that rates were rising.

The Eurodollar futures contract and associated options are traded at the International Monetary Market of the Chicago Mercantile Exchange. When the underlying futures prices change, the exchange opens additional options at new exercise prices to bracket the current futures price. Most option holders choose to get out of their option positions by taking the opposite side of their initial position prior to expiration. Thus, few options are exercised. An initial option buyer will sell the same option rather than exercise it because with time remaining to expiration there is usually some time value that can be realized above the intrinsic value. An option buyer will exercise the option only when it is in the money and its time value is zero.[2] An option that a holder lets expire is typically out of the money.

PROFIT DIAGRAMS

What advantages do options on futures have over futures contracts? When is a trader better off using options? This section introduces profit diagrams that demonstrate key differences between futures and options on futures.[3] Importantly, these diagrams are constructed under the assumption that a trader holds the position until expiration of the options contract. The diagrams are useful in demonstrating the risk and return characteristics of various positions.

EURODOLLAR FUTURES

Section A of Exhibit 11.3 demonstrates when an unhedged futures position is profitable, using the data on Eurodollar futures from Exhibit 11.2. The vertical axis indicates the profit

---

[2]All options traded in the United States (American options) can be exercised anytime prior to expiration.
[3]The discussion follows Koppenhaver (1986) and Kuprianov (1986).

• EXHIBIT 11.3

**PROFIT DIAGRAMS FOR UNHEDGED FUTURES AND OPTIONS ON
FUTURES ASSUMING TRADERS TAKE POSITIONS
USING THE DATA FROM EXHIBIT 11.2**

A. Futures Positions

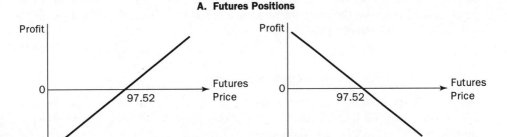

1. Buy June 2002 Eurodollar Futures at 97.52.   2. Sell June 2002 Eurodollar Futures at 97.52.

B. Call Options on Futures

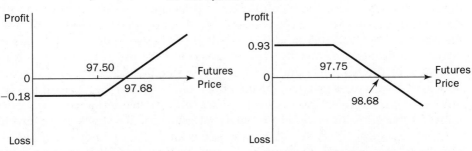

1. Buy a June 2002 Eurodollar Futures Call
Option at 97.50.

2. Sell a Sept. 2002 Eurodollar Futures Call
Option at 97.75.

C. Put Options on Futures

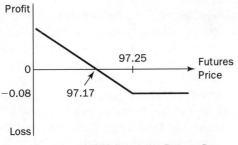

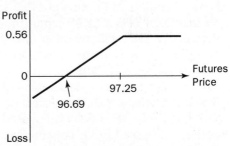

1. Buy a June 2002 Eurodollar Futures Put
Option at 97.25.

2. Sell a Sept. 2002 Eurodollar Futures Put
Option at 97.25.

or loss equal to $25 times the number of basis points indicated. The horizontal axis measures the level of the futures price. As the futures price increases, evidenced by movements to the right on this axis, corresponding futures rates decrease. These figures ignore transactions costs and opportunity gains or losses from margin requirements. According to section A-1, the buyer of a June 2002 Eurodollar futures contract at 97.52 gains when futures prices increase above 97.52 and loses when futures prices fall below 97.52. Because rates and prices vary inversely, this means that a buyer benefits (loses) when the futures rate falls below (exceeds) 2.48 percent. Sellers of futures gain when the futures price falls after the initial transaction. Section A-2 notes the profit profile for the seller of a June 2002 Eurodollar futures contract who gains (loses) when the futures rate rises (falls) above (below) 2.48 percent. Both buyers and sellers can lose an unlimited amount, but given the historical range of futures price movements and the short-term nature of futures contracts, actual prices have not varied all the way to zero or 100.

CALL OPTIONS ON EURODOLLAR FUTURES

Section B-1 of Exhibit 11.3 shows the profit profile of a trader who buys a June 2002 Eurodollar futures call option at 97.50 for 18 basis points. The buyer immediately pays a $450 premium (18 × $25), which represents the maximum loss, or greater cost, if the option expires unexercised. At the time of purchase the futures price of 97.52 is greater than the strike price by 0.02, so the option is in the money. The buyer pays 16 basis points in intrinsic value and two basis points in time value and thus does not earn a profit until the futures price rises above 97.68, which equals the strike price plus the 18 basis point premium.[4] In general, the buyer's profit equals the eventual futures price minus the strike price and the initial call premium. For example, if the buyer exercises the option when the futures price equals 98.25, the profit equals $1,425 [(98.25 − 97.50 − 0.18) or 57 basis points × $25]. In this example, the buyer's profit increases directly with increases in the June Eurodollar futures price (with decreases in futures rates) and is limited only if rates fall to zero. Compared with an unhedged long futures position, the buyer of a call option on the same futures contract faces less risk of loss if futures prices fall yet realizes similar potential gains. At any price above the initial futures price, the buyer of a futures contract gains. In contrast, if the June futures price does not rise above 97.68, the call option holder loses at least a portion of the 18 basis point premium. Thus, large price movements are necessary before a call option increases substantially in value, while small price changes immediately benefit or cost a futures participant.

The seller of a Eurodollar futures call option, or the writer of the call, will gain or lose in similar fashion when futures prices move in the opposite direction. Consider the seller of a September 2002 call option at 97.75 in section B-2 of Exhibit 11.3. The seller immediately receives $2,325 (93 × $25), the maximum possible profit. Only if the September futures price rises above 98.68 will the seller lose. The loss potential, however, is unlimited. This makes selling call options unattractive to most hedgers. The seller earns the full $2,325 if the option expires unexercised. With option exercise, the profit is reduced by the amount by which the eventual futures price exceeds the strike price. For example, if the futures price at exercise of the option equals 98.00, the futures price exceeds the strike price by 0.25 and the seller earns $1,700 ($2,325 − 25 × $25). Compared with a pure short futures position, the seller of a call option has limited profit potential but captures the time value component of the premium (one basis point in the example). A short futures position loses immediately if prices rise above 96.83, the current September 2002 futures price. This price is 185 basis points lower than the break-even point for the seller of a call option of 97.75. Selling a call option is most valuable when interest rates are volatile at the time of sale so that the time value component of the premium is large, but rates remain stable after the date of sale so the option is less likely to increase in value.

---

[4]The analysis assumes that all options are held until expiration. If the buyer sells the call option prior to expiration, the return will reflect the difference between the option premium at the time of sale versus the time of purchase and may be either positive or negative.

PUT OPTIONS ON EURODOLLAR FUTURES

The buyer of a put option gains if futures prices fall or futures rates rise. Consider the purchase of a June 2002 Eurodollar futures put option at a strike price of 97.25. The buyer pays a premium of $200 (8 × $25) for the right to sell June futures at 97.25 when the current futures price equals 97.52. The option is out-of-the money by 27 basis points, or $675. Although the buyer's potential profit is unlimited, the net gain will be positive only if the futures price falls below 97.17, or 35 basis points below its current level. The buyer's maximum loss equals the initial premium of $200. If the eventual futures price at expiration falls between 97.17 and 97.25, the buyer loses less than $200.

Section C-1 illustrates the profit positions of the purchase of a put option on financial futures and is directly comparable to the short sale of a futures contract (section A-2 in Exhibit 11.3). In both cases the position is profitable when futures prices fall but generates losses when futures prices rise. The use of a put option, however, limits losses to the option premium, while a pure futures sale exhibits greater loss potential. Still, the futures position is immediately profitable once futures prices decrease. The buyer of a put option does not gain until the futures price falls below the strike price minus the premium. Thus, large price movements may be necessary before a put option increases substantially in value.

Section C-2 of Exhibit 11.3 summarizes the profit potential for the seller of a September 2002 Eurodollar future put option at 97.25. This option requires the seller to buy a futures contract at 97.25 if the option is exercised. The option is currently in the money because the market price at 96.83 is below the strike price. The intrinsic value is $1,050 (42 basis points), of the 56 basis point premium represents time value. If the futures price exceeds the strike price at expiration, the seller earns the maximum profit equal to the $1,400 premium. If the eventual futures price is below the strike price, the option will be exercised and the seller of a put option will have to buy the futures contract at the higher strike price. If the final market price is below 96.69, the loss from liquidating the obligated futures position will exceed the initial 56 basis point premium and the seller will suffer a net loss. For example, if the futures price is 96.30 at expiration, the seller of an option will have to buy futures at 97.25, and the subsequent 95 basis point loss exceeds the 56 basis point premium initially received, for a net loss of $975 (39 × $25).

The sale of a put option is comparable to the direct purchase of a Eurodollar futures contract (section A-1 in Exhibit 11.3). Both positions face potentially large losses if futures prices fall substantially. Futures prices would have to fall more than 56 basis points, however, before the seller of a September 2002 put option at 97.25 loses, while a long futures position loses as soon as the futures price declines. The maximum profit on the put sale is limited, however, while profit from a long futures position is open-ended when futures prices rise. In general, hedgers do not find short put positions attractive.

THE USE OF OPTIONS ON FUTURES BY COMMERCIAL BANKS

Bank managers can use financial futures options for the same hedging purposes they use financial futures. They follow the same steps introduced in Chapter 10, starting with identifying the bank's relevant interest rate risk position to be hedged. Such risk can be measured on a micro basis, focusing on a specific transaction, or a macro basis, using the bank's funding GAP or duration gap profile. This risk position, in turn, determines what type of risk-offsetting trade is necessary, how many contracts are appropriate, and so on.

POSITIONS THAT PROFIT FROM RISING INTEREST RATES

Suppose that a bank would be adversely affected if the level of interest rates increases. This might occur because the bank is liability sensitive in terms of earnings sensitivity or it simply anticipates issuing new CDs in the near term. Management wants to take a futures or options position so it can earn a profit that offsets the potential loss in the cash market if rates do rise.

A bank has several alternatives that should reduce the overall risk associated with rising interest rates. In terms of the alternatives discussed previously, it can sell financial futures contracts directly, sell call options on financial futures, or buy put options on financial futures. From Chapter 10, it could also enter a basic interest rate swap agreeing to pay a fixed rate and receive a floating rate. The profit diagram for this swap is essentially that for a short futures position (A-2 in Exhibit 11.3). Each of these positions will earn a profit if futures prices fall sufficiently and futures rates increase, or with the swap if the floating rate increases. Each alternative, however, exhibits different risk-return characteristics. The short futures position produces profits as soon as futures rates rise but will generate losses once futures rates decline. Profits and losses are unlimited. Selling a call option also produces profits once futures rates rise but sets a maximum profit equal to the initial call premium received. Potential losses are virtually unlimited if rates fall. Thus, the sale of a call option "protects" a bank only against relatively small interest rate changes and hence is not appropriate as a hedge. The sale is intended to speculatively generate premium income. Buying a put option produces unlimited profits once the futures price falls below the strike price net of the put premium. If rates fall, the bank loses only the put premium, so it does not have the same rate exposure as with a short futures position. The basic swap position differs also. A bank will receive cash from this swap only when the floating rate exceeds the fixed rate. These relationships are summarized in Exhibit 11.4.

PROFITING FROM FALLING INTEREST RATES

Banks that are asset sensitive in terms of earnings sensitivity or that commit to buying fixed-income securities in the future will be adversely affected if the level of interest rates declines. Their appropriate use of futures, basic interest rate swaps, and options on futures will be to take positions that produce profits when futures rates or floating rates decline. Again, a bank has numerous alternatives. It can buy futures directly, buy call options on futures, sell put options on futures, or enter a swap to pay a floating rate and receive a fixed rate. Exhibit 11.4 lists the potential outcomes. Although the futures position offers unlimited gains and losses that are presumably offset by changes in value of the cash position, a purchased call option offers the same approximate gain but limits the loss to the initial call premium. The sale of a put limits the gain and has unrestricted losses. The basic swap, in contrast, produces gains only when the actual floating rate falls below the fixed rate.

The best outcome is not known at the time the trade is initiated, but several general conclusions apply.

1. Futures and basic swap positions produce unlimited gains or losses depending on which direction rates move and this value change occurs immediately with a rate move. Thus, a hedger is protected from adverse rate changes but loses the potential gains if rates move favorably.

2. Buying a put or call option on futures limits the bank's potential losses if rates move adversely. This type of position has been classified as a form of insurance because the option buyer has to pay a premium for this protection. When rates move favorably, a

▪ EXHIBIT 11.4

PROFIT AND LOSS POTENTIAL ON FUTURES, OPTIONS ON FUTURES
POSITIONS, AND BASIC INTEREST RATE SWAPS

Generate Profits if Futures Rates Rise

Transaction	Potential Profit	Potential Loss
Sell financial futures	Unlimited	Unlimited
Sell call options on futures	Limited to call premium	Unlimited
Buy put options on futures	Unlimited	Limited to put premium

Generate Profits if Futures Rates Fall

Transaction	Potential Profit	Potential Loss
Buy financial futures	Unlimited	Unlimited
Buy call options on futures	Unlimited	Limited to call premium
Sell put options on futures	Limited to put premium	Unlimited

Generate Profits if Floating Rates Rise: Basic Interest Rate Swap

Transaction	Potential Profit	Potential Loss
Pay fixed rate, receive floating rate	Unlimited	Unlimited

Generate Profits if Floating Rates Fall: Basic Interest Rate Swaps

Transaction	Potential Profit	Potential Loss
Pay floating rate, receive fixed rate	Unlimited	Unlimited

NOTE: Profits and losses are limited when futures rates equal 0 percent and 100 percent.

bank can realize unlimited gains. Still, rates have to move more than with a futures position for the purchased options to be profitable.

3. Selling a call or put option limits the potential gain but produces unlimited losses if rates move adversely. Selling options is generally speculative and not used for hedging.

4. Determining the best alternative depends on how far management expects rates to change and how much risk of loss is acceptable.

5. A final important distinction is the cash flow requirement of each type of position. The buyer of a call or put option must immediately pay the premium. This can be substantial for in the money options and often discourages a user from selecting these options. However, there are no margin requirements for the long position. The seller of a call or put option immediately receives the premium, but must post initial margin and is subject to margin calls because the loss possibilities are unlimited. All futures positions require margin and swap positions require collateral.

HEDGING BORROWING COSTS

This section provides numerical examples that document the mechanics of straight futures hedges versus using options on futures to differentiate the risk and return trade-off between the alternatives. The anticipated cash transaction being hedged is a bank's issuance of 3-month Eurodollar time deposit liabilities. The scenario is of interest because it indicates problems that bankers frequently confront when pricing loans. Borrowers in the commercial

· **EXHIBIT 11.5**

FUNDING A 1-YEAR LOAN WITH A SERIES OF 3-MONTH
EURODOLLAR TIME DEPOSITS

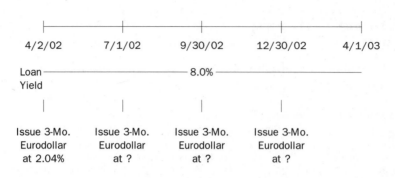

loan market and mortgage market often demand fixed-rate loans. How can a bank agree to make fixed-rate loans when it has floating-rate liabilities and doesn't want to take interest rate risk?

Suppose that on April 2, 2002, your bank agrees to make a $1 million commercial loan with a 1-year maturity. The loan carries an 8 percent fixed rate. The bank initially finances the loan by issuing a $1 million 3-month Eurodollar time deposit paying 2.04 percent. After the first three months, the bank expects to finance the loan by issuing a series of 3-month Eurodollar deposits timed to coincide with the maturity of the preceding deposit. The timeline in Exhibit 11.5 characterizes the anticipated sequence of cash market transactions.

Because the bank chooses to finance the fixed-rate loan with a series of shorter-term deposits, it will lose if 3-month Eurodollar rates increase throughout the year. In particular, the bank has locked-in a 5.96 percent spread for the first 3 months, but does not know what the spread will be after April 2, 2002. If the 3-month Eurodollar rate rises above 8 percent, the bank will pay more in interest than it earns on the loan.

HEDGING WITH 3-MONTH EURODOLLAR FUTURES

One way to reduce the risk of loss with rising interest rates is to sell Eurodollar futures. The bank anticipates issuing 3-month Eurodollar deposits in the cash market at three specific future dates over the next year: July 1, 2002, September 30, 2002, and December 30, 2002. Because the bank loses if Eurodollar rates rise from current levels on these dates, the appropriate strategy is to sell futures contracts. Because the loan amount is $1 million, on April 2 the bank can sell one of each of the September 2002, December 2002, and March 2003 3-month Eurodollar futures contracts to hedge. This assumes a desired hedge ratio of 1-to-1 and that the first futures contract to expire after each of the borrowing dates will have the highest correlation with cash Eurodollar deposit rates. Exhibit 11.6 summarizes the bank's initial position and reports the initial basis with each futures contract using data from Exhibit 10.1. Remember that with futures, the trader assumes basis risk.

Consider the sale of the September 2002 futures contract at 3.17 percent. The contract expires in mid-September and thus is used to hedge the July Eurodollar borrowing. In July the bank issues another Eurodollar deposit, so it must buy a September 2002 futures contract because it is no longer exposed to rate risk with this cash market borrowing. The bank assumes the risk that the basis, represented by the difference between the futures rate and the initial cash rate, will decline between April 2 and July 1. Because the futures contract expiration is two months after the hedge offset, the basis may take on any value.

The bottom of Exhibit 11.6 summarizes the results of the hedged transactions for all dates using hypothetical data. Assume that on July 1, the bank actually issued Eurodollars at 2.90 percent as cash rates increased by 86 basis points. The bank simultaneously offset its September futures position by buying one contract at 3.20 percent. The net effect was a $75 futures profit that partially offset the $2,150 opportunity loss in the cash market. As noted at the bottom of the exhibit, the effective borrowing cost of the July Eurodollar was 2.87 percent. This reflects the fact that the basis actually fell from 113 basis points at initiation of the hedge to 30 basis points at offset.

The basis follows the opposite pattern for the September 30 Eurodollar deposit transaction date. In September, cash rates again rose and the bank issues Eurodollars at 4.08 percent representing an opportunity loss over the initial 2.04 percent rate available in April. The December 2002 futures rate also rises from 3.79 percent in April to 4.71 percent, which produces a profit of $2,300 on the futures. The profit in the futures market is less than the cash market loss, however, as the basis again decreased from 175 basis points to 63 basis points. Thus, the effective borrowing cost of the September Eurodollar was 3.16 percent.

Finally, cash and futures rates increased through December 2002. This produced an opportunity loss in the cash market and a futures profit as of December 30. The futures profit fell short of the cash loss by $4,200 as the basis narrowed from 233 basis points to 67 basis points, and the effective borrowing cost equaled 3.70 percent.

The net result of the hedge with Eurodollar futures is that the bank was able to borrow at an average 2.94 percent. Thus, the net interest spread on the commercial loan averaged 5.06 percent during the year. If the bank had not hedged, it would have paid an average of 3.34 percent on the four cash Eurodollar borrowings producing a smaller net interest spread. On April 2, the 1-year cash Eurodollar rate was 3.99 percent, so attempts to issue longer-term cash Eurodollars would have similarly raised borrowing costs over this hedging alternative. The availability of futures not only enabled the bank to hedge its borrowing costs but even to lower them. The risk again was that the basis could have declined sharply at each repricing. In this situation, the bank's effective borrowing cost would have risen sharply, but the bank would likely have been able to maintain a positive spread.

HEDGING WITH OPTIONS ON EURODOLLAR FUTURES

As indicated in Exhibit 11.4, a participant who wants to reduce the risk associated with rising interest rates can buy put options on financial futures. In the above example with the bank issuing a series of Eurodollars, the bank would want to buy one put option on each of the September 2002, December 2002, and March 2003 Eurodollar futures. The purchase of a put option essentially places a cap on the bank's borrowing cost. If futures rates rise above the strike price plus the premium on the option, the put will produce a profit that offsets dollar-for-dollar the increased cost of cash Eurodollars.[5] If futures rates do not change much or decline, the option may expire unexercised and the bank will have lost a portion or all of the option premium. Along with this, however, cash Eurodollar rates should remain stable or decline so that the borrowing cost does not vary substantially from current rates. In this context, buying a put option is comparable to buying insurance against rising rates. The option premium represents the cost of the insurance.

---

[5]This assumes that Eurodollar cash and futures rates move in the same direction by the same amount.

· EXHIBIT 11.6

USING FUTURES TO HEDGE BORROWING COSTS

3-Month Eurodollar Cash and Futures Rates

April 2, 2002	**Initial Basis**
3-month cash rate = 2.04%	September contract: 3.17% − 2.04% = 1.13%
September 2002 futures rate = 3.17%	December contract: 3.79% − 2.04% = 1.75%
December 2002 futures rate = 3.79%	March contract: 4.37% − 2.04% = 2.33%
March 2003 futures rate = 4.37%	

July 1, 2002

3-month cash rate = 2.90%
September 2002 futures rate = 3.20%

September 30, 2002

3-month cash rate = 4.08%
December 2002 futures rate = 4.71%

December 30, 2002

3-month cash rate = 4.33%
March 2003 futures rate = 5.00%

Date	Cash Market	Futures Market	Basis at Close
4/2/02	Bank issues $1 million in 3-month Eurodollars at 2.04%	Bank sells one September 2002 Eurodollar future at 3.17%; one December 2002 Eurodollar future at 3.79%; one March 2003 Eurodollar future at 4.37%	

7/1/02	Bank issues 1 million in 3-month Eurodollars at 2.90%
	Opportunity loss = 86 × $25
	              = $2,150
		Bank buys one September 2002 Eurodollar future at 3.20%
		Profit = 3 × $25
		      = $75
			0.30%

9/30/02	Bank issues $1 million in 3-month Eurodollars at 4.08% Opportunity loss = 204 × $25 = $5,100	Bank buys one December 2002 Eurodollar future at 4.71% Profit = 92 × $25 = $2,300	0.63%
12/30/02	Bank issues $1 million in 3-month Eurodollars at 4.33% Opportunity loss = 229 × $25 = $5,725	Bank buys one March 2003 Eurodollar future at 5.00% Profit = 63 × $25 = $1,575	0.67%

Effective Cost of Borrowing

Eurodollar Issue Date	Cost = initial cash rate − ΔBasis
4/1/02	2.04%
7/1/02	2.04% − (0.30% − 1.13%) = 2.87%
9/30/02	2.04% − (0.63% − 1.75%) = 3.16%
12/30/02	2.04% − (0.67% − 2.33%) = 3.70%
	Average 2.94%

Assume that the bank decides to buy the September, December, and March put options at the 97.25 strike price as a hedge against the three future borrowings. The nature of the bank's risk profile after buying the options is revealed by the profit diagrams in Exhibit 11.7 assuming

· EXHIBIT 11.7

PROFIT DIAGRAMS FOR PUT OPTIONS ON EURODOLLAR
FUTURES, JANUARY 6, 1994

A. Buy: September 2002 Put Option; Strike Price = 97.25

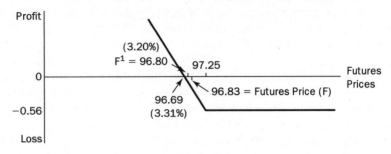

B. Buy: December 2002 Put Option; Strike Price = 97.25*

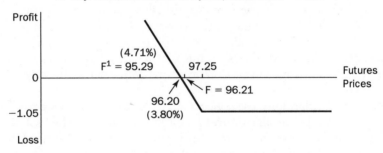

C. Buy: March 2003 Put Option; Strike Price = 97.25*

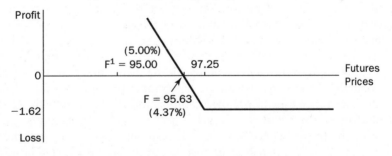

NOTE: F = futures price as of April 2, 2002; F^1 = price when bank offsets the option.

*On April 2, 2002 the premium on the December 2002 option at 97.25 is 1.05; and on the March 2003 option at 97.25 is 1.62.

option premiums of 56, 105, and 162 F^1 basis points, respectively. Section A characterizes the situation with the September put option. With a strike price of 97.25 and premium of 0.56, the break-even price is 96.69. The option will be in the money if the September Eurodollar futures rate remains above 2.75 percent, and will recover its premium only after the futures rate rises above 3.31 percent. Of course, the bank will be better off if all interest rates decline sharply. In this scenario the option will be out of the money, but the cash Eurodollar rates will be very low. The bank will simply lose the option premium, or its "insurance" payment. On April 2, 2002, the September futures price (F) is 96.83 so this option is in the money.

Sections B and C characterize the situations with the December 2002 put option and March 2003 put option, respectively. The December option has a premium of 1.05 and the prevailing December futures price (rate) is 96.21 (3.79 percent). The March option has a premium of 1.62 with an underlying futures price (rate) of 95.63 (4.37 percent). Both options are deep in the money so that most of the premium is time value. The break-even futures rate with the December option is 3.80 percent (2.75 + 1.05), while the break-even rate with the March option is 4.37 percent (2.75 + 1.62). These rates effectively represent caps, or the highest possible rate that each respective borrowing cost might reach. At higher rates, profit from the put option position will fully offset higher cash Eurodollar borrowing rates.

Before examining hedge results, it is important to clarify the types of cash flows expected with this type of hedge. When the bank buys the three options in April, there is a substantial up-front cash outflow as the bank must pay the option premiums. In this example, the bank buys three in the money options with relatively large premiums. The initial premium cost is $9,700 representing the 56, 105, and 162 basis point premiums. If the bank bought deeper in the money options, the premiums would be much higher reflecting the greater intrinsic values. Because the timing of the cash borrowing days falls between contract expiration months, the bank will exit the put option positions by selling each option at the time it issues cash Eurodollars. The profit or loss on the option sale relative to the option purchase price then determines the change in value of the option hedge versus the opportunity gain or loss in the cash market.

Exhibit 11.8 clarifies these concepts by tracking the bank's performance from buying put options on the Eurodollar futures listed in Exhibit 11.7. The cash and futures rates are the same as those in the example from the previous section with Eurodollar futures. Consider the September put option hedge for the July 1 borrowing. On this date, the September Eurodollar futures rate equaled 3.20 percent. Exhibit 11.7 demonstrates that at this rate (price = F^1) the option is in the money. The bank is assumed to be able to sell the option for $1,725 (0.50 premium) representing a 6 basis point loss versus the initial option premium. The effective cost of this borrowing is 2.96 percent represented by the initial 2.04 percent cash rate plus the 86 basis point loss on the cash position and 6 basis point loss on the option position. In this instance, the bank would have had a lower borrowing cost with no hedge.

On September 30, 2002 interest rates rose further such that the bank realized a $5,100 opportunity loss in the cash market with the increase in cash Eurodollar rates to 4.08%. Not surprisingly, with the rise in rates the December put option is farther in the money such that the premium increases to 202 basis points, and the bank sells the December put option for $4,900. The effective cost was thus 3.17 percent or 113 basis points above the initial cash rate representing the difference between the cash opportunity loss and the 91 basis point gain on the option. Finally, interest rates rose again in December. The cash Eurodollar borrowing shows a 229 basis point opportunity loss while the March put option is deep in the money because the futures rate increased to 5.00 percent (F^1 = 95.00). In this example, the cash market opportunity loss of $5,725 is reduced by the $1,575 net gain ([225 − 162] × $25) from the sale of the March option relative to the original option premium. The net borrowing cost was 3.70 percent for the three months.

Over the life of the loan and series of option hedges, the bank's effective 3-month borrowing cost ranged from 2.04 percent to 3.70 percent. The average for the year was 2.97 percent or 3 basis points above the average in the example with Eurodollar futures. This comparison ignores the up-front opportunity cost of buying each option and the cost of meeting margin requirements associated with straight futures positions.

- **EXHIBIT 11.8**

BUYING PUT OPTIONS ON EURODOLLAR FUTURES
TO HEDGE BORROWING COSTS

3-Month Eurodollar Futures Rates and Put Option Premiums for the 97.25 Strike Price

April 2, 2002   **Option Premiums**

September 2002 futures rate = 3.17%   September 2002 Put at 97.25 = 0.83
December 2002 futures rate = 3.79%   December 2002 Put at 97.25 = 1.15
March 2003 futures rate = 4.37%   March 2003 Put at 97.25 = 1.90

July 1, 2002

3-month cash rate = 2.90%   September 2002 Put at 97.25 = 0.69
September 2002 futures rate = 3.20%

September 30, 2002

3-month cash rate = 4.08%   December 2002 Put at 97.25 = 2.02
December 2002 futures rate = 4.71%

December 30, 2002

3-month cash rate = 4.33%   March 2003 Put at 97.25 = 2.55
March 2003 futures rate = 5.00%

Date	Cash Market	Put Options
4/2/02	Bank issues $1 million in 3-month Eurodollars at 2.04%	Bank buys one September 2002 put on Eurodollar futures with strike = 97.25 for 0.56; one December 2002 put on Eurodollar futures with strike = 97.25 for 1.05; one March 2003 put on Eurodollar futures with strike = 97.25 for 1.62.
7/1/02	Bank issues $1 million in 3-month Eurodollars at 2.90% Opportunity loss = 86 × $25 = $2,150	September 2002 Eurodollar futures rate = 3.20% Bank sells September 2002 put option for 0.50; receives $1,250. [Δ value = −.06]
9/30/02	Bank issues $1 million in 3-month Eurodollars at 4.08% Opportunity loss = 204 × $25 = $5,100	December 2002 Eurodollar futures rate = 4.71%; Bank sells December 2002 put option for 1.96; receives $4,900 [Δ value = +.91]
12/30/02	Bank issues $1 million in 3-month Eurodollars at 4.33% Opportunity loss = 229 × $25 = $5,725	March 2003 Eurodollar futures rate = 5.00%; Bank sells March 2003 put option for 2.25; receives $5,625 [Δ value = +0.63]

Effective Cost of Borrowing

Eurodollar Issue Date	Cost: initial cash rate − Δ value of cash − Δ value of option*	
4/2/02	2.04%	
7/1/02	2.04% + 0.86% + 0.06%	= 2.96%
9/30/02	2.04% + 2.04% − 0.91%	= 3.17%
12/30/02	2.04% + 2.29% − 0.63%	= 3.70%
	Average	2.97%

*Measured in basis points; each $25 = 1 basis point. The change in value of the option equals the premium at sale minus the purchase premium.

SENSITIVITY OF THE OPTION PREMIUM TO THE CHANGE IN EURODOLLAR FUTURES PRICE

The previous examples demonstrate that a hedger who uses options can offset the original hedge by reversing the original position. The option produces offsetting cash flows because it changes in value in the opposite direction of the change in value of the cash position. Different types of options will display different price sensitivities and thus may or may not be appropriate for hedging.

Analysts use an option's delta as a measure of how sensitive the option premium is to a change in the value of the underlying asset. In the above examples, delta equals the ratio of the change in option premium to the change in price of the underlying futures. As such, it is a number ranging from 0 to 1 for a call option and from −1 to 0 for a put option. With delta equal to 1, a 10 basis point change in the futures price will be associated with a 10 basis point change in a call option premium in the same direction. A delta of −1 for a put option indicates that a 10 basis point increase in the futures price will be associated with a 10 basis point decrease in the premium, or a one-to-one move in the opposite direction. At a value of zero, the option premium will not change regardless of the change in futures price for both call and put options. An option's delta provides useful information regarding how a future price move will likely affect the value of an option used in hedging. Formally, it is the hedge ratio.

Consider a deep in the money option. Small changes in the Eurodollar futures price will change the intrinsic value of the option on futures on a one-to-one basis, but will not influence the time value of the option. Thus, the option changes in value much like a pure futures contract. The delta equals one. Consider, alternatively, a deep out of the money option. Here, small changes in the underlying futures price do not affect the intrinsic value, which is zero, or the time value and thus will not affect the option premium. The delta equals zero. Which is more useful for hedging? The in the money option will operate like a futures contract, but is more costly because an option buyer must pay the up-front premium, which will be large because of the high intrinsic value. In contrast, the premium for a deep out of the money option will be very small, possibly zero. For the deep out of the money option to experience a large premium change, however, the underlying futures price must change substantially. For hedge purposes, a hedger must trade multiple contracts to obtain a similar absolute dollar value of price move. The implication is that most hedgers do not trade deep out of the money or deep in the money options when they take their initial positions.

One of the practical difficulties in using options is that options contracts do not extend out for any length of time. In other words, there is very little liquidity for trading either puts or calls on financial futures far out in the future. There are also only a limited number of strike prices that are offered. To get around this, many of the larger commercial and investment banks create "synthetic" options and futures positions via dynamic hedging. This consists of using liquid futures, swaps, and options contracts in combination and altering the combination over time to replicate the effect of longer-term options and futures. Such hedged portfolios exhibit pricing characteristics of the caps and floors described in the following section. The mechanic of establishing a dynamic hedge is quite complicated, but it is important to recognize that such innovation frequently appears to resolve a problem with existing financial contracts.[6]

INTEREST RATE CAPS, FLOORS, AND COLLARS

The purchase of a put option on Eurodollar futures essentially places a cap on the bank's borrowing cost. Examine the data from Exhibits 11.7 and 11.8 for the September 2002 put option.

---

[6]The interested reader should examine the articles by Abken (1989) and Mattu (1986) for details regarding dynamic hedging.

Any futures price below 96.69 (rate above 3.31 percent) generates a profit on the option that can be used to offset the cost of higher cash market interest rates. The advantage of a put option in the effort to hedge the bank's borrowing cost is that for a fixed price, the option premium, the bank can set a cap on its borrowing costs, yet retain the possibility of benefiting from rate declines. If the bank is willing to give up some of the profit potential from declining rates, it can reduce the net cost of insurance. It can accomplish this by accepting a floor, or minimum level, for its borrowing cost. The bank might agree to do this because management does not expect rates to decline substantially. In this scenario, a floor would not be binding.

A bank borrower in the above example can establish a floor by selling a call option on Eurodollar futures. The seller of a call receives the option premium, but agrees to sell the call option buyer the underlying Eurodollar futures at the agreed strike price upon exercise. Reviewing section B2 of Exhibit 11.3 demonstrates that the call option seller's maximum profit is the call premium. Losses arise if the futures price rises above the strike price plus option premium, which is consistent with futures rates declining. Conceptually, the bank borrower is using the call option premium to reduce the net cost of a put option premium for a cap. Any decline in futures rates should, in turn, coincide with a decline in cash rates. The floor thus exists because any opportunity gain in the cash market from borrowing at lower rates will be offset by the loss on the sold call option. In essence, the bank has limited its maximum borrowing cost, but also established a floor borrowing cost. The combination of setting a cap rate and floor rate is labeled a collar.

BUYING AN INTEREST RATE CAP

Instead of using options on Eurodollar futures, participants can directly buy or sell caps and floors on specific interest rates. For example, an **interest rate cap** is an agreement between two counterparties that limits the buyer's interest rate exposure to a maximum rate. An **interest rate floor** is an agreement between two counterparties that limits the buyer's interest rate exposure to a minimum rate. The cap is actually the purchase of a call option on an interest rate. The floor is actually the purchase of a put option on an interest rate.

When trading interest rate caps or floors, a participant selects a floating rate index, a term to maturity, a strike (exercise) rate, the frequency of value dates when cash payments are made, and a notional principal amount. Depending on prevailing economic conditions these choices determine the price (premium) at which the option trades.

Consider the two diagrams in Exhibit 11.9. Section A characterizes the payoff diagram for the purchase of a 4 percent cap on 3-month LIBOR. It is the same as a long call option position.[7] An interest rate cap has a maturity and periodic valuation dates, a notional principal amount, and a strike rate that is based on some reference interest rate. The buyer of a cap pays a one-time up-front premium and receives a cash payment from the seller of the cap equal to 3-month LIBOR minus 4 percent multiplied by some notional principal amount on each valuation date, with no payment made if LIBOR is below 4 percent. Formally, the payoff is the maximum of zero or 3-month LIBOR minus 4 percent times the notional principal amount. Thus, if 3-month LIBOR exceeds 4 percent, the buyer receives cash from the seller, and nothing otherwise. At maturity, the cap expires. These payoffs are indicated in section B of Exhibit 11.9.

Consider a cap on 3-month LIBOR at 4 percent based on a $100 million notional principal amount. If LIBOR equals 4.63 percent on the first valuation date and ignoring compounding, the buyer would receive $157,500 (0.0063/4 × $100 million) from the cap seller. If LIBOR is 3.95 percent on the second valuation date, the buyer would receive zero. The obligated payment is a rate differential times the notional principal amount, or zero.

---

[7]Formally, a single call option on an interest rate is referred to as a caplet. An interest rate cap is actually a series of caplets at the same strike rate.

BUYING A CAP ON 3-MONTH **LIBOR** AT 4 PERCENT

A. Cap = Long Call Option on 3-Month LIBOR

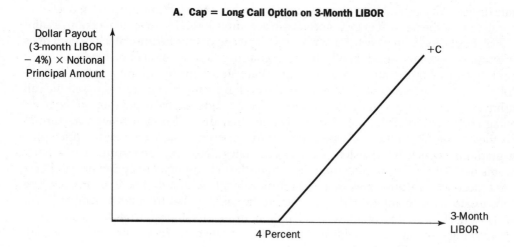

B. Cap Payoff: Strike Rate = 4 Percent*

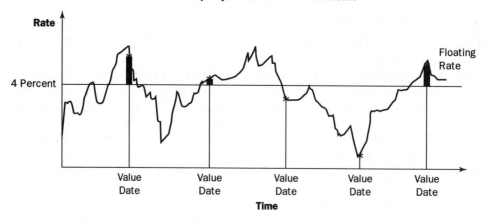

*Payoff at Value Date equals prevailing (LIBOR − 4 percent) × Notional Principal Amount.

An **interest rate cap** is a series of consecutive long call options (caplets) on a specific interest rate at the same strike rate. The buyer selects an interest rate index, such as 3-month LIBOR, the prime rate, 1-month commercial paper rate, T-bill rate or the federal funds rate, a maturity over which the contract will be in place, a strike (exercise) rate that represents the cap rate, and a notional principal amount. By paying an up-front premium, the buyer then locks-in this cap on the underlying interest rate.

The benefits of buying a cap are similar to those of buying any option. The bank as buyer of a cap can set a maximum (cap) rate on its borrowing costs. It can also convert a fixed-rate loan to a floating rate loan. In this context, it gets protection from increasing rates and retains the benefits if rates fall. The primary negative to the buyer is that a cap requires an up-front premium payment. If the buyer wants a cap that is at the money or in the money in a rising rate environment, the premium can be high.

· EXHIBIT 11.10

A. Floor = Long Put Option on 3-Month LIBOR

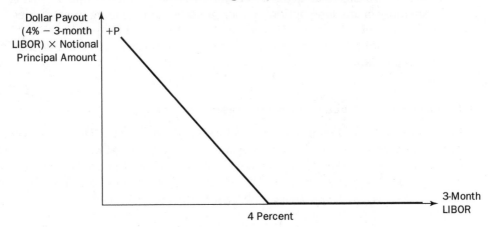

B. Floor Payoff: Strike Rate = 4 Percent*

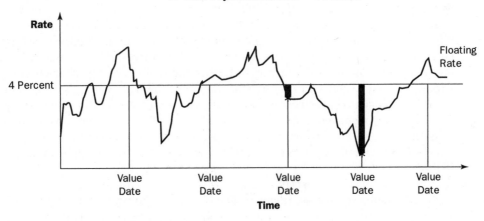

*Payoff at Value Date equals prevailing (4 percent − LIBOR) × Notional Principal Amount.

BUYING AN INTEREST RATE FLOOR

A buyer can also establish a minimum interest rate by buying a floor on an interest rate index. Consider the diagrams in Exhibit 11.10. Section A presents the payoff diagram for buying a 4 percent floor on 3-month LIBOR.[8] Note that the diagram is similar to that for a long put option position. As indicated, the buyer of the floor receives a cash payment equal to the greater of zero or the product of 4 percent minus 3-month LIBOR and a notional principal amount. Thus, if 3-month LIBOR exceeds 4 percent, the buyer of a floor at 4 percent receives nothing. The buyer is paid only if 3-month LIBOR is less than 4 percent. This payoff pattern is indicated in section B of Exhibit 11.10.

---

[8]Formally, a single floor option on an interest rate is referred to as a floorlet. An interest rate floor is actually a series of floorlets at the same strike rate.

An **interest rate floor** is a series of consecutive floorlets at the same strike rate. The buyer of an interest rate floor selects an index, with LIBOR, the prime rate, commercial paper rate, T-bill rate, and federal funds rate again the most popular, a maturity for the agreement, a strike rate, and a notional principal amount. By paying a premium, the buyer of the floor, or series of floorlets, has established a minimum rate on its interest rate exposure. The benefits are again those of any long option. A floor protects against falling interest rates while retaining the benefits of rising rates. The primary negative is that the premium may be high on an at the money or in the money floor, especially if the consensus forecast is that interest rates will fall in the future.

INTEREST RATE COLLAR AND REVERSE COLLAR

In some cases, banks buy interest rate collars or reverse collars. The purchase of an **interest rate collar** is actually the simultaneous purchase of an interest rate cap and sale of an interest rate floor on the same index for the same maturity and notional principal amount. The cap rate is set above the floor rate. The objective of the buyer of a collar is to protect against rising interest rates. The purchase of the cap protects against rising rates while the sale of the floor generates premium income. The motivation for selling the floor is typically to provide income that reduces the cost of the cap. If the index rate rises above the cap, the buyer receives cash from the counterparty equal to the difference between the index rate and the cap (strike) rate. Of course, if the index rate falls below the floor, the collar buyer pays the counterparty the difference between the floor (strike) rate and the reference rate. With falling rates, the buyer of a collar gives up any potential gain from the hedged cash position. A collar creates a band within which the buyer's effective interest rate fluctuates. The buyer is willing to accept a minimum floor rate to reduce the cost of the cap protection or because of a strong belief that rates will rise and the view that the floor will be out of the money. A *zero cost collar* is designed to establish a collar where the buyer has no net premium payment. This requires choosing different cap and floor rates such that the premiums are equal. The benefit is the same as any collar with zero up-front cost. The negative is that the band within which the index rate fluctuates is typically small and the buyer gives up any real gain from falling rates.

A bank can also buy a *reverse collar.* This refers to buying an interest rate floor and simultaneously selling an interest rate cap. The objective is to protect the bank from falling interest rates. The buyer selects the index rate and matches the maturity and notional principal amounts for the floor and cap. The strike rates differ. If the index rate falls below the floor, the buyer of a reverse collar receives cash from the counterparty. If the index rate rises above the cap, the buyer makes cash payment to the counterparty. The motivation for selling the cap is typically to reduce the cost of buying a floor. The net result is that the buyer's interest rate fluctuates within a band. The buyer is willing to accept a maximum rate to reduce the cost of the floor or because it has a strong belief that rates will fall and the cap will be out of the money. Buyers can again construct zero cost reverse collars when it is possible to find floor and cap rates with the same premiums that provide an acceptable band.

One of the most important considerations when evaluating whether to buy caps and floors is the premium cost. Exhibit 11.11 provides summary information for the premiums on various caps and floors on 3-month LIBOR in April 2002. The top part of the exhibit provides the bid and offer premiums for caps and floors at different strike rates. The first column of data in each section indicates the term for the underlying caps and floors. Subsequent columns indicate the premiums. For the caps, the strike rates are 4, 5, and 6 percent. For the floors, the strike rates are 1.50, 2, and 2.50 percent. The bid premium represents what the option seller receives while the offer premium represents what the option buyer pays. At the time of these

▪ EXHIBIT 11.11

PREMIUMS FOR INTEREST RATE CAPS AND FLOORS ON 3-MONTH LIBOR
APRIL 2, 2002

A. Caps/Floors

Term	Bid	Offer	Bid	Offer	Bid	Offer
Caps	4.00%		5.00%		6.00%	
1 year	24	30	3	7	1	2
2 years	81	17	36	43	10	15
3 years	195	205	104	114	27	34
5 years	362	380	185	199	86	95
7 years	533	553	311	334	105	120
10 years	687	720	406	436	177	207
Floors	1.50%		2.00%		2.50%	
1 year	1	2	15	19	57	61
2 years	1	6	32	39	95	102
3 years	7	16	49	58	128	137
5 years	24	39	80	94	190	205
7 years	40	62	102	116	232	254
10 years	90	120	162	192	267	297

NOTE: Caps/Floors are based on 3-month LIBOR; up-front costs in basis points. Figures in bold print represent strike rates.
SOURCE: Bear Stearns

quotes, the cash market 3-month LIBOR equaled 2.04 percent. The 3-month Eurodollar futures rates in Exhibit 10.1 (Chapter 10) indicate the consensus forecast that 3-month LIBOR will rise over time.

The size of these premiums is determined by a wide range of factors. First, the relationship between the strike rate and the prevailing 3-month LIBOR indicates how much LIBOR has to move before the cap or floor is in the money. Specifically, the premiums are highest for in the money options and lower for at the money and out of the money options. With the prevailing LIBOR at 2.04 percent, the floor at 2.50 percent is in the money while the floor at 2 percent is at the money. All other floors and all caps are out of the money. The premiums for the 2.5 percent strike rate will be the highest for the floors because it has an intrinsic value of 46 basis points (2.50–2.04 percent) and any decline in LIBOR immediately increases the expected cash receipts. LIBOR must fall considerably before the 1.5 percent floor is in the money. For the interest rate caps, the premium on the 4 percent strike rate will be highest because LIBOR has to rise the least (196 basis points) before the buyer receives a cash payment. With higher strike rates, LIBOR has to increase sharply before the buyer will receive cash. Note, however, that the Eurodollar futures rates in Exhibit 10.1 indicate an expected sharp increase in rates above 4 percent in March 2003 and over 5 percent by September 2003. Second, the premiums increase with maturity. This reflects the fact that an option seller must be compensated more for committing to a fixed-rate cap or floor for a longer period of time.

Finally, prevailing economic conditions influence premiums via the shape of the associated yield curve and the volatility of interest rates. If the yield curve for Eurodollars is upsloping such that the consensus is that LIBOR will rise in the future, caps will be more expensive than floors. The steeper is the slope of the yield curve, ceteris paribus, the greater are the cap premiums. If the yield curve is flat or inverted, caps will be relatively inexpensive. Floor premiums, in contrast, reveal the opposite relationship. The steeper is the yield curve, the cheaper are floor premiums. If the yield curve is inverted, floor premiums will be relatively expensive. Like all options, the greater is the volatility of rates, the higher will be premiums because there is a greater likelihood that the options may move in the money. Finally, regardless of intrinsic value, maturity, and yield curve shape, a dealer in caps and floors will typically charge a higher premium for substantial positions in large notional principal amounts.

PROTECTING AGAINST FALLING INTEREST RATES

Assume that your bank is asset sensitive such that the bank's net interest income will decrease if interest rates fall. Essentially the bank holds loans priced at prime plus one percent and funds the loans with a 3-year fixed-rate deposit at 2.75 percent. The management team has a strong belief that interest rates will fall over the next three years. It is considering three alternative approaches to reduce risk associated with falling rates: 1) entering into a basic interest rate swap to pay 3-month LIBOR and receive a fixed rate; 2) buying an interest rate floor; and 3) buying a reverse collar. Exhibits 11.12, 11.13, and 11.14 summarize the net results of each position when rates alternatively fall and rise relative to the current environment. Note that initially, the bank holds assets priced off prime and liabilities priced off 3-month LIBOR. For this example, the two rates are assumed to be perfectly correlated.

Exhibit 11.12 compares the results using a basic interest rate swap where the bank agrees to pay 3-month LIBOR and receive 4.55 percent for a 3-year term. There are three interest rate scenarios where rates are constant and rise or fall by 1 percent. Initially, the prime rate equals 5 percent and LIBOR equals 2.04 percent, which generates a spread of 3.25 percent for the loans versus the fixed-rate deposits. With rates constant at these levels, the net cash flow from the swap produces an inflow of 251 basis points for a net interest margin of 5.76 percent as indicated in the first column of data. Examine the second and third columns of data where floating rates are assumed to fall and rise from initial levels. Given the assumed perfect correlation between prime and LIBOR, this margin is constant at 5.76 percent whether rates either fall or rise by one percent. This occurs because any reduction in the spread when prime falls to 5 percent is offset by the gain on the swap as LIBOR falls to 1.04 percent. Similarly, any gain in spread as prime rises to 6 percent is offset by a reduction in the swap receipt as LIBOR rises to 3.04 percent. The use of the swap effectively fixed the spread near the current level, except for basis risk.

Exhibit 11.13 summarizes the outcomes from hedging by buying a floor with a 3-year maturity on 3-month LIBOR at a 2.00 strike rate. The up-front premium is 58 basis points represented by a 21 basis point annual amortization. At current interest rates indicated in the first column of data, the balance sheet interest spread is 3.25 percent which produces a net interest margin of 3.04 percent after subtracting the 21 basis point cost of the floor premium. If rates fall one percent as noted in the second column of data, the spread falls to 2.25 percent, but the floor on LIBOR generates a cash receipt of 75 basis points. Thus, the net interest margin is 3 percent. If rates rise one percent as in the third column of data, the spread widens and the floor falls out of the money such that the margin increases to 4.04 percent. This demonstrates the impact of options on hedge results. If rates fall and the floor is in the money, the increase in option value offsets the loss in the spread position. If rates rise, the option expires worthless, but the value of the cash spread increases. The bank retains benefits from rising rates. The bank is best served if cash market rates move favorably and the floor expires worthless. The floor buyer is protected when bad things (rate declines) happen, but retains the benefit of favorable (rate increases) rate movements. The buyer doesn't want to collect on

· EXHIBIT 11.12

USING A BASIC SWAP TO HEDGE AGGREGATE BALANCE SHEET
RISK OF LOSS FROM FALLING RATES

Bank Swap Terms: Pay LIBOR, Receive 4.55 Percent*

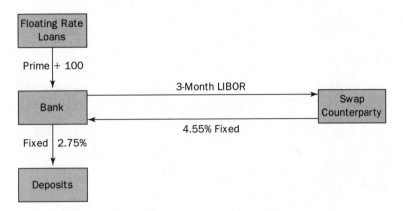

	Current Rates Constant	Rates Fall 100 Basis Points	Rates Rise 100 Basis Points
	PRIME 5.00%	PRIME 4.00%	PRIME 6.00%
	LIBOR 2.04%	LIBOR 1.04%	LIBOR 3.04%
Balance Sheet Flows:			
Loan	6.00%	5.00%	7.00%
Deposit	(2.75%)	(2.75%)	(2.75%)
Spread	3.25%	2.25%	4.25%
Interest Rate Swap Flows:			
Fixed	4.55%	4.55%	4.55%
Floating	(2.04%)	(1.04%)	(3.04%)
Spread	2.51%	3.51%	1.51%
Margin	5.76%	5.76%	5.76%

*Assume swap term is three years and perfect correlation between PRIME and LIBOR.

the insurance. Note that the more rates increase, the higher is the margin for the bank. As such, there is no limit to the upside from this hedged position unlike the swap hedge that fixed the outcome.

Exhibit 11.14 documents the outcomes from simultaneously buying a floor on 3-month LIBOR at 1.50 percent and selling a cap on 3-month LIBOR at 2.50 percent. This reverse collar protects the bank from falling rates but provides a band within which the effective interest margin will fluctuate. The sale of the cap generates a net premium receipt of 27 basis points up-front represented by an annual 10 basis point amortization of premium. At prevailing rates indicated in the first column of data, the net interest margin is expected to be 3.35 percent characterized by the spread plus the 10 basis point premium amortization on the

■ EXHIBIT 11.13

BUYING A FLOOR ON 3-MONTH LIBOR TO HEDGE AGGREGATE BALANCE
SHEET RISK OF LOSS FROM FALLING RATES

Floor Terms: Buy a 2 Percent Floor on 3-Month LIBOR*

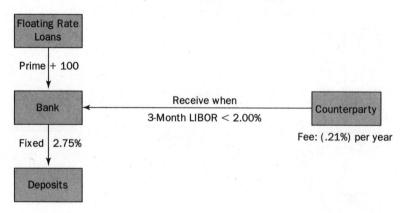

	Current Rates Constant	**Rates Fall 100 Basis Points**	**Rates Rise 100 Basis Points**
	PRIME 5.00%	PRIME 4.00%	PRIME 6.00%
	LIBOR 2.04%	LIBOR 1.04%	LIBOR 3.04%
Balance Sheet Flows:			
Loan	6.00%	5.00%	7.00%
Deposit	(2.75%)	(2.75%)	(2.75%)
Spread	3.25%	2.25%	4.25%
Floor Flows:			
Payout	0.00%	0.96%	0.00%
Fee Amort.	(0.21%)	(0.21%)	(0.21%)
Spread	(0.21%)	0.75%	(0.21%)
Margin	3.04%	3.00%	4.04%

*Assume floor term is three years and perfect correlation between PRIME and LIBOR.

reverse collar. The 1 percent drop in rates summarized in the second column of data produces a net margin of 2.81 percent whereby the 46 basis point receipt from the floor and premium amortization total of 56 basis points and reduce the one percent decline in interest spread. When rates rise (third column of data) the spread widens, but the bank gives back part of the gain by paying 54 basis points on the cap that it sold. Given alternative rates, the bank's realized margin will fluctuate between 2.81 percent and 3.81 percent. Thus, the collar differs from a pure floor by eliminating some of the potential benefits in a rising rate environment. The bank actually receives a net premium up-front, however, rather than having to pay a premium from the outright purchase of a floor in this example.

▪ EXHIBIT 11.14

BUYING A REVERSE COLLAR TO HEDGE AGGREGATE BALANCE SHEET RISK OF LOSS FROM FALLING RATES

Strategy: Buy a Floor on 3-Month LIBOR at 1.50 Percent, and Sell a Cap on 3-Month LIBOR at 2.50 Percent*

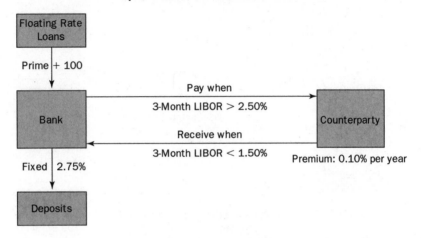

	Current Rates Constant	Rates Fall 100 Basis Points	Rates Rise 100 Basis Points
	PRIME 5.00% LIBOR 2.04%	PRIME 4.00% LIBOR 1.04%	PRIME 6.00% LIBOR 3.04%
Balance Sheet Flows:			
Loan	6.00%	5.00%	7.00%
Deposit	(2.75%)	(2.75%)	(2.75%)
Spread	3.25%	2.25%	4.25%
Reverse Collar Flows:			
Payout	0.00%	0.46%	(0.54%)
Fee Amort.	0.10%	0.10%	0.10%
Spread	0.10%	0.56%	(0.44%)
Margin	3.35%	2.81%	3.81%

*Assume collar term is three years and perfect correlation between PRIME and LIBOR.

PROTECTING AGAINST RISING INTEREST RATES

Assume that a bank has made 3-year fixed rate term loans at 7 percent funded via 3-month Eurodollar deposits for which it pays the prevailing LIBOR minus 0.25 percent. The bank is liability sensitive because it is exposed to loss from rising interest rates. Exhibits 11.15, 11.16, and 11.17 describe the results from three strategies to hedge this risk: 1) enter a basic swap to pay 4.56 percent fixed-rate and receive 3-month LIBOR; 2) buy a cap on 3-month LIBOR with a 3.00 strike rate; and 3) buy a collar on 3-month LIBOR.

▪ EXHIBIT 11.15

USING A BASIC SWAP TO HEDGE AGGREGATE BALANCE
SHEET RISK OF LOSS FROM RISING RATES

Strategy: Pay 4.56 Percent, Receive 3-Month LIBOR*

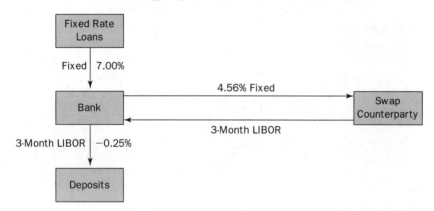

	Current Rates Constant	**Rates Fall 100 Basis Points**	**Rates Rise 100 Basis Points**
	LIBOR 2.04%	LIBOR 1.04%	LIBOR 3.04%
Balance Sheet Flows:			
Loan	7.00%	7.00%	7.00%
Deposit	(1.79%)	(0.79%)	(2.79%)
Spread	5.21%	6.21%	4.21%
Interest Rate Swap Flows:			
Fixed	(4.56%)	(4.56%)	(4.56%)
Floating	2.04%	1.04%	3.04%
Spread	(2.52%)	(3.52%)	1.52%
Margin	2.69%	2.69%	2.69%

*Assume swap term is three years.

The use of the basic swap again effectively fixes a net interest margin. As demonstrated in the first column of data in Exhibit 11.15, the initial interest spread is 5.21 percent and the bank pays 252 basis points on the swap at prevailing rates. This produces a net spread of 2.69 percent. If LIBOR falls 1 percent as noted in the second column of data, the interest spread widens to 6.21 percent but the bank pays out 3.52 percent on the swap. If LIBOR rises one percent as characterized in the third column of data, the spread narrows but the bank pays 1.52 percent on the swap. The net spread or margin is the same 2.69 percent in all cases. Obviously, the consensus forecast is for LIBOR to rise sharply as participants would otherwise refuse to enter this swap with such a large payout if rates remain constant.

· EXHIBIT 11.16

BUY A CAP ON 3-MONTH LIBOR TO HEDGE BALANCE SHEET
RATE RISK OF LOSS FROM RISING RATES

Strategy: Buy a Cap on 3-Month LIBOR at 3.00 Percent*

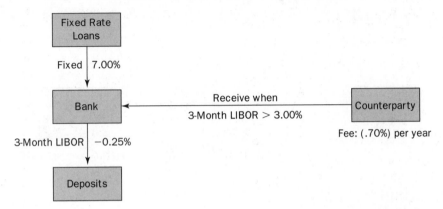

	Current Rates **Constant**	**Rates Fall** **100 Basis Points**	**Rates Rise** **100 Basis Points**
	LIBOR 2.04%	LIBOR 1.04%	LIBOR 3.04%
Balance Sheet **Flows:**			
Loan	7.00%	7.00%	7.00%
Deposit	(1.79%)	(0.79%)	(2.79%)
Spread	5.21%	6.21%	4.21%
Cap **Flows:**			
Payout	0.00%	0.00%	0.04%
Fee Amort.	(0.70%)	(0.70%)	(0.45%)
Spread	(0.70%)	(0.70%)	0.41%
Margin	4.51%	5.51%	3.80%

*Assume cap term is three years.

Buying a 3 percent cap allows the bank to potentially benefit if rates fall, but still protects against loss if rates rise. This is demonstrated in Exhibit 11.16. With an amortized premium cost of the cap at 70 basis points, the initial net interest margin equals 4.51 percent. This is summarized in the first column of data. The subsequent columns indicate the impact if rates vary from initial levels. If rates fall by 1 percent, the net margin increases to 6.21 percent because the interest spread widens and the cap cost remains fixed at 70 basis points. Each subsequent decline in LIBOR will be matched by an increase in the margin. Thus, the bank has unlimited upside in a falling rate environment. If LIBOR rises 1 percent (column three), the cap goes in the money. The interest spread declines consistent with the bank's risk exposure, but the cap position generates a payoff of 4 basis points. The net margin is again 3.80 percent.

■ EXHIBIT 11.17

Strategy: Buy a Cap at 3.00 Percent, and Sell a Floor at 2.00 Percent*

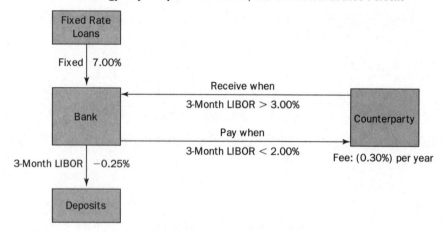

	Current Rates **Constant**	**Rates Fall** **100 Basis Points**	**Rates Rise** **100 Basis Points**
	LIBOR 2.04%	LIBOR 1.04%	LIBOR 3.04%
Balance Sheet **Flows:**			
Loan	7.00%	7.00%	7.00%
Deposit	(1.79%)	(0.79%)	(2.79%)
Spread	5.21%	6.21%	4.21%
Collar **Flows:**			
Payout	0.00%	(0.96%)	0.04%
Fee Amort.	(0.30%)	(0.30%)	(0.30%)
Spread	(0.30%)	(1.26%)	0.26%
Margin	4.91%	4.95%	3.95%

*Assume collar term is three years.

Exhibit 11.17 presents the outcomes from buying a collar on 3-month LIBOR. The combined positions consist of buying a cap at 3 percent and simultaneously selling a floor at 2 percent. The bank thus receives cash if LIBOR rises above 3 percent, but must pay on the floor if LIBOR falls below 2 percent. This effectively creates a band within which the bank's margin will fluctuate. As noted in the three data columns of Exhibit 11.17, the band for the net spread is between 3.95 percent and 4.95 percent. The collar provides similar protection to the straight purchase of a cap, but gives up the potential benefits of falling rates because of the sale of a floor. The net margin declines with each decline in LIBOR. The cost of the collar is just 30 basis points a year rather than the 70 basis points annually for the cap. Not surprisingly, the bank is better off when rates fall and the interest spread is the greatest. It is worse off when rates rise and the spread narrows, but the cap generates a cash receipt.

INTEREST RATE SWAPS WITH OPTIONS

Market participants are constantly looking for ways to improve upon existing risk management efforts. Financial innovation continues to expand both the types of tools available and the nature of applications. Recently, participants have had the opportunity to use interest rate swaps with option features as part of their risk management strategy. The following discussion introduces callable and putable swaps and demonstrates how they can be used to alter the form of borrowing alternatives. The purpose is to provide examples of how these tools represent extensions of plain vanilla swaps and can be used as substitutes for more conventional market activity.[9]

Using Swaps to Reduce Borrowing Costs of a New Debt Issue

The discussion of plain vanilla interest rate swaps in Chapter 10 demonstrated how two financial institutions used a swap to transform fixed-rate debt into floating-rate debt and vice versa, and reduce their effective borrowing cost. In practice, there are a variety of alternatives that can be used and two are demonstrated below. The objective is to obtain fixed-rate financing at the lowest possible cost. The alternative involves issuing cash market debt with options combined with entering into two interest rate swaps. In each case, the alternatives must be compared with straight debt issues to determine which is the cheapest.

Using Interest Rate Swaps with a Call Option

Any firm that wants to obtain fixed-rate financing has a variety of alternatives if it has access to the capital markets. First, it can issue option-free bonds directly. Second, it can issue floating-rate debt that it converts via a basic swap to fixed-rate debt. A third alternative is to issue fixed-rate callable debt, and combine this with an interest rate swap with a call option and a plain vanilla or basic swap.

A firm that issues callable bonds in the cash market has the right to prepay or call the bond prior to maturity at its discretion after a certain amount of time has passed. Typically, the bonds must be called at a premium over par that is established at the initial offering. Investors demand a higher rate for callable bonds compared to option-free bonds to compensate them for the risk that the issuer will call the bonds. This is because the call option will be exercised when interest rates fall, and investors will receive their principal back when similar investment opportunities carry lower yields. The issuer that has the call option effectively pays a price for the option in the form of the higher initial interest rate on the bond versus a noncallable bond.

A **swap with a call option** is much like a basic swap except that the call option holder (buyer) has the right to terminate the swap after a set period of time. Specifically, the swap party that pays a fixed-rate and receives a floating rate has the option to terminate a *callable swap* prior to maturity of the swap. This option may, in turn, be exercised only after some time has elapsed.

Suppose that a firm wants to issue fixed-rate debt with an 8-year maturity. Consider the following terms for its cash market debt obligations and participation in two swaps. Callable bonds have a 4-year deferment period before they can be called. The 10 basis point rate difference in the swap terms reflects the dealer spread for both the callable swap and basic swap.

---

[9]The discussion follows the analysis of Laurie Goodman, "Capital Market Applications of Interest Rate Swaps," in *Interest Rate Swaps*.

Cash Market Alternatives

8-year fixed rate debt: 8.50%
8-year callable fixed-rate debt: 8.80%
6-month floating-rate debt: LIBOR

Interest Rate Swap Terms

Basic Swap: 8-year swap without options: pay 8.55% fixed; receive LIBOR
pay LIBOR; receive 8.45%
Callable Swap: 8-year swap, callable after 4 years: pay LIBOR; receive 8.90% fixed
pay 9.00% fixed; receive LIBOR

The firm's strategy involves three steps implemented simultaneously. It 1) issues callable debt at 8.80 percent, 2) enters into a callable swap paying LIBOR and receiving 8.90 percent, and 3) enters into a basic swap paying 8.55 percent and receiving LIBOR. The first transaction indicates that the firm buys an option in the cash market for 30 basis points because it issues callable debt at 8.80 percent, or 30 basis points more than the cost of noncallable debt. The second transaction indicates that the firm sells the option in the callable swap market because it agrees to pay the floating rate and receive a fixed rate. The third transaction effectively locks in the hedge by locking in the premium (at 35 basis points) for the option sold in the swap markets. The net result is to lock-in a fixed borrowing rate of 8.45 percent for the first four years.

Net Borrowing Cost after Option Exercise

Pay: cash rate + callable swap rate + basic swap rate
    [8.80% + LIBOR + 8.55%]
Receive: callable swap rate + basic swap rate
        −[8.90% + LIBOR]
Net Pay = 8.45%

Note that this is 5 basis points less than the cost of issuing straight debt directly. It is 10 basis points less than issuing 6-month floating-rate debt at LIBOR and entering into a basic swap paying 8.55 percent fixed and receiving LIBOR. What the firm has done is essentially buy a call option in the cash market for 30 basis points (8.8 percent − 8.5 percent), and sell a call option in the swap market for 35 basis points (8.90 percent − 8.55 percent). The 5 basis point difference represents the savings compared with straight debt.

This set of transactions does involve some risk. Specifically, this cost is fixed for the first four years, but there is uncertainty as to what will happen to the call options once they can be exercised after four years. Suppose, for example, that interest rates rise from the date of issue. The issuer of callable debt will not call its bonds, and the holder/buyer of the callable swap (the payer of the 8.90 percent fixed-rate) will not terminate the swap. Thus, the contracts remain outstanding for four additional years and the firm saves 5 basis points each year for the life of the debt. This is the intended result. Suppose, instead, that interest rates fall sharply. Both call options will be exercised. The issuer will repay the outstanding principal on the 8.80 percent callable debt, and the swap counterparty will terminate the callable interest rate swap. The firm that issued the 8-year callable debt now needs funds to payoff the debt and is left with a basic swap position. If the issuer issues floating rate debt at LIBOR plus or minus some spread to obtain funds, it will have effectively locked-in a fixed rate for the last four years of the original term. The net cost can be summarized as:

Net Cost of Borrowing After Option Exercise in Four Years

Basic swap: pay 8.55%; receive LIBOR
New floating-rate debt: pay LIBOR +/− ?
Net cost = 8.55% +/− spread to LIBOR

The issuer's effective cost will equal the 8.55 percent plus or minus the premium that the firm has to pay relative to LIBOR to issue floating rate debt four years after origination of the debt. The 8.55 percent rate is 5 basis points higher than the option-free bond rate currently available. If the firm's credit quality has worsened, the spread will widen and the effective cost will be over 8.55 percent. If the firm's credit quality has improved, the spread will narrow and the effective cost will fall below 8.55 percent. Thus, the firm must accept some credit risk over the last four years of the deal.

USING INTEREST RATE SWAPS WITH A PUT OPTION

The same type of outcome can be obtained by combining the issuance of putable debt with two interest rate swaps, where one carries a put option. A put option gives the holder of a putable swap the right to put the security back to the issuer prior to maturity. With a putable bond an investor can get principal back by requesting payment after a deferment period. This option has value and increases in value when interest rates rise, as investors will put existing bonds and reinvest the proceeds at higher rates. As payment for the option, investors are willing to accept lower yields than those available on otherwise comparable option-free bonds. With a *putable swap,* the party receiving the fixed-rate payment has the option of terminating the swap after a deferment period, and will likely do so when rates increase.

Consider the following terms in conjunction with those provided earlier.

> Putable Bond: 8-year bond, putable after four years: 8.05 percent
> Putable Swap: 8-year swap, putable after four years: pay LIBOR; receive 8.20 percent fixed
> pay 8.30 percent fixed; receive LIBOR

To obtain fixed-rate financing, a firm would pursue three transactions simultaneously: it would 1) issue putable debt at 8.05 percent, 2) enter into a putable swap to pay LIBOR and receive 8.20 percent, and 3) enter into a basic swap to pay 8.55 percent and receive LIBOR. The first transaction has the effect of selling a put option in the cash market for 45 basis points, which equals the difference between the option-free bond rate (8.50 percent) and the put bond rate (8.05 percent). The second transaction involves buying the put option in the putable swap market. The third transaction effectively fixes the price of the put option in the swaps market. The net cost is fixed at 8.40 percent and the firm saves 10 basis points for the first four years.

Net Cost of Borrowing with a Putable Swap for Four Years

Pay: Put bond rate + Put swap rate + Basic swap rate
       [8.05% + LIBOR + 8.55%]
Receive: Put swap rate + Basic swap rate
       −[8.20% + LIBOR]
Net cost = 8.40%

This reflects savings that arise because the firm sells a put option in the cash debt market for 45 basis points (8.50 percent − 8.05 percent) and buys a put option for 35 basis points (8.55 percent − 8.20 percent) in the swaps markets.

The firm is again subject to the risk that its credit quality will deteriorate after four years. If rates fall, neither of the put options will be exercised and all contracts will remain outstanding. The firm would continue to save 10 basis points annually. If, however, rates rise, both options would be exercised and the existing put bond and putable swap would be terminated. The firm would be left with a basic swap. If it issued floating rate debt to obtain the proceeds to payoff the put bonds in the cash market, its net cost the last four years would depend on whether its floating rate debt was priced at a premium or discount relative to LIBOR. In this example, the cost would again equal 8.55 percent adjusted for the premium to LIBOR.

Net Cost of Borrowing after Option Exercise in Four Years

Basic swap: pay 8.55%; receive LIBOR
New floating-rate debt: pay LIBOR +/− ?
Net cost = 8.55% +/− spread to LIBOR

The key point is that a variety of instruments now exist to manage interest rate risk. In addition to these swaps with options, there exist options on swaps, labeled swaptions, and a wide range of other instruments.[10] The analysis of these vehicles is left for other courses.

SUMMARY

This chapter extends the analysis of financial futures, forward contracts, and basic interest rate swaps in Chapter 10 as a means of managing interest rate risk by discussing options on financial futures, interest rate caps, floors and collars, and interest rate swaps with options. Examples are provided that demonstrate the basic features of these instruments and indicate how they can be used to manage risk.

In general, a bank that wants to reduce the risk of loss from falling interest rates can buy call options on financial futures as a hedge, buy an interest rate floor, or buy a reverse collar. A long call option and the purchase of a floor have the advantage of limiting losses if rates move in the bank's favor, yet providing protection if rates fall. The primary drawback is that the buyer must pay the premium as an up-front cost. This cost may be quite high. The reverse collar involves the simultaneous purchase of a floor and sale of a cap and establishes a band within which the bank's effective interest rate fluctuates. The premium is lower than with a floor, but the bank gives up potential gains from rising rates.

A bank that wants to reduce the risk of loss from rising interest rates can buy put options on financial futures, buy an interest rate cap, or buy a collar. The advantage of buying a put option or an interest rate cap is again that losses are limited if rates fall so the bank retains the benefits in falling rate environments, but the option and cap provide protection against rising rates. The primary disadvantage is that the up-front premium cost can be quite high. A collar involves the simultaneous purchase of a cap and sale of a floor and establishes a band within which the bank's effective interest rate fluctuates. The premium is lower, but the bank gives up some of the potential gain from falling rates.

The chapter also discusses selling call and put options. These, however, are not attractive hedging tools for interest rate risk management because they provide for only limited gains when rates move against a bank in the cash market, yet carry unlimited loss potential. Interest rate swaps with options are also traded by swap dealers. They can be used to manage interest rate risk and are commonly linked with basic swaps to fix borrowing costs or asset yields at fixed or floating rates.

QUESTIONS

1. Explain how the buyer of an option on Eurodollar futures can limit loss, but the buyer of Eurodollar futures cannot.

2. Once a bank buys a call option on Eurodollar futures as a hedge, how might it get out of its position? Once a bank buys a put option on Eurodollar futures, how might it exit its position?

---

[10]A swaption is an option that gives a swap party the right to enter into an interest rate swap at a future date. The option can be constructed to give the party to pay either the fixed or floating rate with there being a precise exercise price and expiration date.

3. Using the data from Exhibit 11.2, draw the profit diagram for:
   a. long June put option at 98.00 strike price
   b. sell a September call at 97.00
   c. short September Eurodollar futures position
   d. long June call at 97.25

4. Calculate the intrinsic value and time value of the September call options and September put options from Exhibit 11.2 at the different strike prices. Compare the time values to those of the June call and put options with the same strike prices. Why is there a difference?

5. As the strike price of call options with the same expiration increases, what should happen to:
   a. intrinsic value of options
   b. premium
   c. time value

6. As the strike price of put options with the same expiration increases, what should happen to:
   a. intrinsic value of options
   b. premium
   c. time value

7. As a call or put option's expiration date gets farther into the future, what should happen to:
   a. time value of options with the same strike price
   b. option premiums for the same strike price

8. In each of the following situations, indicate whether a bank should buy a call option on Eurodollar futures or buy a put option on Eurodollar futures to hedge interest rate risk.
   a. In five months the bank expects to sell $5 million of securities from its investment portfolio to meet liquidity needs.
   b. In two months the bank expects to buy short-term securities with funds obtained from a lawsuit.
   c. In six months the bank expects to issue Eurodollar liabilities to fund a new loan.
   d. A bank has a positive cumulative GAP through one year.
   e. A bank has a negative duration gap

9. Use the data from Exhibit 11.11 to answer the following questions:
   a. When will the buyer of a 5-year cap on 3-month LIBOR with a 6 percent strike rate expect to receive cash? What is the cap premium?
   b. When will the buyer of a 3-year floor on 3-month LIBOR with a 2.00 percent strike rate expect to receive cash? What is the floor premium?
   c. Can you construct a zero cost collar on 3-month LIBOR with a 3-year term? If not, what positions at what strike rates might produce a zero cost collar? Use approximations.

10. Explain how the outcome from using a basic interest rate swap to hedge borrowing costs will generally differ from using an interest rate cap and an interest rate collar as hedges. Why is there a difference?

11. In each of the following cases, indicate whether an interest rate cap, floor, collar, or reverse collar is an appropriate position for a hedge. Recommend a specific position.
    a. A bank loan customer wants to borrow at a fixed 8 percent rate and the bank only lends at floating rates.
    b. A bank has agreed to pay a large depositor a fixed 5.5 percent on balances over the next three years regardless of rate moves. The bank expects rates to fall on similar deposits over this period.

c. Your bank owns adjustable rate mortgages (ARMs) that are priced at 3-month LIBOR plus 2 percent. There is an annual cap on the allowable rate increase equal to a maximum of 1 percent a year. Thus, if LIBOR rises by 3 percent, the bank can raise the ARM rate just 1 percent. How can the bank effectively remove this cap?

12. Suppose that the yield curve on Eurodollars is sharply upsloping.
    a. Will premiums on interest rate floors on 3-month LIBOR be high or low? Explain.
    b. Will premiums on interest rate caps on 3-month LIBOR be high or low? Explain.

13. Assume that you bought an interest rate cap on 3-month LIBOR with a 4.50 percent strike rate. The current rate for 3-month LIBOR is 4.28 percent.
    a. What will happen to the premium (value) on this cap if LIBOR rises to 5.16 percent? Explain.
    b. What will happen to the premium (value) on this cap if LIBOR falls to 4.10 percent? Explain.

14. Your bank is asset sensitive and management wants to protect against loss from interest rate changes.
    a. Would an interest rate cap or floor serve as a better hedge? Explain.
    b. Would a collar or reverse collar serve as a better hedge? Explain.
    c. Why would the bank choose a collar or reverse collar over a cap or floor, respectively? Explain.

15. Who controls option exercise with a:
    a. callable swap
    b. putable swap

16. Explain why any market participant would:
    a. sell a call option on Eurodollar futures
    b. sell a put option on Eurodollar futures
    c. sell an interest rate cap
    d. sell an interest rate floor

17. Suppose that you buy an interest rate cap on 3-month LIBOR with a 2-year maturity and simultaneously sell a floor on 3-month LIBOR with a 2-year maturity. Ignore the premiums. Draw a profit diagram that indicates when you will gain and lose on the combined positions. Compare this to different basic interest rate swap and futures positions.

18. Are there margin requirements for the following positions? Explain why or why not.

    a. Buy an interest rate cap
    b. Sell a put option on Eurodollar futures
    c. Sell an interest rate floor
    d. Sell a Eurodollar futures contract

PROBLEMS

I. HEDGING WITH OPTIONS ON EURODOLLAR FUTURES Your bank is a regular borrower in the Eurodollar market. On October 28, 2002, the head of funds management decides to hedge the bank's interest cost on a $10 million 3-month Eurodollar issue scheduled for February 2003. The targeted hedge vehicle is a put option on March 2003 Eurodollar futures. On October 28 the bank could issue $10 million in 3-month Eurodollars at 5.79 percent. The March 2003 Eurodollar futures rate was 6.36 percent. A March 2003 put option at 93.75 carried a premium of 0.44.

1. What is the bank's cash market risk? Should the bank buy or sell the put option to hedge its borrowing cost? Explain how the hedge should work.

2. Calculate the intrinsic value and time value of the March 2003 put option.

3. Suppose that the bank issues $10 million in Eurodollars on February 18, 2003, at 6.43 percent. Coincidentally, it closes out its put option position. On February 18 the March 2003 Eurodollar futures rate equaled 6.55 percent and the put option premium fell to 0.34. Calculate the profit or loss in the cash market, the gain or loss on the options trade, and the effective cost or return of the Eurodollar issue to the bank.

II. CONVERTING FIXED-RATE LOANS TO FLOATING-RATE LOANS Your bank made a 3-year fixed rate loan to Fresh Corp. at 8.50 percent. The ALCO wants only to accept floating rate loans so that it can reduce its liability sensitivity. Using the following information, indicate what position the bank should take to convert this fixed-rate loan to a floating rate loan in the best possible manner. The current prime rate is 8.25 percent and 3-month LIBOR is 5.50 percent.

3-Year Basic Interest Rate Swap: Pay 8.22%   Receive 3-month LIBOR
Pay 3-month LIBOR   Receive 8.17%

	Bid/Offer Premium		
3-Year Interest Rate Cap on Prime Rate	8.25% Cap	8.50% Cap	9.00% Cap
Premium	0.71/0.68	0.52/0.47	0.20/0.15
3-Year Interest Rate Cap on 3-Mth LIBOR	5.50% Cap	5.75% Cap	6.00% Cap
Premium	0.95/0.90	0.70/0.64	0.47/0.42

1. Describe what position you would take with a basic interest rate swap to reduce the bank's risk. Assume that the bank takes this position. What will its risk/return profile be?
   a. Suppose that 3-month LIBOR rises by 1 percent after one year and remains at this higher level the next two years. What will the effective loan yield equal?
   b. Suppose that 3-month LIBOR falls by 0.75 percent after one year and remains at this lower level the next two years. What will the effective loan yield equal?

2. Describe what position you would take with an interest rate cap. Which index (prime or LIBOR) would you use? Explain why. Which strike rate would you use? Explain why. Assume that the bank takes this position.
   a. Suppose that LIBOR and the prime rate rise by 1 percent after one year and remain at these higher levels the next two years. What will the effective loan yield equal?
   b. Suppose that LIBOR and the prime rate fall by 0.75 percent after one year and remain at these lower levels the next two years. What will the effective loan yield equal?

III. INTEREST RATE SWAP WITH OPTIONS You are the chief financial officer for a firm that would like to obtain fixed-rate financing on a long-term bond offering. You are considering four alternatives:

1. Issue 10-year option-free bonds at 9.25 percent

2. Issue 6-month floating rate debt at LIBOR + 0.10 percent, and enter a basic swap

3. Issue 10-year bonds, callable after five years at 9.50 percent, and enter into a basic swap and a callable swap

   4. Issue 10-year bonds, putable after five years at 9.03 percent, and enter into a basic swap
      and a putable swap

The prevailing swap terms are provided below:

Basic Swap:	Pay LIBOR and receive 9.20 percent;
	Pay 9.30 percent, and receive LIBOR
Callable Swap:	Pay LIBOR and receive 9.62 percent;
	Pay 9.72 percent and receive LIBOR
Putable Swap:	Pay LIBOR and receive 9.10 percent;
	Pay 9.21 percent and receive LIBOR

Using these terms, demonstrate the steps involved in each alternative for the firm to obtain
fixed-rate financing. What specific positions will the firm take in the cash market and swaps
markets? Calculate the effective cost of each alternative. Which is the lowest cost? What
credit risk does the firm accept if it chooses alternative 3 or alternative 4.

IV

MANAGING THE COST OF FUNDS, BANK CAPITAL, AND LIQUIDITY

12

Managing Liabilities and the Cost of Funds

Banks have found it increasingly difficult to manage their liabilities in the low interest rate environment of recent years. Dissatisfied with low time deposit and CD yields, individuals have shifted their financial assets to mutual funds, which offer higher promised returns. Between 1982 and 2001, for example, individuals reduced the fraction of their financial resources in bank deposits from 31.9 percent to 12 percent. Mutual funds, in contrast, grew from 4.4 percent to over 15 percent. A crucial concern is whether banks will be able to recapture these low rate deposits when interest rates move higher. After the stock market's significant retreat after March 2001, many banks found themselves inundated with deposits. Whether this move back to bank deposits as a "safe haven" is a shift in consumer thinking has yet to be determined.

With the potential high returns that can be earned in stocks and mutual funds, banks find themselves in a highly competitive situation that requires innovative product development, a high level of customer service, and attention to cost controls. Banks began to pursue individual retail customers in the late 1980s and are even more aggressive today. Individuals, as a group, are generally not as interest rate sensitive as wholesale customers such as commercial firms and government units, but the attractive returns and ease of access to mutual funds is changing this. If banks can attract consumer deposits, however, these funds are likely to remain on the books for longer periods of time and not move as readily as commercial accounts to other banks when rates change. The objective of banks is to build long-term customer relationships and establish a strong core deposit base.

Liability management plays an important role in the risk-return trade-off at commercial banks. Ever since regulators removed interest rate ceilings on liabilities and expanded the types of deposit products banks could offer, liability management decisions have dramatically influenced a bank's profitability and risk position. During the 1980s, for example, many thrift institutions used brokered deposits to finance extraordinary asset growth. In one infamous case Vernon Savings, a small Texas savings and loan, grew from $45 million in assets to $1.1 billion in just three years, financed primarily *by large CDs sold through brokerages. The bank's managers, in turn, speculated on real estate to such an extent that when the thrift failed, 96 percent of its commercial loans were in default.*

Liability management decisions affect profitability by determining interest expense on borrowed funds, noninterest expense associated with check handling costs, personnel costs, and noninterest income from fees and deposit service charges. They affect interest rate risk and liquidity risk by determining the rate sensitivity of liabilities, the stability of deposits toward preventing unanticipated deposit outflows, and the ease of access to purchased funds.

This chapter examines four related issues. First, it examines the risk-return characteristics of various bank liabilities. The second part discusses the appropriate use of average historical costs versus marginal costs and presents a procedure for measuring a bank's weighted marginal cost of funds. Marginal costs for single sources of funds are then compared with average historical costs for a sample commercial bank. Third, it summarizes the relationship between financing events and a bank's liquidity, credit, and interest rate risk position. The final part describes the changing role and nature of federal deposit insurance.

THE COMPOSITION OF BANK LIABILITIES

There are many different types of liabilities. Transaction accounts usually pay relatively low explicit interest rates but have higher noninterest processing costs. Other accounts offer limited check writing capabilities but pay higher rates. Liabilities with long-term fixed maturities typically pay the highest interest rates but have the lowest noninterest transaction costs. Customers who hold each instrument respond differently to interest rate changes. Thus, the composition and maturity/duration of each bank's liabilities are important determinants of the interest cost and liquidity and interest rate risk associated with performance.

Prior to 1960 banks relied on standardized demand and savings deposits as their primary source of funds. Government regulators determined allowable interest rates, and virtually all banks paid the maximum. Banks could compete for funds only by differentiating the quality of service and paying implicit interest through lowering service charges or offering premiums to open accounts. The primary strategy for most retail banks centered on having a well-located home office and branches (where allowed).

In 1961 Citibank, then First National City Bank, introduced the first truly marketable CD by arranging for securities dealers to make a secondary market that provided investors liquidity to trade large CDs after the initial purchase. Regulators still set maximum allowable rates on new issues, but in most periods the market rate fell below the ceiling. The evolution of other market rate instruments similarly followed from bank efforts to circumvent regulation. Whenever regulators attempted to restrict borrowing capabilities via specific liabilities, banks either developed new instruments or expanded their use of alternative liabilities. The credit crunches of the 1960s reveal this tendency. In 1969, for example, regulators let secondary market rates on CDs rise above the maximum allowable rate on new CD issues so that banks found it difficult to roll over or obtain new CD funds. Large banks, in particular, substituted unregulated Eurodollar liabilities and commercial paper for CDs rather than reduce credit availability to loan customers.[1] Thus,

---

[1]Eurodollars are dollar denominated deposits in banks located outside the United States. Domestic banks can acquire the funds either from foreign banks or branches of U.S. banks. Most bank commercial paper is issued by multibank holding companies. Specific features of each are discussed later in the chapter.

while all U.S. banks experienced a net CD outflow of $15.5 billion in 1969, they realized a net $7.4 billion gain in Eurodollar liabilities to foreign banks and a $4.3 billion increase in commercial paper outstanding.

When CD rates were again competitive in 1970, banks resumed their traditional financing by obtaining $23.5 billion in net new CDs and letting Eurodollars and commercial paper run off by a combined $8.3 billion. In similar fashion, large deposit runoffs to money market mutual funds in the early 1980s induced banks to create automatic transfers from savings accounts and retail repurchase agreements. Automatic transfer accounts paid passbook interest on checking accounts while retail RPs paid market rates on short-term savings certificates held by individuals. During the 1990s when deposit rates fell sharply, individuals shifted their resources to mutual funds. Banks reacted by offering mutual funds that they sponsored, or selling other vendors' funds. If they couldn't retain the deposits, at least they would get fees for selling the alternative investments.

Today, virtually all bank liabilities are free of regulatory restrictions on allowable rates, maturities, and minimum denominations. Price competition is the dominant consideration in attracting new funds. Aggressive pricing and the development of electronic funds transfer systems and home banking have reduced the importance of location to the point that many individuals now purchase banking services from firms located outside their home state. By the late 1990s many banks were advertising their CD and money market rates on the Internet. In general, bank CD, savings, and money market accounts have grown slowly in the late 1990s and early 2000s but banks that offer competitive rates can easily attract new funds. The Internet has opened up a new method for banks to gather deposits, and depositors need only search one of the many bank sites that list market yields from all over the country to find the most attractive returns.

RECENT TRENDS FOR LARGE AND SMALL BANKS

Perhaps the most difficult problem facing bank management is how to develop strategies to compete for funding sources. With no interest rate ceilings on deposits or restrictions on maturities, banks can offer any deposit product that customers demand. Although this freedom creates market opportunities, it also presents significant problems. First, bank customers have become much more rate conscious. They shop around for the highest yields and typically pay less attention to long-term bank relationships. From the bank's perspective, liabilities have become more interest elastic, so that small rate changes can produce large fluctuations in outstanding balances. Second, many customers have demonstrated a strong preference for shorter-term deposits. Depositors can reduce their interest rate risk by investing in short-term contracts that almost always trade close to par. The rate sensitivity of liabilities is thus greater, creating difficulties in pricing assets to manage net interest margin and interest rate risk.

Exhibit 12.1 documents recent trends in the composition of bank funds for banks in two different size groupings. Each column represents the percentage of total assets financed by the specific funds source indicated for the average bank in each size group. Regardless of size, banks operated with relatively fewer total deposits, transaction accounts, and core retail deposits and have made up for this shortfall with relatively more time deposits (CDs over $100,000) and equity in 2001 as compared to 1992. In 2001 large banks operated with proportionately *fewer* transaction accounts (NOW, ATS, and other), time deposits over $100,000 and equity, and *more* MMDAs, foreign deposits (CDs over $100,000), and other borrowings compared to smaller banks. Generally speaking, small banks relied proportionally more on core deposits and equity compared to the larger banks. Large banks, in turn, relied proportionally more on volatile funds obtaining more than twice the proportional share of funding from this source versus small banks.

▪ EXHIBIT 12.1

THE PERCENTAGE CONTRIBUTION OF VARIOUS SOURCES OF BANK FUNDS:
A COMPARISON OF LARGE VERSUS SMALL BANKS:
1992 AND 2001 (PERCENTAGE OF TOTAL ASSETS)

Liabilities and Stockholders' Equity	Banks with Assets more than $10B		Banks with Assets less than $100M	
	2001	1992	2001	1992
Number of institutions reporting	80	51	4,486	8,292
Total liabilities	91.23%	93.38%	89.10%	90.62%
Total deposits	63.10	70.37	84.69	88.59
Deposits held in domestic offices	49.71	52.65	84.69	88.56
Transaction accounts	9.49	19.81	24.45	26.54
Demand deposits	8.24	14.42	12.81	12.82
"NOW" accounts	1.25	5.27	11.64	13.34
Nontransaction accounts	40.22	32.84	60.25	62.02
Money market deposit accounts (MMDAs)	19.44	12.04	9.87	11.02
Other savings deposits (excluding MMDAs)	6.58	6.21	7.64	10.59
Total time deposits	41.47	14.59	71.88	40.40
Time deposits of less than $100,000	7.38	9.69	29.62	32.67
Memo: Core (Retail) deposits	42.88	47.75	71.58	80.83
Time deposits of $100,000 or more	6.83	4.90	13.11	7.73
Foreign Offices Deposits	13.39	17.72	0.00	0.03
Noninterest-bearing deposits	0.68	0.88	0.00	0.00
Interest-bearing deposits	12.70	16.84	0.00	0.03
Interest-bearing deposits	49.37	54.27	71.69	75.72
Deposits held in domestic offices	49.71	52.65	84.69	88.56
Federal funds purchased & repurchase agreements	8.64	8.94	0.91	0.78
Trading liabilities	3.97	N/A	0.00	N/A
Other borrowed funds	9.24	6.06	2.69	0.33
Memo: Volatile liabilities	35.75	38.54	14.73	8.94
Subordinated debt	1.93	1.91	0.01	0.02
All other liabilities	4.35	5.11	0.80	0.81
Total liabilities in foreign offices	18.42	22.47	0.00	0.03
Equity capital	8.77	6.62	10.90	9.38
Perpetual preferred stock	0.08	0.04	0.02	0.03
Common stock	0.32	0.72	1.58	1.60
Surplus	4.76	3.28	4.38	3.59
Undivided profits	3.61	2.65	4.92	4.16
Cumulative foreign currency translation adjustment	−0.03	−0.06	0.00	0.00
Memo: Domestic Offices				
Deposit accounts of $100,000 or less	24.96	30.77	58.73	71.31
Total time and savings deposits	41.47	38.22	71.88	75.74
Noninterest-bearing deposits	13.05	15.23	13.00	12.87
Interest-bearing deposits	36.66	37.42	71.69	75.69
IRAs and Keogh plan accounts	1.97	3.20	4.22	5.06
Brokered deposits	4.10	1.23	0.84	0.16
Fully insured	3.04	0.84	0.73	0.16

SOURCE: FDIC Statistics on Banking, www.fdic.gov.

NOW = Negotiable orders of withdrawal; ATS = automatic transfer from savings;
MMDA = money market deposit account.

The decline in transaction accounts reflects the factors discussed earlier. With alternative interest-bearing transactions accounts available, individuals shifted into MMDAs, nonbank money market mutual funds. They can earn higher market rates of interest on these instruments and still have transactions capabilities. Smaller banks' reduction in transaction accounts has been much less than that of the larger banks. Corporate depositors have reduced demand balances at the larger banks through efficient cash management techniques, often taught by banks, such as the use of "sweep accounts" (see Chapter 14) that allow them to minimize nonearning deposits.

With the decline in demand balances, banks raised rates on savings and time deposits to replace lost financing. In many cases, depositors simply moved balances from low-rate to high-rate accounts at the same institution. This increased borrowing costs without increasing the total amount of funds acquired. At the end of 2001, core deposits for banks in the greater than $10-billion-in-assets category funded 42.9 percent of total assets, down 51 percent from 1992. Conceptually, core deposits are stable deposits that customers are less likely to move when interest rates on competing investments rise. They are not as rate sensitive as large-denomination purchased (volatile) liabilities. Core deposits tend to be influenced more by location, availability, price of services, and other factors. Due to highly competitive factors, including the high returns paid by mutual funds, banks have had to pay very attractive rates on small time deposits (less than $100,000).

Bank reliance on liabilities other than core deposits, including federal funds purchased, securities sold under agreement to repurchase, Federal Home Loan Bank (FHLB) advances, borrowings from the Federal Reserve, and deposits in foreign offices declined over the period 1992–2001 for large banks but increased for smaller banks. Except for discount window borrowings, these funds all have large denominations and pay market rates. They typically have relatively short-term maturities except for some FHLB advances that can extend as long as 20 years.

Banks use the term *volatile liabilities* to describe purchased funds from rate-sensitive investors.[2] The types of instruments include federal funds purchased, RPs, jumbo CDs, Eurodollar time deposits, foreign deposits, and any other large-denomination purchased liability. Investors in these instruments will move their funds if other institutions pay higher rates or if it is rumored that the issuing bank has financial difficulties. Such volatile liabilities accounted for 35.8 percent of financing for large banks in 2001 but only 14.7 percent for smaller banks. The net effect is that larger banks are paying market rates on a greater proportion of their liabilities, with less customer loyalty and thus greater liquidity risk.

Comparisons between different-sized banks reveal key differences in operating style. First, money market deposits declined at smaller banks while demand deposits remained the same.[3] Smaller banks had considerably more core deposits in 2001 versis large banks, but the percentage of assets these funds made up fell by 9.3 percent since 1992. Because core deposits typically cost less than nondeposit liabilities, large bank borrowing costs normally exceed small bank costs. In addition, only the large banks obtained significant funds outside the United States, as foreign deposits totaled 13.4 percent of total funding. Finally, large banks used proportionally less equity capital than small banks even though all banks increased their use of equity financing dramatically since 1992. In 2001, common and preferred equity accounted for 8.77 and 10.9 percent of total assets at large and small banks, respectively.

---

[2]The Uniform Bank Performance Report now refers to volatile liabilities as "Short-Term Net-Noncore Funding." Short-term noncore funding is defined as: CDs of $100,000 or more that mature within one year; brokered deposits less than $100,000 maturing in less than one year; other borrowings with maturities of less than one year; repurchase agreements; and demand notes issued by the U.S. Treasury.

[3]Currently many larger banks have "automatic" sweep systems in place, which simply reclassified NOW accounts to MMDAs. These are relative sophisticated systems that move these funds but remain within regulations that require no more than six movements of MMDAs. Hence, NOW accounts may not accurately represent interest-bearing checking accounts at large banks.

• EXHIBIT 12.2

AVERAGE ANNUAL COST OF LIABILITIES: A COMPARISON OF LARGE VERSUS SMALL BANKS, 2001

Liabilities	Banks with Assets from $3 to $10 Billion	Banks with Assets from $10 to $25 Million
	2001	2001
Transaction accounts	1.71%	1.63%
MMDAS and other savings deposits	2.15	2.79
Large CDs	4.94	5.40
All other time deposits	5.06	5.53
Foreign office deposits	0.56	N/A
Total interest-bearing deposits	3.60%	4.29%
Federal funds & RPs	3.57	1.27
Other borrowed funds	5.16	3.37
Subordinated notes and bonds	1.93	N/A
All interest-bearing funds	3.86	4.31

SOURCE: Uniform Bank Performance Report.

Competitive pressures have pushed the average cost of funds between small banks and large banks to be comparable in many categories. Consider the data in Exhibit 12.2. The primary differences between the costs of deposit funds between the small and large banks is in the cost of transactions accounts and MMDAs, large CDs, and other time deposits.[4] While small banks' overall cost of interest-bearing deposits was 69 basis points higher, they paid lower rates on transaction costs and on hot money sources such as federal funds purchased, repurchase agreements, and other borrowed funds. Lower rates on volatile funds and the fact that the smallest banks obtained more funding in the form of transactions costs did not offset the higher cost of interest-bearing deposits, and that meant that their overall cost of interest-bearing funds was 45 basis points higher than the largest banks.

CHARACTERISTICS OF SMALL DENOMINATION LIABILITIES

The characteristics of small denomination (under $100,000) liabilities are fundamentally different from those of large denomination liabilities. Instruments under $100,000 are normally held by individual investors and are not actively traded in the secondary market. Large balance instruments typically carry denominations in multiples of $1 million and can be readily sold in the secondary market. Individuals traditionally had few alternatives to banks when selecting interest-bearing deposits. Today, commercial banks, savings and loans, credit unions, money market mutual funds, investment banks, and insurance companies offer deposit products with similar features. All pay market interest rates. The principal advantage of banks, savings and loans, and credit unions is that deposits are insured up to $100,000 per account by the federal government.

---

[4]Transactions accounts include interest-bearing demand deposit accounts and NOW and ATS accounts.

TRANSACTIONS ACCOUNTS

Individuals and businesses own checking accounts for transactions purposes. Checks are attractive because they are readily accepted and provide formal verification of payment. Most banks offer three different accounts with transactions privileges: demand deposits (DDAs); interest-checking, or formally negotiable orders of withdrawal (NOWs) and automatic transfers from savings (ATS); and money market deposit accounts (MMDAs). Banks differentiate between deposits in the number of checks permitted, the minimum denomination required to open an account, and the interest rate paid. All carry FDIC insurance up to $100,000 per account.

Demand deposits (DDA) are non-interest-bearing checking accounts held by individuals, businesses, and governmental units. Although explicit interest payments are prohibited, there are no regulatory restrictions on the number of checks or minimum balances. Today, commercial customers own most DDAs because, unlike individuals and governments, they cannot hold NOWs. Individuals with sufficiently large balances prefer interest-bearing accounts that provide transactions privileges.

A **NOW account** is simply a demand deposit that pays interest. An **ATS account** is basically the same but the structure is different. With ATSs the customer has both a DDA and savings account, but the bank forces a zero balance in the DDA at the close of each day after transferring just enough funds from savings to cover checks presented for payment. These accounts have been available nationally since 1981 and have attracted considerable funds away from DDAs since that time.[5] Only individuals and nonprofit organizations can hold NOW or ATS accounts. Every bank prices NOWs based on competitive conditions without restriction. Some banks limit the number of checks that can be written without fees and impose minimum balance requirements before paying interest. Some pay tiered interest rates that increase with the size of the deposit. The rationale is to encourage individuals to consolidate accounts. Depositors are better off if they centralize their accounts because they can earn higher yields and pay lower service charges.

Money market deposit accounts (MMDAs) were introduced to provide banks an instrument to compete with money market mutual funds offered by large brokerage firms. Formally, they are time deposits with limited checking privileges.[6] These accounts differ from NOWs in that depositors are limited to six transactions per month, of which only three can be checks.[7] The average size of each MMDA check is thus much larger than for other transactions accounts. Banks find MMDAs attractive because required reserves against them are considerably below required reserves on DDAs and NOWs. Limited check processing and low reserves reduce their effective cost. Banks can thus afford to pay higher rates to attract MMDA funds. Interestingly, banks have rarely paid rates as high as those on money market mutual funds. The primary reason is that customers are willing to accept a lower rate because of deposit insurance and the fact that they can establish personal banking relationships via their deposit business.

---

[5]NOWs were introduced on an experimental basis in 1972 in New England. Murphy and Mandell (1980) document bank performance with NOWs from 1972 to 1980 prior to nationwide authorization in 1981.

[6]Money market deposit accounts are classified as time deposits, not transactions accounts, when calculating required reserves. They are discussed here because they provide limited check-writing capabilities. Minimum balance requirements were initially set at $2,500, then gradually removed.

[7]The Board's Regulation D regarding reserve requirements of depository institutions (12 CFR Part 204) implements this distinction between NOW accounts and MMDAs or savings deposits. Section 204.2(d)(2) of Regulation D defines "savings deposit" to include an account from which: the depositor is permitted or authorized to make no more than six transfers and withdrawals, or a combination of such transfers and withdrawals, per calendar month or statement cycle to another account (including a transactions account) of the depositor at the same institution or to a third party by means of a preauthorized or automatic transfer, or telephonic (including data transmission) agreement, order, or instruction, and no more than three of the six such transfers may be made by check, draft, debit card, or similar order made by the depositor and payable to third parties.

The ownership of transactions accounts is changing rapidly as institutions offer new deposit products and refine their pricing schedules. Individuals, once loyal customers, previously would not withdraw their funds unless a crisis arose. The advent of interest-bearing checking accounts and the Internet, however, has increased interest rate awareness so that customers today move deposits between accounts and institutions depending on which account or firm pays the highest rates.

Pricing strategies influence the composition of accounts via service charges, minimum balance requirements, and interest rates paid. Service charges may be imposed as flat monthly fees, per-check charges, or a combination of both. Many banks specify minimum balance requirements high enough to limit the number of small balance accounts, for which they impose high monthly service charges. Banks often encourage customers to consolidate accounts by offering tiered interest rates that increase with deposit size and club programs that provide a range of transactions services for a fixed monthly fee. Individuals with demand deposits typically cannot meet minimum balance requirements to open a NOW account. Many critics contend that bank pricing of transactions accounts drives low-income individuals to use check cashing outlets to obtain cash and pay bills via money orders. Importantly, the passage of FDICIA required the consistent reporting of interest rates on deposits as indicated in Contemporary Issues: Truth in Savings Act.

ELECTRONIC MONEY

Electronic commerce, in its infancy just a few years ago, has grown quite rapidly. If one considers carefully the impact of technology in banking, it is apparent that almost all products of the financial services industry can be provided electronically. One can pay for goods electronically, apply and receive a loan electronically, even invest and transfer funds electronically. The need for a physical bank location reflects customer preference—it is not a requirement for doing business.

Some analysts believe that smart cards, e-cash, and e-checks will soon replace other mediums as the means of payment for Internet transactions. **E-cash** and **e-checks** are not Federal Reserve money but rather digital "tokens" somewhat like bus tokens or casino chips, only electronic versions. These funds represent encrypted value that is first paid for by credit card or cash and then presented for online purchases. Lauren Bielski argues that e-money "is arguably more of an electronic instruction to pay than true 'electronic money.'"[8] With respect to small payments, e-money has been compared to "prepaid" phone cards in that one "purchases" electronic value that can be used to make payments in a secure fashion. On the large payment side, Electronic Data Interchange (EDI), a paperless exchange of business information between business partners, is used by more than 100,000 companies today.

Those green pieces of paper stuffed in your pocket or wallet, sometimes referred to as money or dollars, are likely going to become cryptographically sealed digital images stored electronically. This "digital" money may be stored on a "smart card," a plastic credit-card–sized card with a microchip, an "electronic wallet," a small wallet-sized reader and loader for smart cards, or even the hard disk of your computer or the bank's computer.

There are basically two types of smart cards: an "intelligent" smart card and a "memory" card. An intelligent smart card contains a microchip with the ability to store and secure information, and makes different responses depending on the requirements of the card issuer's specific application needs. Intelligent cards offer a read and storage capability and new information can be added or updated at anytime; additional funds can be added or the card can be terminated if needed. Memory type cards simply store information. Similar to the stored

---

[8]See Lauren Bielski, "New Wave of E-Money Options Hits the Web." *ABA Banking Journal*, August 2000, http://www.banking.com/aba.

TRUTH IN SAVINGS ACT

Since the passage of FDICIA in 1992, banks have been required to report interest rates on deposits in a new, consistent format. The intent is to eliminate confusion regarding how interest is calculated and establish uniform rules for the reporting of true yields. Banks also must disclose more fees and provide more information in their advertising.

Banks must report the interest rates they pay on deposits in terms of an annual percentage yield, or APY. The APY can be used to calculate what your deposit will be worth if you left it at the bank for one year. For example, an APY of 4.45 percent means that a customer who deposits $10,000 will find the deposit worth $10,445 after one year. In each case the year-ending interest balance equals the amount on deposit times the APY ($10,000 3 .0445 in the above case).

Truth in Savings also requires that banks pay interest on the full customer deposit rather than some fraction of the total. Many banks historically paid interest on investable deposits defined as the amount that appears on the books minus float and minus required reserves the bank must hold against the deposit. With Truth in Savings, the APY is applied against the ledger balance amount that appears on the books. In addition, if a bank plans to change any terms of a time deposit that will adversely affect the depositor, such as offering a lower interest rate, it must give the customer 30 days notice. Many banks believe that this will eliminate the fixed-rate time deposit because notification costs will be high.

Finally, it is illegal for banks to structure a deposit that requires a minimum balance to earn interest, then not pay any interest if your balance falls below the minimum even for just one day. Banks cannot pay interest for the period the balance falls below the minimum, but cannot cancel interest on the actual balance for days it exceeds the minimum.

With fees and advertising banks must reveal more information. When an account is opened, a bank is required to provide a list of fees associated with normal account activity. They may also not use terms such as "free" or "no cost" when they require some minimum balance, or if any maintenance or activity fee may be charged.

---

information on the back of a credit card, a storage card can contain value that the user can spend in a pay phone, a retail store, or a vending machine. Memory type smart cards are popular on college campuses.

Wireless transactions using computers, personal digital assistance (PDAs) and even your cell phone are in limited use in the United States. Cell phones are used to make small payments in Europe to a much greater degree than in the United States. Soft-drink vending machines are connected to a network that makes a drink fall from the machine after one dials in the telephone number listed on the front of the machine! The following is a typical data interchange between a cell phone and the host computer. The question you might ask is, what is the difference between this and the information sent by another electronic payment scheme?

Offhook @ 09/07/01 11:21:08, On-off time = 1.37 seconds, Volt on/off = 50/06 New dialtone, DP-23455551212, X, New ringback = 02, Voice @ 11:21:45 Onhook @ 09/07/01 11:28:57, Call duration: 00:07:49 Ringing @ 09/07/01 14:14:26 R, R, Answered @ 09/07/01 14:14:42, Volt on/off = ++/07 Voice @ 14:14:46 Onhook @ 09/07/01 14:18:25, Call duration: 00:03:43

Moves to a cashless society will not only change the physical way you spend your money, they may alter the way you view your own financial status. For years, many experts have argued that the United States would become a cashless society. Almost all large transactions—the trillions of dollars handled each day by banks, other financial institutions, and the Federal Reserve clearinghouses—are already digital. Although the technology to go "cashless" has been available for many years, paper money is popular and still the preferred means of making transactions by the average consumer. In fact, it is estimated that cash accounted for 82.3 percent of the total volume of payments in 2000. Checks were the second largest in terms of volume at 10.3 percent while electronic payments (ATM, credit cards, and debit cards) accounted for 7.4 percent of all payments. In terms of the value of transactions, however, cash accounted for only 0.3 percent of the total value of transactions, checks were 10.9 percent and electronic payments (ATM, credit cards, and debit cards) accounted for 2.9 percent. The vast majority of large transactions were wholesale wire transfers such as CHIPS and Fed Wire transactions. Although cash dominates the "small" payment end of transactions, it represents a very small fraction of the total value of payments.

Technology may eventually mean, however, that paper money is no longer a viable option. The advent of high-quality color copiers and computer imaging equipment means that the security of paper money is questionable. The costs of doing business with paper money are quite high as well. Paper money must be guarded, insured, physically transported, and there is always the divisibility problem. That is, dollar bills are not always substitutable for quarters in vending machines. According to Donald Gleason, president of the Smart Card Enterprise unit of Electronic Payment Services Inc., "It costs money handlers in the United States alone approximately $60 billion a year to move the stuff, a line item ripe for drastic pruning. The solution is to cram our currency in burn bags and strike some matches. This won't happen all at once, and paper money will probably never go away, but bills and coinage will increasingly be replaced by some sort of electronic equivalent."

An *electronic funds transfer* (EFT) is an electronic movement of financial data, designed to eliminate the paper instruments normally associated with such funds movement. There are many types of EFTs including ACH, POS, ATM, direct deposit, telephone bill paying, automated merchant authorization systems, and preauthorized payments. A *point of sale* (POS) transaction is a sale that is consummated by payment for goods or services received at the point of the sale or a direct debit of the purchase amount to the customer's checking account. That is, funds are transferred at the time the sale is made.[9] An *automated clearing house* (ACH) transaction is an electronically processed payment using a standard data format. A computer network to clear and settle electronic payment transactions links ACH institutions. ACH payments are electronic payments of funds and government securities among financial institutions and businesses. ATMs, or automatic teller machines, have been a popular EFT system for many years. These machines provide customers electronic access to their funds all over the world. Direct deposits of paychecks and social security checks are quite common today as well. Automated merchant and preauthorized payments are actually the other side of direct deposits in which payments are made automatically and electronically. In both cases, direct deposits and automated payments, one level of paper has been eliminated. These payments go directly to the party authorized for payment. For example, rather than a check being written to the employee and deposited in their bank account, the payment is made directly to the employee's bank with instructions to credit the customer's account.

Even though Internet bill payments, telephone bill payments, automatic deposits, and bank drafts are considered to be electronic payments, money may not be. These types of payments seem to be electronic, but in many cases paper checks are still often written on the customer's behalf and mailed to the business. Obviously, these types of payments will most likely become totally electronic in the near future. The question is, will you part with your paper money or will technology force you to give it up?

FUNCTIONAL COST ANALYSIS

Periodically the Federal Reserve System conducts a survey called the *Functional Cost and Profit Analysis (FCA)* report to collect cost and income data on commercial bank operations. It then publishes average data for banks grouped by deposit size. The cost data are somewhat imprecise because banks subjectively allocate expenses to various products and services, but

---

[9]Technically speaking, it can actually take one to three days before the funds are transferred.

they are the best data publicly available for analyzing costs and provide useful comparisons between firms.

According to functional cost analysis data, demand deposits are the least expensive source of funds. Costs are still substantial, however, as most banks employ a large staff to process checks. Functional cost analysis classifies check-processing activities as either deposits (electronic and nonelectronic), withdrawals (electronic and nonelectronic), transit checks deposited, transit checks cashed, account opened or closed, on-us checks cashed, or general account maintenance (truncated and nontruncated). *Electronic transactions* are those that occur through automatic deposits, Internet and telephone bill payment, ATMs, and ACH transactions. *Nonelectronic* are those transactions conducted in person or by mail. *Transit checks deposited* are defined as checks drawn on any bank other than the subject bank. *On-us checks cashed* are checks drawn on the bank's customer's account. *Deposits* represent checks or currency directly deposited in the customer's account. *Account maintenance* refers to general record maintenance and preparing and mailing a periodic statement. A *truncated account* is a checking account in which the physical check is "truncated" at the bank; that is, checks are not returned to the customer. *Official check issued* would be for certified funds. Finally, *net indirect costs* are costs not directly related to the product such as salaries to manage the bank or general overhead.

Exhibit 12.3 summarizes 1999 average cost and revenue information for various types of accounts at banks with deposits between $50 million and $200 million. The first two columns contain data for demand or checking accounts. The next two columns of data are for savings accounts, which are small personal savings accounts with no maturity. Time deposit data, listed in the third two columns, are generally for larger accounts such as CDs with a fixed term to mature. It should be noted that these data are obtained voluntarily, so there may be biases toward the features of the healthiest banks. Also, few very large institutions participate in the survey, so figures may not be applicable to the largest banks.

The first column in each account category indicates the average cost per item for each activity. Examining the first group of data under the category Noninterest Income clearly indicates that service charges and fees are highest for checking (demand) accounts and lowest for time deposit accounts. This is not surprising because transaction expenses associated with checking accounts are much greater than those for savings accounts or time deposits. Transaction activity in savings accounts is also somewhat greater than time accounts (adjusted for account size), hence the slightly higher fees collected on these types of accounts. On the other hand, the average interest cost is highest for time accounts and lowest for checking (demand) accounts. Noninterest expenses are much higher on checking (demand) accounts and lowest on time deposits (as a percentage of average balance). Finally, note that the cost of electronic transactions is but a fraction of the cost of nonelectronic transactions. In fact, if banks could significantly increase the use of electronic transactions by their customers, they would dramatically reduce the cost of servicing these types of accounts. This is one reason why some larger banks have begun to charge a $2–$3 fee for nonelectronic transactions.

Whether these accounts are profitable depends on how much a bank earns from service charges and fees and from investing deposit balances. Estimates of these average monthly revenues are listed at the top of Exhibit 12.3. Interest (investment) income is calculated by multiplying the earnings rate on balances in excess of float and required reserves.[10] Not surprisingly, total revenue varies directly with the average size of the deposit. Net revenue per month is greatest for commercial time deposit accounts and least for demand accounts, ranging from approximately $11.15 to $26.16 per account. It should be noted, however, that these

---

[10]Earnings credit rate is assumed to be 7.5 percent for all accounts. Required reserves are 10 percent for demand accounts, zero for other accounts. Float is assumed to be 5 percent for demand accounts, 2 percent for small savings, and zero for time accounts.

· EXHIBIT 12.3

COST AND REVENUE ANALYSIS OF SELECTED TRANSACTIONS ACCOUNTS: BANKS WITH DEPOSITS OF $50 MILLION TO $200 MILLION

	Demand Accounts		Savings Accounts		Time Deposits	
	Unit Cost	Monthly Income/ Expenses	Unit Cost	Monthly Income/ Expenses	Unit Cost	Monthly Income/ Expenses
Income						
Interest Income (estimated 7.5% earnings credit)		$29.47		$34.04		$121.84
Noninterest Income						
Service charges		2.80		0.44		0.11
Penalty fees		4.32		0.28		0.27
Other		0.63		0.16		0.05
Total Noninterest Income		*$ 7.75*		*$ 0.88*		*$ 0.42*
Expenses						
Activity Charges						
Deposit electronic	$0.0089	$0.02	$0.0502	$0.01	$0.1650	$0.1296
Deposit nonelectronic	0.2219	0.66	0.7777	0.46	3.1425	2.2016
Withdrawal electronic	0.1073	0.43	0.4284	0.07	0.5400	0.2840
Withdrawal nonelectronic	0.2188	3.63	0.7777	0.39	1.4933	0.5875
Transit check deposited	0.1600	1.71	0.5686	1.09		
Transit check cashed	0.2562	0.50				
Account opened	9.46	0.20	33.63	0.53	5.78	1.73
Account closed	5.67	0.07	20.18	0.26	3.38	1.02
On-us checks cashed	0.2412	0.42				
Account maintenance (truncated) monthly	2.42	1.67	4.10	3.56	1.99	1.99
Account maintenance (nontruncated) monthly	8.60	7.03				
Official check issued	1.02					
Total Activity Expense		$16.34		$6.37		$7.94
Net Indirect Expense		$4.35		$1.81		$18.38
Total noninterest expense		20.69		8.18		26.32
Interest Expense	1.25%	5.38	2.96%	13.45	5.18%	69.79
Total Expense		*$26.07*		*$21.63*		*$96.11*
Net Income (expense) Before Earnings Credit		$(18.32)		$(20.75)		$(95.69)
Net Revenue Per Month		11.15		13.29		26.16
Average account balance		$5,515.00		$5,557.00		$19,495.00
Average annual net cost[a]		4.66%		4.57%		5.89%
Average interest cost		1.37		2.96		4.30
Average noninterest cost		5.27		1.80		1.62
Average noninterest income		1.97		0.19		0.03

[a]Required reserves are assumed to be 10 percent for demand accounts and zero for others. Float is assumed to be 5 percent for demand accounts, 2 percent for savings accounts, and zero for time accounts.

SOURCE: *Functional Cost and Profit Analysis*, based on data furnished by participating banks in 12 Federal Reserve Districts, 1999 National Average Report, Commercial Banks.

estimates are based on rather large average balances, from $5,515 for demand checking and $5,557 for small savings to $19,495 for time deposits. Smaller average balances would dramatically affect the bank's profitability on these accounts.

Data for other banks show similar cost and revenue relationships across account categories. Smaller banks generally realize lower costs per account but earn less as revenues are much lower because they handle much smaller accounts. Larger banks have the highest costs but earn more revenue because they handle larger deposits.

Small time deposits have denominations under $100,000, specified maturities ranging from seven days to any longer negotiated term, and substantial interest penalties for early withdrawal. Banks can pay market rates on any account regardless of deposit size. Since 1983 bank customers have had the flexibility to negotiate maturity and rate for any size account maturing beyond 31 days. Banks can control the flow of deposits by offering products with specific maturities and minimum balances and varying the relative rates paid according to these terms. The effective cost of small time deposits is comparable to that for MMDAs. Average interest expense is higher, but operating costs are lower. In today's environment, there is also some difference between small time deposits ($25,000) and the larger, small time deposits ($75,000 to $99,999) as these larger deposits act more like jumbo CDs. They are very interest rate sensitive and typically held by high-income individuals, small companies, and even other financial institutions.

SERVICE CHARGES

For many years banks priced check-handling services below cost. Although competition may have forced this procedure, it was acceptable because banks paid below-market rates on most deposits. This low interest subsidy implicitly covered losses on check handling. The popular view was that the 20 percent of bank customers with the largest deposit balances subsidized the 80 percent with lower balances.

Deregulation removed this subsidy and induced banks to modify their pricing policies. Because banks now pay market rates on deposits, they want all customers to pay at least what the services cost. This has brought about relationship pricing, in which service charges decline and interest rates increase with larger customer deposit balances. Many banks have unbundled services and price each separately. Some charge for services once considered simple courtesies, such as check cashing and balance inquiries. In fact there are even banks that charge a fee to see a real person! For most customers, service charges and fees for banking services have increased substantially in recent years.

Such pricing schemes have essentially created a caste system of banking. Large depositors receive the highest rates, pay the lowest fees, and often get free checking. They do not wait in long teller lines and receive more attention from their personal banker. Small depositors earn lower rates, if any, and pay higher fees, with less personal service. Consider the pricing terms outlined in Exhibit 12.4. Unless an individual keeps a minimum $1,000 in checking balances each month, the monthly service charge equals $15, or $180 per year. Similarly, the bank pays no interest on a NOW account unless the minimum balance is $2,000. The related charges for insufficient funds checks, stop payment orders, and check-cashing for noncustomers are substantial as well. This bank also charges $3 for each balance inquiry made by a customer. The point is that this bank wants small-balance customers only if they generate substantial fee income.

CALCULATING THE NET COST OF TRANSACTION ACCOUNTS

The average historical cost of funds is a measure of average unit borrowing costs for existing funds. Average interest cost for the total portfolio is calculated by dividing total interest expense by the average dollar amount of liabilities outstanding and measures the average percentage cost of a single dollar of debt. Average historical costs for a single source of funds can be calculated as the ratio of interest expense by source to the average outstanding debt for that source during the period. The interest cost rates presented in Chapter 3 represent such costs.

■ EXHIBIT 12.4

INDIVIDUAL TRANSACTION ACCOUNT PRICING

Account Type	Minimum Balance	Monthly Service Charge
Individual DDA	$0 ~ $999	$15
	≥ 1,000	0
NOW	$0 ~ $1,999	$10
	≥ 2,000	0
	No interest is paid on days the balance falls below $2,000.	
MMDA	$0 ~ $4,999	$15
	5,000 ~ 9,999	10
	≥ 10,000	0
	If the balance falls below $2,500, the NOW account rate is paid.	

Selected Charges	Item Charge
Insufficient funds	$30
Stop payment orders	30
Automatic teller machine withdrawal—off premise	1
Automatic teller machine withdrawal—on premise	0
Balance inquiry	3
Check cashing—noncustomer	15

Interest costs alone, however, dramatically understate the effective cost of transaction accounts for several reasons. First, transaction accounts are subject to legal reserve requirements of up to 10 percent of the outstanding balances, which are generally invested in nonearning assets (Federal Reserve deposits or vault cash). This effectively increases the cost of transactional accounts because a reduced portion of the balances can be invested. Nontransactional accounts have no reserve requirements (see Chapter 14 for a discussion of required reserves) and hence are cheaper, ceteris paribus, because 100 percent of the funds can be invested. Second, when depositors write a large number of checks against their balances, there are substantial processing costs. Third, certain fees are charged on some accounts to offset noninterest expenses and this reduces the cost of these funds to the bank.

To estimate the annual historical net cost of bank liabilities simply add historical interest expense with noninterest expense (net of noninterest income) and divide by the investable amount of funds to determine the minimum return required on earning assets:

Historical Net Cost of Bank Liabilities

$$= \frac{\text{Interest Expense} + \text{Noninterest Expense} - \text{Noninterest Income}}{\text{Average Balance net of float} \times (1 - \text{reserve requirement ratio})} \qquad (12.1)$$

The net cost of demand accounts from Exhibit 12.3, assuming 5 percent float and 10 percent reserve requirements, would be:

$$\text{Net cost of demand accounts} = \frac{\$5.38 + \$20.69 - \$7.75}{\$5,515 \times 0.95 \times 0.90} \times 12 = 4.66\%[11]$$

Note that the UBPR, introduced in Chapter 3, would have estimated the interest cost of non-interest-bearing checking accounts at near 0 percent, truly underestimating the cost of

---

[11]We have to multiply by 12 because the cost figures given in Exhibit 12.3 are monthly costs.

these funds to the bank. There are no reserve requirements on savings accounts, so the net cost of these from Exhibit 12.3 (assuming a 2 percent float) would be:

$$\text{Net cost of savings accounts} = \frac{\$13.45 + \$8.18 - \$0.88}{\$5,557 \times 0.98 \times 12} = 4.57\%$$

Although the actual historical cost of the small savings account is less than the demand checking, a low-balance checking account customer could prove to be quite expensive. In fact, if the average account balance on the regular checking account were just $500, the net annual cost would have been 51.42 percent—much higher than that for the savings account.

CHARACTERISTICS OF LARGE DENOMINATION LIABILITIES

In addition to small denomination deposits, banks purchase funds in the money markets. Money center and large regional banks effect most transactions over the telephone, either directly with trading partners or through brokers. Most trades are denominated in $1 million multiples. Smaller banks generally deal directly with customers and have limited access to national and international markets. Some types of liabilities, such as jumbo CDs sold directly by a bank, are viewed as permanent sources of funds, while others are used infrequently. Banks must pay market rates on all sources and can normally attract additional funds by paying a small premium over the current quoted market rate. Because customers move their investments on the basis of small rate differentials, these funds are labeled "hot money," volatile liabilities, or short-term noncore funding.

JUMBO CDS (CDS OVER $100,000)

Large, negotiable certificates of $100,000 or more are referred to as jumbo CDs. These CDs are issued primarily by the largest banks and purchased by businesses and governmental units. Since their introduction in the early 1960s, CDs have grown to be the most popular hot money financing used by the largest banks.

Although CDs come in many varieties, they all possess similar characteristics. First, they have a minimum maturity of seven days. The most common maturities are 30 and 90 days, but recent issues of zero coupon CDs extend the maturity out as long as 10 years. Second, CD interest rates are quoted on the basis of a 360-day year. Except for zeros, CDs are issued at face value and trade as interest-bearing instruments. Thus, trades are settled at market value of the principal plus interest accrued from the original purchase. Third, CDs are insured up to $100,000 per investor per institution. Any balances in excess of $100,000 are at risk to the purchaser. For example, investors in CDs issued by Penn Square Bank of Oklahoma City that failed in 1983 received only 65 cents on the dollar for the uninsured portion of their CDs. Jumbo CDs are considered risky instruments and are traded accordingly. When an issuing bank has financial difficulties, it must pay a stiff premium over current yields, often 2 to 3 percent, to attract funds. When traders perceive that all large banks are experiencing difficulties, as with the Asian financial crisis in 1998, they bid CD rates higher relative to comparable maturity Treasury bill rates.

Banks issue jumbo CDs directly to investors or indirectly through dealers and brokers. Whenever they use an intermediary, banks pay approximately one-eighth of 1 percent, or 12.5 basis points, for the service. Deposits obtained in this manner are labeled **brokered deposits.** The broker essentially places a bank's CDs with investors who demand insured deposits. The advantage is that brokers provide small banks access to purchased funds. They package CDs in $100,000 increments so that all deposits are fully insured, and market them to interested investors. In essence, the broker is selling deposit insurance because the buyer assumes the risk that the government will not pay off insured depositors, which has never happened. Thus, a bank or savings and loan might request that a broker obtain $50 million in CDs, which could be handled by selling 500 $100,000 fully insured CDs.

Not surprisingly, bank regulators argue that brokered CDs are often abused to where there is a link between brokered deposits and problem/failed banks. Banks and thrifts can use the funds to speculate on high-risk assets. If the investments deteriorate and the bank fails, it is the FDIC, not the owners of the bank, that must pay insured depositors. In fact, many failed banks and savings and loans grew too rapidly during the 1980s by buying funds through brokers and making speculative loans. Loan losses subsequently followed. For this reason, Congress restricted the use of brokered deposits to banks with high amounts of equity capital that are less likely to fail.

Large multibank holding companies have successfully marketed large denomination CDs by agreeing to allocate a total investment among affiliate banks in $100,000 increments so that the full amount is insured. Thus, a holding company with 60 subsidiary banks could place $6 million from any single depositor within the group with full insurance coverage. Deposit insurance again provides greater access to funding in this form. Interestingly, pension fund deposits are insured up to $100,000 per individual pensioner, amounts that reach many millions of dollars even at the same institution.

Uncertainty over future interest rates has induced many investors to shorten their investment horizon, making short-term CDs the most popular maturities. Many banks prefer to lengthen CD maturities, thereby reducing rate sensitivity because they currently operate with negative funding GAPs near-term. Banks have gone to extremes to attract long-term CD funds, often creating hybrid CDs that appeal to select investors. Several of these are identified next.

VARIABLE-RATE CDS. Traditionally, CDs were fixed-rate contracts that were renegotiated at 1-, 3-, and 6-month maturities. Since the mid-1970s, large banks have issued variable-rate contracts for longer periods, with rates renegotiated at specified intervals. For example, a bank might issue a CD where the depositor agrees to keep funds on deposit for two years. The bank prices the contract as a series of eight CDs, with the rate renegotiated every three months. The rate paid at each interval is equal to the average of 3-month CD rates quoted by securities dealers.[12] These variable-rate CDs appeal to investors who expect rising rates or want the added rate sensitivity.

CALLABLE CDS. During the late 1990s interest rates increased, bank loan demand was high, and banks were having difficulty funding asset growth. Large CD rates were as high as 8 percent on 2- to 5-year CDs, much higher than rates on comparable maturity Treasury securities. The need for long-term funding, combined with the concern that rates would fall, lead some banks to begin issuing callable 5-year CDs. These CDs typically carried a 2-year deferment period, meaning they could not be called for two years after issue. Afterward, the bank could call the CDs, meaning that it could repay the depositor's principal, at its discretion. These CDs offered attractive rates but provided the bank with lower borrowing costs risk if rates were to fall over the life of the CDs.

ZERO COUPON CDS. Like zero coupon bonds, zero coupon CDs are sold at a steep discount from par and appreciate to face value at maturity. They carry fixed rates and fixed maturities. For example, a bank might issue a CD with a current price of $500,000 that pays

---

[12]A newer twist, popular at smaller banks, is to give the depositor the alternative to keep the original rate or reinvest at a higher rate if rates go up, often called a "jump rate." Because this option transfers all interest rate risk to the issuing bank, a customer should be willing to accept a lower initial yield.

$1 million in six years. The investor receives a fixed 12.24 percent annual return and knows with certainty what the value of the investment is after six years. The primary disadvantage is that the amortized portion of the original ($500,000) discount is subject to federal income taxes each year, even though the investor does not actually receive current income. For this reason, many banks market the zeros to individual retirement or Keogh accounts. Whenever the maturity value is below $100,000, the CD is fully insured. The attraction to issuing banks is in getting longer-term funds. In this case, the bank obtains $500,000 immediately with no corresponding cash outflow for six years. This deposit's effective duration is six years.

STOCK MARKET INDEXED CDS. During the 1990s the U.S. stock market boomed, producing historically high returns for most buy and hold investors. As stock prices rose, yields on CDs fell behind. Many banks tried to capitalize on this phenomenon by offering CDs with yields linked to a stock market index such as the S&P 500. A depositor who opens such an account might receive a yield equal to the higher of a fixed 1 percent or 90 percent of the total return on the S&P 500 index. A bank can offer this CD in part because it can hedge the risk of stock prices rising sharply by selling futures contracts on the S&P 500.

IMMEDIATELY AVAILABLE FUNDS

As the name suggests, immediately available funds are balances that are accepted as a means of payment within one business day on demand. Two types of balances are immediately available: deposit liabilities of Federal Reserve Banks and certain "collected" liabilities of commercial banks that may be transferred or withdrawn during a business day on order of account holders.[13] Through its wire transfer facilities, the Federal Reserve System can electronically move deposits anywhere throughout the United States within 24 hours. Collected balances of banks are ledger balances appearing on a bank's books minus float. All checks written against such accounts, but not yet cleared, have been deducted, and the remaining balances are transferable within one day. Most large transactions are settled in immediately available funds, including maturing CDs, federal funds, and security repurchase agreements.

FEDERAL FUNDS PURCHASED

The term **federal funds** is often used to refer to excess reserve balances that are traded between banks. This is grossly inaccurate, given reserves averaging as a method of computing reserves, different nonbank players in the market, and the motivation behind many trades. In some instances, nonbank participants, such as securities dealers and state governments, trade federal funds. In other cases, bank reserve balances at Federal Reserve Banks do not change ownership. The formal definition of federal funds is unsecured short-term loans that are settled in immediately available funds. They encompass transactions outside the arena of bank reserve trading by including any participant that holds large balances at Federal Reserve Banks or collected liabilities at depository institutions. Thus, thrift institutions, foreign governments, and the U.S. Treasury can trade federal funds.

Most transactions are overnight loans, although maturities are negotiated and can extend up to several weeks. Interest rates are negotiated between trading partners and are quoted on a 360-day basis. The absence of collateral suggests that participants are well known by their trading partners as lenders accept default risk. Large transactions are

---

[13]Immediately available funds are discussed by Lucas, Jones, and Thurston (1977). Deposit liabilities of Federal Reserve Banks to financial institutions constitute the major portion of the banking system's legal required reserves.

denominated in multiples of $1 million and are typically handled by brokers. On the other side of the spectrum, small banks frequently buy and sell federal funds in amounts as low as $50,000. When a bank purchases federal funds, its cost of borrowing equals the interest rate plus the brokerage fee because the bank does not have to hold required reserves against this liability.

The federal funds market is important to monetary policy because the federal funds rate is a key target variable for the Federal Reserve System. Federal Reserve policies, particularly Federal Open Market Committee purchases and sales of securities, directly alter the bank reserves component of immediately available funds, increasing or decreasing the federal funds rate. Increases in bank reserves reduce borrowing pressure relative to desired lending of immediately available funds, and the federal funds rate declines over the near term. The opposite occurs with decreases in bank reserves.

SECURITY REPURCHASE AGREEMENTS

Security repurchase agreements (RPs or repos) are short-term loans secured by government securities that are settled in immediately available funds. They are virtually identical to federal funds in function and form except they are collateralized. Technically, the loans embody a sale of securities with a simultaneous agreement to buy them back later at a fixed price plus accrued interest. The later date is normally the next day, as most RPs have 24-hour maturities. Some loans are for longer periods, with maturity and rate negotiated. Although securities dealers dominate the market, any institution can trade RPs as long as it meets collateral and balance requirements.

For example, if City National Bank used an RP to acquire immediately available funds, it would have to post securities as collateral against the borrowing. Whenever the collateral is U.S. government or agency securities, the funds obtained are free of reserves. In market terminology, the lender's transaction is a reverse RP. Banks participate both as borrowers and lenders directly or as securities dealers.

In most cases, the market value of the collateral is set above the loan amount when the contract is negotiated. This difference is labeled the *margin*. If, for example, City National pledged $1.1 million of U.S. government securities against its $1 million borrowing, the margin equals $100,000. Positive margin protects the lender from potential decreases in collateral value if interest rates increase. This protection makes RPs less risky compared to unsecured federal funds transactions and thus RP rates are less than federal funds rates for similar maturity contracts.

Such collateral proved inadequate in 1982, when two government securities dealers, Drysdale Government Securities and Lombard-Wall Inc., were forced into bankruptcy when they could not pay accrued interest owed on heavy borrowings via RPs when the loans came due. As a result, Chase Manhattan Bank and Manufacturers Hanover took losses from Drysdale alone equal to $285 million and $21 million, respectively. Although both banks initially disclaimed liability, they eventually made good on losses their customers otherwise would have incurred because the banks arranged the RP transactions.

In 1985 E.S.M. Group Inc. similarly collapsed after suffering losses trading RPs, bringing about the failure of Home State Savings in Ohio and the closing of over 70 thrifts that faced losses from a massive run on deposits. Deposits at Home State and the thrifts were privately insured, but the insurance pool was insufficient to meet payment obligations. The closed thrifts ultimately reopened with federal deposit insurance coverage.[14]

---

[14]A series of articles from "Repurchase Agreements: Taking a Closer Look at Safety" (Federal Reserve Bank of Atlanta, September 1985) discuss the structure of the RP market and factors influencing credit and interest rate risk.

These failures increased regulatory scrutiny of the RP market and focused attention on the true legal status of a repo. In particular, creditors of Drysdale and Lombard-Wall who held RP collateral sold the securities. If, in fact, RPs are secured loans, bankruptcy law prohibits creditors from selling any assets owned by the failed firms. If RPs are separate contracts to sell and repurchase securities, creditors can liquidate the securities. Technically, the securities are the lenders because the borrower failed to repurchase them. Court rulings appear to side with the creditors, allowing them to liquidate security holdings.

FOREIGN OFFICE DEPOSITS

Most large U.S. commercial banks compete aggressively in international markets. They borrow from and extend credit to foreign-based individuals, corporations, and governments. In recent years international financial markets and multinational businesses have become increasingly sophisticated to the point where bank customers go overseas for cheaper financing and feel unfettered by national boundaries.

Transactions in short-term international markets often take place in the Eurocurrency market. The term **Eurocurrency** refers to a financial claim denominated in a currency other than that of the country where the issuing institution is located. The most important Eurocurrency is the **Eurodollar,** a dollar-denominated financial claim at a bank outside the United States. The banks may be foreign-owned or foreign branches of U.S. banks. The Eurodollar market comprises both loans and deposits, each with different characteristics and participants.

Eurodollar deposits are dollar-denominated deposits in banks outside the United States. They are virtually identical to time deposits issued directly by domestic banks, except for the country of issue. In all cases, dollar deposits at U.S. banks support the creation of a Eurodollar deposit. These deposits never physically leave the United States, only the ownership does. Maturities range from call to five years, and most deposits are traded in denominations of $1 million or more. Eurodollar CDs, the counterpart of domestic CDs, are the most popular Eurodollar deposit. They carry short-term maturities, typically three to six months, and can be traded in the secondary market prior to maturity. Although most Eurodollar CDs pay fixed rates, floating-rate instruments are becoming increasingly popular. Eurodollar rates are quoted on an interest-bearing basis, assuming a 360-day year. Eurodollar deposit rates must be competitive with rates on comparable maturity instruments, such as federal funds and jumbo CDs.[15] Otherwise, the deposits would not attract funds away from U.S.-based instruments.

Eurodollar depositors include individuals, businesses, and governments from around the world. Many transactions, in fact, are merely interbank deposits. Exhibit 12.5 characterizes the origination of Eurodollar deposits and the eventual path to a Eurodollar loan. It summarizes activities of four groups and encompasses three stages of transactions. In the first stage, a U.S. manufacturing corporation based in New York opens a Eurodollar deposit at the Bank of England in London and effectively transfers ownership of a demand balance held at a U.S. Money Center Bank in New York. The terms of the Eurodollar deposit are negotiated as discussed above. At the end of this transaction, $10 million in Eurodollar deposits has been created. The amount of demand deposits at U.S. banks, however, is unchanged. Only the ownership has changed, from the U.S. manufacturer to the Bank of England.

During Stage II, the Bank of England redeposits the dollars with the U.S. Money Center Bank's London office. Ownership of the original demand balance at the New York bank again changes, but the deposit does not physically leave the United States. Another $10 million in Eurodollar deposits has been created with no change in total demand deposits at U.S. banks.

---

[15]Goodfriend (1981) discusses these relationships and general Eurodollar characteristics in detail.

■ EXHIBIT 12.5

THE ORIGIN AND EXPANSION OF EURODOLLAR DEPOSITS

Stage I: U.S. manufacturer opens $10 million Eurodollar account at Bank of England, London (BE-L).
Stage II: Bank of England, London, opens Eurodollar account at U.S. Money Center Bank, London (MCB-L).
Stage III: U.S. Money Center Bank, London, extends $10 million Eurodollar loan to British corporation in London (MCB-NY).

U.S. Manufacturer, New York		U.S. Money Center Bank, New York		U.S. Money Center Bank, London		Bank of England, London	
ΔASSETS	ΔLIABILITIES	ΔASSETS	ΔLIABILITIES	ΔASSETS	ΔLIABILITIES	ΔASSETS	ΔLIABILITIES
Stage I:							
Demand deposits due from MCB-NY −$10 million			Demand deposits due to U.S. manuf.-NY −$10 million			Demand deposit due from MCB-NY +$10 million	Eurodollar deposit due to U.S manuf.-NY +$10 million
Eurodollar deposit due from BE-L +$10 million			Demand deposit due to BE-L +$10 million				
Stage II:			Demand deposit due to BE-L −$10 million	Demand deposit due from MCB-NY +$10 million	Eurodollar deposit due to BE-L +$10 million	Demand deposit due from MCB-NY −$10 million	
			Demand deposit due to MCB-L +$10 million			Eurodollar deposit due from MCB-L +$10 million	
Stage III:			Demand deposit due to MCB-L −$10 million	Demand deposit due from MCB-NY −$10 million			
British Corp., London			Demand deposit due to British corp. +$10 million	Eurodollar loan to British corp. +$10 million			
ΔASSETS	LIABILITIES						
Demand deposit due from MCB-NY +$10 million	Eurodollar loan from MCB-L +$10 million						

Stage III documents a Eurodollar loan made to a British corporation such that the foreign firm ultimately owns the original demand deposit. This intermediation among banks permits the multiple expansion of Eurodollar deposits based on a fixed demand deposit at a U.S. bank. There are no reserve requirements on Eurodollar deposits, and a bank will move the entire balance as long as it can earn a profitable spread. The base rate paid on interbank deposits (Stage II) is termed the London Interbank Offer Rate (LIBOR). Additional interbank deposits are typically made at spreads of 0.125 to 0.25 percent. Thus if the initial deposit at the Bank of England paid 8 percent, the Bank of England would require at least 8.125 percent on its redeposit. The spread on a Eurodollar loan to the ultimate borrower is considerably greater.

INDIVIDUAL RETIREMENT ACCOUNTS

Individual retirement accounts (IRAs) are savings plans for wage earners and their spouses. The plans encompass many types of savings vehicles with varied maturities, interest rates, and other earnings features. Individuals can choose between different financial services companies and many different products. Commercial banks, thrift institutions, brokerage houses, and insurance companies dominate IRA investments. Investor options range from small time deposits and MMDAs at banks and savings and loans to common stocks, zero coupon Treasury securities, and shares in limited real estate partnerships offered by brokerages.

The primary attraction of IRAs is their tax benefits. Each wage earner can invest up to $3,000 ($3,500 if aged 50 or more) of earned income annually in an IRA. Prior to 1987, the principal contribution was tax deductible, and any accumulated earnings in the account were tax deferred until withdrawn. The Tax Reform Act of 1986 removed the tax deductibility of contributions for individuals already covered by qualified pension plans if they earned enough income.[16] Funds withdrawn before age 59 1/2 are subject to a 10 percent IRS penalty. Investors can change investments prior to this age but must pay another penalty if the change does not occur when the underlying savings vehicle matures. These features make IRAs an attractive source of long-term funds for commercial banks and other issuers that can be used to balance the rate sensitivity of longer-term assets. Customers opening accounts are less likely to move them as long as the bank pays competitive rates.

These traditional IRAs are attractive because all funds contributed to the IRA are tax deductible. Taxes are paid when the funds are withdrawn, hence the investor will earn interest on what they would have had to pay in taxes. A new IRA, the Roth IRA, is similarly attractive but has different tax treatment. With a Roth IRA, contributions are made from after-tax dollars, but income accumulates tax-free. When the individual eventually withdraws Roth IRA proceeds, the entire amount is not taxed.

Commercial banks and thrifts offer IRA products related to small time deposits with fixed maturities and MMDAs. These deposits are federally insured, which appeals to many individuals. Money market deposit accounts are the most rate sensitive, as banks change rates at least every 30 days. Banks can typically induce customers to lengthen deposit maturities by paying higher rates on longer-term instruments. Small CDs carrying variable rates tied to external indexes have become increasingly popular with the greater uncertainty over future interest rate movements.

FEDERAL HOME LOAN BANK ADVANCES

With the competition for core deposits so strong, many banks today rely heavily on advances (borrowings) from one of the Federal Home Loan Banks (FHLBs). The FHLB system is a government-sponsored enterprise that was originally created to assist individuals in home buying. Today, the FHLB system is one of the largest U.S. financial institutions, which is rated AAA (Aaa) because of the government sponsorship. It borrows cheaply and either buys government securities or makes loans to other institutions. These loans represent a source of financing to many banks.

---

[16]Beginning in 1997, the total combined contributions that can be made to each spouse's IRA, even if one spouse had little or no compensation, can be as much as $4,000 for the year. Previously, if a wage earner's spouse has no earned income, a couple could contribute a combined $2,250 in two separate IRAs. Prior to January 1982, individuals covered by qualified business or government retirement plans were prohibited from opening IRAs. The Tax Reform Act of 1986 eliminated the deduction for making a contribution if couples filing jointly reported adjusted gross income of at least $40,000 ($25,000 for singles) and were covered by a pension plan. Interest income from an IRA investment remains exempt until withdrawn.

Any bank can become a member of the FHLB system by buying FHLB stock. If it has the available collateral, primarily real-estate-related loans, it can borrow from the FHLB. The Gramm-Leach-Bliley Act of 1999, however, made is much easier for smaller banks to borrow with the funds used for non-real-estate-related loans. In particular, this act allows banks with less than $500 million in assets to use long-term advances for loans to small businesses, small farms, and small agribusinesses. The act also establishes a new permanent capital structure for the Federal Home Loan Banks with two classes of stock authorized, redeemable on 6-months' and 5-years' notice. The greater competition for funds and the authorization of new uses for FHLB advances has resulted in rapid growth in the number of banks with FHLB borrowing and the dollar amount of these borrowings. Exhibit 12.6 tracks the growth in commercial banks with FHLB advances and the dollar amount of these advances.

These borrowings come in the form of advances, which take a variety of forms. Advances can have maturities as short as one day or as long as 20 years. Banks with temporary funding needs (typically linked to increases in home lending) often use short-term advances with maturities from 30- to 90-days. A more recent trend has seen banks use longer-term advances as a more permanent source of funding for loan growth. In many instances, the interest cost compares favorably with the cost of jumbo CDs and other purchased liabilities. The range of potential maturities further allows banks to better manage their interest rate risk by helping them adjust effective maturities or durations of their funding and match them with assets. In addition, banks can borrow virtually any amount as long as they have the qualifying collateral. The interesting issue is whether these advances are truly a permanent source of funds and thus comparable to core deposits, or whether they are hot money.

Some of these FHLB advances are callable in the sense that the FHLB has the right to call the advance prior to maturity, typically after a predetermined deferment period. For example, a 5-year callable advance may be called after one year. By agreeing to an advance with this call feature, a bank sells an option to the FHLB and receives value by paying a lower initial interest rate. Of course, if rates increase, the FHLB will call the loan and the bank will be forced to replace the funds at a higher rate.

MEASURING THE COST OF FUNDS

It is extremely important that banks continuously monitor the cost of their funding sources. Changes in interest rates and the composition of liabilities and equity alter financing costs and may reduce available liquidity. Changes in financing costs require corresponding changes in asset yields to maintain profit margins. With increased competition among financial services companies, both the frequency and magnitude of these changes have increased significantly.

Managing liabilities used to be relatively routine for most commercial banks as federal regulators dictated maximum rates banks could pay on deposits, and customers had few alternatives for their savings. Banks competed for depositors primarily through location and personal service. Customers were quite loyal. These factors gave rise to the well-known 3-6-3 method of running a bank: pay 3 percent on deposits, charge 6 percent on loans, and hit the golf course at 3 o'clock!

Reading any newspaper or financial publication shows how different the environment is today. Most noticeably, deposit rate ceilings no longer exist. Banks have almost unlimited opportunities to develop new deposit products with any maturity that pay market rates, but they must now compete with a variety of firms offering similar products and services. Any individual wishing to open a simple transaction account can use a commercial bank, credit union, savings and loan, and money market mutual fund offered by a brokerage house, American Express, or traditionally nonbank firms such as State Farm and USAA. Although this choice is attractive to consumers, it creates considerable uncertainty for banks regarding the availability and cost of funding sources.

- **EXHIBIT 12.6**

COMMERCIAL BANKS WITH FHLB ADVANCES: 1991–2001

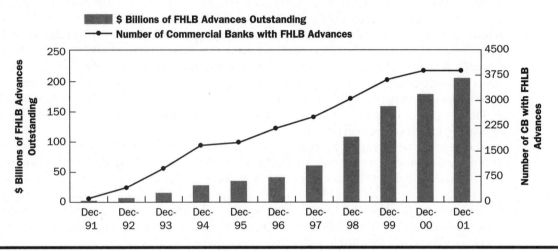

SOURCE: FHLB. Available from the FDIC's Quarter Banking Profile, http://www.fdic.gov/.

EVALUATING THE COST OF BANK FUNDS

It is important that management understand how to measure the cost of financing bank operations. Accurate cost measurement allows the bank to compare prices between alternative funding sources and to assure that assets are priced high enough to cover costs and pay shareholders a required return. The following analysis describes two approaches to estimating the cost of total bank funds. Before doing so, it summarizes differences in the concepts of average and marginal cost of funds.

THE AVERAGE HISTORICAL COST OF FUNDS

Many banks incorrectly use average historical costs, developed earlier in the chapter, in their pricing decisions. They simply add historical interest expense with noninterest expense (net of noninterest income) and divide by the investable amount of funds to determine the minimum return required on earning assets. Any profit is represented as a markup.

The primary problem with historical costs is that they provide no information as to whether future interest costs will rise or fall. When interest rates rise, average historical costs understate the actual cost of issuing new debt. Fixed-rate asset yields based on historical costs will not be high enough to cover costs and meet profit targets.[17] When interest rates fall, the opposite occurs. Average historical costs overstate actual interest costs on new debt so that fixed-rate loans might be priced too high to be competitive. The use of average costs assumes that interest rates will be constant at historical levels during the current pricing period.

---

[17]Many analysts attributed the failure of Franklin National Bank in 1974 to its failure to distinguish between average and marginal costs. Franklin's management, using average historical costs to project borrowing costs in a rising interest rate environment, invested in fixed-rate assets yielding less than the incremental cost of new debt. Rose (1974) provides details.

Pricing decisions should be based on marginal costs compared with marginal revenues. Suppose that a bank can make a new, 1-year loan at 10 percent. The bank's simple average cost of funds equals 6 percent. If the bank compares the new loan rate (marginal revenue rate) with the average cost of funds to determine whether it will make the loan, it estimates a 4 percent spread and accepts the loan. Suppose that it must finance the loan at the margin by issuing a new, 1-year jumbo CD at 11 percent. This represents the marginal interest cost of a single source of new funds. If the bank compares the marginal loan rate with the marginal CD rate, it estimates a negative 1 percent spread and rejects the loan. Because pricing new loans is an incremental decision, it should be based on incremental (marginal) funding costs, not historical average costs. If the bank makes the loan, it loses at least 1 percent on the transaction because its incremental interest expense will exceed its incremental interest income by at least 1 percent of the loan amount.

The best use of average historical costs is in evaluating past performance. It is relatively easy to understand, after the fact, why a bank's expenses and profits differ from peer banks' by comparing average borrowing costs and asset yields. Average costs for noninterest expenses, such as check handling and brokerage fees, can also be evaluated and applied toward measuring expected new debt costs. Typically, these outlays increase by predictable amounts with inflation. Contemporary Issues: Marginal versus Average clarifies the differences between these measures.

THE MARGINAL COST OF FUNDS

The **marginal cost of debt** is a measure of the borrowing cost paid to acquire one additional unit of investable funds. The **marginal cost of equity capital** is a measure of the minimum acceptable rate of return required by shareholders. Together, the marginal costs of debt and equity constitute the **marginal cost of funds,** which can be viewed as independent sources or as a pool of funds.[18] Independent sources of funds have distinct marginal costs that vary with market interest rates, handling costs, and reserve requirements. These independent costs can then be combined to yield an overall weighted marginal cost estimate for all new funds. When interest rates are expected to rise, marginal costs exceed historical costs. When rates are expected to fall, marginal costs are lower.

Marginal costs are especially useful in pricing decisions. If these costs are known, a bank can set asset yields at some markup over marginal costs to lock in a profitable spread. Presumably, the markup reflects default risk as well as the required return to shareholders. Marginal costs also serve as indicators of the relative cost of different funds, which banks can use to target the least expensive sources for financing growth.

COSTS OF INDEPENDENT SOURCES OF FUNDS. Unfortunately, it is difficult to measure marginal costs precisely. Management must include both interest and noninterest costs it expects to pay and identify which portion of the acquired funds can be invested in earning assets. There is also considerable disagreement on whether equity costs are relevant and, ultimately, how to measure equity costs. One researcher introduced a formula similar to that listed below for measuring the explicit marginal cost of a single source of bank liabilities.[19]

---

[18]Banking terminology generally refers to the average or marginal cost of funds as the associated cost of liabilities alone. The cost of equity is incorporated as a required spread over the cost of debt necessary for a bank to meet profit targets and pay shareholders their required return.

[19]Watson (1978) subtracts service charge income from the sum of costs listed in the numerator as presented earlier in the chapter. This analysis distinguishes between revenues and costs associated with obtaining various sources of funds. This makes it easier to implement the individual account profitability analysis described in Chapter 18.

MARGINAL VERSUS AVERAGE

Confusion over the terms average and marginal makes it difficult to evaluate performance measures and understand pricing rules. This is especially true for average costs and weighted marginal costs, which are similar sounding concepts. With cost and pricing data, readers should view simple averages as referring to historical values. The marginal concept, in contrast, refers to incremental or new values.

Consider, for example, a baseball player's batting average. The press reports a historical average representing the summary performance measure over all games played and a marginal average representing the last game. Suppose that during the first two games in a year, the player gets three hits out of 10 batting attempts. His average is 3 divided by 10, or .300. Common usage omits the reference to percent, so the batter is "hitting 300." During the next game, the player gets two hits in five at-bats. His marginal average for the five incremental at-bats is

.400, which raises his overall (historical) average to .333 (five hits in 15 at-bats). The player's overall average increases because the marginal performance (.400) exceeded the previous historical average (.300). If the player gets no hits in his next five at-bats (.000 marginal average), his historical average will drop to .250.

Marginal cost

$$= \frac{\text{Interest rate} + \text{Servicing costs} + \text{Acquisition costs} + \text{Insurance}}{1 - \% \text{ of funds in nonearning assets}} \quad \textbf{(12. 2)}$$

All elements of the numerator are expected costs annualized as a percentage of each dollar obtained. The denominator measures the fraction of liabilities that can be invested to generate interest income. With transactions accounts, for example, the fraction in nonearning assets will reflect legal reserve requirements plus any allocation to such nonearning assets as float or correspondent balances. A bank may also add indirect costs to the numerator, such as the implicit cost of increased risk associated with higher leverage, to obtain an effective marginal cost estimate. Of these costs, only acquisition costs that primarily reflect marketing expenses are truly discretionary. Interest rates are largely determined by market conditions as banks are price takers, servicing costs are determined by the volume of check processing business handled by a bank, and deposit insurance costs are set by the FDIC.

Consider the following marginal cost estimates associated with obtaining additional NOW account funding:

$$\text{market interest rate} = 2.5\%$$

$$\text{servicing costs} = 4.1\% \text{ of balances}$$

$$\text{acquisition costs} = 1.0\% \text{ of balances}$$

$$\text{deposit insurance costs} = 0.25\% \text{ of balances}$$

$$\text{percentage in nonearning assets} = 15.0\% \ (10\% \text{ required reserves and 5\% float})$$

Equation 12.2 indicates that the estimated marginal cost of obtaining additional NOW balances equals 9.24 percent.

$$\text{marginal cost} = \frac{0.025 + 0.041 + 0.01 + 0.0025}{0.85} = 0.0924$$

Intuitively, this cost estimate is the all-inclusive incremental cost of obtaining the investable balances from additional NOW funds.

Two problems create potentially large measurement errors. First, the relevant interest rate must be forecast over the entire planning horizon, a task made difficult by volatile interest rates. Thus, forecasts need to be frequently modified.[20] Second, a bank must rely on its comptroller or cost accountant to generate meaningful estimates of noninterest costs associated with each debt source. This involves allocating overhead, advertising outlays, and the cost of employee time to handling checks, servicing customer complaints, posting account information, and bidding for public funds. In practice, many banks simply rely on the *Functional Cost Analysis* averages provided by the Federal Reserve as discussed earlier in the chapter. Note that some of these costs may be fixed and thus not vary with additional funding. They are still important in pricing issues because asset yields must then be set at a markup over the marginal cost of funds to cover the outlays.

The following discussion summarizes general procedures used to estimate the pretax marginal cost of various sources of bank funds. Tax implications are not considered for convenience and because pretax cost estimates are used in asset pricing decisions.

COST OF DEBT. The marginal cost of different types of debt varies according to the magnitudes of each type of liability. High-volume transactions accounts generate substantial servicing costs and have the highest reserve requirements and float. The advantage of low interest is offset by other costs and the fact that banks can invest a smaller percentage of investable funds. Purchased funds, in contrast, pay higher rates but carry smaller transactions costs and require lower reserves with greater investable balances.

The cost of long-term nondeposit debt equals the effective cost of borrowing from each source, including interest expense and transactions costs. Traditional analysis suggests that this cost is the discount rate that equates the present value of expected interest and principal payments with the net proceeds to the bank from the issue. Suppose, for example, a bank issues $10 million in par value subordinated notes paying $700,000 in annual interest and carrying a 7-year maturity. It must pay $100,000 in flotation costs to an underwriter. In this case, the effective cost of borrowing (k_d), where t equals the time period for each cash flow, is:

$$\$9,900,000 = \sum_{t=1}^{7} \frac{\$700,000}{(1 + k_d)^t} + \frac{\$10,000,000}{(1 + k_d)^7}$$

or

$$k_d = 7.19\%$$

COST OF EQUITY. Conceptually, the marginal cost of equity equals the required return to shareholders. It is not directly measurable because dividend payments are not mandatory. Still, several methods are commonly used to approximate this required return, including the dividend valuation model, capital asset pricing model (CAPM), and targeted return on equity model.

DIVIDEND VALUATION MODEL. Returns to common stockholders take the form of periodic dividend receipts and changes in share price during the interval of stock ownership. Dividend valuation models discount the expected cash flows from owning stock in determining a reasonable return to shareholders. The cost of equity equals the discount rate (required return) used to convert future cash flows to their present value equivalent. Specifically, the price of common stock (P) equals the present value of expected dividends

---

[20]For comparative purposes, all interest rates should be measured identically. Effective rates that recognize differences in discrete and continuous compounding and interest bearing versus discount instruments should be used. The fact that the Truth in Savings Act requires banks to report an annual percentage yield (APY) to customers makes this easier.

over the life of the stock. This holds because the market price at any future point equals the discounted value of expected dividends beyond that point. Recognizing that common stock is issued in perpetuity, the value of a firm's stock is determined by the following formula:

$$P = \sum_{t=1}^{\infty} \frac{D_t}{(1 + k_e)^t} \tag{12.3}$$

where

D_t = the dollar value of the expected dividend in period t
k_e = cost of equity, and
t = time period

The dividend valuation model applies for all patterns of expected dividends. A simplified solution to Equation 12.3 exists, however, if dividends are expected to grow at a constant rate in each period.[21] If the periodic growth rate (g) is assumed to be a constant and less than k_e, Equation 12.3 reduces to:

$$k_e = \frac{D_0(1 + g)}{P} + g \tag{12.4}$$

where

D_0 = the expected percentage dividend yield during the next period
g = the expected growth in firm earnings, dividend payments, and stock price appreciation.[22]

There are many difficulties in applying Equations 12.3 and 12.4 in solving for the required rate of return. No precise estimate of future dividends exists, so different shareholders often have substantially different expectations regarding the firm's prospects. Furthermore, many banks' stock is not actively traded. Dividend streams and quoted share prices may not reflect a true measure of returns to owners who extract benefits from the banks' paying extraordinary expenses. The general model does, however, provide an approximation of required shareholder returns.

Consider, for example, a bank's stock that currently trades at $24 per share and pays a $1 annual dividend. It is generally agreed that analysts' forecasts represent the best estimate of future dividends. Suppose that their consensus forecast is that the bank's annual dividends will increase by an average 10 percent annually. With this expectation, the estimated equity cost is:

$$k_e = \frac{\$1(1 + 0.10)}{\$24} + 0.10$$
$$= 14.58\%$$

The 14.58 percent represents a payment from after-tax dollars. For pricing purposes, it should be converted to a pretax equivalent. This can be accomplished by dividing by 1 minus the relevant marginal tax rate. Assuming a 34 per-cent corporate tax rate, the pretax expected return equals $0.1458/(1 - 0.34)$, or 22.10 percent.

---

[21]This stock valuation model, developed by Myron Gordon, assumes a constant growth rate in dividend payments. Most corporate finance textbooks analyze the features of this model in detail.

[22]A formal derivation of these equations appears in most corporate finance books. Brigham (1997) analyzes a wide range of modified versions with applications. Analysts frequently distinguish between the cost of retained earnings and the cost of new common stock issues. Equation 12.3 represents the cost of retained earnings. New common stock issues cost more than retained earnings because of flotation costs. The cost of new common stock (k_e^*) is determined via Equations 12.3 and 12.4 using the share price net of flotation costs (P_n) such that $k_e^* = \frac{D_0(1 + g)}{P_n} + g$

CAPITAL ASSET PRICING MODEL (CAPM). Large institutions with publicly traded stock can obtain an estimate of their cost of equity from the CAPM. This model relates market risk, measured by Beta (β), to shareholders' required returns. Formally, the required return to shareholders (k'_e) equals the riskless rate of return (r_f) plus a risk premium (ρ) on common stock reflecting nondiversifiable market risk:

$$k'_e = r_f + \rho \tag{12.5}$$

The risk premium equals the product of a security's Beta and the difference between the expected return on the market portfolio (k_m) and the expected riskless rate of return (r_f). Beta measures a stock's historical price volatility relative to the price volatility of the market portfolio as:

$$\beta_i = \frac{\text{Covariance [individual security (i) return, market return]}}{\text{Variance (market return)}} \tag{12.6}$$

where

i = individual security.

Covariance represents a statistical measure of how closely two variables move together. If changes in one variable are associated with changes in another variable in the same direction and magnitude, the covariance is high. If β equals one over any estimation period, the individual security exhibits the same systematic price volatility as the market portfolio. Here, the covariance of the individual security's return and the market index equals the variance in the market index. If β is greater than one, the stock's systematic price volatility exceeds the market portfolio's and vice versa. Generally, the greater the absolute value of β, the greater the relative systematic price volatility and market risk.[23]

Banks can use historical β estimates from Equation 12.6 and a projection of the market premium ($k_m - r_f$) to estimate the required return to shareholders for individual securities:

$$k'_{e,i} = r_f + \beta_i(k_m - r_f) \tag{12.7}$$

Most large bank stocks exhibited β's near 1 through the early 1980s. Since the early 1980s, beta estimates for banks have taken a wider range of values with many greater than one—reflecting greater market risk.

The application of Equation 12.7 is straightforward. Suppose that a bank's β estimate equals 1.42. This means that the bank's stock varies 42 percent more in price relative to the market portfolio over the base period. If the differential between the market return (k_m) and risk-free return (r_f)—proxied by Standard & Poor's 500 stock composite index minus the 3-month Treasury bill rate—is expected to average 5 percent with the Treasury bill rate expected to equal 6 percent, the CAPM estimate for the bank's cost of equity is:

$$k_e = 0.06 + 1.42(0.05) = 13.1\%$$

This cost of equity should again be converted to a pretax equivalent that equals 19.85 percent, using an assumed 34 percent marginal tax rate.

TARGETED RETURN ON EQUITY MODEL. Investors require higher pretax returns on common stock than on debt issues because of the greater assumed credit risk. Depending on the business cycle, the differential in returns ranges from 3 to 8 percent. As an approximation,

---

[23]Systematic price volatility refers to variation in returns on a security caused by factors that influence the market in general. As such, it is nondiversifiable. Such variation is normally distinguished from nonsystematic price volatility, which is unique to a specific company and is diversifiable.

a firm's cost of equity should exceed its cost of debt by some positive differential. Many banks use a *targeted return on equity* guideline based on the cost of debt plus a premium to evaluate the cost of equity. This method simply requires that owners and managers specify a desirable return to shareholders in terms of return on equity. This return is then converted to a pretax equivalent yield. It assumes that the market value of bank equity equals the book value of equity.

Assume that a bank's *targeted* ROE, derived from a comparison of the bank's cost of debt versus the expected return on equity to shareholders, equals 15 percent and its marginal tax rate equals 34 percent. The *pretax required return on bank equity* can be determined by:

$$\text{Targeted ROE} = \frac{\text{Targeted net income}}{\text{Stockholders' Equity}} = 15\%$$

$$\text{Targeted ROE} = \frac{\text{Targeted income before taxes }(1 - 0.34)}{\text{Stockholders' Equity}} = 15\%$$

$$\text{Pretax required return} = \frac{\text{Targeted income before taxes}}{\text{Stockholders' Equity}} = \frac{15\%}{(1 - 0.34)} = 22.73\%$$

Although this measure has deficiencies, it is easy to calculate for banks without publicly traded stock and serves as a benchmark for other cost of equity approximations.

COST OF PREFERRED STOCK. Preferred stock has characteristics of debt and common equity. It represents ownership with investors' claims superior to those of common stockholders but subordinated to those of debtholders. Like common stock, preferred stock pays dividends that may be deferred when management determines that earnings are too low. Like long-term bonds, preferred stock stipulates contractual dividend payments over the life of the security and often provides call protection and sinking fund contributions. Recently, preferred issues paying variable-rate dividends have become increasingly common.

The marginal cost of preferred stock (k_p) equals the required return to stockholders and can be approximated in the same manner as the return on common equity from Equation 12.4. In this case, however, dividend growth is zero. Consider the case of noncallable, nonsinking fund preferred stock sold at par with a fixed-dividend payment. With dividend payments contractually fixed, expected dividend growth equals 0 and

$$k_p = \frac{D_p}{P_p} \tag{12.8}$$

where

D_p = contractual dividend payment,
P_p = net price of preferred stock,

and D_p is constant over the life of the issue. Management must estimate D_p for variable rate preferred by forecasting changes in the pricing index, such as the 10-year Treasury bond yield, and estimate k_p using an equation similar to Equation 12.3. As with new common stock issues, P_p is net of placement costs from taking a new issue to market.[24]

---

[24] The effective cost of common and preferred stock should also reflect the portion of these funds that is allocated to nonearning assets. Although reserves are not required, banks typically allocate fixed assets and intangibles to equity sources. Computationally, management divides the equity marginal cost estimate by 1 minus the percentage in nonearning assets. To calculate the marginal cost of common and preferred stock when dividends are not constant, the reader should review examples provided in any current corporate finance textbook.

TRUST PREFERRED STOCK. A recent innovation in capital financing is the introduction of **trust preferred stock,** which is a hybrid form of equity capital at banks. It is attractive because it effectively pays dividends that are tax deductible. To issue the securities, a bank or bank holding company establishes a trust company. The trust company sells preferred stock to investors and loans the proceeds of the issue to the bank. Interest on the loan equals dividends paid on the preferred stock. This loan interest is tax deductible such that the bank effectively gets to deduct dividend payments on the preferred stock. The after-tax cost of trust preferred stock would be:

$$k_{tp} = \frac{D_{tp}(1 - t)}{P_{tp}}$$

(12.9)

where

D_{tp} = contractual dividend payment on trust preferred, equivalently interest on the loan to the trust,

P_{tp} = net price of trust preferred stock,

and D_{tp} is constant over the life of the issue. As is true of common and preferred stock, P_{tp} is net of placement cost from taking a new issue to market.

Weighted Marginal Cost of Total Funds

Many banks price loans using the marginal cost of a single source of debt funds as the base rate. For example, prime commercial customers are often allowed to choose the interest rate they pay as some mark-up over the marginal cost of either CDs, the London Interbank Offer Rate (LIBOR), or federal funds. Obviously, the customer selects the base rate expected to be the lowest over the credit period. Unfortunately, the cost of any single source of funds may change more or less than the cost of other sources and thus vary substantially from the bank's composite cost of financing.

The best cost measure for asset-pricing purposes is a weighted marginal cost of total funds (WMC). This measure recognizes both explicit and implicit costs associated with any single source of funds. It assumes that all assets are financed from a pool of funds and that specific sources of funds are not tied directly with specific uses of funds.

WMC is computed in three stages:

1. Forecast the desired dollar amount of financing to be obtained from each individual debt and equity source.
2. Estimate the marginal cost of each independent source of funds.
3. Combine the individual estimates to project the weighted cost, which equals the sum of the weighted component costs across all sources.

First, management must forecast the desired dollar amount of financing to be obtained from each individual debt and equity source. This requires that the bank specify a planning horizon, such as one year, and identify significant changes in composition of liabilities and equity over time. Management should determine a marketing strategy and allocate employees' time to the different account generating functions. Second, management must estimate the marginal cost of each independent source of funds. It should allocate fund-raising and processing costs among the different liability and equity components and project interest and dividend costs for each source, recognizing any perceived changes in risk associated with changes in financial leverage. Each cost estimate should also reflect management's assignment of nonearning assets per Equation 12.2 that indicates the percentage of investable funds. Third, management should combine the individual estimates to project the weighted cost, which equals the sum of the weighted component costs across all sources. Each source's weight (w_j) equals the expected dollar amount of financing from that source divided by the dollar amount of total liabilities and equity. Thus, if k_j equals the single-source j component marginal cost of financing, where there are m liabilities plus equity,

$$WMC = \sum_{j=1}^{m} w_j k_j \qquad (12.9)$$

MARGINAL COST ANALYSIS: AN APPLICATION

The following analysis demonstrates the procedures for measuring a bank's cost of funds. The analysis consists of projecting the bank's balance sheet composition and marginal costs in order to generate a weighted marginal cost of total funds.

Suppose that you are the cashier for Community State Bank and a member of the bank's ALCO. The ALCO has just completed its monthly meeting and asked you to generate an estimate of the bank's weighted marginal cost of funds for the next year. For the first time in several years, there was a consensus among the senior officers that the economy would experience moderate growth throughout the year, which the Federal Reserve would accommodate. Inflation was expected to remain stable around 3 percent and interest rates would increase only slightly. As part of the meeting, the committee approved a preliminary budget that projected income, net of dividends, equal to $1,200,000, representing a lower return on equity and return on assets compared with the prior year. Total average assets were projected to grow by $7 million, of which $6 million was new loans. Liabilities were expected to grow proportionately relative to the past year except that the bank would rely proportionately more on CDs.

Exhibit 12.7 summarizes the ALCO's consensus forecast for the next year. Columns (a) and (b) list the projected composition of funding between debt and equity sources over the next year in dollar amount and percentage. Column (c) lists the interest rates expected to prevail during the year as projected by the senior investment officer. Processing and acquisition costs for each type of liability and the investable percentages are based on the bank controller's estimates, and are reported in columns (d) and (e). The expected marginal cost for each source, using these projections as defined in Equation 12.1 is presented in column (f). The weighted marginal cost of funds, obtained by summing the products of figures in columns (b) and (f) for each component, is calculated in column (g) and reported at the bottom of the column; 8.39 percent for the year. This projected marginal cost exceeds historical costs because the bank forecasts an increase in interest rates and expects to obtain a higher percentage of funds from more expensive sources.

The marginal cost of funds estimate should be applied carefully in pricing decisions. The bank in this example should charge at least 8.39 percent on loans (assets) of average risk to cover the marginal costs of debt and pay shareholders a reasonable return. The bank should add a risk premium for loans of greater than average default risk to compensate for the increased probability of greater charge-offs. Chapter 18 describes loan pricing models in detail. Whether a bank meets its aggregate profit target depends on the bank's ability to price assets to meet this hurdle rate, its actual default experience, and whether noninterest income covers noninterest expense net of costs allocated to attracting and handling liabilities.

Assume, for the moment, that as an ALCO member you have serious reservations that economic stability will persist. The worldwide economic crisis may well spread to the United States and the economy is somewhat fragile. As a result, the Federal Reserve is under increased pressure to accelerate money growth. Loan problems at many large regional banks spooked foreign institutions and investors last year to the point where a serious national liquidity crisis might arise if a single, large U.S. bank failed and foreign depositors withdrew their funds. If this occurred, interest rates would rise well above the ALCO's forecast, and the bank would have difficulty issuing new CDs.

· EXHIBIT 12.7

FORECAST OF THE WEIGHTED MARGINAL COST OF FUNDS: PROJECTED FIGURES FOR
COMMUNITY STATE BANK FOR 2001

Liabilities and Equity	(a) Average Amount	(b) Percent Amount	(c) Interest of Total	(d) Processing and Acquisition Cost	(e) Costs	(f) Component Nonearning Percentage	(g) Weighted Marginal Cost Marginal Costs	Marginal Cost of Funds (b) × (f)
Demand deposits	$28,210	31.0%		8.0%		18.0%	9.76%	0.0302
Interest checking	5,551	6.1	2.5%	6.5		15.0	10.59	0.0065
Money market demand accounts	13,832	15.2	3.5	3.0		3.0	6.70	0.0102
Other savings accounts	3,640	4.0	4.5	1.2		1.5	5.79	0.0023
Time deposits < $100,000	18,382	20.2	4.9	1.4		1.0	6.36	0.0129
Time deposits > $100,000	9,055	10.0	5.0	0.3		0.5	5.34	0.0053
Total deposits	$78,670	86.5						
Federal funds purchased	$ 180	0.2	5.0	0.0		0.0	5.00	0.0001
Other liabilities	$ 4,550	5.0		0.0		40.0	0.00	
Total liabilities	$83,402	91.7						
Stockholders' equity	$ 7,680	8.4	18.9*			4.0	19.69	0.0164
Total liabilities and equity	$91,000	100.0						
Weighted marginal cost of capital								→ 8.39%

NOTE: Balance sheet and income statement data for the previous year appear in Exhibits 3.1 and 3.2.

* Required pretax return.

Differences in the weighted marginal cost projection generally reflect different interest rate scenarios and variations in the composition of liabilities. Exhibit 12.8 provides a revised cost calculation, assuming higher interest rates and greater shifts of bank financing from lower cost demand, savings, and small time deposits into interest checking, MMDAs, and CDs. The funds shift and rate increase both have an adverse impact on financing costs. In this scenario, the weighted marginal cost of funds equals 9.16 percent, or almost than 1 percent higher than the ALCO projection. If the bank acquired fixed-rate assets at 9 percent with the expectation that financing costs would average 8.39 percent, its net interest income would drop with the environment characterized in Exhibit 12.8. Obviously, management should monitor its funding operation and project marginal costs regularly to detect significant deviations from plan.

Although this analysis is quite simple, once figures on costs and the composition of liabilities are obtained, it glosses over many controversial issues, such as how cost estimates are obtained. In particular, it is extremely difficult to allocate processing and acquisition costs between different liabilities. What is the annual cost of an automatic teller machine? How much of a teller's salary should be allocated to the marginal cost of taking deposits? How should utility expenses be allocated among different account categories? It should be recognized that the procedure for estimating marginal costs is not exact. Useful decisions can be made, however, as long as the data are reported and analyzed in a consistent manner.

FUNDING COSTS AND BANKING RISK

Banks face two fundamental problems in managing their liabilities: uncertainty over what rates they must pay to retain and attract funds; and uncertainty over the likelihood that customers will withdraw their money regardless of rates. The basic fear is that they will be vulnerable to

▪ EXHIBIT 12.8

REVISED FORECAST OF THE WEIGHTED COST OF FUNDS

Liabilities and Equity	Average Amount	Percent of Total	Interest Cost	Component Marginal Costs	Weighted Marginal Cost of Funds
Demand deposits	$25,890	28.5%		9.8%	0.0278
Interest checking	6,461	7.1	4.0%	12.4	0.0088
Money market demand accounts	12,831	14.1	4.8	8.0	0.0113
Other savings accounts	3,640	4.0	5.8	7.1	0.0028
Time deposits < $100,000	19,383	21.3	6.3	7.8	0.0166
Time deposits > $100,000	10,465	11.5	6.5	6.8	0.0079
Total deposits	$78,670	86.5			
Federal funds purchased	$ 182	0.2	6.5	6.5	0.0001
Other liabilities	4,550	5.0		0.0	0.0000
Total liabilities	$83,402	91.7			
Stockholders' equity	$ 7,599	8.4	18.9*	19.7	0.0164
Total liabilities and equity	$91.001	100.0			
Weighted marginal cost of capital ⟶					9.16%

* Required pretax return.

a liquidity crisis arising from unanticipated deposit withdrawals. Banks must have the capacity to borrow in financial markets to replace deposit outflows and remain solvent. Liquidity problems have grown with the increased reliance on "hot money" and brokered deposits. When a bank is perceived to have asset quality problems, customers with uninsured balances move their deposits. The problem bank must then pay substantial premiums to attract replacement funds or rely on regulatory agencies to extend emergency credit.

During the years that deposit rates were regulated and banks paid the maximum rates allowed, deposits were relatively stable and liquidity was less of a problem. Interest rate deregulation and bank competition have since increased depositors' rate awareness so that many individuals and firms move funds to institutions paying the highest rates. Customer loyalty is closely tied to deposit size and the quality of bank service. Small balance depositors are generally more loyal than large balance depositors, especially if they receive consistently good service. All customers are more loyal if they purchase a bundle of credit, deposit, and other services.

The previous examples demonstrate the difficulty of accurately projecting funding costs. Unanticipated changes in interest rates and the composition of bank liabilities can significantly raise or lower bank profits as interest expense rises or falls more than interest income. The same changes also affect a bank's risk position. This section examines the relationship between the composition of bank funds and banking risk, identifying differences between small and large banks.

FUNDING SOURCES AND INTEREST RATE RISK

During the 1980s, most banks experienced a shift in composition of liabilities away from demand deposits into interest-bearing time deposits and other borrowed funds. This reflects three phenomena: the removal of Regulation Q interest rate ceilings, a volatile interest rate environment, and the development of new deposit and money market products. The cumulative effect was to increase the interest sensitivity of funding operations. Today, many depositors and investors prefer short-term instruments that can be quickly rolled over as interest rates change. Banks must offer substantial premiums to induce depositors to lengthen maturities and assume interest rate risk. Many banks choose not to pay the premiums and subsequently reprice liabilities more frequently than in past years.

These changes affect a bank's interest rate risk position to the extent that they do not adjust their asset rate sensitivity. A bank operating with a zero GAP in the late 1990s would today be liability sensitive and have substantial negative GAPs within one year if it did not acquire more rate-sensitive assets. For this reason, many institutions attempt to price all loans on a floating-rate basis and no longer purchase bonds for their investment portfolios with maturities beyond five to seven years.

One widely recognized strategy to reduce interest rate risk and the long-term cost of bank funds, is to aggressively compete for retail core deposits. Individuals are generally not as rate sensitive as corporate depositors. Once a bank attracts deposit business, many individuals will maintain their balances through rate cycles as long as the banks provide good service and pay attention to them. Such deposits are thus more stable than money market liabilities. Core deposits carry an additional advantage to banks because interest rates are lower, but still cost more to handle.

FUNDING SOURCES AND LIQUIDITY RISK

Liquidity risk associated with a bank's deposit base is a function of many factors, including the number of depositors, average size of accounts, location of the depositor, and specific maturity and rate characteristics of each account. These features are customer-driven, and banks cannot dictate the terms of deposit contracts. But banks can monitor potential deposit outflows if they are aware of seasonal patterns in outstanding balances and the timing of large transactions such as payroll draws on commercial accounts and maturing large-balance CDs. They can periodically contact large depositors to provide rate quotes and assess the probability of the customer reinvesting the funds.

Equally important is the *interest elasticity* of customer demand for each funding source. How much can market interest rates change before the bank experiences deposit outflows? If the bank increases its rates, how many new funds will it attract? Ideally, a bank would like to lower its customers' rate sensitivity. It can do so by packaging deposit products with other services or privileges so that withdrawals deprive the customer of all services or by developing personal relationships with depositors. In this way management can determine the base funding level (core deposit base) below which outstanding balances never fall.

The liquidity risk associated with all liabilities has risen dramatically in recent years. Depositors often simply compare rates and move their funds between investment vehicles to earn the highest yields. It is increasingly difficult to establish long-term customer relationships that withstand rate differentials, a problem compounded in virtually every banking market that has at least one firm that pays premium rates at all maturities. These firms are often brokerage companies who offer non-FDIC-insured money market and stock mutual funds. Credit unions often offer higher rates afforded by their significant tax advantages over banks. Commercial banks feel they are at a competitive disadvantage and, without matching the offered rates, have trouble keeping deposit customers.

The largest banks that rely on jumbo CDs and Eurodollars face similar problems. Investors in these instruments are highly rate sensitive. They normally prefer short-term maturities and will move their balances for slightly higher yields elsewhere. Large depositors with uninsured balances, especially foreign investors, frequently react to rumors of financial distress by shifting their funds into less risky Treasury securities until the crisis passes. For this reason, the largest U.S. banking organizations maintain dealer operations in London, Singapore, and Hong Kong to guarantee access to financial markets 24 hours a day.

The liquidity risk facing any one bank depends on the competitive environment. Many smaller banks operate in communities with only a few competitors that tacitly price deposits comparably. Customers like to invest their funds locally so they can conveniently contact their banker with questions or easily withdraw or move balances. Liquidity risk is relatively low and deposit outflows are predictable. As indicated earlier, many community banks view the FHLB as a primary source of liquidity. Banks in larger communities normally face more aggressive competition, which increases liquidity risk, and must monitor the composition of funds more closely. Again, it is important to note the liquidity advantage that stable core deposits provide an acquiring bank.

Most banks try to build a liquidity buffer into their deposit base. Small banks with limited access to national financial markets promote customer service to expand core deposits and reduce liability interest elasticity. Many large banks periodically borrow more funds than they need to guarantee access to deposit sources.[25] When the bank does not need the funds, it still borrows and simply invests in short-term loans. Comparing a bank's current borrowings to its maximum debt outstanding over the previous year can approximate the amount of liquidity available to large banks via purchased funds.

Funding Sources and Credit Risk

Changes in the composition and cost of bank funds can indirectly affect a bank's credit risk by forcing it to reduce asset quality. For example, banks that have substituted purchased funds for lost demand deposits have seen their cost of funds rise. They have not been able to reprice existing high quality assets to offset this rise because of competitive pressures. Rather than let their interest margins deteriorate, many banks make riskier loans at higher promised yields. Although they might maintain their margins in the near-term, later loan losses typically rise with the decline in asset quality. This effect is greatest at small banks with limited opportunities to supplement earnings in other ways.

Funding Sources and Bank Safety

Changes in the composition and cost of bank funds have clearly lowered traditional earnings. This decrease slows capital growth and increases leverage ratios. Borrowing costs will ultimately increase unless noninterest income offsets this decline or banks obtain new external capital. Bank safety has thus declined in the aggregate.

BORROWING FROM THE FEDERAL RESERVE

Federal Reserve Banks are authorized to make loans to depository institutions to help them meet reserve requirements. Before 1980, only commercial banks that were members of the Federal Reserve System could borrow under normal circumstances. DIDMCA opened borrowing to any depository institution that offers transactions accounts subject to reserve requirements. The borrowing facility is called the **discount window.** All Federal Reserve Banks charge a fixed rate, known as the discount rate, which is formally set by the district Federal Reserve Banks and approved by the Board of Governors. In practice, the board determines when rate changes are necessary and requests approval from district representatives.

---

[25]Bailey (1984) documents several banks' strategies in dealing with potential liquidity problems.

The Federal Reserve establishes conditions and procedures for borrowing. Banks must apply and provide acceptable collateral before a loan is granted. Eligible collateral includes U.S. government securities, bankers' acceptances, and qualifying short-term commercial or government paper. Frequent borrowers typically use U.S. Treasury securities already held in bookkeeping form at Federal Reserve Banks. Federal Reserve Regulation A states that borrowing is a privilege and banks should view the Federal Reserve as a lender of last resort. Banks subsequently borrow to meet temporary reserve deficiencies, not to obtain permanent financing.

Discount window loans directly increase a member bank's reserve assets. Advances are loans secured by qualifying collateral. Discounts refer to member banks temporarily selling eligible loans to the Federal Reserve. The Federal Reserve agrees to return the loan to the bank at maturity. The discount rate charged determines the interest payment in both cases and is set by the Federal Reserve in light of current economic conditions. Frequently, the discount rate is below the current federal funds rate. The Federal Reserve prohibits arbitrage by not allowing banks to sell federal funds and borrow at the discount window simultaneously.

Federal Reserve policies distinguish among three types of loans. The first, *short-term adjustment loans*, are made to banks experiencing unexpected deposit outflows or overdrafts caused by computer problems. Banks that use adjustment credit typically borrow for very short periods until the problem disappears. Small banks are also permitted to borrow under a *seasonal borrowing privilege* if they can demonstrate that they experience systematic and predictable deposit withdrawals or new loan demand. Banks serving agricultural or resort communities often qualify. The needs must persist for at least eight weeks, so seasonal loans have considerably longer maturities. The final loan type, *extended credit*, receives the most attention but is the least prevalent. These loans are granted to banks that are experiencing more permanent deposit outflows typically associated with a run on the bank. In July 1984, for example, the Federal Reserve extended $4 billion in credit to Continental Illinois of Chicago to offset deposit losses of customers fearful that the bank was about to fail.

Each Federal Reserve Bank employs a discount officer who has the authority to accept or reject borrowing requests. If a bank borrows infrequently, the request is normally granted. The officer restricts overuse of the discount window either by a discreet telephone call to senior management indicating that the request will be denied or by raising the indirect costs of the loan. Indirect costs include delays in processing paperwork and increased uncertainty over future access to borrowings. As such, most banks are reluctant to borrow without a crisis.

FEDERAL DEPOSIT INSURANCE

The Banking Act of 1933 established the FDIC and authorized federal insurance for bank deposits up to $2,500. The Federal Savings and Loan Insurance Corporation (FSLIC) was established in 1934 to replicate federal assistance for savings and loan associations.[26] Both insurance funds were funded via premiums paid by member banks. Fund expenses included operating costs and payouts mandated when banks failed and regulators paid insured depositors.

The enactment of the Banking Act of 1933 followed three years in which more than 5,000 banks failed and investors lost confidence in the country's financial system. There were approximately 4,000 failures in 1933 alone. The initial objectives of deposit insurance were to prevent liquidity crises caused by large-scale deposit withdrawals and to protect depositors of modest means against a bank failure. With insurance, depositors' funds were safe, even if the bank failed.

---

[26]The National Credit Union Share Insurance Fund (NCUSIF) insures credit unions.

Deposit insurance worked well until the early 1980s, as there were few depositor runs on federally insured banks and bank failures were negligible. In fact during the period from 1950 to 1980, less than seven banks failed, on average, each year. After 1980, however, bank failures increase once again and there were 220 bank failures in 1988. In fact, the FSLIC was no longer solvent by the late 1980s and the FDIC's insurance fund was depleted by 1990.

The Financial Institution Reform, Recovery, and Enforcement Act of 1989 (FIRREA) eliminated the FSLIC and created two new insurance funds, the **Savings Association Insurance Fund (SAIF)** and the **Bank Insurance Fund (BIF),** to replace the old funds with both to be controlled by the FDIC. The Deposit Insurance Funds Act of 1996 (DIFA) mandated the ultimate elimination of the BIF and SAIF funds by merging them into a new Deposit Insurance Fund.[27]

DEPOSITOR PROTECTION AND HANDLING PROBLEM INSTITUTIONS

When an insured bank fails, all insured depositors are either paid off or their deposits are merged into a new institution. When an insured institution fails, the FDIC has five basic options.

- **Purchase and assumption.** Bids are accepted by healthy banks for the failed bank's good loans and other assets. The FDIC can also sell the "Whole" bank that would include all the assets. Usually the bidding bank would bid a negative amount. In either case, insured depositors will have accounts at the new bank rather than being paid off by the FDIC.

- **Open bank assistance.** An acquiring bank is provided financial assistance by the FDIC in acquiring a failing bank. Typically the FDIC will take notes or preferred stock. The failing bank is not closed, hence depositors are paid off, and their deposits are transferred to another institution.

- **Insured deposit assumption or transfer.** Insured deposits are transferred to a healthy bank rather than the FDIC directly paying off the depositors.

- **Bridge bank.** The FDIC will operate the bank for a "short" period of time until it can find the appropriate buyer. In this case all insured depositors continue to have accounts at the bank.

- **Payout option.** The FDIC immediately (one week) pays depositors the full amount of their insured funds. The FDIC assumes the depositors' claims and becomes a general creditor of the bank. It also serves as receiver and liquidates the failed bank's assets, from which it pays uninsured deposit holders and other creditors. Payments frequently total 60 to 80 percent of the claim and can be delayed several years because of lawsuits.

Under the *purchase and assumption option*, the FDIC negotiates a merger of the failed bank with a solvent firm. The acquiring bank assumes all deposits and other nonsubordinated liabilities. It uses these funds to purchase selected assets of the failed bank, including fixed assets, government securities, and performing loans. It also receives or pays an amount of cash, less the purchase premium, equal to the amount necessary for the acquired assets to equal the assumed liabilities. The FDIC owns all rejected assets, typically problem loans with limited repayment prospects. In this case, uninsured depositors and other creditors lose nothing. Instead, they receive claims on the new bank's assets equal to their prior claims on the failed bank. Shareholders lose the full amount of their investment under both options.

---

[27]For a complete discussion of FDIC assessment rates and the problems with FDIC insurance see Chapter 13, The Effective Use of Bank Capital.

THE EXTENT OF DEPOSIT INSURANCE COVERAGE

It pays to understand deposit insurance. Do you? As a test, answer the following questions. Both banks carry deposit insurance.

1. You have $100,000 in a CD at First National Bank, and another $100,000 in a CD at First State Bank. Are both deposits fully insured?

2. Your parents are concerned about their health and managing their resources if one becomes incapacitated. They own two $75,000 CDs at First National Bank jointly. Are both deposits fully insured?

3. Your grandfather has a joint account with your father for $60,000, another joint account with your sister for $50,000, and another joint account with you for $50,000 all at First State Bank. Are all deposits fully insured?

4. You own a $100,000 CD from First State Bank and your grandmother opened a trust account in your name for another $100,000. Are both accounts fully insured?

5. You own a $94,000 CD at First National Bank. At the time the bank fails, you are owed the $94,000 plus $9,000 in interest. How much will you be paid from deposit insurance?

Account balances held by the same individual in his or her name are insured up to $100,000, including both principal and interest, per institution. The $100,000 coverage extends to total deposit balances summing across all types.

Joint accounts held by the same individuals are combined to determine insurance coverage, with $100,000 maximum coverage. It does not matter whether the underlying deposit accounts differ in form or if the individuals list their names in different orders. The insurance funds assume equal ownership among joint owners. Suppose that two parents own a $100,000 account jointly, another

$90,000 jointly ($30,000 each) with a daughter, and another $90,000 jointly with a son. With equal ownership, the father and mother own $110,000 each for insurance purposes so that $10,000 in not insured for each. Each child's $30,000 balance is fully insured.

With trust accounts, each account is insured separately for each beneficiary and each owner. Thus two parents with two children can establish $400,000 in trust balances that are fully insured. The father sets up a trust for each child in his name for $100,000 and the mother sets up a trust in her name for each child for $100,000. Individual retirement accounts (IRAs) and Keogh accounts are treated separately for deposit insurance purposes. [Answers: 1. Yes 2. No 3. Yes 5. no]

Under a *deposit transfer*, regulators transfer all insured deposits plus a fraction less than 100 percent of uninsured deposits of a failing bank to an acquiring bank. The fraction of insured deposits that is transferred is based on the regulators' assessment of what they would collect from the failing bank's assets, and thus what the likely payout to uninsured creditors would equal. Typically, regulators create a *bridge bank* when they expect the value of the bridge bank will increase during the time of the initial closing and final take over by a solvent bank, and that the process would allow the regulators to force uninsured creditors of bank holding companies to take losses. The latter would presumably force these creditors to carefully scrutinize their investments in problem institutions and thus impose market discipline in the pricing of bank stocks and bonds. The bridge bank concept was used in the closing of both First RepublicBank Corp. and MCorp. in Texas during 1988 and 1989, which were eventually taken over by NCNB (now BankAmerica) and Bank One, respectively. (See Contemporary Issues: Regulatory Policy Toward Large Bank Failures in Chapter 13.)

The FDIC chooses the option that minimizes costs to the insurance fund. In virtually all cases, FDIC payouts involve small banks that, because of location or limited deposit base, are not attractive to investors. Large bank failures are normally handled via purchase and assumption. This option costs less because the acquirer pays a premium for the "going concern" value of the bank that disappears under a payout. See the following chapter for additional details on deposit insurance.

SUMMARY

This chapter focuses on characteristics of various bank liabilities and the measurement of costs associated with these liabilities and equity capital. Small denomination instruments exhibit fundamentally different risk-return features compared with those of large denomination liabilities. In both cases, price competition is considerably more important today than in previous years. The chapter introduces the specific features of immediately available funds, repurchase agreements, Eurodollars, and borrowings from the Federal Home Loan Banks and Federal Reserve Banks as sources of funds. It describes the difference between the average cost of funds and marginal cost of funds and demonstrates the appropriate calculations. Finally, it analyzes the role of deposit insurance in bank failures and problems associated with maintaining the viability of the FDIC insurance funds with past failures.

In the section on measuring the cost of funds, the differences in average and marginal costs and their application to understanding historical bank performance are discussed. The chapter then focuses on estimating marginal costs that are used in pricing decisions. Marginal costs represent the incremental cost of obtaining financing. Each individual source of debt funds has a distinct cost that reflects interest expense, acquisition and processing costs, and restrictions regarding the amount of funds a bank can invest. Equity capital has a marginal cost that reflects shareholders' required returns. Individual cost estimates are combined into a weighted marginal cost of capital, which is used in pricing. The chapter provides applications of the estimation process.

QUESTIONS

1. Rank the following types of bank liabilities first according to their level of liquidity risk, and then according to their interest rate risk. Then rank them according to their current cost to the bank. Explain why they vary.
   DDAs
   NOW accounts
   MMDAs
   small time deposits
   jumbo CDs
   Federal funds purchased
   Eurodollar liabilities
   Federal Home Loan Bank advances

2. Indicate how a bank's core deposits differ from its hot money or volatile liabilities in terms of interest elasticity. What factors are relatively more important to attracting and retaining core deposits as compared to purchased funds?

3. Using the data from Exhibit 12.3, determine the average monthly cost of servicing the typical student's demand deposit account, which generates 27 withdrawals (15 electronic), two transit checks deposited, two transit checks cashed, two deposits (one electronic), and one on-us check cashed per month. Assume there is one account maintenance for an account in which checks are not returned and that net indirect expenses apply. Assume that the bank can invest 85 percent of the deposit balance at 7 percent and charges the student $4.50 in fees monthly. What is the break-even deposit balance the bank must hold for its revenues to cover its costs? Compare your average balance with the break-even balance you calculate and determine whether your account would be profitable to the bank. What is your bank's insufficient funds charge (NSF), and how will these fees influence account profitability?

4. Explain why it is or is not reasonable for a bank to charge an explicit fee for balance inquiries (calling to request balance verification).

5. True or false: Federal funds transactions involve an exchange of bank reserves held at Federal Reserve Banks. Explain your reasoning.

6. Assume the following transactions occur sequentially:
   a. The TIB Corp., based in New Orleans, converts a $3 million demand deposit held at the New York Money Center Bank to a $3 million Eurodollar deposit held at Barclays Bank in London.
   b. Barclays Bank opens a $3 million Eurodollar deposit at the Bank of England in London.
   c. The Bank of England makes a $3 million Eurodollar loan to Pflug & Co. in England. Provide T-accounts for TIB, New York Money Center Bank, Barclays Bank, and the Bank of England that describe each set of transactions. Explain how many Eurodollar deposit liabilities were created at each stage and what happened to the original demand deposit held by TIB.

7. As a potential jumbo CD depositor, what would your circumstances have to be for you to prefer a variable-rate CD over a fixed-rate CD? What would the circumstances be for you to prefer a zero coupon CD over a variable-rate CD?

8. Many banks compete aggressively for retail time deposits. What marketing strategies will attract large volumes of deposits from individuals? Why are retail deposits attractive to banks?

9. As the FDIC fund dropped in size, regulators and Congress realized that there were basic problems with deposit insurance. With perfect hindsight, identify these problems and recommend policies to correct the problems.

10. How large would Barnett's uninsured deposits be in these FDIC insured banks if the funds were held at the same point in time?
    a. Barnett owns a joint account with his sister for $175,000 in Metro Bank.
    b. Barnett owns an account in his name only for $80,000 in Metro Bank.
    c. Barnett owns a joint account with his wife for $455,000 in Rural Bank.
    d. Barnett owns a joint account with his parents for $530,000 in Rural Bank.

11. When a bank fails, regulators have a choice of ways to resolve all claims. In one type of resolution uninsured depositors get full reimbursement of their deposits, but in another type they only receive their share of residual claims beyond the insured deposit amount.
    a. Explain how the two different systems work. Who are the uninsured depositors?
    b. Is the different treatment of uninsured deposits unfair? If so, who is treated unfairly?
    c. Explain how the concept of Too-Big-to-Fail is related to the issue of FDIC insurance premiums and bank failure policy. Are small banks discriminated against?

12. Identify whether you should use an average cost of bank funds or a marginal cost of funds in the following situations.
    a. Setting the rate on a new loan
    b. Evaluating the profitability of a long-standing customer's relationship
    c. Calculating the bank's income tax liability
    d. Deciding whether to build a new building or refurbish the old one
    e. Deciding whether to advertise the bank's jumbo CDs or borrow funds in the Eurodollar market

13. What are the consequences of a bank mistakenly pricing loans based on the historical cost of funds? Do they differ in a rising rate environment versus a falling rate environment?

14. What types of bank liabilities generate the highest servicing costs? What types generate the highest acquisition costs?

15. Use the following information to estimate the marginal cost of issuing a $100,000 CD paying 6.2 percent interest. It has a 1-year maturity and the following estimates apply relative to the balance obtained:
   Acquisition costs = 1/8 of 1 percent
   FDIC insurance = 1/12 of 1 percent
   Required reserves percentage = 0 percent

16. Calculate the following single source marginal costs.
   a. A bank plans to issue $20 million in 10-year subordinated notes. The issue is priced at a discount to provide $19.3 million to the bank. The notes will pay $1.4 million in coupon interest at the end of each year. Flotation costs will total $160,000.
   b. A bank plans to issue perpetual preferred stock carrying a $40 share price and paying $3.20 in annual dividends. Flotation costs are expected to be $1.65 per share. The stock is noncallable with no sinking fund.
   c. The common stock of a major bank currently sells for $43.50 per share and pays a $1.40 annual dividend. Most analysts expect the bank to increase its dividends by 9 percent over each of the next five years. Flotation costs of the new issues will average $1.50 per share.

17. The weighted marginal cost of funds is used in pricing decisions. Explain how it should be used if the loan being priced exhibits average risk. How should the weighted marginal cost of funds be used if the loan carries above-average risk?

18. You have collected the following information, at least some of which you think will be useful in estimating the pretax cost of issuing new common stock for your bank. What is that estimated cost?

T-bill rate = 5%	S&P 500 rate = 12%
Bank's CD rate = 5.5%	Bank's stock price = $30
Bank's bond rate = 7.1%	Bank's stock beta = 1.25
Bank's marginal tax rate = 34%	

PROBLEMS

I. ANALYZING PROFITABILITY

A senior bank officer has asked you to analyze the profitability of selected customer deposit relationships. The procedure is to estimate the total expense associated with account activity and compare this with projected revenues. Use the data from Exhibit 12.3 to answer the following questions.

1. The typical low-balance customer at your bank with an average monthly demand deposit balance under $175 exhibits the following monthly activity: 35 withdrawals (11 electronic), two transit checks deposited, one transit check cashed, two deposits (one electronic), and one on-us check cashed per month. Assume there is one account maintenance for an account in which checks are not returned and that net indirect expenses apply.
   a. Use the unit cost data to estimate the average monthly expense for the bank to service this account.
   b. Suppose the bank can earn an average 6.5 percent annually on investable deposits (ledger balances minus float minus required reserves). The typical customer keeps an average monthly balance net of float equal to $116 in the account and pays a $3.25 monthly service charge. The bank must hold 10 percent required reserves against the average balance and thus can invest 90 percent of the balance. Determine whether the account is profitable for the bank.

2. The typical high-balance NOW account customer at your bank maintains a monthly balance of $1,250 net of float, writes 34 checks or withdrawals (21 electronic), four transit checks deposited, two transit checks cashed, two deposits (one electronic), and one on-us check cashed per month. Assume there is one account maintenance for an account in which checks are not returned and that net indirect expenses apply. Interest is paid on the account at an annual 2.5 percent rate. Use the unit cost information to determine whether this account is profitable. Assume the bank collects no service charges and can again earn 6.5 percent on investable balances net of 10 percent required reserves.

II. WEIGHTED MARGINAL COST OF FUNDS

The table below provides information that can be used to estimate Northwestern National Bank's weighted marginal cost of funds for 2001. The estimates represent a best-guess forecast of the funding sources and associated costs for the year. Follow the format in Exhibit 12.7 and calculate the bank's forecasted weighted marginal cost of funds.

Liabilities and Equity	Average Amount	Interest Cost	Processing and Acquisition Costs	Nonearning Percentage
Demand deposits	$ 44,500	0.0%	7.2%	17.0%
Interest checking	69,900	2.1	5.0	14.0
Money market demand accounts	49,800	2.8	3.2	3.0
Other savings accounts	25,100	3.0	1.0	2.0
Time deposits < $100,000	187,600	4.1	1.5	2.0
Time deposits ≥ $100,000	63,000	4.8	0.3	3.0
Total deposits	$439,900			
Federal funds purchased	18,000	2.0	0.0	0.0
Other liabilities	7,500		0.0	50.0
Total liabilities	$465,400			
Stockholders' equity	$ 34,600	20.08%*		5.0
Total liabilities and equity	$500,000			

*Required return

ACTIVITIES

1. Evaluate the activity you generated in your checking account last month. How many home debits, transit checks, and deposits did you create? Include an estimate of how many times you used an automated teller machine (ATM). What interest did you earn on your balance and what fees did you pay? Use the data from Exhibit 12.3 to determine the bank's break-even deposit balance without insufficient funds (NSF) check charges. Given the amount of your bank's NSF charge per item, how many NSF check charges must a bank collect for your account to be profitable?

2. Take a survey of local banks regarding the pricing of transactions accounts. Include a list of all fees associated with these account relationships. Compare the different types of pricing strategies and identify the type of customer (low/high balance, low/high activity, etc.) that each bank appears to be targeting. Which account appears to be most attractive to the average college student?

13

THE EFFECTIVE USE OF CAPITAL

Inadequate bank capital is like pornography. You can't accurately define it or measure it. You simply know it when you see it.

— ANONYMOUS BANK REGULATOR

The large number of bank failures, the decline in FDIC insurance fund reserves in the early 1990s, recent increases in loan charge-offs and problem loans, as well as the creation of new product powers have focused increased attention on the adequacy of bank capital. Regulators want high capital requirements to better protect depositors and the viability of the insurance fund, and to reduce overall risk-taking. Historically, bankers have preferred lower capital requirements, which increase financial leverage and the multiplier effect on ROE. Low capital requirements also allow for substantial asset growth. In an environment of increased competition and consolidation, however, the market rewards banks with substantial capital by valuing their stock highly because they are viewed as the firms most likely to survive as acquirers. In the early 1990s, the Federal Reserve Board of Governors (FED), Federal Deposit Insurance Corp. (FDIC), and Office of the Comptroller (OCC) imposed minimum risk-based capital (RBC) standards that help control bank risk-taking. These RBC standards mean that higher levels of capital are required against higher risk bank assets. The Federal Deposit Insurance Corporation Improvement Act of 1991 (FDICIA) established a system of prompt regulatory action with sanctions for undercapitalized institutions. These requirements have expedited consolidation within the banking industry and increased the cost of offering banking services. During 2001, bank regulators around the globe were considering imposing new risk-based standards.

Capital plays a significant role in the risk-return trade-off at banks. Increasing capital reduces risk by cushioning the volatility of earnings, restricting growth opportunities, and lowering the probability of bank failure. It also reduces expected returns to shareholders, as equity is more expensive than debt. The fundamental asset and liability management decision regarding capital thus focuses on how much capital is optimal. Firms with greater capital can borrow at lower rates, make larger loans, and expand faster through acquisitions or internal growth. In general, they can pursue riskier investments. A second important decision concerns the form in which new capital is obtained, because regulators allow certain types of debt and preferred stock to qualify as capital to meet the requirements. These decisions are examined in this chapter in light of the regulatory definition of capital, its function, and cost.

WHY WORRY ABOUT BANK CAPITAL?

Bank regulators' primary objective is to ensure the safety and soundness of the U.S. financial system. It is generally believed that failures of individual banks, particularly large institutions, might erode public confidence in the financial system. The federal government attempts to limit the magnitude and scope of bank failures and ensure confidence in the banking system by imposing minimum capital requirements for individual banks. Requirements are met when banks obtain an acceptable amount of financing in the form of qualifying equity capital and related long-term debt sources. Such capital reduces the risk of failure by acting as a cushion against losses, providing access to financial markets to meet liquidity needs, and limiting growth.

Bank supervision has reached the point where regulators now specify minimum amounts of equity and other qualifying capital that banks must obtain to continue operations.[1] Historically, regulators stipulated minimum capital-to-asset ratios but did not worry about the quality of bank assets. While bank capital-to-asset ratios averaged near 20 percent at the turn of the century, comparable ratios today are closer to 8 percent. Capital trends since the 1930s are shown in Exhibit 13.1.

Clearly, solvency risk in the banking system has increased in the aggregate over time because asset quality has not improved sufficiently to compensate for the lower percentages of capital. More importantly, under the old capital regulation two banks of the same size would have to operate with the same amount of capital, independent of their risk profiles. Thus, a bank that held only Treasury securities needed the same amount of capital as the same size bank that held speculative real estate loans. Does this seem reasonable? The answer depends on the role that capital is expected to serve and how regulators want to control bank risk.

Capital-to-asset ratios at commercial banks and savings and loans are below similar ratios at other financial institutions and well below capital ratios at other nonfinancial businesses. This difference reflects the intermediation function of depository institutions and thus is not remarkable. High financial leverage, however, increases the relative riskiness of operations by providing less protection to creditors upon liquidation of the firm. Bankers also recognize that high leverage increases potential profitability, so they attempt to minimize external equity financing. Regulators, in contrast, want to increase bank equity financing and focus on balancing solvency risks with an individual bank's profit potential.

This chapter introduces the risk-based capital requirements that banks have been subject to since the end of 1992. It then examines the functions of bank capital and its impact on

---

[1]The International Lending Supervision Act of 1983 empowered the Federal Reserve, Federal Deposit Insurance Corp., Office of the Comptroller of the Currency, and Federal Home Loan Bank Board to mandate legally binding minimum capital requirements. Most banks acceded to prior guidelines even though the legal requirement did not exist.

· EXHIBIT 13.1

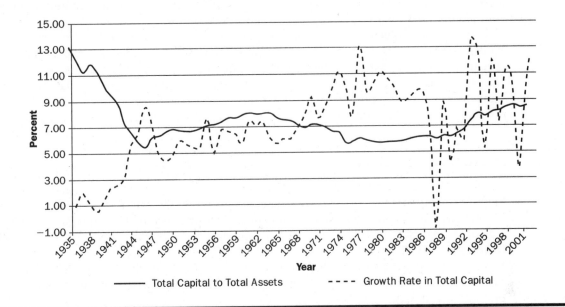

commercial bank operations. It addresses the following issues: (1) What constitutes bank capital? (2) What functions do capital accounts serve? (3) How much capital is adequate? (4) What is the impact of regulatory capital requirements on bank operating policies? (5) What are the advantages and disadvantages of various sources of internal and external capital? These issues are important because federal regulators appear intent on raising or maintaining high capital standards for banks and other institutions over time. The last section describes the framework for new capital standards as proposed in 2001.

RISK-BASED CAPITAL STANDARDS

Historically, bank regulators specified minimum capital standards for banks that were independent of the riskiness of each institution. During the 1970s, the regulatory agencies established capital adequacy by creating bank peer groups, setting target capital ratios for each group, and then adjusting those targets on a case-by-case basis with no specific minimum capital requirement. During this period, capital ratios declined steadily as the capital ratios of many large banks declined, and several large banks failed. In 1981, the Federal Reserve Board and the Comptroller of the Currency adopted explicit numerical capital standards for two of three groups established based on asset size. The three groups were defined as multinational, regional, and community. The largest multinationals were treated on a case-by-case basis with no explicit capital ratio requirement but with the expectation that they would increase their capital positions or explicit requirements would be put in place. Regional banks (assets between $1 billion and $15 billion) and community banks (assets below $1 billion) were required to maintain a primary capital-to-asset ratio of at least 5 percent and 6 percent, respectively. **Primary capital** consisted of common and perpetual preferred stock, surplus, undivided profits, contingency and other capital reserves, mandatory convertible debt, and the allowance for loan and lease losses.[2] Regulators recognized **secondary capital** to include balance sheet items such as long-term subordinated debt and limited-life preferred stock.[3] Primary plus secondary capital equaled total capital, with the minimum set at 6 percent of total bank assets.

One notable problem was that these requirements were established without regard to a bank's asset quality, liquidity risk, and interest rate risk. Thus, when banks fell under pressure to increase earnings, as in the case of declining net interest margins, capital requirements imposed no constraints to risk-taking other than limiting growth. Bank regulators did force banks to have more capital than the minimums when they perceived bank risk to be excessive, but this determination often occurred long after management made risky loans.

THE BASEL AGREEMENT

In 1986, U.S. bank regulators proposed that banks be required to maintain minimum amounts of capital that reflect the riskiness of bank assets. By the time it was implemented, the proposal included risk-based capital standards for banks in 12 industrialized nations. U.S. bank regulators phased in the requirements starting in 1990 with the regulations in place by the end of 1992. Importantly, savings and loans have been required to meet the same risk-based capital standards since 1992. Today, countries that are members of the Organization for Economic Cooperation and Development (OECD) enforce similar risk-based requirements on their own banks.

Although the terms varied between nations, primarily in terms of what constitutes capital, the Basel Agreement contained several important elements. First, a bank's minimum capital requirement is linked, by formula, to its credit risk as determined by the composition of assets. The greater is credit risk, the greater is required capital. Second, stockholders' equity is deemed the most critical type of capital. As such, each bank is expected to operate with a minimum amount of equity based on the amount of credit risk. Third, the minimum total capital requirement increased to 8 percent of risk-adjusted assets. Finally, the capital requirements were approximately standardized between countries to "level the playing field;" that is, to remove competitive advantages that banks in one country might have over banks in other countries because of regulatory or accounting differences.

RISK-BASED ELEMENTS OF THE PLAN

To determine minimum capital requirements for a bank to be adequately capitalized, bank managers follow a four-step process.

1. Classify assets into one of four risk categories, appropriate to the obligor, collateral, or guarantor of the asset.

2. Convert off-balance sheet commitments and guarantees to their on-balance sheet "credit equivalent" values and classify them in the appropriate risk categories.[4]

---

[2] Perpetual preferred stock has no set maturity date; mandatory convertible debt refers to bonds that must contractually be converted into either common stock or preferred stock; and the allowance for loan and lease losses refers to the contra-asset account appearing on a bank's balance sheet which represents management's estimate of uncollectible loans.

[3] Subordinated debt refers to bonds where the claims of bondholders are paid only after insured and uninsured depositors are paid in the case of a bank failure.

[4] Banks have been required to hold capital against off-balance shed activities long before the Enron collapse.

3. Multiply the dollar amount of assets in each risk category by the appropriate risk weight; this equals risk-weighted assets.

4. Multiply risk-weighted assets by the minimum capital percentages, either 4 percent for Tier 1 capital or 8 percent for total capital for a U.S. bank to be adequately capitalized.

The process ensures that assets with the highest perceived credit risk have the highest risk weights and require the most capital. In addition to these credit risk-based standards, the Fed, FDIC, and OCC adopted measures related to the supervisory treatment of interest rate risk and market risk capital requirements, which are described in the following sections "Capital Requirements for Interest Rate Risk" and "Capital Requirements for Market Risk Using Internal Models."

Consider the data in Exhibit 13.2 for Regional National Bank (RNB). As indicated in the first column of data, total assets for the bank were just under $5 billion and the bank had almost $656 million in off-balance sheet items. Under the former capital standards, RNB would have needed 6 percent total capital or approximately $299.6 million in primary and secondary capital. The exhibit demonstrates that the risk-based capital requirements are slightly higher for total capital.

Exhibit 13.3 lists the four risk categories and the general types of assets that fall into each category for RNB. Exhibit 13.4 demonstrates the application of step 2, which involves converting off-balance sheet activity into a balance sheet equivalent value. Exhibit 13.5 provides a summary list of the balance sheet items in each category.

Note that the lowest risk category carries a zero weight because there is no default risk (or very little) with direct obligations of the federal government, such as cash, Treasury securities, and U.S. agency securities issued by the Government National Mortgage Association (GNMA).[5] Assets in each of the subsequent categories are assumed to exhibit increased default risk. Thus, assets in category 2 are subject to a 20 percent risk weight and an *effective* total-capital-to-total-assets ratio of 1.6 percent (0.2×8 percent). Category 2 assets are short-term and often carry U.S. government agency guarantees; e.g., U.S. agency securities, general obligation municipal bonds, interest-bearing depository institution deposits, and federal funds sold, among other assets. Each type is low in default risk so that the risk weight is slightly above that for zero default risk assets. First mortgages, collateralized mortgage obligations (CMOs), and municipal revenue bonds comprise the bulk of the 50 percent risk weight assets under category 3, which carry a 4 percent effective total capital ratio (0.5×8 percent). The final category includes assets with the highest default risk, such as commercial loans and real estate loans other than first mortgages, and thus these assets carry a risk weight of 100 percent.

An important element of the risk-based standards is that a bank's off-balance sheet items must be supported by capital. A bank that exposes its operations to risk by making long-term loan commitments, offering letter of credit guarantees, and participating in interest rate swaps and forward or futures transactions must hold capital against the exposure. Management first converts the dollar value of each off-balance sheet item to an on-balance sheet *credit equivalent* amount, as indicated in the second column of Exhibit 13.4, using the conversion factors in Exhibit 13.6. The converted credit equivalent amount is then assigned to the appropriate risk category, based on the obligor, collateral, or guarantor of the asset, and then multiplied by the associated risk weight to calculate risk-adjusted assets. Exhibit 13.4 indicates that long-term loan commitments greater than one year (364,920) are classified as 50 percent conversion items, while standby letters of credit or direct credit substitutes (165,905), futures and forward contracts (50,000), and interest rate swaps (75,000) are converted using a 100 percent conversion

---

[5]For RNB, trading account securities consist solely of U.S. Treasury securities.

▪ EXHIBIT 13.2

REGIONAL NATIONAL BANK (RNB), RISK-BASED CAPITAL (MILLIONS OF DOLLARS)

	Assets $1,000	Risk Weight	Risk Weighted Assets
Category 1: Zero Percent			
Cash & reserve	104,525	0.00%	0
Trading account	830	0.00%	0
U.S. Treasury & agency secs.	45,882	0.00%	0
Federal reserve stock	5,916	0.00%	0
Total category 1	157,153		0
Category 2: 20 Percent			
Due form banks/in process	303,610	20.00%	60,722
Int. bearing dep./Fed. funds sold	497,623	20.00%	99,525
Domestic dep. institutions	38,171	20.00%	7,634
Repurchase agreements (U.S. Treas. & agency)	329,309	20.00%	65,862
U.S. agencies (govt. sponsored)	412,100	20.00%	82,420
State & municipal secured tax authority	87,515	20.00%	17,503
C.M.O. backed by agency secs.	90,020	20.00%	18,004
SBAs (govt. guaranteed portion)	29,266	20.00%	5,853
Other category 2 assets	0	20.00%	0
Total category 2	1,787,614		357,523
Category 3: 50 Percent			
C.M.O. backed by mtge. loans	10,000	50.00%	5,000
State & Muni's/all other	68,514	50.00%	34,257
Real estate: 1–4 family	324,422	50.00%	162,211
Other category 3 assets	0	50.00%	0
Total category 3	402,936		201,468
Category 4: 100 Percent			
Loans: comm./ag./inst./leases	1,966,276	100.00%	1,966,276
Real estate, all other	388,456	100.00%	388,456
Allowance credit loss	(70,505)	0.00%	0
Other investments	168,519	100.00%	168,519
Premises, equity, other assets	194,400	100.00%	194,400
Other category 4 assets	0	100.00%	0
Total category 4	2,647,146		2,717,651
Total assets before off-balance sheet	4,994,849		3,276,642
Off-Balance Sheet Contingencies			
0% collateral category	0	0.00%	0
20% collateral category	0	20.00%	0
50% collateral category	364,920	50.00%	182,460
100% collateral category	290,905	100.00%	290,905
Total contingencies	655,825		473,365
Total assets and contingencies before allowance for loan and lease losses and ATR	5,468,214		3,750,007
Less: Excess allowance for loan and lease losses (amount that exceeds 1.25% of gross RAA)			(2,152)
Total assets and contingencies	5,468,214		3,747,854

Capital Requirements (Adequately Capitalized)	Actual Capital	Minimum Required Capital (%)	Required Capital (Adequate)
Tier 1	199,794	4.00%	149,914
Total capital	399,588	8.00%	299,828

▪ EXHIBIT 13.3

GENERAL DESCRIPTION OF ASSETS IN EACH OF THE FOUR RISK CATEGORIES

Asset Category	Risk Weight	Effective Total Capital Requirement*	Obligor, Collateral, or Guarantor of the Asset
1	0%	0%	Generally, direct obligations of OCED central government or the U.S. federal government; e.g., currency and coin, government securities, and unconditional government guaranteed claims. Also, balances due or guaranteed by depository institutions.
2	20%	1.6%	Generally, indirect obligations of OCED central government or the U.S. federal government; e.g., most federal agency securities, full faith and credit municipal securities, and domestic depository institutions. Also, assets collateralized by federal government obligations are generally included in this category; e.g., repurchase agreements (when Treasuries serve as collateral) and CMOs backed by government agency securities.
3	50%	4%	Generally, loans secured by 1–4 family properties and municipal bonds secured by revenues of a specific project (revenue bonds).
4	100%	8%	All other claims on private borrowers; e.g., most bank loans, premises, and other assets.

*Equals 8% of equivalent risk-weighted assets and represents the minimum requirement to be adequately capitalized.

▪ EXHIBIT 13.4

REGIONAL NATIONAL BANK (RNB), OFF-BALANCE SHEET CONVERSION WORKSHEET

	$ Amount	Credit Conversion Factor	Credit Equivalent $ Amount
Contingencies 100% conversion factor			
Direct credit substitutes	165,905	100.00%	165,905
Acquisition of participations in BA, direct credit substitutes*	0	100.00%	0
Assets sold w/recourse	0	100.00%	0
Futures & forward contracts	50,000	100.00%	50,000
Interest rate swaps	75,000	100.00%	75,000
Other 100% collateral category	0	100.00%	0
Total 100% collateral category	290,905		290,905
Contingencies 50% conversion factor			
Transaction-related contingencies	0	50.00%	0
Unused commitments > 1 year	364,920	50.00%	182,460
Revolving underwriting facilities (RUFs)	0	50.00%	0
Other 50% collateral category	0	50.00%	0
Total 50% collateral category	364,920		182,460
Contingencies 20% conversion factor			
Short-term trade-related contingencies	0	20.00%	0
Other 20% collateral category	0	20.00%	0
Total 20% collateral category	0		0
Contingencies 0% conversion factor			
Loan commitments < 1 year	0	0.00%	0
Other 0% collateral category	0	100.00%	0
Total 0% collateral category	0		0
Total Off-Balance sheet commitment	655,825		473,365

*BA refers to bankers acceptance.

· EXHIBIT 13.5

Risk Weights and Risk Categories for Specific Balance Sheet Items*

Category 1: 0%

(1) Currency and coin (domestic and foreign) held in the bank or in transit
(2) Securities issued by the U.S. government and other OECD central governments (including U.S. Treasury securities)
(3) Claims that are unconditionally guaranteed by the U.S. government and its agencies and other OECD central governments (including GNMA and SBA securities and loans guaranteed by the Export-Import Bank)
(4) Gold bullion held in the bank's vaults or in another's vaults on an allocated basis, to the extent offset by gold bullion liabilities
(5) Credit equivalent amount of those off-balance sheet direct claims on, or claims unconditionally guaranteed by the U.S. government and other OECD central governments

Category 2: 20%

(1) Cash items in the process of collection (CIPC)
(2) Balances due from (claims guaranteed by) U.S. depository institutions and other OECD banks
(3) Short-term (one year or less) claims guaranteed by non-OECD banks
(4) Securities, loans, local currency, and other claims conditionally guaranteed by the U.S. government and its agencies and other OECD central governments (e.g., VA and FHA mortgage loans and student loans on which the U.S. Department of Education acts as a reinsurer)
(5) Claims on, guaranteed, or collateralized by securities issued by U.S. government-sponsored agencies (e.g., loans collateralized by FHLMC pass-through securities) or official multilateral lending institutions or regional development banks (e.g., the World Bank including the International Finance Corporation)
(6) Certain privately issued mortgage-backed securities representing indirect ownership of U.S. government agency or U.S. government-sponsored agency mortgage-backed securities (e.g., GNMA, FNMA, and FHLMC pass-through securities)

NOTE: For more details, see the Federal Financial Institutions Examination Council FFIEC Report Forms available on the Internet at www.ffiec.gov.

*Several of the risk weight categories refer to claims against OECD countries; i.e., the Organization for Economic Cooperation and Development. The following countries are members of the OECD: Australia, Austria, Belgium, Canada, the Czech Republic, Denmark, Finland, France, Germany, Greece, Hungary, Iceland, Ireland, Italy, Japan, Korea, Luxembourg, Mexico, the Netherlands, New Zealand, Norway, Poland, Portugal, Slovak Republic, Spain, Sweden, Switzerland, Turkey, the United Kingdom, and the United States. In addition, Saudi Arabia should be treated as an OECD country. All other countries should be treated as non-OECD countries.

factor.[6] Figures in the final column represent converted amounts. Once converted to on-balance sheet equivalents, all of these commitments are classified as category 4 assets subject to a 100 percent risk weighting.

The second and third columns of Exhibit 13.2 indicate the associated risk weight and the dollar value of each balance sheet figure, respectively for RNB. Risk-weighted assets are calculated by multiplying the dollar value of assets in column one by its respective risk weight. Total risk-weighted assets are the sum of risk-weighted assets in each category, including off-balance sheet items. Total risk-weighted assets for RNB thus equaled $3.75 billion. Finally, RNB's minimum capital requirements are specified as a fraction of total risk-weighted assets. Figures at the bottom of Exhibit 13.2 are for RNB to be adequately capitalized.

The next section describes the components of bank capital under the standards. At this point, it is sufficient to know that banks must simultaneously meet three capital standards. To be adequately capitalized a bank's Tier 1 capital must equal no less than 4 percent of risk-weighted assets, total capital must equal at least 8 percent of risk-weighted assets, and

---

[6]Values for futures, forwards, and interest rate swaps represent the sum of the mark-to-market value plus the potential future increase in credit exposure. See Exhibit 13.5.

(7) General obligation claims on (municipal securities), and the portion of claims that are guaranteed by the full faith and credit of local governments and political subdivisions in the U.S. and other OECD local governments

(8) Credit equivalent amount for those off-balance sheet items that are risk weighted at 20 percent; e.g., credit equivalent amount of claims collateralized by cash on deposit (standby letters of credit collateralized by cash)

Category 3: 50%

(1) Loans that are fully secured by first liens on 1–4 family residential properties and loans fully secured by first liens on multifamily residential properties that have been prudently underwritten

(2) Privately issued mortgage-backed securities representing direct and indirect ownership of the mortgage loans (if the mortgages are prudently underwritten and are not restructured, past due, or in nonaccrual status)

(3) Revenue bonds (municipal revenue securities) or similar claims that are obligations of U.S. state or local governments, or other OECD local governments, for which the government is committed to repay the debt only out of revenues from the facilities financed

(4) Credit equivalent amount, for those *off-balance sheet items* that are to be risk weighted at 50 percent; e.g., credit equivalent amounts of interest rate and foreign exchange rate contracts that are not accorded a lower risk weight as a result of the counterparty, collateral, or a guarantee

Category 4: 100%

(1) All other loans, debt securities, and other claims where the counterparty is a private obligor

(2) Premises and fixed assets

(3) Margin accounts on futures contracts

(4) Other real estate owned

(5) All other assets not already reported above

(6) Credit equivalent amounts of those off-balance sheet items where the counterparty is a private obligor and which are not accorded a lower risk weight as a result of collateral or a guarantee

leverage capital must equal no less than 3 percent of adjusted total assets. Figures at the bottom of Exhibit 13.2 indicate that RNB must have at least $149.914 million in Tier 1 capital and $299.828 million in total capital based on risk-adjusted assets. Leverage capital is discussed later.

WHAT CONSTITUTES BANK CAPITAL?

According to the accounting definition, **capital** or **net worth** equals the cumulative value of assets minus the cumulative value of liabilities and represents ownership interest in a firm. It is traditionally measured on a book value basis where assets and liabilities are listed in terms of historical cost.[7] In banking, the regulatory concept of bank capital differs substantially from accounting capital. Specifically, regulators include certain forms of debt and loan

---

[7]FASB 115 requires banks to mark-to-market those securities that are not classified as held to maturity. Because marking securities to market value will directly affect equity capital, capital listed on a bank's balance sheet is a hybrid between book value and market value.

■ EXHIBIT 13.6

SUMMARY OF OFF-BALANCE SHEET CONVERSION FACTORS
FOR RISK-BASED CAPITAL REQUIREMENTS

100% Conversion Factor

1. Direct credit substitutes (general guarantees of indebtedness and guarantee-type instruments, including standby letters of credit serving as financial guarantees for, or supporting, loans and securities)
2. Risk participations in bankers' acceptances and participations in direct credit substitutes (for example, standby letters of credit)
3. Sale and repurchase agreements and asset sales with recourse, if not already included on the balance sheet
4. Forward agreements (that is, contractual obligations) to purchase assets, including financing facilities with certain drawdown

50% Conversion Factor

1. Transaction-related contingencies (for example, bid bonds, performance bonds, warranties, and standby letters of credit related to a particular transaction)
2. Unused commitments with an original maturity exceeding one year, including underwriting commitments and commercial credit lines
3. Revolving underwriting facilities (RUFs), note issuance facilities (NIFs), and other similar arrangements

20% Conversion Factor

1. Short-term, self-liquidating trade-related contingencies, including commercial letters of credit

0% Conversion Factor

1. Unused commitments with an original maturity of one year or less, or that are unconditionally cancelable at any time

Credit conversion process for off-balance sheet interest rate, foreign exchange, equity derivative, and commodity and other contracts—

In general, to calculate the credit equivalent amount for these contracts, a bank should, for each contract, add:
(1) The mark-to-market value (only if a positive value) of the contract; i.e., the contract's current credit exposure or replacement cost, and
(2) An estimate of the *potential future increase in credit exposure* over the remaining life of the instrument.
For risk-based capital purposes, *potential future credit exposure* of a contract is determined by multiplying the notional principal amount of the contract (even if the contract had a negative mark-to-market value) by the appropriate credit conversion factor from the chart presented below (existence of a legally enforceable bilateral netting agreement between the reporting bank and a counterparty may be taken into consideration when determining both the current credit exposure and the potential future exposure of off-balance sheet derivative contracts.)

Remaining Maturity	Interest Rate Contracts	Foreign Exchange and Gold Contracts	Equity Derivative Contracts	Precious Metals (Except Gold)	Other Commodity Contracts
One year or less	0.0%	1.0%	6.0%	7.0%	10.0%
More than one year through five years	0.5%	5.0%	8.0%	7.0%	12.0%
More than five years	1.5%	7.5%	10.0%	8.0%	15.0%

SOURCE: Federal Financial Institutions Examination Council FFIEC Report Forms available on the Internet at http://www.ffiec.gov/.

loss reserves when measuring capital adequacy. This policy raises numerous issues regarding bank capital's function and optimal mix.

Accounting capital includes the book value of common equity and preferred stock outstanding. **Total equity capital** equals the sum of common stock, surplus, undivided profits, and capital reserves, and net unrealized holding gains (losses) on available-for-sale securities, cumulative foreign currency translation adjustments, and perpetual preferred stock as defined below:

- **Common stock** equals par value of common stock outstanding; thus, if there are one million shares outstanding with par value of $10 per share, common stock will show $10 million.

- **Surplus** equals the excess over par value at which common stock was issued plus the value of undivided profits allocated to surplus. Suppose, in the above case, that one million common stock shares were originally sold in the market place to net a bank $15 per share. The excess, $5 per share or $5 million, would be allocated to surplus.

- **Undivided Profits** equal the value of cumulative retained earnings minus transfers to surplus. Retained earnings increase when a bank reports net income that exceeds dividend payments, and decreases when net income is less than dividends or the bank reports a loss.

- **Capital reserves** for contingencies and other capital reserves equal the value of cumulative reserves established for deferred taxes or contingencies. Contingencies include expected payments to retire outstanding preferred stock, settle lawsuits, and satisfy other extraordinary obligations. These reserves have been combined with undivided profits for reporting purposes since 1978.

- **Net unrealized holding gains (losses) on available-for-sale securities.** For risk-based capital purposes, common stockholders' equity capital includes any net unrealized holding losses on available-for-sale equity securities with readily determinable fair values, but excludes other net unrealized holding gains (losses) on available-for-sale securities. FASB 115 requires banks and other firms to mark certain available-for-sale securities to their market value. These unrealized losses (gains) directly affect equity reported on the balance sheet, but do not affect qualifying capital for risk-based calculations.

- **Preferred stock** includes the book value of aggregate preferred stock outstanding. While it exhibits many of the same characteristics as long-term bonds, preferred stock represents ownership in a firm with claims superior to common stock but subordinated to all debt holders. It is issued either in **perpetuity** or with a **fixed maturity** (limited life). Most issues are callable, and some are convertible to common stock. Dividend payments may be fixed, much like coupon payments on bonds, or may vary with some market index over the life of the issue. Unlike coupon payments, dividends are not deductible for corporate income tax purposes.

Regulatory capital ratios focus at least in part on the **book value of equity,** which equals the book value of bank assets minus the book value of total liabilities. Most analysts try to estimate the market value of bank equity when assessing financial performance and risk. This can be done in several ways. One procedure is to multiply the number of outstanding shares of stock by the most recent stock price per share. Another procedure requires estimating the market value of bank assets and subtracting the market value of bank liabilities. As discussed in Chapter 10, the market value of equity is an important measure of performance in interest rate risk management. Claims of equity stockholders are paid in the case of failure after the claims of all debt holders and preferred stockholders.

Regulators also include long-term **subordinated debt** in Tier 2 capital, which is part of the broader definition of total bank capital (Tier 1 and Tier 2). The term *subordinated* means that claims of the debt holders are paid only after the claims of depositors. Subordinated debt takes many forms. It includes straight bonds with long maturities that carry fixed rates. It also includes variable rate bonds, capital notes, or bonds that are convertible into the bank's common or preferred stock. The fact that nonequity accounts constitute capital relates to regulatory perceptions of capital's function. Mandatory convertible debt and subordinated long-term debt are included because they carry relatively long-term maturities and creditors' claims are subordinated to those of depositors. These funding sources, therefore, provide solvency protection for insured depositors and the insurance funds.

Risk-based capital standards utilize two measures of qualifying bank capital as summarized in Exhibit 13.7. **Tier 1** or **core capital** consists of common stockholders' equity, noncumulative perpetual preferred stock and any related surplus, and minority interests in equity capital accounts of consolidated subsidiaries, minus intangible assets like goodwill and disallowed deferred tax assets. For most banks, Tier 1 capital will equal common stockholders' equity capital less any net unrealized holding gains or losses on available-for-sale equity securities. **Tier 2** or **supplementary capital** is limited to 100 percent of Tier 1 capital and consists of cumulative perpetual preferred stock and any related surplus, long-term preferred stock, limited amounts of term subordinated debt and intermediate-term preferred stock, and a limited amount of the allowance for loan and lease losses (up to 1.25 percent of gross risk-weighted assets).[8]

Regulators are also concerned that a bank could acquire a sufficient dollar amount of low risk assets (federal government securities) such that risk-based capital requirements would be negligible. Suppose, for example, that RNB from Exhibit 13.2 held all of its assets in the form of cash and due balances and Treasury securities. In this case, its risk-weighted assets would equal zero and its Tier 1 and total capital requirements would be zero. This would allow (at least theoretically) RNB to operate with no equity capital! To prevent this from occurring, regulators impose a minimum 3 percent **leverage capital ratio,** defined as Tier 1 capital divided by total assets net of goodwill, other disallowed intangible assets, and disallowed deferred tax assets. The impact is that all banks must maintain some minimum amount of equity capital relative to their total assets in recognition of risks other than default risk.

Exhibit 13.8 compares the average capital ratios for different-sized banks in 2001. Regardless of how the averages are calculated, three implications stand out. First, capital ratios at banks of all sizes exceeded the regulatory minimums. Second, capital ratios at small banks greatly exceeded those at larger banks, on average. This reflects greater regulatory pressure on small banks, which presumably carry less diversified asset portfolios, and the impact of record profits during the mid- to late-1990s. Finally, as seen in Exhibit 13.1, capital ratios have generally increased since 1980 as banks moved to strengthen their financial positions. The Contemporary Issues segment describes capital ratios at Japanese banks in the 1990s.

FDICIA AND BANK CAPITAL STANDARDS

Effective December 1991, Congress passed the Federal Deposit Insurance Improvement Act (FDICIA) with the intent of revising bank capital requirements to emphasize the importance of capital and authorize early regulatory intervention in problem institutions. The act also authorized regulators to measure interest rate risk at banks and require additional capital when risk is deemed excessive. The focal point of the act is the system of **prompt regulatory action,** which divides banks into categories or zones according to their capital positions and mandates action when capital minimums are not met.

---

[8]The definitions of Tier 1 and Tier 2 capital are from *Instructions for Preparation of Consolidated Reports of Condition and Income (FFIEC 031, 032, 033, and 034),* Federal Financial Institutions Examination Council. FFIEC Report Forms are available on the Internet at http://www.ffiec.gov/.

▪ EXHIBIT 13.7

Components	Minimum Requirements
Tier 1 (Core)Capital	Must equal or exceed 4 percent of risk-weighted assets
Common stockholders' equity*	No limit
Noncumulative perpetual preferred stock and any related surplus	No limit, regulatory caution against *undue reliance*
Minority interests in equity capital accounts of consolidated subsidiaries	No limit, regulatory caution against *undue reliance*
Less: goodwill, other disallowed intangible assets, and disallowed deferred tax assets, and any other amounts that are deducted in determining Tier 1 capital in accordance with the capital standards issued by the reporting bank's primary federal supervisory authority	
Tier 2 (Supplementary)Capital	Total of Tier 2 is limited to 100 percent of Tier 1[†]
Cumulative perpetual preferred stock and any related surplus	
Long-term preferred stock (original maturity of 20 years or more) and any related surplus (discounted for capital purposes as it approaches maturity)	No limit within Tier 2
Auction rate and similar preferred stock (both cumulative and noncumulative)	No limit within Tier 2
Hybrid capital instruments (including mandatory convertible debt securities)	Subordinated debt and intermediate-term preferred stock are limited to 50 percent of Tier 1, amortized for capital purposes as they approach maturity.
Term subordinated debt and intermediate-term preferred stock (original weighted average maturity of five years or more)	50 percent of Tier 1 capital (and discounted for capital purposes as they approach maturity)
Allowance for loan and lease losses	Lesser of the balance of the allowance account or 1.25 percent of gross risk-weighted assets
Tier 3 (Capital Allocated for Market Risk)	
Applicable only to banks that are subject to the market risk capital guidelines	May not be used to support credit risk
	Tier 3 capital allocated for market risk plus Tier 2 capital allocated for market risk are limited to 71.4 percent of a bank's measure for market risk.
Deductions	
Deductions are made for:	As a general rule, one-half of aggregate investments would be deducted from Tier 1 capital and one-half from Tier 2 capital.
investments in banking and finance subsidiaries that are not consolidated for regulatory capital purposes; intentional reciprocal cross-holdings of banking organizations' capital instruments; and other deductions as determined by the reporting bank's primary federal supervisory authority	
Total Capital (Tier 1 + Tier 2 − Deductions)	Must equal or exceed 8 percent of risk-weighted assets For most banks, total risk-based capital will equal the sum of Tier 1 capital and Tier 2 capital.

*For risk-based capital purposes, common stockholders' equity capital includes any net unrealized holding losses on available-for-sale equity securities with readily determinable fair values, but excludes other net unrealized holding gains (losses) on available-for-sale securities.

[†]Amounts in excess of limitations are permitted but do not qualify as capital.

SOURCE: Federal Financial Institutions Examination Council FFIEC Report Forms available on the Internet at www.ffiec.gov.

• EXHIBIT 13.8

RISK-BASED CAPITAL RATIOS FOR DIFFERENT-SIZED U.S. COMMERCIAL BANKS, JUNE 1995–2001

			Asset Size			
	Year	< $100 Million	$100 Million to $1 Billion	$1 to $10 Billion	> $10 Billion	All Commercial Banks
Number of institutions reporting	2001	4,486	3,194	320	80	8,080
	2000	4,842	3,078	313	82	8,315
	1999	5,156	3,030	318	76	8,580
	1997	5,853	2,922	301	66	9,142
	1995	6,658	2,861	346	75	9,940
Equity capital ratio (percent)	2001	10.9	9.68	9.76	8.77	9.09
	2000	11.08	9.6	8.99	8.05	8.49
	1999	10.68	9.24	9.09	7.87	8.37
	1997	10.81	9.62	9.16	7.58	8.33
	1995	10.42	9.39	8.57	7.19	8.11
Return on equity (percent)	2001	8.07	12.24	13.77	13.43	13.1
Core capital (leverage) ratio (percent)	2001	10.63	9.17	8.74	7.23	7.79
Tier 1 risk-based capital ratio (percent)	2001	15.87	12.88	11.83	8.86	9.9
Total risk-based capital ratio (percent)	2001	16.96	14.06	13.77	12.16	12.72

SOURCE: FDIC, Quarter Banking Profile, http://www2.fdic.gov/qbp/.

As shown in Exhibit 13.9, there are five capital categories, with the first two representing well-capitalized and adequately capitalized banks. Because of their strong capital positions, **well-capitalized banks** are not subject to any regulatory directives regarding capital. For this reason, most banks make every effort to meet the 6 percent, 10 percent, and 5 percent minimum ratios. **Adequately capitalized** banks also have strong capital, but are restricted from obtaining brokered deposits without FDIC approval. While this provision may not seem too restrictive, it has the potential to create problems. Today, regulators designate any bank deposit liability as a brokered deposit if the issuing bank pays an above-market rate. The deposit does not have to arise via a broker. Suppose that a bank competes in a three-bank community and all banks currently pay 2 percent on interest-checking accounts. If the two competitors lower their rates to 1.25 percent, the bank finds that it is paying a 75 basis point premium. Regulators may now label these interest-checking accounts as brokered deposits and disallow them (or make the bank pay a lower rate). Does this make sense?

Banks that fall into one of the bottom three categories prompt some explicit regulatory action. **Undercapitalized banks** are institutions that do not meet at least one of the three minimum capital requirements. **Significantly undercapitalized** banks have capital that falls significantly below at least one of the three standards. Finally, **critically undercapitalized** banks do not meet minimum threshold levels for the three capital ratios.

Exhibit 13.9 documents the specific definitions and associated regulatory actions as summarized by the Federal Reserve Board of Governors in late 1997. The top panel lists the minimum capital ratios that a bank must meet to qualify in each category or zone. Each of these ratios must be met simultaneously. The bottom panel lists mandatory and discretionary provisions within each classification. Note the restrictive nature of the mandatory actions. A bank that is undercapitalized must limit its asset growth, suspend dividends, and offer a capital restoration plan among other requirements. For a bank that is significantly undercapitalized, regulators can specify deposit rates and the pay of bank officers, clearly decisions that

JAPANESE BANK CAPITAL RATIOS

International risk-based capital requirements were originally agreed upon by the regulatory authorities in 12 industrialized nations. There are now 31. While Tier 1 capital components are quite comparable, Tier 2 components vary substantially between banks in different countries. Consider the requirements for Japanese banks, which account for many of the largest banks in the world. Japanese banks can own equities. As part of Tier 2 capital, Japan's banks can include 45 percent of unrealized gains on stock investments. When stock prices rise, the banks' capital positions improve while capital declines when stock prices fall.

From December 1989 through April 2001, the Nikkei Index, a broad-based index of Japanese stocks, fell almost 75 percent. This decline produced an $85 billion capital loss for just the five largest Japanese banks. Not surprisingly, growth opportunities were sharply curtailed and Japan's banks were under serious pressure to increase earnings to supplement their capital positions. Between 1990 and 2001, Japanese stock prices first rose then fell sharply again, ultimately worsening Japanese banks' capital positions even further. The point is that volatility in Japanese stocks translates into volatility in Japanese bank capital positions and makes it difficult to manage overall risk. The decline in stock prices and the general recession in Asia in the late 1990s through 2001 put the Japanese banking system in a very similar position as the United States savings and loan crisis of the mid-1980s.

senior management normally makes in the general course of business operation. Critically undercapitalized banks are near failure and treated accordingly. Once a bank reaches this stage, regulators can place them under receivership within 90 days. A review of the top panel reveals that such banks can have positive tangible equity capital equal to almost 2 percent of assets, be technically solvent, and still be closed by regulators.

The impact of FDICIA is much broader than that suggested by these provisions. Clearly, problem or undercapitalized institutions must obtain capital to remain in business. This often requires entering into a merger or acquisition because it is difficult to enter the primary markets and issue new capital. Similarly, bank managers know that if they maintain strong capital positions the regulators will let them operate without much restriction. Of course, the capital standards in Exhibit 13.9 are minimums. If the regulators believe that risk is above average for any reason, they can impose additional requirements.

TIER 3 CAPITAL REQUIREMENTS FOR MARKET RISK

Many large banks have dramatically increased the size and activity of their trading accounts, resulting in greater exposure to market risk. **Market risk** is the risk of loss to the bank from fluctuations in interest rates, equity prices, foreign exchange rates, commodity prices, and exposure to specific risk associated with debt and equity positions in the bank's trading portfolio. Market risk exposure is, therefore, a function of the *volatility* of these rates and prices and the corresponding sensitivity of the bank's trading assets and liabilities.

In response to the FDICIA stipulation that regulators systematically measure and monitor a bank's market risk position, risk-based capital standards require all banks with significant market risk to measure their market risk exposure and hold sufficient capital to mitigate this exposure. A bank is subject to the market risk capital guidelines if its consolidated trading activity, defined as the sum of trading assets and liabilities for the previous quarter, equals 10 percent or more of the bank's total assets for the previous quarter, or $1 billion or more in total dollar value. The primary federal supervisory authority, however, may exempt or include a bank if necessary or appropriate for safe and sound banking practices. Banks subject to the market risk capital guidelines must maintain an overall minimum 8 percent ratio

■ **EXHIBIT 13.9**

CAPITAL CATEGORIES AND PROMPT REGULATORY ACTION UNDER **FDICIA**

A. Minimum Capital Requirements across Capital Categories

	Total Risk-Based Ratio		Tier 1 Risk-Based Ratio		Tier 1 Leverage Ratio	Capital Directive/Requirement
Well capitalized	≥10%	and	≥6%	and	≥5%	Not subject to a capital directive to meet a specific level for any capital measure
Adequately capitalized	≥8%	and	≥4%	and	≥4%*	Does not meet the definition of well capitalized
Undercapitalized	≥6%	and	≥3%	and	≥3%†	
Significantly undercapitalized	<6%	or	<3%	or	<3%	
Critically undercapitalized	Ratio of tangible equity to total assets is ≤ 2%†					

B. Provisions for Prompt Corrective Action

Category	Mandatory Provisions	Discretionary Provisions
1.) Well capitalized	None	None
2.) Adequately capitalized	1. No brokered deposits, except with FDIC approval	None
3.) Undercapitalized	1. Suspend dividends and management fees 2. Require capital restoration plan 3. Restrict asset growth 4. Approval required for acquisitions, branching, and new activities 5. No brokered deposits	1. Order recapitalization 2. Restrict interaffiliate transactions 3. Restrict deposit interest rates 4. Restrict certain other activities 5. Any other action that would better carry out prompt corrective action
4.) Significantly undercapitalized	1. Same as for Category 3 2. Order recapitalization§ 3. Restrict interaffiliate transactions§ 4. Restrict deposit interest rates§ 5. Pay of officers restricted	1. Any Zone 3 discretionary actions 2. Conservatorship or receivership if fails to submit or implement plan or recapitalize pursuant to order 3. Any other Zone 5 provision, if such action is necessary to carry out prompt corrective action
5.) Critically undercapitalized	1. Same as for Category 4 2. Receiver/conservator within 90 days§ 3. Receiver if still in Category 5 four quarters after becoming critically undercapitalized 4. Suspend payments on subordinated debt§ 5. Restrict certain other activities	

*Three percent or above for composite one-rated banks and savings associations that are not experiencing or anticipating significant growth.

†Under 3 percent for composite one-rated banks and savings associations that are not experiencing or anticipating significant growth.

†Staff is proposing to define tangible equity as core capital elements plus cumulative perpetual preferred stock, net of all intangibles except limited amounts of purchased mortgage servicing rights.

§Not required if primary supervisor determines action would not serve purpose of prompt corrective action or if certain other conditions are met.

SOURCE: FDIC.

of total qualifying capital [the sum of Tier 1 capital (both allocated and excess), Tier 2 capital (both allocated and excess), and Tier 3 capital (allocated for market risk), net of all deductions] to risk-weighted assets and market risk equivalent assets. Tier 3 capital allocated for market risk plus Tier 2 capital allocated for market risk are limited to 71.4 percent of a bank's measure for market risk.

CAPITAL REQUIREMENTS FOR MARKET RISK USING INTERNAL MODELS

The market risk capital rules require that an institution measure its general market risk using an internally generated risk measurement model. This model is then used to calculate a **value-at-risk** (VAR) based capital charge. VAR is an estimate of the amount by which a bank's positions in a risk category could decline due to expected losses in the bank's portfolio due to market movements during a given period, measured with a specified confidence level. An institution may measure its specific risk through a valid internal model or by the so-called "standardized approach." The standardized approach uses a risk-weighting process developed by the Basel Committee on Banking Supervision.[9] The VAR of a bank's covered positions should be used to determine the bank's measure for market risk. **Covered positions** include all positions in a bank's trading account as well as foreign exchange and commodity positions, whether or not they are in the trading account. A bank's measure for market risk equals the sum of its VAR-based capital charge, the specific risk add-on (if any), and the capital charge for *de minimus* exposures (if any). A bank's market risk equivalent assets equal its measure for market risk multiplied by 12.5 (the reciprocal of the minimum 8.0 percent capital ratio).[10]

Regulatory requirements propose that an institution electing to use an internal model approach to measure market risk be subject to the following eight standards:

1. Value-at-risk should be computed each business day and should be based on a 99 percent (one-tailed) confidence level of estimated maximum loss.
2. The assumed holding period used for the VAR measure must be 10 business days.
3. The model must measure all material risks incurred by the institution.
4. The model may utilize historical correlations within broad categories of risk factors (interest rates, exchange rates, and equity and commodity prices), but not among these categories. That is, the consolidated value-at-risk is the sum of the individual VARs measured for each broad category.
5. The nonlinear price characteristics of options must be adequately addressed.
6. The historical observation period used to estimate future price and rate changes must have a minimum length of one year.
7. Data must be updated no less frequently than once every three months and more frequently if market conditions warrant.
8. Each yield curve in a major currency must be modeled using at least six risk factors, selected to reflect the characteristics of the interest rate-sensitive instruments that the institution trades. The model must also take account of spread risk.

The explicit market risk capital requirements are designed to capture both general market risk as well as specific market risks. **General market risk** refers to changes in the market value of on-balance sheet assets and off-balance sheet items resulting from broad market movements. General market risk includes risk common to all securities, such as changes in

---

[9]Chapter 4 of the Basel Committee on Banking Supervision demonstrates the VAR concept in general terms.

[10]See *Regulator Capital Guidelines*, FDIC, http://www.fdic.gov.

the general level of interest rates, exchange rates, commodity prices, or stock prices. **Specific market risks** are those risks specific to a particular security issue such as the underlying credit risk of the firm who issued a bond.[11]

The market risk capital standards also impose a set of qualitative standards in addition to the quantitative measure discussed above. The qualitative standards are designed to ensure that banks using internal models to measure market risk have conceptually sound risk management systems and that these systems are implemented with integrity. In particular, there are three qualitative elements required:

- The bank's internal risk measurement model should be closely integrated in the daily risk management process and serve as a basis for reporting of risk exposures to senior officers.

- The bank should routinely evaluate its exposures to highly stressful events via stress tests to identify the circumstances to which their particular trading portfolios are most vulnerable.

- The bank's risk control unit should be completely independent of the business units that generate the market risk exposures.

Banks and regulators are in the early stages of developing these internal market risk models. These models must undergo back-testing and verification and may eventually be expanded to help analyze credit, operational, and even legal risk in the future.

THE NEW BASEL CAPITAL ACCORD (BASEL II) AND OPERATIONAL RISK

The events of September 11, 2001 tragically demonstrated the need for banks to protect themselves against operational risk to their systems and people. The new Basel Capital requirements will require them to make capital charges for operational risk. Starting in 2005, regulators will begin calculating bank capital according to the recently adopted Basel II Accord for capital adequacy. The new focus of Basel II is operational risk. The focus is on the optimum use of capital in the technology and business process operations areas of a financial institution. The Basel Committee defines **operational risk** as "the risk of loss resulting from inadequate or failed internal processes, people, and systems, or from external events." From a capital adequacy point of view, this covers technology risks, management- and people-related operational risks, and legal risks. The new accord's focus on these areas is comprehensive.

The original Basel Accord's approach to capital requirements was primarily based on credit risk. Although it set appropriate protections from a market- and credit-risk perspective, it did not address operational or other types of risk. Operational risk itself is not new to financial institutions. It's the first risk a bank must manage, even before making its first loan or executing its first trade. What is new is that by 2005, a bank's regulatory capital needs could increase significantly—up to 20 percent of total risk-based capital—as a result of its exposure to operational risk. Banks can reduce that charge, however, by gathering substantial data and performance metrics on the institution's business processes. The more sophisticated and risk-sensitive a bank's approach to gathering this data, the lower its capital requirements can be.

---

[11]Hendricks and Hirtle (1997) suggest that these two types of risk are analogous to systematic and nonsystematic risk in a capital asset pricing model. See Hendricks, Darryll, and Hirtle, Beverly, "Regulatory Minimum Capital Standards for Banks: Current Status and Future Prospects," Conference on Bank Structure and Competition (1997 : 33rd).

• EXHIBIT 13.10

COMPARATIVE BALANCE SHEETS: MANUFACTURING FIRM VERSUS COMMERCIAL BANK

Manufacturing Firm		Commercial Bank	
Assets		**Assets**	
Cash	4%	Cash	8%
Accounts receivable	26%	Short-term securities	17%
Inventory	30%	Short-term loans	50%
Total Current Assets	60%	Total Current Assets	75%
		Long-term securities	5%
		Long-term loans	18%
Plant and equipment	40%	Plant and equipment	2%
Total Assets	100%	Total Assets	100%
Liabilities		**Liabilities**	
Accounts payable	20%	Short-term deposits	60%
Short-term notes payable	10%	Short-term borrowings	20%
Total Current Liabilities	30%	Total Current Liabilities	80%
Long-term debt	30%	Long-term debt	12%
Stockholders' equity	40%	Stockholders' equity	8%
Total Liabilities and Equity	100%	Total Liabilities and Equity	100%

WHAT IS THE FUNCTION OF BANK CAPITAL?

Much confusion exists over what purposes bank capital serves. The traditional corporate finance view is that capital reduces the risk of failure by providing protection against operating and extraordinary losses. While this holds for nonfinancial firms that rely on long-term debt with relatively low financial leverage, it is less applicable to commercial banks.

From the regulators' perspective, bank capital serves to protect the deposit insurance funds in the case of bank failures. When a bank fails, regulators can either pay-off insured depositors or arrange a purchase of the failed bank by a healthy bank.[12] The greater is a bank's capital, the lower is the cost of arranging a merger or paying depositors. An additional benefit of minimum capital requirements is that the owners of equity and long-term debt impose market discipline on bank managers because they closely monitor bank performance. Excessive risk taking lowers stock prices and increases borrowing costs, which adversely affect the wealth of these monitoring parties.

The function of bank capital is thus to reduce bank risk. It does so in three basic ways:

- It provides a cushion for firms to absorb losses and remain solvent.
- It provides ready access to financial markets and thus guards against liquidity problems caused by deposit outflows.
- It constrains growth and limits risk taking.

Bank capital provides a cushion to absorb losses. Consider the balance sheets for two hypothetical firms in Exhibit 13.10. The manufacturing firm has 60 percent current assets and 40 percent fixed assets. Its financing is composed of 60 percent debt and 40 percent equity.

---

[12]See Chapter 12 for alternative options available to the FDIC when a bank fails.

Exactly one-half of the debt is short-term, such that its current ratio equals 2. The commercial bank, in contrast, operates with very few fixed assets and finances 92 percent of its assets with debt and just 8 percent with equity. Its current ratio is less than 1. The value of the manufacturing firm's assets would have to decline by more than 40 percent before the firm sees its equity fall below zero and is technically insolvent. An 8 percent decline in asset values would similarly make the bank insolvent. Equity reduces the risk of failure by increasing the proportion of allowable problem assets that can default before equity is depleted.

The issue, however, is not this simple. For example, why do creditors allow banks to operate with far greater financial leverage than manufacturers? One reason is that banks exhibit little operating risk because fixed assets are low. Yet, several factors suggest that banks should have more equity. First, the market value of bank assets is more volatile than the value of assets at a typical manufacturing firm. Market values change whenever interest rates change and whenever bank borrowers experience difficulties. Manufacturing companies own proportionately fewer financial assets and are not as sensitive to interest rate fluctuations. Second, banks rely proportionately more on volatile sources of short-term debt, many of which can be withdrawn on demand. It seems reasonably probable that banks might be forced to liquidate assets at relatively low values. On the positive side, however, most of a bank's assets are financial and hence are generally more liquid and less risky (everything else equal) than the real assets held by nonfinancial companies. After all, it is often easier to sell Treasury securities and high-quality bank loans than an automobile assembly plant!

This capital discrepancy can be largely explained by federal deposit insurance and bank regulatory policy.[13] Depositors' funds at each member institution are insured up to $100,000. Even if a bank fails, an insured depositor is fully reimbursed. This system prevents massive withdrawals of small denomination deposits and makes uninsured creditors the arbiters of bank risk. Just as significantly, bank regulators provided de facto insurance for uninsured creditors at the largest financial institutions. Rather than let these banks fail, regulators arranged mergers or acquisitions that allowed such firms to continue operations without liquidation. In the case of Continental Illinois in 1984 and First City Bancorporation in 1987, the U.S. government effectively guaranteed the claims of both debt holders and preferred stockholders who lost little when the banks collapsed.[14] In these extreme cases, no private capital is technically required for the banks to continue operations. In general, deposit insurance and regulatory policy increase bank liquidity, which reduces the amount of equity financing required.

Interestingly, bank regulators shifted their policy with the failures of First Republic Bank Corp. in 1988 and MCorp. in 1989. These bank holding companies had $27 billion and $16 billion in assets, respectively, at the time they failed. Still, the regulators created bridge banks that took over the subsidiary banks and stripped the holding companies of their assets. This left common and preferred stockholders to file claims behind bondholders and other uninsured creditors for what little remained. For the first time, investors in the nation's largest banks suffered substantial losses.

---

[13]See the section at the end of this chapter on Federal Deposit Insurance for a more detailed discussion of Bank Capital and FDIC insurance.

[14]In 1984, C. T. Conover, the Comptroller of the Currency, suggested indirectly that regulators would not allow the 11 largest banking organizations in the United States to fail. These banks controlled 23 percent of all assets at the end of 1983. Feldman and Rolnick (1997) suggest that in 1997 dollars, regulators might view the top 21 banks, which controlled 38 percent of assets, as being too big to fail. In 1997, there were 24 commercial banks and S&Ls larger than $35 billion in assets. The large number of bank megamergers in the late 1990s has meant that the largest banks have gotten even larger and the number of large banks has increased. There were 33 (31 in current dollars) commercial banks and S&Ls larger than $35 million ($38.2 million current dollars) at the end of 2000.

The role of capital as a buffer against loan losses is clear when put in the context of cash flows rather than accounting capital. Consider a bank whose customers default on their loans. Defaults immediately reduce operating cash inflows because the bank no longer receives interest and principal payments. Cash outflows are largely unaffected except for incremental collection costs. The bank remains operationally solvent as long as its overall operating cash inflows exceed its cash outflows. Capital serves as a buffer because it reduces obligated outflows. Banks can defer dividends on preferred and common stock without being in default. Interest payments on bank debt, in contrast, are mandatory. Banks with sufficient capital can, in turn, issue new debt or stock to replace lost cash inflows and buy time until any asset problems are corrected. Thus the greater is a bank's equity capital, the greater is the magnitude of assets that can default before the firm is technically insolvent and the lower is bank risk.

Bank capital provides ready access to financial markets. Adequate bank capital minimizes operating problems by providing ready access to financial markets. As long as a bank's capital exceeds the regulatory minimums, it can stay open and has the potential to generate earnings to cover losses and expand. FDICIA demonstrates that banks with the greatest capital-to-risk asset ratios will have the greatest opportunities to operate without restraint and to enter new businesses. Capital enables the bank to borrow from traditional sources at reasonable rates. As such, depositors will not remove their funds and asset losses will be minimized. Any losses that arise can be charged against current earnings or, ultimately, against equity.

Research on the link between bank capital and the risk of failure suggests mixed conclusions.[15] Some analysts attribute failures to bad management and argue that well-managed banks should be allowed to operate with low capital-to-asset ratios. In these studies, banks with low capital-to-asset ratios do not exhibit any greater tendency toward insolvency, compared to banks with higher capital ratios. Other researchers attribute failures to liquidity problems and generally ignore capital. When depositors withdraw their funds, a bank must either liquidate assets from its portfolio or replace the deposit outflows with new borrowings. Forced asset sales can be accomplished only through lowering asset prices. These losses, in turn, would be charged against equity, bringing the bank closer to insolvency. Most banks therefore rely on substitute debt sources. If, however, the volume of required financing is large, the bank must pay an interest premium, which reduces current earnings and depresses potential equity.

Uncertainty regarding the link between capital and liquidity problems and bank failure reflects a misunderstanding of accounting versus economic value. What is important is the market value of bank capital, not its accounting value. As long as the market value is positive, banks can issue debt to offset liquidity problems. This is true regardless of whether accounting capital is positive or negative. If the market value of capital were negative, no private lender would extend credit. Failures, then, are tied directly to market values, not accounting values.

Regulatory interference confuses the true purpose of capital. When regulators guarantee bank debt or create artificial capital, they improve liquidity. The intent is to postpone problems until the firms are self-sufficient. Capital, as such, is meaningless to the firm's continued operation. Capital serves the same purpose as federal guarantees when regulatory assistance is not openly provided.

Capital constrains growth and reduces risk. By limiting the amount of new assets that a bank can acquire through debt financing, capital constrains growth. As indicated in Exhibit 13.9, regulators impose equity capital requirements as a fraction of aggregate bank assets. If banks choose to expand loans or acquire other assets, they must support the growth with

---

[15]Wall (1985) summarizes the conclusions of several studies suggesting both that capital is and is not linked directly to bank failures.

additional equity financing. Because new equity is expensive, expected asset returns must be high to justify the financing. This restriction is extremely important because many bank failures in the 1980s were linked to speculative asset growth financed by brokered deposits. Rigid capital requirements reduce the likelihood that banks will expand beyond their ability to manage their assets successfully and thus save to reduce risk.

HOW MUCH CAPITAL IS ADEQUATE?

The issue of bank capital adequacy has long pitted regulators against bank management. Regulators, concerned primarily with the safety of banks, the viability of the insurance fund, and stability of financial markets, prefer more capital. This reduces the likelihood of failure and increases bank liquidity. Bankers, on the other hand, generally prefer to operate with less capital. As indicated in Chapter 3, the smaller is a bank's equity base, the greater is its financial leverage and equity multiplier. High leverage converts a normal return on assets into a high return on equity (ROE). Exhibit 13.10 illustrates this point. Suppose that the manufacturing firm and commercial bank each earn 1 percent on assets during the year. The firms' equity multipliers (ratio of total assets to stockholders' equity) equal 2.5 and 12.5, respectively. This difference in leverage produces a 2.5 percent ROE for the manufacturer that equals only one-fifth of the 12.5 percent ROE for the bank. Alternatively, the manufacturer must generate an ROA equal to five times that for the bank, 5 percent in this example, to produce the same ROE. Leverage thus improves profitability when earnings are positive.

Whether a specific bank's capital is adequate depends on how much risk the bank assumes. Banks with low-quality assets, limited access to liquid funds, severe mismatches in asset and liability maturities and durations, or high operational risk should have more capital. Low-risk firms should be allowed to increase financial leverage.

The regulatory agencies periodically assess specific bank risks through on-site examinations. A thorough review includes an evaluation of the bank's asset quality—particularly the probability of defaults on interest and principal payments in the loan portfolio—loan review policies, interest rate risk profile, liquidity profile, cash management and internal audit procedures, and management quality. The FDIC rates banks according to the Uniform Financial Institutions Rating System, which encompasses six general categories of performance, labeled CAMELS: C = capital adequacy, A = asset quality, M = management quality, E = earnings, L = liquidity, S = sensitivity to market risk. The FDIC numerically rates every bank on each factor, ranging from the highest quality (1) to the lowest quality (5). It also assigns a composite rating for the bank's entire operation. A composite ranking of 1 or 2 indicates a fundamentally sound bank, while a ranking of 3, 4, or 5 signifies a problem bank with some near-term potential for failure.

WEAKNESSES OF THE RISK-BASED CAPITAL STANDARDS

There are three fundamental weaknesses of the risk-based capital requirements. First, as indicated earlier, the formal standards do not account for any risks other than credit risk, except for market risk at large banks with extensive trading operations. Certainly a bank that assumes extraordinary amounts of interest rate risk in volatile rate environments or high liquidity risk with a heavy reliance on Eurodollar or other purchased liabilities, has an abnormal chance of failing. Nevertheless, the bank's formal capital requirement is determined by its asset composition. Regulators can, of course, identify risk takers and raise required capital above the minimums, but this system is somewhat subjective and would most likely happen after problems became apparent. Furthermore, large banks subject to market risk capital requirements using a value-at-risk system report the results of their own model to the regulators. This means that regulators generally accept the model and risk assessment rather than doing their own independent evaluation. The new operational risk standards, scheduled to be implemented by 2005, are designed to directly address this weakness.

A second weakness is that the book value of capital is not the most meaningful measure of soundness. Among other problems, it ignores changes in the market value of assets, the value of unrealized gains or losses on held-to-maturity bank investments, the value of a bank charter, and the value of federal deposit insurance. Trading account securities must be marked-to-market and unrealized gains and losses reported on the income statement, but other bank assets and liabilities are generally listed at book value with the possible exception of bank loans. The contra-asset account, loan loss allowance, is a crude measure of anticipated default losses but does not generally take into account the change in value of the loans from changes in interest rates. In practice, book values can be manipulated through accounting ploys and often overstate the firm's true market value. Ideally, regulators would obtain and use the market value of stockholders' equity accounting for the market value of assets, liabilities, and off-balance sheet factors in monitoring a bank's risk exposure.

Third, by the end of 2001, almost 93 percent of commercial banks and over 90 percent of S&Ls were considered to be well capitalized. This means, for the most part, that the risk-based capital requirements are not "binding" for almost all banks. Hence, once a bank achieves the status of "well capitalized," there are really few risk-based incentives for the bank to control risk.

A related criticism is that many banks have actually seen their capital requirements decrease under the risk-based standards. In fact, a bank with extremely low-risk assets could conceivably get by with very little capital. To see this, remember that a bank with only cash assets and short-term U.S. Treasury securities, which are zero-risk weight assets, is subject only to the minimum leverage capital ratio requirement introduced earlier (3 percent). In fact, banks that bump up against the regulatory capital minimums today find that this leverage capital ratio is the only binding one.

THE EFFECT OF CAPITAL REQUIREMENTS ON BANK OPERATING POLICIES

Regulatory efforts to increase capital impose significant restrictions on bank operating policies. Many large banks with access to national markets can issue common stock, preferred stock, or subordinated capital notes to support continued growth and are relatively unaffected by minimum capital ratios. Smaller banks, however, do not have the same opportunities. They lack a national reputation, and investors generally shy away from purchasing their securities. These banks often rely instead on internally generated capital and find their activities constrained by a deficiency in retained earnings.

LIMITING ASSET GROWTH

Minimum capital requirements restrict a bank's ability to grow. Additions to assets mandate additions to capital for a bank to continue to meet minimum capital-to-asset ratios imposed by regulators. Each bank must limit its asset growth to some percentage of retained earnings plus new external capital.

Consider the $100 million bank in Exhibit 13.11 that just meets the minimum 8 percent total capital requirement. Initially, the bank has $8 million in capital, of which $4 million is undivided profits and $4 million is other capital. Various effects of planned asset growth are shown in the following columns of data, which represent projections of balance sheet and

■ **EXHIBIT 13.11**

MAINTAINING CAPITAL RATIOS WITH ASSET GROWTH: APPLICATION
OF EQUATION 13.1 AND EQUATION 13.2

Ratio	Initial Position	Case 1 Initial 8% Asset Growth	Case 2 12% Growth: ↑ROA	Case 3 12% Growth: ↓Dividend	Case 4 12% Growth: ↑External Capital
Asset growth rate (percent)		8.00%	12.00%	12.00%	12.00%
Asset size (millions of $)	100.00	108.00	112.00	112.00	112.00
ROA (percent)*		0.99%	1.43%	0.99%	0.99%
Dividend payout rate (percent)		40.00%	40.00%	13.42%	40.00%
Undivided profits (millions of $)	4.00	4.64	4.96	4.96	4.665
Total capital less undivided profits (millions of $)	4.00	4.00	4.00	4.00	4.295
Total capital/total assets (percent)	8.00%	8.00%	8.00%	8.00%	8.00%

Application of Equation 13.2

Case 1: 8% asset growth, dividend payout = 40%, and capital ratio = 8%.
 What is ROA?

$$0.08 = \frac{ROA(1 - 0.40) + 0}{0.08 - ROA(1 - 0.40)}$$

Solve for ROA = 0.99%

Case 2: 12% asset growth, dividend payout = 40%, and capital ratio = 8%.
 What is the required ROA to support 12% asset growth?

$$0.12 = \frac{ROA(1 - 0.40) + 0}{0.08 - ROA(1 - 0.40)}$$

Solve for ROA = 1.43%

Case 3: ROA = 0.99%, 12% asset growth, and capital ratio = 8%.
 What is the required dividend payout ratio (DR) to support asset growth?

$$0.12 = \frac{0.0099(1 - DR) + 0}{0.08 - 0.0099(1 - DR)}$$

Solve for DR = 13.42%

Case 4: ROA = 0.99%, 12% asset growth, capital ratio = 8%, and dividend payout = 40%.
 What is the required increase in external capital to support 12% asset growth?

$$0.12 = \frac{0.0099(1 - 0.40) + \Delta EC/TA_1}{0.08 - 0.0099(1 - 0.40)}$$

Solve for $\Delta EC/TA$ = 0.29%
 ΔEC = $294,720

*ROA = Return on Assets

NOTE: Equations 13.1 and 13.2 appear on the following page.

income statement data for the upcoming year. The bank's initial plan, designated as Case 1, calls for 8 percent asset growth with a projected 0.99 percent ROA and 40 percent dividend payout rate. In this scenario, the bank would have $108 million in assets and $641,520 in retained earnings for the year. The 8 percent target capital ratio would be just met.

Suppose that profitable credit opportunities are available to generate 12 percent asset growth within acceptable risk limits. The last three columns of data identify three distinct strategies to grow and still meet minimum capital requirements. One option (Case 2) is for the bank to generate a higher ROA. This bank would need $960,000 in additional retained earnings to support the $112 million in assets:

$undivided profits = total assets × ROA × (1 − dividend payout rate)

$960,000 = $112,000,000 × 0.0143 × (1 − 0.40)

Because competition prevents banks from raising yield spreads on high quality loans, they can achieve higher returns only by acquiring riskier assets or generating greater fee income from services. This sample bank would have to increase its ROA by 0.44 basis points to 1.43 percent if it did not change its dividend policy or obtain additional capital externally. If banks substitute riskier loans for lower yielding and less risky assets, the benefit from increased profits may be offset by future loan losses or higher capital requirements.

A second option is for the bank to increase retained earnings by decreasing dividends (Case 3). In this scenario, the bank must lower its 40 percent payment rate to 13.42 percent with the same 0.99 percent ROA, to leave capital ratios unchanged. This option is often unattractive because any unanticipated dividend reduction encourages shareholders to sell stock, which lowers share prices immediately. It would then be extremely difficult and costly to issue stock anytime in the near future. The final option (Case 4) is to finance part of the asset growth with new capital, such as new common stock or perpetual preferred stock. Here the growth in retained earnings would total $665,280, so $294,720 in new external capital would be needed. Such equity is considerably more expensive than debt if the bank actually has access to the stock market.

In practice, a bank would likely pursue some combination of these strategies, or may simply choose not to grow. If the bank in this example decides not to alter its initial policies, asset growth is restricted to 12.5 (100/8) times the addition to retained earnings. In other words, each dollar of retained profits can support $12.50 in new assets.

The relationship for internally generated capital can be summarized by the following constraints.[16]

Let: **TA** = total assets

   EQ = equity capital

   ROA = return on assets

   DR = dividend payout rate

   EC = new external capital

and the subscripts refer to the beginning of the period (1) or the end of the period (2). Capital constraints require that the asset growth rate equal the rate of growth in equity capital:

$$\Delta TA/TA_1 = \Delta EQ/EQ_1 \tag{13.1}$$

Recall that new capital comes from two sources: internal or retained earnings and external or new stock issues. Equation 13.1 can be restated as providing the following sustainable growth rate in assets:

$$\Delta TA/TA_1 = (EQ_2 - EQ_1)/EQ_1$$

$$= \frac{EQ_1 + ROA(1 - DR) \times TA_2 + \Delta EC - EQ_1}{EQ_1}$$

$$= \frac{ROA(1 - DR) + \Delta EC}{[EQ_2 - ROA(1 - DR) \times TA_2]/TA_2}$$

$$\Delta TA/TA_1 = \frac{ROA(1 - DR) + \Delta EC}{EQ_2/TA_2 - ROA(1 - DR)} \tag{13.2}$$

---

[16]See the discussion by Bernon (1978). A simple approximation to Equation 13.2 is $\Delta TA/TA_1 = (ROA[1 - DR])/(TA_2/EQ_2)$, or the rate of asset growth equals the product of ROA, the earnings retention rate, and the leverage ratio.

The numerator equals ROA times the earnings retention rate plus any additions to equity from external sources.

Equation 13.2 demonstrates the effect of minimum equity capital ratios on asset growth, earnings requirements, dividend payout rates, and new stock issues. For example, a bank that does not plan on issuing new stock and targets an 8 percent capital ratio, a 1.2 percent ROA, and a 35 percent dividend payout rate, can increase assets by over 10.8 percent. Hence, banks without access to the capital markets can essentially grow only at the rate of growth in equity from retained earnings. If, on the other hand, the bank also obtains new external capital equal to 0.3 percent of the original assets ($300,000), asset growth can again equal 12 percent, with a 0.99 percent ROA, an 8 percent equity-to-asset ratio, and a 40 percent dividend payout rate. Equation 13.2 is applied at the bottom of Exhibit 13.10 using the data for each case.

CHANGING THE CAPITAL MIX

Banks that choose to grow faster than the rate allowed with internally generated capital alone must raise additional capital externally. Here, large banks operate with a competitive advantage over smaller banks. In particular, large banks can obtain capital nationally through public offerings of securities. Their name recognition is high and investors willingly purchase the instruments of quality organizations. Small banks, in contrast, can generally only issue capital securities to a limited number of investors, such as existing shareholders, bank customers, and upstream correspondent banks. Limits to growth are far more rigid. One solution often pursued by small bank shareholders is to sell their stock to a holding company with greater access to funding sources.

Many large banks responded to the increased capital requirements and FDICIA by issuing new capital securities. The most popular forms were long-term debt requiring conversion to common stock and adjustable-rate, perpetual preferred stock. With the strong stock market for bank stocks during the 1992 to 1999 period, many large banks issued large volumes of common stock under shelf registration opportunities as well. Several banks also entered into sale and leaseback arrangements with bank real estate properties to generate one-time infusions of capital. This arrangement typically costs relatively little and can be easily implemented to acquire large amounts of capital. The aggregate effect has been to gradually increase the proportion of total capital represented by common and preferred stock and their hybrids.

CHANGING ASSET COMPOSITION

Banks may respond to risk-based capital requirements by changing their asset composition. Managers that are risk averse may shift assets from high-risk categories such as commercial loans with a 100 percent risk weight to lower risk categories. The natural consequence is that while required risk-based capital declines, potential profitability declines as well. The fear among regulators, however, is that other banks facing higher capital requirements may actually shift assets into higher risk categories or off-balance sheet commitments in pursuit of extraordinary returns. This would increase the overall risk profile of the banking industry in contrast to what the regulators desire.

PRICING POLICIES

One of the advantages of risk-based capital requirements is that they explicitly recognize that some investments are riskier than others are. The riskiest investments require the greatest equity capital support. Banks have been forced to reprice assets to reflect these mandatory equity allocations. For example, if a bank has to hold capital in support of a loan commitment, it should raise the fee it charges to compensate for the greater cost of providing that service compared to the time when capital was not required. In fact, all off-balance sheet items should now be priced higher. Remember that equity is expensive. Thus, a bank should also raise loan rates on it highest risk assets that require the greatest capital relative to other asset yields.

SHRINKING THE BANK

Historically, banks tried to circumvent capital requirements by moving assets off the books. Interest rate and product deregulation encouraged banks to transfer risks off the balance sheet by creating contingent liabilities that produce fee income but do not show up as assets in financial reports. Because off-balance sheet activity increases risk, bank regulators included off-balance sheet items in the base when calculating risk weighted assets. In today's banking environment, the greater a bank's off-balance sheet commitments the greater are its capital requirements. In actuality, regulators examine a bank's off-balance sheet exposure and may selectively request additional capital above the risk-based standards when the exposure is deemed to be great.

Alternatively, banks can meet the new standards by shrinking in size. As such, existing capital represents a higher fraction of the smaller asset base. The problem is that a shrinking bank has difficulty generating earnings growth and thus paying shareholders a reasonable risk-adjusted return. Not surprisingly, banks with capital problems often look to merge with stronger banks and may only survive as part of another firm.

CHARACTERISTICS OF EXTERNAL CAPITAL SOURCES

Internally generated capital can support asset growth at a rate implied by Equation 13.2. Banks that choose to expand more rapidly must obtain additional capital from external sources, a capability determined by asset size. Large banks tap the capital markets regularly, but small banks must pay a stiff premium to obtain capital, if it is available at all. While there are many different types of capital sources, they can be grouped into one of four categories: subordinated debt, common stock, preferred stock, and leases. Each carries advantages and disadvantages.

SUBORDINATED DEBT

For the past 25 years, banks have been able to use subordinated debt to meet capital requirements. This debt constitutes capital because of its relatively long maturities and funding permanence. It does not qualify as Tier 1 or core capital because it eventually matures and must be replenished, unlike common equity. It also imposes an interest expense burden on the bank when earnings are low. Subordinated debt must possess several specific features before the regulators accept it as capital. First, debt holders' claims must be subordinated to depositors' claims. If the bank fails, insured depositors are paid first, followed by uninsured depositors, then subordinated debt holders. Second, only debt with an original weighted average maturity of at least seven years qualifies as capital.

Subordinated debt offers several advantages to banks. Most important, interest payments are tax deductible, so the cost of financing is below that for equity sources. Because they are debt instruments, shareholders do not reduce their proportionate ownership interest, and earnings are not immediately diluted. Furthermore, this type of debt generates additional profits for shareholders as long as earnings before interest and taxes exceed interest payments. Thus, shareholders may receive higher dividends, and greater retained earnings may increase the capital base. Fixed-rate debt accentuates this profit potential.

Subordinated debt also has shortcomings. Interest and principal payments are mandatory and, if missed, constitute default. In addition, many issues require sinking funds that increase liquidity pressures as banks allocate funds to repay principal. Finally, from the regulators' perspective, debt is worse than equity because it has fixed maturities and banks cannot charge losses against it. Subordinated debt and equity, however, protect depositors and the FDIC equally.

Some subordinated debt pays variable rates that fluctuate with selected interest rate indexes. These securities subsequently trade close to par, as the yield changes when market rates change. Banks can pay initial rates below those for comparable fixed-rate debt because they are assuming the interest rate risk. Many bank holding companies also issue mandatory convertible debt in the form of either equity commitment notes or mandatory convertible notes. Both types require that banks issue common stock, perpetual preferred stock, or other primary capital securities to redeem the convertible debt. The average convertible debt issue carries floating rates, matures in 12 years, and contains an option for the debtor to redeem the security anytime after four years.

COMMON STOCK

Common stock is preferred by regulators as a source of external capital. It has no fixed maturity and thus represents a permanent source of funds. Dividend payments are also discretionary, so that common stock does not require fixed charges against earnings. Losses can be charged against equity, not debt, so common stock better protects the FDIC.

Common stock is not as attractive from the bank's perspective due to its high cost. Because dividends are not tax deductible, they must be paid out of after-tax earnings. They are also variable in the sense that shareholders expect per share dividend rates to rise with increases in bank earnings. Transactions costs on new issues exceed comparable costs on debt, and shareholders are sensitive to earnings dilution and possible loss of control in ownership. Most firms wait until share prices are high and earnings performance is strong before selling stock. A positive feature of the Tax Reform Act of 1986 is that it makes common stock relatively more attractive to a firm than before. By lowering corporate marginal income tax rates, the act increased the cost of tax-deductible interest on debt relative to the nondeductible dividend cost of common stock.

Issuing common stock is frequently not a viable alternative for a bank that needs capital. If the current share price is far below book value, new issues dilute the ownership interests of existing shareholders. Stocks of the largest banks are traded in national markets with substantial liquidity. Bank managers attempt to increase share prices through strong earnings, consistent dividend policy, and adequate disclosure of performance to security analysts. Even with these efforts, however, stock prices often fall with adverse economic conditions or market disfavor with the industry. At these times, other capital sources are less expensive.[17] When stock prices are low, many large banks issue debt that is convertible into common stock. Investors accept lower interest payments in lieu of the option to convert the security into common stock. The conversion price is normally set 20 to 25 percent above the share price at time of issue so that eventual conversions are not as costly.

Small bank stocks are traded over the counter, with far fewer annual transactions. Still, a market for new issues does exist within local communities. Banks can often sell new shares to existing stockholders or current customers. Share prices are less volatile but sensitive to deviations in current versus historical earnings.

---

[17]Many large holding company banks raise new equity by issuing securities via private placements outside the United States. They can lower underwriting fees by as much as 25 percent and shorten the length of time to place an issue.

PREFERRED STOCK

Preferred stock is a form of equity in which investors' claims are senior to those of common stockholders. As with common stock, preferred stock pays nondeductible dividends out of after-tax dollars. One significant difference is that corporate investors in preferred stock pay taxes on only 20 percent of dividends. For this reason, institutional investors dominate the market. New issues are effectively restricted to large, well-known banking organizations that are familiar to institutional investors while smaller banks are excluded.

Since 1982, preferred stock has been an attractive source of primary capital for large banks. Most issues take the form of adjustable-rate perpetual stock. The dividend rate changes quarterly according to a Treasury yield formula. Investors earn a return equal to some spread above or below the highest of the 3-month Treasury bill rate and the 10- or 20-year constant maturity Treasury rates. The size of the spread and whether it is above or below the base yield reflects the perceived quality of the issuing bank.

Investors are attracted to adjustable-rate preferred stock because they earn a yield that reflects the highest point on the Treasury yield curve under all market conditions. This removes guesswork as to whether short-term yields will move more or less than long-term yields and whether they will all move in the same direction. Unlike fixed-rate issues, these securities trade close to par and thus are more liquid. They effectively represent 3-month securities and have been sold to individuals as well as corporations.

Preferred stock has the same disadvantages as common stock, but there are instances when it is more attractive. First, if a bank's common stock is priced below book value and has a low price-to-earnings ratio, new equity issues dilute earnings. This earnings dilution is less with perpetual preferred stock than with common stock, so that the cost of common shares is relatively higher. Second, aggregate dividend payments on preferred stock will be less than dividends on common stock over time for any bank that regularly increases common stock dividends. Cash flow requirements on perpetual preferred shares will also be lower because no sinking fund allocations are required to repay principal.

TRUST PREFERRED STOCK

A recent innovation in capital financing is the introduction of **trust preferred** stock, which is a hybrid form of equity capital at banks. It is attractive because it effectively pays dividends that are tax deductible. To issue the securities, a bank or bank holding company establishes a trust company. The trust company sells preferred stock to investors and loans the proceeds of the issue to the bank. Interest on the loan equals dividends paid on the preferred stock. This loan interest is tax deductible such that the bank effectively gets to deduct dividend payments of the preferred stock. As a bonus, the preferred stock counts as Tier 1 capital under the RBC guidelines. In addition, the bank can miss a dividend payment and not be forced into bankruptcy. The net effect is that trust preferred stock costs less than common equity, but has the same value for regulatory purposes. Not surprisingly, most large banks, as well as a few community banks, have issued trust preferred stock.

LEASING ARRANGEMENTS

Many banks entered into sale and leaseback arrangements as a source of immediate capital. Most transactions involve selling bank-owned headquarters and other real estate and simultaneously leasing it back from the buyer. The terms of the lease can be structured to allow the bank to maintain complete control of the property, as if the title never changes hands, yet receive large amounts of cash at low cost. Lease rates run 1 to 2 percent below rates on subordinated debt. A sale-leaseback transaction effectively converts the appreciated value of real estate listed on the bank's books at cost to cash. The price appreciation is taxed at normal income tax rates, with most of the gain flowing to the bottom line as increased earnings. The transaction can be effected quickly when a buyer is located and avoids the high placement costs of stocks and bonds.[18]

CAPITAL PLANNING

Capital planning is part of the overall asset and liability management process. Bank management makes decisions regarding the amount of risk assumed in operations and potential returns. The amount and type of capital required is determined simultaneously with the expected composition of assets and liabilities and forecasts of income and expenses. The greater is assumed risk and asset growth, the greater is required capital.

Capital planning begins with management generating pro forma balance sheets and income statements for the next several years. The bank projects the dollar funding available from alternative deposit and nondeposit sources and the likely asset composition, given the bank's product mix and expertise. Assuming various interest rate scenarios and projections of noninterest income and expense, management forecasts earnings. Asset growth in excess of that financed with new debt or internally generated capital must be financed with external capital. Once a bank recognizes that it needs to obtain additional capital externally, it evaluates the costs and benefits of each source.

The planning process can be summarized in three steps:

1. Generate pro forma balance sheets and income statements for the bank.
2. Select a dividend payout.
3. Analyze the costs and benefits of alternative sources of external capital.

The first step provides an estimate of how much capital is needed to finance assets. Total equity capital required equals the residual between expected assets and expected debt. The amount of qualifying primary and secondary capital must be at least equal the regulatory minimums. If management chooses to shrink the bank by liquidating assets, it may find that total capital required declines. Typically, additional equity capital is needed. Step 2 identifies how much capital will be generated internally and what amount of external capital is necessary. Dividend payments reduce the amount of retained earnings and add pressure for external capital funding. The third step involves evaluating alternatives. Management should project bank needs over several years so that it can develop a long-term plan. To be flexible, it should not rely extensively on any single source of capital in the short run, so that it can retain that option in future years. If, for example, a bank is leveraged to the maximum, it may be forced to issue new stock at a time when its share price is low. Chapter 12 introduces quantitative measures of the costs of different capital components.

APPLICATIONS

Bank capital planning used to be a simple process. Management projected asset growth and retained earnings to show that capital ratios would be strong. Today, capital plans are typically an outgrowth of sophisticated asset and liability management planning models. They are carefully scrutinized by regulators to verify those essential assumptions regarding asset

---

[18]If the sale conforms to FASB statement #13, the operating lease does not require capitalization and the transaction further provides off-balance sheet financing.

· EXHIBIT 13.12

CAPITAL PLANNING: FORECAST PERFORMANCE MEASURES
FOR A BANK WITH DEFICIENT CAPITAL RATIOS

	2001	2002	2003	2004	2005
Historical 10% Growth in Assets: $250,000 in Dividends					
Total assets	$ 80.00	$ 88.00	$ 96.80	$ 106.48	$ 117.13
Net interest margin	4.40%	4.40%	4.50%	4.60%	4.70%
ROA	0.45%	0.45%	0.60%	0.65%	0.75%
Total capital	$ 5.60	$ 5.75	$ 6.08	$ 6.52	$ 7.15
Capital ratio	7.00%	6.53%	6.28%	6.12%	6.10%
Shrink the Bank, reduce assets by $1 million a year: $250,000 in Dividends					
Total assets	$ 80.00	$ 79.00	$ 78.00	$ 77.00	$ 76.00
Net interest margin	4.40%	4.40%	4.50%	4.60%	4.70%
ROA	0.45%	0.45%	0.60%	0.65%	0.75%
Total capital	$ 5.60	$ 5.71	$ 5.92	$ 6.17	$ 6.49
Capital ratio	7.00%	7.22%	7.59%	8.02%	8.54%
Slow Growth, $2 million increase in assets each year: No Dividends					
Total assets	$ 80.00	$ 82.00	$ 84.00	$ 86.00	$ 88.00
Net interest margin	4.40%	4.40%	4.50%	4.60%	4.70%
ROA	0.45%	0.45%	0.60%	0.65%	0.75%
Total capital	$ 5.60	$ 5.97	$ 6.47	$ 7.03	$ 7.69
Capital ratio	7.00%	7.28%	7.71%	8.18%	8.74%
Slow Growth, $2 million increase in assets each year:					
$250,000 in Dividends, $800,000 External Capital Injection in 2004					
Total assets	$ 80.00	$ 82.00	$ 84.00	$ 86.00	$ 88.00
Net interest margin	4.40%	4.40%	4.50%	4.60%	4.70%
ROA	0.45%	0.45%	0.60%	0.65%	0.75%
Total capital	$ 5.60	$ 5.72	$ 5.97	$ 7.08	$ 7.49
Capital ratio	7.00%	6.97%	7.11%	8.23%	8.51%

NOTE: Figures are in millions of dollars.

quality, loan losses, and net interest margins are realistic. The output itself is the same pro forma balance sheet and income statement data presented in traditional performance reports. (See Chapter 3.)

Capital planning can be illustrated using the reporting framework of Exhibit 13.11. Consider a bank that has exhibited a deteriorating profit trend. Classified assets and loan-loss provisions are rising, and earnings prospects are relatively bleak, given the economic environment. Federal regulators who recently examined the bank indicated that the bank should increase its primary capital-to-asset ratio to 8.5 percent within four years from its current 7 percent.

The planning process consists of generating pro forma balance sheets and income statements over the next four years. Because regulators closely examine historical earnings and are keenly aware of asset problems, the initial pro forma statements should incorporate recent earnings trends slowly, moving the bank toward peer bank averages for key ratios. Often bankers conclude that their bank will meet capital guidelines easily because they overstate earnings. Regulators quickly point out the deficiencies and recommend substantial adjustments.

Suppose that the hypothetical bank reported the summary performance measures listed in Exhibit 13.12 for 2001. Because of asset quality problems, the $80 million bank reported an ROA of just 0.45 percent, less than one-half its average over the past five years. The current capital ratio is 7 percent, or 1.5 percent less than the regulatory target. During each of the past five years, the bank paid $250,000 in common dividends.

The first part of the exhibit simply extrapolates historical asset growth of 10 percent through 2005, assuming that earnings slowly rise to where ROA equals 0.75 percent in the fourth year. Under these conditions and the assumed continued dividend payout, the bank's total capital ratio would decrease to 6.1 percent by 2005. This is clearly unacceptable under the regulatory directive.

The following three parts identify different strategies to meet the required 8.5 percent capital ratio by 2005 and present summary performance measures. The second section examines the impact of shrinking the bank. The quickest way to increase a capital ratio is to reduce the denominator, or shrink the bank's asset base. Shrinkage can normally be achieved by reducing the bank's loan exposure and letting high cost purchased liabilities run off. In this example, the bank gradually reduces its assets by $1 million per year until 2005, when the capital ratio reaches 8.54 percent. The capital ratio increases continuously because the denominator (total assets) is falling while the numerator (capital) is rising with the growth in retained earnings.

A bank can also increase its capital by cutting its dividend payments. The third section projects the bank's capital position assuming slow asset growth at $2 million annually while eliminating the $250,000 dividend payment. Retained earnings increase more than total assets producing a capital ratio of 8.74 percent in 2005, which exceeds the target.

The final alternative proposes that the bank grow slowly and maintain its dividend, but issue $800,000 in common stock to meet its capital requirement. In this case, the bank would wait until its earnings position had improved sufficiently, 2004 in this pro forma, before issuing external capital. Again, the projected capital ratio just exceeds the regulatory target by 2005.

In practice, a bank's asset and liability management committee will consider numerous other alternatives by varying assumptions until it determines the best plan. What is best depends on a comparison of the costs of each alternative. Eliminating dividends, for example, reduces stock prices and makes it extremely difficult and costly to raise external capital later. If the bank plans to add capital externally, it must carefully measure placement costs and their subsequent impact on share prices. For instance, if a bank issues subordinated debt, it must estimate the direct transactions costs and set aside a portion of future cash flows to service the debt. The same would apply to common stock issues and dividend payments.

FEDERAL DEPOSIT INSURANCE

The Banking Act of 1933 established the FDIC and authorized federal insurance for bank deposits up to $2,500. The Federal Savings and Loan Insurance Corporation (FSLIC) was established in 1934 to replicate federal assistance for savings and loan associations.[19] Both insurance funds were funded via premiums paid by member banks. Fund expenses included operating costs and payouts mandated when banks failed and regulators paid insured depositors.

The Banking Act of 1933 (in which FDIC insurance was established) followed three years in which more than 5,000 banks failed and investors lost confidence in the country's financial system. There were approximately 4,000 failures in 1933 alone. The initial objectives of deposit insurance were to prevent liquidity crises caused by large-scale deposit withdrawals and to protect depositors of modest means against a bank failure. With insurance, depositors' funds were safe, even if the bank failed.

---

[19]The National Credit Union Share Insurance Fund (NCUSIF) insures credit unions.

• EXHIBIT 13.13

FDIC RESERVE RATIOS, FUND BALANCE , AND INSURED DEPOSITS

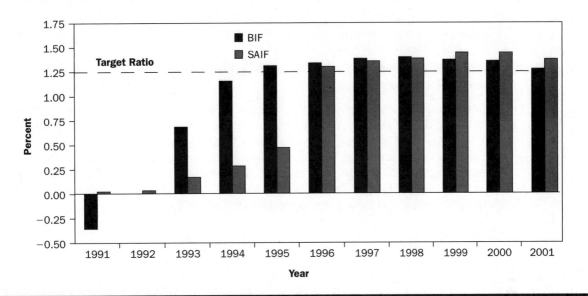

SOURCE: FDIC Quarterly Banking Profile, http://www.fdic.gov/.

NOTE: Insurance fund balance as a percent of total issued deposits.

Federal deposit insurance facilitated stability in the U.S. financial system throughout its early history and worked well until the early 1980s. There were few depositor runs on federally insured banks and bank failures were negligible. In fact, during the period from 1950 to 1980, fewer than seven banks failed, on average, each year. After 1980, however, bank failures increase once again and there were 280 bank failures in 1988. By the late 1980s, in fact, the FSLIC was no longer solvent and the FDIC's insurance fund was depleted by 1990. So many savings and loans failed or were taken over by solvent firms with federal assistance in the 1980s that the FSLIC fund went bankrupt. Data on the FDIC insurance fund in Exhibit 13.13 reveals similar problems for the FDIC fund in the early 1990s. By 1998, however, the number of bank failures had fallen substantially. In fact, there was only one bank failure in 1997. The number of bank failures increased slightly during the late 1990s and there were six failures in 2000 and only 3 failed banks in 2001.

The large number of failures in the late 1980s and early 1990s put pressure on the FDIC by slowly depleting the reserve fund. As indicated in Chapter 2, the Financial Institution Reform, Recovery and Enforcement Act of 1989 (FIRREA) authorized the issuance of bonds to finance the bailout of the FSLIC and provide resources to close problem thrifts. The act also created two new insurance funds, the Savings Association Insurance Fund (SAIF) and the Bank Insurance Fund (BIF), to replace the old funds with both controlled by the FDIC. It further created the Resolution Trust Corporation to handle failed thrifts.

To make the insurance funds solvent, federal regulators increased bank deposit insurance premiums to $0.23 per $100 of insured deposits to keep pace with losses from closing failed institutions. During 1991 and 1992, the bank fund ran a deficit and had to borrow from the Treasury. FDICIA authorized risk-based deposit insurance premiums ranging from $0.23 to $0.27 per $100 depending on a bank's capital position. By 1993, the reduction in failures and increased premiums allowed the FDIC to pay off the debt and put the fund in the black.

The Deposit Insurance Funds Act of 1996 (DIFA) was enacted on September 30, 1996, and had three main components:

- Included both a one-time assessment on SAIF deposits to capitalize the SAIF fund to the mandated 1.25 percent reserve ratio (insurance reserves to insured deposits)
- Required the repayment of the Financing Corporation (FICO) bonds be shared by both banks and thrifts
- Mandated the ultimate elimination of the BIF and SAIF funds by merging them into a new Deposit Insurance Fund[20]

Deposit insurance assessment rates (insurance premiums) for some SAIF members fell to zero for the first time January 1, 1997. It is anticipated, under current favorable conditions, that FDIC investment earnings will be sufficient to cover each fund's expenses for the near future, so that most banks and savings and loans will pay no deposit insurance premiums. Assessment rates for 2002 were still zero for well-capitalized banks, which constituted about 93 percent of banks. The FDIC's risk-based premium system, however, still requires institutions not in the most favorable category to pay assessments.

RISK-BASED DEPOSIT INSURANCE

FDIC insurance premiums are assessed based on a Risk-Based Deposit Insurance system—required by the FDIC Improvement Act of 1991 and adopted in September 1992. Deposit insurance assessment rates for both BIF and SAIF are reviewed semiannually by the FDIC to ensure that premiums appropriately reflect the risks posed to the insurance funds and that fund reserve ratios are maintained at or above the target Designated Reserve Ratio (DRR) of 1.25 percent of insured deposits. Deposit insurance premiums are assessed as basis points per $100 of insured deposits.[21]

Annual assessment rates for insured depository institutions are assigned based on an assessment of risk using a risk classification system. Each institution's assessment risk classification is composed of two parts: a capital adequacy group and supervisory subgroup.

Each institution is first assigned to one of three capital groups — well capitalized, adequately capitalized, and undercapitalized (the three lower capital categories) — using the minimum capital ratios in Exhibit 13.9.

Within each capital group, each institution will be assigned to one of three subgroups based on supervisory evaluations provided by the institution's primary federal regulator. The three supervisory subgroups are:

Subgroup A: Financially sound institutions with only a few minor weaknesses and generally corresponds to the primary federal regulator's composite rating of "1" or "2."

Subgroup B: Institutions that demonstrate weaknesses that, if not corrected, could result in significant deterioration of the institution and increased risk of loss to the BIF or SAIF. This subgroup assignment generally corresponds to the primary federal regulator's composite rating of "3."

---

[20]The BIF and SAIF were supposed to merge effective January 1, 1999, subject to the condition that no insured savings association existed on this date. The merger was postponed indefinitely because insured savings associations still exist and the thrift charter has considerable value beyond a bank charter.

[21]Recall that a basis point (bp) is 1/100 of one percent. An FDIC assessment of 20 basis points amount to 20 cents per 100 dollars of insured deposits, or 0.2 percent.

Subgroup C: Institutions that pose a substantial probability of loss to the BIF or the SAIF unless effective corrective action is taken. This subgroup assignment generally corresponds to the primary federal regulator's composite rating of "4" or "5."[22]

Based on this system, there are nine different risk categories. The current assessment rate schedule for BIF-insured and SAIF-insured institutions is as follows:

| | Supervisory Subgroups | | |
Capital Group	A	B	C
1. Well capitalized	0 bp	3 bp	17 bp
2. Adequately capitalized	3 bp	10 bp	24 bp
3. Undercapitalized	10 bp	24 bp	27 bp

Approximately 93 percent of all BIF-insured institutions are currently listed in the lowest risk category and pay no assessment. The BIF reserve ratio (fund balance to estimated insured deposits) was 1.27 percent in December 2001, while the SAIF reserve ratio stood at 1.37 percent. Based upon the latest available data and projections from the FDIC, the existing rate schedule is expected to maintain the fund reserve ratios at or above the target DRR through year-end 2002.

PROBLEMS WITH DEPOSIT INSURANCE

Government backed deposit insurance provides for stability of the financial system by reducing or preventing banking panics and protecting the less sophisticated depositor — but this come at a price. First, deposit insurance acts similarly to bank capital and is a substitute for some functions of bank capital. In noninsured industries, investors or depositors look to the company's capital as a safety net in the event of failure. All else equal, lower capital levels mean that the company must pay a risk premium to attract funds or they will find it very difficult if not impossible to borrow money. In banking, a large portion of borrowed funds come from insured depositors who do not look to the bank's capital position in the event of default — rather to the FDIC insurance fund. A large number of depositors, therefore, do not require a risk premium to be paid by the bank. Normal market discipline in which higher risk requires the bank to pay a risk premium does not apply to all providers of funds.

In addition to insured depositors, many large banks are considered to be **"too-big-to-fail"** (TBTF). As such, any creditor of a large bank would receive de facto 100 percent insurance coverage regardless of the size or type of liability.[23] This means that depositors at large banks most likely know that they have de facto 100 percent coverage and would not be as concerned about the bank's capital cushion. Hence, the larger the coverage and scope of deposit insurance, the less capital the market would demand the bank hold. See Contemporary Issues: Regulatory Policy Toward Large Bank Failures.

Second, deposit insurance has historically ignored the riskiness of a bank's operations, which represents the critical factor that leads to failure. Thus, two banks with equal amounts of domestic deposits paid the same insurance premium, even though one invested heavily in

---

[22]Details of the FDIC assessment procedures can be found on the FDIC Web site at http://www.fdic.gov, (http://www.fdic.gov/deposit/insurance/).

[23]The Federal Deposit Insurance Corp. Improvement Act (FDICIA) addressed the issue of TBTF but allows for full protection when regulators determine that the bank's failure could significantly impair the rest of the industry and the overall economy.

REGULATORY POLICY TOWARD LARGE BANK FAILURES

In July 1988, bank regulators declared First RepublicBank Corp. of Texas insolvent and turned over management of its subsidiary banks to NCNB. In contrast to prior failures of large bank holding companies, the terms of closing wiped out the claims of all stockholders and left bondholders to fight with other creditors for the remains of the holding company. Regulators used a bridge bank to handle the closing, which fostered numerous lawsuits claiming that the rights of investors in First RepublicBank were violated. Consider the following sequence of events.

- March 17, 1988: The FDIC loaned $1 billion to First RepublicBank Corp. to help meet deposit outflows. This was a 6-month loan secured by stock in each of First RepublicBank's subsidiary banks.
- July 29, 1988: The FDIC announced that it would not renew the 6-month loan when it came due in September. As prearranged, the Federal Reserve advised First RepublicBank that it would refuse to lend any additional funds via the discount window and the bank would have to repay the $3.5 billion it owed. Because First RepublicBank could not pay, the Comptroller of the

Currency declared that the bank had formally failed. The FDIC then called its $1 billion loan. When First Republic-Bank Corp. did not pay, the FDIC charged the amount of each subsidiary bank's guarantee against its capital, which then made each subsidiary bank insolvent.
- July 29, 1988: The FDIC created a bridge bank owned jointly with NCNB that took over and managed the failed subsidiary banks. NCNB paid approximately $200 million for 20 percent ownership with the right to buy the remaining 80 percent over the next five years. NCNB retained the right to put problem loans back to the FDIC so that its risk was lowered, and received enough federal tax benefits to pay for the entire bridge bank in a few years.
- October 15, 1988: In a bankruptcy filing, First RepublicBank Corp. indicated that it had $3.5 billion in liabilities and just $300,000 in assets.

In March 1989, bank regulators failed several subsidiary banks of MCorp., another large Texas bank holding company. Although the events followed the pattern with First RepublicBank Corp., MCorp.'s managers essentially held the regulators hostage. Prior to the failures,

MCorp.'s problems were well known. Regulators had strongly encouraged the holding company to downstream $400 million in funds to its subsidiary banks to shore up their capital. MCorp.'s management realized that once it made the transfer the regulators would fail the firm and it would lose any leverage they had in negotiating their own failure resolution plan. The holding company thus did not transfer the $400 million. Eventually, the regulators called loans to the holding company's lead bank and charged the losses when it could not pay off MCorp.'s subsidiaries based on their federal funds loans to the lead bank and other interbank deposits. The 20 subsidiaries with losses in excess of their capital subsequently failed and were taken over by the FDIC. Again the FDIC created a bridge bank that was soon sold to Bank One.

Bondholders and other creditors sued claiming that the regulators discriminated against the bank's creditors and effectively manufactured the failures of solvent subsidiary banks. As part of FIRREA, Congress in turn instituted a system of cross guarantees where subsidiaries of bank holding companies must effectively guarantee the performance of all other subsidiaries.

---

risky loans and had no uninsured deposits while the other owned only U.S. government securities and just 50 percent of its deposits were fully insured. This created a **moral hazard** problem whereby bank managers had an incentive to increase risk. For example, suppose that a bank had a large portfolio of problem assets that was generating little revenue. Managers could use deposit insurance to access funds via brokered CDs in $100,000 blocks. Buyers of the CDs were not concerned about the quality of the underlying bank because their funds were fully insured, hence they did not impose market discipline in the form of higher rates to be paid for additional risk. The bank's managers were able to use these funds to speculate on risky projects, in essence, betting the bank. If the risky investments succeeded, managers could use the returns to pay the depositors and offset the lack of revenue from the problem assets. In fact, if the bank obtained enough deposits, it could make enough loans to swamp the problem assets. If the risky investments went bankrupt, the bank would fail but the deposit insurance fund would have to pay creditors.[24]

Third, deposit insurance funds were always viewed as providing basic insurance coverage. Yet, there were three fundamental problems with the pricing of deposit insurance. First, premium levels were not sufficient to cover potential payouts. The FDIC and FSLIC were initially expected to establish reserves amounting to 5 percent of covered deposits funded by premiums. Unfortunately, actual reserves never exceeded two percent of insured deposits as Congress kept increasing coverage while insurance premiums remained constant. For example, the standard insurance premium was a flat one-twelfth of 1 percent of insured deposits. Yet, deposit insurance coverage slowly increased from $15,000 per account per institution in 1966 to $20,000 in 1969, $40,000 in 1974, and $100,000 in 1980. Even then, customers could obtain multiple account coverage at any single institution by carefully structuring ownership of each account. The high rate of failures during the 1980s and the insurance funds demonstrate that premiums were inadequate.

The final historical problem with deposit insurance is that premiums were not assessed against all of a bank's insured liabilities. There were many liabilities that the federal government effectively guaranteed or where the holders had a prior claim on bank assets, that should have required insurance premiums. For example, insured deposits consisted only of domestic deposits while foreign deposits were exempt. Why? If a large bank failure would severely disrupt the smooth functioning of financial markets, regulators would allow de facto 100 percent insurance coverage regardless of the size or type of liability. This too-big-to-fail doctrine toward large banks means that large banks would have coverage on 100 percent of their deposits but pay for the same coverage as if they only had $100,000 coverage as smaller banks do. This means that regulators were much more willing to fail smaller banks and force uninsured depositors and other creditors to take losses. If a bank's liabilities were covered by federal insurance, the firm should have paid insurance premiums. The argument for not charging premiums against foreign deposits is that U.S. banks would be less competitive with foreign bank competitors.

WEAKNESS OF THE CURRENT RISK-BASED DEPOSIT INSURANCE SYSTEM

Risk-based deposit insurance has addressed some of these issues but not all of them. First, the risk-based deposit system is based on capital and risk. Hence, banks that hold higher capital, everything else equal, pay lower premiums. Lower risk banks will pay lower premiums. Alternatively, approximately 93 percent of all BIF-insured institutions are currently listed in the lowest risk category and pay no assessment. Consequently, 93 percent of all banks pay a flat-rate assessment that was zero in 2001. The fund's growth is determined largely by investment income.

The second issue is that of too-big-to-fail. The FDIC must follow the "least cost" alternative in the resolution of a failed bank. As such, the FDIC must consider all alternatives and choose the one that is the lowest cost to the insurance fund and this has definitely lead to a reduction of coverage of uninsured depositors. Exhibit 13.14 demonstrates that in the late 1980s and early 1990s, the FDIC provided protection to more than 80 percent of the uninsured assets at failed commercial banks. In contrast, many fewer uninsured assets have been covered since 1991.

FDICIA, however, still allows for the coverage of uninsured deposits, as indicated by the solid bars in Exhibit 13.14, which represent the proportion of failed banks where uninsured

---

[24]This represents a classic principal/agent problem in finance. The intent of bank regulation and periodic examination is to limit bank risk-taking and reduce the incentives of deposit insurance.

PERCENTAGE OF FAILED COMMERCIAL BANKS BY UNINSURED
DEPOSITOR TREATMENT, 1986–1996

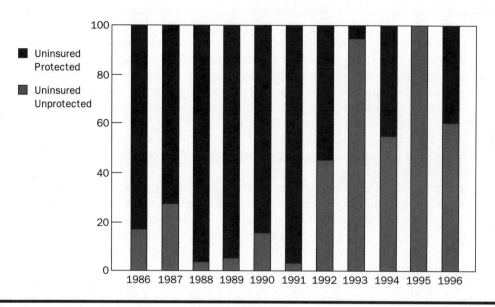

NOTE: Percentage of banks by assets.

SOURCE: "Fixing FDICIA," 1997 *Annual Report*, Federal Reserve Bank of Minneapolis, March 1998, Ron J. Feldman and Arthur J. Rolnic. Available on the Internet at http://woodrow.mpls.frb.fed/pubs/ar/ar1997.html.

deposits were paid in full at failure. FDICIA provides for full coverage if the Secretary of the Treasury determines that the least cost alternative would have serious adverse effects on financial stability or economic conditions and that 100 percent coverage would avoid or reduce these effects. The decrease requires approval of two-thirds of the Board of Governors of the Federal Reserve System and two-thirds of the directors of the FDIC.

PROPOSALS TO IMPROVE DEPOSIT INSURANCE

When the number of failures was small, bank regulators were not concerned about deposit insurance. The large number of thrift and bank failures of the 1980s and incredible cost of bailing out the insurance funds focused considerable attention on how regulators handle failures and how to restructure the insurance system. Although FDICIA has addressed some of the problems with deposit insurance, the issue of too-big-to-fail, effective risk-based insurance premiums, and inadequate insurance fund remain to one degree or another.[25]

In response to these criticisms, many proposals have been offered to protect the viability of the insurance funds and ensure the safety and soundness of the banking system. FDICIA provides for early intervention, which allows regulators to close a problem institution once its capital falls below a minimum fraction of risk assets. Early closings force managers to

[25]An excellent summary of proposals to fix the FDICIA is "Fixing FDICIA," *1997 Annual Report*, Federal Reserve Bank of Minneapolis, March 1998, Ron J. Feldman and Arthur J. Rolnic. Available on the Internet at http://woodrow.mpls.frb.fed/pubs/ar/ar1997.html. The FDIC also publishes a Deposit Insurance Initiative on their Web site: http://www.fdic.gov.

monitor risks more closely and raise new capital when they approach the minimum. FDICIA also provides for higher insurance premiums for banks with riskier operations relative to their capital base. FDICIA also addressed too-big-to-fail, but the federal government still provides for coverage of some of the nation's largest banks. With all the merger activity, more and more banks will likely be considered too-big-to-fail—hence the scope of coverage is increasing.

Other prominent proposals include:

1. Limit immediate payouts to all large depositors in failed institutions to some fraction on the dollar, regardless of whether the payout or purchase and assumption option is used.

2. Coinsurance of Deposits. Establish a maximum loss rate such as 10 or 20 percent. Private insurance companies have used this method very effectively to address the moral hazard problem of insurance.

3. Limit insurance coverage to $100,000 per depositor or lower, and not per insured account.

4. Narrow bank. Only insure deposits that are used to support government guaranteed assets or risk-free assets. All other liabilities would need to be insured privately, if at all.

5. Implementing market-based risk adjusted insurance assessments using the risk premiums implicit in rates paid on uninsured deposits.

6. Privatize deposit insurance. Premiums would be based on a bank's overall risk profile as determined by private insurance companies.

The motivation behind each proposal is obvious. Each proposal would presumably impose market discipline on institutional risk-taking. Any limits on deposit insurance coverage or payouts at failure would force creditors to closely monitor their investments and move their balances from high-risk banks because they share in losses. Brokers currently funnel deposits in $100,000 increments throughout the country to the highest bidders. Banks and savings and loans can obtain these fully insured funds at subsidized rates to finance whatever speculative ventures they choose. Regulators now restrict undercapitalized banks from soliciting brokered deposits. The last two proposals suggest that the insurance system should be put on a sound financial basis by charging market-determined premiums.

The primary weakness of these proposals is that they require bank customers to perform a detailed analysis of each bank's riskiness. Particularly hurt would be smaller institutions where customers typically do not evaluate performance measures but rely on management. Deposits would likely flow to large firms that analysts rate as low risk. Risk-adjusted premiums would also raise borrowing costs for risky banks that charge higher insurance costs to depositors, making them less competitive and indirectly reducing the attractiveness of risky investments. In practice, there is no easy method to measure bank risk accurately. Current failure prediction models are only partially successful in identifying problem banks.[26] What is needed is the consistent application of regulatory review with the tools already available to the regulators.

The lack of a consistent plan to handle continued bank failures has forced regulators to control banking risk by other means and to consider other options. One alternative is to increase regulatory capital requirements. If banks are forced to operate with more equity capital, their financial risk will decrease and there will be fewer failed banks.

---

[26]David Cates, president of Cates Consulting Analysts, says that his firm uses no less than 70 ratios when analyzing bank performance (Cates, 1984). The FDIC's proposed risk assessment model is based on three ratios. Such a system will likely produce highly distorted risk classifications.

SUMMARY

This chapter addresses eight basic issues: What are the features of the risk-based capital standards? What constitutes bank capital? How did FDICIA use capital standards to control bank activities? What function does capital serve? How much capital is adequate? What effect do regulatory capital requirements have on bank operating policies? What considerations are important in capital planning? Finally, how are FDIC deposit insurance and bank capital related?

Bank capital fulfills three basic functions. It serves as a cushion against loan losses and helps protect the interests of depositors and the FDIC. It provides access to financial markets so that management can borrow to offset liquidity problems. It also limits growth by forcing banks to add capital in support of asset expansion. Each purpose serves to reduce bank risk directly, and ultimately to protect the viability of the deposit insurance funds.

Because of these functions, federal regulators consider bank capital to be much broader than accounting capital. Regulatory capital therefore includes certain debt and loss reserve components. Effective in 1992, the FDIC, OCC, and Federal Reserve System changed bank capital standards to conform uniformly to risk-based capital requirements. Each bank must hold common equity as a minimum 4 percent of risk-weighted assets and total capital cannot fall below 8 percent of risk-weighted assets. For the first time, regulators tied capital asset requirements to the perceived default risk of bank assets and off-balance sheet commitments. Procedures to incorporate excessive market risk were put in place by 1995 and market risk capital requirements took effect in January 1998 for those banks with large trading accounts. Banks with special problems, however, must increase capital according to specific regulatory directives.

The passage of FDICIA in 1991 further categorized banks as being well capitalized, adequately capitalized, or undercapitalized, and imposed operating restrictions on undercapitalized institutions. This act, and the specific minimum capital requirements, forced banks to slow growth, limit their loan exposure, change their asset composition, and find new methods of generating profits and obtaining external capital during the early 1990s. Capital levels have increased dramatically in the late 1990s, due to good profitability, such that risk-based capital requirements have not been binding. A final impact is that banks now actively prepare and analyze capital plans as part of their annual risk-return performance review.

QUESTIONS

1. What are the advantages and disadvantages of using financial leverage? Answer from the banker's view and then from a bank regulator's view.

2. Provide the general outline of existing risk-based capital requirements. Is there a difference between default risk, interest rate risk, and liquidity risk?

3. Explain how capital reduces banking risks. Discuss the importance of cash flows and economic value rather than accounting value.

4. Many analysts argue that risk-based capital requirements should force banks to raise loan rates. Explain this by assuming that a bank's management sets loan rates to earn a 16 percent return on equity. How does the allocation of equity to a loan affect loan pricing?

5. Suppose that a bank wants to grow during the next year but does not want to issue any new external capital. Its current financial plan projects a return on assets of 1.25 percent, a dividend payout rate of 35 percent, and an equity-to-asset ratio of 8 percent. Calculate the allowable growth in the bank's assets supported by these projections.

What growth rate could be supported if the bank issued additional common stock equal to 1 percent of bank assets, with the same earnings projections?

6. Many regulators would like to see bank capital requirements raised. Consider a proposal to increase the minimum Tier 1 and total capital ratios to 6 percent and 12 percent, respectively. What impact would this have on bank risk? Would small banks and large banks have equal opportunity in meeting these requirements? What impact would this have on banking industry consolidation?

7. Regulators put great pressure on banks to reduce their common dividend payments when asset problems appear. Discuss the costs and benefits of cutting dividends.

8. Two competing commercial banks situated in the same community have comparable asset portfolios, but one operates with a total capital ratio of 8 percent, while the other operates with a ratio of 10 percent. Compare the opportunities and risk profiles of the two banks.

9. Explain why increased regulatory capital requirements lead to a greater consolidation of banking firms via mergers and acquisitions.

10. Risk-based capital requirements may induce bank managers to change their asset composition. Explain why. Determine how a shift from any of the following should affect a bank's required capital. How will each shift affect the bank's profit potential?
   a. from consumer loans to 1–4 family mortgages
   b. from U.S. agency securities to construction loans
   c. from FNMA-sponsored mortgage-backed securities to municipal revenue bonds

11. A bank has decided it must raise external capital. Discuss the advantages and disadvantages of each of the following choices:
   a. subordinated debt at 7.7 percent
   b. preferred stock at a 10 percent dividend yield
   c. common stock

12. What is the leverage capital ratio and why do regulators specify a minimum for it?

13. FDICIA imposes increasingly severe operating restrictions on undercapitalized banks (those in zones 3, 4, and 5). Explain why these restrictions are appropriate. Describe how managers should respond to these restrictions if they manage an undercapitalized bank.

14. Although FDICIA calls for risk-based insurance premiums, why do many argue that we still have a flat deposit insurance system?

PROBLEMS

I. FIRST STUDENT BANK
First Student Bank (FSB) has the following balance sheet:

Assets		Liabilities and Equity	
Cash	$100	Transactions accounts	$700
Treasury bills (30 days)	$190	CDs	$220
Treasury bonds (5 years)	$30	Subordinated debt	$7
Repos	$10	Preferred stock	$5
Student tuition loans	$500	Retained earnings	$48
Student home mortgages	$100	Common stock	$5
Building and furniture	$110	Surplus	$15
Loan loss reserves	$(40)		
Total	$1,000	Total	$1,000

The bank is only two years old and is desperately trying to break into the local market for student loans. Consequently, it has followed the policy of guaranteeing tuition loans for three additional years to every student who promptly paid off his or her first-year loan. This policy has been a success, and the bank has signed agreements guaranteeing $800 in loans. The bank has also tried to encourage the building of 1–4 family homes near campus. The bank is willing to lend money on these properties and to commit to repurchasing the homes when the students graduate. The repurchase price is settled at the time the mortgage is written, such that the whole package is expected to be profitable for the bank. Currently, the bank has obligated itself to spend $75 to repurchase homes.

1. This is a student-owned-and-run bank and does not operate in international markets. Does it need to comply with the risk-based capital rules?

2. How many dollars of common equity capital does this bank have? How many dollars of Tier 1 capital does it have?

3. How many dollars of total capital does this bank have?

4. Categorize the bank's assets by risk category. How many dollars of Category 1 assets, Category 2 assets, and so on, does the bank have?

5. How many dollars of contingencies does this bank have (after applying the appropriate conversion factor)?

6. How many dollars of risk-weighted assets does FSB own?

7. Does FSB have adequate Tier 1 capital? Adequate total capital?

II. ONE-YEAR BANK GROWTH

Consider a bank with $500 million in assets and $30 million in total capital. Its minimum total capital-to-asset ratio must equal 6 percent. At the beginning of the year, senior management and the board of directors project that the bank will likely earn 0.86 percent on assets, will pay a 30 percent dividend, and will not obtain any external capital. In this environment, how large can the bank grow by the end of the year?

1. Assume that the bank would like to grow its assets by 15 percent during the year. If the dividend rate is 30 percent and no external capital is obtained, what must the bank's ROA equal?

2. Assume that the bank wants to grow assets by 15 percent with an ROA of 0.85 percent, and will not obtain external capital. What dividend payout rate will support 15 percent growth? What are the costs and benefits of changing dividends in this direction?

3. What increase in external capital is necessary to support 15 percent asset growth with ROA equal to 0.85 percent and a dividend payout rate of 30 percent?

14

LIQUIDITY PLANNING AND MANAGING CASH ASSETS

Have you ever written a check against an account balance that you didn't have, then scrambled to deposit funds before the check cleared? Have you ever charged certain expenses on your credit card, then been shocked at how much you owed when the bill came due? Consider the shock at Bank of New York when its deposit balance at the Federal Reserve went negative. On November 20, 1985, officers at the Bank of New York, a $16 billion firm, determined that the bank was deficient in its required reserve holdings by $23.6 billion. The deficiency resulted from a computer malfunction that did not permit the bank to collect payments from other banks for transferring government securities. Although checks drawn on it cleared, it received few of the deposits it expected. The Federal Reserve Bank of New York subsequently stepped in and loaned the bank $23.6 billion overnight (with interest) to cover the deficiency. This sum represented the largest single discount window loan in history.

During the early 1980s, Home State Savings Bank in Cincinnati, Ohio, dealt closely with E.S.M. Government Securities Inc. in the market for repurchase agreements. Home State, a $1.4 billion thrift institution, bought and sold securities through E.S.M., speculating on short-run interest rate movements. On March 4, 1985, the Securities and Exchange Commission (SEC) closed E.S.M., citing huge losses on speculative securities trades. That same week, Home State's depositors withdrew approximately $90 million out of concern that E.S.M.'s problems would harm the thrift. On March 10, the regulators closed Home State.

Home State was one of 72 thrifts that were privately insured by the Ohio Deposit Guarantee Fund and not the Federal Savings and Loan Insurance Corp. or the Federal Deposit Insurance Corp. At that time, the insurance fund had only $136 million in reserves. The fund allocated $45 million to Home State before the thrift closed, which helped create the impression that private deposit insurance and the fund itself were insufficient to cover customer deposits. Before long, depositors were lining up at the 71 other privately insured thrifts in Ohio to withdraw their deposits. Two weeks after E.S.M. failed, Ohio's governor invoked emergency powers to close the remaining 71 thrifts temporarily until the viability of the private insurance fund and consumer confidence could be restored.

THE RELATIONSHIP BETWEEN CASH AND LIQUIDITY REQUIREMENTS

The amount of cash that management chooses to hold is heavily influenced by the bank's liquidity requirements. The potential size and volatility of cash requirements, in turn, affect the liquidity position of the bank. Transactions that reduce cash holdings normally force a bank to replenish cash assets by issuing new debt or selling assets. Transactions that increase cash holdings provide new investable funds. From the opposite perspective, banks with ready access to borrowed funds can enter into more transactions because they can borrow quickly and at low cost to meet cash requirements.

Liquidity needs arise from net deposit outflows as balances held with Federal Reserve Banks or correspondent banks decline. Most withdrawals are predictable because they are either contractually based or follow well-defined patterns. For example, banks that purchase securities typically pay for them with immediately available funds. Maturing investments similarly are credited to deposit balances held at the Federal Reserve. Transactions accounts normally exhibit weekly or monthly patterns that follow the payroll and billing activities of large commercial customers.

Still, some outflows are totally unexpected. Often, management does not know whether customers will reinvest maturing CDs and keep the funds with the bank or withdraw them. Management also cannot predict when loan customers will borrow against open credit lines. This uncertainty increases the risk that a bank may not have adequate sources of funds available to meet payments requirements. This risk, in turn, forces management to structure its portfolio to access liquid funds easily, which lowers potential profits.

Exhibit 14.1 portrays the effects of customer deposit withdrawals and loan usage on a bank's deposit balances at the Federal Reserve. The first part indicates that a maturing CD is not rolled over directly and immediately reduces a bank's reserves. Here the CD holder directs the Federal Reserve to transfer the funds by wire to another institution, which directly lowers CDs outstanding as well as deposit balances held at the Federal Reserve. Loan usage produces the same result. In the second part, a loan customer borrows $250,000 against an outstanding credit line by requesting a wire transfer to cover the purchase of some good or service. The bank authorizes the payment, lowering its deposit balance at the Federal Reserve by $250,000 while simultaneously booking the loan. In the last part, the bank first allocates $500,000 in loan proceeds to the borrower's account. The bank's deposit at the Federal Reserve falls when the customer writes a check against the proceeds and the check clears after being deposited in another bank. Each transaction reduces immediately available funds, creating the possibility that the bank is reserves deficient and, perhaps, short of balances needed to cover future deposit outflows.

This chapter examines the issues of liquidity planning and cash management. The first part examines the nature of cash assets and the rationale for holding each type of cash asset. It looks at legal reserve requirements, the source and impact of float, and the pricing of correspondent balances. This discussion provides a background for the following sections that outline the link between liquidity, banking risks, and returns. The second part of the chapter describes the strengths and weaknesses of traditional measures of liquidity. The final section applies bank liquidity planning to reserves management and estimates of longer-term funds requirements. The Appendix to this chapter presents a case study of Continental Illinois National Bank & Trust's liquidity crisis and the regulatory response.

• EXHIBIT 14.1

EFFECT OF MATURING CERTIFICATES OF DEPOSIT AND LOAN USE ON A
BANK'S DEPOSIT BALANCES AT THE FEDERAL RESERVE

Maturing Certificate of Deposit Not Rolled Over
Commercial Bank

ΔASSETS	ΔLIABILITIES	
Demand deposit at Federal Reserve −$100,000	Certificate of deposit −$100,000	CD not rolled over; CD holder directs the Federal Reserve to wire funds to another institution.

Loan Customer Borrows against a Credit Line
Commercial Bank

ΔASSETS	ΔLIABILITIES	
Commercial loans +$250,000 Demand deposit at Federal Reserve −$250,000		Customer borrows against outstanding credit line. Wire transfer to cover purchase of goods or services.

Borrowing against a New Term Loan
Commercial Bank

ΔASSETS	ΔLIABILITIES	
Commercial loan +$500,000 Demand deposit at Federal Reserve −$500,000	Demand deposit +$500,000 Demand deposit −$500,000	Bank grants loan and deposits proceeds in customer's account. Customer spends full amount of loan proceeds by writing check.

CASH VERSUS LIQUID ASSETS

Banks own four types of cash assets: vault cash, demand deposit balances at Federal Reserve Banks, demand deposit balances at private financial institutions, and cash items in the process of collection (CIPC). Cash assets do not earn any interest, so the entire allocation of funds represents a substantial opportunity cost for banks. Banks, therefore, want to minimize the amount of cash assets held and hold only those required by law or for operational needs.

Why do banks hold cash assets? Banks hold cash assets to satisfy four objectives. First, banks supply coin and currency to meet customers' regular transactions needs. The amount of cash in a bank's vault corresponds to customer cash deposits and the demand for cash withdrawals. Both exhibit seasonal fluctuations, rising prior to holidays such as Christmas and falling immediately thereafter. Second, regulatory agencies mandate legal reserve requirements that can only be met by holding qualifying cash assets. Third, banks serve as a clearinghouse for the nation's check payment system. Each bank must hold sufficient balances at Federal Reserve Banks or other financial institutions so that checks written by its depositors will clear when presented for payment. Finally, banks use cash balances to purchase services from correspondent banks.

A **liquid asset** is one that can be easily and quickly converted into cash with minimum loss. Contrary to popular notion, however, "cash assets" do not generally satisfy a bank's liquidity needs. To understand this, recall that a bank will hold the minimum amount of cash assets required. If the bank experiences an unexpected drain on vault cash, the bank must immediately replace the cash or it would have less vault cash than required for legal or operational needs. Cash assets are liquid assets only to the extent that a bank holds more than the minimum required. It is interesting to note that while cash is the most liquid asset, it is not a viable long-term source of liquidity for the bank.

If cash assets are not really a source of liquidity for a bank, what assets are? Liquid assets are generally considered to be cash and due from banks in excess of requirements, federal funds sold and reverse repurchase agreements, short-term Treasury and agency obligations, high-quality short-term corporate and municipal securities, and some government-guaranteed loans that can be readily sold. These assets are liquid because they can be quickly converted into immediately available funds with limited price depreciation.

For a financial institution that regularly borrows in the financial markets, liquidity takes on the added dimension of the ability to borrow funds at minimum cost or even issue stock. This view of liquidity explicitly recognizes that firms can acquire liquidity in three distinct ways: by selling assets, new borrowings, and new stock issues. Bank liquidity, therefore, more generally refers to a bank's capacity to acquire immediately available funds at a reasonable price. It encompasses the potential sale of liquid assets, borrowing in the form of federal funds purchases and Federal Home Loan Bank advances, new issues of CDs, Eurodollars, subordinated debt, and new stock offerings. These liabilities similarly represent liquid sources of funds if a bank can easily borrow at rates comparable to those paid by peers. Common and preferred stock are liquid only if there is a ready market for these instruments with little delay and cost associated with new funds.

Liquidity planning is an important facet of asset and liability management. Although public confidence is essential for preventing deposit runs, there are steps managers can take to reduce the likelihood of unanticipated deposit outflows and gain access to additional sources of cash assets. Managers must be able to estimate liquidity needs accurately and structure their bank's portfolio to meet the anticipated needs.

OBJECTIVES OF CASH MANAGEMENT

Banks prefer to hold as few cash assets as possible without creating transactions problems. Because cash assets do not generate interest income, excess holdings have a high opportunity cost represented by the interest that could be earned on an alternative investment. As the level of interest rates rises, so does the opportunity cost and the incentive to economize on cash assets. There are, however, significant risks in holding too little cash. Imagine depositors' concerns if they were told that their bank did not have enough currency on hand for withdrawals. A bank must similarly keep enough deposit balances at other banks and the Federal Reserve to cover deposit outflows or it will be forced to replenish its balances under duress. Owning too few cash assets potentially creates liquidity problems and increases borrowing costs. Continued deficiencies are attributed to poor management, which ultimately leads to close regulatory scrutiny and deteriorating business relationships.

Fortunately, vault cash needs are fairly predictable. Local businesses make regular cash deposits and bank customers generally withdraw cash at predictable intervals near weekends, holidays, and when they receive their paychecks. Vault cash shortages can be avoided by requesting a currency shipment from the closest Federal Reserve Bank or correspondent bank.

It is much more difficult to accurately predict the timing and magnitude of deposit inflows and outflows that influence deposits held at Federal Reserve Banks and other financial institutions. Deposit inflows raise legal reserve requirements but also increase actual reserve assets and correspondent deposits. Deposit outflows lower reserve requirements and reduce actual deposit holdings. Because deposit flows are determined by customer credit and payment transactions, banks cannot directly control the timing of clearings and float. When projecting cash needs, management is thus continually aiming at a moving target.

When banks realize unexpected deposit shortages, they must have access to balances at Federal Reserve or correspondent banks via either new borrowings or the sale of noncash assets. Unfortunately, borrowing costs typically increase and funding sources disappear when a bank experiences credit problems or operating difficulties. Similarly, assets that can be easily sold near par value typically earn lower yields. A bank's cash needs are thus closely related to its liquidity requirements and sources. The fundamental management goal underlying cash and liquidity management is to accurately forecast cash needs and arrange for readily available sources of cash at minimal cost.

RESERVE BALANCES AT THE FEDERAL RESERVE BANK

Banks hold deposits at the Federal Reserve in part because the Federal Reserve imposes legal reserve requirements and deposit balances qualify as legal reserves. Banks also hold deposits to help process deposit inflows and outflows caused by check clearings, maturing time deposits and securities, wire transfers, and other transactions. Deposit flows are the link between a bank's cash position and its liquidity requirements.

Consider the T-account at the top of Exhibit 14.1, which documents the impact of a $100,000 maturing CD (not rolled over) that clears through the bank's reserve account at the Federal Reserve. The outflow may represent a daily net clearing drain, where the value of checks written on deposits at the sample bank exceeds the value of checks drawn on other banks which are deposited at the sample bank and presented to the Federal Reserve for payment. The offsetting adjustment to the deposit loss is a $100,000 decrease in reserve balances at the Federal Reserve. In this simplified example, required reserves do not decline because reserves are not required against CD balances. A liquidity problem arises, however, because actual deposit balances held at the Federal Reserve decrease by $100,000 million. If the bank was holding the minimum reserve required (no excess reserves), the bank would be deficient $100,000 in required reserves. This represents its immediate liquidity needs. It is interesting to note that even though the required reserve balance at the Federal Reserve satisfied the bank's clearing requirements, these funds would have to be replaced; i.e., required reserves do not provide the bank a longer-term liquidity source. If, however, the bank had excess reserve balances at the Fed of $100,000, the deposit outflow would have reduced the bank's reserves at the Fed by $100,000 but no immediate liquidity need arises. All such deposit outflows directly reduce a bank's deposit balances either at the Federal Reserve or correspondent banks and raise its liquidity needs. A deposit inflow has the opposite impact.

REQUIRED RESERVES AND MONETARY POLICY

The purpose of required reserves is to enable the Federal Reserve to control the nation's money supply. By requiring banks and other depository institutions to hold deposit balances in support of transactions accounts, the Federal Reserve hopes to control credit availability and thereby influence general economic conditions.

There are basically three distinct monetary policy tools: open market operations, changes in the discount rate, and changes in the required reserve ratio. **Open market operations** are conducted by the Federal Reserve Bank of New York under the direction of the Federal Open Market Committee (FOMC). The sale or purchase of U.S. government securities in the "open market" or secondary market is the Federal Reserve's most flexible means of carrying out its policy objectives. Through the purchase or sale of short-term government securities, the Fed can adjust the level of reserves in the banking system. Through open market operations, the Fed can offset or support changes in reserve requirements, changes in the discount rate, as well as seasonal or international shifts of funds and thereby influence short-term interest rates and the growth of the money supply. Fed open market purchases increase liquidity, hence reserves in the banking system, by increasing a bank's deposit balances at the Fed. Fed open market sales of securities decrease bank reserves and liquidity by lowering deposit balances at the Fed.

Banks can borrow deposit balances, or required reserves, directly from Federal Reserve Banks with the discount rate representing the interest rate that banks pay. **Changes in the discount rate** directly affect the cost of borrowing. When the Fed raises the discount rate it discourages borrowing by making it more expensive. Fed decreases in the discount rate make borrowing less expensive. Most economists argue that the Fed changes the discount rate primarily to signal future policy toward monetary ease or tightness rather than to change bank borrowing activity. Changes in the discount rate are formally announced and trumpeted among the financial press so that market participants recognize that the Fed will likely be adding liquidity or taking liquidity out of the banking system.

Changes in reserve requirements directly affect the amount of legal required reserves and thus change the amount of money a bank can lend out. For example, a required reserve ratio of 10 percent means that a bank with $100 in demand deposit liabilities outstanding must hold $10 in legal required reserves in support of the DDAs. The bank can thus lend only 90 percent of its DDAs. When the Fed increases (decreases) reserve requirements, it formally increases (decreases) the required reserve ratio which directly reduces (raises) the amount of money a bank can lend. Thus, lower reserve requirements increase bank liquidity and lending capacity while higher reserve requirements decrease bank liquidity and lending capacity.[1]

The Federal Reserve sets required reserves for member banks equal to a fraction of the dollar amount of selected bank liabilities. Assume that the legal reserve requirement equals 10 percent for demand deposits and 0 percent for all time deposits. (Actual percentage requirements are introduced in Exhibit 14.4.) A bank with $100 million in demand deposits and $500 million in time deposits will have to hold required reserves of $10 million, which is the minimum amount the bank must keep as vault cash or on deposit at the Federal Reserve. If this bank actually holds $12 million in deposits at the Fed plus vault cash, it has $2 million in excess reserves, which represents a source of liquidity. If the volume of outstanding demand deposits at the bank were to increase to $120 million, the bank's required reserves would rise to $12 million and there would be no excess reserves. In general, when deposit liabilities increase (decrease), a bank's required reserves increase (decrease). Thus, the amount of deposit balances a bank holds at the Federal Reserve will vary directly with the magnitude of reservable bank liabilities.

The use of reserve requirements as a policy tool has declined in the United States and in other industrialized countries in recent years because reserve requirement changes are no longer considered an essential tool of monetary policy. As discussed later, banks can circumvent the requirements by substituting liabilities that are not subject to the requirements for those that are. The Fed can also control the money supply and credit availability in other ways.[2] Sellon and Weiner (1998) suggest that the reduced role of reserve requirements as a monetary tool is the result of three factors: the change in Federal Reserve policy emphasizing the control of short-term interest rates; the recognition that reserve requirements are a tax on banks in the form of an interest-free loan to the Federal Reserve; which puts them at a competitive disadvantage with other financial institutions; and the active use of "sweep accounts" that have reduced required reserve balances to their lowest level in 30 years.

---

[1]Changing reserve requirement ratios has a significant announcement effect because of the dramatic impact it has on all member financial institutions. It has the additional advantage of affecting all institutions simultaneously in a predictable magnitude.

[2]At least three countries—Canada, New Zealand, and the United Kingdom—conduct monetary policy without reserve requirements. See Sellon and Weiner (1998).

GROWTH OF SWEEPS TRANSACTION DEPOSITS INTO MMDAs

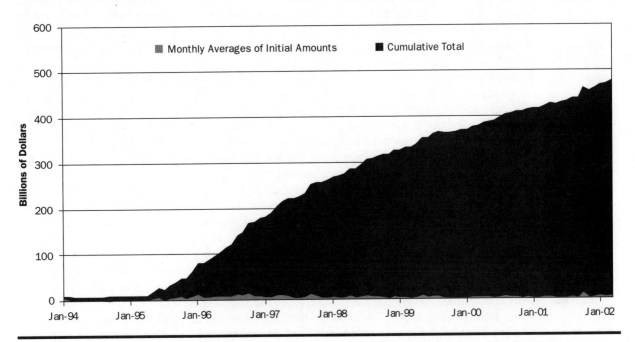

■ Monthly Averages of Initial Amounts   ■ Cumulative Total

SOURCE: Federal Reserve Board Data on OCD Sweep Account Programs, http://www.stls.frb.org/research/swdata.html.

THE IMPACT OF SWEEP ACCOUNTS ON REQUIRED RESERVE BALANCES

Under the Federal Reserve's Regulation D, checkable deposit accounts such as demand deposits, ATS, NOW, and other checkable deposit accounts have a 10 percent reserve requirement, but money market deposit accounts (MMDAs) are considered to be personal saving deposits and have a zero reserve requirement ratio.[3] In January 1994, the Federal Reserve Board permitted commercial banks to use computerized sweep programs. A sweep account is an account that enables a depository institution to shift funds from transaction accounts, which are reservable, to MMDAs or other accounts, which are not reservable. For example, a retail sweep account is an account in which the bank's computer "sweeps" excess funds into an MMDA from a demand deposit account. The bank determines the amount of excess funds. Essentially, a bank must designate only an amount of funds necessary to meet daily check clearings as the DDA balance. It could transfer any excess balances daily, thereby forcing a zero daily balance in the DDA. Although it would appear that banks are "moving" a customer's balance from one account to another, in reality the computer software actually dynamically "reclassifies" the customer's balance from a reservable account to a nonreservable account. This effectively reduces a bank's statutory required reserves while leaving the customer's account balance unchanged. Because customers are not very sensitive to the rates paid on these accounts, the bank's interest costs may not be much higher while it reduces required reserves.[4] Exhibit 14.2 demonstrates the rapid growth of retail sweep account programs at commercial banks since 1994.

---

[3]Regulation D and statutory reserve requirements are discussed in the following section. For a good discussion of sweep accounts, see Anderson, Richard G. and Rasche, Robert H., "Retail Sweep Programs and Bank Reserves, 1994–1999, *Federal Reserve Bank of St. Louis Review,* January/February 2001.

[4]The interesting question is whether banks inform each customer as to whether it is sweeping the customer's deposits into an MMDA.

There are generally two types of retail sweep programs in use today. The first is a weekend program. This account reclassifies transaction deposits as savings deposits at the close of business on Friday and back to transactions accounts on Monday. On average, this means that on Friday, Saturday, and Sunday (occasionally on a Monday holiday), or three-sevenths of the week, required reserves on these deposits are zero. Because reserve requirements are computed on the basis of a seven-day week, this would come close to cutting required reserves in half.[5] A second type of sweep account is the minimum threshold account. In these accounts, the bank's computer moves the customer's account balance to an MMDA when the dollar amount of funds exceeds some minimum and returns the funds as needed. It is interesting to note how sophisticated bank computer systems have become. Prior to the extensive use of computers in banks, these types of programs were only available to the largest and most profitable customers because of the time and effort required to calculate and move funds.

Although the number of transfers into the MMDA account is unlimited, Regulation D limits the number of withdrawals or transfers out of an MMDA to no more than six each month. If the number exceeds six, the MMDA is classified as an ATS (automatic transfer to savings) account and reserve requirements apply. The second type of sweep account, then, is limited in that the full amount of funds must be moved back into the transaction account on the sixth transfer of the month.

These retail sweep programs should not be confused with business sweep programs initiated by banks during the 1960s and 1970s. Business sweep account programs are very popular today and are also offered by nonbank financial service companies such as securities firms and mutual funds. Regulation Q (under the Banking Acts of 1933 and 1935) prohibits banks from paying explicit interest on business demand deposit accounts. A commercial sweep account sweeps excess funds from business demand deposits overnight (typically) into nondeposit, interest-earning assets such as repurchase agreements and money market mutual funds. These accounts are not bank deposit accounts and are not FDIC insured; hence they are not subject to reserve requirements.

MEETING LEGAL RESERVE REQUIREMENTS

The actual computation of legal reserve requirements is more complex than that suggested above. Reserve percentages are multiplied by outstanding deposit balances, but not all deposits are subject to reserves. Banks reduce the volume of liabilities subject to required reserves by subtracting correspondent balances, and vault cash qualifies as a reserve asset. Most importantly, required reserves can be met over a two-week period, so a bank does not have to hold a specific amount of cash assets on each day. Beginning in July 1998, the Fed required banks to hold reserves against outstanding deposit balances from three to five weeks earlier. Banks pushed hard for this change because it dramatically reduces their error in reserve planning. On the negative side, this lagged reserve accounting system reduces the Fed's ability to control the money supply and may increase the volatility of interest rates. This section analyzes current reserve requirements in detail and provides a comprehensive example. Important terminology is introduced in Exhibit 14.3.

---

[5]Some consultants offering sweep account programs claim that a bank can reduce its effective reserve requirement to 1 percent rather than the statutory 10 percent of reservable balances. Alan Greenspan, in his July 1995 Humphrey-Hawkins testimony, cited that sweep programs had reduced other checkable deposit balances by about $12 billion and required reserves by about $1.2 billion. Because some of the reduction in required reserves occurred at smaller banks that satisfy most of their required reserves with vault cash, balances at Federal Reserve Banks decreased less. In addition, balances at the Fed might not fall as much because even though most sweep programs have been implemented by larger institutions subject to a 10 percent marginal reserve requirement, smaller institutions have started sweep programs as well and are subject to only a 3 percent requirement.

• EXHIBIT 14.3

Base computation period: The 14-day period during which a bank's outstanding liabilities determine the amount of required reserves to be held during the reserve maintenance period.

Collected balances: The dollar value of ledger balances minus float.

Correspondent bank: A bank that provides services to other financial institutions and receives payment in the form of either deposit balances or direct user fees.

Daylight overdrafts: The process of authorizing payments within a business day from deposit accounts held at the Federal Reserve or correspondent banks in excess of actual balances held.

Deferred availability credit items: The dollar amount of checks deposited at the Federal Reserve Bank for which the Federal Reserve has not yet granted credit.

Earnings credit: The assumed interest rate at which a bank can invest customer deposit balances to earn interest income.

Investable balances: The dollar value of collected balances minus required reserves.

Reserve maintenance period: The 14-day period during which a bank must hold sufficient deposit balances at the Federal Reserve to meet its legal reserve requirement.

Respondent bank: A bank that buys services from other financial institutions and pays by holding nonearning deposit balances at the correspondent bank or via direct user fees.

Transactions accounts: All deposits on which the account holder is allowed to make withdrawals by negotiable instruments and more than three monthly telephone and preauthorized funds transfers.

Federal Reserve Regulations D and M specify minimum reserve requirements for commercial banks. The regulations stipulate that each bank must hold cash reserves equal to a fraction of its base liabilities. There are three elements of required reserves: the dollar magnitude of base liabilities, the required reserve fraction, and the dollar magnitude of qualifying cash assets. Base liabilities are comprised of *net transactions accounts* in which the holder is permitted to make withdrawals by negotiable or transferable instruments, payment orders, and telephone and preauthorized transfers in excess of three per month. MMDAs are not classified as transactions accounts. The dollar amount equals the sum of the balances that are listed on the bank's books, referred to as ledger balances, minus the sum of a bank's cash items in the process of collection (CIPC) and collected balances due from private depository institutions. No reserves are required against any other liability.

A bank's qualifying reserve assets include vault cash and demand deposits due from Federal Reserve Banks. The relevant percentages, or required reserve ratios, appear in Exhibit 14.4. In 2002, each bank was required to hold zero reserves against its first $5.7 million of daily average net transactions accounts, 3 percent on the amounts between $5.7 and $41.3 million, and 10 percent on any amount over $41.3 million.[6] The Board of Governors can vary these reserve ratios within established regulatory limits. In recent years, the Board has generally lowered reserve ratios and expanded the list of liabilities not subject to reserves.

RECENT PROBLEMS WITH RESERVE REQUIREMENTS

Historically, commercial bank reserve requirements varied with the type of bank charter and each bank's geographic location. Different states stipulated reserve requirements for banks that were not members of the Federal Reserve System (state-chartered nonmembers), which

---

[6]Financial institutions that are not members of the Federal Reserve System can use pass-through balances to meet reserve requirements. Pass-through balances are deposits held at either the Federal Home Loan Bank, the National Credit Union Administration Central Liquidity Facility, or any bank that keeps balances at the Federal Reserve Bank. The exempt amount increases each year as a fraction of the increase in aggregate reservable liabilities.

· EXHIBIT 14.4

RESERVE REQUIREMENT PERCENTAGES FOR DEPOSITORY INSTITUTIONS

Type of Deposit		Percentage	Effective Date of Applicable Percentages
Net transactions accounts*			
Exempt amount[†]	$ 5.70 million	0.00	1/1/2002
Up to	$ 41.30 million	3.00	1/1/2002
Over	$ 41.30 million	10.00	1/1/2002
All other liabilities		0.00	1/1/2002

Effective 2002.

*Demand deposits are deposits that are payable on demand, or a deposit issued with an original maturity or required notice period of less than seven days, or a deposit representing funds for which the depository institution does not reserve the right to require at least seven days' written notice of an intended withdrawal. Demand deposits may be in the form of checking accounts; certified, cashier's, and officer's checks; traveler's checks and money orders; letters of credit sold for cash; certain withheld funds (taxes); time deposits that have matured; and obligations to pay, on demand or within six days. MMDAs are not transaction accounts.

[†]Exemption from reserve requirements: Each depository institution, Edge or agreement corporation, and U.S. branch or agency of a foreign bank is subject to a zero percent reserve requirement on an amount of its transaction accounts not in excess of $5.7 million. This amount increases annually by 80 percent of the increase in total reservable liabilities at all depository institutions.

SOURCE: Federal Reserve Board, in Title 12, Chapter II of the Code of Federal Regulations (12 CFR 204), Reserve Requirements of Depository Institutions, Reg. D, http://www.federalreserve.gov/Regulations/CG/regDcg.htm.

were generally less restrictive than those for members. Nonmember reserve ratios were lower, and more assets, even interest-bearing government securities, often qualified as legal reserves. Only vault cash and demand balances held at the Federal Reserve constituted reserves for member banks. Thus, nonmembers could invest more funds in earning assets than similar member banks. This discrepancy represented a substantive opportunity cost of Federal Reserve membership, which was compounded further because nonmembers had access to Federal Reserve services through correspondent bank relationships.

Not surprisingly, many member banks switched charters and withdrew their Federal Reserve memberships. This withdrawal peaked during 1977 to 1979, when the level of interest rates reached historical highs and the opportunity cost became prohibitive. Congress eliminated this problem by passing the Depository Institutions Deregulation and Monetary Control Act (DIDMCA) in 1980. DIDMCA mandated that all depository institutions offering transaction accounts be subject to uniform reserve requirements, regardless of charter. The figures in Exhibit 14.4 now apply to member and nonmember banks, savings and loans, and credit unions.

During the late 1970s, the Federal Reserve experienced problems in controlling the banking system's aggregate reserves. This trouble resulted from its reserve accounting system and monetary policy operating strategy. From 1968 through February 1984, the Federal Reserve employed **lagged reserve accounting (LRA)**, under which an individual bank held reserves against its deposit liabilities outstanding two weeks earlier. It could average its actual reserve holdings over a 7-day period (the reserve maintenance week) based on its actual liabilities outstanding during the 7-day base period two weeks prior. Each bank knew its total reserve requirement with certainty during the entire maintenance week because changes in deposit liabilities during the week did not alter reserve needs until two weeks later. A bank simply had to manage its clearing balances to avoid problems.

The Fed moved to a **contemporaneous reserve accounting (CRA)** system in 1984. During the period from 1984 until 1998, open market operations affected both the current deposit levels and required reserves coincidentally. Banks disliked this contemporaneous system because the amount of reserves that must be held is not known until the period is almost over. In July 1998, the Federal Reserve moved back to a lagged reserve account (LRA) system. Under the current LRA system, reserves are held over a 2-week period against deposit liabilities held for the 2-week period ending almost three weeks earlier. This system makes it more difficult for the Federal Reserve to control the money supply when it is targeting monetary aggregates rather than short-term interest rates, but helps banks manage their reserves more accurately. With LRA, Federal Reserve purchases or sales of securities immediately altered the amount of total reserves in the system but do not affect required reserves. Banks know that the cost of reserves varies depending on the amount of excess reserves available, but they do not have to alter their required holdings until about three weeks later, when deposit fluctuations affect reserve requirements.

LAGGED RESERVE ACCOUNTING

Under the current lagged reserve accounting procedure, weekly reporting institutions maintain reserves on their reservable liabilities with a 30-day lag.[7] That is, the reserve maintenance period for a weekly reporter begins 30 days after the beginning of a reserve computation period. In particular, banks must maintain reserves—on a daily average basis—for a 14-day period beginning on the third Thursday following the computation period. A **computation period** consists of two 1-week **reporting periods** and, therefore, consists of 14 consecutive days beginning on a Tuesday and ending on the second Monday thereafter. A **maintenance period** consists of 14 consecutive days beginning on a Thursday and ending on the second Wednesday thereafter. The reserve balance requirement to be maintained in any given 14-day maintenance period ending on Wednesday is measured by:

- the reserve requirement on reservable liabilities calculated as of the computation period that ended 17 days prior to the start of the associated maintenance period;
- less vault cash as of the same computation period used to calculate the reserve requirement—i.e., the 14-day computation period ending 17 days before the start of the associated maintenance period.

Both vault cash and Federal Reserve deposit balances qualify as reserves, but the timing varies. Daily average balances determine the amount of vault cash that qualifies over the 2-week computation period that ends 17 days prior to the maintenance period, while reserve balances are held during the reserve maintenance period. The institution must satisfy its reserve requirement in the form of vault cash or balances maintained either directly with a Reserve Bank or in a pass-through account (correspondent bank account). The portion of the reserve requirement that is not satisfied by vault cash holdings is called the reserve balance requirement.

Exhibit 14.5 demonstrates the timing of these intervals. Note that Friday balances carry over to Saturday and Sunday such that they have a 3-day impact on the daily average. Because transaction balances are determined (for reserve purposes) about two and one-half weeks in advance and vault cash is determined three days in advance of the reserve maintenance period, a bank can manage its deposit balances at the Fed with a much greater degree of certainty as compared to the contemporaneous system.

---

[7]Smaller banks (generally less than $15 million in reservable liabilities) compute and meet reserve requirements quarterly.

· EXHIBIT 14.5

RELATIONSHIP BETWEEN THE RESERVE MAINTENANCE AND BASE COMPUTATION
PERIODS UNDER LAGGED RESERVE ACCOUNTING

Sun	Mon	Tue	Wed	Thu	Fri	Sat
July 8	9	10	11	12	13	14
15	16	17	18	19	20	21
22	23	24	25	26	27	28
29	30	31	Aug 1	2	3	4
5	6	7	8	9	10	11
12	13	14	15	16	17	18
19	20	21	22	23	24	25

■ Lagged Reserve Computation Period
⊟ Vault Cash Computation Period
▨ Reserve Maintenance Period

The procedure to determine required reserves involves multiplying the percentages from Exhibit 14.4 by the daily average amount outstanding for each reservable liability during the base computation period. Banks can vary from the daily average requirement on any day of the maintenance period as long as their average reserve holdings meet the minimum daily requirement over the entire period. Both vault cash and demand balances at the Federal Reserve qualify as reserve assets. Vault cash held during the lagged computation period that ended 17 days prior to the start of the associated maintenance period is used to offset reserve balance requirements. For example, if a bank's daily average required reserves based on reservable liabilities total $20 million during the reserve maintenance period, then required demand balances at the Federal Reserve would equal $18 million if the bank held an average $2 million in vault cash during the computation period.

Finally, actual reserve holdings during the maintenance period can deviate slightly from the exact percentage requirement, with any excess or deficiency carried forward to the next period. The present allowance is 4 percent of daily average required reserves before past excesses or deficiencies and the vault cash offset, or $50,000, whichever is greater. If a bank is deficient by more than this amount, it must pay a nondeductible interest penalty equal to the discount rate plus 2 percent times the extraordinary deficiency. More importantly, if a bank consistently holds too few reserves, the Federal Reserve will penalize it further by restricting its operating procedures and allowable business activities. If a bank holds more reserves than the allowable excess, it cannot carry this difference forward and thus loses any interest income it could have earned by investing the balances. The timing of these requirements places a premium on Wednesday's transactions just prior to the end of the maintenance week. Because federal funds are an important source of reserves, federal funds trading is very active on Wednesdays and the federal funds rate is typically more volatile compared to other days.

AN APPLICATION: RESERVE CALCULATION UNDER LRA

Reserve maintenance requirements can be best demonstrated through an example. Consider the time frame outlined in Exhibit 14.5, with August 9 to August 22 representing the 14-day reserve maintenance period. Exhibit 14.6 presents daily balances for vault cash and net transactions accounts during the lagged reserve computation period for a sample bank. The final columns list the cumulative totals for each balance sheet item over the 2-week period and the daily average balances.[8] Note that the base period for net transactions accounts begins on July 10, almost four and one-half weeks before the maintenance period starts.

Exhibit 14.7 demonstrates the required reserves calculation. The procedure has four steps:

- Calculate daily average balances outstanding during the lagged computation period.
- Apply the reserve percentages.
- Subtract vault cash.
- Add or subtract the allowable reserve carried forward from the prior period.

Daily average balances equal the cumulative total divided by 14, the number of days in the base period. Weekends count even if a bank is not open for business. These daily average balances are then multiplied by the percentages from Exhibit 14.4. The first $5.7 million of net transactions accounts is exempt from required reserves, while the next $35.6 million is subject to the lower 3 percent requirement.

For this sample bank, total daily average gross required reserves equal $88.595 million. Average vault cash of $32.214 million during the lagged computation period is then subtracted to yield a net requirement of $56.381 million. Banks can deviate from the exact requirement as long as they make up deficiencies in the following maintenance period. Excess reserve holdings or surpluses of up to 4 percent of gross required reserves can be carried forward to reduce the next period's minimum requirement. The computation in Exhibit 14.7 assumes that the prior period deficiency totaled $2.276 million. The sample bank must hold minimum reserves equal to the net requirement plus any daily deficiency—a total of $58.657 million. The last item in the exhibit, maximum reserves at the Federal Reserve, equals the minimum requirement plus 4 percent of $88.595 million—or $62.201 million. Of course, there is no limit on how much in balances a bank may hold at the Federal Reserve. The term maximum refers to the fact that no more than a 4 percent surplus can be used to reduce future balance requirements.

The calculations would be slightly different if the bank carried forward a surplus from the previous maintenance period. In this case, a bank is allowed to be deficient by 4 percent of gross reserves during the current maintenance period. If, for example, the bank in Exhibit 14.7 reported a carry-forward surplus of $1 million, it could have used the $1 million to reduce its total requirement and still be deficient 4 percent more. Thus, the minimum point in the target range would equal $55.381 million.

---

[8]Banks can report balance sheet figures to the nearest thousand dollars. Exhibit 14.6 rounds figures to the nearest million.

■ EXHIBIT 14.6

REPORT OF RESERVABLE LIABILITIES AND OFFSETTING ASSET BALANCES

Balances at Close of Business Day

Lagged Computation Period	Tue 10-Jul	Wed 11-Jul	Thu 12-Jul	Fri 13-Jul	Sat 14-Jul	Sun 15-Jul	Mon 16-Jul	Tue 17-Jul	Wed 18-Jul	Thu 19-Jul	Fri 20-Jul	Sat 21-Jul	Sun 22-Jul	Mon 23-Jul	Two-Week Total	Daily Average
DDA's	992	995	956	954	954	954	989	996	960	959	958	958	958	990	$13,573	$969.50
Auto trans. from savings	0	0	0	0	0	0	0	0	0	0	0	0	0	0	$ —	$ —
NOW and Super NOW	221	221	222	223	223	223	223	224	225	225	225	225	225	225	$ 3,130	$223.57
Deductions:															$ —	$ —
DD bal from U.S. dep.	163	281	190	186	186	186	159	159	274	178	182	182	182	164	$ 2,672	$190.86
CIPC	96	96	78	78	78	78	95	98	92	79	81	81	81	88	$ 1,199	$ 85.64
Net trans. accounts	954	839	910	913	913	913	958	963	819	927	920	920	920	963	$12,832	$916.57
Vault Cash	28	30	31	33	33	33	38	30	31	32	32	32	32	36	$ 451	$ 32.21

NOTE: Figures are in millions of dollars.

CIPC is cash items in process of collection.

· EXHIBIT 14.7

REQUIRED RESERVES REPORT: AUGUST 9–22.

Reservable Liabilities for:	Daily Average Deposit Liab.	Reserve Percentage	Daily Average Requirement
July 10–23			
Net trans. accounts			
Exempt up to $5.70 million	$ 5.70	0.0%	$ 0.000
Over 5.7 up to $41.30 million	35.60	3.0%	$ 1.068
Over $41.30 million	875.27	10.0%	$87.527
Total	$ 916.57		
Gross reserve requirement			$88.595
Daily average vault cash			$32.214
Net reserve requirement			$56.381
Reserve carry-forward (prior period)			($ 2.276)
Minimum reserves to be maintained with Federal Reserve			$58.657
Maximum reserves to be maintained			$62.201
(0.04 × 88.595) + 58.657			
If a surplus carry-forward of $1,000:			
Minimum reserves to be maintained with Federal Reserve			$55.381
Carry-forward (4% of gross reserve requirement)			$ 3.544
Maximum reserves to be maintained			$58.925
(0.04 × 88.595) + 55.381			

NOTE: Figures in millions of dollars.

RESERVES PLANNING

Prior to the recent change to lagged reserve accounting, the greatest difficulty in meeting reserve requirements came from not knowing what the average periodic requirement would be during the first 12 days of the maintenance period. Unlike LRA, changes in the volume of net transaction accounts under a contemporaneous reserve system simultaneously changed actual reserve requirements. The bank was required to continuously monitor its deposit inflows and outflows and make corresponding adjustments to its cash position. Typically, weekly patterns reflect large commercial deposit inflows from weekend transactions or regular payroll payments. Changes in float naturally follow. Management had to incorporate these systematic funds flows into a planning model to time federal funds sales and purchases. Under today's lagged reserve accounting system, management knows the amount of required reserves with certainty, but the lag time increases the challenges to the Federal Reserve system when managing the money supply.

Every bank should manage reserves to keep actual Federal Reserve balances within the range represented by the theoretical minimum and maximum of Exhibit 14.7. In this case, every dollar of reserves counts. Deficiencies and interest penalties are avoided, while all excesses reduce future requirements. This means that banks should alternate between deficiencies and excesses over successive maintenance periods. If a bank is deficient, it must liquidate assets, such as Treasury bills, or borrow cash balances, such as in the federal funds or repo markets. If a bank has a surplus, it will invest the excess balances.

· **EXHIBIT 14.8**

FACTORS AFFECTING DAILY RESERVES HELD AT THE FEDERAL RESERVE

Factors Increasing Reserves	Factors Decreasing Reserves
Nondiscretionary	*Nondiscretionary*
Yesterday's immediate cash letter	Remittances charged
Deferred availability items	Deficit in local clearinghouse
Excess from local clearinghouse	Treasury tax and loan account calls
Deposits from U.S. Treasury	Maturing certificates of deposit, Eurodollars not rolled over
Discretionary	*Discretionary*
Currency/coin shipped to Federal Reserve	Currency and coin received from Federal Reserve
Security sales	Security purchases
Borrowing from Federal Reserve	Payment on loans from Federal Reserve
Federal funds purchased	Federal funds sold
Securities sold under agreement to repurchase	Securities purchased under agreement to resell
Interest payments on securities	
New certificates of deposit, Eurodollar issues	

LIQUIDITY PLANNING OVER THE RESERVE MAINTENANCE PERIOD

The fundamental objective in managing a legal reserve position is to meet the minimum requirement at the lowest cost. Because vault cash needs are determined by customer preferences, they vary largely with the payments patterns of the bank's customers and local businesses. They also exhibit well-defined seasonal patterns that are easily forecasted. When a bank needs additional vault cash, it simply requests a cash delivery from its local Federal Reserve Bank or a correspondent bank. It similarly ships any excess cash when appropriate. The primary difficulty in meeting required reserves derives from forecasting required deposit balances at the Federal Reserve resulting from volatile shifts in bank liabilities. The process involves forecasting daily clearing balances and either investing any excess at the highest yield or obtaining additional balances at the lowest cost to cover any deficits. The change to a lagged reserve account system has made this process somewhat easier.

Exhibit 14.8 identifies several factors that alter a bank's actual and required reserve assets. These factors are separated into nondiscretionary items, over which a bank has virtually no control, and discretionary items, over which it has at least partial control. The most important nondiscretionary items are checks presented for payment. Exhibit 14.8 differentiates between the Federal Reserve's cash letter and local clearings.[9] Because the Federal Reserve provides a schedule for the timing of clearings, a bank knows when previously deferred items will be available. Check clearings are uncontrollable in that bank customers determine the timing and magnitude of check payments. Customers do not normally notify a bank at the time of payment or prior to making deposits.

This uncontrolled activity presents planning problems when large withdrawals or new deposits catch a bank unaware and force it to scramble for additional reserves or to invest newfound funds. Good data management and communications systems from tellers and ATMs to management are essential. Interest of 5 percent on $10 million over the weekend is $4,110, a substantial opportunity cost of poor planning! Managers should monitor activity in large deposit accounts routinely. They should know when large CDs mature, when the

---

[9] A cash letter is a letter or data tape on which a bank lists and describes transit checks.

Treasury transfers deposits to the Federal Reserve, and when loan customers make large loan payments. They should also identify any weekly or monthly patterns in deposit flows that arise from normal business activity. This may allow them to use balances from inflows during one part of the maintenance period to offset outflows during another part, rather than jump in and out of federal funds trading.

When managers need to adjust a bank's reserve assets they use the discretionary items listed in Exhibit 14.8. Managers have some control over these transactions and use them to complement uncontrollable deposit flows. In most cases, a bank receives information on clearing surpluses or deficiencies twice daily. Summary figures from yesterday's check clearings are available each morning, along with balances from federal funds trades and securities transactions. In most urban areas, local clearinghouses report net clearings each afternoon from checks submitted that day. Once this information is available, managers may actively increase or decrease daily reserves by choosing among the items in Exhibit 14.8. Although federal funds and RP transactions are the most popular, the choice depends on a comparison of costs and returns.

MANAGING FLOAT

During any single day, more than $100 million in checks drawn on U.S. commercial banks is waiting to be processed. Individuals, businesses, and governments deposit the checks but cannot use the proceeds until banks give their approval, typically in several days. Checks in process of collection, called float, are a source of both income and expense to banks.

THE PAYMENT SYSTEM

To understand float management and recent criticism of bank policies, it is necessary to explain the bank payment system. Payments between banks can be made either by check or electronically. Checks drawn against transactions accounts are presented to the customer's bank for payment and ultimately "cleared" by reducing the bank's deposit balance at the Federal Reserve or a correspondent bank. Payments made electronically directly and immediately alter balances held at Federal Reserve Banks. This network for transferring funds electronically is called the Fedwire.

The standard check-clearing process is outlined in Exhibit 14.9. An individual visiting San Jose, California, purchases goods from a local business for $500 by writing a check on his demand deposit held at Community National Bank (CNB) in Portland, Oregon. The check-clearing process begins when the business deposits this check at the Bay Area National Bank (BANB). Because BANB assumes the risk that the check may not be good, it does not allow the depositor to use the funds immediately. Normally, a bank places a hold on the check until it verifies that the check writer has enough funds on deposit to cover the draft. BANB thus increases the ledger balances of the business's demand deposit account and its own CIPC. The business's usable collected balances, ledger balances minus float, are unchanged.

During stage 2, BANB forwards the check to its upstream correspondent, the Bank of California (BOC) in San Francisco. This bank replicates BANB's procedures, deferring credit to BANB for several days until the check clears. In stage 3, BOC presents the check to the Federal Reserve Bank of San Francisco. The Federal Reserve follows a timetable indicating how long a bank must wait before it can receive credit on deposited items. The dollar amount of deferred credit is labeled deferred availability credit items (DACI). Until the Federal Reserve provides credit, it increases its CIPC and DACI equally so that Federal Reserve float (CIPC − DACI) equals zero.

■ **EXHIBIT 14.9**

EXAMPLE OF THE CHECK-CLEARING PROCESS

Bay Area National Bank, San Jose					Bank of California, San Francisco			
Δ**ASSETS**		Δ**LIABILITIES**			Δ**ASSETS**		Δ**LIABILITIES**	
1. CIPC	+$500	Demand deposit owed the business	+$500		2. CIPC	+$500	Demand deposit (BANB)	+$500
4. CIPC	−$500				5. CIPC	−$500		
Demand deposit at BOC	+$500				Demand deposit at FRB of San Francisco	+$500		

Federal Reserve Bank of San Francisco					Community National Bank, Portland			
Δ**ASSETS**		Δ**LIABILITIES**			Δ**ASSETS**		Δ**LIABILITIES**	
3. CIPC	+$500	DACI	+$500		6. Demand deposit at FRB of San Francisco	−$500	Demand deposit owed the individual	−$500
5.		DACI	−$500					
		Demand deposit (BOC)	+$500					
6. CIPC	−$500	Demand deposit (CNB)	−$500					

NOTE: CIPC indicates checks in the process of collection; BOC, Bank of California; FRB, Federal Reserve Bank; BANB, Bay Area National Bank; DACI, deferred credit availability items; and CNB, Community National Bank.

Up to this point, no depositor can spend its funds, and the check has not been presented to CNB for payment. Frequently, correspondent banks and the Federal Reserve give credit on checks deposited by other banks prior to actually verifying that the checks are good. This is indicated as stages 4 and 5 in Exhibit 14.9. BANB, however, does not provide the same credit to the business depositor until the check clears. After stage 4, BANB can invest its deposit at BOC while it defers crediting the business account. BOC, in turn, receives reserve credit before the check actually clears. During stage 6, the Federal Reserve Bank presents the original check to CNB, which verifies that the individual has enough funds on deposit to cover the payment.

Most checks complete this trip in two to six days. The actual length of time varies with the number of financial institutions that handle an item and the geographic distance between banks. The greater the number of handlers and distance, the longer it takes to transfer and verify a check. To accelerate the process, banks encode checks with magnetic numbers that can be read by high-speed machines and often move checks via overnight couriers between destinations. Unfortunately, the process does not work as quickly in reverse. If the bank on which the original check is drawn (CNB in the above example) discovers that the check writer has insufficient funds to cover the draft, it sends the check back to the bank accepting the initial deposit (BANB in the example). In most instances, the check must again go through each intermediate institution that handled it earlier.[10] This may take another 7 to 14 days because returned checks are physically analyzed for endorsements.

---

[10]The Federal Reserve Bank of Dallas implemented a test program in 1984 for the final payer bank to return items directly to the bank of first deposit without following the chain of endorsements. The payer bank is required to notify the first bank within three business days of a check's receipt if a check is not honored. Notification is required for all checks over $2,500. Failure to notify makes the payer bank liable.

Many payments are effected electronically without any checks. Customers simply advise their banks to transfer funds via telephone or computer hook-ups between institutions. The exchange is completed on the same day as payment authorization using immediately available funds. Customers who use the Federal Reserve's wire transfer system pay a fee to their bank. Most large denomination transactions are handled via the Fedwire. Consider the payment outlined in Exhibit 14.9. In this case, the individual could have authorized CNB to have the Federal Reserve immediately transfer $500 from CNB's reserve account to BANB's reserve account. The Federal Reserve's computer records the funds transfer and notifies BANB of payment.[11] Reserve credit is immediate because the payment comes from immediately available funds.

HOLDS ON DEPOSITED CHECKS

A bank that accepts a deposit accepts the risk that supporting funds will eventually appear. If the individual in Exhibit 14.9 does not have sufficient funds to cover the $500 draft, BANB must collect from its business depositor and may suffer losses. To reduce this risk, banks typically place a hold on deposited funds. Essentially, they do not let depositors spend the proceeds until there is reasonable certainty the deposit is good.

Consumer groups and legislators have long criticized banks for lengthy delays in making deposits available. Prior to 1989, banks often forced customers to wait 20 business days for availability. Averages for checks drawn on out-of-state banks typically ranged from 8 to 10 days. Because banks can normally invest deposited items in two to three days, they earned substantial amounts of interest while delaying availability and interest payments on deposits. In the previous example, BANB may be able to invest the initial deposit after two days via its correspondent bank. It may coincidentally delay availability to the depositor for six or more days, during which time it pays no interest and prohibits transactions.[12]

Effective in September 1990, Congress passed the Expedited Funds Availability Act, which stipulated maximum time limits under Regulation CC for banks to make funds available on deposited checks. There are several basic limits that all banks must meet. Local checks must be cleared in no more than two business days. A local check is one written on a firm in the same metropolitan area or within the same Federal Reserve check processing region. Nonlocal checks must be cleared in no more than five business days. Funds deposited in the form of government checks, certified checks, and cashiers checks must be available by 9 A.M. the next day.

There are exceptions to these schedules, such as with habitual check bouncers, but the law generally indicates the longest time that account holders will have to wait to access their funds. The act also required banks to disclose their hold policy to all transaction account owners, required banks to start accruing interest when the firm receives credit for its deposited checks, and established penalties for failure to comply with the provisions.

DAYLIGHT OVERDRAFTS

Most individuals at one time or another have played the float game, writing checks against insufficient balances, then rushing to deposit funds that permit the checks to clear. Banks play the same game with electronic funds transfers—for far greater dollar amounts—by authorizing payments from deposits held at the Federal Reserve or correspondent banks in

---

[11]Large payments involving international participants are handled through the New York Clearing House Interbank Payment System (CHIPS).

[12]Interest is applicable only on NOW and MMDA accounts. If the business had immediate availability and liquidated the deposit, BANB's actual reserves would decline, forcing the bank to replenish nonearning assets.

excess of their balances. In doing so, they drive their collected balances below zero. These negative balances are called daylight overdrafts. Normally, enough funds are transferred into the account by the end of each day to cover the overdraft.[13] In November 1985, the Federal Reserve was forced to loan the Bank of New York $23.6 billion to cover overdrafts caused by a computer malfunction. (See Contemporary Issues: A $24 Billion Overdraft.) The Fed has taken steps since then to reduce its exposure.

These overdrafts could potentially close down the electronic payments system. The primary risk is that some financial institution might fail because it cannot meet a payments obligation. A failure might produce liquidity problems at other banks and have a ripple effect, generating other losses and failures. Suppose, for example, that CNB from Exhibit 14.9 transfers funds over the Fedwire to BANB before the individual makes sufficient balances available to cover the original $500 check to the San Jose business. Once the wire transfer is received, BANB can release funds to the business without risk. Settlement is immediate and final. If the individual does not provide the underlying balances, CNB could lose the amount of the transfer. When extended to all transactions, any single bank may have daylight overdrafts two or three times larger than its capital base.

There are two main electronic funds transfer networks: the Fedwire and CHIPS (Clearing House Interbank Payment System). Most of the transactions on Fedwire involve transfers of immediately available funds between financial institutions and balance adjustments from the purchase or sale of government securities. Most of the wire transfers on CHIPS involve either transfers of Eurodollar balances or foreign exchange trading. Although participants are required to maintain positive balances at the Federal Reserve and correspondent banks at the end of each business day, they may create negative balances during a day by transferring funds in excess of their initial balance before any deposits are received. This negative balance is a daylight overdraft. Conceptually, the overdraft is a loan, but under current regulation it is costless to the deficient bank because no interest or fees are paid. It may be intentional or unintentional but clearly imposes risk to the Federal Reserve or CHIPS system. The Fed assumes risk because recipients of wire transfers retain legal title to the funds. The Fed thus essentially guarantees wire transfers.

The Federal Reserve endorsed guidelines on overdrafts in 1986, which limited the size of daylight overdrafts while transferring funds over the Fedwire. Van Hoose and Sellon (1989) describe the types of policies the Fed uses to control payment system risk over the Fedwire and CHIPS. The policies consist primarily of caps on the size of any single firms overdrafts. Interestingly, the Fed chooses not to use the price mechanism by charging interest on overdrafts to influence their usage. Still, the Fed identifies large overdrafts on the Fedwire and discusses the potential risks with the guilty bank's senior management. If the overdrafts arise because of computer problems, it will extend discount window credit at the current discount rate plus 2 percent. Its ultimate weapon, however, is to restrict bank operations.

PRICING FEDERAL RESERVE CHECK-CLEARING SERVICES

One important facet of DIDMCA (Depository Institutions and Monetary Control Act) of 1980 was to promote competition in check-clearing services. Prior to the act, the Federal Reserve provided free check collection to member banks. Banks did pay indirectly through owning nonearning reserve deposits. Still, many banks also chose to clear checks through correspondent banks. Correspondents generally provided deposit credit sooner than the Federal Reserve, and banks could invest funds earlier.

---

[13]Richard Smoot (1985) discusses overdrafts arising over the major wire transfer systems and analyzes the risks assumed in each case.

A $24 BILLION OVERDRAFT

The Bank of New York serves as a clearing agent for numerous brokers that buy and sell U.S. government securities, transferring ownership of securities between buyers and sellers. Normally, sellers of securities route the instruments through the Bank's securities account at the Federal Reserve Bank of New York and simultaneously receive payment through debits against the Bank of New York's reserve account. The Bank of New York promptly routes the securities to the buyers, from whom it collects payment.

On November 20, 1985, the bank experienced a computer malfunction that short-circuited the normal sequence of transactions. Although the computer allowed sellers to route securities to the bank's account and debit the bank's reserves in payment, it did not allow the bank to route the same securities to the ultimate buyers. Thus, the bank saw its reserves decline, but it could not generate sufficient cash receipts to replenish the deductions. By the end of the day, the bank reported a $22.6 billion overdraft in its reserve account. The Federal Reserve Bank of New York stepped in and made a $22.6 billion overnight discount window loan at 7.5 percent. Later, it was determined that the actual deficiency was $23.6 billion, and the bank was charged interest on an additional $1 billion loan.

The $23.6 billion loan was 2,300 percent of the bank's capital, and it cost the bank almost $5 million in unanticipated interest expense. If a bank were unable to cover its exposure, it could lose an amount far in excess of its capital and thus quickly become insolvent. Because Bank of New York's loan was fully collateralized with U.S. government securities, the Federal Reserve was never at risk of loss. In response to the bank's problems, the Federal Reserve imposed operational standards on the allowable size of daylight overdrafts that clearing banks could run. The applicable interest charge was also increased to 2 percent over the prevailing discount rate.

DIDMCA authorized the Federal Reserve to price float by charging interest at the federal funds rate for reserves that banks received in the form of float. The catalyst was the rise in Federal Reserve float during the late 1970s, when interest rates rose to historical highs. At the time, corporate cash managers set up remote disbursement facilities, which allowed them to write checks on remotely located banks. This method increased the time it took for checks to clear (increased CIPC) and simultaneously increased Federal Reserve float. Unpredictable changes in float, in turn, made it more difficult for the Federal Reserve to control the nation's money supply. Banks now pay for float on a per item basis, which has substantially lowered Federal Reserve float.

After this pricing began in 1981, correspondent banks argued that the Federal Reserve was undercutting private sector prices to maintain its market share. By 1984, the debate had subsided, after the Federal Reserve reported a $25 million surplus on check-collection services. This surplus came after direct operating expenses, the cost of float, and a private sector adjustment factor were netted out. The adjustment factor is a cost surcharge the Federal Reserve recoups in pricing to cover capital requirements, that is, to pay a targeted return on equity, and taxes it would pay if it operated privately. The Federal Reserve earns a profit of several million dollars on its services.

MANAGING CORRESPONDENT BALANCES

In addition to holding deposit balances at the Federal Reserve, most banks maintain demand deposit accounts at other financial institutions. The balances are held as payment for services purchased from the issuing bank. This interbank deposit network links the activities of small and large banks and banks located in different geographic areas. A bank that owns deposit balances is a respondent bank. A bank that accepts deposits is a correspondent bank. Larger banks typically fill both roles, providing basic services to smaller banks and buying services from large firms that are either located in other geographic markets or able to offer a broader range of services.

CORRESPONDENT BANKING SERVICES

Correspondent banking is the system of interbank relationships in which one bank sells services to other financial institutions. The institution providing the services is the **correspondent bank** or upstream correspondent, while the institution buying the services is the **respondent bank** or downstream correspondent.

Respondent banks purchase services from correspondents for a variety of reasons. Some services, such as check collection, carry advantages over those provided directly by the Federal Reserve System, which generally takes longer to grant credit. Other services are either too expensive to provide independently or cannot be provided because of regulatory constraints. Small banks, for example, want to offer a full range of services to their customers, but the demand for specialty transactions is sporadic. It would be too costly to invest in the technology and manpower for international transactions or investment banking advice on mergers and acquisitions if those services were used infrequently. These services can only be provided in large volume to take advantage of economies of scale, which lower unit costs. Even when priced at a markup over correspondents' costs, these services are cheaper than if provided independently. Respondent banks similarly sell loan participations to correspondent banks when individual loans exceed a bank's legal lending limit.

The correspondent banking system evolved before the establishment of the Federal Reserve, largely to help process checks. Respondent banks paid for the service by maintaining balances above those needed to clear items. Correspondent banks could invest the excess, with interest income covering their costs. The fundamental relationships are the same today. Respondent banks choose services they need from menus provided by correspondents. They shop around for quality service at the lowest available price and hold balances that pay for the supplier's costs plus profit.

The most common correspondent banking services are:

- Check collection, wire transfer, coin and currency supply
- Loan participation assistance
- Data processing services
- Portfolio analysis and investment advice
- Federal funds trading
- Securities safekeeping
- Arrangement of purchase or sale of securities
- Investment banking services: swaps, futures, mergers, and acquisitions
- Loans to directors and officers
- International financial transactions

The predominant services purchased can be grouped into three broad categories: check clearing and related cash transactions, investment services, and credit-related transactions. Check-clearing services are attractive because respondent banks can reduce float. Correspondent banks often make funds available for respondent investment before the Federal Reserve's scheduled availability. Additional interest earned more than compensates for the required compensating balances.

Respondents purchase other services when the price is below the unit cost of supplying the service directly. Small banks with a limited customer base cannot justify large investments in equipment or manpower to provide infrequently used services. They must, however, be able to provide these services to remain a full-service bank, and it is cheaper to buy them on demand. Many large banks, in contrast, view correspondent banking as a profit center. The demand for basic correspondent services and related leasing, international banking, stock brokerage, and real estate services by other banks and their customers is sufficiently large to justify offering these services worldwide.

PAYMENT FOR SERVICES

Many banks act as both a correspondent and respondent bank as determined by size and geographic market. Small banks typically purchase services from larger correspondents, which take advantage of scale economies, and from banks located in distant geographic markets where bank customers do significant business. Respondents pay for services either with explicit fees or by maintaining deposit balances at the correspondent. In most cases, compensation takes the form of demand deposit balances, which provide an investment return to the correspondent. These due-to and due-from relationships represent the lifeblood of correspondent banking.

Correspondent banking traditionally relied on personal friendships among bankers. Increased competition resulting from deregulation and interstate mergers and acquisitions, however, has shrunk the pool of commercial bank respondents and put pressure on profit margins. Banks that acquire a firm in another state no longer need the same services previously obtained through a correspondent. In response, many correspondent banks no longer provide a full range of services and have scaled back the size of their correspondent departments, focusing only on profitable product lines. Other correspondents have aggressively gone after business from savings banks and credit unions. Small banks have also become increasingly sensitive to competition from correspondent banks for the small bank customers' business.

A community banker who acquaints an upstream correspondent with his or her customer base will frequently discover that the correspondent has tried to market services directly to the customer and completely circumvent the respondent bank. This situation has produced two results. First, respondents now unbundle the services of upstream correspondents, purchasing different services from different correspondents rather than dealing with only one firm. Second, community banks are forming and buying services from cooperative institutions known as **bankers' banks,** which are owned by independent commercial banks in a state and are authorized to provide services only to financial institutions. They do not market services directly to bank customers and compete only with other correspondent banks. Bankers' banks maintain a staff that handles check collection, analyzes the credit quality of loan participations, trades in government and corporate securities for investments, and offers other services, such as discount brokerage, leasing, and data processing at competitive prices. Independent bankers serve as directors and offer guidance regarding product selection, pricing, and portfolio policies. There are different bankers' banks in different states throughout the United States. In recent years, several of these bankers' banks have helped community banks form the equivalent of reverse holding companies that offer trust services. Community banks thus jointly own a firm that offers trust services to each of their customers. The attraction is that this correspondent bank is not in direct competition with each community bank and will not try to steal its customers.

COMPUTING BALANCE REQUIREMENTS

It is relatively easy to calculate the dollar amount of balances required to pay for correspondent services. Important variables include the volume and type of services used, unit prices charged by the correspondent, direct fees paid for specific services, and the applicable

· EXHIBIT 14.10

PRICING CORRESPONDENT SERVICES: MONTHLY ANALYSIS

A. Services Provided: June

Check clearing	
10,540 items at $0.045 per item	$474.30
Wire transfers	
28 items at $1.50 per item	42.00
Security safekeeping	
7 items at $3.00 per item	21.00
Data processing services/microcomputer software	100.00
Total monthly cost	$637.30

B. Correspondent Bank Revenues

Fees for computer services	$100.00
Required investment income from compensating balances	537.30
Total	$637.30

C. Required Ledger Balances (B)

Investment income = (Earnings credit)(30/365)(Ledger balances − Float − Required reserves)

If earnings credit = 8%, average float = $7,200, and required reserves = 10% of collected balances;

$537.30 = (.08)(30/365)(.90)(B − 7,200)$

$B = \$97,994$

(assumed) earnings rate applied to investable balances. Consider the pricing analysis presented in Exhibit 14.10. The respondent bank uses services valued at $637.30 for the month of June. Of this total, $100 is covered by fees, so that the correspondent needs to earn $537.30 in interest on balances to meet costs. Section C calculates the respondent's required ledger balances, assuming an 8 percent earnings credit applied to ledger balances less $7,200 float and 10 percent required reserves. During the month, the respondent should have maintained approximately $98,000 in balances to pay for its services.

Of course, several elements are subject to negotiation, particularly unit costs for each service applied by the correspondent and the applicable earnings credit. Respondent banks prefer lower costs and higher assumed investment yields. Normally, the earnings credit floats with money market yields and is often specified as the monthly average federal funds or Treasury bill rate. High-volume purchasers can further obtain unit cost discounts to lower balance requirements. In recent years, correspondent banks have tried to move to fee-based pricing of correspondent services. Respondent banks, however, have generally resisted, so that less than 10 percent of all correspondent relationships currently use direct fee pricing. Competition continues to dictate payment in the form of demand deposit balances.

LIQUIDITY PLANNING

Banks actively engage in liquidity planning at two levels. The first relates to managing the required reserve position. The previous sections describe the reserve accounting requirements and the procedure for calculating legal requirements. The planning horizon is two weeks, during which a bank must hold a minimum amount of deposit balances at the Federal Reserve. Actual balances vary daily, with many transactions affecting outstanding liabilities and the investment portfolio but these transactions occurred over two weeks before and are therefore known. Short-term liquidity planning focuses on forecasting closing balances at the Federal

Reserve relative to potential legal reserves. The second stage involves forecasting net funds needs derived from seasonal or cyclical phenomena and overall bank growth. The planning horizon is considerably longer, encompassing monthly intervals throughout an entire year.

THE DEVELOPMENT OF LIQUIDITY STRATEGIES

Historically, liquidity management focused on assets and was closely tied to lending policies. Under the commercial loan theory prior to 1930, banks were encouraged to make only short-term, self-liquidating loans. Such loans closely matched the maturity of bank deposits and enabled banks to meet deposit withdrawals with funds from maturing loans. An inventory loan, for example, would be repaid when the borrower sold the items that coincided with the need for financing to accumulate additional inventory. A bank was liquid if its loan portfolio consisted of short-term loans.

The **shiftability theory** represented the next extension by recognizing that any liquid asset could be used to meet deposit withdrawals. In particular, a bank could satisfy its liquidity requirements if it held loans and securities that could be sold in the secondary market prior to maturity. The ability to sell government securities and eligible paper effectively substituted for illiquid, longer-term loans with infrequent principal payments. Not surprisingly, the application of this theory coincided with the growth of the U.S. government securities market after 1930. The effect was to lengthen loan maturities and expand bank portfolios to include marketable securities.

Around 1950, the focus shifted to the **anticipated income theory,** which suggested that liquidity requirements and thus loan payments should be tied to a borrower's expected income. Banks were still encouraged to invest in marketable instruments but now structured loans so that the timing of principal and interest payments matched the borrower's ability to repay from income. The primary contribution was the emphasis on cash flow characteristics of different instruments because a borrower's cash flow generally varied closely with his or her income. This encouraged the growth in amortized loans with periodic interest and principal payments and staggered maturities in a bank's bond portfolio.

More recently, banks have focused on liabilities. According to the **liability management theory,** banks can satisfy liquidity needs by borrowing in the money and capital markets. When they need immediately available funds, they can simply borrow via federal funds purchased, RPs, jumbo CDs, commercial paper, and Eurodollars. This theory became increasingly popular as banks gained the ability to pay market interest rates on large liabilities. The fundamental contribution was to consider both sides of a bank's balance sheet as sources of liquidity.

Today, banks use both assets and liabilities to meet liquidity needs. Available liquidity sources are identified and compared to expected needs by a bank's asset and liability management committee (ALCO). Management considers all potential deposit outflows and inflows when deciding how to allocate assets and finance operations. Key considerations include maintaining high asset quality and a strong capital base that both reduces liquidity needs and improves a bank's access to funds at low cost.

LIQUIDITY VERSUS PROFITABILITY

There is a short-run trade-off between liquidity and profitability. The more liquid a bank is, the lower are its return on equity and return on assets, all other things being equal. Both asset and liability liquidity contribute to this relationship. Asset liquidity is influenced by the composition and maturity of funds. Large holdings of cash assets clearly decrease profits because of the opportunity loss of interest income. In terms of the investment portfolio, short-term securities normally carry lower yields than comparable longer-term securities. Investors value price stability, so long-term securities pay a yield premium to induce investors to extend maturities. Banks that purchase short-term securities thus increase liquidity, but at the expense of higher potential returns. Consider an environment where market expectations are for short-term Treasury yields to remain constant at present levels. The Treasury yield curve will slope upwards, reflecting liquidity premiums that increase with maturity.[14] A bank that buys 6-month bills at 5 percent rather than a 1-year bill at 5.2 percent gives up 20 basis points for the greater price stability (lower risk).

A bank's loan portfolio displays the same trade-off. Loans carrying the highest yields are the least liquid. Yields are high because default risk or interest rate risk is substantial and the loan administration expense is high. Loans that can be readily sold usually are short-term credits to well-known corporations or government-guaranteed instruments and thus carry minimal spreads. Amortized loans, in contrast, may improve liquidity even though they are frequently long-term because the periodic payments increase near-term cash flow.

In terms of liability liquidity, banks with the best asset quality and highest equity capital have greater access to purchased funds. They also pay lower interest rates and generally report lower returns in the short run. Promised yields on loans and securities increase with the perceived default risk of the underlying issuer. Banks that acquire low default risk assets, such as U.S. government securities, forgo the risk premium that could be earned. Interestingly, many banks buy U.S. agency securities because the incremental yield more than compensates for perceived differences in default risk relative to U.S. Treasuries. Similarly, banks with greater equity financing exhibit lower equity multipliers (total assets/total equity) and thus generate lower returns on equity, even with identical returns on assets. These banks can borrow funds cheaper because a greater portion of their assets have to be in default before they might fail.

Liquidity planning focuses on guaranteeing that immediately available funds are available at the lowest cost. Management must determine whether liquidity and default risk premiums more than compensate for the additional risk on longer-term and lower-quality bank investments. If management is successful, long-term earnings will exceed peer banks' earnings, as will bank capital and overall liquidity. The market value of bank equity will increase relative to peers as investors bid up stock prices.

LIQUIDITY, CREDIT, AND INTEREST RATE RISK

Liquidity management is a day-to-day responsibility. Banks routinely experience fluctuations in their cash assets, depending on the timing and magnitude of unexpected deposit outflows. Deviations from expectations can normally be attributed to large payments or deposits that clear through the Federal Reserve or local clearinghouse. Most shortages can be met by accelerating planned borrowings or deferring asset purchases. Excess cash can be easily invested in earning assets. A well-managed bank monitors its cash position carefully and maintains low liquidity risk.

Liquidity risk for a poorly managed bank closely follows credit and interest rate risk. In fact, banks that experience large deposit outflows can often trace the source to either credit problems or earnings declines from interest rate gambles that backfired. The normal sequence of events underlying liquidity problems is:

- Bank management assumes substantial risk by mismatching asset and liability maturities and durations or by extending credit to high risk borrowers.
- The bank reports reduced earnings.

---

[14]Research by Cook et al. (1987) and Toevs (1986) demonstrates that Treasury bill rates include a liquidity or term premium through at least one year.

- The media publicizes the credit and interest rate difficulties.
- The bank must pay higher rates to attract and keep deposits and other purchased funds.
- Bank earnings decline further with reduced interest margins and nonaccruing loans, and uninsured depositors move their funds, forcing the bank to sell assets at fire sale prices and obtain temporary financing from government sources until a merger can be arranged or the bank fails.

Few banks can replace lost deposits independently if an outright run on the bank arises. Liquidity planning forces management to monitor the overall risk position of the bank such that credit risk partially offsets interest rate risk assumed in the bank's overall asset and liability management strategy. If credit risk is high, interest rate risk should be low and vice versa. Potential liquidity needs must reflect estimates of new loan demand and potential deposit losses. The following list identifies factors affecting certain liquidity needs:

NEW LOAN DEMAND

- Unused commercial credit lines outstanding
- Consumer credit available on bank-issued cards
- Business activity and growth in the bank's trade area
- The aggressiveness of the bank's loan officer call programs

POTENTIAL DEPOSIT LOSSES

- The composition of liabilities
- Insured versus uninsured deposits
- Deposit ownership between: money fund traders, trust fund traders, public institutions, commercial banks by size, corporations by size, individuals, foreign investors, and Treasury tax and loan accounts
- Large deposits held by any single entity
- Seasonal or cyclical patterns in deposits
- The sensitivity of deposits to changes in the level of interest rates

Each of the factors under new loan demand signifies a potential increase in borrowing that might deplete a bank's cash reserves. Suppose, for example, that the Federal Reserve tightens credit policy and pushes short-term interest rates higher. Businesses often choose to borrow under outstanding loan commitments rather than use commercial paper, so that bank loans increase. During recessions, individuals might similarly increase outstanding borrowings under credit card agreements. Loan demand closely follows the economic development and growth in a community such that good economic times accelerate borrowing requests. Finally, some banks require loan officers to systematically call on customers to solicit new business. If such call programs are successful, loan demand will increase accordingly.

The factors under potential deposit losses similarly convey information regarding potential cash deficiencies. Banks with substantial core deposits and few purchased liabilities will experience smaller proportionate deposit losses. If the majority of the deposits are federally insured, unanticipated outflows will decline further. Large purchased liabilities are also more sensitive to changes in market interest rates. When rates rise, for example, a bank must increase the rate it pays on these rate-sensitive balances or customers will quickly move their balances in search of higher yields. Finally, many banks are located in markets that experience seasonal or cyclical deposit outflows that track changes in regional economic conditions. Consider a bank in a resort community. Deposits flow into the bank during resort season, but flow out afterwards. Managers must thus monitor these influences in order to plan for cash needs.

TRADITIONAL MEASURES OF LIQUIDITY

As described earlier, banks rely on both assets and liabilities as sources of liquidity. Small banks generally have limited access to purchased funds and thus rely primarily on short-term assets. Larger banks, in contrast, obtain liquid funds mainly via liabilities rather than selling assets. Traditional liquidity measures focus on balance sheet accounts and measure liquidity in terms of financial ratios.

ASSET LIQUIDITY MEASURES

Asset liquidity refers to the ease of converting an asset to cash with a minimum of loss. The most liquid assets mature near term and are highly marketable. Liquidity measures are normally expressed in percentage terms as a fraction of total assets. Most small banks maintain substantial investments in highly liquid assets because they provide liquidity in times of duress. Highly liquid assets include:

1. Cash and due from banks in excess of required holdings
2. Due from banks—interest bearing; these typically have short maturities
3. Federal funds sold and reverse repurchase agreements
4. U.S. Treasury securities maturing within one year
5. U.S. agency obligations maturing within one year
6. Corporate obligations maturing within one year, rated Baa and above
7. Municipal securities maturing within one year, rated Baa and above
8. Loans that can be readily sold and/or securitized

In general, the most marketable assets exhibit low default risk, short maturities, and large trading volume in the secondary market. Cash and due from banks is liquid in the sense that a bank needs clearing balances to process transactions on a daily basis. Without deposits at the Federal Reserve or other financial institutions, a bank could not conduct business. Banks normally minimize cash holdings because they do not earn interest. Only excess cash is truly liquid. This excess includes balances held above legal reserve requirements and the amounts required by correspondent banks for services. Cash balances can decline during any single day without presenting serious problems but must be quickly replenished to sustain operations. Thus, cash and due meets daily liquidity requirements, but banks rely on other assets for longer-term or permanent liquidity needs.

Federal funds and reverse RPs typically mature overnight and increase cash and due at maturity if they are not rolled over. The other securities exhibit low default risk and short maturities. Thus, they typically trade at prices close to par and if sold, have a negligible impact on noninterest income. Treasury obligations are backed by federal taxing authority and borrowing capability. U.S. agency securities are issued by quasi-public entities, such as the Federal Home Loan Mortgage Corporation and Federal Land Bank, and have a long history of low defaults. Liquid corporate and municipal securities are high-rated, investment grade obligations (Baa rated and above) that are well known nationally. Other securities are similarly liquid if their current market value exceeds their book value. This results from management's willingness to sell securities at a gain, which adds to reported net income, but unwillingness to take losses. Finally, standardized loans such as credit card receivables may be liquid if a bank regularly packages these assets and securitizes them.

Historically, banks and regulators focused on loan-to-deposit ratios. Because loans are relatively illiquid in general, the greater is a bank's loan-to-deposit ratio, the lower is the assumed liquidity. As discussed below, the key issue is whether loans generate cash inflows and exhibit high or low default risk.

PLEDGING REQUIREMENTS. Not all of a bank's securities can be easily sold. Like their credit customers, banks are required to pledge collateral against certain types of borrowing. U.S. Treasuries or municipals normally constitute the least cost collateral and, if pledged against a debt, cannot be sold until the bank removes the claim or substitutes other collateral. Collateral is required against four different liabilities: securities sold under agreement to repurchase, borrowing from Federal Reserve Banks at the discount window, public deposits owned by the U.S. Treasury or any state or municipal government unit, and FHLB advances. With public deposits, each depositor stipulates which assets qualify as collateral and what the pledging ratio is. For example, cities often stipulate that a local bank can pledge either U.S. Treasury securities or municipals against 100 percent of the city's uninsured deposits at the bank. Treasuries are valued at par, while A-rated or better in-state municipal securities are valued at 110 percent of par. A third-party trustee holds this collateral. Although these terms favor municipal securities, the bank can choose among its securities to pledge long-term bonds. Pledging requirements against RPs and discount window borrowing establish Treasury securities as preferred collateral against 100 percent of qualifying liabilities. The FHLB, in turn, requires banks to pledge real estate-related loans or securities as collateral against its advances. All pledged securities should be subtracted from the above list of liquid assets to obtain the dollar value of net liquid assets.

LOANS. Many banks and bank analysts monitor loan-to-deposit ratios as a general measure of liquidity. Loans are presumably the least liquid of assets, while deposits are the primary source of funds. A high ratio indicates illiquidity because a bank is fully loaned up relative to its stable funding. Implicitly, new loans or other asset purchases must be financed with large, purchased liabilities. A low ratio suggests that a bank has additional liquidity because it can grant new loans financed with stable deposits.

The loan-to-deposit ratio is not as meaningful as it first appears. It ignores the composition of loans and deposits. Some loans, such as dealer call loans and government-guaranteed credits, either mature soon or can be easily sold if needed. Others are longer term, with deferred payments, and can be sold only at a substantial discount. Two banks with identical deposits and loan-to-deposit ratios may have substantially different loan liquidity if one bank has highly marketable loans while the other has risky, long-term loans. An aggregate loan figure similarly ignores the timing of cash flows from interest and principal payments. Installment contracts generate cash faster than balloon notes, which defer the principal payment until maturity. The same is true for a bank's deposit base. Some deposits, such as long-term nonnegotiable time deposits, are more stable than others, so there is less risk of withdrawal. Aggregate ratios thus ignore the difference in composition of both assets and liabilities and their cash flow characteristics.

Finally, loan-to-deposit ratios have generally increased recently with interest rate deregulation. Although ratios averaged 60 to 70 percent in the 1970s, many banks run ratios near 100 percent or more today. This increase results from the loss of demand and savings deposits and the increased reliance on purchased funds. The corresponding pressure on net interest margins induces many banks to seek more loans, which are only assets offering high enough yields to maintain interest spreads. It is thus difficult to compare loan-to-deposit ratios over time.

In summary, the best measures of asset liquidity identify the dollar amounts of unpledged liquid assets as a fraction of total assets. The greater is the fraction, the greater is the ability to sell assets to meet cash needs. Alternatively, liquid assets as a fraction of purchased liabilities conveys whether net liquidity sources are available from assets. In particular, this ratio should exceed unity indicating that if the bank experiences a run-off of all purchased funds, liquid assets will be sufficient to cover the cash loss.

LIABILITY LIQUIDITY MEASURES

Liability liquidity refers to the ease with which a bank can issue new debt to acquire clearing balances at reasonable costs. Measures typically reflect a bank's asset quality, capital base, and composition of outstanding deposits and other liabilities. The following ratios are commonly cited:

1. Total equity to total assets
2. Loans to deposits
3. Loan losses to net loans
4. Reserve for loan losses to net loans
5. The percentage composition of deposits
6. Total deposits to total assets
7. Core deposits to total assets
8. Federal funds purchased and RPs to total assets
9. Commercial paper and other short-term borrowings to total assets

A bank's ability to borrow at reasonable rates of interest is closely linked to the market's perception of asset quality. Banks with high-quality assets and a large capital base can issue more debt at relatively low rates, compared with peers. The reason is that investors believe there is little chance that such banks will fail. Thus, analysts focus on measures of loan quality and risk assets along with a bank's equity base when assessing future borrowing capabilities.

Banks with stable deposits such as transactions accounts, savings certificates, and nonnegotiable time deposits generally have the same widespread access to borrowed funds at relatively low rates. Those that rely heavily on purchased funds, in contrast, must pay higher rates and experience greater volatility in the composition and average cost of liabilities. For this reason, most banks today compete aggressively for retail core deposits. **Core deposits** are funds that management feels are not rate sensitive and will remain on deposit regardless of economic conditions or seasonal trends. They are typically associated with retail customers who exhibit greater loyalty and prefer to deal with one institution. It is well known that individuals exhibit considerable inertia in their choice of banks as long as they perceive that the bank offers quality, friendly service. The last five ratios listed above provide information regarding the breakdown of liabilities between core deposits and noncore, purchased liabilities.

One procedure to estimate the magnitude of stable, core deposits is diagrammed in Exhibit 14.11. The procedure involves plotting total deposits against time and drawing a line through the low points in the graph. This base line represents core deposits equal to the minimum trend deposit level under which actual deposits never fall. Future stable deposits can be forecast by extending the base line on trend. **Volatile deposits** equal the difference between actual current deposits and the base estimate of core deposits. Implicitly, these are a bank's highly rate-sensitive deposits that customers withdraw as interest rates vary. A curved base line is used in Exhibit 14.11 to emphasize the lack of growth in stable deposits. Many banks calculate liquidity ratios that use an estimate of volatile deposits as the base.

It is also important to recognize that different institutions have different access to specific funding sources. Allen, Peristiani, and Saunders (1989) demonstrate, for example, that banks over $1 billion in assets are the largest proportionate purchasers of federal funds. Regardless of size, banks located in primary banking centers are heavier federal funds borrowers. In the RP market, however, the smallest banks are the largest net borrowers.

The real difficulty in managing liabilities is estimating the interest elasticity of different sources of funds. Management would like to know the quantity response to a change in the level of rates. For example, if interest rates increase by an average of 1 percent during the next 6 months, how much will demand deposits and NOW accounts change? Similarly, if a bank pays one-half of 1 percent more on CDs relative to competitors, how many new funds will it

• EXHIBIT 14.11

MEASURING CORE DEPOSITS

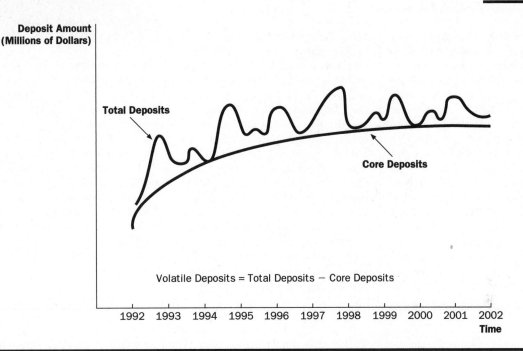

Deposit Amount (Millions of Dollars)

Total Deposits

Core Deposits

Volatile Deposits = Total Deposits − Core Deposits

1992 1993 1994 1995 1996 1997 1998 1999 2000 2001 2002

Time

attract? Some information is available from historical relationships. Management can document the magnitude of disintermediation when interest rates rose in past years as an approximation of potential deposit losses, given expected rate changes. Management can also periodically conduct market tests of rate sensitivity by offering yield premiums on selected liabilities independently and observing the quantity response. These estimates are imprecise, however, and actual rate-sensitivity can change quickly with economic conditions or changes in the public's evaluation of the bank's financial health. If the market perceives that a bank is not sound, most borrowing sources immediately dry up regardless of the rate premiums paid. In response, many banks aggressively solicit retail deposits using innovative marketing strategies (see Contemporary Issues: Competing for Retail Deposits: Gifts for Cash Using Federal Deposit Insurance) because individuals are less rate sensitive and the deposits are more stable.

Large banks attempt to maintain a base of unused borrowing capacity. Many simply expand their funding sources beyond routine loan needs and invest any excess at other banks. When their loan demand increases, the financing is there. A bank's unused borrowing capacity by source can be approximated as the maximum amount ever borrowed minus current borrowings. Banks occasionally use all sources, even though they do not have extraordinary funding needs, just to keep channels open.

LIQUIDITY ANALYSIS OF PNC BANK AND COMMUNITY NATIONAL BANK

Small banks rely on different sources of liquidity compared to larger money center banks. This section analyzes liquidity measures for PNC Bank with almost $63 billion in assets and Community National Bank (CNB) with $156 million in assets using the balance sheet and risk figures from Exhibits 3.2, 3.6, and 3.8 of Chapter 3. The relevant ratios appear in Exhibit 14.12.

COMPETING FOR RETAIL DEPOSITS: GIFTS FOR CASH USING FEDERAL DEPOSIT INSURANCE

With the collapse in energy prices during the early 1980s, First City Bancorporation of Texas saw its asset quality deteriorate and its ability to attract funds on Wall Street virtually disappear. Recognizing that it needed a more stable deposit base, the group's management introduced several innovative deposit programs that offered luxury gift items to customers who made large cash deposits. All gifts were in addition to interest earned.

For opening a 5-year CD of $6 million in 1986, a customer could select either a 1986 Rolls-Royce Corniche convertible, valued at $164,000, or a 40-foot Hatteras motor yacht, valued near $200,000. First City was a bank holding company with 63 subsidiary banks in Texas and one in South Dakota. To improve the CDs' marketability, it allocated the deposits among its subsidiary banks in $100,000 increments so that a single customer's entire $6 million was fully insured by the FDIC. Customers wishing to make smaller deposits could receive a Procraft bass boat with trailer ($500,000 for five years), a Honda three-wheeler ($75,000 for five years), an RCA video camcorder ($20,000 for five years), and many other gifts for simply opening a savings account.

The incentive for First City was obvious: Gift items attract long-term deposits, which should remain with the group of banks until its problems disappear. Depositors, in turn, viewed the gifts as implicit interest and compared the total return to that available on competing instruments. First City's gift program for the prior year attracted more than $300 million. Clearly, the attractiveness of these programs depends on FDIC insurance and the holding company system of ownership.

Consider first the asset liquidity measures. As indicated in Exhibit 14.12, PNC holds fewer of its assets as cash and due, federal funds sold and repos, plus nonmunicipal securities. Cumulatively, PNC holds only 7.11 percent while the smaller CNB holds 24.85 percent of total assets in these types of liquid assets. Small banks generally rely proportionately more on short-term Treasury securities to meet normal liquidity needs. The percentage of gross liquid assets for CNB exceeds that for PNC by almost 18 percent. The lower cash and due percentage for PNC reflects two phenomena. First, many large banks now hold relatively few or no legal reserves because of the use of sweep accounts. Prior to the recent rise in the use of retail sweep accounts, large banks held proportionately more legal reserves because the first $5.7 million of net transactions accounts was reservable at 10 percent and the next $35.6 million was reservable at only 3 percent. The higher 10 percent requirement thus applied to proportionately fewer of a small bank's outstanding accounts. This effect has been reduced as larger banks use more sweep accounts to avoid reserve requirements altogether.[15] Second, large banks hold more interbank deposits to support national and international correspondent relationships. Cash balances do not provide much liquidity to meet permanent needs, and the independent bank owns less cash, more securities, and more federal funds sold. PNC is actually a net purchaser of Fed funds.

The data in rows 1e through 1f adjust the gross liquid asset ratios by identifying unpledged securities with maturities of one year or less. The contribution of federal funds sold is offset by subtracting any overnight borrowing via federal funds purchased. With these adjustments, CNB owns 21.78 percent of its assets in liquid form, or 17.04 percent more than PNC. When cash and due balances are subtracted, the small bank has 15.64 percent liquid assets, while PNC actually has a negative balance of −0.76 percent. These differences clearly reflect the greater borrowing capacity of PNC as compared to Community National. PNC relies substantially more on its ability to borrow liquidity and therefore holds few liquid assets.

---

[15]See the previous discussion on sweep accounts.

• EXHIBIT 14.12

LIQUIDITY MEASURES FOR PNC BANK AND COMMUNITY NATIONAL BANK, 2001

	PNC Bank (%)	First Community Bank (%)
Asset Liquidity Measures		
1. Percentage of total assets		
a. Cash and due from banks	5.50%	6.14%
b. Due from banks (interest bearing)	0.20	0.14
c. Federal funds sold and reverse repurchase agreements	0.58	7.79
d. Treasuries and U.S. agencies*	0.83	10.78
Total gross liquid assets (a + b + c + d)	7.11	24.85
e. Unpledged U.S. Treasuries, agencies, and municipal securities (maturity < 1 year)[†]	0.74	8.40
f. Federal funds sold and reverse RPs minus federal funds purchased and RPs	−1.70	7.10
Total (a + b + e + f)	4.74	21.78
Total (b + e + f)	−0.76	15.64
2. Percentage of total deposits		
a. Net loans	96.81	70.86
Liability Liquidity Measures		
1. Percentage of total assets		
a. Total deposits	70.93%	91.65%
b. Federal funds purchased and RPs	2.28	0.69
c. Other borrowed funds < 1 year	2.79	0.00
2. Percentage of total deposits		
a. Demand deposits	10.95	35.20
b. All NOW & ATS accounts	1.96	7.16
c. Insured money market deposit accounts	33.11	18.01
d. Other savings deposits	2.95	4.21
e. Time deposits < $100,000	14.77	16.27
f. Time deposits (CDs) > $100,000	4.37	10.80
3. Total equity to total assets	8.25	7.29
4. Noncurrent loans to total loans	1.05	2.91
5. Net loan charge-offs to total loans	2.11	0.24
6. Reserve for loan losses to total loans	1.49	0.82
7. Core deposits to total assets	63.74	80.85
8. Volatile liabilities to total assets	11.02	10.30

NOTE: PNC Bank and Community National Bank were introduced in Exhibit 3.1.

*Ignores trading account securities.

[†]Figures obtained from the UBPR. Separate data for Treasury, municipal, and CMO pledging requirements are not available. The unpledged securities figure assumes that the same pledging percentage applies equally to all securities—which may not be the case.

The larger PNC has a substantially higher loan-to-deposit ratio at almost 97 percent (down substantially from 2000's 113 percent), while Community National's is only 71 percent. The high loan-to-deposit ratio for PNC reflects its greater reliance on purchased funds and fewer core deposits. Still, it is difficult to assess actual loan liquidity without knowing all contract terms including the cash flow characteristics of specific loans, whether any loans can be securitized, and whether any loans are government guaranteed.

Liability measures focus on the composition of funding sources. As indicated, CNB relies proportionately more on deposits, while PNC obtains more of its funding from nondeposit liabilities such as federal funds and commercial paper. More of the PNC's deposit base consists of demand deposits, interest checking, money market deposit accounts, and small time deposits, while less comes in the form of demand deposits, interest checking, money market deposit accounts, and small time deposits. The core deposit base contributes about 17 percent more and noncore liabilities contribute more than 0.7 percent less at CNB as compared to PNC, which is consistent with aggregate figures nationally. Surprisingly, Community National operates with less equity. Consistent with national averages, however, Community National has fewer past due and nonaccrual loans, and lower loan losses. The higher equity level at PNC is somewhat unusual. Smaller banks generally operate with more equity capital since they have less access to national markets. The low capital level at Community National is an indicator of a lower relative borrowing capacity and thus less liquidity.

LIQUIDITY PLANNING: MONTHLY INTERVALS

The second stage of liquidity planning involves projecting funds needs over the coming year and beyond if necessary. ALCO members are responsible for forecasting deposit growth and loan demand and arranging for adequate liquidity sources to meet potential needs. Projections are separated into three categories: base trend, short-term seasonal, and cyclical values. The analysis assesses a bank's liquidity gap, measured as the difference between potential uses of funds and anticipated sources of funds, over monthly intervals. In practice, many large banks perform their analysis weekly. Deposit and loan data are aggregated to supply the calculations.

Exhibit 14.13 summarizes the basic procedure for projecting liquidity needs over a 12-month planning horizon. The sample bank's year-end balance sheet, which serves as the reference point in the planning model, is provided at the top. Total deposits and loans are forecast monthly during the year at the bottom, with the deposit forecast excluding CDs. The base trend forecast examines the regular annual growth component of deposits or loans. Deposits are expected to grow at a 6 percent annual rate and loans at 12 percent. These growth rates are calculated from historical data consistent with drawing a trend growth line through annual December figures, as in Exhibit 14.11. The estimates indicate what the monthly balances would equal if no seasonal or cyclical fluctuations existed and trend growth continued.

Seasonal influences net of trend are identified in the third column of data. Column 2 provides a seasonal index for each month relative to December totals. This index represents the average of the monthly figure relative to the average of the December figure over the past five years. Independent of trend, January deposits average 99 percent of December deposits while January loans equal 101 percent of December loans. Column 3 lists the difference between the monthly seasonal estimate and the respective December deposit or loan figure. Finally, column 4 measures cyclical deposits and loans as monthly deviations of the prior year's actual deposit or loan balance and the implied trend plus seasonal component. In this example, the January trend plus seasonal estimate for loans equaled $6 million less than the actual balance. This $6 million represents the next year's forecast of unanticipated cyclical loan needs. The final column lists the forecast of total deposits and total loans, respectively, equal to the sum of figures in Columns 1, 3, and 4.

Exhibit 14.14 presents summary estimates of monthly liquidity needs. The cumulative liquidity needed equals the forecast change in loans plus required reserves minus the forecast change in deposits.

Liquidity needs = Forecasted Δloans + ΔRequired reserves − Forecasted Δdeposits

A positive figure means the bank needs additional liquid funds. A negative figure suggests that the bank will have surplus funds to invest.

Although this analysis is somewhat general, it can be used to identify longer-term trends in fund flows. In practice, forecasts are prepared for each distinct deposit account and loan

· EXHIBIT 14.13

FORECASTS OF TREND, SEASONAL, AND CYCLICAL
COMPONENTS OF DEPOSITS AND LOANS

Reference Balance Sheet (Millions of Dollars)

Assets		Liabilities	
Cash and due from banks	$ 160	Transaction accounts and nonnegotiable deposits	$1,600
Loans	1,400	Certificates of deposit and other borrowing	280
Investment securities	400	Stockholders' equity	120
Other assets	40	Total	$2,000
Total	$2,000		

Deposit Forecast

End of Month	(1) Trend Deposits*	(2) Seasonal Deposit Index[†]	(3) Seasonal Deposits— December Deposits	(4) Cyclical Deposits	(5) Total
January	$1,608	99%	−$16	−$3	$1,589
February	1,616	102	+32	+8	1,656
March	1,623	105	+80	+7	1,710
April	1,631	107	+112	+10	1,753
May	1,639	101	+16	+1	1,656
June	1,647	96	−64	−8	1,575
July	1,655	93	−112	−15	1,528
August	1,663	95	−80	−9	1,574
September	1,671	97	−48	−4	1,619
October	1,680	101	+16	0	1,696
November	1,688	104	+64	+3	1,755
December	1,696	100	0	0	1,696

Loan Forecast

End of Month	Trend Loans*	Seasonal Loan Index[†]	Seasonal Loans— December Loans	Cyclical Loans	Total
January	$1,413	101%	$14	$6	$1,433
February	1,427	97	−42	−9	1,376
March	1,440	95	−70	−18	1,352
April	1,454	94	−84	−21	1,349
May	1,467	97	−42	−15	1,410
June	1,481	102	+28	−3	1,506
July	1,495	108	+112	+9	1,616
August	1,510	106	+84	+17	1,611
September	1,524	103	+42	+11	1,577
October	1,538	99	−14	+5	1,529
November	1,553	98	−28	0	1,525
December	1,568	100	0	0	1,568

*Growth trend for December to December averaged 6 percent for deposits and 12 percent for loans over the past 5 years.
[†]Multiply by the preceding December figure.

▪ EXHIBIT 14.14

ESTIMATES OF LIQUIDITY NEEDS (MILLIONS OF DOLLARS)

End of Month	ΔDeposits	ΔRequired Reserves	ΔLoans	Liquidity Needs*
January	−$ 11.0	−$ 1.1	$ 33.0	$ 42.9
February	56.0	5.6	−24.0	−74.4
March	110.0	11.0	−48.0	−147.0
April	153.0	15.3	−51.0	−188.7
May	56.0	5.6	10.0	−40.4
June	−25.0	−2.5	106.0	128.5
July	−72.0	−7.2	216.0	280.8
August	−26.0	−2.6	211.0	234.4
September	19.0	1.9	177.0	159.9
October	96.0	9.6	129.0	42.6
November	155.0	15.5	125.0	−14.5
December	96.0	9.6	168.0	81.6

*Estimates of liquidity needs equal the change in loans plus change in required reserves minus the change in deposits. The reserve ratio equals 10 percent. A positive figure represents a shortage, while a negative figure means the bank has surplus funds to invest.

category, then summed to yield a total estimate. This allows management to incorporate different trend and seasonal patterns for demand deposits, NOWs, MMDAs, and thus reduce the aggregate forecast error. For example, demand deposit growth has slowed in recent years while the growth in MMDAs, IRAs, and other deposits has accelerated. Separate estimates capture this diverse behavior.

Management can supplement this analysis by including projected changes in purchased funds and investments with specific loan and deposit flows. One procedure is to calculate a liquidity gap measure over different time intervals. This format is comparable to the funding GAP analysis introduced in Chapters 3 and 8. It begins by classifying potential uses and sources of funds into separate time frames according to their cash flow characteristics. The liquidity gap for each interval equals the dollar value of uses of funds minus the dollar value of sources of funds.

Exhibit 14.15 demonstrates this format for a hypothetical bank. By using specific account information, managers can trace the source of any significant outflow or inflow and take remedial action. Consider the data representing the next 30 days for the hypothetical bank. The bank has $50 million in maturing CDs and Eurodollars and $5.5 million in small time deposits that mature. It expects to fund $113 million in new loans and see transactions accounts fall by $4.5 million for a total $173 million in uses. Expected sources of funds include $18 million in maturing securities and $80 million in loan principal payments. The liquidity gap for the next 30 days thus equals $75 million. The bank needs to replace the maturing CDs and Eurodollars plus find an additional $25 million in liquid funds to finance this loan growth.

Comparable figures for 31 to 90 days out and 91 to 365 days out are also shown in the exhibit. The cumulative gap summarizes the total liquidity position from the present to the farthest day within each time interval. The bank expects to experience a liquidity surplus two to three months out and a $208 million liquidity shortage for the entire year.

Once normal liquidity needs are forecast, a bank should compare the estimates with potential funding sources and extraordinary funds needs. One researcher introduced a simple format, modified as Exhibit 14.16, that requires each bank to project its borrowing

> ▪ **EXHIBIT 14.15**

LIQUIDITY GAP ESTIMATES

	0 to 30 Days	31 to 90 Days	91 to 365 Days
Potential Uses of Funds			
Add: Maturing time deposits			
Small time deposits	$ 5.5	$ 8.0	$ 34.0
Certificates of deposit over $100,000	40.0	70.0	100.0
Eurodollar deposits	10.0	10.0	30.0
Plus: Forecast new loans			
Commercial loans	60.0	112.0	686.0
Consumer loans	22.0	46.0	210.0
Real estate and other loans	31.0	23.0	223.0
Minus: Forecast net change in transactional accounts*			
Demand deposits	−6.5	105.5	10.0
NOW accounts	0.4	5.5	7.0
Money market deposit accounts	1.6	3.0	6.0
Total uses	$173.0	$155.0	$1,260.0
Potential Sources of Funds			
Add: Maturing investments			
Money market instruments	$ 8.0	$ 16.5	$ 36.5
U.S. Treasury and agency securities	7.5	10.5	40.0
Municipal securities	2.5	1.0	12.5
Plus: Principal payments on loans	80.0	262.0	903.0
Total sources	$98.0	$290.0	$992.0
Periodic Liquidity GAP[†]	75.0	−135.0	268.0
Cumulative Liquidity GAP	75.0	−60.0	208.0

NOTE: Figures are in millions of dollars.

*Net of required reserves.

†Potential uses of funds minus potential sources of funds.

capacity via federal funds purchased, RPs, and unused CDs and combine it with funds available from reducing federal funds sold and selling loan participations, money market securities, and unpledged securities.[16] This total is then compared with potential draws against unused loan commitments and letters of credit. Of course, no bank wants to utilize its borrowing capacity fully or sell all of its available assets. It should always leave some potential funding available for extraordinary events.

Applying the data from Exhibit 14.16 to the 30-day gap in Exhibit 14.15, the sample bank has considerable flexibility in meeting its liquidity need. First, it could simply replace the maturing CDs and Eurodollars with similar borrowings, for which it has an estimated $90 million capacity. Second, the bank could borrow via federal funds or RPs, eliminate federal funds sold, and make up the difference with new CDs. The best alternative is the one with the lowest cost. In general, large banks prefer to borrow rather than liquidate assets, while small banks sell assets or restrict growth. The best use of this information is to conduct

---

[16]See Temple (1983).

■ EXHIBIT 14.16

POTENTIAL FUNDING SOURCES

	Time Frame		
	0 to 30 Days	**31 to 90 Days**	**91 to 365 Days**
Purchased Funds Capacity			
Federal funds purchased (overnight and term)	$ 20	$ 20	$ 30
Repurchase agreements	10	10	10
Negotiable certificates of deposit			
Local	50	50	60
National	20	20	25
Eurodollar certificates of deposit	20	20	20
Total	$120	$120	$145
Additional Funding Sources			
Reductions in federal funds sold	$ 5	$ 5	$ 5
Loan participations	20	20	20
Sale of money market securities	5	5	5
Sale of unpledged securities	10	10	10
Total	$ 40	$ 40	$ 40
Potential Funding Sources*	$160	$160	$185
Potential Extraordinary Funding Needs			
50% of outstanding letters of credit	5	10	15
20% of unfunded loan commitments	25	30	35
Total	$ 30	$ 40	$ 50
Excess Potential Funding Sources	$130	$120	$135

NOTE: Figures are in millions of dollars.

*Purchased funds capacity plus additional funding sources.

"what-if" analysis to determine the cost implications of various alternatives and assess how much flexibility management has in adjusting its cash position. Large banks with international operations should perform this liquidity analysis in each currency in which they operate since their liquidity position might vary by currency.

CONSIDERATIONS IN SELECTING LIQUIDITY SOURCES

The previous analysis focuses on estimating the dollar magnitude of liquidity needs. Implicit in the discussion is the assumption that the bank has adequate liquidity sources. For most banks, loan growth exceeds deposit growth net of CDs and Eurodollars. In the short run, banks have the option of financing this net growth either by selling securities or obtaining new deposits. In the long run, this net growth must be financed out of purchased liabilities because banks own a limited amount of securities. Yet most banks have limited access to new purchased funds because they are small with no market reputation, or they have exhausted their borrowing capacity in terms of their capital base and earnings potential. There are two possible solutions to this dilemma. Management can either restrict asset growth or seek additional core deposits or equity. Regulatory actions to raise bank capital requirements, discussed in Chapter 13, have the beneficial side effect of improving access to the money and capital markets.

Banks with options in meeting liquidity needs evaluate the characteristics of various sources to minimize costs. The following factors should be considered in asset sales or new borrowings:

ASSET SALES

1. Brokerage fees
2. Securities gains or losses
3. Foregone interest income
4. Any increase or decrease in taxes
5. Any increase or decrease in interest receipts

NEW BORROWINGS

1. Brokerage fees
2. Required reserves
3. FDIC insurance premiums
4. Servicing or promotion costs
5. Interest expense

The costs should be evaluated in present value terms because interest income and interest expense may arise over substantially different time periods. The choice of one source over another often involves an implicit interest rate forecast.

Suppose, for example, that a bank temporarily needs funds for six months. Management has decided to sell $1 million of Treasuries from the bank's portfolio. The choice is between securities with either one year or five years remaining to maturity. Both securities sell at par and earn 5.5 percent annually. If the bank sells the 1-year security, it implicitly assumes that the level of short-term Treasury rates is going to fall far enough below 5.5 percent so that any eventual reinvestment of funds would yield less than that on a 5-year security. If the bank sells the 5-year bond, it assumes that the level of short-term rates will rise above 5.5 percent, on average.

Suppose instead that the bank decides to issue either a 6-month CD or a 1-month CD. Clearly, the 6-month CD locks in interest expense and requires only one transaction. A 1-month CD will need to be rolled over, with uncertain future interest expense. Transactions costs will also be higher. The rationale for issuing any shorter-term CD can only be that the present value of expected interest expense plus transactions costs will be lower with this alternative.[17]

SUMMARY

Banks manage their cash position to minimize required holdings because cash assets do not generate interest income. Vault cash is held to meet customer transaction needs. Banks hold demand deposit balances at the Federal Reserve and other financial institutions to meet the Federal Reserve's legal reserve requirements and to purchase services such as check clearing. Float, or checks in the process of collection, is a natural product of the check-clearing process.

---

[17]The yield curve incorporates both liquidity premiums and interest rate expectations. Thus, 1-month yields at 5 percent and 6-month yields at 5.2 percent signify that traders expect 1-month rates to increase. By issuing a 1-month security, the borrower implicitly assumes that rates will not increase as much as that implied by the yield curve.

This chapter examines the characteristics of cash and liquid assets and explains why banks hold each type and how the magnitudes can be minimized. Liquid assets generally include federal funds sold and RPs, short-term unpledged Treasury and other highly marketable securities, and loans that can be readily sold at predictable prices. Their primary advantage over cash is that they earn interest. Liquidity planning is an ongoing part of a bank's asset and liability management strategy. In the short run, it focuses on meeting legal reserve requirements. It specifically involves monitoring net deposit outflows and inflows and deciding how to finance deficiencies or invest excess funds. This chapter examines two different stages of liquidity planning. The first focuses on managing a bank's required reserve position over the two-week maintenance period. The second analyzes monthly liquidity gaps as measures of liquidity risk throughout the next year. A bank's liquidity gap measures the difference between the dollar value of expected cash outflows and expected cash inflows within a given time interval. Positive liquidity gaps indicate a net liquidity need, while negative liquidity gaps indicate surplus investable funds. Planning models for each stage of analysis are applied to a hypothetical bank's data.

QUESTIONS

1. What are the different types of cash assets and the basic objectives for holding each?
2. The determination of cash requirements is closely associated with a bank's liquidity requirements. Explain why.
3. What are the advantages and disadvantages for a bank contemplating holding more cash?
4. Monetary theory examines the role of excess reserves (actual reserves minus required reserves) in influencing economic activity and Federal Reserve monetary policy. Viewed in the context of a single bank, excess reserves are difficult to measure. Explain what amount of a bank's actual reserve assets are excess reserves during any single day in the reserve maintenance period under lagged reserve accounting.
5. Under a contemporaneous reserve accounting, Federal Reserve open market operations affect a bank's required reserves and actual reserves simultaneously. Explain how and why this improves the Federal Reserve's ability to influence general economic conditions. Why is the Fed hampered under lagged reserve accounting?
6. Which of the following activities will affect a bank's required reserves?
   a. The local Girl Scout troop collects coins and currency to buy a new camping stove. They deposit $250 in coins and open a small time deposit.
   b. You decide to move $200 from your MMDA to your NOW account.
   c. You sell your car to the teller at your bank for $3,000. The teller pays with a check drawn on the bank, and you deposit the check immediately into your checking account at the bank.
   d. The local university takes one-half of the fall tuition receipts and buys a 3-month CD.
   e. Ford Motor Company opens an assembly plant outside town and opens a checking account at the local bank for $100,000 with a check drawn on its bank in Detroit.
7. In many cases, banks do not permit depositors to spend the proceeds of a deposit until several days have elapsed. What risks do banks face in the check-clearing process? Does this justify holds on checks?

8. Define a daylight overdraft and outline the nature of the risks it poses to the Federal Reserve System. What policies might be implemented to control these risks? How does a daylight overdraft differ from float?

9. What is the difference between a correspondent, respondent, and bankers' bank?

10. A corporate customer borrows $150,000 against the firm's credit line at a local bank. Indicate with a T-account how the transaction will affect the bank's deposit balances held at the Federal Reserve when the firm spends the proceeds.

11. What are the fundamental differences and similarities between the commercial loan theory, shiftability theory, anticipated income theory, and liability management theory regarding liquidity?

12. Liquidity planning requires monitoring deposit outflows. In each of the following situations, which of the outflows are discretionary and which are not? If the outflow is not discretionary, is it predictable or unexpected?
    a. In April, a farmer draws down his line of credit in order to purchase seed.
    b. Students borrow to pay fall tuition.
    c. The bank makes a preferred stock dividend payment.
    d. A fire destroys a portion of the local business district and many firms apply for reconstruction loans.
    e. The rent on the bank's offices is paid.
    f. On the Friday before the citywide festival, all ATMs in town have been drained of cash.
    g. A New York bank has just opened a local banking office and is offering a VCR to anyone who transfers funds from a CD at another bank.
    h. The bank buys most of the newly issued local municipal securities.

13. What do the terms core deposits and volatile, or noncore, deposits mean? Explain how a bank might estimate the magnitude of each.

14. Liquidity measures and potential sources of liquidity differ for large multinational banks and small community banks. List the key differences and explain why they appear.

15. Explain how each of the following will affect a bank's deposit balances at the Federal Reserve:
    a. The bank ships excess vault cash to the Federal Reserve.
    b. The bank buys U.S. government securities in the open market.
    c. The bank realizes a surplus in its local clearinghouse processing.
    d. The bank sells federal funds.
    e. A $100,000 certificate of deposit at the bank matures and is not rolled over.
    f. Local businesses deposit tax payments in the Treasury's account at the local bank.

16. Banks must pledge collateral against four different types of liabilities. Which liabilities require collateral, what type of collateral is required, and what impact do the pledging requirements have on a bank's asset liquidity?

17. Explain how a bank's credit risk and interest rate risk can affect its liquidity risk.

18. Rank the following types of depositors by the liquidity risk they typically pose for a bank.
    a. A CD depositor attracted through a stockbroker
    b. Foreign investors trading with a local corporation
    c. Local schoolchildren
    d. A two wage earner family with $38,000 in annual salaries and with three children

19. A traditional measure of liquidity risk is a bank's loan-to-deposit ratio. Give two reasons why this is a poor measure of risk. Give one reason why it is a good measure.

20. What can a bank do to increase its core deposits? What are the costs and benefits of such efforts? Generally, how might management estimate the relative interest elasticity of various deposit liabilities of a bank?

21. Your bank's estimated liquidity gap over the next 90 days equals $180 million. You estimate that projected funding sources over the same 90 days will equal only $150 million. What planning and policy requirements does this impose on your $3 billion bank?

22. What are the conceptual differences between the trend, seasonal, and cyclical components of a bank's loans and deposits? Discuss why a bank should examine each component rather than simply look at total loans and deposits.

23. Discuss the relative importance of liquidity versus capital problems in causing bank failures. Explain the normal sequence of events leading to failure and the importance of market value measures.

PROBLEMS

I. CALCULATION OF REQUIRED RESERVES

At the close of business on Wednesday, Gene Wandling was reviewing whether Hawkeye National Bank was successful in meeting its legal reserve requirements at the Federal Reserve. The bank had just completed the 2-week reserve maintenance period, during which it held a daily average of $238 million in reserve deposits with the Federal Reserve. The bank had a daily average reserve deficiency the previous maintenance period of $3.75 million, which was within the allowable 4 percent limit.

Hawkeye National Bank's daily average net transactions accounts for the base computation period along with balances for selected assets are listed below.

Daily average (millions of dollars)	
Net transactions accounts	3,257
Demand deposits due from U.S. depository institutions	366
Cash items in process of collection	181

Hawkeye National Bank could use daily average vault cash holdings of $31 million to offset its reserve requirement. Using the reserve percentages from Exhibit 14.4, calculate the bank's daily average required reserve holdings during the maintenance period. Did Hawkeye meet its reserve target? If the bank had carried forward a daily reserve surplus of $2.1 million instead of a deficiency, would it have met its target? What are the costs to a bank if its reserves fall outside the target range?

II. PRICING CORRESPONDENT SERVICES

In addition to his other duties, Gene Wandling is responsible for analyzing the profitability of Hawkeye National Bank's respondent bank account relationships. Like most of its competitors, Hawkeye priced correspondent services monthly, using cost allocations obtained from its own accounting department. Respondent banks paid for services by maintaining demand deposit balances with Hawkeye, which was quite firm in its pricing. Hawkeye had to hold 10 percent reserves against demand deposits and gave an earnings credit equal to the average 3-month Treasury bill rate during the month applied to its customers' investable balances.

Gene was concerned that one bank in particular, Valley State Bank, was not keeping sufficient balances at Hawkeye to pay for its correspondent services. He decided to review the bank's account relationship for the past month. Using the relevant data for April provided below, determine whether Hawkeye's revenues from the account covered its cost of services. If the revenues were deficient, calculate how much Valley State Bank would have to increase its correspondent balances to cover the cost of services.

Services Provided	Cost per Item
Check clearing—14,785 items	$ 0.0031
Wire transfers—43 items	2.00
Currency shipment—1 item	75.00
Security safekeeping—11 items	4.50
Data processing—1 item	150.00
Letters of credit—2 items	100.00

Memoranda

Valley State's average ledger balance was $107,500.
Average float associated with the account was $35,808.
Fee income generated by Hawkeye was $150.
Applicable earnings credit was 7.1 percent.

ACTIVITY

Determine how long it takes your bank to process your checks. Find some old checks you wrote to people locally and in a different Federal Reserve district. Note the date on which you wrote the check and then find the date on your monthly account statement when the bank deducted the amount from your account. How might you use this information to manage your personal float? Compare this with the funds availability schedule at your bank.

APPENDIX

CONTINENTAL ILLINOIS: THE MAKING OF A LIQUIDITY CRISIS

On Friday, May 11, 1984, Continental Illinois National Bank & Trust Co. of Chicago borrowed $3.6 billion from the Federal Reserve System to replace overnight deposits at the bank that could not be rolled over. The largest run ever on a single bank had begun. By the end of 1984, Continental's deposit base had shrunk by almost $12 billion and the bank had been effectively nationalized. The story behind Continental's problems is a simple one: bad loans produced earnings problems, which decreased the market value of bank equity, undermined customer confidence, and subsequently brought about net deposit outflows. The story behind Continental's rescue demonstrates the inconsistencies of current regulatory policy.

THE LOAN PROBLEMS

Continental's problems largely reflect management's pursuit of growth through aggressive lending initiated in the early 1970s. Roger Anderson, named chairman in 1973, targeted the

· EXHIBIT A.1

COMPARISON OF PERFORMANCE MEASURES: CONTINENTAL ILLINOIS VERSUS PEER BANKS

Ratios	1977–1981		1982		1983	
	Continental	Peers	Continental	Peers	Continental	Peers
Growth*						
Loan growth	19.82%	14.67	2.70%	9.26	−7.15	5.99
Asset growth	16.41	13.04	−8.67	7.56	−1.87	4.59
Earnings growth	14.74	18.26	−69.41	4.19	39.07	10.79
Profitability						
Return on equity	14.38	12.65	4.56	11.53	5.95	11.15
Return on assets	0.54	0.50	0.18	0.49	0.26	0.52
Capital Adequacy						
Equity/Total assets Peers	4.36	4.55	4.81	4.86	5.17	5.39
Equity/Total loans Peers	6.16	7.00	5.26	6.98	6.03	7.62
Asset Quality						
Net charge-offs/Total loans	0.33	0.45	1.28	0.55	1.37	0.64
Allowable for possible loan losses/Total loans	0.97	1.01	1.15	1.08	1.24	1.21
Nonperforming assets/Total assets	1.4	1.4	4.6	2.1	4.5	2.3
(Liquid assets − Volatile liabilities)/Total assets	−43.83	−23.63	−58.16	−31.51	−52.61	−30.88

NOTE: Peer banks' data are averages for the 16 largest U.S. banking organizations at year-end 1983, excluding Continental Illinois.

*Average annual growth rates.

bank as one of the top three domestic lenders in the United States. Loan officers were given considerable leeway in booking new credits. Individual officers had authority to approve larger loans than their counterparts at other banks and often offered lower rates to win new business. If the bank was part of a loan syndicate, it often insisted on a disproportionately large share of the credit.[18] Not surprisingly, Continental's loan growth far outpaced that at other multinational banks. From 1977 to 1981, Continental's loans grew at a 19.8 percent average annual rate, while the comparable rate for peer banks was 14.7 percent. Exhibit A.1 compares Continental's performance ratios with peer banks.[19] It indicates that through 1981, Continental was a high-performance bank, operating with greater leverage and earning more with comparable loan quality.

Still, the reported profit figures disguised potentially serious earnings and liquidity problems in funding the loan growth. Unlike other large banks, Continental had few core deposits. The state of Illinois imposed strict limits on branch banking, which gave Continental a relatively small stable consumer deposit base. The bank subsequently financed its loan growth with short-term CDs, Eurodollars, and overnight borrowings from commercial customers and

---

[18]In most cases, syndicate partners split the credit into shares in proportion to each bank's relative asset size.

[19]The comparisons are between Continental Illinois Corp. (Continental Bank's holding company) and other large bank holding companies. The data are from *Inquiry into Continental Illinois*, 1984. Peer banks are the 16 largest U.S. multinational banking organizations, not including Continental Illinois.

financial institutions. Through 1981, its net reliance on this "hot money" was almost double that of comparable banks, indicated by the liquidity measure net of these volatile liabilities at the bottom of Exhibit A.1.

The bank's reported earnings also masked problems with loan quality. Aggressive lending in a volatile economic environment like the late 1970s virtually mandates that a bank take on marginal credits. Ultimately, Continental had heavy loan exposure to problem companies like Braniff, International Harvester, Nucorp Energy, and Wickes. Still, energy lending fueled much of the loan growth, an area where Continental had a long-standing interest and recognized expertise. Lending in this area coincided nicely with the oil boom's rising prices, and profitable-looking borrowers, which included major oil companies, wildcat drillers, and oil field servicing operators.

With the downturn in oil prices, many energy customers began having serious problems. Continental subsequently had problems with its own customers, as did Penn Square Bank, a downstream respondent in Oklahoma City. By 1981, Continental had purchased more than $600 million in loan participations from Penn Square Bank. In many cases, loan officers failed to obtain or review loan documentation. This documentation provides collateral information, cash flow projections, and the reason for granting the loan. Bank auditors often did not verify that collateral existed, and bank lawyers did not complete the paperwork to ensure the bank's security interest. When Penn Square Bank failed in July 1982, Continental held more than $1 billion in loans originated by Penn Square. By December 1982, Continental had written off or listed as nonperforming more than $500 million of this total. Losses on other marginal credits followed.

Exhibit A.1 documents the deterioration in Continental's performance during 1982 and 1983. Earnings fell by more than 60 percent as the bank charged off more loans and restricted its growth. Nonperforming assets (those with interest payments more than 90 days past due) increased to 4.6 percent of total assets, more than double that of peer banks. Even with the decrease in loans and other assets in 1983, the bank's liquidity position worsened to where volatile liabilities exceeded liquid assets by almost 53 percent of total assets.

Two events foretold Continental's eventual liquidity trouble. First, in July 1982, Continental's CDs were removed from the list of CDs traded "on the run." This list represents CDs of the largest, well-known U.S. banking organizations that are traded interchangeably by dealers without reference to the specific underlying banks. Removal reduced the effective demand for Continental's CDs and increased the bank's borrowing costs. It also signified that investors were not eager to acquire Continental's CDs. Second, the bank announced in response that it would rely more heavily on Eurodollars. Continental was then paying a premium on its deposits, and investors demanded much shorter maturities.

THE LIQUIDITY CRUNCH

The Penn Square failure forced Continental to closely examine its loan policies and asset quality. Regulators pressured the bank to clean up its operations while management played down its problems. Nonperforming loans increased to $1.9 billion at the end of 1983, leading to the early retirement of chairman Anderson in February 1984. During the first three months of 1984, problem loans rose to $2.3 billion, net interest income fell $80 million below that for the first quarter of 1983, and the bank reported an operating loss. Many of the newer problem loans were to Third World borrowers. Although the bank's loan loss reserve increased, it equaled only the industry norm. To report a quarterly profit and pay dividends, Continental sold its credit card operation to Chemical Bank of New York. The economic value of shareholder equity was deteriorating rapidly.

Continental's deposit-gathering problems surfaced during this period. As of December 31, 1983, the bank obtained only 25 percent of its borrowings from relatively stable, domestic sources. An incredible 64 percent came from CDs, Eurodollars, commercial paper, and overnight borrowings, as indicated below.

Funding Source	Percentage of Liabilities
Noninterest bearing accounts	9.8%
Domestic time and savings deposits, nonnegotiable	15.5%
Commercial CDs	8.8%
Time deposits in foreign branches	38.1%
Federal funds purchased and RPs	15.5%
Commercial paper	1.3%
Other interest-bearing debt	11.0%
	100.0%

The market was constantly bombarded with Continental's problems. When rumors circulated on May 8, 1984, that the bank was about to fail, foreign banks called in credit lines extended to Continental and refused to buy the bank's new CDs. Over the next few days, depositors refused to roll over maturing CDs and Eurodollars, and Continental had to borrow $3.6 billion from the Federal Reserve to replace the deposit outflow. In short, the market had lost confidence in Continental's future.

THE RESCUE

The first step in Continental's rescue was to calm the money markets. Without public confidence, Continental could not sell its CDs or borrow unsecured federal funds overnight. A group of banks led by Morgan Guaranty Trust Co. quickly put together a $4.5 billion line of credit to Continental. The Federal Reserve allocated $17 billion of Continental's assets deposited with it as collateral against potential borrowing. Still, this was not enough to stem the panic. On May 17, regulators stepped in with a four-part, government-arranged rescue. First, the FDIC guaranteed all of Continental's depositors and general creditors against any loss, regardless of size. This effectively removed the $100,000 per account limit on FDIC insurance. Second, the FDIC and seven large banks injected $2 billion into the bank's capital base.[20] Third, the initial private bank credit line was extended to $5.5 billion with 28 banks participating. Finally, the Federal Reserve pledged to continue funding Continental's discount window borrowing.

This package represented only a temporary solution as the deposit outflow continued even with this support. In early July, after liquidating $5 billion in assets, Continental still owed $4 billion to the Federal Reserve, $4 billion to the 28 banks, and $2 billion to the FDIC. In just two months, the bank had lost around $15 billion in deposits.[21]

---

[20]The Federal Deposit Insurance Corp. stated that its capital contribution would be available only until Continental obtained permanent capital "by merger or otherwise."

[21]Investor uncertainty explains why depositors pulled their funds even with a government guarantee. The initial guarantee was extremely vague, providing no detail for a formal legal challenge if necessary. If Continental failed, depositors did not know whether they would lose interest until restitution or how long their funds would be tied up. If Continental were sold, there was no assurance the government guarantee would still apply. The premium for rolling over deposits was not worth the worry.

PERMANENT FINANCIAL RESTRUCTURING

In July 1984, the regulators proposed a permanent restructuring of Continental that was later approved by shareholders. This agreement made the FDIC an owner in Continental through a complex series of transactions, yet it forced the bank's existing shareholders to bear most of the risk of loss. The plan contained the following elements:

1. The FDIC immediately purchased $3 billion (book value) of Continental's problem loans. The FDIC paid for the loans by assuming $2 billion of Continental's existing debt from the Federal Reserve. It immediately charged off $1 billion as a loss, which reduced the book value of its capital to $800 million.

2. Continental retained the option to sell an additional $1.5 billion in problem loans during the next three years.

3. The FDIC purchased $1 billion of newly issued preferred stock in Continental, convertible into 160 million common shares. Holders of Continental's existing 40 million shares exchanged their shares for stock in a newly created holding company, which owned the remaining 40 million shares. The FDIC thus immediately owned 80 percent of the bank.[22]

4. The FDIC kept the right to purchase the 40 million shares in the new holding company, depending on its losses on the problem loans it purchased. The FDIC's total loss, including interest expense paid to the Federal Reserve and collection costs, will be calculated after five years. The FDIC could repurchase one share, for one one-thousandth of a cent, for each $20 in loss.[23]

5. Existing shareholders received one right for each share owned to purchase a share in Continental for $4.50 within 60 days and for $6 afterwards.

In addition to these changes, Continental continued to borrow from private banks and the Federal Reserve. It was essentially nationalized even though it changed management and the FDIC did not play a role in supervising day-to-day operations.

From 1985 through 1989, Continental Illinois reported profits. It shrunk its asset base to $29 billion in 1990, one-third less than the asset base in 1981. In 1986, Continental's management announced, with the FDIC's approval, its intent to purchase several Chicago area suburban banks with cumulative assets of over $150 million. The strategy was to start building a stable retail deposit base. From 1987 to 1989, Continental redirected its business strategy by focusing on commercial lending, particularly highly leveraged transactions, and offering investment advisory services in the area of futures and options through its First Options Corp. subsidiary. During 1990, Continental's management announced that it was selling First Options, cutting 900 employees representing 13 percent of its total, and it reported a doubling of its nonperforming loans to more than $450 million. New management came in and refocused on large commercial business customers. In January 1994, BankAmerica announced that it had purchased Continental and would headquarter its business operations in Chicago.

---

[22]Interestingly, in 1932, the Reconstruction Finance Corp., a federal government agency, purchased $50 million of preferred stock in Continental under similar circumstances to help prevent the bank's failure.

[23]If the total loss reached $800 million, the Federal Deposit Insurance Corp. could repurchase all 40 million shares and effectively own 100 percent of the bank. This ignored the rights offer to existing shareholders that was part of the agreement. Even if all rights were exercised, the FDIC would still own over 83 percent of Continental.

PUBLIC POLICY ISSUES

The FDIC's bailout of Continental raises numerous policy issues. Should the bank have been allowed to fail? Throughout the crisis, the regulators guaranteed that none of Continental's depositors or other creditors would lose anything. This promise conflicts directly with the modified-payout solution imposed at other bank failures, in which uninsured depositors lost their investment. Because most failures involve small banks, Continental's special treatment constitutes discrimination against small banks. The rescue also leaves unanswered what the consequences would have been had Continental failed. The regulators argued that failure would have led to a chain-reaction of small bank failures because so many banks held correspondent balances with Continental. Finally, what is the ultimate cost of this type of bailout to the U.S. Treasury? What is the impact on the federal deficit?

Another lesson for bank managers is the value of a stable deposit base. Banks that rely heavily on large, purchased liabilities subject the firm to the whims of creditors with little allegiance. These investors are quite willing to move their funds when a bank reports problems or another institution offers higher rates. Extreme reliance on hot money increases a bank's liquidity risk and risk for the entire banking system. Many banks have had to seek stable retail deposits, limit their asset growth, and generally increase their capital base to reduce potential funding problems.

EXTENDING CREDIT TO BUSINESSES AND INDIVIDUALS

15

OVERVIEW OF CREDIT POLICY AND
LOAN CHARACTERISTICS

For most people in commercial banking, lending represents the heart of the industry. Loans dominate assets at most banks and generate the largest share of operating income. Loan officers are among the most visible bank employees, while loan policies typically determine how fast a community grows and what type of business develops. Historically, senior management has selected future replacements from the lending staff.

The increased competition among commercial banks, savings banks, credit unions, finance companies and investment banks has lead to changes in lending policies and loan portfolios. Following World War II through the 1970s, commercial banks controlled commercial lending in the United States. When confronted with earnings pressure, they often raised loan-to-asset ratios by extending credit to marginal borrowers in the search for higher returns. Increasing loan losses necessarily followed, in many cases causing banks to fail. The credit environment during the 1980s and early 1990s consisted of too many high-risk loans, few creditworthy customers, historically high loan losses, and aggressive pricing producing low risk-adjusted returns. Not surprisingly, banks in the aggregate reduced the size of their loan portfolios and substituted marketable securities. In 1992 bank investment securities were 22 percent of total assets and net loans were down to 56 percent of total assets. As the U.S. economy moved out of the recession, banks slowly grew their loan portfolios along with the growth in consumer confidence and spending. By 2001, investment securities were down to 18 percent of total bank assets while total loans were up to 58.2 percent of total assets.[1] Loan growth and loan demand were so great by early 2001 that regulators had begun to express concerns about the quality of banks' loan portfolios. The U.S. and world economies slowed appreciably by the end of 2001. This economic slow down, combined with the tragic events of September 11, 2001, meant that loan losses and problem loans were once again on the rise.

---

[1]From the FDIC Institutions Directory, available on the Internet at http://www.fdic.gov.

Different management teams pursue different lending strategies. Many banks concentrate on niches in which they restrict new loans to well-defined markets where they have specialized experience. They consciously limit growth in hopes of building capital to support future expansion. At one end, some larger banks have gravitated toward investment banking, underwriting securities, and making loans but moving the loans off-balance sheet by selling them to other investors and earning a profit from servicing fees. Other banks see loan growth as their primary path to long-term survival and aggressively court new consumer and commercial business. Many hope to eventually be allowed to make an equity investment in some of the companies to whom they currently lend.

This chapter provides an overview of the credit process and the types of credit extended by commercial banks. It describes recent problems banks have faced in certain credit areas and issues related to default risk and interest rate risk. Finally, it explains the trend toward increased involvement in off-balance sheet activities including loans by introducing credit derivatives.

RECENT TRENDS IN LOAN GROWTH AND QUALITY

Commercial banks extend credit to different types of borrowers for many different purposes. For most customers, bank credit is the primary source of available debt financing. For banks, good loans are the most profitable assets. As with any investment, extending loans to businesses and individuals involves taking risks to earn high returns. Returns come in the form of loan interest, fee income, and investment income from new deposits. Banks also use loans to cross sell other fee-generating services. The most prominent assumed risk is credit risk. Many factors can lead to loan defaults. An entire industry, such as energy, agriculture, or real estate, can decline because of general economic events. Firm-specific problems may arise from changing technology, labor strikes, shifts in consumer preferences, or bad management. Individual borrowers find that their ability to repay closely follows the business cycle as personal income rises and falls. Loans as a group thus exhibit the highest charge-offs among bank assets, so banks regularly set aside substantial reserves against anticipated losses.

Interest rate risk also arises from credit decisions. Loan maturities, pricing, and the form of principal repayment affect the timing and magnitude of a bank's cash inflows. Floating-rate and variable-rate loans, for example, generate cash flows that vary closely with borrowing costs. Fixed-rate balloon payment loans, in contrast, generate fewer cash flows. Longer-term consumer loans need to be funded with stable deposits to reduce exposure to rate changes.

Loans are the dominant asset in most banks' portfolios, comprising on average 50 to 75 percent of total assets. Loan composition varies between banks depending on size, location, trade area, and lending expertise. Exhibit 15.1 summarizes proportionate differences among general loan categories for different-sized banks at the end of 2001. Several trends stand out. First, with the exception of the banks over $1 billion, the ratio of loans to assets generally increases with bank size. The range is from 61 percent for banks with assets under $100 million to 66 percent for banks from $500 million to $1 billion. Second, real estate loans represent the largest single loan category for all banks and is highest for savings banks. Third, of the real estate loans, residential 1–4 family loans (mostly mortgage products) contribute the largest amount. Fourth, commercial and industrial loans represent the second highest concentration of loans at banks with assets greater than $10 billion, but

EXHIBIT 15.1

COMMERCIAL BANK LOANS AS A PERCENTAGE OF TOTAL ASSETS, 2001.

	Commercial Banks with Asset Size							
	Less than $100 Million	$100 to $300 Million	$300 to $500 Million	$500 to 1 Billion	$1 to $10 Billion	Greater than $10 Billion	All Commercial Banks	All Savings Institutions
Number of institutions reporting	4486	2350	509	335	320	80	8080	1533
Net loans and leases	60.22%	63.39%	64.20%	65.05%	60.58%	56.59%	58.20%	66.49%
Plus: Loan Loss Allowance	0.86	0.89	0.91	1.02	1.11	1.14	1.10	0.59
Total loans & leases	61.08	64.28	65.12	66.08	61.69	57.73	59.30	67.08
Plus: Unearned income	0.07	0.08	0.08	0.06	0.06	0.04	0.05	0.01
Loans and leases, gross	61.15	64.36	65.19	66.14	61.75	57.77	59.34	67.09
All real estate loans	35.86	42.57	44.27	42.65	34.97	22.80	27.46	58.38
Real estate loans in domestic offices:	35.86	42.57	44.26	42.65	34.94	22.01	26.90	58.38
Construction and land development	3.38	4.78	5.81	5.87	4.57	2.17	2.94	2.96
Commercial real estate	10.45	15.62	17.63	16.92	12.36	5.13	7.73	4.84
Multifamily residential real estate	0.81	1.20	1.61	1.72	1.53	0.79	0.98	4.54
1-4 family residential	16.73	18.64	17.62	17.19	16.02	13.77	14.71	46.02
Home equity loans	0.99	1.61	2.09	2.16	2.15	2.54	2.35	2.31
Farmland	4.50	2.33	1.59	0.95	0.45	0.15	0.54	0.02
Real estate loans in foreign offices	0.00	0.00	0.01	0.00	0.04	0.79	0.56	0.00
Farm loans	6.31	2.52	1.63	1.15	0.61	0.27	0.73	0.04
Commercial and industrial loans	10.51	11.17	11.27	12.47	12.43	16.27	14.96	2.83
To non-U.S. addressees	0.00	0.07	0.11	0.19	0.30	3.11	2.24	0.00
Loans to individuals	7.61	7.00	6.67	7.72	10.76	9.92	9.61	5.34
Credit cards and related plans	0.18	0.54	0.94	1.31	4.05	4.08	3.54	1.34
Related Plans	0.13	0.15	0.25	0.27	0.41	0.48	0.42	0.03
Other loans to individuals	7.30	6.32	5.48	6.14	6.30	5.36	5.65	3.97
Total other loans and leases	0.87	1.09	1.35	2.15	2.97	8.51	6.60	0.50
Acceptances of other banks	0.00	0.00	0.00	0.02	0.02	0.16	0.11	0.00
Loans to foreign governments & official institutions	0.31	0.35	0.41	0.37	0.45	0.34	0.36	0.01
Obligations of states & political subdivisions in the U.S.	0.28	0.35	0.38	0.60	0.87	2.23	1.75	0.12
Other loans	0.24	0.30	0.32	0.87	1.11	3.37	2.59	0.35
Lease financing receivables	0.00	0.00	0.00	0.00	0.04	0.54	0.38	0.00
Of non-U.S. addressees								
Loans to depository institutions and acceptances of other banks	0.04	0.10	0.24	0.29	0.52	2.40	1.78	0.02
Memoranda:								
Commercial real estate loans not secured by real estate	0.12	0.15	0.17	0.15	0.39	0.94	0.74	0.02
Restructured loans and leases, total	0.05	0.05	0.03	0.04	0.02	0.01	0.02	0.13
Loans secured by real estate to non-U.S. addressees	0.00	0.00	0.02	0.11	0.06	0.64	0.46	0.01
Total loans & leases in foreign offices	0.00	0.08	0.03	0.22	0.32	6.34	4.51	0.00

SOURCE: FDIC Statistics on Depository Institutions, http://www.fdic.gov/.

▪ **EXHIBIT 15.2**

CREDIT RISK DIVERSIFICATION, CONSUMER LOANS VERSUS
LOANS TO COMMERCIAL BORROWERS: 1988–2001

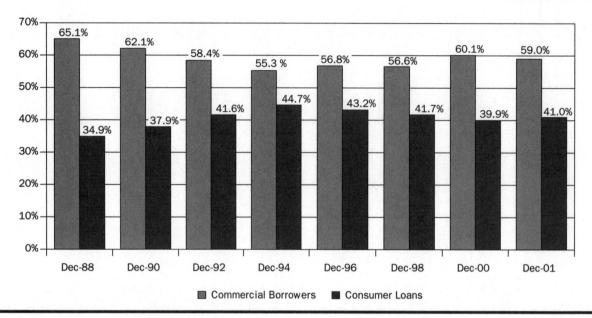

■ Commercial Borrowers   ■ Consumer Loans

NOTE: Ratios shown are as a percent of loans and leases.

SOURCE: FDIC Quarterly Banking Profile, Fourth Quarter 2001, http://www.fdic.gov/.

contribute proportionately less elsewhere. Fifth, farm loans make up a significant portion of the smallest banks' loans but are negligible at larger banks. Sixth, banks invest from 7 to 11 percent of their loans to finance consumer expenditures. Finally, other loans and leases are significant only at the largest banks. Other loans include primarily loans to other financial institutions, international loans, and lease receivables.

A popular way to categorize banks reflects their orientation to business or individual borrowers. Those that emphasize business lending are labeled **wholesale banks** while those that emphasize lending to individuals are labeled **retail banks.** Of course, most banks make loans to both types of borrowers, so the distinction is one of degrees. Exhibit 15.2 presents data comparing banks' aggregate commercial and consumer lending. Interestingly, the relative importance of consumer loans has generally increased from 35 percent of total loans in 1988 to 41 percent by 2001.[2] The trend toward increase in consumer loans, however, ended in 1995 as consumer bankruptcy filings increased—reaching record levels in 1998 and again in 2000. The percentage of consumer loans is highest at banks with between $500 million and $10 billion in assets due primarily to the credit card operations of these banks.[3] The different focuses reflect different risk and return profiles. Individuals are less rate sensitive and thus less likely to move their business due to rate differentials. Consumer loans are smaller in denomination so that it costs more to manage a retail portfolio. Offsetting this is the fact that many consumer loans carry the highest promised interest rates even after higher expected charge-offs.

---

[2]Consumer loans are defined as 1–4 family residential mortgages, home equity, and loans to individuals. Loans to commercial borrowers include construction and development, commercial real estate, multifamily residential real estate, farmland, other real estate loans, commercial and industrial loans, farm loans, and other loans and leases.

[3]Many large banks, such as Citigroup and BancOne, operate independent credit card banks.

RELATIVE IMPORTANCE OF LOANS, INVESTMENT SECURITIES, AND
CASH ASSETS AT COMMERCIAL BANKS, 1935–2001

Percent of Total Assets

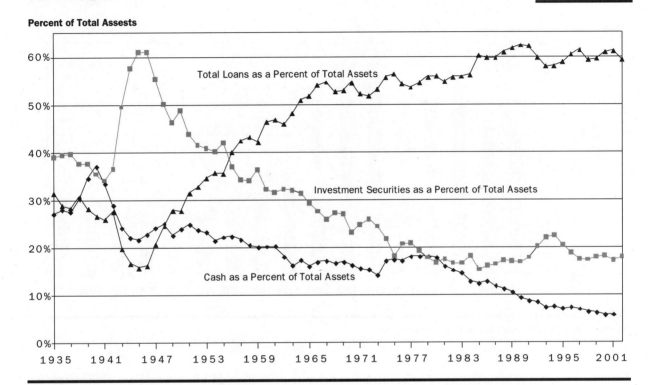

SOURCE: FDIC Historical Statistics, http://www.fdic.gov/.

These static comparisons, however, mask several important trends in bank lending. First, bank loans vary with the business cycle. Exhibit 15.3 demonstrates that loans, as a percentage of total assets, have grown sharply since the late 1940s with only slight dips during recession years. This ratio leveled off and declined between 1985 and 1992 as banks substituted lower risk investment securities for loans, then reversed course with loans again growing at historical rates. Second, problem loans and loan losses also vary with the business cycle. Exhibit 15.4 documents the credit problems of the late 1980s and early 1990s where the fraction of noncurrent loans to total loans increased sharply from 1984 through 1990. Not until 1993 did noncurrent loans return to more reasonable levels. By the late 1990s loan losses were at historically low levels.

Exhibit 15.5 compares noncurrent loan rates and net loan charge-off rates across types of loans from 1984 through 2000. Noncurrent loans are loans and leases past due 90 days or more and still accruing interest plus all loans and leases in a nonaccrual status.[4] Net charge-offs, in turn, represent the dollar amount of loans that are formally charged-off as uncollectible minus the dollar value of recoveries on loans previously charged off. Note how performance varied between different types of loans. Noncurrent loans for the category "total real estate loans" jumped dramatically from 1986 to 1987 as a direct result of overbuilding, and the Tax Reform

---

[4]Nonaccrual loans and leases are those that (a) are maintained on a cash basis because of deterioration in the financial position of the borrower, (b) where full payment of interest and principal is not expected, or (c) where principal or interest has been in default for a period of 90 days or more, unless the obligation is both well secured and in the process of collection.

■ **EXHIBIT 15.4**

NONCURRENT LOANS AS A PERCENT OF TOTAL LOANS,
ALL COMMERCIAL BANKS, 1984–2001

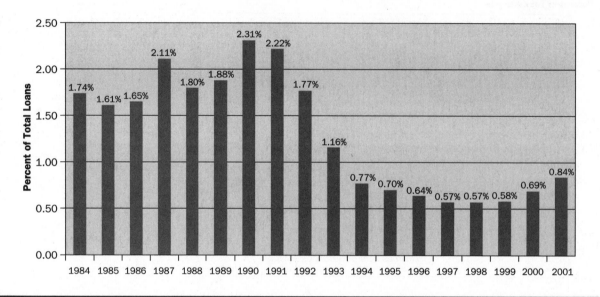

SOURCE: FDIC Historical Statistics, http://www.fdic.gov/.

Act of 1986. Foreign loan problems and charge-offs followed a few years later. Noncurrent real estate loans jumped the most from 1988 to 1991, as did charge-off rates. Noncurrent consumer loans were relatively constant, but charge-off rates increased systematically through 1991, fell somewhat through 1994, and increased to historical highs in 1998 and 2000. Most of this increase can be attributed to credit card losses and the dramatic increase in personal bankruptcies. Exhibit 15.6 shows this dramatic increase in credit card charge-off rates and personal bankruptcy filings in the late 1990s.

With the exception of loans to individuals, noncurrent and charge-off rates have generally dropped since 1991, indicative of an improving U.S. economy. The stock market meltdown of 2000 and the economic slowdown of 2001, combined with the tragic events of September 11, 2001, however, have led to an increase in charge-offs. Recent regulation has increased the importance of lending to overall performance. In response to interest rate deregulation during the early 1980s, most banks raised their loan-to-asset ratios. Because banks now pay market rates on their liabilities, their cost of funds is more volatile. As customers move deposits to stocks and mutual funds, bank cannot easily grow their low-cost core deposits. They continue to borrow more via purchased liabilities and FHLB advances such that they must earn higher yields on investments to maintain a positive spread and grow their net interest income. Loans offer the highest promised yields. If banks can find enough good loans and price them appropriately, they can continue historical earnings growth. The problem that banks face is increased competition from other lenders, many of whom price credits aggressively to establish a market presence and increase market share. Many quality borrowers also have access to alternative sources of funds by directly borrowing in the commercial paper or long-term bond markets. Alternatively, banks must increase services to generate additional fee income. Banks that securitize loans essentially prefer income from loan origination fees to interest income from holding loans in their portfolio. They are also subject to less credit risk.

▪ EXHIBIT 15.5

NONCURRENT LOAN RATES AND NET CHARGE-OFFS BY LOAN
TYPE AT U.S. COMMERCIAL BANKS, 1985–2001

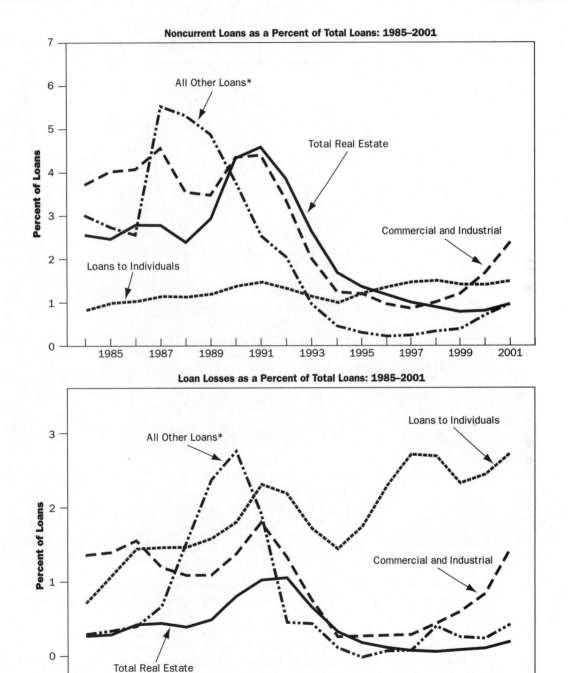

NOTE: Noncurrent loan rates represent the percentage of loans that are past due 90 days or more or are in nonaccrual status.
*Includes loans to foreign governments, depository institutions, and lease receivables.
SOURCE: FDIC Quarterly Banking Profile, Fourth Quarter 2001, http://www.fdic.gov/.

CREDIT CARD LOSS RATE AND PERSONAL
BANKRUPTCY FILINGS, 1984–2001

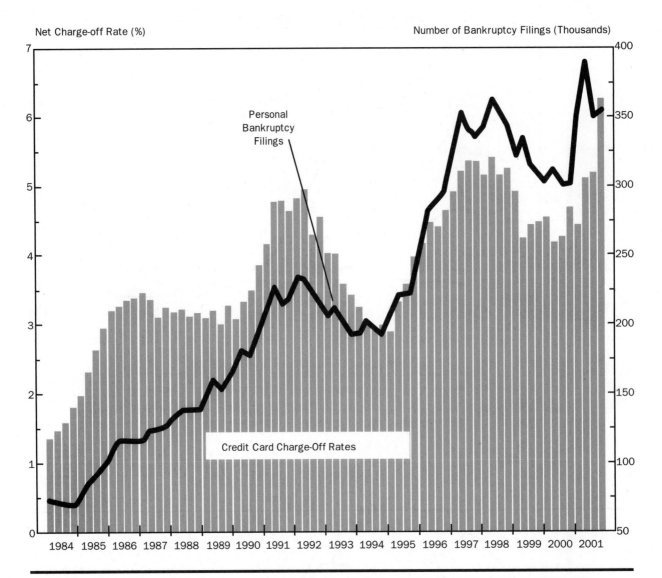

Net Charge-off Rate (%)

Number of Bankruptcy Filings (Thousands)

SOURCE: Bankruptcies—Administrative Office of the United States Courts; Charge-Off Rates—Commercial Bank Call Reports.

Today's widespread use of credit scoring by lenders and the securitization of consumer and small business loans and leases puts additional pressure on interest rates. **Credit scoring,** which is discussed in Chapter 17 for consumer loans, is a statistical process that assigns a score to a borrower based on characteristics of the borrower that indicate a high or low likelihood of loan repayment. Widespread use of credit scoring standardizes the perceived quality of different types of loans, such as pools of mortgages, credit card receivables, home equity loans, and small business loans. As more lenders originate these loans and securitize them, the supply of credit increases. This lowers market interest rates, ceteris paribus.

ARE CAR DEALERS THE NEWEST BANKERS?

New and used car dealers not only offer to sell automobiles but will arrange financing for you as well. Often, a car dealer makes more money arranging financing for you than it does selling you the car! When a car dealer "arranges" financing for the customer, he or she fills out a relatively uniform credit application and faxes this to one of several underwriters in town; e.g., local banks, General Motors Acceptance Corporation, Ford Motor Credit, and other credit corporations from Daimler Chrysler, Toyota, Nissan, and so on. Typically, the dealer will accept the best rate from the first few underwriters who respond to the fax.

Most often, the rate the underwriter will lend money for on the credit application is not the rate the dealer quotes the customer. For example, on a $20,000 loan, the dealer might get a 4-year loan rate quote of 9 percent. This dealer will then offer the customer financing at 13 percent. If customers don't know they can obtain cheaper financing elsewhere, they will often accept the terms, and the dealer has just made a $1,561.14 profit on this loan. The monthly payments on the $20,000 loan at 13 per-

cent for four years would be $536.55 to the customer. The dealer will sell this 13 percent loan to the bank (or auto finance company) for a premium, because the bank quoted the note at only 9 percent to the dealer. The bank would earn a 9 percent return on a 4-year loan paying $536.55 if it paid $21,561.14 to the car dealer for a $20,000 note! Hence, the dealer sells the $20,000 note to the bank for an instant profit of $1,561.14.

The Internet has also led to smaller spreads for the more standardized loan products. Many banks and nonbanks advertise auto loan, credit card, mortgage, and home equity rates on the Internet. Consumers have much greater access to information on loan rates from across the country and can readily shop for the lowest rate, putting even more pressure on spreads. Finally, several firms have introduced automated loan machines (ALMs) that are designed to work like ATMs. Instead, the customer provides background information, typically via a credit or debit card, a loan is credit scored, and the borrower receives an automated response to the loan request. If ALMs are ever widely accepted, the availability of credit will increase again.

In addition to increased competition, risk-based capital standards require that banks hold a minimum amount of equity capital for each loan kept on the books (see Chapter 13). More generally, strict capital ratios restrict loan growth and force banks to change the pricing based on increased capital required to support loans. The bottom line is that bank's choosing to make loans and keep the loans in their portfolio must obtain additional capital to continue growing. Many banks have responded by acting as loan brokers rather than keeping all loans on their books. This process involves making large loans or large volumes of loans and selling parts to other depository institutions or other investors. Banks earn fees for originating the loans and servicing the payments. In many cases, they can sell part of the loan at a lower interest rate than that negotiated with the borrower. If so, the bank keeps a portion of the interest payment as well as the loan fee. Loan sales increase earnings but do not adversely affect the capital position.

Banks can supplement earnings and circumvent capital requirements by engaging in off-balance sheet lending arrangements and financial guarantees. Here a bank does not directly extend credit but either serves as an underwriter arranging financing or attaches a letter of credit to a loan agreement. In both cases, the bank earns a fee for its role but retains a contingent liability. If the borrower defaults, the bank must take over the asset and make the obligated payments. Even with the current risk-based capital requirements, not all contingent liabilities are converted to on-balance sheet equivalents at 100 percent (see Chapter 13). Many off-balance sheet liabilities do not appear on the balance sheet and thus do not affect the capital-to-asset ratio calculated from balance sheet items. The recent experiences of ENRON and PNC clearly demonstrate that not all risks are reflected in total assets.

TRENDS IN COMPETITIONS FOR LOAN BUSINESS

Robert Morris chartered the first commercial bank in the United States in 1781 called the Bank of North America. This bank did business principally with the federal government and merchants. There were almost 14,500 banks by 1984 and less than 8,080 by the beginning of 2002. This reduction in the number of banks is a direct result of the relaxation of branching restrictions and increased competition (see Chapter 2). Banks today face tremendous competition for business that they were previously uniquely qualified for. This has forced consolidation as banks have attempted to lower costs and provide a broader base of services.

Although banks have historically been the primary lenders to business, most firms can obtain loans from many different sources today, such as credit unions, commercial finance companies (AT&T Capital, Commercial Credit, and GE Capital Corporation), life insurance companies, commercial paper, and the issuance of junk bonds. Reduced regulation, financial innovation, increased consumer awareness, and new technology has made it easier to obtain loans from a variety of sources. Junk bonds (bonds rates below BBB) have become "acceptable" thereby providing a viable funding source for smaller or new businesses. Commercial paper is very inexpensive to issue and most investment bankers can arrange private placements of debt quite easily.

Banks, however, still have the required expertise, experience, and customer focus to make them the preferred lender for many types of loans. Lending is not just a matter of making the loan and waiting for payment. Loans must be monitored and closely supervised to prevent losses. This requires an administrative staff for which banks are well suited. Not all loans can be standardized, credit scored, and securitized (sold in marketable packages). The most commonly securitized loans are those with the most standard features: mortgages, government-guaranteed student loans, small business loans sponsored by the Small Business Administration (SBA), credit cards, and auto loans. Many other loans are more difficult to credit score and securitize. For example, many farm and small business loans are designed to meet a specific business need. Repayment schedules and collateral are often customized so that they do not conform to some standard. Medium to large businesses will have specialized needs as well. Not surprisingly this is the area of lending that is still dominated by commercial banks and the area in which the bank is uniquely qualified for. A **structured note** is such a loan that is specifically designed to meet the needs of one or a few companies but has been packaged for resale. It may have common features, but an investor has to review the terms and covenants carefully to fully understand the payment patterns and inherent risks.

THE CREDIT PROCESS

The fundamental objective of commercial and consumer lending is to make profitable loans with minimal risk. Management should target specific industries or markets in which lending officers have expertise. The somewhat competing goals of loan volume and loan quality must be balanced with the bank's liquidity requirements, capital constraints, and rate of return objectives. The credit process relies on each bank's systems and controls that allow management and credit officers to evaluate risk and return trade-offs.

The credit process includes three functions: business development and credit analysis, underwriting or credit execution and administration, and credit review (Exhibit 15.7). Each reflects the bank's written loan policy as determined by the board of directors. A **loan policy** formalizes lending guidelines that employees follow to conduct bank business. It identifies preferred loan qualities and establishes procedures for granting, documenting, and reviewing loans.[5] Specific elements within each function are listed in the exhibit.

---

[5]In their periodic examinations, regulators evaluate each bank's written loan policy to see if existing loans conform to management's objectives and acceptable guidelines.

Business Development and Credit Analysis	Credit Execution and Administration	Credit Review
■ Market research ■ Advertising, public relations ■ Officer call programs ■ Obtain formal loan request ■ Obtain financial statements, borrowing resolution, credit reports ■ Financial statement and cash flow analysis ■ Evaluate collateral ■ Line officer makes recommendation on accepting/rejecting loan	■ Loan committee reviews proposal/recommendation ■ Accept/reject decision made, terms negotiated ■ Loan agreement prepared with collateral documentation ■ Borrower signs agreement, turns over collateral, receives loan proceeds ■ Perfect security interest ■ File materials in credit file ■ Process loan payments, obtain periodic financial statements, call on borrower	■ Review loan documentation ■ Monitor compliance with loan agreement: Positive and negative loan covenants Delinquencies in loan payments Discuss nature of delinquency or other problems with borrower ■ Institute corrective action: Modify credit terms Obtain additional capital, collateral, guarantees Call loan

Management's **credit philosophy** determines how much risk the bank will take and in what form. Under the label **credit culture,** banks evidence large differences in their lending philosophy. This term refers to the fundamental principles that drive lending activity and how management analyzes risk. There are three potentially different credit cultures: values-driven, current-profit driven, and market-share driven.

VALUES-DRIVEN
Focus is on credit quality with strong risk management systems and controls.
Primary emphasis is on bank soundness and stability and a consistent market presence.
Underwriting is conservative and significant loan concentrations are not allowed.
Typical outcome is lower current profit from loans with fewer loan losses.

CURRENT-PROFIT DRIVEN
Focus is on short-term earnings.
Primary emphasis is bank's annual profit plan.
Management is often attracted to high-risk and high-return borrowers.
Outcome is typically higher profit in good times, followed by lower profit in bad times when loan losses increase.

MARKET-SHARE DRIVEN
Focus is on having the highest market share of loans among competitors.
Primary emphasis is on loan volume and growth with the intent of being the largest bank.
Underwriting is very aggressive and management accepts loan concentrations and above-average credit risk.
Outcome is that loan quality suffers over time, while profit is modest because loan growth comes from below-market pricing.

Exhibit 15.8 documents elements of a strong values-driven credit culture that encourages management to maintain asset quality amid pressures to chase bad deals. This credit culture is set and enforced by the chief executive officer. Most of the elements address the systematic approach to risk-taking that forces loan officers to focus on long-term performance, consider a wide range of possible outcomes, and be accountable for actual earnings and loss performance.

■ **EXHIBIT 15.8**

20 ESSENTIALS OF GOOD BANKING FOSTERED
BY A STRONG CREDIT CULTURE

1. Commitment to excellence
2. Philosophical framework for day-to-day decision making
3. Sound value system that will cope with change
4. Uniform approach to risk-taking that provides stability and consistence
5. Development of a common credit language
6. Historical perspective on the bank's credit experience
7. Bank comes first and ahead of every profit center
8. Candor and good communication at all levels
9. Awareness of every transaction's effect on the bank
10. A portfolio with integrity and an appreciation of what properly belongs in it
11. Accountability for decisions and actions
12. Long-term view as well as a short-term view
13. Respect for credit basics
14. Reconciliation of market practice with common sense
15. Use of independent judgment and not the herd instinct
16. Constant mindfulness of the bank's risk-taking parameters
17. Realistic approach to markets and budgeting
18. An understanding of what the bank expects and the reasons behind its policies
19. Credit system with early warning capabilities
20. Appreciation that in risk-taking there are no surprises, only ignorance

SOURCE: P. Henry Mueller, "Risk Management and the Credit Culture—Necessary Interaction." *Journal of Commercial Lending* (May 1993). Copyright 1993 by Robert Morris Associates. Reprinted with permission from the *Journal of Commercial Lending*.

BUSINESS DEVELOPMENT AND CREDIT ANALYSIS

Where would a bank be without customers? Business development is the process of marketing bank services to existing and potential customers. With lending, it involves identifying new credit customers and soliciting their banking business, as well as maintaining relationships with current customers and cross-selling noncredit services. Every bank employee, from tellers handling drive-up facilities to members of the board of directors, is responsible for business development. Each employee regularly comes into contact with potential customers and can sell bank services. To encourage marketing efforts, many banks use cash bonuses or other incentive plans to reward employees who successfully cross-sell services or bring new business into the bank.

The normal starting point for any business development effort is market research. Management should establish targets for loan composition and identify areas of potential business. The research may formally analyze economic conditions, local demographic trends, and customer surveys. Alternatively, it may simply evolve from normal customer contacts and developing a communications link with local businesses about forthcoming opportunities. The purpose is to forecast the demand for bank services. The second step is to train employees regarding what products are available, what customers are likely to need or products they want, and how they should communicate with customers. Finally, the bank should make customers aware of its services. The most obvious means is through effective advertising and public relations. Many banks also incorporate formal officer call programs, in which lending officers are required to make regular face-to-face contact with current and potential borrowers. Borrowers are often hesitant to reveal personal details or business financial backgrounds. Before doing so, they like to know and trust the bank official with whom they are dealing.

Call programs require constant personal contact with potential borrowers, either through civic groups and trade associations or direct appointments. Formal programs involve bank-determined numerical objectives and officer implementation of customer contact procedures.

The numerical objectives often stipulate a minimum number of calls each month. Some are directed at current customers, while others target potential customers identified through research. The calling officer establishes the personal contact, makes the call, and files a report. After each call, the officer logs the date and time of the meeting, the issues discussed, and notes the opportunities for obtaining new business. Typically, officers must call on new customers several times before an opportunity develops. The bank is essentially positioning itself for the times when customers become dissatisfied with their prior bank relationship or qualify as good credits.

CREDIT ANALYSIS. Once a customer requests a loan, bank officers analyze all available information to determine whether the loan meets the bank's risk-return objectives. Credit analysis is essentially default risk analysis in which a loan officer attempts to evaluate a borrower's ability and willingness to repay. Eric Compton identified three distinct areas of commercial risk analysis related to the following questions:[6]

1. What risks are inherent in the operations of the business?
2. What have managers done or failed to do in mitigating those risks?
3. How can a lender structure and control its own risks in supplying funds?

The first question forces the credit analyst to generate a list of factors that indicate what could harm a borrower's ability to repay. The second recognizes that repayment is largely a function of decisions made by a borrower. Is management aware of the important risks and has it responded? The last question forces the analyst to specify how risks can be controlled so the bank can structure an acceptable loan agreement.

Traditionally, key risk factors have been classified according to the five Cs of credit: character, capital, capacity, conditions, and collateral. *Character* refers to the borrower's honesty and trustworthiness. An analyst must assess the borrower's integrity and subsequent intent to repay. If there are any serious doubts, the loan should be rejected. *Capital* refers to the borrower's wealth position measured by financial soundness and market standing. Can the firm or individual withstand any deterioration in its financial position? Capital helps cushion losses and reduces the likelihood of bankruptcy. *Capacity* involves both the borrower's legal standing and management's expertise in maintaining operations so the firm or individual can repay its debt obligations. A business must have identifiable cash flow or alternative sources of cash to repay debt. An individual must be able to generate income. *Conditions* refers to the economic environment or industry-specific supply, production, and distribution factors influencing a firm's operations. Repayment sources of cash often vary with the business cycle or consumer demand. Finally, *collateral* is the lender's secondary source of repayment or security in the case of default. Having an asset that the bank can seize and liquidate when a borrower defaults reduces loss, but does not justify lending proceeds when the credit decision is originally made.

Golden and Walker further identify the five Cs of *bad* credit, representing things to guard against to help prevent problems.[7] These include complacency, carelessness, communication breakdown, contingencies, and competition. *Complacency* refers to the tendency to assume that because things were good in the past they will be good in the future. Common examples are an overreliance on guarantors, reported net worth, or past loan repayment success because it's always worked out in the past. *Carelessness* involves poor underwriting typically evidenced by inadequate loan documentation, a lack of current financial information or other

---

[6]The discussion is based on Compton, 1985.

[7]Golden, Sam, and Harry Walker, "The Ten Commandments of Commercial Credit: The Cs of Good and Bad Loans," *Journal of Commercial Bank Lending,* January 1993.

pertinent information in the credit files, and a lack of protective covenants in the loan agreement. Each of these makes it difficult to monitor a borrower's progress and identify problems before they are unmanageable. Loan problems often arise when a bank's credit objectives and policies are not clearly *communicated*. Management should articulate and enforce loan policies, and loan officers should make management aware of specific problems with existing loans as soon as they appear. *Contingencies* refers to lenders tendency to play down or ignore circumstances in which a loan might default. The focus is on trying to make a deal work rather than identifying downside risk. Finally, *competition* involves following competitors' behavior rather than maintaining the bank's own credit standards. Doing something because the bank down the street is doing it does not mean it's good.

The formal credit analysis procedure includes a subjective evaluation of the borrower's request and a detailed review of all financial statements. Credit department employees may perform the initial quantitative analysis for the loan officer. The process consists of:

1. Collecting information for the credit file; such as credit history and performance
2. Evaluating management, the company, and the industry in which it operates; *i.e.,* evaluation of internal and external factors
3. Spreading financial statements; *i.e.,* financial statement analysis
4. Projecting the borrower's cash flow and thus its ability to service the debt
5. Evaluating collateral or the secondary source of repayment
6. Writing a summary analysis and making a recommendation

The credit file contains background information on the borrower, including call report summaries, past and present financial statements, pertinent credit reports, and supporting schedules such as an aging of receivables, a breakdown of current inventory and equipment, and a summary of insurance coverage. If the customer is a previous borrower, the file should also contain copies of the past loan agreement, cash flow projections, collateral agreements and security documents, any narrative comments provided by prior loan officers, and copies of all correspondence with the customer. One of the most important aspects of lending is determining the customers *desire to repay the loan*. Although this is critically important, it is difficult to measure. Information in the credit file will give the credit officer information on the customer's repayment history.

The credit analyst also uses the credit file data to spread the financial statements, project cash flow, and evaluate collateral.[8] An evaluation of management, the company, and industry is also needed to insure the safety and soundness of the loan. The last step is to submit a written report summarizing the loan request, loan purpose, and the borrower's comparative financial performance with industry standards, and to make a recommendation.

The loan officer evaluates the report and discusses any errors, omissions, and extensions with the analyst. If the credit (loan) does not satisfy the bank's risk criteria, the officer notifies the borrower that the original request has been denied. The officer may suggest procedures that would improve the borrower's condition and repayment prospects and solicit another proposal if circumstances improve. If the credit satisfies acceptable risk limits, the officer negotiates specific preliminary credit terms including the loan amount, maturity, pricing, collateral requirements, and repayment schedule.

Many small banks do not have formal credit departments and full-time analysts to prepare financial histories. Loan officers personally complete the steps outlined above before accepting or rejecting a loan. Often loan requests are received without detailed information on the

---

[8]This detailed data analysis is discussed in Chapter 16 for commercial loans and Chapter 17 for consumer loans, with several examples.

borrower's condition. Financial statements may be handwritten or unaudited and may not meet generally accepted accounting principles. Yet the borrower may possess good character and substantial net worth. In such instances, the loan officer works with the borrower to prepare a formal loan request and obtain the best financial information possible. This may mean personally auditing the borrower's receipts, expenditures, receivables, and inventory.

CREDIT EXECUTION AND ADMINISTRATION

The formal credit decision can be made individually, by an independent underwriting department, or by committee, depending on a bank's organizational structure. This structure varies with a bank's size, number of employees, and the type of loans handled. A bank's board of directors normally has the final say over which loans are approved. Typically, each lending officer has independent authority to approve loans up to some fixed dollar amount. Junior officers at a large bank might have authority to approve loans no larger than $100,000, while senior lending officers might independently approve loans up to $500,000. A *loan committee* made up of the bank's senior loan officers often formally reviews larger loans. This committee reviews each step of the credit analysis as presented by the loan officer and supporting analysts and makes a collective decision. Loan committees meet regularly to monitor the credit approval process and asset quality problems when they arise. When required, the board of directors or a directors' loan committee reviews this decision and grants final approval.

Many larger banks employ a centralized underwriting department. *Centralized underwriting* uses a relationship manager (RM), who sources new business and manages existing relationships within the portfolio. On new credit requests, the RM advises the client on the required information to process the request, evaluates and prescreens the request when the information is received, and if the request has a good probability of approval, will prepare the package and send it to the loan center. If the request has a remote probability of approval, the RM will advise the customer of that prospect—a de facto decline of the loan. Credit specialists in central underwriting make the final loan decision, but some banks allow for market overrides if the RM can mitigate the reasons for decline. Most large banks use computer software to quantitatively spread and evaluate the credit requests. Approvals from the computer system are considered one of the required signatures. The RM's signature will be the second required signature (up to officer's authority).

Once a loan has been approved, the officer notifies the borrower and prepares a **loan agreement.** This agreement formalizes the purpose of the loan, the terms, repayment schedule, collateral required, and any loan covenants. It also states what conditions bring about default by the borrower. These conditions may include conditions such as late principal and interest payments, the sale of substantial assets, a declaration of bankruptcy, and breaking any restrictive loan covenant. The officer then checks that all loan documentation is present and in order. The borrower signs the agreement along with other guarantors, turns over the collateral if necessary, and receives the loan proceeds.

DOCUMENTATION. A critical feature of executing any loan involves perfecting the bank's security interest in collateral. A security interest is the legal claim on property that secures payment on a debt or performance of an obligation. When the bank's claim is superior to that of other creditors and the borrower, its security interest is said to be *perfected.*[9]

---

[9]The Uniform Commercial Code (UCC) establishes what documentation is required to obtain a security interest in commercial lending. The UCC applies in every state, although various states have revised certain conditions. Each lending officer must understand what conditions apply wherever the bank conducts business.

Because there are many different types of borrowers and collateral, there are different methods of perfecting a security interest. In most cases, the bank requires borrowers to sign a security agreement that assigns qualifying collateral to the bank. This agreement describes the collateral and relevant covenants or warranties. Formal closure may involve getting the signature of a third-party guarantor on a loan agreement or having a key individual assign the cash value of a life insurance policy to the bank. In other cases, a bank may need to obtain title to equipment or vehicles. Whenever all parties sign a security agreement and the bank holds the collateral, the security interest is perfected. When the borrower holds the collateral, the bank must file a financing statement with the state that describes the collateral and the rights of the bank and borrower. It must be signed to establish the bank's superior interest.

Losses are a normal part of lending. They can only be totally eliminated by taking no credit risk. Banks have many procedures that help limit their loss exposure. The primary strategic tool is to have a formal loan policy that establishes exposure limits to any single borrower or group of borrowers. Such maximum exposures will not put the bank at risk of failure if the entire exposure goes unpaid. Other specific procedures include position limits, risk rating loans, and loan covenants.

POSITION LIMITS. Position limits are the maximum allowable credit exposures to any single borrower, industry, or geographic locale. The size of the exposure indicates the amount of the bank's equity capital that it is willing to put at risk. It should be lower for single borrowers and industries with the greatest loss potential. The objective is to avoid catastrophic losses.

RISK RATING LOANS. Another procedure to limit risk is for banks to strategically grade individual loans and counterparties. Risk grading involves evaluating characteristics of the borrower and loan to assess the likelihood of default and the amount of loss in the event of default (LIED). The grades may be assigned subjectively or by formal quantitative credit scoring models. Chapter 16 introduces such a risk rating scale for commercial loans. Loans are rated from low risk to high risk and vary sharply across industries, types of borrowers, different regions of the United States, and different countries. Obviously, charge-offs will be higher for the highest risk loans and banks must price these loans much higher relative to their costs.

LOAN COVENANTS. Once a bank lends funds to a customer, the bank and borrower effectively become partners. The bank wants the customer to repay the debt and purchase other bank services. The customer looks to the bank to provide useful accounting, financial, and tax advice.

Both the bank and borrower should recognize this partnership when negotiating credit terms. Still, it is important that each party protect its interests. For this reason, the bank often includes covenants in the loan agreement. Covenants may either be negative, indicating financial limitations and prohibited events, or positive, indicating specific provisions to which the borrower must adhere. The intent is to protect against substantive changes in the borrower's operating environment that damage the bank's interests. Most covenants address target financial ratios, limitations on asset sales, and maintenance of management quality. Exhibit 15.9 provides a partial list of covenants. The first three negative covenants, for example, attempt to limit discretionary cash payments by a firm. If effective, more cash is available for debt service. The first affirmative covenant prevents management from altering a firm's balance sheet adversely. Others stipulate actions that will protect the bank if key personnel die or performance deteriorates.

SAMPLE LOAN COVENANTS

Negative	Affirmative
■ Capital outlays cannot exceed $3 million annually	■ Borrower must maintain following financial ratios:
■ Cash dividends cannot exceed 60 percent of periodic earnings	Current ratio > 1.0
	Days receivables outstanding < 50 days
■ Total officers' salaries cannot exceed $500,000 annually	Inventory turnover > 4.5 times
	Debt to total assets < 70 percent
■ No liens on assets beyond existing liens	Net worth > $1 million
■ No mergers, consolidations, or acquisitions without bank approval	Fixed charge coverage > 1.3 times
	Cash flow from operations > dividends + current maturities of long-term debt
■ No sale, lease, or transfer of more than 10 percent of existing assets	■ Certified financial statements must be provided within 60 days of end of each fiscal year
■ No change in senior management	■ Borrower will maintain $500,000 key man life insurance policy on company president, with bank named as beneficiary
■ No additional debt without bank approval	■ Bank will be allowed to inspect inventory, receivables, and property periodically
	■ Borrower must pay all taxes and government fees, unless contested in good faith, and comply with all laws
	■ Borrower must inform bank of any litigation or claim that might materially affect its performance
	■ Borrower must maintain all property in good condition and repair

CREDIT REVIEW

The loan review effort is directed at reducing credit risk as well as handling problem loans and liquidating assets of failed borrowers. Effective credit management separates loan review from credit analysis, execution, and administration. The review process can be divided into two functions: monitoring the performance of existing loans and handling problem loans. Many banks have a formal loan review committee, independent of calling officers, that reports directly to the chief executive officer and directors' loan committee. Loan review personnel audit current loans to verify that the borrower's financial condition is acceptable, loan documentation is in place, and pricing meets return objectives. If the audit uncovers problems, the committee initiates corrective action. Removing the problem may simply involve getting signatures on omitted forms or filing required documents with the state. If the borrower has violated any loan covenants, the loan is in default. The bank can then force the borrower to correct the violation or it can call the loan. Calling a loan is normally a last resort and done only when the borrower does not voluntarily correct the problem. It allows the bank to request full payment before repayment prospects worsen.

The problem is much more serious when the borrower's financial condition deteriorates. These loans are classified as problem loans and require special treatment. In many cases, the bank has to modify the terms of the loan agreement to increase the probability of full repayment. Modifications include deferring interest and principal payments, lengthening maturities, and liquidating unnecessary assets. Often the bank requests additional collateral or guarantees and asks the borrower to contribute additional capital. The purpose is to buy time until the borrower's condition improves. Banks often separate loan work-out specialists from traditional loan officers because they are liquidation oriented and frequently involved in intense negotiations.

CHARACTERISTICS OF DIFFERENT TYPES OF LOANS

This section describes the basic characteristics of commercial bank loans. Although there are many ways to classify loans, the analysis focuses on the use of loan proceeds and maturity. Each type of loan has different features that necessitate different repayment schemes, collateral, and loan covenants. The Uniform Bank Performance Report (UBPR) classifies loans into one of six types: real estate loans, commercial loans, individual loans, agricultural loans, other loans and leases in domestic offices, and loans and leases in foreign offices.[10]

REAL ESTATE LOANS

The UBPR (Uniform Bank Performance Report) defines real estate loans as domestic-office loans secured by real estate. In particular, real estate loans are generally classified into seven subcategories: construction and development loans, commercial real estate, multifamily residential real estate, 1–4 family residential, home equity, farmland, and other real estate loans. Exhibit 15.1 indicates that real estate loans represent a high percentage of total loans at most commercial banks. They are classified separately from commercial and consumer loans because the collateral is some form of real property and the loans are subject to different risks and regulation. During prosperous times, short-term real estate loans are among the most profitable investments and are extremely attractive to growth-oriented banks. Many banks also extend long-term mortgage credit to residential homeowners or to holders of commercial property.

Real estate loans can be highly speculative, however, if banks lend against properties that do not generate predictable cash flows. Many banks, savings and loans, insurance companies, and pension funds, in fact, have owned significant amounts of real estate with other credits still on the books that are not producing sufficient cash to service debt. Often the underlying real estate is commercial property built under the assumption that lease rates and occupancy would quickly rise. Banks can only sell the properties at depressed prices, so they keep them on their books to avoid taking losses. The failures of numerous banks, such as the Bank of New England in 1991, have been attributed largely to problem real estate loans.

COMMERCIAL REAL ESTATE LOANS. Commercial real estate loans are generally short-term loans consisting of construction and real estate development loans, land development loans, and commercial properties loans such as shopping centers and office buildings. Many banks lend heavily to businesses for new building construction and land development. *Construction loans* represent interim financing on commercial, industrial, and multifamily residential property. A bank extends credit to a builder to pay for the materials and labor necessary to complete a project. Funds are usually disbursed on an irregular basis, such as upon the completion of certain phases of the construction process (foundation poured, framed, dry-wall, etc.) or based on actual supplier and subcontractor bills presented to the banker. The builder repays the entire loan when the project is completed, and permanent (long-term) financing is arranged. Construction loans are interim loans. *Interim loans* provide financing

---

[10]Information on the UBPR can be found in Chapter 3 and on the Internet at http://www.ffiec.gov/UBPR.htm.

only for a limited time until permanent financing is arranged; for example, long-term mortgage or direct financing from insurance companies or pension funds. Land development loans finance the construction of roads and public utilities in areas where developers plan to build houses. *Land development* loans are also interim loans as the developer will repay the loan as homeowners or investors buy lots. Maturities on these loans normally range from 12 months to two years but are often extended when developers cannot find permanent financing. Interest rates on interim loans can be high for some borrowers but are typically priced at a floating rate over prime or other base role. The bank may also charge an origination fee to make the original loan.

The credit analysis of construction and land development loans follows that described in Chapter 16.[11] There are, however, peculiar features of these projects that deserve mention. Most importantly, these loans may be extremely risky. Individual projects such as the construction of an office building in a metropolitan area's downtown business district are often quite costly. Few banks choose to assume that risk alone, so most enter into joint financing agreements. The primary source of repayment is permanent financing provided by a third party. If this is not forthcoming, the bank must look either to the developer's cash flow from other projects or, ultimately, the outright sale of the building. If the developer defaults on the loan before construction is completed, the bank must pay for someone else to finish the project. Banks prefer a project in which customers have already committed to lease space and the developer has arranged for a takeout commitment. A *takeout commitment* is an agreement whereby a different lender, such as a life insurance company or pension fund, agrees to provide long-term financing after construction is finished. The construction loan is speculative when the builder does not have a commitment or the ultimate owner of the structure is not known.

Most banks attempt to limit their risk by working closely with a select group of developers and by requiring third-party appraisals of projects. A bank that makes a construction loan essentially underwrites the developer. Maintaining a close working relationship allows the bank to assess whether the developer can complete a specific project and has cash flow from other projects to cover losses if this one fails. Third-party appraisals provide an estimate of the project's value at completion and offer assurance that the structure's value can cover loan payments in the event of default.[12]

Banks try to compensate for high default risk by requiring up-front fees and pricing construction loans at substantial markups over their funding costs. It is not uncommon, for example, for a bank to charge an *origination fee* of 1 percent of the loan and float the interest rate at 4 percent over the bank's base rate. Interest rate risk is lessened because interest income varies with changes in the level of interest rates. Still, if the structure is not sold or adequately leased, cash flows will not cover debt service requirements.

The quality of these loans closely follows the business cycle. During the first half of the 1980s, many developers overbuilt office space in major metropolitan areas. Normal business growth did not absorb the new construction, and many borrowers defaulted because of high vacancy rates. These problems resulted, in part, from liberal lending policies pursued by savings banks and some commercial banks. Lenders and their developers speculatively built apartments and office buildings with little or no preleased space. In many cases, banks even loaned funds for origination fees and loan interest in addition to normal materials and labor

---

[11]The financial statements of developers differ markedly from those of most nonfinancial businesses. Analysts must be familiar with how specific firms allocate costs for projects under construction and how they report gross profit. Generally accepted accounting principles allow builders to estimate profit on unfinished projects. An analyst must know what portion of gross profit can be attributed to completed contracts and should compare this with past estimates to assess the efficiency of the builder's historical profit estimates.

[12]Unfortunately, there is no guarantee that appraisals are meaningful. Appraisers are not regulated, and many instances of abuse are known. Bank of America, for example, charged off $95 million in the last three months of 1984 based on faulty mortgages involving inflated property appraisals.

costs. Developers were often not even required to invest any of their own equity in the projects. Banks expected to be repaid when the developer sold the project at completion of construction or when the project generated sufficient cash flow from rentals. High vacancy rates lowered real estate values and the quality of these loans.

RESIDENTIAL MORTGAGE LOANS. Most bank real estate loans are long-term mortgages, primarily on single-family houses. A **mortgage** is a legal document through which a borrower gives a lender a lien on real property as collateral against a debt. The borrower gets to use the property as long as the scheduled interest and principal payments are met. If the borrower defaults, the lender can exercise the lien and claim the property. Generally a borrower has the right of redemption, whereby foreclosure is prevented if the debt is repaid within a reasonable time after default.

Banks can make conventional mortgages or mortgages insured by the Federal Housing Authority or Veterans Administration. These last two carry long maturities and require small down payments by borrowers. They are costly in terms of officer time because management must complete considerable paperwork before the loans are officially approved.

The *1–4 family residential mortgage loans* are attractive investments when priced correctly. When their deposit base was relatively stable, banks made fixed-rate loans with 30-year maturities. They paid below-market rates on their deposits but effectively passed on some of the savings by charging artificially low fixed rates on mortgages. Mortgage rates did not include large-term premiums because deposit rates could not rise above regulatory ceilings. Such banks operated with negative funding GAPs but were not penalized as long as interest rates remained low.[13] With the gradual removal of deposit rate ceilings and the increased volatility of interest rates in the 1970s, banks at times found that they were paying 15 to 18 percent on CDs and money market certificates, while their mortgages earned 6 to 9 percent.

Not surprisingly, lenders have developed contracts that increase the rate sensitivity of their mortgage portfolio to reduce the bank's interest rate risk exposure. Mortgages now may provide for (1) periodic adjustments in the interest rate, (2) adjustments in periodic principal payments, or (3) the lender sharing in any price appreciation of the underlying structure at sale. The purpose is to increase cash flow when the level of interest rates rises or inflation accelerates.[14] Most banks now offer borrowers a choice between fixed-rate and adjustable-rate mortgages. Because borrowers assume interest rate risk with rate-sensitive mortgages, banks offer inducements, such as lower initial rates and caps on how high the rate might go, to increase their attractiveness.

The credit analysis of single family residential mortgages resembles that of any consumer loan. Most mortgages are *amortized* with monthly payments including both principal and interest. Because of the long maturity, banks look carefully at the borrower's cash flow, character, and willingness to repay. The evaluation concentrates on three significant features of the loan: the appraised property value, the borrower's down payment, and the borrower's cash flow relative to required interest and principal payments. Banks assume less credit risk when the down payment is high and debt service payments are small relative to the buyer's income.

---

[13]See Chapters 8 and 9 for more details about interest rate risk and funding GAP. A negative funding GAP means that the bank has fewer rate-sensitive assets than rate-sensitive liabilities. Hence when interest rates increase, the cost of bank funds increases faster than the yields on the longer-term assets. The value of equity typically falls as well because longer-term securities are more sensitive to changes in interest rates than shorter-term securities.

[14]Many types of adjustable-rate mortgages have evolved. Some tie the interest rate to an index that changes when the general level of rates changes. Others establish rates that change according to a fixed schedule. Principal payments may likewise be indexed to inflation.

THE SECONDARY MORTGAGE MARKET. Real estate lending is popular, in part, due to the growth of the secondary mortgage market. Today, there is a large number of players in the mortgage banking business who originate and service mortgages. One newly developed segment is the market for subprime, or higher risk, mortgage borrowers. The secondary mortgage market involves the trading of previously originated residential mortgages. Lenders who originate mortgages can either sell them directly to interested investors or package them into mortgage pools. With a mortgage pool, the original lender issues long-term securities that evidence a claim on the mortgages in the pool. Investors in the securities receive the interest and principal payments on the underlying mortgages net of servicing fees. In most cases, the pool originator collects the mortgage payments from home buyers, keeping a portion as a servicing fee, pays the relevant property taxes, and apportions the remainder to insurers and holders of the securities.

With risk-based capital requirements, many banks follow a strategy of originating mortgages for the purpose of securitizing them. Their earnings come from origination and servicing fees. Chapter 19 documents recent growth in the secondary mortgage market including the nature of securities created by the securitization process.

HOME EQUITY LOANS. The Tax Reform Act of 1986 gradually phased out the deductibility of interest on consumer debt when computing federal income taxes, except for mortgages. As might be expected, lenders quickly packaged home equity loans that quickly substituted for many traditional forms of consumer borrowing. *Home equity loans* are actually a second mortgage secured by real estate so that any interest payments meet the requirement for deductibility. *Second mortgages* are usually shorter term, 3 to 10 years, and have a subordinated claim to the first residential mortgage. They have been structured to resemble direct installments loans, but even more so like credit lines in which an individual has a credit limit and can borrow up to the limit for any purpose.

From the lender's perspective, home equity loans were fully secured and thus low risk. In reality, the loans have actually encouraged many consumers to spend beyond their normal ability to generate income so that borrowers did default on loans. In addition, because the claims of the home equity loan are secondary to the first mortgage, it is more difficult for the bank holding the second mortgage to bring about foreclosure. With declining property values in the late 1980s and early 1990s, lenders tightened standards because of concern over their risk exposure and the economic downturn. Through 2000 few banks charged off unexpectedly large losses on home equity loans so they appear not to have been abused by borrowers.

EQUITY INVESTMENTS IN REAL ESTATE. For many years government regulations prevented commercial banks from owning real estate except for their corporate office or property involved in foreclosure. State-chartered savings and loan associations and insurance companies, in contrast, have long been able to take equity positions in real estate projects. This enabled them to charge lower loan rates in exchange for unlimited profit potential from price appreciation. Federal regulators want banks to engage in these more speculative real estate activities only through separate subsidiaries, if at all. Many states have passed laws permitting state-chartered banks to invest in real estate, in many cases restricting the dollar investment to a fixed percentage of assets.

COMMERCIAL LOANS

There are as many types of commercial loans as there are business borrowers. The UBPR defines commercial loans as domestic-office commercial and industrial loans, loans to depository institutions, acceptances of other banks, and obligations (other than securities) of states and political subdivisions. Commercial loans are made to business to assist in financing working capital needs (accounts receivables and inventory), plant and equipment needs, and other legitimate business purposes. Banks lend large amounts to manufacturing companies, service companies, farmers, securities dealers, and other financial institutions. The loans may finance short-term uses such as temporary working capital needs and construction expenses in which the borrower has obtained a commitment for long-term financing from another lender, or long-term uses such as new equipment purchases and plant expansion. Short-term business loans often take the form of loan commitments or line of credit agreements. These loans may be formal or informal and operate much like a credit card arrangement. A bank and borrower agree in advance that the customer can draw against the line as needed up to some maximum credit limit. The borrower determines the timing of borrowings and the actual amount. The obvious advantage to the borrower is flexibility. For example, the firm may only need temporary financing as it accumulates inventory prior to its major sales period. Once sales occur, it can repay the loan. These loans also take up less of the loan officer's time. Bankers must, however, still complete a detailed analysis before extending credit. Prior to formal approval, the loan officer evaluates the purpose and repayment prospects and negotiates the size of the commitment, the term the commitment is outstanding, any fees or compensating balance requirements, and the interest rate charged.

Because many commercial loans finance current assets (primarily accounts receivables and inventory), the following discussion analyzes normal working capital requirements and several types of loans associated with this financing. The previous section addressed commercial real estate loans and the following sections analyze the general features of term commercial loans and agriculture loans. Often, commercial and industrial loans are linked to commercial real estate loans with the only real distinguishing characteristic being whether the loans are secured by real estate or other assets of the company.

WORKING CAPITAL REQUIREMENTS. A company's (net) working capital equals its current assets minus its current liabilities. For most firms, working capital is positive, suggesting that current assets are financed partially by current debt and partially by long-term debt and equity. If current assets are liquidated, the proceeds from the sale of the current assets will exceed current liabilities. Working capital, therefore, is a net liquidity measure.

Consider the daily average balance sheet information in Exhibit 15.10 for Simplex Corp., which has $300 in net working capital ($1,280 − $980). Implicitly, $300 of long-term debt and equity is financing $300 of cash, receivables, and inventory, and the firm's current assets cover its current liabilities. Note that $450 of the current liabilities are notes payable to a bank indicating short-term financing currently provided for operating purposes.

Virtually all businesses must invest in current assets to operate. Manufacturers purchase materials to produce goods that are often sold on credit. Retail firms purchase display merchandise and often rely on credit sales to stimulate business. Service companies need operating cash and small inventories of supplies. Each type of business relies on different financing methods depending on its operating policies and growth. If the financing needs are truly short term, a working capital loan is appropriate.

The bottom of Exhibit 15.10 and Exhibit 15.11 summarize the normal working capital cycle for a manufacturing firm using the data for Simplex Corp. This cycle compares the timing difference between converting current assets to cash and making cash payments on normal operating expenses. Supplementary income statement data are provided in Exhibit 15.10 and used to calculate the timing difference. All sales are assumed to be credit sales and the data are viewed in daily average terms. Initially, a firm accumulates operating cash. It then invests in inventory by purchasing materials that are converted into finished goods. Accounts receivable appear when the firm sells the inventory on credit. Finally, the receivables revert to cash

■ **EXHIBIT 15.10**

BALANCE SHEET AND INCOME STATEMENT DATA FOR SIMPLEX CORPORATION

Assets		Liabilities and Equity		Selected Income Statement Data*	
Cash	80	Accts. payable	400	Net Sales	9,125
Accts receivable	700	Acc. Expenses	80	COGS	6,100
Inventory	500	Notes Pay—Bank	450	Oper Expense	2,550
Current Assets	1,280	CMLTD	50	Purchases	6,430
Fixed Assets	1,220	Current Liab	980	Avg Daily Sales	25.00
Total Assets	2,500			Avg Daily COGS	16.71
		Long-term Debt	550	Avg Daily Oper. Expense	6.99
		Equity	970	Avg Daily Purchases	17.62
		Total Liab & Eq	2,500		

Working Capital Cycle†

Current Assets		Current Liabilities	
Days Cash	3.20 = 80 / 25.00	Days Payable	22.71 = 400 / 17.62
Days Receivable	28.00 = 700 / 25.00	Days Accruals	11.45 = 80 / 6.99
Days Inventory	29.92 = 500 / 16.71		
Days Asset Cycle	61.12	Days Liability Cycle	34.16

Difference in cash-to-cash cycles = (61.12 − 34.16) = 26.96
Working capital needs = 26.96 × 16.71 = 450.53

*Assumes a 365-day year; CMLTD refers to current maturity of long-term debt; COGS refers to cost of goods sold.
†Ratio definitions:
Days cash = cash / (sales / 365)
Days receivables = accounts receivable / (sales / 365)
Days inventory = inventory / (COGS / 365)
Days payables = accounts payable / (purchases / 365)
Days accruals = accruals / (operating expenses / 365)

as customers pay off their credit purchases. Many factors influence how long it takes to complete the cycle, including the complexity of the production process, the terms of credit sales, and the firm's collection efforts on outstanding receivables. The longer it takes to produce a finished good, sell it, and collect on the sale, the longer the firm has to wait to get its cash investment back. If a timing difference exists between the number of days in the asset cycle and cash payments on liabilities, a loan may be necessary to help a firm manage the mismatch in cash flows.

In most industries, the *cash-to-cash asset cycle* takes longer than the comparable cycle for nonbank current liabilities. The *cash-to-cash liability cycle* essentially measures how long a firm can obtain interest-free financing from suppliers in the form of accounts payable and accrued expenses.[15] Firms use trade credit to finance materials purchases temporarily, but must normally pay their suppliers within 30 days to receive any discounts. Even when they can ride suppliers longer, they still pay down accounts payable well before their current asset cycle is completed. Firms may also be able to accrue expenses rather than make immediate cash payments, but the deferment period is quite short. The net effect is that most businesses receive

---

[15]Actually the term "interest-free" may not be totally correct. If discounts for early payment are offered and not taken, the effective interest cost of paying late (after the discount period) could be quite high.

· EXHIBIT 15.11

CASH-TO-CASH WORKING CAPITAL CYCLE FOR SIMPLEX CORPORATION

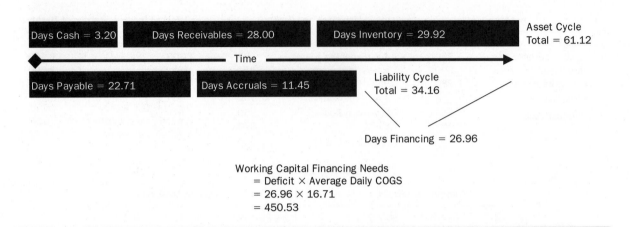

cash from an asset sale long after they have paid suppliers, associated labor costs, and other operating expenses. With the timing discrepancy, firms must rely on bank credit or long-term debt to finance current assets during this period of mismatched cash flows.

This cash-to-cash comparison is demonstrated at the bottom of Exhibits 15.10 and Exhibit 15.11. In Exhibit 15.10 the days cash-to-cash for assets indicates that it takes over 61 days for Simplex's current assets to turn over. In comparison, the company rides its suppliers for an average of 23 days and defers operating expenses for 11 days. Notes payable to the bank and long-term debt finance this 27-day deficiency in underlying cash flows.

One procedure for estimating working capital loan needs is to multiply the number of days deficiency between the asset and liability cash-to-cash cycles by the firm's average daily cost of goods sold. In this example the product equals 450.53 (26.96 × 16.7), which is close to the amount of the notes payable currently outstanding ($450). Of course, this calculation ignores the firm's capital structure. If a company has above average equity or more long-term debt financing than the norm, working capital financing needs can be met by these more permanent sources of funds. In this case, the estimate based on the above calculation will overstate true short-term funding needs.

SEASONAL VERSUS PERMANENT WORKING CAPITAL NEEDS. Many businesses find that their working capital fluctuates over time. This may be caused by events such as an unexpected increase in credit sales relative to cash sales, an increase in inventory resulting from defective materials, or changes in payment patterns to suppliers. Working capital may also vary during the year because of seasonal sales. Businesses temporarily build up inventories and pay higher operating expenses prior to the peak sales season. Working capital needs rise because accounts payable increase at a slower pace. The deficiency increases further with an increase in receivables, then declines to normal as the firm collects on receivables and inventory contracts. An important facet of working capital financing is thus to assess any seasonal pattern in inventory accumulation, production, sales, and collection of receivables. If seasonal patterns exist, a lender must obtain interim financial statements that reveal peak holdings of current assets. Consider, for example, a company that manufactures fireworks or a restaurant in a ski resort area. The maximum working capital loan will normally apply during or just preceding their peak business activity.

Most businesses have a stable amount of working capital that persists regardless of unexpected events and seasonal fluctuations. That is to say, most businesses have some level of

· EXHIBIT 15.12

TRENDS IN WORKING CAPITAL NEEDS

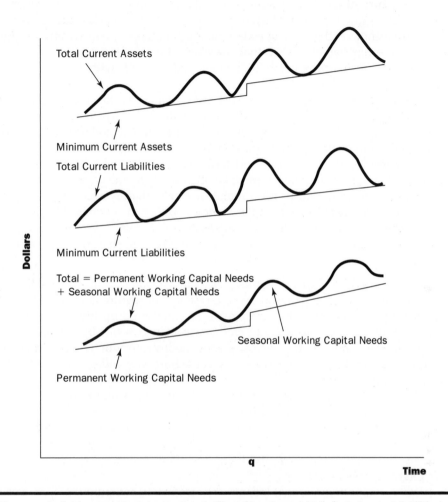

NOTE: Current liabilities are net of notes payable and current maturities of long-term debt (adjusted current liabilities).

accounts receivable, inventory, and accounts payable that are a permanent part of the business. One customer's accounts receivable will be paid off but a new receivable will replace it, hence, some dollar amount of accounts receivables will always be with the firm. This base or **permanent working capital** need equals the minimum level of current assets minus the minimum level of current liabilities net of short-term bank credit and current maturities of long-term debt (adjusted current liabilities) throughout each year. It is important that businesses and their lenders recognize this permanent need because it represents the amount of long-term debt or equity financing required for current assets. Firms should try to raise funds for these permanent needs in the bond or stock market as banks are reluctant to make term loans for this purpose. Any working capital requirement in excess of this base amount would be financed with short-term credit.

A time series plot of a firm's working capital position helps quantify permanent and temporary needs. It also identifies any seasonal patterns that appear. Exhibit 15.12 shows this concept graphically. The base trend lines, through the minimum amounts of current assets and adjusted current liabilities, designate the permanent components of these balance sheet items. These amounts jump at period q when the firm is assumed to expand its physical plant. The curved lines represent total current assets and total current liabilities. The peak value of current liabilities comes before the peak in current assets, reflecting the fact that receivables growth typically lags behind increases in inventory and trade credit.

Permanent working capital needs equal the difference between minimum current assets and adjusted current liabilities. **Seasonal working capital** needs equal the difference in total current assets and adjusted current liabilities. Peak needs coincide with the peak level of current assets.

SHORT-TERM COMMERCIAL LOANS. Banks try to match credit terms with a borrower's specific needs. The loan officer estimates the purpose and amount of the proposed loan, the expected source of repayment, and the value of collateral. The loan amount, maturity, and repayment schedule are negotiated to coincide with the projections. Short-term funding needs are financed by short-term loans, while long-term needs are financed by term loans with longer maturities. A mistake often made by the young credit analysts is making a loan for a larger amount or for a longer maturity than is necessary for a "good" customer. The issue is not whether to loan the money to the good customer but to ensure that the bank meets the customer's need and minimizes its risk. If you loan more money than the customer needs, the customer may spend the money unwisely, such as to purchase unnecessary assets (corporate jets) on which the bank does not hold a lien.

Seasonal Working Capital Loans. Seasonal working capital loans finance a temporary increase in net current assets above the permanent requirement (Exhibit 15.12). A borrower uses the proceeds to purchase raw materials and build up inventories of finished goods in anticipation of later sales. Trade credit also increases but by a smaller amount. Funding requirements persist as the borrower sells the inventory on credit and accounts receivables remain outstanding. The loan declines as the borrower collects on the receivables and stops accumulating inventory.

This type of loan is *seasonal* if the need arises on a regular basis and if the cycle completes itself within one year. It is *self-liquidating* in the sense that repayment derives from sales of the finished goods that are financed. Because the loan proceeds finance an increase in inventories and receivables, banks try to secure the loan with these assets. Seasonal working capital loans are often unsecured because the risk to the lender is relatively low.

When evaluating seasonal loans it is necessary to compare the borrower's working capital position over time (Exhibit 15.12). If the bank only obtained year-end historical financial statements when current assets were at seasonal lows, an analysis would demonstrate that the borrower did not need seasonal financing. To estimate maximum seasonal needs, the bank needs comparative statements for periods when current assets are at their highs and lows. The difference in total working capital needs between the two periods equals the maximum seasonal loan requirement. This means that the bank must request interim financial statements. Suppose, for example, that the balance sheet data for Simplex Corp. in Exhibit 15.10 represent the company's minimal seasonal working capital needs. If the peak needs arise four months later when current assets equal $1,800 and current liabilities equal $1,200, the maximum seasonal requirements total $600.

Open Credit Lines. Seasonal loans often take the form of open credit lines.[16] Under these arrangements, the bank makes a certain amount of funds available to a borrower for a set

---

[16]Credit lines are used to meet many types of temporary needs in addition to seasonal needs. One popular type is the backup credit line used by large corporations that regularly issue commercial paper. This credit is available to pay investors when commercial paper matures if the corporation does not or cannot roll over its outstanding paper.

period of time. The customer determines the timing of actual borrowings, or "takedowns." Typically, borrowing gradually increases with the inventory buildup, then declines with the collection of receivables. The bank likes to see the loan fully repaid at least once during each year. This confirms that the needs are truly seasonal.

The terms of credit lines vary between borrowers and whether arrangements are informal or contractual. Informal lines are not legally binding but represent a promise that the bank will advance credit. The customer pays for the service only by paying interest on the funds actually borrowed. A contractual or formal credit line is legally binding even though no written agreement is signed. The bank charges a *commitment fee* for making credit available, regardless of whether the customer actually uses the line. The customer also pays interest on actual borrowings. In both cases, credit lines are renegotiated each year when the bank reassesses the firm's credit needs. Borrowers pay interest at variable rates and often must hold compensating deposit balances with the bank as part of the arrangement. These pricing characteristics are discussed in Chapter 18.

Asset-Based Loans. In theory, any loan secured by a company's assets is an asset-based loan. One very popular type of asset-based short-term loan would be those secured by inventories or accounts receivable. Loans to finance leveraged buyouts are also classified in this category. In the case of inventory loans, the security consists of raw materials, goods in process, and finished products. The value of the inventory depends on the marketability of each component if the borrower goes out of business. Banks will lend from 40 to 60 percent against raw materials that are common among businesses and finished goods that are marketable, and nothing against unfinished inventory. With receivables, the security consists of paper assets that presumably represent sales. The quality of the collateral depends on the borrower's integrity in reporting actual sales and the credibility of billings.

Even though all loans secured by a company's assets could be considered asset-based loans, asset-based lending today generally refers to loans where substantially more weight is given to the collateral than cash flow when evaluating the loan request. Payoff from collateral liquidation is more likely to occur in an asset-based loan than in other secured loans, hence the need for good estimates of current and future value of the collateral. Asset-based lending grew in the mid-1980s when many of the large Texas banks were lending off the value of proven oil reserves. During this time, many of the banks were lending 60 percent of a "low" price of oil. For example, when oil prices were $40 a barrel, banks were lending up to $24 per barrel of reserves. Most of the bank's customers thought they were being extremely conservative. No one believed that the price of oil would ever drop to $10 a barrel, which it did. When the price of oil dropped this low, all equipment and industries related to the oil industry crashed. One example was that a $1.6 million drilling rig was only worth $38,000 after the crash because that was the value of scrap metal!

Making asset-based loans requires a loan officer to examine the asset. For example, the loan officer should examine the inventory on site and personally confirm that the customer's figures for receivables are purged of uncollectible or nonexistent accounts. A bank normally lends against 50 to 80 percent of a borrower's receivables depending on the accounts receivable aging schedule and collection experience. An **accounts receivable aging schedule** is a list of accounts receivables segregated according to the month in which the invoice is dated (invoice aging) or in which the invoice is payable (due date aging). An analyst can quickly determine the volume of past-due accounts and trends in collection experience by comparing the fraction of total receivables in each month over time.

Banks frequently require lockbox arrangements to assure that borrowers repay receivables loans when payments are received. With a **lockbox** the borrower requests that its customers mail payments directly to a post office box number controlled by the bank. The bank processes the payments and reduces the borrower's loan balance but charges the borrower for handling the items. Furthermore, because banks spend more time monitoring asset-based loans, they charge rates above those available on open credit lines. The standard interest pricing is a rate that floats from 2 to 6 percent above a bank's base rate.[17]

Highly Leveraged Transactions. During the early 1980s, one growth area in asset-based lending was leveraged buyouts (LBOs). A **leveraged buyout** involves a group of investors, often part of the existing management team, buying a target company and taking it private with a minimum amount of equity and large amount of debt. Target companies are generally those with undervalued hard assets. The investors often sell off specific assets or subsidiaries to pay down much of the debt quickly. If key assets have been undervalued, the investors may own a downsized company whose earnings prospects have improved and whose stock has increased in value. The investors sell the company or take it public once the market perceives its greater value. If investors misforecast and pay too much, the target company goes bankrupt.

Many of the earliest LBOs produced returns as high as 50 percent. The availability of junk bond financing during the early 1980s subsequently gave corporate raiders the capacity to make takeovers a real threat so that both friendly and hostile takeovers were common. As more players entered the game, prices increased and the returns declined. By the late 1980s the junk bond market collapsed and takeover financing was restricted for all but the soundest deals. Many large corporations, such as the Campeau group and Revco, declared bankruptcy. The descriptions of the Allied-Signal and RJR LBOs in the Contemporary Issues segments demonstrate the risks and returns of two well-known transactions. During the mid- to late 1990s, LBO activity rebounded as the junk bond market strengthened and these securities were again readily used for financing.

With the bidding wars and onslaught of bankruptcies in the 1980s, lenders and bank regulators grew concerned with the credit risks that banks were assuming in these transactions. Bank regulators eventually grouped LBOs with other transactions involving extensive borrowings under the label highly leveraged transactions (HLTs). HLTs arise from three types of transactions:

- LBOs in which debt is substituted for privately held equity
- Leveraged recapitalizations in which borrowers use loan proceeds to pay large dividends to shareholders
- Leveraged acquisitions in which a cash purchase of another related company produces an increase in the buyer's debt structure

According to regulatory definition, an HLT must involve the buyout, recapitalization, or acquisition of a firm in which either:

1. The firm's subsequent leverage ratio exceeds 75 percent.
2. The transaction more than doubles the borrower's liabilities and produces a leverage ratio over 50 percent.
3. The regulators or firm that syndicates the loans declares the transaction an HLT.

Commercial banks play a variety of roles in leveraged buyouts. They may act as investment bankers in putting deals together by obtaining commitments from wealthy individuals, pension funds, and insurance companies for financing. More typically, they extend credit directly in support of the buyer's equity investment. These loans are asset-based because they are secured by the firm's underlying assets and thus represent senior debt in HLTs. It is these loans

---

[17]The term **base rate** refers to an index rate used to price loans. The index can be any rate that approximates a bank's cost of debt financing, including the federal funds rate, CD rate, weighted marginal cost of debt, and a bank's own prime rate. Historically, loans were priced as a markup over prime. The term base rate has generally replaced *prime rate* in loan agreements.

that have increased problem loans and adversely affected bank profits in recent years. Most HLTs also involve **mezzanine financing,** a type of credit that is subordinated to the claims of bank debt but senior to the investor's common stock. It is appealing because it usually carries an equity participation option. As the number of leveraged buyouts increases, however, the riskiness of the deals also increases. There are more potential buyers, prices get bid higher, financing costs increase, and fewer deals generate the necessary cash flow to service the debt.

TERM COMMERCIAL LOANS. Many businesses have credit needs that persist beyond one year. Term commercial loans, which have an original maturity of more than one year, are normally used in these cases. Most term loans have maturities from one to seven years and are granted to finance either the purchase of depreciable assets, start-up costs for a new venture, or a permanent increase in the level of working capital. Because repayment comes over several years, lenders focus more on the borrower's periodic income and cash flow rather than the balance sheet. Chapter 16 examines the traditional credit analysis underlying a term loan from basic ratio analysis to cash flow projections. Term loans often require collateral, but this represents a secondary source of repayment in case the borrower defaults.

The characteristics of term loans vary with the use of the proceeds. For asset purchases, the loan principal is advanced in its entirety after an agreement is signed. The amount equals the net purchase price on the asset acquired. The maturity is determined by the asset's useful life and the borrower's ability to generate cash to repay principal and interest. The interest charged reflects the bank's cost of funds plus a risk premium to compensate for default risk and interest rate risk. Virtually all term loans use formal loan agreements that stipulate what is expected of each party and provide remedies when the agreement is breached. They are necessary because most term loans are too complex to comprehend over several years, during which time the principals tend to forget the initial negotiated terms.

Loan payments are structured in several forms. Many are scheduled over several years so that the borrower's cash flow is sufficient to cover the interest and principal in each year. Many term loans are repaid on an installment basis and fully amortized. Each periodic payment includes interest plus principal in varying amounts. Other term loans may use equal annual principal payments with interest computed on the declining principal balance. Occasionally, term loans will call for balloon payments of principal. In these cases, the borrower pays only the periodic interest until maturity, when the full principal comes due (bullet loan), or makes amortized principal and interest payments based on a very long maturity (30 years), with the remaining principal paid at maturity (five years). The normal source of repayment is cash flow generated from a company's operations.

For new ventures and permanent increases in working capital, banks advance the loan principal as needed. If the borrower needs different amounts over time, a bank usually structures the agreement as a loan commitment during the early stages, then converts the outstanding principal to a term loan. With this type of term loan—often called a revolving credit—repayment still derives from future cash flows and the agreement is priced at higher yields because of the greater risk.

REVOLVING CREDITS. Revolving credits are a hybrid of short-term working capital loans and term loans. They often involve a commitment of funds (the borrowing base) for one to five years. At the end of some interim period, the outstanding principal converts to a term loan. During the interim period, the borrower determines usage much like a credit line. Mandatory principal payments begin once the commitment converts to a term loan. The revolver has a fixed maturity and often requires the borrower to pay a fee at the time of conversion to a term loan. This agreement reduces paperwork and simplifies loan servicing for creditworthy customers, who like its flexibility during the interim period. Revolvers have often substituted for commercial paper or corporate bond issues.

CONTEMPORARY ISSUES

RJR—Deleveraging an LBO

At the end of 1988, Kohlberg Kravis Roberts & Co. (KKR) acquired RJR Nabisco for $24.7 billion, the largest LBO in history. In October 1988, RJR's chairman and other insiders offered to buy the firm for $75 a share. After an aggressive bidding war that ended two months later, the eventual sales price was the equivalent of $114 in securities per share. RJR obtained $24.7 billion in financing and immediately announced a plan to sell corporate assets to pay down the debt. The following chart demonstrates how RJR's stock price reacted initially versus prices on its outstanding bonds with a 13-year maturity. The stock price rose over the offer price because arbitrageurs bought shares in anticipation of a bidding war for the company. The bond prices plummeted because any firm that acquired RJR would load up on debt to finance the purchase. Existing bondholders' claims would be adversely affected

and RJR's ability to service interest and principal payments on debt would be hampered. In fact, when KKR announced a $1.25 billion senior note offering in January 1989, Moody's rated the bonds as speculative thereby raising KKR's borrowing costs based on the firm's reduced ability to cover debt payments.

By 1991 KKR was concentrating its efforts on deleveraging, or substituting equity for debt. Asset sales had gone slower than expected and prices were generally lower than expected. To reduce interest payments KKR decided to inject $1.18 billion in equity with the proceeds used to pay down its debt. KKR had gone full circle from increasing leverage to decreasing leverage. Through 1998 the firm's stock price was still low, particularly because tobacco products were subject to extreme price pressure, and the firm had too much debt. KKR was con-

sidering dividing the company into two companies, a food products group and a tobacco group, to try to increase market value.

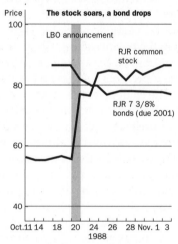

The stock soars, a bond drops

SOURCE: Diana Fortier (1989).

AGRICULTURE LOANS

Agriculture loans are similar to commercial and industrial loans in that short-term credit finances seasonal operating expenses, in this case those associated with planting and harvesting crops. Much like working capital loans, the proceeds are used to purchase inventory in the form of seed, fertilizer, and pesticides and to pay other production costs. Farm operators expect to repay the debt when the crops are harvested and sold. Long-term credit finances livestock, equipment, and land purchases. The fundamental source of repayment is cash flow from the sale of livestock and harvested crops in excess of operating expenses. These loans differ, however, because agriculture is perceived to be a vital national industry. The federal government lends considerable sums to farmers through its farm credit system. Federal agencies involved with agriculture lending include the Farmers Home Administration, the Farm Credit Banks, and Federal Land Banks. Commercial banks often work with these agencies to keep farmers operating, even when it appears that they will sustain large near-term losses.

The profitability of agriculture loans follows cyclical trends in the farm economy. During the 1970s when inflation was high, farm land values more than doubled in many regions of the United States. Using land as collateral, banks encouraged farmers to expand their operations, financed with term loans. Both farmers and banks expected land values to continue rising and virtually ignored whether cash flow from production was sufficient to cover the debt service. A series of events—beginning with the Soviet grain embargo in 1980, the worldwide recession in 1982, and the strong U.S. dollar lowering net exports—reversed the trend. Farm commodity prices fell so far that farm revenues were frequently less than the cost of seed, fertilizer, and loan interest. Land values fell with this negative operating cash flow, reducing the farmer's borrowing base just when he needed more credit for operating expenses.

The problem was that banks loaned against the perceived value of land, but farmers never expected to sell the land to repay the debt. As cash flow deteriorated from 1984 to 1987, land values fell and the loans were undercollateralized. The obvious lesson is that farm loans, like term commercial loans, are repaid out of cash flow. Before lending, a bank should verify that cash flows will be sufficient to service debt under most circumstances.

From 1984 to 1987 many small agriculture banks throughout the United States experienced severe credit problems with their farm loans. During this time over 40 percent of the nation's bank failures were agriculture banks, and many that did not fail had more problem loans than capital.[18] In 1985 the Farm Credit System, which consists of 12 Federal Land Banks, 12 Federal Intermediate Credit Banks, 13 Banks for Co-ops, and affiliated associations, lost $2.7 billion in loan and mortgage defaults on a portfolio of approximately $70 billion. The U.S. Congress had to reorganize the system and give it access to Treasury credit. Even with these losses, many commercial banks and the government's farm lending agencies deferred charging off more loans by extending credit to borrowers, with little chance of repayment. Agriculture lenders and farmers are constantly working through the cycle where commodity prices rise and fall depending on the demand from foreign and U.S. markets and changes in supply from improved or reduced production. The cycles can be extremely volatile. Again, in 1998 commodity prices plummeted and small farmers with hog and cattle operations took a beating in the marketplace.

CONSUMER LOANS

Nonmortgage consumer loans differ substantially from commercial loans. Their usual purpose is to finance the purchase of durable goods, although many individuals borrow to finance education, medical care, and other expenses. The average loan to each borrower is relatively small. Most loans have maturities from one to four years, are repaid in installments, and carry fixed interest rates. In recent years, most states have removed usury ceilings that set maximum rates banks can charge so that consumer loan rates are now high relative to historical norms. This leads to different risk and return features than with other loans. In general, an individual borrower's default risk is greater than a commercial customer's. Consumer loan rates are thus higher to compensate for the greater losses.

Although most consumer loans carry fixed rates, installment payments increase their rate sensitivity so their average duration is relatively short. Long-term loans, however, may subject banks to considerable interest rate risk. Finally, consumer loans are relatively illiquid. Banks generally cannot sell them near face value because no secondary market exists. This is slowly changing, however, as more banks attempt to securitize automobile loans and credit card receivables. (See Chapter 2.)

Consumer loans are normally classified as either installment, credit card, or noninstallment credit. Installment loans require a partial payment of principal plus interest periodically until maturity. Other consumer loans require either a single payment of all interest plus principal or a gradual repayment at the borrower's discretion, as with a credit line. Banks' share of the consumer credit market has fallen over time, but even with many competitors, commercial banks held around 38 percent of the total credit outstanding in the late 1990s and were the largest single holders of automobile loans, mobile home loans, and all other types.

---

[18]McCoy and Charlier (1985) describe farm loan delinquencies and farm bank problems during the early 1980s.

Noninstallment loans are for special purposes in which the individual normally expects a large cash receipt to repay the debt, such as a temporary bridge loan for the down payment on a house that is repaid from the sale of the previous house. Chapter 17 discusses additional features of consumer loans and selected credit analysis procedures. Pools of securitized assets are the second largest holder of consumer credit with almost 28 percent of total consumer credit at the end of the 1990s. Pools of securitized assets were the largest single holder of revolving credit (credit card or overdraft loans), having surpassed banks in 1997.

VENTURE CAPITAL. Due to the high leverage and risk involved, as well as regulatory requirements, banks generally do not participate directly in venture capital deals. Some banks, however, do have subsidiaries that finance certain types of equity participations and venture capital deals, but their participation is limited. Venture capital (VC) is a broad term use to describe funding acquired in the earlier stages of a firm's economic life. This type of funding is usually acquired during the period in which the company is growing faster than its ability to generate internal financing and before the company has achieved the size needed to be efficient. Generally speaking, venture capital provides long-term, risk-sharing equity capital or debt to assist non–publicly traded companies with their growth opportunities. VC firms attempt to add value to the firm without taking majority control. Although many venture capital deals are in the form of debt, venture capital investors often take a minority equity participation in the firm as owners must sell a minority share in their companies to attract the venture backer. The VC firm will most likely seek a nonexecutive board position and attend monthly board meetings. Often, VC firms not only provide financing but experience, expertise, contacts, and advice when required. There are many types of venture financing. Early stages of financing come in the form *seed* or *start-up capital*. These are highly levered transactions in which the VC firm will lend money for a percentage stake in the firm. Rarely, if ever, do banks participate as VCs at this stage. Later-stage development capital takes the form of *expansion and replacement financing*, *recapitalization* or *turnaround financing*, *buy-out or buy-in financing*, and even *mezzanine financing*. Banks do participate in these rounds of financing, but if the company is overleveraged at the onset, the banks will be effectively excluded from these later rounds of financing.

Mezzanine financing became quite popular during the technology boom of the late 1990s and provides a company the funds to continue to grow at a rapid pace. It is usually the second, third, or fourth round of financing. This type of financing is popular because VCs are investing in later-rounds of financing; such that the firms have a track record upon which to base their investment decisions. Some venture capital firms focus on particular industries, while others may focus on specific types of mezzanine financing, such as financing used to take a company public or acquisition financing.

SUMMARY

Lending involves more risk than virtually any other banking activity. Management, therefore, analyzes the nature of risks carefully before extending credit. The credit process includes three functions: business development and credit analysis, credit execution and administration, and credit review. Business development activities concentrate on identifying profitable customers and encouraging credit relationships. Credit analysis is the process of assessing risk and includes a review of financial data and subjective evaluation of the borrower's character. The credit staff formally accepts or rejects a loan request and executes the necessary documents with approvals. Finally, loan officers periodically review each outstanding loan, especially when it comes up for renewal or reaches workout status. At times, loan terms may need to be modified to recognize a change in the borrower's status.

Banks make many different types of loans, which are the dominant asset in most bank portfolios. This chapter describes the basic features of short-term working capital loans, asset-based loans, real estate loans, consumer loans, and agriculture loans. It analyzes many banks' efforts to move assets off the balance sheet or directly enter into off-balance sheet activities to supplement earnings.

QUESTIONS

1. Discuss the importance of a bank's credit culture in managing credit risk.

2. Describe the basic features of the three functions underlying the credit process at commercial banks.

3. What are the five Cs of credit? Discuss their importance in credit analysis. Describe the five Cs of bad credit introduced in the text.

4. How does a bank make a profit on loans? Discuss the importance of loans in attracting a borrower's other business with a financial institution.

5. Discuss reasons why banks might choose to include the following covenants in a loan agreement:
   a. Cash dividends cannot exceed 60 percent of pretax income.
   b. Interim financial statements must be provided monthly.
   c. Inventory turnover must be greater than five times annually.
   d. Capital expenditures may not exceed $10 million annually.

6. Explain how a company's permanent working capital needs differ from its seasonal working capital needs.

7. Explain how banks move loans off the balance sheet. What motivates different types of off-balance sheet activities? Discuss the risks these actions involve.

8. What motivation encourages commercial banks to make adjustable-rate mortgages? Why are adjustable mortgage rates normally below fixed mortgage rates? As the level of rates declines, would you expect banks to increase or decrease the adjustable rate proportion of their mortgage portfolios?

9. You are considering making a working capital loan to a company that manufactures and distributes fad items for convenience and department stores. The loan will be secured by the firm's inventory and receivables. What risks are associated with this type of collateral? How would you minimize the risk and periodically determine that the firm's performance was not deteriorating?

10. Discuss whether each of the following types of loans can be easily securitized. Explain why or why not.
    a. Residential mortgages
    b. Small business loans
    c. Pools of credit card loans
    d. Pools of home equity loans
    e. Loans to farmers for production

11. Describe the basic features of:
    a. Open credit lines
    b. Asset-based loans
    c. Term commercial loans
    d. Short-term real estate loans

12. Why do firms or individuals involved in farming need to borrow? What type of inventory does a farmer need? What type of receivables does a farmer typically have? What collateral is typically available? In addition to general economic conditions, what should a banker be watchful of before extending credit to a farmer?

13. Many banks compete aggressively for business in consumer credit cards. What is the particular attraction of this type of lending?

14. Suppose that you are considering making a working capital loan to a business customer of your bank. You do the cash-to-cash cycle analysis and determine that the days cash-to-cash for assets is 35 while the days cash-to-cash for liabilities is 48. The firm's daily average cost of goods sold is $50,000. What does this mean?

15. Describe how each of the following helps a bank control its credit risk.
    a. Loan covenants
    b Risk rating systems
    c. Position limits

PROBLEMS

LOAN TO BOOK PUBLISHER   Suppose that RSM Publishing Co., a children's book publisher, has approached your bank and wants to borrow $250,000 in working capital. The firm provides you with the following balance sheet and income statement data:

Assets		Liabilities & Equity	
Cash	$50,000	Accounts payable	$166,000
Accounts receivable	$375,000	Accrued expenses	$37,000
Inventory	$510,000	Notes payable	$75,000
Fixed assets	$925,000	Current maturity of long-term debt	$25,000
Total Assets	$1,860,000	Long-term debt	$475,000
		Equity	$1,082,000
		Total Liabilities	$1,860,000

Sales: $4,622,800
Cost of goods sold: $3,504,100
Operating expenses: $893,000
Purchases: $ 3,116,000

1. What fraction of the firm's current assets is being funded with long-term debt or equity?

2. Assuming a 365-day year, calculate the firm's asset cash-to-cash cycle, liability cash-to-cash cycle, and days deficiency. Using this information and the procedure described in the text, estimate the firm's working capital loan needs.

3. What general concerns might you have regarding this loan request?

4. Suppose that the typical publishing firm in this industry has just one-half the amount of equity that RSM has. How will this affect key industry ratios and the estimate of working capital needs by this procedure, in general?

ACTIVITY

Obtain copies of the annual reports for several community banks in your area and at least one large regional or nationwide bank. Compare the size of the loan portfolios as a fraction of total assets. Compare the composition of their loan portfolios. What impact should the differences have on each bank's risk position and earnings? Examine the footnotes to determine the loan loss experience for each type of loan. Why do differences appear?

16

Evaluating Commercial Loan Requests

Though my bottom line is black, I am flat upon my back,
 My cash flows out and customers pay slow.
The growth of my receivables is almost unbelievable;
 The result is certain-unremitting woe!
And I hear the banker utter an ominous low mutter,
 "Watch cash flow."

— HERBERT S. BAILEY JR., WITH APOLOGIES TO "THE RAVEN" BY EDGAR ALLAN POE[1]

The financial press pays great attention to corporate earnings announcements as indicators of past performance and future growth opportunities. Most analysts, however, recognize that cash flow information is equally important when evaluating a firm's prospects. Reported earnings and earnings per share can be manipulated by management and may not depict the firm's true ability to meet payments obligations. Debts are repaid out of cash flow, not earnings.

Most firms, for example, record credit sales as revenues, even though no cash is immediately generated. A firm with large increases in receivables might report increasing profits but have no cash to cover operating expenses. Similarly, some companies report their share of undistributed profits in companies in which they have a limited equity interest as income, even though no cash is received. In 2001 and 2002, the SEC determined that many telecom companies inappropriately exchanged service rights, which did not affect cash flow, but were reported as sales, thereby increasing reported earnings. Cash flow used in conjunction with trends in net income is critically important to determining the quality, and thus permanence, of earnings.

This chapter provides guidelines for evaluating commercial credit requests. It briefly considers the qualitative aspects of lending such as the quality of data, quality of management, the borrower's character and desire to repay a loan, and the quality of the company's product. These qualitative issues and other economic and industry specific factors can be as important as the quantitative factors

---

[1]Cited in R. Green, "Are More Chryslers in the Offing?" *Forbes*, February 2, 1981.

associated with the loan decision. An evaluation of these qualitative factors requires experience and "hands-on knowledge," difficult to acquire in a textbook. Instead, this chapter focuses on a company's ability to repay a loan and related quantitative factors associated with the loan decision. As Bailey's banker advised, "Watch cash flow" is an important motto.

The basic objective of credit analysis is to assess the risks involved in extending credit (making a loan). As used here, risk refers to the volatility in earnings. Lenders are particularly concerned with adverse fluctuations in net income, or more importantly cash flow, which hinder a borrower's ability to service or repay a loan. Such risk manifests itself to the bank by a borrower defaulting, or not making timely interest and/or principal payments. Credit analysis assigns a probability to the likelihood of default based on quantitative and qualitative factors. Some risks can be measured with historical and projected financial data. Other risks, such as those associated with the borrower's character and willingness to repay a loan, are not directly measurable. When deciding whether or not to approve a loan, the bank ultimately compares the various risks with the potential benefits to the bank (income) from making the loan. A formal comparison of loan revenues with loan expenses and estimated risk expense, called loan profitability analysis, appears in Chapter 18.

---

his chapter introduces a four-step procedure to analyze the quantifiable aspects of commercial credit requests. The procedure incorporates an objective and systematic interpretation of management and operations as well as financial data. It focuses on issues that typically arise when determining creditworthiness. The results supplement qualitative information regarding the borrower's character and history of financial responsibility. After analyzing a loan request, a loan officer should have a firm grasp on the answers to the following key questions:

1. What is the character of the borrower and quality of information provided?
2. What are the loan proceeds going to be used for?
3. How much does the customer need to borrow?
4. What is the primary source of repayment, and when will the loan be repaid?
5. What is the secondary source of repayment; i.e., what collateral or guarantees are available?

The first section discusses these questions in detail. The second section introduces an objective evaluation procedure. The final section provides an application and interpretation of the analysis for a hypothetical loan request. The appendices review basic terminology and discuss sources of financial data.

FUNDAMENTAL CREDIT ISSUES

Virtually every business in the United States has a credit relationship with a financial institution. Some firms only use backup credit lines in support of commercial paper issues. Some rely on periodic short-term loans to finance temporary working capital needs. Others primarily use term loans with a maturity beyond one year to finance capital expenditures, new acquisitions, or permanent increases in working capital. Regardless of the type of loan, all credit requests mandate a systematic analysis of the borrower's ability to repay.

When evaluating loan requests, bankers can make two types of errors in judgment. The first is extending credit to a customer who ultimately defaults. The second is denying a loan to a customer who ultimately would repay the debt. In both cases, the bank loses a customer and its profits are less. Many bankers focus on eliminating the first type of error, applying rigid credit evaluation criteria and rejecting applicants who do not fit the mold of the ideal borrower. A well-known axiom in banking is that the only time borrowers can get financing is when they really do not need the funds. Unfortunately, as many bankers have discovered, turning down good loans is unprofitable as well. The purpose of credit analysis is to identify the meaningful, probable circumstances under which the bank might lose. Lenders also use credit analysis to restructure a weak loan application into a good loan when the borrower is strong, but does not fully understand the true borrowing needs.

CHARACTER OF THE BORROWER AND QUALITY OF DATA PROVIDED

The foremost issue in assessing credit risk is determining a borrower's commitment and ability to repay debts in accordance with the terms of a loan agreement. An individual's honesty, integrity, and work ethic typically evidence commitment. For a business, commitment is evidenced by the owners and senior management. Bankers who argue that they make many quick credit decisions implicitly state that many potential borrowers are of dubious character. Even if the numbers look acceptable, a bank should lend nothing if the borrower appears dishonest. Whenever there is deception or a lack of credibility, a bank should not do business with the borrower.

It is often difficult to identify dishonest borrowers. The best indicators are the borrower's financial history and personal references. When a borrower has missed past debt service payments or been involved in a default or bankruptcy, a lender should carefully document why, to determine if the causes were reasonable. Borrowers with a history of credit problems are more likely to see the same problems arise later. Similarly, borrowers with a good credit history will have established personal and banking relationships that indicate whether they fully disclose meaningful information and deal with subordinates and suppliers honestly. A loan officer should begin the credit analysis by analyzing the firm's prior banking relationships, dealings with suppliers and customers, and current record from appropriate credit bureaus.

Lenders often look for signals of a borrower's condition beyond basic balance sheet and income statement data. For example, negative signals may appear in the following forms.

- A borrower's name consistently appears on the list of bank customers who have overdrawn their accounts.

- A borrower makes a significant change in the structure of the business, such as a change in accountant or change in key manager or adviser.

- A borrower appears to be consistently short of cash, which might be indicated by frequent requests for small loans or keeping small balances in checking accounts when net worth is high.

- A borrower's personal habits have changed for the worse; red flags include behavior suggesting drug use, heavy gambling, alcoholism, or marital breakup.

- A firm's goals are incompatible with those of stockholders, employees, and customers.[2]

The quality of data used in the analysis is critical. Many small companies use less sophisticated accounting techniques and their financial statements are unaudited. Audited financial statements are preferred because accounting rules are well established so that an analyst can

---

[2]See Thomas Bennett (1987) for a lender's view of these issues. Conrad Newburgh (1991) presents procedures for evaluating character and maintaining control of the lending agreement.

better understand the underlying factors that affect the entries. Just because a company has audited financial statements, however, does not mean the reported data are not manipulated. Management has considerable discretion within the guidelines of generally accepted accounting principles and thus can "window dress" financial statements to make the results look better. An analyst should review the following to assess accounting data quality:

- Areas of accounting choices in which estimates and judgments are required inputs.
- Periods in which a change in account principle, method, or assumption has occurred.
- Extraordinary and discretionary expenditures, as well as nonrecurring transactions.
- Income and expense recognition that do not closely track cash flow.
- Nonoperating income, gains, and losses.

In addition to character and assessment of data quality, four additional fundamental issues must be resolved prior to extending credit: the use of loan proceeds, loan amount, source and timing of repayment, and collateral. These issues draw attention to specific features of each loan that can be addressed when structuring the loan agreement terms.

USE OF LOAN PROCEEDS

The range of business loan needs is unlimited. Firms may need cash for operating purposes to pay overdue suppliers, make a tax payment, or pay employee salaries. Similarly, they may need funds to pay off maturing debt obligations or to acquire new fixed assets. Although the question of what the borrowed funds will be used for seems simple enough, frequently a firm recognizes that it is short of cash but cannot identify specifically why.

Loan proceeds should be used for legitimate business operating purposes, including seasonal and permanent working capital needs, the purchase of depreciable assets, physical plant expansion, acquisition of other firms, and extraordinary operating expenses. Speculative asset purchases and debt substitutions should be avoided. The use of the loan proceeds can either enhance the ability of the firm to repay the loan or make it more risky. Financing illegal activities or unprofitable operations can actually increase the losses of the firm and hence reduce the possibility of repayment. The true need and use of the loan proceeds determines the loan maturity, the anticipated source and timing of repayment, and the appropriate collateral.

Many commercial loans are made for working capital purposes. As such, they bridge the gap between the expenditure of funds to purchase raw materials or inventory and pay employees with the sale of those goods on credit and the ultimate collection of the cash on the credit sales. The analyst must determine whether the bank is financing an increase in inventory or receivables, or replacing outstanding payables and debt. Banks all too often originate working capital loans as seasonal credits, only to find that they are never fully repaid as anticipated. In this case, the banker discovers that the loan was not a seasonal need but rather a replacement of outstanding payables or financing a permanent increase in working capital needs. Term loans should be made for permanent increases in working capital needs and asset acquisitions with an economic life beyond one year. These types of loans require a longer repayment schedule. One common pitfall is to focus too much on collateral and end up financing a firm's long-term needs with short-term notes. A careful review of a firm's financial data reveals why a company needs financing.

LOAN AMOUNT

In many cases, borrowers request a loan before they clearly understand how much external financing is actually needed and how much is available internally. The amount of credit required depends on the use of the proceeds and the availability of internal sources of funds. For example, if a firm wants to finance new equipment, the loan request is typically for the purchase price less the resale value of any replaced assets. For a shorter-term loan, the amount might equal the temporary seasonal increase in receivables and inventory net of that supported by increased accounts payable. With term loans, the amount can be determined via *pro forma* analysis.[3] Borrowers often ask for too little in requesting a loan and return later for more funds. The lender should not only estimate how much the borrower will need today but also in the future. Failure to recognize that lending only a portion of the funds needed may actually reduce the borrower's ability to pay the loan back is a mistake often made by inexperienced lenders. A half-built warehouse will not produce revenue but will be a revenue drain. The lender's job is to help determine the correct amount, such that a borrower has enough cash to operate effectively but not too much to spend wastefully.

Once a loan is approved, the amount of credit actually extended depends on the borrower's future performance. If the borrower's cash flows are insufficient to meet operating expenses and debt service on the loan, the bank will be called upon to lend more and possibly lengthen the loan maturity. If cash flows are substantial, the initial loan outstanding might decline rapidly and even be repaid early. The required loan amount is thus a function of the initial cash deficiency and the pattern of future cash flows.

THE PRIMARY SOURCE AND TIMING OF REPAYMENT

Loans are repaid from cash flows. The four basic sources of cash flow are: the liquidation of assets, cash flow from normal operations, new debt issues, and new equity issues. Credit analysis evaluates the risk that a borrower's future cash flows will not be sufficient to meet mandatory expenditures for continued operations and interest and principal payments on the loan.

Specific sources of cash are generally associated with certain types of loans. Short-term, seasonal working capital loans are normally repaid from the liquidation of receivables or reductions in inventory. Term loans are typically repaid out of cash flows from operations, specifically earnings and noncash charges in excess of net working capital needs and capital expenditures needed to maintain the existing fixed asset base. A comparison of projected cash flow from operations with interest and principal payments on prospective loans indicates how much debt can be serviced and the appropriate maturity. Unless specifically identified in the loan agreement, it is inappropriate to rely on new equity from investors or new debt from other creditors for repayment. Too often these external sources of cash disappear if the firm's profitability declines or economic conditions deteriorate.

The primary source of repayment on the loan can also determine the risk of the loan. The general rule is not to count on the acquired asset or underlying collateral as the primary source of repayment. If you lend money for someone to buy 1,000 shares of IBM stock and they have no other source of income to pay you back, the primary source of repayment is the acquired asset. If the stock does well, the borrower makes money and repays the loan. If the stock does poorly, the borrower declares bankruptcy and you will not be fully repaid. Obviously, this was not a loan but venture capital disguised as a loan. This is not to say that you would never lend money for someone to buy IBM stock or that an acquired asset cannot be expected to help pay back the loan. They are just not the primary source of repayment.

---

[3]*Pro forma* analysis is the projecting or forecasting of a company's financial statements into the future. The use of income statement, balance sheet, and cash flow projections allows an analyst to assess the amount of the loan needed, the purpose of the loan proceeds, when the loan will be paid back, and what collateral is available.

COLLATERAL

It is not by chance that the question of collateral is the last question to be addressed. If something goes wrong, a bank wants all the collateral it can get, but it generally does not want to take possession of the collateral. Taking the collateral means that the borrower is unable to continue operations. If the collateral is inventory or uncollected receivables, why would the bank be better able to liquidate the assets than the managers who know the industry? It is also costly to maintain and sell collateral, and foreclosures do not build long-term relationships with the customers.

Banks can, however, lower the risk of loss on a loan by requiring backup support beyond normal cash flow. This can take the form of assets held by the borrower or an explicit guarantee by a related firm or key individual. Collateral is the security a bank has in assets owned and pledged by the borrower against a debt in the event of default. Banks look to collateral as a secondary source of repayment when primary cash flows are insufficient to meet debt service requirements. Banks should select collateral that will retain its value over the business cycle. Receivables and marketable inventory are preferred because of their liquidity. Plant, equipment, and real estate are also potentially valuable.

Virtually any asset, or the general capacity to generate cash flow, can be used as collateral. From a lender's perspective, however, collateral must exhibit three features. First, its value should always exceed the outstanding principal on a loan. Any lender that must take possession of the collateral can then sell it for more than the balance due and losses are reduced. Imagine lending for the purchase of an automobile where the value of the car is less than the outstanding loan balance. The borrower may have a financial incentive to default on the loan. Second, a lender should be able to easily take possession of collateral and have a ready market for sale. Highly illiquid assets are worth far less because they are not portable and often are of real value only to the original borrower. Third, a lender must be able to clearly mark collateral as its own. This means that the claim must be legal and clear. Careful loan documentation is required to perfect the bank's interest in the collateral.

When physical collateral is not readily available, banks often look for personal guarantees. They generally rely on the borrower's cash flow to cover debt service with the borrower's net worth in reserve. Banks attempt to protect themselves against adverse changes in a borrower's financial condition by imposing loan covenants in the loan agreement that restrict a borrower's ability to make extreme decisions and thereby alter its fundamental operating profile. When the borrower's cash flow is problematic, a bank can request that the borrower find a co-signer who agrees to assume the debt in the event of default.

Liquidating collateral is clearly a second best source of repayment for three reasons. First, there are significant transactions costs associated with foreclosure. Banks must often allocate considerable employee time and pay large legal expenses that reduce the collateral's net value. Thus, when negotiating loan agreements, the bank should select collateral with a value above the anticipated loan amount. Second, bankruptcy laws allow borrowers to retain possession of the collateral long after they have defaulted. During that time, the collateral often disappears or deteriorates in value. Third, when the bank takes possession of the collateral, it deprives the borrower of the opportunity to salvage the company. The bank must hire new managers or manage the firm temporarily with its own personnel until sale, a poor alternative.

In general, a loan should *not* be approved on the basis of collateral alone. Unless the loan is secured by collateral held by the bank, such as bank CDs, there is risk involved in collection. In most cases, it is essential that lenders periodically examine the quality of collateral to determine whether it truly exists or has deteriorated over time. This involves on-site inspections of a borrower's inventory, receivables, and operating facilities. In addition to assessing collateral, the lender can reevaluate the borrower's character by the nature of the business and collateral. Collateral improves the bank's position by lowering its net exposure. It does not improve the borrower's ability to generate cash to repay the loan.

In addition to these issues, credit analysis should examine risks that are unique to each loan. Each analysis should identify questions regarding the quality of management, the soundness of the business, sensitivity to economic conditions, the firm's relationship with other creditors, and any other information that is not available in the financial statements.

EVALUATING CREDIT RESOURCES: A FOUR-PART PROCESS

The purpose of credit analysis is to identify and define the lender's risk in making a loan. There is a four-stage process for evaluating the financial aspects of commercial loans:

1. Overview of management, operations, and the firm's industry
2. Common size and financial ratio analysis
3. Analysis of cash flow
4. Projections and analysis of the borrower's financial condition

During all phases, the analyst should examine facts that are relevant to the credit decision and recognize information that is important but unavailable. The analyst should prepare a list of questions to be presented to the borrower for clarification. Financial calculations, using historical data, should examine the absolute magnitudes of ratios and funds flows and pertinent changes in the magnitudes over time (trend analysis), and compare these measures to industry averages for the firm's competitors. Much of the information is available from the bank's credit files and conversations with the firm's management and chief financial officer. Sources of financial data on comparable firms are described in Appendix II to this chapter.

Financial projections (*pro forma*) involve making reasonable assumptions about a firm's future sales, working capital needs, capital expenditures, operating expenses, taxes, and dividends. A company may need to borrow funds today (and possibly more in the future), but those funds will be paid back with future cash flows. Projections of the borrower's financial condition are used to forecast cash flows and determine answers to the questions discussed above: how much is needed, what are the funds going to be used for, what is the primary source of repayment, and when will the funds be repaid? These projected cash flows are formally compared with expected interest and principal payments on all debt obligations and other mandatory cash expenditures. The same ratio analysis can then be performed using the projected data as a check on the reasonableness of the forecasts.

OVERVIEW OF MANAGEMENT, OPERATIONS, AND THE FIRM'S INDUSTRY

Before analyzing financial data, the analyst should gather background information on the firm's operations, including specific characteristics of the business and intensity of industry competition, management character and quality, the nature of the loan request, and the data quality. Relevant historical developments and recent trends should also be examined.

This evaluation usually begins with an analysis of the organizational and business structure of the borrower. Is it a holding company with subsidiaries or a single entity? Does it operate as a corporation or partnership? Is the firm privately or publicly held? When did the firm begin operations, and in what geographic markets does it now compete? The evaluation should also identify the products or services provided and the firm's competitive position in the marketplace as measured by market share, degree of product differentiation, presence of economies of scale or scope in the cost structure, and the bargaining power of buyers and sellers that the firm deals with.[4]

The next step is usually to write a brief *Business and Industry Outlook* report. The analyst should examine historical sales growth, the relationship between industry sales and the business cycle, and an implied forecast for the industry. The analyst should also address related questions. How many firms offer competitive products? Are there differences in product quality or life? A logical extension is to evaluate suppliers and the production process. Has the firm contracted for the appropriate raw materials at good prices? How many suppliers can provide the necessary materials? What is the quality of the firm's labor force and employee relations? Are the firm's fixed assets obsolete?

Particular attention should be focused on management character and quality. The backgrounds of the chief executive, financial, and operating officers should be examined in terms of key individuals' ages, experience in the business, service with the company, and apparent line of succession. Businesses frequently are dominated by one individual even though others hold officer titles. When possible, it is useful to identify the top officers' equity interest in the firm and the type of compensation received. This helps identify motivating factors underlying firm decisions.

Finally, the overview should recognize the nature of the borrower's loan request and the quality of the financial data provided. It should indicate the proposed use and amount of credit requested and the borrower's anticipated source of repayment. It should specify whether the financial statements are audited and, if so, the type of opinion issued. A brief discussion of generally accepted accounting principles and audited statements appears in Appendix I to this chapter.

COMMON SIZE AND FINANCIAL RATIO ANALYSIS

Most banks initiate the data analysis using a financial analysis spreadsheet, which arranges the borrower's balance sheet and income statement data into a consistent format for comparison over time and against industry standards. Balance sheet and income statement data for Prism Industries are presented in Exhibits 16.1 and 16.2, respectively. Data for each reporting period are provided in three columns. The first column lists the percentage change in the value from the previous year. The second column contains the actual dollar value of the accounting entry. The third column converts the figure to a common size ratio by dividing by total assets (balance sheet) or net sales (income statement). Comparable peer figures for 2001 are listed in the column labeled "Peer Group Ratios."[5]

Prism Industries is a small manufacturer of outdoor storage buildings. Prism's sales increased by almost 17 percent in 2001. Management indicates that the strong economic environment and its high quality product have lead to the recent success. Examining the balance sheet data presented in Exhibit 16.1 indicates that Prism's accounts receivable increased in 2001 but remained below the industry norms (as a percentage of assets). Inventory actually decreased in 2001 and was also below industry norms. Net fixed assets, on the other had, were well above industry standards in each year. In terms of financing, Prism relied more on stockholders' equity and used less debt. Prism used slightly more short-term bank debt and less trade credit (accounts payable) than the industry average. Prism also used somewhat less long-term debt than peer average. Prism appears to have financed much of its growth using internally generated funds; i.e., retained earnings.

---

[4]Arnold (1988) describes how the intensity of competition affects a firm's business risk. Lenders should incorporate the results of this analysis in their forecasts of sales, costs, and product pricing.

[5]See Appendix II for an overview of available peer group data sources.

▪ EXHIBIT 16.1

COMPARATIVE BALANCE SHEET FOR PRISM INDUSTRIES, 2000–2001

	2000		2001			Peer Group Ratios
	$1,000	Percent of Total	Percentage Change	$1,000	Percent of Total	
ASSETS						
Cash and marketable securities	85	8.1%	5.9%	90	8.2%	5.5%
Accounts receivable	141	13.4%	18.4%	167	15.2%	18.2%
Inventory	306	29.1%	−3.6%	295	26.8%	29.3%
Prepaid expenses	22	2.1%	−18.2%	18	1.6%	
Current assets	554	52.8%	2.9%	570	51.8%	53.0%
Gross fixed assets	575	54.8%	12.2%	645	58.6%	
Less accumulated depreciation	115	11.0%	39.1%	160	14.5%	
Net fixed assets	460	43.8%	5.4%	485	44.1%	38.2%
Long-term investments	36	3.4%	25.0%	45	4.1%	
Total Assets	1,050	100.0%	4.8%	1,100	100.0%	100.0%
LIABILITIES & EQUITY						
Notes payable — bank	50	4.8%	40.0%	70	6.4%	6.0%
Accounts payable	99	9.4%	7.1%	106	9.6%	11.2%
Accrued expenses	15	1.4%	113.3%	32	2.9%	
Income tax payable	6	0.6%	100.0%	12	1.1%	1.7%
Current maturity – LTD	35	3.3%	14.3%	40	3.6%	3.6%
Current liabilities	205	19.5%	26.8%	260	23.6%	27.5%
Long-term debt (LTD)	280	26.7%	−14.3%	240	21.8%	22.8%
Total liabilities	485	46.2%	3.1%	500	45.5%	57.5%
Common stock — par	325	31.0%	0.0%	325	29.5%	
Retained earnings	240	22.9%	14.6%	275	25.0%	
Stockholder's equity	565	53.8%	6.2%	600	54.5%	42.5%
Total Liabilities and Equity	1,050	100.0%	4.8%	1,100	100.0%	100.0%

NOTE: Figures are in thousands of dollars; LTD refers to long-term debt. Prism's first year of operations was 2000.

Common size values of the income statement for Prism are provided in Exhibit 16.2. Examining profitability we find that Prism's profit before taxes increased in 2001, but it was less profitable than the industry average. Lower profitability is due to a much higher cost of goods sold (COGS), reflecting either a higher cost of goods or lower markups on finished products. Prism's COGS, as a percent of sales, fell in 2001 but remains above the industry average. This higher COGS was offset somewhat by Prism's lower operating expenses but the net effect is that the firm earns proportionately less before taxes than comparable firms.

Common size ratio comparisons are valuable because they adjust for size and thus enable comparisons across firms in the same industry or line of business. The figures can be distorted, however, if a firm has one balance sheet or income statement item that differs sharply from industry standards. For example, a firm that leases fixed assets will report a sharply different asset composition than firms in an industry where most firms own fixed assets. To address this issue, analysts should move to the next step, which is to calculate a series of ratios that indicate performance variances.

· EXHIBIT 16.2

COMPARATIVE INCOME STATEMENT FOR PRISM INDUSTRIES, 2000–2001

	2000		2001			Peer Group Ratios
	$1,000	Percent of Total	Percentage Change	$1,000	Percent of Total	
NET SALES	2,400	100.0%	16.67%	2,800	100.0%	100.0%
Cost of goods sold	2,050	85.4%	16.10%	2,380	85.0%	82.2%
Gross profit	350	14.6%	20.00%	420	15.0%	17.8%
Selling expenses	195	8.1%	7.69%	210	7.5%	
Depreciation & amortization	42	1.8%	21.43%	51	1.8%	
Other operating expenses	0	0.0%	#N/A	40	1.4%	
Total operating expenses	237	9.9%	27.00%	301	10.8%	12.5%
Operating profit	113	4.7%	5.31%	119	4.3%	5.3%
Interest expense	38	1.6%	−10.53%	34	1.2%	
All other expenses	7	0.3%	71.43%	12	0.4%	
All other income	9	0.4%	22.22%	11	0.4%	
Total All Other Expenses (Income)	36	1.5%	−2.78%	35	1.3%	1.4%
Profit before taxes	77	3.2%	9.09%	84	3.0%	3.9%
Income taxes	25	1.0%	16.00%	29	1.0%	
NET INCOME	52	2.2%	5.77%	55	2.0%	
Dividends	15	0.6%	33.33%	20	0.7%	
ΔRetained earnings	37	1.5%	−5.41%	35	1.3%	

NOTE: Figures are in thousands of dollars. Lease payments are included in other operating expenses and were $2,200 in 2001.

Most analysts differentiate between at least four categories of ratios: liquidity, activity, leverage, and profitability.[6] *Liquidity ratios* indicate a firm's ability to meet its short-term obligations and continue operations. *Activity ratios* signal how efficiently a firm uses assets to generate sales. *Leverage ratios* indicate the mix of the firm's financing between debt and equity and potential earnings volatility. Finally, *profitability ratios* provide evidence of the firm's sales and earnings performance.

LIQUIDITY AND ACTIVITY RATIOS. Evaluating liquidity risk requires an understanding of a firm's operating cycle. Recall that the typical business buys raw materials or finished goods for resale on credit. It then uses labor and other operating expenses to produce a final product, often paying cash for these services. The product is then sold, typically on credit. Trade credit rarely provides enough financing to cover the time it takes to collect on credit sales. So the proceeds of short-term loans are often used to finance current assets or to reduce other current liabilities. Notes are repaid by systematically reducing inventories following increases in sales and reducing receivables following the collection of credit sales. Measures of net working capital, current and quick ratios, inventory turnover, accounts receivables collection period, days accounts payables outstanding, and the days cash-to-cash cycle, help indicate whether current assets will support current liabilities.

The **current ratio** (current assets/current liabilities) is a gross measure of liquidity. Historically, analysts have viewed a current ratio of about 2.0 to be consistent with adequate

---

[6]Key ratios are defined in Appendix II. Activity ratios are grouped with liquidity ratios in this discussion.

liquidity. This means that firms hold twice as much cash, inventory, and accounts receivable as current liabilities coming due in the next year. Thus, the firm has good ability to pay off the current obligations as they come due. Caution should be exercised here, however, especially when examining the data for smaller firms. A high current ratio could indicate that inventory and/or accounts receivable are high, but this does not mean the firm is liquid unless the inventory and accounts receivable are of high quality. If the firm has obsolete or damaged inventory or overdue accounts receivables, a high current ratio could also indicate a lack of liquidity, hence, the need to carefully examine inventory turnover and days accounts receivables collection period. Faster turnover generally indicates sound inventory levels and good collection of receivables.

A more conservative measure of liquidity is the **quick ratio** [(cash + accounts receivable)/current liabilities]. By eliminating inventories, prepaid expenses, and other current assets, which are generally less liquid, the quick ratio provides a more conservative measure of aggregate liquidity.

Activity ratios measure the efficiency of the firm as well as the liquidity of current assets. A highly efficient firm, for example, will report a **sales to asset ratio** that exceeds industry norms—indicating that its asset base produces proportionately more revenue. A low ratio indicates that the asset mix is not efficient in the sense that too much is allocated to that asset. For example, **days accounts receivables collection period** (accounts receivables/average daily credit sales) indicates the average number of days required to convert accounts receivable into cash. This ratio provides information about a company's credit policy as well as its ability to collect on these accounts. Hence, it is a measure of how efficient the firm is in using this asset as well as how liquid these assets are respectively. **Days inventory on hand** (inventory/average daily purchases) and **inventory turnover** (COGS/inventory) similarly measure the efficiency of the firm in managing its inventory. High days inventory and low turnover relative to industry norms indicate less efficient inventory management and/or less liquidity.

On the other side of the balance sheet, **days accounts payable outstanding** (accounts payable/average daily purchases) measures the firm's efficiency in using trade credit to finance its working capital needs.[7] The greater the days payable, *ceteris paribus*, the more efficient is the firm and the less bank financing needed. Caution is appropriate, however, because all else may not be equal. A high days payable figure may indicate the firm has serious liquidity problems and may be in danger of being "cut off" by its supplier. If this happens, the need for additional bank debt will increase dramatically. Also, a high days payable figure may mean that the firm is giving up early payment discounts, hence, using trade credit financing which is more expensive than bank debt.

Financial ratios for Prism are presented in Exhibit 16.3. Current and quick ratios are low and have declined over the last two years. Days accounts receivable is about six days shorter than the industry norm such that receivables turn over 17 times a year as compared to the industry norm of 13 times. Days inventory and inventory turnover indicate that Prism was slightly more efficient than peers in 2001 in managing inventory. Days accounts payable is much lower at 16.3 days outstanding in 2001 compared to the industry norm of 26.1 days. This indicates that Prism is not using as much financing from trade creditors as the industry average.

LEVERAGE RATIOS. Leverage ratios indicate the mix of the firm's financing between debt and equity and potential earnings volatility resulting from debt financing. The greater is a firm's level of debt, the higher are its fixed interest payments and the more likely it is to generate insufficient earnings (cash flow) to cover debt payments. Thus, the greater is a firm's leverage, the more volatile its net profit (or losses) because certain sales are required to cover

---

[7]Recall the accounting relationship: purchase = COGS + Δ inventory.

■ EXHIBIT 16.3

FINANCIAL RATIO ANALYSIS FOR PRISM INDUSTRIES, 2000–2001

BALANCE SHEET	2000 $1,000		2001 $1,000		Peer Group Ratios	
Liquidity Ratios						
Current Ratio	2.70		2.19		2.10	
Quick Ratio	1.10		0.99		1.01	
	Days	Times	Days	Times	Days	Times
Days Cash	12.93	28.24×	11.73	31.11×		
Accounts Receivable Collection Turnover	21.44	17.02×	21.77	16.77×	28.0	13.0×
Inventory Turnover	54.48	6.70×	45.24	8.07×	48.2	7.6×
Days AP Outstanding	17.49	20.87×	16.33	22.35×	26.1	14.0×
Days Assets Cash to Cash Cycle	88.85	4.11×	78.74	4.64×		
Est. Working Capital Financing Needs	$499.00		$513.00			
Leverage Ratios						
Debt to Tangible Net Worth		0.86×		0.83×		1.4×
Times Interest Earned		3.03×		3.47×		3.1×
Fixed Charge Coverage		3.03×		3.32×		2.4×
Net Fixed Assets to Tangible Net Worth	81.42%		80.83%		63.0%	
Profitability Ratios						
Return on Equity (ROE)	9.20%		9.17%			
Profit Before Taxes to Equity	13.63%		14.00%		19.8%	
Return on Assets (ROA)	4.95%		5.00%			
Profit Before Taxes to Total Assets	7.33%		7.64%		8.3%	
Equity Multiplier (Leverage = Total Assets/ Total Equity)		1.86×		1.83×		2.4×
Income						
Total Asset Turnover (Net Sales/Total Assets)		2.29×		2.55×		2.4×
All Other Income/Total Assets	0.86%		1.00%			
Expenses						
Net Profit Margin (Net Income/Net Sales)	2.17%		1.96%			
COGS/Net Sales	85.42%		85.00%		82.2%	
Operating Expenses/Net Sales	9.88%		10.75%		12.5%	
Income Taxes to Earnings Before Taxes	32.47%		34.52%			
Sales/Net Fixed Assets		5.22×		5.77×		
Cash Flow Ratios*						
CFO/(DIV + last CMLTD)	2.33×		2.27×			
CFO/(DIV + last CMLTD + S.T. Debt)	0.54		1.00			

*CFO, DIV, and CMLTD refer to cash flow from operations, cash dividends, and current maturities of long-term debt, respectively; CM Term

fixed interest charges. An analyst should examine a firm's leverage with respect to both the firm's ability to service debt (principal and interest payments) and the amount of debt relative to the size of the firm.

Ratios derived primarily from the income statement, such as times interest earned and fixed charge coverage, measure a firm's ability to service debt or meet interest and lease payments with current earnings. **Times interest earned** (earnings before interest and taxes (EBIT)/interest expense) measures the number of times the company can pay the interest payments on it outstanding debt.[8] The **fixed charge coverage ratio** [(EBIT + lease payments)/(Interest expense + lease payments)] ratio measures the number of times the firm can pay interest and other fixed charges (such as lease payments) with current earnings. Obviously, the greater the number of times the firm can cover these required fixed payments, the greater is the firm's ability to service existing debt. Prism's earnings coverage of required interest payments increased to 3.47 times and fixed charge coverage increased to 3.32 times in 2001. This represents good coverage and both ratios exceed peer group averages.

Ratios derived primarily from the balance sheet, such as debt to total assets and net fixed assets to tangible net worth, can be used to measure the amount of debt relative to the size of the firm. The greater the existing **debt to total assets ratio,** the more limited is the firm's future growth potential and the greater is the likelihood the firm will be unable to meet future principal payments on the debt. High debt levels restrict a firm's growth because the firm needs additional funds to finance the growth. If the firm is heavily debt ridden, expansion using additional debt may not be possible. **Net fixed assets to tangible net worth** is an indicator of the proportion of the firm's least liquid assets financed by net worth. The greater is this ratio, the more likely it is that liquidation proceeds will fall short of net worth in the event of failure. Finally, a firm's **dividend payout** (cash dividends/net income) ratio measures the fraction of earnings a firm pays out in cash to stockholders and thus is not retained. The higher the ratio, the lower are retained earnings which potentially increases future financing needs were the firm to run into financial problems.

Leverage ratios for Prism Industries are presented in Exhibit 16.3. Debt is only 83 percent of tangible net worth—well below the industry average. Lower levels of debt and greater earnings coverage, times interest earned and fixed charge coverage, confirm the common size analysis of much greater equity and less financial leverage risk.

PROFITABILITY ANALYSIS. Basic profitability ratios include the firm's return on equity (ROE), return on assets (ROA), profit margin (PM), asset utilization (AU or asset turnover), and sales growth rate. **ROE** indicates the percentage return to stockholders for each dollar of equity. Prism's ROE fell slightly in 2001 and indicates that stockholders only earned 9.17 percent on funds invested in the firm. This ratio can be decomposed into two components: the average return per dollar of assets invested (ROA) and the equity multiplier (EM):[9]

$$\textbf{ROE} \text{ (NI/Equity)} = \textbf{ROA} \text{ (NI/Total assets)} \times \textbf{EM} \text{ (Total assets/Equity)}$$

Where NI is net income. **Return on assets** (ROA) measures the percentage return on assets while the **equity multiplier** (EM) measures the degree of financial leverage employed. The greater is the return on invested assets, the greater is the return to shareholders. By the same token, the greater is the degree of leverage (the more debt rather than equity is used to finance these assets), the greater the returns to shareholders. Recall, however, that a greater degree of leverage is also an indicator of risk. Very high leverage means that the firm is less likely to meet its debt payment requirements if it has an off year. Prism's lower return to shareholders (ROE) was a result of both lower profit on invested assets (ROA) and much higher equity, hence a lower equity multiplier (EM). Prism's ROA was only 5 percent and its equity multiplier was 1.8 times compared to the industry average of 2.4 times.

Recall that net income is simply gross income (sales plus other revenue) minus expenses (COGS, operating expenses, other expenses, and taxes). Hence, ROA can be broken down

---

[8]EBIT is a proxy for cash flow and equals earnings before interest expense and taxes.

[9]This is, of course, the familiar Dupont Analysis introduced in Chapter 3 for banks now applied to non-financial companies.

into **profit margin** (PM), a measure of expense control, and **asset utilization** (AU) which reveals the gross yield on assets:

$$\text{ROA (NI/Total assets)} = \text{PM (NI/Sales)} \times \text{AU (Sales/Total assets)}$$

PM measures aggregate expense control at the firm and actually equals one minus the expense ratio:

$$\text{PM} = (\text{Sales} - \text{Expenses})/\text{Sales}$$
$$= 1 - \text{Expenses/Sales}$$

The major expenses are: COGS, operating expenses, other expenses, and taxes. Hence, we can measure the company's specific strengths or weaknesses in controlling these expenses by decomposing PM and comparing the following common size ratios to industry averages:

$$\text{PM} = 1 - (\text{COGS/Sales}) - (\text{Operating expenses/Sales})$$
$$- (\text{Other expenses/Sales}) - (\text{Taxes/Sales})$$

Finally, **sales growth** figures demonstrate whether the firm is expanding or contracting and provide evidence of industry competitiveness. Examining growth rates for COGS and other expenses and comparing these to sales growth provides an estimate of the relative efficiency of growth.

The profitability ratios, presented in Exhibit 16.3, indicate that Prism's profits before taxes were below the industry standard relative to both equity and total assets. Although reported dollar profits increase in 2001, due to the 16.7 percent increase in net sales, Prism's profits before taxes to total assets (similar to ROA) were below industry averages in 2001 due to much higher COGS. Profits before taxes to total assets fell as well in 2001 because Prism's operating expenses increased from 9.9 percent to 10.8 percent of sales. Even though operating expenses increased in 2001, they were still below those of peers, but the much higher COGS led to lower profits relative to total assets. This combined with the higher level of equity also meant that profits before taxes to tangible net worth was lower.

The analyst should evaluate these ratios with a critical eye, trying to identify firm strengths and weaknesses. All ratios should be evaluated over time to detect shifts in competitiveness and/or firm strategy, and relative to industry standards. The latter comparison indicates where significant deviations occur, both positively and negatively. When reviewing the ratios, the analyst should prepare a list of questions to ask the firm's managers, suppliers, and creditors that fill in information not revealed by the data.

CASH FLOW ANALYSIS

Most analysts focus on cash flow when evaluating a nonfinancial firm's performance. Bank regulators require banks to support credit decisions with cash flow information for each borrower. This section presents a framework for calculating a firm's cash flow from operations that essentially converts a company's income statement to a cash basis. Cash flow estimates are subsequently compared to principal and interest payments and discretionary cash expenditures to assess a firm's borrowing capacity and financial strength.

Accounting standards mandate that the statement of cash flows be divided into four parts: operating activities, investing activities, financing activities, and cash. The intent is to allow the reader to distinguish between reported accounting profits (net income) and cash flow from operations (cash net income) as well as other financing and investing activities which affect cash flow but are not reported on the income statement. The direct method of reporting cash flow converts or reconciles the income statement to its cash equivalent.[10]

The **cash-based income statement** introduced in this chapter is a modified form of a direct statement of cash flows. It is essentially a statement of changes reconciled to cash, which combines elements of the income statement and balance sheet. In general, a statement of changes records changes in balance sheet accounts over a specific time period, indicating the source or use of cash. Its purpose is to indicate how new assets are financed or how liabilities are repaid. Actual funds flows are measured by the absolute differences between balance sheet entries in two different time periods, such as year-end 2001 versus year-end 2000. Recall that the balance sheet is a stock measure. To convert the balance sheet into a flow, we must calculate the change in the stock amount. Because the income statement represents flows over time, income statement data can be combined by adding the revenues and subtracting the expenses that determine net income as well as subtracting cash dividends for the change in retained earnings on the balance sheet. A generalized cash-based income statement, which identifies the sources of data and nature of calculations, appears as Appendix III.

The key element in the analysis is to determine how much cash flow a firm generates from its normal business activity, that is, cash flow from operations. This cash flow must be sufficient to make interest and principal payments on debt. It may differ substantially from reported profits, as Charter Co. revealed (see Contemporary Issues: Illusory Profits at Charter Co.). A cash-based income statement also provides insights into whether a firm has adequately structured its financing. In a normal operating environment, a firm should repay short-term debt by liquidating its receivables and inventory. Long-term debt, in contrast, should be repaid from operating cash flow in excess of financing costs and funds needed to maintain capital assets.

CASH FLOW STATEMENT FORMAT. Because most firms prepare financial statements on an accrual rather than cash basis, revenues and expenses are recognized when earned or incurred rather than when a cash payment is made. Thus, reported net income may differ substantially from operational cash flow. Consider the balance sheet and income statements for Prism Industries in Exhibits 16.1 and 16.2. These data are used to generate the statement of changes reconciled to cash for Prism presented in Exhibit 16.4. This format combines traditional income statement and changes in balance sheet figures to produce a cash-based income statement. It emphasizes cash flow from operations, not reported net income.

The following items are included in each of the four sections of a cash flow statement:

- *Operations Section*—income statement items and the change in current assets and current liabilities (except bank debt)
- *Investments Section*—the change in all long-term assets
- *Financing Section*—payments for debt and dividends, the change in all long term liabilities, the change in short term bank debt, and any new stock issues
- *Cash Section*—the change in cash and marketable securities

---

[10]Actually, two types of cash flow statements are used in the industry: the direct and indirect method. The indirect method is required disclosure where the direct method is generally considered optional. The indirect method of cash flow reporting begins with net income and adjusts for changes in current assets and liabilities to derive cash flow from operations. The direct method, in contrast, closely follows the income statement and adjusts each income statement category to produce a cash equivalent; e.g., cash sales, cash purchases, cash operating expenses, etc. This method is most useful to analysts and is widely used in banking. We, therefore, use the direct cash flow method in this chapter.

■ **EXHIBIT 16.4**

STATEMENT OF CHANGES RECONCILED TO CASH
FOR PRISM INDUSTRIES, 2001

CASH-BASED INCOME STATEMENT	2001	Cash Flow Impact	
Net sales	2,800	Source	Revenue
Change in accounts receivable	(26)	Use	Asset increase
Cash receipts from sales	2,774		
Cost of goods sold	(2,380)	Use	Expense
Change in inventory	11	Source	Asset increase
Change in accounts payable	7	Source	Liability increase
Cash purchases	(2,362)		
Cash margin	412		
Total operating expenses	(301)	Use	Expense
Depreciation & amortization	51	Source	Noncash expense
Change in prepaid expenses	4	Source	Asset decrease
Change in accrued expenses	17	Source	Liability increase
Cash operating expenses	(229)		
Cash operating profit	183		
All other expenses & income (net)	(1)	Use	Expense
Cash before interest & taxes	182		
Interest expense	(34)	Use	Expense
Income taxes reported	(29)	Use	Expense
Change in income tax payable	6	Source	Liability increase
Change in other current assets and liabilities	0		
Cash flow from operations (CFO)	125		
Capital exp. and leasehold improvements	(76)	Use	Asset increase
Change in long-term investments	(9)	Use	Asset increase
Change in other noncurrent assets	0		
Cash used for investments	(85)		
Payment for last period's CMLTD	(35)	Use	Payment for financing
Dividends paid (DIV)	(20)	Use	Payment for financing
Payments for financing	(55)		
Cash before external financing	(15)		
Change in short-term bank debt	20	Source	Liability increase
Change in LT debt + end of period CMLTD	0		
Change in stock & surplus	0		
Change in other noncurrent liabilities	0		
External financing	20		
Change in cash & mktbl. securities	**5**		

NOTE: Figures are in thousands of dollars.

With a statement of changes reconciled to cash (cash-based income statement), a source of funds is any transaction that increases cash (or cash-equivalent) assets. A use of funds is any transaction that decreases cash assets. As noted below, sources of funds include any decrease in a noncash asset, increase in liability, any noncash expense, or any revenue item. Selling receivables or issuing new debt subsequently represent sources of cash. Uses of funds include any increase in a noncash asset, decrease in a liability, and any cash expense item. Thus, the purchase of a building or principal payment on debt is a use of cash.

CONTEMPORARY ISSUES

ILLUSORY PROFITS AT MICROSTRATEGY

In March 2000 at the peak of the Internet and technology stock market boom, management of Microstrategy Inc. announced that the firm would restate its sales and earnings for 1998 and 1999. Microstrategy was in the business of providing business intelligence software and consulting, training, and support services. At the time, the firm would bundle its software with services for long-term projects, but record the entire value of software sold as up-front revenue. In restating its sales and earnings, Microstrategy announced that it would subsequently record software revenue gradually over the life of the contract, rather than all at once. This latter method conforms with generally accepted accounting principles, while the previous method did not.

The impact was enormous. Microstrategy initially reported sales of $106.4 million in 1998 and $205.3 million in 1999. Rather than reporting large profits, earnings fell to just $7 million in 1998 and a loss of $34 million in 1999. Investors immediately punished Microstrategy by driving the share price from $330 at the time of the announcement to just $30 three days later for a loss of $11.9 billion to stockholders. By May 2002, the share price had fallen to $1.30.

Regardless of how Microstrategy chose to report its sales, its cash flow from operations was dramatically less than reported earnings. Market participants, investors and Microstrategy's lenders, who focused on earnings rather than cash flow were misled by the revenue reporting effects.

Sources of funds must equal uses of funds. Equivalently, the balance sheet identity requires that the sum of the changes in each asset must equal the sum of the changes in each liability and the change in net worth (stockholders' equity). Let:

A_i = the dollar value of the ith type of asset (A)

L_j = the dollar value of the jth type of liability (L)

NW = the dollar value of net worth

There are n different assets and m different liabilities. Then:

$$\sum_{i=1}^{n} \Delta A_i = \sum_{j=1}^{m} \Delta L_j + \Delta NW \tag{16.1}$$

We know that ΔNW equals net income (NI) minus cash dividends paid (DIV) plus the change in common and preferred stock (stock) outstanding plus the change in paid-in surplus (surplus). Thus, if we designate the first asset as cash, A_1, and solve 16.1 for the change in cash, Equation 16.1 can be written as:

$$\Delta A_1 = \sum_{j=1}^{m} \Delta L_j - \sum_{i=2}^{n} \Delta A_i + \Delta stock + \Delta surplus + NI - DIV \tag{16.2}$$

Cash flow from operations is derived using Equation 16.2 and the components of net income from the income statement. Each source of cash has a positive sign and each use of cash has a negative sign. The statement of changes format simply rearranges the elements of Equation 16.2 in terms of a cash-based income statement. Because net income (NI) equals revenues minus expenses and taxes, substituting into Equation 16.2 yields:

$$\Delta A_1 = \sum_{j=1}^{m} \Delta L_j - \sum_{i=2}^{n} \Delta A_i + \Delta stock + \Delta surplus$$
$$+ \text{Revenues} - \text{Expenses} - \text{Taxes} - \text{DIV} \tag{16.3}$$

As the signs before each element indicate, any increase in a liability or decrease in a noncash asset is a source of cash. A decrease in a liability or increase in a noncash asset is a use of cash.

Issues of stock or positive additions to surplus represent a source of cash. Finally, revenues are a source of cash, while cash expenses, taxes paid, and cash dividends are a use of cash. These general relationships are summarized below:

Sources of Cash	Uses of Cash
Increase in any liability	Decrease in any liability
Decrease in any noncash asset	Increase in any noncash asset
New issue of stock	Repayments/buy back stock
Additions to surplus	Deductions from surplus
Revenues	Cash expenses
	Taxes
	Cash dividends

APPLICATION TO PRISM INDUSTRIES

The cash flow statement is presented in Exhibit 16.4 using the balance sheet and income statement data from Exhibits 16.1 and 16.2 for Prism Industries. The focal point is the firm's cash flow from operations. The far right column identifies the type of cash flow impact in terms of Equation 16.3 for each entry. The top part of the statement shows why reported net income for Prism differs from cash flow from operations.

CASH FLOW FROM OPERATIONS. The first item listed is net sales. Prism collected less in credit sales than it billed its customers because outstanding accounts receivable increased from 2000 to 2001. Thus, net sales are offset by the $26,000 increase in receivables to obtain actual cash receipts. Had receivables declined, actual cash receipts from sales would have exceeded the reported sales figure. Accounts receivable will increase with sales growth and a more lenient credit policy. Days accounts receivables outstanding (credit policy) increased only slightly from 2000 to 2001 so the use of cash in accounts receivable was primarily to support sales growth, not a more lax credit policy.

The next series of figures recognizes that actual cash purchases differs from reported cost of goods sold (COGS). Actual cash purchases differs for two basic accounting reasons. First, COGS does not represent actual purchases of inventory during the year. That is, reported COGS only represents the cost of goods sold during the period, not the actual purchases of inventory the company made. Second, some purchases are financed by increases in accounts payable (trade credit) while others are paid for in cash. If the company's inventory increased (decreased) over the year, purchases will exceed (be less than) COGS. From accounting we know that:

$$\text{Purchases} = \text{COGS} + \Delta\text{inventory}. \tag{16.4}$$

For Prism, purchases equaled $2,369,000 in 2001 as indicated by the following calculation and the application of Equation 16.4.

Production Budget Summary for 2001 (Thousands of Dollars)

Beginning inventory	$306
+ Purchases	$2,369
= Goods available for sale	$2,675
− Cost of goods sold	$2,380
= Ending inventory	$295
or Purchases = 2,380 + (295 − 306) = 2,369	

Prism started 2001 with $306,000 in inventory. During 2001 the firm purchased $2,369,000 from suppliers such that after cost of goods sold was subtracted, it held $295,000 in inventory at the end of the year. The statement of changes adds the change in inventory to the cost of goods sold to get total purchases. If inventory decreases, as it does for Prism, actual cash purchases are less than cost of goods sold, and vice versa. The reduction in inventory was a source of cash as Prism's inventory turnover was faster in 2001 (8.07 times) as compared to 2000 (6.70 times).

The cash flow statement then subtracts the change in outstanding accounts payable from total purchases to get actual cash purchases. For Prism, the $7,000 increase in payables indicates that a portion of purchases is financed by additional trade credit provided by suppliers. Prism's cash purchases thus equaled $2,362,000 ($2,369,000 − $7,000). In general, net cash purchases equals the cost of goods sold adjusted for inventory accumulation not financed by additional trade credit:

$$\text{Cash purchases} = -(\text{COGS} + \Delta\text{inventory} - \Delta\text{accounts payable}) \tag{16.5}$$

Cost of goods sold is reported on the income statement while cash purchases represents the actual amount of cash used to purchase goods for resale. Using the relationship shown in Equation 16.5 and reviewing Exhibit 16.4, we know that four factors directly affect cash purchases: sales growth, gross margin, inventory policy, and trade credit policy. Holding other factors constant, we know that COGS will increase proportionate to sales. Hence, cash purchases will increase proportionate to sales.

Because the statement format presented mimics an income statement, the next step is to subtract cash operating expenses. Reported operating expenses typically overstate actual cash expenses by the amount of noncash charges, including depreciation and amortization. The format subtracts total operating expenses, which includes all noncash charges, then adds noncash charges back to yield a net figure for cash expenses. In this example, depreciation is the only noncash expense such that total operating expense equals $301,000 before the adjustment. Note that depreciation reported in the income statement ($51,000) differs from the change in accumulated depreciation from the balance sheet ($45,000). This typically occurs when a firm sells assets that have been at least partially depreciated. The difference can be attributed to the fact that, under these circumstances, the change in gross fixed assets on the balance sheet understates true capital outlays. Specifically:

$$\Delta\text{Net fixed assets} = \Delta\text{Gross fixed assets} - \Delta\text{Accumulated depreciation} \tag{16.6}$$

and

$$\Delta\text{Net fixed assets} = \text{Capital expenditures} - \text{Depreciation} \tag{16.7}$$

The best procedure is to use the depreciation figure from the income statement or cash flow statement and obtain the capital expenditure figure from Equation 16.7.

Prism's prepaid expenses fell in 2001 as it paid more in expenses than that reported on the income statement. The increase in accrued expenses further indicates that Prism paid $17,000 less in cash than costs incurred. Combining the changes in prepaid and accrued expenses with total operating expenses adjusted for noncash charges produces cash operating profit. The resulting figure is then adjusted by income on marketable securities and long term investments and other noninterest expense and income that arise from normal business activity.

Finally, actual interest expense and an estimate of income taxes paid are subtracted to obtain cash flow from operations. The data indicate that income taxes reported on the income statement exceeded actual taxes paid. This typically occurs because firms take greater deductions for tax purposes than they report in published statements. Tax payments are effectively deferred, and the net tax expense is $23,000 or $6,000 less than that reported.

The resulting net figure, **cash flow from operations,** indicates whether Prism was able to service its debt and is useful in forecasting whether the firm can assume additional debt. As Contemporary Issues: The Many Faces of Cash Flow suggests, cash flow from operations is one of many cash flow measures. As a rule, any transaction representing a normal business activity should be recognized prior to calculating cash flow from operations.

THE MANY FACES OF CASH FLOW

What is cash flow? The classic definition is net income plus depreciation, amortization, and deferred taxes. According to a statement of changes reconciled to cash, cash flow from operations approximately equals classic cash flow adjusted for changes in working capital. In practice, the meaning of cash flow varies according to which analyst reviews the data.

Four commonly accepted definitions of cash flow are listed below, along with the associated value, using the data for Prism Industries in 2001 (in thousands of dollars):

1. Net income + (Depreciation + Amortization + ΔDeferred tax liability): $55 + $51 = $106
2. [No. 1] − All capital expenditures: $106 − $76 = $30

3. [No. 2] − ΔAccounts receivable − ΔInventory − ΔPrepaid expenses + ΔAccounts payable + ΔAccruals: $30 − $26 + $11 + $4 + $7 + $17 = $43
4. Pretax income + (Depreciation + Amortization) − Maintenance capital expenditures: $84 + $51 − $70 = $65

Maintenance capital expenditures equal that portion of capital outlays that maintain production operations at the current level (*assumed* equal to $70 for Prism). This last measure is often referred to as **free cash flow.** Prism's cash flow from operations is calculated before subtracting capital expenditures and thus at $125 exceeds values obtained for cash flow according to definitions 2, 3, and 4.

Which is the best measure? Like most data analysis, there is no obvi-

ous answer. Definitions 3 and 4 provide the best estimates of how much new debt a firm can support with existing cash flow. However, firms can generally manipulate both balance sheet and income statement data and thus bias cash flow estimates. The statement of changes format incorporates all balance sheet and income statement data. When viewed comprehensively, an analyst can examine transactions relationships across the entire portfolio. Cash flow from operations is the appropriate estimate but must be compared with dividends, mandatory principal payments, and capital expenditures to determine debt service capabilities.

The items listed in Exhibit 16.4 do not represent all items that potentially appear in a balance sheet or income statement, as financial statements contain different line items for different firms. When constructing a cash-based income statement, it is important to recognize that every balance sheet and income statement account or item must appear somewhere.[11] The key criterion is that the cash flow impact of normal activities are listed above cash flow from operations while extraordinary items should be listed after cash flow from operations. Thus, if other income arises from a one-time sale of real estate, it should appear below cash flow from operations.

At a minimum, cash flow from operations must be sufficient to cover cash dividends and mandatory principal payments. These required principal payments for the upcoming year are indicated by current maturities of long-term debt (CMLTD). Thus, when looking back on historical performance for a period, cash flow from operations should cover current maturities of long-term debt outstanding at the beginning of the period. For Prism, the amount is $35,000 as listed in Exhibit 16.1 as the balance sheet value for CMCTD at year-end 2000. Other cash flows are unpredictable and cannot be relied on. In the case of Prism, cash flow from operations of $125,000 in 2001 exceeded cash dividends paid and the principal payment on long-term debt by $70,000 ($125,000 − $20,000 − $35,000). The excess cash flow, along with an increase in short-term debt, was essentially used to purchase new capital assets ($76,000) and increase long-term investments ($9,000). In this example, the $76,000 capital expenditure is obtained from Equation 16.7 and equals the change in net fixed assets

---

[11]Exceptions to this would be net income from the income statement and retained earnings from the balance sheet, as these items are already included.

plus depreciation from the income statement. If a firm sells fixed assets, capital expenditures will exceed the change in gross fixed assets reported on the balance sheet.

CASH FROM INVESTING ACTIVITIES. There are many cash expenditures not directly reflected in financial statements. In particular, capital expenditures and long-term investments require cash but are not reflected on the income statement. If cash flow from operations is insufficient to cover capital expenditures and new long-term investments, additional financing will be required. Because capital expenditures are not listed on the income statement or the balance sheet they must be estimated. One measure of capital expenditures is simply the change in gross fixed assets. This is appropriate, however, only when a firm has not sold any fixed assets during the period. If the firm sells an asset, accounting procedures will reduce accumulated depreciation by the amount of accumulated depreciation attributable to the asset sold. According to Equation 16.7, the change in gross fixed assets will then underestimate actual capital expenditures. Equation 16.7 adjusts for this. In addition to the $76,000 in capital expenditures, Prism had another $9,000 in new long-term investments that represented a cash outflow. Total cash used for investments was $85,000. Subtracting this from cash flow from operations produced a positive $40,000 in cash before principal debt and dividend payments.

CASH FROM FINANCING ACTIVITIES. The bottom of the statement indicates the firm's payments for financing and how a firm obtains financing from external sources. Although cash flow statements group payments for financing below the investment section, this is somewhat misleading. Payments for financing generally take precedence over capital expenditures and increases in long-term investments. After subtracting the required principal payment on long-term debt (last period's current maturity of long-term debt) and cash dividends, Prism's cash shortage is $15,000 before external financing. Note that cash flow from operations was sufficient to make the required debt and dividend payments but was insufficient to cover the capital expenditures.

Prism's cash shortfall must be financed by external sources or by reducing cash balances. Although Prism's balance sheet indicates there is enough cash to cover this shortfall, cash is required in the operations of the business. A firm cannot bring cash levels to zero as some minimum amount of cash is necessary to make change in the cash registers, pay bills and employee salaries. Typical external sources of financing include new issues of long-term debt, common stock, or preferred stock, increases in notes payable to banks or other short-term liabilities, or issues of other hybrid instruments. In this example, Prism actually increased its notes payable to the bank by $20,000, which represented a cash inflow accounting for all its external financing.

CHANGE IN CASH. The last element of the cash-based income statement is the change in cash and marketable securities, or the left hand side item (ΔCash) in Equation 16.3. This equals cash flow from operations adjusted for cash used for investments, payments for financing, and external financing. For Prism Industries, cash flow from operations plus discretionary expenditures produced a $15,000 deficiency. The $20,000 in external financing generated a $5,000 net cash inflow for the year. The cash-based income statement balances by reconciliation to the change in cash because this $5,000 inflow equals the change in cash and marketable securities calculated from the 2000 and 2001 balance sheet figures ($90,000 − $85,000). Because the cash-based income statement is a sources and uses summary reconciled to cash and marketable securities, an analyst can verify the aggregate calculations by comparing the bottom line change in cash and marketable securities obtained from the statement with the simple change in the balance sheet figures. If the two figures are not equal, at least one of the components of the statement is incorrect.

INTERPRETING CASH FLOW FROM OPERATIONS. While short-term debt is typically rolled over, cash flow from operations might ultimately be needed to cover these maturing obligations as well as certain cash expenditures. In 2001 Prism's cash flow from operations ($125,000) was sufficient to pay $20,000 in cash dividends, $35,000 in maturing principal on long-term debt, and the entire $70,000 in notes payable outstanding at the end of the year. Thus, Prism was in excellent operating condition and could have supported new borrowing, *ceteris paribus*.

This analysis suggests that two additional ratios may be useful in evaluating a firm's cash flow condition and whether it has the ability to service additional debt:

1. Cash flow from operations (CFO) divided by the sum of dividends paid (DIV) and last period's current maturities of long-term debt (CMLTD). In the following ratios, the subscripts t and t−1 refer to values for the period being examined (2001 for Prism) and the preceding period (2000 for Prism), respectively:

$$CFO_t/(DIV_t + CMLTD_{t-1}) \text{ and}$$

2. Cash flow from operations divided by the same two terms plus short-term debt outstanding at the beginning of the year.

$$CFO_t/(DIV_t + CMLTD_{t-1} + \text{S.T. Debt}_t)$$

The denominator in the first ratio represents mandatory principal payments owed on outstanding long-term debt plus discretionary cash dividends. The second ratio adds outstanding principal on other short-term debt. If these ratios exceed 1, as is the case with Prism at 2.27x and 1.00x, respectively, the firm's operational cash flows can pay off existing debt and support new borrowing. If these numbers are less than one or negative, the firm's operational cash flows are not sufficient to repay the required principal payments or the balance of short-term notes.

$$\$125,000/(\$20,000 + \$35,000) = 2.27$$
$$\$125,000/(\$20,000 + \$35,000 + \$70,000) = 1.00$$

Some analysts construct a third ratio that adds maintenance capital expenditures to the denominator. Maintenance capital expenditures are generally viewed as the amount of outlays that is necessary to replace the firm's depreciating capital assets. As such, it is investigated internally.

FINANCIAL PROJECTIONS

The three-stage process described previously enables a credit analyst to evaluate the historical performance of a potential borrower. The final step in evaluating a loan request, generating *pro forma* statements, addresses the basic issues introduced at the beginning of the chapter. Projections of the borrower's financial condition reveal what the loan proceeds are needed for, how much financing is required, how much cash flow can be generated from operations to service new debt, and when, if at all, a loan can be repaid. In order to understand the range of potential outcomes, an analyst should make forecasts that incorporate different assumptions about sales, inventory turnover, the level of interest rates, and the growth in operating expenses.

Consider the prospective use of loan proceeds. Firms with a legitimate need for working capital financing would demonstrate a decline in cash flow from operations caused by some combination of increased receivables and inventory or decreased accounts payable and accruals. Seasonal needs should appear from interim (within year) financial statements. Firms with positive and stable cash flow from operations do not generally need working capital financing but do have the capacity to service new debt. Specific cash outflows associated with term loans are easily identified in the bottom part of the statement of changes as discretionary expenditures increase or external financing declines. The amount of financing required and the source and timing of repayment can be similarly determined with financial projections. In essence, each element of the cash flow statement is projected over the future.

PRO FORMA ASSUMPTIONS. Projecting financial statements typically begins with sales projections. The key driver is sales growth which determines how fast sales will increase or decrease in the future. Next periods sales (t+1) is estimated as:

$$\text{Sales}_{t+1} = \text{Sales}_t \times (1 + \boldsymbol{g_{sales}})$$

The required input, or parameter, needed to project sales is the growth rate in sales (g_{sales}) and is listed in **bold italic.** Estimates are commonly obtained by evaluating the average growth expected in the industry, what is going on with respect to the company's market share and even the company's own profit plan and capital budget. Sales growth, along with all other change-related parameters, should be based on the analyst's best estimate of what the company will actually do. Often, an inexperienced analyst views his or her job as projecting the financials such that the company will qualify (or not qualify) for a loan. However, the true purpose of *pro forma* analysis is to provide an objective method of examining potential positive or negative events that might affect a company's ability to repay the loan.

Cost of goods sold is critically related to sales and the expected markup on goods sold. COGS is usually estimated as:

$$\text{COGS}_{t+1} = \text{Sales}_{t+1} \times \boldsymbol{COGS \text{ \% of Sales}}$$

The *pro forma* parameter, **COGS as a percent of sales,** is estimated by past data, industry averages, expected future competitive strengths and weaknesses, and the analyst's best estimates of what COGS will be in the future. Other operating expenses are projected by using a growth rate assumption or a percent of sales assumption. Selling expenses, for example, are usually considered variable costs and would most likely be estimated as a percent of sales. General and administrative expenses could be estimated by either a growth rate assumption or as a percent of sales.

Many balance sheet items are also associated with sales or obtained directly from external sources such as capital budgets. For example, current assets frequently equal a relatively constant percentage of sales or exhibit a stable turnover rate. Accounts receivable are a function of sales growth and the firm's credit policy, while inventory is linked to COGS, a predictable fraction of sales. Projecting accounts receivable thus requires forecasts of sales growth and the *pro forma* parameter **days accounts receivable outstanding:**

$$\text{Accounts receivables}_{t+1} = \boldsymbol{Days \text{ } A/R \text{ } outstanding} \times \text{Average Daily Sales}_{t+1}$$

Inventory is projected similarly using the parameter inventory turnover:

$$\text{Inventory}_{t+1} = \text{COGS}_{t+1}/\boldsymbol{Inventory \text{ } turnover}$$

The analyst can determine the approximate turnover rates from historical data or comparable firm standards. Purchases and trade credit financing are tied to inventory growth. Accounts payable, therefore, will also vary with sales forecasts:

$$\text{Accounts payable}_{t+1} = \boldsymbol{Days \text{ } AP \text{ } outstanding} \times \text{Average Daily purchases}_{t+}$$
$$= \boldsymbol{Days \text{ } AP \text{ } outstanding} \times [(\text{COGS}_{t+1} + \Delta\text{Inventory}_{t+1})/365]$$

Contractual principal payments on debt are known and planned fixed asset purchases can be obtained from the capital budget. Other accounting principles apply as well. For example, accumulated depreciation is simply last period's accumulated depreciation plus the current period's depreciation expense. Retained earnings on the balance sheet increase each year by the difference between net income and dividends paid. The follow section, "Credit Analysis: An Application," applies these relationships in more detail to Wade's Office Furniture.

One obvious exception to the sales link is interest expense, which is based on the amount of debt a borrower has or is expected to have outstanding and the underlying interest rates. Forecasts must incorporate expectations regarding outstanding debt and loan balances and projected interest rates. This can be cumbersome as many loans carry floating rates and the projections must include an interest rate forecast as well. Based on this model, net income will vary directly with sales in a stable environment.

PROJECTING NOTES PAYABLE TO BANKS. During the *pro forma* process, assets, liabilities, and equity are forecast separately. Rarely will the balance sheet balance in the initial round of *pro forma* forecasts. To reconcile this, there must be a balancing item, which is often called a "plug" figure. When projected assets exceed projected liabilities plus equity, additional debt is required. When projected assets are less than projected liabilities plus equity, no new debt is required and existing debt could be reduced or excess funds invested in marketable securities (also a "plug" figure). Typically any new debt is considered to be a firm's line of credit or short-term debt requirement. The difference in the projected asset base and total funding without new debt, therefore, indicates how much additional credit is required at each future interval. This is an iterative procedure as new debt, in turn, increases projected interest expense and lowers net income. Lower net income means lower retained earnings, hence greater levels of debt.

Working capital financing projections should be made using peak and trough estimates of current asset needs over the next year. This enables an analyst to determine maximum and minimum borrowing requirements when there are seasonal patterns in the borrower's business that should be reflected in balance sheet or income statement items. For term loans, projections should be made over several years or as long as the debt will remain outstanding. The projected loan need must approach zero within a reasonable time period or the firm will have to restructure its existing financing and operations to service new debt. The effective maturity of a loan is revealed in the *pro forma* data as the period when the additional debt requirement, or "plug" figure, approaches zero. This estimate will vary with the assumptions that generate the *pro forma* estimates.

SENSITIVITY ANALYSIS. *Pro forma* analysis is a form of sensitivity analysis. The analyst formulates a set of assumptions that establishes the relationships between different balance sheet and income statement items. At a minimum, three alternative scenarios or sets of assumptions should be considered:

- A *best case scenario* in which optimistic improvements in planned performance and the economy are realized;
- A *worst case scenario* that represents the environment with the greatest potential negative impact on sales, earnings, and the balance sheet; and
- A *most likely scenario* representing the most reasonable sequence of economic events and performance trends.

The three alternative forecasts of loan needs and cash flow establish a range of likely results, which indicates the riskiness of the credit. The analysts can use these alternative scenarios to determine if the loan will be paid back in a reasonable time under less than favorable conditions.

Rating Category	Rating Scale	Collateral Support	Descriptive Indicators of Loan Quality
Highest Quality	1	Gov't. securities; cash	Highest quality borrowers. 5 years of historic cash flow data. Strong balance sheet and liquidity.
	2	Agency & high-quality municipal securities; insured CDs	Highest quality; differs from class 1 only by degree of financial strength.
	3	Uninsured CDs; high-quality stocks & bonds	Highest quality; cash flow average is slightly below classes 1 and 2.
Acceptable Quality	4	Gov't. guaranteed loans; may be unsecured	High degree of liquidity; assets readily convertible to cash; unused credit facilities. Strong equity capital and management.
	5	Secured by trading assets (A/R & Inv.) and/or real estate	Adequate liquidity; adequate equity capital with comfortable cash flow coverage; proactive management; cyclical industry with smaller margins.
	6	Heavily dependent on collateral and/or guarantees	Partially strained liquidity; limited equity so that leverage exceeds industry norms; limited management strength; business is cyclically vulnerable.
Poor Quality	7	Inadequate collateral	Strained liquidity, inadequate capital, and weak management. Adverse trends in industry and borrower financials.
	8	Inadequate collateral	Same as class 7, except financials are weaker.
	9	Inadequate collateral	Totally inadequate profile; well-defined weaknesses.

RISK-CLASSIFICATION SCHEME

Most banks use a risk-classification scheme as part of the analysis process for commercial loans. After evaluating the borrower's risk profile along all dimensions, a loan is placed in a rating category ranked according to the degree of risk. Such a system, used for credit granting and pricing decisions, is presented in the table presented above.

The actual risk rating assigned by lenders will reflect an evaluation of the borrower's historical performance along the lines of the analysis introduced earlier and a critique of the borrower's pro forma operating profile. The evaluation will look at key trends in historical performance and the current profit and risk profile relative to industry norms. *Pro forma* analysis will determine the adequacy of the firm's cash flow from operations coverage of debt service requirements if the firm requests a term loan, or the adequacy of cash flow from liquidating trading assets and collateral if the firm requests a working capital loan. Banks do not generally make new loans to firms rated 7 through 9 because they are high risk, but borrowers may be downgraded to these lower ratings if their condition deteriorates.

CREDIT ANALYSIS: AN APPLICATION

The following analysis presents a systematic application of the credit evaluation procedure just described. It emphasizes using the procedure to evaluate a term loan request that requires forecasts of cash flow from operations. It focuses on how to interpret data and make a loan decision rather than on how the model works. Each of the four key issues is addressed. The nonquantitative aspects of the evaluation are generally ignored.

On March 1, 2002, Marcus Wade, president and majority owner of Wade's Office Furniture, met with you and requested an increase in the company's credit line from $900,000 to $1.2 million and a term loan of $400,000 for the purchase of new equipment. Wade's Office Furniture is a small manufacturer of metal office furniture. It has been in business for over

25 years and has been a good customer of the bank for the last 10 years. Mr. Wade was very positive about the firm's present condition, having just reported a 50 percent increase in sales for 2001 after two consecutive years of slow growth. He attributed this recent success to a new product line and marketing program and claimed it would continue evidenced by back-logged orders totaling $250,000. In support of his request, he provided you with three years of historical balance sheet and income statement data for 1999–2001 as well as two years of *pro forma* data (2002–2003), which appear in Exhibits 16.5 and 16.6.[12] Wade projected sales to increase another 50 percent in 2002 and felt that this would quickly reduce the outstanding note payable to the bank and help repay the term loan.

COMMON SIZE AND FINANCIAL RATIOS ANALYSIS: WADE'S OFFICE FURNITURE

The analysis begins with an evaluation of common size ratios from the balance sheet and income statement (Exhibits 16.5 and 16.6). Comparable figures from the *Annual Statement Studies* by Robert Morris Associates (RMA) for 2001 are listed in the column labeled "RMA." The balance sheet data in Exhibit 16.5 indicate that Wade's accounts receivables and inventory substantially exceeded the industry norms in 2001 and increased each year from 1999 to 2001. Net fixed assets, on the other hand, were well below industry standards in each year. After further exploration, you discover that Wade's leases a much larger portion of its fixed assets than the industry norm. One weakness of common size ratios is that they may be distorted by any one account that takes an extreme value. The fact that Wade's leases a disproportionately large amount of equipment necessarily increases the relative proportion of current assets. For this reason, the analyst must carefully compare the implications of common size ratios and other financial ratios before drawing conclusions. Finally, in terms of financing, Wade's relied almost twice as much as the industry norm on accounts payable and short-term bank loans and less on long-term debt than comparable firms. The firm's net worth-to-asset ratio was 8 percent less than the industry norm in 2001, which indicates that Wade's has financed much of its growth using debt.

Wade's balance sheet is typical of a small company exhibiting short-term rapid sales growth. Most of the growth in sales, which has lead to a large increase in accounts receivables and inventory, was financed by a short-term line of credit. Cash has fallen to a minimum level, and Wade's is likely pushing the upper limit of its short-term line of credit. A cash shortage may be one of the reasons Wade's is making the loan request.

A review of the income statement in Exhibit 16.6 reveals two important factors. First, cost of goods sold was a substantially lower percentage of sales compared with the industry average, reflecting either lower cost of goods or higher mark-ups on finished products. This is very positive in light of the most recent 50 percent sales growth. Second, Wade's operating expenses far exceeded the industry norm. This may reflect a large salary for Marcus Wade in that the firm pays no dividends and the company provides his only source of income. The net effect is that the firm earns proportionately less before taxes than comparable firms.

Financial ratios for Wade's are presented in Exhibit 16.7. Current and quick ratios are low and have been fairly stable over the preceding three years. Days accounts receivable is about 11 days longer than the industry norm and inventory turns over only 4.7 times a year compared to the industry norm of 5.6 times. The low current and quick ratios tend to indicate a lower value of current assets, but the common size and ratio analysis indicate that the level of accounts receivable and inventory is above peers. Remember that the common size ratios are distorted (too high for current assets) relative to peers due to the high amount of leased fixed assets.

---

[12]Actually, the *pro forma* data provided in Exhibits 16.5 and 16.6 are assumed not to have been provided by Wade's, rather by the credit analysts. These data will be discussed below.

EXHIBIT 16.5

COMPARATIVE BALANCE SHEET FOR WADE'S OFFICE FURNITURE, 1999–2003

Unaudited: SIC #2522	[—HISTORICAL—] 1999 $1,000	Percent of Total	[—HISTORICAL—] Percent Change	2000 $1,000	Percent of Total	[—HISTORICAL—] Percent Change	2001 $1,000	Percent of Total	RMA 2001	[—PRO FORMA—] Percent Change	2002 $1,000	Percent of Total	[—PRO FORMA—] Percent Change	2003 $1,000	Percent of Total
ASSETS															
Cash	141	4.3%	-5.7%	133	3.9%	-45.9%	72	1.6%	5.5%	66.7%	120	2.3%	0.0%	120	2.1%
Marketable securities	0	0.0%	N/A	0	0.0%	N/A	0	0.0%		N/A	0	0.0%	N/A	0	0.0%
Accounts receivable	1,254	38.4%	11.6%	1,399	40.8%	35.5%	1,896	42.3%	28.8%	7.8%	2,043	38.7%	10.4%	2,256	39.6%
Inventory	1,160	35.6%	3.9%	1,205	35.2%	46.4%	1,764	39.4%	29.7%	17.3%	2,070	39.2%	15.3%	2,387	41.9%
Prepaid expenses	47	1.4%	6.4%	50	1.5%	-70.0%	15	0.3%		33.3%	20	0.4%	25.0%	25	0.4%
Other current assets	0	0.0%	N/A	0	0.0%	N/A	0	0.0%	2.4%	N/A	0	0.0%	N/A	0	0.0%
Current assets	2,602	79.7%	7.1%	2,787	81.4%	34.4%	3,747	83.6%	66.4%	13.5%	4,253	80.6%	12.6%	4,787	84.0%
Gross fixed assets	629	19.3%	7.2%	674	19.7%	17.4%	791	17.7%		50.6%	1,191	22.6%	0.0%	1,191	20.9%
Leasehold improvements	198	6.1%	2.0%	202	5.9%	17.8%	238	5.3%		0.0%	238	4.5%	0.0%	238	4.2%
Less acc. deprec.	206	6.3%	34.5%	277	8.1%	24.9%	346	7.7%		31.8%	456	8.6%	24.1%	566	9.9%
Net fixed assets	621	19.0%	-3.5%	599	17.5%	14.0%	683	15.2%	28.2%	42.5%	973	18.4%	-11.3%	863	15.1%
Intangible assets	40	1.2%	-2.5%	39	1.1%	28.2%	50	1.1%	0.4%	0.0%	50	0.9%	0.0%	50	0.9%
Other noncurrent assets	0	0.0%	N/A	0	0.0%	N/A	0	0.0%	5.0%	N/A	0	0.0%	N/A	0	0.0%
Total Assets	3,263	100.0%	5.0%	3,425	100.0%	30.8%	4,480	100.0%	100.0%	17.8%	5,276	100.0%	8.0%	5,700	100.0%
LIABILITIES & EQUITY															
Notes payable - bank	643	19.7%	-9.5%	582	17.0%	53.3%	892	19.9%	6.0%	-21.8%	697	13.2%	-48.5%	359	6.3%
Accounts payable	836	25.6%	8.6%	908	26.5%	41.2%	1,282	28.6%	14.0%	18.3%	1,517	28.8%	19.5%	1,813	31.8%
Accrued expenses	205	6.3%	25.9%	258	7.5%	34.9%	348	7.8%		5.7%	368	7.0%	5.4%	388	6.8%
Income tax payable	41	1.3%	51.2%	62	1.8%	27.4%	79	1.8%	1.7%	27.4%	101	1.9%	27.4%	128	2.3%
Current maturity—Term notes	0	0.0%	N/A	0	0.0%	N/A	0	0.0%		N/A	50	0.9%	0.0%	50	0.9%
Current maturity—LTD	75	2.3%	0.0%	75	2.2%	0.0%	75	1.7%	3.6%	0.0%	75	1.4%	0.0%	75	1.3%
Other current liabilities	0	0.0%	N/A	0	0.0%	N/A	0	0.0%	11.8%	N/A	0	0.0%	N/A	0	0.0%
Current liabilities	1,800	55.2%	4.7%	1,885	55.0%	42.0%	2,676	59.7%	37.1%	4.9%	2,808	53.2%	0.2%	2,814	49.4%
Term notes	0	0.0%	N/A	0	0.0%	N/A	0	0.0%		N/A	350	6.6%	-14.3%	300	5.3%
Long-term debt (LTD)	450	13.8%	-16.7%	375	10.9%	-20.0%	300	6.7%	20.1%	-25.0%	225	4.3%	-33.3%	150	2.6%
Other noncurrent liabilities	0	0.0%	N/A	0	0.0%	N/A	0	0.0%	0.9%	N/A	0	0.0%	N/A	0	0.0%
Total liabilities	2,250	69.0%	0.4%	2,260	66.0%	31.7%	2,976	66.4%	58.1%	13.7%	3,383	64.1%	-3.5%	3,264	57.3%
Common stock—par	600	18.4%	0.0%	600	17.5%	0.0%	600	13.4%		0.0%	600	11.4%	0.0%	600	10.5%
Paid-in surplus	100	3.1%	0.0%	100	2.9%	0.0%	100	2.2%		0.0%	100	1.9%	0.0%	100	1.8%
Retained earnings	313	9.6%	48.6%	465	13.6%	72.9%	804	17.9%		48.4%	1,193	22.6%	45.5%	1,737	30.5%
Stockholders' equity	1,013	31.0%	15.0%	1,165	34.0%	29.1%	1,504	33.6%	41.9%	25.9%	1,893	35.9%	28.7%	2,437	42.7%
Total Liabilities and Equity	3,263	100.0%	5.0%	3,425	100.0%	30.8%	4,480	100.0%	100.0%	17.8%	5,276	100.0%	8.0%	5,700	100.0%

NOTE: Figures are in thousands of dollars. The liability "term notes" in 2002 and 2003 represent the term loan granted Wade's, with $50,000 principal due in each year for 8 years.

■ EXHIBIT 16.6

COMPARATIVE INCOME STATEMENT FOR WADE'S OFFICE FURNITURE, 1999–2003

Unaudited: SIC #2522	[—HISTORICAL—] 1999 $1,000	Percent of Total	[—HISTORICAL—] Percent Change	2000 $1,000	Percent of Total	[—HISTORICAL—] Percent Change	2001 $1,000	Percent of Total	RMA 2001	[—PRO FORMA—] Percent Change	2002 $1,000	Percent of Total	[—PRO FORMA—] Percent Change	2003 $1,000	Percent of Total
Net sales	7,571	100.0%	8.1%	8,184	100.0%	51.9%	12,430	100.0%	100.0%	20.0%	14,916	100.0%	20.0%	17,899	100.0%
Cost of goods sold	5,089	67.2%	6.6%	5,424	66.3%	52.2%	8,255	66.4%	67.3%	22.9%	10,143	68.0%	20.0%	12,171	68.0%
Gross profit	2,482	32.8%	11.2%	2,760	33.7%	51.3%	4,175	33.6%	32.7%	14.3%	4,773	32.0%	20.0%	5,728	32.0%
Selling expenses	906	12.0%	13.2%	1,026	12.5%	58.7%	1,628	13.1%		19.1%	1,939	13.0%	20.0%	2,327	13.0%
General & admin. expenses	1,019	13.5%	18.8%	1,211	14.8%	39.5%	1,689	13.6%		7.7%	1,820	12.2%	20.0%	2,184	12.2%
Depreciation & amortization	70	0.9%	1.4%	71	0.9%	2.8%	73	0.6%		50.7%	110	0.7%	0.0%	110	0.6%
Other operating expenses	0	0.0%	N/A	0	0.0%	N/A	0	0.0%		N/A	0	0.0%	N/A	0	0.0%
Total operating expenses	1,995	26.4%	15.7%	2,308	28.2%	46.9%	3,390	27.3%	25.7%	14.1%	3,869	25.9%	19.4%	4,621	25.8%
Operating profit	487	6.4%	-7.2%	452	5.5%	73.7%	785	6.3%	7.0%	15.2%	904	6.1%	22.4%	1,107	6.2%
Int. exp.–Bank notes	141	1.9%	-15.6%	119	1.5%	31.9%	157	1.3%		-35.6%	101	0.7%	-48.5%	52	0.3%
Int. exp.–Term notes + LTD	0	0.0%	N/A	0	0.0%	N/A	0	0.0%		N/A	85	0.6%	-16.5%	71	0.4%
All other expenses	63	0.8%	36.5%	86	1.1%	17.4%	101	0.8%		8.9%	110	0.7%	22.7%	135	0.8%
All other income	0	0.0%	N/A	0	0.0%	N/A	0	0.0%		N/A	0	0.0%	N/A	0	0.0%
Total (Expenses)	(204)	-2.7%	0.5%	(205)	-2.5%	25.9%	(258)	-2.1%		14.8%	(296)	-2.0%	-12.8%	(258)	-1.4%
Profit before taxes	283	3.7%	-12.7%	247	3.0%	113.4%	527	4.2%	6.2%	15.4%	608	4.1%	39.6%	849	4.7%
Income taxes	100	1.3%	-5.0%	95	1.2%	97.9%	188	1.5%		16.5%	219	1.5%	39.6%	306	1.7%
Extraordinary*	0	0.0%	N/A	0	0.0%	N/A	0	0.0%		N/A	0	0.0%	N/A	0	0.0%
Net income	183	2.4%	-16.9%	152	1.9%	123.0%	339	2.7%		14.8%	389	2.6%	39.6%	543	3.0%
Dividends	0	0.0%	N/A	0	0.0%	N/A	0	0.0%		N/A	0	0.0%	N/A	0	0.0%
Retained earnings	183	2.4%	-16.9%	152	1.9%	123.0%	339	2.7%		14.8%	389	2.6%	39.6%	543	3.0%

NOTE: Figures are in thousands of dollars. Lease payments of $154, $192, and $325 were included in total operating expenses for the years 1999, 2000, and 2001.

*Extraordinary and other income (exp.).

Examination of days accounts payable further explains the conflicting information. Days accounts payable is much higher at 53 days outstanding as compared to the industry norm of only 32 days. This indicates that accounts payable exceeded that for peers relative to purchases. Thus, it is the denominator of the current and quick ratios (current liabilities) that lowers the current and quick ratios rather than the denominator. High accounts payable suggest that Wade's is riding its creditors for long periods and may be at risk of being put on a "cash basis" by the creditors.

The set of leverage ratios in Exhibit 16.7 confirms the common size analysis in that minimal net worth supports the firm's operations. Debt exceeds tangible net worth by almost 100 percent in each year, well above the RMA average. Both the times interest earned and fixed charge coverage are low compared with competitors, indicating greater interest expense and lease payments on equipment relative to earnings.

The profitability ratios, presented in Exhibit 16.7, indicate that Wade's profits before taxes exceeded the standard relative to net worth but fell below the standard relative to total assets. This again evidences the firm's relatively high degree of financial leverage. Reported profits did increase substantially in 2001, due in large part to the dramatic increase in net sales. However, Wade's lower profits before taxes to total assets (similar to ROA) was due to the higher operating expenses relative to industry norm; 27.3 percent for Wade's versus 25.7 percent for the industry. Lower profits were obtained even though Wade's cost of goods sold was lower than peers at 66.4 percent of total sales, versus the peer average of 67.3 percent. The lower profitability was due principally to higher operating expenses. Still, Wade's reported a ROE of 22.54 percent in 2001, which was a substantial improvement over prior years.

In summary, Wade's has invested more in receivables and inventory and less in fixed assets than comparable firms. It likewise relies proportionately more on trade credit and short-term bank loans and less on long-term debt for financing. Its net worth is also substantially lower. These ratios are important because they suggest areas in which additional information must be obtained. Here the focus should be on Wade's current and fixed assets. Possible explanations are that the firm's terms of credit sales are too lenient or that the firm has poor collection policies. Some of the receivables might be uncollectable because they are outdated. Thus, a receivables aging schedule seems necessary. Similarly, Wade's may hold obsolete inventory or simply acquire it too far in advance of sales. Profitability has been relatively low, adversely affecting the equity base. On the positive side, the firm's sales growth and mark-up on sales are excellent. If the receivables and inventory are of good quality, Wade's exhibits excellent potential. It is important, however, for the banker to obtain a receivables aging schedule and personally audit the composition and quality of inventory.

The data suggest two specific risks. First, if suppliers refuse to grant Wade's the same volume of trade credit in the future, the firm will need additional bank loans to support operations. In particular, accounts payable provided $1,282,000 in financing for 2001. If suppliers were to put the company on a cash basis (cash on delivery), Wade's would have to pay off this $1,282,000 and come up with additional funds to buy its inventory. If the firm is having a problem with its suppliers, Marcus Wade would probably return to the bank for additional financing! Second, the firm's low net worth and high debt provide limited support for the planned growth and expose the firm to declining profits if interest rates rise. Wade's profitability has not been high enough to continue to support a 50 percent per year growth in sales using only debt. The firm must either slow its growth or additional equity will be required. On the positive side, however, Wade's could slow the growth in sales by either restricting credit sales, reducing inventory, or even increasing price. All of these would improve Wade's cash position.

■ EXHIBIT 16.7

FINANCIAL RATION ANALYSIS FOR WADE'S OFFICE FURNITURE, 1999–2003

	—HISTORICAL— 1999		—HISTORICAL— 2000		—HISTORICAL— 2001		RMA 2001		—PRO FORMA— 2002		—PRO FORMA— 2003	
Liquidity and Activity Ratios												
Current Ratio	1.45		1.48		1.40		1.70		1.51		1.70	
Quick Ratio	0.78		0.81		0.74		0.90		0.77		0.84	
	Days	Times	Days	Times	Days	Times	Days	Times	Days	Times	Days	Times
Days Cash	6.80	53.70×	5.93	61.53×	2.11	172.64×			2.94	124.30×	2.45	149.16×
Days Accounts Receivable	60.46	6.04×	62.39	5.85×	78.00	4.68×	65.0	5.6×	74.49	4.90×	71.57	5.10×
Days Inventory (turnover)	83.20	4.39×	81.09	4.50×	55.67	6.56×	45.0	8.1×	50.00	7.30×	46.00	7.93×
Days Accounts Payable Outstanding	N/A	N/A	60.60	6.02×	53.09	6.88×	32.0	11.3×	53.00	6.89×	53.00	6.89×
Days Cash to Cash Cycle	101.62	3.59×	88.81	4.11×	82.70	4.41×			74.43	4.90×	67.02	5.45×
Est. Working Capital Financing Needs	$1,417		$1,320		$1,870				$2,068		$2,235	
Leverage Ratios												
Debt to Tangible Net Worth	2.31×		2.01×		2.05×		1.7×		1.84×		1.37×	
Times Interest Earned	3.01×		3.08×		4.36×		5.3×		4.27×		7.90×	
Fixed Charge Coverage	1.96×		1.79×		2.09×		2.8×		2.19×		2.89×	
Net Fixed Assets to Tangible Net Worth	63.82%		53.20%		46.97%		50.0%		52.79%		36.16%	
Dividend Payout	0.00%		0.00%		0.00%				0.00%		0.00%	
Profitability Ratios												
Return on Equity (ROE)	18.07%		13.05%		22.54%				20.56%		22.30%	
Profit Before Taxes to Equity	29.09%		21.94%		36.24%		27.7%		33.00%		35.58%	
Return on Assets (ROA)	5.61%		4.44%		7.57%				7.38%		9.53%	
Profit Before Taxes to Total Assets	8.67%		7.21%		11.76%		12.1%		11.53%		14.90%	
Equity Multiplier (leverage = TA/TE)	3.22×		2.94×		2.98×		2.4×		2.79×		2.34×	
Income												
Tot. Asset Turnover (net sales/total assets)	2.32×		2.39×		2.77×		2.1×		2.83×		3.14×	
All Other Income/Total Assets	0.00%		0.00%		0.00%				0.00%		0.00%	
Expenses												
Net Profit Margin (net income/net sales)	2.42%		1.86%		2.73%				2.61%		3.04%	
COGS/Net Sales	67.22%		66.28%		66.41%		67.3%		68.00%		68.00%	
Operating Expenses/Net Sales	26.35%		28.20%		27.27%		25.7%		25.94%		25.81%	
Income Taxes to Earnings Before Taxes	35.34%		38.46%		35.67%				36.00%		36.00%	
Sales/Net Fixed Assets	12.19×		13.66×		18.20×				15.33×		20.74×	
Cash Flow Ratios												
CFO/(DIV + last CMLTD)	2.35				−1.71				4.24		6.17	
CFO/(DIV + last CMLTD + S.T. Debt)	0.27				−0.13				0.41		1.07	
CFO/(DIV + last CMLTD & CM Term + bnk Notes)	0.27				−0.13				0.39		0.96	

CASH-BASED INCOME STATEMENT: WADE'S OFFICE FURNITURE

Exhibit 16.8 presents a cash-based income statement for Wade's and documents changes in cash flow from operations (CFO). Consider the first two columns of historical data. In 2000 cash flow from operations equaled $176,000, which was $24,000 more than reported net income. CFO fell to −$128,000 in 2001, however, even though sales increased by over $4 million and profits increased by 123 percent. A close examination of the statement reveals that the decline in CFO for 2001 was caused by a combined increase in receivables and inventory of almost $1.1 million. The $374,000 increase in accounts payable, while substantial, left $682,000 in new trading assets (change in accounts receivable plus the change in inventory less the change in accounts payable) to be financed either externally or out of cash flow. The cash margin did increase by $851,000 but cash operating expenses increased by over $1 million, leading to a decline in cash operating profit. Increases in noninterest and interest expense and income taxes paid then produced the negative cash flow from operations. The additional $310,000 in notes payable to the bank financed a portion of this cash deficiency. Payments for maturing principal on term debt and $157,000 in capital expenditures added to the cash deficiency as well. The residual financing came from reduced cash holdings.

Consider the following implications. Wade's collected less on credit sales than it billed its customers in 2000 and 2001 as shown by an increase in accounts receivable outstanding from 1999 to 2001. Thus, net sales were offset by the $497 million increase in receivables to obtain actual cash receipts. Had receivables declined, actual cash receipts from sales would have exceeded the reported sales figure. Sales increased by almost 52 percent from 2000 to 2001 while accounts receivables only increased by 35.5 percent. The liquidity and activity ratios in Exhibit 16.7 indicate that Wade's credit policy tightened from 2000 to 2001 as days accounts receivable fell by almost 7 days from 62.39 to 55.67. If Wade's credit policy had not improved over this period, cash flow from operations would have been approximately $229,000 lower.[13] The improvement in collection of receivables is a positive sign for Wade's and has reduced the amount of financing Wade's otherwise would have needed at the end of 2001. Wade's profitability (gross margin) improved in 2000 but deteriorated in 2001—indicating cash flow from operations would be higher relative to net income in 2000, but the lower gross margin in 2001 was a use of cash. Wade's inventory turnover improved in 2000 (4.50×) and 2001 (4.68×). The improved inventory turnover means that inventory growth was less than the growth in sales. The company's more efficient utilization of inventory means that Wade's used proportionately less cash to finance sales growth than it would have had inventory turnover not improved, again positive news. The fact that days accounts payable outstanding decreased in 2001 means cash was used to reduce trade credit obligations as well.

On the positive side, Wade's accounts receivable and inventory growth, although substantial, was less than the growth in sales. Wade's cash needs to finance the increase in working capital was not a result of a more lax credit or inventory policy, but instead was primarily driven by sales growth. If these credit sales and inventory are of high quality, this will provide cash flow in the future as Wade's collects on credit sales. Wade's also reduced its days accounts payable outstanding in 2001, thus improving its position with suppliers.

In summary, Wade's cash flow from operations in 2000 of $176,000 exceeded capital expenditures ($49,000) and the principal payment on long-term debt ($75,000) by $53,000. This excess cash flow, along with $8,000 in cash, was essentially used to pay $61,000 on the amount of short-term debt owed. In 2001, however, cash flow from operations was negative (−$128,000) and hence insufficient to cover current principal payments on long-term debt

---

[13]If credit policy had not changed, then accounts receivable would have been $2,125,000 [($12,430,000/ 365) × 62.39], hence the change in accounts receivables would have been $726,000 ($2,125,000 − 1,399,000).

▪ EXHIBIT 16.8

STATEMENT OF CHANGES RECONCILED TO CASH FOR WADE'S
OFFICE FURNITURE, 2000–2003

| | [—HISTORICAL—] | | [—PRO FORMA—] | |
| | 2000 | 2001 | 2002 | 2003 |
CASH-BASED INCOME STATEMENT	$1,000	$1,000	$1,000	$1,000
Net sales	8,184	12,430	14,916	17,899
Change in accounts receivable	(145)	(497)	(147)	(213)
Cash receipts from sales	8,039	11,933	14,769	17,687
Cost of goods sold	(5,424)	(8,255)	(10,143)	(12,171)
Change in inventory	(45)	(559)	(306)	(317)
Change in accounts payable	72	374	235	296
Cash purchases	(5,397)	(8,440)	(10,214)	(12,192)
Cash margin	2,642	3,493	4,555	5,495
Total operating expenses	(2,308)	(3,390)	(3,869)	(4,621)
Depreciation & amortization	71	73	110	110
Change in prepaid expenses	(3)	35	(5)	(5)
Change in accruals	53	90	20	20
Change in other current assets & liab.	0	0	0	0
Cash operating expenses	(2,187)	(3,192)	(3,744)	(4,496)
Cash operating profit	455	301	811	999
Interest on marketable securities	0	0	0	0
Income on long term investments	0	0	0	0
All other expenses & income (net)	(86)	(101)	(110)	(135)
Cash before interest & taxes	369	200	701	864
Interest expense—Bank notes	(119)	(157)	(101)	(52)
Interest expense—Term notes and LTD	0	0	(85)	(71)
Income taxes reported	(95)	(188)	(219)	(306)
Change in income tax payable	21	17	22	28
Change in deferred income taxes	0	0	0	0
Cash flow from operations (CFO)	**176**	**(128)**	**318**	**463**
Capital exp. and leasehold improvements	(49)	(157)	(400)	0
Change in long-term investments	0	0	0	0
Change in intangible assets	1	(11)	0	0
Change in other noncurrent assets	0	0	0	0
Cash used for investments	**(48)**	**(168)**	**(400)**	**0**
Payment for last period's CM Term note	0	0	0	(50)
Payment for last period's CMLTD	(75)	(75)	(75)	(75)
Dividends paid (DIV)	0	0	0	0
Payments for financing	**(75)**	**(75)**	**(75)**	**(125)**
Cash before external financing	53	(371)	(157)	338
Change in short-term bank debt	(61)	310	(195)	(338)
Change in term notes & EOP CM term notes	0	0	400	0
Change in LT debt + EOP CMLTD	0	0	0	0
Change in stock & surplus	0	0	0	0
Change in other noncurrent liabilities	0	0	0	0
External financing	**(61)**	**310**	**205**	**(338)**
Change in cash & mktbl securities	**(8)**	**(61)**	**48**	**0**

NOTE: Figures are in thousands of dollars.

LTD, CM, and EOP refer to long-term debt, current maturity, and end-of-period, respectively.

($75,000) and capital expenditures ($157,000). Cash flow before external financing was also negative (−$371,000) in 2001. Wade's borrowed an additional $310,000 in short-term debt and used $61,000 in cash to fund this deficit.

Wade's generated good profits but these profits did not materialize as cash profits. Why? In essence, the increase in receivables and inventory exceeded the increase in accounts payable. While Wade's provided $73,000 from noncash expenditures (depreciation) and $142,000 from a reduction in prepaid expenses and increase in accrued expenses and income tax payables, this was less than that needed to finance current operations. Wade's profit of $339,000 provided all but $128,000 of this deficiency. Thus, most of the $310,000 in additional financing was used to finance the increase in working capital needs.

The ratios at the bottom of Exhibit 16.7 demonstrate that Wade's generated enough cash from operations to pay off current maturities of long-term debt in 2000 but fell far short in 2001. The negative cash flow from operations in 2001 indicates that the firm should not take on additional debt unless it can successfully restructure its operating policies.

Negative cash flow does not necessarily eliminate the possibility that the bank may want to make a loan. Under proper operating policies, Wade's may be able to expand and pay off new debt on a timely basis. Recall that Wade's negative cash flow was primarily driven by the 50 percent growth in sales. If sales growth slows, Wade's use of cash for accounts receivables and inventory will fall dramatically—most likely producing positive cash flow from operations. Exhibits 16.9 and 16.10 outline a set of financial projections that describes a *most likely* set of circumstances regarding the economic environment and revisions in Wade's operating policies. In this case, the loan should be repaid.

Each of these *pro forma* assumptions (parameters) reflects a conservative but realistic estimate of future performance moving Wade's operating ratios closer to industry norms. In making the loan decision, the bank will lend money only if Wade's restricts its growth in current assets by tightening credit policies and slowing inventory growth. The loan officer cannot, however, require Wade's to restrict sales in any formal document or the bank may be held responsible if the company does not perform well. Rather, the officer must be convinced, based on discussions with Wade and an assessment of his character, that Wade agrees that this plan is in the best interest of the company. This is just one of the many aspects of the more qualitative issues that must be addressed to finalize a loan decision. Restrictions on credit sales are assumed to lower sales below Marcus Wade's forecast and to decrease the effective markup over cost of goods sold. Both receivables and inventory turnover will increase closer to the industry norm by 2003. Net profit will increase proportionately because of decreases in expenses as Wade's salary is unchanged and nonoperating expenses decline proportionately.

Balance sheet and income statement projections for 2002 and 2003 appear in Exhibits 16.5 and 16.6, respectively. These projections are based on the explicit assumptions in Exhibits 16.9 and 16.10. The resulting projected cash-based income statement is presented in Exhibit 16.8. If projected cash flow from operations is realized, it will total $318,000 in 2002 and $463,000 in 2003, considerably more than current maturities of long-term debt. Cash flow from operations increases with sales because new trading assets are presumably financed almost entirely by additional trade credit. Thus, the cash margin increases more than cash operating expense, interest expense, and taxes paid. The bank's short-term loan exposure will decrease in 2002 and 2003 to $697,000 and $359,000, respectively. Of course, the total bank loan outstanding will equal almost $1.1 million at the end of 2002 and $709,000 at the end of 2003. This is substantially less than the requested $1.6 million.

In 2002, cash flow from operations of $318,000 is forecast to exceed principal and interest payments by $243,000. Capital expenditures of $400,000 were financed with a term loan of an equal amount leaving surplus cash flow after payment on long term debt of $195,000. This excess was used to pay down the short-term bank debt. The excess cash flow is forecast to reach $338,000 in 2003. Both estimates reveal that Wade's has the ability to take on additional debt.

In this scenario, the loan proceeds would be used to finance the new equipment and Wade's continued need for working capital financing. The projected decrease in notes payable, however, represents a reduced working capital financing need. Effectively, the bank

· **EXHIBIT 16.9**

FINANCIAL PROJECTIONS: ASSUMPTIONS FOR MOST LIKELY CIRCUMSTANCES
AT WADE'S FURNITURE, 2002 AND 2003

1. Sales increase by 20 percent annually. All sales are credit sales. Wade's forecasts a 50 percent rise.

2. Cost of goods sold equals 68 percent of sales.

3. Selling expenses average 13 percent of sales, general and administrative expenses average 12.2 percent of sales, and depreciation equals $110,000 annually.

4. Noninterest expense equals $110,000 in 2002 and $135,000 in 2003.

5. Interest expense equals 14.5 percent of outstanding bank and term debt and 9 percent of other long-term debt.

6. Income taxes equal 36 percent of earnings before taxes; income tax payable increases annually by the rate of change in 2001.

7. Receivables collection improves so that days receivables outstanding equals 50 in 2002 and 46 in 2003.

8. Inventory turnover increases to 4.9 times in 2002 and 5.1 times in 2003.

9. Days accounts payable outstanding remains constant at 53.

10. Prepaid expenses and accruals increase by $5,000 and $20,000 annually, in 2002 and 2003 respectively.

11. No dividends are paid.

12. $400,000 is loaned to purchase new equipment, with the principal repaid over eight years in equal annual installments. The first payment is due March 1, 2002.

13. Reported depreciation on the new equipment equals $40,000 a year for 10 years. Depreciation on old assets will be $70,000 per year.

14. The minimum cash required is $120,000.

15. Other assets remain constant at $50,000.

---

has restructured Wade's debt to include more term debt and less of the short-term line of credit. Alternatively, the bank could shorten the maturity of the term loan and increase the annual principal payment. At the end of 2003, Wade's is producing about $338,000 in excess cash flow to repay the outstanding loans. If this continues, the remaining bank debt of $709,000 ($359,000 + $50,000 + $300,000) could effectively be repaid in just over two additional years; i.e., by 2005. The projections simply provide an estimate of total loan needs; the composition is determined through negotiations. If the assumed conditions hold for several years, the entire loan could be repaid from internal cash flow by 2005, shown by projecting the statement items through that year.

It is further likely that the bank would secure both the short-term and term loans with all available collateral, including receivables, inventory, and new equipment. The bank must subsequently determine the quality of Wade's trading assets. Again, a receivables aging schedule and an inventory evaluation are required.[14]

---

[14]An aging schedule is a listing of accounts receivable grouped according to the month in which the invoice is either dated or payable. A comparison of aging schedules indicates whether the volume of past due accounts is rising or falling and whether the general quality of receivables is deteriorating.

- **EXHIBIT 16.10**

PRO FORMA MODEL USED TO PROJECT WADE'S INCOME STATEMENT

$$\text{Sales}_{2002} = \text{Sales}_{2001} \times (1 + \textbf{\textit{g}}_{\textbf{\textit{sales}}})$$
$$= \$12,430 \times (1 + \textbf{\textit{0.20}}) = \$14,916$$

$$\text{COGS}_{2002} = \text{Sales}_{2002} \times \textbf{\textit{COGS \% of Sales}}$$
$$= \$14,916 \times \textbf{\textit{0.68}} = \$10,143$$

$$\text{Selling Exp}_{2002} = \text{Sales}_{2002} \times \textbf{\textit{Selling Exp. \% of Sales}}$$
$$= \$14,916 \times \textbf{\textit{0.13}} = \$1,939$$

$$\text{G\&A Exp}_{2002} = \text{Sales}_{2002} \times \textbf{\textit{G\&A Exp. \% of Sales}}$$
$$= \$14,916 \times \textbf{\textit{0.122}} = \$1,820$$

$$\text{Interest Exp}_{2002} = (\text{Bank debt}_{2002} \times \textbf{\textit{rate on bank debt and term debt}})$$
$$+ (\text{L.T. debt}_{2002} \times \textbf{\textit{rate on L.T. debt}})$$
$$= [\$697 + \$50 + \$350] \times \textbf{\textit{0.145}} + [(\$75 + \$225) \times \textbf{\textit{0.09}}] = \$186$$

Pro forma values on the balance sheet are calculated as follows:

$$\text{Accounts rec}_{2002} = \textbf{\textit{Days A/R outstanding}} \times \text{Average Daily Sales}_{2002}$$
$$= \textbf{\textit{50}} \times (\$14,916/365) = \$2,043$$

$$\text{Inventory}_{2002} = \text{COGS}_{2002}/\textbf{\textit{Inventory turnover}}$$
$$= \$10,143/\textbf{\textit{4.9}} = \$2,070$$

$$\text{Gross fixed}_{2002} = \text{Gross fixed}_{2001} + \textbf{\textit{Capital Expenditures}}_{\textbf{\textit{2002}}}$$
$$= \$791 + \textbf{\textit{\$400}} = \$1,191$$

$$\text{Accumulated dep}_{2002} = \text{Accumulated depreciation}_{2001} + \text{Depreciation}_{2002}$$
$$= \$346 + \$110 = \$456$$

$$\text{Notes payable}_{2002} = \textbf{\textit{"Plug figure"}} = \text{Assets}_{2002} - (\text{Liabilities}_{2002} + \text{Net worth}_{2002})$$

$$\text{Accounts pay}_{2002} = \textbf{\textit{Days AP outstanding}} \times \text{Average Daily purchases}_{2002}$$
$$= \textbf{\textit{Days AP outstanding}} \times [(\text{COGS}_{2002} + \Delta\text{Inventory}_{2002})/365]$$
$$= 53 \times [(\$10,143 + (\$2,070 - \$1,764))/365] = \$1,517$$

$$\text{LTD}_{2002} = \text{LTD}_{2001} - \textbf{\textit{Current Maturity (CM) LTD}}_{\textbf{\textit{2002}}} + \textbf{\textit{New issues of LTD}}_{\textbf{\textit{2002}}}$$
$$= \$300 - \textbf{\textit{\$75}} + \textbf{\textit{\$0}} = \$225$$

$$\text{Term notes}_{2002} = \text{Term notes}_{2001} - \textbf{\textit{Current Maturity (CM) Term notes}}_{\textbf{\textit{2002}}}$$
$$+ \textbf{\textit{New issues of Term notes}}_{\textbf{\textit{2002}}}$$
$$= \textbf{\textit{\$0}} - \textbf{\textit{\$50}} + \textbf{\textit{\$400}} = \$350$$

$$\text{Retained earn}_{2002} = \text{Retained earnings}_{2001} + (\text{Net income}_{2002} - \textbf{\textit{Dividends}}_{\textbf{\textit{2002}}})$$
$$= \$804 + (\$339 - \textbf{\textit{\$0}}) = \$1,193$$

NOTE: Figures are in thousands of dollars. Values in **_bold italic_** are parameters that the analyst must provide.

Exhibit 16.11 represents a summary of Wade's **borrowing base.** The borrowing base is an estimate of the available collateral on a company's current assets. Accounts receivables are purged of accounts 60 days or more past due and credit is given for 70 percent of the remaining accounts. The percentage of credit given will vary by bank policy as well as the analyst's estimate of the general quality of the accounts. Inventory value is reduced by the amount of payables, because trade creditors will generally have a superior claim to the bank. In this example, inventory is credited at 50 percent of its value. Again, the credit rate will vary by

■ **EXHIBIT 16.11**

BORROWING BASE CERTIFICATE FOR WADE'S OFFICE FURNITURE, 2001

Borrowing Base	$1,000
Accounts receivables	$ 1,896
Less: accounts over 60 days	$ (192)
Subtotal	$ 1,704
Total eligible @ 70%	$ 1,193
Inventory	$ 1,764
Less: accounts payable	$(1,282)
Subtotal	$ 482
Total eligible @ 50%	$ 241
Total debt (less LTD secured by real estate)	$ (892)
Excess (deficit)	$ 542

NOTE: Figures are in thousands of dollars. The $192,000 presented for accounts over 60 days is an estimate.

bank policy and quality of inventory. Total debt not secured by real estate is then removed to determine the company's excess (deficit) of collateral available. As revealed in Exhibit 16.11, Wade's has sufficient collateral to support the current loan in 2001 by an excess of $542,000.

SENSITIVITY ANALYSIS

The financial forecasts previously presented represent only one possible outcome. In all likelihood, Wade's performance in 2002 and 2003 will differ materially from that described above. A lender should always perform sensitivity analysis by adjusting assumptions regarding key factors, such as sales growth and receivables collection, and recalculating the projected financial statements. If the above projections are a most likely scenario, management should compare the results with worst-case and best-case scenarios. This generates a range of projected outcomes for the loan magnitude and repayment schedule. For example, if Wade's accounts receivable collection remained stable at its 2001 pace, its projected short-term loan requirement would exceed $800,000 at about $953,000 in 2002 and $908,000 in 2003. Further projections indicate that it would take until about 2008 to repay the loan. The bank ultimately assigns probabilities (at least implicitly) to each potential outcome to arrive at an expected result. A worst-case scenario is extremely useful because it identifies all contingencies that a lender should consider when considering downside risk.

Note that when forecasting a firm's financial condition, a lender does not know what interest rates will prevail. Most commercial loans will be priced on a floating rate basis such that the rate a borrower pays will vary with changes in some base rate. Thus, the actual interest due will typically not be known before a loan is approved. To address this, a bank should include as part of the sensitivity analysis a comparison of forecasts of *cash flow from operations before interest* with expected principal and interest payments plus cash dividends. Cash flow from operations before interest equals cash flow from operations prior to any adjustment for interest expense on any new debt. Expected interest payments will then vary under scenarios of rising, falling, and constant interest rates. A bank can thus assess the extent to which rising interest rates may create problems for the borrower.

SUMMARY

Credit analysis is the evaluation of risk associated with a borrower's willingness and ability to repay debts. Before analyzing financial data, the analyst should assess the borrower's character and the quality of management. The subsequent financial analysis consists of spreading the financial statements, which involves analyzing common size balance sheet and income statement data and calculating liquidity, activity, leverage and profit ratios, determining cash flow from operations using historical data, followed by a review of *pro forma* balance sheet and income statement data. The entire procedure provides a framework for determining how large a loan is needed, what the proceeds will finance, how and when the loan should be repaid, and what collateral is available. This information and answers to specific questions about the firm's production process, supply relationships, and related concerns generally enable the lending officer to determine whether the credit request falls within acceptable risk limits.

One important facet of the analysis is evaluating cash flow. Principal and interest payments on debt plus dividends and a portion of other discretionary expenditures should be paid out of cash flow from operations. Term loans should generally not be approved unless the analysis indicates that projected cash flow will be sufficient to cover debt service requirements. Term loan analysis requires *pro forma* analysis. A statement of changes reconciled to cash generates cash flow estimates by constructing a cash-based income statement. The ratio of cash flow from operations to dividends and principal payments on loans reveals whether the firm's underlying operating position is healthy.

QUESTIONS

1. Rank the importance of the five basic credit issues described in the text.
2. Explain why collateral alone does not justify extending credit. Cite examples using real estate or agriculture products as collateral.
3. Which of the following loan requests by an off-campus pizza parlor would be unacceptable, and why?
   a. to buy cheese for inventory
   b. to buy a pizza heating oven
   c. to buy a car for the owner
   d. to repay the original long-term mortgage used to buy the pizza ovens
   e. to pay employees due to a temporary cash flow problem
   f. to buy stock in the company that supplies cheese to the parlor
4. Standard ratio analysis distinguishes between four categories of ratios. Describe how ratios in each category indicate strength or weakness in the underlying firm's performance.
5. Explain how it is possible for a firm to report rising net income each year yet continue to need more working capital financing from a bank.
6. Indicate whether each of the following is a source of cash, use of cash, or has no cash impact.
   a. Firm issues new long-term debt
   b. Firm prepays operating costs

    c. Because a firm buys another firm it amortizes goodwill

    d. Firm sells outdated computer equipment

    e. Firm pays a stock dividend

    f. Firm sells its product on credit

    g. Firm buys a new fleet of trucks

7. Suppose that you generate a cash-based income statement and determine that cash flow from operations equals 75 percent of cash dividends paid and payments on current maturities of long-term debt. What is the significance of this in terms of the firm's cash flow position?

8. Should a firm's cash flow from operations generally exceed capital expenditures?

9. Suppose that you have generated the estimates listed below from a *pro forma* analysis for a manufacturing company that had requested a 3-year term loan. The loan is a $1.5 million term loan with equal annual principal payments. Principal and interest are payable at the end of each year with interest calculated against outstanding principal at a rate of prime plus 2 percent.

	Year 1	Year 2	Year 3
Capital expenditures	$250,000	$125,000	$75,000
Cash dividends	140,000	140,000	140,000
Cash flow from operations before interest expense	750,000	780,000	800,000

    a. If prime averages 8 percent each year, will the firm's cash flow from operations before interest be sufficient to meet debt service requirements and other mandatory expenditures?

    b. If prime averages 8 percent, 9 percent, and 10 percent over the three years, respectively, will cash flow be sufficient?

10. Develop a list of questions that a loan officer should ask Marcus Wade, from the example in the text, to gain a better understanding of the risks in lending to Wade's Office Furniture.

PROBLEMS

I. SOUTHWEST TRADING COMPANY, TAOS, NEW MEXICO

Summer is approaching and Steven and Sue Mayall have finally decided that their idea of a successful southwest furniture, art, and jewelry trading company has come of age. They know that summer is a popular tourist time in New Mexico and could be the best time to start this new business. The Mayalls have had a longtime interest in southwestern art and furniture. Steven graduated from college with an economics degree about 15 years ago and received his MBA in finance three years later. He has been working in Dallas, Texas, as the controller of a major wholesale distributor company for many years. His wife, Sue, who is a full partner in the business, spent the first 10 years of her career in retail sales. Over the last several years she has assumed more administrative duties with the group she works with.

    Steven and Sue know they bring the expertise and skill to run a successful business, but to ensure success they have been researching the market for over five years. They also know that they must be very careful and thoroughly research the business and industry they are pursuing. They have traveled extensively to New Mexico and spent a good deal of time getting to know the local artists (primarily ski "bums"). They believe that there is a great demand for southwestern furniture throughout the Southwest and prices are currently high.

They have informal commitments from local craftsmen to supply them with goods that they will display and sell. They have also made tentative arrangements with a large and reliable firm to supply the furniture and art pieces they will need to run the business.

The Mayalls have decided to open a shop in Taos, New Mexico, under the name Southwest Trading Company, operating as both a supplier to furniture and art outlets and seller in the retail shop. Steven's extensive contacts with business in Dallas and Houston have given him the orders needed to get the business off the ground as soon as they begin shipping the goods. Sue has already begun marketing the southwestern products. The arrangements with the local craftsmen will allow very aggressive pricing of the goods to retail establishments in the Southwest. This aggressive pricing has been well received and tentative orders are already in place.

Steven has found an ideal location for the shop that is currently available. The owner is asking $275,000 for the space but Southwest Trading has a contract, contingent on financing, for $250,000. Based on remodeling bids, Steven and Sue estimate that they will be able to fix up the place for about $45,000. Although they will purchase the building, the land is leased on a transferable lease with 65 years remaining. The Mayalls have decided to invest $235,000, which represents most of their savings, into the venture to ensure success. Sue's sister is also lending Southwest Trading Company $90,000. Repayment on the note is not expected to begin for five years. The Mayalls estimate that they will need $130,000 in inventory to start the business and will pay for the inventory in cash to build goodwill with the local craftsmen. They also estimate that they will need a minimum cash balance of $20,000 to conduct day-to-day operations and pay bills.

Steven has approached Cary Farmer, the senior loan officer at Santa Fe National Bank in Santa Fe, New Mexico, for financing. Steven's background in finance has allowed him to put together the following assumptions for Southwest's preliminary business plan. He believes that all renovations to the building and inventory can be in place by June 30, 2002.

1. Sales are expected to be a bit lower through 2002 because of Southwest's newness and it takes time for any firm to establish a market presence. Sales are expected to grow significantly in 2003 and 2004 with lower growth rates in 2005. Sales are expected to be $275,000 in the final six months of 2002, and $675,000, $800,000, and $900,000 during the three full years of operations (2003, 2004, and 2005). Sales are expected to level off at $900,000 after 2005.

2. Based on tentative agreements and orders, it is expected that cost of goods sold will average 63 percent of sales.

3. General and administrative expenses are expected to be $70,000 for the six months in 2002, increase to $100,000 in 2003, and level off at $120,000 from 2004 on. The land lease expenses and interest expenses are included in operational expenses.

4. Selling expenses are expected to be 12 percent of sales and Sue is expecting to undertake extensive marketing and promotion efforts throughout the Southwest immediately after the business is opened. These additional promotional expenses will be $30,000 in 2002 only.

5. Southwest will use 10-year straight-line depreciation of the building and improvements.

6. Southwest's effective tax rate is expected to be 34 percent.

7. A relatively large portion of business is expected to be on credit such that Southwest will carry about 48 days of accounts receivables. Based on the type of business they are entering, Steven and Sue expect to turn their inventory three times a year.

8. Based on the negotiations they have had with their craftsmen, suppliers, and other wholesale distributors, they estimate that they can count on about 28 days of accounts payable to help finance the business.

In preparing to go to the bank for the necessary loan, the Mayalls want to prepare projected financial statements for Southwest Trading Company showing the company can make a profit and pay back the loan. They also want to know more precisely how much they will need to borrow from the bank to open the doors for business and help finance the initial years of business. The Mayalls plan to prepare five years of balance sheet, income statement, and cash budget data for the bank. They must also develop an opening balance sheet as of the day they plan to open the doors, June 30, 2002. These *pro forma* financial statements will aid them and the bank officer in answering many questions including:

1. How much financing will be needed to open the doors of the business in July of 2002?

2. Five years of *pro forma* balance sheet and income statement data must be prepared to determine if additional financing is needed. If so, how much? Steven's finance background tells him that the estimated financing needed each year will be an accounting plug figure to ensure that the balance sheet balances. If projected assets exceed liabilities and equity, the difference will be the bank borrowing needs. If liabilities and equity exceeds projected assets purchases, these funds will be used to pay off debt or increase cash or marketable securities.

3. Because this is a start-up business, it is important to identify what the loan proceeds will be used for, what the primary source of repayment is, and when to estimate the total loan proceeds will be repaid. Using the *pro forma* projections, the primary source of repayment and when the loan will be repaid.

4. A cash budget or cash based income statement needs to be prepared because Steven knows the only thing that matters to the bank is cash. Prepare these for each year.

5. Finally, Steven needs to prepare a collateral schedule. He knows that the banker does not want the collateral but will need all he can get if the business is not as successful as expected.

6. Prepare a list of questions you would need to answer. Be sure to explain the specifics of the questions as they relate to this case.
    a. What types of loan covenants would you require?
    b. Identify the bank's largest risks in making this loan.
    c. How would you structure the loan to protect the bank?

You should conduct the analysis suggested in the above questions. What is your recommendation concerning the loan request?

II. PERFORMANCE OF CHEM-CO COATINGS

Table 1 presents balance sheet and income statement data for Chem-Co, a producer of specialty chemical coatings, that recently bought a small manufacturer of outdoor pools. During 2001 the firm instituted a national marketing campaign to inform individuals of the firm's new products related to home pool management. Chief Executive Officer Wynona Presley was pleased with sales in 2001, noting the 30 percent increase over 2000 sales. As the U.S. economy continues to expand, Presley is considering marketing Chem-Co's products outside the United States.

1. Using the data in Table 1, generate a cash-based income statement for Chem-Co for 2001.

2. Interpret the figures by evaluating the firm's cash flow from operations and key financial ratios.

3. Identify potential problems that the firm faces.

▪ TABLE 1

BALANCE SHEET AND INCOME STATEMENT DATA FOR CHEM-CO

Balance Sheet	2000	2001	Income Statement	2001
Assets				
Cash and marketable securities	$30	$6	Net sales	$861
Accounts receivable	102	215	Cost of goods sold	680
Merchandise inventory	65	104	Gross margin	181
Prepaid expenses	8	5	Selling expenses	64
Gross fixed assets	120	149	General & adm. expenses	60
Less accumulated depreciation	40	57	Depreciation	26
Net fixed assets	80	92	Operating profit	31
Intangible assets	4	3	Interest income	6
Total	$289	$425	Interest expense	18
Liabilities and Net Worth				
Notes payable-bank	$106	$223	Profit before taxes	19
Current maturities of long-term debt	9	11	Income taxes	5
Accounts payable	33	50	Net profit	14
Accruals	2	9		
Federal income tax payable	3	4		
Long-term mortgage	16	15		
Long-term debt	43	32		
Liabilities	$212	$344		
Common stock	40	40		
Retained earnings	37	41		
Net worth*	77	81		
Total liabilities and equity	$289	$425		

*Net worth reconciliation
Beginning net worth	77
=+ Net profit	14
Dividends paid (cash)	10
Ending net worth	81

NOTE: Figures are in millions of dollars.

APPENDIX I

BACKGROUND INFORMATION FOR FINANCIAL ANALYSIS

A quantitative analysis of financial data serves as the basis for most credit decisions. Its effectiveness depends largely on the quality of the data. Before proceeding with the ratio and cash flow evaluation, an analyst should examine the nature of available information and its completeness. This appendix summarizes background information regarding financial analysis.

FINANCIAL STATEMENTS

Accountants prepare formal financial statements with an eye toward "generally accepted accounting principles" (GAAP). The intent of GAAP is to establish a set of policies and procedures that require the consistent, systematic presentation of accounting information. Even with GAAP, however, two problems frequently arise. First, many financial statements are prepared by individuals who are not familiar with GAAP, let alone fundamental accounting identities such as assets equal liabilities plus net worth. Thus asset classifications and expenses claimed in many reports vary from allowable provisions. Second, even GAAP allow different procedures for presenting information. For example, if a company sells a product under an installment contract, it can book sales when the order is signed or when delivery is actually made. Similarly, a company has a choice in how it accounts for inventory. Last-in-first-out systems have far different reporting and cash flow impacts than first-in-first-out systems.

The implication is that an analyst must examine the nature of financial data before spreading statements. Following are some recommended guidelines:

1. Determine who prepared the statements.

2. Determine if the statements are audited.

3. If audited, assess what type of opinion was issued and the nature of any qualification or disclaimer. In general, an unqualified opinion means that the auditor determined that the reported statements conformed with GAAP. A qualified opinion means that either some item in the report does not conform to GAAP or selected figures cannot be determined with a reasonable degree of certainty. The second case occurs, for example, when the value of inventory cannot be adequately determined. Adverse opinion means that the financial statements are not presented in accordance with GAAP, and a disclaimer appears when the auditor expresses no opinion.

4. Determine areas where a firm has used its discretion to select a particular accounting policy within GAAP that might significantly affect reported figures. This requires the careful examination of footnotes to financial statements. Discretionary policies frequently arise in the areas of revenue recognition, income tax reconciliation, inventory valuation, accounts receivable classification, depreciation of plant and equipment, goodwill, consolidation of entities, and pension, profit sharing, and stock option plans.

5. Determine all outstanding commitments and contingent claims.

6. Identify any unusual balance sheet entries or transactions.

APPENDIX II

CALCULATION OF FINANCIAL RATIOS[15]

LIQUIDITY RATIOS

1. Current ratio = Current assets/Current liabilities

2. Quick ratio = $\dfrac{\text{Cash + Accounts receivable}}{\text{Current liabilities}}$

3. Accounts receivable aging schedule: a comparison of the dollar amount and percentage of total receivables outstanding across the number of days they have been outstanding (less than 30, 31–60, etc.)

ACTIVITY RATIOS

1. Days cash = Cash/Average daily sales

2. Days inventory on hand = Inventory/Average daily COGS

3. Inventory turnover = 365/Days inventory

4. Accounts receivable collection period (Days A/R)
   = Accounts receivables/Average daily sales

5. Accounts receivable turnover = 365/Days A/R

6. Days cash-to-cash asset cycle = Days cash + days accounts receivables outstanding + days inventory outstanding

7. Days accounts payable outstanding
   = Accounts payable/Average daily purchases
   = Accounts payable/[(COGS + Δinventory)/365]

8. Sales to net fixed assets = Sales/Net fixed assets

LEVERAGE RATIOS

1. Debt to tangible net worth = Total liabilities/Net worth

2. Times interest earned = EBIT/Interest expense

3. EBIT = earnings before taxes + interest expense

4. Fixed charge coverage = (EBIT + lease payments)/(Interest expense + lease payments)

5. Net fixed assets to tangible net worth = Net fixed assets/Tangible net worth

6. Dividend payout = Cash dividends paid/Net profit

PROFITABILITY RATIOS

1. Return on Equity (ROE) = Net income/Total equity

2. Profit before taxes to net worth = Profit before taxes/Tangible net worth

3. Return on average net worth = Net income/Tangible net worth

4. Return on Assets (ROA) = Net income/Total Assets

---

[15]An interpretation of each ratio along with its corresponding deficiencies can be found in Robert Morris Associates' *Annual Statement Studies.* EBIT refers to earnings before interest and taxes.

5. Profit before taxes to total assets = Profit before taxes/Total assets

6. Asset utilization (or asset turnover) = Sales/Total assets

7. Profit margin (PM) = Net income/Sales

8. Sales growth = Change in sales/Last period's sales

9. Income taxes to profit before taxes = Reported income tax/Profit before taxes

REFERENCES

Annual Statement Studies, RMA, published annual. (http://www.rmahq.org) Provides common size balance sheet and income statement data as well as ratio data by four-digit SIC code. Data for all companies are provided for the last five years and current peer group data provided by size using total assets and total sales. Median and upper and lower quartiles for each ratio are also provided.

Industry Norms and Key Business Ratios, Dun & Bradstreet, published annually. (http://www.dnb.com) Common size balance sheet and income statement data as well as industry ratios using four-digit SIC code. Common size data are presented using total assets or total sales and the median value must be used to calculate the percentage of total values. Data are presented for the current year only but median and upper and lower quartiles are provided for each ratio.

Analyst's Handbook, Standard & Poors Corporation, published annual. (http://www.mcgraw-hill.com/financial-markets and /http://www.compustat.com)

Industry Surveys, Standard & Poors Corporation, (http://www.compustat.com)

Almanac of Business and Industrial Ratios, Leo Troy, annual.

Edgar Database of Corporate Information, Securities and Exchange Commission, available online at (http://www.sec.gov). Features a large and searchable database of corporate filings include 10Ks and 10Qs.

INVESTMENT AND FINANCIAL RESOURCES

Corporation Records, The Outlook, and *Stock Reports,* Standard & Poors, (http://www.mcgraw-hill.com).

Moody's Manuals, Moody's Investor Service, Inc., (http://www. moodys.com)

The Value Line Investment Survey, Value Line, Inc., (http://www.valueline.com)

APPENDIX III

GENERALIZED CASH-BASED INCOME STATEMENT FORMAT

Cash Flow Statement Section	Row Number	Cash-Based Income Statement	Income Statement Equivalent	Factors Determining the Difference between the Income Statement and Cash-Based Income Statement
Operations	(1)	+ Sales	Sales	Sales growth Credit policy
	(2)	− ΔAccounts receivables		
	(3) =(1)+(2)	= Cash Sales		
	(4)	− COGS	COGS	Sales growth Gross margin Inventory turnover Trade credit policy and relationship
	(5)	− ΔInventory		
	(6)	+ ΔAccounts payable		
	(7) =(4)+(5)+(6)	= Cash purchases		
	(8) =(3)+(7)	= Cash Gross Margin	Gross Margin	All factors listed above
	(9)	− Operating Expenses	Operating Expenses	Accounting methods Operating expense payment policies
	(10)	+ Depreciation	Depreciation	
	(11)	− ΔPrepaid Expenses		
	(12)	+ ΔAccrued Expenses		
	(13) = (9)+(10)+(11)+(12)	= Cash Operating Expenses		
	(14)	+ Other Income	Other Income	Changes in other current assets and liabilities
	(15)	− Other Expenses	Other Expenses	
	(16)	− Interest Expense	Interest Expenses	
	(17)	− ΔOther Current Assets		
	(18)	+ ΔOther Current Liabilities		
	(19) =(13)+sum(14 to 18)	= Cash Profit Before Taxes	Profit Before Taxes	All factors listed above
	(20)	− Income Taxes Reported	Income Taxes	Accounting methods Tax laws
	(21)	+ ΔIncome Tax Payable		
	(22)	+ ΔDeferred Income Taxes		
	(23) =(20)+(21)+(22)	= Cash Taxes Paid		
	(24) =(19)+(23)	**= Cash Flow from Operations**	**Net Income**	**All factors listed above**

continued

Investment

(25)	− Capital Expenditures	Actual capital expenditures
	= − (ΔNet Fixed Assets + Dep. Expense)	Additions to long-term investments
		Changes in all other long-term assets
(26)	− ΔLong-term Investments	
(27)	− ΔAll Other Noncurrent Assets	
(28) =(25)+(26)+(27)	= Cash Used for Investments	
(29)	− Payment for last period's CMLTD	Loan principal repayment schedule

Financing

(30)	− Dividends paid (DIV)	Dividend policy
(31) =(29)+(30)	= Payments for financing	
(32)	+ ΔShort-term Bank Debt	Level of short-term bank debt and working capital needs, long-term debt, capital expenditures, and capital structure decisions
(33)	+ ΔLT debt + end of period CMLTD	
(34)	+ ΔCommon and Preferred Stock	
(35)	+ ΔOther Equities and Noncurrent Liabilities	
(36)	= External Financing	
=(32)+(33)+(34)+(36)		

Cash

(37)	= Δ(Cash and Mkt. Securities)	All factors listed above
=(24)+(28)+(31)+(36)		

17

EVALUATING CONSUMER LOANS

In 1995, Lawrence B. Lindsey, a member of the Federal Reserve Board of Governors that oversees monetary policy in the United States and regulates banks, applied for a Toys 'R' Us credit card. He was 41 years old, earned $121,100 annually from his position with the Fed, and had no record of bad credit. When he received his letter from Bank of New York, the card issuer, he was surprised to read "We have received your new account application. We regret that we are not able to approve it at this time."[1]

Why was a Fed governor with a clean credit record denied a basic credit card? The answer lies in one of the popular methods of evaluating the risk of consumer loans, credit scoring. The application was mechanically graded and given a numerical score using characteristics regarding Lindsey's financial and work history. The denial was based on the fact that "multiple companies requested your credit report in the past six months." Statistical analysis of prior good and bad loans had demonstrated that applicants with seven or eight voluntary credit bureau inquiries over this time interval initiated by the prospective borrower are three times as risky as the average applicant and six times as risky as applicants who have no inquiries.

Credit scoring represents one of the dominant trends in consumer lending as more lenders use statistical models to predict which individuals are good and bad credit risks. Another trend is the rapid consolidation of the credit card business with fewer card issuers controlling an increasing share of credit card receivables. At year-end 2001, for example, the 10 largest general purpose credit card issuers held over $492 billion in receivables, or approximately 85 percent of all credit card loans. A third trend is the move to subprime lending, where banks court the business of higher risk individuals. It is popular because banks credit score these loans and thus feel comfortable pricing them at much higher rates than prime loans. Because loans are credit scored, there is a standardized way of making

---

[1]Information and quotes are from "A Man Who Governs Credit Is Denied a Toys 'R' Us Card." *Wall Street Journal* (December 14, 1995).

loan decisions that is understood by investors. Thus, firms that originate the loans can securitize them and transfer the credit risk to investors in the securities.

Lenders, ranging from credit unions to investment banks and finance companies, compete aggressively with commercial banks for consumer credit. In part, this reflects the extraordinary profitability of most consumer loans during the 1980s and 1990s. It also reflects the attraction of relatively low-cost, stable consumer deposits. This chapter analyzes the characteristics and profitability of different types of consumer loans and introduces general credit evaluation techniques to assess risk. In doing so, it demonstrates why consumer banking relationships are attractive to banks.

For many years, banks viewed consumer loans with skepticism. Commercial loans were available in large volume, net yields were high, and the loans were highly visible investments. Consumer loans, in contrast, involved small dollar amounts, a large staff to handle accounts, and there was less prestige associated with lending to individuals. This perception changed with the decline in profitability of commercial loans. In recent years, competition among lenders has lowered spreads on commercial loans to where potential profits are small relative to credit risk. Most states no longer have effective usury ceilings on consumer loans so that lenders have increased interest rates and risk-adjusted returns have exceeded those on commercial loans. Even with high relative default rates, consumer loans in the aggregate currently produce greater percentage profits than commercial loans.

Today, many banks target individuals as the primary source of growth in attracting new business. This reflects the attraction of consumer deposits as well as consumer loans. Interest rate deregulation forced banks to pay market rates on virtually all their liabilities. Corporate cash managers, who are especially price sensitive, routinely move their balances in search of higher yields. Individuals' balances are much more stable largely because they are federally insured up to $100,000 per account. Although individuals are price sensitive, a bank can generally retain deposits by varying rates offered on different maturity time deposits to meet the customer's needs. Consumers also hold substantial demand deposits and NOW accounts that are relatively inexpensive to the bank and normally are not held to meet compensating balance requirements. A consumer who maintains a deposit relationship and borrows from the same institution is typically quite loyal.

From a lender's perspective, the analysis of consumer loans differs from that of commercial loans. First, the quality of financial data is lower. Personal financial statements are typically unaudited so that it is easy for borrowers to hide other loans. It is similarly easy to inflate asset values. Second, the primary source of repayment is current income, primarily from wages, salaries, dividends, and interest. This may be highly volatile depending on the nature of the individual's work experience and history. The net effect is that character is more difficult to assess, but extremely important.

TYPES OF CONSUMER LOANS

When evaluating the measurable aspects of consumer loan requests, an analyst addresses the same issues discussed with commercial loans: the character of the borrower, the use of loan proceeds, the amount needed, and the primary and secondary source of repayment. However, consumer loans differ so much in design that no comprehensive analytical format applies to all loans. With credit cards, for example, a bank does not know what the loan proceeds will be used for or how much the customer will borrow at any point in time. In contrast, a boat loan with fixed installment payments has a maximum borrowing amount and regular repayment schedule. Credit analysis thus differs across loan types. Many banks mass market their credit cards knowing that losses will increase but hoping to price this risk accordingly and to attract enough affluent customers to offset charge-offs. There is no formal analysis of individual borrower characteristics unless the lender uses a credit scoring model. In contrast, lenders treat installment loans made directly in negotiation with the borrower much like commercial loans. Each facet of the credit request, such as estimating discretionary income (cash flow) relative to debt service requirements is evaluated similarly to commercial loans.

As discussed in Chapter 15, consumer loans can be classified into one of three types: installment loans, credit cards or revolving credit lines, and noninstallment loans. Each type requires a different approach for credit analysis and provides different answers to the fundamental credit issues.

INSTALLMENT LOANS

Installment loans require the periodic payment of principal and interest. In most cases, a customer borrows to purchase durable goods or cover extraordinary expenses and agrees to repay the loan in monthly installments.[2] Although the average dollar amount of the loan is quite small, some may be much larger, depending on the use of the proceeds. It is not unusual, for example, to see loans for aircraft, boats, and personal investments exceed $250,000. The typical maturity ranges from two to five years. Except for revolving credit, most consumer loans are secured.

Installment loans may be either direct or indirect loans. A *direct loan* is negotiated between the bank and ultimate user of the funds. An individual who borrows from a bank to finance an automobile must formally request credit and provide supporting personal financial information. The loan officer analyzes the information and approves or rejects the request. An *indirect loan* is funded by a bank through a separate retailer that sells merchandise to a customer. The retailer, such as an automobile dealer, takes the credit application, negotiates terms with the individual, and presents the agreement to the bank. If the bank approves the loan, it buys the loan from the retailer under prearranged terms. Automobile loans exceed any other type of installment loans at banks, followed by revolving credit and mobile home loans. Approximately 60 percent of automobile loans are indirect loans purchased from dealers. The figure for indirect mobile home loans is considerably higher.

REVENUES AND COSTS FROM INSTALLMENT CREDIT. Installment loans can be extremely profitable. Exhibit 17.1 summarizes revenue and cost data for different-sized banks from the Federal Reserve's 1999 *Functional Cost Analysis*. In 1999, the average size of a loan was between $5,104 and $5,448, depending on the size of the bank, and it cost from $85 to $202 to originate each installment loan with electronic loan costs the lowest for larger banks. Origination costs include salaries, occupancy, computer, and marketing expenses associated with soliciting, approving, and processing loan applications. It also cost from $17 to $22 to collect payments, and the bank charged off an average of $27 to $31 per loan per month.

Even though these costs are high, banks were able to earn reasonable spreads on the average loan. Loan income, for example, ranged from 9.35 percent to 10.11 percent of the outstanding loan. After subtracting acquisition costs, collection costs, and net charge-offs, the net yield ranged from 5.01 percent for the smaller banks to 5.25 percent for banks with more than

---

[2]Credit card loans and overdraft lines are formally installment loans because they require periodic monthly payments. They are discussed separately because their other features differ widely from other installment loans.

▪ EXHIBIT 17.1

COSTS AND RETURNS ON CONSUMER INSTALLMENT LOANS:
FUNCTIONAL COST ANALYSIS DATA FOR 1999

	Deposit Size (Millions of Dollars)	
	<$200	>$200
Data		
Average size of loan	$5,104	$5,448
Average number of loans	1,146	6,729
Number of banks surveyed	70	49
Costs per Loan		
Cost to make a loan:		
Electronic	$202.42	$84.56
Nonelectronic	152.17	137.49
Cost to maintain a loan (monthly)		
Electronic	$19.21	$16.96
Nonelectronic	21.74	20.07
Loan loss (average size loan)	27.05	31.05
Total	$422.59	$290.13
As a Percent of Total Loans Outstanding		
Loan income*	10.11%	9.35%
Expenses		
Direct	3.60	2.83
Net indirect	0.97	0.70
Loan loss rate (3-year average)	0.53	0.57
Total	5.10	4.10
Net yield	5.01	5.25
Cost of funds	3.28	3.31
Net spread	1.73%	1.94%

*Includes installment plus noninterest income.

$200 million in deposits. Because the average cost of financing the loans averaged around 3.3 percent, the net spread ranged from 1.73 percent to 1.94 percent, depending on the size of the bank. Anything over 1 percent exceeds historical norms, and thus the average consumer installment loan was very profitable in 1999 for all the sample banks.

CREDIT CARDS AND OTHER REVOLVING CREDIT. Credit cards and overlines tied to checking accounts are the two most popular forms of revolving credit agreements. In 2001, consumers charged almost $650 billion on credit cards. Many pay only a fraction of their monthly bill and thus incur finance charges on the remainder. Thomas Durkin reported that 35 percent of card users hardly ever paid their outstanding balance in full each month.[3] Credit lines against demand deposit accounts at banks are less common but function identically to credit cards. Customers can write checks in excess of actual balances held but must pay interest on the overdraft, usually against lump sums at $50 or $100 increments.

Banks offer a variety of credit cards. Although some banks issue cards with their own logo and supported by their own marketing effort, most operate as franchises of MasterCard or

---

[3]See "Credit Cards: Use and Consumer Attitudes, 1970–2000," Federal Reserve Bulletin, September 2000.

DEBIT CARDS, SMART CARDS, AND PREPAID CARDS

Banks throughout the world are investing in technologies that promote *debit cards, smart cards,* and *prepaid cards.* Debit cards are widely available and becoming increasingly attractive to consumers. As the name suggests, when an individual uses the card his or her balance at a bank is immediately debited; that is, funds are instantaneously transferred from the card user's account to the account of the retailer. The obvious disadvantage to a consumer is the loss of float. Some retailers also charge fees when a customer uses a debit card. Banks prefer that customers use debit cards over checks because they have lower processing costs compared with checks and ATM transactions.

A smart card is an extension of the debit and credit cards that contains a computer memory chip that stores and manipulates information. Such a chip can store more than 500 times the data of a magnetic-stripe credit or debit card. When inserted in a terminal, the cardholder can pay for goods and services, dial the telephone, make airline arrangements, and authorize currency exchanges. It is programmable so users can store information regarding their complete financial history, and recall this information when effecting transactions. These electronic checkbooks can effectively handle virtually all purchasing that consumers prefer. Although smart cards are very popular in Europe and Japan, they have only modestly penetrated the United States with just 2 percent of worldwide usage. This largely reflects the U.S. consumer's satisfaction with existing technology and banks' unwillingness to invest in the computer terminals necessary to process transactions.

There are several reasons why smart card usage will likely take off in the United States in the near future. First, firms can offer a much wider range of services. This provides greater sources of noninterest income. Second, smart cards represent a link between the Internet and real economic activity. Smart cards are an alternative to digital money, or E-cash, used to buy items via the Internet with security advantages to the user. Finally, suppliers of smart cards are standardizing the formats so that all cards work on the same systems.

Prepaid cards are a hybrid of debit cards in which customers prepay for services to be rendered and receive a card against which purchases are charged. The subway system in Washington, D.C., for example, lets customers prepay for access cards, then use the cards to pay for subway rides. Many universities and businesses, in turn, let students and employees prepay for books and meals then charge their purchases against the card. The primary advantage to the bank is that processing costs are low and there is little risk of loss.

Visa. To become part of either group's system, a bank must pay a one-time membership fee plus an annual charge determined by the number of its customers actively using the cards. MasterCard and Visa, in turn, handle the national marketing effort. All cards prominently display the MasterCard and Visa logos with the issuing bank's name. Recently, both MasterCard and Visa have allowed banks to increase the size of the bank's name and reduce the size of the logo to emphasize which bank actually issues the card. The primary advantage of membership is that an individual bank's card is accepted nationally and internationally at most retail stores without each bank negotiating a separate agreement with every retailer. While U.S. banks have pushed consumers to use debit cards, they have not been aggressive in developing alternatives like the smart card, which is currently dominated by foreign competitors. (See Contemporary Issues: Debit Cards, Smart Cards, and Prepaid Cards.)

Credit cards are attractive because they typically provide higher risk-adjusted returns than other types of loans. Card issuers earn income from three sources: charging cardholders fees, charging interest on outstanding loan balances, and discounting the charges that merchants accept on purchases. In 2001, annual fees to maintain an account averaged almost $15 per account, annual interest rates averaged around 10 percent, and the discount to merchants ranged from 2 to 5 percent. Even though other interest rates may fall, credit card rates are notoriously sticky. Thus, the spread between the rate charged and a bank's cost of funds widens. This has generated criticism that banks use credit cards to gouge customers. In fact, as banks have increased their focus they have begun to lower loan rates and annual fees such that many customers can avoid fees entirely and pay interest at rates 1 to 4 percent above the Wall Street prime rate. Still, in order to generate more revenue, card issuers have been raising late-payment fees, when they do not receive the monthly payment by the due date, to around $28 per month.

Credit card lending involves issuing plastic cards to qualifying customers. The cards have preauthorized credit limits that restrict the maximum amount of debt outstanding at any time. An individual can use the card to purchase goods and services from any merchant that accepts the card. Thus, the individual determines the timing and amount of actual borrowing. Many cards can be used in electronic banking devices, such as automatic teller machines, and to make deposits or withdrawals from existing transactions accounts at a bank.

The recent regulatory and competitive environment has made credit cards extremely attractive. Many banks view credit cards as a vehicle to generate a nationwide customer base. They offer extraordinary incentives to induce consumers to accept cards in the hope that they can cross-sell mortgages, insurance products, and eventually securities. Some banks also use the card relationship to solicit money market deposits or small CDs. Credit cards are profitable because many customers are price insensitive. Most banks charge annual user fees, and credit card interest rates are among the highest rates quoted. Still, many borrowers look primarily at the minimum monthly payment required rather than the quoted interest rate. People simply like the convenience of buying goods whenever they wish, and many believe that the periodic interest is too small to give up the spending convenience.

One negative with credit cards is that losses are among the highest of all loan types. Fraud is prevalent, and many individuals eventually default on their debts because their incomes do not cover their spending habits. The data in Exhibit 17.2 document recent trends in charge-off rates on credit cards that banks keep on their books and the number of personal bankruptcy filings. Note the increase in both charge-offs and the number of personal bankruptcies during the recession in 1990–1991. The surprising trend is the sharp increase in both measures after 1994. This occurred during a strong period of growth in the U.S. economy when loan quality typically improves and more people are working and in relatively strong financial condition. Many analysts believe that individuals' access to credit card debt is too easy and that culturally, the stigmatism associated with filing for bankruptcy has been largely eliminated. Credit cards represent a low-cost way to start over. Not surprisingly, both credit card losses and personal bankruptcies increased in 2001, when the U.S. economy fell into recession and Congress attempted to tighten existing bankruptcy laws.

Interestingly, the charge-off data are even worse when loss rates on securitized credit card loans are recognized. Securitized credit cards account for approximately 40 percent of all credit card debt, and according to Moodys, charge-off rates are around 1.5 percent higher. Also, the data are potentially misleading because there are no industry standards regarding when to recognize a loss. Legally, lenders can wait up to 209 days after an account is bankrupt to charge it off. Some lenders charge off bankrupt accounts immediately while others wait the maximum 209 days.

CREDIT CARD SYSTEMS AND PROFITABILITY. The returns to credit card lending depend on the specific roles that a bank plays. According to Federal Reserve classifications, a bank is called a card bank if it administers its own credit card plan or serves as the primary regional agent of a major credit card operation, such as Visa or MasterCard. In contrast, a noncard bank operates under the auspices of a regional card bank and does not issue its own card. Noncard banks do not generate significant revenues from credit cards.

The types of revenues available are described in Exhibit 17.3, which summarizes the clearing process for a credit card transaction. Once a customer uses a card, the retail outlet submits the sales receipt to its local merchant bank for credit. A retailer may physically deposit

U.S. CREDIT CARD LOSS RATES AND PERSONAL BANKRUPTCY FILINGS, 1984–2001

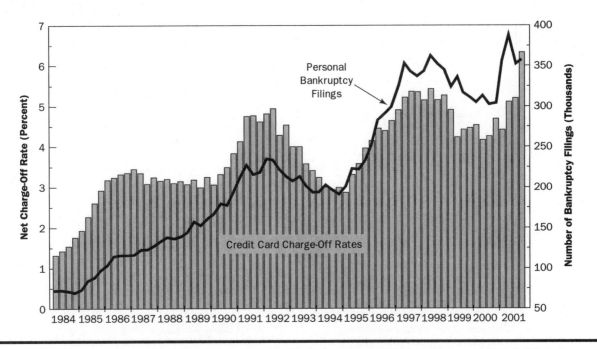

SOURCES: Bankruptcies — Administrative Office of the United States Courts. Charge-Off Rates—Commercial Bank Call Reports. Diagram from FDIC Quarterly Banking Profile, Third Quarter, 2001 www.FDIC.GOV./DATABANK.

the slip or electronically transfer the information via a card-reading terminal at the time of sale. The merchant bank discounts the sales receipt by 2 to 5 percent as its fee. Thus, a retailer will receive only $97 credit for each $100 sales receipt if the discount is 3 percent. If a merchant bank did not issue the card, it sends the receipt to the card-issuing bank through a clearing network, paying an interchange fee. The card-issuing bank then bills the customer for the purchase. Most card revenues come from issuing the card that a customer uses. The bank earns interest at rates ranging from 2.9 percent to 22 percent and normally charges each individual an annual fee for use of the card. As mentioned earlier, interest rates are sticky. When money market rates decline and lower a bank's cost of funds, the net return on credit card loans increases because credit card rates do not fall coincidentally. Interest income and annual fees comprise approximately 80 percent of credit card revenues. The remaining 20 percent are merchant discounts.

OVERDRAFT PROTECTION AND OPEN CREDIT LINES. Revolving credit also takes the form of overdraft protection against checking accounts. A bank authorizes qualifying individuals to write checks in excess of actual balances held in a checking account up to a pre-specified limit. The customer must pay interest on the loan from the date of the draft's receipt and can repay the loan either by making direct deposits or by periodic payments. One relatively recent innovation is to offer open credit lines to affluent individuals whether or not they have an existing account relationship. These loans are the functional equivalent of loan commitments to commercial customers. In most instances, the bank provides customers with special checks that activate a loan when presented for payment. The maximum credit available typically exceeds that for overdraft lines, and the interest rate floats with the bank's base rate.

■ **EXHIBIT 17.3**

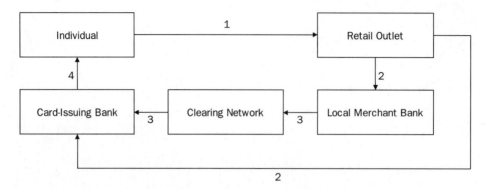

Steps	Fees
1. Individual uses a credit card to purchase merchandise from a retail outlet.	1. None
2. Retail outlet deposits the sales slip or electronically transmits the purchase data at its local bank.	2. The merchant bank discounts the sales receipt. A 3 percent discount indicates the bank gives the retailer $97 in credit for each $100 receipt.
3. Local merchant bank forwards the transaction information to a clearing network, which routes the data to the bank that issued the credit card to the individual.	3. The card-issuing bank charges the merchant bank an interchange fee equal to 1 to 1.5 percent of the transaction amount for each item handled.
4. The card-issuing bank sends the individual an itemized bill for all purchases.	4. The card-issuing bank charges the customer interest and an annual fee for the privilege of using the card. A card-issuing bank also serves as a merchant bank.

SOURCE: Michael Weinstein, "Credit Card Business Mushrooms at Large Banks." *American Banker* (August 14, 1986).

HOME EQUITY LOANS AND CREDIT CARDS. Home equity loans grew from virtually nothing in the mid-1980s to over $220 billion in 2001, spurred by the Tax Reform Act of 1986, which limited deductions for consumer loan interest paid by individuals unless the loan was real estate related. Home equity loans meet the tax deductibility requirements (with some limits) because they are secured by equity in an individual's home. The bulk of these loans are structured as open credit lines where a consumer can borrow up to 75 percent of the market value of the property less the principal outstanding on the first mortgage. Individuals borrow simply by writing checks, pay interest only on the amount borrowed, pay 1 to 2 percent of the outstanding principal each month and can repay the remaining principal at their discretion. In most cases, the loans carry adjustable rates tied to the bank's base rate.

The Tax Reform Act of 1986 accelerated the use of home equity loans by eliminating the deductibility of interest paid on traditional consumer debt, such as credit cards and car loans, but retaining the deductibility of interest on debt secured by the equity in an individual's home. Many banks subsequently introduced home equity credit lines that, in some cases, can be accessed by using a credit card. Because consumers can take out only one such loan, the lender that initiates the credit relationship has locked in a long-term customer.

These credit arrangements combine the risks of a second mortgage with the temptation of a credit card, a potentially dangerous combination. Home equity loans place a second lien on a borrower's home. If the individual defaults, the creditor can foreclose so that the borrower loses his or her home. Still, ready access to the financing through credit cards encourages consumers to spend and ultimately take on too much debt. Federal Reserve studies have generally shown that consumers borrow primarily to improve their existing home, consolidate debts, or finance a child's college education. In either case, the typical home equity loan represents a large initial borrowing that is paid down over several years.

In order to attract customers, many banks price these loans at prime or just 1 to 2 percent over prime, which is well below other consumer loan rates. Some require only interest payments during the first few years. Low rates have been justified by historically low losses and good collateral, which is a home. Of course, delinquency rates increase during economic downturns when real estate values often decline. In addition, there is always the risk that customers will borrow the maximum, especially under credit card arrangements, for short-run lifestyle expenses. If they take on too much debt and interest rates increase or housing values decline, many borrowers may default and lenders will see losses increase.

NONINSTALLMENT LOANS

A limited number of consumer loans require a single principal and interest payment. Typically, the individual's borrowing needs are temporary. Credit is extended in anticipation of repayment from a well-defined future cash inflow. Bridge loans are representative of single payment consumer loans. Bridge loans often arise when an individual borrows funds for the down payment on a new house. The loan is repaid when the borrower sells an existing home, hence the term bridge. The quality of the loan depends on the certainty of the timing and amount of the anticipated net cash inflow from the sale.

SUBPRIME LOANS

Many lenders long ago recognized that they could earn high risk-adjusted returns by lending to riskier borrowers. Large bank holding companies and firms like GE Capital have bought consumer finance subsidiaries that make loans to individuals that a bank would not traditionally make and keep on balance sheet. Of course, subprime lenders charge higher rates and have more restrictive covenants.

During the 1990s, one of the hottest growth areas was subprime lending. These higher-risk loans were labeled "B," "C," and "D" credits, and were especially popular in auto, home equity, and mortgage lending. These are the same risk loans as those originated through consumer finance companies. Although no precise definitions exist, "B," "C," and "D" credits exhibit increasingly greater risk and must be priced consistently higher than prime-grade loans. Paul Finfer of Franklin Acceptance Corp., a subprime auto lender, provided the following definitions:[4]

> B: Typically, scores 600+ under the Fair Isaac credit scoring system (FICO); has some 90-day past dues but is now current. When extended credit, delinquencies are 2–5 percent; repossessions are 2.5–6 percent; and losses are 1.5–3 percent.

---

[4]Definitions appear in Cocheo, Steve. "Give Me Your Delinquents, Your Former Bankrupts, Yearning to Borrow." *ABA Banking Journal* (August 1996).

C: Typically scores between 500 and 600 under the Fair Isaac System and has had write-offs and judgments. The borrower has made subsequent payments of some or all of the loans. When extended credit, delinquencies are 5–10 percent; repos are 5–20 percent; and losses are 3–10 percent.

D: Typically scores between 440 and 500 under the Fair Isaac System; has charge-offs and judgments that have not been repaid; and has not made payments on these loans. When extended credit, delinquencies are 10–20 percent; repos are 16–40 percent; losses are 10–20 percent.

Finfer stated that "this is not a business for the faint of heart." As might be expected, many of these loans are "story loans." In other words, a lender must listen to the applicant's story to assess whether past problems reflect a one-time problem or represent a willingness to walk away from debt.

During the latter half of the 1990s and early 2000s, many lenders upped the stakes by making "high LTV" (loan-to-value) loans based on the equity in a borrower's home. Where traditional home equity loans are capped at 75 percent of appraised value minus the outstanding principal balance, high LTV loans equal as much as 125 percent of the value of a home. For example, suppose that an individual owned a home worth $100,000 and owed $85,000 on the first mortgage. A lender would be willing to lend another $40,000 (1.25 times $100,000, minus $85,000). The loan rate is typically set between the prevailing first mortgage rate and a base credit card rate to make the loan attractive to the borrower. The marketing efforts focus on getting borrowers to use these loans to consolidate their debt and lower their monthly payments. The risk is that default leaves the lender exposed to the amount in excess of the home's (collateral's) true value after expenses. What makes this a lucrative business is that many investment banks buy these loans and securitize them. Originators can earn from 4 to 8 percent origination fees.

CONSUMER CREDIT REGULATIONS

The federal government has approved a wide range of regulations to protect individuals when obtaining credit. Most of the regulations address discrimination, billing practices, customer liability, and the proper disclosure of finance charges and reasons for denying credit. The need for such regulation arose from abuses of the credit system. At one time, many lenders refused to extend credit to women who did not have a personal credit record because loans were credited to a husband. Loans were sometimes denied because of the borrower's race or age. Lenders would refuse to extend credit in deteriorating neighborhoods and made it difficult for borrowers to determine the effective cost of credit. This section discusses several important regulations that addressed these abuses.

EQUAL CREDIT OPPORTUNITY

Ideally, credit will be available to any borrower who satisfies acceptable risk criteria. To ensure this, Congress passed the Equal Credit Opportunity Act (ECOA), which makes it illegal for lenders to discriminate against potential borrowers because of race, religion, sex, marital status, age, or national origin. The Federal Reserve's Regulation B specifies conditions that must be met in structuring credit applications and establishing creditworthiness. In doing so, it focuses on three different aspects of credit transactions. First, it indicates what information a creditor may not request. Implicitly, this information is not relevant to the credit evaluation and would, if available, be used primarily to discriminate. Second, it specifies how certain information can be used in credit scoring systems. Credit scoring models are discussed later in the chapter. Finally, it provides for proper credit reporting. For example, lenders must include spouses in the credit records whenever a spouse is jointly liable for any debts. Lenders must also notify applicants of adverse action on a loan within 30 days of the request. The following list identifies specific items that are prohibited or required.

PROHIBITED INFORMATION REQUESTS

1. Lenders may not request information about the applicant's marital status unless credit is being requested jointly, the spouse's assets will be used to repay the loan, or the applicant lives in a community property state.[5] This popularized the term *cohabitant* on many application forms.

2. Lenders may not request information about whether alimony, child support, and public assistance payments are included in an applicant's reported income. Applicants can voluntarily provide this information if they believe it will improve perceived creditworthiness.

3. Lenders may not request information about a woman's childbearing capability and plans, or birth control practices.

4. Lenders may not request information about whether an applicant has a telephone.

CREDIT SCORING SYSTEMS

1. Credit scoring systems are acceptable if they do not require prohibited information and are statistically justified. The statistical soundness should be systematically reviewed and updated.

2. Credit scoring systems can use information about age, sex, and marital status as long as these factors contribute positively to the applicant's creditworthiness.

CREDIT REPORTING

1. Lenders must report credit extended jointly to married couples in both spouses' names. This enables both individuals to build a credit history.

2. Whenever lenders reject a loan, they must notify applicants of the credit denial within 30 days and indicate why the request was turned down. An applicant may request written notification, and the lender must comply.

In practice, the ECOA includes many complex provisions that are difficult to comprehend. To make compliance easier, the Federal Reserve provides model loan application forms that conform to Regulation B.

TRUTH IN LENDING

The intent underlying truth in lending legislation is for lenders to disclose consumer loan finance charges and interest rates in a standardized format. This enables borrowers to compare credit terms and the cost of credit between loans and between lenders. Truth in lending

---

[5]In community property states, couples own assets jointly. Assets listed on an application are often only partly owned by a married applicant, which would restrict a lender's access to collateral.

regulations apply to all loans up to $25,000 extended to individuals, where the borrower's primary residence does not serve as collateral.[6]

Legislation arose because lenders quoted interest rates in many different ways and often included supplemental charges in a loan that substantially increased the actual cost. Consumers could not easily determine how much they were paying and what the effective interest rate was on a loan. This confused borrowers and potentially led to inferior credit decisions.

Historically, consumer loan rates were quoted as add-on rates, discount rates, or simple interest rates. **Add-on rates** are applied against the entire principal of installment loans. The gross interest is added to the principal with the total divided by the number of periodic payments to determine the size of each payment. For example, suppose that a customer borrows $3,000 for one year at a 12 percent add-on rate with the loan to be repaid in 12 equal monthly installments. Total interest equals $360, the monthly payment equals $280, and the effective annual interest cost is approximately 21.5 percent. Exhibit 17.4 presents these calculations and similar ones for discount rate and simple interest examples.

With the **discount rate** method, the quoted rate is applied against the sum of principal and interest, yet the borrower gets to use only the principal, as interest is immediately deducted from the total loan. Exhibit 17.4 considers a 1-year loan with a single $3,000 payment at maturity. The borrower receives only $2,640, or the total loan minus 12 percent discount rate interest. The effective annual percentage rate, or APR, equals 13.64 percent. The bottom part of Exhibit 17.4 demonstrates simple interest calculations. **Simple interest** is interest paid on only the principal sum. A $3,000 loan at 12 percent simple interest per year produces $360 in interest, or a 12 percent effective rate. At the bottom of the exhibit, the quoted rate is adjusted to its monthly equivalent, which is applied against the unpaid principal balance on a loan. A $3,000 loan, repaid in 12 monthly installments at 1 percent monthly simple interest, produces interest under $200. The monthly interest rate equals 1 percent of the outstanding principal balance at each interval. Depending on how it is quoted, a 12 percent rate exhibits a noticeably different effective rate, ranging from 12 percent to 21.5 percent in the examples.

Truth in lending legislation requires that lenders disclose to potential borrowers both the total finance charge and an annual percentage rate (APR). The **total finance charge** equals the dollar amount of interest costs plus all supplemental charges that are imposed as part of a loan, including loan origination fees, service charges, and insurance premiums if the lender demands the customer take out a policy as part of the agreement. The **annual percentage rate** (APR) equals the total finance charge computed against the loan balance as a simple annual interest rate equivalent.

The regulations also stipulate that advertisements must include all relevant terms of a loan if any single payment or pricing feature is mentioned. These terms include the finance charge, APR, the dollar magnitude of any down payment requirement, the number of payments, and final maturity. This prevents a lender from using one very attractive feature, such as no required down payment, to lure customers without disclosing all terms. Assuming the borrower does not pay additional fees, the effective interest rates in Exhibit 17.4 are APRs.

FAIR CREDIT REPORTING

Lenders can obtain information on an individual's prior credit relationships from local credit bureaus when evaluating consumer loan requests. The Fair Credit Reporting Act enables

---

[6]The Truth in Lending Act, passed in 1968, is implemented through the Federal Reserve's Regulation Z. Originally, it applied to agriculture loans as well as personal credit, but in 1980, Congress exempted agriculture from the reporting requirements.

▪ EXHIBIT 17.4

Add-On Rate
$3,000 loan for 1 year, 12% add-on rate, repaid in 12 equal monthly installments
Interest charge: $360

$$\text{Monthly payment: } \frac{[0.12(\$3,000) + \$3,000]}{12} = \frac{\$3,360}{12} = \$280$$

$$\text{Effective interest rate (i): } \sum_{t=1}^{12} \frac{\$280}{(\$1+i)^t} = \$3,000$$

$$i = 1.796\%$$

Annual percentage rate (APR) = 21.55%

Discount Rate
$3,000 to be repaid at the end of 1 year, 12% discount rate

Interest charge: 0.12($3,000) = $360
Year-end payment: $3,000

$$\text{Annual percentage rate (APR) } (i_n)\text{: } \$2,640 = \frac{\$3,000}{(1 + i_n)}$$

$$i_n = 13.64\%$$

Simple Interest Rate
$3,000 loan for 1 year, 12% simple interest, repaid at end of year in one payment

$$\text{Interest } (i_s)\text{: } = \$3,000(0.12)(1) = \$360$$

$$\$3,000 = \frac{\$3,360}{(1 + i_s)}$$

$$i_s = 12\%$$

$3,000 loan for 1 year, 1% monthly simple interest rate, repaid in 12 equal monthly installments

Repayment Schedule

End of Month	Monthly Payment	Interest Portion	Principal	Outstanding Principal Balance
January	$ 266.55	$ 30.00	$ 236.55	$2,763.45
February	266.55	27.63	238.92	2,524.53
March	266.55	25.25	241.30	2,283.23
April	266.55	22.83	243.72	2,039.51
May	266.55	20.40	246.15	1,793.36
June	266.55	17.93	248.62	1,544.74
July	266.55	15.45	251.10	1,293.64
August	266.55	12.94	253.61	1,040.03
September	266.55	10.40	256.15	783.88
October	266.55	7.84	258.71	525.17
November	266.55	5.25	261.30	263.87
December	266.51	2.64	263.87	0.00
Total	$3,198.56	$198.56	$3,000.00	

Effective interest rate: Monthly rate = 1%
Annual percentage rate (APR) = 12%

$$\text{Monthly payment} = \$3,000 / \sum_{i=1}^{12} \frac{1}{(1.01)^t}$$

individuals to examine their credit reports provided by credit bureaus. If any information is incorrect, the individual can have the bureau make changes and notify all lenders who obtained the inaccurate data. If the accuracy of the information is disputed, an individual can permanently enter into the credit file his or her interpretation of the error. The credit bureau, when requested, must also notify an individual which lenders have received credit reports.

CONTEMPORARY ISSUES

ERRORS IN CREDIT REPORTING

Garbage in, garbage out is a fair description of the information contained in many individuals' credit reports. Credit bureaus, such as Equifax, Experian, and Trans Union, process millions of credit reports to financial institutions and retailers each month without spending much effort to verify the accuracy of the data. Thus, there is a surprisingly high probability that there are errors in a credit report.

In 1991, National Data Retrieval, a firm that collects data used to construct individuals' credit histories, hired Margaret Herr and her son to collect information from public records for residents in the town of Norwich, Vermont. The firm paid them 25 cents per name for information collected regarding who was delinquent in their local property tax payments. Herr and her son, who received virtually no training, misread the tax records by identifying those who had paid their taxes as those who were delinquent. When they passed the information on to TRW (now Experian), virtually all of Norwich's 1,500 residents were designated as having been delinquent on their taxes and thus found their credit records damaged. The town clerk notified TRW, but got no response. Only after the state of Vermont sued TRW were the credit reports corrected.

SOURCE: Peter Kuper, "Garbage Out," *Smart Money* (October 1996).

There are three primary credit reporting agencies: Equifax, Experian, and Trans Union. Unfortunately, the credit reports that they produce are quite often wrong. In 1996, Trans Union reported that 50 percent of the 2.5 million individuals who requested a copy of their credit report disputed or questioned part of the reported credit history. One problem is that these credit bureaus make little effort to verify the information they receive from retailers, banks, and finance companies. Consider the problems of Norwich, Vermont, residents in 1991. (See Contemporary Issues: Errors in Credit Reporting.) In addition, the credit bureaus do not rush to correct their record when errors are found. A study by the U.S. Public Interest Research Group determined that consumers spent an average of 32 weeks after initial contact negotiating with credit bureaus to get incorrect information removed, before they contacted federal officials.

Exhibit 17.5 provides a sample credit report for a hypothetical John Doe. It lists the names of companies that provide credit, the account numbers, the type of credit — whether it is for an individual, joint account, and so on — how many months of activity are reviewed, the date of the last activity, the highest amount charged over the time period or the maximum amount of credit available, and the key items as of the date reported. This section indicates the balance outstanding at the time of the report, the status of the account, such as how long it is past due or whether it is delinquent or a charged-off account, and the reporting date. Lenders are especially interested in this part of the borrower's credit history as it indicates the historical record of payment and a borrower's propensity to be late or not pay. Just below this is a summary of the number of times the applicant was past due and the date of the most recent delinquencies and their severity. The courthouse record similarly indicates whether the applicant has declared bankruptcy or whether any liens or judgments have been filed against him or her. Finally, the bottom indicates the companies that have requested the applicant's credit history and the dates of inquiry. Too many voluntary inquiries, where the applicant requests a credit card, often indicate a high risk credit.[7]

---

[7]Individuals can readily obtain a copy of their personal credit report over the Internet. They can also find descriptions as to how to read a credit report and improve their credit score. See http://www.myvesta.com and http://www.fairisaac.com.

· EXHIBIT 17.5

Please address all future
correspondence to the address
shown on the right

CREDIT REPORTING OFFICE
BUSINESS ADDRESS
CITY, STATE 00000
PHONE NUMBER

JOHN DOE
123 HOME STATE
CITY, STATE 00000

DATE 06/04/93
SOCIAL SECURITY NUMBER 123-45-6789
DATE OF BIRTH 04/19/57
SPOUSE JANE

CREDIT HISTORY

What it tells you

If this was your credit report, this is what this line of information would tell you:
You have an individual account with Citibank that was opened in November of
1991. It was last used in November of 1995 and the balance is paid in full.

B	C	D	E	F	G	H	I	Items as of Date Reported			M
Company Name	Account Number	Whose Acct.	Date Opened	Months Reviewed	Date of Last Activity	High Credit	Terms	Balance	Past Due	Status	Date Reported
SEARS	11251514	J	05/91	66	10/96	3500		0		R1	12/97
CITIBANK	12345678901236578	I	11/91	48	11/95	9388	48M	0		I1	11/97
AMEX	123456789070	A	06/92	24	10/96	500		0		O1	12/97
CHASE	1234567	I	05/90	48	10/96	5000	340	3000	680	R3	12/97

>>> PRIOR PAYING HISTORY — 30(03) 60 (04) 90+(01) 08/90-R2, 02/89-R3, 10/88-R4 <<<

>>> COLLECTION REPORTED 06/91, ASSIGNED 09/90 TO PRO COLL (800) 555-1234 CLIENT-ABC
HOSPITAL; AMOUNT-$978; STAT UNPAID 06/91; BALANCE — $978 06/91; DATE OF LAST ACTIVITY
09/90; INDIVIDUAL; ACCOUNT NUMBER 123456789B

>>>>>>>>>>>>>>>>>>>>>>>>>>> COLLECTION AGENCY TELEPHONE NUMBER(S) <<<<<<<<<<<<<<<<<<<<<<<

PRO COLL (800) 555-1234

*************************** COURTHOUSE RECORDS ***************************

>>> LIEN FILLED 03/88; FULTON CITY; CASE NUMBER — 32114; AMOUNT — $26667; CLASS — CITY/
COUNTY; PERSONAL; INDIVIDUAL; SIRCHARGED; ASSETS — $780

>>> BANKRUPTCY FILED 12/89; NORTHERN DIST CT; CASE NUMBER — 673HC12; LIABILITIES — $15787;
PERSONAL; INDIVIDUAL; DISCHARGED; ASSETS — $780

>>> JUDGEMENT FILED 07/87; FULTON CTY; CASE NUMBER-898872; DEFENDANT-JOHN DOE AMOUNT —
$8984; PLAINTIFF — ABC REAL ESTATE; SATISFIED 03/89; VERIFIED 05/90

*************************** ADDITIONAL INFORMATION ***************************

FORMER ADDRESS 456 JUPITER RD, ATLANTA, GA 30245

FORMER ADDRESS P.O. BOX 2134, SAVANNAH, GA 31406

CURRENT EMPLOYMENT ENGINEER, SPACE PATROL

*********** COMPANIES THAT REQUESTED YOUR CREDIT HISTORY ******************

05/03/93 EQUIFAX	02/12/93 MACYS
12/16/92 PRM VISA	08/01 92 AM CITIBANK
06/11/92 NATIONS BANK	04/29/92 GE CAPITAL
07/17/92 JC PENNEY	02/12/94 AR SEARS

ABC's of a credit report

A. The name and address of the office you should contact if you have any questions or disagreement with your credit report.

B. Identifies the business that is reporting the information

C. Your account number with the company reporting

D. Indicates who is responsible and type of payment participation with the account

E. Month and year account is opened with the credit grantor

F. Number of months account payment history has been reported

G. Date of last activity on the account and may be the date of last payment or the date of last change

H. Highest amount charged or the credit limit

I. Represents number of installments (M=months) or monthly payments

J. Amount owed on the account at the time it was reported

K. Indicates any amount past due at the time the information was reported

L. Status and type of account, and timeliness of payment

M. Date of last account update

N. Number of times account was either 30/60/90 days past due

O. Date two most recent delinquencies occurred plus date of most severe delinquency

COMMUNITY REINVESTMENT

The Community Reinvestment Act (CRA) was passed in 1977 to prohibit redlining and to encourage lenders to extend credit within their immediate trade area and the markets where they collect deposits. *Redlining* is the practice of not extending credit within geographic areas that are believed to be deteriorating. Its name comes from the reputed practice of outlining in red those areas of a city where a lender would automatically refuse credit because of location. It discriminates against borrowers from economically declining neighborhoods that represent the redlined areas. These areas typically represent low-income and minority neighborhoods. Community reinvestment has played an important role in the interstate banking movement. Out-of-state banks that acquire local banks must commit to continued lending in the area and not use acquired banks simply as deposit gatherers.

The Financial Institutions Reform, Recovery and Enforcement Act (FIRREA) of 1989 raised the profile of the CRA by mandating public disclosure of bank lending policies and regulatory ratings of bank compliance. Specifically, regulators now rate banks as outstanding, satisfactory, needs improvement, or in substantial noncompliance in terms of their compliance with nondiscriminatory lending practices. These ratings are publicized to put pressure on banks that are not in compliance out of fear that negative publicity will harm their image and subsequent performance. Historically, few banks have been rated as outstanding and only a very small number have been rated in substantial noncompliance. Many bankers cite these ratings in arguing that the costs of CRA compliance exceed the benefits to aggrieved consumers. Consumer groups, in contrast, argue that the regulators are too lenient in classifying banks.

Regulators must also take lending performance into account when evaluating a bank's request to charter a new bank, acquire a bank, open a branch, or merge with another institution. Consumer groups now routinely use claims of noncompliance under CRA to delay such requests, forcing the bank to demonstrate how performance will be improved. It is both good business and appropriate for every bank to comply with nondiscrimination legislation.

BANKRUPTCY REFORM

Individuals who cannot repay their debts on time can file for bankruptcy and receive court protection against creditors. Court protection takes the form of exempting selected personal assets from creditors' claims and providing for an orderly repayment of debts. In 1978 and 1985, Congress modified the Federal Bankruptcy Code. The 1978 legislation liberalized the volume and type of assets that individuals could exempt and made unsecured loans extremely risky.

Individuals can file for bankruptcy under Chapter 7 or Chapter 13. Chapter 7 authorizes individuals to liquidate qualified assets and distribute the proceeds to creditors. The 1978 Bankruptcy Reform Act specifically exempted such assets as an automobile, household furnishings, some jewelry, and a fraction of the individuals' equity in a primary residence from liquidation. In some states, exemptions are even more liberal, and individuals can take advantage of the broadest exemptions.[8] An individual must pay all taxes, alimony, and child support owed in full. Cash received from the sale of nonexempt assets is allocated to other creditors on a pro rata basis, with secured creditors paid first. Because the list of exemptions was so broad after 1978, unsecured creditors rarely received any payment. Once the cash is distributed, the remaining debts are discharged.

---

[8]The 1978 regulations actually allowed one spouse to file for bankruptcy in state court while the other filed in federal court, thereby doubling their exemptions. The 1985 provisions force a couple to file in only one jurisdiction.

Under Chapter 13, an individual works out a repayment plan with court supervision. The individual gets to keep his or her assets but commits to repay selected debts out of future earnings according to a schedule approved by all secured creditors. Once the scheduled debts are repaid, the remaining debt is discharged. Under the 1978 regulations, unsecured creditors again had no recourse and often received nothing under Chapter 13.

Reforms to the bankruptcy code in 1985 made it more costly for an individual to walk away from outstanding debt. Under Chapter 13 plans, lenders can obtain a court order that assigns a large fraction of a debtor's income to repay debt for three years after the date of filing. The reforms shortened the list of exempt assets and permitted the court to switch a Chapter 7 filing to Chapter 13 when it determined that an individual, who was financially able, was using bankruptcy simply to avoid paying all debts. Unsecured lenders were also protected by provisions that forced borrowers to repay all credit card purchases made during the three weeks prior to filing for bankruptcy.

In 1995, Congress created a bankruptcy commission that would recommend changes in bankruptcy law. By 1997, approximately 70 percent of bankruptcy filers selected Chapter 7 with the remaining 30 percent selecting Chapter 13. Clearly, many individuals used bankruptcy as a financial planning tool to get out of debt. The stigma was largely gone. This presents serious problems for lenders given recent consumer loan charge-off experience and the increase in bankruptcy filings noted in Exhibit 17.2. In March 2001, the U.S. House and Senate passed bills that would have made it more difficult for borrowers to file for bankruptcy protection. The subsequent recession and September 11 terrorist attack on the World Trade Center stopped the legislation before any compromise could be reached. Many analysts believe that the U.S. bankruptcy process is abused too frequently, with up to 10 percent of filings being fraudulent and annual losses around $4 billion. The proposed reforms would make it more difficult to file, as filers would be forced to provide details on their spending habits and would have to earn below median income in their home state to qualify for the best protection.

CREDIT ANALYSIS

The objective of consumer credit analysis is to assess the risks associated with lending to individuals. Not surprisingly, these risks differ substantially from those of commercial loans. Most consumer loans are quite small, averaging around $7,500 in 2001. Because the fixed costs of servicing consumer loans are high, banks must generate substantial loan volume to reduce unit costs. This means dealing with a large number of distinct borrowers with different personalities and financial characteristics.

When evaluating loans, bankers cite the five Cs of credit: character, capital, capacity, conditions, and collateral. The most important—yet difficult to assess—is character. A loan officer essentially must determine the customer's desire to repay a loan. The only quantitative information available is the borrower's application and credit record. If the borrower is a bank customer, the officer can examine internal information regarding the customer's historical account relationship. If the borrower is not a current customer, the officer must solicit information from local credit bureaus or other businesses that have extended credit to the individual. The ECOA stipulates what information can be required and prohibits discrimination. It also mandates how lenders must report information to the credit reporting agencies. Banks also rely heavily on subjective appraisals of the borrower's character. They normally obtain personal references, verify employment, and check the accuracy of the application. This is necessary because fraud is prevalent, and it is relatively easy for an individual to disguise past behavior. If the officer determines that a potential customer is dishonest, the loan is rejected automatically.

Capital refers to the individual's wealth position and is closely related to capacity, an individual's financial ability to meet loan payments in addition to normal living expenses and other debt obligations. For almost all consumer loans, the individual's income serves as the primary source of repayment. A loan officer projects what income will be available after other expenses and compares this with periodic principal and interest payments on the new loan. To assure adequate coverage, the lender often imposes minimum down payment requirements and maximum allowable debt-service to income ratios. The loan officer verifies that the borrower's income equals that stated on the application and assesses the stability of the income source. Conditions refers to the impact of economic events on the borrower's capacity to pay when some income sources disappear as business activity declines.

The importance of collateral is in providing a secondary source of repayment. Collateral may be the asset financed by the loan, other assets owned by the individual, or the personal guarantee of a cosigner on the loan. Collateral gives a bank another source of repayment if the borrower's income is insufficient. Normally, a loan is not approved simply because the collateral appears solid. Often the collateral disappears or deteriorates in value prior to the bank taking possession, as with a damaged or older automobile. Finally, the bankruptcy code enables individuals to protect a wide range of assets from creditors, and it may be difficult to obtain a judgment.

Two additional Cs have been added reflecting customer relationships and competition.[9] A bank's prior relationship with a customer reveals information about past credit and deposit experience that is useful in assessing willingness and ability to repay. Competition has an impact by affecting the pricing of a loan. All loans should generate positive risk-adjusted returns. However, lenders periodically react to competitive pressures by undercutting competitors' rates in order to attract new business. Still, such competition should not affect the accept/reject decision.

POLICY GUIDELINES

Consumer loans are extended for a variety of purposes. The most common purposes are for the purchase of automobiles, mobile homes, home improvement, furniture and appliances, and home equity loans. Before approving any loan, a lending officer requests information regarding the borrower's employment status, periodic income, the value of assets owned, outstanding debts, personal references, and specific terms of the expenditure that generates the loan request. The officer verifies the information and assesses the borrower's character and financial capacity to repay the loan. Because borrowers' personal and financial characteristics differ widely, most banks have formalized lending guidelines. As an example, guidelines for acceptable and unacceptable loans might appear as listed below.

ACCEPTABLE LOANS

Automobile

1. Limited to current year models or models less than five years old.

2. Made on an amortizing basis with a minimum 10 percent down payment.

3. Advances against used models should not exceed National Automobile Dealer Association loan value.

---

[9]See Larry White (1990) for a general discussion of the 7 Cs of credit.

4. New automobiles for business purposes are limited to 30-month amortization.

5. Insurance must be obtained and verified with a $250 maximum deductible.

Boat

1. Limited to current year models or models less than three years old.

2. Made on an amortizing basis with a minimum 20 percent down payment.

3. Marine survey must be obtained with large craft.

4. Insurance must be obtained and verified.

Home Improvement

1. Loans in excess of $2,500 should be secured by a lien.

2. Loans in excess of $10,000 require a property appraisal and title search.

3. A third lien position is not acceptable.

4. Bank should retain the right to cancel in all cases.

Personal — Unsecured

1. Minimum loan is $2,500.

2. Made only to deposit customers.

3. Limited to 1/12 of the applicant's annual income.

Single Payment

1. Limited to extraordinary purposes.

2. Require a verified, near-term source of repayment.

3. Insurance claims, pending estate settlements, and lawsuit settlements are not acceptable sources of repayment.

Cosigned

1. Applicant exhibits the potential to be a qualified, long-term bank customer.

2. Both the applicant and cosigner are depositors of the bank.

3. Applicant does not have an established credit history but does have the capacity to pay.

4. Cosigner has qualified credit history and the capacity to pay.

5. Cosigner is informed that the bank is relying totally on the cosigner for repayment in case of default.

Unacceptable Loans

1. Loans for speculative purposes.

2. Loans secured by a second lien, other than home improvement or home equity loans.

3. Any participation with a correspondent bank in a loan that the bank would not normally approve.

4. Accommodation loans to a poor credit risk based on the strength of the cosigner.

5. Single payment automobile or boat loans.

6. Loans secured by existing home furnishings.

7. Loans for skydiving equipment and hang gliders.

EVALUATION PROCEDURES: JUDGMENTAL AND CREDIT SCORING

Banks employ judgmental procedures and quantitative credit scoring procedures when evaluating consumer loans. In both cases, a lending officer collects information regarding the borrower's character, capacity, and collateral. With a pure judgmental analysis, the loan officer subjectively interprets the information in light of the bank's lending guidelines and accepts or rejects the loan. This assessment can often be completed shortly after receiving the loan application and visiting with the applicant. With a pure quantitative analysis, or credit scoring model, the loan officer grades the loan request according to a statistically sound model that assigns points to selected characteristics of the prospective borrower. The model tallies the points — or score — and compares the total with statistically determined accept/reject thresholds.[10] If the total exceeds the accept threshold, the officer approves the loan. If the total is below the reject threshold, the officer denies the loan. Thus, high scores signify low risk while low scores signify higher risk. A lender can specify these thresholds consistent with how much risk it is willing to accept. Typically, there is a gap between the reject and accept scores representing an inconclusive evaluation of characteristics. If the total falls within this gap, the officer makes a decision based on judgmental factors.

When developing the accept/reject scores, banks must obtain data on applicant characteristics when loans were originally requested, for both accepted and rejected loans. Actual performance on the loans is then evaluated to determine the extent to which different factors influenced the individual's ability to repay. Specifically, the analysis identifies borrower characteristics that have predictive power in determining when loans will be repaid or when borrowers will default. Good models assign high scores to a high fraction of performing loans and low scores to a high fraction of nonperforming loans. The importance of different factors is determined by the weights in the credit scoring formula. Information is generally obtained from prior loan applications and from credit bureaus. For nonmortgage consumer loans, the common borrower characteristics used include the applicant's monthly income, length of employment, outstanding debt and debt-service requirements, liquid financial asset holdings, whether the applicant owns a home or rents, the nature and number of bank accounts and relationships, the existence and frequency of prior delinquencies and/or defaults, and the number of voluntary credit inquiries. Most of these credit scoring models rely on eight to 12 factors.

Clearly, credit scoring procedures are more objective than judgmental evaluations. Credit decisions can be made quickly once the information is verified, often in less than 10 minutes when computers are used. Discrimination is largely eliminated because the ECOA does not allow credit scoring models to grade race, religion, or national origin. The benefits include lower costs if scoring and decision making are done mechanically, timely decisions, and avoidance of discrimination. The primary difficulty is that credit scoring models must be statistically verified and continually updated, which can be expensive. In fact, many small banks are precluded from developing their own models because of the high cost and a limited database.

A 1996 Federal Reserve survey of senior loan officers reported that of banks using consumer credit scoring, 82 percent used it to identify individuals from whom they would solicit applications and 97 percent used it to assess whose loan applications to approve.[11] Some

---

[10]Credit scoring systems and accept/reject scores are empirically derived from either multiple regression analysis or multiple discriminate analysis. These statistical techniques use historical data regarding a bank's good and bad consumer loans to assess what characteristics identify a high percentage of good or bad borrowers. The accept/reject scores represent the weighted value of borrowers' characteristics. Recent efforts involve using option-pricing models and neural networks to assign scores. See Loretta Mester, "What's the Point of Credit Scoring?" *Business Review* (Federal Reserve Bank of Philadelphia, September–October 1997) for a summary of these techniques.

[11]Mester (1997) provides an excellent summary of consumer and small business credit scoring models.

nonbank institutions, such as insurance companies, have also discovered that an individual's credit score can be used to identify high and low insurance risks for property-casualty (particularly automobile and medical) insurance.

AN APPLICATION: CREDIT SCORING A CONSUMER LOAN

Credit scoring models are based on historical data obtained from applicants who actually received loans.[12] Statistical techniques assign weights to various borrower characteristics that represent each factor's contribution toward distinguishing between good loans that were repaid on time and problem loans that produced losses. These weights are then used as predictors of high-risk and low-risk loans, using data from new loan applications.

The use of credit scoring models can be demonstrated with an example. Suppose that a bank officer receives a loan application for the purchase of an automobile, as outlined in Exhibit 17.6. In the loan request, Melanie Groome wants to buy a 2000 Jeep Cherokee. The application identifies the purpose, amount, and maturity of the loan as well as information regarding the applicant's personal and financial circumstances and recognizes ECOA guidelines. Before providing any information, Groome indicates that she is applying for individual credit and not relying on alimony, child support, or government income maintenance payments to repay the debt. The bank, therefore, cannot demand information regarding her marital status or information about joint applicants or cosigners.

THE CREDIT SCORE. Exhibit 17.7 lists the factors and corresponding weights for the bank's credit scoring model. A loan is automatically approved if the applicant's total score equals at least 200. The applicant is denied credit if the total score falls below 150. Scores in between these accept/reject values are indeterminate. The weights indicate the relative importance of each characteristic. At University National Bank, five factors, including employment status, principal residence, monthly debt relative to monthly income, total income, and banking references, are weighted heaviest. Not surprisingly, these characteristics represent financial capacity and personal stability, which are important in determining repayment prospects. The bank also uses a local retail merchants association and a similar national association to check credit histories. Subsequent reports reveal the applicant's current list of outstanding debts, the highest balance outstanding at any one point, and whether the individual was ever late in making payments.

Groome's credit score totals 185, as the sum of the scores in the darkened-areas from her application within each category in Exhibit 17.7 indicates. Given the accept/reject scores, the model provides an inconclusive evaluation of the credit risk, and the loan officer must rely on judgmental factors. When discussing the application, Groome revealed that she moved to Denver after her husband, who worked for an oil field services company, died in an automobile accident. After searching for two months, she found work as a dental assistant with a dentist who had recently started his own business. She had experience in this field before she met her husband but quit her job to stay at home with their son. She is currently attending evening classes at a local university to complete a degree in accounting. She further indicated that the total cost of the Jeep she wanted to purchase was $17,500 but she intended to make a $5,000 down payment. This would lower her savings balance at the bank to $1,200. The loan officer verified this and determined that Groome's monthly checking account balance averaged around $150. Her monthly rent payment was $550. She had outstanding loans on a VISA card and to Sears that she was paying off over time.

---

[12]The fact that the sample excludes applications that were rejected biases the model parameters because the characteristics of these applicants are ignored. The extent of the bias depends on whether good borrowers who would have repaid the loan on a timely basis were eliminated or whether all rejects were bad credits.

■ **EXHIBIT 17.6**

CREDIT APPLICATION, UNIVERSITY NATIONAL BANK

IMPORTANT: Please read these directions before completing this Application, and check (✔) the appropriate box below.

☒ If you are applying for individual credit in your own name, are not married, and are not relying on alimony, child support, or separate maintenance payments or on the income or assets of another person as the basis for repayment of the credit requested, complete only Sections A and D. If the requested credit is to be secured, also complete Section E.

☐ In all other situations, complete all Sections except E, providing information in B about your spouse, a joint applicant or user, or the person on whose alimony, support, or maintenance payments or income or assets you are relying. If the requested credit is to be secured, also complete Section E.

AMOUNT REQUESTED	PAYMENT DATE DESIRED	PROCEEDS OF CREDIT TO BE USED FOR
$ 12,500	Nov. 15, 2001	Purchase of a 2000 Jeep Cherokee

SECTION A — INFORMATION REGARDING APPLICANT

FULL NAME		AGE	BIRTH DATE	SOCIAL SECURITY NO
Melanie Groome		28	July 12, 1973	496-62-0448

PRESENT ADDRESS (Street, City, State, & Zip)	How Long At Present Address?	HOME PHONE
#115 Woodhaven Lane Apts., Denver, Colo.	10 mths	765-1191

PREVIOUS ADDRESS (Street, City, State, & Zip)	How Long At Previous Address?
Circle Townhouses, #820A, Broken Arrow, Oklahoma	2 years

PRESENT EMPLOYER (Company Name & Address)
James O'Malley, DDS 650 University Avenue, Denver, Colo.

How Long With Present Employer?	YOUR POSITION OR TITLE	NAME OF SUPERVISOR	BUSINESS PHONE
8 mths	Dental assistant	James O'Malley	765-8014

PREVIOUS EMPLOYER (Company Name & Address)
Homemaker

Your Present Gross Salary or Commission	Your Present Net Salary or Commission	No. Dependents	Ages of Dependents
$28,500 PER year	$1820 PER month	1	

Alimony, child support, or separate maintenance income need not be revealed if you do not wish to have it considered as a basis for repaying this obligation. Alimony, child support, separate maintenance received under: ☐ Court Order ☐ Written Agreement ☐ Oral Understanding

OTHER INCOME	SOURCES OF OTHER INCOME
$ 160 PER year	savings interest

Is any income listed in this Section likely to be reduced before the credit requested is paid off? ☒ No ☐ Yes (Explain)

Have you ever received ☒ No credit from us? ☐ Yes — When?	Checking Account No 355 0114 8	Where? UNB
	Savings Account No 457 1988	Where? UNB

NAME & ADDRESS OF NEAREST RELATIVE NOT LIVING WITH YOU	RELATIONSHIP
Albert F. Johnson, RR#10, Adair, Oklahoma	Uncle

OUTSTANDING DEBTS (Include charge accounts, installment contracts, credit cards, rent, mortgages, etc. Use separate sheet if necessary)

CREDITOR	BALANCE	PAYMENT	PAID OFF ACCOUNTS
Visa	$1,108	open	
Sears	$920	$120/mth	

SECTION B — INFORMATION REGARDING JOINT APPLICANT OR OTHER PARTY

FULL NAME	BIRTH DATE	RELATIONSHIP

ADDRESS	PHONE NUMBER

PRESENT EMPLOYER — ADDRESS	PHONE NUMBER

HOW LONG	PREVIOUS EMPLOYER	HOW LONG	SOCIAL SECURITY NUMBER

GROSS SALARY	SOURCE AND AMOUNT OF OTHER INCOME
$ PER	$ PER

NAME & ADDRESS OF NEAREST RELATIVE NOT LIVING WITH YOU

Alimony, child support, or separate maintenance income need not be revealed if you do not wish to have it considered as a basis for repaying this obligation. Alimony, child support, separate maintenance received under ☐ Court Order ☐ Written Agreement ☐ Oral Understanding

SECTION C — MARITAL STATUS

APPLICANT	☐ Married	☐ Separated	☐ Unmarried, including single, divorced, and widowed
OTHER PARTY	☐ Married	☐ Separated	☐ Unmarried, incluing single, divorced, and widowed

Are you a co-maker, endorser, or guarantor on any loan or contract? ☐ No ☐ Yes — For Whom? To Whom?

Are there any unsatisfied judgements against you? ☐ No ☐ Yes — Amount $ If "Yes", To Whom Owed?

SECTION D — ASSET & DEBT INFORMATION

If Section B has been completed, this Section should be completed, giving information about both the Applicant and Joint Applicant or Other Person. Please mark Applicant- related information with an "A". If Section B was not completed, only give information about the Applicant in this section.

ASSETS OWNED (Use separate sheet if necessary)

DESCRIPTION OF ASSETS	VALUE	SUBJECT TO DEBTS	NAMES OF OWNERS
Cash	$		
Automobiles 1 1992 Ford Taurus	800	No	Melanie Groome
2			
3			

Landlord or Mortgage Holder	☒ Rent Payment ☐ Mortgage	Name Account Carried		Balance	Monthly Payment	Past Due
Woodhaven Lane Apts		Melanie Groome	$	$	$550	$ 0

SECTION E — SECURED CREDIT (Complete only if credit is to be secured.) Briefly describe the property to be given as security:

Property Description
2000 Jeep Cherokee

NAMES AND ADDRESSES OF ALL CO-OWNERS OF THE PROPERTY

IF THE SECURITY IS REAL ESTATE GIVE THE FULL NAME OF YOUR SPOUSE (If any)

SIGNATURES

EXHIBIT 17.7

CREDIT SCORING SYSTEM, UNIVERSITY NATIONAL BANK, APPLIED TO CREDIT APPLICATION FOR PURCHASE OF A 2000 JEEP

Category | **Characteristics/Weights**

Category					
Annual Gross Income	<$10,000 5	$10,000–$20,000 15	$20,000–$40,000 30	$40,000–60,000 45	>$60,000 60
Monthly Debt Payment / Monthly Net Income	>40% 0	30–40% 5	20–30% 20	10–20% 30	<10% 50
Bank Relationship Checking/Saving	None 0	Checking Only 30	Saving only 30	Checking & Saving 40	No answer 0
Major Credit Cards	None 0	1 or more 30	No answer 0		
Credit History	Any derogatory within 7 yrs. −10		No record 0		Met obligated payments 30
Applicant's Age	<50 yrs. 5	>50 yrs. 25	No answer 0		
Residence	Rent 15	Own/Buying 40	Own outright 50	No answer 15	
Residence Stability	<1 yr. 0	1–2 yrs. 15	2–4 yrs. 35	>4 yrs. 50	No answer 0
Job Stability	<1 yr. 5	1–2 yrs. 20	2–4 yrs. 50	>4 yrs. 70	Unemployed 5 / Retired 70

NOTE: Minimum score for automatic credit approval is 200; score for judgmental evaluation, 150 to 195; score for automatic credit denial is less than 150. Melanie Groome's credit score is 185.

THE CREDIT DECISION. The credit decision rests on the loan officer's evaluation of the applicant's character and capacity to repay the debt. The officer estimates that the monthly installment payment on the loan at current rates would equal $275 for the next four years. The officer ponders the following questions. Will the applicant remain in Denver long enough to repay the loan? How stable is her job and income? Is her income high enough to cover normal monthly living expenses, debt payments, and extraordinary expenses? Should the officer reject the loan and encourage the applicant to reapply with a cosigner?

The loan officer has numerous grounds to deny credit. The applicant's credit history is limited to a Sears credit card, her local residence was established too recently, and she was employed too recently to establish job stability. Even if she were to get a cosigner, such as her employer, experience shows that many co-signers renege on their commitments. On the positive side, Groome appears to be a hard worker who is the victim of circumstances resulting from her husband's death. It is also unlikely that anyone who puts almost 30 percent down on a new model is going to walk away from a debt. The bank will likely lose Groome as a depositor if it denies the application. The resolution depends on the careful weighting of the costs and benefits. What would you recommend?

YOUR BEACON/FICO CREDIT SCORE

In today's world, a FICO score summarizes in one number an individual's credit history.[13] Lenders often use this number when evaluating whether to approve a consumer loan or mortgage, and many insurance companies consider the score when determining whether to offer insurance coverage and how to price the insurance. Generally, the scores range from 300 to 850 with a higher figure indicating a better credit history and thus, the more likely a lender or insurer sees the individual as making the promised payments in a timely manner. The national average is in the upper 600s. If, for example, an individual's FICO score is 670, the probability that the individual will be delinquent on one or more credit accounts is over 3 times greater than that for the average scorer. A lender typically views this prospective borrower as much riskier than someone with a much higher score.

In late 2001, Fair, Isaac, and Company, the firm that provides the statistical model that produces the FICO score, reported the distribution of scores provided in the top panel of Exhibit 17.8. Note that 60 percent of individuals had scores of 700 or more. The bottom panel lists delinquency rates, measured as the fraction of borrowers with a loan payment that was 90 days or more past due, over the same ranges of scores. As suggested, delinquency rates decline as the credit score increases to where just one percent of accounts with scores of 800 or more were delinquent. Imagine the interest rate differential that a lender would have to charge on low-scoring accounts versus high-scoring accounts to cover expected losses.

An individual's credit score is based on five broad factors: payment history (35%), amounts owed (30%), length of credit history (15%), new credit (10%), and type of credit in use (10%). As such, a score is determined by whether an individual has made promised principal and interest payments on prior debts on time, the amount of outstanding balances and available credit, how long the individual has been a borrower, recent trends in borrowing and payment activity, and the mix of loans. A lender who solicits a prospective borrower receives a list of reasons why the score is not higher along with the actual credit score. Such reasons range from 'serious delinquency' to 'too many accounts with outstanding balances.' A lender then evaluates the score and reasons to assess whether to make the loan and if so, how to price the loan.

---

[13]Information in this section is based largely on data provided by Fair, Isaac, and Company (FICO) on their Web site, www.fairisaac.com.

• EXHIBIT 17.8

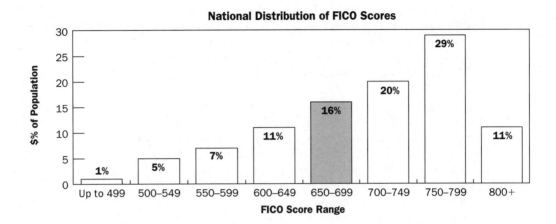

National Distribution of FICO Scores

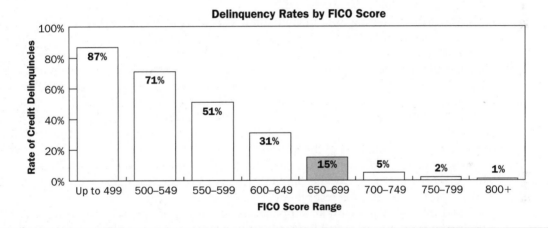

Delinquency Rates by FICO Score

SOURCE: http://www.fairisaac.com/.

If you are active in your spending and borrowing, it is important to review your credit score at least annually. It is not uncommon for erroneous information to find its way into a credit report and it is often difficult to have it removed. It is also valuable to know how to improve your credit score as your future borrowing potential and cost of borrowing will depend on your credit history as summarized in this figure.

AN APPLICATION: INDIRECT LENDING

Indirect lending is an attractive form of consumer lending when a bank deals with reputable retailers. A retailer sells merchandise and takes the credit application when the consumer decides to finance the purchase. Because many firms do not have the resources to carry their receivables, they sell the loans to banks or other financial institutions. In most instances, a bank analyzes the credit application and makes the credit decision. These loans are collectively referred to as dealer paper. Banks aggressively compete for paper originated by well-established automobile, mobile home, and furniture dealers.

Most banks involved in indirect lending provide a wide range of services to dealers in addition to buying their paper. For example, automobile dealers often finance their display inventory under floor plan arrangements. When the dealer sells a vehicle, the bank buys the paper and reduces the dealer's inventory loan by the loan value of the vehicle.

Dealers negotiate finance charges directly with their customers. A bank, in turn, agrees to purchase the paper at predetermined rates that vary with the default risk assumed by the bank, the quality of the assets sold, and the maturity of the consumer loan. A dealer normally negotiates a higher rate with the car buyer than the determined rate charged by the bank. This differential varies with competitive conditions but potentially represents a significant source of dealer profit.

Most indirect loan arrangements provide for dealer reserves that reduce the risk in indirect lending. The reserves are derived from the differential between the normal, or contract, loan rate and bank rate and help protect the bank against customer defaults and refunds. Consumers make their loan payments directly to the bank. Instead of immediately giving up the dealer's share of interest, a bank retains the interest in reserve. The reserve is used to cover defaults and the unearned portion of the dealer's share of interest. If the dealer chooses to approve a loan at a rate below the predetermined rate set by the bank for a preferred customer, this negative interest earned also reduces the reserve. A bank refunds a dealer's share of the differential only after the reserve equals some minimum amount, normally a negotiated fraction of total loans purchased.

Consider the following example in Exhibit 17.9 using automobile dealer paper. The dealer charges a customer a 15 percent annual percentage rate (APR)—1.25 percent monthly—to finance the purchase of an automobile for $8,000. The bank has evaluated the credit application, and the transaction qualifies for a discounted 12 percent rate. By agreement, the bank retains 25 percent of the interest differential and transfers 75 percent to the dealer's account. The loan is written for three years, with 36 monthly payments of $277.32. The borrower pays $1,983.52 in total interest expense, of which $1,565.72 is credited to the bank, to yield 12 percent. Of the $417.80 interest differential, 75 percent is immediately allocated to the dealer, while 25 percent is retained in the reserve.

The reserve serves primarily to cover charge-offs. If the borrower defaults on the loan, the bank reduces the reserve by the unpaid principal outstanding. This ultimately lowers the dealer's profits because the reserve must be replenished. The reserve also covers rebates of unearned interest. For example, suppose that the dealer charges the borrower a 9 percent add-on rate for three years and the bank discounts it at a 7 percent add-on rate. With add-on interest, a lender receives some unearned interest if the borrower prepays. Interest rebates are commonly calculated according to the rule of 78s, which determines the fraction of total interest to be refunded at a point in time prior to maturity.[14] Applicable rebate percentages at the end of each year are determined at the bottom of Exhibit 17.9 in the second column, assuming 36 monthly payments. A 3-year loan prepaid after two years indicates that 11.71 percent of the interest is unearned (88.29 percent is earned). If, in this example, a borrower prepays the entire loan after two years and the bank takes interest into income by the sum of the digits method, the bank must rebate $252.93 to the customer at the 9 percent add-on rate. Because the bank earns interest at the 7 percent add-on rate, its unearned interest income equals only $196.73 after two years. The $56.20 difference between the rebate amount and

---

[14]According to the rule of 78s, the applicable rebate percentage equals the sum of the integers from one to the number of payments remaining after prepayment, divided by the sum of integers from one to the total number of payments in the loan. The number 78 equals the sum of integers 1 through 12 and thus serves as the denominator for rebate fractions on all 1-year, monthly payment loans. For example, a 1-year loan with 12 monthly payments that is prepaid after the seventh month produces a rebate percentage of $(1 + 2 + 3 + 4 + 5)/(1 + 2 + \ldots + 12) = 19.23$ percent. The lender would take 80.77 percent of the finance charge and rebate 19.23 percent to the borrower.

• EXHIBIT 17.9

ROLE OF DEALER RESERVES IN INDIRECT LENDING: AUTOMOBILE PAPER

Terms of the Dealer Agreement

Bank buys dealer paper at a 12 percent rate. Dealer charges customers a higher rate (15 percent APR), with 25 percent of difference allocated to a reserve.

Sample Automobile Loan

Principal   = $8,000
Maturity   = 3 years, 36 monthly installments
Loan rate   = 15% annual percentage rate (APR)
Monthly payment = $8,000/[(1/.0125) − (1/.0125(1.0125)^{36})] = $277.32

Allocation to the Dealer Reserve

Total interest expense to customer = $1,983.52
Total interest income for bank   = 1,565.72
Differential interest   = $ 417.80

75% allocated to dealer: 0.75(417.80) = $313.35
25% allocated to reserve: 0.25(417.80) = $104.45

Interest Refunds on Prepayments with Add-on Rates

Loan is written on a precomputed basis, and bank accrues interest using "rule of 78s."*
Interest expense to customer = 0.09($8,000)(3) = $2,160
Interest income for bank   = 0.07($8,000)(3) = 1,680
Differential interest   = $ 480
75% allocated to dealer: 0.75($480) = $360
25% allocated to reserve: 0.25($480) = $120

End of Year	Interest Earned*	Total	Bank	Difference
1	54.96%	$1,187.14	$ 923.33	$263.81
2	33.33	719.33	559.94	159.99
3	11.71	252.93	196.73	56.20
	100.00%	$2,160.00	$1,680.00	$480.00

*Rule of 78s factors are 366/666, 222/666, and 78/666, respectively.

unearned bank interest would be charged against the reserve. The rule of 78s penalizes borrowers by assuming that earned interest is greater than that actually generated on a loan's outstanding principal. For short-term loans, however, the error is small.

There are many different reserve agreements, the most common being full recourse and no recourse arrangements. As the name suggests, *full recourse agreements* place the dealer at risk. If a borrower defaults, the dealer absorbs the loss by either reducing the reserve at the bank or paying off the note on the bank's terms. *No recourse agreements,* in contrast, stipulate that banks assume the credit risk. All losses are charged directly against bank earnings. Finally, some reserve arrangements involve limited recourse. A bank may negotiate a plan whereby dealers are liable for any losses only during the first three months of the loan. Although these losses are immediately charged to the reserve, later losses are absorbed by the bank. The above example represents a full recourse arrangement.

Banks prefer to deal with well-established retailers that generate paper (loans) of predictable quality. Banks vary the predetermined discount rate according to the dealer's reputation and the nature of the recourse agreement. They charge lower rates under full recourse plans because they assume less credit risk. Dealers that have the capability to assess credit quality prefer these arrangements because their profits are potentially greater. Under no recourse arrangements, banks charge higher rates and review each application carefully, as if the loan were a direct one.

RECENT RISK AND RETURN CHARACTERISTICS OF CONSUMER LOANS

Historically, banks have viewed themselves as being either wholesale or retail institutions, focusing on commercial and individual customers, respectively. Recent developments, however, have blurred the distinction, as traditional wholesale banks have aggressively entered the consumer market. The attraction is twofold. First, competition for commercial customers narrowed commercial loan yields so that returns fell relative to potential risks. As indicated earlier, consumer loans now provide some of the highest net yields for banks. Second, developing loan and deposit relationships with individuals presumably represents a strategic response to deregulation. The removal of interest rate ceilings substantially reduced banks' core deposits by making high-balance customers more price sensitive. On average, individuals hold small balances and move deposit accounts less frequently, providing a more stable deposit base. Thus, liquidity risk declines as a bank's retail deposit base increases.

REVENUES FROM CONSUMER LOANS

Banks earn significant revenues from interest on loans and associated fees. Because many usury ceilings have been eliminated or are no longer effective, banks can ration credit via price rather than by altering nonprice credit terms. This permits banks to quickly raise consumer loan rates as conditions require. When conditions permit, banks also delay lowering rates when their borrowing costs decline.

Consumer loan rates have been among the highest rates quoted at banks in recent years. Most consumer loans are made at fixed rates that banks do not change frequently. In a declining rate environment, consumer loans thus yield a larger spread relative to the bank's borrowing cost. When short-term rates rise, the spread narrows until banks raise loan rates. During the 1980s and early 1990s, the spread widened with the general decline in interest rates. However, the spread narrowed with the increased competition for consumer loans after the 1991 recession. With aggressive marketing campaigns at many banks and nonbank competitors, consumers are becoming increasingly sensitive to price such that credit card loan rates and fees now follow bank funding costs more closely.

Consumer groups still argue that consumer loan rates are too high, especially when the prime stays constant as other rates decline. They claim that lenders must be conspiring to fix prices. There are many reasons for large spreads, however. First, consumer loans are typically smaller in size and cost more to administer on a unit basis than commercial loans. Still, to eliminate "excess" profits that banks might earn when rates fall and the spread widens, noninterest costs from handling consumer loans would have to increase. There is no explanation for this. Second, consumer loans are longer-term and often carry fixed rates. New car loans, for example, now average between four and five years until maturity. Banks include a premium in longer-term, fixed-rate loans to compensate for the risks of inflation and volatile funding costs. Third, individuals are more likely to default than businesses. The spread should be large enough to cover greater losses. Finally, many lenders still face state usury ceilings that may not be lifted when rates increase. These banks essentially make up for reduced profits during high rate environments by keeping loan rates high when their financing costs fall. In response to this criticism, many banks now offer variable-rate credit cards as alternatives to fixed-rate cards. (See Contemporary Issues: Variable-Rate Credit Cards.)

In addition to interest income, banks generate substantial noninterest revenues from consumer loans. With traditional installment credit, banks often encourage borrowers to purchase credit life insurance on which the bank may earn premium income. Credit card operations also provide different types of fee income. Most banks now impose annual fees, ranging from $10 to $40 per customer, for the right to use the card and for access to related

VARIABLE-RATE CREDIT CARDS

Politicians and some consumers routinely criticize banks for raising loan rates too quickly when interest rates increase in general, but not lowering loan rates when interest rates fall. This is particularly true with consumer credit. For example, regardless of movements in federal funds and the prime rate, credit card rates generally range from 9 to 20 percent.

Banks respond by pointing out that both the cost of making consumer loans and consumer loan losses are high. Exhibit 17.2 demon-strates that credit card losses in 1998 represented over 5 percent of out-standing loans. Nominal interest rates have to be high to compensate for the large losses.

Some banks have responded to the criticisms by introducing vari-able-rate and floating-rate credit cards. Rates generally change quar-terly with changes in a bank's cost of funds or are tied to some base rate, such as prime. The most aggressive banks, however, have used these cards to attract affluent card users. These banks offer vari-able rates on premium cards that are set below the fixed rate on tradi-tional credit cards. Loan losses on premium cards average less than 1 percent, which justifies a lower rate. Premium card users tend to charge more with their cards and leave a larger unpaid balance. They are also considerably more price sensitive. Variable-rate premium cards thus reduce interest rate risk and help attract affluent customers.

bank services. The customer essentially receives a line of credit with travel-related services, debit card privileges, and merchandise discounts also available. Banks bill cardholders monthly and expect the customer to repay the debt on a revolving credit basis with mini-mum payments equal to 5 percent of the outstanding balance. Historically, customers have had the option to repay the entire balance within a specified grace period, such as 25 days, and avoid any interest. Experience has demonstrated that just under one-third of all cus-tomers take advantage of this interest-free period. Many banks have eliminated this option by charging interest on each transaction from the date of posting. Banks often impose other fees for late payments and cash advances and may impose a fee if customers do not charge sufficient amounts.

CONSUMER LOAN LOSSES

Losses on consumer loans are normally the highest among all categories of bank credit. This reflects highly cyclical patterns in personal income as well as extensive fraud. Losses are anticipated because of mass marketing efforts pursued by many lenders, particularly with credit cards. In 2001, the consumer credit card charge-off rate averaged 6.5 percent such that losses amounted to just under $10 billion, of which 80 percent historically represent outright defaults and 20 percent fraud. Not surprisingly, both losses and delinquent accounts rise dur-ing recessions and decline during high growth periods. Many lenders simply factor losses into their pricing as a part of doing business.[15]

Credit card fraud arises out of the traditional lender-merchant relationship. In most cases, banks give merchants credit for sales long before they are reimbursed by cardholders. In 2001, the estimated time lag averaged around 36 days. This allows fraudulent merchants to set up a temporary operation, bill card-issuing banks for bogus sales, and escape with the proceeds before cardholders recognize billing errors.

To perpetrate the fraud, thieves need access to a retail business and cardholder account information. Frequently, the business front is nothing more than a telephone-based mail-order

---

[15]See Merwin (1985). Peterson (1985) provides a detailed analysis of issues related to pricing consumer loans and individual transactions accounts.

operation. Callers tell cardholders that they have won prizes but must provide account numbers, expiration dates, and billing addresses to collect. Alternatively, thieves can obtain credit card information by stealing credit cards or by copying information from carbons of card charges at various legitimate businesses. Thieves use the information to make purchases or receive cash advances during the 40-day lag period. Unsuspecting cardholders eventually discover that fraudulent charges appear on their monthly statements. By the time the card-issuing bank recognizes the fraud, the thief has closed down the business and moved to greener pastures.

INTEREST RATE AND LIQUIDITY RISK WITH CONSUMER CREDIT

The majority of consumer loans are priced at fixed rates. New auto loans typically carry 4-year maturities, and credit card loans exhibit an average 15- to 18-month maturity. In most cases, the borrower can prepay a loan without any penalty when rates decline. This creates difficult problems in trying to match fund the consumer portfolio.

Bankers have responded in two ways. First, they price more consumer loans on a floating rate basis. Such policies have been relatively successful in the mortgage market but require substantial discounts below fixed-rate loans to attract interest. Second, commercial and investment banks have created a secondary market in consumer loans that allows loan originators to sell a package of loans to investors with longer-term holding periods. The first efforts appeared in early 1985, when Marine Midland Bank, in conjunction with Salomon Brothers, sold automobile loans to secondary market investors. Salomon Brothers sold the loans in the form of collateralized securities, conveniently labeled certificates of automobile receivables (CARs). As with mortgage banking operations, Marine Midland agreed to service the loans for which it receives servicing income. Banks now routinely sell certificates supported by credit card receivables and other consumer credit as a means of moving assets off the balance sheet, reducing capital requirements, and increasing noninterest income.

SUMMARY

Commercial banks aggressively compete for consumer loans for a variety of reasons. For many types of loans, net yields exceed those on commercial loans. Default rates are above those on other loans, but the gross yield charged more than compensates for the higher losses. When rates decline, net profits on credit card and other fixed-rate loans rise sharply because consumer loan rates are relatively sticky. Individuals also typically maintain deposit accounts where they borrow. Retail deposits are relatively low cost and not nearly as interest rate sensitive as commercial deposits. Thus, the more liquidity risk is reduced, the greater is the volume of consumer deposits at a bank. Consumer loans, however, exhibit greater interest rate risk than commercial loans. Most are fixed-rate loans, and many carry 3- to 5-year maturities. Banks wishing to reduce interest rate risk often try to match fund these loans with longer-term deposits.

Loan officers consider the same basic issues applicable to commercial loans when evaluating the riskiness of consumer loans: use of proceeds, size of loan, cash flow repayment sources, collateral, and the borrower's character. The fundamental difference is that personal financial statements are generally unaudited and it is more difficult to forecast net cash flow. Evaluation procedures may involve the subjective interpretation of financial information provided directly by an individual on a credit application and obtained indirectly from credit bureaus and references. Alternatively, banks may use credit scoring models based on a numerical assessment of an acceptable-risk borrower's profile. This chapter introduces a basic credit scoring model and describes the risk and return features of various types of consumer loans, such as credit card transactions and the purchase of dealer paper. It also summarizes the factors that the most popular models incorporate in their scoring systems. A significant trend is that credit scoring has moved to small business loans. If such loans can be successfully securitized, they may become commodities more like mortgages and their yields will decline. This will be especially problematic for community banks where small business loans often account for a substantial portion of annual profits.

QUESTIONS

1. Explain how an installment loan differs from revolving credit in terms of risk and the nature of the return to the lender.

2. What are the major expenses associated with making consumer loans? What is the average size of consumer installment loans at small banks? How does loan size affect loan rates that banks charge on consumer loans?

3. Examine credit card loss rates and personal bankruptcy filings in Exhibit 17.2. What might explain the increase in both measures after 1994 in a period when economic growth in the United States was strong and unemployment was low and again in 2001? What will likely occur to losses and personal bankruptcies during the next recession?

4. Why are home equity loans attractive today relative to before the Tax Reform Act of 1986? How do some banks tie home equity loans to their credit card? How are home equity lines generally priced (what rates apply)?

5. Explain how a direct installment loan differs from an indirect installment loan.

6. What are the key provisions of the Equal Credit Opportunity Act? Why was such legislation necessary?

7. Describe how a bank should apply an objective credit scoring model when evaluating consumer loan requests. Given the information in Exhibits 17.6 and 17.7 and information in the text, indicate why you would or would not approve Melanie Groome's loan request.

8. Given the distribution of FICO credit scores and the associated delinquency rates in Exhibit 17.8, describe how lenders might price loans to borrowers with lower scores versus borrowers with higher scores in terms of rates and fees charged.

9. What different sources of revenue are available from credit card lending? Outline the clearing process with a credit card transaction. What is the biggest risk in credit card loans?

10. The differential between fixed-rate credit card rates and a bank's cost of funds typically varies over the interest rate cycle. What is this relationship and why does it exist? Does the differential between commercial loan rates and a bank's cost of funds behave similarly?

11. Calculate the effective annual rate on each of the following loans:
    a. A $5,000 loan for two years, 10 percent simple annual interest with principal repayment at the end of the second year.
    b. A $5,000 loan for two years, 10 percent add-on interest, paid in 24 equal monthly installments.
    c. A $5,000 loan to be repaid at the end of two years, 10 percent discount rate.

12. What is the purpose of a dealer reserve in indirect lending? When is a bank at risk with indirect loans?

13. What is the goal of the Community Reinvestment Act? How do regulators enforce its provisions?

14. Subprime loans have higher loss rates than many other types of loans. Explain why lenders offer subprime loans. Describe the characteristics of the typical borrower in a subprime consumer loan.

15. Explain generally how smart cards, debit cards, and prepaid cards differ from traditional credit cards.

PROBLEMS

I. BUYING PAPER FROM A USED CAR DEALER

Dealer reserves in indirect lending serve to protect a bank against loan losses and prepayments. Suppose that a bank enters into an agreement with a used car dealer to buy dealer paper at a 5.5 percent add-on rate, and retain 25 percent of the interest differential relative to the rate the dealer charges the car buyer. Under the agreement, the bank charges losses and prepayments against the reserve, transferring any excess to the dealer periodically. Interest rebates on prepayments are computed according to the rule of 78s.

Consider the case where the dealer charges a customer a 7.5 percent add-on rate for the purchase of a $15,000 automobile to be financed over 36 months. Calculate the effective annual percentage rate (APR), the total interest expense to the customer, the bank's share, and the interest differential allocated to the dealer reserve. Suppose that the customer prepays the entire loan after 13 months. Determine how much interest the bank must rebate to the car buyer and any charge to the dealer reserve.

II. CREDIT REPORT

1. Examine the sample credit report provided in Exhibit 17.5. From a lender's perspective, explain the importance of information regarding:
   a. Number and type of businesses that report credit information
   b. Date the account was opened
   c. Date of last activity on the account
   d. Highest credit amount and terms
   e. Balance outstanding, amount past due, and status

2. Explain the meaning of the following status measures: R1, I1, O1, and R3.

3. How would you interpret the information provided for John Doe in the section of the report on courthouse records?

ACTIVITIES

I. CREDIT CARDS

Collect the following information on three nationally advertised credit cards and three locally offered credit cards. You can use the Internet to search for the best terms.

1. Annual fee

2. Interest rate and grace period

3. Additional services to credit availability

Is there a pattern between the national versus local cards? Which card appeals most to you? Explain why.

II. CREDIT REPORTING AND SECURITY

Go to the Web sites, http://www.myvesta.com and http://www.fairisaac.com. Review the most recent delinquency rates by FICO score. What differential interest rates do lenders charge for different FICO scores? Provide reasoning for differential rates.

18

CUSTOMER PROFITABILITY ANALYSIS AND LOAN PRICING

A *popular view among bankers is that 20 percent of a bank's customers account for 80 percent of the bank's profits. More than one-half of accounts generate losses. If true, this raises several questions. First, how do banks measure customer profitability? Second, does the bank recognize all relationships or products that a customer uses and does it fully allocate all costs, such as overhead, to assess profitability? Third, if so many customers are unprofitable, why doesn't the bank change its pricing to ensure that more accounts are profitable? It may also be the case that banks cannot adequately measure customer profitability.*

Many bankers have reacted to these findings by using incentives to encourage traditionally unprofitable customers to use low-cost delivery systems, such as ATMs, telephone banking, or the Internet. At the high end, they are packaging services and offering low or no fees to customers who generate substantial profits for the bank. Efforts are directed at cross-selling services to both segments.

Bank managers are similarly confronted with many issues related to pricing. Should they make variable-rate loans or fixed-rate loans? Should they quote their own local bank prime rate or use a prime rate quoted by other banks? Is the bank willing to lose a customer's business if it raises the rate charged on a loan? Is charging fees better than requiring a borrower to maintain a deposit account at the bank? How does a loan officer adjust the pricing of a borrower's credit relationship when the customer insists on reducing compensating balance requirements? These are key issues confronting commercial bankers in today's environment of deregulated interest rates and intense price competition for credit services.

Most banks use a generalized customer profitability analysis framework as a guideline to address these issues. Although strategic decisions regarding deposit and loan pricing should not be based solely on a mechanical system, the framework does demonstrate the relationships between revenues, expenses, and a bank's target return to shareholders for a customer's total account relationship. The examples in this chapter focus on loans. They demonstrate why banks often underprice loans and provide a basis for resolving each of the above questions and other related pricing problems.

For many years, managers looked at their bank's aggregate profitability measures to determine whether strategies were appropriately conceived and implemented. Frequently, they did not know the cost of providing services and thus set prices artificially high or low. Deregulation changed this practice. Declining net interest margins forced banks to reassess their expenses and revenues in search of better cost control and more efficient pricing. Today, most banks use formal customer profitability analysis procedures to meet these objectives.

Customer profitability analysis is a decision tool used to evaluate the profitability of a customer relationship. Historically, it has been used to determine the cost of deposit services and subsequent balance requirements, along with how to price specific products such as loans. It is used here, instead, to evaluate all relevant expenses and revenues associated with a customer's total banking relationship. The analysis enables management to estimate the net profit from a given account and provides a framework for repricing specific products to meet profit objectives.

The analysis procedure compels banks to be aware of the full range of services purchased by each customer and to generate meaningful cost estimates for providing each service. It identifies the various sources of income and expense, and dollar charges by category. If performed systematically, the analysis can help a bank identify when and why profitability declines and what steps must be taken to correct any deterioration in the relationship. For example, a commercial customer may reduce deposit balances because it is unable to get trade credit or sales are declining. A corresponding decrease in the bank's revenues from the account is easily recognizable and a red flag is raised. Alternatively, the procedure assists banks in negotiating terms. In many instances, bank officers antagonize credit customers by rejecting their requests for lower interest rates without fully comprehending the total profit relationship. This analysis indicates what repricing flexibility exists.

The applicability of customer profitability analysis has been questioned in recent years with the move toward unbundling services. Bank customers often selectively purchase single products from different institutions and thus maintain relationships with several banks. It is important for banks to allocate their costs across different products and price each accordingly. As such, each product can stand alone in generating revenues to cover associated expenses and add to profits. A similar type of analysis, labeled segment or line of business profitability analysis, was introduced in Chapter 4 and used a return on risk-adjusted capital (RORAC) framework to address whether specific lines of business generate acceptable risk-adjusted returns on allocated capital. If specific products or services are underpriced, it will show up in the RORAC calculations. RORAC analysis combined with customer profitability analysis ensures that both products and customer relationships meet a bank's target return criteria.

This chapter examines the contributing factors in customer profitability and account analysis. The first part describes a general framework and important terminology. The next part provides an application, using data from a hypothetical commercial account. The final part shows extended applications of the framework to pricing new loan agreements and determining minimum acceptable balances and maturities on installment loan contracts. The loan pricing analysis provides a framework for projecting a required interest charge, emphasizing the role of base lending rates. Both applications reveal the format of and difficulties with segment profitability analysis.

ACCOUNT ANALYSIS FRAMEWORK

Customer profitability analysis is used to evaluate whether net revenue from an account meets a bank's profit objectives. It is generally performed using monthly or quarterly historical data so that pricing can be modified where appropriate. The procedure involves comparing revenues from all services provided a customer with associated costs and the bank's target profit. Although the analysis applies particularly well to loan customers, it can be easily modified to evaluate noncredit activities. The appropriate comparison is:

$$\text{Account revenues} \gtreqless \text{Account expenses} + \text{Target profit} \qquad (18.1)$$

If revenues exceed the sum of expenses and the target profit, the account generates a return in excess of the minimum return required by the bank. If revenues equal expenses plus the target profit, the account just meets the required return objective. There are two other possible outcomes. If revenues fall short of expenses, the account is clearly unprofitable. When revenues exceed expenses but are less than the sum of expenses and target profit, the account is profitable but does not generate the minimum acceptable return to the bank. The following discussion summarizes the components to each element in Equation 18.1.

EXPENSE COMPONENTS

The first step is to identify the full list of services used by a customer. The list normally includes transactions account activity, extension of credit, security safekeeping, and related items such as wire transfers, safety deposit boxes, and letters of credit. The next step is to assess the cost of providing each service. Unit costs can be determined from the bank's cost accounting system or approximated from Federal Reserve *Functional Cost Analysis* data. Unfortunately, FCA data are not available after 1999. Often, specific figures vary substantially between banks because they allocate fixed costs and overhead differently. There is no best method for allocating fixed costs, so estimated unit expenses are, at best, an approximation. Banks that do not have formal customer profitability models typically attribute it to the inability to allocate costs due to systems limitations.

NONCREDIT SERVICES. Aggregate cost estimates for noncredit services are obtained by multiplying the unit cost of each service by the corresponding activity level. If, for example, it costs $7 to facilitate a wire transfer and the customer authorized eight such transfers, the total periodic wire transfer expense to the bank is $56 for that account. In general, check processing expenses are the major noncredit cost item for commercial customers. If priced separately, service charge income should at least equal this aggregate cost.

CREDIT SERVICES. Cost estimates for credit services represent the largest expense and are typically related to the size of the loan. These costs include the interest cost of financing the loan, loan administration or handling costs, and risk expense associated with potential default. The first two are actual cash expenses, while default risk expense is a noncash expense.

Cost of Funds. The cost of funds estimate may be a bank's weighted marginal cost of pooled debt or its weighted marginal cost of capital at the time the loan was made. Most banks distinguish between their cost of debt and cost of stockholders' equity, which together comprise the cost of capital, by separately calculating a target return to shareholders representing the cost of equity. As such, the cost of funds typically refers to the weighted marginal cost of pooled debt. This calculation follows that described in Chapter 12. A bank computes the effective marginal cost of each debt source and divides the estimate by the proportion of investable balances from that source. The weights then reflect the anticipated proportion of financing for each source from the bank's target capital structure. Because equity is excluded, the weights sum to 1 minus the targeted percentage financing from equity. Alternatively, banks can use the weighted marginal cost of capital, which incorporates the cost of both debt and equity. In this case, a separate target profit measure would count equity twice, and thus is excluded.

Loan Administration. Loan administration expense is the cost of a loan's credit analysis and execution. It includes personnel and overhead costs as well as direct costs for sending interest bills, processing payments, and maintaining collateral. The charge may be imposed on a per item basis, determined by the unit cost of handling a loan times the number of notes outstanding, or computed as a fixed percentage of the loan amount.

Default Risk Expense. A formal allocation of default risk expense represents one method of handling the impact of potential loan losses. Many banks categorize loans according to their risk characteristics at the time of issue. Low-risk loans, which typically have short-term maturities, are those extended to borrowers with strong financial statements, adequate cash flow and collateral, and sound management. High-risk loans, which generally have longer maturities, are extended to borrowers with weaker financial statements, low cash flow, and collateral that potentially fluctuates widely in value. Management first ranks loans by these characteristics and historical default experience, assigning each credit to a particular risk class. This risk rating system allows different charges for potential loss in the event of default for loans with different likelihoods of default and different magnitudes of loss when in default. The actual risk expense measure equals the historical default percentage for loans in that risk class times the outstanding loan balance.[1]

Exhibit 18.1 shows a simplified risk rating classification, using hypothetical data and only four loan categories. The historical default percentage serves as a proxy for the expected percentage of charge-offs on existing loans. A 1-year $400,000 loan assigned to the second risk class is charged a $2,440 risk expense, for example, because average loss experience on loans of this type equals 61 cents per $100. This risk estimate recognizes that the bank expects to charge off $2,440 on the average $400,000 loan of this type. The relationship should thus be priced to reflect this anticipated loss. If the loan was categorized in risk class 4, the risk expense charge would equal $7,760 because average losses are greater.

Rather than charge directly for default risk, some banks formally recognize different default risks on different loans by allocating varying proportions of equity financing in the cost of funds estimate. Because equity costs more than debt, riskier loans are assigned a higher percentage of equity funding. For example, a bank might assume 8 percent equity financing for a loan in the lowest risk class and 15 percent equity financing for a loan in the highest risk class. This raises the cost of capital or target return requirement, and thus the minimum revenue necessary for an account to be profitable.

TARGET PROFIT

The separate recognition of a target return forces management to allocate equity in support of each account relationship. The target profit is then based on a minimum required return to

---

[1]When pricing loans, many banks levy risk charges that increase systematically with the presumed riskiness of loans. Thus, loans in category 1 of Exhibit 18.1 might be charged 25 basis points for risk, loans in category 2 might be charged 50 basis points, and so forth, to where loans in category 4 are charged 100 basis points. There are many problems with this, particularly the fact that average default losses are not linear. Loans in the highest risk class will normally exhibit default loss rates that are exponentially greater than default loss rates in the lowest risk class. The last section indicates how this technique leads to mispricing loans.

· EXHIBIT 18.1

COMMERCIAL LOAN CLASSIFICATION BY RISK CATEGORY

Risk Class	Characteristics	Historical Default Percentage
1	Short-term working capital loans secured with accounts receivable and inventory	0.22%
2	Short-term real estate loans secured by facility and borrower's cash flow from total operations	0.61
3	Term plant and equipment loans secured by physical plant and other real estate	1.30
4	Other loans	1.94

NOTE: Percentage is average of loan charge-offs divided by total loans in that risk class during the past five years.

shareholders per account. Equity capital can be readily allocated to credit relationships on the basis of a bank's financial leverage. For an average-risk loan, the appropriate percentage equals the ratio of a bank's average equity to total assets.[2] A bank with an 8 percent equity-to-asset ratio, for example, implicitly finances 8 percent of every dollar loaned out with equity and 92 percent with debt. The dollar magnitude of the required pretax target profit equals the product of this equity to asset percentage, the percentage target return to shareholders, and the dollar amount of the borrower's outstanding loan. The general formula applicable to a credit relationship is:

$$\text{Target profit} = \left(\frac{\text{Equity}}{\text{Total assets}} \right) \left(\begin{array}{c} \text{Target return to} \\ \text{shareholders} \end{array} \right) (\text{Loan amount}) \qquad \textbf{(18.2)}$$

The target return to shareholders can be determined from a dividend valuation model, capital asset pricing model framework, or cost of debt plus risk premium analysis. Each measure is discussed in Chapter 12, with sample calculations.

REVENUE COMPONENTS

Banks generate three types of revenue from customer accounts: investment income from the customer's deposit balances held at the bank, fee income from services, and interest and fee income on loans. Account profitability analysis provides a pricing framework that compares the sum of these revenues with expenses and the target profit.

INVESTMENT INCOME FROM DEPOSIT BALANCES. Every deposit that customers hold generates investment income for the bank. In cases involving transactions accounts, banks must set aside legal reserves as a percentage of deposits, but they can invest remaining balances that exceed customer float on the account. Many customers are net depositors; their balances exceed any loans the bank has extended them. Other customers are net borrowers; their outstanding loans are greater than their total deposits. This account analysis procedure treats investment income on balances separately from loan interest. As such, a

---

[2]It is not appropriate to divide this percentage by the ratio of a bank's earning assets unless the marginal cost of funds and target return to shareholders calculations are not adjusted by the investable portion of bank assets. See Chapter 12.

customer does not borrow his own deposits, but rather all funding comes from all pooled debt and equity.[3] Implicitly, customer deposits are viewed as part of a bank's total available funds. Thus, the cost of financing a loan equals the weighted cost of debt times the full amount of the loan plus the cost of equity, which is the target return to shareholders. Investment income is allocated using an *earnings credit* as an estimate of the interest a bank can earn on the customer's investable balances.

Estimating investment income from balances involves four steps.

1. The bank determines the average *ledger (book) balances* in the account during the reporting period.

2. The average transactions float—uncollected funds that still appear as part of the customer's ledger deposit—is subtracted from the ledger amount. This difference equals *collected balances.*

3. The bank deducts required reserves that must be maintained against collected balances to arrive at *investable balances.*

4. Management applies an earnings credit rate against investable balances to determine the average interest revenue earned on the customer's account.

This earnings credit rate is subjectively determined. As such, banks and their customers frequently debate what the appropriate rate should be. Banks argue that the rate should reflect the customer's opportunity cost of funds, measured as the best alternative rate available on a comparable money market investment. Many banks thus use a moving average of 3-month Treasury bill or CD rates. Customers, in contrast, argue that the rate should reflect a higher rate charged on the customer's loan or, at worst, the bank's average interest yield on earning assets. The ultimate rate used depends on each side's bargaining position and negotiation skills.

Exhibit 18.2 demonstrates the computation of investment income generated from a corporation's investable deposits during a single month. The firm's ledger balances of $335,000 were reduced by $92,500 in float and $24,250 in reserves at 10 percent to yield net investable balances of $218,250. The bank applied an earnings credit rate of 4.21 percent to yield $755.20 in investment income over the 30-day period. If the corporation also held a CD at the bank, the net investable portion would simply be added to the $218,250.

COMPENSATING BALANCES. In many commercial credit relationships, borrowers maintain compensating deposit balances with the bank as part of the loan agreement. The term "compensating" indicates that the balances are used, in part, to compensate the bank for services rendered. Typically, the qualifying balances must be demand deposits, with the minimum amount stipulated as some percentage of the loan. This minimum may stipulate that the balance cannot fall below this figure during the month or quarter, or that the average balance must exceed this figure. The agreement further specifies whether the minimum is stated in terms of ledger, collected, or investable balances. *Ledger balances* are those listed on the bank's books. *Collected balances* equal ledger balances minus float associated with the account. *Investable balances* are collected balances minus required reserves.

Consider a $1 million credit line. A bank that does not know the magnitude and timing of the customer's draws against the line might negotiate compensating balance requirements equal to 5 percent of the available credit plus 3 percent of the actual amount borrowed (5 + 3 balances). A customer who borrowed an average of $800,000 against the line would be

---

[3]Some procedures assume that a borrower's deposit balances at a bank directly fund the associated loan. This assumes that interest is paid on the deposit at the same rate as interest earned on the loan. In this case, no separate earnings credit would apply.

· EXHIBIT 18.2

CALCULATION OF INVESTMENT INCOME FROM DEMAND DEPOSIT BALANCES

Analysis of Demand Deposits: Corporation's Outstanding Balances for November
Average ledger balances = $335,000
Average float = $92,500
Collected balance = $335,000 − $92,500 = $242,500
Required reserves = (0.10) $242,500 = $24,250
Investable balance = $218,250

Earnings Credit Rate:
Average 90-day CD rate for November = 4.21%

Investment Income from Balances: November

$$\text{Investment Income} = 0.0421 \frac{(30)}{(365)} (\$218,250) = \$755.20$$

required to hold $74,000 ($50,000 + $24,000) in qualifying demand deposits. Suppose that float averages $35,000 during any month. Note that 10 percent required reserves equal $3,900 or 10 percent of the $39,000 in collected balances. If the balance requirement was stipulated in terms of ledger balances, a customer who maintained $74,000 in ledger balances would actually have only $39,000 in collected balances and $35,100 in investable balances with a 10 percent reserve ratio. If, instead, the balance requirement was stipulated in terms of collected balances, a 5 + 3 balance requirement would necessitate $109,000 in ledger balances so that after subtracting float, collected balances would equal $74,000 ($109,000 ledger − $35,000 float). In this case, investable balances would equal $66,600. Obviously, a bank could earn more interest with $74,000 in collected balances versus ledger balances. Finally, if the requirement was stipulated in terms of investable balances, the minimum investable funds would equal $74,000 and the corresponding ledger amount would rise to $117,222.[4]

A bank can raise the effective cost of balances to the customer, or yield to the bank, in several ways. First, it can simply raise the percentages applied against the line. Instead of 5 + 3 balances, it could require 8 + 5 balances. Second, it can shift from ledger balance requirements to having either collected or investable balances qualify, keeping the same percentage requirement. Finally, it can encourage increased borrowing against the line. A customer that borrowed the full amount in the above example would see balance requirements increase to $80,000. A customer's actual borrowing or usage against a line can often be influenced by fees in that higher fees against unused credit encourage borrowing.

Compensating balances are increasingly unpopular among corporate customers. Using sophisticated cash management techniques, financial officers can calculate and invest excess cash balances in earning assets rather than leave them in nonearning demand deposits at a bank. Many borrowers prefer to pay fixed fees that create an opportunity for increased income if the level of interest rates rises. The opportunity cost of compensating balances, in contrast, varies directly with the level of interest rates. In response, many banks now allow customers to meet balance requirements with time deposits. Thus, the opportunity cost to the borrower equals the loan rate minus the time deposit rate.

Both borrowers and the bank benefit from eliminating balance requirements when the bank lends the customer the deposits to meet balance requirements. This anomaly results from eliminating reserve requirements. Suppose, for example, that a bank charged 13 percent on $800,000 of actual borrowings in the above $1 million credit line and that the customer

---

[4]$74,000/(1 − .10) + $35,000 = $117,222.

needed only a $675,000 loan for operating purposes. The remaining $125,000 loan went to meet balance requirements. The following data reveal the comparative return to the bank and cost to the borrower with and without balance requirements.

$125,000 Ledger Balances Required	No Balances Required
Cost to borrower: $\dfrac{0.13(\$800,000)}{\$675,000} = 15.41\%$	$\dfrac{0.1541(\$675,000)}{\$675,000} = 15.41\%$
Return to bank: $\dfrac{0.13(\$800,000)}{\$675,000 + \$9,000} = 15.20\%$	$\dfrac{0.1541(\$675,000)}{\$675,000} = 15.41\%$

With balance requirements, the borrower paid $104,000 in interest during the year for an effective rate of 15.41 percent. The bank, in turn, allocated $675,000 for the loan but also had to increase its required reserves by 10 percent of $90,000, or $9,000. The bank earned $104,000 in interest on a net investment of $684,000, for a net yield of 15.2 percent. If, alternatively, the bank charged 15.41 percent with no balance requirements on a loan of $675,000, the cost to the borrower and return to the bank would equal 15.41 percent. Both the bank and borrower would have been better off if compensating balances were eliminated and the bank charged a rate between 15.2 and 15.41 percent on a $675,000 loan.

There are instances, however, when a borrower will move balances from another institution to the lending bank to meet balance requirements. In these cases, the lending bank has additional investable funds equal to the new deposit less float and required reserves against the deposit. Over time, firms tend to reduce their deposits to the minimum necessary to handle transactions requirements. Investment income from such transferred deposits is thus frequently short-lived.

FEE INCOME. Banks increasingly rely on fee income to supplement earnings. Competition among savings banks, credit unions, brokerage houses, insurance companies, and other commercial banks has increased borrowing costs relative to yields available on loans. This pressure on net interest margins and growth constraints from capital restrictions make new products and fee income the most promising source of earnings growth. Many corporate customers, in turn, are so efficient in minimizing their deposit balances that fees represent a better source of income than interest income from compensating balances.

When analyzing a customer's account relationship, fee income from all services rendered is included in total revenue. Fees are frequently charged on a per item basis, as with Federal Reserve wire transfers, or as a fixed periodic charge for a bundle of services, regardless of usage rates. Fees for servicing mortgage loans supported by pass-through securities and providing letters of credit, financial guarantees, data processing, and cash management have recently risen at banks, which aggressively market these services.

With credit relationships, banks often negotiate loan fees and compensating balance requirements. Three fees merit attention. Banks that extend formal loan commitments to corporate borrowers normally charge for making credit available. The loan commitment represents a line of credit that can be accessed at the borrower's discretion. If the customer chooses not to borrow, a bank earns no income from the service except for fees. The most common fee selected is a *facility fee*, which ranges from one-eighth of 1 percent to one-half of 1 percent of the total credit available. The fee applies regardless of actual borrowings because it is a charge for making funds available. For example, finance companies need back-up credit lines when their outstanding commercial paper matures, and a facility fee is the price for guaranteed bank financing.

Importantly, banks that make loan commitments are exposed to significant risks and facility fees do not cover potential losses. For example, late in 2001, both Enron and K-mart filed for bankruptcy. Prior to filing, investors refused to buy these firms' commercial paper. Thus, both Enron and K-mart increased their borrowings against outstanding loan commitments right before declaring bankruptcy. Banks that extended the commitments absorbed the losses soon after the borrowing. J.P. Morgan Chase, one of the lenders burned with loan commitments to Enron and K-mart, withdrew from the loan commitment business in 2002.

A *commitment fee* serves the same purpose but is imposed against the unused portion of the line. Because it applies only to committed funds that are not actually borrowed, it represents a penalty charge for not borrowing. A customer that fully uses the available funds pays no commitment fee. The last fee is selectively applied to loan commitments that convert to a term loan after a specified period. Called a *conversion fee,* it equals as much as one-half of 1 percent of the loan principal converted to a term loan and is paid at the time of conversion.

Determining the impact of these fees on revenues is straightforward. Suppose that each fee equals one-fourth of 1 percent and applies to the $1 million credit line previously discussed. The customer borrows $800,000, which is converted to a term loan at the end of the year. The annual facility fee, commitment fee, and conversion fee amount to $2,500, $500, and $2,000, respectively.

LOAN INTEREST AND BASE LENDING RATES. Loans are the dominant asset in bank portfolios, and loan interest is the primary revenue source. The actual interest earned depends on the contractual loan rate and the outstanding principal. Although banks quote many different loan rates to customers, several general features stand out. Most banks price commercial loans off of base rates, which serve as indexes of a bank's cost of funds. Common base rate alternatives include the federal funds rate, CD rate, commercial paper rate, the London Interbank Offer Rate (LIBOR), the LIBOR swap curve, Wall Street prime, and a bank's own weighted cost of funds. The contractual loan rate is set at some mark-up over the base rate, so that interest income varies directly with movements in the level of borrowing costs. Such floating-rate loans are popular at banks because they increase the rate sensitivity of loans in line with the increased rate sensitivity of bank liabilities. Also, the magnitude of the mark-up reflects differences in perceived default and liquidity risk associated with the borrower. The mark-up increases with loans in higher risk classes and with maturity as there is more time for the borrower's condition to deteriorate.[5] Finally, a substantial portion of commercial loans and most consumer loans carry fixed rates. In each case, the contractual rates should reflect the estimated cost of bank funds, perceived default risk, and a term liquidity and interest rate risk premium over the life of the agreement.

The use of different base rates masks the traditional role filled by the prime rate. Prior to the mid-1970s, banks tied most commercial loan rates to prime, which they described as the lowest loan rate available for the best commercial borrowers. (See Contemporary Issues: The Prime Rate Controversy.) Prime was an administered rate that banks changed in response to longer-term fundamental changes in money market rates. Prime rate changes occurred infrequently, but signaled permanent movements in interest rate levels.

There are, in fact, many different prime rates. A national prime rate quoted by the money center banks receives most of the attention. These banks compete in the same national and international markets, so that when one bank changes its prime, the others quickly follow. Large regional banks and smaller banks typically quote their own local prime rates that reflect their own institutions' cost of funds. The money center and international banks serve as price leaders, but most other banks change their local prime with a lag, depending on local market conditions. If customers insist, they may tie their base rate to New York prime or the prime rate of a specific large regional bank. This creates problems, however, because banks other than the lender may control base rate changes and thus the yield on many loans. In this

---

[5]When a comprehensive customer profitability analysis is used, the mark-up reflects either default risk or required interest to cover expenses and to meet profit targets. Many banks price loans independent from other account activity.

THE PRIME RATE CONTROVERSY

For many years banks described the prime rate as the rate they charged their best corporate customers. It was the lowest rate available to corporate borrowers, with most commercial loans carrying rates set at a mark-up over prime. This environment deterred price competition between the money center banks that administered the rate. When money market rates increased, a money center bank serving as a price leader would raise its prime. The others would follow closely. When market rates fell, another price leader would lead the group in lowering quoted prime.

Eventually, the money center banks broke with traditional prime rate pricing. In the mid-1970s, the best large corporate borrowers developed cheaper funding sources in the commercial paper market and with foreign banks that based loan rates at narrow margins over LIBOR. Rather than lower prime, and thus the effective yield on all floating-rate loans, U.S. banks simply priced selected loans below prime where competition demanded it. The result was that prime rate borrowers were not paying the lowest rate available.

In 1980, Jackie Kleiner sued the First National Bank of Atlanta claiming that, by definition, the bank's prime rate was its lowest rate.

Because other borrowers paid less than his prime rate loan, he argued that the prime rate was a fraud. First Atlanta settled the suit for an estimated $12 million. Other similar cases were quickly filed, most of which were settled out of court at considerable expense to banks. Most banks now substitute the generic term "base rate" for "prime rate" in their loan agreements. Those that still use "prime" explicitly define it as the bank's quoted commercial loan rate or add a disclaimer that it is not always the lowest rate.

environment, loan rates may not change coincidentally with a bank's own cost of funds. Small banks have subsequently moved to using their own prime rate whenever possible.

The prime rate remains a popular index for pricing loans, and it is increasingly applied to consumer loans, such as home equity loans and credit card loans. Individuals who borrow in these forms typically pay a floating rate that changes when the prime rate changes. Prime is less attractive to large corporate customers of banks. Many of these firms have direct access to the money and capital markets such that they can borrow at rates well below prime. Why should they borrow at prime? Banks recognize this and often allow these firms to borrow at floating rates tied to other indexes, such as the federal funds rate, commercial paper rate, LIBOR, or the 1-year constant maturity Treasury rate. This has induced banks to keep prime constant when rates fall in general. Customers that have market power benefit from falling money market (and bank loan) rates because their loans are tied to money market indexes. Customers without market power, individuals and small businesses, continue to pay rates tied to the higher prime rate.

Clearly, the prime rate has decreased in importance to the point where it now represents just another potential base rate. Large banks generally allow financially strong corporations to select their own base rate from CDs, commercial paper, federal funds, and LIBOR. LIBOR pricing is particularly popular because the market is very liquid and many customers routinely deal in international markets. Banks also favor LIBOR pricing because they and their customers can readily hedge risk with interest rate futures, options, swaps, caps, and floors that are based on different LIBOR contracts. The federal funds rate is more volatile because it represents a target variable of the Federal Reserve's monetary policy and prime rates change too slowly at a bank's discretion. When borrowers choose these alternatives, the bank's effective yield is invariably below its prime rate. Thus, such high quality borrowers view prime minus some rate (below prime rates) as a competitive alternative. Prime rate pricing at prime plus some mark-up now applies almost exclusively to small businesses and individuals. Banks that use prime rate pricing effectively segment borrowers in terms of their alternative credit sources. Borrowers with direct access to money markets pay below prime rates, as banks act as price takers. Borrowers with no alternatives to bank credit pay higher rates set by banks.

▪ EXHIBIT 18.3

ACCOUNT ACTIVITY FOR BANKEN INDUSTRIES, JANUARY THROUGH MARCH

Loan Agreement

Revolver: $5 million commitment that converts to term loan after three years

Interest rate: Bank's average 90-day CD rate + 2%

Fees: 0.125% facility fee; 0.25% conversion fee

Compensating balances: 3% of facility + 2% of actual borrowing; collected balances

Account Activity	Activity (No. of Items)	Item Cost
Demand deposit activity		
Home debits	4,187	$0.23
Transit items	15,906	0.12
Deposits	90	0.35
Account maintenance	3	6.75
Returned items	33	3.50
Wire transfers	336	2.00
Security safekeeping	13	4.00
Payroll processing	3	1,500.00
Loan and Deposit Activity: January 1–March 31		
Average borrowing	$4.1 million	
Contractual interest rate	10.00%	
Loan administration (annual)	0.70%	
Risk expense (annual)	1.00%	
Average ledger demand deposit balance	$174,516	
Average float	$ 60,112	
Required reserve ratio	10.00%	
Earnings credit rate	5.80%	
Weighted marginal cost of debt	6.48%	
Bank tax rate	35.00%	

NOTE: Weighted marginal cost of debt is calculated assuming 92 percent of the loan financing is in the form of debt. Thus, .0648 = .92 times the weighted average cost of debt of 7.04 percent.

The net result is that the prime rate no longer tracks money market rates as closely during periods of declining rates. When money market rates increase, borrowing costs also increase and banks raise prime with a short lag. When money market rates decrease, banks are slow to lower prime. This behavior helps maintain interest spreads when rates increase and widen spreads when rates decrease.

CUSTOMER PROFITABILITY ANALYSIS: AN APPLICATION TO COMMERCIAL ACCOUNTS

The following analysis applies the customer profitability characteristics discussed previously. The bank's account manager has collected information regarding services used by Banken Industries, which designs, manufactures, and distributes home fragrance products, for the first three months of the year. During this time, the company borrowed $4.1 million of a $5 million credit line. Exhibit 18.3 lists pertinent information on the loan and other services provided. Exhibit 18.4 formally compares the bank's expenses and target profit with revenues from the total account relationship.

The loan is a revolving credit agreement in which Banken Industries has the option after three years of converting its outstanding loan to a term loan with fixed principal payments.

• EXHIBIT 18.4

CUSTOMER PROFITABILITY ANALYSIS FOR BANKEN
INDUSTRIES, JANUARY THROUGH MARCH

Expenses

Demand deposit expense			
Home debit	4,187 @ $0.23	$ 963.01	
Transit items	15,906 @ $0.12	1,908.72	
Deposits	90 @ $40.35	31.50	
Returned items	33 @ $43.50	115.50	
Account maintenance	3 @ $6.75	20.25	
Total			$ 3,039
Wire transfers	336 @ $2.00		672
Security safekeeping	13 @ $4.00		52
Payroll processing	3 @ $1,500.00		4,500
Loan expense			
Loan administration: (0.007)(90/365)($4.1 million)			7,077
Risk expense: (0.01)(90/365)($4.1 million)			10,110
Interest expense on pooled debt financing:			
(0.0704)(90/365)(0.92)($4.1 million)			65,478
Total expenses			$ 90,928

Target Profit

Target pretax return to shareholders = 18%
Relevant financing percentage: 8% equity, 92% debt

Target profit: (0.18)(90/365)(0.08)($4.1 million)	$ 14,558
Expenses + Target Profit	$105,486

Revenues

Investment income from balances		
Ledger balances	$174,516	
Minus float	60,112	
Collected balance	$114,404	
Minus required reserves @ 10%	11,440	
Investable balances	$102,964	
Investment income: (0.051)(90/365)($102,964)		$ 1,295
Fee income: (0.00125)(90/365)($5 million)		1,541
Loan interest: (0.10)(90/365)($4.1 million)		101,096
Total revenues		$103,932
Revenues − (Expenses + Target Profit)		−$ 1,554

It will pay a conversion fee only if it converts the line to a term loan. Compensating balances are set at 3 percent of the facility plus 2 percent of borrowings. Banken Industries used a variety of check-clearing services, wire-transferred funds between banks, and had the bank hold securities for safekeeping in addition to borrowing funds. The bank also processed Banken's payroll at a cost of $1,500 per month.

The breakdown of expenses and revenues is readily apparent when Banken's loan and deposit account relationship is viewed in terms of the bank's T-account.

Asset	Liability
Loan to Banken	Demand Deposit—Banken
$4.1 million	$174,516

Banken Industries is clearly a net borrower of funds. Exhibit 18.3 lists specific loan and deposit activity for January through March, and each item produces expenses and/or revenues. The general framework of the profitability analysis assumes that 92 percent of the $4.1 million loan is financed by debt with the remaining 8 percent financed by equity.

Expenses during the quarter totaled $90,928. Of this total, approximately 72 percent related to financing the loan, with the remainder attributable primarily to processing checks and Banken's payroll. Check-handling expenses, while measurable, do not represent direct cash outlays. The cost of processing checks includes labor costs, processing equipment, repairs, overhead, and an allocation for fixed costs. Security safekeeping and loan handling add to personnel expenses. Risk expense on the loan is a noncash charge based on historical loan loss experience. Interest expense on borrowed funds totals $65,478 and is obtained by multiplying the bank's weighted marginal cost of debt by the amount of the loan (92 percent) that is financed by debt.

The bank's target profit is expressed as a percentage of the loan. The percentage, derived from Equation 18.2, assumes an 18 percent pretax target return to shareholders determined by management, with 8 percent of the financing coming from equity. Based on $4.1 million borrowed, the target profit over 90 days equals $14,558. The sum of target profit and expenses—$105,486—represents the minimum revenue that must be generated for the bank to cover expenses and meet profit objectives. Some banks include a mark-up over costs in their unit cost estimates. If so, this sum overstates the true revenue requirement.

Revenues are separated into three components. Investment income from Banken's demand deposit balances equals $1,295. This is obtained by multiplying the periodic earnings credit rate of 5.1 percent by investable balances of $102,964. Note that Banken Industries actually held an average $114,404 in collected balances, while the 3 + 2 compensating balance requirement mandated $232,000 [(.03 × $5 million + .02 × $4.1 million)]. If the company increased its collected balances to meet the minimum balance requirement, investment income from balances would have equaled $2,917, an increase of $1,622 over that credited. Facility fee income contributed $1,541, and loan interest $101,096, for total revenue of $103,932. This fell short of expenses plus the target profit by $1,554. The Banken Industries account thus generated profits in excess of the bank's estimated expenses but did not meet its 18 percent targeted pretax return to shareholders. Importantly, if Banken had met its minimum compensating balance requirement, the bank would have met its profit target with the account. The account officer should call on Banken to resolve the deficient balance problem.

PRICING NEW COMMERCIAL LOANS

The same framework can also be used to price new loan agreements. The approach is the same, equating revenues with expenses plus target profit, but now the loan officer must forecast borrower behavior. Hence, marginal analysis is appropriate using incremental data, not historical data. For loan commitments this involves projecting the magnitude and timing of actual borrowings, compensating balances held, and the volume of services consumed. For other loans the amount borrowed is known. Once projections are formalized, the officer can solve for the loan interest rate that equates expected revenues with expected expenses. The analysis assumes that the contractual loan rate is set at a mark-up over the bank's weighted marginal cost of funds and thus varies coincidentally with borrowing costs.

Suppose that a bank is analyzing a request for a new 1-year $7 million working capital line of credit. The prospective borrower has no prior relationship with the bank. The officer handling the account forecasts that the customer will borrow an average $5.25 million during the year and that the annual cost of deposit services will equal $68,000. The bank will charge a commitment fee of one-half of 1 percent on the unused line, its weighted marginal cost of debt equals 7.4 percent, and its pretax target profit equals 18 percent. The loan is financed 7 percent by equity and 93 percent by debt. The combined risk and loan administration expense is projected at 1.3 percent of the loan. The issue is, what loan rate and compensating balance requirement will cover expected costs? For simplicity, the customer is required to hold a specified percentage of the loan in investable compensating balances and will receive a 4 percent earnings credit rate.[6]

Exhibit 18.5 summarizes two pricing alternatives. Estimated expenses and target profit based on 75 percent usage total $590,900 for the year. Option A requires 4 + 4 investable balances or $490,000 net of account float and required reserves. With this amount in investable balances, commitment fee and investment income equal $28,350, leaving $562,550 in loan interest that must be earned for total revenues to equal $590,900. The required loan rate of 10.72 percent is calculated by dividing required loan interest by the $5.25 million estimated loan.

Many influential borrowers refuse to maintain substantial balances at a bank and instead prefer to pay explicit fees. Option B in this example assumes that the customer holds no compensating balances, but instead pays a facility fee of one-fourth of 1 percent. In this environment, the bank would need to increase the loan rate by 0.20 percent to 10.92 percent. In essence, the bank expects to earn nothing in investment income from balances, which is offset by higher fee income and loan interest. In both cases, the required loan rate will vary directly with the bank's cost of funds.

The usefulness of the pricing procedure is that it provides a basis for understanding costs and revenues and negotiating terms. A bank is largely indifferent as to how revenues are obtained as long as the total covers expected costs.

RISK-ADJUSTED RETURNS ON LOANS

When deciding what rate to charge, loan officers attempt to forecast default losses over the life of a loan. Credit risk, in turn, can be divided into expected losses and unexpected losses. *Expected losses* might be reasonably based on mean historical loss rates, much like the summary ratios in Exhibit 18.1. *Unexpected losses*, in contrast, should be measured by computing the standard deviation of realized losses from the historical mean. Ideally, the interest rate on a loan will encompass both expected and unexpected losses.

Unfortunately, many banks ignore these risk components entirely. A common loan pricing scheme is for banks to classify loans into risk categories like that in Exhibit 18.1 based on mean historical loss rates. Low-risk loans have low default rates while default rates on higher-risk loans increase systematically. Risk expense, or the charge for potential default losses, is then levied in an approximate linear fashion with perceived riskiness. For example, the incremental risk charge might increase by 25 basis points per category from the lowest to the highest risk types.

There are two problems with this approach. First, expected losses do not normally vary in a linear fashion. Mean loss rates in each successive risk class typically increase by a greater amount from the lowest to highest risk categories. The loss rates in Exhibit 18.1 support this. A 25 basis point risk charge for risk class 1 loans exceeds the mean loss rate. A 50 basis point risk charge for risk class 2 loans is less than the mean loss rate because the default percentage increased by 39 basis points rather than just 25. The default percentage rises by an increased amount from risk class 2 to 3 and from risk class 3 to 4 as well. Any risk charge should thus increase nonlinearly. Second, even if expected losses vary linearly, unexpected losses typically do not. Suppose, for example, that the default percentages in the four risk classes varied at 25 basis point increments from .25 percent to 1 percent. The normal situation is that the highest risk loans will exhibit the greatest volatility of loss rates such that the standard deviation of unexpected loss is greatest. These loans are thus riskier yet, and this incremental risk should be priced.

---

[6]If ledger or collected balances were required, the bank would also have to forecast float and required reserves.

• EXHIBIT 18.5

Expenses

Deposit activity	$ 68,000	
Loan administration and risk	68,250	(0.013 × $5.25 million)
Interest on borrowed funds	388,500	(0.074 × $5.25 million)
	$524,750	
Target Profit	66,150	(0.18 × 0.07 × $5.25 million)
Total	$590,900	

Revenues

Option A: Compensating balances set at 4 + 4 investable balances
($490,000); earnings credit rate = 4%; 1/2 of 1% commitment fee
Option B: 1/4 of 1% facility fee, no balances required

	Option A	Option B
Fee income	$ 8,750	$ 17,500
Investment income from balances	19,600	0
Required loan interest	562,550	573,400
Total	$590,900	$590,900
Required loan rate	10.72%	10.92%

NOTE: Required loan rate is $562,550/5,250,000 = 10.72 percent; 573,400/5,250,000 = 10.92 percent.

Some banks now calculate a risk-adjusted return on equity for individual loans using the volatility in unexpected loan loss rates to allocate equity to each type of loan. Rose (1991) documents an application where a bank allocates equity to each class of loans equal to one standard deviation of unexpected losses. The risk-adjusted return is then calculated as the net profit divided by allocated equity. The procedure adjusts for risk because loans with highly volatile unexpected losses are allocated large amounts of equity, while loans with little volatility in unexpected losses are allocated little equity. When the procedure was applied to historical loan performance, the results indicated that the highest quality loans produced the highest risk-adjusted returns. Even though the dollar amount of net profit was small per loan, losses were so low that the equity allocation was similarly small.

Chapter 4 introduced EVA analysis as described by Stern Stewart. This approach to analyzing whether a transaction contributes to maximizing shareholder value can also be applied directly to individual loans and a bank's loan portfolio. Some banks, such as Centura (part of Royal Bank of Canada), use the EVA framework to price and evaluate the profitability of individual loans. In this application, each loan officer incorporates the descriptive information for each loan request in the EVA model and, given the riskiness of this class of loans (in general), determines a revenue amount and loan interest that will add value to the bank's stockholders.

Today, commercial loans are frequently underpriced at banks, especially when competition for loans is strong, because lenders appear to systematically understate risk. The appropriate procedure is to identify both expected and unexpected losses and incorporate both in determining the appropriate risk charge. This does not appear to be the case with many other types of loans at banks. Witness the substantial profits banks have earned on consumer credit cards. Nonbank financial institutions similarly have had greater success in pricing loans. Consumer finance companies, for example, experience higher default rates but charge much higher loan rates than banks so that net profits and returns to stockholders exceed that at most banks. At the extreme are pawn shops. A study of pawn shops in five states determined that the effective APRs paid by consumers ranged from 36 percent to 240 percent in 1987 and 1988, high enough to cover default rates as high as 20 percent.[7]

FIXED RATES VERSUS FLOATING RATES

When interest rates were relatively stable and the yield curve was upsloping, banks were willing to make loans at fixed rates above those being paid on shorter-term liabilities. Even though it was liability sensitive in that earnings would fall with a rate increase, a bank could continually roll over deposits at relatively low rates and maintain a positive spread. In a volatile rate environment with an increased reliance on market rate liabilities, banks prefer floating-rate loans and short loan maturities. Floating-rate loans increase the rate sensitivity of bank assets, increase asset sensitivity, and reduce potential net interest income losses from rising interest rates.

In the above situation, floating-rate loans effectively transfer interest rate risk from the bank to the borrower. Although this is normally desirable, it may eventually return to haunt the bank in the form of higher credit risk. Rising interest rates increase a borrower's interest expense. If corporate cash flow from operations or personal income do not increase accordingly, the borrower may be unable to meet debt service requirements.

This scenario became real in 1980 and 1981 for small businesses and again in 1985 for residential mortgages. When the prime rate rose above 20 percent in 1980 and 1981, small business' cash flow could not support the high interest payments and failures followed. During the late 1970s, housing prices rose by more than 10 percent annually. Many individuals, fearing that housing might not be affordable if they waited, stretched themselves to the limit financially to purchase a home. This often meant paying as little as 5 percent down and negotiating some form of adjustable-rate mortgage for the remainder of the purchase price. After 1980, U.S. housing values increased at roughly the rate of inflation but personal income did not increase fast enough to meet rising mortgage payments. Homebuyers, in turn, started defaulting on their mortgages. By 1985, payments on more than 6 percent of all mortgages were delinquent, and foreclosures had reached almost 0.25 percent of outstanding mortgages. In subsequent years, conditions improved but by 1990, the cycle repeated itself, and mortgage delinquencies rose sharply to 6 or 7 percent. While delinquencies dropped to historical lows in 1998, they increased again in 2001 with the economic slowdown.

Given equivalent rates, most borrowers prefer fixed-rate loans in which the bank assumes all interest rate risk. Banks frequently offer two types of inducements to encourage floating-rate pricing. First, floating rates are initially set below fixed rates for borrowers with a choice. The discount may be as high as 3 percent, depending on the current level of rates. A bank essentially charges a term premium to cover the added risk on fixed-rate loans. The size of the discount is, of course, constrained by a bank's cost of funds and required return. Second, a bank may establish an interest rate cap on floating-rate loans to limit the possible increase in periodic payments. A cap represents the maximum interest rate that will be applied at any interval, or it may be fixed over the entire maturity. Common caps with adjustable rate mortgages are a 1 percent annual cap and 5 percent lifetime cap, or a 2 percent annual cap with a 6 percent lifetime cap. For example, suppose that a borrower agreed to a mortgage with the initial rate equal to 6 percent for the first year but adjusted each year based on some index. With the first cap described, the maximum loan rate that would apply one year after origination is 7 percent (6 percent + 1 percent annual cap), and the maximum rate that would ever apply is 11 percent (6 percent + 5 percent lifetime cap) regardless of how high rates moved.

---

[7]Caskey and Zikmund (1990) document the performance of pawnshops in Indiana, New Jersey, Oklahoma, Oregon, and Pennsylvania.

A borrower pays the negotiated floating rate until the cap is reached. Although cap rate agreements improve a bank's ability to market floating-rate loans, they lower revenues when interest rates rise. Lenders recognize the inherent risk of such caps and incorporate their impact in their modeling of interest rate risk (see Chapters 8 and 9). Lenders and borrowers can hedge this risk by entering into interest rate swap, futures, and caps.

Although many commercial loans carry floating rates, it has been difficult for banks to market floating-rate consumer loans except for real estate. Since 1992, adjustable-rate mortgages have comprised more than one-half of new mortgages. It appears, however, that floating-rate installment loan pricing will evolve slowly. Banks that market variable-rate consumer loans generally follow these guidelines.

1. Select an index or base rate that varies closely with the bank's cost of funds. The bank's weighted cost of funds is preferred, assuming the bank can adequately explain it to customers. Borrowers, however, may prefer a more visible, publicly quoted index.

2. Link variation in the floating rate with the timing of index changes. If the index on consumer credit lines changes monthly, for example, vary the floating rate monthly.

3. Offer both fixed-rate and floating-rate options. Price the fixed rate at a premium large enough to protect against possible increases in the cost of funds. Impose prepayment penalties on all fixed-rate contracts.

4. Use interest rate caps sparingly. If they are used, hedge the risk exposure in the interest rate cap or swap markets.

MATCHED FUNDING AND HEDGING. Some banks make fixed-rate loans and attempt to control interest rate risk by matched funding or using interest rate swaps and financial futures. Matched funding involves negotiating loans and purchasing funds with identical maturities. If, for example, a customer requests a 1-year fixed-rate loan, a bank would issue 1-year CDs to fund it. If the loan is priced at a positive spread over the CDs and the timing of interest payments coincides, the bank assumes no additional interest rate risk. This strategy is limited to large banks with an extensive customer base that can generate different maturity deposits on demand. Chapter 4 outlines the mechanics of transfer pricing systems, which are flexible enough to hedge interest rate risk via matched funding.

In recent years, Federal Home Loan Banks have provided funding to banks via advances, which have greatly expanded the range of loans that community banks can offer with limited interest rate risk. Specifically, most FHLBs offer advances with long maturities of up to 15–20 years. Banks borrowing in this form can match the advances with loans of similar maturities priced at a positive spread. The remaining risk is that the loan might prepay. FHLBs also offer amortizing advances that banks match with amortizing loans with maturities of up to 15 years. Both amortization schedules are the same, so prepayment risk remains.

Chapters 10 and 11 cover off-balance sheet hedging tools and strategies that banks can use to manage interest rate risk. With financial futures, it is possible to make fixed-rate loans and hedge against potential losses from higher future borrowing costs by selling futures contracts or buying put options on financial futures. It is also possible to enter into interest rate swaps by agreeing to make fixed rate payments in return for floating rate receipts, or to directly buy interest rate caps. Hedging can be applied either to a bank's funding GAP or earnings sensitivity, duration gap or market value of equity sensitivity, or individual transactions. Details for the various hedging strategies are provided in these earlier chapters.

Both matched funding and the use of interest rate swaps and financial futures entail certain risks. A bank will lose in both instances if a borrower prepays a loan. Prepayments normally occur when interest rates fall. With matched funding, a bank will still pay interest on its liabilities at the original rates but must reinvest the proceeds at lower rates. Any "fixed" spread will decline and possibly even become negative. With interest rate swaps and futures,

■ EXHIBIT 18.6

PRICING ALTERNATIVES OVER VARIOUS BASE RATES

	6-Year Revolver/Term Loan Pricing Options			
	Years	CD +	LIBOR +	Weighted Cost of Debt +
Revolver	1–2	1	⅞	¼
Term	3–4	1⅛	1	½
Term	5–6	1⅜	1¼	¾

the bank will have a loss on its swap contract or short futures position. This necessitates prohibiting prepayments or imposing substantial prepayment penalties.

BASE RATE ALTERNATIVES

Contractual loan rates for commercial customers are determined through negotiation. As Exhibit 18.5 demonstrates, banks take into account projected expenses, compensating balances, fee income, and profit objectives. The two parties often negotiate the base rate as well in floating-rate loans. Large, multinational borrowers can virtually dictate terms. Frequently, a major customer will circulate a loan request among several financial institutions and accept bids on the loan terms. It is common for the borrower to retain the option to price the loan off of several potential base rates. The actual base rate is determined not when the agreement is signed, but when the borrower actually takes down the funds. Thus, a borrower can wait until the funds are needed to determine which alternative will likely provide the lowest-cost alternative.

For example, a large bank has agreed to extend a 6-year $50 million revolver/term loan to a Fortune 500 company with domestic and overseas operations. The revolver portion extends two years with the 4-year term portion also divided into consecutive two-year agreements. Because of its market power, the borrower is granted three base rate options: the bank's 3-month CD rate, 3-month LIBOR, or the bank's weighted cost of debt. Exhibit 18.6 indicates the size of premium over each base rate.

Chapter 12 describes the weighted cost of debt calculation. The CD base rate is normally the quoted nominal rate adjusted for required reserves and the cost of Federal Deposit Insurance Corp. insurance. LIBOR represents the quoted rate, as neither reserves nor insurance is required. The customer selects which alternative is lowest cost at the time funds are borrowed under the revolver. At the end of each following quarter, the customer can reset the base rate according to the cost comparison. Obviously, the customer will select the base rate and premium that it forecasts will provide the lowest-cost alternative.

Smaller corporations do not possess the same financial flexibility and thus do not receive the same treatment. Banks are moving toward using their own weighted marginal cost of debt as the preferred base rate for these customers. This rate represents the effective marginal cost of bank borrowing. Loans priced at a positive spread over this cost of funds lock in a return as long as the borrower does not default. Still, two issues continually arise. What is the best measure of the bank's cost of funds and subsequent base rate for pricing purposes? How can the bank readily communicate its base rate computation to customers?

THE WEIGHTED COST OF FUNDS AND BASE RATE. Chapter 12 introduced a procedure to estimate the weighted marginal cost of total bank funds, including debt and equity. In loan pricing, the cost of equity represents the bank's target profit. Base rate analysis focuses on the cost of debt plus target return.

· EXHIBIT 18.7

Loanable Market Rate Debt	Amount	%	Current Rates	Weighted Cost
Money market deposit accounts	$16.8	19%	4.50%	0.86%
Small time deposits (6-mo.)	19.5	22	5.00	1.10
Small time deposits (30-mo.)	21.3	24	6.80	1.63
Jumbo CDs	25.6	29	6.60	1.91
Federal funds purchased	5.3	6	5.15	0.31
Total	$88.5	100%		5.81%
Base Rate Calculation:				
Weighted cost of market rate debt	5.81%			
Target net interest margin	4.50			
Target loan rate	10.31%			
Maximum premium over base rate	−2.50			
Base rate	7.81%			

NOTE: Figures are in millions of dollars.

The following calculation of a base rate is an attempt to ensure that loans are priced to cover bank costs. It rests on several assumptions that guarantee a base rate estimate above a bank's weighted marginal cost of total debt. First, core deposits are not available to fund loans. This is justified because loans presumably do not exceed deposits, and long-term funds should finance long-term bank assets. Second, deposits paying below-market rates will continue to decrease as a funding source. For these reasons, the cost of debt calculation excludes core deposits, such as demand deposits, NOW accounts, and savings deposits as funding sources for loans.

Exhibit 18.7 provides an estimate of a hypothetical bank's weighted cost of market-rate debt. The bank currently operates with $88.5 million in MMDAs, time deposits, CDs, and federal funds purchased. The weighted cost of 5.81 percent is calculated as the sum of the proportionate financing from each source times the corresponding current market interest rate across components. Current interest rates are adjusted for reserves and FDIC insurance.

The base rate quotation uses this weighted cost as the primary input. A bank's target loan rate equals this composite cost plus a premium that reflects the bank's target net interest margin. This net interest margin includes coverage for anticipated expenses, taxes, and target profit. Finally, most borrowers resent paying too large of a premium over any base rate. This reflects the perception that loans priced at a bank's base rate are available only to the most creditworthy borrowers. The base rate quote is set at the target loan rate minus the maximum premium acceptable to normal risk customers, 10.31 percent minus 2.50 percent in this example. The quoted rate would thus be 7.75 percent rounded to the nearest quarter of a percent.

Communicating any base rate to customers can be confusing. Borrowers constantly hear references to the national prime rate and federal funds rates following the weekly money supply announcement. The natural tendency is to compare base rates, and normally the rate calculated from Exhibit 18.7 is above the national prime rate. A bank must clearly indicate why its cost of funds does not match a money center bank's, and focus on the fact that the bank's own base rate tracks its cost of market rate funds. Most discussions eventually focus on the benefits from this bank's personal relationship and quality of service.

CUSTOMER PROFITABILITY ANALYSIS: CONSUMER INSTALLMENT LOANS

The previous applications focused on commercial accounts. In general, banks can use the same format in evaluating the profitability of individual accounts. However, there are two significant differences that alter the analysis: consumer loans are much smaller than commercial loans, on average, and processing costs per dollar of loan are much higher for consumer than commercial loans. In 1996, for example, the average installment loan at banks with $50 million to $200 million in deposits equaled only $6,031, ranging from $1,035 for check credit plans to $20,929 under floor plan arrangements. Each consumer loan officer made an average of 428 loans at a cost of $185 per loan, and it cost almost $11 to collect each payment.[8] Loans will not generate enough interest to cover costs if they are too small or the maturity is too short, even with high loan rates. Banks thus set pricing targets with regard to minimum loan size, maturity, and the contract interest rate.[9]

The profitability framework discussed below recognizes this trade-off between size, maturity, and rate. It establishes break-even values for each pricing element based on average unit costs associated with consumer installment loans, assuming values for the other pricing elements. The break-even relationship is based on the objective that loan interest revenues, net of funding costs and losses, equal loan costs:

$$\text{Net Interest income} = \text{Interest expense} + \text{Loan losses} + \text{Acquisition costs} + \text{Collection costs} \tag{18.3}$$

More generally, if:

r = annual percentage loan rate (%)

d = interest cost of debt (%)

l = average loan loss rate (%)

S = initial loan size

B = average loan balance outstanding (% of initial loan)

M = number of monthly payments

C_a = loan acquisition cost, and

C_c = collection cost per payment

then

$$(r - d - l)SB(M/12) = C_a + (C_c)(M) \tag{18.4}$$

The left side of the equality represents total net interest revenue over the life of the loan. The right side represents the initial cost of making the loan plus the cost of collecting all payments.

Two applications of Equation 18.4 are provided in Exhibit 18.8, using 1999 *Functional Cost Analysis* data.[10] A 2-year loan with 24 monthly payments priced at a 12 percent annual percentage rate (APR) required a minimum $6,932 initial loan to cover costs. A similar $4,000 loan over two years requires a 17.95 percent APR for the bank to break even.

---

[8]The information is drawn from the Federal Reserve's *Functional Cost Analysis* data for 1999 for banks with deposits from $50 million to $200 million.

[9]Peterson (1985) provides a comprehensive analysis of consumer loan and deposit pricing issues.

[10]Equation 18.4 approximates the true relationship. In fact, the average loan outstanding varies with the true interest rate and maturity. A precise equation appears in *Functional Cost Analysis*.

· EXHIBIT 18.8

BREAK-EVEN ANALYSIS: NONELECTRONIC CONSUMER INSTALLMENT LOANS: BANKS WITH MORE THAN $200 MILLION IN DEPOSITS

Average Costs: 1999 Functional Cost Analysis Data

Acquisition cost per loan	$C_a = \$137.49$
Collection cost per payment	$C_c = \$20.07$
Interest cost of debt	$d = 3.31\%$
Loan loss rate (3-year average)	$l = 0.57\%$

Break-Even Loan Size (S)

Assume:

No. of monthly payments	$M = 24$
Annual percentage loan rate	$r = 12\%$
Average loan balance outstanding (%)	$B = 55\%$

$$(0.12 - 0.0331 - 0.0057)S(0.55)(24/12) = \$137.49 + \$20.07(24)$$
$$S = \$6,932$$

Break-Even Loan Rate (r*)

Assume:

$M = 24$
$S = \$4,000$
$B = 55\%$
$$(r^* - 0.0331 - 0.0057)(\$4,000)(0.55)2 = \$137.49 + \$20.07(24)$$
$$r = 17.95\%$$

Although these examples are simplistic, they show the procedure to calculate break-even costs and returns. In practice, banks must include other expenses that the federal data omit, such as costs from overhead, credit reports, advertising, and repossession. They should also recognize income from late-payment charges, fractions of months interest, and the effect of rebates, and then compare the difference between income and expenses with their target return.

SUMMARY

Customer profitability analysis is a procedure for analyzing the profitability of existing account relationships using historical data. It compares revenues generated from fees, investment income from a customer's deposit balances, and loan interest to expenses associated with extending credit and providing noncredit services plus a target return to shareholders. If revenues exceed or equal the sum of expenses and target profit, the account relationship at least meets the bank's minimum acceptable rate of return criteria. If revenues are less than expenses, the relationship is clearly unprofitable. If revenues exceed expenses but are less than expenses plus the target profit, the account covers costs but does not meet the minimum return objectives. These last two relationships subsequently need to be repriced.

The same framework using marginal or forecast data can be used to price commercial loans. It further demonstrates the trade-off between desired loan interest income, fee income, and compensating balance requirements in pricing decisions. In today's environment, fees are preferred to compensating balances because banks must hold reserves against balances, which lowers the net yield on the account relationship. Corporate treasurers spend considerable time and effort minimizing balances, and they prefer explicit pricing via fees. There is a general concern among analysts and regulators that, in recent years, bank loan yields have been too low, on average, relative to the risk assumed on many commercial loans. Banks are trying to better estimate the risk of loans and aggregate loan portfolios and allocate risk capital to reflect this risk. In doing so, RAROC and EVA methods are often used to assess loan profitability.

Consumer loan pricing is based on break-even analysis regarding the minimum acceptable size of loan or minimum acceptable rate of return. Because most loans are relatively small and do not generate significant fees or investment income from balances, consumer loan rates are relatively high. Viewed alternatively, banks need to increase the minimum size of consumer installment loan before revenues cover the cost of making the loan and processing payments.

In terms of loan pricing, most banks prefer to make floating-rate loans that increase the rate sensitivity of assets. Banks now price floating-rate loans off of many different base rates, including money market rates, a money center bank's prime rate, and their own local bank prime rate. The latter alternative assures a bank that loan yields will vary with its marginal cost of funds. Banks can generally lock in a spread and transfer interest rate risk to borrowers.

QUESTIONS

1. Explain how ledger deposit balances differ from collected balances and investable balances. Which is more restrictive to a borrower in meeting compensating balance requirements?

2. Loan officers and borrowers negotiate the earnings credit rate applicable to the borrower's deposit balances. What rate is appropriate theoretically? Analyze this from both the banker's and borrower's position.

3. What potential problems might arise from a bank making loans that are tied to (float with) the prime rate quoted by large multinational banks and not making loans tied to the bank's own prime rate?

4. List the three primary sources of revenue from a commercial customer's account. In today's economic environment, indicate whether each is growing or declining in use and explain why.

5. Are the following statements true or false? Explain why.
   a. The prime rate is the rate a bank charges its best (lowest risk) commercial borrowers.
   b. Commercial banks and borrowers are both better off with zero compensating balance requirements and a higher loan rate if the bank has to lend the borrower the compensating balances.
   c. Banks should make variable-rate loans in a rising interest rate environment and fixed-rate loans in a declining interest rate environment.
   d. Banks are typically quick to lower prime when money market rates fall and slow to raise prime when money market rates rise.

6. Why is LIBOR an attractive base rate for many banks and their corporate borrowers?

7. What is the difference between a bank's marginal cost of debt and its marginal cost of capital? Which should be used in estimating a bank's expenses and/or target profit when analyzing the profitability of a customer's account relationship?

8. Explain why a bank might prefer to charge a commitment fee instead of a facility fee.

9. Suppose that a borrower needs $80,000. A bank gives the borrower a choice of two pricing schemes. The first is a $100,000 loan with 20 percent compensating balance requirements (funded from the loan) priced at 10 percent. The second is an $80,000 loan with no balance requirements priced at 12.5 percent. Calculate the effective cost

to the borrower of each alternative. Assuming the bank must hold 12 percent required reserves against customer deposits, calculate the effective return to the bank of each alternative. Which pricing scheme is preferred for the bank?

10. If consumer loans tend to have longer maturities than commercial loans, why are fewer consumer loans priced on a floating rate basis?

11. Categorizing loans by risk category can be deceiving if the bank prices each higher risk category with a constant marginal premium. Explain what is wrong with this approach.

12. In each of the following situations, evaluate the profitability of the customer's account relationship with the bank. Did profits meet expectations? The expense figure includes the cost of debt but not the cost of equity. Figures are in millions of dollars.

	Expenses	Revenue	Target Profit
a. Class Action Corp	$11.45	$12.98	$1.50
b. Zisk Drive	131.81	130.27	4.66
c. Gonzo Ltd.	88.35	93.77	6.58

PROBLEMS

I. CONDUCTING A PRICING ANALYSIS

The chief financial officer for Vardon Drugs just requested an increase in the firm's credit line to $2 million from the present $1 million. As the first step in the pricing analysis, you collected information concerning Vardon's account relationship with the bank during the past year (Table 1). During the year, Vardon Drugs borrowed the full $1 million and maintained relatively small compensating balances that were set at 3 + 3 collected balances.

1. Using the information in Table 1, determine whether bank revenues from the account covered expenses during the year and met the bank's profit target of an 18 percent pretax return on equity.

2. Assume that Vardon's expenses other than interest increase by 10 percent during the next year and that all other items remain constant except the weighted cost of debt, which is expected to equal 9.8 percent. Determine the nominal loan rate the bank should charge to cover expenses plus meet the 18 percent pretax profit target.

3. Assume that Vardon will not hold any compensating balances. Relative to your analysis in question 2, what nominal interest rate should the bank charge to cover expenses and meet its target profit?

II. IDENTIFYING A NONPRODUCTIVE ACCOUNT

You are responsible for identifying customer accounts that are not meeting the bank's profit target of a 20 percent pretax return to shareholders. Applicable direct expenses and revenue factors are listed below for Michala's Marina for 2002.

- Actual borrowing: $827,000 of a $1,000,000 loan commitment
- Deposit activity expense: $14,336
- Loan risk expense: 1.05%
- Loan handling expense: 0.80%
- Pooled cost of debt financing the loan: 7.60%
- Bank commitment fee: 0.25%

▪ TABLE 1

ACCOUNT ACTIVITY FOR VARDON DRUGS IN THE PREVIOUS 12 MONTHS

	No. of Items	Item Cost
Account Activity		
Demand deposit activity		
Home debits	9,144	$ 0.22
Transit items	22,307	0.18
Deposits	406	0.64
Account maintenance	12	9.00
Wire transfers	58	3.00
Payroll processing	12	750
Loan and Deposit Activity		
Average loan outstanding: $1 million		
Average contract loan rate: 10.13%		
Loan administration expense: 0.65%		
Loan risk expense: 1.10%		
Average ledger demand deposit balance: $90,580		
Average account float: $24,900		
Bank required reserve ratio: 10%		
Weighted marginal cost of debt: 9.16%		
Facility fee: 0.25%		
Earnings credit rate: 5%		
Bank marginal tax rate: 35%		
Bank target capital structure: debt = 92%; equity = 8%		

- Michala's investable deposit balances: $39,850
- Bank interest income on the loan: $74,121

The bank pays taxes at the 35 percent rate, provides a 3.0 percent earnings credit, and allocates 6 percent equity and 94 percent debt financing to all loans. The pooled cost of debt estimate incorporates the 94 percent debt financing assumption. Did this account generate enough revenue to cover bank expenses and pay shareholders a 20 percent pretax return? How much did the bank earn or lose on the account?

III. DETERMINING MAXIMUM REVENUE

A senior officer at your bank estimates that the annual expenses and target profit of a customer's account relationship will total $334,000 for the next year. The customer is expected to borrow $2.6 million of a $3 million credit line. The bank will charge a facility fee of one-fourth of 1 percent. The customer has a choice of two pricing schemes:

	A	B
Compensating balances:	4% + 0% ledger balances	3% + 3% investable balances
Loan interest:	prime rate + 2%	prime rate + 1.25%
Earnings credit:	4%	4%

1. If the customer's average deposit float equals $44,000, the prime rate averages 8 percent, and the bank must hold 10 percent required reserves against collected balances, determine which alternative will produce the greatest revenue for the bank.

2. Using the data for pricing scheme A, determine the interest rate the bank should charge for total revenues to exactly equal expenses plus the target profit.

IV. DETERMINING AN INTEREST RATE

Laverneus Best recently stopped by the bank to request a $95,000 loan to buy a sailboat. He indicated that he would put $18,000 down and wants to borrow the remainder over three years with monthly payments. Use the following information and assume that Laverneus is an acceptable credit risk to determine the interest rate you would charge on the loan.

Cost of processing the loan application	$425
Collection cost per payment	$17
Loan loss rate on collateralized sailboat loans	0.72%
Weighted marginal cost of bank funds	8.5%

The proposed loan is an installment loan with 36 monthly payments. On average, the outstanding loan balance will equal 55 percent of the initial loan.

MANAGING THE INVESTMENT PORTFOLIO AND SPECIAL TOPICS

19

THE INVESTMENT PORTFOLIO
AND POLICY GUIDELINES

The world of bank investments has changed dramatically since 1986. At that time, Congress changed the tax laws so banks no longer found most municipal bonds to be attractive. Because banks had historically invested substantial sums in municipals, the tax change forced a fundamental restructuring of the composition of bank investments. Today there are few tax-sheltered investments remaining. Banks subsequently rely on taxable investments to meet their portfolio objectives.

This situation has presented both problems and opportunities. Problems generally center around the fact that many banks purchase securities without fully understanding their risk and yield features. For example, banks in the aggregate have purchased large amounts of callable agency and mortgage-backed securities in a variety of forms. Unfortunately, the call feature of the agency securities and the prepayment option for the mortgage borrower underlying mortgage-backed securities make it extremely difficult to accurately forecast both the magnitude of interest and principal payments and when they will be received. How then does an investor understand the risk and return trade-off? Opportunities exist with other innovative investment alternatives, such as mutual funds and securities backed by car loans, leases, and credit card receivables, to further complicate the investment decision.

This chapter examines why banks own marketable securities. It discusses the motivation behind trading account securities versus securities held as investments and provides an overview of the risk and return factors that influence the choice of securities and the basic features of securities held in the investment portfolio. As such, it follows the discussions of security pricing and interest rates in Chapters 6 and 7. It further introduces policy guidelines that should help identify the appropriate investment decisions. Chapter 20 critiques various investment strategies that banks typically follow.

Many commercial banks concentrate their asset management efforts on meeting loan customers' credit needs. Because this involves detailed credit analysis and direct negotiation of terms with borrowers, they maintain a large staff of loan officers. Managing investment securities typically plays a secondary role, especially at small banks. Banks operate as price-takers because security yields are normally determined nationally in the money and capital markets. Basic investment decisions, including what amount and type of securities to purchase, can be determined by senior management and implemented by a smaller staff.

The securities activities of large banks and small banks are fundamentally different. Historically, small banks have purchased securities and held them until maturity. In many cases, they work with large correspondent banks or bankers' banks in deciding which securities to buy and how many. Large banks, in contrast, not only buy securities for their own portfolios, but also trade them more actively prior to maturity in an effort to make a profit. They also may manage a securities trading account, such that they buy and sell securities in the secondary market, and may operate an underwriting subsidiary that helps municipalities and businesses issue debt in the money and capital markets. These activities are commonly grouped under a single division, which is also responsible for the bank's funding and interest rate risk management.

Historically, bank regulators have emphasized the risks associated with owning securities. Investment policy guidelines thus focus on controlling credit and interest rate risk within the securities portfolio. Regulators generally prohibit banks from purchasing common stock for income purposes and effectively limit investments in debt instruments to investment grade securities (designated as bonds rated Baa or above).[1] To provide greater liquidity, many banks keep security maturities or durations short-term because of the lower price volatility. Some banks pursue passive investment strategies, under which managers react to events, rather than active strategies involving buying and selling securities prior to maturity for profit in anticipation of changing economic conditions.

Interest rate deregulation and low spreads on loans, however, have encouraged an increasing number of banks to pursue active strategies in managing investments. Bank managers now look to marketable securities to generate more interest income and periodic gains from sales prior to maturity. Consequently, they manage their portfolio maturity/duration and composition more aggressively relative to their preferred interest rate risk position. The following analysis describes the function of bank trading accounts, characteristics of the most popular taxable and tax-exempt securities, and then outlines the objectives and structure of the investment portfolio. The final section identifies the key facets and importance of a bank's formal investment policy statement.

DEALER OPERATIONS AND THE SECURITIES TRADING ACCOUNT

When banks buy securities they must indicate the underlying objective for accounting purposes. The alternative classifications include held to maturity, available for sale, and trading purposes. *Held to maturity* securities are recorded at amortized cost on the balance sheet with changes in value having no impact on the income statement. Unless the underlying quality of the securities changes dramatically, banks must hold these securities until they mature. *Available for sale* securities are reported at market value. Any increases or decreases in market

---

[1]In certain situations, such as when common stock is taken as collateral against a loan, commercial banks can own equities. However, they must liquidate equities within a reasonable period of time. Banks can also own noninvestment grade securities but must show they are comparable in quality to similar investment grade instruments.

value associated with interest rate changes are balanced by an entry in stockholders' equity that recognizes unrealized gains and losses on securities. Again, there is no income statement impact. Banks can sell these securities at any time. Securities held for *trading* purposes are part of a trading account. A trading account represents an inventory of securities that a bank holds for resale to other investors. The securities can be of any type including Treasury, agency, and municipal securities, but the bank expects to own them only briefly until a long-term buyer is found. Such securities are listed separately on a bank's balance sheet as trading account securities and are marked to market. The bank profits from this activity by buying the securities at prices below the sales price, which is referred to as a trading profit and appears on the income statement.

In this capacity, banks operate both as primary dealers with the Federal Reserve and as market makers with other participants. As a primary dealer, a bank (or bank subsidiary) normally buys U.S. Treasury securities at auction and in the secondary market and sells the securities to its customers. The Federal Reserve System trades only with primary dealers through its New York Bank when implementing open market purchases and sales. As market makers, banks perform the same service with U.S. Treasury, agency, and selected municipal securities, trading with all interested parties.

Banks perform three basic functions within their trading activities. First, they offer investment advice and assistance to customers managing their own portfolios. With their market expertise they can help a smaller bank determine the appropriate type of investment and select specific instruments. If a customer needs to sell a security, they stand willing to buy. Second, they maintain an inventory of securities for possible sale to investors. The willingness to buy and sell securities is called making a market. Third, traders speculate on short-term interest rate movements by taking positions in various securities.

Banks earn profits from their trading activities in several ways. When making a market, they price securities at an expected positive spread, charging a higher price (lower interest rate) on securities sold than the price paid on securities purchased. Thus, a customer who contacts a bank's trading department will get two price quotes for the same instrument: a bid price, reflecting what the dealer is willing to pay and an ask or offer price, representing the price at which a dealer will sell. Profits arise from a positive spread between the ask minus the bid prices.

Traders can also earn profits if they correctly anticipate interest rate movements. This is accomplished by taking long (ownership) and short (borrowed) positions consistent with their expectations or by adjusting maturities on repurchase agreements (RPs). Both long and short positions are normally financed via RPs. When traders expect interest rates to decline (prices to rise), they want to own securities, so they take a long position in selected instruments. In most cases, overnight financing is used so that the bank earns net interest from the spread between the yield on the asset owned and the cost of financing, as well as being able to sell the asset for a price above that initially paid. When traders expect interest rates to rise, they want to sell securities or go short (sell securities not owned) to avoid holding assets that depreciate in value. Traders typically negotiate reverse RPs to obtain securities to short, and earn interest that varies daily with financing costs on the short position. The bank profits if rates rise and traders buy back the securities shorted at a lower price than that initially paid.

OBJECTIVES OF THE INVESTMENT PORTFOLIO

A bank's investment portfolio differs markedly from a trading account as investment securities are held to meet one of six general objectives:

1. Safety or preservation of capital
2. Liquidity
3. Yield

4. Credit risk diversification

5. Help in managing interest rate risk exposure

6. Assistance in meeting pledging requirements

Not surprisingly, securities with different return and risk features meet each objective differently so that the average portfolio is quite varied in terms of composition and price sensitivity. Banks generally hold these securities for longer periods of time than trading account securities. Periodic interest payments appear on the income statement as interest income while any gains or losses from sale prior to maturity appear as noninterest income.

ACCOUNTING FOR INVESTMENT SECURITIES

Decisions regarding the types of securities that banks buy and the length of time they are held in portfolio are driven, in part, by market value accounting rules that were put in place effective January 1994. These rules link the presumed motive for buying investment securities to the accounting for value on the balance sheet and for income on the income statement. Specifically, the Financial Accounting Standards Board's Statement 115 (FASB 115) requires banks to divide their securities holdings into three categories: Trading, Held to Maturity, and Available for Sale, with the following accounting treatment.

- Trading: Securities purchased with the intent to sell in the near term; carried at market value on the balance sheet with unrealized gains and losses included in income.

- Held to Maturity: Securities purchased with the intent to hold to final maturity; carried at amortized cost (historical cost adjusted for principal payments) on the balance sheet; unrealized gains and losses have no income statement impact.

- Available for Sale: Securities that are not classified in either of the previous categories; carried at market value on the balance sheet with unrealized gains and losses included as a component of capital.

The distinction between motives is important because of the accounting impact. Remember that changes in interest rates can dramatically affect the market value of a fixed-rate security. A fixed-rate bond without options will sell at par if the market rate equals the coupon rate on the bond. If the market rate is above (below) the coupon rate, the market value is below (above) par value. This difference between market value and par value equals the unrealized gain or loss on the security, assuming a purchase at par value,

$$\text{Market value} - \text{par value} = \text{unrealized gain (if positive)}$$
$$= \text{unrealized loss (if negative)} \tag{19.1}$$

If a bank plans to hold a security to maturity, changes in interest rates after purchase—and thus unrealized gains or losses—do not affect the accounting for the security either on the balance sheet or income statement. However, FASB 115 requires that banks carry all other securities at market value. Thus, if rates rise and there is an unrealized loss, the value of the security will decline on the balance sheet. For trading securities, the bank will report a loss on the income statement; for securities available for sale, the bank will report a direct reduction in its capital account. If rates fall and there is an unrealized gain, the value of the security will rise on the balance sheet with a corresponding increase in earnings (trading) or a bank's capital account (available for sale).[2] Importantly, the change in bank capital due to unrealized gains and losses on securities available for sale does not affect risk-based capital ratios.

---

[2]The presumed objective of market value accounting is to improve investors' and regulators' ability to evaluate the economic worth of a bank. Regulators see the added benefit of forcing banks to more closely monitor how much interest rate risk they assume in their investment portfolios. If banks choose to minimize the adverse accounting effects, they will likely take less risk by buying shorter-term securities.

The primary impact is that a bank's net income and equity capital position will be more volatile when securities are accounted for in market value terms. Investors see volatility as inherently bad, and often require a risk premium as compensation. A bank's cost of capital will likely be higher with market value accounting, to the extent that investors do not already incorporate market values in their analysis.

SAFETY OR PRESERVATION OF CAPITAL

Banks assume considerable default risk in their commercial and consumer loan portfolios. They typically balance this by accepting much lower default risk in their investment portfolio. Thus, a primary objective is to preserve capital by purchasing securities where there is only a small risk of principal loss. Regulators encourage this policy by requiring that banks concentrate their holdings in investment grade securities, those rated Baa or higher (See Exhibit 7.8). When they buy nonrated securities, banks must maintain a credit file which indicates that management periodically evaluates the borrowers' ability to meet debt service requirements, and this profile is consistent with an investment grade credit. Still, banks occasionally report losses on defaulted securities.

LIQUIDITY

Commercial banks purchase debt securities to help meet liquidity requirements. Liquidity needs are determined by unanticipated deposit outflows and unanticipated loan demand. Many banks, particularly small institutions that do not have ready access to the money and capital markets to borrow funds, rely on selling securities if a liquidity shortage appears. Because securities are more marketable than most commercial and consumer loans, banks often designate a portion of their investment portfolio as a liquidity reserve. This reliance on securities for liquidity has become less important as banks have joined the Federal Home Loan Bank system and rely on FHLB advances to meet liquidity needs.

As indicated in Chapter 14, securities with maturities under one year can be readily sold for cash near par value and are classified as liquid investments. In reality, most securities with a market value above book value can also be quickly converted to cash, regardless of maturity. Although at first glance a security's market value may not appear to affect its liquidity, in practice most banks choose not to sell securities if their market values are below book values. The rationale is that they would have to report securities losses on the income statement, which would reduce net income and the bank's aggregate profit ratios. In contrast, they are much more willing to sell securities at a gain when market values exceed book values, and thus artificially inflate periodic net income.[3]

When evaluating the potential liquidity in a bank's investment portfolio, most managers simply compare a security's current market value with its book value. If it trades at a premium, it is liquid. Consider the four securities summarized in Exhibit 19.1. As indicated, the bonds were purchased 8 to 13 years before the statement data. Because market interest rates changed significantly during the interim, the Treasury note and the State of Illinois municipal sell at a premium, while the other two sell at a discount. If the bank sold the premium bonds on September 30, 2002, it would report a gain from securities sales under noninterest income in its income statement. If the bank held the premium bonds but sold either of the discount bonds, it would report a loss from securities sales. Because securities losses lower reported net income in the short run, most banks are unwilling to sell securities at a discount.

---

[3]The costs and benefits of selling securities for a gain versus a loss and reinvesting the proceeds are discussed in Chapter 20 in the section on security swaps. In general, selling to realize short-term gains is short-sighted because a bank sacrifices greater longer-term cash flow.

• EXHIBIT 19.1

INVESTMENT PORTFOLIO FOR A HYPOTHETICAL COMMERCIAL BANK

Current Date: September 30, 2002

Purchase Date	Book Value	Description	Annual Coupon Income	Market Value
12/15/90	$4,000,000	$4,000,000 par value U.S. Treasury note at 11%, due 11/15/03	$440,000	$4,099,000
10/15/90	2,000,000	$2,000,000 par value Federal National Mortgage Association bonds at 8.75%, due 10/15/10	175,000	1,824,000
6/6/94	500,000	$500,000 par value Allegheny County, PA, A-rated general obligations at 5.15%, due 3/1/06	25,750	482,500
10/1/89	1,000,000	$1,000,000 par value State of Illinois Aaa-rated general obligations at 11%, due 10/1/14	110,000	1,190,000

Liquid securities are often viewed as only those that can be sold at a gain, regardless of the remaining term to maturity, credit quality, and issue size. This again ignores the fact that low-rate, discount securities often carry an opportunity loss in the form of reduced interest income. As described below, securities pledged as collateral cannot be readily sold so they are not liquid regardless of their market value.

YIELD

To be attractive, investment securities must pay a reasonable return for the risks assumed. The return may come in the form of price appreciation or periodic coupon interest. It may be fully taxable, or exempt from federal income taxes and/or state and local income taxes. Chapter 6 documents how yields are quoted on different types of securities, and Chapter 7 explains why yields differ across securities depending on default risk, marketability, tax treatment, maturity, and whether the securities carry call or put features. Clearly, bank managers must evaluate each security to determine whether its yield is attractive given its other features and the overall profile of the bank's portfolio. As discussed in Chapter 6, portfolio managers that actively trade securities generally look at total return, not yield to maturity, when evaluating the risk and return trade-off.

DIVERSIFY CREDIT RISK

The diversification objective is closely linked to the safety objective and difficulties that banks have with diversifying their loan portfolios. Too often, particularly at small banks, loans are concentrated in one industry, such as agriculture, energy, or real estate, which reflects the specific economic conditions of the bank's trade area. In these situations, the loan portfolio is not adequately diversified even when loans are not concentrated among single borrowers because its value will deteriorate if conditions adversely affect the industry in question. Banks view the securities portfolio as an opportunity to spread credit risk outside their geographic region and across other industries.

HELP MANAGE INTEREST RATE RISK EXPOSURE

Investment securities are very flexible instruments in managing a bank's overall interest rate risk exposure. Although some are private placements by the borrower directly with a lender as may be the case with a local municipal bond, most are standardized contracts purchased through brokers. Thus, banks can select terms that meet their specific needs without fear of antagonizing the borrower. They can readily sell the security if their needs change. For example, if management chooses to become more liability sensitive in anticipation of falling rates, the bank can easily and quickly lengthen the maturity or duration of its securities portfolio. Contrast this with the difficulty in adjusting commercial or consumer loan terms, or calling a loan with undesirable pricing features. As a consequence, managers can change the composition and price sensitivity of the investment portfolio at the margin to achieve the desired rate sensitivity profile.

PLEDGING REQUIREMENTS

By law, commercial banks must pledge collateral against certain types of liabilities. Banks that obtain financing via RPs essentially pledge some of their securities' holdings against this debt. Similarly, banks that borrow at the discount window or from the Federal Home Loan Bank must collateralize the loan with qualifying assets. While some loans meet the collateral requirements, most banks pledge Treasury securities which are already registered at the Federal Reserve in bookkeeping form, for discount window borrowings. For advances, banks typically pledge real estate related loans. Finally, banks that accept public deposits must also pledge government securities against the uninsured portion of deposits. Under federal regulations, 100 percent of uninsured federal deposits must be secured with Treasury and agency obligations valued at par or with municipals valued at 80 to 90 percent of par for collateral purposes. Pledging requirements for state and local government deposits vary according to specific regulations established by each deposit holder. In many instances, the public depositor values local municipal securities above par while valuing Treasury and agency securities at less than par for collateral purposes. The intent is to increase the attractiveness of local issues to potential bank investors.

TRADE-OFFS BETWEEN OBJECTIVES

Many investment managers, particularly at community banks, argue that securities are held to meet liquidity requirements as needed. Whenever the bank experiences unanticipated deposit outflows, they want the ability to sell securities quickly with minimal price risk. They do not buy securities subject to large amounts of default risk or interest rate risk. They do not actively trade securities to take advantage of perceived changes in interest rates.

For many such community banks, FASB 115 creates problems. Management generally does not want to report securities at market value because the added volatility of asset values, earnings, and capital can create confusion among depositors and investors. The fundamental issue is thus to determine which securities are best for liquidity and yield purposes and how to account for them with minimal adverse impact. If management knew that it would not have to sell any securities prior to maturity, it could simply classify all as held to maturity. There would be no market value accounting. Of course, a bank choosing this approach might find that if it ever sells a security before it matures, the regulators would force it to restate prior period earnings and capital and go to full market value accounting. If management chooses to classify all securities as available for sale, it is subject to the volatility that goes with full market value accounting.

The ideal approach is to classify only those securities that will eventually be sold before maturity as available for sale. Of course, this is not known with certainty at the time of purchase when the classification is made. Many banks hold tax-exempt municipal bonds for yield purposes such that they classify them as held to maturity. They minimize potential liquidity problems by classifying most other securities in the available for sale category. With the general decline in interest rates from 1994 to 1999, banks were typically able to report securities gains and increases in market values on balance sheet, followed by some securities losses as rates rose in 2000.

COMPOSITION OF THE INVESTMENT PORTFOLIO

A commercial bank's investment portfolio consists of many different types of instruments. Money market instruments with short maturities and durations include Treasury bills, large negotiable CDs and Eurodollars, bankers acceptances, commercial paper, security repurchase agreements, and tax anticipation notes. Capital market instruments with longer maturities and durations include long-term U.S. Treasury securities, obligations of U.S. government agencies, obligations of state and local governments and their political subdivisions labeled municipals, mortgage-backed securities backed both by government and private guarantees, corporate bonds, foreign bonds, and other asset-backed securities. At the end of 2000, U.S. banks in the aggregate owned over $1.04 trillion of fixed-income investment securities and another $24.8 billion of corporate equities and mutual fund shares. They also held almost $40 billion of securities in inventory for trading account purposes.

The top part of Exhibit 19.2 documents the changing composition of bank investments from 1965 through 2000 in four broad categories by issuer. There are several obvious trends. First, the investment portfolio consistently fell as a fraction of total bank assets from a high of 31.1 percent in 1965 to just 20 percent in 1990 where it has remained relatively constant. This coincides with an increase in the proportionate contribution of loans. Second, municipal securities were the dominant bank investment through 1985, after which bank holdings fell sharply. As discussed later, this reflects the impact of the Tax Reform Act of 1986, which induced banks to withdraw as investors in most municipal securities. In 2000 less than 2 percent of bank financial assets were municipals. Third, since 1965 banks have slowly reduced their proportionate investment in Treasury securities to where they represent under 3 percent of financial assets in 2000. Finally, both agency and corporate/foreign securities increased sharply after 1985 as a fraction of financial assets, because banks sought out alternatives to municipals following the Tax Reform Act of 1986. The growth in agency securities is due to the growth of both callable bonds and mortgage-backed securities, which have far different characteristics than traditional bank investments.

The bottom part of the exhibit indicates the proportionate security holdings of different-sized U.S. banks at the end of 2000. Note that the securities are divided into those held for investment purposes and trading account securities. Not surprisingly, the 10 largest banks account for most of the trading account securities because they are generally active market makers. For investment securities, the figures document significant differences including the fact that the proportionate size of the portfolio decreases with bank size, ranging from over 25 percent of total assets at the smallest banks to just over 17 percent at banks ranked 11 to 100 in size. This is not surprising because smaller banks rely more heavily on securities to meet liquidity needs. Money center and large regional banks routinely borrow in the money markets to help meet deposit outflows and finance incremental loan demand. In addition, U.S. government agency securities, which include most mortgage-backed securities, are the dominant category at banks of all sizes comprising from 6.6 percent to 17 percent of assets. The combination of U.S. Treasury and agency securities accounts for 75 percent of the smallest

· EXHIBIT 19.2

COMPOSITION OF U.S. COMMERCIAL BANK INVESTMENTS: 1965–2000*

A. All Banks Over Time

	Percentage of Total Financial Assets							
	1965	1970	1975	1980	1985	1990	1995	2000*
U.S. Treasury securities	17.6%	12.1%	9.8%	7.8%	8.3%	5.4%	6.2%	2.80%
Agency securities	1.7	2.7	3.9	4.1	3.2	8.4	10.4	11.2
Municipal securities	11.4	13.6	11.6	10.0	9.7	3.5	2.1	1.8
Corporate & foreign securities	0.4	0.6	0.9	0.5	1.0	2.7	2.5	4.3
	31.1%	29.0%	26.4%	22.4%	22.2%	20.0%	21.2%	20.1%
Total financial assets (billions of dollars)	$342	$517	$886	$1,482	$2,375	$3,334	$4,488	$6,455.6

B. Percentage of Total Consolidated Assets, December 31, 2000

	Commercial Banks Ranked by Assets			
	10 Largest	11–100 Largest	101–1,000 Largest	>1,000 Largest
Investment securities				
U.S. Treasury securities	1.96%	1.12%	1.81%	2.12%
U.S. Gov't. agency & corporate securities	6.59	9.71	15.56	16.95
Private mortgage-backed securities	0.51	1.66	0.99	0.23
Municipal securities	0.51	0.96	2.91	4.64
Other securities	3.47	2.06	2.18	0.88
Equities	0.68	0.60	0.79	0.56
Total investment securities	13.72%	16.11%	24.24%	25.38%
Trading account securities	5.26	1.22	0.09	0.02
Total	18.98%	17.33%	24.33%	25.40%

*Data are for December 31 each year.

SOURCES: Flow of Funds Accounts, Board of Governors of the Federal Reserve System; *Federal Reserve Bulletin*, Board of Governors.

banks investment securities and 45 percent of the 10 largest banks' investment securities holdings. Municipals represent significant investments at all but the 100 largest banks. The concentration in municipals reflects the high demand for tax-exempt interest income at all banks. The ratio of municipals to total assets is greater at small banks because they do not use other means to shelter income. Large banks shelter proportionately more income via tax credits and accelerated depreciation generated from foreign operations and leasing activities. Other securities, including corporate and foreign bonds and equities, are significant as the 1000 largest banks, but comprise a small portion of the investment portfolio at the smallest banks.

THE RISK RETURN CHARACTERISTICS OF INVESTMENT SECURITIES

The fundamental objective of the investment portfolio is to maximize earnings while limiting risk within guidelines set by management. Earnings come in the form of periodic interest income, reinvestment income, and capital gains or losses. Managing returns involves selecting the appropriate mix of taxable and tax-exempt securities, optimal maturities/durations, and the timing of purchases and sales. Portfolio risk is evidenced by deviations in actual returns from that expected. Such deviations may result from unanticipated changes in interest rates, defaults on promised interest and principal payments, and unanticipated inflation. Managing risk focuses on ensuring the safety of principal, guaranteeing access to cash to meet liquidity needs, and timing security purchases relative to the business cycle. It also involves diversifying the portfolio with different types of securities, issuers, and issue maturities or durations.

GENERAL RETURN CHARACTERISTICS

Bank investments contribute to earnings in the form of periodic interest income, reinvestment income, and principal appreciation or depreciation, which represent the cash flows when calculating total return (see Chapter 6). Most debt instruments either accrue interest at fixed rates against the principal invested with a lump sum distribution at maturity, or carry fixed coupon payments with the return of principal at final maturity. Some securities, such as Treasury bills, are purchased at a discount and pay interest in the form of principal appreciation. Mortgage-backed and other asset-backed securities produce cash flows that represent the periodic payment of both principal and interest. In recent years banks have acquired larger amounts of variable-rate securities, whose returns fluctuate with market conditions.

Chapter 6 describes how different securities generate periodic income and the nature of their associated yield calculations. It is important to note that returns vary substantially across securities. In order to accurately compare returns an analyst must know how interest accrues, the frequency of compounding, whether yields are quoted on a 360- or 365-day basis, and whether the interest is subject to taxes or is tax-exempt.

Aggregate returns are also affected by capital gains and losses on securities sold before maturity. Realized principal appreciation or depreciation is reported separately under non-interest income on the income statement as a securities gain or loss. Whether securities increase or decrease in value after purchase depends on the general movement in the level of interest rates and specific features of individual securities. If market interest rates on comparable debt securities increase after purchase, the market value of fixed-rate option-free debt decreases. If comparable interest rates decrease, market value increases. These relationships potentially differ for securities with embedded options. For example, the price of a callable bond will not increase much over par when interest rates fall because the bond will generally be called at par once the issuer can call the bond. Investors know that if they purchase the bond above par and the bond is called, they will realize capital losses. Similarly, a mortgage-backed security that is subject to prepayment risk will produce dramatically different cash flows (interest plus reinvestment income) in rising versus falling interest rate environments. Thus, no simple, standard relationship exists between rate changes and price changes for these securities with options.

Variable-rate debt instruments normally trade at prices close to maturity value because periodic interest payments change directly with the level of interest rates. The magnitude of reported gains or losses on these securities depends on whether portfolio managers buy them at interest rate peaks or troughs and whether they sell them prior to maturity to realize principal appreciation or depreciation. Only if a bank sells securities from its portfolio will it report a securities gain or loss.

In general, bank managers are reluctant to report securities losses, even in the face of superior reinvestment opportunities. Securities losses directly lower reported profits and, in the near term, earnings may appear depressed. In reality, market values are low because interest rates on comparable securities are higher than when the securities owned were originally purchased. By not selling low-rate instruments, banks accept the opportunity loss of higher interest income over future reporting periods. Management substitutes reduced net interest income for not reporting securities losses, even though the bank may gain by improving its current cash flow and later profits. Chapter 20 demonstrates that there are often substantial long-term benefits from selling securities at a loss and reinvesting the proceeds, while there are typically long-term losses associated with selling securities for a near-term gain.

GENERAL RISK CHARACTERISTICS

Portfolio managers attempt to maximize returns while controlling risk, which is evidenced by variations in cash inflows. The real concern, however, is that actual returns will fall short of expected returns. Expected returns reflect promised interest and principal payments, a real rate of return after inflation, and potential returns available when interest rates fluctuate. Specific risk factors are discussed briefly in the following sections.

CREDIT RISK. Credit risk is the potential variability in returns resulting from debt issuers not making promised principal and interest payments. Such nonpayment is normally caused by deterioration in general economic conditions. Because most banks concentrate their investments in federal, agency, or state and local government securities, actual defaults occur infrequently. Still, banks purchase some corporate and foreign bonds for which nonpayment is a real possibility, and municipal borrowers occasionally default because of deficient revenues supporting the bonds.

Most banks do not directly analyze the probability of timely repayment attributable to potential default for different corporate and municipal securities. Instead they rely on quality assessments provided by private agencies, such as Standard & Poor's Corp. and Moody's Investors Service. Ratings are based on a corporation's or municipality's financial condition, demographic trends, the local economic base, and the tax and borrowing powers of issuers. Exhibit 7.14 summarizes the various ratings provided by Standard & Poor's and Moody's for municipal bonds. The lowest risk, Aaa- or AAA-rated securities offer the lowest promised yields, while noninvestment grade securities offer the highest promised yields.

Regulators strongly encourage banks to restrict their investments to the four top categories, which are labeled investment grade securities. Many securities are not rated, usually because the issuer is small and unwilling to pay the required fees. In some cases the issuer can place its debt privately with a local institution. Regulators permit banks to purchase these nonrated securities, but the banks must maintain a credit file on the issuer and be able to demonstrate the economic soundness of the investment. Sound investments require the same detailed credit analysis normally associated with commercial loans.

PURCHASING POWER RISK. Purchasing power risk refers to the potential variability in returns caused by unanticipated changes in inflation. It arises when actual inflation does not equal expected inflation. Investors who buy fixed-rate securities lose purchasing power when the actual inflation rate exceeds the after-tax expected rate of return from interest and principal payments was made. They have deferred consumption expenditures by purchasing securities, yet their realized return buys less when it is actually received. Accordingly, banks like other investors should require a nominal after-tax return on investments that exceeds the expected inflation rate. Purchasing power risk at banks is mitigated by the intermediation function. As long as depositors' inflation expectations are identical to bank management's, both asset yields and interest costs of liabilities incorporate the same inflation premiums. Inflation poses serious problems to a bank when its inflation expectations are below those of its depositors and actual inflation is high. In this instance, a bank is willing to accept lower yields on its investments (a smaller spread) relative to its deposit rates. Higher than expected inflation reduces the spread even more, and a bank's profitability worsens. Investors who are concerned with inflation can now buy Treasury Inflation Protection securities (TIPs) that pay a real interest rate that is fixed at issue, plus an inflation premium that tracks actual price changes after purchase. (See Chapter 7.)

INTEREST RATE RISK. Interest rate risk in the investment portfolio is the potential variability in returns caused by changes in the level of interest rates. Interest rate changes affect returns in two ways. First, the market values of option-free, fixed-rate security holdings change in the opposite direction of interest rate changes on comparable securities. Second, investors are subject to reinvestment risk on securities that make periodic coupon payments. If the level of interest rates decreases, an investor must reinvest the coupon payments at lower rates over the life of the security to maintain the same quality of investment. This is especially important for securities with embedded options.

These two facets of interest rate risk are embodied in the concepts of duration and convexity, which signify the overall price sensitivity of a security to changing interest rates. In general, the longer the duration, the greater is the percentage fluctuation in a security's market value for a given change in interest rates. A security's duration is, in turn, closely linked to its coupon rate. Consider the case of option-free bonds. Zero coupon securities that pay no periodic interest have a Macaulay's duration equal to final maturity, while coupon-bearing securities have a duration less than maturity. Thus, a 5-year maturity bond that pays semi-annual interest at 4 percent (8 percent annually) will have a shorter duration than a 5-year zero coupon security paying 4 percent semiannually. There is no reinvestment risk with the zero coupon security because there are no interim cash flows that must be reinvested. In general, high coupon securities have relatively short durations while low coupon securities have longer durations, *ceteris paribus*. Thus, high coupon securities exhibit relatively stable prices compared with otherwise similar low coupon securities.

Exhibit 19.3 demonstrates the general price sensitivity of option-free bonds with the same final maturity but different-sized periodic payments. The vertical axis measures the percentage price change on various securities when interest rates rise by 2 percent and fall by 2 percent, respectively. The securities are positioned from highest coupon (high coupon corporate bond) to lowest coupon (zero coupon Treasury bond). Regardless of the direction of rate changes, low coupon instruments change proportionately more in price than high coupon instruments for a given change in interest rates.

In most cases, the variation in returns caused by securities gains or losses is at least partially offset by the variation in reinvestment returns. If, for example, interest rates increase and the portfolio manager sells bonds at less than cost, part of the loss can be recovered by reinvesting the proceeds and future coupon payments at the higher rates. The opposite occurs when rates decrease and investors sell securities at a gain. Part of the gain is lost because reinvestment income drops with the lower rates. Thus, price risk and reinvestment risk must be viewed jointly. If desired, portfolio managers can "immunize" their portfolio through the use of duration analysis.[4] This is accomplished by acquiring securities with a combined duration equal to the bank's planned holding period. If the bank holds the securities as planned, changes in interest rates will not affect the portfolio's expected total return because price changes will be exactly offset by changes in reinvestment income. Of course, a bank with an immunized portfolio will not realize speculative gains.

Securities with embedded options, such as call and put features, may exhibit substantially different price sensitivities than option-free securities. Mortgage-backed securities, for example, may vary widely in price due to sharp swings in mortgage prepayments as a result of rising or falling interest rates. In essence, securities' durations may change substantially when interest rates change so that the relative price sensitivity varies widely with rate movements. The concepts of effective duration and effective convexity are used to characterize these variations in price sensitivity. They are applied to securities with options in Chapter 20.

---

[4]Chapter 6 introduces Macaulay's duration and Chapter 9 applies it to managing a bank's total balance sheet. The duration concept can be applied to the investment portfolio alone. See Bierwag, Kaufman, and Toevs (1983) and Fabozzi (1996) for a discussion and applications.

IMPACT OF INTEREST RATE CHANGES ON FIXED-RATE, OPTION-FREE BOND PRICES

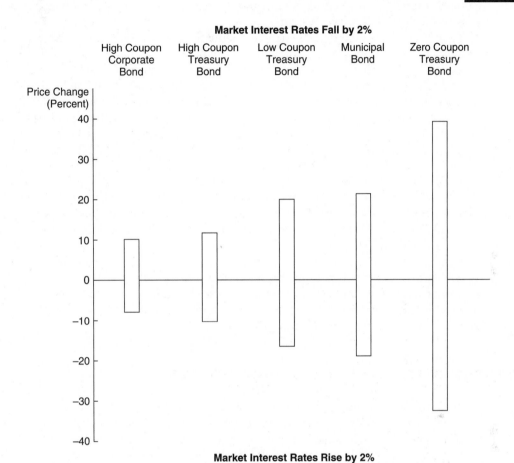

Market Interest Rates Fall by 2%

| High Coupon Corporate Bond | High Coupon Treasury Bond | Low Coupon Treasury Bond | Municipal Bond | Zero Coupon Treasury Bond |

Price Change (Percent)

Market Interest Rates Rise by 2%

All bonds have the same final maturity. For a given change in interest rates, low coupon securities change proportionately more in price than high coupon securities with the same final maturity.

LIQUIDITY AND MARKETABILITY RISK. Some securities cannot be easily traded prior to maturity. This may occur because the security is small in size and nonrated. To induce another investor to buy it, the owner may have to substantially lower the price. The risk of potential variability in returns caused by this lack of marketability represents a component of liquidity risk.

Liquidity risk is also affected by pledging requirements that limit the pool of securities that banks can sell to obtain cash. In most cases, pledged securities are held by a third-party trustee. Banks must substitute other collateral before selling a pledged security. For this reason, banks normally pledge securities that they intend to hold for long periods. The key point, however, is that any pledged security is illiquid over the near term. Finally, banks cannot effectively sell securities that are classified as held to maturity unless there has been a material change in the quality of the security.

REGULATORY GUIDELINES

Bank investments differ markedly in their risk-return features. Regulators attempt to limit the range of options by specifying what securities qualify as investments and conducting periodic examinations. Regulators identify three classes of securities for banks that are members of the Federal Reserve System.

Type I securities include U.S. Treasury, federal agency, and general obligation municipal obligations, which presumably carry the lowest default risk. Banks can own unlimited quantities of these securities and underwrite new issues or make a market in outstanding obligations. Type II securities consist of obligations issued by quasi-public federal and municipal agencies such as the International Bank for Reconstruction and Development, the Tennessee Valley Authority, and selected state agencies associated with housing and general university projects. The amount owned from any single issuer is limited to 15 percent of a bank's capital plus surplus. However, banks can underwrite and deal in these obligations. Type III securities include all other investment grade equivalent obligations. While there is no specific restriction to a BBB/Baa or better rating, this grouping is normally followed. Banks can invest only 10 percent of capital and surplus in any single issue and are not allowed to underwrite or deal in these securities unless they've obtained prior regulatory approval.[5] As indicated in Exhibit 19.2, banks concentrate their Type III investments in municipal, corporate, and foreign bonds.

Regulators do not directly restrict banks in their maturity choices. Banks are required, however, to understand their overall interest rate risk position as part of the regular examination process. Remember that banks are required to hold capital in support of default risk associated with securities.[6] If regulators believe that a bank has taken on too much interest rate risk, they will require additional capital.

CHARACTERISTICS OF TAXABLE SECURITIES

Banks own a substantial amount of securities on which the interest is subject to federal income taxes. In order to meet liquidity and pledging requirements and earn a reasonable return, banks hold significant amounts of government and corporate securities that mature within one year, labeled money market instruments. Most are highly liquid because they are issued by well-known borrowers and because a deep secondary market exists. Banks own a larger amount of longer-term taxable securities, labeled capital market instruments. The following sections describe the basic characteristics of each. Key terminology is presented in Exhibit 19.4.

MONEY MARKET INVESTMENTS

REPURCHASE AGREEMENTS (RPS OR REPOS). RPs involve a loan between two parties, with one typically either a securities dealer or commercial bank. The lender or investor buys securities from the borrower and simultaneously agrees to sell the securities back at a later date at an agreed-upon price plus interest. The transaction represents a short-

---

[5]Recall the discussion of bank underwriting activities in Chapter 2. Banks with Section 20 affiliates who've obtained regulatory approval can underwrite corporate and municipal securities.

[6]Chapter 13 documents the specific risk classifications for different bank assets. It is sufficient to note here that Treasury securities are in the zero risk class, while other government-guaranteed securities are in the 20 percent risk class. Municipal revenue bonds are in the 50 percent risk class.

• EXHIBIT 19.4

IMPORTANT TERMINOLOGY

ARM: Adjustable rate mortgage—a mortgage where the contractual interest rate is tied to some index of interest rates and changes when supply and demand conditions alter the underlying index.

CBO: Collateralized Bond Obligation—a security backed by a pool of noninvestment grade (junk) bonds.

CD: Certificate of deposit—a large, negotiable time deposit issued by a financial institution.

CMO: Collateralized Mortgage Obligation—a security backed by a pool of mortgages and structured to fall within an estimated maturity range (tranche) based on the timing of allocated interest and principal payments on the underlying mortgages.

Conventional Mortgage: A mortgage or deed of trust that is not obtained under a government-insured program.

FHA: Federal Housing Administration—a federal agency that insures mortgages.

FHLMC: Federal Home Loan Mortgage Corporation (Freddie Mac)—a private corporation, operating with an implicit federal guarantee, that buys mortgages financed largely by mortgage-backed securities.

FNMA: Federal National Mortgage Association (Fannie Mae)—a private corporation, operating with an implicit federal guarantee, that buys mortgages financed largely by mortgage-backed securities.

GNMA: Government National Mortgage Association (Ginnie Mae)—a government entity that buys mortgages for low income housing and guarantees mortgage-backed securities issued by private lenders.

GO: General Obligation bond—municipal bond issued by a state or local government where the promised principal and interest payments are backed by the full faith, credit, and taxing authority of the issuer.

GSE: Government Sponsored Enterprise—a quasi-public federal agency that is federally sponsored, but privately owned. Examples include the Farm Credit Bank, Federal Home Loan Banks (FHLBs), Federal Home Loan Mortgage Corporation (Freddie Mac), and Federal National Mortgage Association (Fannie Mae).

IDB: Industrial Development Bond—a municipal bond issued by a state or local government political subdivision in which the proceeds are used to finance expenditures of private corporations.

IO: Interest only security representing the interest portion of a stripped Treasury or stripped mortgage-backed security.

MBS: Mortgage-backed security—a security that evidences an undivided interest in the ownership of a pool of mortgages.

PAC: Planned amortization class CMO—a security that is retired according to a planned amortization schedule, while payments to other classes of securities are slowed or accelerated. The objective is to ensure that PACs exhibit highly predictable maturities and cash flows.

PO: Principal only security representing the principal portion of a stripped Treasury or stripped mortgage-backed security.

Revenue Bond: A municipal bond in which the promised principal and interest payments are backed by revenues from whatever facility or project the bond proceeds are used to finance.

RP: Repurchase agreement (Repo)—an agreement by one party to buy back, under certain terms, the item that is originally sold to a second party. The underlying item is generally a U.S. Treasury, agency, or mortgage-backed security.

Secured Investor Trusts: Bonds secured by the cash flow from pieces of CMOs or related securities placed in trust. In most cases the securities are high-risk instruments subject to substantial prepayment risk. The securities are labeled "kitchen-sink bonds" because they are backed by everything but the kitchen sink.

Tranche: The principal amount related to a specific class of stated maturities on a CMO.

VA: Veterans Administration—a federal agency that insures mortgages.

Z-Tranche: The final class of securities in a CMO exhibiting the longest maturity and greatest price volatility. These securities often accrue interest until all other classes are retired.

term loan collateralized by the securities because the borrower receives the principal in the form of immediately available funds, while the lender earns interest on the investment. If the borrower defaults, the lender gets title to the securities.

Consider an overnight RP transaction for $1 million at 5.4 percent between a bank as lender and a foreign government as borrower. RP rates are quoted on an add-on basis assuming a 360-day year. The bank would book an asset, securities purchased under agreement to resell, and would lose deposit balances held at the Fed equal to $1 million. After one day the transaction would reverse, as deposit balances would increase by $1 million and the RP loan would disappear; also, the foreign government would pay the bank $150 in interest.

$$\text{Interest} = \$1,000,000 \times (.054/360) = \$150 \tag{19.2}$$

If the foreign government defaults, the bank retains the securities as collateral on the loan. This transaction is technically labeled a reverse RP because the bank is the lender while another party is the borrower. In a regular repurchase agreement a bank or securities dealer sells securities under an agreement to repurchase at a later date, and thus represents the borrower. Every RP transaction involves both a regular RP and reverse RP depending on whether its viewed from the lender's or borrower's perspective.[7]

Banks operate on both sides of the RP market as borrowers and lenders. Although any securities can serve as collateral, most RPs involve Treasury or U.S. agency securities. Typically small banks lend funds aggressively in the RP market because they operate their reserves position more conservatively with positive excess reserves, and own proportionately more of these securities available as collateral. Every RP transaction is negotiated separately between parties. The minimum denomination is generally $1 million with maturities ranging from one day to one year. The rate on one day RPs is referred to as the overnight RP rate which plays an important role in arbitrage transactions associated with financial futures and options. Longer-term transactions are referred to as term RPs and the associated rate the term RP rate. The RP rate varies from 15 to 50 basis points below the comparable federal funds rate because RP transactions are secured.

TREASURY BILLS. At the end of 2001, commercial banks owned approximately $163 billion in securities issued directly by the United States. Although no precise breakdown is available, banks are significant investors both in short-term Treasury bills and longer-term Treasury notes and bonds. Banks find Treasuries attractive because they pay market rates of interest, are free of default risk, and can be easily sold in the secondary market. Because they are default risk-free, Treasury securities pay a lower pretax yield than otherwise comparable taxable securities. They carry a tax advantage, however, because all interest is subject to federal income taxes but is exempt from state and local income taxes. In addition, the primary and secondary market for Treasury instruments is very competitive. Dealers keep bid-ask spreads low and maintain substantial inventories. This ease of purchase and sale lowers transactions costs and makes Treasuries highly liquid.

Treasury bills are marketable obligations of the U.S. Treasury that carry original maturities of one year or less. They exist only in book-entry form, with the investor simply holding a dated receipt. Treasury bills are discount instruments, and the entire return is represented by price appreciation as maturity approaches.

Each week the Treasury auctions bills with 13-week and 26-week maturities. Investors submit either competitive or noncompetitive bids. With a competitive bid, the purchaser indicates the maturity amount of bills desired and the discount price offered. Noncompetitive bidders indicate only how much they want to acquire. They agree to pay the average price posted for all competitive offers that the Treasury accepts but are limited to no more than $500,000 in maturity value. The auctions are closed in that sealed bids must be submitted by 1:30 P.M. each Monday, the normal sale date. The Treasury accepts all noncompetitive bids. It then ranks the competitive bids from the highest discounted price offered to

---

[7]Market terminology for RP transactions is viewed from the perspective of the Federal Reserve's relationship with securities dealers or banks. Reverse RPs are formally labeled matched sales-purchase agreements because they involve the Fed initially selling securities to banks or securities dealers to contract the reserve base, then buying them back.

T-BILL AUCTION RESULTS AND SELECTED YIELDS, MAY 20, 2002

T-Bill Auction Results for May 20, 2002

	13-Week	26-Week
Applications	$35,879,782,000	$32,156,863,000
Accepted bids	$17,000,105,000	$15,000,055,000
Accepted noncomp	$1,438,237,000	$1,087,195,000
Accepted frgn non	$175,000,000	$75,000,000
Auction price (Rate)	99.563 (1.730%)	99.039 (1.900%)
Coupon equivalent	1.760%	7.946%
Bids at market yield	58.13%	25.09%
Cusip number	912795KX8	912795LL3

Both issues are dated May 20, 2002. The 13-week bills mature Aug. 22, 2002, and the 26-week bills mature Nov. 21, 2002.

Yield Comparisons

Based on Merrill Lynch Bond Indexes, priced as of midafternoon Eastern time.

	5/20	5/17	52 Week High	Low
Corp.-Govt. Master	5.20%	5.27%	5.77%	4.35%
Treasury 1-10yr	3.72	3.79	4.72	2.92
10+ yr	5.69	5.74	5.96	4.83
Agencies 1-10yr	4.17	4.23	5.28	3.25
10+ yr	6.21	6.27	6.52	5.38
Corporate				
1-10 yr High Qlty	5.02	5.09	5.82	4.20
Med Qlty	6.48	6.55	6.67	5.52
10+ yr High Qlty	6.96	7.02	7.21	6.27
Med Qlty	7.85	7.90	7.93	7.08
Yankee Bonds (1)	5.91	5.97	6.45	5.10
Current-coupon mortgages (2)				
GNMA 6.50%	6.31	6.33	6.77	5.75
FNMA 6.50%	6.28	6.33	6.93	5.65
FHLMC 6.50%	6.31	6.36	6.96	5.65
High-yield corporates	11.16	11.16	13.70	10.92
Tax-Exempt Bonds				
7-12-yr G.O. (AA)	4.31	4.32	4.62	3.84
12-22-yr G.O. (AA)	5.19	5.20	5.32	4.67
22+ yr revenue (A)	5.35	5.36	5.46	4.91

Note: High quality rated AAA-AA; medium quality A-BBB/Baa; high yield, BB/Ba-C.
(1) Dollar-denominated, SEC-registered bonds of foreign issuers sold in the U.S. (2) Reflects the 52-week high and low of mortgage-backed securities indexes rather than the individual securities shown.

SOURCE: *The Wall Street Journal.*

continued

• EXHIBIT 19.5

CONTINUED

Money Rates

Monday, May 20, 2002

The key U. S. and foreign annual interest rates below are a guide to general levels but don't al-ways represent actual transactions.

Commercial Paper

Yields paid by corporations for short-term financing, typically for daily operation

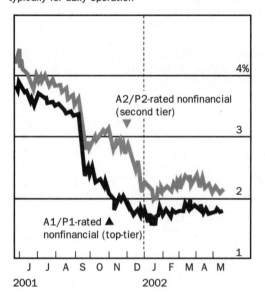

A2/P2-rated nonfinancial (second tier)

A1/P1-rated ▲ nonfinancial (top-tier)

4%

3

2

1

J J A S O N D J F M A M
2001   2002

SOURCE: Federal Reserve.

Prime Rate: 4.75% (effective 12/12/01).

Discount Rate: 1.25% (effective 12/11/01).

Federal Funds: 1.938% high, 1.563% low, 1.750% near closing bid, 1.938% offered. Effective rate: 1.71%. Source: Prebon Yamane (USA) Inc. Federal-funds target rate 1.750% (effective 12/11/01).

Call Money: 3.50% (effective 12/12/01). SOURCE: Reuters.

Commercial Paper: Placed directly by General Electric Capital Corp.: 1.77% 30 to 59 days; 1.78% 60 to 89 days; 1.81% 90 to 119 days; 1.86% 120 to 149 days; 1.92% 150 to 179 days; 2.00% 180 to 209 days; 2.08% 210 to 239 days; 2.19% 240 to 262 days; 2.28% 263 to 270 days.

Euro Commercial Paper: Not available.

Dealer Commercial Paper: High-grade unsecured notes sold through dealers by major corporations: 1.74% 30 days; 1.75% 60 days; 1.78% 90 days.

Certificates of Deposit: 1.80% one month; 1.83% three months; 2.04% six months.

Bankers Acceptances: 1.84% 30 days; 1.85% 60 days; 1.86% 90 days; 1.92% 120 days; 2.00% 150 days; 2.07% 180 days. SOURCE: Reuters.

Eurodollars: 1.81%–1.69% one month; 1.88%–1.75% two months; 1.88%–1.75% three months; 2.00%–1.88% four months; 2.06%–1.94% five months; 2.13%–2.00% six months.

London Interbank Offered Rates (LIBOR): 1.8400% one month; 1.9075% three months; 2.12313% six months; 2.7200% one year. Effective rate for contracts entered into two days from date appearing at top of this column.

Euro LIBOR: 3.42000% one month; 3.52213% three months; 3.71200% six months; 4.08313% one year. Effective rate for contracts entered into two days from date appearing at top of this column.

Euro Interbank Offered Rates (EURIBOR): 3.415% one month; 3.524% three months; 3.716% six months; 4.090% one year.

Foreign Prime Rates: Canada 4.00%; Germany 3.25%; Japan 1.375%; Switzerland 3.25 ; Britain 4.00%.

Treasury Bills: Results of the Monday, May 20, 2002, auction of short-term U.S. government bills, sold at a discount from face value in units of $1,000 to $1 million: 1.745% 13 weeks; 1.900% 26 weeks. Tuesday, May 14, 2002 auction: 1.745% 4 weeks.

Overnight Repurchase Rate: 1.71%. SOURCE: Reuters.

Freddie Mac: Posted yields on 30-year mortgage commitments. Delivery within 30 days 6.51%, 60 days 6.61%, standard conventional fixed-rate mortgages: 3.625%,' 2% rate capped one-year adjustable rate mortgages. SOURCE: Reuters.

Fannie Mae: Posted yields on 30 year mortgage commitments (priced at par) for delivery within 30 days 6.65%, 60 days 6.74%, standard conventional fixed-rate mortgages; 4.45%, 6/2 rate capped one-year adjustable rate mortgages. Constant Maturity Debt Index: 1.801% three months; 1.979% six months; 2.546% one year. SOURCE: Reuters.

Merrill Lynch Ready Assets Trust: 1.49%.

Consumer Price Index: April, 179.8; up 1.6% from a year ago. Bureau of Labor Statistics.

the lowest price and accepts bids until the desired financing objective is met. Noncompetitive bidders then pay the average price of the accepted competitive bids. Exhibit 19.5 documents the auction results for the May 20, 2002, Treasury auction. On this date, the Treasury sold over $32 billion in T-bills at an average rate of 1.73 percent and 1.90 percent for the 13-week and 26-week bills, respectively. Approximately 3.1 percent of the accepted bids were noncompetitive. Occasionally, the Treasury offers cash management bills with maturities under 18 weeks that supplement the regular bill offerings.

Banks participate in the auction process in two ways, by buying bills directly for their own portfolios or by buying bills for inventory in their securities trading activity. Treasury bills are purchased on a discount basis so that the investor's income equals price appreciation. As with most money market yields, the Treasury bill discount rate (dr) is quoted in terms of a 360-day year, as indicated below:

$$dr = \frac{FV - P}{FV} (360/n) \qquad (19.3)$$

Where FV is the dollar amount of face value, P is the dollar purchase price, and n equals the number of days to maturity.

For example, a bank that purchases $1 million in face value of the 26-week (182-day) bills at $990,390, the auction price in Exhibit 19.5, earns a discount yield of 1.90 percent.[8]

$$dr = \frac{\$1,000,000 - \$990,390}{\$1,000,000} (360/182)$$

$$= 0.0190$$

The bank reports interest of $9,610 over the 182 days if the bill is redeemed at maturity.

CERTIFICATES OF DEPOSIT AND EURODOLLARS. Many commercial banks buy negotiable certificates of deposit (CDs) and Eurodollars issued by other commercial banks. Domestic CDs are dollar-denominated deposits issued by U.S. banks with fixed maturities ranging from 14 days to several years. They are attractive because they pay yields above Treasury bills and, if issued by a well-known bank, can be easily sold in the secondary market prior to maturity. As with federal funds, interest is quoted on an add-on basis assuming a 360-day year. Eurodollars are dollar-denominated deposits issued by foreign branches of U.S. banks or by foreign banks outside the United States. Because only the largest banks can tap this market, the secondary market is quite deep. The Eurodollar market is less regulated than the domestic market so that the perceived riskiness is greater. Eurodollar rates subsequently exceed domestic CD rates for comparable banks.

Investing banks can choose from a variety of CDs in terms of yield characteristics and issuer. Although most CDs pay fixed rates to term, some carry floating rates that are pegged to an index such as LIBOR or a commercial paper rate. An investor commits the funds for up to five years but the rate is reset periodically according to a pre-established formula. For example, a floating rate CD may carry a rate equal to the prevailing 3-month commercial paper rate plus 50 basis points, with interest paid quarterly, at which time the rate is reset. Two other CDs that pay above average rates are Yankee CDs and Asian Dollar CDs. Yankee CDs are dollar-denominated deposits issued by branches of foreign banks in the United States, while Asian Dollar CDs are issued by banks in Singapore that pay interest in dollars which varies with the Singapore interbank offer rate (SIBOR) as an index. Even though the

---

[8]Alternatively, a known discount rate (dr) produces a purchase price (P):

$$P = FV [1 - dr (n / 360)]$$

The discount rate understates the true percentage yield to an investor. *The Wall Street Journal* publishes a bond coupon-equivalent yield for Treasury bills at each auction, calculated in terms of Equation 19.3, but which instead compares the dollar return to the actual purchase price and uses a 365-day year. The coupon-equivalent rate (cer) for the 182-day bills in the example equals 1.946 percent.

$$cer = \frac{(\$1,000,000 - \$990,390)(365/182)}{\$990,390} = 0.01946$$

The true (effective) yield is even greater, calculated generally as

$$\text{Effective yield} = \left[1 + \frac{(FV - P)}{P}\right]^{365/k} - 1$$

where k = the number of days until maturity. In this example, the effective yield equals 1.956 percent.

issuers are well-known institutions, investors demand a risk premium over rates paid by the safest domestic institutions. In recent years, many banks have offered stock market indexed CDs where the interest rate is tied to some measure of an aggregate stock index, such as the S&P 500 index. This presumably allows investors to benefit from increases in general stock prices without taking some of the price risk.

COMMERCIAL PAPER. Commercial paper refers to unsecured promissory notes issued by corporations that use the proceeds to finance short-term working capital needs. Because these instruments are neither insured nor backed by collateral, the issuers are presumably the highest quality firms. However, several commercial issues have defaulted. In fact, the market is extremely sensitive to deterioration in any well-known borrower's financial condition. When a large firm is known to be in distress, virtually all issuers of new commercial paper must pay a substantial premium over T-bills to place their debt regardless of their financial condition.[9] Most commercial paper is rated by different rating agencies to help investors gauge default risk. Issuers also typically obtain an irrevocable letter of credit from a bank that guarantees payment is case the issuer defaults. This guarantee mitigates default risk and improves marketability. Still, most investors hold commercial paper to maturity because the secondary market is thin.

Small banks purchase large amounts of commercial paper as investments. The minimum denomination is $10,000, and maturities range from three to 270 days. Interest rates are fixed to term and quoted on a discount basis, as with T-bills. Thus, the market price is always less than face value and the entire principal plus interest is paid at maturity. The primary attraction is the yield premium over T-bills and the ability to match specific commercial paper maturities with the bank's planned holding period.

BANKERS ACCEPTANCES. According to Federal Reserve Board Regulation A, a bankers acceptance is a "draft or bill of exchange . . . accepted by a bank or trust company, or a firm, company, or corporation engaged generally in the business of granting bankers acceptance credits." In essence it is a draft drawn on a bank by a firm that either exports or imports goods and services. Chapter 21 describes in detail how a bankers acceptance arises to assist in financing international trade.

From an investor's perspective, a bankers acceptance is a short-term interest-bearing time draft created by a high-quality bank. The acceptance has a fixed maturity ranging up to nine months and is priced as a discount instrument, like T-bills. Because default risk is relatively low, the promised rate is only slightly above the rate on a comparable maturity T-bill. Banks find bankers acceptances attractive investments because they exhibit low default risk, pay a premium over T-bills, and can be used as collateral against discount window borrowings. Various money market rates as of May 20, 2002, appear in Exhibit 19.5.

CAPITAL MARKET INVESTMENTS

The largest portion of bank securities consists of instruments with original maturities greater than one year that are labeled capital market instruments. By regulation, banks are restricted to investment-grade securities—those rated Baa or above—and thus do not buy junk bonds. The long-term taxable portfolio is subsequently dominated by Treasury and U.S. agency securities, corporate and foreign bonds, and mortgage-backed securities. Each of these

---

[9]There are two basic types of commercial paper—direct paper and dealer paper. Direct paper comprises the bulk of new commercial paper and is issued primarily by finance companies and large bank holding companies. Thus firms such as General Motors Acceptance Corp., Ford Motor Credit Corp., and the Associates Corp., along with the nation's largest bank holding companies, borrow heavily in this market. Dealer paper (or industrial paper) refers to commercial paper issued primarily by nonfinancial firms through securities dealers.

exhibits broadly different risk and return features. Selected capital market rates appear at the end of Exhibit 19.5.

TREASURY NOTES AND BONDS. These long-term Treasury securities differ from Treasury bills in terms of original maturity and the form of interest payment. Notes have original maturities of one to 10 years. Bonds can carry any original maturity but typically are issued to mature well beyond 10 years. Most notes and bonds pay coupon interest semiannually. Since 1985 the Treasury has also issued zero coupon discount bonds that are comparable in form to bills. These zeros, labeled STRIPS (separate trading of registered interest and principal of securities), typically mature 20 to 30 years from origination and carry reported yields that assume semiannual compounding.

Like bills, Treasury notes and bonds are sold via closed auctions. In most cases, securities with a variety of maturities and coupon payments are sold, with buyers submitting either competitive or noncompetitive bids. The auctions normally take place every three months when large amounts of outstanding notes and bonds mature. The secondary market is extremely deep, due to the large volume of securities outstanding, low default risk, and wide range of investors who trade these securities. Banks buy these notes and bonds both in the auction and secondary markets. They are attractive because they exhibit low default risk, are highly liquid, and pay a market return.

Unlike T-bill rates, yields are quoted on a coupon-bearing basis with prices expressed in thirty-seconds of a point. Each thirty-second is worth $31.25 per $1,000 face value ($1,000/32). Coupon interest is paid semiannually. For example, an investor might obtain a price quote of 96.24 on a 10 percent coupon, $10,000 par value Treasury note with exactly two years remaining to maturity. Interest equals five percent semiannually so that the investor receives four coupon payments of $500 at 6-month intervals and $10,000 principal after two years. The quoted price equals 96.75 percent (96 plus 24/32) of par value or $9,675. The effective pretax yield to maturity can be calculated from the present value formula presented in Chapter 6 and equals 11.87 percent.[10]

During recent years, many banks have purchased zero coupon Treasury securities as part of their interest rate risk management strategies. Since 1985 the U.S. Treasury has allowed any Treasury with an original maturity of at least 10 years to be "stripped" into its component interest and principal pieces and traded via the Federal Reserve wire transfer system. Each component interest or principal payment thus constitutes a separate zero coupon security and can be traded separately from the other payments.

Consider a 10-year, $1 million par value Treasury bond that pays 9 percent coupon interest or 4.5 percent semiannually ($45,000 every six months). This security can be stripped into 20 separate interest payments of $45,000 each and a single $1 million principal payment, or 21 separate zero coupon securities.

---

[10]The yield to maturity (y) formula follows Equation (6.8) from Chapter 6 and can be expressed solving for y, as

$$P_O = \sum_{t=1}^{n} \frac{C_t}{(1 + y)^t} + \frac{P_n}{(1 + y)^n}$$

where
P_O = current price,
P_n = cash flow at maturity,
C_t = dollar value of the cash flow (interest payment) received in period t,
n = number of periods until the final cash flow, and
y = periodic yield to maturity.
Applied to the Treasury note, the annualized yield to maturity (y*) is determined:

$$\$9,675 = \sum_{t=1}^{4} \frac{\$500}{(1 + y^*/2)^t} + \frac{\$10,000}{(1 + y^*/2)^4} \text{, or}$$

$$y^* = 11.87\%$$

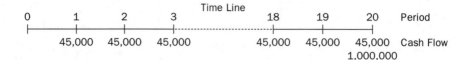

Each zero coupon security is priced by discounting the promised cash flow at the appropriate interest rate. If the market rate on the 2-year zero—fourth periodic cash flow—equals 8 percent (4 percent semiannually), the associated price of the $45,000 promised payment would equal $38,466.[11]

The primary advantage of zero coupon Treasury securities is that a bank can lock in a fixed interest payment and yield for whatever maturity is selected. The above 2-year zero, for example, would pay $45,000 at maturity thus providing $6,534 in interest. Because there are no interim cash flows, there is no reinvestment risk and the bank can be assured of receiving its promised yield of 8 percent. In terms of interest rate risk management advantages, the Macaulay duration of zero coupon securities equals maturity so a bank can more precisely balance its earnings sensitivity or duration gap profile with such STRIPS.

U.S. GOVERNMENT AGENCY SECURITIES. In December 2001, commercial banks owned $781 billion in U.S. government agency securities. The bulk of these securities exhibit characteristics similar to those of U.S. Treasury securities, which is why they are attractive investments. Others, such as mortgage-backed securities, exhibit characteristics that are more comparable to corporate bonds. The wide range of mortgage-backed securities is described in the next section.

Federal agencies can be separated into two groups. Members in the first group are formally part of the federal government. As such, they obtain operating funds from the Treasury and borrow from the Federal Financing Bank, a political subdivision of the Treasury that borrows from the Treasury and lends to selected agencies. This intermediation function enables agencies to borrow at the Treasury rate but also raises total Treasury financing requirements. These agencies, including the Federal Housing Administration, Export-Import Bank, and Government National Mortgage Association (Ginnie Mae), are effectively owned by the U.S. government.

Members in the second group are government-sponsored enterprises (GSEs) that are quasi-public entities. The quasi-public label represents the fact that even though the agencies are federally authorized and chartered, they are privately owned and often have publicly traded stock. They operate like any private corporation, issuing debt and acquiring assets that presumably provide revenues to cover operating expenses, pay interest and dividends, and add to capital. The U.S. government sponsors the agencies by encouraging and often subsidizing activities in favored markets such as housing and agriculture. Sponsorship also involves an implied guarantee to bail out any agency with financial problems. GSE securities are not direct obligations of the Treasury and thus are not backed by the Treasury's tax and credit authority. Default risk is considered low, however, because investors believe that the U.S. Congress has a moral obligation to provide financial aid in the event of problems at specific agencies. These agency issues normally carry a risk premium of 10 to 100 basis points over comparable maturity direct Treasury obligations due to this lack of a direct guarantee.

Exhibit 19.6 lists the major U.S. agencies and their status. Those marked with the superscript † are true agencies of the federal government and not sponsored. The agencies listed are generally active in the areas of housing, agriculture, education, and small business. During the late 1980s and early 1990s, a variety of agency securities were offered by the Financing

---

[11]$45,000/(1.04)^4$

· EXHIBIT 19.6

FEDERAL STATUS OF U.S. GOVERNMENT AGENCY SECURITIES

Agency	Full Faith and Credit of the U.S. Government	Authority to Borrow from the Federal Treasury	Interest on Bonds Generally Exempt from State and Local Taxes
Farm Credit System	No	Yes—$260 million revolving line of credit.	Yes
Farm Credit System Financial Assistance Corporation (FCSFAC)	Yes	Yes—FCSFAC began issuing bonds in late 1988.	Yes
Federal Home Loan Banks (FHLB)	No	Yes—the Treasury is authorized to purchase up to $4 billion of FHLB securities.	Yes
Federal Home Loan Mortgage Corporation (Freddie Mac)*	No	Yes—indirect line of credit through the FHLBs.	No
Federal National Mortgage Association (FNMA) (Fannie Mae)*	No	Yes—at FNMA request the Treasury may purchase $2.25 billion of FNMA securities.	No
Financing Corporation (FICO)	No	No	Yes
Student Loan Marketing Association (Sallie Mae)	Not since 1/9/82	Yes—at its discretion the Treasury may purchase $1 billion of Sallie Mae obligations.	Yes
United States Postal Service†	Guarantee may be extended if Postal Service requests and Treasury determines this to be in the public interest.	Yes—the Postal Service may require the Treasury to purchase up to $2 billion of its obligations.	Yes
Resolution Funding Corporation (RefCorp)	No	No	Yes
Farmers Home Administration† (FmHA) CBOs	Yes	No	No
Federal Financing Bank (FFB)	Yes	Yes—FFB can require the Treasury to purchase up to $5 billion of its obligations. The Treasury Secretary is authorized to purchase any amount of FFB obligations at his or her discretion.	Yes
General Services Administration† (GSA)	Yes	No	Yes
Government National Mortgage Association† (GNMA)	Yes	No	No
Maritime Administration Guaranteed Ship Financing Bonds issued after 1972	Yes	No	No
Small Business Administration (SBA)	Yes	No	No, with exceptions
Tennessee Valley Authority (TVA)	No	Yes—up to $150 million.	Yes
Washington Metropolitan Area Transit Authority (WMATA) Bonds	Yes	No	No, except for states involved in the interstate compact

*Fully modified pass-through mortgage-backed securities and certain mortgage-backed bonds of Freddie Mac and Fannie Mae are guaranteed by Ginnie Mae as to timely payment of principal and interest.
†True federal agencies.
SOURCE: *Handbook of Securities of the United States Government and Federal Agencies*, First Boston Corporation, 1988.

Corporation (FICO) and the Resolution Funding Corporation (RefCorp) to assist in the bailout of troubled savings and loans. These agencies generally borrow in both the money and capital markets. Most money market instruments are discount securities comparable to Treasury bills. Capital market instruments are similar to Treasury notes and bonds, except that original maturities are typically shorter. They represent attractive investments because of the low default risk, high marketability, and attractive yields relative to Treasury securities.

CALLABLE AGENCY BONDS. One of the most popular bank investments during the 1990s has been callable agency bonds. These are securities issued by GSEs in which the issuer has the option to call, or redeem, the bonds prior to final maturity. Typically, there is a call deferment period during which the bonds cannot be called. Such bonds contain an explicit call option where the issuer, such as a FHLB, buys the option to call the bonds and investors sell the option. The issuer pays by offering a higher promised yield relative to comparable noncallable bonds. The present value of this rate differential essentially represents the call premium. Banks find these securities attractive because they initially pay a higher yield than otherwise similar noncallable bonds. Of course, the premium reflects call risk. If rates fall sufficiently, the issuer will redeem the bonds early, refinancing at lower rates, and the investor gets the principal back early which must then be invested at lower yields for the same risk profile.

Consider the following callable agency bonds.

Issuer	Final Maturity	Call Deferment	Yield to Maturity	Price
FNMA	7 years	1 year	6.42%	99.91
FHLB	5 years	3 months	5.84	100.00
FHLMC	10 years	1 year	6.55	99.625
FHLMC	10 years	2 years	6.37	99.10
FHLB	3 years	1 year	5.78	99.97
FHLMC	3 years	1 year	5.62	99.4375

The first column of data lists the final maturity while the second column indicates how much time must elapse before the issuer can call the security. The final two columns note the prevailing yield to maturity and market price per $100 par value. At this time, the Treasury yield curve was slightly upward sloping. Note two things about these promised yields. First, as suggested by the FHLMC securities, the yield is lower the longer is the call deferment period. Investors know that they have call protection for a longer period, so they accept a lower yield, ceteris paribus. Second, the final two securities differ primarily by the amount of the discount from par. The call option is in the money when rates fall, such that the price rises above or equals 100. The greater is the discount, the more yields have to fall to move the call option into the money. These securities are thus more attractive, ceteris paribus. Chapter 20 critiques these securities in terms of bank investment strategies.

CONVENTIONAL MORTGAGE-BACKED SECURITIES. Since passage of the Tax Reform Act of 1986 and implementation of risk-based capital standards, banks have been aggressive buyers of mortgage-backed securities (MBSs). Banks find MBSs attractive because default risk is generally low and the securities offer higher promised yields than other instruments with comparable average maturities. The problem is that mortgage-backed securities exhibit fundamentally different interest rate risk features than other investments due to mortgage prepayments. The following discussion thus focuses on the characteristics of different MBSs and the nature of prepayment risk.

In order to understand prepayment risk, it is necessary to understand the characteristics of mortgages. Formally, a mortgage is the pledge of property, typically real estate, to secure a debt. Thus, a mortgage on a house represents the pledge of the house as payment for the

• EXHIBIT 19.7

STRUCTURE OF THE GNMA MORTGAGE-BACKED PASS-THROUGH
SECURITY ISSUANCE PROCESS

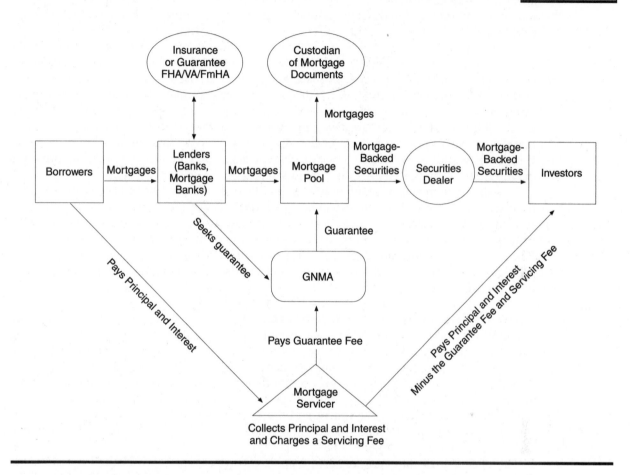

loan in case of default by the borrower. Mortgage loans generally take the form either of fixed-rate loans where the associated interest rate is constant over the life of the loan, or adjustable-rate loans where the interest rate varies over time based on movements in market interest rates. Mortgages are typically amortized, with monthly payments that include both interest and principal. For example, a 30-year fixed rate mortgage will have a constant monthly payment where the interest portion is quite high during the early years of the loan because the outstanding loan balance is large, but declines with each successive payment as the outstanding principal declines. The principal portion of the fixed payment similarly rises over the life of the loan.

A mortgage-backed security is any security that evidences an undivided interest in the ownership of mortgage loans. The most common form of MBS is the pass-through security in which traditional fixed-rate mortgages are pooled and investors buy an interest in the pool in the form of certificates or securities. Exhibit 19.7 demonstrates how a GNMA guaranteed mortgage pass-through security is created based on residential mortgages. The originator of the mortgages makes the initial loans to individuals and contracts for the promised principal and interest payments. At this point the mortgages may be insured or guaranteed by the Federal Housing Authority (FHA), Veterans Administration (VA), or Farm Home

Administration (FmHA). The originator packages the mortgages into a pool and securitizes the pool. This involves working with a securities dealer to create securities that are collateralized by the original mortgages. Typically, the creator of the pool gets a federal government agency, such as GNMA, to guarantee the borrowers' interest and principal payments. A custodian is similarly designated to maintain the mortgage documents. The securities are then sold to investors.

Operationally, a mortgage servicer collects principal and interest payments on the underlying mortgages, pays the guarantor a fee (around 5 basis points of the principal balance), charges a fee for processing and record-keeping (around 12.5–25 basis points), and passes through the remaining interest and principal payments to investors. Thus, the term pass-through indicates that actual principal and interest payments minus fees are passed-through to investors. Investors, in turn, receive a pro rata share of the payments that reflects their fractional ownership of the pool. If, for example, five investors each owned one-fifth of the securities, each would receive 20 percent of the total principal and interest payments. If borrowers default in this example, GNMA steps in and makes the promised payments.

This structure creates substantial differences in the features of different types of mortgage-backed securities as well as differences between MBSs and conventional bonds. In contrast to conventional bonds, each payment on a MBS includes scheduled principal and interest plus principal prepayments. In addition, MBS payments occur monthly rather than semiannually. Finally, there are significant differences in price volatility due to prepayment risk on most MBSs that does not appear with conventional bonds. Characteristics of the most popular forms of MBSs are discussed below.

GNMA PASS-THROUGH SECURITIES. The Government National Mortgage Association (GNMA or Ginnie Mae) was established as part of the Department of Housing and Urban Development to provide support for the residential mortgage market. It does so primarily by guaranteeing the timely payment of interest and principal to the holders of pass-through securities, regardless of whether the promised mortgage payments are made.[12] As such, even though GNMA pass-through securities are issued by private institutions, they are backed by the federal government and thus exhibit low default risk and high liquidity. Investors willingly pay for this guarantee so yields on GNMA pass-throughs are lower than yields on otherwise comparable MBSs.

The underlying mortgages in GNMA pools consist of mortgages insured by either the Federal Housing Association (FHA), Veterans Administration (VA), or Farmers Home Administration (FmHA). They can be of virtually any form including both fixed payment and adjustable rate mortgages (ARMs). Generally, mortgages in the pool are quite homogeneous in that they are issued at roughly the same time, have approximately the same maturity, and carry rates that are similar.

FHLMC SECURITIES. The Federal Home Loan Mortgage Corporation (FHLMC or Freddie Mac) was established to support the market for conventional mortgages. Unlike GNMA, FHLMC is a private corporation, albeit one that operates with an implicit federal guarantee. Although its stock is publicly traded today, it was originally owned by the Federal Home Loan Banks and member savings and loans, and Congress still selects a portion of its Board of Directors that helps set policy. FHLMC provides support by buying mortgages in the secondary market. It finances its purchases by issuing a variety of securities. It is these securities that banks and others purchase as investments.

---

[12]The term *modified pass-through* is used to describe this guarantee feature of securities. GNMA also directly purchases mortgages at below market interest rates where the mortgages are used to finance low income housing.

FHLMC Participation Certificates are pass-through securities issued by FHLMC that are secured by conventional residential mortgages. Each participation certificate (PC) represents an undivided interest in the mortgages that comprise the mortgage pool used as collateral. FHLMC guarantees monthly interest and principal payments to security holders whether or not the payments are actually received on the underlying mortgages. This is not the same as a federal guarantee so investors demand a risk premium. The risk premium can be volatile due to uncertainty regarding the credit quality of FHLMC's mortgage portfolio and questions about the viability of the implied federal guarantee.

FHLMC Guaranteed Mortgage Certificates are mortgage-backed securities issued by FHLMC that are similar to bonds. Interest and principal payments on the certificates are again backed by a pool of mortgages, but interest is paid just semiannually and principal is repaid annually. FHLMC also backs these payments with its guarantee.

FHLMC Collateralized Mortgage Obligations are debt issues originated by FHLMC that are secured by a pool of mortgages, but with the securities are grouped into classes according to estimated stated maturities. The purpose of these classes is described in the discussion of collateralized mortgage obligations (CMOs). Investors in all classes of CMOs receive semiannual interest payments until maturity.[13] Principal payments are also semiannual but are allocated initially to the class of CMOs with the shortest stated maturity, then sequentially to the remaining outstanding classes by maturity. Investors find CMOs attractive because they can better estimate the effective maturity of the securities compared with other types of pass-throughs.

FNMA SECURITIES. The Federal National Mortgage Association (FNMA or Fannie Mae) was created by the federal government in 1938 to support housing, but today is another private corporation GSE that operates with an implicit federal guarantee. It operates much like FHLMC, buying mortgages and financing the mortgages with securities backed by pools of mortgages with features similar to FHLMC's participation certificates. FNMA similarly guarantees timely interest and principal payments so that default risk is generally perceived to be low.

PRIVATELY ISSUED PASS-THROUGHS. Commercial banks, savings and loans, and mortgage banks also issue mortgage-backed pass-through securities secured by pools of mortgages. The primary difference with federal agency MBSs is that there is no actual or implied guarantee by the federal government or agency. Instead, private issuers purchase mortgage insurance either in the form of pool insurance by such groups as the Mortgage Guarantee Insurance Corporation or via letters of credit. In most cases, it is more profitable for mortgage lenders to use the agency programs. With certain mortgages, such as large mortgages where the outstanding principal balance exceeds the acceptable maximum set by the agencies, a private pass-through program is the only one available.

PREPAYMENT RISK ON MORTGAGE-BACKED SECURITIES

As indicated earlier, most mortgage-backed securities carry a guarantee that principal and interest payments will be made to investors regardless of whether the payment on the underlying mortgages is made. Despite these guarantees, MBSs exhibit considerable risk because they may fluctuate widely in price when interest rates change. This results from uncertainty over the timing of prepayments and thus what cash flows will actually be passed through to investors at various points in time.

---

[13]Holders of certain classes of interest accrual securities do not receive any interest payments until all interest and principal payments are made on the other classes of bonds. Interest continues to accrue, however, until received.

Remember that investors receive the actual principal and interest payments made by borrowers on the underlying mortgages minus a servicing fee. These borrowers, in fact, may prepay the outstanding mortgage principal at any point in time, for any reason, and often without penalty. Prepayments generally occur because of fundamental demographic trends as well as from movements in interest rates. Demographic phenomena include factors affecting general labor mobility as individuals change jobs with fluctuations in regional economic activity, as well as changes in family structure attributable to events such as children leaving home or divorce. The important point is that the prepayment feature represents an option and is quite valuable to the borrower who buys the option and chooses when to exercise (prepay). It is risky to an investor who sells the option because the cash flows are unpredictable.

Consider the case where an investor buys a Ginnie Mae MBS based on a pool of mortgages paying 8.5 percent. Current mortgage rates are lower so that the security trades at a substantial premium for a promised yield of 8 percent. If rates remain constant, an investor might receive interest on the outstanding principal at the higher rate for seven or eight years. Suppose instead that mortgage rates fall sharply. Some mortgage borrowers will exercise their option and refinance their properties with new mortgages at lower rates because they can save on monthly interest payments. They subsequently prepay principal on the 8.5 percent mortgages so that MBS investors receive smaller interest payments. If prepayments are substantial, all outstanding principal may be quickly repaid so that the MBS effectively matures. Investors lose because they paid a premium expecting to receive high interest payments for several years. With the decline in rates, they not only receive considerably less interest over a shorter period of time, but they have to reinvest their cash receipts at lower rates. If prepayments are high enough, they may not even recover the premium paid. The total return can be negative.

Suppose, alternatively, that mortgage rates rise substantially. Prepayments will either slow or remain constant because fewer individuals will move and interest rates will induce fewer refinancings. The effect on investors in MBSs is threefold. First, the outstanding principal will be higher than originally anticipated. Thus, interest received will be higher as repayment slows. Second, the security will remain outstanding longer so that interest payments will be received for more periods. This lengthening of final maturity is labeled extension risk. Third, all cash receipts can be reinvested at higher rates. Of course, the increase in rates at least partly offsets this by lowering the market value of the MBS.

Panel A of Exhibit 19.8 demonstrates the general interest sensitivity of a MBS. The vertical axis represents the market value of a $100,000 interest in a pool of 30-year mortgages carrying 9 percent rates. Assume that the expected rate of prepayments over the life of the mortgages is 6 percent per year. This type of constant prepayment rate (CPR) is typically measured as the annualized fraction of principal prepaid during a specific period, such as a year.[14] The dashed line represents the value of the MBS if the prepayment rate remains at 6 percent regardless of the level of mortgage rates. The solid line indicates the value of the MBS if the prepayment rate varies from 6 percent at different interest rate levels. At a current market rate of 9 percent, the MBS is valued at $100,000. As interest rates rise or fall, the value of the MBS declines or rises, respectively. Note, however, the differences in the two values at different rate levels. An increase in rates lowers the actual price of the MBS below the price at a constant prepayment rate because prepayments will slow and an investor will receive below market interest payments for a longer period of time than originally anticipated. A decrease in rates raises value, but the sharp increase in prepayments at low rates limits the

---

[14]Suppose that a pool of mortgages contained $100 million in principal. A 6 percent annual CPR means that prepayments equal $6 million during the first year, $5.64 million (.06 × $94) during the second year, etc. If $6 million in principal was prepaid during the first three months, the annualized CPR would equal 24 percent. CPR does not include normal amortization.

- EXHIBIT 19.8

PREPAYMENT RISK ON MORTGAGE-BACKED SECURITIES

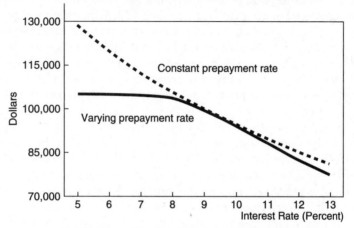

A. The Interest Sensitivity of Mortgage Pass-Throughs
(Dollar Value of $100,000 Share in a Mortgage Pool)

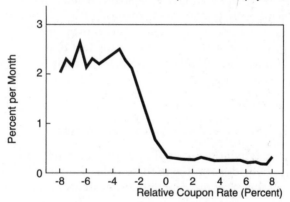

B. The Effect of Relative Coupon on the Prepayment Rate

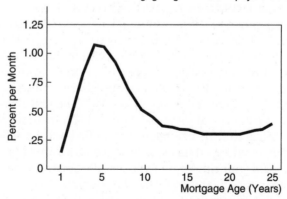

C. The Effect of Mortgage Age on the Prepayment Rate

SOURCE: Sean Becketti, "The Prepayment Risk of Mortgage-Backed Securities." *Economic Review* (Federal Reserve Bank of Kansas City, February 1989).

price appreciation. Thus, prepayments increase potential capital losses to investors while they decrease potential capital gains.

This would not be a problem if investors could accurately forecast prepayments. Unfortunately, this is difficult to do. Pools of mortgages differ by geographic region, by the type of home or commercial property financed, by the age of the mortgages or how long they have been in existence, and by the actual interest rates on the underlying mortgages. Fixed-rate mortgages prepay at different rates than adjustable-rate mortgages. Thus, prepayment experience will vary widely between pools of mortgages even at the same point in time. This problem is mitigated somewhat by the fact that the federal government collects and reports data on the prepayment experience of selected mortgage pools. Securities dealers similarly track prepayment experience to assist investors when buying MBSs. While such information helps distinguish between pools, past prepayment experience is not always useful in predicting prepayments.

The bottom two panels of Exhibit 19.8 document the relationship between the prepayment rate on the vertical axis and different coupon rates on the underlying mortgages and mortgage age. The horizontal axis in panel B indicates the difference between the current rate on new mortgages and the rate on the underlying mortgages, while mortgage age in panel C refers to the length of time the mortgages have been outstanding since origination. Not surprisingly, prepayment rates rise sharply when mortgage rates fall. Prepayments are relatively low until mortgage rates fall where they fluctuate between two and three percent per month. Prepayments are virtually unchanged when rates rise because there are no rate-induced prepayments, only prepayments resulting from demographic events. According to panel C, prepayment experience is low on new mortgages, but rises consistently through five years after which it declines. This reflects the fact that rate changes are typically small near term and that most individuals must remain in their home for a while before they can cover the costs of refinancing.

UNCONVENTIONAL MORTGAGE-BACKED SECURITIES

The existence of prepayment risk complicates the valuation and marketing of MBSs. Issuers have created many hybrids to mitigate these risks and structure MBSs that appeal to more investors. Several of the more prominent hybrids are introduced below.

COLLATERALIZED MORTGAGE OBLIGATIONS.

Freddie Mac first introduced CMOs in 1983 to try and circumvent some of the prepayment risk associated with the traditional pass-through security. This was accomplished by converting pass-throughs to securities with more predictable maturity and yield features comparable to those of well-known fixed-income securities. CMOs are essentially bonds. An originator combines various mortgage pools together that serve as collateral and creates classes of bonds with different maturities secured by the collateral. Consider a *sequential CMO*. The first class of bonds, or *tranche*, has the shortest maturity because all principal payments on the underlying mortgages are allocated to these securities so that repayment occurs first and on schedule. Interest is paid on these and most other bonds at all times that the securities are outstanding. Once these bonds have been fully repaid, principal payments are allocated to a second class (or tranche) of bonds until they are paid off, and so forth. The primary advantage is that bonds in the first CMO tranches exhibit less prepayment uncertainty. An investor can subsequently better forecast the effective maturity and overall yield. In some instances the last class, a Z-tranche, consists of an accrual bond in which no interest or principal is paid until all other classes of bonds have been repaid. These securities are higher risk and represent a hybrid form of zero coupon bond.

As an example, consider the CMO prospectus in Exhibit 19.9. These CMO bonds were issued by Freddie Mac in January 1990, have $896 million in principal, and are divided into four tranches. The underwriters, led by Prudential-Bache Capital Funding, are listed at the bottom. Bonds in the first tranche (Series 123) carry a coupon rate of 8.25 percent but are priced to yield slightly more because the price is below 100. Note that the final payment date is listed at February 1995, roughly five years after issue. This is an approximate maturity date assuming no prepayments of principal. According to the structure of this issue, investors in first tranche bonds receive all principal payments, including prepayments, until the $330 million is repaid. Because there will be some prepayments, five years represents the longest an investor would have to wait for a return of all principal. After these bonds are retired, all principal payments are next allocated to the second tranche (Series 124) bonds until they are retired. The estimated longest final maturity here is seven years, assuming no prepayments. The process continues until bonds in the third and fourth tranches are paid off. As such, the bonds evidence a sequential (SEQ) repayment pattern. The longest possible maturity for the Series 126 bonds is 25 years.

The structure essentially creates four classes of bonds with different maturities and cash flow features. The coupon rates and promised yields increase with estimated maturity to compensate investors for the additional risk. The bonds are guaranteed by Freddie Mac such that investors assume little default risk. There is, however, still substantial interest rate risk with uncertain prepayments. It is relatively low for the first tranche bonds, but increases with bonds in each successive tranche.

There are many different types of CMOs. The least risky are *planned amortization classes* (PACs) in which principal payments are allocated according to a fixed amortization schedule. Specifically, as long as prepayments fall within a predetermined range, the principal of a PAC will be repaid in a predictable, timely fashion. If actual prepayment rates fall outside this range, principal allocated to other nonplanned amortization class tranches is reduced or accelerated to ensure that the PAC CMO is paid as scheduled. Such non-PAC CMOs are labeled *support (SUP) tranches.* The result is that PAC bonds exhibit relatively low prepayment risk, as long as the PAC prepayment range (band) is wide, but the non-PAC tranches exhibit great prepayment risk. Exhibit 19.10 summarizes the general terms for a Freddie Mac CMO with $340 million in principal issued in September 2001 with 15 different classes (tranches) of bonds, including PACs, SEQs, SUPs, and other forms. Generally, the bonds listed first have a prior claim on principal payments versus bonds listed later. Note that some of the CMOs are zero coupon securities.

CMOs provide advantages over traditional MBSs in a variety of ways. First, they exhibit less prepayment risk. Second, by segmenting the securities into maturity classes, CMOs appeal to different investors who have different maturity preferences. Banks, for example, often prefer first tranche securities because the short maturities and durations better match their cash flow obligations with deposit liabilities. Insurance companies, in contrast, often prefer later tranches where the bonds have much longer effective maturities. Third, CMOs exhibit little default risk because the collateral backing the bonds are generally agency securities that carry explicit guarantees, or the issuer purchases private insurance. Thus, many CMOs are Aaa- and Aa-rated. In addition, many early classes of bonds are overcollateralized because the actual cash flows from the collateral exceed cash flow required to pay bondholders. Fourth, like MBSs, CMOs are priced at a spread over Treasury securities so that changes in yields are fairly predictable.

CMOs have several disadvantages. They are less liquid because the secondary market is less developed. Transactions costs are subsequently higher. In addition, an investor may find it difficult to obtain an accurate price quote when trying to sell a CMO. This is particularly true for the latter tranches, which exhibit far greater price volatility. Banks and other investors have had serious trouble estimating prepayment speeds and thus the interest rate risk with CMOs

New Issue

$896,000,000

Freddie
Mac

Federal Home Loan Mortgage Corporation

Multifamily Plan C REMIC
Mortgage Participation Certificates
(Guaranteed), Series 123 through 126

Series 123
$330,000,000   8.25% Class 123-A Final Payment Date February 15, 1995 — Price 99.781250%

Series 124
$307,000,000   8.50% Class 124-A Final Payment Date March 15, 1997   — Price 99.093750%

Series 125
$220,000,000   8.75% Class 125-A Final Payment Date March 15, 2000   — Price 99.031250%

Series 126
$ 39,000,000   9.00% Class 126-A Final Payment Date March 15, 2005   — Price 99.390625%
(plus accrued interest at the applicable rate from January 15, 1990)

Freddie Mac, in its corporate capacity, will be contractually obligated to pay PC Yield Maintenance Premiums, if any, to each Holder of the Class 123-A, Class 124-A, Class 125-A and Class 126-A Plan C REMIC PCs.

The obligations of Freddie Mac under its guarantee of the Plan C REMIC PCs, and its obligations to pay PC Yield Maintenance Premiums, are obligations of Freddie Mac only and are not backed by the full faith and credit of the United States.

The residual interest for each Plan C REMIC PC Pool is not offered by the Offering Circular Supplement and the related Offering Circular and will initially be retained by Freddie Mac.

The Class 123-A, Class 124-A, Class 125-A and Class 126-A Plan C REMIC PCs will each be a regular interest in one of the Plan C REMIC PC Pools.

Elections will be made to treat the Plan C REMIC PC Pools as REMICs.

Copies of the Offering Circular Supplement and the related Offering Circular describing these securities and the business of the Corporation may be obtained from any of the undersigned in States in which such underwriters may legally offer these securities. This announcement is neither an offer to sell nor a solicitation of an offer to buy these securities. This offer is made only by the Offering Circular Supplement and the related Offering Circular.

Prudential–Bache Capital Funding

The First Boston Corporation

Goldman, Sachs & Co.

Merrill Lynch Capital Markets

Salomon Brothers Inc

Shearson Lehman Hutton Inc.

BT Securities Corporation   Bear, Stearns & Co. Inc.   Citicorp Securities Markets, Inc.

Donaldson, Lufkin & Jenrette   Drexel Burnham Lambert

Freddie Mac Security Sales and Trading Group   Greenwich Capital Markets, Inc.

Kidder, Peabody & Co.   J.P. Morgan Securities Inc.   Morgan Stanley & Co.

Nomura Securities International, Inc.   PaineWebber Incorporated   UBS Securities Inc.

January 9, 1990

- **EXHIBIT 19.10**

DIFFERENT CLASSES (TRANCHES) OF CMO BONDS ISSUED BY THE FEDERAL HOME LOAN MORTGAGE CORPORATION, SEPTEMBER 2001

Class	Orig. Amt (000s)	Coupon	Orig. WAL*	Orig. Maturity	Description**
1) B	100,000	6.00	4.00	2/15/31	TAC(11)
2) C	34,900	6.00	4.60	9/15/31	SEQ
3) LL	10,944	6.25	16.00	9/15/31	SEQ, RTL
4) LO	456	0.00	16.00	9/15/31	PD, SEQ
5) TW	40,912	6.50	4.00	9/15/31	SCH(22)
6) ZA	3,700	6.00	11.90	3/15/31	Z, SUP
7) MC	159,088	6.50	8.50	9/15/31	EXCH, PZ, SUP, PAC
8) R	0	0.00		9/15/31	R, NPR
9) KA	34,282	6.50	2.50	7/15/18	PAC(11)
10) KB	47,270	6.50	6.00	7/15/26	PAC(11)
11) KC	38,898	6.50	11.00	6/15/30	PAC(11)
12) KD	15,923	6.50	19.10	9/15/31	PAC(11)
13) KD	11,380	6.50	2.10	9/15/31	SUP
14) KZ	11,335	6.50	15.80	9/15/31	Z, SUP
15) KE	136,373	6.50	8.10	9/15/31	EXCH, PAC

* WAL refers to weighted average life in years.

** TAC (Targeted amortization class), SEQ (Sequential), PO (Principal only), SUP (Support), PAC (Planned amortization class), Z (Z-tranche), and others. See Bloomberg's description.

SOURCE: Bloomberg Description of CMO Structure, FHR 2365.

has been extraordinary. Regulators have tried to limit the riskiness of a CMO for banks by forcing banks to mark-to-market all CMOs that do not meet well-defined price and extension volatility criteria. Finally, all CMO interest is taxable at both the federal and state and local government levels, unlike Treasury securities, which are subject only to federal income taxes.

STRIPPED MORTGAGE-BACKED SECURITIES. Stripped Treasury securities, introduced earlier, are nothing more than zero coupon instruments that represent either a principal payment or coupon interest payment on a Treasury obligation. The general label is principal only (PO) and interest only (IO) security. The previous time line for the 10-year Treasury reveals 20 distinct IOs paying $45,000 each at maturity and one PO of $1 million. These stripped Treasury securities exhibit no default risk and no interest rate risk if held to final maturity. An investor can therefore lock-in a guaranteed return if he or she matches the holding period with a stripped Treasury of the same maturity.

Stripped mortgage-backed securities are much more complicated in terms of their structure and pricing characteristics. This reflects the design of mortgage contracts and the impact of mortgage prepayments. Consider a 30-year, 12 percent fixed-rate mortgage that is fully amortized. There will be 360 scheduled principal and interest payments equal to a fixed dollar amount per month (PY). The following time line demonstrates the cash flow pattern of interest (I) and principal (P) payments where the subscripts refer to the month in which the payment is made.

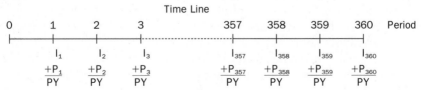

Time Line

| 0 | 1 | 2 | 3 | | 357 | 358 | 359 | 360 | Period |

I_1 I_2 I_3 I_{357} I_{358} I_{359} I_{360}
$+P_1$ $+P_2$ $+P_3$ $+P_{357}$ $+P_{358}$ $+P_{359}$ $+P_{360}$
PY PY PY PY PY PY PY

Loan amortization requires that the early period principal payments are small relative to the total payment so that $P_1 < P_2 < \ldots < P_{360}$. Interest payments are large during the early periods when the outstanding principal is high, and decline over time and the principal is reduced. Thus $I_1 > I_2 > \ldots > I_{360}$.

Unlike Treasury securities, there is more than one principal component as each payment is part principal. Furthermore, MBSs are typically stripped into just two securities with the PO representing the entire stream of principal payments, and the IO representing the entire stream of interest payments. Thus, each payment is not a separate security and the strips are no longer simple zero coupon instruments. More importantly, MBSs are subject to prepayment risk which affects the underlying principal and interest payments and thus makes mortgage-backed POs and IOs highly interest sensitive.

Suppose that an investor purchased the PO security represented by the stream of principal payments in the above time line when the market rate and coupon rate both equaled 10 percent. Given normal demographic trends, prepayments are expected to equal 6 percent annually. Now suppose that the prevailing mortgage rate drops to 8 percent so that prepayments accelerate and the CPR jumps to 20 percent. The investor will receive principal payments earlier than originally anticipated. In addition, the payments will be discounted at a lower rate so that the price of the PO will rise substantially. Similarly a rise in mortgage rates will not slow prepayments because they are already at the minimum 6 percent, but the cash flows will be discounted at a higher rate so the price of the PO will fall. If the PO originally carried a higher coupon rate, prepayments would have slowed and the price decline would be even greater. In short, a mortgage-backed PO behaves much like a typical MBS or conventional bond except it is more price sensitive.

Suppose that another investor bought the IO security represented by the stream of interest payments at the 10 percent coupon rate. A decline in the market rate to 8 percent would accelerate principal payments and the outstanding principal balance would fall below that anticipated. The IO investor would thus receive much lower interest payments than originally anticipated. In the extreme case when the entire outstanding principal balance is repaid, the IO investor would receive no interest payments. Not surprisingly, the price of an IO is quite volatile. If prepayments are high enough, the drop in the dollar value of interest received can swamp any effect from discounting at a lower rate so that the price of an IO will fall. In a similar vein, suppose that the investor purchased the IO when the prevailing mortgage rate was 6 percent, or four percent below the 10 percent coupon rate on the underlying mortgages. The initial forecast would call for a high prepayment speed such that the IO could be purchased at a relatively low price. If the market rate increased to 8 percent, prepayments would slow substantially, outstanding principal would be greater than that initially anticipated, and interest payments would rise sharply. If the prepayment effect was large enough, it could swamp discounting at a higher rate such that the value of the IO might rise. These IO instruments can have prices that move in the same direction as market interest rates.

The essential point is that mortgage-backed IOs are extremely price sensitive to changes in interest rates and the price/yield relationship may be positive. When prepayments rise sharply with a drop in rates compared to that anticipated, the value of the IO similarly falls. When prepayments fall sharply with an increase in rates relative to expectations, the value of the IO will similarly rise. Thus, IOs may vary in price in the opposite direction of that normally observed for traditional fixed income securities. In securities parlance, these IOs exhibit negative convexity. The concept of convexity is described and applied to mortgage-backed securities in Chapter 20. To compensate for their high risk, IOs often carry yields that are 4 to 5 percent above comparable duration Treasury yields.

Unfortunately, many investors, including banks and savings and loans, purchased IOs for interest rate hedges without understanding their features. Certain high coupon IOs could presumably be used to hedge a negative GAP or positive duration gap because a bank with this risk profile would lose when interest rates increased. An IO would presumably rise in value as rates increased as an offset. Of course, if rates fell a bank would win with its GAP profile, but this would be off-set by losses on the IO. The success of IOs as hedges, however, depends on wide swings in rates. Small rate changes typically move IO prices in the same direction as a bank's cash flows from normal operations so that no hedge is in place.

It is extremely difficult to predict prepayments and thus the value of IOs and POs when rates change. They are extremely risky because they are extremely interest sensitive. There are many better hedging tools, such as interest rate swaps and options on futures, with more predictable cash flows and changes in value. Bank regulators have subsequently encouraged banks to stay away from IOs.

CORPORATE, FOREIGN, AND TAXABLE MUNICIPAL BONDS

Banks also purchase taxable fixed income securities in the form of corporate bonds and foreign govern-ment bonds. By year-end 2001, they held $372 billion, which more than tripled their holdings of munici-pals. Banks do not purchase junk bonds because they are restricted to investment grade securities. Banks are also constrained by regulation concerning legal lending limits to investing no more than 10 percent of capital in the securities of any single firm. These bonds typically pay interest semiannually and return the entire principal at maturity. In most cases, banks purchase securities that mature within 10 years.

Occasionally, banks also purchase municipal bonds that pay taxable interest. The Tax Reform Act of 1986 eliminated the tax-exempt status of certain types of municipal revenue bonds. These entities have subse-quently issued debt that pays taxable interest to meet their financing needs. The pretax yields are compa-rable to those on corporate securities even though the borrower is affiliated with a municipal government. Exhibit 19.11 compares the features of corporate securities with Treasury securities and pass-throughs.

ASSET-BACKED SECURITIES

One of the dominant trends in financial markets is the securitization of bank loans. Chapter 1 describes the process and rationale given the returns that are available and the recent increase in regulatory capital requirements. Although some banks have been active in securitizing nontraditional types of loans, others view these securities as potential investments. Conceptually, an asset-backed security is comparable to a mortgage-backed security in structure. The securities are effectively pass-throughs because promised inter-est and principal payments are secured by the payments on the specific loans pledged as collateral.

Two of the more popular forms of asset-backed securities are collateralized automobile receivables (CARS) and certificates for amortizing revolving debt (CARDS).[15] As the names suggest, CARS are securi-ties backed by automobile loans to individuals. CARDS are, in turn, securities backed by credit card loans to individuals. Exhibit 19.12 documents the composition of the asset-backed securities market at year-end 2000 and the first quarter of 2001. Note that credit card loans and retail auto loans represented the largest types of securitized loans in 2000 with other types, primarily home equity loans and auto or equipment leases, a substantial portion of the $312 billion market.

CARS may be structured either as conventional pass-throughs or CMOs. Automobile loans represent-ing installment contracts with maturities up to 60 months are placed in a trust. CARS represent an undi-vided interest in the trust. An investor receives the underlying monthly principal and interest payments less a servicing fee. As with CMOs, CARS may be multiple class instruments in which cash flows pay inter-est to all security holders, but repay principal sequentially from the first class of bonds to the last. Default risk is reduced because the issuer may either set up a reserve fund out of the payments to cover losses, pur-chase insurance, or obtain a letter of credit. Such credit enhancements typically provide the securities the

---

[15]CARS and CARDS are formally the labels copyrighted by Salomon Brothers for their specific issues of asset-backed securities, but will be used generically in the discussion to refer to any similar securities.

■ **EXHIBIT 19.11**

FEATURES OF PASS-THROUGH, GOVERNMENT, AND CORPORATE SECURITIES

	Pass-Throughs	Treasuries	Corporates	Stripped Treasuries
Credit risk	Generally high grade; range from government guaranteed to A (private pass-throughs).	Government guaranteed.	High grade to speculative.	Backed by government securities.
Liquidity	Good for agency issued/guaranteed pass-through.	Excellent.	Generally limited.	Fair.
Range of coupons (discount to premium)	Full range.	Full range.	Full range for a few issuers.	Zero coupons (discount securities).
Range of maturities	Medium and long term (fast-paying and seasoned pools can provide shorter maturities than stated).	Full range.	Full range.	Full range.
Call protection	Complex prepayment pattern; investor can limit through selection variables, such as coupon seasoning, and program.	Noncallable (except certain 30-year bonds).	Generally callable after initial limited period of 5 to 10 years.	Noncallable.
Frequency of payment	Monthly payments of principal and interest.	Semiannual interest payment.	Semiannual interest (except Eurobonds, which pay interest annually).	No payments until maturity.
Average life	Lower than for bonds of comparable maturity; can only be estimated due to prepayment risk.	Estimate only for small number of callable issues; otherwise, known with certainty.	Minimum average life known, otherwise a function of call risk.	Known with certainty.
Duration/interest rate risk	Function of prepayment risk; can only be estimated; can be negative when prepayment risk is high.	Unless callable, a simple function of yield, coupon, and maturity; is known with certainty.	Function of call risk; can be negative when call risk is high.	Known with certainty; no interest rate risk if held to maturity.
Basis for yield quotes	Cash flow yield based on monthly prepayments and constant CPR assumption (usually most recent three-month historical prepayment experience).	Based on semiannual coupon payments and 365-day year.	Based on semi-annual coupon payments and 360-day year of twelve 30-day months.	Bond equivalent yield based on either 360- or 365-day year depending on sponsor.
Settlement	Once a month.	Any business day.	Any business day.	Any business day.

SOURCE: *Handbook of Securities of the United States Government and Federal Agencies*, First Boston Corporation, 1988.

· EXHIBIT 19.12

U.S. MARKET FOR ASSET-BASED SECURITIES,

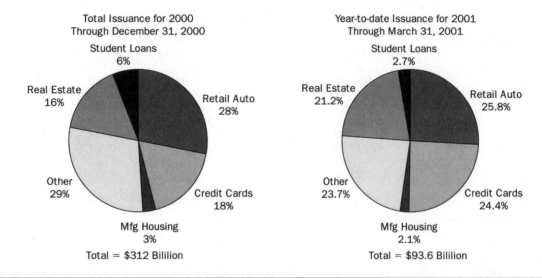

Total Issuance for 2000
Through December 31, 2000

Student Loans 6%
Real Estate 16%
Retail Auto 28%
Other 29%
Credit Cards 18%
Mfg Housing 3%

Total = $312 Bililion

Year-to-date Issuance for 2001
Through March 31, 2001

Student Loans 2.7%
Real Estate 21.2%
Retail Auto 25.8%
Other 23.7%
Credit Cards 24.4%
Mfg Housing 2.1%

Total = $93.6 Bililion

Aaa credit rating. CARS are attractive to investors because they have maturities of five years or less, exhibit little prepayment risk, and carry rates that are approximately 1 percent over rates on comparable duration Treasury securities. Prepayment risk is low because automobile loan rates are somewhat sticky and there are limited incentives to prepay. The primary negative is that liquidity is reduced compared with many other securities.

Exhibit 19.13 documents the features of automobile-backed securities issued by First Security Corp. in 1999. There are five classes of securities where Class B clearly supports the much larger Class A-1 to A-4 securities. The collateral consists of both new and used cars with the owners concentrated in Washington, Idaho, and Utah; an average outstanding principal balance of almost $14,000, and a remaining maturity of 58 months. The credit enhancement is such that an initial deposit and reserve collected from the borrowers' payments support potential defaults. The Class A-1 securities are short-term and rated A-1 with a yield 4 basis points below the matched duration Treasury yield. The Class A-2, A-5, and A-4 securities carry a AAA rating and pay yields that are 20 to 78 basis points over the matched duration Treasury yield.

CARDS are structured much like CARS except that the collateral is credit card receivables. An issuer places credit card accounts in a trust and sells participations. The securities generally have stated maturities around five years with only interest being paid monthly during the first one and one-half to two years. Principal payments begin thereafter. Because many cardholders repay their debts quickly, the principal may be repaid well before the stated maturity. Thus prepayment risk is higher for CARDS than CARS. Still, issuers establish a reserve fund or obtain explicit guarantees via letters of credit so that the securities are similarly rated Aaa.

MUTUAL FUNDS. In recent years, regulators have allowed banks to purchase certain types of mutual fund shares as an investment. The shares must be in funds that purchase only securities that banks would be allowed to own directly for their own account, such as Treasury and agency obligations, mortgage-backed securities, and investment grade corporates. The

CHARACTERISTICS OF FIRST SECURITY AUTO
OWNER TRUST 1999-1 CARS

	Class A				Class B
Transaction Structure	*A-1*	*A-2*	*A-3*	*A-4*	*B*
Face amount	$170,000,000	$300,800,000	$240,000,000	$252,000,000	$45,347,000
Percent of initial pool balance	16.8%	29.9%	23.8%	25.0%	4.5%
Ratings	A-1+/P-1	AAA	AAA	AAA	A
Credit enhancement	Reserve Acct: 4.5%	Reserve Acct: 4.5%	Reserve Acct: 4.5%	Reserve Acct: 4.5%	Reserve Acct: 4.5%
	Class B: 4.5%	Class B: 4.5%	Class B: 4.5%	Class B: 4.5%	
Spread	−4 bps	+20 bps	+72 bps	+78 bps	+115 bps
Expected final maturity	March 2000	April 2002	June 2003	June 2004	March 2005
Legal final					
Average life (@ 1.5 ABS) to 10% clean-up call	.225 yrs.	.997 yrs.	2.02 yrs.	3.21 yrs.	2.01 yrs.
ERISA eligible	Yes	Yes	Yes	Yes	Yes

Collateral Information		
Aggregate principal balance	$1,008,147,000	
Number of receivables	73,355	
Average principal balance	$13,743.40	
Weighted average original term	64.20 months	
Weighted average remaining term	57.84 months	
Weighted average contract rate	9.931%	
New	36.40%	
Used	63.60%	
Geographic concentrations	26.57% WA	10.20% OR
	20.71% ID	8.74% NV
	19.99% UT	

presumed benefit is that small banks might be able to better diversify credit risk because they would own shares in a pool of securities rather than individual securities. Regulators further limit mutual fund purchases to no more than 10 percent of a bank's capital plus surplus.

After initial interest during the latter 1980s, banks generally ignored mutual funds through 1996, but increased their holdings from almost $14 billion in 1996 to over $20 billion by year-end 2001. The primary reason is that regulations require that mutual fund shares be marked to market rather than reported at book values. Funds that do not have fixed share prices fluctuate in value with changes in interest rates, which translates into fluctuating values reported on a bank's balance sheet. Such volatility looks bad in periodic financial statements because it presents an appearance of high risk.

CHARACTERISTICS OF MUNICIPAL SECURITIES

At year-end 1985 commercial banks owned $232 billion in municipal securities or 35 percent of total municipals outstanding, more than any other investor group. By year-end 2001, bank municipal holdings had fallen to around $120 billion, or around 7 percent of outstandings. This reflects changes in federal income tax laws to where many municipals yield less to banks than comparable maturity and risk taxable bonds.

Municipals are generally attractive investments because their interest is exempt from federal income taxes. Interest on in-state issues is also normally exempt from state or local income taxes. This tax treatment lowers quoted yields below pretax yields on taxable securities of comparable maturity and risk because municipal yields effectively represent after-tax returns. Such investments also support local business development and growth, in addition to essential public services.

Municipal securities are formally issued by state and local governments and their political subdivisions, such as school corporations, water treatment authorities, and river authorities. Nonprofit organizations and nonfinancial corporations also effectively issue municipals because they get the use of the proceeds at reduced rates, even though a municipal unit's name actually goes on the debt. Government units distinguish between short-term and long-term municipals because they are used for different purposes and are subject to different restrictions. Short-term securities are used to finance temporary imbalances between the timing of operating receipts and expenditures or to provide interim financing of construction outlays. By law, most governmental units are forced to run balanced operating budgets meaning that current operating revenues must be sufficient to cover operating expenses. State and local governments are not allowed to issue long-term bonds to finance short-term operating budget deficits.

Today, long-term municipals are used primarily to finance capital expenditures for such purposes as education facilities, hospitals, housing, and public utilities. The benefits to these facilities presumably arise over long periods so that future taxes that should cover the interest and principal payments. The intent is that higher taxes will be paid by those who benefit. *General obligation* bonds are municipals in which principal and interest payments are backed by the full faith, credit, and taxing authority of the issuer. As such, they are the closest thing to a Treasury bond because the issuer can raise taxes or issue new debt to repay the bonds. *Revenue* bonds are municipals in which principal and interest payments are backed by revenues generated from whatever facility or project the bond proceeds are used to finance. An example is bonds issued by a water treatment facility which are backed by fees or assessments on user of the treated water. For a pure revenue bond, no tax receipts back the promised payments. For many years a large share of long-term municipal debt effectively financed the expenditures of private corporations in the form of *industrial development* bonds, a special form of revenue bond. For example, it was not unusual for Kmart to negotiate a deal with a municipality to locate a store within the city limits if the municipality would form a local economic development unit, have the unit issue debt, and then let Kmart pay the debt service with lease payments to the economic development unit. The advantage to Kmart was that it could effectively borrow at lower tax-exempt interest rates. The advantage to the community was that it had attracted a new business which presumably brought jobs and services. The Tax Reform Act of 1986 sharply reduced the issuance of tax-exempt industrial development bonds so that they now comprise a much smaller share of the municipal market.

Most long-term municipals are serial bonds, with a fraction of the total principal maturing in consecutive years. This is shown in Exhibit 19.14 for the $30 million issue by the Sequoia Union High School District. This new issue indicates that the offering has 25 serial components of different amounts that mature annually from 2003 through the year 2026. Serialization enables a municipality to spread out principal and interest payments to stay within annual debt service capability. Issues may also have term components where the entire principal comes due at a set maturity. The state of Washington issue has a separate term component of bonds with $8.65 million in principal that matures in 2031, 29 years after the issue date. The firms listed at the top with Salomon Smith Barney as the lead, are the investment banks that served as underwriters.

From a bank's perspective, serial issues allow portfolio managers to select instruments with the precise maturities that best meet the bank's risk and return preferences. For example, a bank with many short-term liabilities may choose to concentrate investments near

SUMMARY OF TERMS FOR A MUNICIPAL SCHOOL BOND

Sequoia Union High School District
$30,000,000

General Obligation Bonds Election of 2001
Dated: May 1, 2002
Due: July 1, 2003 through July 1, 2031
Callable: July 1, 2011 at 102.0% of par, declining to par as of July 1, 2013
Winning Bid: Salomon Smith Barney, at 100.0000,
     True interest cost (TIC) of 5.0189%

Other Managers: Bear, Stearns & Co., Inc., CIBC World Markets Corp.,

Due Date	Amount	Coupon	Yield
7/1/03	$225,000	7.00%	2.00%
7/1/04	$520,000	7.00%	2.50%
7/1/05	$545,000	7.00%	3.00%
7/1/06	$575,000	7.00%	3.25%
7/1/07	$605,000	7.00%	3.50%
7/1/08	$635,000	7.00%	3.70%
7/1/09	$665,000	7.00%	3.80%
7/1/10	$700,000	4.00%	3.90%
7/1/11	$735,000	4.00%	4.00%
7/1/12	$765,000	4.125%	4.125%
7/1/13	$800,000	4.25%	4.25%
7/1/14	$835,000	4.375%	4.375%
7/1/15	$870,000	4.50%	4.50%
7/1/16	$910,000	4.60%	4.60%
7/1/17	$950,000	4.70%	4.70%
7/1/18	$995,000	4.80%	4.80%
7/1/19	$1,045,000	4.90%	4.90%
7/1/20	$1,095,000	5.00%	5.00%
7/1/21	$1,150,000	5.00%	5.00%
7/1/22	$1,210,000	5.00%	5.00%
7/1/23	$1,270,000	5.00%	5.00%
7/1/24	$1,335,000	5.00%	5.00%
7/1/25	$1,405,000	5.00%	5.20%
7/1/26	$1,480,000	5.00%	5.21%
7/1/31	$8,650,000	5.125%	5.21%

SOURCE: The Bond Buyer, Results of Competitive Sales, April 25, 2002.

term. Similarly, banks that choose to use municipals to lengthen their asset rate sensitivity profile may select longer-term issues. With a serial issue, the manager can simply select the appropriate maturity instrument because credit and liquidity risk is held constant.

MONEY MARKET MUNICIPALS

Municipal notes are issued to provide operating funds for government units. Tax and revenue anticipation notes are issued in anticipation of tax receipts or other revenue generation, typically from the federal government. These securities enable governments to continue to spend funds even when operating revenues decline, then repay the debt as revenues are received. Bond anticipation notes provide interim financing for capital projects that will ultimately be financed with long-term bonds. For example, a school district may begin construction of new schools with note proceeds because it believes that current long-term municipal rates are temporarily high. Long-term bonds will be issued after rates decline, with the proceeds used to retire the notes. Most notes carry a minimum denomination of $25,000, with maturities ranging from 30 days to one year. Maturities on bond anticipation notes may extend to three years.

Project notes and tax-exempt commercial paper also play important roles in the municipal market. Local housing authorities issue project notes to finance federal expenditures for urban renewal, local neighborhood development, and low-income housing. The notes are repaid out of revenues from the projects financed. In the event that revenues are not forthcoming, the Department of Housing and Urban Development agrees to make the obligated interest and principal payments, so the notes carry an implied federal guarantee. Tax-exempt commercial paper is issued by the largest municipalities, which regularly need blocks of funds in $1 million multiples for operating purposes. Because only large, well-known borrowers issue this paper, yields are below those quoted on comparably rated municipal notes.

Banks buy large amounts of short-term municipals. They often work closely with municipalities in placing these securities and have a built-in need for short-term liquidity given that most bank liabilities are highly rate sensitive near term. Thus short-term municipals are in high demand, and short-term municipal rates are relatively low compared with rates on longer-term municipals. The Sequoia Union High School District issue in Exhibit 19.14 demonstrates this rate relationship. Consider the serial bond issues that mature from 2003 through 2026. The coupon column refers to the coupon rate while the yield column indicates the market rate. A coupon rate equal to the market rate means that the security sells at par. A coupon rate above (below) the market rate indicates that the bond sells at a premium (discount). Note that the one-year serial bond pays 2 percent, which is lower than all other market rates, which generally increase with maturity. Long-term municipals carry higher yields than short-term municipals.

CAPITAL MARKET MUNICIPALS

GENERAL OBLIGATION BONDS.
Interest and principal payments on general obligation bonds are backed by the full faith, credit, and taxing power of the issuer. This backing represents the strongest commitment a government can make in support of its debt. At the extreme, governments promise to raise taxes, attach real property, and issue new debt to meet promised debt service payments. The state of Washington issue in Exhibit 19.13 is such a bond. Because this guarantee is so broad, issuers must generally obtain voter approval via referendum to issue new general obligation debt. Actual default risk depends on the viability of the issuer's tax base and its willingness to live up to the terms of the debt.

Occasionally, a municipality's taxing authority is limited, typically by a maximum allowable tax rate. In these cases, the bonds are still classified as general obligations but are referred to as *limited tax* bonds. In addition, municipalities often issue general obligations that are also secured by revenues independent of issuer general funds. Such bonds are referred to as *double barrel* bonds because of the dual backing.

REVENUE BONDS. Revenue bonds are issued to finance projects whose revenues are the primary source of repayment. An example is bonds issued to finance airport expansion that are supported by fees obtained from the sale of landing rights and the city's share of parking and concessions. Other common public purpose revenue bond projects include toll roads and bridges, port facilities, hospital facilities, university dormitories, and water/sewer treatment plants. The revenue sources of these bonds can be identified by a label: tolls, port entry and exit charges, hospital charges, student fees, and water/sewer user charges, respectively. In general, revenue bonds exhibit greater default risk than general obligations. The risk associated with specific bonds, however, depends on the strength of the revenue source supporting each project. Thus, some revenue bonds supported by substantial cash flows trade at rates below those on general obligations. Many revenue bonds are sufficiently complex that an investor must read the bond prospectus carefully to determine what the primary revenue source is and what group is ultimately responsible for ensuring that investors are paid. Unlike general obligations bonds, revenue bonds do not need voter approval prior to issue.

Banks buy both general obligation and revenue bonds. The only restriction is that the bonds be investment grade or equivalent. Banks generally have a preference, however, for general obligations because they are more marketable and more closely associated with essential public purposes. Since the Tax Reform Act of 1986, banks no longer buy IDBs because they carry no tax advantage.

CREDIT RISK IN THE MUNICIPAL PORTFOLIO

Until the 1970s, few municipal securities went into default. This was followed by deteriorating conditions in many large cities that ultimately resulted in defaults by New York City (1975) and Cleveland (1978). The Washington Public Power & Supply System (WHOOPS) similarly defaulted in 1983 on $2.25 billion of bonds issued to finance two nuclear power plants.[16] During the decade of the 1980s, over 600 distinct municipals went into default. Past defaults and deteriorating economic conditions during the early 1990s raised investor concerns regarding the quality of municipal issues and the accuracy of bond ratings. Since WHOOPS's difficulties, the rating agencies have intensified their periodic reviews of issuer characteristics and conditions and revised their ratings with greater frequency after initial issue. Since 1990, Standard & Poor's Corporation has downgraded almost three times as many municipal issues as it has upgraded.

Unfortunately, the diversity of municipal borrowers and disparate types of issues make it difficult to categorize municipal securities. Many issuers do not purchase bond ratings, so their securities are nonrated. Although these securities may be low risk, an investing bank is responsible for documenting that they are equivalent to investment grade securities. Much like the rating agencies, banks must examine the issuer's existing debt burden, the soundness of the operating budget, the strength of the tax base, cash flow support for revenue issues, and local demographic trends, all of which is recorded in a credit file. With many securities, it is extremely difficult for an investor to trace the web of revenue sources and guarantees to determine which group is ultimately responsible for meeting debt service requirements. Thus, it is often difficult to assess the credit risk associated with nonrated issues.

Many municipal issuers purchase bond insurance to reduce perceived default risk and increase the marketability of their debt. The insurance is an unconditional guarantee by a property and casualty insurance company to pay promised coupon interest and principal if

---

[16]The WHOOPS bonds were rated A+ and A1 by Standard & Poor's and Moody's respectively, at the time of default.

the issuer defaults. The municipality pays for the insurance when the securities are issued, and the policy is nonrefundable and noncancelable over the life of the securities. During 1997 approximately 50 percent of new issues carried some form of insurance or third-party guarantee. Municipalities that purchase insurance benefit from reduced interest costs because ratings on most insured bonds improve to the triple-A or double-A level. Such issues paid rates 10 to 25 basis points below rates on otherwise comparable noninsured bonds, which can alternatively be viewed as the price investors pay for the reduced credit risk. Of course, the value of the guarantee is only as good as the insurance company. Three well-known insurers, the American Municipal Bond Assurance Corp. (AMBAC), the Municipal Bond Insurance Association (MBIA), and Financial Guarantee (FGIC), provide most insurance coverage in the municipal market.

LIQUIDITY RISK

Municipals exhibit substantially lower liquidity than Treasury or agency securities. The secondary market for municipals is fundamentally an over-the-counter market. Small, nonrated issues trade infrequently and at relatively large bid-ask dealer spreads. Large issues of nationally known municipalities, state agencies, and states trade more actively at smaller spreads. Name recognition is critical, as investors are more comfortable when they can identify the issuer with a specific location. Insurance also helps by improving the rating and by association with a known property and casualty insurer.

Still, municipals are less volatile in price than Treasury securities. This is generally attributed to the peculiar tax features of municipals.[17] The municipal market is segmented. On the supply side, municipalities cannot shift between short- and long-term securities to take advantage of yield differences because of constitutional restrictions on balanced operating budgets. Thus long-term bonds cannot be substituted for short-term municipals to finance operating expenses. On the demand side, banks once dominated the market for short-term municipals so that their rates were a set fraction of Treasury rates. Today, individuals via tax-exempt money market mutual funds dominate the short maturity spectrum. The investment activity of banks and money market mutual funds at the short end stabilizes municipal bond prices because these groups purchase most of the short-term municipals offered. This does not hold at longer maturities where individuals represent the marginal investor. As such, short-term municipals do not vary sharply in price over time relative to short-term Treasuries.

ESTABLISHING INVESTMENT POLICY GUIDELINES

Each bank's asset and liability or risk management committee (ALCO) is responsible for establishing investment policy guidelines. These guidelines define the parameters within which investment decisions help meet overall return and risk objectives. Because securities are impersonal loans that are easily bought and sold, they can be used at the margin to help achieve a bank's liquidity, credit risk, and earnings sensitivity or duration gap targets. Investment guidelines identify specific goals and constraints regarding the composition of investments, preferred maturities or durations, quality ratings, pledging requirements, and strategies underlying any portfolio adjustments.

---

[17]Stock and Schrems (1987) compare the relative price volatility of municipals and Treasuries. They conclude that the volatility of short-term municipals is much lower, which is attributed to substantial short-term municipals investments by commercial banks. Relative volatility with longer-term securities is more similar.

RETURN OBJECTIVES

A bank's ALCO policy statement specifies overall return objectives in terms of return on equity, return on assets, and net interest margin. Investment policy guidelines complement this by identifying what portion of interest income should be generated by securities. In particular, they establish targets for the contribution of both taxable interest and tax-exempt interest to net income. Guidelines also outline the potential costs and benefits of taking tax losses or gains on security sales. The guidelines generally assume that the bank has an interest rate forecast and structures its portfolio to take advantage of rate changes.

PORTFOLIO COMPOSITION

Investment guidelines concerning portfolio composition directly address the bank's targeted liquidity, credit risk, and interest rate risk position. The guidelines generally specify the types of securities that can be purchased, acceptable credit ratings, acceptable maturity ranges at different stages of the interest rate cycle, and those that securities should be pledged as collateral against public deposits. Examples of areas for specific guidelines follow.

LIQUIDITY CONSIDERATIONS

1. What volume of federal funds transactions is desirable?
2. To what financial institutions should the bank sell federal funds, and from what institutions should the bank purchase security RPs?
3. Which Treasury, agency, or municipal securities should the bank pledge as collateral?
4. What amount of short-term securities (under one year) should be held as a potential liquidity reserve?
5. With which banks or securities dealers should the bank establish a trading relationship?

CREDIT RISK CONSIDERATIONS

1. What amount of municipal, corporate, and foreign securities is optimal?
2. How much (what percentage) should the bank hold in each of the top four rating categories?
3. What is the maximum amount that can be invested in any one issuer's securities?
4. What information should credit files for nonrated municipals and all corporate and foreign bonds contain?
5. Which issuer's securities should be avoided?
6. Should the bank purchase insured municipals?

INTEREST RATE RISK CONSIDERATIONS

1. What maturity distribution of Treasuries, agencies, and municipals (separately) is desired?
2. What duration characteristics are desirable?
3. What planned holding period is desirable?
4. To what extent should the bank purchase discount (or zero coupon) securities?

5. What prepayment probabilities are associated with specific mortgage-backed securities?

6. What is the convexity of specific mortgage-backed securities, and how does it vary according to the underlying coupon rate on the mortgages?

TOTAL RETURN VERSUS CURRENT INCOME

1. To what extent will the bank actively manage its securities portfolio? Will management attempt to time interest rate movements relative to the business cycle?

2. Will management look to total return or yield to maturity (current income) as the measure of performance?

3. How will reinvestment income be calculated? Should management forecasts or forward rates be used for expected reinvestment rates?

GENERAL PORTFOLIO CONSIDERATIONS

Investment policies must be flexible because no bank can exactly forecast its operating environment. Interest rates rise and fall, the yield curve changes shape, loan demand fluctuates, and the risk features of securities change when issuers' economic circumstances improve or deteriorate. A bank should establish guidelines that specify what and when portfolio adjustments are appropriate. Adjustments normally take the form of lengthening or shortening acceptable maturities, swapping securities, and security sales. Chapter 20 examines these adjustment strategies in detail. The following items influence each portfolio decision.

OPTIMUM SIZE OF THE LOAN PORTFOLIO

Except perhaps for the largest banks, most bankers consider meeting the credit needs of businesses and individuals within risk guidelines the most important part of asset management. Thus, considerable effort is directed at determining the optimal size of the loan portfolio. Obvious factors that influence the decision include international, national, and regional economic conditions, the seasonality of loan demand, local demographic trends characterizing population growth and new business formation, and specific risks and returns associated with individual credits. Decisions regarding how much to invest in securities and what specific instruments to buy typically follow after credit decisions are made.

The issue is often couched in terms of the optimum loan-to-deposit ratio. Core deposits presumably measure the stable source of bank funds, which can support loans. The greater are loans as a fraction of core deposits, the greater is the presumed default risk of assets and the greater is liquidity risk. Aggressive banks in high growth areas frequently report loan to deposit ratios above 100 percent. Obviously, a high ratio indicates that a bank will own proportionately fewer securities. In addition, however, the composition of securities will reflect the presumed riskiness of loans as banks with high loan-to-deposit ratios will generally hold more shorter-term and higher-rated securities to balance overall risk.

STABILITY OF DEPOSITS

The stability of a bank's deposits affects the investment portfolio by raising or lowering liquidity risk. A bank with a large amount of stable, core deposits does not experience the same unanticipated deposit outflows as a bank with fewer core deposits. The more stable is the deposit base, the less management has to rely on securities to meet liquidity needs. Such a bank can make more loans, hold longer duration securities, and potentially hold lower rated investment grade securities in search of higher promised yields.

OPTIMAL FEDERAL FUNDS POSITION

As indicated in Chapter 12, federal funds refer to immediately available funds (certain collected deposits) at Federal Reserve Banks and financial institutions. Banks buy and sell federal funds as part of managing their reserve positions. The transactions usually involve overnight loans in some multiple of $1 million. Large banks typically borrow federal funds from smaller banks as a permanent source of financing. Small banks, in turn, lend federal funds to earn interest on otherwise idle balances.

Two aspects of a bank's federal funds position affect the investment portfolio: whether the bank borrows or lends federal funds, and the size of the position. Lenders (federal funds sold) actually treat the loans as short-term investments. It is the ultimate rate-sensitive asset, for it reprices daily. When the federal funds rate rises, interest income rises, and when the rate falls, interest income falls. Not surprisingly, during tight money periods when short-term rates are pushed higher, sellers of federal funds do quite well. This was evidenced from 1979 to 1981 as many small banks earned considerable interest by selling federal funds to large banks when the federal funds rate varied from 17 percent to 22 percent. Borrowers, in turn, view federal funds purchased as volatile, noncore liabilities that can disappear quickly. Banks with a large exposure often reduce the risk of their securities portfolio by holding highly liquid, highly rated instruments that can be readily sold to obtain cash. The essential point is that banks should use the investment portfolio to balance the bank's overall risk and return profile.

CAPITAL REQUIREMENTS

Risk-based capital standards require different amounts of equity and total capital in support of different bank assets. Because loans are generally in a higher risk class than securities, the standards impart a bias for banks to increase their securities portfolios at the expense of loans. The preferential treatment of certain low-risk class securities, in turn, induces banks to direct a greater share of their investments to these instruments. Thus, banks have purchased large amounts of government-guaranteed mortgage backed securities that require only 20 percent capital backing. In general, capital requirements influence the allocation of bank investments because banks operate as price takers and cannot independently raise security yields to offset the higher capital requirements.

SUMMARY

Bank investment activities consist of two distinct functions. Large banking organizations manage trading accounts in which they offer investment advice to other market participants, make a market in government securities, and speculatively trade instruments in the short run to take advantage of perceived changes in interest rates. All banks, regardless of size, also own marketable securities for their own portfolios and generate substantial interest income that supplements earnings from their loan portfolios. FASB 115 forces banks to classify investment securities either as trading securities, held to maturity, or available for sale, with each category subject to different accounting treatment. Held to maturity securities are valued at amortized cost, while all others must be reported at market values.

From 1965 through 1990 banks slowly reduced their security holdings as a fraction of assets. During the early 1990s with the recession and recent problem loan experience, banks added substantially to their security holdings at the expense of loans. Historically, commercial banks were the dominant investors in municipal securities. They also owned large amounts of U.S. Treasury and agency securities. With the Tax Reform Act of 1986 banks shifted the composition of investments more toward mortgage-backed and straight corporate securities. By year-end 1998, federal agency securities including mortgage-backed securities were the dominant instruments owned, followed by U.S. Treasuries.

This chapter examines the general risk and return features of different instruments and general policy guidelines for assessing their liquidity, credit, and interest rate risk characteristics. It introduces the characteristics of different types of mortgage-backed securities, callable agency bonds, and municipal bonds that make them attractive to banks and risky as investments.

QUESTIONS

1. Describe how a bank makes a profit with its securities trading account. What are the risks?

2. Explain why bank managers often refuse to sell securities at a loss relative to book value. What is the cost of continuing to hold discount instruments? What are the costs of selling securities at a gain?

3. Explain how zero coupon securities differ from coupon securities. Which are more liquid, in general? Which are more price sensitive? What is the advantage of a zero coupon security in terms of total return?

4. What types of securities are banks prohibited from buying for investment purposes?

5. Explain how the composition of a small community bank's investment portfolio differs, in general, from the composition of a large bank's portfolio. Why might mutual funds be attractive to banks?

6. Examine the data in Exhibit 19.2. Identify key trends and explain the driving force behind each. Why might banks prefer agency securities over Treasury securities?

7. What is the option in a callable agency bond? What impact does the call deferment period have on a callable bond's promised yield? What is the primary advantage of a discount callable bond versus one trading at par?

8. List the objectives that banks have for buying securities. Explain the motive for each.

9. Explain how a reverse RP differs from federal funds sold as an income producing asset.

10. How do banks judge the credit risk in the investment portfolio? What information is available that helps?

11. FASB 115 requires certain classifications within a bank's securities portfolio. What is the accounting treatment of securities within each classification? Describe why full market value accounting might adversely affect a bank's reported capital. How should management classify the bank's securities to minimize potential reporting problems?

12. Discuss the impact of each of the following on prepayment risk for a mortgage-backed pass-through security (MBS).
   a. High coupon interest MBS versus low coupon interest MBS.
   b. MBS issued six years prior versus MBS issued this year.
   c. Demographic trends in different areas of the country.

13. Explain how the design of a CMO supposedly helps to manage prepayment risk for investors. What is a tranche?

14. Suppose that you own a 4-year maturity Treasury bond that pays $100,000 in principal at maturity and $3,000 every six months in coupon interest. Use the features of the bond to explain what Treasury IOs and POs are.

15. Consider a $100 million pool of conventional mortgages paying 8 percent interest. Suppose that you create one PO and one IO for this entire pool. Describe what a PO and IO would look like for this mortgage pool.

16. Using the data in Exhibit 19.13, explain what a CAR is in terms of an asset-backed security. Why is the spread (0.48 percent) on the Class A security lower than the spread (0.63 percent) on the Class B security in terms of the features of the two instruments?

17. Explain why municipal securities have default risk if they are issued by government units.

18. What group within a bank sets the investment policy? What issues does the policy address?

19. Explain how a bank's loan-to-deposit ratio is likely to affect both the size and composition of the investment portfolio. Does management first decide how many loans to make, and then allocate remaining funds to investments?

20. Large banks often borrow heavily in the federal funds market and maintain small investment portfolios relative to their asset size. Are these offsetting risk positions? Why do large banks organize themselves this way?

PROBLEMS

I. LEARN MORE ABOUT YOUR LOCAL BANK

Obtain a copy of a local community bank's annual report and the annual report of a large bank. Determine the extent to which each of the banks:

1. Operates a trading account
2. Reports gains or losses on securities trades
3. Invests in municipal securities
4. Invests in mortgage-backed securities
5. Reports a change in capital due to its securities holdings

II. EXPLAIN BOND RISKS

Obtain a copy of *The Wall Street Journal*. Compare the price and yield characteristics of corporate bonds, municipal bonds, Treasury bonds, and mortgage-backed securities in the Money and Investing section under "Interest Rates and Bonds." Explain what general risks are associated with each and why the quoted rates differ as they appear.

ACTIVE INVESTMENT STRATEGIES

Suppose that you make the investment decisions for your bank and currently have $25 million to invest in Treasury securities. You determine that the appropriate holding period is five years. The current yield curve is upsloping with 1-year Treasuries yielding 5.5 percent, 5-year Treasuries yielding 6 percent, and 10-year Treasuries yielding 7 percent. Based on your reading of economic conditions, you believe that interest rates will rise in the foreseeable future. Which Treasury security should you buy? You could buy a 1-year security and reinvest the maturing proceeds each year until five years elapse. You could buy a 5-year security, which matches your holding period. Alternatively, you could buy a 10-year security and sell it after five years when it still has five years remaining until it matures. When do you win and when do you lose with each alternative?

One tendency is to buy the 5-year security because its maturity matches your holding period. You will automatically get your principal back when you want it. Another tendency is to buy the 10-year security because it offers the highest promised yield among these alternatives. In fact, if the yield curve is correct in the sense that forward rates accurately forecast future cash market rates, then your choice of investment doesn't matter. Your return over five years from buying the 6 percent 5-year bond will exactly match the return from buying a 1-year Treasury at 5.5 percent and reinvesting the proceeds each year in another 1-year Treasury. If forward rates are accurate forecasts, both returns will match that from buying a 10-year Treasury at 7 percent and selling it after five years. The only case in which you can earn an above-average return is when forward rates are incorrect, and you are able to out predict the market. This involves speculating when rates will exceed forward rates and staying short, or speculating that rates will be lower than forward rates and going long-term.

Commercial banks, like individual investors, constantly search for good investments to supplement earnings. As in the above situation, portfolio managers often speculate on short-term interest rate changes in the hope of guessing correctly. They also alter the composition of the portfolio as circumstances dictate. A bank that experiences large unanticipated loan losses, for example, may no longer need to shelter as much income with municipal securities. Another bank may want to shift its portfolio into higher-rated *instruments when quality spreads are low or shorten maturities when interest rates are expected to rise. Successful implementation depends on using the flexibility inherent in the investment portfolio to alter strategies. Two important developments have complicated the decision making at banks. First, many securities carry embedded options that can cause the security's market value to rise or fall sharply as rates change. Second, most non-Treasury securities are priced off of zero coupon Treasury securities or LIBOR swaps such that investors must constantly be aware of forward rates on the zeros or Eurodollars and the size of the spreads or markups that indicate the prevailing yields on non-Treasury securities.*

This chapter addresses several basic questions facing investment portfolio managers. What maturity securities should be acquired? What are the specific risks and interest rate bets if the bank buys securities with embedded options? How do after-tax yields on tax-sheltered municipal bonds differ from those on taxable bonds? How should a bank change its portfolio risk and return profile when economic conditions change? Specific strategies with applications cover each of these topics. The discussion focuses on distinctions between active and passive investment strategies and the costs or benefits of each.

Unlike loans and deposits, which have negotiated terms, bank investments generally represent impersonal financial instruments. As such, portfolio managers can buy or sell securities at the margin to achieve aggregate risk and return objectives without the worry of adversely affecting long-term depositor or borrower relationships. Investment strategies can subsequently play an integral role in meeting overall asset and liability management goals regarding interest rate risk, liquidity risk, credit risk, the bank's tax position, expected net income, and capital adequacy.

Unfortunately, not all banks view their securities portfolio in light of these opportunities. Many smaller banks passively manage their portfolios using simple buy and hold strategies. The purported advantages are that such a policy requires limited investment expertise and virtually no management time, lowers transaction costs, and provides for predictable liquidity. Regulators reinforce this approach by emphasizing the risk features of investments and not available returns. For example, the *Comptroller's Handbook* states that "the investment account is primarily a secondary reserve for liquidity rather than a vehicle to generate speculative profits. Speculation in marginal securities to generate more favorable yields is an unsound banking practice."[1] Other banks actively manage their portfolios by adjusting maturities, changing the composition of taxable versus tax-exempt securities, and swapping securities to meet risk and return objectives that change with the external environment. The presumed advantage is that active portfolio managers can earn above-average returns by capturing pricing discrepancies in the marketplace. The disadvantages are that managers must consistently outpredict the market for the strategies to be successful, and transactions costs are high.

The remainder of this chapter examines general factors that affect most investment decisions and active portfolio strategies that help achieve specific risk and return objectives. The analysis begins with a discussion of the traditional interest rate cycle and maturity/duration strategies to take advantage of broad-based rate movements. It then describes the impact of interest rates on mortgage prepayments, the likelihood that callable bonds will be called, and the subsequent impact on price. The following sections address how to determine the after-tax yields and optimal holdings of taxable and tax-exempt securities, and the use of security swaps as a strategy to meet risk and return targets.

---

[1]See the *Comptroller's Handbook for National Bank Examiners*, section 203.1, U.S. Department of Treasury, Washington, DC. Related publications are available at http://www.occ.ustreas.gov/.

THE MATURITY OR DURATION CHOICE
FOR LONG-TERM SECURITIES

Portfolio managers consider many factors when determining which securities to buy or sell. Perhaps the most difficult to quantify is the optimal maturity or duration. Difficulties arise because it is virtually impossible to systematically forecast interest rates better than the forecasts embodied in forward rates. Management must also be aware of the bank's overall interest rate risk position to make investments that will achieve the targeted risk and return profile. Many managers justify passive buy and hold strategies because they lack the time and expertise to evaluate investment alternatives and monitor performance in an attempt to outperform the market. As a result, they select securities with maturities that they hope will generate average returns over the entire business cycle. Other managers actively trade securities in an effort to earn above average returns.

PASSIVE MATURITY STRATEGIES

Specific policies frequently follow one of two models. The first model, the *laddered* (or *staggered*) *maturity strategy,* stipulates that management should initially specify a maximum acceptable maturity or holding period. Securities are held to maturity, and managers acquire bonds expecting to earn fixed yields over the life of the instruments. Under this strategy, securities are spaced approximately evenly throughout the maturity range so that an equal proportion of the entire portfolio matures each year. Bonds near maturity represent a liquidity buffer, with the proceeds simply reinvested at maturity in securities with the longest acceptable maturity, regardless of prevailing yields. If, for example, management wants all securities to mature within 10 years, it will have 10 percent of the portfolio maturing each year. As securities mature, the proceeds will be reinvested in new 10-year maturity instruments. The only decision involves selecting 10-year securities of acceptable credit quality. As such, managers do not attempt to forecast interest rates but rather recognize that the bank earns average yields over the interest rate cycle.[2]

The second model, the *barbell maturity strategy,* differentiates between bonds purchased primarily for liquidity versus income purposes. Management invests a fraction of the portfolio, typically 25 to 40 percent, in short-term securities that pay market rates and normally trade at prices close to par. These instruments are held primarily to meet liquidity requirements. All remaining funds are invested at long-term maturities, typically 10 to 15 years, to maximize coupon interest income. The long-term bonds are sold prior to maturity and the proceeds reinvested long-term once the remaining maturity falls into the intermediate range. With an upward-sloping yield curve, long-term securities pay higher initial yields. If the level of interest rates does not increase, banks sell the securities at a capital gain when less than 10 years remain to maturity, thereby increasing the total return.[3] During relatively stable interest rate environments, this barbell, or short and long strategy, increases the total return from holding short- and long-term bonds above that for the laddered maturity strategy because coupon interest is higher, reinvestment income is greater, and the long-term bonds are sold for a gain.

Exhibit 20.1 graphically demonstrates the differences between the two strategies. With the laddered maturity strategy, a constant portion of the portfolio matures each year. With the barbell strategy, short and long maturities dominate, as most of the portfolio matures at these extreme periods. The first strategy simply picks yields off the long maturities whenever a bond matures. The second picks yields off the short and long end of the maturity spectrum

---

[2]This strategy earns average yields as long as the yield curve does not change, which is highly unlikely.

[3]Total return is the zero coupon equivalent return an investor receives from the coupon payments, the reinvestment income on these coupons, and the price appreciation or depreciation at sale or maturity. See Chapter 6 for details.

• EXHIBIT 20.1

COMPARISON OF LADDERED AND BARBELL MATURITY STRATEGIES

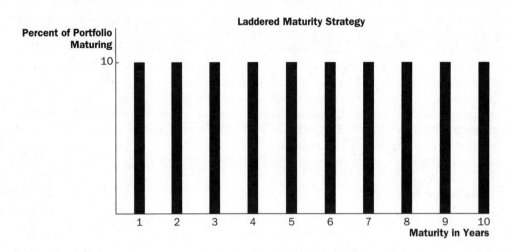

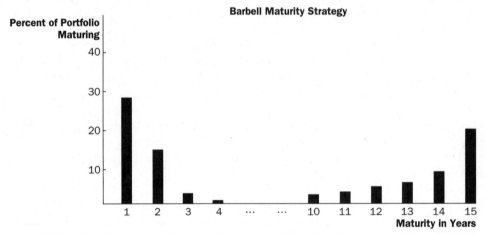

so managers are reinvesting proceeds more frequently. Both strategies are mechanical and have the advantage of reducing transactions costs over active portfolio management. In addition, there is little likelihood that losses will arise from selling securities prior to maturity. The disadvantage is that banks that follow these strategies sacrifice short-term returns for risk reduction, so extraordinary profit opportunities may be missed.

ACTIVE MATURITY STRATEGIES

Today, many banks actively manage their portfolios in response to the general economic climate and their interest rate risk position. Active portfolio management involves taking risks to improve total returns by adjusting maturities, swapping securities, and periodically liquidating discount instruments. To do this successfully, a bank should exhibit a strong capital base and broad-based earnings power. It must also avoid the trap of aggressively buying fixed-income securities at relatively low rates when loan demand is low and liquidity is high.

As indicated in Chapter 19, current accounting rules require banks to designate their securities as Trading, Held to Maturity, and Available for Sale. Banks that actively buy and sell securities must be acutely aware of the potential impact on earnings and stockholders equity. Securities held for trading purposes are carried at market value on the balance sheet, with unrealized gains and losses included in income. Although rate changes could alter their market values sharply, these securities are generally held only briefly as part of the bank's inventory in making a market for the securities with potential investors and sellers. Securities designated as Held to Maturity are carried at amortized cost (historical cost adjusted for principal payments) on the balance sheet, while unrealized gains and losses have no income statement impact. A bank will find itself in serious trouble if it sells these securities prior to maturity because the sale will directly contradict the classification. While it is not known how regulators will handle this, it seems likely that such a bank will have to restate prior period earnings and capital and be forced to classify all future securities holdings as Available for Sale. Instruments in this final category are carried at market value on the balance sheet with unrealized gains and losses included as a component of capital. Thus, an integral part of active portfolio management is the correct classification of securities and having a substantial amount of securities classified as available for sale.

Much like the previous examples, active portfolio strategies recognize both liquidity needs and income requirements. A primary focus is liquidity, in which a bank maintains a portion of its portfolio with market values at or above book values. Such instruments can always be sold at par or a gain, regardless of maturity. While this is not always easily accomplished, banks can keep their portfolios trading near par if they purchase instruments of short maturity or duration or variable rate instruments, or if they willingly sell securities at a loss and reinvest the proceeds in other marketable securities when rates increase. The primary advantage of this liquidity focus is that a bank can substitute between long and short duration instruments as long as a portion of the portfolio exhibits price appreciation. If an acceptable amount of long-term securities is currently priced above book value, management can invest any remaining funds at maturities or durations consistent with its interest rate forecasts and desired risk position. The primary disadvantage is that losses may arise from inaccurate forecasts.

One strategy has banks actively adjust their GAP and earnings sensitivity profile in line with interest rate forecasts. Regular ALCO meetings identify the portfolio interest sensitivity and potential volatility of the bank's net interest margin to rate changes. Banks that are liability sensitive or have a positive duration gap may reduce their earnings sensitivity or shorten the aggregate duration of assets by purchasing short duration securities if they intend to reduce their risk exposure. This would be consistent with an environment where rates are expected to rise above those suggested by the market. Alternatively, such banks may choose to increase their exposure by buying long-term or long duration securities, thereby increasing the degree of liability sensitivity and the duration gap. This might occur when the bank has sufficient liquidity and management forecasts a long-term decrease in interest rates. Banks that are asset sensitive or have a negative duration gap might similarly buy long duration securities to reduce their risk exposure when rates are expected to decline, or do the opposite when rates are expected to rise. The key point is that a bank's maturity or duration choice depends on its aggregate goals for interest rate risk and return. By adjusting security maturities and durations it may be speculating on future rate movements. If management consciously assumes greater risk in the security portfolio, it assumes that it can forecast rates better than the market such that its interest rate forecast is better than forward rates implied by current yields.

RIDING THE YIELD CURVE. Another example might be a portfolio manager who attempts to ride the yield curve. It works best when the yield curve is upward-sloping and rates are stable. The strategy involves buying securities with a maturity longer than the planned holding period and selling the securities prior to maturity. There are three basic steps.

EFFECT OF RIDING THE YIELD CURVE ON TOTAL RETURN
WHEN INTEREST RATES ARE STABLE

Initial conditions and assumptions: Bank has a planned 5-year investment horizon. The yield curve is upward-sloping, with 5-year securities yielding 7.6 percent and 10-year securities yielding 8 percent. Coupon interest is payable annually and can be reinvested at 7 percent annually. The investment choice is to invest $100,000 in a 5-year security and hold it until maturity or to invest $100,000 in a 10-year security and sell it after 5 years.
Objective: Compare total return and choose the higher-yielding alternative.

Cash Flows

	Buy a 5-Year Security		Buy a 10-Year Security and Sell It after 5 Years	
Period: Year-End	Coupon Interest	Reinvestment Income at 7%	Coupon Interest	Reinvestment Income at 7%
1	$ 7,600	—	$ 8,000	—
2	7,600	$ 532	8,000	$ 560
3	7,600	1,101	8,000	1,159
4	7,600	1,710	8,000	1,800
5	7,600	2,362	8,000	2,486
Total	$38,000	$5,705	$40,000	$6,005
5	Principal at Maturity = $100,000		Price at Sale after 5 years = $101,615 when rate = 7.6%	

Expected total return:*

5-Year Security:

$$i = \left[\frac{(100,000 + 38,000 + 5,705)}{100,000} \right]^{1/5} - 1$$

$$i = 0.752$$

10-Year Security:

$$y = \left[\frac{(101,615 + 40,000 + 6,005)}{100,000} \right]^{1/5} - 1$$

$$y = 0.810$$

Difference in Total Returns: $y - i = .0058$

*Realized yield with an assumed reinvestment rate different from the yield to maturity.

First, identify the appropriate investment horizon, such as five years. Second, buy a par value security with a maturity longer than the investment horizon where the coupon yield is high in relation to the overall yield curve. Third, sell the security at the end of the holding period when time still remains until maturity. If market rates stay relatively constant or fall, the total return will exceed that from simply buying the security that matches the planned investment horizon. The reason is that the holder receives more in coupon interest, reinvests the higher coupons to earn greater reinvestment income, and probably sells the security at a gain.

Consider the example summarized in Exhibit 20.2. A portfolio manager has a 5-year invest-ment horizon or holding period. A risk reduction strategy might involve buying a 5-year secu-rity yielding 7.6 percent and holding it to maturity. Alternatively, if the manager felt that rates would remain roughly constant over the next five years, another alternative would be to buy a 10-year security paying 8 percent, and sell the security after five years. If rates are stable, a 5-year security will yield the same 7.6 percent in five years and the bond can be sold at a gain. In addition, the 10-year security carries a higher coupon so that periodic interest payments are higher and reinvestment income will be greater. As indicated, the 5-year security pays $7,600 in interest each year that is assumed to be reinvested each year at 7 percent. The 10-year security, in contrast, pays $8,000 in annual interest so that actual coupon and reinvestment income will be greater with the same assumed 7 percent annual reinvestment rate. After five years, the 5-year bond returns principal of $100,000. If rates are constant, the 10-year bond sells for $101,615 with five years remaining to maturity. The bottom part of the exhibit demonstrates that the total return from riding the yield curve is 58 basis points greater than the total return for the matched holding period strategy. Of course, this active strategy involves greater risk. If rates rise substantially, the bond would have to be sold for a loss that could potentially wipe out the incremental coupon and reinvestment income earned.

To implement active investment strategies, portfolio managers must understand the interest rate environment in which they operate. They should continuously monitor recent movements in the level of rates and the magnitude of various rate differentials to formulate an interest rate forecast. Most importantly, portfolio managers must understand their bank's specific risk and return objectives and current financial position. No one can accurately forecast specific interest rates over long periods of time. However, managers can often position their portfolios to take advantage of long-term trends in rates.

INTEREST RATES AND THE BUSINESS CYCLE

Most portfolio managers structure security maturities relative to the business cycle. Exhibit 7.6 from Chapter 7 is reproduced here as Exhibit 20.3 with additional data that characterizes the general relationship between when the yield curve first inverts and the length of time until a U.S. recession begins. The exhibit suggests that the term-structure of Treasury yields follows predictable patterns within the business cycle. Generally, the Fed and analysts look at the 1-year Treasury rate versus the 10-year Treasury rate. If the 10-year rate exceeds the 1-year rate, the yield curve is upward-sloping. This generally occurs during periods that coincide with monetary ease and short-term rates are low. The 1-year rate exceeds the 10-year rate (the yield curve is inverted) when rates increase to their cyclical peak and thereafter as the Federal Reserve restricts money growth. The consensus is that the shape of the yield curve contains information regarding the market's consensus forecast of interest rates.[4] When the yield curve is upward-sloping, the market forecast is that short-term rates are going to rise from their relatively low levels. Because long-term rates represent an average of current and expected short-term rates, they too will increase with expected increases in short-term rates. When the yield curve is inverted or downward-sloping, the market forecast is that short-term rates will decline, thus lowering long-term rates.

Data at the bottom of Exhibit 20.3 demonstrate that in each of the five recent times noted that the U.S. Treasury yield curve inverted, a recession followed in the United States within 8 to 20 months. The average length of time was 14 months. The implication is that the 10-year to 1-year Treasury yield differential serves as a good indicator of an economic downturn.

Consensus forecasts obviously represent averages. Individual traders may have substantially different views of economic conditions and the likely movement in interest rates. As they take different positions, the yield curve shifts to reflect the new, market-driven consensus. Thus, any implied interest rate forecast simply reflects the market's current guess about future rates, based on prevailing information.

---

[4]Three theories of yield curves, the unbiased expectations theory, the liquidity premium theory, and the market segmentation theory, are described in Chapter 7. This analysis focuses only on the role of expected interest rates. Chapter 7 demonstrates how to derive forward rates from prevailing yields. In 2001, the U.S. Treasury stopped the regular auction of 1-year Treasury securities, but it is still possible to use an impacted 1-year yield in the analysis.

· EXHIBIT 20.3

INTEREST RATES OVER THE BUSINESS CYCLE WITH
CONSTANT INFLATION EXPECTATIONS

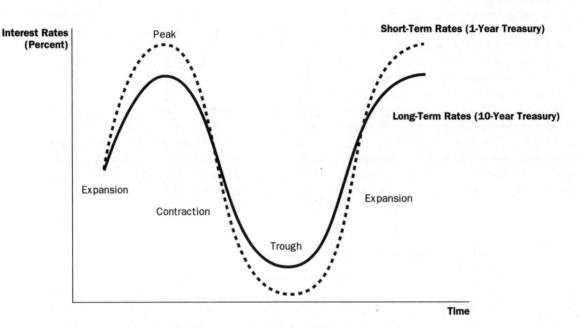

The inverted U.S. Treasury yield curve has predicted these recessions:

Date when 1-Year Rate First Exceeds 10-Year Rate	Length of Time until Start of Next Recession
April 1968	20 months (December 1969)
March 1973	8 months (November 1973)
September 1978	16 months (January 1980)
September 1980	10 months (July 1981)
February 1989	17 months (July 1990)
December 2000*	3 months (March 2001)
	12.3 months average

*3-month Rate First Exceeded 10-Year Rate

PASSIVE STRATEGIES OVER THE BUSINESS CYCLE. One popular passive investment strategy follows from the traditional belief that a bank's securities portfolio should consist of primary reserves and secondary reserves. This view suggests that banks hold short-term, highly marketable securities primarily to meet unanticipated loan demand and deposit withdrawals. Once these primary liquidity reserves are established, banks invest any residual funds in long-term securities that are less liquid but offer higher yields. These residual investments, or secondary reserves, thus focus on generating income.

A problem arises because banks normally have excess liquidity during contractionary periods when consumer spending is low, loan demand is declining, unemployment is rising, and the Fed starts to pump reserves into the banking system. Interest rates are thus relatively low. Banks employing this strategy add to their secondary reserve by buying long-term securities near the low point in the interest rate cycle. Long-term rates are typically above short-term rates, but all rates are relatively low. With a buy and hold orientation, these banks lock themselves into securities that depreciate in value as interest rates move higher. Bankers who follow these passive strategies are often unwilling to sell securities at a loss. They end up holding the low-coupon securities until maturity, thereby forgoing opportunities to enhance investment returns.

Passive investment strategies can avoid these difficulties only if the bank buys securities when yields are at cyclical peaks or if the bank restricts its purchases to securities with short maturities. In both cases the bank will find that the market value of its portfolio consistently exceeds or at least equals its cost. At rate peaks, the economy is growing rapidly as spending and loan demands are high. The Fed, concerned about rising inflation expectations, slows reserves growth such that short-term rates move above long-term rates as rates increase. With high loan demand, banks do not have sufficient funds to invest in securities in the belief that meeting loan demand is more important than buying securities. Of course, it is extremely difficult to accurately forecast interest rate turns, so banks cannot systematically time investments at interest rate peaks. The fundamental problem with short-term investments is that interest income is relatively unpredictable beyond one year. The bank also forgoes any opportunity to earn above average returns by locking in high coupon yields or selling securities with substantial price appreciation.

ACTIVE STRATEGIES AND THE BUSINESS CYCLE. Many portfolio managers attempt to time major movements in the level of interest rates relative to the business cycle and adjust security maturities accordingly. Some try to time interest rate peaks by following a contracyclical investment strategy defined by changes in loan demand. The strategy entails both expanding the investment portfolio and lengthening maturities when loan demand is high, and alternatively contracting the portfolio and shortening maturities when loan demand is weak. As such, the bank goes against the credit (lending) cycle. A review of Exhibit 20.3 indicates that the yield curve generally inverts when rates are at their peak prior to a recession. Note the data at the bottom of the exhibit, which relate the date when the 1-year Treasury rate first exceeded the 10-year Treasury rate. In all but one instance since World War II, a recession followed within 20 months after the Treasury yield curve inverted.[5] In 1967, the 1-year rate exceeded the 10-year rate and a recession did not follow. This date coincided with the Vietnam War such that many analysts attribute the lack of a recession to massive federal government spending.

A contracyclical strategy involves buying long-term securities when the yield curve is inverted. The yield curve inversion signals a gradual decline in rates that active portfolio managers try to anticipate by substituting bonds for loans and lengthening bond maturities with impending recession. If a recession is likely, banks should reduce their loan exposure because loan charge-offs will eventually increase. A bank that follows such a contracyclical strategy is much more likely to purchase securities when the level of interest rates is high. These yields can in turn be locked in for long periods of time. The disadvantage is that a bank either has to restrict credit to loan customers or rely on relatively expensive, short-term debt instruments such as federal funds to finance the loans. Because the yield curve is inverted, many investment officers feel pressure to continue buying short-term securities due to their higher yields. If rates follow the cycle, these high short-term rates will be only temporary. Investment officers also feel pressure from lenders who are being asked not to make loans when loan demand is strong. Of course, if a recession follows, loan problems typically increase and effective loan yields after charge-offs fall.

---

[5] The yield curve did invert in 1999 when the U.S. Treasury announced a program to use federal budget surpluses to repurchase outstanding long-term Treasury securities. Not surprisingly, participants immediately bid long-term rates lower in anticipation of future Treasury purchases. Thus, the yield curve inversion was materially independent of general economic conditions. Current analysis focused on a comparison of the 3-month yield with the 10-year yield as the Treasury no longer regularly issues 1-year securities.

AN INTEREST RATE GAMBLE THAT LOST

There are many ways to bet the bank. During the 1980s, senior management of First Bank System, Inc., of Minneapolis chose to speculate on interest movements in its bond portfolio. In 1986 the bank sold enough government securities to report a gain of almost $400 million, which just exceeded it loan losses of $385 million. For the year, it reported a record profit over $200 million—not bad for a $25 billion bank that had loan quality problems. The gamble consisted of buying long-term securities and hoping that interest rates remained stable or fell. In this case it worked. So willing was the bank to take risk that it did not hedge its position.

In April 1987, interest rates climbed higher, pushing the value of fixed-rate bonds lower. By September 1987, First Bank System reported $640 million in unrealized paper losses on its $8 billion bond portfolio. Again, it chose not to hedge believing that interest rates would soon fall.

After the dust settled in 1988, First Bank System reported a $500 million pretax loss. This arose from a combination of loan losses and the sale of over 50 percent of its investment portfolio. To shore up capital, the bank sold a 50 percent interest in its headquarters building in Minneapolis, laid off employees, and shrunk the bank's asset base. By 1989, both the president and chief executive officer had resigned. The basic lesson is that high risk involves greater volatility in earnings, potentially to the detriment of the investor.

The contracyclical strategy also suggests that when loan demand is weak, banks should keep investments short-term. This is a time of relatively low yields indicated by the trough in Exhibit 20.3. The obvious problem is that without loans banks need to find higher yielding investments to maintain net interest income. Thus, the tendency is to lengthen maturities because the yield curve is upward-sloping and banks are in search of higher yields. If rates do increase, the bank will ultimately have to sell the securities at a loss or keep them in its portfolio and simply not realize the loss but earn a below-market yield.

It is important to remember that efforts to time interest rate changes are risky. If management guesses incorrectly and positions the bank accordingly, it may have to take capital losses when it sells securities or it will forgo income that it could have earned alternatively. Because it is a riskier strategy, the volatility of returns will be greater than with passive strategies. Contemporary Issues: An Interest Rate Gamble That Lost demonstrates how one institution, First Bank System, Inc., of Minneapolis, gambled heavily on interest rates and lost.

THE IMPACT OF INTEREST RATES ON THE VALUE OF SECURITIES WITH EMBEDDED OPTIONS

During the 1990s, banks were heavy buyers of a wide range of mortgage-backed securities and callable agency securities. Each of these carries embedded options in the sense that the security issuers (borrowers) can prepay the outstanding principal at their discretion. This feature makes it more difficult for an investor to value the security because the value will depend on the likelihood that the option will be exercised and the terms of exercise. The following discussion addresses issues that must be considered when deciding whether to buy such securities and how valuable the securities are.

ISSUES FOR SECURITIES WITH EMBEDDED OPTIONS

Whenever a bank buys a callable agency security or mortgage-backed security, it must value the embedded option to know the risk and return profile of the instrument. There are three direct questions to address. First, is the investor the buyer or seller of the option?

Second, how much does the option cost or how much is the seller being compensated? Third, when will the option be exercised and what is the likelihood of exercise? Answers to each of these indicate how the option affects the security's value.

The answer to the first question is straightforward. The buyer of the option is the party that controls the option exercise. In the case of a callable bond or MBS, the borrower chooses when to exercise the option, that is, when to call the bond or refinance the underlying mortgage. Thus, the investor sells the option to the borrower. How does the investor get paid? Generally, the investor receives a higher yield on a security with an option compared to a similar security without the option. Several models exist to estimate how much the option is worth and help an investor decide whether to buy the security. A model that uses option-adjusted spread (OAS) analysis is introduced later in the chapter. Finally, these embedded options will generally be exercised when they are in the money and it is in the borrower's best interest to refinance or prepay. In the case of callable agencies and MBSs, option exercise normally occurs when interest rates fall sufficiently below the current coupon and borrowers can replace the existing debt with lower cost debt. Uncertainty regarding when these options will be in the money and exercised makes it more difficult to estimate the market value of such securities.

Consider the FHLB bond introduced in Chapter 19. This bond was callable at $100 par value, had a 3-year final maturity the issuer could not call the bond for 1 year, and was priced at 99.97 to yield 5.78 percent. The top part of Exhibit 20.4 indicates its general price-yield relationship. At the quoted price and yield, the option is at the money. Note that if market rates rise, the bond's price will fall, much like an option-free bond. However, as rates fall, the call option moves in the money. Because the bond cannot be called for one year, the price may rise above $100, but it will not increase much above par and will move toward the $100 call price as the call deferment period ends. Unlike an option-free bond, there is little potential price appreciation for this bond because an investor knows it will be called when possible if rates fall. A noncallable FHLB bond with a 3-year maturity will carry a lower initial yield, but would increase in price were rates to fall. Thus, the value and price sensitivity of the callable bond versus the noncallable bond will vary sharply depending on whether rates rise or fall over time and whether the bond is called.

Now consider the high coupon, interest-only (IO) MBS with the price-yield relationship characterized in section B of Exhibit 20.4. This security carries a 9.5 percent coupon, but the prevailing mortgage rate is 7 percent. Given the rate differential, the mortgages underlying the IO are prepaying at a CPR of 30 percent, which produces a market price of P*. At this CPR, the IO has an estimated life of just 1.5 years, so an investor will receive the high coupon interest only briefly. If the rate on the underlying mortgages rises, prepayments will slow and the investor will receive the high coupons for a longer period of time than the 1.5 years currently expected. The price of the IO will typically increase in this situation. However, if the underlying mortgage rate decreases, the prepayment rate will increase and the coupons will be received for a shorter time period. Not surprisingly, the IO's price will generally fall. Over the range of mortgage rates below 9.5 percent, the IO's price varies directly with changes in the mortgage rate.

How different is this from option-free bonds where the price of fixed-income securities varies inversely with market interest rates? At mortgage rates above 9.5 percent, the IO will decline in price as the CPR falls toward 6 percent and the expected cash flows are discounted at higher rates. Again, the point is that the value and price sensitivity of the IO varies with whether the option is in the money and the likelihood that it will move in or out of the money.

THE ROLES OF DURATION AND CONVEXITY IN ANALYZING BOND PRICE VOLATILITY

Most option-free bonds exhibit predictable price-yield relationships because valuation involves straightforward present value analysis of promised cash flows. The analysis is complicated when bonds with call and put options are valued. Prepayments with MBSs make

• EXHIBIT 20.4

PRICE-YIELD RELATIONSHIP FOR SECURITIES WITH EMBEDDED OPTIONS

A. Callable Agency Bond

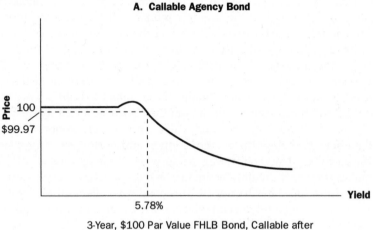

3-Year, $100 Par Value FHLB Bond, Callable after
One Year, Priced at $99.97

B. High-Coupon, Interest-Only Mortgage-Backed Security

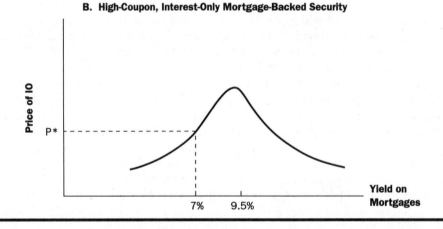

pricing difficult because prepayment effects can swamp discounting effects resulting from the same change in interest rates. The case where an IO decreases in value when mortgage rates decrease serves as an example. Many bond analysts use the concepts of duration and convexity to measure price sensitivity.

Duration for option-free securities measures the weighted average of the time until cash flows are made on a security. The weights equal the present value of each cash flow divided by the price of the security. Alternatively, duration is an approximate elasticity measure. As such, it measures the relative price sensitivity of a security to a change in the underlying interest rate. Consider a three-year, $10,000 par bond with a 10 percent coupon, that pays $500 interest at six-month intervals and $10,000 at maturity. The bond is option-free. The curved line in Exhibit 20.5 shows the relationship between the bond's price and market yield according to the present value formula. Notice that the shape of the curve is nonlinear. The Macaulay duration of the bond appears at the bottom of the exhibit and is

· EXHIBIT 20.5

PRICE-YIELD RELATIONSHIPS AND DURATION FOR AN OPTION-FREE BOND

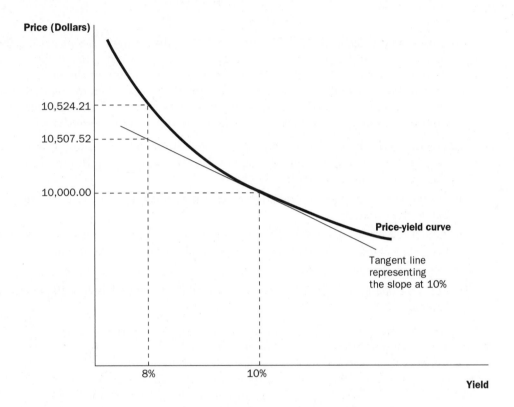

Yield	Price	Price − $10,000	Duration*
8%	$10,524.21	$524.21	5.349
9	10,257.89	257.89	5.339
10	10,000.00	0.00	5.329
11	9,750.00	(249.78)	5.320
12	9,508.27	(491.73)	5.310

*Macaulay's duration in semiannual periods.

SOURCE: Timothy Koch, "The Roles of Duration and Convexity in Analyzing Bond Price Volatility." *Bank Asset/Liability Management.* New York: Warren, Gorham & Lamond, 1989.

measured in semiannual periods. Duration can be represented by the slope of the price-yield relationship at various yields, and approximated by the following equation:

$$\text{Duration} \cong - \frac{\Delta P/P}{\Delta i/(1 + i)} \tag{20.1}$$

where P equals the price of the bond and i equals the market yield. Rearranging terms,

$$\Delta P \cong - \text{Duration} \, [\Delta i/(1 + i)]P \tag{20.2}$$

Equation 20.2 can be applied in the following manner. Suppose that the prevailing yield on the bond is 10 percent so that duration equals 5.329 six-month periods (2.665 years). If the underlying market rate falls to 8 percent, the bond's price increases to $10,524.21 according to the present value formula. Equation 20.2 approximates the price change as:

$$\Delta P = -5.329(-0.01/1.05) \; \$10,000$$

$$= \$507.52$$

The estimated price of $10,507.52 can be read off the straight line in Exhibit 20.5 representing the slope of the price-yield curve at a 10 percent yield. The pricing error is thus $16.69. Interestingly, a 2 percent increase in market rate will lower the bond price by only $491.73, which is less in absolute value than the price increase when the market rate fell by 2 percent. The pricing error ($15.79 in this instance) is also lower when rates increase.

A careful inspection of Exhibit 20.5 reveals several important conclusions:

- The difference between the actual price-yield curve and the straight line representing duration at the point of tangency equals the error in applying duration to estimate the change in bond price at each new yield.

- For both rate increases and rate decreases, the estimated price based on duration will be below the actual price.

- Actual price increases are greater and price declines less than that suggested by duration when interest rates fall or rise, respectively, for option-free bonds.

- For small changes in yield, such as yields near 10 percent, the error is small.

- For large changes in yield, such as yields well above or well below 10 percent, the error is large.

The fundamental implication is that duration reasonably approximates price volatility on an option-free bond only when yield changes are small.

Convexity, in contrast, characterizes the rate of change in duration when yields change. It attempts to improve upon duration as an approximation of price volatility. Notice from Exhibit 20.5 that the slope of a line tangent to the price-yield curve will increase as yields fall below 10 percent, and will decrease as yields rise above 10 percent. In essence, the duration of the bond lengthens as yields fall and shortens as yields rise. The percentage price decrease is smaller, in turn, than the percentage price increase for the same change in rates. This characteristic is called *positive convexity*, signifying that the underlying bond becomes more price sensitive when yields decline and less price sensitive when yields rise, and this is a good feature of price sensitivity.

Formally, convexity can be defined as the second derivative of a bond's price with respect to the interest rate, divided by the bond's price. A bond's convexity can be combined with duration to better estimate true price volatility from yield changes. The additional convexity measure captures a portion of the error associated with using duration alone. The previous example demonstrates the value of convexity. From 10 percent to 8 percent, the estimated price change due to duration equals $507.52 as described earlier. At 10 percent, the estimated convexity of the bond in Exhibit 20.5 is 16.23 semiannual periods. The estimated price change due to convexity thus equals $16.23 with the assumed 1 percent decline in the semiannual rate.

$$\Delta P \text{ due to convexity} = \text{convexity} \; (\Delta i)^2 P \qquad\qquad \textbf{(20.3)}$$

or

$$= 16.23 \; (.01)^2 \; \$10,000$$

$$= \$16.23$$

The estimated price change due to duration and convexity together equals $523.75, or just $0.46 less than the actual price change. Knowing a bond's duration and convexity allows for improved forecasts of price sensitivity even when yields change substantially.

IMPACT OF PREPAYMENTS ON DURATION AND YIELD FOR BONDS WITH OPTIONS

The previous discussion about duration and convexity addresses option-free securities. Securities with options potentially exhibit far different price sensitivities as indicated in Exhibit 20.4. These embedded options affect the estimated duration and convexity of such securities.

Even though participants cannot forecast prepayments precisely, it is important to know how they affect the duration and thus the price and yield of MBSs. In general, market participants price mortgage-backed securities by following a 3-step procedure. First, participants estimate the duration of the MBS based on an assumed interest rate environment and the corresponding prepayment speed. Second, they identify a zero coupon Treasury security with the same (approximate) duration. Third, the MBS is priced at a markup over the Treasury. Specifically, the MBS yield is set equal to the yield on the same duration Treasury plus a positive spread. This spread can range from 20 basis points to 3 percent depending on market conditions. Thus, MBS yields reflect the zero coupon Treasury yield curve plus a premium.[6]

Different MBSs will exhibit different durations and different price sensitivities depending on their specific characteristics. The most important characteristics are those that influence the prepayment rate, and include the coupon rate, mortgage age, and related demographic factors. The coupon rate is important because it is generally just below the rate that borrowers pay on the underlying mortgages. If the current mortgage rate is substantially below the coupon rate, prepayments should be substantial. The greater the prepayments, the shorter a security's duration, because an investor receives the underlying principal and interest payments earlier. If prepayments slow, duration lengthens because larger cash flows are received later. Mortgage age is important because most borrowers won't refinance immediately after taking out a new mortgage. Specifically, during the first 30 months after origination, mortgage prepayments are relatively low and increase slowly over time. Without any special rate inducements prepayments typically increase through five years, then slowly decline. Finally, demographic factors affect prepayments because of labor mobility and the age of the underlying population. A younger population is normally more mobile as is the entire labor force when a specific geographic labor market is booming.

Exhibit 20.6 documents differences in the pricing and yields of a GNMA pass-through MBS on March 1, 1999, in which the underlying mortgages carry an 8 percent weighted-average coupon (WAC). This WAC and weighted-average maturity (WAM) of 28 years and 4 months are listed at the top right of the exhibit. The data capture the yield sensitivity of a MBS that is just 20 months old after issue. Consider the information in the first column of data indicating different prices for the MBS that vary by 2/32nds. Each subsequent column of data indicates the estimated yield of the MBS at a different prepayment speed. In this exhibit, prepayment speeds are cited as some multiple of PSA.[7] At the bottom of the exhibit are listed the estimated average life of the security in each scenario and its associated modified duration. The average life of a MBS is the average time until receipt of principal payments where time is weighted by the amount of the scheduling payment or forecast principal prepayment as a fraction to total principal outstanding. The middle row of data indicates the corresponding yields at the prevailing market price of 102 and 17/32nds. Thus,

---

[6]Alternatively, securities with options may be priced off of the LIBOR interest rate swap curve such that yields are quoted as a spread to the swap curve.

[7]PSA refers to the Public Securities Association, which has standardized how prepayment speeds are quoted. For mortgages that have been outstanding at least 30 months, 100 PSA indicates a prepayment speed of 6 percent (CPR equal to 6 percent). This prepayment rate indicates that 6 percent of the remaining principal is prepaid annually, in addition to normal authorization. Higher multiples indicate faster prepayment speeds, while lower multiples indicate slower prepayment speeds. Importantly, for securities that have been outstanding less than 30 months, such as the one in Exhibit 20.6, 100 PSA is some factor less than 6 percent, which increases with mortgage age.

· EXHIBIT 20.6

IMPACT OF PREPAYMENTS ON MODIFIED DURATION AND PRICE OF A GNMA PASS-THROUGH SECURITY

M Bloomberg
MEDIAN PREPAYMENTS

GG <GD>

GNSF 7 1/2   Generic: GNMA I   7.5%

GNSF 7.5 A   8.000 (340) 20 WAC (UAM) CAGE

				Age	1: 8
1mo	592.P	30.7C		WAM*	28: 4
3mo	587	35.4		WAC*	8.00
6mo	671	31.7			
12mo	524	26.6			
Life	203	13.3			

next pay	4/15/99 (monthly)
rcd date	3/31/99 (14 Delay)
accrual	3/1/99 - 3/31/99

3/1/99

YIELD TABLE

B: Median:
Vary 2. 1 32

PRICE	+300bp 94 PSA	+200bp 113 PSA	+100bp 152 PSA	0bp 258 PSA	-100bp 602 PSA	-200bp 817 PSA	-300bp 921 PSA
102-11	7.214	7.187	7.128	6.958	6.326	5.866	5.622
102-13	7.205	7.177	7.117	6.943	6.296	5.826	5.576
102-15	7.196	7.167	7.105	6.927	6.266	5.786	5.530
102-17	7.186	7.157	7.094	6.912	6.236	5.745	5.484
102-19	7.177	7.147	7.083	6.897	6.207	5.705	5.438
102-21	7.168	7.137	7.071	6.882	6.177	5.665	5.392
102-23	7.158	7.127	7.060	6.867	6.147	5.625	5.346
AvgLife	11.12	10.10	8.42	5.57	2.39	1.68	1.45
Mod Dur	6.54	6.12	5.39	4.01	2.05	1.51	1.33

*WAC is the weighted average mortgage rate of loans in the pool of mortgages where the weights are the amounts of each mortgage outstanding as a fraction of the pool's total mortgage value. WAM is the weighted average maturity, which equals the remaining months until maturity for each loan weighted by the amount of the outstanding mortgage as a fraction of the total.

source: Bloomberg.

at the time of the analysis (0 basis point change in rates), the estimated prepayment speed is 258 PSA, average life is 5.57 years, and modified duration is 4.01 years, producing a yield of 6.912 percent. At higher market rates of +300, +200, and +100 basis points, the estimated prepayment speeds slow considerably, while the estimated average life and modified duration lengthen. At lower market rates of −100, −200, and −300 basis points, the reverse occurs. Note that as duration lengthens (shortens), the yield generally moves in the same direction. For example, an investor who bought the GNMA at 102 and 17/32nds to yield 6.912 percent would find that the yield dropped to 5.745 percent were prepayments to immediately rise to 817 PSA with declining rates. The yield would similarly rise to 7.157 percent were rates to rise and the prepayments slow to 113 PSA. Both yield changes reflect the impact of greater or lesser prepayments and the corresponding reduction or increase in interest earned. Under these different rate environments, modified duration ranges from 1.33 years to 6.54 years. The implication is that if prepayments slow, an investor might end up owning this MBS much longer than originally anticipated.

Chapter 6 demonstrated that option-free securities have well-defined price and yield relationships. This is not true for securities with embedded options. Specifically, as rates rise (fall), Macaulay's duration for an option-free security declines (increases). Option-free securities exhibit *positive convexity* because as rates rise the percentage price decline is less than the percentage price increase associated with the same rate decline. Securities with embedded options may exhibit *negative convexity*. This characteristic means that the percentage price increase is less than the percentage price decrease for equal negative and positive changes in rates. The callable bond and high-coupon IO described in Exhibit 20.4 reveal such negative convexity. In fact, as market rates fall and the option moves in the money, in both cases the duration of the security declines and the price either stays unchanged (callable FHLB bond) or falls (high coupon IO).

Analysts use measures of *effective duration* and *effective convexity*, provided in Equations 20.4 and 20.5, to describe the price sensitivity of securities with options

$$\text{Effective Duration} = \frac{P^- - P^+}{P^*(i^+ - i^-)} \tag{20.4}$$

$$\text{Effective Convexity} = \frac{P^- + P^+ - 2P^*}{P^*[0.5(i^+ - i^-)]^2} \tag{20.5}$$

where P^- = price if the market rate falls by z basis points,

P^+ = price if the market rate rises by z basis points,

P^* = initial price,

i^- = initial market rate minus z basis points, and

i^+ = initial market rate plus z basis points.

Consider the data for the GNMA pass-through in Exhibit 20.6, which is initially priced at 102 and 17/32nds to yield 6.912 percent at an estimated 258 PSA. At this price and PSA, the MBS has an estimated average life of 5.57 years and modified duration of 4.01 years. Ignoring the other data in the exhibit, assume that a 1 percent rate decline will accelerate prepayments and lead to a price of 102 while a 1 percent rate increase will slow prepayments and produce a price of 103. The effective duration and convexity for this security are:

$$\text{Effective GNMA duration} = [102 - 103]/102.53125(.02) = -0.4877$$

$$\text{Effective GNMA convexity} = \frac{102 + 103 - 2(102.53125)}{102.53125(0.5)^2(.02)^2}$$

$$= -6.096$$

This suggests that over this range of rates, duration shortens as rates fall and lengthens as rates rise, which is attributed to the change in prepayments. Also, the percentage price decline in the GNMA is not more than offset by the percentage price increase when rates rise.

TOTAL RETURN AND OPTION-ADJUSTED SPREAD ANALYSIS OF SECURITIES WITH OPTIONS

When buying securities with options, many investors conduct *total return analysis* to estimate the potential return on the security. This is valuable because investors do not know when the options may move in-the-money and how cash flows may change from that expected. Such cash flow changes may, in turn, dramatically influence the return actually realized. Investors also frequently consider a security's *option-adjusted spread* as an estimate of the value of the option that is being sold to the security issuer.

TOTAL RETURN ANALYSIS. An investor's actual realized return should reflect the coupon interest, reinvestment income, and value of the security at maturity or sale at the end of the holding period. When the security carries embedded options, such as the prepayment option with mortgage-backed securities, these component cash flows will vary in different interest rate environments. For example, if rates fall and borrowers prepay faster than originally expected, coupon interest will fall as the outstanding principal falls, reinvestment income will fall because rates are lower when the proceeds are reinvested and less coupon interest is received, and the price at sale (end of the holding period) may rise or fall depending on the speed of prepayments. When rates rise, borrowers prepay slower so that coupon income increases, reinvestment income increases, and the price at sale (end of the holding period) again may rise or fall.

Consider the total return analysis for the Federal Home Loan Bank bond in Panel A of Exhibit 20.7. On May 10, 2001, the bond had seven years until maturity and was callable at par anytime after three years. It was priced at 100 and 33/64ths to yield 5.685 percent. The data provide the results of a rate shock analysis in which the Treasury yield curve is assumed to shift up and down by 50, 100, and 150 basis points from prevailing levels (0 yield shift position) as represented by the different rows of data. Focus on the two columns of data under the heading "Total Return." The first column under "Bond" indicates the estimated total return on the callable FHLB bond, while the second column under "2 YR" indicates the total return on a 2-year, option-free Treasury as an alternative investment. The horizon notation indicates that the assumed holding period is one year from settlement. The column of data under "S/A Reinv" indicates the assumed reinvestment rate, and the data under "Price" indicate the estimated price of the FHLB bond at different interest rate levels.

Compare the two total returns at different rate levels. If rates stay constant over the year, the callable bond's total return will equal 5.69 percent. while the Treasury's total return will equal 4.13 percent. If rates fall as indicated by the negative values for the yield shift, both total returns will be higher due to the increased price for each bond. The FHLB bond is assumed to be priced to its call date in three years. If rates rise as indicated in the bottom three rows of data, both total returns fall over the year due to the falling prices. The analysis indicates in general what an investors "bet " is if he or she buys the callable bond versus a 2-year Treasury. Specifically, with a 1-year holding period, the investor would be better off buying the callable bond if rates ranged between 150 basis points lower and 50 basis points higher. The result largely reflects the three years of call protection afforded.

▪ EXHIBIT 20.7

TOTAL RETURN ANALYSIS FOR A CALLABLE **FHLB** BOND

Panel A

Total Return Analysis for   FHLB5 ⅞ 05/08

Settlement **5/21/01** Price **100.516** Yield **5.685** to **5/21/04** @ **100**

YLD SHFT	S/A Reinv	Pricing at Traded to			5/12/02 HORIZON SPRD*	Yield	Price	Total Return Bond	2 YR	%PROB
-150	4.19	CALL	5/21/04	100	+137.6	4.185	103.25	8.52	5.53	1.8
-100	4.69	CALL	5/21/04	100	+137.6	4.685	102.27	7.57	5.08	10.4
-50	5.19	CALL	5/21/04	100	+137.6	5.185	101.31	6.62	4.59	24.8
0	5.69	CALL	5/21/04	100	+137.6	5.685	100.36	5.69	4.13	29.6
50	6.19	MTY	5/21/08	100	+ 76.7	6.185	98.456	3.80	3.66	20.4
100	6.69	MTY	5/21/08	100	+ 76.7	6.685	96.032	1.36	3.20	9.2
150	7.19	MTY	5/21/08	100	+ 76.7	7.185	93.679	-1.03	2.74	3.8
ExVal	5.68				117.3	5.681	99.807	5.13	4.13	

Mode: **U** (Trad'l/OAS)   Fixed Yld Convention? **V**

BOND TOTAL RETURN vs TSY YLD SHIFT

BMK TSY YLD 11:02	
10YR	5.218
5 YR	4.703
5 YR	4.703
2 YR	4.108

Probabilities **V**
C-Custom
V-Yld Std Dev at
66 bp/year Log?**V**
15.5% Yld Volat.

View **U**
T-TotRet,C-CVX,D-DUR

* SPRDS done to interpolated BMRK Curve

Panel B

Total Return Analysis for   FHLB5 ⅞ 05/08

Settlement **5/21/01** Price **100.516** Yield **5.685** to **5/21/04** @ **100**

YLD SHFT	S/A Reinv	Pricing at Traded to			5/12/03 HORIZON SPRD*	Yield	Price	Total Return Bond	5 YR	%PROB
-150	4.19	CALL	5/21/04	100	+137.6	4.185	101.68	6.31	6.68	7.6
-100	4.69	CALL	5/21/04	100	+137.6	4.685	101.18	6.10	6.03	14.1
-50	5.19	CALL	5/21/04	100	+137.6	5.185	100.68	5.89	5.38	20.6
0	5.69	CALL	5/21/04	100	+137.6	5.685	100.18	5.69	4.74	21.1
50	6.19	MTY	5/21/08	100	+ 76.7	6.185	98.674	5.00	4.10	16.4
100	6.69	MTY	5/21/08	100	+ 76.7	6.685	96.586	4.04	3.47	10.3
150	7.19	MTY	5/21/08	100	+ 76.7	7.185	94.551	3.09	2.84	9.8
ExVal	5.66				115.3	5.659	99.369	5.30	4.78	

Mode: **U** (Trad'l/OAS)   Fixed Yld Convention? **V**

BOND TOTAL RETURN vs TSY YLD SHIFT

BMK TSY YLD 11:02	
10YR	5.218
5 YR	4.703
5 YR	4.703
2 YR	4.108

Probabilities **V**
C-Custom
V-Yld Std Dev at
66 bp/year Log?**V**
15.5% Yld Volat.

View **U**
T-TotRet,C-CVX,D-DUR

* SPRDS done to interpolated BMRK Curve

Consider now the data in Panel B, which are generated in similar fashion to the data in Panel A except the assumed investment horizon is two years or just one year before the first call date. The comparison of total returns between the FHLB bond and 5-year, option-free Treasury now indicates that an investor would be better off buying the callable bond if rates ranged between 100 basis points lower and 150 basis points higher. The callable bond's return is lower when rates fall 150 basis points due to "premium resistance," which refers to the limited increase in price associated with the high probability of the bond being called one year after the holding period. If the same analysis was conducted over a 3-year horizon, the callable bond would dominate only if rates stayed constant or rose 50 basis points. The analysis reflects the fact that the bond would trade at par on the call date in a falling rate environment compared with a noncallable Treasury that would increase in price. The call option is in the money so the investor gives up the higher potential return. Total return analysis allows an investor to better gauge the risk and return trade-off between securities.

OPTION-ADJUSTED SPREAD. The previous discussion demonstrates that the standard calculation of yield to maturity is inappropriate with prepayment risk. Many analysts instead use an option-adjusted spread (OAS) approach when pricing callable agency and mortgage-backed securities that accounts for factors that potentially affect the likelihood and frequency of call and prepayments.[8] Before discussing OAS, it is important to understand *static spread*, which is commonly used to describe the yield on a security with options versus that of an option-free Treasury. Specifically, the static spread is the yield premium, in percent, that when added to Treasury spot rates (zero coupon Treasury rates) along the yield curve, equates the present value of the estimated cash flows for the security with options to the prevailing price of the matched-maturity Treasury. It is an average spread over the entire spot yield curve that indicates the incremental yield to an investor in the security relative to yields on zero coupon Treasuries with options. It does not directly take into account the value of the option or its frequency of exercise.

OAS analysis is one procedure to estimate how much an investor is being compensated for selling an option to the issuer of a security with options. Stephen Smith (1991) summarizes the process via the diagram in Exhibit 20.8 for mortgage-backed securities. Briefly, the approach starts with estimating Treasury spot rates (zero coupon Treasury rates) using a probability distribution and Monte Carlo simulation, identifying a large number of possible interest rate scenarios over the time period that the security's cash flows will appear. The analysis then assigns probabilities to various cash flows based on the different interest rate scenarios. For mortgages, one needs a prepayment model and for callable bonds, one needs rules and prices indicating when the bonds will be called and at what values. OAS analysis involves three basic calculations.

1. For each scenario, a yield premium is added to the Treasury spot rate (matched maturity zero coupon Treasury rate) and used to discount the cash flows.

2. For every interest rate scenario, the average present value of the security's cash flows is calculated.

3. The yield premium that equates the average present value of the cash flows from the security with options to the prevailing price of the security without options is the OAS.

Conceptually, OAS represents the incremental yield earned by investors from a security with options over the Treasury spot curve, after accounting for when and at what price the embedded options will be exercised. The advantage is that an option-adjusted spread reflects

---

[8]Frank Fabozzi provides an excellent summary of static spread and OAS applied to CMOs in *CMOs: Structure and Analysis*, FJF Associates, 1996.

· EXHIBIT 20.8

STEPS IN OPTION-ADJUSTED SPREAD CALCULATION

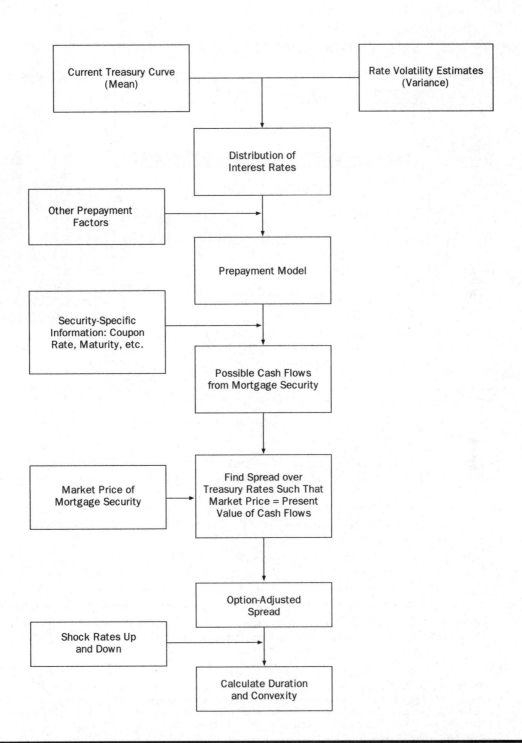

SOURCE: Stephen Smith, "Mortgage-Backed Securities: Analyzing Risk and Return." *Economic Review* (Federal Reserve Bank of Atlanta, January/February 1991).

■ EXHIBIT 20.9

OPTION-ADJUSTED SPREAD ANALYSIS FOR A CALLABLE FHLB BOND

OPTION-ADJUSTED SPREAD ANALYSIS

FED HOME LN BANK FHLB 5 ⅞ 08-04   100.5053/100.5053   (5.69/5.69) BFV   @17:04

| Calculate (P,O,V) ⬤ | **Price** P) 100.505304 | **OAS (bp)** O) +55.1 | **Volatility** V) 16.58 | 2 <GO> Customize Curve CMT   Semi Const Mty Tsy Crv 5/10/2001 |

Cusip / ID#   EC3887782   Option Value : 1.92 (33 BP)

Settle 5/21/2001

Spread : 107.6bp vs5Y T 4 ⅝ 05/15/06   @99-20   (4.710)

Shift   +0(bps)
Yield Spread

{NUM}<GO> for: 3) Call Schedule 5/21/ 4 100.00		OAS Method	Option Free	To Call on 5/21/2004	To Mty
	Yld		5.454	5.689	5.786
	Sprd		54.0	138.0	87.3
	M Dur	4.55		2.72	5.68
	Risk	4.57		2.73	5.71
	Cnvx	-0.28		0.09	0.39

	Yield Spread
3m	3.690
6m	3.604
1y	3.620
2y	4.122
3y	4.309
4y	4.509
5y	4.709
7y	4.913
10y	5.240
20y	5.463
30y	5.707

Model ▪ Assumptions

L=Lognormal
B=Black-Derman-Toy
N=Normal Mean Reverting
R=Lognormal w/Mean Rev
Exercise Premium 0.00

consensus expectations regarding the interest rate environment. Importantly, OAS allows a comparison of the attractiveness of callable agencies and MBSs relative to Treasuries over different time periods.[9]

Exhibit 20.9 provides data related to calculating the OAS for the 7-year maturity FHLB bond that was callable after 3 years. In May 2001, the bond was priced at a 107.6 basis point spread over the yield to maturity on a 5-year Treasury. Using the constant maturity Treasury curve (CMT) as the benchmark, OAS was estimated at 55.1 basis points assuming a 16.58 percent volatility in rate.[10] This OAS figure suggests that an investor might expect to earn a 55 basis point yield premium over the Treasury spot curve given the current level and volatility of rates and the likelihood that the bond will be called prior to maturity. The issue is whether this premium is sufficient to compensate the investor for the greater risk and cost, in terms of required capital, of owning the callable bond.

---

[9]OAS analysis is also frequently applied using the LIBOR swap curve as the benchmark rather than the Treasury spot curve. In recent years, the slope of the Treasury spot curve was downsloping while the slope of the LIBOR swap curve was upsloping. The different slopes reflected, in part, the Treasury's buyback program at long maturities. At the time, the OAS calculated against the Treasury benchmark was much higher, on average, than the OAS using the LIBOR swap curve.

[10]Changing the assumed volatility in interest rates can have a dramatic effect on OAS. Conceptually, the call option will have greater value when rates are more volatile. As such, increasing (decreasing) the assumed volatility of rates will lower (raise) the OAS given the fixed price at which the bond is purchased and against which OAS is calculated.

COMPARATIVE YIELDS ON TAXABLE VERSUS TAX-EXEMPT SECURITIES

A bank's effective return from investing in securities depends on the amount of interest income, reinvestment income, potential capital gains or losses, whether the income is tax-exempt or taxable, and whether the issuer defaults on interest and principal payments. When making investment decisions, portfolio managers compare expected risk-adjusted, after-tax returns from alternative investments. They purchase securities that provide the highest expected risk-adjusted return.

Interest on most municipal securities is exempt from federal income taxes and, depending on state law, from state income taxes.[11] Some states exempt all municipal interest. Most states selectively exempt interest from municipals issued in-state but tax interest on out-of-state issues. Other states either tax all municipal interest or do not impose an income tax. Capital gains on municipals are taxed as ordinary income under the federal income tax code. This makes discount municipals less attractive than par municipals because a portion of the return, the price appreciation, is fully taxable.

The net effect of the tax treatment is that municipal securities trade at yields well below yields on comparable-risk taxable securities. Thus, when a 10-year taxable yields 8 percent, a comparable risk 10-year municipal might yield just 6 percent. The difference in pretax yields reflects the tax benefit to an investor in municipals.

AFTER-TAX AND TAX-EQUIVALENT YIELDS

The importance of income taxes on yields can be easily shown. Suppose that we are comparing yields on two securities of comparable maturity and risk. For the moment, ignore state and local income taxes as well. Let

R_m = pretax yield on a municipal security

R_t = pretax yield on a taxable security

t = investor's marginal federal income tax rate

Once an investor has determined the appropriate maturity and risk security, the investment decision involves selecting the security with the highest after-tax yield. The relevant yield comparison is

$$R_m \gtreqless R_t (1 - t) \qquad (20.6)$$

Using the 6 percent and 8 percent pretax yields for R_m and R_t, respectively, an investor who pays taxes at the 36 percent rate would buy the municipal because it pays 0.6 percent more after taxes.

$$6\% > 8\% (1 - .36) = 5.12\%$$

An investor who pays taxes at the 15 percent rate would prefer the taxable security because it offers 0.80 percent more in yield.

$$6\% < 8\% (1 - .15) = 6.80\%$$

Municipals are often marketed to investors using a modified form of relationship 20.6. Consider the following question. What tax rate would make an investor indifferent between buying a taxable or municipal security? Indifference here means that the after-tax yields are

---

[11]Some securities issued by states and local governments and their political subdivisions, while still municipal bonds, pay interest that is subject to federal income taxes. They are labeled taxable municipals.

equal. The answer is obtained by solving relationship 20.6 as an equality. Using the above data, an investor would be indifferent at the margin if his or her tax rate was 25 percent. In general, this indifference tax rate (t*) is solved by Equation 20.7.

$$t^* = 1 - \frac{R_m}{R_t} \qquad (20.7)$$

The investment decision is then made by comparing an investor's actual marginal tax rate with the indifference rate. The following rules determine the appropriate choice.

If $t > t^*$, then buy the municipal

If $t < t^*$, then buy the taxable

If $t = t^*$, indifferent because after-tax yields are equal.

With R_m equal to 6 percent and R_t equal to 8 percent, any investor with a marginal tax rate over 25 percent prefers municipals while any investor with a tax rate below 25 percent prefers taxables.

The analysis is complicated only slightly when state and local income taxes are taken into account. Let t_m equal the marginal state and local tax rate on municipal interest and taxable interest. Then the relevant yield comparison is

$$R_m(1 - t_m) \gtreqless R_t [1 - (t_m + t)] \qquad (20.8)$$

Suppose that t_m equals 5 percent in the above case where the marginal federal income tax rate equals 36 percent. The after-tax yield comparison now becomes

$$6\% \, (1 - .05) > 8\% \, (1 - .41)$$
$$5.70\% > 4.72\%$$

The municipal now yields 0.98 percent more.

Many analysts compare returns on municipals with taxables in terms of tax-equivalent yields. This involves nothing more than restating relationships 20.6 and 20.8 when the equality of after-tax yields is enforced. Specifically, municipal yields are converted to their tax-equivalent values by solving Equation 20.9.

$$\text{tax-equivalent yield} = \frac{R_m \, (1 - t_m)}{[1 - (t_m + t)]} \qquad (20.9)$$

In the above example, the tax-equivalent municipal yield equals 8.91 percent $[.06(1 - .05)/(1 - .36)]$. This figure means that the investor would have to earn 8.91 percent on a comparable taxable security to produce the same 7.125 percent after-tax yield.[12]

THE YIELD COMPARISON FOR COMMERCIAL BANKS

Suppose that a bank portfolio manager wants to compare potential returns between a taxable security and a municipal security that currently yield 10 percent and 8 percent, respectively. Both securities are new issues trading at $10,000 par with identical maturities, call treatment, and default risk. The primary difference is that the bank pays federal income taxes at a 34 percent marginal rate on the taxable security while municipal interest is entirely exempt.

---

[12]In most published reports, taxes on municipal interest are ignored (t_m is set equal to zero) so that the reported tax-equivalent yield equals the municipal rate divided by one minus the federal income tax rate. In this example, such a tax-equivalent yield would equal 9.38% $[6\%/(1 - .36)]$. This clearly understates the true tax-equivalent yield.

• EXHIBIT 20.10

A COMPARISON OF AFTER-TAX RETURNS ON TAXABLE AND TAX-EXEMPT SECURITIES FOR A BANK AS INVESTOR

A. After-Tax Interest Earned on Taxable versus Exempt Municipal Securities

	Taxable Security	Municipal Security
Par value	$10,000	$10,000
Coupon rate	10%	8%
Annual coupon interest	$ 1,000	$ 800
Federal income taxes at 34%	$ 340	Exempt
After-tax interest income	$ 660	$ 800

B. Disallowing Deduction of Interest on Indebtedness to Finance Municipal Purchases for a Bank: Total Portfolio and Income Statement Effect

Factors affecting allowable deduction for 2002.
- Total interest expense paid in 2002: $1,500,000
- Average amount of assets owned during 2002: $20,000,000
- Average amount of tax-exempt securities owned that were acquired after the change in tax laws affecting interest deductibility: $800,000
- Weighted-average cost of financing assets: $\dfrac{\$1,500,000}{\$20,000,000} = 7.5\%$

Nondeductible interest expense:
- Pro rata share of interest expense to carry municipals purchased after 1982:

  $\dfrac{\$800,000}{\$20,000,000} = 4\%$

- Nondeductible interest expense at 20 percent: $1,500,000(.04)(0.2) = $12,000

Deductible interest expense: $1,500,000 − $12,000 = $1,488,000

C. After-Tax Interest Earned, Recognizing Partial Deductibility of Interest Expense: Individual Asset

	Taxable Security	Municipal Security
Par value	$10,000	$10,000
Coupon rate	10%	8%
Annual coupon interest	$ 1,000	$ 800
Federal income taxes at 34%	$ 340	Exempt
Pooled interest expense (rate = 7.5%)	$ 750	$ 750
Lost interest deduction (20%)	$ 0	$ 150
Increased tax liability at 34%	$ 0	$ 51
Effective after-tax interest income	$ 660	$ 749

Section A of Exhibit 20.10 shows that the portfolio manager would earn $140 more in after-tax interest from buying the municipal.

Applying Equation 20.8 using this data, the yield comparison is

$$8\%(1 - 0) = 8\% > 10\%(1 - 0.34) = 6.6\%$$

The after-tax yield differential times the principal invested produces the $140 difference in after-tax income. The tax-equivalent yield, which essentially converts the municipal yield to a pretax yield that would produce an after-tax return equal to that on an otherwise identical taxable security, equals 12.12 percent from Equation 20.9.

THE EFFECTIVE TAX ON INCREMENTAL MUNICIPAL INTEREST EARNED BY COMMERCIAL BANKS

Prior to 1983, commercial banks could invest in tax-exempt securities and deduct the full amount of interest paid on liabilities used to finance their purchases. Virtually all other investors, including individuals, were (and are still) denied a deduction for any indebtedness to carry or purchase tax-exempts. The deduction enabled many banks to do a tax arbitrage between the after-tax cost of borrowing and municipal yields at the margin to supplement earnings and reduce their effective income tax liability.

In 1983, Congress rewrote the tax law to deny banks a deduction for 15 percent of their interest expense allocated to indebtedness for the purpose of acquiring and holding new municipal issues. This nondeductible portion was increased to 20 percent in 1985. The Tax Reform Act of 1986 went one step farther and eliminated the deduction for most municipal bonds.

The following calculations demonstrate the impact of a lost deduction on a bank's total after-tax income and on the effective yield on municipal securities. For income tax purposes, interest expense allocated to municipal investments is prorated against total interest expense. The applicable fraction equals the amount of tax-exempt securities purchased after the change in tax laws divided by total assets. Section B of Exhibit 20.10 provides an example that uses data on a bank's total portfolio and calculates the total amount of lost deductions for the year assuming 20 percent lost interest deductibility. The bank is relatively small with only $20 million in average assets. During 1998 the bank paid $1.5 million in total interest expense so that its weighted average cost of financing assets equaled 7.5 percent. The amount of interest expense that is nondeductible depends on how many bonds the bank owns that were purchased after the tax change, $800,000 in this example. Because the bank's post-tax reform municipal holdings amount to 4 percent of average assets, a 4 percent pro rata share of total interest expense is allocated to municipal financing costs. This produces a disallowed deduction of $12,000. The remaining $1.488 million in interest was tax deductible. The $12,000 lost deduction has a tax value of $4,080 (.34 × $12,000), which represents the increase in taxes owed by the bank.[13]

Section C of Exhibit 20.10 indicates the effect of this lost interest deductibility on the expected return from municipal investments. It replicates section A except that the bank as an investor can deduct only 80 percent of its interest expense applicable to financing the municipal security. The analysis is identical through the federal income tax calculation. Beyond that, the bank pays a pooled interest cost of 7.5 percent (the same as in section B; $1.5 million/$20 million). Thus, interest paid to finance the $10,000 in municipals equals $750, of which $150 is nondeductible. This lost deduction raises the bank's effective tax liability by $51 (34 percent of $150) and reduces the realized return on the municipal to $749, or 7.49 percent.

The lost interest deduction essentially represents a tax on incremental municipal interest. A good analogy is a homebuyer who obtains a mortgage to finance the purchase. Each month the homeowner makes a mortgage payment that includes interest on the debt. Suppose that Congress suddenly changed the tax laws and no longer allowed individuals to deduct home mortgage interest. The homeowner would still make the obligated mortgage payments, but could no longer itemize the interest deduction on his or her income tax statement. The lost deduction essentially represents an increase in taxes owed because reported taxable income increases without any additional cash receipts. The cost of owning a home would increase, or alternatively, the after-tax return from owning a home would decrease.

---

[13]Note that the bank must pay the entire $1.5 million in interest, which represents its actual cash outflow. However, it is allowed a deduction for just $1.488 million, so its reported income is $12,000 higher. This produces the $4,080 additional tax payment.

In order to compare yields on municipal and taxable securities, the lost interest deduction is converted to a marginal tax on municipal interest. Setting

c = bank's pooled interest cost rate

n = the nondeductible portion of interest expense

t_c = the marginal corporate income tax rate.

the tax value of the lost interest deduction equals the product of c, n, and t_c, divided by the pretax municipal rate (R_m). When state and local income taxes are added, the effective bank tax rate on municipal interest (t_b) can be expressed as

$$t_b = \frac{c\,(n)\,t_c}{R_m} + \text{state and local income tax rate} \qquad (20.10)$$

Applying the data from section C with no state and local income taxes,

$$t_b = \frac{[0.34(0.2)(0.075)]}{0.08} = 0.06375$$

and

$$8\%(1 - 0.06375) = 7.49\% > 10\%(1 - 0.34) = 6.6\%$$

The true tax-equivalent municipal yield for this bank paying no state and local income taxes is 11.35 percent.[14]

THE IMPACT OF THE TAX REFORM ACT OF 1986

The Tax Reform Act of 1986 dramatically altered commercial banks' investment strategies and the attractiveness of different types of securities. This section describes factors that lowered returns on most municipal securities. In general, the act reduced the pool of municipal securities that kept their tax exemption and eliminated banks' ability to deduct carrying costs on new municipal purchases except for qualifying small issues that meet essential public purpose requirements. The discussion focuses only on commercial banks as the distinction between qualified and nonqualified issues does not apply to other investors.

QUALIFIED VERSUS NONQUALIFIED MUNICIPALS

All municipal interest is still tax-exempt for federal income tax purposes. There are, however, a variety of ways in which banks may be subject to tax when they buy municipals. The Tax Reform Act created different categories of municipal bonds. The more essential a given type of bond is for states and localities, the broader is its tax exemption. The first distinction is between municipals issued before and after August 7, 1986. Municipals issued before this date retain their tax exemption. They are essentially grandfathered in because banks can still deduct 80 percent of their associated financing costs regardless of the Act. Securities issued after this date are categorized as bank qualified or nonqualified, depending on whether they meet certain criteria.

QUALIFIED MUNICIPALS. Banks can still deduct 80 percent of their carrying costs associated with the purchase of certain essential, public-purpose bonds. There are two important criteria for bonds to qualify. First, the proceeds must be used to finance essential

---

[14]$[0.08\,(1 - 0.06375)/(1 - 0.34)] = 0.1135.$

government services including schools, highways, sewer systems, and so forth. In most cases, traditional general obligation bonds meet this standard. Second, the municipality cannot issue more than $10 million in municipal securities per year. Thus, only small issue municipals qualify. Such instruments are labeled *bank qualified* municipals. State government issues do not qualify regardless of total debt issuance. The purpose of this special treatment is to help small governmental units obtain financing. In many communities banks are the only investors in local government securities because they are the only ones with the resources and knowledge of the financial condition of the borrower. If this exception to the lost deduction had not been granted, it was feared that many governmental units would be forced to cut services drastically.

The effective bank tax rate against qualified municipals from Equation 20.7 uses a nondeductible portion of interest equal to 20 percent (n = 0.20). Thus, the after-tax yield calculation in Exhibit 20.9 and the above examples assumes that the municipal is bank qualified. The net impact is that even though banks lose a portion of their interest deductibility, with n = 0.20 the bank tax rate on municipal interest is so low that qualified municipals still yield more than fully taxed alternative investments. As such, qualified municipals are attractive investments for profitable banks. The problem is that transactions costs are high when banks search out qualified municipals. This occurs because only smaller, lesser-known municipalities can issue qualifying debt.

NONQUALIFIED MUNICIPALS. All municipals that do not meet the criteria as bank qualified bonds are labeled nonqualified municipals. If banks buy these securities, they can deduct none of their associated carrying costs. In terms of Exhibit 20.10 and the after-tax yield comparison, nondeductible interest on nonqualified municipals equals 100 percent. This sharply raises the effective tax rate on nonqualified municipals purchased by banks to such an extent that they are no longer viable investments. If the 8 percent municipal bond in Exhibit 20.10 (section C) was nonqualified, the lost interest deduction would have totaled $750 and the tax liability would have increased to $255 ($t_b$ = 0.3188). The effective after-tax income would have equaled only $545, or $115 less than that from the taxable security.

$$R_m (1 - t_b) = 8\% \left(1 - \frac{.075 \ (1.0) \ .34}{.08}\right) = 5.45\%$$

As demonstrated, the effective bank tax rate on nonqualified municipal interest is quite high. Because these securities are still attractive to nonbank investors looking for tax-sheltered income, they continue to carry yields below those on comparable taxable securities. The combination of tax-exempt yields and a high effective tax rate makes nonqualified municipals unattractive to banks. Banks no longer buy nonqualified municipals because they can get higher yields elsewhere.

A second important change under the act is the expanded alternative minimum tax (AMT). Banks must now compute their tax liability in two ways, according to regular income tax guidelines and according to minimum tax rules, which add preference items back to normal taxable income and apply a 20 percent minimum tax rate. Banks pay the higher of the two taxes. The importance for the investment portfolio is that tax-exempt interest is a preference item and banks must include one-half of tax-exempt interest earned in the taxable base. Thus, the effective tax on qualified, essential public-purpose bond interest potentially rises by 10 percent.

The Tax Reform Act of 1986 has had several other structural effects on bank investments and relative security yields. First, pretax municipal yields have risen relative to taxable yields to reflect reduced demand by commercial banks. This is particularly true at short maturities. Second, banks have shifted their investment portfolios to taxable securities, such as mortgage-backed pass-through securities and CMOs, to earn higher risk-adjusted yields. Finally, large banks have found it difficult to locate enough bank-qualified municipals to fully meet the demand for tax-sheltered interest income. They now look to other tax-sheltered vehicles to take the place of municipal interest income.

STRATEGIES UNDERLYING SECURITY SWAPS

Active portfolio strategies also enable banks to sell securities prior to maturity whenever economic conditions dictate that additional returns can be earned without a significant increase in risk, or risk can be lowered without reducing expected returns. In most cases, banks reinvest the sale proceeds in securities that differ in terms of maturity, credit quality, or even tax treatment.[15] Such portfolio restructuring improves long-term profitability beyond that available from buy and hold strategies.

Banks are generally willing to sell securities that have appreciated in price yet are unwilling to sell depreciated securities. Although gains are quite popular and enhance earnings, senior bank officers usually believe that stockholders will attribute security losses to poor management. They are thus extremely reluctant to take any losses. This philosophy, however, does not prevent the same banks from taking securities gains to supplement normal operating income and capital in low-profit periods.

This is perverse behavior. The reason that a security is priced at a discount is that the prevailing market rate exceeds the coupon rate on the security. The bank is earning below market interest. A security is priced at a premium when its coupon rate exceeds the market rate so that the holder earns an above-average coupon. An investor who holds a security to maturity may suffer an opportunity loss by not selling the security at a loss, or may give up substantial value by selling at a premium to capture the gain. The appropriate financial decision can be viewed as a straightforward capital budgeting problem.

ANALYSIS OF A CLASSIC SECURITY SWAP

In its classic form, a security swap involves the sale of a depreciated bond and the simultaneous purchase of a similar par bond to improve long-term earnings. The basic principle is to take advantage of the tax laws and the time value of money. Consider the two bonds identified in section A of Exhibit 20.11. A bank currently owns the 10.5 percent Treasury with three years remaining maturity and is considering buying a 3-year FHLMC bond yielding 12.2 percent. If the bank sells the Treasury, it gives up $105,000 in semiannual interest and realizes a capital loss of $73,760. This loss directly lowers taxable income, as banks do not distinguish between the tax treatment of short- and long-term capital gains or losses. A loss results because comparable instruments yield 12 percent annually, or 1.5 percent more than the Treasury coupon rate. The paper loss, in turn, produces a tax savings of $25,816, which can be reinvested with the direct proceeds from the sale in a FHLMC security at par that pays $119,075 in semiannual interest. The cost to the bank includes transactions costs plus potential negative ramifications from the reported capital loss. The benefits include the $14,075 increase in semiannual interest.

---

[15]The following discussion focuses on securities that banks hold as part of their investment portfolio classified as Available for Sale, as opposed to trading account securities. Investment securities generate a return via coupon interest or price appreciation on discount instruments. Current accounting procedures record these securities at market value with unrealized gains or losses as a component of capital.

■ EXHIBIT 20.11

EVALUATION OF SECURITY SWAPS

	Par Value	Market Value	Remaining Maturity	Semiannual Coupon Income	Yield to Maturity
A. Classic Swap Description					
Sell U.S. Treasury bonds at 10.5%	$2,000,000	$1,926,240	3 yrs.	$105,000	12.0%
Buy FHLMC bonds at 12.2%*	1,952,056†	1,952,056	3 yrs.	119,075	12.2
Incremental coupon income				$ 14,075	
B. Swap with Minimal Tax Effects					
Sell U.S. Treasury bonds at 10.5%	$2,000,000	$1,926,240	3 yrs.	$105,000	12
Sell FNMA at 13.8%	3,000,000	3,073,060	4 yrs.	207,000	13
Total	$5,000,000	$4,999,300		$312,000	
Buy FNMA at 13%	$5,000,000	$5,000,000	1 yr.	$325,000	12
				$ 13,000	

C. Present-Value Analysis

Time Line: Semiannual Periods

Period	0	1	2	3	4	5	6

Incremental
Cash Flows
Treasury: $1,926,240 $−105,000 $−105,000 $−105,000 $−105,000 $−105,000 $−2,105,000
Tax saving: 25,816

FHLMC: $−1,952,056 $119,075 $119,075 $119,075 $119,075 $119,075 $2,071,131
Difference: 0 $14,075 $14,075 $14,075 $14,075 $14,075 $−33,869

Present value calculation: discounted at 6.1 percent§

$$\sum_{t=1}^{5} \frac{\$14,075}{(1.061)^t} - \frac{\$33,869}{(1.061)^6} = \$35,380$$

---

*FHLMC indicates Federal Home Loan Mortgage Corporation; FNMA indicates Federal National Mortgage Association.

†Reported security loss equals $73,760, which generates a tax savings of $25,816 at 35 percent. The loss recovery period equals $47,944/$14,075 at 3.4 periods, where the loss equals $73,760 − $25,816.

§12.2%/2 = 6.1%.

The simple net present value analysis in section C of the exhibit demonstrates how much value the swap adds for the slightly greater default risk and adverse reporting consequences. The calculation essentially compares the cash flow from the Treasury if the bank held it to maturity with the cash from selling the Treasury and buying the FHLMC bond. Note that this computation reduces to a comparison of the present value of the incremental coupon payments versus the lower principal received at the end of the three years. In this case, the net present value equals $35,380, using a discount rate equal to the yield on the FHLMC bond.

The attractiveness of such a swap is often viewed in terms of a calculated loss-recovery period for the combined transaction. This is comparable to payback analysis in capital budgeting, which ignores the time value of money. Still, in this example, the after-tax security loss equals $47,944, which the bank can recover entirely in four semiannual periods ($47,944/$14,075). Obviously, the net benefits would increase if the bank chose to reinvest the proceeds in a riskier asset, such as a loan that offered an even higher yield. A bank could also search out higher yields by lengthening maturities with an upsloping yield curve. Alternatively, a bank in need of tax-sheltered income could reinvest the proceeds in a municipal bond of similar maturity that offers a higher after-tax yield.

These alternatives point out the attractiveness of security swaps. In general, banks can effectively improve their portfolios by

1. Upgrading bond credit quality by shifting into high-grade instruments when quality yield spreads are low;
2. Lengthening maturities when yields are expected to level off or decline;
3. Obtaining greater call protection when management expects rates to fall;
4. Improving diversification when management expects economic conditions to deteriorate;
5. Generally increasing current yields by taking advantage of the tax savings;
6. Shifting into taxable securities from municipals when management expects losses.

Any swap transaction requires a comprehensive assessment of a bank's overall risk position and explicit interest rate forecast. As a rule, banks normally lengthen maturities when they expect market rates to decline and shorten maturities when they expect market rates to rise. They shift into higher quality securities when they expect economic conditions to deteriorate and lower quality securities when conditions are expected to improve.

Consider, alternatively, a swap that involves the sale of a security at a gain and the simultaneous purchase of another security at par. A gain produces an increased tax liability so that the seller receives more than cost, but less than the market price after-taxes. Because the government gets its cut up front, there are fewer funds to invest. The reason there was a gain is that prevailing interest rates are below the liquidated bond's coupon rate. Thus, periodic interest income from the reinvested proceeds will decline from that generated by the bond alone. The net present value comparison is again straightforward. Is the present value of the incremental principal cash flow at maturity greater than the present value of the negative interim cash flows? In most cases, the answer is no. It does not add value to sell securities at a gain and reinvest in a like instrument.

SWAP WITH MINIMAL TAX EFFECTS

Because most banks are reluctant to take capital losses regardless of the financial opportunities, swaps can occasionally be constructed that have no tax or reporting impacts. Section B of Exhibit 20.11 outlines a swap where the net tax impact is negligible. This possibility arises because the bank acquired securities at different times in the past. Over time, rates have changed, so some securities have appreciated in value relative to cost while others have depreciated. The simultaneous sale of two such instruments minimizes any tax effects and frees up funds for reinvestment. In the example, the bank sells a Treasury bond at a pretax loss of $73,760 and a Federal National Mortgage Association (FNMA) bond at a pretax gain of $73,060. The net loss equals only $700, and the bank has almost $5 million to reinvest. Because management anticipates rising rates, it reinvests the proceeds in a 1-year FNMA security yielding 13%, thereby shortening the maturity and duration of its assets. It is difficult to conduct a net present value analysis until management specifies what it will do with the proceeds after the first year. Of course, sensitivity analysis involving a variety of rate forecasts is extremely relevant here.

The essential point is that with swaps active portfolio management allows a bank to adjust its interest rate risk, liquidity risk, and credit risk profile via buying and selling securities. Portfolio managers must also recognize that not selling securities because they are priced at a discount entail losses in the form of reduced periodic interest income. Similarly, securities sold for a gain typically involve a substitution of a larger current period cash inflow for reduced interest income in later periods.

LEVERAGED ARBITRAGE STRATEGY

During the mid- to late-1990s, many bank managers believed that their banks were under-leveraged. Too little debt relative to stockholders' equity lowered the equity multiplier and reduced ROE, given the strong ROAs that were being generated. To increase earnings and make the bank more expensive if an acquirer was interested in buying the bank, some portfolio managers implemented a leveraged arbitrage strategy involving borrowing from the Federal Home Loan Bank and using the proceeds to buy securities. The specific strategy consists of matching the maturity of FHLB advances with the call dates of callable agency bonds and the maturity dates of securities currently held in the investment portfolio.

Consider a bank with $100 million in assets and $12 million in stockholders' equity that expects to earn $1.5 million, or 1.5 percent on assets. With its equity base, the bank would report an equity multiplier of 8.33 and an ROE of 12.5 percent. The bank currently owns $3 million of Treasury securities yielding 5.4 percent that mature in one year, and $3 million in Farm Credit Bank bonds yielding 5.7 percent that mature in 18 months. It can borrow from the FHLB for one year at 6 percent and for 18 months at 6.2 percent. The leveraged arbitrage strategy involves borrowing from the FHLB at these maturities and buying callable agency bonds with call dates at one year and 18 months, respectively. For example, assume that a 5-year maturity bond, noncallable for one year, yields 7 percent, while a 7-year bond that is noncallable for 18 months yields 7.25 percent. The spread between the respective advances and callable agencies is

	Agency Interest	−	FHLB Advance Interest	=	Spread
5 NC 1 year	7%	−	6%	=	1%
7 NC 18 mo.	7.25%	−	6.2%	=	1.05%

If the transactions amounts were the same $3 million, the bank would earn an additional $61,500 in net interest income over the year. This would lower the bank's ROA to 1.45 percent, but increase the bank's ROE to 12.84 percent.[16] If the transactions amounts were at $10 million each, the bank would earn an additional $205,000. This would lower the ROA to 1.36 percent, but raise the ROE to 13.63 percent.[17]

The risk of this strategy is associated with potential liquidity problems and the specific interest rate bet. If rates fall after the FHLB borrowing and purchase of callable agencies, the agencies will likely be called. The bank would use the proceeds from the bonds being called to pay off the advances. It would then be out of all transactions. The net effect is that the bank would earn the incremental income over the next year and 18 months. Suppose instead that rates stay constant or increase in which case the bonds will not likely be called. To pay off the advances the bank would have to use proceeds from securities or loans that mature or proceeds from new deposit offerings. In this example, the bank has mitigated this liquidity problem by having two $3 million Treasury securities that mature in 1 year and 18 months, respectively. If rates rise, the callable bonds will trade at a discount and the bank will own securities that earn below-market yields for potentially five and seven years, unless management chooses to sell them. The bet underlying this strategy is that rates will fall to avoid the liquidity problems. It is highly unusual that the seller of an option (the bank) wants the option to be exercised (agency bonds to be called) as it appears with this strategy.

---

[16]Assume that the bank's top rate is 34 percent and all incremental income is paid out as dividends so that equity is unchanged. The incremental net income equals $40,590 ($61,500 × 0.66) such that ROA equals $1,540,590/$106,000,000 and ROE equals $1,540,590/$12,000,000.

[17]ROA = $1,635,300/$120,000,000 = 0.0136

SUMMARY

With the changing competitive environment, commercial banks are looking to manage their investment portfolios more aggressively. Passive strategies, which view the portfolio as a simple supplement to loans, earn average returns over time relative to the interest rate cycle. Active strategies, if implemented carefully, can enhance returns by taking advantage of perceived changes in interest rates and required adjustments in portfolio composition. Still, taking large speculative positions based on interest rate forecasts is inappropriate. The higher risk will inevitably come back to haunt managers in the form of losses.

Banks can generally improve the timing of their investments if they buy securities contracyclically, when loan demand is high. If successful, they will earn above-average coupon interest and be able to sell securities later at a gain. Most active investment strategies involve looking at a security's total return. This is especially difficult, however, when securities have embedded options, such as the call option in a callable agency bond and the prepayment option in mortgage-backed securities. This chapter provides examples of how total return analysis can assist in evaluating these securities. It also describes the impact of these embedded options on a security's duration, convexity, and general price sensitivity. It demonstrates why banks should hold municipal securities to shelter as much income as possible due to their higher after-tax yields than otherwise comparable taxable securities. Unfortunately, only bank-qualified municipals are attractive on a yield basis and they are in limited supply. Finally, portfolio managers should recognize that holding low-rate discount instruments produces opportunity losses in the form of reduced interest income in future years. If possible, they should take advantage of security swaps, which allow a bank to realign its overall risk and return position.

QUESTIONS

1. Describe the characteristics of the laddered investment strategy and compare them to the barbell investment strategy. Why should the barbell strategy outperform the laddered maturity strategy in a stable or declining interest rate environment? Why should the laddered strategy outperform the barbell strategy in a rising rate environment?

2. The term-structure of U.S. Treasury interest rates generally exhibits certain shapes during different stages of the business cycle. Discuss this relationship and explain why it holds, on average. What shape does the yield curve take prior to a recession in the United States?

3. What rationale suggests that a contracyclical investment strategy should outperform the market, on average? Is it possible to consistently earn above-average returns by timing security purchases?

4. Suppose that the U.S. Treasury yield curve is continuously downsloping. Should a bank portfolio manager buy securities with maturities under one year or securities with maturities of 10 years to maximize interest income over the next 10 years? Explain what factors should be used to make a decision.

5. Provide one reason for using the bank's investment portfolio to speculate on interest rate movements. Provide one reason against. What do you believe about efficient markets and how does this influence your opinion of speculating? Can investors accurately forecast the direction of future interest rate movements?

6. Suppose that a bank's ALCO reports that the bank is too liability sensitive in that earnings will fall more than desired should rates rise. You have been asked to reduce the bank's earnings sensitivity. What specific strategies might the investment manager pursue? Identify the cost and benefit of each. Is each an active or passive strategy and is it speculating?

7. Describe the basic strategy in riding the yield curve. Can you ride the yield curve if the yield curve is downsloping with short-term rates above long-term rates?

8. In each of the following cases, identify the buyer and seller of the option, how the value of the option is indicated, and when (in what interest rate environment) the option will be exercised.
   a. A bank buys a 5-year maturity FNMA bond that is callable at par after 1 year, yielding 6.88 percent. The matched duration Treasury zero coupon rate is 6.11 percent.
   b. A bank buys a FHLMC pass-through MBS at par yielding 7.47 percent. The matched duration Treasury zero coupon rate is 6.48 percent.

9. Use the characteristics of interest only (IO) mortgage-backed securities and the diagram in section B of Exhibit 20.4 to answer the following.
   a. Explain why the price of this IO will fall if market rates on mortgages rise above 9.5 percent.
   b. Suppose the current market rate on mortgages is 8 percent. If these rates fall, what will happen to the price of the IO? If these rates rise to 9 percent, what will happen to the price of the IO? Explain why in each instance.

10. What do the terms positive convexity and negative convexity mean? Using the diagrams in Exhibit 20.4, do these securities exhibit positive convexity, negative convexity, or both? Explain.

11. Explain why the modified durations of the GNMA pass-through security in Exhibit 20.6:
    a. Increase when rates rise above the initial level.
    b. Decrease when rates fall below the initial level.

12. Explain conceptually how effective duration differs from Macaulay's duration for a bond with options.

13. Suppose that you own a callable U.S. agency bond like that in Exhibit 20.7. Explain why your total return will fall when interest rates rise. Identify changes in return associated with each component of total return. Why will total return rise when rates fall?

14. Describe conceptually how static spread differs from option-adjusted spread for a callable bond?

15. Suppose that a bank currently owns a $5 million par value Treasury bond, purchased at par, with four years remaining to maturity that pays $200,000 in interest every six months. Its current market value is $5.23 million. If the bank sold the bond and reinvested the proceeds in a similar maturity taxable security, it could earn 6.6 percent annually. Determine the incremental cash flow effects for the bank if it sold the Treasury note and reinvested the full after-tax proceeds from the sale in a 6.6 percent 3-year taxable security, assuming a 34 percent tax rate.

16. Suppose that the above bank also owns a $1 million par value Treasury bond, purchased at par, with two years to maturity, paying $29,000 in semiannual interest, with a market value of $960,000. Determine the incremental cash flow effects if the bank sold this note and bought a 2-year taxable security yielding 6.2 percent with the proceeds.

17. You pay federal income taxes at a 28 percent marginal tax rate. You have the choice of buying either a taxable corporate bond paying 7.10 percent coupon interest or a similar maturity and risk municipal bond paying 5.90 percent coupon interest.
    a. Which bond offers the higher after-tax yield?
    b. If you also pay a state income tax on taxable coupon interest at a 9 percent rate but no tax on municipal interest, which bond offers the higher after-tax yield?

18. Your bank is considering borrowing $1 million in 1-year funds from the Federal Home Loan Bank at 6.42 percent and buying a $1 million par value 5 NC 1 agency bond yielding 7.55 percent. The current Treasury yield curve is moderately upsloping. You currently own a Treasury bill that pays $1 million at maturity in one year.
    a. Describe the interest rate risk that you assume in this matched transaction.
    b. Describe the liquidity risk associated with this matched transaction.

PROBLEMS

I. RIDING THE YIELD CURVE

Victory Bank plans to invest $1 million in Treasury bonds and has a 4-year investment horizon. It is considering two choices: a 4-year bond currently yielding 5.3 percent annually and an 8-year bond yielding 6.54 percent annually. Coupon interest is payable semiannually and can be reinvested at 5 percent (2.5 percent semiannually). If the bank buys the 8-year bond, it will sell it after four years. In four years a 4-year bond is expected to yield 6 percent. Follow the example in Exhibit 20.2 and answer the following questions.

1. Calculate the total coupon interest, reinvestment income, and principal returned at maturity expected from investing $1 million in the 4-year bond. What is the bank's expected total return?

2. Calculate the total coupon interest, reinvestment income, and sale value after four years expected from investing $1 million in the 8-year bond and selling it prior to maturity. What is the bank's expected total return?

3. Determine which investment promises the higher return. What risks are involved in this strategy?

4. Suppose that instead of yielding 6 percent after four years, the market rate on a 4-year bond is 7.4 percent. What will the total return be for the strategy of buying an 8-year bond and selling it after four years?

II. EFFECTIVE DURATION AND CONVEXITY

You own a 7-year final maturity callable agency bond that is currently priced at 100.15 per $100 par value to yield 7.63 percent. If the prevailing market yield on this bond rises to 8.30 percent, the price will fall to 99.45. If the prevailing market yield on this bond falls to 6.93 percent, the price will fall to par value.
    a. What is the effective duration of this bond?
    b. What is the effective convexity of this bond?
    c. Does this bond exhibit positive or negative convexity? Why?

III. SECURITY SWAP

The ALCO members of Jackson County Bank have just reached a consensus that market interest rates are going to rise by 100 to 200 basis points during the upcoming year. Committee members decided to swap securities in the bank's investment portfolio to make it more rate sensitive. Below are listed selected security holdings and market interest rates currently available on Treasury and agency instruments.

Security	Par Value	Market Value	Semiannual Coupon
2-year U.S. Treasury note	$2,000,000	$2,094,600	$ 60,000
10-year U.S. Treasury bond	$3,000,000	$3,277,525	$148,200
4-year Federal National Mortgage Assoc. bond	$2,000,000	$1,902,880	$ 52,000
4-year Federal Land Bank (FLB) bond	$2,000,000	$2,105,425	$ 76,000
*Current Market Rates**			
6-month Treasury bills: 3.88%			
52-week Treasury bills: 4.57%			
2-year Treasury note: 5.40%			
3-year FLB: 6.05%			

*The bank's marginal income tax rate equals 35 percent.

1. What will the incremental cash flow effects be over the next year if the bank sells both 4-year bonds from its portfolio and invests the entire after-tax proceeds in a new 3-year FLB bond? Is this a positive or negative net present value project? What are the advantages and disadvantages of the bank doing this?

2. Suppose the bank sells the 2-year Treasury note, the 10-year Treasury bond, and the 4-year FNMA bond. Determine what dollar amount the bank will report under securities gains or losses. Analyze the incremental cash flow effects if the bank uses the proceeds after taxes to (a) buy 6- month T-bills, (b) buy 52-week T-bills, and (c) buy 2-year Treasury notes. In each case explain how the bank's risk profile will have changed.

3. Suppose that the bank also owned CMOs with an estimated life of 4.5 years that currently produced 8 percent coupon interest. At current interest rates the prepayment speed was 25 percent faster than normal. Discuss the pros and cons of selling these CMOs in a rising rate environment.

ACTIVITY

Obtain a copy of a large bank's most recent annual report. Analyze data for the securities portfolio and footnotes to the balance sheet and income statement to determine:

1. How the bank accounts for its security holdings (review the amounts designated as trading securities, held to maturity, and available for sale);

2. Whether the market value of securities held to maturity exceeds or falls below the book value;

3. How much the impact of changing interest rates either increased or decreased reported bank capital.

21

GLOBAL BANKING ACTIVITIES

By the end of 2001, U.S. banks had experienced 11 consecutive years of record profits, due largely to substantial increases in noninterest income, limited growth in noninterest expense, high but slightly declining net interest margins, and reduced loan losses. Many issued new stock, which along with an increase in retained earnings, raised capital ratios to recent record levels. Generally, large U.S. banks positioned themselves to better compete globally by increasing their capital and expanding the range of products and services offered.

Given the wide range of economic and structural changes around the world, including a unified Germany, the expansion of the European Community, the privatization of Eastern Europe, and the growth of global powerhouse banking organizations, banks in the industrialized countries are trying to expand their trade areas and compete for global business. The elimination of interstate branching restrictions and deregulation of the U. S. banking system with the Gramm-Leach-Bliley Act of 1999 dramatically reshaped the international banking scene. Restrictions on interstate branching and a limited product line (a result of the Glass-Steagall Act) meant that U.S. banks were smaller and offered fewer products compared with banks around the world. For example, Glass-Steagall did not allow banks operating inside the U.S. to engage in insurance or underwriting corporate securities. Banks headquartered outside the U.S. have not been subject to these same limitations. U.S. banks were also restricted by individual state law, that often restricted branching to within the home state, county, or city. As a result, no U.S. bank was among the ten largest in terms of size in 1996. However, after the passage and full implementation of the Riegle-Neal Interstate Banking and Branching Efficiency Act of 1994, which allowed U.S. banks to branch across state lines, U.S. banking companies represented 3 of the 10 largest banks, including Citigroup at number one.[1]

---

[1]One problem with comparing U.S. banks with banks from around the world is that U.S. reporting requirements are much more stringent with respect to disclosure and timing. Publicly-owned U.S. companies must make an annual report within 90 days after the end of their fiscal year. U.S. banks must file their quarterly reports within 30 days while companies based outside the U.S. do not have the same restrictions. For example, in Germany, companies have nine months to report.

GLOBAL BANKING PARTICIPANTS

One clear trend in the evolution of financial institutions and markets is the expansion of activities across national boundaries. Technology has made it possible to conduct business around the world with relative ease and minimal cost. Producers recognize that export markets are as important as domestic markets, and that the range of competitors includes both domestic and foreign operatives. This is increasingly apparent in agriculture, textiles, steel, and microelectronics. Many financial institutions have similarly expanded their activities internationally while developing financial instruments to facilitate trade and funds flows.

Global banking activities involve both traditional commercial and investment banking products. U.S. commercial banks now accept deposits, make loans, provide letters of credit, trade bonds and foreign exchange, and underwrite debt and equity securities in dollars and other currencies. With the globalization of financial markets, all firms compete directly with other major commercial and investment banks throughout the world. Foreign banks offer the same products and services denominated in their domestic currencies and in U.S. dollars. Still, it was not always this way.

U.S. banks, although a dominant player in some world markets, have not been considered "large" by international standards. Exhibit 21.1 lists the largest banking companies by assets as of year-end 1996, and Exhibit 22.2 reports the largest banking companies by assets at year-end 2000 (latest data available internationally).[2] Restrictive branching laws, restrictions on the types of activities U.S. banks could engage in, and other regulatory factors generally meant that U.S. banks were greater in number, but smaller in size.

The Riegle-Neal Interstate Banking and Branching Efficiency Act of 1994 effectively eliminated interstate branching restrictions in the U.S. such that interstate branching became fully effective in 1997. In early 1994, there were 10 U.S. banks with 30 interstate branches. By June 2001, there were 288 U.S. banks with 19,298 interstate branches. U.S. banks were also hampered in their ability to compete internationally by the Glass-Steagall Act, which effectively separated commercial banking from investment banking. As such, U.S. commercial banks essentially provided two products: loans and FDIC-insured deposits. Glass-Steagall, however, left open the possibility of banks engaging in the investment banking business through the use of Section 20 affiliates so long as the bank was not "principally engaged" in these activities. In 1987, commercial banks received permission from the Federal Reserve to underwrite and deal in securities. The Fed initially resolved the issue of what "principally engaged" means by allowing banks to earn up to 5 percent of their revenue in their securities affiliates. This fraction was raised to 10 percent in 1989, and to 25 percent in 1997. By the beginning of 1998, there were 45 Section 20 companies. In November 1999, the U.S. Congress passed the Gramm-Leach-Bliley Act which, for the first time, allowed U.S. banks to fully compete with the largest global diversified financial companies by offering the same broad range of products. The Gramm-Leach-Bliley Act of 1999 repealed restrictions on banks affiliating with securities firms contained in Sections 20 and 32 of the Glass-Steagall Act and modified portions of the Bank Holding Company Act to allow affiliations between banks and insurance underwriters. While it preserved the authority of states to regulate insurance, the act prohibited state actions that prevent bank-affiliated firms from selling insurance on an equal basis with other insurance agents. The act further created a new financial holding company authorized to engage in underwriting, selling insurance and securities, conducting both commercial and merchant banking, investing in and developing real estate, and other "complementary activities."

---

[2]Exhibits 21.1 and 21.2 convert foreign assets and equity into U.S. dollars. When the value of the dollar declines (rises) relative to a foreign currency, the dollar-valued magnitude of foreign assets and equity rises (declines). Thus, comparisons between countries incorporate fluctuations in the relative prices of currencies.

▪ EXHIBIT 21.1

RANKINGS OF WORLD BANKING COMPANIES PRIOR TO FULL ENACTMENT OF RIEGLE-
NEAL INTERSTATE BANKING AND BRANCHING EFFICIENCY ACT: 1996

Rank	Company Name	12/31/1996
1	Bank of Tokyo-Mitsubishi Ltd., Tokyo, Japan	$648,161.00
2	Deutsche Bank AG, Frankfurt, Germany	575,072.00
3	Credit Agricole Mutual, Paris, France (2)	479,963.00
4	Credit Suisse Group, Zurich, Switzerland (1)	463,751.40
5	Dai-Ichi Kangyo Bank Ltd., Tokyo, Japan	434,115.00
6	Fuji Bank Ltd., Tokyo, Japan	432,992.00
7	Sanwa Bank Ltd., Osaka, Japan	427,689.00
8	Sumitomo Bank Ltd., Osaka, Japan	426,103.00
9	Sakura Bank Ltd., Tokyo, Japan	423,017.00
10	HSBC Holdings, Plc., London, United Kingdom	404,979.00
11	Norin Chunkin Bank, Tokyo, Japan	375,210.00
12	Dresdner Bank, Frankfurt, Germany	358,829.00
13	Banque Nationale de Paris, France (2)	357,322.00
14	Industrial Bank of Japan Ltd., Tokyo, Japan	350,468.00
15	ABN-AMRO Bank N.V., Amsterdam, Netherlands	341,916.00
16	Societe Generale, Paris, France	341,867.00
17	**Chase Manhattan Corp., New York, United States**	**333,777.00**
18	Union Bank of Switzerland, Zurich, Switzerland (a)	326,190.00
19	NatWest Group, London, United Kingdom	317,295.00
20	Credit Lyonnais, Paris, France	311,747.00
21	BarclaysBank Plc., London, United Kingdom	308,710.00
22	Westdeutsche Landesbank Girozentrale, Duesseldorf, Germany	298,455.00
23	Compagnie Financiere de Paribas, Paris, France	292,320.00
24	Commerzbank, Frankfurt, Germany	290,300.00
25	Mitsubishi Trust & Banking Corp., Tokyo, Japan	284,528.00
26	**Citicorp, New York, United States (b)**	**278,941.00**
27	Tokai Bank Ltd., Nagoya, Japan	273,430.00
28	Swiss Bank Corporation, Basel, Switzerland (a)	268,519.00
29	Bayerische Vereinsbank AG, Munich, Germany	260,848.00
30	Mitsui Trust & Banking Co., Ltd., Tokyo, Japan	254,189.00

NOTE: Assets are in billions of dollars.
SOURCE: *The American Banker:* http://www.americanbanker.com.

The merger between Citicorp and Travelers created Citigroup, the first diversified financial services company in the U.S. The merger, however, was not completely permissible at the
time it was approved under provisions of the Glass-Steagall Act. The passage of the Gramm-
Leach-Bliley Act (GLB) made this merger permissible and thereby allowed Citigroup to
legally be the world's largest banking company. Had the GLB not become law, Citigroup
would have had from two and five years to divest itself of Travelers' insurance underwriting. Citigroup formed a financial holding company under the provisions of GLB and became
one of the first integrated financial services companies engaged in investment services, asset
management, life insurance and property casualty insurance, and consumer lending. Its
operating companies include Salomon Smith Barney, Salomon Smith Barney Asset
Management, Travelers Life & Annuity, Primerica Financial Services, Travelers Property
Casualty Corp., and Commercial Credit.[3]

---

[3]In 2002, Citigroup sold 20 percent of its Travelers Property & Casualty company and indicated it would later spin
off the remaining 80 percent to its stockholders.

■ EXHIBIT 21.2

WORLD RANKINGS OF FINANCIAL COMPANIES (BY ASSETS) AFTER MERGERS, THE FULL
ENACTMENT OF RIEGLE-NEAL INTERSTATE BANKING AND BRANCHING
EFFICIENCY ACT AND GRAMM-LEACH-BLILEY ACT: 2000.

2000 Rank	Company Name	Total Assets Year-end 2000	Total Assets Year-end 1999	% Change
1	**Citigroup Inc, New York**	**$902,210.00**	**$716,937.00**	**25.84%**
2	Deutsche Bank, Frankfurt, Germany	872,626.68	829,155.67	5.24
3	Bank Of Tokyo-Mitsubishi Ltd., Tokyo	720,808.94	638,926.83	12.82
4	**J.P. Morgan Chase & Co., New York**	**715,348.00**	**406,105.00**	**76.15**
5	UBS, Zurich	673,705.58	615,324.33	9.49
6	HSBCHoldings, London	673,475.21	600,680.41	12.12
7	BNP Paribas, Paris	651,431.86	702,370.25	−7.25
8	**Bank of America Corp., Charlotte, NC**	**642,191.00**	**632,574.00**	**1.52**
9	Credit Suisse Group, Zurich	612,098.13	451,062.77	35.70
10	Fuji Bank Ltd., Tokyo	557,111.70	467,410.23	19.19
11	Sumitomo Bank*, Osaka, Japan	515,238.07	440,136.88	17.06
12	ABN Amro Holding, Amsterdam	512,004.48	460,405.73	11.21
13	Dai-Ichi Kangyo Bank Ltd., Tokyo	499,407.99	442,555.31	12.85
14	Norinchukin Bank, Tokyo	498,437.70	416,825.83	19.58
15	Royal Bank of Scotland Group, London	477,618.77	146,379.23	226.29
16	Barclays, London	471,918.76	411,620.64	14.65
17	Sakura Bank Ltd.*, Tokyo	464,952.80	396,525.34	17.26
18	Dresdner Bank, Frankfurt	454,802.86	399,262.66	13.91
19	Sanwa Bank Ltd., Osaka, Japan	450,034.22	403,124.35	11.64
20	Societe Generale, Paris	429,598.47	409,690.37	4.86
21	Commerzbank, Frankfurt	428,751.08	371,285.44	15.48
22	Industrial Bank of Japan Ltd., Tokyo	408,786.63	371,899.82	9.92
23	Lloyds TSB Group, London	325,305.06	284,420.23	14.37
24	Banco Santander Central Hispanoamerican, Santander	321,204.41	254,616.58	26.15
25	Abbey National, London	305,018.46	291,993.74	4.46
26	Tokai Bank Ltd., Nagoya, Japan	293,689.17	259,112.93	13.34
27	Asahi Bank Ltd., Tokyo	276,584.24	237,385.94	16.51
28	**Wells Fargo & Co., San Francisco**	**272,426.00**	**218,103.00**	**24.91**
29	**Bank One Corp., Chicago**	**269,300.00**	**269,425.00**	**−0.05**
30	**First Union Corp., Charlotte, NC**	**254,170.00**	**253,024.00**	**0.45**

NOTE: Assets are in billions of dollars.
SOURCE: *The American Banker*, as of August 24, 2001, http://www.americanbanker.com/.

Today, the product offerings of Citigroup are similar to those of Deutsche Bank in Germany. Prior to the merger between Citibank and Travelers, however, Citibank's product line was much more limited. Outside the U.S., Citibank was able to offer a diversified set of products using an Edge Act corporation. Edge Act corporations are domestic subsidiaries of banking organizations chartered by the Federal Reserve. All "Edges" are located in the United States and may be established by U.S. or foreign banks and bank holding companies, but are limited to activities involving foreign customers. They can establish overseas branches and international banking facilities (IBFs) and own foreign subsidiaries. Domestic and foreign banking organizations can subsequently conduct international business in the locales where their customers do their business. Inside the U.S., Citibank operated under more restrictions because it was limited in the range of products and services it could offer and geographically where it could locate its banking offices.

Many community banks located along the nation's borders also rely heavily on businesses and individuals based outside the U.S., as such groups represent large depositors and borrowers. These banks typically conduct business in multiple currencies, especially those near Mexico, and face additional risks with the devaluation of foreign currencies when foreign business slows.[4] Banks generally find that it is advantageous

■ EXHIBIT 21.3

COMPARISON OF MARKET SHARE DATA FOR U.S. OFFICES OF DOMESTICALLY
AND FOREIGN-OWNED COMMERCIAL BANKS IN THE UNITED STATES:
TOTAL ASSETS AND DEPOSITS, 1973–2001

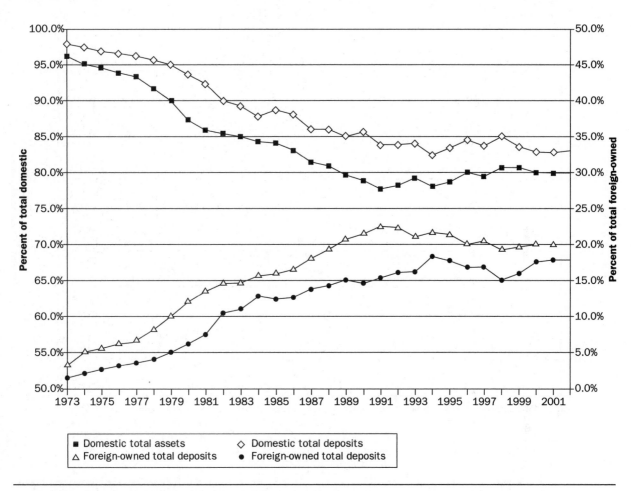

■ Domestic total assets   ◇ Domestic total deposits
△ Foreign-owned total deposits   ● Foreign-owned total deposits

SOURCE: Federal Reserve Board, Share Data for U.S. Offices of Foreign Banks, http://www.federalreserve.gov/
or http://www.federalreserve.gov/releases/iba/.

to follow firms and individuals that the bank already feels comfortable with, so banks will
often enter into contracts denominated in foreign currencies and hedge the foreign exchange
risk with these customers.

Foreign banks operating through their American banking offices have also aggressively
pursued U.S. business. Exhibit 21.3 indicates the dramatic change in market share data for
U.S. offices of foreign banks. In 1973, U.S. offices of foreign banks controlled only 3.8 percent
of U.S. banking assets and 1.6 percent of deposits. This increased dramatically over the next
28 years to where U.S. offices of foreign banks controlled 20.2 percent of assets and 17.4 percent of deposits by year-end 2001. Market share peaked at 22.6 percent of banking assets in

---

[4]The term devaluation refers to the situation in which a government administratively resets the value of its currency
to a lower level relative to other currencies. Thus, the same amount of the domestic currency buys less.

■ EXHIBIT 21.4

COMPARISON OF MARKET SHARE DATA FOR U.S. OFFICES OF DOMESTICALLY
AND FOREIGN-OWNED COMMERCIAL BANKS IN THE UNITED STATES:
TOTAL LOANS AND TOTAL BUSINESS LOANS, 1973–2001

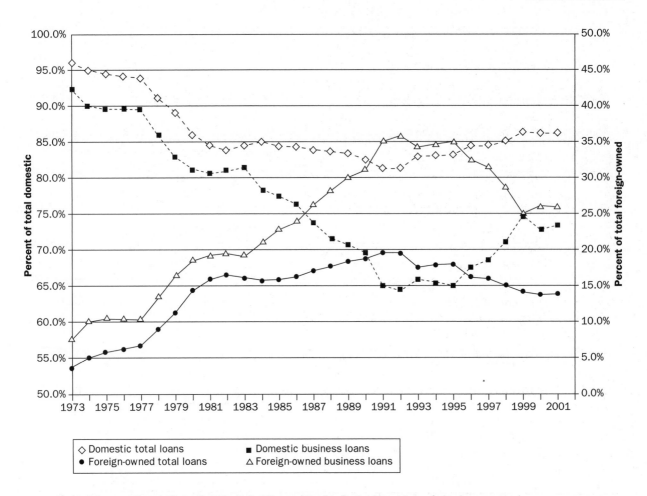

SOURCE: Federal Reserve Board, Share Data for U.S. Offices of Foreign Banks, http://www.federalreserve.gov/
or http://www.federalreserve.gov/releases/iba/.

1991, and 18.3 percent of deposits in 1994. The most active foreign banks operating in the U.S. have been those headquartered in Japan and Taiwan, with extensive operations along the West Coast, and banks headquartered in western Europe and Hong Kong, with operations primarily in the Midwest and along the East Coast. Given its status as a financial center, many foreign offices and branches are located in New York City.

Global banks often follow different strategies. Some U.S. banks, such as Citigroup, have aggressively located offices outside the U.S. and attempted to establish their brand with extensive marketing efforts. Many foreign banks have, in contrast, been content to take silent participations in deals originated by U.S. banks with little fanfare. Domestic borrowers that might object to negotiating a credit agreement with a foreign bank are often unaware that the originating U.S. bank sells part of the loan. Foreign banks, in addition, are extremely aggressive in underwriting Eurobonds and engaging in off-balance sheet activities, including interest rate swaps, standby letters of credit, and municipal bond guarantees. This provides

· EXHIBIT 21.5

LARGEST U.S. BANKS FOREIGN BANKING ACTIVITY ABROAD: FOREIGN OFFICE DEPOSITS, LOANS AND BRANCHES, 2001

Name	Total Assets	Deposits Held in: Domestic Offices	Foreign Offices $ M	%TA	Net Loans and Leases in: Domestic Offices	Foreign Offices $ M	%TA	Number of U.S. Branches
Citibank NA, New York, NY	452,343	98,899	208,024	46.0%	121,901	157,462	34.8%	277
J.P. Morgan Chase Bk, New York, NY	537,826	160,102	120,371	22.4%	135,872	39,022	7.3%	612
Bank of America NA, Charlotte, NC	551,691	334,909	56,634	10.3%	287,364	20,867	3.8%	4,350
Fleet NA Bk, Providence, RI	187,949	110,148	22,316	11.9%	102,956	19,737	10.5%	1,709
Bank of New York, New York, NY	78,019	28,786	27,024	34.6%	19,822	16,879	21.6%	362
Bank One NA, Chicago, IL	161,023	81,020	26,358	16.4%	76,440	4,991	3.1%	804
MBNA America Bk NA, Wilmington, DE	43,066	26,187	1,448	3.4%	18,733	4,123	9.6%	3
First Union NB, Charlotte, NC	232,785	135,276	12,473	5.4%	118,053	3,479	1.5%	2,143
State Street B&TC, Boston, MA	65,410	12,137	26,718	40.8%	4,519	1,402	2.1%	1
Wachovia Bk NA, Winston-Salem, NC	71,555	42,684	3,627	5.1%	45,434	807	1.1%	790
Keybank NA, Cleveland, OH	71,526	40,010	2,721	3.8%	54,047	785	1.1%	980
PNC Bk NA, Pittsburgh, PA	62,610	44,079	2,307	3.7%	39,072	777	1.2%	735
Mellon Bk NA, Pittsburgh, PA	27,813	9,947	4,949	17.8%	6,269	548	2.0%	346
Bank of Hawaii, Honolulu, HI	10,493	5,621	1,369	13.0%	5,312	495	4.7%	78
Northern Trust Co, Chicago, IL	32,758	10,380	9,424	28.8%	11,331	397	1.2%	1
National City Bk, Cleveland, OH	39,214	20,464	1,007	2.6%	31,022	154	0.4%	353
Wells Fargo Bk NA, San Francisco, CA	140,675	73,644	5,433	3.9%	93,799	20	0.0%	939
Wells Fargo Bk MN NA, Minneapolis, MN	52,428	26,311	7,459	14.2%	34,277	1	0.0%	169

NOTE: Millions of dollars
SOURCE: Sheshunoff BankSearch, ® 2002 Sheshunoff Information Services, a division of Thomson Financial Media.

instant credibility and a foothold when negotiating loans later. Exhibit 21.4 shows the growth in market share of U.S. offices of foreign banks in total loans and business loans. In 1973, U.S. offices of foreign banks controlled 3.7 percent of total loans and 7.6 percent of business loans within the U.S. This again peaked in 1992 at 18.9 percent market share of total loans and 35.6 percent market share of business loans. The market share of U.S. offices of foreign banks has fallen steadily since 1992, and these offices controlled just 13.4 percent of total loans and 26.4 percent of business loans by year-end 2001.

Some of the largest U.S. banks allocate a significant portion of their assets internationally and generate considerable earnings through these activities. Exhibit 21.5 provides details on the largest U.S. banks that have any significant international operations. Citibank is clearly the dominant player in foreign office banking with $157 billion in foreign office loans, 35 percent of total assets and $208 billion in deposits held in foreign offices, which is 46 percent of total assets. It also has 297 foreign branches. While their lending activity dwarfs that of other banks in terms of foreign office loans, J.P. Morgan Chase has about $120 billion in foreign office deposits. Together, Citibank, J.P. Morgan Chase, Bank of America, Fleet, and Bank of New York conduct the vast majority of foreign lending for U.S.-owned banks.

Exhibit 21.6 lists the largest "foreign-owned" banks operating in the U.S. HSBC bank, owned by HSBC Holdings in London, is the largest foreign bank operating in the U.S. if one measures these banks independently. ABN Amro, an Amsterdam-based holding company, however, owns both Lasalle Bank, Chicago, and Standard Federal, Troy, MI. Together these two banks control almost $97 billion in assets. With the exception of Puerto Rican Banks, the foreign owned banks operating in the U.S. operate primarily U.S. branches. Foreign operations are generally handled through banks operated in the banks' domestic country.

· EXHIBIT 21.6

Rank by Assets	Name	Total Assets	Deposits Held in Domestic Offices	Deposits Held in Foreign Offices	Loans in Foreign Offices
1	HSBC Bank USA, Buffalo, NY	84,230	37,067	21,153	3,194
2	LaSalle Bank NA, Chicago, IL	54,731	24,963	4,226	0
3	Bankers Trust Co., New York, NY	42,678	11,423	10,000	253
4	Standard Federal Bank NA, Troy, MI	42,088	19,702	624	0
5	Union Bank of CA NA, San Francisco, CA	35,591	26,518	3,305	1,041
6	Banco Popular De PR, San Juan, PR	20,477	11,459	190	10,306
7	Harris T&SB, Chicago, IL	19,673	9,498	1,708	151
8	Allfirst Bank, Baltimore, MD	17,762	12,758	545	249
9	RBC Centura Bank, Rocky Mount, NC	13,732	7,388	273	0
10	Bank of the West, San Francisco, CA	13,412	9,212	N/A	0
11	United CA Bank, San Francisco, CA	10,524	8,285	428	0
12	First Hawaiian Bank, Honolulu, HI	8,682	5,691	463	364
13	Firstbank PR, San Juan, PR	8,143	4,117	N/A	0
14	Banco Santander PR, Hato Rey, PR	7,656	4,811	0	0
15	TD Waterhouse Bank NA Jersey City, NJ	6,069	5,546	N/A	0
16	Israel Discount Bank of New York, New York, NY	6,021	2,112	2,094	415
17	Westernbank Puerto Rico, Mayaguez, PR	5,887	3,214	N/A	0
18	Banco Popular North America, New York, NY	5,606	4,761	0	0
19	Safra NB, New York, NY	5,010	2,548	320	875
20	Banco Bilaro Vizcaya Argenta, San Juan, PR	4,801	2,971	N/A	0
21	Bank of Tokyo Mitsubishi TC, New York, NY	4,337	1,491	1,310	46
22	Bank Leumi USA, New York, NY	4,082	1,496	1,800	169
23	R-G Premier Bank of PR, San Juan, PR	3,963	2,115	N/A	0
24	Doral Bank, San Juan, PR	3,486	1,528	N/A	0
25	Laredo NB, Laredo, TX	2,349	2,029	N/A	0

NOTE: Millions of dollars

SOURCE: Sheshunoff BankSearch, ®2002 Sheshunoff Information Services, a division of Thomson Financial Media.

THE EUROPEAN COMMUNITY

In 1985, the countries of Western Europe started a process to design a plan for economic stability and growth in the region. The effort created the European Community, or EC, which is a confederation of countries that have negotiated the removal of trade barriers to enhance competition. The objective is to increase national output and employment by creating a unified economic engine that can better compete with Japan, the United States, and Eastern Europe. Today, these countries support a common currency—the Euro (European Unified Currency)—which is usable in wholesale financial transactions in Belgium, Germany, Spain, France, Ireland, Italy, Luxembourg, The Netherlands, Austria, Portugal, Finland, and Greece. Coins and currency Euros are now circulating in the market with monetary policy for the single currency set by the European Central Bank, based in Frankfurt, Germany.

The 16 countries in the EC—Austria, Belgium, Denmark, Finland, France, Germany, Greece, Ireland, Italy, Luxembourg, the Netherlands, Norway, Portugal, Spain, Sweden, and the United Kingdom—have generally agreed on rules that allow the following:[5]

---

[5]Several countries are also considered closely tied to the EC: Andorra, Cyprus, Greenland, Iceland, Liechtenstein, Malta, Monaco, San Marino, Turkey, and the Vatican.

LARGEST FOREIGN OWNED BANKS OPERATING IN THE U.S.:
FOREIGN OFFICE DEPOSITS, LOANS AND BRANCHES, 2001

Top Holding Company	Percent Foreign- Owned	Number of U.S. Branches	Number of Foreign Branches
HSBC Holdings PLC, London NA	100	440	19
ABN Amro, Amsterdam NA	100	122	2
Taunus Corporation, New York, NY	100	4	14
ABN AmRO Amsterdam NA	100	385	2
Bank of Tokyo-Mitsubishi, Tokyo NA	66	286	6
Popular Inc., San Juan, PR	100	2	20
Bank of Montreal, Montreal NA	100	57	2
Allied Irish Banks Limited, Dublin NA	100	270	2
Royal Bank of Canada, Montreal NA	100	241	1
Bancwest Corporation, Honolulu, HI	44	193	0
Sarwa Bank Limited, Osaka NA	100	121	1
Bancwest Corporation, Honolulu, HI	44	56	6
First Bancorp, San Juan, PR	100	1	49
Banco Santander SA, Santander NA	80	1	72
TD Waterhouse Holdings, Inc., New York, NY	80	2	0
Israel Discount Bank Limited,Tel-Aviv NA	100	7	1
W. Holding Company, Inc., Mayaguez, PR	100	1	35
Popular Inc., San Juan, PR	100	98	0
SNBNY Holdings Limited, Marina Bay NA	99	2	1
BBVAPR Holding Corporation, San Juan, PR	100	1	61
Bank of Tokyo-Mitsubishi, Tokyo NA	100	1	1
Bank Leumi Le Israel B.M., Tel-Aviv NA	99	8	1
R&G Financial Corporation, San Juan, PR	100	1	25
Doral Financial Corporation, San Juan, PR	100	1	26
Incus Co., Ltd., Road Town NA	71	24	0

- Free flow of capital across borders
- Elimination of customs formalities
- Establishment of a central bank, which creates the potential for a single currency

Although there have been short-term disruptions in the original plans, the expected long-term result is an environment where trade quotas will no longer exist, where the removal of tariffs and license restrictions will lower production costs and ultimately prices to consumers, and where national output will soar.

The implications for the banking industry are wide ranging. First, trade restrictions have generally protected European banks from outside competition. Banks in France, for example, reported efficiency ratios of 60 to 70 percent during the 1990s, while U.S. banks reported ratios closer to 55 to 60 percent. In order to improve their competitive opportunities, many banks have merged with banks in other countries. U.S. banks similarly view the EC as an opportunity to expand their market presence, and many are forming joint ventures with European banks. In addition, any benefits to consumers in the form of lower prices or enhanced output will benefit all lenders, regardless of where the home office is located.

The remainder of this chapter examines the basic features of international banking. The analysis begins with a description of the different types of organizational units that engage in international activities. The following sections analyze the Eurocurrency and Eurobond markets, international lending activities, fee-based services, and foreign exchange operations. Improved communications systems and the development of innovative securities permit market participants to look globally before making investment or borrowing decisions. Participants benefit greatly from the increased liquidity and lower interest rates, that would otherwise not exist. The final section describes foreign exchange risk and price risk associated with bank activities in multiple currencies.

UNIVERSAL BANKING MODEL

Universal banks have long dominated banking in most of continental Europe. As the label suggests, universal banks engage in everything from insurance to investment banking and retail banking—similar to U.S. banks prior to the enactment of the Banking Act of 1933 and Glass-Steagall provisions, and now *post* the passage of the Gramm-Leach-Bliley Act of 1999. Universal banks can also own shares (common stock) in industrial firms. Universal banking is the conduct of a variety of financial services such as the trading of financial instruments, foreign exchange activities, underwriting new debt and equity issues, investment management, insurance, as well as extension of credit and deposit gathering.

Three events changed the development of banking in the United States. The first was the stock market crash of 1929 and the ensuing Great Depression. Many people blamed the banks and universal banking activities for the problems, although there is no strong evidence to link the speculative activities of banks with the crash. The second was the enactment of the Banking Act of 1933 and the Glass-Steagall provision, which separated commercial banking from investment banking activities. The third was the increasing importance of the federal government in financial markets. Prior to these events, the U.S. banking system operated more or less under a universal banking system.

Universal banks, like Deutsche Bank in Germany and Credit Lyonnais in France, grew to prominence in the 19th century and were an integral part of the industrialization that began to sweep over Europe in the 1830s and 1840s. European governments have, in many circumstances, actively promoted the growth of big banks believing they would better serve national economic interests. As part of this trend, European banks are now actively merging or striking alliances with large insurance companies.

One reason universal banking has worked well in continental Europe is because European banks are able to induce corporate customers into using them for a broad range of business. Banks have thus developed expertise in traditional banking, investment banking, and insurance activities. However, while banks in Europe have tied investment banking and lending activities with the same customer, this has not generally been permissible in the United States until the passage of GLB, and even now there are restrictions. There are other drawbacks to universal banking as well. First, it has slowed consolidation in most European countries, with the exception of Spain and France, such that many European markets have highly fragmented banking systems. Second, banks with the capability of handling all types of financial transactions have failed to excel or become innovative in any one field. Thus, Europe has few investment banks that dominate any product market even though they compete in a wide range of markets around the world. For example, many European investment banks have not grown as fast in their own countries as U.S. institutions—such as Morgan Stanley, Goldman Sachs, Merrill Lynch, and J.P. Morgan Chase—have.

Proponents, however, promote the advantages of a more flexible banking model, particularly risk diversification and expanded business opportunities. A universal bank can spread its costs over a broader base of activities and generate more revenues by offering a bundle of products. Diversification, in turn, reduces risk. In November 1999, the United States made a dramatic change in its banking system and implemented a type of universal banking that will be similar to, but distinct from, the European model. GLB repealed Glass-Steagall and effectively allowed U.S. banks to operate in the business of commercial banking, investment banking, and insurance. Although there are many restrictions, particularly in terms of how banks will be functionally regulated, U.S. banks can now, for the first time since the passage of the Glass-Steagall Act, allowed to compete with foreign banks on equal footing. Other financial companies—such as insurance companies, investment banks, and other suppliers of financial services—are moving toward building financial conglomerates, while technology firms, such as Microsoft, are hammering away at banks' networks, building the electronic gateways into financial services.

The United States moved away from a universal banking system in the 1930s because of problems in separating commerce from finance, in which there is an inherent conflict of interest. A universal bank might use pressure tactics to coerce a corporation into using its underwriting services or buy insurance from its subsidiary by threatening to cut off credit facilities. It could force a borrower in financial difficulty to issue risky securities in order to pay off loans. A universal bank could also abuse confidential information supplied by a company issuing securities as well. Some of the most complicated aspects of GLB are functional regulation, privacy provisions, and what banks are allowed to do versus what the bank's "Financial Holding Company" is allowed to do. Under GLB, the Federal Reserve is the primary regulator of the Financial Holding Company. The act further streamlines bank holding company supervision by establishing the Federal Reserve as the umbrella holding company supervisor, while State and other Federal regulators 'functionally' regulate the various affiliates of the holding company. The new authorities permitted within the scope of the legislation allow banks to engage in securities, insurance, and commerce businesses, provide for a rulemaking and resolution process between the SEC and the Federal Reserve, and allow multi-state insurance agency licensing.

Under the U.S. system, Financial Holding Companies (FHC) are distinct entities from bank holding companies (BHC). A company can form a BHC, an FHC, or both. The primary advantage to forming an FHC is that the organizer can engage in a wide range of financial activities not permitted in the bank or within a BHC. Some of these activities include insurance and securities underwriting and agency activities, merchant banking, and insurance company portfolio investment activities. Activities that are "complementary" to financial activities also are authorized. The primary disadvantage in forming an FHC, or converting a BHC to an FHC, is that the Federal Reserve may not permit a company to form a financial holding company if any of its insured depository institution subsidiaries are not well capitalized and well managed, or did not receive at least a satisfactory rating in their most recent CRA exam. More importantly, if any of the insured depository institutions or affiliates of a FHC received less than a satisfactory rating in its most recent CRA exam, the appropriate Federal banking agency may not approve any additional new activities or acquisitions under the authorities granted under the act. This is considered a severe penalty, which has made many banks cautious about converting their BHC to an FHC.

The Federal Reserve Board regulates allowable nonbank activities that are "closely related to banking," in which bank holding companies may acquire subsidiaries. Restrictions came about for three reasons. First, it was feared that large financial conglomerates would control the financial system because they would have a competitive advantage. Second, there was concern that banks would require customers to buy nonbank services in order to obtain loans. Third, some critics simply did not believe that bank holding companies should engage in businesses that were not allowed banks because these businesses were less regulated and considered more risky.

Special ties between large banks, commercial firms, and regulators have often characterized the Japanese financial system. Most of these firms owned stock in their related parties and were engaged in joint business activities. While the system worked well in the past, Japanese banks and other members of keiretsus (conglomerations of closely-tied firms) are currently experiencing severe problems that the system makes more difficult to resolve. If one firm fails, several firms in the same keiretsu may fail.

Every year, the U.S. Congress considers legislation that proposes an expansion of the powers of U.S. banks. If passed, such legislation would generally allow banks, securities firms, and insurance companies to offer new products and services in areas in which they were not previously permitted, and to enter into currently unauthorized business combinations.

ORGANIZATIONAL STRUCTURE OF U.S. BANKS

U.S. commercial banks conduct their international activities through a variety of units. Small- and medium-sized banks typically do business strictly through the bank's head office. Large banks and multibank holding companies typically operate a variety of representative offices, foreign branches, foreign subsidiaries, Edge Act and Agreement corporations, and export trading companies. These units differ in terms of where they are located, what products they can offer, with whom they can conduct business, and how they are regulated.

HEAD OFFICE. U.S. banks involved in international activities normally have an international division or department as part of the home office's organizational structure. Division managers supervise all international activities, with the possible exception of funding responsibilities if a bank has a funds management division. These activities include direct commercial and retail lending, lease financing, and securities operations. Other international units report to senior management through this division.

REPRESENTATIVE OFFICE. A representative office is usually the first type of international office that a bank forms outside the country. The term "representative" indicates that the office does not conduct normal banking business but simply represents the corporation. Employees cannot accept deposits or make loans. The purpose is to promote the corporation's name and, therefore, develop business that can be funneled to the home office. Banks that establish these offices are trying to assess whether it is feasible to pursue normal banking activities in that location. Because they are exploratory in nature, representative offices have few employees until their transition to full-service banking units.

FOREIGN BRANCH. U.S. banks conduct an estimated 60 percent of their international business through foreign branches. Branch offices are legally part of the home bank but are subject to the laws and regulations of the host nation. Foreign branches are either shell offices or full-service banks. Shell branches normally do not solicit business from local individuals, companies, or governments. Instead, they serve as conduits for Eurodollar activities that originate in the head office. Since December 1981, banks have been allowed to engage in the same activities as shell branches via International Banking Facilities (IBFs). IBFs provide cheaper access to the Eurodollar market, reducing the value of pure shell branches. Full-services branches operate much like domestic banks. They accept deposits, make loans, trade securities, and provide fee-based services. Most large U.S. banks have a branch located in London, the center of Eurodollar activity.

FOREIGN SUBSIDIARY. Domestic commercial banks can acquire an ownership interest in foreign banks. A bank holding company or Edge Act corporation can acquire both foreign banks and qualifying nonbank subsidiaries. Unlike branches, subsidiaries are distinct organizations from the parent bank with their own sets of books.

Most nonbank subsidiaries serve the same functions as their domestic counterparts: commercial and consumer financing, data processing, and leasing. The largest U.S. bank holding companies have also formed investment banking subsidiaries (merchant banks) that underwrite a broad range of stocks and bonds in full competition with foreign investment banks. Foreign bank subsidiaries operate much like foreign branches, concentrating on loans and deposits.[6]

---

[6]U.S. banks are also involved in joint ventures with foreign organizations, including consortium banks that are jointly owned by several foreign banks. The primary purpose is to share credit expertise in loan syndications.

EDGE ACT AND AGREEMENT CORPORATIONS. Edge Act corporations are domestic subsidiaries of banking organizations chartered by the Federal Reserve. All "Edges" are located in the United States but may be established by U.S. or foreign banks and bank holding companies.[7] Agreement corporations are the state-chartered equivalents of an Edge. Both types of firms are limited to activities involving foreign customers. These include accepting demand and time deposits, extending credit, and other activities incidental to international business.[8] The primary advantage of Edge Act corporations is that they can locate anywhere in the United States, independently of branching restrictions. They can establish overseas branches and IBFs and own foreign subsidiaries. Domestic and foreign banking organizations can subsequently conduct international business near their sources.

Edge Act corporations account for a very small share of total claims on foreign entities. Most of this activity involves firms in New York and Miami, where many international businesses set up offices. Approximately 70 percent of total Edge assets originated at either Miami or New York firms. Still, Edge Act corporations primarily represent deposit gatherers as they do not keep many commercial loans on their books.

INTERNATIONAL BANKING FACILITIES (IBFs). Many international banking units were formed expressly to circumvent U.S. regulations. Shell branches are a prime example. By channeling Eurodollar transactions through shell branches, domestic banks could avoid legal reserve requirements, Regulation Q interest ceilings where applicable, and FDIC insurance payments. IBFs were created to make it easier for U.S. banks to conduct international business without the cost and effort of avoiding regulatory requirements through shell units. Thus, IBFs are not required to have legal reserves or pay FDIC insurance.[9]

Much like Edge Act corporations, IBFs accept deposits from and extend credit to foreign entities. They also engage in numerous transactions with Edge Act corporations, foreign banks, and other IBFs. IBFs, in fact, are part of other banking organizations because they exist simply as a set of accounting entries. The organizing unit—a domestic commercial bank or savings and loan, U.S. branch or agency of a foreign bank, or an Edge corporation—makes all the financial decisions, as it does with a shell branch.

Four basic restrictions on IBF activities are intended to distinguish IBF transactions from domestic money market operations.[10] First, IBFs cannot offer transactions accounts to nonbank customers. Deposit maturities must thus be a minimum of two business days. Second, IBFs cannot issue large, negotiable CDs that would be competitive with CDs offered by domestic depository institutions. Third, $100,000 is the minimum acceptable transaction amount. This limits IBF customers to major wholesale participants, including corporations and governments. Finally, loans and deposits must be directly tied to a customer's foreign activity such that direct competitors are those involved in international trade.

EXPORT TRADING COMPANIES. Under federal legislation, an export trading company is "exclusively engaged in activities related to international trade and is organized and operated principally for purposes of exporting goods and services produced in the United States by unaffiliated persons."[11] Bank holding companies can acquire export trading companies as part of

---

[7]Nonbank banks, such as Merrill Lynch and American Express Bank Ltd., are also own Edge corporations.

[8]In October 1985, the Federal Reserve allowed Edge corporations to provide full banking services to international businesses. Previously, Edges needed to verify that all deposits from a foreign firm and credit granted were for the sole purpose of carrying out international transactions.

[9]A parent company of an IBF must hold reserves against any borrowings from the IBF.

[10]See Chrystal (1984), "International Banking Facilities," *Review* (Federal Reserve Bank of St. Louis).

[11]Edge Act and Agreement subsidiaries of bank holding companies, as well as bankers' banks, can similarly purchase export trading companies. Park and Zwick (1985) describe the legislation that authorized this investment.

their international business efforts and extend them credit within limits. These subsidiaries enable banks to expand the range of services offered companies, including handling transportation and shipping documentation, field warehousing, and insurance coverage. Export trading companies can also take title to trade items, which a bank is not permitted to do directly.

AGENCIES OF FOREIGN BANKS. Foreign banks compete in the United States through their head offices, U.S. branches, subsidiaries, Edge Act and Agreement corporations, agencies, and investment companies. The first four types of facilities are structured and operate much like U.S. facilities. Agencies and investment companies, in contrast, can offer only a limited range of banking services.[12] They cannot accept transactions deposits from U.S. residents or issue CDs, but must deal exclusively with commercial customers. Their primary purpose is to finance trade originating from firms in their own country. Agencies also actively participate in interbank credit markets and in lending to U.S. corporations. Agencies and investment companies can accept credit deposit balances, much like correspondent balances from commercial customers, if the account is directly tied to the commercial services provided.

INTERNATIONAL FINANCIAL MARKETS

International banking activities have grown along with the growth in international trade. The development of international financial instruments and markets has necessarily followed. Firms that export or import goods and services and banks that finance these activities transact business in many different currencies under different sets of regulations. International financial markets have evolved to facilitate the flow of funds and reduce the risk of doing business outside the home country.

International banks are active in soliciting deposits and lending funds outside their domestic borders. The market in which banks and their international facilities obtain international deposits is labeled the **Eurocurrency market.** The market for long-term international securities is the **Eurobond market.** Term lending activities tied to Eurocurrency operations occur in the **Eurocredit market.**

THE EUROCURRENCY MARKET

A Eurocurrency is a deposit liability denominated in any currency except that of the country in which the bank is located. Two features identify qualifying Eurocurrencies. First, a bank or one of its international facilities must accept the deposit. Second, the accepting bank must be located outside the country that issues the currency. Thus, a BankAmerica branch located in London that accepts U.S. dollar deposits is dealing in Eurodollars, one type of Eurocurrency. The same bank that accepts a sterling deposit is not operating in the Eurocurrency market. Banks that issue Eurocurrency claims are called **Eurobanks.**

Eurodollar deposits are the dominant type of Eurocurrency. Eurodollars are dollar-denominated deposits at banks located outside the United States. Functionally, deposits at IBFs are equivalent and are often included as Eurodollars. Chapter 11 introduces Eurodollars and Exhibit 11.6 describes how Eurodollars originate. Briefly, they arise when the owner of a dollar deposit at a U.S. bank moves the deposit outside the United States. The Eurobank accepting the deposit receives a dollar claim on the U.S. bank from which the funds were transferred. The Eurodollar and Eurocurrency markets consist of a series of transactions leading to the eventual extension of a loan.

---

[12]New York State charters foreign agencies as investment companies. These companies are granted powers similar to federally chartered agencies of foreign banks.

Eurodollar deposits are equivalent to domestic CDs from the depositor's perspective. They are issued in large denominations, typically some multiple of $1 million, have fixed maturities, and pay interest at rates slightly above rates on comparable-maturity CDs issued by U.S. banks. The deposits take the form of both nonnegotiable time deposits and negotiable CDs.[13] Issuing banks do not hold reserves against Eurodollar liabilities and do not pay deposit insurance, which justifies the higher interest rates.

Because Eurobanks that issue Eurodollars pay interest but receive a nonearning U.S. demand deposit, they are eager to reinvest the funds. Eurobanks without immediate credit demand for U.S. dollars simply redeposit the Eurodollar proceeds in another Eurobank. Normally, this deposit is made at a small spread over the initial Eurodollar rate paid. The second Eurobank that accepts the deposit either lends dollars to a commercial or government unit or also redeposits the proceeds. Such pyramiding of deposits continues until a loan is granted. The initial or base rate at which a Eurodollar deposit is accepted is called the **London Interbank Offer Rate** (LIBOR). Each redeposit is priced at a mark-up over LIBOR, as is the final loan. Many U.S. banks also price loans to domestic firms at a premium over LIBOR, in recognition of the fact that dollars obtained outside the country are identical to dollars obtained domestically.

The markets for other types of Eurocurrencies are similarly structured. **Eurosterling** represents claims on deposits denominated in pounds sterling at banks located outside the United Kingdom. A nonfinancial firm or bank that needs sterling can borrow in either the Eurosterling market or from Great Britain's domestic banks at a mark-up over LIBOR. The size of each Eurocurrency market reflects the underlying demand for that currency. The Eurodollar market dominates because U.S. dollars are accepted as a means of payment throughout the world.

THE EUROBOND MARKET

Many international banks are active in the Eurobond market. Traditional corporate bonds are long-term instruments, underwritten by well-known investment banks that are subject to the securities laws of the country in which they are issued. The U.S. Securities and Exchange Commission, for example, requires extensive disclosure regarding the terms of the offering before it will approve a bond issue. Eurobonds are similar in form but subject to virtually no regulation. They can be denominated in any currency or international currency units. As Park and Zwick state, "Eurobonds are issued in the international Euromarket, underwritten by an international banking syndicate not subject to any one country's securities laws, and denominated in any major national currency or even in an artificial currency unit such as the Special Drawing Right, Eurco, the European Unit of Account, and the European Currency Unit."[14]

The primary issuers of Eurobonds are nonfinancial corporations that view them as alternatives to traditional corporate bonds and direct international loans from banks. International banks with investment banking subsidiaries underwrite the bond offerings and often engage in secondary market trading activities. Some international banks issue a hybrid form of Eurobonds structured as a floating-rate note. Floating-rate notes are issued in denominations as low as $5,000, with maturities ranging from two to five years, and carry interest rates that vary with LIBOR. Typically, the interest rate floats every six months at a fixed spread over 6-month LIBOR. Through floating-rate notes, an issuing bank can obtain long-term financing by paying short-term rates. These markets should continue to grow with the move toward syndications among financial institutions and the gradual removal of regulatory restrictions. Borrowers benefit because interest rates are generally lower than they would be without Euromarket opportunities.

---

[13]A small amount of Eurodollars is callable on demand by the depositor. Because the funds have an effective 24-hour maturity, they earn much lower rates than time deposits or CDs.

[14]See Park and Zwick (1985).

Consumers and borrowers benefit from the increased competition. More services are available and interest rates are lower because spreads are smaller. Some critics claim, however, that foreign institutions compete in the United States without the same opportunities available to U.S. firms abroad. Discrepancies in different nations' regulations create inequities, which are slowly disappearing.

EUROCREDITS

Banks that accept Eurocurrency deposits face the same asset and liability management decisions that derive from other funding sources. The fundamental difficulty is in managing interest rate risk. This problem disappears when a bank re-deposits Eurodollars because it matches the asset maturity with that of the initial deposit. When a bank makes a commercial loan, however, it often mismatches the loan maturity with the deposit maturity.

This risk was especially evident during the credit crunches of the 1960s. U.S. banks that could not issue domestic CDs were forced to go to the Eurodollar market for funding. During these periods, Eurodollar rates rose above ceiling rates on new-issue domestic CDs with the competition for funds and credit tightening efforts of the Federal Reserve. Eurobanks subsequently faced a dilemma. Although dollar borrowers generally required term loan financing, Eurobanks did not want to make fixed-rate term loans funded by short-term deposits representing hot money. Borrowing costs could potentially rise above the fixed loan rate if depositors moved their funds.

One solution was the development of **Eurocredits,** term loans priced at a premium over LIBOR. In most cases, the loan rate floats every three or six months, thereby reducing the mismatch between asset and liability maturities. For large loans, banks form a syndicate of international banks in which each member takes a share of the loan and participates in the negotiation of terms. Because both credit and interest rate risks are reduced, Eurocredits are generally priced at spreads as low as 10 basis points over LIBOR.

INTERNATIONAL LENDING

International loans exhibit many of the same characteristics as domestic loans. Individuals, multinational businesses with offices in the United States and overseas, domestic export/import companies, foreign businesses, and foreign governments constitute the basic borrowing groups. The use of proceeds ranges from working capital lines to production loans that facilitate a country's long-term economic development. The difference with international loans is that they entail unique risks. Historically, many large banks have found these risks attractive. Many U.S. money center banks generate more than 50 percent of their earnings from international operations. Citibank, a part of Citigroup, earns almost two-thirds of its earnings in global activities.

In 1987, and again in 1989, most of the largest U.S. banks charged off significant portions (up to 25 percent) of their loans to Latin American and other foreign borrowers, and subsequently reported net losses. In 1998, the economic meltdown in Asia and Russia's default on its outstanding debts caused many U.S. and foreign banks to suffer losses. In 2001, problems in Argentina produced substantial losses at Fleet Boston, Citicorp, and J.P. Morgan Chase. After the fact, some of these banking organizations came to the conclusion that foreign loans effectively produced few profits because the losses offset earlier earnings. In response, many U.S. banks no longer aggressively pursue international loans. Banks that continue to be aggressive are those that follow U.S. customers as they expand outside the United States or those that have strategically decided to become truly global universal banking organizations.

Foreign banks have experienced the same volatility in performance because loans outside their home countries initially produce profits only to lead to later losses. Japanese and European banks were exposed to the Asian and Russian problems, while Spain's largest banks suffered losses from their exposures in Brazil and other parts of South America. Lending across national boundaries introduces country risk and foreign exchange risk. **Country risk** refers to default risk associated with loans to borrowers outside the home country. It exists because lenders and borrowers face different regulations and because of differing political considerations in each country. Country risk increases with government controls over business and individuals, internal politics that potentially disrupt payments, the elimination or reduction of subsidies, and general market disruptions. **Foreign exchange risk** refers to the current and potential volatility in earnings and stockholders' equity due to changes in foreign exchange rates. This risk is discussed in the last section.

The previous section introduced Eurocredits. U.S. banks are also heavily involved in financing foreign trade and making direct loans to major commercial customers. The characteristics of these loans are described below.

SHORT-TERM FOREIGN TRADE FINANCING

International trade and international trade financing are considerably more complex than simply dealing with trading partners within the same country. Not only is the importer located apart from the exporter, but the two parties usually operate under different rules and regulations and may be totally unfamiliar with each other's financial stability and credit rating. Frequently, they transact business in different currencies. To facilitate trade, someone must enter the transaction and assume the risk that the importer may not pay. Commercial banks fulfill this role through bankers acceptance financing.[15] Trading partners must also have the opportunity to convert one currency into another, which creates a demand for foreign exchange services as well.

A **bankers acceptance** is a time draft that represents an order to pay a specified amount of money at a designated future date. A bank accepts the draft when it stamps the word "accepted" across the document. This approval represents a guarantee under which the accepting bank agrees to remit the face value of the draft at maturity. Acceptances are attractive because a bank substitutes its credit rating for that of the importer. The maturity date is far enough forward to allow the goods being financed to be shipped and inspected before the draft matures. Bankers acceptances are negotiable instruments, with maturities ranging from one to six months. Most bankers acceptance transactions are associated with letters of credit, documents that stipulate the contract terms and duties of all parties and authorize an exporter to draw a time draft on a participating bank. The draft is then converted to a negotiable instrument when it is accepted.

Exhibit 21.7 illustrates the mechanics of how a bankers acceptance is created and used to finance trade.[16] Drafts accepted by U.S. banks are used almost exclusively to finance either U.S. imports or U.S. exports. A small portion finances the warehousing of goods in transit. The trade activity outlined in the exhibit involves a U.S. importer, but the sequence of events is similar for all types of transactions. After agreeing to terms with the exporter (Stage 1), the U.S. importer applies for a letter of credit (LOC) from a U.S. bank (Stage 2). Upon approving the request, the U.S. bank issues an LOC, which authorizes the exporter to draw a time draft

---

[15]Exporters who are familiar with an importer often extend credit on open account and receive payment after the goods have been delivered. In other cases, an exporter may demand payment from the importer directly before shipping the goods.

[16]Exhibit 21.8 is taken from Duffield and Summers (1981). The following discussion is based on their explanation of the transactions underlying the exhibit.

■ EXHIBIT 21.7

BANKERS ACCEPTANCE FINANCING OF U.S. IMPORTS: A BANKERS ACCEPTANCE
IS CREATED, DISCOUNTED, SOLD, AND PAID AT MATURITY

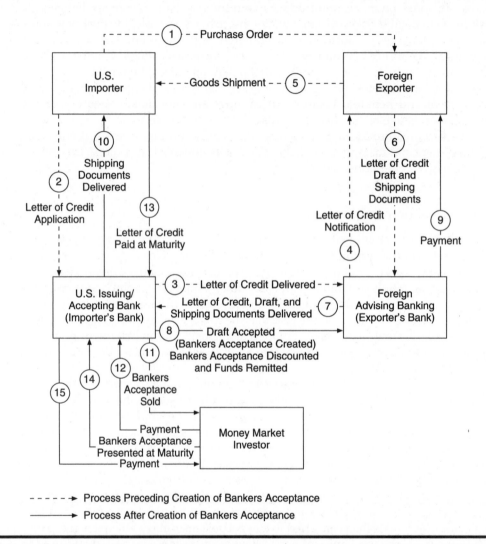

SOURCE: J. Duffield and B. Summers, "Bankers Acceptances," in *Instruments of the Money Market*, T. Cook and B. Summers, eds., (Richmond, VA: Federal Reserve Bank of Richmond, 1981).

against the U.S. bank, and delivers it to the exporter's bank (Stage 3). The foreign bank then notifies the exporter, who ships the goods and submits the LOC, time draft, and shipping documents, which it forwards to the U.S. bank. When the U.S. bank accepts the draft, it creates a bankers acceptance (Stage 8).

The bankers acceptance has a face value and fixed maturity. The exporter discounts the draft with the issuing bank and receives immediate payment (Stage 9). If, for example, the bankers acceptance carried a face value of $1 million and 90-day maturity, the discounted price would equal $980,000 at an 8 percent discount rate.[17] This covers the purchase price of

---

[17]Price = $[1 - (90/360)(0.08)]$ ($1 million) = $980,000.

the goods, although the importer will remit the full face value at maturity. The accepting bank delivers the shipping documents to the importer (Stage 10), who can then legally obtain the goods.

Use of the acceptance enables the exporter to be paid before the importer receives the goods, and the importer to effectively borrow the purchase price. If the issuing bank keeps possession of the bankers acceptance, it essentially finances the importer's purchase, much like a direct loan. In most cases, the issuing bank will sell the acceptance to a third-party investor in the money market (Stage 11). If the bank receives the same discount value, $980,000 in this example, it has no funds committed to the financing. It must, however, pay off the acceptance at maturity (Stages 13 to 15), when it presumably receives payment from the importer.

The issuing bank makes a profit in several ways. First, it levies a fee on the importer for accepting the draft and providing its guarantee. Second, it earns the discounted value of the draft, $20,000 in this example, if it simply keeps the acceptance in its portfolio. Finally, it can earn additional profits if it sells the acceptance prior to maturity at a price below the original discounted value ($980,000). Of course, the sale eliminates any interest income.

Historically, exporters and importers originated most of the time drafts that evolved into bankers acceptances. Since the early 1970s, however, many bankers acceptances have refinanced credits of foreign banks that wanted to liquidate their direct financing of foreign trade. These bank-drawn drafts are known as **refinancing acceptances** or **accommodations.**

DIRECT INTERNATIONAL LOANS

International loans originate from international departments of domestic banks, Edge Act corporations, and the credit offices of foreign branches and subsidiaries. Eurodollar loans to foreign governments and well-established multinational corporations are generally low risk. Defaults are extremely rare, so that the loans are priced at a small mark-up over LIBOR. Some loans are extended to private corporations but carry an explicit guarantee from the source country's government. These loans carry higher risk because some governments have reneged on their guarantees. Loans that have received the greatest attention recently are made within less-developed countries (LDCs). LDC credit extended to both private borrowers and governmental units has generally shown a poor repayment history over the long term. With increasing frequency, regulators and bank shareholders express concern about U.S. banks' exposure to potential foreign loan losses. International loans to LDCs, in fact, clearly contributed to regulators' demand that U.S. money center banks increase their capital-to-asset ratios.

Unfortunately, nonperforming loans do not completely reflect potential losses. Many loans are not classified as nonperforming because U.S. banks have loaned the borrowers funds to make interest and principal payments on existing loans to keep the loans current. Several Latin American governments, including those of Brazil, Peru, and Mexico, have called for a moratorium on debt service to U.S. and foreign banks when they are short of funds. The risk is that these countries may and often do unilaterally determine that borrowers, including governments, should suspend interest and principal payments until their revenues increase sufficiently.

To assess risk, the analyst must understand the relationship between large financial institutions and the U.S. government. International loans are part of the price banks pay for the U.S. government's implied guarantee that they will not be allowed to fail. If the banks were to demand payment on defaulted foreign loans or charge off loans as uncollectible and refuse to extend additional credit, economic conditions in LDCs would clearly worsen. Not wanting to bring about a collapse of world trade and financial markets, governments encouraged the largest banks to renegotiate existing agreements and continue lending.

Through 1986, U.S. banks generally acceded to the government's request and continued lending to LDCs. In May 1987, however, Citicorp reversed the trend by allocating $3 billion to its loan loss reserve for possible loan charge-offs with Latin American borrowers. The transfer produced a quarterly loss near $2.5 billion. Other money center banks quickly increased their associated loss reserves. The reserve allocations enabled the banks to recognize discounts on the loans so that they could sell the loans in the secondary market and engage in debt for equity swaps with foreign borrowers. In essence, U.S. banks acknowledged that the financial markets realized LDC debts would not be paid in a timely fashion. Banks prefer foreign exposure in the form of equity investments rather than long-term, constantly renegotiated loans to foreign central banks.

CREDIT ANALYSIS. It is difficult to evaluate international loans from a traditional credit analysis viewpoint. In addition to analyzing the borrower's financial condition, a lender must assess country risk. Many foreign governments rely heavily on single industries or products as a source of reserves to pay off their debt. Mexico, with its reliance on oil revenues, is a prime example. When oil prices were rising in the late 1970s and early 1980s, Mexico increased its foreign borrowing to finance internal economic development. The subsequent steep drop in oil prices eliminated its source of foreign currency and forced a total restructuring of the country's international debt obligations. The recent passage of NAFTA again made Mexico an attractive place to invest such that new ventures and funding have moved into the country in anticipation of expanded trade and the growth that typically coincides.

Credit analysis for international loans generally follows the same systematic procedures outlined previously for domestic loans. Analysts evaluate the required loan amount, use of the proceeds, source and timing of expected repayment, and availability of secondary collateral sources. What makes international lending different is a series of additional risks associated with debt repayment prospects and constraints. If, for example, a bank accepts payment in a currency other than its own country's monetary unit and does not hedge, it assumes foreign exchange risk. If the value of the foreign currency declines relative to the domestic currency, the value of the debt service declines, even though all payments might be received on a timely basis. Other potential problems are also created with country risk, which includes economic and political risks introduced earlier. Economic risks are readily quantifiable, reflecting the considerations discussed above. Political risks are much more difficult to assess. Bankers frequently analyze **sovereign risk,** which refers to the likelihood that foreign governments will unilaterally alter their debt service payments, regardless of the formal repayment schedule. In 1985, for example, governments in Nigeria and Peru both capped the amount of interest their countries would pay toward international debt obligations. In general, banks have little recourse in the event that a foreign government restricts debt service payments in dollars, because the legal systems of different countries do not allow a resolution of the default.

Many banks have developed credit scoring systems for assessing country risk. One bank's system measures country risk by using discriminant analysis to quantify economic risks and subjective checklists to quantify political risks.[18] The evaluation produces an index that ranks different countries according to their riskiness in rescheduling debt payments. In this application, economic risk is measured by debt management factors and economic indexes. The best indicators of risk were a country's current debt service ratio, defined as the sum of debt service and short-term debt outstanding divided by total exports; total debt divided by exports; and basic economic measures such as per capita income, real growth in a gross domestic product, and the inflation rate. Political risk was measured according to a subjective political rating model and structural factors. The political model assesses both political stability and general government characteristics (Exhibit 21.8). Each country receives a weighted score representing its cumulative risk profile. The bank determines appropriate loan limits or concentrations in different countries according to these rankings.

---

[18]Morgan, 1985, describes the inputs and evaluation procedures in detail.

• EXHIBIT 21.8

POLITICAL RATING MODELS

Government Characteristics, Country *ABC*

What classification best describes the current government?

Government Type (0 to 10)   6

- 0 Despot, dictator
- 2 Military dictator
- 4 Monarchy, family rule
- 6 One-party democracy or nonviable multiparty democracy
- 8 Multiparty (coalition) democracy
- 10 Viable two-party democracy

Latest change in government (0 to 10)   8

- 0 Bloody and violent coup d'etat
- 2 Bloodless coup d'etat
- 4 Peaceful dictator change
- 6 Monarch change, change in colonial status
- 8 Elections, one candidate only
- 10 Peaceful elections, two or more candidates

Relations with United States (0 to 10)   4

- 0 Considered a threat to U.S. security
- 2 Anti-American policies
- 4 Nonaligned, but leaning to the East
- 5 Nonaligned
- 6 Nonaligned, but leaning to the West
- 8 Supports most U.S. foreign policies
- 10 Strongly pro-American, supports all U.S. policies

Government's Role in Economy (0 to 10)   6

- 0 Government controls all aspects of economy (communism)
- 2 Government influences all aspects of economy
- 4 Socialist type of economy
- 6 General agreement between capitalists and government
- 8 Capitalism with minor government intervention
- 10 Strongly capitalistic, free enterprise

Stability of Present Government (0 to 10)   6

- 0 Violent coup d'etat imminent
- 2 Overthrow of government likely
- 4 Unexpected change in government possible (i.e., death of leader)
- 6 Government could lose in next election
- 8 Likely change in government, political power remains intact
- 10 Government unlikely to lose in next elections

Political Stability, Country *ABC*

What are the chances of the following events in the short term and medium term?*

	Short Term	Medium Term
Destabilizing riots, civil unrest	3	2
Increased terrorist activities	3	2
Guerrilla activity, armed rebels	3	2
Civil war	4	4
Government overthrow, coup d'etat	4	3
Foreign war, border skirmishes	4	4
Political moratorium of debt	4	4
Nationalization of major industries	3	3
Socialistic party comes to power	3	3
Communist party comes to power	4	4
Total	35	31

Probabilities

5 Extremely unlikely	2 Likely
4 Unlikely	1 Extremely likely
3 Neutral	0 Present situation

Government characteristics	30
Political stability (short term/medium term)	35/31
Total political rating	65/61

---

*Short-term is within one year; long-term is between one and five years.

SOURCE: John Morgan, "Assessing Country Risk at Texas Commerce." Reprinted with permission from *Bankers Magazine,* May–June 1985, Vol. 168, No. 3. Copyright © 1985, Warren, Gorham & Lamont, Inc., 210 South Street, Boston, MA 02111. All Rights Reserved.

FOREIGN EXCHANGE ACTIVITIES

Because different countries use different monetary units, traders must be able to convert one unit into another. Foreign exchange markets are where these monetary units are traded. **Foreign exchange** refers to currency other than the monetary unit of the home country, and an **exchange rate** is the price of one currency in terms of another currency. For example, Japanese yen represent foreign exchange in the United States, such that one U.S. dollar may be worth 128 yen if exchanged today. Banks participate in foreign exchange markets by buying and selling currencies from participants who use different currencies in their business or travels. They also coordinate foreign exchange hedges for bank customers, enter arbitrage transactions, and speculate on currency price movements for their own account by taking unhedged positions.

FOREIGN EXCHANGE RISK

Foreign exchange risk is the current and potential risk to earnings and stockholders' equity arising from changes in foreign exchange rates. It is found in assets and liabilities denominated in different currencies that are held on a bank's balance sheet and in certain off-balance sheet activities where the commitments or guarantees are denominated in different currencies. It is evidenced when changing exchange rates affect a bank's cash inflows differently than cash outflows associated with these positions denominated in different currencies.

Banks also make markets in foreign currencies and take positions buying and selling currencies for their own account. The change in values of these positions due to changing foreign exchange rates is labeled *price risk*. It is a component of the sensitivity to market risk (S in a bank's CAMELS rating) evaluated by bank regulators.

Foreign exchange risk can be high if a bank holds assets and issues liabilities denominated in different currencies where the amounts are substantially different. In this case, changes in exchange rates will produce changes in earnings and the market value of stockholders' equity. Consider the situation faced by Commerce Bank (CB) whose home country is Poland and home currency is the zloty. The current (spot) exchange rate is $1 equals 150 zlotys. Commerce Bank's balance sheet position in U.S. dollars is such that the bank has $1,000 in loans and $250 in liabilities. Assume that all loans and liabilities have the same maturity and there are no embedded options. In terms of zlotys, CB's assets are worth 150,000 zlotys and its liabilities are worth 37,500 zlotys at the prevailing exchange rate.

- If the exchange rate moved to $1 equals 160 zlotys, the assets would increase in value by 10,000 zlotys, while the liabilities would increase in value by 2,500 zlotys. The bank would gain 7,500 in zlotys, holding everything else constant, such that stockholders' equity would increase by 7,500 zlotys.

- If the exchange rate moved to $1 equals 140 zlotys, the assets would decrease in value by 10,000 zlotys, while the liabilities would decrease by 2,500 zlotys. In this case, the bank would see stockholders' equity decrease by 7,500 zlotys.

These same exposures exist for off-balance sheet commitments and guarantees when counterparties effect the at-risk transactions or activities.

A bank's risk managers analyze aggregate foreign exchange risk by currency. The basic approach is to calculate a bank's net balance sheet exposure by currency and relate this to the potential change in value given changes in the associated exchange rate.

$$\text{Let } A_j = \text{amount of assets denominated in currency j, and}$$
$$L_j = \text{amount of liabilities denominated in currency j.}$$

A bank's net balance sheet exposure in currency **j** ($NEXP_j$) is the amount of assets minus the amount of liabilities denominated in currency j:

$$NEXP_j = A_j - L_j \tag{21.1}$$

If $NEXP_j > 0$, the bank is long on currency j on its balance sheet. If $NEXP_j < 0$, the bank is short on currency j on its balance sheet. The bank will lose if it is long on a currency and the currency depreciates in value (the currency buys less of another currency). The bank will lose if it is short on a currency and the currency appreciates in value (the currency buys more of another currency). CB, which was long U.S. dollars, would thus lose if the dollar depreciates as indicated by the movement in the exchange rate to $1 equals 140 zlotys. CB would gain if the dollar appreciates as indicated by the exchange rate change to $1 equals 160 zlotys. The gain or loss in a position with a currency is indicated by:

$$\text{Gain/Loss in a Position with Currency } j = NEXP_j \times \Delta \text{spot exchange rate} \tag{21.2}$$

where the spot exchange rate is measured as the number of units of the home currency for one unit of the foreign currency. In the case of CB, the bank's loss from a move to $1 equals 140 zlotys is:

$$Loss = (1,000 - 250) \times (140 - 150)$$
$$= -7,500 \text{ zlotys}$$

Risk managers must assess their foreign exchange risk for each currency in which the bank has significant balance sheet and off-balance sheet exposures. They should also assess interest rate risk and liquidity risks in each currency. They can choose to speculate or hedge this risk. Many banks use currency forward, futures, and swap contracts to manage this risk.

CURRENCY EXCHANGE

A fundamental responsibility of international banks is to facilitate funds transfers between trading partners who deal in different currencies. Most transactions are settled by exchanging deposits, so banks must maintain either correspondent bank relationships or operate their own foreign bank offices to have access to Eurocurrencies. Each funds transfer may require a conversion of deposits to another currency and thus may affect exchange rates if banks choose to realign their inventories.

Suppose, for example, that a U.S. retail outlet negotiates the purchase of video recording equipment for $500,000 from a Japanese manufacturer. If the purchase is invoiced in yen, the buyer will convert U.S. dollars to yen at $1 to 128 yen and exchange 64 million yen for the goods. The hypothetical transaction is summarized in Exhibit 21.9, assuming that the traders deal with Western Bank and Fuji Bank Ltd. After the purchase, Western Bank's inventory of currencies has changed because it holds 64 million fewer yen than previously. The bank will have to buy yen to bring its foreign exchange holdings back to the initial position. If the transaction was denominated in dollars, Fuji Bank would hold $500,000 more and would need to sell dollars to reach its initial foreign exchange position. Both the purchase of yen by Western Bank and sale of dollars by Fuji Bank would put pressure on the dollar to decrease in value (increased supply of dollars) and the yen to increase in value (increased demand for yen). Current exchange rates will thus be affected when transactions force a realignment of foreign exchange holdings.

In actuality, there is a spot market, forward market, futures markets, and markets for options on futures for foreign exchange. The **spot market** is the exchange of currencies for immediate delivery. The **forward market** comprises transactions that represent a commitment to exchange currencies at a specified time in the future at an exchange rate determined at the time the contract is signed. For example, a bank might commit to buy 1 million yen 90 days forward for $8,000. After 90 days, the bank pays $8,000 and receives 1 million yen, regardless of movements in exchange rates during the 90-day period. The 90-day forward rate in this

■ **EXHIBIT 21.9**

FACILITATING FUNDS TRANSFERS OF DIFFERENT CURRENCY-DENOMINATED DEPOSITS

U.S. retailer imports $500,000 in video equipment from Japanese manufacturer. Spot exchange rate is $1 = 105 yen.

Western Bank		Fuji Bank Ltd.	
Δ*ASSETS*	Δ*LIABILITIES*	Δ*ASSETS*	Δ*LIABILITIES*
1. Deposit at Fuji Bank −52.5 million yen	Deposit of U.S. retailer −$500,000		1. Deposit of U.S. retailer +52.5 million yen Deposit of Western Bank −52.5 million yen
			2. Deposit of U.S. retailer −52.5 million yen Deposit of Japanese manufacturer +52.5 million yen

1. U.S. retailer buys yen from Western Bank and deposits balance at Fuji Bank in Tokyo.
2. U.S. retailer pays Japanese manufacturer for goods.

case is different from the spot rate quoted earlier because $1 equals 125 yen. Foreign exchange trading also occurs in organized markets for **futures** and **options on futures,** which enables traders to hedge spot transactions or speculate on future exchange rate changes.[19]

Banks that buy or sell currencies for customers normally charge a commission. Alternatively, they may enter into forward contracts with customers and speculatively trade for their own account. For example, suppose that the current dollar-to-yen spot rate is $1 equals 128 yen, and the 90-day forward rate is $1 equals 125 yen. If a bank buys 100 million yen with dollars 90 days forward, it agrees to pay $800,000 for the yen when the forward contract comes due, even though the current exchange rate sets the value at $781,250. If the position is unhedged, the bank assumes the risk that dollars will increase in value relative to yen or stay above the forward rate during the 90-day interval. It will gain if dollars fall more in value than that suggested by the forward-to-spot rate differential (below 125 yen).

A spot rate of $1 to 129 yen at the time of delivery of the forward contract would indicate that the dollar rose in value and the bank could have purchased 100 million yen for only $775,194. A spot rate of $1 to 124 yen at delivery would require a price of $806,452, which exceeds the contracted price by over $6,000. When the forward price of a foreign currency is higher than its spot price, the foreign currency is priced at a forward premium. When the forward price is lower, the foreign currency is priced at a forward discount. In the above case, the yen is priced at a forward premium against the dollar.

THE RELATIONSHIP BETWEEN FOREIGN EXCHANGE RATES AND INTEREST RATES

The relationship between spot rates and forward rates is determined by the same factors that influence relative interest rates between countries. Arbitrage transactions essentially guarantee that interest rate changes produce changes in foreign exchange rates, and vice versa. Suppose that a trader can borrow U.S. dollars for one year at 9 percent at the same time that

---

[19]Chrystal (1984), describes the rudiments of foreign exchange futures and options in "A Guide to Foreign Exchange Markets," *Review* (Federal Reserve Bank of St. Louis).

1-year maturity, risk-free, Swiss franc-denominated securities yield 10 percent. The trader can convert dollars to francs at the spot rate of $1 for 1.7 francs and sell francs for dollars one year forward at $1 = 1.667 francs.

The series of transactions is demonstrated in Exhibit 21.10. A trader borrows $1 million and agrees to repay $1.09 million one year later. Simultaneously, the trader sells the dollars for francs, buys a Swiss security, and sells the expected amount of francs at maturity for dollars one year forward. As indicated, the trader can earn a riskless profit of $31,776 for each $1 million borrowed. The profit is riskless because the trader has borrowed in one currency yet covered the transaction by selling the expected foreign exchange after investment for the original currency in the forward market. A profit is available because the interest rate differential between securities in the two countries is out of line with the spot-to-forward exchange rate differential. This series of trades is called **covered interest arbitrage.**[20]

If the exchange rates and interest rates were this far out of line and the large profit was available, arbitrageurs would quickly negotiate the same series of transactions until prices moved back in line to eliminate (net of transactions costs) the riskless return. Interest rate parity exists when covered interest arbitrage profit potential is eliminated. Letting:

i_1 = annual interest rate in Country 1
i_2 = annual interest rate in Country 2
$s_{1,2}$ = spot exchange rate equal to the number of units of Country 2's currency for one unit of Country 1's currency
$f_{1,2}$ = 1-year forward exchange rate equal to the number of units of Country 2's currency for one unit of Country 1's currency

interest rate parity implies: $\dfrac{1 + i_2}{1 + i_1}\left(\dfrac{s_{1,2}}{f_{1,2}}\right) = 1$, or   **(21.3)**

$$\frac{i_2 - i_1}{1 + i_1} = \frac{f_{1,2} - s_{1,2}}{s_{1,2}} \qquad \textbf{(21.4)}$$

The equilibrium condition, expressed in Equation 21.4, suggests that the forward exchange rate differential as a fraction of the spot rate should equal the interest rate differential relative to 1 plus an interest factor to eliminate arbitrage profits. If i_1 is 9 percent, i_2 is 10 percent, and $s_{1,2}$ is 1.7 in the previous example, then $f_{1,2}$ should equal 1.7156:

$$\frac{0.10 - 0.09}{1 + 0.09} = \frac{f_{1,2} - 1.7}{1.7}, \text{ or}$$

$$f_{1,2} = 1.7156$$

Conceptually, if interest rates are relatively low in one country, that country's currency should sell at a forward premium. Any gain from borrowing at low rates and investing at higher rates (0.01/1.09) is exactly offset (0.0156/1.7) when the borrower attempts to sell the investment proceeds forward at a premium price.

PRICE RISK WITH FOREIGN CURRENCIES

International banks actively trade most foreign currencies. They buy and sell foreign exchange for customers by request, to hedge transactions for customers and themselves, to earn arbitrage profits by taking advantage of temporary price discrepancies, and to trade speculatively for their own account. Foreign exchange gains often supplement normal operating earnings for many banks. Risk managers continually assess a bank's exposure to the risk of loss from these trading positions associated with adverse changes in foreign exchange rates. Regulators refer to this as price risk and require large banks to formally measure their

---

[20]If the calculation showed a loss, reversing the direction of transactions by borrowing in the opposite currency and converting it in a similar fashion could make a profit.

COVERED INTEREST ARBITRAGE

2. Convert dollars to francs at $1 = 1.7 francs

3. Invest in Swiss securities yielding 10 percent

$$\left[\frac{\$1,090,000}{1 + 0.09}\right](1.7) = 1.7 \text{ million francs} \qquad \left[\frac{\$1,090,000}{1 + 0.09}\right](1.7)(1.10) = 1.87 \text{ million francs}$$

$$\left[\frac{\$1,090,000}{1 + 0.09}\right] = \$1,000,000 \qquad \left[\frac{\$1,090,000}{1 + 0.09}\right]\frac{(1.7)(1.10)}{1.667} = \$1,121,776$$

1. Borrow dollars at 9 percent

4. Sell francs for dollars one year forward at $1 = 1.667 francs

Sample Transaction: Borrow $1,000,000.
1. Borrow $1,000,000 at 9 percent; agree to repay $1,090,000 in one year.
2. Convert $1,000,000 to 1.7 million francs in spot market at $1 = 1.7 francs.
3. Invest 1.7 million francs in 1-year security yielding 10 percent; will receive 1.87 million francs after 1 year.
4. Sell 1.87 million francs 1 year forward for $1,121,776 at $1 = 1.667 francs.
Net profit = $1,121,776 − $1,090,000 = $31,776

exposure or sensitivity to market risk from all potential price moves. In terms of measuring this risk, a bank can identify its net exposure in each currency much like that in Equation 21.1 except that the amounts represent the value of a bank's long positions and short positions in each currency from these speculative positions or customer positions in each of the currencies. The gain or loss can be similarly measured by Equation 21.2. Regulators, however, require that the largest banks perform a value-at-risk (VAR) analysis of their entire trading positions that they then require capital to support.

SUMMARY

Large international banks effectively operate as commercial banks and investment banks. They accept foreign deposits and make loans to foreign borrowers. They act as brokers, dealers, and underwriters in negotiating Eurobond issues, floating-rate note issues, interest rate and currency swaps, and foreign equity issues. Many banks located outside the United States are more heavily capitalized and thus better able to compete globally. The largest U.S. banks, in turn, are aggressively pursuing business outside the U.S. as well as within the U.S. Citigroup and J.P. Morgan Chase, for example, have well-defined strategies to actively pursue commercial and investment banking business in Western Europe and elsewhere and generate a considerable portion of their overall profits from activities outside the U.S.

Because of large losses on international loans and the difficulty in assessing country risk, many large banks have substantially reduced their international commercial loan exposure. This is true for both U.S. and non-U.S. banks who have experienced substantial losses in recent years. In 2002, there is real concern that Japanese banks do not have adequate control over asset quality even within Japan. As such, Japanese banks have largely withdrawn from engaging in business outside of Asia. Many U.S. banks that pursue business outside the U.S. prefer to do mergers, acquisitions, and security underwriting rather than straight commercial lending.

International banks operate a wide range of offices to conduct foreign banking business. These offices generally provide access to the Eurocurrency markets and Eurocredits. Loans to foreign governments and businesses entail two additional risks compared with loans to domestic borrowers. Country risk involves both economic risk that the borrower's ability to repay may deteriorate, and political risk that the underlying government may simply renege on contracted debt service payments. International loans may also involve foreign exchange risk when lenders receive payment in a currency other than their own. Banks also assume foreign exchange and price risk if they hold unequal amounts of assets and liabilities denominated in different currencies or have trading positions where long and short positions are not equal. As such, changes in exchange rates can sharply increase or lower bank profits and the market value of stockholders' equity.

QUESTIONS

1. Discuss the differences between Eurocurrency, Eurobonds, and Eurocredits.

2. Why were international banking facilities created? How do they differ from Edge Act and Agreement corporations?

3. Explain how you would measure country risk in international lending. Can you get a precise statistical measure?

4. Identify several large foreign institutions that are major lenders in the United States. Do any have a basic competitive advantage over U.S. banks? Explain why.

5. Which of the following types of foreign banking operations would best suit the circumstance described?
   a. A major customer of a U.S. bank requests a loan to finance growing export activity in Mexico.
   b. Management notices that an increasing number of its business customers have located offices in Moscow. Although the bank cannot justify a permanent office in Moscow, it wants to provide loans to these international activities.
   c. Indonesia has just announced the privatization of many small banks. Your bank is going to buy one of the banks to establish a local lending and deposit base.

6. What is a bankers acceptance? Explain by setting up an example of how one is created.

7. U.S. banks can underwrite corporate bonds and stocks outside the United States, but not in the United States. Does this seem reasonable? Why do you think such a restriction exists?

8. Explain how the forward market for foreign exchange differs from the spot market. When will forward exchange rates be at a premium or discount to spot exchange rates?

9. Suppose that the following exchange rates and interest rates prevail:

   Spot exchange rate: $1 = 121 yen

   1-year forward rate: $1 = 130 yen

   1-year interest rates: U.S. = 5.54%, Japan = 6.98%

   Can a trader earn covered interest arbitrage profits? If not, explain why not. If possible, determine what the likely directional impact on each rate would be if arbitrageurs took advantage of the profit potential.

10. Assume that the forward exchange rate is for 90 days forward and the interest rates are annualized 90-day rates in Question 9. Can a trader earn covered interest arbitrage profits?

11. Suppose that Commerce Bank in Poland holds $400 in assets and $1,000 in liabilities denominated in dollars. The home currency is the zloty, and the current spot exchange rate is $1 = 145 zlotys.

   a. What is the bank's net exposure in dollars?

   b. Will the bank gain or lose if the spot exchange rate changes to $1 = 152 zlotys? Calculate the gain or loss.

   c. Will the bank gain or lose if the spot exchange rate changes to $1 = 141 zlotys? Calculate the gain or loss.

22

FINANCIAL INSTITUTION MERGERS AND ACQUISITIONS

Mergers and acquisitions continue to be a significant force in the restructuring of the financial services industry. The largest U.S. institutions continue to buy smaller institutions such that the number of banks has declined from 14,451 at the end of 1982 to only 8,080 by year-end 2001. During this same period, however, the total number of branch offices grew from 34,791 to 64,087. Fewer banks control a greater fraction of banking resources. Banks with more than $10 billion in assets make up less than one percent of banks but control over 70 percent of bank assets. These same trends have occurred outside the U.S. as well, although most countries don't have as many independent banks as the U.S. does.

Many factors have led to the merger mania in U.S. banking. The 1980s and 1990s experienced unprecedented growth in the economy. After a large number of failures in the 1980s, banks experienced record profits from 1990 through 2001. Stock prices soared and this provided valuable currency for banks in acquisitions. Most importantly, however, interstate branching restrictions were removed and the Riegle-Neal Interstate Branching and Efficiency Act became fully effective by June 1997. Prior to the Riegle-Neal Act, each state determined the degree to which banks could branch across state lines, and many states did not allow interstate branching. Riegle-Neal allowed for nationwide interstate branching. Savings institutions, on the other hand, have historically been allowed to branch across state lines. The impact on the liberalization of interstate branching restrictions can be seen in Exhibit 22.1. The number of banks with interstate branches and the number of interstate branches of commercial banks increased significantly while the number of banks declined as they collapsed independent banks into branches of the home office. The number of interstate savings institutions branches, with their more liberal interstate branching laws, actually declined somewhat until finally increasing again in 2001.

The liberalization of branching restrictions combined with a rapidly growing economy provided banks the opportunity to consolidate and grow dramatically in size. At the end of 1996, prior to the enactment of Riegle-Neal, the largest U.S. bank was Chase Manhattan Corp., ranked number 17 in the world by assets ($333.8 billion). The next largest U.S. banks were: Citicorp, ranked number 21, J.P. Morgan & Co.

• EXHIBIT 22.1

NUMBER OF INTERSTATE BRANCHES OPERATED BY FDIC-INSURED COMMERCIAL
BANKS AND SAVINGS INSTITUTIONS: 1994–2001

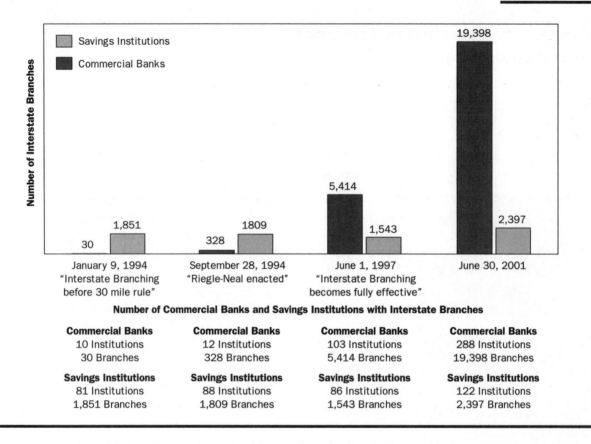

January 9, 1994	September 28, 1994	June 1, 1997	June 30, 2001
"Interstate Branching before 30 mile rule"	"Riegle-Neal enacted"	"Interstate Branching becomes fully effective"	

Number of Commercial Banks and Savings Institutions with Interstate Branches

Commercial Banks	**Commercial Banks**	**Commercial Banks**	**Commercial Banks**
10 Institutions	12 Institutions	103 Institutions	288 Institutions
30 Branches	328 Branches	5,414 Branches	19,398 Branches
Savings Institutions	**Savings Institutions**	**Savings Institutions**	**Savings Institutions**
81 Institutions	88 Institutions	86 Institutions	122 Institutions
1,851 Branches	1,809 Branches	1,543 Branches	2,397 Branches

Inc., ranked number 29, and BankAmerica Corp, ranked number 30. At the end of 1996, six of the ten largest banks in the world were headquartered in Japan. By the end of 2001, the largest banking company in the world was Citigroup at just under one-trillion dollars in assets, and three of the largest ten banking companies in the world were U.S.-based. Details on different global banks can be found in Chapter 21.

Although the pace of acquisitions slowed in 2000–2001, a few large deals still occurred. Chase Manhattan Corp. acquired J.P. Morgan & Co. in December of 2000, Firstar Corp. acquired U.S. Bancorp in February of 2001, First Union Corporation acquired Wachovia Corporation in September of 2001, and Citigroup announced its acquisition of Great Western in May 2002. Acquisitions have also moved outside traditional product lines and across international borders. Exhibit 22.2 lists the largest line of business acquisitions from 1998 to 2001. Most noticeably, banks and investment banks were slowly combining.

■

With the rapidly changing competitive environment, senior management is constantly evaluating whether the firm should acquire other firms, or whether it should position itself for sale. Each of the transactions listed in Exhibits 22.2 and 22.3 was motivated by strategic decisions to expand the firm's domestic and international presence as well as expand product and service lines to enter non-traditional fee-generating businesses. Banks that buy securities firms gain instant market share and credibility. More importantly, the fees and

EXHIBIT 22.2

TOP LINE-OF-BUSINESS ACQUISITIONS ANNOUNCED IN **1998–2001**

Buyer Name	Seller Name	Announce Date	Assets Purchased	Type Of Transaction
Chase Manhattan Corp., New York	Morgan Stanley Dean Witter & Co., New York	7-May-98	400,000	Trust Services
Bank of New York Co. Inc.	Charles Schwab Corp San Francisco	18-Apr-01	348,000	Trust Services
Washington Mutual Inc Seattle	FleetBoston Financial Corp Boston	2-Apr-01	143,900	Mortgage Banking Oper.
Citigroup, Inc. New York	Associates First Capital Corp. Irving, Tex.	6-Sep-00	87,701	Specialty Finance
Chase Manhattan Corp., New York	PNC Bank Corp., Pittsburgh	4-Aug-98	55,000	Trust Services
FleetBoston Financial Corp Boston	Liberty Financial Cos Boston	4-Jun-01	51,000	Investment Advisory
Mellon Financial Corp Pittsburgh	Standish, Ayer & Wood Boston	26-Apr-01	41,000	Investment Advisory
Investors Financial Services	BankBoston Corp.	20-Jul-98	41,000	Trust Services
Wells Fargo & Co. San Francisco	First Union Corp. Charlotte, NC	28-Jun-00	35,700	Servicing Portfolio
Chase Manhattan Corp., New York	BT Funds Management Sydney	14-Sep-00	33,380	Trust Services
GMAC Mortgage Corp., PA	Wells Fargo & Co., San Francisco	2-Apr-98	28,100	Mortgage Banking Oper.
State Street Corp. Boston	Nationwide Mutual Insurance Co Columbus, Ohio	17-Jul-01	25,000	Investment Advisory
PNC Bank Corp., Pittsburgh	Midland Loan Services, MO	28-Jan-98	25,000	Mortgage Servicing
Chase Manhattan Corp., New York	First Tennessee National Corp. Memphis	19-Oct-00	20,000	Trust Services
J.P. Morgan Chase & Co., New York	Advanta Corp Spring House, PA	8-Jan-01	15,800	Mortgage Banking Oper.
Bank of New York Co. Inc.	FleetBoston Financial Corp Boston	6-Mar-01	15,700	Trust Services
Bank of New York Co.	LTCB Trust Co.	22-Jul-99	15,600	Trust Services
GMAC Mortgage Corp.	Mellon Financial Corp.	1-Apr-99	14,000	Mortgage Servicing
First Union Corp. Charlotte, NC	First Albany Companies Inc. Albany, NY	9-May-00	11,400	Securities Brokerage
Wachovia Corp.	Offitbank Holdings Inc.	13-May-99	11,000	Trust Services
National Australia Bank Ltd.	Bank One Corp.	4-Mar-99	10,000	Mortgage Servicing
Unionbancal Corp.	Imperial Bancorp	23-Apr-99	10,000	Trust Services
Bank of New York Co.	Royal Bank of Scotland Group	23-Mar-99	9,500	Trust Services
Chase Manhattan Corp., New York	Colonial BancGroup, Inc. Montgomery, Ala.	16-Feb-00	9,000	Servicing Portfolio
Bank of New York Co. Inc. New York	Bank of America Corp. Charlotte, NC	23-Aug-00	9,000	Trust Services
Bank of New York Co.	First American Corp., Nashville, Tenn.	28-Jul-98	8,000	Trust Services
Chase Manhattan Corp., New York	Robert Fleming Holdings Limited London	11-Apr-00	N/A	Investment Advisory
ReliaStar Financial Corp.	Pilgrim Capital Corp.	22-Jul-99	7,600	Investment Advisory
Bank One Corp Chicago	Wachovia Corp Winston-Salem, NC	9-Apr-01	7,500	Credit Card Portfolios/Oper.
Wells Fargo & Co. San Francisco	FleetBoston Financial Corp. Boston	5-Jul-00	7,500	Servicing Portfolio
Washington Mutual, Inc. Seattle	PNC Financial Services Group Pittsburgh	2-Oct-00	7,000	Mortgage Banking Oper.
Fleet Financial Group Inc., Boston	Sanwa Bank Ltd., Tokyo	23-Nov-98	6,500	Specialty Finance
MBNA Corp. Wilmington, Del.	First Union Corp. Charlotte, NC	14-Aug-00	5,500	Credit Card Portfolios/Oper.
Ameritrade Holding Corp Omaha	Deutsche Bank AG Frankfurt	31-Jul-01	6,300	Securities Brokerage
Coast to Coast Financial Corp., Nevada	FirstPlus Financial Group, Dallas	15-Oct-98	6,000	Mortgage Servicing
J.P. Morgan Chase & Co. New York	Mellon Financial Corp Pittsburgh	21-Dec-01	6,000	Securities Brokerage
PNC Financial Services Group Pittsburgh	FleetBoston Financial Corp. Boston	7-Jun-00	5,200	Servicing Portfolio
National Australia Bank Ltd., Melbourne	People's Mutual Holdings, Bridgeport, Conn.	3-Dec-98	5,000	Mortgage Servicing
National Australia Bank Ltd., Melbourne, Australia	Colonial BancGroup, Inc. Montgomery, Ala.	17-Jul-00	5,000	Servicing Portfolio
Chase Manhattan Corp., New York	Fuji Bank, Limited Tokyo	19-Sep-00	5,000	Trust Services
Chase Manhattan Corp., New York	Dai-Ichi Kangyo Bank, Ltd. Tokyo	27-Dec-00	5,000	Trust Services
Bank One Corp., Columbus, Ohio	Chevy Chase Bank, Chevy Chase, MD	3-Sep-98	4,900	Credit Card Portfolios/Oper.
Travelers Group Inc., New York	J.P. Morgan & Co. Inc., New York	23-Jun-98	4,800	Investment Advisory
Ocwen Financial Corp West Palm Beach, Fla.	New Century Financial Corp Irvine, Calif.	1-Mar-01	4,800	Servicing Portfolio
First Defiance Financial Corp., Ohio	Leader Mortgage Co., Ohio	13-Apr-98	4,700	Mortgage Banking Oper.
GreenPoint Financial Corp., New York	Headlands Mortgage Co., Larkspur, Calif.	8-Dec-98	4,400	Mortgage Banking Oper.
Wintrust Financial Corp Lake Forest, Ill.	Wayne Hummer Inc Chicago	26-Dec-01	4,100	Investment Advisory
Investor Group	BankAmerica Corp., San Francisco	19-Nov-98	4,000	Investment Advisory
City National Corp., Beverly Hills, Calif.	North American Trust Co., Calif.	24-Sep-98	4,000	Trust Services
Bank of New York Co. Inc. New York	Dai-Ichi Kangyo Bank, Ltd. Tokyo	15-Jun-00	4,000	Trust Services

SOURCE: *The Amercan Banker* and Thomson Financial Sheshunoff Information Services (www.sheshunoff.com)

■ EXHIBIT 22.3

LARGEST COMPLETED BANK MERGERS 1998–2001

Rank 1998–2001	Rank in Year	Buyer	Seller	Closed	Price at closing	Closing Price to equity
1	1	NationsBank Corp., Charlotte, NC	BankAmerica Corp., San Francisco	30-Sep-98	$42,215,100	2.09
2	2	Travelers Group, New York	Citicorp, New York	7-Oct-98	$38,197,700	1.74
3	3	Norwest Corp., Minneapolis	Wells Fargo & Co. San Francisco	2-Nov-98	$32,273,300	2.42
4	1	Chase Manhattan Corp., New York	J.P. Morgan & Co. New York	31-Dec-00	$29,524,804	2.31
5	1	Firstar Corp. Milwaukee	U.S. Bancorp Minneapolis	27-Feb-01	$22,294,488	2.58
6	4	First Union Corp., Charlotte, NC	CoreStates Financial Corp., Philadelphia	27-Apr-98	$20,202,400	6.14
7	5	Banc One Corp., Columbus, Ohio	First Chicago NBD Corp.	1-Oct-98	$19,092,200	2.24
8	6	NationsBank Corp., Charlotte, NC	Barnett Banks Inc., Jacksonville, Fla.	9-Jan-98	$14,700,000	3.71
9	2	First Union Corporation, Charlotte, NC	Wachovia Corporation, Winston-Salem, NC	1-Sep-01	14,231,883	2.18
10	1	Fleet Financial Group Inc.	BankBoston Corp.	1-Oct-99	$13,037,000	2.54
11	2	HSBC USA Inc.	Republic New York Corp.	31-Dec-99	$9,850,000	2.33
12	3	Deutsche Bank AG	Bankers Trust Corp.	4-Jun-99	$9,378,700	1.96
13	4	Firstar Corp.	Mercantile Bancorp.	20-Sep-99	$8,301,400	2.67
14	7	Star Banc Corp., Cincinnati	Firstar Corp., Milwaukee	19-Nov-98	$8,106,900	4.32
15	8	National City Corp., Cleveland	First of America Bank Corp., Kalamazoo, Mich.	31-Mar-98	$7,827,300	4.09
16	3	FleetBoston Financial Corp. Boston	Summit Bancorp Princeton, NJ	1-Mar-01	7,427,644	2.42
17	9	Washington Mutual Inc., Seattle	H.F. Ahmanson & Co., Irwindale, Calif.	1-Oct-98	$6,320,300	1.69
18	4	Fifth Third Bancorp Cincinnati	Old Kent Financial Corp. Grand Rapids, Mich.	2-Apr-01	5,513,703	3.10
19	5	Amsouth Bancorp.	First American Corp.	1-Oct-99	$5,190,400	2.89
20	10	Bank One Corp., Columbus, Ohio	First Commerce Corp., New Orleans	12-Jun-98	$3,464,100	3.94
21	2	Charles Schwab Corp. (The) San Francisco	U.S. Trust Corp. New York	31-May-00	3,068,062	8.45
22	3	Wells Fargo & Co. San Francisco	First Security Corp. Salt Lake City	25-Oct-00	2,997,025	1.71
23	5	ABN Amro North America Inc. Chicago	Michigan National Corp. Farmington Hills, Mich.	31-Mar-01	2,750,000	1.94
24	11	Regions Financial Corp., Birmingham, Ala.	First Commercial Corp., Little Rock, Ark.	31-Jul-98	$2,628,900	4.13
25	6	Fifth Third Bancorp	CNB Bancshares	29-Oct-99	$2,470,300	4.70
26	6	BNP Paribas Paris	BancWest Corp. Honolulu	19-Dec-01	2,451,132	2.04
27	7	Washington Mutual Inc. Seattle	Bank United Corp. Houston	9-Feb-01	2,393,383	2.51
28	12	First American Corp., Nashville	Deposit Guaranty Corp., Jackson, Miss.	30-Apr-98	$2,382,400	3.71
29	13	Union Planters Corp., Memphis	Magna Group, St. Louis	30-Jun-98	$2,117,000	3.17
30	8	Royal Bank of Canada, Toronto	Centura Banks Inc. Rocky Mount, NC	5-Jun-01	2,092,241	2.10
31	9	Citigroup Inc. New York	European American Bank Uniondale, NY	17-Jul-01	1,950,000	2.72
32	14	California Federal Bank, San Francisco	Golden State Bancorp, Glendale, Calif.	11-Sep-98	$1,800,000	1.66
33	4	National Commerce Bancorp., Memphis	CCB Financial Corp., Durham, NC	3-Jul-00	1,541,022	2.13
34	5	Citizens Financial Group Providence, R.I.	UST Corp. Boston	11-Jan-00	1,406,839	2.51
35	10	Comerica Inc. Detroit	Imperial Bancorp Inglewood, Calif.	29-Jan-01	1,315,624	2.51
36	15	Astoria Financial Corp., Lake Success, NY	Long Island Bancorp, Melville, NY	30-Sep-98	$1,232,200	2.03
37	11	New York Community Bancorp, Flushing	Richmond County Financial Corp New York	31-Jul-01	1,219,079	3.56
38	6	M&T Bank Corp., Buffalo	Keystone Financial Harrisburg, PA	6-Oct-00	1,186,476	2.10
39	7	Wells Fargo & Co. San Francisco	National Bancorp of Alaska, Anchorage	14-Jul-00	1,183,495	2.57
40	12	BB&T Corp. Winston-Salem, NC	F & M National Corp. Winchester, VA	9-Aug-01	1,177,304	2.82
41	8	BB&T Corp. Winston-Salem, NC	One Valley Bancorp, Inc. Charleston, WV	6-Jul-00	1,132,006	1.95
42	16	National City Corp., Cleveland	Fort Wayne National Corp., Indiana	30-Mar-98	$1,048,500	3.42
43	7	U.S. Bancorp	Western Bancorp	15-Nov-99	$1,047,400	2.84
44	9	E*Trade Group Palo Alto, Calif.	Telebanc Financial Corp. Arlington, VA	12-Jan-00	1,040,226	1.82
45	17	North Fork Bancorp, Melville, NY	New York Bancorp	27-Mar-98	$1,036,000	5.81
46	18	First Hawaiian Inc., Honolulu	BancWest Corp., San Francisco	1-Nov-98	$1,032,800	2.51
47	19	M&T Bank Corp., Buffalo	Onbancorp, Syracuse, NY	31-Mar-98	$1,002,900	3.02
48	20	Charter One Financial Inc., Cleveland	Albank Financial Corp., Albany, NY	30-Nov-98	$963,100	10.43
49	21	H.F. Ahmanson & Co., Irwindale, Calif.	Coast Savings, Newport Beach, Calif.	13-Feb-98	$949,200	1.85
50	8	Charter One Financial Inc.	St. Paul Bancorp	1-Oct-99	$945,200	1.81

SOURCE: *The American Banker* and Thomson Financial Sheshunoff Information Services (www.sheshunoff.com)

other noninterest income generated represent a potential source of profit growth that will off-set stable or declining net interest margins.

Very large banks have been the order of business as the largest banks merge. Citigroup, formed by the merger of Citicorp and Travelers, had around $1.1 trillion in assets by year-end 2001. J.P. Morgan Chase, created by the mergers of Chemical Bank with Manufacturers Hanover, which was acquired by Chase Manhattan, which then acquired J.P. Morgan & Co., reported around $800 billion in assets. The new BankAmerica, which was created by numer-ous acquisitions including the purchase of Boatmen's, Montgomery Securities, Barnett Banks, and finally BankAmerica by NationsBank, operated as a $640 billion organization at the end of 2001. Additional acquisitions along with internal assets growth at reasonable rates will likely produce more $1 trillion organizations in the near future.

Mergers among foreign banks and cross-border mergers are increasingly common as well. Banco Santander and Banco Bilbao Vizcaya, two of Spain's largest financial institutions, have a strong market share after acquiring banks in Latin America. ABN Amro and ING Group, two large Dutch financial institutions, have been buying banks and securities firms through-out Europe and the United States. Deutsche Bank AG, Germany, with the acquisition of Bankers Trust (U.S.) in 1999, created the world's largest banking organization at the time. Which bank is actually the largest, Citigroup or Deutsche Bank, depends on how one meas-ures the banks—by asset size or market capitalization, and if one measures the holding com-pany or just the bank. Record profits during the 1990s, and the resulting strong market values, will sharply increase the likelihood that U.S. banks will expand overseas and over-seas banks will expand in the U.S. Citigroup, J.P. Morgan, Chase, and BankAmerica have sig-nificant international operations and will continue to look to Europe. HSBC, ABN Amro, and others already have substantial operations in the U.S. and will likely expand there.

The most fundamental issue faced by a bank's board of directors and senior managers is how to maximize shareholder value. One important facet of the associated strategic plan is whether the bank should buy other banks, remain independent, or position itself for sale. Each alternative has dramatically different implications regarding future growth in earnings, the security of employees' jobs, and the nature of services provided the bank's customers.

During the 1970s and early 1980s, many individuals chartered banks or purchased groups of community banks in anticipation of selling the package to a large multibank holding com-pany. Because of restrictions against interstate banking and branching, it was a seller's mar-ket, and those willing to part with the franchise could often extract large premiums. The latter part of the 1980s brought about a reevaluation of acquisition strategies. With the large number of bank and thrift failures, acquirers had several options to enter new markets. They could buy a failed institution outright or simply purchase its deposits, purchase a healthy firm, or enter via a new charter. More restrictive regulatory capital requirements, in turn, raised the cost of doing business.

Many banks with problem assets, and especially smaller banks with limited access to new capital, discovered that becoming part of a financial conglomerate offered an attractive alter-native to remaining independent. In many cases, it was their only alternative. In the early 1990s, it was a buyer's market in which banks with adequate capital could dictate terms. Premiums subsequently declined as acquirers cherry-picked the best deals. With the boom in bank stock prices throughout the 1990s, large banks could issue new capital to finance the purchase of additional banks and nonbank institutions. By early 2002, banks were coming off eleven years of record profits. Capital was at historically high levels and it was once again a seller's market. Some merger prices exceeded four and even six times the seller's book value, a historically high premium. The largest completed deals from 1998 to 2001 are listed in Exhibit 22.3. As one might guess by the number of large mergers, many considered this to be "merger mania." There were several record-setting deals in 1998—including Charter One Financial Inc., Cleveland's acquisition of Albank Financial Corp., Albany, NY at 10.4 times equity; Charles Schwab Corp.'s purchase of U.S. Trust Corp. at 8.5 times book equity; and First Union's acquisition of CoreStates at 6.14 times book value—that are historically high premiums to book value.

This chapter examines the merger and acquisition phenomenon in recent years. It focuses on three key issues: Why are mergers increasingly common and how do mergers add value? How do you value a bank for acquisition or sale? What nonmonetary considerations affect the valuation and post-merger success of the new firm?

Bankers are sensitive to the issue of size. Community bank employees often take pride in annual asset growth and working for the biggest bank in town. Size connotes market power and influence. Why else do bankers continually build larger and taller buildings than competitors? Regional banks also put a premium on being the biggest bank in a state or region, and ultimately reaching the top 50 or 100 banks in the country. In the old days, banks would try to bulk up their balance sheets just prior to the end of each quarter when they filed financial reports so that assets would be as large as possible. The largest regional banks, labeled super regionals, and money center banks similarly compare their size and growth to comparable institutions and multinational banks throughout the world. From senior management's perspective, being among the largest institutions means increased compensation and prestige.

Today, with interstate banking made permissible by the Riegle-Neal Interstate Branching and Efficiency Act and the repeal of Glass-Steagall by the Gramm-Leach-Bliley Act, the push is to have a nationwide or even globalwide bank and to provide a full range of financial products. The NationsBank-BankAmerica merger produced the first large-scale, coast-to-coast banking franchise in the U.S. and the Norwest-Wells Fargo deal produced the second—doing significant business in all 50 states. The merger of Bank One and First Chicago produced one of the largest credit card banks. NationsBank and BankAmerica both purchased securities firms in 1997, dramatically expanding the potential services these organizations could offer. The merger between Citicorp and Travelers produced the first large-scale combination of insurance underwriting and banking—a financial institution with a global reach, a commercial and investment bank, and insurance.

Why is size so important? Historically, managers of the largest banks in a market had considerable influence and received extraordinary attention. They were compensated well, based to some degree on the size of the empire they controlled rather than bank profitability. They served on community, state, and national boards that set policy and lobbied legislators. The traditional benefits of economies of scale and scope in business have been:

- Size, product diversity, and brand identification, which generate benefits from cross-selling more products to more customers

- A reduction in the large fixed costs required for brand identification, distribution of a large variety of products and services, and a massive technology expenditure requirement

- Enhanced operating leverage that results from spreading fixed overhead cost across a larger operating and revenue base

- Reduced earnings risk, which enhances the value of a franchise by creating a more diversified product and earnings base

Even though the rapid consolidation has improved efficiency ratios in the U.S. banking industry, these benefits have yet to be realized by the largest banks as compared with other smaller banks.[1] The evidence, however, suggests that *average unit costs* are flat across different-sized banks.[2] Size essentially represents prestige and financial power.

Summary performance measures are presented for different-sized banks in Exhibit 22.4. With the exception of the efficiency ratio for the smallest banks, the average efficiency ratio and net interest margin for banks in each size category have decreased dramatically since 1992. This result arises from a general improvement in overhead expense control and noninterest income with a general decline in interest margins. Contrary to popular belief, however, the best overall performance based on these general performance ratios was generated by banks in the $100 million to $10 billion asset range. Performance for the smallest banks ranks the lowest, while banks with $1 to $10 billion in assets produce the best ROAs, followed closely by the banks with $300 to $500 million and $500 million to $1 billion in assets. Banks with $1 to $10 billion in assets produce the highest ROEs, again followed closely by banks in the $300 to $500 million range and the largest banks. The largest banks' performance falls in the middle in terms of performance with one notable exception—the generation of noninterest income.

After the Riegle-Neal Act, many banks have consolidated their bank activities. The dramatic reduction in the number of banks in the 1990s is primarily a result of a bank holding company or parent bank converting a bank, in which they own 100 percent, to a branch. Exhibit 22.5 shows the dramatic reduction in the number of banks and corresponding increase in the number of branches. Formally, a merger is a combination of two or more separate enterprises typically involving the issuance of new securities. A *consolidation* is the combination of two or more separate enterprises in which there is no change in ownership, as when an out-of-state bank collapses its independent banking operations into a branch of the home office. An *acquisition* occurs when one firm purchases the stock of another firm. There is a clear buyer and seller in the transaction terms and structure of the surviving entity. Prior to the 1980s, geographic restrictions limited where and how banks could compete. Interstate branching and banking was prohibited. Many states further restricted in-state branching, limiting it to either local counties or cities or prohibiting it altogether. Mergers and acquisitions were a natural response to penetrate new markets, particularly in states with no branching. Without branching, the only way that banks could expand was via multibank holding companies, which were formed to acquire banks in different markets. During this period, the demand for acquisitions raised serious concerns that some markets would be controlled by monopolistic competitors. Regulators evaluated all transactions closely to ensure that the acquiring firm did not gain too large a market share in any geographic area. (See Contemporary Issues: Merger Antitrust Analysis.)

Exhibit 22.6 documents trends in the number of banks from mergers, failures, and new charters from 1980 through 2001. As discussed earlier, the number of deals increased throughout most of the 1990s and is high relative to the previous decade. Surprisingly, as the number of mergers slowed in the late 1990s, the number of new charters increased. In fact, the ratio of mergers to new charters is now about 2 to 1. By the end of 2001, both merger activity as well as new charters slowed significantly. Still, the most dramatic impact has been on the consolidation of assets and deposits at the largest banks. Exhibit 22.7 shows that from 1993 to 2001, the proportion of assets controlled by banks with more than $10 billion in assets has increased from 43 percent to over 70 percent. Similar deposit consolidation has occurred with the largest banks' share of deposits increasing from 40 percent to more than

---

[1] Recall from Chapter 3 that the efficiency ratio is noninterest expense/net operating income and measures a bank's ability to control overhead expenses relative to income.

[2] There is little evidence that scale economies exist beyond very small banks. Humphrey (1990) documents the results of recent studies and concludes that "the average cost curve in banking reflects a relatively flat U-shape at the firm level, with significant economies at small banks, but small and significant diseconomies at the largest [banks]." Later studies have documented economies of scale and scope for banks as large as $1 billion to $2 billion in assets.

EXHIBIT 22.4

SUMMARY PERFORMANCE MEASURES BY COMMERCIAL BANK SIZE: 1992–2001

Bank Size	< $100M		$100M to $300M		$300M to $500M		$500M to $1B		$1B to $10B		> $10B		All Banks	
Year	2001	1992	2001	1992	2001	1992	2001	1992	2001	1992	2001	1992	2001	1992
Number of institutions	4,486	8,292	2,350	2,141	509	397	335	252	320	329	80	51	8,080	11,462
Total assets (in billions)	221.6	346.0	396.8	350.9	195.0	151.9	227.6	177.4	915.4	1,034.2	4,612.8	1,445.3	6,569.2	3,505.7
Total deposits (in billions)	187.7	306.5	331.2	308.3	158.7	130.3	178.5	148.6	625.0	787.9	2,910.5	1,017.1	4,391.6	2,698.7
Net income (in millions)	1,912	3,487	4,364	3,611	2,351	1,445	2,607	1,611	11,518	10,322	51,559	11,510	74,310	31,987
% of unprofitable institutions	11.19	6.83	3.40	5.93	1.77	8.06	2.09	7.54	3.12	11.25	1.25	7.84	7.54	6.85
% of institutions with earn gains	49.53	78.69	63.28	81.83	71.91	75.82	71.04	80.56	69.06	79.33	62.50	86.27	56.73	79.27
Performance ratios (%)														
Return on equity	8.07	11.10	11.62	12.60	13.41	12.26	12.38	12.33	13.77	13.74	13.43	13.33	13.10	12.98
Return on assets	0.91	1.04	1.16	1.06	1.28	0.98	1.20	0.93	1.31	1.02	1.13	0.81	1.16	0.93
Equity capital ratio	10.90	9.38	9.83	8.48	9.45	8.06	9.63	7.75	9.76	7.68	8.77	6.62	9.09	7.51
Net interest margin	4.23	4.74	4.35	4.71	4.37	4.72	4.39	4.83	4.31	4.71	3.71	3.94	3.90	4.41
Yield on earning assets	7.83	8.55	7.93	8.41	7.87	8.32	7.90	8.32	7.76	8.19	7.06	8.62	7.29	8.43
Cost of funding earn assets	3.61	3.81	3.58	3.71	3.50	3.60	3.52	3.49	3.45	3.47	3.35	4.68	3.40	4.02
Earning assets to total assets	91.39	91.16	91.26	91.21	90.88	90.84	91.17	89.69	89.49	88.41	83.03	85.87	85.23	88.08
Efficiency ratio	69.59	66.85	63.70	64.98	62.14	63.82	62.07	64.36	55.75	62.53	56.83	65.96	57.72	64.68
Noninterest inc to earn assets	1.11	1.05	1.42	1.28	1.94	1.27	2.04	1.49	2.62	2.47	3.19	2.64	2.85	2.17
Noninterest exp to earn assets	3.74	3.90	3.71	3.92	3.98	3.87	4.07	4.13	4.02	4.59	4.07	4.42	4.03	4.33
LN&LS loss provision to assets	0.30	0.35	0.34	0.45	0.35	0.57	0.46	0.69	0.66	0.91	0.74	0.85	0.67	0.76
Asset Quality (%)														
Net charge-offs to LN&LS	0.34	0.57	0.38	0.64	0.40	0.75	0.48	0.96	1.03	1.38	1.06	1.57	0.94	1.27
Loss allow to Noncurr LN&LS	128.1	114.2	142.3	104.4	161.0	105.9	161.1	102.0	167.7	108.7	123.5	73.3	131.0	87.6
Loss allowance to LN&LS	1.41	1.79	1.39	1.80	1.40	1.85	1.55	2.12	1.79	2.77	1.97	3.16	1.85	2.68
Net LN&LS to deposits	71.11	57.22	75.93	61.35	78.91	67.21	82.95	69.51	88.72	76.10	89.68	80.87	87.06	73.28
Capital Ratios (%)														
Core capital (leverage) ratio	10.63	9.37	9.40	8.43	8.93	7.94	8.98	7.57	8.74	7.38	7.23	6.17	7.79	7.21
Tier 1 risk-based capital ratio	15.87	16.33	13.52	13.98	12.50	12.32	12.15	11.48	11.83	10.41	8.86	7.39	9.90	9.84
Total risk-based capital ratio	16.96	17.51	14.66	15.19	13.69	13.61	13.38	12.91	13.77	12.37	12.16	10.75	12.72	12.30

SOURCE: FDIC Statistics on Depository Institutions (SDI), www.fdic.gov (http://www3.fdic.gov/sdi/index.asp).

NOTE: M refers to million; B refers to billion.

· EXHIBIT 22.5

DECLINE IN THE NUMBER OF BANKS AND INCREASE IN THE
NUMBER OF BRANCHES: 1960–2001

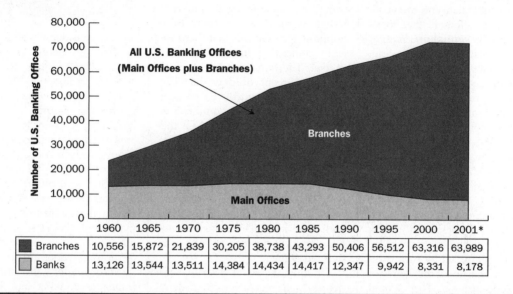

	1960	1965	1970	1975	1980	1985	1990	1995	2000	2001*
Branches	10,556	15,872	21,839	30,205	38,738	43,293	50,406	56,512	63,316	63,989
Banks	13,126	13,544	13,511	14,384	14,434	14,417	12,347	9,942	8,331	8,178

*Data for 2001 is as of June 2001.

SOURCE: FDIC Historical Statistics, http://www.fdic.gov/.

· EXHIBIT 22.6

CHANGES IN THE NUMBER OF BANKS THROUGH MERGERS,
FAILURES AND NEW CHARTERS: 1980–2001

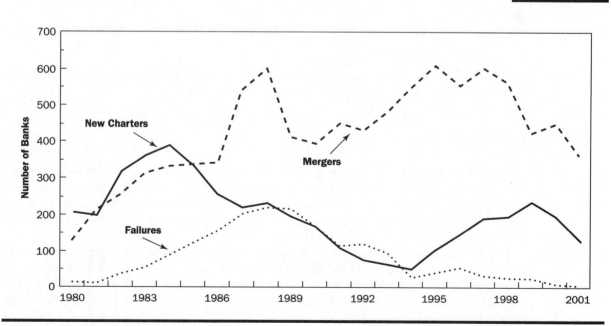

SOURCE: FDIC Historical Statistics, www.fdic.gov.

MERGER ANTITRUST ANALYSIS

There once was great concern that mergers might violate anti-trust provisions, which stipulate that firms should not gain control of a market and then pursue monopolistic pricing and output policies. The decision as to whether a proposed acquisition would be approved was largely based on a simple calculation.

The first step was to define the trade area of the target bank, such as the metropolitan area or county where the bank was located. The second step was to identify the number of competing firms within the area. Regulators then calculated a Herfindahl-Hirschmann Index (HHI), based on the fractional share of deposits controlled by each competitor, as a measure of the degree of market concentration. They would determine whether the transactions violated anticompetitive guidelines by comparing the index before and after the proposed acquisition. The standard was the 1,800/200 rule. If the post-acquisition HHI was less than 1,800 and increased by less than 200, the transaction would generally be approved.

The HHI is calculated by summing the squares of the market shares of each distinct competitor. Suppose, for example, that there are eight competing institutions in a market. The two largest control 25 and 15 percent of deposits. The remaining six control 10 percent each. The HHI would equal 625 + 225 + 600, or 1,450. If the largest and smallest banks were to merge, the post-merger HHI would equal 1,950 (1,225 + 225 + 500). According to the rule, the post-merger HHI would exceed 1,800 and the increase would equal 500, thereby violating both conditions. Thus, the transaction would be deemed anticompetitive and denied.

Of course, even if the rule was not violated, regulators could deny the transaction if competition would be better enhanced in other ways. It was often argued that the buyer would enter by new charter if it was not allowed to buy an existing firm. Because this would increase competition even more, the original acquisition would be denied.

In today's environment, regula-tors are considerably less aggressive in denying mergers and acquisitions. This perspective can be achieved in line with the numerical formula by lowering the existing market share figures. To do this, one need only expand the geographic area used to identify competitors. Alternatively, one could expand the types of firms viewed as competitors by including thrift and credit union deposits in the base deposit figure. Both of these adjustments have been made and the HHI standard has effectively been ignored so that fewer transactions are now denied.

Still, under the Riegle-Neal Interstate Banking and Branching Efficiency Act of 1994, mergers are subject to concentration limits. The limits generally mean that a merger cannot result in a bank controlling more than 20 to 30 percent of deposits in a state, with a 10 percent limit nationwide. Mergers are also subject to state laws and good community reinvestment (CRA) evaluations.

66 percent over the same period. In fact, only the largest and middle categories of banks saw an increase in the dollar amount of deposits over this period.

HOW DO MERGERS ADD VALUE?

It is not uncommon for two banks to announce a merger and for stock analysts to immediately praise the transaction as enhancing value or criticize it for making little sense for shareholders. Why the difference? Is it possible to get a quick sense of whether a transaction is inherently good or bad? The following discussion outlines various factors that both enhance value and diminish value.

It is easy to specify, in abstract terms, when a merger is beneficial. Simply compare the market value of the combined firm after the transaction with the sum of the market values of the independent firms prior to the transaction. If the combined value exceeds the pre-merger value, the merger is value-enhancing. Otherwise, value declines. The obvious question is, how does an acquisition increase the combined value?

Value is created in two ways. The first is that the combined bank might be able to immediately generate increased earnings (or cash flow) on a per share or otherwise comparable

• EXHIBIT 22.7

CONCENTRATION IN THE NUMBER OF BANKS, TOTAL ASSETS AND
TOTAL DEPOSITS BY BANK ASSET SIZE: 1993–2001

Number of Banks, Year-End

	Total	< $100 M	$100M–$1B	$1B–$10B	> $10B
1993	11,330	8,215	2,741	322	52
		72.51%	24.19%	2.84%	0.46%
1995	10,242	7,123	2,741	331	63
		69.55%	26.76%	3.23%	0.62%
1997	9,451	6,147	2,900	331	73
		65.04%	30.68%	3.50%	0.77%
1999	8,580	5,157	3,029	318	76
		60.10%	35.30%	3.71%	0.89%
2001	8,080	4,486	3,194	320	80
		55.52%	39.53%	3.96%	0.99%

Total Assets ($ billions), Year-End

	Total	< $100 M	$100M–$1B	$1B–$10B	> $10B
1993	3,514	345	669	1,005	1,495
		9.81%	19.05%	28.59%	42.55%
1995	4,116	310	668	1,077	2,061
		7.54%	16.22%	26.17%	50.07%
1997	4,642	277	711	995	2,658
		5.97%	15.32%	21.45%	57.27%
1999	5,735	243	755	915	3,823
		4.23%	13.16%	15.96%	66.65%
2001	6,569	222	819	915	4,613
		3.37%	12.47%	13.93%	70.22%

Total Deposits ($ billions)

	Total	< $100 M	$100M–$1B	$1B–$10B	> $10B
1993	2,778	302	592	783	1,100
		10.88%	21.32%	28.19%	39.61%
1995	3,028	259	586	734	1,448
		8.55%	19.36%	24.25%	47.84%
1997	3,422	230	602	625	1,965
		6.73%	17.60%	18.25%	57.42%
1999	3,831	206	612	625	2,389
		5.37%	15.97%	16.31%	62.35%
2001	4,392	188	668	625	2,911
		4.27%	15.22%	14.23%	66.27%

NOTE: M refers to millions, B refers to billions.
SOURCE: FDIC Quarterly Banking Profile, www.fdic.gov (http://www2.fdic.gov/qbp/).

basis, compared to historical norms. The second is through the increase in market share and product depth, which eventually led to increased earnings. The sources of these potential gains are wide-ranging and include:

Economies of Scale, Cost Cutting

- Consolidation of data processing and backroom operations
- Consolidation, diversification, and streamlining of investment departments and the securities portfolio

- Consolidation of the credit department, including loan documentation and preparation
- Consolidation of loan review and audit operations
- Consolidation of branch delivery systems, including use of the Internet
- Other scale economies

Increased Market Share

- Brand identification
- Political and market power enhancements
- Removal of a competitor

Enhanced Product Lines

- Stronger and more diversified product lines
- Improved marketing/distribution of products

Entry into Attractive New Markets

- Entrance into new growth markets
- Easier access to faster growth markets

Improved Managerial Capabilities and Increased Financial Leverage

- Improve profitability through loan purchase and maintenance of loan quality
- Alternative to paying dividends
- Increased financial coverage, buyers rarely pay a premium for excess capital

Financial and Operating Leverage

- Expansion into other lines of business and achievement of additional operating leverage
- Fixed cost of technology distributed over a larger customer base

Cost cutting often receives considerable attention because the acquirer has some direct control of noninterest expense. Banks with excess data processing capacity, for example, often view acquisitions as a way of generating activity that lowers unit costs by spreading fixed technology costs across more items. As mentioned earlier, however, there is mixed evidence on whether banks realize significant economies of scale or scope by expanding. True cost cutting arises when the acquirer and target have duplicate facilities, operations, staff, and general over-capacity. A merger allows the combined firm to offer the same quality and level of service with fewer people and fewer capital assets than two separate banks. For this reason, the mergers that make the most sense are in-market transactions. One bank's excess systems capacity and employees can service the customers of both merger parties such that the duplicate noninterest expense can be eliminated. This cost reduction goes directly to the bottom line and, more importantly, represents an annuity. Where else can banks, especially the large super-regional and regional banks, increase profits so quickly?

Value is created a second way by increasing market share. The high costs related to brand identification can be spread over a larger revenue stream. Larger market share also has the potential of reducing competition. Nevertheless, even if earnings rates remain unchanged after a merger, a bank can position itself as a future acquisition target by capturing a greater share of its deposit market. Buyers value a target's customer base and will pay a premium to obtain core deposits and profitable customers. Thus, a bank's deposit market share and customer relationship profiles are an important determinant of value in an acquisition.

Increasing market share can also lead to an enhanced product line and open new markets. Large product lines can bring economies of scale and scope. Cross-selling opportunities and enhanced delivery channels for existing and new products make size attractive as well. When growth in a bank's primary market slows, an acquisition can provide a bank with growth opportunities that may not be present in its original market.

Most banks also attempt to achieve additional operating and financial leverage. By 2001, banks had finished eleven straight years of record profits and high capital levels. Banks with excess capital can buy back stock—thereby increasing share prices—pay increased dividends, expand into other related activities, or acquire other banks or financial services companies. Greater operating leverage can be achieved by eliminating the duplication of services and spreading the fixed cost of delivery over a larger base of customers and products. Finally, increasing a company's product and earnings base can reduce earnings risk and thereby enhance the value of the franchise.

To enhance value, the acquirer would like to retain the best employees of the target bank, retain the target's best customers, and preserve the best parts of the target's culture. In general, employees and directors of an acquired bank often leave because they perceive either that they will not have the same opportunities as before or that they will be eventually let go. Customers also often move their relationships. They may be frustrated at the buyer bank being from out-of-state and prefer to conduct business with a locally owned bank. They may also follow the officer with whom they had previously conducted business when that officer leaves. With this uncertainty, earnings forecasts are highly suspect, especially for the near term.

PROBLEM MERGERS

What makes a merger unattractive? In financial terms, mergers are problematic when the buyer does not earn the expected return on investment in a reasonable period of time. One broad standard of performance is that a merger should not produce any dilution in earnings per share (EPS) for the acquiring bank greater than 5 percent. In fact, some acquirers will not pay a price that dilutes earnings at all. The essential message then is that earnings dilution is bad!

Formally, EPS dilution is measured as:

EPS dilution =

$$\frac{\text{current EPS of acquiring bank} - pro\ forma \text{ EPS of consolidated entity}}{\text{current EPS of acquiring bank}} \quad \text{(22.1)}$$

The *pro forma* consolidated EPS is a forecast value for the upcoming period. The 5 percent standard suggests that some dilution is acceptable because most transactions are financed by an exchange of stock and the EPSs for both the target and acquirer are not the same initially. However, many mergers dilute the acquirer's EPS and the question is how long will it take to overcome the dilution.

A second hurdle is whether the acquisition, when treated as an investment, earns the expected rate of return over time. EPS dilution analysis focuses on short-run performance. Many firms perform a workout time analysis that focuses on long-run results. The analysis essentially computes the time necessary for the acquirer to earn enough to pay for the initial investment and meet the cumulative target return objective. Obviously, the less the acquirer pays and the greater the earnings growth, the shorter the time required to generate the target return.

Sanchez (1990) documents the average workout time for bank mergers from 1986 through 1990.[3] Over this period, the average workout time was 22 years, hardly a quick return on investment. The trend, however, is that average workout time has slowly shortened. This is

---

[3]Sanchez (1990) analyzes trends in the pattern of premiums and expected workout time as described by SNL Securities.

consistent with the lower premiums paid after the 1987 stock market crash. Banks may also be improving their ability to grow earnings from target banks. For example, the average workout period for Bank One, an extremely aggressive acquirer in its hey day, was less than 10 years. It is estimated that it takes more than 18 months today just to integrate two banks' computer systems. In general, problems arise when the estimated workout time exceeds 20 years. Beyond this point, acquirers overpay according to financial performance.

VALUE ADDED FROM BUYING FAILED THRIFTS

Several of the largest banks in the country pursued an aggressive strategy of buying failed thrifts in the late 1980s and early 1990s. Rather than assume all the thrift's assets, most transactions were structured where the buyer got to screen loans and buy only ones that met its standards. For example, in 1989, NCNB Texas (NationsBank) acquired University Savings Association and got $3.5 billion in deposits. As part of the deal, it agreed to buy just 15 percent of the savings and loan's assets. From January 1989 through June 1990, NCNB bought 18 failed savings banks in Texas. It obtained almost $7 billion in core deposits, but never bought more that 15 percent of a failed thrift's assets. The Resolution Trust Corp., as seller, kept the remaining assets, which had the lowest prospects for collection.

Clearly, the failed institution's core deposit base made the deals attractive. Buyers knew that the government wanted to move its inventory and thus often got the deposits cheaply. A study of 287 failed thrift purchases through October 1990 revealed that the average premium paid on deposits equaled 2.1 percent.[4] As might be expected, the average premium varied substantially by state, from a low of 0.43 percent in Colorado to 4.53 percent in Illinois. In general, states with the strongest economies, such as California and Illinois, garnered the highest premiums while states with weaker economies or limited demand for the deposits produced lower premiums.

Purchasing deposits adds value for the same reasons that buying a healthy bank adds value. The deposits can be used to grow earnings and increase the buyer's market share. These deposits are core deposits in the sense that they are noninterest-bearing demand balances and small time and savings balances that are relatively stable. They also carry the lowest interest rates. An acquirer must be able to reinvest these funds at a positive spread to increase earnings. In many recent deposit transactions, buyers have simply used the proceeds to buy securities rather than make new loans.

VALUATION PROCEDURES

A merger or acquisition involving financially sound banks is successful if it maximizes shareholder wealth for stockholders of both banks. Transactions terms should reflect a combined firm value that exceeds the sum of firm values when viewed independently. This greater synergistic value is derived from potential benefits via improved profitability that is attributable to an improved earning asset mix, improved pricing, reductions in operating costs, the opportunity to enter new markets and offer new products, and access to core deposits. All of these factors should be incorporated in the analysis of what price an acquirer should pay for a target, or what minimum price a seller will accept.

---

[4]See Rehm (1990). When buying deposits, the acquirer assumes the liability to each deposit owner. What then does the buyer actually pay? If the premium is 2 percent, the buyer effectively pays $2 cash for each $100 in deposits assumed. In actuality, the RTC gives the bank $98 per $100 in liabilities assumed. If the bank buys assets, it receives even less.

Before calculating a purchase price, both buyer and seller should evaluate the other's risk and return profile using historical financial data. The common approach is the ROE framework outlined in Chapter 3, along with the analysis of the bank's credit, liquidity, interest rate, capital, operational, and solvency risk position. Although the ratios simply reflect historical performance, they are important indicators of the bank's financial strengths and weaknesses and help determine the economic value of the firm.

Stockholders in the target bank focus on the premium offered relative to the price of the stock prior to the announcement. In a cash transaction, the premium represents the realized increase in value from the transaction. If the acquirer proposes to exchange stock in the acquiring firm for stock in the target, target stockholders gain if the value of the new stock exceeds the value of stock in the target without the merger. This represents an increase in value if the stock can be immediately liquidated for more than the value of the target's stock, or if expected cash flows from holding the new stock exceed that from holding just the target's stock. In this case, the correct valuation depends on the expected dividend payments and price of the stock when it is eventually sold.

As discussed above, any merger or acquisition should be treated as an investment and evaluated accordingly. Thus, the theoretically correct procedure for determining value is to discount expected cash flows from the new entity at the appropriate discount rate. Because this approach involves estimating many key components of the present value model, market participants often use a variety of less rigorous techniques to obtain a range of fair price estimates. This range of potential prices is then used in negotiations with the other party. The final result will reflect these prices plus each party's bargaining strength and the nonpecuniary benefits that the negotiators include in the price, such as public recognition, ego, and so on. Different valuation procedures produce different benchmark price estimates, as described below.[5]

LEVELS OR TYPES OF VALUE

There are actually several types or levels of value[6]. The **controlling interest value** is the value of the enterprise as a whole assuming that the stock is freely traded in a public market and includes a control premium. The *control premium* reflects the incremental value associated with the risks and rewards of a majority or controlling interest. A controlling interest is assumed to have control power over the minority interests. A **minority interest value** represents the value of a minority interest "as if freely tradable" in a public market. A *minority interest discount* represents the reduction in value from an absence of control of the enterprise. Both controlling interest value and minority interest value assume that the interest is freely tradable in a public market. If the entity were closely held with no (or little) active market for the shares or interest in the company, then a *nonmarketability discount* would be subtracted from the value.

NONMARKETABILIY DISCOUNTS. The Internal Revenue Service defines lack of marketability as "the absences of a ready or existing market for the sale or purchase of securities being valued." The discount represents the reduction in value from a marketable interest

---

[5]This discussion follows the framework of Bullington (1981) and Cates (1985). In addition, many tax and accounting considerations are ignored in this analysis. Issues such as the costs and benefits of purchase accounting versus pooling-of-interests accounting are critical to the evaluation and success of mergers. The reader is referred to Koch and Baker (1983) for a general discussion of the issues. See Contemporary Issues: Pooling Versus Purchase Accounting.

[6]We wish to thank Wade Schuessler, Managing Director, SAMCO Capital Markets, for his assistance in the following sections of the book. Needless to say, the views expressed do not reflect those of Mr. Schuessler or SAMCO. All errors remain the responsibility of the authors.

POOLING VERSUS PURCHASE ACCOUNTING

In May 2001, the Financial Accounting Standards Board ended five years of deliberation by eliminating pooling-of-interests accounting for mergers and imposing a system that would require combining companies to recognize goodwill on their balance sheets. **Goodwill** is the difference between the purchase price of an acquired company and the net value of its assets. Companies are subject to an impairment test on goodwill. If the test determines that goodwill has fallen permanently in value, it would then have to be amortized. According to FASB, the elimination of pooling-of-interests in favor of purchase accounting was done to make financial statements more transparent for investors.

Under **pooling-of-interests accounting,** the book values of both companies are combined such that no goodwill is created. Under the **purchase method,** the acquiring company reports the difference between the purchase price and the book value of the acquired company as an intangible asset—goodwill. Some experts have argued that the elimination of pooling-of-interest accounting would slow down merger activity. In contrast, many academics and other specialists argue that the accounting method

used in a merger is not relevant because it does not affect cash flow.

Purchase accounting almost always resulted in lower reported earnings than pooling accounting. The price paid above the fair value of the book assets of the acquired company using purchase accounting is booked as goodwill and periodically amortized against income over a period as long as 40 years. The problem with writing off goodwill is that it reduces reported earnings. Using pooling accounting, the book value of the acquired company is carried over with no goodwill, no amortization. Nevertheless, since goodwill amortization is a non-cash charge, both methods result in identical cash flows. So, what is the debate? Salomon Smith Barny concluded in The *CPA Journal,* September 1999, that "The evidence from the stock market valuations and from stock market reactions to transaction announcements strongly demonstrates that purchase accounting does not adversely affect firm valuations." On the other hand, Martin Lipton, in *Mergers: Past, Present and Future,* January 2001, suggests that "The availability of pooling accounting for mergers has been a significant factor in the 1990s merger activity.

In theory, therefore, the accounting method does not affect cash flow

and, hence, does not affect value. In a recent article, authors McNish, Harper, and Williams suggest that the "...adoption of purchase accounting treatment does not destroy value. Substantial evidence suggests that analysts, investors and ultimately capital markets see through accounting treatment—the form of accounting for business combinations has no impact on shareholder value." They suggest "Pooling accounting, however, actually destroys value in terms of both hard costs and a range of hidden costs. Companies very visibly spend hard dollars to qualify for pooling treatment, but the real costs of pooling lie beneath the surface. The first of these hidden costs are those associated with bad financing decisions, the second with bad operating decisions."[7] To qualify for pooling treatment, the deal almost always had to be stock-for-stock, so pooling probably led to the high prices paid for bank stocks in the late 1990s.

The new proposed method by the FSAB board, however, could be the best of both worlds. Companies must use purchase accounting, which creates goodwill, but they will only have to amortize the goodwill if the value of that goodwill falls.

---

level of value to compensate an investor for illiquidity of the security, all else equal. The size of the discount varies based on: relative liquidity (such as the size of the shareholder base); the dividend yield; expected growth in value and holding period; and firm-specific issues such as an imminent or pending initial public offering (IPO) of stock to be freely traded on a public market.

---

[7]McNish, Rob, Neil Harper, and Zane Williams. "The Demise Of Pooling—A Blessing In Disguise For M&A," *Corporate Finance.* 17–21. 2000 Nov.

VALUATION METHODS

Several methods of valuation exist but generally fall into two broad categories: comparable analysis and discounted cash flow analysis. **Comparable analysis** (often referred to as "comps") uses a direct comparison of the target bank with similar banks engaged in the same or similar lines of business. Comparables (similar banks) are "filtered" for similar lines of business, asset size, geographic location, profitability characteristics, as well as other factors specific to the target. Minority interest values are determined using a *comparable companies analysis* in which the target bank is compared with the actively traded stocks of banks engaged in similar lines of business, size, and geographic location. *Controlling interest values* are obtained using a *comparable acquisitions analysis* in which comparisons are made with acquisitions of banks engaged in similar lines of business, size, and geographic location. The comparable companies analysis is applicable only to *minority interest values,* both marketable and nonmarketable, while comparable acquisitions analysis is applied only to controlling interest values.

Discounted cash flow analysis (often referred to as DCF) has been applied in finance to almost all income-producing assets, such as valuing a business, and income-producing real estate property. When market participants make an investment, they are looking for future income or cash flow. Thus, the value of any investment is the present value of all future economic benefits (cash earnings) that will come to the investors in the future. To apply this valuation method to a bank, an analyst must estimate the dollar amount of earnings available to investors (the parent bank), the volatility of the earnings and their longevity, and the certainty of the earnings. These earnings are "discounted" to the present using an appropriate risky discount rate, similar to present value calculations preformed on other types of investments such as bonds and stocks. The only true difference is the greater uncertainty evolved in estimating earnings.

COMPARABLE ANALYSIS

PRICE TO BOOK VALUE

Most bankers and market analysts discuss merger prices in terms of book values. Formally, the book value of a share of stock equals the book value of a firm's stockholders' equity divided by the number of shares outstanding. The book value of stockholders' equity is based on reported balance sheet values and equals the dollar amount of assets minus the dollar amount of liabilities. The premium to book value in a transaction compares the per share price offered to target bank stockholders with the book value of the target's stock. Letting:

MP_t = per share market price offered for target's stock, and

BV_t = per share book value of target's stock, then

$$\text{the premium to book value} = \frac{MP_t - BV_t}{BV_t} \tag{22.2}$$

Thus, if the target bank's book value per share is $12.2 and an acquirer offers $22.2 per share, the premium to book value equals 81.97 percent ([22.2 − 12.2]/12.2).

In order to use this concept in valuing a bank, participants simply calculate the average premium offered for similar banks and extrapolate an equivalent price for the target if the same premium is applied. Average premiums for minority interests are found by using a *comparable companies analysis* in which comparable companies are those in similar lines of business with similar asset size and similar profitability characteristics. When value for controlling interest is needed, average premiums are calculated using data from successful acquisitions of similar type using a *comparable acquisitions analysis*. Formally, the transaction price per share of target stock under this approach (P_{bv}) is determined by:

$$P_{bv} = \left[\frac{MP_t}{BV_t}\right]_{avg} \times BV_t \tag{22.3}$$

Thus, if the average premium on comparable transactions is 100 percent (twice book value), the average purchase price to book value multiple will equal 2.0x and the transactions price for the target bank's stock should equal $24.4 (2.0 × $12.2) in the above example.

Merger terms are also described in terms of exchange ratios, or the number of shares of the acquiring bank's stock that target bank stockholders receive for each share in the target bank. Letting:

$$e = \text{exchange ratio, and}$$

$$MP_a = \text{per share market price of the acquirer's stock, then}$$

$$e = \frac{P_{bv}}{MP_a} = \frac{BV_t(1 + \text{premium})}{MP_a} \tag{22.4}$$

Using the previous example, if the premium on comparable transactions is 100 percent and the price of the acquirer's stock is $55, then the exchange ratio is 0.4463:

$$0.4463 = \frac{\$24.4}{\$55} = \frac{\$12.2(1 + 100\%)}{\$55}$$

NORMALIZED EQUITY CAPITAL. One surprise to potential sellers of banks is the impact of "excess" capital. The 1990s produced record profits in the banking industry and many successful banks found that their capital to asset levels rose well over 10 percent. Because capital, in excess of what is "required" to satisfy regulatory requirements and ensure success of the bank, can be acquired by simply issuing stock or injecting this capital into the bank, potential acquirers will often not pay more than a dollar for dollar for "excess" capital. Capital levels at the target bank are "normalized" to a minimum level of capital, and then excess capital is purchased dollar for dollar. Although what is considered normal capital varies, 8 to 10 percent has recently been considered a general guideline. One approach that recognizes the impact of excess capital involves assigning a value to 'excess capital' that is different from the value assigned to other capital. In this case, multiplying the average price to book premium offered for similar banks by the "normalized" equity ratio for the target bank (8 percent in this discussion) and then adding back "excess" capital, dollar for dollar, determines value. The normalized book value of equity (BV^{norm}) and excess equity are found by:

$$(BV^{norm}) = \text{total assets of target bank} \times \text{normalized equity ratio}$$

$$\text{Excess equity} = \text{total equity} - \text{normalized equity}$$

The transaction price per share of target stock under this approach (P_{nbv}) is determined by:

$$P_{nbv} = \left[\frac{MP_t}{BV_t}\right]_{avg} \times BV_t^{norm} + \$ \text{ excess equity} \tag{22.5}$$

For example, assume the target bank has 3 million shares, $338 million in assets, $35.5 million in equity, the normalized equity ratio is 8 percent, and the average price to book multiple is 2x. Then, normal equity is $27 million and excess equity is $8.5 million. The price per share of the company (assuming 1 million shares of stock) is:

$$P_{nbv} = \$20.83 \text{ share} = [2 \times (\$27 \text{ million}/3 \text{ million shares})] + (\$8.5 \text{ million}/3 \text{ million shares})$$

The price to book value procedure outlined above has many weaknesses. The most obvious is that book value may not closely resemble a bank's true economic value. Suppose that a bank systematically understates problem loans. Reported loan values will overstate true values and book value will be artificially large. Suppose also that the bank has a severe interest rate mismatch between rate-sensitive assets and liabilities in a volatile interest rate environment. Book values do not reflect this risk. Alternatively, book values may understate true value. Consider a bank that operates a large mortgage-servicing portfolio. This value does not appear on-balance sheet, and thus book value understates economic value. The essential point is that book values can be misleading because the market value of assets and liabilities may differ widely from that reported in periodic financial statements, and off-balance sheet items are ignored.

Another weakness is that premiums paid on other bank acquisitions have no relation to the rate of return that an acquirer can potentially earn on the investment, and they completely ignore risk. Market prices incorporate nonpecuniary values that both acquiring and target bank managers place on doing the deal. These values may not be those of participants in the proposed deal. In general, you can justify a premium over book value when expected returns are high relative to the associated risk or when the acquisition provides benefits that are not directly measurable.

ADJUSTMENTS TO BOOK VALUE. Because reported book value may differ substantially from true economic value, it is appropriate to compute an adjusted book value of equity for the target bank that recognizes the measurement error. A comparison of the market price to adjusted book value then provides a better measure of the premium paid. Adjusted book value may be greater than or less than book value. It can be obtained by adding or subtracting the following items from stated book value:

- **Change in loan loss reserve.** If asset quality is lower than that reported, the loan loss reserve should be restated higher such that the net loans amount is lower than that reported. If asset quality is higher than that reported, the loss reserve should be adjusted downward such that the net loans amount is higher.

- **Change in market value of investments.** The portion of the investment portfolio that is *held-to-maturity* is listed at amortized cost.[8] If market values of securities differ sharply from cost because interest rates have either risen or fallen, any difference between market and book values should be added to book value.

- **Change in other asset appraisals.** Occasionally, banks own real estate and other assets that have market values far different from the cost, which appears on the balance sheet. A bank may own stock acquired in a foreclosure that has risen in value, or land with proven oil reserves that is not currently in production. If the market value is above (below) book value, the difference should be added to the book value of equity.

- **Value of off-balance sheet activities.** The earning power or risk of off-balance sheet items is generally not reflected on the balance sheet. The value of mortgage servicing from bank-originated mortgages is such an item. If these activities are valuable, an estimate of the market value should be added to (subtracted from) the book value of equity.

- **Value of core deposits.** Core deposits are attractive because they are relatively stable. An acquirer can leverage them by selling additional services to existing deposit holders. This value also incorporates the franchise value of the bank, or its value as an ongoing concern. Unfortunately, the value is difficult to estimate, but it should be added to the book value of equity.

---

[8]Recall that FASB 115 requires the bank to mark its trading account assets (investments) and available-for-sale securities to market. Hence, this adjustment generally applies only to held-to-maturity securities, which are listed at historical cost.

PRICE TO EARNINGS PER SHARE (EPS)

Many analysts prefer to focus on earnings rather than balance sheet values when estimating a market price to pay for a target bank. As such, the key variable is earnings per share of the target. The valuation approach involves computing the average purchase price to EPS ratio for similar banks and then multiplying this mean ratio by the target bank's earnings per share (EPS$_t$). Average price to EPS ratios for minority interests are found by using a *comparable companies analysis* in which comparable companies are those in similar lines of business, with similar asset sizes and similar profitability characteristics. When value for controlling interest is needed, average price to EPS ratios are calculated using data from successful acquisitions of similar type using a *comparable acquisitions analysis*. The transactions price per share under this approach (P$_{eps}$) is determined from:

$$P_{eps} = \left[\frac{MP_t}{EPS_t} \right]_{avg} \times EPS_t \qquad (22.6)$$

In this case, the premium equals:

$$\text{premium to EPS} = \frac{MP_t - EPS_t}{EPS_t} \qquad (22.7)$$

and the exchange ratio equals:

$$e = \frac{P_{eps}}{MP_a} = \frac{EPS_t \times (1 + \text{Premium})}{MP_a} \qquad (22.8)$$

The use of a one period earnings measure as a base has numerous weaknesses. First, an appropriate earnings measure should reflect the volatility of earnings that gives some indication of the riskiness of the bank's operations. Second, it is not clear what time interval is appropriate. The current year's EPS may be dramatically different from EPS over the past few years, and different still from expected EPS. Analysts get around these problems by using a weighted average of historical earnings per share figures, and then using a forecast average value of EPS over the near future.

EPS DILUTION CONSTRAINTS. Most bank acquisitions have a negative short-term effect on earnings largely because the acquiring bank pays a premium for the target. This decline in EPS should be of negligible size and short-lived for a merger to be attractive to the purchaser. The earlier discussion of problem mergers noted that banks have historically been unwilling to close deals where EPS dilution exceeds 5 percent. David Cates notes, in fact, that such acquisitions are termed "dilutions of grandeur."[9] The difficulty with excessive EPS dilution is that the purchase price is so high that it takes forever for the acquiring bank to improve performance to where it earns a reasonable risk-adjusted return on investment.

Consider the case summarized in Exhibit 22.8 where Bank ABC has proposed buying Bank XYZ in a 2-for-1 stock exchange. The top panel indicates that, prior to the acquisition, Bank ABC reports an EPS of $5, while Bank XYZ has an EPS of $3.50 on net income of $14 million with 4 million shares outstanding. Bank XYZ is less than 10 percent of the size of Bank ABC, but has a higher return on assets. The bottom panel demonstrates the EPS dilution when net income for each bank is forecast to grow by 10 percent in the upcoming year and the acquisition goes through as planned. Without any transaction, Bank ABC's EPS would have increased by the same 10 percent to $5.50. The consolidated firm, however, is expected to

---

[9]Cates (1985).

• EXHIBIT 22.8

ANALYSIS OF EARNINGS-PER-SHARE DILUTION

A. Pre-Acquisition: December 31, 2001	Bank ABC	Bank XYZ
Net income ($millions)	$160.0	$14.0
Number of shares outstanding (millions)	32	4
Earnings per share	$5.00	$3.50
Total assets ($billions)	$22.2	$1.5

B. Forecasts for 2002

Assume: i) Net income for both banks increases by 10 percent.

ii) Bank ABC offers a 2-for-1 stock exchange whereby Bank XYZ stockholders receive 2 shares in Bank ABC for every share of Bank XYZ .

	Bank ABC	Bank XYZ	Consolidated
Net income ($millions)	$176.0	$15.4	$191.40
Number of shares outstanding (millions)	32	8	40
Earnings per share	$5.500	$1.925	$4.785
EPS dilution	$\dfrac{\$5.500 - \$4.785}{\$5.500} = 13.0\%$		

Summary

1. With no acquisition, Bank ABC's EPS would increase to $8.05 by 2006.
2. Earnings at Bank XYZ would have to increase to $64.4 million in 2006 to increase its EPS to the same $8.05 by 2006. Thus, earnings would have to grow at a 35.7 percent annual rate for dilution to be recovered within five years.

report $191.4 million in net income on 40 million shares, for an EPS of $4.785. This dilutes Bank ABC's EPS by 13 percent:

$$\text{EPS dilution} = \frac{\text{EPS without transaction} - \text{Consolidated EPS}}{\text{EPS without transaction}} = 13.0\% = \frac{\$5.500 - \$4.785}{\$5.500}$$

which exceeds the 5 percent threshold viewed as maximum acceptable dilution.

Cates introduced a micro-dilution framework that provides even clearer evidence of problem acquisitions. The term **micro-dilution** refers to EPS dilution of the target. In the bottom panel of Exhibit 22.8, this amounts to computing the earnings per issued share for Bank XYZ of $1.925 from a projected $14.4 million net income with 8 million shares outstanding. This contrasts with Bank ABC's projected EPS of $5.50. Suppose that no acquisition occurred. If Bank ABC's earnings grew 10 percent annually for five years, its EPS would grow to $8.05. In order for the dilution in the above example to be temporary, Bank XYZ's EPS must also grow to $8.05 by the fifth year. This means that after the acquisition, Bank XYZ's net income would have to increase at a 35.7 percent annual rate. It is highly unlikely than any bank's earnings will increase at such a rate under normal circumstances. This transaction is of highly questionable value because dilution is permanent, unless there is some strategic value to the purchase that is not revealed by the earnings data.

PRICE TO TOTAL ASSETS

A bank uses the funds provided by stockholders and depositors to invest in the assets of the bank. Theoretically, the assets of the bank create value. Hence, analysts often focus on total assets as a determinant of value. The ratio of average price per share to total assets per share for similar banks is calculated using comparable analysis and these average ratios are multiplied by the target bank's total assets to determine value. Formally, if we define TA as total assets per share, the transaction price per share of target stock under this approach (P_{ta}) is determined by:

$$P_{ta} = \left[\frac{MP_t}{TA_t} \right]_{avg} \times TA_t \qquad (22.9)$$

To use this concept in valuing a bank, participants simply calculate the average total asset premium offered for similar banks and extrapolate an equivalent price for the target if the same premium is applied. Average asset premiums for minority interests are found by using a *comparable companies analysis* in which comparable companies are those in similar lines of business, with similar asset size and similar profitability characteristics. When value for controlling interest is needed, average premiums are calculated using data from successful acquisitions of similar type using a *comparable acquisitions analysis*.

Using the data from the previous example where the target bank has: 3 million shares, $338 million in assets, and $35.5 million in equity—and assuming the median price to total asset multiple is 19.3 percent—the price per share of the company (assuming 1 million shares of stock) is:

$$P_{ta} = \$21.7 \text{ share} = [0.193 \times (\$338 \text{ / } 3 \text{ million shares})]$$

The price to total assets approach also suffers from many weaknesses. Many of these weaknesses are similar to those of the price to book value procedure outlined above. First, reported total assets may not represent true economic value. Loan values might overstate the true value such that the book value of assets would be artificially large. The book value of assets may be artificially small as well in that many banks have significant "off-balance sheet" activities which enhance value (but could also pose risk not included in total assets). Furthermore, the true strength of banks is in generating fee income, ideally without a commitment to new asset holdings. Hence, assets may not represent the value of a banking firm. The essential point is that book value of assets can be misleading because the market value of assets and liabilities may differ widely from that reported in periodic financial statements, and off-balance sheet items are ignored.

Another weakness is that the prices paid on other bank acquisitions of total assets have no relation to the rate of return that an acquirer can potentially earn on the investment, and they ignore differences in risk. One bank may have a significant portfolio of Treasury securities and Fed Funds sold. Obviously, these types of assets are easily acquired and would involve no premium payment. On the other hand, high quality loans with good yields would carry a premium and low quality loans with lower relative yields would carry a discount.

PRICE TO TOTAL DEPOSITS

Inexpensive core deposits are often seen as a bank's greatest resource and source of core earnings. The growth in core deposits is on the decline today as investors continue to move their money to mutual funds and direct equity investments. When the stock market was rising, many banks experienced a slow growth in core deposits. When the stock market fell sharply after March 2000, many banks saw their core deposits increase as customers moved funds back to the safe haven of insured deposits. In general, a bank can enhance value as a future acquisition target by capturing a greater share of its deposit market. Buyers value a target's customer base and will pay a premium to obtain core deposits. A larger deposit market share can also lead to an enhanced product line and open new markets. Large product lines can bring economies of scale and scope. Cross-selling opportunities and enhanced delivery channels for existing and new products make size attractive as well. When growth in a bank's primary market slows, an acquisition can provide a bank with growth opportunities that may not be present in its original market.

Purchasing deposits adds value because these deposits can be used to grow earnings and increase the buyer's market share. Core deposits are relatively stable and carry the lowest interest rates. An acquirer will reinvest these funds at a positive spread to increase earnings. Hence, the final comparable analysis valuation procedure is to compute a price to total deposits premium. Using this method, the average price per share to total deposits per share for similar banks is calculated using comparable analysis and these average ratios are multiplied by the target bank's total deposits to determine value. Formally, if we define TD as total deposits per share, the transaction price per share of target stock under this approach (P_{td}) is determined by:

$$P_{td} = \left[\frac{MP_t}{TD_t} \right]_{avg} \times TD_t \qquad (22.10)$$

To use this concept in valuing a bank, participants simply calculate the average total deposit premium offered for similar banks and extrapolate an equivalent price for the target if the same premium is applied. Average deposit premiums for minority interests are found by using a *comparable companies analysis* in which comparable companies are those in similar lines of business, with similar asset sizes and similar profitability characteristics. When value for controlling interest is needed, average premiums are calculated using data from successful acquisitions of similar type using a *comparable acquisitions analysis*.

Using the data from the previous example in which the target bank has 3 million shares, $338 million in assets, $35.5 million in equity, $279 million in total deposits and assuming the median price to total deposits ratio of 24.6 percent, the price per share of the company (assuming 1 million shares of stock) is:

$$P_{td} = \$22.9 \text{ share} = [0.246 \times (\$279 / 3 \text{ million shares})]$$

The price to total deposit approach suffers from the same previously-mentioned weaknesses. Reported total deposits may not represent true core deposits. The bank may have obtained their deposits as brokered deposits or by offering a premium rate over the Internet. Since brokered deposits and premium Internet deposits are not unique, they do not carry the same value as true core deposits. Recall that the bank is seeking inexpensive core deposits that are relatively stable local deposits. Another weakness is that just because a bank acquires core deposits, these deposits will only enhance the acquiring bank's profitability if they are successful in holding on to these funds and reinvesting these funds at a profitable spread and these deposits remain with the bank.

DISCOUNTED CASH FLOW (DCF)

This approach views the purchase of a bank's stock as an investment and compares the expected present (discounted) value of stockholders' equity, discounted at some target rate of return, with the current equity value. If the discounted value exceeds the current equity value, the net present value of the stock purchase is positive and the investment meets the minimum required return. The expected present value of stockholders' equity is determined by adding up the present value of forecasted cash earnings.

The real value of this procedure is that it provides an estimate of economic value. The estimated value or premium to be paid for the target bank's stock is often lower as compared to other approaches because only realized cash flows are incorporated in the analysis. Thus, sellers often ignore this analysis when they have any market power. Buyers can use it to assess the true economic premium that can be justified in terms of the required return on investment.

VALUING FUTURE EARNINGS

When investors make an investment, they are looking for future income. Thus, the value of any investment is the present value of all future economic benefits (cash earnings) that will come to the investors in the future. This method of value has been applied in finance to almost all income-producing assets, such as valuing a business and real estate lease property. To apply this method to a bank, analysts must estimate the dollar amount of earnings available to investors, the volatility of the earnings, their longevity, and the certainty of the earnings.

The price (or value) bank investors are willing to pay, in this framework, is the present value of all future income available to investors.

$$\text{bank value} = \text{PV [Expected cash income available to parent bank]} \qquad \text{(22.11)}$$

In practice, the value to an investor is the present value of expected future cash income plus the terminal or salvage value the investor would receive at the end of the investment's life:

$$\text{bank value} = \text{PV [expected cash income available to parent over } n \text{ years]}$$
$$+ \text{ PV [terminal value (TV) in year } n] \qquad \text{(22.12)}$$

Application of this method requires estimates of expected future cash earnings available to the parent bank, the number of years the income is expected, the terminal value or salvage value of the bank in the future, and the required return or discount rate of investors. Expected future cash income available to investors (FCF) can, under certain conditions, be estimated by:

$$\text{FCF} = \text{NI} + \text{depreciation} - \text{required capital additions} \qquad \text{(22.13)}$$

Recall that a bank has very few operating assets such as accounts receivable and inventory. Thus, net income after tax (net of cash taxes) is generally a close approximation of cash flow.[10] Because a bank has few real assets subject to depreciation, we can generally ignore depreciation as well. Banks are somewhat unique in that they have minimum capital requirements. Once a bank is purchased, the parent will presumably try to minimize capital at the subsidiary bank such that the parent can maximize its return on investment (equity). Hence, required capital additions are a function of existing equity (TE_{t-1}), earnings (NI), total asset (TA) growth, and the required capital to asset ratio. Required capital additions are estimated as:

$$\text{required capital additions} = \left[\text{required capital asset ratio} - \frac{\text{TE}_{t-1}}{\text{TA}_t}\right] \text{TA}_t + \text{new equity[11]} \qquad \text{(22.14)}$$

Ignoring depreciation and new equity issues and using Equation 22.14, future cash income available to investors (FCF) can be approximated by:

$$\text{FCF}_t = \text{NI}_t - \left[\text{required capital asset ratio} - \frac{\text{TE}_{t-1}}{\text{TA}_t}\right] \text{TA}_t \qquad \text{(22.15)}$$

ESTIMATING TERMINAL VALUE

The second issue that must be addressed is the life expectancy of the bank. This is usually unknown or indefinite, so that the terminal value of the investment is difficult to determine. There are two approaches to this problem. The first is to ignore income beyond a

---

[10]Larger banks' cash flow may be affected by significant operating assets, depreciation, and amortization. In this case, it is important to examine each bank's cash flow statement to get a more accurate measure of cash flow.

[11]It is generally assumed that new equity would be invested only if net income was insufficient to maintain minimum capital ratios at the bank. Without loss of generality, we generally assume that income is sufficient to maintain minimum equity and, hence, new equity is zero.

certain time period. This method assumes that estimates will not be perfectly accurate and accuracy will diminish over time, and that the use of present value reduces the degree of the error. For example, the present value of $1 per year as a perpetuity (infinite number of years) discounted at 15 percent is $6.67 ($1/0.15). The present value of this flow for only 20 years (ignoring all flows after 20 years) at a 15 percent discount rate is $6.26. This is only a 6.1 percent error.

The second approach used to approximate the terminal value (TV) is to employ the mathematical solution to an infinite stream of future income. Recall that the value of a current *constant* infinite stream of income (FCF_t), discounted at the investor required return **(r)**, is:

$$TV_t = \frac{FCF}{r} \tag{22.16}$$

If we assume that the infinite stream of income *increases at a constant rate* **(g)**, the terminal value would be:

$$TV_t = \frac{FCF_t(1 + g)}{r - g} = \frac{FCF_{t+1}}{r - g} \tag{22.17}$$

Note here that the free cash flow value equals next period's expected cash flow (current free cash flow times one plus the expected growth rate). This second method is functionally useful as well because the target bank's FCF may fluctuate a great deal in the short run and be more difficult to predict explicitly in the future. We can break the problem into two parts: the first, in which explicit FCF estimates are made, and the second, in which a stabilized income is projected to grow at a constant rate into the indefinite future:

$$\text{bank value} = \sum_{t=1}^{n} \frac{FCF_t}{(1 + r)^t} + \frac{TV_n}{(1 + r)^n} \tag{22.18}$$

If we assume that the target bank's stabilized income will grow at a constant rate, **g,** then the terminal value can be approximated by Equation 22.17. We can rewrite Equation 22.18 as:

$$\text{bank value} = \sum_{t=1}^{n} \frac{FCF_t}{(1 + r)^t} + \frac{\left[\dfrac{FCF_{n+1}}{r - g}\right]}{(1 + r)^n} \tag{22.19}$$

Applying Equation 22.19 means that the bank's value is estimated using explicit earnings forecasts for the next **n** years, plus the value of future earnings, expected to grow at a constant rate, for the indefinite future. These earnings are then discounted back at the investors' required return, **r.** The biggest advantage of the income method is that value is determined by the investors' estimates of expected returns. Banks with high and growing expected future earnings will be valued very highly. Banks with low earnings and low expectations for growth in those earnings, on the other hand, will not be valued as high.

AN APPLICATION

The following analysis demonstrates the application of the valuation procedures described above. Each procedure is addressed using the balance sheet and income statement data for acquirer, Western Plains National Bank (WPNB), and the target, Citizens Trust Bank (CTB) found in Exhibits 22.9 through 22.12. Data for the banks appear in the exhibits that follow. The nonquantitative aspects of the analysis are ignored. Western Plains National Bank is considering buying a controlling interest (100 percent) of CBT's stock. Although the most appropriate comparative valuation method would be the Comparative Acquisitions Analysis, the

BALANCE SHEET FOR WESTERN PLAINS NATIONAL BANK (WPNB)

	2000	% TA	2001	% TA
Assets				
Cash and due from banks	$107	7.0%	$111	6.9%
Interest-bearing deposits with banks	46	3.0%	63	3.9%
Investment securities:				
Treasury & U.S. agency	152	10.0%	123	7.6%
Corporate & mortgage-backed securities	60	3.9%	74	4.6%
Municipals	71	4.7%	67	4.2%
Total loans and leases	993	65.1%	1,070	66.5%
Less reserve for losses	14	0.9%	17	1.1%
Net loans and leases	$979	64.2%	$1,053	65.4%
Real estate owned	22	1.4%	27	1.7%
Premises and equipment	27	1.8%	28	1.7%
Other assets	62	4.1%	64	4.0%
Total assets	$1,526	100.0%	$1,610	100.0%
Liabilities				
Demand deposits	$235	15.4%	$240	14.9%
Savings deposits	358	23.5%	369	22.9%
Time deposits	504	33.0%	549	34.1%
Total deposits	$1,097	71.9%	$1,158	71.9%
Borrowed funds:				
Federal funds purchased & RPs	166	10.9%	166	10.3%
Other borrowed funds	113	7.4%	128	8.0%
Acceptances and other liabilities	48	3.1%	52	3.2%
Total liabilities	$1,424	93.3%	$1,504	93.4%
Stockholders' Equity				
Common stock	10	0.7%	10	0.6%
Paid-in capital	40	2.6%	40	2.5%
Retained earnings	52	3.4%	56	3.5%
Total stockholders' equity	$102	6.7%	$106	6.6%
Total liabilities and equity	$1,526	100.0%	$1,610	100.0%

NOTE: Figures are in millions of dollars.

Comparative Companies Analysis is provided for demonstration purposes. The discounted cash flow model is also presented. Note that WPNB's stock price is currently $60 while CBT's stock price is $15. Book values for each bank can be obtained from the balance sheet.

Exhibit 22.13 provides information on each bank's earnings per share and dividends per share in the two most recent years. WPNB's management is also unwilling to accept EPS dilution beyond 5 percent. Net income for WPNB is forecast to be $22.6 million in 2002, while net income for CTB is forecast at $5.2 million. The problem is to determine a range of acquisition prices for CTB by applying each of the valuation procedures described earlier. When evaluating EPS dilution, assume that WPNB is considering a 0.5-for-1 stock exchange where CTB stockholders will get one share of WPNB stock for every two shares of CTB stock. Using the discounted cash flow approach, a minimum acceptable rate of return of 15 percent per year is assumed.

· EXHIBIT 22.10

INCOME STATEMENT FOR WESTERN PLAINS NATIONAL BANK (WPNB)

	2000	Rate	2001	Rate
Interest Income				
Loans and losses (includes fees)	$97.9	10.0%	$89.5	8.5%
Interest-bearing deposits	2.3	5.0%	2.2	3.5%
Treasury & U.S. agency securities	7.9	5.2%	4.6	3.7%
Corporate & mortgage backed securities	4.1	6.8%	3.9	5.3%
Municipals	3.0	4.2%	2.1	3.1%
Total interest income	$115.2		$102.3	
Interest Expense				
Deposits	43.1	5.0%	29.4	3.2%
Federal funds purchased & RPs	7.6	4.6%	5.0	3.0%
Other borrowed funds	6.8	6.0%	5.4	4.2%
Total interest expense	$ 57.5		$ 39.7	
Net Interest Income	57.7		62.5	
		% TL		**% TL**
Provisions for loan losses	4.9	0.5%	5.3	0.5%
Net interest for income after provisions	$ 52.8		$ 57.3	
		% TA		**% TA**
NonInterest Income	30.5	2.0%	32.2	2.0%
NonInterest Expense				
Salaries & benefits	32.0	2.1%	30.6	1.9%
Other expense	35.1	2.3%	35.4	2.2%
Total noninterest expense	$67.1		$66.0	
Income before taxes	16.1		23.5	
Provision for income taxes (avg tax rate)	3.4	21.0%	4.8	20.5%
Net Income	$12.7		$18.6	
Dividends paid to parent	$0		$15	
Retained Earnings	$13		$4	

NOTE: Figures are in millions of dollars. TL is total loan and TA is total asset.

HISTORICAL PERFORMANCE ANALYSIS

The first stage of the valuation process involves familiarizing oneself with the historical profitability and risk profile of the prospective parties to the transaction. Exhibit 22.14 summarizes the basic components of the ROE model for 2001 using balance sheet data for both banks. Several brief conclusions are offered. First, WPNB was comparatively more profitable than CTB in 2001, and above its peers in terms of ROE. CBT and WPNB, however, reported lower ROAs as compared with peers, indicating that WPNB's ROE was higher because it used greater financial leverage. WPNB's expense ratio was below peers but higher than CTB's. Although WPNB's asset utilization was well above CTB, it was significantly below peers. CTB and WPNB exhibited greater expense control than peers, but reported a lower yield on earning assets. WPNB and CTB both have higher noninterest expense relative to peers. Provisions for loan losses are low for both banks. In terms of assets, WPNB earns less in interest and noninterest income than peers. Interest income is below peers while noninterest income is above

· EXHIBIT 22.11

BALANCE SHEET FOR CITIZENS TRUST BANK (CTB)

	2000	%TA	2001	%TA
Assets				
Cash and due from banks	$23	7.1%	$23	6.9%
Interest-bearing deposits with banks	18	5.4%	19	5.5%
Investment securities:				
Treasury & U.S. agency	40	12.3%	40	11.8%
Corporate & mortgage-backed securities	17	5.2%	18	5.4%
Municipals	19	5.7%	20	5.9%
Total loans and leases	187	57.7%	196	58.0%
Less reserve for losses	3	1.0%	4	1.1%
Net loans and leases	$184	56.8%	$192	56.9%
Real estate owned	3	1.0%	4	1.1%
Premises and equipment	7	2.1%	7	2.2%
Other assets	14	4.4%	15	4.3%
Total assets	$324	100.0%	$338	100.0%
Liabilities				
Demand deposits	$67	20.7%	$70	20.8%
Savings deposits	99	30.5%	106	31.3%
Time deposits	97	30.0%	103	30.5%
Total deposits	$263	81.2%	$279	82.6%
Borrowed funds:				
Federal funds purchased & RPs	21	6.5%	14	4.0%
Other borrowed funds	3	1.0%	4	1.3%
Acceptances and other liabilities	5	1.5%	5	1.6%
Total liabilities	$292	90.2%	$302	89.5%
Stockholders Equity				
Common stock	15	4.6%	15	4.4%
Retained earnings	17	5.2%	21	6.1%
Total stockholders' equity	$32	9.9%	$36	10.5%
Total liability and equity	$324	100%	$338	100.0%

NOTE: Figures are in millions of dollars.

peers for CTB. WPNB's lower interest expense, however, led to a higher net interest margin than peers and that of CTB.

Key risk ratios are not available, so it is difficult to get a clear picture of the bank's overall risk and return profile. Still, several potential sources of difficulty for CTB appear to be its relatively lower interest and noninterest earnings and a smaller earning asset base. CTB's assets do not appear to be accruing interest as they should, which could be attributed to poor loan quality, an investment portfolio earning below market coupon interest, or other problems. CTB's high equity base and lower earning assets could indicate a slow growth or low opportunity loan market, which could mean their deposits could be invested more effectively.

VALUATION BASED ON ALTERNATIVE PROCEDURES

The first step is to calculate the book value of CTB's stock. The second step is to conduct a comparative analysis of similar banks and completed acquisitions, which have recently

- **EXHIBIT 22.12**

INCOME STATEMENT FOR CITIZENS TRUST BANK (CTB)

	2000	Rate	2001	Rate
Interest Income				
Loans and losses (includes fees)	$16.2	8.8%	$15.2	7.9%
Interest-bearing deposits	0.7	4.1%	0.6	3.2%
Treasury & U.S. agency securities	1.7	4.2%	1.3	3.3%
Corporate & mortgage-backed securities	1.3	7.8%	1.2	6.8%
Municipals	0.7	3.9%	0.7	3.3%
Total interest income	$20.6		$19.0	
Interest Expense				
Deposits	7.3	3.7%	6.3	3.0%
Federal funds purchased & RPs	0.9	4.5%	0.5	3.6%
Other borrowed funds	0.2	5.9%	0.2	5.0%
Total interest expense	$8.4		$7.0	
Net Interest Income	12.3		12.0	
		% TL		***% TL***
Provisions for loan losses	0.9	0.5%	1.2	0.6%
Net interest income after provisions	$11.3	***% TA***	$10.9	***% TA***
Noninterest Income	6.2	1.9%	6.8	2.0%
Noninterest Expense				
Salaries & benefits	6.5	2.0%	6.4	1.9%
Other expense	6.5	2.0%	7.1	2.1%
Total noninterest expense	$13.0		$13.5	
Income before taxes	4.5		4.1	
Provision for income taxes (avg tax rate)	0.6	13.8%	0.6	13.9%
Net Income	$3.9		$3.5	

NOTE: Figures are in millions of dollars. TL is total loans and TA is total assets.

occurred. According to Exhibit 22.13, stockholders' equity at CTB at the end of 2001 is $35.5 million, or $11.85 per share. For comparative purposes, WPNB's book value per share equals $26.43 in 2001. Estimated per share offering prices for CBT can be obtained using the average multiples for comparable companies which appear in Panel A of Exhibit 22.15 and average multiples for recently completed transactions appear in Panel B.[12] The prices per share using median multiples for comparable companies (Panel B) are:[13]

Comparable Companies Analysis: Valuing Minority Interests

Price/Share	Premium over Book
P_{ta} = $17.12 = (0.152) $\times$ $112.64	44.48%
P_{bv}^{norm} = $18.33 = (1.719) $\times$ $9.01 + 2.84	54.68%
P_{eps} = $15.47 = (13.085) $\times$ $1.182	30.55%

[12]Comparable mergers data were provided by SNL Securities (with permission). The authors wish to thank Scott Reed of Bear Stearns for the valuable assistance in providing the data.

[13]The following analysis assumes a normalized book value of equity of 8 percent.

■ EXHIBIT 22.13   SUMMARY PROFIT, DIVIDEND, ASSET, DEPOSIT, AND EQUITY DATA FOR WPNB AND CTB

A. Summary Profit and Dividend Figures

	WPNB				CTB			
	2000	Per Share	2001	Per Share	2000	Per Share	2001	Per Share
Number of shares outstanding	4,000,000		4,000,000		3,000,000		3,000,000	
Net income	$ 12,743,490	$ 3.19	$ 18,645,135	$ 4.66	$ 3,905,666	$ 1.30	$ 3,545,737	$ 1.18
Dividends	$ 5,000,000	$ 1.25	$ 14,916,108	$ 3.73	$ 1,950,000	$ 0.65	$ 1,950,000	$ 0.65
Total assets	$ 1,526,000,000	$381.50	$ 1,610,000,000	$402.50	$324,000,000	$108.00	$337,932,000	$112.64
Deposits	$ 1,097,000,000	$274.25	$ 1,158,000,000	$289.50	$263,107,786	$ 87.70	$279,131,832	$ 93.04
Excess Equity Calculation								
Book value of equity	$ 102,000,000	$ 25.50	$ 105,729,027	$ 26.43	$ 32,000,000	$ 10.67	$ 35,545,737	$ 11.85
Pro forma equity / Total assets							8.00%	
Implied normalized equity	$ 102,000,000					$ 10.67	$ 27,034,560	$ 9.01
Implied excess equity	$ 32,000,000						$ 8,511,177	$ 2.84

· EXHIBIT 22.14

PERFORMANCE RATIOS FOR WPNB, CITIZENS TRUST, AND PEER BANKS, 2001

	Citizens Trust	Peer Group: $300M to $500M in Assets	WPNB	Peer Group: $1B to $10B in Assets
ROE	10.04%	13.41%	17.63%	13.77%
ROA	1.06%	1.28%	1.16%	1.31%
Equity multiplier	9.50×	10.58×	15.23×	10.25×
Profit margin (Net income/Total revenue)	13.87%	14.22%	13.87%	14.00%
Expense ratio (expenses excluding taxes/TA)	6.39%	7.18%	6.89%	7.35%
Asset utilization (Total revenue/Total assets)	7.62%	9.00%	8.35%	9.36%
Yield on earning assets	6.58%	7.87%	7.41%	7.76%
Cost of funding earning assets	2.40%	3.50%	2.88%	3.45%
Net interest margin	4.17%	4.37%	4.53%	4.31%
Interest expense/Total assets	2.05%	3.19%	2.47%	3.09%
Noninterest expense/Total assets	4.00%	3.64%	4.10%	3.60%
Provisions for loan losses/Total assets	0.34%	0.35%	0.33%	0.66%
Efficiency ratio	71.83%	62.14%	69.68%	55.75%
Interest income/Total assets	5.62%	7.19%	6.35%	6.95%
Noninterest income/Total assets	2.00%	1.77%	2.00%	2.35%
Earning assets/Total assets	85.50%	90.87%	85.71%	89.27%

NOTE: M refers to millions; B refers to billions.

The prices per share using median multiples for comparable acquisitions (Panel A) are:

Comparable Acquisitions Analysis: Valuing Controlling Interest

Price/Share		Premium over Book
P_{ta}	$= \$21.73 = (0.193) \times \$112.64$	83.38%
P_{bv}^{norm}	$= \$19.56 = (1.855) \times \$9.01 + 2.84$	65.06%
P_{eps}	$= \$22.41 = (18.96) \times \$1.182$	89.11%
P_{td}	$= \$22.89 = (0.246) \times \$93.04$	93.16%

According to these procedures, the prospective offering price for a share of CTB's stock ranges from $15.47 with the price-to-earnings per share value approach for minority interest to $22.89 based on the price-to-total deposits approach using an acquisitions analysis. The column of data under "Premium over Book" indicates the percentage premium that each share price represents to the book value share price. These estimates actually provide a wide range of values when considering minority values but a somewhat narrower range when evaluating controlling interest value. Earnings and "core deposits" are clearly driving the market today and CTB's core deposits provide the highest value of all the methods.

EPS DILUTION. WPNB's management has stipulated that dilution will not be allowed to exceed 5 percent. Recall that EPS for WPNB is expected to be $5.65 ($22.6 million / 4 million) in 2002. This constraint means that EPS of the consolidated bank after acquisition cannot fall below $5.3675. From Equation 22.1:

$$\frac{(5.65 - \text{consolidated EPS})}{\$5.65} = 0.05$$

or

$$\text{consolidated EPS} = \$5.3675$$

Recalling that WPNB is currently trading at $60 a share, the exchange ratios consistent with the four valuation procedures range from 0.2578 to 1 up to 0.3815 to 1.

■ EXHIBIT 22.15

NATIONAL COMPARABLE MERGERS DATA

A. Summary Comparable Companies Data, 2001

Comparable Acquisition Analysis

Transaction Group	Number of Transactions	2001 Transaction Multiples				Implied Per Share Values Citizens Trust Bank			
		Price / EPS (LTM)	Price / Book	Price / Assets	Price / Deposits	Price / EPS (LTM)	Price / Book*	Price / Assets	Price / Deposits
National Medians (All transactions)	240	18.90	1.65	0.17	0.20	$22.34	$17.72	$18.86	$18.93
Southern Banks, Assets between $100M and $1.0 billion	42	19.62	2.06	0.19	0.24	$23.19	$21.39	$21.41	$22.42
All Banks between $100M and $1.0B and ROA Greater than 1.25%	31	16.62	2.16	0.21	0.26	$19.64	$22.30	$24.13	$24.18
All Banks between $100M and $1.0B and Equity/Assets Greater than 10%	36	19.01	1.49	0.20	0.25	$22.47	$16.25	$22.04	$23.35
High		19.62	216.0%	21.42%	25.99%	23.19	$22.30	$24.13	$24.18
Average		18.54	184.0%	19.19%	23.89%	21.91	$19.42	$21.61	$22.22
Median		18.96	185.5%	19.29%	24.60%	22.41	$19.56	$21.73	$22.89
Low		16.62	148.9%	16.74%	20.35%	19.64	$16.25	$18.86	$18.93

*Normalized book value, assuming 8 percent equity as 'normal.'
SOURCE: SNL Securities, 2002.
Southern U.S. includes: AL, AR, FL, GA, LA, MS, NC, OK, SC, TN, TX, VA, and WV.

B. Summary Comparable Acquisitions Data, 2001

Comparable Companies Analysis

Statistics on Comparable Companies Multiple of Market Value

	High	Low	Mean	Median
LTM				
Total Assets	0.359×	0.093×	0.162×	0.152×
Tangible Book Value*	2.490×	1.155×	1.688×	1.719×
LTM EPS	85.000×	10.131×	17.181×	13.085×
2002 Est EPS	28.333×	9.350×	13.037×	12.195×
2003 Est EPS	14.856×	8.611×	11.288×	11.255×

Citizens Trust Bank

	Per Share 3,000,000	Actual Values	Implied Per Share Equity Value			
			High	Low	Mean	Median
Total Assets	112.64	$337,932,000	40.44	10.48	18.25	17.12
Tangible Book Value*	11.85	$ 35,545,737	25.28	13.25	18.05	18.33
LTM EPS	1.182	$ 3,545,737	100.46	11.97	20.31	15.47
2002 Est EPS	1.724	$ 5,172,415	48.85	16.12	22.48	21.03
2003 Est EPS	1.961	$ 5,883,841	29.14	16.89	22.14	22.07

*Normalized book value, assuming 8 percent equity as 'normal.'
SOURCE: SNL Securities, 2002 (Pricing as of 3/25/2002).
Summary of 21 comparable banking companies with similar assets, capital, and profitability characteristics.

Valuing Minority Interests	Valuing Controlling Interest
$\dfrac{P_{ta}}{MP_a} = \dfrac{\$17.12}{\$60} = 0.2853$	$\dfrac{P_{ta}}{MP_a} = \dfrac{\$21.73}{\$60} = 0.3622$
$\dfrac{P_{bv}}{MP_a} = \dfrac{\$18.33}{\$60} = 0.3055$	$\dfrac{P_{bv}}{MP_a} = \dfrac{\$19.56}{\$60} = 0.3260$
$\dfrac{P_{eps}}{MP_a} = \dfrac{\$15.47}{\$60} = 0.2578$	$\dfrac{P_{eps}}{MP_a} = \dfrac{\$22.41}{\$60} = 0.3735$
	$\dfrac{P_{td}}{MP_a} = \dfrac{\$22.89}{\$60} = 0.3815$

Assuming a 0.5-for-1 stock exchange where holders of CTB stock get one-half of a share of WPNB stock for each share of CTB stock, the number of shares outstanding in the combined firm would total 5.5 million. Given forecasted net income of $22.6 million and $5.2 million for WPNB and CTB respectively, the combined EPS would equal $5.0545 for 2002. This is well below the $5.3675 minimum established by WPNB's management and actually represents 10.54 percent dilution. If management sticks to this restriction, it must offer a less than 0.5-for-1 stock exchange. (Holders of CTB stock must exchange more than 2 shares for each one share of WPNB.) In fact, the maximum stock exchange rate to keep EPS dilution at 5 percent is 39.31 shares of WPNB's stock for each 100 shares in Citizens Trust Bank (exchange 2.54 shares of CTB for 1 share of WPNB). This is obtained by solving for the maximum number of shares that can be outstanding (n) if projected income is $27.8 million for the combined firm.

$$\frac{\$5.65 - \$27,800,000/n}{\$5.65} = 0.05$$

or

$$n = 5.17932 \text{ million}$$

Thus, CTB stockholders can receive no more than 1.17932 million shares in WPNB or 22.77 percent of total outstanding shares. Whether this will be acceptable depends on the increase in value provided to CTB's stockholders. If CTB's current stock price equalled $15, then with 3 million shares their market capitalization would be $45 million. The value of a share in WPNB after the acquisition would have to be at least $38.16 ($45 million / 1.17932 million) for stockholders to be indifferent on a strictly cash basis. Because this price is well below WPNB's current $60 stock price, the exchange may be attractive to CTB's shareholders.

DISCOUNTED CASH FLOW APPROACH. The discounted cash flow (DCF) approach is based on the notion that investors will value a bank based on the present value of future cash earnings they expect to receive from the purchased bank over the life of the investment. Exhibits 22.16 and 22.17 contain projections of CTB's balance sheet and income statement. Assets at CTB are expected to grow at 10 and 11 percent in 2002 and 2003, respectively. Asset growth is then expected to slow back down to 7 percent and reach a more normal 5 percent by 2005 and thereafter. The percentage of assets invested in net loans at CTB is expected to increase from 57.5 percent to 60 percent by 2004. Interest rates are expected to increase somewhat over the next three years and CTB is expected to control noninterest expense and increase noninterest income slightly. Return on the book value of equity is projected to be 17.4%, 17.8%, and 18.25% percent from 2002 to 2004, respectively. While return on equity (ROE) is expected to be approximately 18.4 percent from 2005 and beyond. CTB is expected to maintain a minimum

EXHIBIT 22.16 PRO FORMA BALANCE SHEET FOR CITIZENS TRUST BANK (CTB)

	2002	% TA	2003	% TA	Pro Forma 2004	% TA	2005	% TA	2006	% TA	2007	% TA
Assets												
Cash and due from banks	$24	6.5%	$25	6.0%	$26	6.0%	$28	6.0%	$29	6.0%	$31	6.0%
interest bearing deposits with banks	22	5.8%	25	6.0%	27	6.2%	29	6.2%	30	6.2%	32	6.2%
Investment securities:												
Treasury & U.S. agency	43	11.5%	41	10.0%	40	9.0%	42	9.0%	44	9.0%	46	9.0%
Corporate & mortgage-backed securities	19	5.0%	21	5.0%	22	5.0%	23	5.0%	24	5.0%	26	5.0%
Municipals	22	6.0%	25	6.0%	26	6.0%	28	6.0%	29	6.0%	31	6.0%
Total loans and leases	221	59.5%	253	61.2%	274	62.0%	287	62.0%	302	62.0%	317	62.0%
Less reserve for losses	7	2.0%	8	2.0%	9	2.0%	9	2.0%	10	2.0%	10	2.0%
Net loans and leases	$214	57.5%	$244	59.2%	$265	60.0%	$278	60.0%	$292	60.0%	$307	60.0%
Real estate owned	4	1.1%	5	1.1%	5	1.1%	5	1.1%	5	1.1%	6	1.1%
Premises and equipment	9	2.3%	10	2.4%	11	2.5%	12	2.5%	12	2.5%	13	2.5%
Other assets	16	4.3%	18	4.3%	19	4.3%	20	4.3%	21	4.3%	22	4.3%
Total assets	$372	100.0%	$413	100.0%	$441	100%	$464	100%	$487	100%	$511	100%
Liabilities												
Demand deposits	$78	21.0%	$87	21.0%	$93	21.0%	$97	21.0%	$102	21.0%	$107	21.0%
Savings deposits	119	32.1%	132	32.1%	142	32.1%	149	32.1%	156	32.1%	164	32.1%
Time deposits	121	32.5%	134	32.5%	143	32.5%	151	32.5%	158	32.5%	166	32.5%
Total deposits	$318	85.6%	$353	85.6%	$378	85.6%	$397	85.6%	$417	85.6%	$437	85.6%
Borrowed funds:												
Federal funds purchased & RPs	8	2.2%	9	2.2%	10	2.2%	10	2.2%	11	2.2%	11	2.2%
Other borrowed funds	4	1.2%	5	1.2%	5	1.2%	6	1.2%	6	1.2%	6	1.2%
Acceptances and other liabilities	11	3.0%	12	3.0%	13	3.0%	14	3.0%	15	3.0%	15	3.0%
Total liabilities	$342	92.0%	$380	92.0%	$406	92.0%	$426	92.0%	$448	92.0%	$470	92.0%
Stockholders Equity												
Common stock	15	4.0%	15	3.6%	15	3.4%	15	3.2%	15	3.1%	15	2.9%
Retained earnings	15	4.0%	18	4.4%	20	4.6%	22	4.8%	24	4.9%	26	5.1%
Total stockholders' equity	$30	8.0%	$33	8.0%	$35	8.0%	$37	8.0%	$39	8.0%	$41	8.0%
Total liability and equity	$372	100.0%	$413	100.0%	$441	100.0%	$464	100.0%	$487	100.0%	$511	100.0%

NOTE: Figures are in millions of dollars.

PRO FORMA INCOME STATEMENT FOR CITIZENS TRUST BANK (CTB)

EXHIBIT 22.17

	2002	Rate	2003	Rate	2004	Rate	2005	Rate	2006	Rate	2007	Rate
Interest Income												
Loans and losses (includes fees)	$17.5	8.2%	$20.8	8.5%	$22.5	8.5%	$23.6	8.5%	$24.8	8.5%	$26.1	8.5%
Interest-bearing deposits	0.8	3.6%	1.0	3.9%	1.1	3.9%	1.1	3.9%	1.2	3.9%	1.2	3.9%
Treasury & U.S. agency securities	2.3	5.3%	2.3	5.6%	2.2	5.6%	2.3	5.6%	2.5	5.6%	2.6	5.6%
Corporate & mortgage-backed securities	1.3	7.1%	1.5	7.4%	1.6	7.4%	1.7	7.4%	1.8	7.4%	1.9	7.4%
Municipals	0.8	3.7%	1.0	4.0%	1.1	4.0%	1.1	4.0%	1.2	4.0%	1.2	4.0%
Total interest income	$22.7		$26.6		$28.5		$29.9		$31.4		$33.0	
Interest Expense												
Deposits	8.2	3.3%	10.2	3.7%	10.8	3.7%	11.3	3.7%	11.8	3.7%	12.4	3.7%
Federal funds purchased & RPs	0.3	3.8%	0.4	4.1%	0.4	4.1%	0.4	4.1%	0.4	4.1%	0.5	4.1%
Other borrowed funds	0.2	5.4%	0.3	5.6%	0.3	5.6%	0.3	5.6%	0.3	5.6%	0.3	5.6%
Total interest expense	$8.7		$10.8		$11.5		$12.0		$12.6		$13.2	
Net Interest Income	14.0		15.7		17.0		17.9		18.8		19.8	
		% TA		% TA		% TA		% TA		% TA		% TA
Provisions for loan losses	1.3	0.6%	1.5	0.6%	1.6	0.6%	1.7	0.6%	1.8	0.6%	1.8	0.6%
Net interest income after provisions	$12.7		$14.3		$15.4		$16.3		$17.1		$17.9	
Noninterest Income	8.2	2.2%	9.1	2.2%	9.7	2.2%	10.2	2.2%	10.7	2.2%	11.2	2.2%
Noninterest Expense												
Salaries & benefits	7.1	1.9%	7.8	1.9%	8.4	1.9%	8.8	1.9%	9.2	1.9%	9.7	1.9%
Other expense	7.8	2.1%	8.7	2.1%	9.3	2.1%	9.7	2.1%	10.2	2.1%	10.7	2.1%
Total noninterest expense	$14.9		$16.5		$17.7		$18.5		$19.5		$20.4	
Income before taxes	6.0		6.8		7.5		7.9		8.3		8.7	
Provision for income taxes (avg tax rate)	0.8	13.9%	0.9	13.9%	1.0	14.0%	1.1	14.0%	1.2	14.0%	1.2	14.0%
Net Income	$5.2		$5.9		$6.4		$6.8		$7.2		$7.5	

NOTE: Figures are in millions of dollars.

	2002	2003	2004	2005	2006	2007
Growth in total assets	10.0%	11.0%	7.0%	5.0%	5.0%	5.0%
Return on equity	17.4%	17.8%	18.25%	18.40%	18.40%	18.40%
Return on assets	1.39%	1.43%	1.46%	1.47%	1.47%	1.47%
Retained earnings	−5.81	3.27	2.31	1.77	1.85	1.95
Dividends paid to parent	10.98	2.61	4.13	5.06	5.31	5.57
Dividend per share to parent	3.66	0.87	1.38	1.69	1.77	1.86
Growth in earnings to parent	N/A	−76.2%	58.23%	22.30%	5.00%	5.00%
Required return	15.0%	15.0%	15.0%	15.0%	15.0%	15.0%
Present value of dividends per share to parent	3.18	0.66	0.91	0.96	0.88	0.80

capital-to-asset ratio of 8 percent. Based on Citizen's projections, dividends or earnings available to WPNB after required additions to capital are expected to be:

	2001	2002	2003	2004	2005	2006
Dividends paid to parent ($ millions)	$ 10.98	$ 2.61	$ 4.13	$ 5.06	$ 5.31	$ 5.57
Dividends per share to parent	$ 3.66	$ 0.87	$ 1.38	$ 1.69	$ 1.77	$ 1.86
Growth in earnings to parent	N/A	−76.21%	58.23%	22.30%	5.00%	5.00%
Required return	15%	15%	15%	15%	15%	15%
Present value of dividends per share to parent	$ 3.18	$ 0.66	$ 0.91	$ 0.96	$ 0.88	$ 0.80

Note that beginning in 2006, the growth in earnings available to WPNB (the parent bank) stabilizes around 5 percent. If we break this problem into two parts, we would use the period from 2002 through 2005 as our explicit forecast period and the period from 2006 and beyond as the implicit forecast period. Earnings are expected to grow at approximately 5 percent beyond 2005 and the bank's required return is 15 percent. Applying Equation 22.19 produces a market value of equity of $45.39 million or $15.13 per share:

$$Bank\ Value\ per\ share = \$15.83 = \frac{3.66}{1.15} + \frac{0.87}{1.15^2} + \frac{1.38}{1.15^3} + \frac{1.69}{1.15^4} + \frac{\left[\frac{1.77}{0.15 - 0.05}\right]}{1.15^4}$$

This value represents a 1.336 multiple over book value for the bank, below the 2001 market determined price-to-book values of 1.855 times for controlling interest and the 1.719 minority interest. It is generally assumed that a minority shareholder cannot change the interim cash flows due to a lack of control. A higher DCF value could easily be obtained if we credit the acquirer with controlling interest in which they could credit the seller (CTB) with some of the cost savings expected as a result of the acquisition. Basically, for the market to justify the prices actually paid for U.S. and foreign banks in 2001, significant cost savings or dramatic increases in earnings must be expected! Unfortunately, many times these expected cost savings, because of controlling interest, do not always materialize. Second, since the transaction is stock for stock, the transaction prices could well be higher if the stock price of WPNB is 'high' relative to its discounted cash flow value. DCF analysis assumes a 'cash' value where most multiples used in the industry assume stock for stock transactions.

IMPLICATIONS

The previous analysis suggests a range of potential prices for CTB stock. The final resolution will depend on the negotiating strength of each party as well as nonfinancial considerations that have not been addressed. The relationships observed among the various procedures are representative of results in many applications. From an economic perspective, the present value approach often produces the lowest price estimate. If a transaction can be negotiated close to this price, the acquirer will experience the smallest EPS dilution and will be able to reach its earnings objectives soonest. Not surprisingly, sellers prefer to focus on historical premium-to-book value and premium-to-earnings valuation approaches.

NONFINANCIAL CONSIDERATIONS THAT AFFECT MERGERS AND ACQUISITIONS

The previous discussion focused on financial aspects of analyzing a prospective merger or acquisition. In every transaction, there are nonfinancial considerations that are even more important. Managers of buyers and sellers have fundamental objectives, opportunities, and fears that can be beneficially served or seriously harmed by such deals. At the forefront are the egos of the senior managers for both acquirer and target. Even in the case where there is a presumed **merger of equals,** where the two institutions are comparable in size, one group generally gains at the expense of the other and egos must be accommodated accordingly. It is difficult for a bank CEO or president to willingly give up control of an organization that he or she once dominated, even if it is best for shareholders. Thus, friendly transactions are difficult to complete unless serious personnel issues are successfully resolved. Of course, in a hostile takeover, the seller's most senior management team is generally removed. The mergers of Citicorp and Travelers as well as NationsBank and Bank America are such examples of a presumed merger of equals where senior management in one firm quickly left after the transaction was complete.

Although price is the most important consideration in most transactions, buyers and sellers have important nonprice objectives. Buyers typically want to:

- Avoid post-merger financial and operational complications
- Retain the best employees of the acquired bank
- Keep the acquired bank's best customers
- Maintain the beneficial aspects of the acquired bank's culture

In many cases, the banks have different computer systems and software, but the acquirer wants to convert the target bank to its system to cut costs. If there are operational snags, customers are relatively impatient and will move their relationships.

Key employees are also difficult to retain. Those who are exceptional will have alternatives to move, often at a substantial increase in pay. These same employees may be able to move profitable accounts with them. This routinely occurs when bankers at acquired institutions leave and charter a new community bank. They criticize the previous organization for forgetting the individual and commit to serving customers on a personal basis. Any loss of key personnel and accounts makes it difficult to grow earnings and can damage the bank's public image. Of course, the seller's lower level employees are often frightened about job security. Many acquisitions are motivated in large part by perceived cost savings. These savings are typically derived from shrinking personnel expense. Thus, even if employees keep their jobs, the potential increase in salary is unknown and the benefits package may worsen. The essential point is that uncertainty creates tremendous anxiety.

Sellers in a friendly transaction typically want to walk away from the deal without any residual risk. This means they want to be indemnified against yet unrevealed liabilities or losses that might arise from decisions under their tenure. They are primarily concerned, however, with the size of the premium offered. In a cash transaction, the subsequent issue is when the cash payment will be made. In a securities transaction, the key issue is the value and marketability of the securities. Sellers of community banks are also concerned about whether a deal will adversely affect the local community. Many will try to exact concessions from acquirers to keep employees, not move data processing facilities out of the community, and keep supporting local community projects.

SUMMARY

The relaxation of regulatory constraints, enactment of interstate branching, and record profitability leading to high capital levels at banks have spurred the consolidation of banking organizations. Banks with strong equity capital positions have been on a buying spree. As the nation's largest banks strategically identify the geographic markets in which they want to compete and the value of increased market penetration for their portfolio of financial products and services, they will continue to buy both bank and nonbank firms.

This chapter describes the financial and nonfinancial factors that buyers and sellers must consider when deciding whether to negotiate a deal, and if so, at what price. Participants generally use several different procedures for establishing a value for the acquired bank. The most appropriate procedure views the purchase of bank stock as an investment. The buyer projects future earnings (cash flows) that are discounted at the minimum required rate of return to determine the true economic value. Other procedures focus on recently completed transactions and average premium-to-book value or earnings ratios. These historical averages are then applied to a bank's financial measures to estimate a range of prices. In general, these latter procedures produce higher price estimates than discounting future cash flows.

Participants also consider nonfinancial issues when negotiating a merger or acquisition. The most important concern in a friendly transaction is whether the two cultures match and whether senior officers can work together. It is also important to recognize what impact efforts to cut noninterest expense will have on employee attitudes and opportunities. Mergers generally have both beneficial and harmful aspects depending on the relative perspectives of stockholders, bank employees, or bank customers.

QUESTIONS

1. How does a bank merger differ from a bank acquisition?

2. Assume that you work for a large, regional bank as a junior loan officer. Your supervising officer informs you that your bank has just been acquired by a larger commercial banking organization. Assume that the other bank is located in another region of the country and has limited business activity in your geographic market.
    a. How might the acquisition affect your responsibilities? Will it differ if you are a commercial lender or a consumer lender?
    b. How might the acquisition affect you if you were instead involved in marketing, personnel, or data processing?
    c. Suppose, instead, that the acquiring bank was headquartered in a neighboring state and has extensive lending activity in your state. How would your answers to the above questions differ, if at all?
    d. Suppose, instead, that your bank acquires another large bank. How will your answers to the above questions change, if at all?

3. The value of an acquisition is difficult to assess before the fact. Identify the factors that can potentially increase value. In each case, indicate where difficulties might arise in realizing the increased value.

4. Provide a list of cost savings that might be available from a merger. How will it differ if the merger is in-market (firms serve same geographic markets with similar products) versus out-of-market?

5. What types of bank risk should be considered when evaluating a merger or acquisition?

6. Describe what earnings dilution is in an acquisition. Explain what it means when EPS dilution is a high figure.

7. Describe what impact each of the following will have on a bank's adjusted book value.
    a. Bank owns common stock that is currently worth $90 per share, but is listed at its original acquired value of $10 per share.
    b. Bank has more problem loans than it has reported.
    c. Bank has just lost a lawsuit and will be forced to make a cash payment of $1.25 per share.

8. Explain why an investor would be willing to pay more than book value for a bank's stock.

PROBLEMS

1. Bayou Bank is considering the acquisition of Crawfish Bank. During the past three years, Bayou Bank has bought four small banks with the following average bids relative to the acquired bank's ratios:
   a. Bid price per share/book value per share = 2.03
   b. Bid price per share/adjusted book value per share = 2.353
   c. Bid price per share/earnings per share = 16.43
   d. Bid price per share/preannouncement price per share = 1.863

   Bayou has collected the following information for Crawfish Bank. Use it to determine a range of stock prices that Bayou Bank could offer in a tender offer, according to the procedures described in the chapter. Bayou Bank requires a 15 percent return on equity for any acquisition of this type.

   Total assets = $560 million
   Total liabilities = $510 million
   Number of shares outstanding = 4,000,000
   Book (market) value of investments = $100 million ($102.5 million)
   Market value of off-balance sheet activities = $3 million
   Anticipated loan losses not reflected on-balance sheet = $25 million
   Market price of stock = $13.20
   Net income (estimate for next year) = 6.55 million
   Forecast return on equity:
   next year = 13.5%; next three years = 14.5%; thereafter = 16% annually

2. A takeover attempt has been made for the bank in which you are a stockholder. There are two offers on the table. One is a cash tender offer for $50 a share if shares are tendered within one month. The other is a stock swap in the acquiring bank in which you would get three shares of the acquiring bank for each two shares of your bank tendered. The acquiring bank's stock is currently selling for $36 per share. Before the offers were made, your bank's stock was selling for $40 per share. Which of the offers is better? What should your bank's stock price equal now at a minimum?

3. Coastal Bank is considering buying Valley Bank. Valley Bank's stockholder will receive two shares of Coastal Bank's stock for every one share of Valley Bank's stock they own. Valley's revenues are growing at 12 percent annually while its expenses are growing at 10 percent. Coastal Bank's revenues and expenses are both growing at 10 percent a year. Given the following information, what current EPS dilution and dilution in one year will occur with this merger if the combined firm's net income grows at 1.5 percent? Calculate the micro-dilution EPS. Will EPS be restored for Coastal's stockholders within five years?

4. First State Bank is looking for a potential acquisition on which it will require a return of 20 percent. It is considering the purchase of City Bank, which currently has a stock price with $18 book value and 1 million shares outstanding. City Bank is expected to earn a 15 percent ROE for the next four years and an 18 percent ROE for the next six years. Using the discounted cash flow procedure, determine what price is warranted for City Bank's stock. Explain why First State Bank might reasonably have to pay a premium over this price.

5. Bigtime Bank (BB) is considering making an offer on Local Lender (LL), a small community bank. BB has collected the following information:

Balance Sheet (in millions)

	BB		LL	
	20×1	20×2	20×1	20×2
Assets				
Cash and near cash	$100	$110	$40	$50
Investments	200	200	10	15
Gross loans	1,000	1,100	400	400
Less: reserves	50	55	40	50
Net loans	950	1,045	360	350
Other assets	50	50	10	10
Total	$1,300	$1,405	$420	$425
Liabilities				
Deposits	1,000	1,100	300	350
Borrowed funds	100	85	65	20
Equity	200	220	55	55

Other Balance Sheet Considerations	BB	LL
Additional provisions for losses	60	—
Securities depreciation	20	—
Franchise value (2% of core deposits)	4	4
Number of shares (millions)	5	3

Income Statement (in millions)

	BB		LL	
	20×1	20×2	20×1	20×2
Interest income	$150	$160	$60	$50
Interest expense	70	75	20	18
Noninterest income	30	40	5	5
Noninterest expense	60	65	45	40
Taxes	20	20	—	—
Net income	30	40	0	(3)

	BB	LL
Net income forecast for 20×3	45	0
Net income forecast if merger succeeds	44	8

BB management has already made these decisions:

- Two LL shares (currently at $20/share) will trade for one BB share (currently at $34/share).
- EPS dilution must be restricted to 4 percent.
- Required return on investments of this risk is 14 percent.

With the following additional information, perform a historical analysis of both BB and LL. Start by completing the following table.

BB	LL	Peer
ROE		15%
ROA		1%
Total assets/Equity		153
Total assets/Interest income		103
Interest expense/Interest income		50%
Noninterest expense/Total assets		1%

a. Calculate the book value per share and the adjusted book value per share for both banks. Use the "Other Balance Sheet Considerations" section of data to do the adjusting.

b. Using the following ratios taken from recent mergers and acquisitions, what range of prices is reasonable for LL?
   1. bid price per share/book value per share   1.5×
   2. bid price per share/adjusted book value   1.9×
   3. bid price per share/EPS   14×
   4. bid price per share/preannouncement stock price   1.8×

c. Because management has specified that earnings dilution must be limited to 4 percent, what is the minimum EPS acceptable to BB after a merger?

d. What exchange ratios would be fair if BB stock is worth $45 and LL stock is worth the following "true" values?

   $20

   $25

   $30

   $35

   Which of these exchange ratios would be best for BB stockholders? Would the same be the best for LL stockholders? At the proposed rate of two LL for one BB, would you expect the merger to receive approval?

e. If the merger is consummated at 2-for-1 and projected earnings materialize, will BB produce an acceptable EPS after dilution?

f. Why might the earnings forecast differ with a merger as opposed to without a merger?

Bank Structure and Regulation

"History of the Eighties–Lessons for the Future," a study prepared by the FDIC's Division of Research and Statistics, December 1997. http://www.fdic.gov/databank/hist80/contents.html.

"Better Than Basle." *Economist*, 06/19/99, Vol, 351 Issue 8124, P80, 1p.

"A Brief History of Deposit Insurance in the United States," prepared for the International Conference on Deposit Insurance, Washington, D.C., September 1998. http://www.fdic.gov/databank/brhist/brhist.pdf.

"New Directions in Interstate Banking." *Economic Review*, Federal Reserve Bank of Atlanta, special issue, January 1985.

"The Depository Institutions Deregulation and Monetary Control Act of 1980." *Economic Perspectives*, Federal Reserve Bank of Chicago, September– October, 1980.

"The Garn–St Germain Depository Institutions Act of 1982." *Economic Perspectives*, Federal Reserve Bank of Chicago, March–April, 1983.

"Payment Systems in the Global Economy: Risks and Opportunities." *Economic Perspectives*, 1998 1st Quarter, Vol. 22 Issue 1.

Aguilar, Linda. "Still Toe-to-Toe: Banks and Nonbanks at the End of the '80s." *Economic Perspectives*, Federal Reserve Bank of Chicago, January–February 1990.

Barsness, Robert N. "The Impact on Community Bankers." *Region* (Federal Reserve Bank Of Minneapolis), Mar 2000, Vol. 14, Issue 1, P23, 4p.

Barth, James and Dan Brumbaugh. *Financing Prosperity in the Next Century*. The Jerome Levy Economics Institute of Bard College, 1993.

Barth, James and Dan Brumbaugh, eds. *The Reform of Federal Deposit Insurance*. New York: HarperBusiness, 1992.

Barth, James, Genston, George and Philip Wiest. "The Financial Institutions Reform, Recovery and Enforcement Act of 1989: Description, Effects and Implications." *Issues in Bank Regulation*, Winter 1990.

Becketti, Sean. "The Truth About Junk Bonds." *Economic Review*, Federal Reserve Bank of Kansas City, July–August 1990.

Bennett, Barbara. "Bank Regulation and Deposit Insurance: Controlling the FDIC's Losses." *Economic Review*, Federal Reserve Bank of San Francisco, Spring 1984.

Benston, George. "Scale Economies in Banking: A Restructuring and Reassessment." *Journal of Money, Credit and Banking*, November 1982.

Berger, Allen, David Humphrey, and Lawrence B. Pulley. "Do Consumers Pay for One-Stop Banking? Evidence from an Alternative Revenue Function." *Journal of Banking & Finance*, November 1996.

Billett, Matthew T., Jon A. Garfinkel, and Edward S. O'Neal. "The Cost of Market versus Regulatory Discipline in Banking." *Journal of Financial Economics*, June 1998.

Brady, Nicholas. "Global Competition: A Catalyst for Restructuring U.S. Financial Services." *Issues in Bank Regulation*, Summer 1990.

Brenner, Lynn. "Credit Card Deal May Be Model for Securitization." *American Banker*, April 14, 1986.

Brenner, Lynn. "Turning Assets into Securities is Knotty Problem, Panel Says." *American Banker*, May 2, 1986.

Brewer III, Elijah; Evanoff, Douglas D.. "Changing Financial Industry Structure and Regulation." *Chicago Fed Letter*, Sep2000 Special Issue 157a.

Brewer III, Elijah; Evanoff, Douglas D.. "Global Financial Crisis: Implications for Banking and Regulation." *Chicago Fed Letter*, Aug99 Special Issue 144a.

Burke, Sarah A. "Privacy Matters: Payment Cards Center Workshop on the Right to Privacy and the Financial Services Industry." *Business Review*, Federal Reseve Bank of Philadelphia, Fourth Quarter 2001.

Bush, Vanessa and Katherine Morall. "FIRREA Slows Deregulation and Closes the Gap Between Commercial Banks and Savings Institutions." *Savings Institutions*, October 1989.

Calem, Paul. "The New Bank Deposit Markets: Goodbye to Regulation Q." *Business Review*, Federal Reserve Bank of Philadelphia, November–December 1985.

Carron, Andrew. *The Plight of the Thrift Industry*. Washington, D.C.: The Brookings Institute, 1982.

Cerda, Oscar; Brewer III, Elijah; Evanoff, Douglas D.. "The Financial Safety Net: Costs, Benefits and Implications." *Chicago Fed Letter*, Nov2001, Issue 171a.

Cocheo, Steve. "Anatomy of an Examination." *ABA Banking Journal*, February 1986.

Davis, Richard. "The Recent Performance of the Commercial Banking Industry." *Quarterly Review*, Federal Reserve Bank of New York, Summer 1986.

DeFerrari, Lisa M. and David E. Palmer. "Supervision of Large Complex Banking Organizations." *Federal Reserve Bulletin*, Board of Governors of the Federal Reserve System, February 2001.

DeYoung, Robert, Iftekhar Hasan, and Bruce Kirchhoff. "The Impact of Out-of-State Entry on the Cost Efficiency of Local Commercial Banks." *Journal of Economics & Business*, March–April 1998.

Eisenbeis, Robert. "Inflation and Regulation: The Effects on Financial Institutions and Structure." Chapter 3 in *Handbook For Banking Strategy*, Richard Aspinwall and Robert Eisenbeis, eds. New York: John Wiley & Sons, 1985.

Evanoff, Douglas D; Wall, Larry D. "Subordinated Debt and Bank Capital Reform." *Working Paper Series* (Federal Reserve Bank Of Atlanta), Nov2000, Vol. 2000 Issue 24, P1.

Evanoff, Douglas, and Diana Fortier. "The Impact of Geographic Expansion in Banking: Some Axioms to Grind." *Economic Perspectives*, Federal Reserve Bank of Chicago, May–June 1986.

Frieder, Larry. "Toward Nationwide Banks." *Economic Perspectives*, Federal Reserve Bank of Chicago, Special Issue, 1986.

Furlong, Fred and Simon Kwan. "Deposit Insurance Reform – When Half a Loaf is Better." *Economic Letter*, Federal Reserve Bank of San Francisco, No. 2002-14, May 10, 2002.

Garver, Rob. "Opening Moves on Agency Revamp." *American Banker*, February 19, 2002.

Guzman, Mark G.. "The Economic Impact of Bank Structure: A Review of Recent Literature." *Economic & Financial Review*, 2000 2nd Quarter.

Hancock, Diana and James Wilcox. "The 'Credit Crunch' and the Availability of Credit to Small Business." *Journal of Banking & Finance*, August 1998.

Haubrich, Joseph. "Bank Diversification: Laws and Fallacies of Large Numbers." *Economic Review*, Federal Reserve Bank of Cleveland, Second Quarter, 1998.

Hirtle, Beverly and Jose Lopez. "Supervisory Information and the Frequency of Bank Examinations." *Economic Policy Review*, Federal Reserve Bank of New York, April 1999.

Hoenig, Thomas M. "Rethinking Financial Regulation." *Economic Review*, Federal Reserve Bank of Kansas City, Second Quarter, 1996.

Hoenig, Thomas. "Bank Regulation: Asking the Right Questions." *Economic Review*, Federal Reserve Bank of Kansas City, First Quarter, 1997.

Jayaratne, Jith and Philip Strahan. "Entry Restrictions, Industry Evolution, and Dynamic Efficiency: Evidence from Commercial Banking." *Journal of Law & Economic*, April 1998.

Kane, Edward. "Accelerating Inflation, Technological Innovation, and the Decreasing Effectiveness of Banking Regulation." *Journal of Finance*, May 1981.

Kane, Edward. "Good Intentions and Unintended Evil: The Case Against Selective Credit Allocation." *Journal of Money Credit and Banking*, February 1977.

Kaufman, George G. and Larry R. Mote. "Is Banking a Declining Industry? A Historical Perspective." *Economic Perspectives*, Federal Reserve Bank of Chicago, May–June 1994.

Keeton, William R. "Are Rural Banks Facing Increased Funding Pressures? Evidence from Tenth District States." *Economic Review*, Federal Reserve Bank of Kansas City, Spring 1998.

Krainer, John and Jose Lopez. "Off-Site Monitoring of Bank Holding Companies." *Economic Letter*, Federal Reserve Bank of San Francisco, No. 2002-15, May 17, 2002.

Kroszner, Randall and Raghuram Rajan. "Organizational Structure and Credibility: Evidence from Commercial Bank Securities Activities before the Glass-Steagall Act." *Journal of Monetary Economics*, August 1997.

Kwan, Simon. "Financial Modernization and Banking Theories." *Economic Letter*, No. 2001-37, Federal Reserve Bank of San Francisco, December 21, 2001.

Liang, Nellie and Donald Savage. "The Nonbank Activities of Bank Holding Companies." *Federal Reserve Bulletin*, Board of Governors of the Federal Reserve System, May 1990.

Maclachlan, Fiona C. "Market Discipline in Bank Regulation." *Independent Review*, Fall 2001, Vol. 6 Issue 2.

Marquis, Milton. "What's Different About Banks – Still?" *Economic Letter*, No. 2001-09, Federal Reserve Bank of San Francisco, April 6, 2001.

Mester, Loretta. "Repealing Glass-Steagall: The Past Points the Way to the Future." *Business Review*, Federal Reserve Bank of Philadephia, July–August 1996.

Miller, Merton. "Financial Innovation: The Last Twenty Years and the Next." *Journal of Financial and Quantitative Analysis*, December 1986.

Nathans, Leah and William Glasgall. "Japan's Waiting Game on Wall Street." *Business Week*, February 19, 1990.

Orr, Bill. "International Debt Problem Clarified." *ABA Banking Journal*, May 1986.

Pavel, Christine. "Securitization." *Economic Perspectives*, Federal Reserve Bank of Chicago, July–August 1986.

Pozdena, Randall. "Securitization and Banking." *Weekly Letter*, Federal Reserve Bank of San Francisco, July 4, 1986.

Rose, John T. "Commercial Banks as Financial Intermediaries and Current Trends in Banking: A Pedagogical Framework." *Financial Practice and Education*, Fall 1993.

Rowe III, Robert and Kenneth Guenther. "The Erosion of the Glass-Steagall Act and the Bank Holding Company Act." *Banking Law Journal*, July–August 1998.

Savage, Donald. "Interstate Banking: A Status Report." *Federal Reserve Bulletin,* Board of Governors of the Federal Reserve System, December 1993.

Santomero, Anthony M. "The Causes and Effects of Financial Modernization." *Business Review,* Federal Reserve Bank of Philadelphia, Fourth Quarter 2001.

Santos, Joao. "Banking and Commerce: How Does the United States Compare to Other Countries?" *Economic Review,* Federal Reserve Bank of Cleveland, Fourth Quarter, 1998.

Sheehan, Kevin, P. "Electronic Cash." *FDIC Banking Review,* 1998, Vol. 11, No. 2. Available on the FDIC Internet Web site at http://www.fdic.gov/.

Stern, Gary H. "Managing Moral Hazard With Market Signals: How Regulation Should Change With Banking." *Region* (Federal Reserve Bank Of Minneapolis), Jun 99, Vol. 13, Issue 2, P28, 7p.

U.S. Department of the Treasury. "An Introduction to Electronic Money Issues." Washington, D.C., 1997.

Van Walleghem, Joe. "Financial Modernization: A New World or Status Quo?" *Financial Industry Perspectives 2001,* Federal Reserve Bank of Kansas City, December 2001.

Wright, Don. *The Effective Bank Director.* Reston, Va.: Reston Publishing Co., 1985.

Performance Analysis

Aggeler, Heidi and Ron Feldman. "Banking: Record Bank Profitability: How, Who and What Does it Mean?" *Fedgazette,* April 1998.

Asher, Joe. "Can Efficiency Go Too Far?" *ABA Banking Journal,* September 1994.

Atlas, Riva D. "They're Betting the Bank on a Comeback at J. P. Morgan." *New York Times,* 5/3/2002, Vol. 151 Issue 52107, Pc1, 0p, 2c, 1bw.

"Bank Performance." *Economic Trends* (Federal Reserve Bank Of Cleveland), December 1999.

Bassett, William F. and Egon Zakrajsek. "Profits and Balance Sheet Developments at U.S. Commercial Banks in 1999." *Federal Reserve Bulletin,* Board of Governors of the Federal Reserve System, June 2000.

Bassett, William F. and Egon Zakrajsek. "Profits and Balance Sheet Developments at U.S. Commercial Banks in 2000." *Federal Reserve Bulletin,* Board of Governors of the Federal Reserve System, June 2001.

Bassett, William F. and Thomas F. Brady. "The Economic Performance of Small Banks, 1985–2000." *Federal Reserve Bulletin,* Board of Governors of the Federal Reserve System, November 2001.

Beckett, Paul. "Citigroup to Split Off Travelers Property Unit." *Wall Street Journal,* December 20, 2001.

Bielski, Lauren. "The Great Risk Debate." *ABA Banking Online.* http://www.banking.com, May 9, 2002.

Cline, Kenneth. "A Matter of Scale." *Banking Strategies,* May–June 1998.

Cocheo, Steve, executive editor. *Community Bank Competitiveness Survey.* A supplement to the *ABA Banking Journal,* February 2000.

Cocheo, Steve, executive editor. *Community Bank Competitiveness Survey.* A supplement to the *ABA Banking Journal,* February 2002.

Cole, David W. "A Return-on-Equity Model for Banks." *The Bankers Magazine,* Summer 1972.

Community Banking: Practical Insights for Today's Market. *American Banker Special Report,* March 2002.

Condon, Bernard. "Sharepopper." Forbes, January 8, 2001.

Costanzo, Chris. "First Manhattan: 70% of Web Accounts Unprofitable." *American Banker,* December 14, 1999.

Creswell, Julie. "Covering their Assets." *Fortune,* March 4, 2002.

Crews, Joseph M. "Monitoring Bank Risks: New Requirements Yield Useful Ratios." *Magazine of Bank Administration,* October 1986.

Danielson, Arnold and Karen Holliday. "The Worst of Times is Over—Almost." *Bank Management,* September 1993.

Davidson, Steven. "Beyond the Efficiency Ratio." *America's Community Banker,* June 1995.

Davidson, Steven. "Measuring Profitability." *America's Community Banker,* October 1997.

Davidson, Steven. "Measuring Your Marketing ROI." *America's Community Banker,* March 1998.

DeNicola, Nino. "Making the Grade." *Bank Marketing,* November 1996.

"The Economic Performance of Small Banks, 1985–2000." *Federal Reserve Bulletin,* Nov2001, Vol. 87 Issue 11, P719, 10p.

Eden, Dov; Moriah, Leah. "Impact of Internal Auditing On Branch Bank Performance: A Field Experiment." *Organizational Behavior & Human Decision Processes,* Dec96, Vol. 68 Issue 3, P262.

Evanoff, Douglas. "Assessing the Impact of Regulation on Bank Cost Efficiency." *Economic Perspective,* Federal Reserve Bank of Chicago, Second Quarter 1998.

Fairley, Juliette. "What to do with the 'losers.' *ABA Banking Journal,* October 2000.

Federal Deposit Insurance Corporation. *FDIC Quarterly Banking Profile,* Office of Research and Statistics, Washington, D.C.

Furlong, Fred and Simon Kwan. "Rising Bank Risk?" *Economic Letter,* Federal Reserve Bank of San Francisco, No. 99-32, October 22, 1999.

Gamble, Richard. "Will Your Banks Clear the Bar? Measures of Financial Strength." *Corporate Cashflow,* November 1991.

Genay, Hesna. "Assessing the Condition of Japanese Banks: How Informative are Accounting Earnings?" *Economic Perspectives,* Federal Reserve Bank of Chicago, Fourth Quarter 1998.

Gup, Benton, and John Walters. "Top Performing Small Banks: Making Money the Old-Fashioned Way." *Economic Review,* Federal Reserve Bank of Richmond, November–December 1989.

Hannan, Timothy. "Retail Fees of Depository Institutions, 1994–1999." *Federal Reserve Bulletin,* Board of Governors of the Federal Reserve System, January 2001.

Harris, Shaun. "Quietly Staking Out the Future." *Finance Week,* May 21–27, 1998.

Harris, Shaun. "Showing Off its Market Approval." *Finance Week,* July 23–29, 1998.

Holliday, Karen. "Forget 'Cost-Cutting' Think Low-Cost Revenue Growth." *ABA Banking Journal,* November 2000.

Jayaratne, Jith; Strahan, Philip E. "Entry Restrictions, Industry Evolution, and Dynamic Efficiency: Evidence from Commercial Banking." *Journal Of Law & Economics,* Apr 98, Vol. 41 Issue 1, P239, 35p.

Jayaratne, Jith; Strahan, Philip E. "The Benefits of Branching Deregulation." *Economic Policy Review* (Federal Reserve Bank Of New York), Dec97, Vol. 3 Issue 4, P13, 17p.

Jorion, Phillippe. *Value at Risk.* Chicago: Irwin, 1997.

Kaplan, Robert and David Norton. *The Balanced Scorecard.* Boston: Harvard Business School Press, 1996.

Kessler, Lance. "Bank Performance: The Path to Sustainable High Performance." *Bank Marketing,* December 1998.

Kimball, Ralph. "Innovations in Performance Measurement in Banking." *New England Economic Review,* Federal Reserve Bank of Boston, May–June 1997.

Kimball, Ralph. "Economic Profit and Performance Measurement in Banking." *New England Economic Review,* Federal Reserve Bank of Boston, July–August 1998.

Kleege, Stephen. "Midsize Banks Score Best in Profit-Per-Client Study." *American Banker,* December 10, 1999.

Kwan, Simon.. "Has Bank Performance Peaked?." *FRBSF Economic Letter,* 10/27/2000, Vol. 2000 Issue 32.

Lee, W.A. "Credit Card Profitability Improved Again Last Year." *American Banker,* January 9, 2001.

Lopez, Jose. "What is Operational Risk?" *Economic Letter,* No. 2002–02, Federal Reserve Bank of San Francisco, January 25, 2002.

Mandaro, Laura. "New Accounting Change A Potential EPS Blow." *American Banker Market Monitor,* April 1, 2002.

Marshall, Jeffrey. "This Little Engine Can." *United States Banker,* May 1997.

Mathis, F John. "Impact of the Asia Crisis on Bank Performance." *Journal of Lending & Credit Risk Management,* October 1998.

McCandless, Thomas D. "Bank Performance 1998: Trouble Ahead?" *Banking Strategies,* January–February 1998.

Mester, Loretta. "Owners versus Managers: Who Controls the Bank?" *Business Review,* Federal Reserve Bank of Philadelphia, May–June 1989.

Michael, Nancy. "Banking's Top Performers 2002." *ABA Banking Journal,* June 2002.

Neely, Michelle Clark; Wheelock, David C. "Why Does Bank Performance Vary Across States?" (Cover Story), *Review* (Federal Reserve Bank of Saint Louis), Mar/Apr97, Vol. 79 Issue 2.

Milligan, John W. "Reaching for the Top." *United States Banker,* May 1997.

Molyneux, Philip and Seth Rama. "Foreign Banks, Profits and Commercial Credit Extension in the United States." *Applied Financial Economics,* October 1998.

Nelson, William R. and Ann L. Owen. "Profits and Balance Sheet Developments at U.S. Commercial Banks in 1996." *Federal Reserve Bulletin,* June 1997.

Nussbaum, Philip. "Is the UBPR Utterly Broken?" *ABA Banking Journal,* May 1998.

Patjens, Greg. "The Credit Department–A Source of Noninterest Income." *Journal of Commercial Bank Lending,* August 1991.

Prouse, Stephen. "Alternative Methods of Corporate Control in Commercial Banks." *Economic Review,* Federal Reserve Bank of Dallas, Third Quarter 1995.

Rose, Peter S. "The Local and Statewide Market-Share Advantages of Interstate Banking Firms." *Antitrust Bulletin,* Summer99, Vol. 44 Issue 2, P285, 28p.

Rogers, Kevin E. "Nontraditional Activities and the Efficiency of U.S. Commercial Banks." *Journal of Banking & Finance,* May 1998.

Schulz, Ellen E. and Theo Francis. "Why Are Workers in the Dark?" *Wall Street Journal,* April 24, 2002.

Shearer, Angus and Lawrence Forest Jr. "Improving Quantification of Risk-Adjusted Performance within Financial Institutions." *Commercial Lending Review,* Summer 1998.

Siems, Thomas and Jeffrey Clark. "Rethinking Bank Efficiency and Regulation: How Off-Balance-Sheet Activities Make a Difference." *Financial Industry Studies,* Federal Reserve Bank of Dallas, December 1997.

"Revisiting Efficiency Ratios." *United States Banker,* January 1999.

Toevs, Alden, and Robert Zizka. "Straight Talk on Bank Efficiency." *Journal of Retail Banking,* Summer 1994.

Uyemura, Dennis and Charles Kantor. "Mind Muscle." *Banking Strategies,* January–February 1997.

Uyemura, Dennis, Charles Kantor, and J. Pettit. "EVA for Banks: Value Creation, Risk Management, and Profitability Measurement." *Journal of Applied Corporate Finance,* Summer 1996.

Whalen, Gary. "The Impact of the Growth of Large, Multistate Banking Organizations on Community Bank Profitability." *Economic and Policy Analysis Working Paper 2001–5,* Office of the Comptroller of the Currency, December 2001.

Wilson, Caroline. "Investment Services: A Weapon in our Bank's Arsenal." *Community Banker*, August 2001.

Wilson, Caroline. "Fee Generation Strategies." *Community Banker*, November 2001.

Yeager, Timothy. "Down, But Not Out: The Future of Community Banks." *The Regional Economist*, Federal Reserve Bank of St. Louis, October 1999.

Asset and Liability Management

Angbazo, Lazarus. "Commercial Bank Net Interest Margins, Default Risk, Interest-Rate Risk, and Off-Balance Sheet Banking." *Journal of Banking & Finance*, January 1997.

Arditti, Fred. *Derivatives*. Boston: Harvard Business School Press, 1996.

"The Basle Committee Looks at Management of Interest Rate Risk." *World of Banking*, Spring 1997.

Babbel, David F., Craig Merrill, and William Panning. "Default Risk and the Effective Duration of Bonds." *Financial Analysts Journal*, January–February 1997.

Bessis, Joel. *Risk Management in Banking*. Chicheser, U.K.: John Wiley & Sons, 1998.

Bohlen, Bruce D. "Managing Risk with Derivatives: A Guide for Bankers and Their Customers." *Government Finance Review*, December 1996.

Breeden, Doug. "Complexities of Hedging Mortgages." *Journal of Fixed Income*, December 1994.

Brewer III, Elijah; Jackson III, William E.; Moser, James T. "The Value of Using Interest Rate Derivatives to Manage Risk at U.S. Banking Organizations. *Economic Perspectives*, 2001 3rd Quarter, Vol. 25 Issue 3, P49.

Britt, Phil. "The Return of Prepayment Penalties." *America's Community Banker*, August 1997.

Buhler, Wolfgang, Marliese Uhrig-Homburg, Ulrich Walter and Thomas Weber. "An Empirical Comparison of Forward-Rate and Spot-Rate Models for Valuing Interest-Rate Options." *Journal of Finance*, February 1999.

Cagan, Penny. "Financial Risk Management Sources." *Econtent*, Dec99, Vol. 22 Issue 6, P16.

Casson, Peter. "The Management of Interest-Rate Risk." *Financial Regulation Report*, March 1997.

Chew, Lillian. *Managing Derivative Risks: The Use and Abuse of Leverage*, New York: John Wiley & Sons, 1996.

Choi, Jongmoo and Elyas Elyasiani. "Derivative Exposure and the Interest Rate and Exchange Rate Risks of U.S. Banks." *Journal of Financial Services Research*, October–December 1997.

Clayton, Michelle. "OFHEO to Add Stress Tests to Risk-Based Capital Standards." *America's Community Banker*, August 1997.

Colvin, Robert. "New Rule Marks Major Shift in Investment Policy." *ABA Banking Journal*, July 1998.

Condon, Bernard. "Who's Minding the Branches at BofA?," *Forbes*, 09/06/99, Vol. 164 Issue 5, P58.

Culp, Christopher, L. Neves and M. Andrea. "Credit and Interest Rate Risk in the Business of Banking." *Derivatives Quarterly*, Summer 1998.

Cummins, J. David, Richard Phillips, and Stephen Smith. "The Rise of Risk Management." *Economic Review*, Federal Reserve Bank of Atlanta, First Quarter 1998.

Danielsson, Jon; De Vries, Casper G; Jorgensen, Bjorn N; Christoffersen, Peter F; Diebold, Francis X; Schuermann, Til; Lopez, Jose A; Hirtle, Beverly. "Issues in Value-At-Risk Modeling and Evaluation." *Economic Policy Review* (Federal Reserve Bank of New York), Oct98, Vol. 4 Issue 3.

Davidson, Steven. "Measuring Interest Rate Risk." *America's Community Banker*, October 1996.

Derivatives Engineering. Chicago: The Globecon Group, Ltd., Irwin Publishing, 1995.

Doner, Gregory W. "Interest Rate Risk: Measurement in a Shifting World." *Bankers Magazine*, May–June 1997.

Edwards, G. and G. Eller. "Overview of Derivatives Disclosures by Major U.S. Banks." *Federal Reserve Bulletin*, September 1995.

Evanoff, Douglas D; Wall, Larry D. "Subordinated Debt and Bank Capital Reform." *Working Paper Series* (Federal Reserve Bank of Atlanta), Nov 2000, Vol. 2000 Issue 24.

Fabozzi, Frank. *Valuation of Fixed Income Securities and Derivatives*. New Hope, Pa.: Frank J. Fabozzi Associates, 1995.

Faulstitch, James R. "Banks Get More Adept at Using Home Loan Bank Funding." *ABA Banking Journal*, June 1997.

Figlewski, Steve. "How to Lose Money in Derivatives." *Journal of Derivatives*, Winter 1994.

Flannery, Mark J., Allaudeen S. Hameed and Richard H. Harjes. "Asset Pricing, Time-Varying Risk Premia and Interest Rate Risk." *Journal of Banking & Finance*, March 1997.

Gendreau, Brian C. "Risk Structure of Postbellum U.S. Deposit Rates." *Explorations in Economic History*, Oct 99, Vol. 36 Issue 4.

Guven, S. and E. Persentili. "A Linear Programming Model for Bank Balance Sheet Management." *Omega*, August 1997.

Haight, G. Timothy and Stephen O. Morrell. "Using Derivatives to Manage Foreign Exchange Risk." *Bankers Magazine*, November–December 1996.

Haubenstock, Michael. "Organizing a Financial Institution to Deliver Enterprise-Wide Risk Management." *Journal of Lending & Credit Risk Management*, February 1999.

Haubrich, Joseph G. "Bank Diversification: Laws and Fallacies of Large Numbers." *Economic Review* (Federal Reserve Bank Of Cleveland), 1998 2nd Quarter, Vol. 34 Issue 2.

Hazen, Julie. "Helping Small and Midsized Companies Clear International Business Hurdles." *Commercial Lending Review,* Fall 1998.

Hopper, Gregory P. "Value at Risk: A New Methodology for Measuring Portfolio Risk." *Business Review,* Federal Reserve Bank of Philadelphia, July–August 1996.

Huang, C. and W. Xia. "Modeling ARM Prepayments." *Journal of Fixed Income,* March 1996.

Kambhu, John; Mosser, Patricia C. "The Effect of Interest Rate Options Hedging On Term-Structure Dynamics." *Economic Policy Review.* (Federal Reserve Bank of New York), Dec 2001, Vol. 7 Issue 3.

Kildegaard, Arne; Williams, Pete. "Banks, Systematic Risk, and Industrial Concentration: Theory and Evidence." *Journal of Economic Behavior & Organization,* Apr2002, Vol. 47, Issue 4.

Levonian, Mark E. "Bank Capital Standards for Foreign Exchange and other Market Risks." *Economic Review,* Federal Reserve Bank of San Francisco, 1994.

Longstaff, Francis. "Hedging Interest Rate Risk with Options on Average Interest Rates." *Journal of Fixed Income,* March 1995.

Lopez, Jose A. "Methods for Evaluating Value-At-Risk Estimates." *Economic Review* (Federal Reserve Bank Of San Francisco), 1999, Issue 2.

Mattey, Joe. "Measuring Interest Rate Risk for Mortgage-Related Assets." *FRBSF Economic Letter,* Jan 14, 2000, Vol. 2000 Issue 1.

McKinnon, Ronald and Huw Pil. "International Overborrowing: A Decomposition of Credit and Currency Risks." *World Development,* July 1998.

Ludwig, Eugene A. "Supervision by Risk." *Journal of Commercial Lending,* November 1995.

Lynch, Thomas E. "Interest Rate Swaps." *The Internal Auditor,* August 1996.

McKenzie, George. "Interest-Rate Risk Policies Revised." *Financial Regulation Report,* October 1996.

Moynihan, Brendan. "Real Interesting: Is a Low Real Yield Good News for the Economy?" *Bloomberg Personal Finance,* November 2001.

"New Supervisory Framework for Derivatives Activities of Banks and Securities Firms." *World of Banking,* Spring 1996.

Putnam, Bluford. "Lessons in Quantitative Risk Management." *Global Investor,* February 1996.

Putnam, Bluford. "The Long-Term Lessons of Long-Term Capital." *Global Investor,* November 1998.

Rieker, Matthias. "Looking at Who Will Gain When Interest Rates Rise." *American Banker*, April 5, 2002.

Rieker, Matthias. "Bracing for a Downturn in Net Interest Margins." *American Banker,* May 13, 2002.

"Risks Associated with Derivatives." *Federal Reserve Bulletin,* September 1995.

Robinson, Kenneth and Kelly Klemme. "Does Greater Mortgage Activity Lead to Greater Interest Rate Risk? Evidence from Bank Holding Companies." *Financial Industry Studies,* Federal Reserve Bank of Dallas, August 1996.

Sacks, Jonathan. "Managing Market Risk: Science versus Art or Science and Art?" *Bankers Magazine,* May–June 1997.

Santomero, Anthony. "Commercial Bank Risk Management: An Analysis of the Process." *Journal of Financial Services Research,* December 1997.

Shay, Rodger. "Balancing Interest-Rate Risk." *America's Community Banker,* November 1996.

Shay, Rodger. "Buying IRR Insurance." *America's Community Banker,* June 1997.

Shay, Rodger. "Hot under the 'Collar'." *America's Community Banker,* May 1997.

Shay, Rodger. "Investment Management: Caps or Swaps?" *America's Community Banker,* July 1997.

Shilling, A. Gary. "Buy Zeros Now." *Forbes,* 02/22/99, Vol. 163 Issue 4.

Simons, Katerina. "Interest Rate Derivatives and Asset-Liability Management by Commercial Banks." *New England Economic Review,* Federal Reserve Bank of Boston, January–February 1995.

Smithson, Charles, Clifford Smith Jr., and D. Sykes Wilford. *Managing Financial Risk,* Burr Ridge, Ill.: Irwin Publishing, 1995.

Stern, Gary S. "Market Discipline as Bank Regulator." *Region* (Federal Reserve Bank of Minneapolis), Jun 98, Vol. 12, Issue 2, P2, 2p, 1bw.

Strauss, Mel. "Examining FAS 133: Managing the Balance Sheet." *U.S. Banker,* September 1998.

"Survey of Foreign Exchange Risk Management in U.S." *World of Banking,* August–September 1995.

Talmor, Sharona. "The Limits of Limits Systems." *The Banker,* February 1998.

"Using Value at Risk to Evaluate Foreign Exchange Risk." *Tma Journal,* March–April 1996.

Van Horne, James. *Financial Market Rates and Flows,* Fifth Edition. Saddle River, N.J.: Prentice Hall, 1998.

Van Wyk, Antonie. "How to Soften Interest Rate Blows." *Finance Week,* June 18–24, 1998.

Walker, Townsend. "Using Derivatives to Manage Interest Rate Risk." *Business Credit,* January 1997.

Wong, Pong Kit. "On the Determinants of Bank Interest Margins Under Credit and Interest Rate Risks." *Journal of Banking & Finance,* February 1997.

Capital and Liquidity Management

Aggarwal, Raj and Kevin T. Jacques. "Assessing the Impact of Prompt Corrective Action on Bank Capital and Risk." *Economic Policy Review,* October 1998.

Allen, Linda, Stavros Peristiani, and Anthony Saunders. "Bank Size, Collateral, and Net Purchase Behavior in the Federal Funds Market: Empirical Evidence." *Journal of Business*, October 1989.

Amihud, Yakov; Miller, Geoffrey, eds. "Bank Mergers and Acquisitions." *New York University Salomon Center Series on Financial Markets and Institutions*, Vol. 3. Boston; Dordrecht and London: Kluwer Academic, 1998.

Ashley, Lisa, Elijah Brewer, and Nancy Vincent. "Access to FHLBank Advances and the Performance of Thrift Institutions." *Economic Perspectives*, Second Quarter 1998.

Beatty, Anne L.; Gron, Anne. "Capital, Portfolio, and Growth: Bank Behavior Under Risk-Based Capital Guidelines." *Journal of Financial Services Research*, v20 n1 (September 2001): 5-31.

Bauer, Paul. "Efficiency and Technical Progress in Check Processing." *Economic Review*, Federal Reserve Bank of Cleveland, Third Quarter 1993.

Bender, Roxanne. "Bank Liquidity: Learning to Love It." *Bankers Monthly*, December 1985.

Bender, Michael. "Trust Preferred Issuers Race to Beat Congress." *Investment Dealers Digest*, January 6, 1997.

Benink, Harald; Wihlborg, Clas. "The New Basel Capital Accord: Making It Effective with Stronger Market Discipline." *European Financial Management*, v8 n1 (March 2002): 103-15.

Bentson, George and George Kaufman. "Deposit Insurance Reform in the FDIC Improvement Act: The Experience to Date." *Economic Perspectives*, Federal Reserve Bank of Chicago, Second Quarter 1998.

Bernon, David G. "Capacity for Asset Growth Model: A Tool for Internal Bank Management and External Bank Analysis." *The Magazine of Bank Administration*, August 1978.

Brooks, Robert; Gup, Benton E. "Embedded Options Impact on Interest Rate Risk and Capital Adequacy." *Journal of Applied Business Research*, v15 n4 (Fall 1999): 11-20.

Calem, Paul. "The New Bank Deposit Markets: Goodbye to Regulation Q." *Business Review*, Federal Reserve Bank of Philadelphia, November–December 1985.

Calem, Paul and Rafael Rob. "The Impact of Capital-Based Regulation on Bank Risk-Taking." *Journal of Financial Intermediation*, v8 n4 (October 1999): 317-52.

Carraro, Kenneth and Daniel Thornton. "The Cost of Checkable Deposits in the United States." *Review*, Federal Reserve Bank of St. Louis, April 1986.

Cates, David. "Liquidity Lessons for the '90s." *Bank Management*, April 1990.

Charlton, William. "The Pricing Effects of the Risk-Based Capital Regulations." *Journal of Commercial Bank Lending*, April 1991.

"Closing of Ohio S&Ls after Run on Deposits is One for the Books." *The Wall Street Journal*, March 18, 1985.

Cocheo, Steve. "Program Allows Ag Banks to Have Loan and 'Sell' It Too." *ABA Banking Journal*, August 1998.

Colby, Mary. "Truth in Savings' Marketing Morass." *Bank Management*, March 1993.

Cole, C. Alexander and Gerald Fischer. "Risk-Based Capital: A Loan and Credit Officer's Primer." *Journal of Commercial Bank Lending*, August 1988.

Cole, Leonard. *Management Accounting in Banks*. Rolling Meadows, Ill.: Bank Administration Institute, Bankers Publishing Company, 1988.

"Continental Illinois: How Bad Judgments and Big Egos Did It In." *The Wall Street Journal*, July 30, 1984.

Cooper, Russell and Thomas W. Ross. "Bank Runs: Liquidity Costs and Investment Distortions." *Journal of Monetary Economics*, February 1998.

Cornett, Marcia Millon; Mehran, Hamid; Tehranian, Hassan. "The Impact of Risk-Based Premiums on FDIC-Insured Institutions." *Journal of Financial Services Research*, v13 n2 (April 1998): 153–69 .

Cumming, Christine. "Federal Deposit Insurance and Deposits at Foreign Branches of U.S. Banks." *Quarterly Review*, Federal Reserve Bank of New York, Autumn 1985.

Diamond, Douglas W.; Rajan, Raghuram G. "A Theory of Bank Capital." *The Journal of Finance*, 55 no. 6 (2000): 2431–2465 (35 pages).

Dotsey, Michael and Anatoli Kuprianov. "Reforming Deposit Insurance: Lessons from the Savings and Loan Crisis." *Economic Review*, Federal Reserve Bank of Richmond, March–April 1990.

Dowd, Kevin. "Bank Capital Adequacy versus Deposit Insurance." *Journal of Financial Services Research*, 17 no. 1 (2000): 7–15 (9 pages).

Drzik, John, Peter Nakada, and Til Schuremann. "Risk, Capital, and Value Measurement in Financial Institutions." *Journal of Lending & Credit Risk Management*, September 1998.

Dyl, Edward. "The Marginal Cost of Funds Controversy." *Journal of Bank Research*, Autumn 1978.

Ely, Bert. "Technology, Regulation and the Financial Services Industry in the Year 2000." *Issues in Bank Regulation*, Fall 1988.

Estrella, Arturo; Park, Sangkyun; Peristiani, Stavros. "Capital Ratios as Predictors of Bank Failure." *Federal Reserve Bank of New York Economic Policy Review*, v6 n2 (July 2000): 33–52 .

Evanoff, Douglas. "Daylight Overdrafts: Rationale and Risks." *Economic Perspectives*, Federal Reserve Bank of Chicago, May–June 1988.

Evanoff, Douglas. "Priced Services: The Fed's Impact on Correspondent Banking." *Economic Perspective*, Federal Reserve Bank of Chicago, September–October 1985.

Fasbee, Pamela. "Bankers' Banks: An Institution whose Time has Come." *Economic Review*, Federal Reserve Bank of Atlanta, April 1984.

Feddis, Nessa. "Analyzing the Revised Reg CC." *ABA Banking Journal*, July 1988.

Federal Deposit Insurance Corp. *Regulators Statement on the Permanent Assistance Program for Continental Illinois National Bank and Trust Co.* Washington, D.C.: July 26, 1984.

Federal Reserve System. *Functional Cost Analysis: 1996 Average Banks.* Washington, D.C.: Government Printing Office, 1996.

Feldman, Ron J. and Arthur J. Rolnic. "Fixing FDICIA." *1997 Annual Report*, Federal Reserve Bank of Minneapolis, March 1998. Available on the Internet at http://woodrow.mpls.frb.fed/pubs/ar/ar1997.html.

Flood, Mark. "On the Use of Option Pricing Models to Analyze Deposit Insurance." *Economic Review*, Federal Reserve Bank of St. Louis, January–February 1990.

Gendreau, Brian and Scott Prince. "The Private Costs of Bank Failure." *Business Review*, Federal Reserve Bank of Philadelphia, March–April 1986.

Gilbert, Alton. "Payments System Risk: What is It and What Will Happen If We Try to Reduce It?" *Review*, Federal Reserve Bank of St. Louis, January–February 1989.

Goodfriend, Marvin. "Discount Window Borrowing, Monetary Policy, and the Post–October 6, 1979 Federal Reserve Operating Procedure." *Journal of Monetary Economics*, Volume 12, 1983.

Goodfriend, Marvin. "The Promises and Pitfalls of Contemporaneous Reserve Requirements for the Implementation of Monetary Policy." *Economic Review*, Federal Reserve Bank of Richmond, May–June 1984.

Gregor, William and Robert Hedges. "Alternative Strategies for Successful Cost Management." *The Bankers Magazine*, May–June 1990.

Gupta, Atul. "The Value of a Regulatory Seal of Approval." *Journal of Financial Research*, Spring 1997.

Hameeteman, Daphne; Scholtens, Bert. "Size, Growth, and Variance among the World's Largest Non-merged Banks." *International Journal of the Economics of Business*, 7 no. 3 (2000): 313–323.

Harvey, James and Kenneth Spong. "The Decline in Core Deposits: What Can Banks Do?" *Financial Industry Perspectives*, Federal Reserve Bank of Kansas City, December 2001.

Hendricks, Darryll and Beverly Hirtle. "Bank Capital Requirements for Market Risk: The Internal Models Approach." *Economic Policy Review*, Federal Reserve Bank of New York, December 1997.

Hendricks, Darryll and Beverly Hirtle. "Bank Capital Requirements for Market Risk: The Internal Models Approach." *Economic Policy Review*, December 1997.

Hirtle, Beverly J., et al. "Using Credit Risk Models for Regulatory Capital: Issues and Options." *Federal Reserve Bank of New York Economic Policy Review*, v7 n1 (March 2001): 19–36.

Hovakimian, Armen; Kane, Edward J. "Effectiveness of Capital Regulation at U.S. Commercial Banks, 1985 to 1994." *The Journal of Finance*, 55 no. 1 (2000): 451–468 (18 pages).

Horowitz, Jed. "Manny Hanny, Chemical: Does Marriage Make Sense?" *American Banker*, March 5, 1991.

Horvitz, Paul. "FDIC's Solution for Continental Illinois was a Masterful Deal." *American Banker*, August 28, 1984.

Humphrey, Thomas. "Lender of Last Resort: The Concept in History." *Economic Review*, Federal Reserve Bank of Richmond, March/April 1989.

Inquiry into Continental Illinois Corp. and Continental Illinois National Bank. Hearings Before the Subcommittee on Financial Institutions Supervision, Regulation, and Insurance of the Committee on Banking, Finance, and Urban Affairs, House of Representatives, 98th Congress, second session. Washington, D.C., September 18 and 19 and October 4, 1984.

Jackson, Patricia, David J. Maude, and William Perraudin. "Bank Capital and Value at Risk." *Journal of Derivatives*, Spring 1997.

Jones, David. "Emerging Problems with the Basel Capital Accord: Regulatory Capital Arbitrage and Related Issues." *Journal of Banking and Finance*, v24 n1-2 (January 2000): 35–58.

Jones, David; Mingo, John. "Credit Risk Modeling and Internal Capital Allocation Processes: Keeley, Michael. Bank Capital Regulation in the 1980s: Effective or Ineffective?" *Economic Review*, Federal Reserve Bank of San Francisco, Winter 1988.

Implications for a Models-Based Regulatory Bank Capital Standard." *Journal of Economics and Business*, v51 n2 (March-April 1999): 79–108.

Keeton, William. "Deposit Insurance and the Deregulation of Deposit Rates." *Economic Review*, Federal Reserve Bank of Kansas City, April 1984.

Keeton, William. "The New Risk-Based Capital Plan For Commercial Banks." *Economic Review*, Federal Reserve Bank of Kansas City, December 1989.

Lopez, Jose A. "Methods for Evaluating Value-at-Risk Estimates." Federal Reserve Bank of San Francisco Economic *Review*, v0 n2 (1999): 3–17.

Lucas, Charles, Marcus Jones, and Thom Thurston. "Federal Funds and Repurchase Agreements." *Quarterly Review*, Federal Reserve Bank of New York, Summer 1977.

Luckett, Dudley. "Approaches to Bank Liquidity Management." *Economic Review*, Federal Reserve Bank of Kansas City, March 1980.

Matten, Chris. *Managing Bank Capital.* New York: John Wiley & Sons, 1996.

McAndrews, James. "Network Issues and Payment Systems." *Business Review*, Federal Reserve Bank of Philadelphia, November–December 1997.

McKinney, George. "A Perspective on the Use of Models in the Management of Bank Funds." *Journal of Bank Research*, Summer 1977.

Medlin, John G. Jr. "A Timely Discussion of Capital Requirements." *Journal of Lending & Credit Risk Management*, February 1998.

Mengle, David. "Daylight Overdrafts and Payment System Risks." *Economic Review*, Federal Reserve Bank of Richmond, May–June 1985.

Mengle, David. "The Discount Window." *Economic Review*, Federal Reserve Bank of Richmond, May–June 1986.

Milne, Alistair. "Bank Capital Regulation as an Incentive Mechanism: Implications for Portfolio Choice." *Journal of Banking and Finance*, v26 n1 (January 2002): 1–23.

Mohanty, Sunil. "Noncredit risks subsidization in the international capital standards." *Applied Financial Economics*, 11 no. 1 (2001): 9–16.

Muckenfuss, Cantwell, Robert Eager, and Clark Nielsen. "The Federal Insurance Corporation Improvement Act of 1991." *Bank Management*, January 1992.

Mueller, P. Henry. "Bank Liquidity, Short Memories & Inescapable Basics." *Journal of Lending & Credit Risk Management*, September 1998.

"New Era Dawns for Bank Capital." *Euroweek, UK Capital Markets: Into the Emu Era Supplement*, March 1998.

Peek, Joe and Eric S. Rosengren. "How Well Capitalized Are Well-Capitalized Banks?" *New England Economic Review*, September–October 1997.

Ratti, Ronald. "Pledging Requirements and Bank Asset Portfolios." *Economic Review*, Federal Reserve Bank of Kansas City, September–October 1979.

Reosti, John. "CD Tied to S&P 500 Not Living Up to Promise." *American Banker*, June 21, 2001.

"Repurchase Agreements: Taking a Closer Look at Safety." *Economic Review*, Federal Reserve Bank of Atlanta, September 1985.

Robinson, Anthony. "Wipeout in Moscow." *The Banker*, October 1998.

Ruby P. Kishan Timothy P. "Opiela. "Bank Size, Bank Capital, and the Bank Lending Channel." *Journal of Money, Credit, and Banking*, 32 no. 1 (2000): 121–141.

Ruempler, Henry. "Trust-Preferred Interests Can Combine Tax Deductions with Tier 1 Capital Status." *Journal of Bank Taxation*, Summer 1997.

Santos, João A. C. "Bank Capital Regulation in Contemporary Banking Theory: A Review of the Literature." *Financial Markets, Institutions and Instruments*, 10 no. 2 (2001): 41–84 (44 pages).

Saunders, Anthony; Wilson, Berry. "An Analysis of Bank Charter Value and Its Risk-Constraining Incentives." *Journal of Financial Services Research*, 19 no. 2/3 (2001): 185–195 (11 pages).

Shaffer, Sherrill. "Capital Requirements and Rational Discount-Window Borrowing." *Journal of Money, Credit and Banking*, November 1998.

Shaffer, Sherrill. "The Discount Window and Credit Availability." *Journal of Banking and Finance*, v23 n9 (September 1999): 1383–1406.

Smoot, Richard L. "Billion-Dollar Overdrafts: A Payments Risk Challenge." *Business Review*, Federal Reserve Bank of Philadelphia, January–February 1985.

Stevens, E.J. "Seasonal Borrowing and Open Market Operations." *Economic Review*, Federal Reserve Bank of Cleveland, Second Quarter, 1990.

Temple, W. Robert. "Bank Liquidity: Where Are We?" *American Banker*, March 8, 1983.

Temzelides, Ted. "Are Bank Runs Contagious?" *Business Review*, Federal Reserve Bank of Philadelphia, November–December 1997.

Thomson, Jason. "Using Market Incentives to Reform Bank Regulation and Federal Deposit Insurance." *Economic Review*, Federal Reserve Bank of Cleveland, First Quarter, 1990.

VanHoose, David and Gordon Sellon Jr. "Daylight Overdrafts, Payments System Risk, and Public Policy." *Economic Review*, Federal Reserve Bank of Kansas City, September–October 1989.

Vojta, George. *Bank Capital Adequacy*. New York: First National City Bank, 1973.

Wall, Larry and David Peterson. "The Effect of Capital Adequacy Guidelines on Large Bank Holding Companies." *Journal of Banking and Finance*, December 1987.

Wall, Larry, John Pringle, and James McNulty. "Capital Requirements for Interest-Rate and Foreign-Exchange Hedges." *Economic Review*, Federal Reserve Bank of Atlanta, May–June 1990.

Wall, Larry. "Regulation of Banks' Equity Capital." *Economic Review*, Federal Reserve Bank of Atlanta, November 1985.

Wall, Larry. "Too-Big-to-Fail after FDICIA." *Economic Review*, Federal Reserve Bank of Atlanta, January–February 1993.

Wall, Larry, David Peterson and Pamela Peterson. "Banks' Responses to Binding Regulatory Capital Requirements." *Federal Reserve Bank of Atlanta*, Economic Review, 1998.

Wall, Larry D. and Pamela P. Peterson. "The Choice of Capital Instruments." *Economic Review,* Federal Reserve Bank of Atlanta, March–April 1998.

Wallin, Michelle. "Argentina's Galicia Bank Turns to Private Creditors for Help." *Wall Street Journal,* February 26, 2002.

Watson, Ronald. "Estimating the Cost of Your Bank's Funds." *Business Review,* Federal Reserve Bank of Philadelphia, May–June 1978.

Young, John E. "The Rise and Fall of Federal Reserve Float." *Economic Review,* Federal Reserve Bank of Kansas City, February 1986.

Credit Management

"How Banks Lend." *The Economist,* February 4, 1989.

"Issuance by the Basel Committee of Papers Providing Guidance on Credit Risk in Banking." *Federal Reserve Bulletin,* Sep 99, Vol. 85 Issue 9, P635, 2p.

Alcott, Kathleen. "An Agricultural Loan Rating System." *Journal of Commercial Bank Lending,* February 1985.

Allen W.R. "Measuring Credit Risk Capital Requirements." *The Journal of Lending & Credit Risk Management,* December 1996.

Asarnow, Elliot. "Their $51 Billion World." *Journal of Lending & Credit Risk Management,* September 1998.

Asher, Joseph. "Credit Derivatives: A Red-Hot Growth Area." *ABA Banking Journal,* August 1998.

Avery, Robert, Raphael Bostic, Paul Calem, and Glenn Canner. "Credit Risk, Credit Scoring, and the Performance of Home Mortgages." *Federal Reserve Bulletin,* July 1996.

Avery, Robert, Raphael Bostic, Paul Calem, and Glenn Canner. "Trends in Home Purchase Lending: Consolidation and the Community Reinvestment Act." *Federal Reserve Bulletin,* February 1999.

Barrickman, John, Dana Bauer, and John McKinley. "Predicting Portfolio Credit Quality." *Journal of Lending & Credit Risk Management,* July 1998.

Berger, Allen N., Anthony Saunders, Joseph M. Scalise, and Gregory F. Udell. "The Effects of Bank Mergers and Acquisitions on Small Business Lending." *Journal of Financial Economics,* November 1998.

Charitou, Andreas. "An Analysis of the Components of the Cash Flow Statement: The Case of Campeau Corporation." *Journal of Commercial Bank Lending,* January 1993.

Cocheo, Steve. "Give Me Your Delinquents, Your Former Bankrupts, Yearning to Borrow." *ABA Banking Journal,* August 1996.

Coleman, A. "Restructuring the Statement of Changes in Financial Position." *Financial Executive,* January 1979.

Comiskey, Eugene E. and Charles W. Mulford. "Analyzing Small-Company Financial Statements: Some Guidance for Lenders." *Commercial Lending Review,* Summer 1998.

Compton, Eric N. "Credit Analysis is Risk Analysis." *The Bankers Magazine,* March–April 1985.

Conner, Glenn and Charles Luckett. "Mortgage Refinancing." *Federal Reserve Bulletin,* Board of Governors of the Federal Reserve System, August 1990.

Cocheo, Steve. "Community Bank Credit Check." *ABA Banking Journal,* January 1999.

Durkin, Thomas A. "Credit Cards: Use and Consumer Attitudes, 1970 – 2000, *Federal Reserve Bulletin,* Board of Governors of the Federal Reserve System, September 2000.

Economic Perspectives. A series of articles on the farm credit crunch. Federal Reserve Bank of Chicago, November–December 1985.

Emmanuel, Christine. "Cash Flow Reporting, Part 2: Importance of Cash Flow Data in Credit Analysis." *Journal of Commercial Bank Lending,* June 1988.

Foglia, A., P. Laviola, and Marullo P. Reedtz. "Multiple Banking Relationships and the Fragility of Corporate Borrowers." *Journal of Banking & Finance,* October 1998.

Gahlon, James and Robert Vigeland. "Early Warning Signs of Bankruptcy Using Cash Flow Analysis." *Journal of Commercial Bank Lending,* December 1988.

Golden, Sam and Harry Walker. "The Ten Commandments of Commercial Credit: The Cs of Good and Bad Loans." *Journal of Commercial Bank Lending,* January 1993.

Greene, R. "Are More Chryslers in the Offing?" *Forbes,* February 2, 1981.

Gupton, Gred. "The New Talk of the Town: CreditMetrics™, a Credit Value-at-Risk Approach." *Journal of Lending & Credit Risk Management,* August 1997.

Hall, John and Timothy J. Yeager. "Community Ties: Does 'Relationship Lending' Protect Small Banks When the Local Economy Stumbles?" *The Regional Economist,* Federal Reserve Bank of St. Louis, April 2002. At http://www.stls.frb.org.

Henry, David. "The Numbers Game." *Business Week,* May 14, 2001.

Hirtle, Beverly J; Levonian, Mark; Saidenberg, Marc; Walter, Stefan. "Using Credit Risk Models for Regulatory Capital: Issues and Options." *Economic Policy Review* (Federal Reserve Bank Of New York), Mar2001, Vol. 7 Issue 1, P19.

Hunter, Maura. "How to Identify and Evaluate Industry Risk in a Loan Portfolio: A Five-Step Approach." *Journal of Lending & Credit Risk Management,* November 1998.

Iannuccilli, Joseph. "Asset-Based Lending: An Overview." *Journal of Commercial Bank Lending*, March 1988.

Jones, David; Mingo, John; Gray, Brian; Wilson, Thomas C; Nishiguchi, Kenji; Kawai, Hiroshi; Sazaki, Takanori; Perraudin, William. "Credit Risk Modeling." *Economic Policy Review* (Federal Reserve Bank Of New York), Oct98, Vol. 4 Issue 3.

Kester, George and Thomas Bixler. "Why 90-Day Working Capital Loans Are Not Repaid on Time." *Journal of Commercial Bank Lending*, August 1990.

Kohl, David. "Lending to Agribusiness." *Journal of Commercial Bank Lending*, April 1990.

Largay, James and Clyde Stickney. "Cash Flows, Ratio Analysis, and the W.T. Grant Company Bankruptcy." *Financial Analysts Journal*, July–August 1980.

Lopez, Jose A. "Modeling Credit Risk for Commercial Loans." *FRBSF Economic Letter*, 04/27/2001, Vol. 2001 Issue 12, P1.

Kazuhiko, Ohashi. "Making the Most of the Financial Revolution." *Look Japan*, Oct 99, Vol. 45 Issue 523, P24, 3p, 3c.

Mays, Elizabeth, ed. *Credit Risk Modeling: Design and Application*. Chicago: Glenlake Publishing, 1998.

Mester, Loretta J. "Is the Personal Bankruptcy System Bankrupt?" *Business Review*, Federal Reserve Bank of Philadelphia, Q1, 2002.

Neal, R. "Credit Derivatives: New Financial Instruments for Controlling Credit Risk." *Economc Review*, Federal Reserve Bank of Kansas City, Second Quarter 1996.

Newburgh, Conrad. "Character Assessment in the Lending Process." *Journal of Commercial Bank Lending*, April 1991.

O'Connell, J. Brian. "How Inventory Appraisals Are Done." *Journal of Commercial Bank Lending*, April 1990.

O'Connor, J. and A. Weinman. "Benchmarking Small Business Credit Scoring and Portfolio Management Practices." *Journal of Lending & Credit Risk Management*, January 1999.

O'Leary, Carolyn. "Cash Flow Reporting, Part 1: An Overview of SFAS 95." *Journal of Commercial Bank Lending*, May 1988.

O'Sullivan, Orla. "New Ball Game, New Score." *ABA Banking Journal*, January 1998.

Pilloff, Steven and Robin Prager. "Thrift Involvement in Commercial and Industrial Lending." *Federal Reserve Bulletin*, December 1998.

Piramuthu, Selwyn. "Feature Selection for Financial Credit-Risk Evaluation Decisions." *Journal On Computing*, Summer 99, Vol. 11 Issue 3, P258.

Rizzi, Joseph V. "Managing the Risks of Lending to Growth Firms." *Commercial Lending Review*, Summer 1998.

Sorenson, Richard. "Why Real Estate Projects Fail." *Journal of Commercial Bank Lending*, April 1990.

Strahan, Philip E. and James P. Weston. "Small Business Lending and the Changing Structure of the Banking Industry." *Journal of Banking & Finance*, August 1998.

Strischek, Dev. "Assessing Creditworthiness: Importance of Evaluating Company Management." *Journal of Commercial Bank Management*, March 1990.

Tavakoli, Janet. *Credit Derivatives*. New York: John Wiley & Sons, 1998.

Treacy, William. "Credit Risk Rating at Large U.S. Banks." *Federal Reserve Bulletin*, November 1998.

Viscione, Jerry A. "Assessing Financial Distress." *The Journal of Commercial Bank Lending*, July 1985.

Westergaard, Richard. "Securitizing Small Business Loans." *Bank Management*, September–October 1995.

White, Larry. "Credit Analysis: Two More 'Cs' of Credit." *Journal of Commercial Bank Lending*, October 1990.

Whiting, Rick. "Financial Update: MicroStrategy to Restate Earnings." *www.informationweek.com*, March 27, 2000.

Whittaker, Gregg. "An Introduction to Credit Derivatives." *Journal of Lending & Credit Risk Management*, May 1997.

Wick, Thomas. "Real Estate Basics for Commercial Lenders." *Journal of Commercial Bank Lending*, July 1993.

Investments

Abken, Peter A. "Inflation and the Yield Curve." *Economic Review*, Federal Reserve Bank of Atlanta, May–June 1993.

Altman, Edward. "How 1989 Change the Hierarchy of Fixed Income Security Performance." *Financial Analysts Journal*, May–June 1990.

Altman, Edward. "Revisiting the High-Yield Bond Market." *Financial Management*, Summer 1992.

Becketti, Sean. "The Truth About Junk Bonds." *Economic Review*, The Federal Reserve Bank of Kansas City, July–August 1990.

Carrington, Samantha and Robert Crouch. "Interest Rate Differentials on Short-Term Securities and Rational Expectations of Inflation." *Journal of Banking and Finance*, September 1987.

Choi, S. "Effective Durations for Mortgage-Backed Securities: Recipes for Improvement." *Journal of Fixed Income*, March 1996.

Darby, Michael. "The Financial and Tax Effects of Monetary Policy on Interest Rates." *Economic Inquiry*, June 1975.

Elder, E. Craig and Paul Nathan. "The Basics of Fixed Income Investing." *Fixed Income Research*, Morgan Keegan, January 29, 2002.

Fabozzi, Frank. *Fixed Income Mathematics*. Chicago: Probus Publishing, 1993.

Fabozzi, Frank. *Bond Markets, Analysis and Strategies*, Third Edition. Saddle River, N.J.: Prentice Hall, 1996.

Fabozzi, Frank, ed. *Managing Fixed Income Portfolios.* New Hope, Pa.: Frank J. Fabozzi Associates, 1997.

Fama, Eugene and Robert Bliss. "The Information in Long Maturity Forward Rates." *American Economic Review,* September 1987.

Fama, Eugene. "Short-Term Interest Rates as Predictors of Inflation." *American Economic Review,* June 1975.

Feldstein, Martin. "Inflation, Income Taxes and the Rate of Interest: A Theoretical Analysis." *American Economic Review,* December 1976.

Fisher, Irving. "Appreciation and Interest." *Publications of the American Economic Association,* August 1896.

Fisher, Irving. *The Theory of Interest.* New York, N: Macmillan, 1930.

Garfinkel, Michelle. "What is an 'Acceptable' Rate of Inflation?–A Review of the Issues." *Review,* Federal Reserve Bank of St. Louis, July–August 1989.

Goodman, Laurie and Jeffrey Ho. "Callable Pass-Throughs: Exercise History." *Journal of Fixed Income,* December 1998.

Hafer, R.W. and Scott Hein. "Comparing Futures and Survey Forecasts of Near-Term Treasury Bill Rates." *Review,* Federal Reserve Bank of St. Louis, May–June 1989.

Hakkio, Craig. "Interest Rates and Exchange Rates–What is the Relationship?" *Economic Review,* Federal Reserve Bank of Kansas City, November 1986.

Harvey, Campbell. "The Term Structure and World Economic Growth." *Journal of Fixed Income,* June 1991.

Humphrey, Thomas. "The Early History of the Real/Nominal Interest Rate Relationship." *Economic Review,* Federal Reserve Bank of Richmond, May–June 1983.

Kool, Clemens and John Tatom. "International Linkages in the Term Structure of Interest Rates." *Review,* Federal Reserve Bank of St. Louis, July–August 1988.

Lim, K. and Miles Livingston. "Stripping of Treasury Securities and Segmentation in the Treasury Securities Market." *Journal of Fixed Income,* March 1995.

Litterman, Robert and Jose Scheinkman. "Common Factors Affecting Bond Returns." *Journal of Fixed Income,* June 1991.

Malkiel, Burton. *The Term Structure of Interest Rates: Theory, Empirical Evidence, and Applications.* New York: Silver Burdett, 1970.

McCulloch, Huston. "The Monotonicity of the Term Premium." *Journal of Financial Economics,* March 1987.

MicroStrategy's Brown Discusses Revenue Decline. *Bloomberg News Archive,* May 29, 2002.

Mundell, Robert. "Inflation and Real Interest." *Journal of Political Economy,* June 1963.

Santoni, G.J. and Courtenay Stone. "Navigating Through the Interest Rate Morass: Some Basis Principles." *Economic Review,* Federal Reserve Bank of St. Louis, March 1981.

Siegel, Jeremy. "The Equity Premium: Stock and Bond Returns since 1802." *Financial Analysts Journal,* January–February 1992.

Sparks, A. and F. Sund. "Prepayment Convexity and Duration." *Journal of Fixed Income,* March 1995.

Tobin, James. "Money and Economic Growth." *Econometrica,* October 1965.

Tuckman, Bruce. *Fixed Income Securities.* New York: John Wiley & Sons, 1996.

Wigmore, Barrie. "The Decline in Credit Quality of New-Issue Junk Bonds." *Financial Analysts Journal,* September–October 1990.

Wood, John. "Are Yield Curves Normally Upward Sloping? The Term Structure of Interest Rates, 1862–1982." *Economic Perspectives,* Federal Reserve Bank of Chicago, July–August 1983.

Bank Mergers

"A Merger Chain Reaction." *United States Banker,* May 1998.

Altunbas, Yener, Philip Molyneux, and John Thornton. "Big-Bank Mergers in Europe: An Analysis of the Cost Implications." *Economica,* May 1997.

Barfield, Richard. "Creating Value through Mergers." *The Banker,* July 1998.

Bary, Andrew. "Betting on Banks." *Barrons,* April 20, 1998.

Berger, Allen N. "The Efficiency Effects of Bank Mergers and Acquisitions: A Preliminary Look at the 1990s Data." *Bank Mergers & Acquisitions,* Yakov Amihud and Geoffrey Miller, editors, Kluwer Academic Publishers, 1998.

Berger, Allen, Rebecca Demsetz, and Philip Strahan. "The Consolidation of the Financial Services Industry: Causes, Consequences, and Implications for the Future." *Journal of Banking and Finance,* February 1999.

Blackwell, Rob and Jennifer A. Kingson. "Wal-Mart's Designs on Processing." *American Banker,* May 17, 2002.

Blanden, Michael. "Size Does Matter." *The Banker,* June 1998.

Briddell, E Talbot. "Surprise, Surprise: Borrowers Won't Suffer as a Result of Bank Consolidation." *Secured Lender,* September–October 1998.

Broaddus, Alfred Jr. "The Bank Merger Wave: Causes and Consequences." *Economic Quarterly,* Federal Reserve Bank of Richmond, Summer 1998.

Cetorelli, Nicola. "Competitive Analysis in Banking: Appraisal of the Methodologies." *Economic Perspectives,* Federal Reserve Bank of Chicago, First Quarter 1999.

"Chase Manhattan: Building a Global Bank through Mergers." *Investment Dealers Digest,* November 25, 1996.

Cyrnak, Anthony W. "Bank Merger Policy and the New CRA Data." *Federal Reserve Bulletin,* September 1998.

Foust, Dean. "If This Safety Net Snaps, Who Pays?" *Business Week,* April 27, 1998.

Gold, Jacqueline S. "Ken Do." *Institutional Investor,* June 2001.

Heggestad, Arnold. "Fundamentals of Mergers and Acquisitions" in *Handbook for Banking Strategy,* Richard Aspinwall and Robert Eisenbeis, eds. New York: John Wiley & Sons, Inc., 1985.

Jackson, Ben. "M&A Watchers: Economy Isn't Main Reason for Dip." *American Banker,* April 12, 2002.

Koretz, Gene. "Bank Mergers: Who Benefits?" *Business Week,* July 20, 1998.

Liebich, Kim. "How to Value a Bank." *ABA Banking Journal,* August 1995.

"M&A 2000 Annual Roundup." *American Banker Special Report,* February 12, 2001.

Mandell, Mel. "Euro Means More Bank Mergers." *World Trade,* February 1999.

Marshall, Jeffrey. "U.S. Banker 1998 M&A Rankings: Big, Bigger, Biggest." *United States Banker,* September 1998.

Marshall, Jeffrey. "What Makes a Merger a Winner?" *United States Banker,* June 1998.

Meyerowitz, Steven A. "Mergers." *The Banking Law Journal,* 2 (Banking Law Journal Digest), 1998.

Parkinson, Kenneth L. and Joyce R. Ochs. "The Impact of Banking Mergers on Corporations." *Business Credit,* July–August 1998.

Prager, Robin and Timothy Hannan. "Do Substantial Horizontal Mergers Generate Significant Price Effects? Evidence from the Banking Industry." *Journal of Industrial Economics,* December 1998.

Prince, C.J. "Cool Hand Kovacevich." *CEO Magazine,* May 2001.

Radigan, Joseph. "Buying into New Markets: U.S. Banker 1997 M&A Rankings." *United States Banker,* September 1997.

Schmerken, Ivy. "The Big Gamble: Mergers & Technology." *Wall Street & Technology,* July 1998.

Silverman, Freddi. "Introducing the Sleeker, Smarter Community Bank." *Bank Marketing,* July 1997.

"Special Article: Big Banks: The Trials of Megabanks." *Economist,* October 31, 1998.

Turton, Jonathan. "Corporates Ride Out the Banks' Merger Mania." *Corporate Finance,* September 1998.

Webber, Susan. "Is Bigger Banking Better?" *United States Banker,* September 1998.

Wilcox, James A. "A New View on Cost Savings in Bank Mergers." *Economic Letter,* Federal Reserve Bank of San Francisco, August 20, 1999.

Other Topics

Baer, Herbert. "Foreign Competition in U.S. Banking Markets." *Economic Perspectives,* Federal Reserve Bank of Chicago, May–June 1990.

Bullington, Robert and Arnold Jensen. "Pricing a Bank." *The Bankers Magazine,* May–June 1981.

Buying and Selling Banks: A Guide to Making it Work. Arthur Anderson & Co., August 1989.

Cates, David. "Bank Analysis for a Takeover Era." *Bank Administration,* December 1988.

Cates, David. "Prices Paid for Banks." *Economic Review,* Federal Reserve Bank of Atlanta, January 1985.

Chrystal, K. Alec. "A Guide to Foreign Exchange Markets." *Review,* Federal Reserve Bank of St. Louis, March 1984.

Chrystal, K. Alec. "International Banking Facilities." *Review,* Federal Reserve Bank of St. Louis, April 1984.

Dufey, Gunter and Ian Giddy. *The International Money Market,* Englewood Cliffs, N.J.: Prentice Hall International, 1994.

Duffield, J.G. and B.J. Summers. "Bankers' Acceptances" in *Instruments of the Money Market,* Timothy Cook and Bruce Summers, eds. Richmond, Va.: Federal Reserve Bank of Richmond, 1981.

Freeman, Scott and Joseph Haslag. "Should Bank Reserves Earn Interest?" *Economic Review,* Federal Reserve Bank of Dallas, Fourth Quarter 1995.

Gasser, William and David Roberts. "Bank Lending to Developing Countries: Problems and Prospects." *Quarterly Review,* Federal Reserve Bank of New York, Autumn 1982.

Gillis, Art. "The Future of Outsourcing." *ABA Banking Journal,* February 2002.

Gorton, Gary and Andrew Winton. "Banking in Transition Economies: Does Efficiency Require Instability?" *Journal of Money, Credit and Banking,* August 1998.

Hechinger, John. "Check it Out: Online Banking is Finally Succeeding Thanks to an Added Ingredient: People." *Wall Street Journal,* February 21, 2001.

Hervey, Jack. "Bankers' Acceptances Revisited." *Economic Perspectives,* Federal Reserve Bank of Chicago, May–June 1985.

Humphrey, David. "Why Do Estimates of Bank Scale Economies Differ?" *Economic Review,* Federal Reserve Bank of Richmond, September–October 1990.

Jensen, Frederick and Patrick Parkinson. "Recent Developments in the Bankers Acceptance Market." *Federal Reserve Bulletin,* Washington, D.C.: Board of Governors of the Federal Reserve System, January 1986).

Jordan, John. "Resolving a Banking Crisis: What Worked in New England." *Economic Review,* Federal Reserve Bank of Boston, September–October 1998.

Kehrer, Kenneth and Rob Shore. "Bank Life Sales are Looking Up." *ABA Banking Journal*, November 2001.

Key, Sydney. "The Internationalization of U.S. Banking" in *Handbook for Banking Strategy*, Richard Aspinwall and Robert Eisenbeis, eds. New York: John Wiley & Sons, 1985.

King, Ralph and Steven Lipin. "Corporate Banking, Given Up for Dead, Is Reinventing Itself." *The Wall Street Journal*, January 31, 1994.

Koch, Donald and Robert Baker. "Purchase Accounting and the Quality of Bank Earnings." *Economic Review*, Federal Reserve Bank of Atlanta, April 1983.

Lynn, Matthew. "Could the Internet Destroy Banks?" *http://www.Bloomberg.com*, November 11, 1999.

MacPhee, William. "Bankers' Acceptance Finance." *The Journal of Commercial Bank Lending*, February 1978.

Matthews, Gordon and Karen Talley. "Mellon to Acquire Dreyfus, Joining Ranks of Fund Giants." *American Banker*, December 7, 1993.

Miller, William D. *Commercial Bank Valuation*, New York: John Wiley & Sons Inc., 1995.

Mills, Rodney. "Foreign Lending by Banks: A Guide to International and U.S. Statistics." *Federal Reserve Bulletin*, Washington, D.C.: Board of Governors of the Federal Reserve System, October 1986.

Morgan, John. "Assessing Country Risk at Texas Commerce." *The Bankers Magazine*, May–June 1985.

Neely, Walter. "Banking Acquisitions: Acquirer and Target Shareholder Returns." *Financial Management*, Winter 1987.

Orr, Bill. "E-banking: What's Next?" *ABA Banking Journal*, December 2001.

Park, Yoon and Jack Zwick. *International Banking in Theory and Practice*, Reading, Mass.: Addison-Wesley Publishing, 1985.

Pavel, Christine and John McElravey. *Globalization in the Financial Services Industry Economic Perspectives*, Federal Reserve Bank of Chicago, May–June 1990.

Reich-Hale, David. "Big Arrival for Banks' Insurance Sales Payoff." *American Banker*, January 22, 2001.

Rehm, Barbara. "Paltry 2.1% Is Average Premium On Sales of Seized Thrift Deposits." *American Banker*, November 19, 1990.

Sanchez, Joseph. "Workout Time Proves Key Measure." *American Banker*, November 14, 1990.

Sarver, Eugene. *The Eurocurrency Market Handbook*, New York: New York Institute of Finance, 1988.

Sullivan, Richard J. "Performance and Operation of Commercial Bank Web Sites." *Financial Perspectives 2001*, Federal Reserve Bank of Kansas City, December 2001.

"Tech Trends a 5-Year Scan." *A supplement of ABA Banking Journal*, edited by Lauren Bielski, December 2001.

Accelerated depreciation
A method of computing depreciation deductions for income taxes that permits deductions in early years greater than those under straight line depreciation.

Account activity Transactions associated with a deposit account, including home debits, transit checks, deposits, and account maintenance.

Account analysis An analytical procedure for determining whether a customer's deposit account or entire credit-deposit relationship with a bank is profitable. The procedure compares revenues from the account with the cost of providing services.

Account executive A representative of a brokerage firm who processes orders to buy and sell stocks, options, etc. for a customer's account.

Account maintenance The overhead cost associated with collecting information and mailing periodic statements to depositors.

Accounts payable Funds owed to a firm's suppliers.

Accounts receivable Funds owed a firm by customers to whom the firm sells goods and services.

Accounts receivable turnover Credit sales divided by average accounts receivable outstanding.

Accrual The accumulation of income earned or expense incurred, regardless of when the underlying cash flow is actually received or paid.

Accrual bond A bond that accrues interest but does not pay interest to the investor until maturity when accrued interest is paid with the principal outstanding.

Accrued interest Interest income that is earned but not yet received.

Acid-test ratio A measure of liquidity from reported balance sheet figures with a targeted minimum value of 1. Calculated as the sum of cash and marketable securities divided by current liabilities.

Active portfolio management An investment policy whereby managers buy and sell securities prior to final maturity to speculate on future interest rate movements.

Activity charge A service charge based on the number of checks written by a depositor.

Add-on rate A method of calculating interest charges by applying the quoted rate to the entire amount advanced to a borrower times the number of financing periods. An 8 percent add-on rate indicates $80 interest per $1,000 for 1 year, $160 for 2 years, and so forth. The effective interest rate is higher than the add-on rate because the borrower makes installment payments and cannot use the entire loan proceeds for the full maturity.

Adjustable rate mortgage
A mortgage with an interest rate that can be adjusted with changes in a base rate or reference index. The index generally varies with market interest rates.

ADR American Depository Receipt: A certificate issued by a U.S. bank which evidences ownership in foreign shares of stock held by the bank.

Advance A payment to a borrower under a loan agreement.

Advance commitment An agreement to sell an asset prior to the seller holding a commitment to purchase the asset.

Affiliate Any organization owned or controlled by a bank or bank holding company, the stockholders, or executive officers.

Affinity card A credit card that is offered to all individuals who are part of a common group or who share a common bond.

After-tax real return The after-tax rate of return on an asset minus the rate of inflation.

Agency A trust account in which title to property remains in the owner's name.

Agency securities Fixed-income securities issued by agencies owned or sponsored by the federal government. The most common securities are issued by the Federal Home Loan Bank, Federal National Mortgage Association, Government National Mortgage Association, and Farm Credit System.

Aging accounts receivable
A procedure for analyzing a firm's accounts receivable by dividing them into groups according to whether they are current or 30, 60, or over 90 days past due.

All-in-cost The weighted average cost of funds for a bank calculated by making adjustments for required reserves and deposit insurance costs. The sum of explicit and implicit costs.

Allowance for loan losses
A balance sheet account representing a contra-asset, or reduction in gross loans. It is established in recognition that some loans will not be repaid. Also called a loan loss reserve.

Alternative Minimum Tax (AMT)
A federal tax against income intended to ensure that taxpayers pay some tax even when they use tax-shelters to shield income.

Amortize To reduce a debt gradually by making equal periodic payments that cover interest and principal owed.

Amortizing swap An interest rate swap in which the outstanding notional principal amount declines over time.

Annual percentage rate
The effective annual cost of credit expressed as a percent inclusive of the amount financed, the loan maturity, and the finance charge.

Annuity A constant payment made for multiple periods of time.

Anticipated income theory
A theory that the timing of loan payments should be tied to the timing of a borrower's expected income.

Appreciation An increase in the market value of an asset.

Arbitrage The simultaneous trading (purchase and sale) of assets to take advantage of price differentials.

ARM Adjustable rate mortgage—a mortgage in which the contractual interest rate is tied to some index of interest rates and changes when supply and demand conditions change the underlying index.

Arrears An overdue outstanding debt.

Ask price The price at which an asset is offered for sale.

Asset-backed security A security with promised principal and interest payments backed or collateralized by cash flows originating from a portfolio of assets that generate the cash flows.

Asset-based financing Financing in which the lender relies primarily on cash flows generated by the asset financed to repay the loan.

Asset-liability management The management of a bank's entire balance sheet to achieve desired risk-return objectives and to maximize the market value of stockholders' equity.

Asset sensitive A bank is classified as asset sensitive if its GAP is positive.

Asset utilization Ratio of total operating income to total assets; a measure of the gross yield earned on assets.

Assignment The transfer of the legal right or interest on an asset to another party.

At-the-money An option where the price of the underlying instrument or contract is approximately equal to the option's exercise price.

Automated clearinghouse A facility that processes interbank debits and credits electronically.

Automated loan machine A machine that serves as a computer terminal and allows a customer to apply for a loan and, if approved, automatically deposits proceeds into an account designated by the customer.

Automated teller machine A machine that serves as a computer terminal and allows a customer to access account balances and information at a bank.

Backwardization The situation in which futures prices on futures contracts that expire farther in the future are below prices of nearby futures contracts.

Bad debts Loans that are due but are uncollectable.

Balance inquiry A request by a depositor or borrower to obtain the current balance in his or her account.

Balance sheet A financial statement that indicates the type and amount of assets, liabilities, and net worth of a firm or individual at a point in time.

Balloon loan A loan that requires small payments that are insufficient to pay off the entire loan so that a large final payment is necessary at termination.

Bankers acceptance A draft drawn on a bank and accepted, which makes it a negotiable instrument.

Bankers bank A firm that provides correspondent banking services to commercial banks and not to commercial or retail deposit and loan customers.

Bank holding company Any firm that owns or controls at least one commercial bank.

Bankrupt The situation in which a borrower is unable to pay obligated debts.

Barbell An investment portfolio in which a large fraction of securities mature near-term and another large fraction of securities mature longer-term.

Base rate An interest rate used as an index to price loans; typically associated with a bank's weighted marginal cost of funds.

Basic swap A plain vanilla interest rate swap in which one party pays a fixed interest rate and receives a floating rate, while the other party pays a floating rate and receives a fixed rate with all rates applied to the same, constant notional principal amount.

Basis With financial futures contracts, the futures rate minus the cash rate.

Basis point 1/100th of 1 percent, or 0.0001; 100 basis points equal 1 percent.

Basis risk The uncertainty that the futures rate minus the cash rate will vary from that expected.

Bearer bonds Bonds held by the investor (owner) in physical form. The investor receives interest payments by submitting coupons from the bond to the paying agent.

Benchmark rate The key driver rate used in sensitivity analysis or simulation models to assess interest rate risk. Other model rates are linked to the benchmark rate in terms of how they change when the benchmark rate changes.

Beneficiary The recipient of the balance in a trust account upon termination of the trust.

Best efforts underwriting The underwriter of securities commits to selling as many securities as possible and returns all unsold shares or units to the issuer.

Beta An estimate of the systematic or market risk of an asset within the capital asset pricing model (CAPM) framework.

Beta GAP The adjusted GAP figure in a basic earnings sensitivity analysis derived from multiplying the amount of rate-sensitive assets by the associated beta factors and summing across all rate-sensitive assets, and subtracting the amount of rate-sensitive liabilities multiplied by the associated beta factors summed across all rate-sensitive liabilities.

Bid price The price at which someone has offered to buy an asset.

BIF Bank Insurance Fund that insures deposits at commercial banks.

Blank check A signed check with no amount indicated.

Board of directors Individuals elected by stockholders to manage and oversee a firm's operations.

Board of Governors of the Federal Reserve System The policy-setting representatives of the Federal Reserve System in charge of setting the discount rate, required reserves, and general policies designed to affect growth in the banking system's reserves and U.S. money supply.

Bond An interest-bearing security representing a debt obligation of the issuer.

Bond broker A broker who trades bonds on an exchange.

Bond fund A mutual fund that invests in debt instruments.

Bond rating The subjective assessment of the likelihood that a borrower will make timely interest and principal payments as scheduled. Letters are assigned to a security by rating agencies to reflect estimated creditworthiness.

Book value Accounting value typically measured as historical cost minus depreciation.

Book value of equity Total assets minus total liabilities reported on the balance sheet.

Bounce a check A depositor writes a check which is returned to the bank and by the bank to the depositor because of insufficient funds.

Branch banking An organizational structure in which a bank maintains facilities that are part of the bank in offices different from its home office. Some states allow banks to set up branches through the state, county, or city. Others prohibit branches.

Bridge loan A loan issued to fund a temporary need from the time a security is redeemed to the time another security is issued.

Broker An individual who executes orders for customers for which he/she receives a commission.

Brokered deposits Deposits acquired through a money broker (typically an investment bank) in the national markets.

Bulge bracket firms Firms in an underwriting syndicate that have the highest commitment to assist in placing the underlying securities.

Bullet loan A loan that requires payment of the entire principal at maturity.

Burden Noninterest expense minus noninterest income.

Callable bond A bond in which the issuer has the option to call the bond from the investor, that is, to prepay the outstanding principal prior to maturity.

Call loan A loan that is callable on 24 hours' notice.

Call protection The feature which does not allow a bond to be called for some (deferment) period.

Call provision A provision in a bond that allows the issuer to redeem the bond, typically at a premium over par, prior to maturity.

Call option An agreement in which the buyer has the right to buy a fixed amount of the underlying asset at a set price for a specified period of time.

CAMELS An acronym that refers to the regulatory rating system for bank performance: C = capital adequacy, A = asset quality, M = management quality, E = earnings quality, L = liquidity, and S = sensitivity to market risk.

Cap Use of options to place a ceiling on a firm's borrowing costs.

Capital Funds subscribed and paid by stockholders representing ownership in a bank. Regulatory capital also includes debt components and loss reserves.

Capital gain (loss) Profit (loss) resulting from the sale of an asset for more (less) than its purchase price.

Capital market Market for securities with maturities beyond one year.

Captive finance company A finance company owned by a manufacturer that provides financing to buyers of the firm's products.

Card bank Bank that administers its own credit card plan or serves as a primary regional agent of a national credit card operation.

CARs Collateralized automoblile receivables—a form of asset-backed security in which the collateral is automobile receivables.

Cash basis The accounting procedure that recognizes revenues when cash is actually received and expenses when cash is actually paid.

Cash budget A comparison of cash receipts and cash expenditures over a period of time.

Cash flow from operations A firm's net cash flow from normal business operating activities used to assess the firm's ability to service existing and new debt and other fixed payment obligations.

Cashier's check A bank check that is drawn on the bank issuing the check and signed by a bank officer.

Cash letter Transit letter on tape that lists items submitted between banks for collection.

Cash market The spot market for the immediate exchange of goods and services for immediate payment.

Cash settlement The form for settling futures contracts where the parties exchange cash rather than have one party deliver the underlying asset.

Cash-to-cash asset cycle The time it takes to accumulate cash, purchase inventory, produce a finished good, sell it, and collect on the sale.

Cash-to-cash liability cycle The length of time to obtain interest-free financing from suppliers in the form of accounts payable and accrued expenses.

Cash-to-cash working capital cycle The timing difference between the cash-to-cash asset cycle and the cash-to-cash liability cycle.

Central bank The main bank in a country responsible for issuing currency and setting and managing monetary policy.

Certificate of deposit (CD) A large-denomination time deposit representing the receipt of funds for deposit at a bank.

Certified check A check guaranteed by a bank where funds are immediately withdrawn.

Certified Financial Planner (CFP) A designation earned by individuals who have passed the examination sponsored by the Certified Financial Planner Board. Such individuals have studied banking, investment, insurance, estate planning, and tax planning to assist in managing client financial needs.

Charge-off The act of writing off a loan to its present value in recognition that the asset has decreased in value.

Charter A document that authorizes a bank to conduct business.

Chartered Financial Analyst (CFA) A designation earned by individuals who have passed a three-part examination sponsored by the Institute of Chartered Financial Analysts. Topics include economics, finance, security analysis, and financial accounting to assist in security analysis and portfolio management.

Check kiting The process of writing checks against uncollected deposits while checks are in the process of collection, thereby using funds (float) not actually available.

Chinese wall The imaginary barrier that ensures a trust department will manage trust assets for the benefit of the trust beneficiaries, not for other departments in the bank.

Clearinghouse association
A voluntary association of banks formed to assist the daily exchange of checks among member institutions.

CMO Collateralized mortgage obligation—a security backed by a pool of mortgages that is structured to fall within an estimated maturity range (tranche), based on the timing of allocated interest and principal payments on the underlying mortgages.

Collar Use of options to place a cap and floor on a firm's borrowing costs.

Collateral Property a borrower pledges as security against a loan for repayment if the borrower defaults.

Collected balances Ledger balances minus float.

Commercial loan theory
A theory suggesting that banks make only short-term, self-liquidating loans that match the maturity of bank deposits.

Commercial paper A short-term unsecured promissory note of a prime corporation.

Commitment fee Fee charged for making a line of credit available to a borrower.

Common stock Securities (equities) that evidence ownership in a company for which the holder received discretionary dividends and realizes price appreciation/depreciation.

Compensating balance A deposit balance required as compensation for services provided by a lender or correspondent bank.

Compounding Earning interest on interest.

Conservator An individual or trust department appointed by a court to manage the property of an incapacitated individual.

Consolidated balance sheet
A balance sheet showing the aggregate financial condition of a firm and its subsidiaries, netting out all intracompany transactions.

Consumer bank A bank that does not make commercial loans.

Contingent liabilities Items, such as guarantees or related contracts, that may become liabilities if certain developments arise.

Conventional mortgage
A mortgage or deed or trust that is not obtained under a government-insured program.

Conversion fee Fee charged for converting a loan commitment to a term loan.

Convertible debt A bond that may be exchanged for common stock in the same firm.

Core capital Tier 1 capital consisting primarily of stockholder's equity.

Core deposits A base level of deposits a bank expects to remain on deposit, regardless of the economic environment.

Correspondent bank A bank that provides services, typically check clearing, to other banks.

Country risk The credit risk that government or private borrowers in a specific country will refuse to repay their debts as obligated for other than pure economic reasons.

Coupon rate The ratio of the dollar-valued coupon payment to a security's par value.

Covenant An element of a loan agreement whereby the borrower agrees to meet specific performance requirements or refrain from certain behavior.

Credit bureau An association that collects and provides information on the credit (payment) histories of borrowers.

Credit check Efforts by a lender to verify the accuracy of information provided by potential borrowers.

Credit department The bank department where credit information is collected and analyzed to make credit decisions.

Credit enhancement A guarantee or letter of credit backing for a loan, which improves the creditworthiness of the contract.

Credit file Information related to a borrower's loan request, including application, record of past performance, loan documentation, and analyst opinions.

Credit limit The maximum amount that a borrower is allowed to borrow against a loan commitment or credit line.

Credit risk Potential variation in net income and market value of equity resulting from the nonpayment of interest and principal.

Credit scoring The use of a statistical model based on applicant attributes to assess whether a loan automatically meets minimum credit standards. The model assigns values to potential borrowers' attributes, with the sum of the values compared to a threshold.

Credit union A non-profit organization that offers financial services to qualifying members. Credit unions do not pay state and federal income taxes and thus operate at a competitive advantage to other depository institutions.

Cross hedge Use of a futures contract for a specific asset that differs from the cash asset being hedged.

Currency swap An agreement to exchange payments denominated in one currency for payments denominated in a different currency.

Current ratio The ratio of current liabilities that indicates a firm's ability to pay current debts when they come due.

Current yield The coupon rate on a bond divided by the current market price of the bond.

Customer information file
A record of the services used by each customer.

Customer profitability analysis A procedure that compares revenues with expenses and the bank's target profit from a customer's total account relationship.

Cyclical liquidity needs An estimate of liquid funds needed to cover deposit outflows or loan demand in excess of trend or seasonal factors.

Daylight overdrafts Bank payments from deposits held at a Federal Reserve bank or correspondent bank in excess of actual collected balances during a day.

de novo branch A newly opened branch.

Dealer reserve An account established by a bank and dealer used to assign the interest that accrues to dealers as they sell loans to a bank.

Debenture A long-term bond that is secured by the general performance of the issuer.

Debit card A plastic card that, when used, immediately reduces the balance in a customer's transactions deposit.

Debtor-in-possession financing
A loan made to a firm which has filed for Chapter 11 bankruptcy protection.

Debt service The amount needed to pay principal and interest on a loan.

Defalcation The misappropriation of funds or property by an individual.

Default The failure to make obligated interest and principal payments on a loan.

Deferred availability credit items
Checks received for collection for which a bank has not provided credit to the depositor.

Delinquent account
An account that is past due because the account holder has not made the obligated payment on time.

Delivery date Specific day that a futures contract expires.

Delta The change in an option's price divided by the change in the price of the underlying instrument or contract.

Demand deposit Transactions account, payable on demand, that pays no interest to the depositor.

Depreciation Writing down the value of a capital asset, reported as an expense. Also, a decrease in the market value of a financial asset.

Derivative A financial instrument whose value is determined by the specific features of the underlying asset or instrument.

Direct loan Loan with terms negotiated directly between the lender and actual user of the funds.

Discount broker A brokerage firm that offers a limited range of retail services and charges lower fees than full-service brokers.

Discount rate Interest rate charged by Federal Reserve banks for borrowing from the discount window.

Discount window The process of Federal Reserve banks lending to member institutions.

Dividend A payment made to holders of a firm's common stock and/or preferred stock. Cash dividends are paid in cash while stock dividends are paid in stock.

Draft A written order requesting one party to make payment to another party at a specified point in time.

Dual banking system System in the U.S. in which a group trying to obtain a charter to open a bank can apply to the state banking department or the Office of the Comptroller of the Currency – the national banking agency.

Duration The weighted average of time until cash flows generated by an asset are expected to be received (paid). The weights are the present value of each cash flow as a fraction of the asset's current price.

Duration gap The weighted duration of assets minus the product of the weighted duration of liabilities and the ratio of total liabilities to total assets.

Early withdrawal penalty An interest penalty a depositor pays for withdrawing funds from a deposit account prior to maturity.

Earning assets Income-earning assets held by a bank; typically include interest-bearing balances, investment securities, and loans.

Earnings credit Interest rate applied to investable balances.

Earnings dilution A decrease in earnings per share after one bank acquires another.

Earnings per share Net income divided by the number of outstanding shares of common stock.

EBIT Earnings before interest and taxes.

EBITDA Earnings before interest, taxes, depreciation, and amortization.

Economic value added (EVA) A measure of financial performance trade-marked by Stern, Stewart & Co. equal to a firm's net operating profit after tax (NOPAT) minus a capital charge representing the required return to shareholders.

Economies of scale Cost efficiencies evidenced by low operating costs per unit of output.

ECU European Currency Unit.

Edge corporation A bank subsidiary that engages in international banking activities.

Effective convexity The value for convexity that reflects the price impact of embedded options in different interest rate environments.

Effective duration The value for duration reflecting the price impact of embedded options when interest rates rise versus fall.

Efficiency ratio Noninterest expense divided by the sum of net interest income and noninterest income.

Elasticity A measure of the relative quantity response to a change in price, income, interest rate, or other variable.

EMU European Monetary Union.

Enterprise value The value of a firm equal to the market capitalization (number of shares of stock times the current stock price) plus the market value of outstanding debt.

Equity Ownership interest in a firm represented by common and preferred stockholders.

Equity multiplier Ratio of total assets to equity; a measure of financial leverage.

Euro The European currency unit introduced in January 1999.

Eurocurrency A financial claim denominated in a currency other than the one where the issuing institution is located.

Eurodollars Dollar-denominated deposits at banks located outside the United States.

Exchange rate Price of one currency in terms of another.

Executor An individual or trust department responsible for handling a settlement.

Extension risk The risk that the holder of a mortgage-backed security will receive outstanding principal payments later than originally anticipated. Later principal payments result from interest rates rising and prepayments occuring slower than expected.

Facility fee Fee imposed for making a line of credit available.

Factoring An advance of credit whereby one party purchases the accounts receivable of another party at a discount, without recourse.

Fannie Mae Name referring to the Federal National Mortgage Association.

Federal Financing Bank A federal agency that borrows from the U.S. Treasury and lends funds to various federal agencies.

Federal funds Unsecured short-term loans that are settled in immediately available funds.

Federal Reserve Bank One of the 12 district federal reserve banks that make up the Federal Reserve System.

FHA Federal Housing Administration—a federal agency that insures mortgages.

FHLMC Federal Home Loan Mortgage Corporation (Freddie Mac)—a private corporation operating with an implicit federal guarantee; buys mortgages financed largely by mortgage-backed securities.

Fidelity bond A contract that covers losses associated with employee dishonesty, typically embezzlement and forgery at banks.

Fiduciary An individual or trust department responsible for acting in the best interests of a designated third party.

Finance charge Under Regulation Z, the sum of "all charges payable directly or indirectly by the borrower and imposed directly or indirectly by the lender as an incident to or as an extension of credit."

Finance company A firm that borrows from the money and capital markets to make loans to individuals and commercial enterprises.

Financial futures contract A commitment between two parties to exchange a standardized financial asset through an organized exchange at a specified price for future delivery. The price of futures contracts changes prior to delivery, and participants must settle daily changes in contract value.

Financial innovation The continuous development of new products, services, and technology to deliver products and services.

Financial leverage Relationship between the amount of debt versus equity financing.

Financial risk Potential variation in income before interest and taxes associated with fixed interest payments on debt and lease payments.

Financial services holding company A parent company that owns a bank holding company plus other subsidiaries, such as a thrift holding company and insurance subsidiary.

Fixed rate An interest rate that does not change during a specified period of time.

Float Dollar amount of checks in process of collection, net of deferred availability amounts, to depositors.

Floating rate An interest rate tied to a base rate that changes over time as market conditions dictate.

Floating-rate note (FRN) A short-term note whose interest payment varies with a short-term interest rate.

Floor Use of options to establish a minimum borrowing cost.

FNMA Federal National Mortgage Association (Fannie Mae)—a private corporation operating with an implicit federal guarantee; buys mortgages financed by mortgage-backed securities.

Foreclosure Selling property in order to apply the proceeds in payment of a debt.

Foreign exchange Currency of a foreign country acceptable as a medium of exchange.

Foreign exchange risk The risk that the value of a position denominated in a foreign currency may decline due to a change in exchange rates.

Foreign tax credit Income taxes paid to a foreign country that can be claimed as a tax credit against a domestic tax liability.

Forward contract A commitment between two parties to exchange a nonstandardized asset at a fixed price for future delivery. The price of the contract does not change prior to delivery, and no interim payments are required.

Forward rate Yield on a forward contract. Also, break even yield calculated under pure expectations theory according to prevailing interest rates.

Forward rate agreement A forward contract in which the two parties establish an interest rate to be paid by one party to the other at a set date in the future. If the actual rate on that date differs from the predetermined rate, one party makes a cash payment to the other party.

Full-service broker A brokerage that provides a full range of services to customers including advice on which securities to buy and/or sell.

GAAP Generally Accepted Accounting Principles representing the standard rules and procedures that accountants follow when reporting financial information.

GAP Dollar value of rate-sensitive assets minus the dollar value of rate-sensitive liabilities.

Garnishment A court directive authorizing a bank to withold funds from a borrower.

General obligation bonds Municipal bonds secured by the full faith, credit, and taxing power of the issuing state or local government.

Ginnie Mae Name referring to the Government National Mortgage Association.

Glass-Steagall Act The 1933 act that separated lending activities from investment banking activities at commercial banks by prohibiting commercial banks from underwriting corporate securities.

GNMA Government National Mortgage Association (Ginnie Mae)—a government entity that buys mortgages for low-income housing and guarantees mortgage-backed securities issued by private lenders.

Gold standard A monetary system where the value of a country's currency is determined by the value of the gold content in the currency.

Goodwill An intangible asset representing the difference between the book value of an asset or a firm and the actual sales price.

Grace period The time period for a credit card statement representing the time from when the statement is generated to the last day full payment can be made and still avoid a finance charge.

Grandfather clause A legislative provision that exempts parties previously engaged in activities prohibited by new legislation.

Gross Domestic Product The market value of goods and services produced over a period of time including the sum of consumer expenditures, investment expenditures, government expenditures, and net exports (exports minus imports).

Guarantee Make oneself liable for the debts of another.

Guaranteed investment contract (GIC) A financial contract in which the writer of a policy agrees to pay a fixed amount at maturity after receiving a fixed, single premium up front.

Guardian An individual or a trust department appointed by a court to manage a minor's property or personal affairs.

Hedge Take a position in the forward futures, or swaps, market to offset risk associated with cash market activity.

Highly leveraged transaction (HLT) Transaction in which borrower's debt increases sharply after the asset exchange, such as an LBO.

Historical cost The value for certain balance sheet items reflecting the original cost or amortized cost.

Holding period return The annualized rate of return expected or realized from holding a security over a specific period of time.

Home banking Actions involving the conduct of banking business taking place in customers' homes, including telephone and computer transactions.

Home debit A check drawn on a bank that is presented to the same bank for deposit or payment.

Home equity loan Loan secured by an individual's equity in a home.

Hot money Funds that move between institutions quickly in search of higher yields or greater safety.

Hypothecation In a contract, commiting property to secure a loan.

Illiquid An asset that is not easily or readily converted into cash.

Immediately available funds Collected deposits held at Federal Reserve banks or certain collected liabilities or private financial institutions.

Immunize To fully hedge against interest rate risk.

Implied volatility The expected volatility in return on an underlying asset or contract derived from an option pricing model.

Independent bank A bank operating in one locality that is not part of a large multibank holding company or group of banks.

Index rate The rate that serves as a base rate when pricing certain mortgages and variable rate loans.

Indirect loan Loan in which a retailer takes the credit application and negotiates terms with the actual borrower. The lender then purchases the loan from the retailer under prearranged terms.

Individual retirement account A retirement account available to individuals to defer income taxes.

Industrial revenue bond (IRB) A bond issued by a state government, local government, or political subdivision for the express benefit of a business that will effectively use the proceeds.

Initial public offering (IPO) The initial offering of stock of a private company.

Insolvent The financial position of a firm whose market value of stockholders' equity is less than or equal to zero. A firm is technically insolvent when the book value of stockholders' equity is less than or equal to zero.

Installment loan A loan that is payable in periodic, partial installments.

Interbank loan Credit extended from one bank to another.

Interest-on-interest Interest earned on interest, or reinvestment interest income.

Interest rate cap A contract in which payments are made from the seller who receives an up-front premium to the buyer when a reference index rate exceeds a strike rate.

Interest rate floor A contract in which payments are made from the seller who receives an up-front premium to the buyer when a reference index rate is less than a strike rate.

Interest rate risk Potential variability in a bank's net interest income and market value of equity caused by changes in the level of interest rates.

Interest rate swap A contract in which two parties (counterparties) agree to exchange fixed rate interest payments for floating rate interest payments over a specific period of time based on some notional principal amount.

Internal audit Routine examination of a bank's accounting records.

Inter vivos Phrase referring to "between living persons."

In-the-money An option that has a positive intrinsic value. A call option in which the actual price is above the exercise price; a put option in which the actual price is below the exercise price.

Intrinsic value The net value obtained from exercising an option.

Inverted yield curve Yield curve with long-term rates below short-term rates.

Investable balances Ledger balances minus float minus required reserves against associated deposit balances.

Investment banking Activity involving securities underwriting, making a market in securities, and arranging mergers and acquisitions.

IO Interest-only security representing the interest portion of a stripped Treasury or stripped mortgage-backed security.

Judgment Legal ruling regarding the final payment of a court-determined transfer of assets.

Judgmental credit analysis Subjective assessment of a borrower's ability and willingness to repay debts.

Junk bond A bond with a credit rating below investment grade, below Baa for Moody's, and below BBB for S&P, or a bond that is not rated.

Keogh plan A pension plan for the self-employed which allows them to make contributions and defer taxes until the funds are withdrawn.

Kite Writing checks against uncollected deposits in the process of clearing through the banking system.

Ladder strategy When investing bonds, allocating roughly equivalent amounts (portions) to different maturities.

Lagged reserve accounting System of reserve requirements based on deposits outstanding prior to the reserve maintenance period.

LBO Leveraged buyout.

Lease A contract in which the owner of a property allows another party to use the property if certain terms are met and lease payments (rent) are made.

Ledger balances Dollar value of deposit balances appearing on a bank's books.

Legal lending limit The maximum amount that can be loaned to any one borrower or any group of related borrowers.

Lender liability Circumstances in which the courts have found lenders liable to their borrowers for fraud, deception, breached fiduciary activities, broken promises, and good faith negotiations.

Lessee The party that rents or leases an asset from another party.

Lessor The party that owns an asset and leases or rents it to another party.

Letter of credit A bank's guarantee of payment, indicated by a document that describes the handling of a specific transaction.

Leveraged buyout (LBO) An acquisition where the firm buying another firm contributes a small amount of equity and finances the bulk of the purchase price with debt.

Liability management theory A theory that focuses on banks issuing liabilities to meet liquidity needs.

Liability sensitive A bank is classified as liability sensitive if its GAP is negative.

LIBOR London Interbank Offer Rate, which represents a money market rate offered by banks for the placement of Eurodollars.

Lien Legal right granted by the court to attach property until a legal claim is paid.

Limited branching Provisions that restrict branching to a geographic area smaller than an entire state.

Line of credit A lending agreement between a bank and borrower in which the bank makes a fixed amount of funds available to the borrower for a specified period of time. The customer determines the timing of actual borrowing.

Liquidity premium The premium included in longer-term interest rates to compensate investors for price risk associated with volatile interest rates.

Liquidity risk The variation in net income and market value of bank equity caused by a bank's difficulty in obtaining immediately available funds, either by borrowing or selling assets.

Loan commitment Formal agreement between a bank and borrower to provide a fixed amount of credit for a specified period.

Loan participation Credit extended to a borrower in which members of a group of lenders each provide a fraction of the total financing; typically arises because individual banks are limited in the amount of credit they can extend to a single customer.

Loan syndication An arrangement where several lenders make a loan jointly to a borrower.

Loan-to-value ratio The loan amount divided by the appraised value of the underlying collateral.

London Interbank Offer Rate (LIBOR) Interest rate at which banks deposit Eurodollars with other banks outside the United States.

Long hedge The purchase of a futures contract to reduce the risk of an increase in the price of a cash asset.

Long position Market position in which an investor actually owns an asset.

Long-term securities Securities with maturities in excess of one year.

Macrohedge A hedge strategy designed to reduce risk associated with a bank's entire balance sheet position.

Maintenance margin The minimum amount of funds in a margin account that must be maintained at all times. When the customer's balance falls below this amount, the broker will require an additional deposit or may close the account.

Make a market Stand ready to buy or sell particular assets.

Make-whole clause A provision which requires that the borrower make a payment to a lender after a loan is called or prepaid. The amount of the payment equals the net present value of the lost interest and principal payments.

Margin Deposit with a broker that protects the broker from losses arising from customer transactions.

Marginal cost of funds The incremental cost of additional funds to finance firm operations.

Marginal tax rate Tax rate applied to the last increment of taxable income.

Market value The actual value indicating what an asset can be currently sold for.

Mark to market The daily reconciliation of a future trader's margin account in which gains and losses on the position are added and subtracted, respectively.

Maturity The date at which the principal of a note, draft, or bond becomes due and payable.

MBS Mortgage-backed security—a security that evidences an undivided interest in the ownership of a pool of mortgages.

Merger A combination of two firms, generally where the assets and liabilities of the seller are combined with the assets and liabilities of the buyer.

Microhedge A hedge strategy designed to reduce risk associated with a specific transaction.

Modified duration Macaulay's duration divided by one plus the prevailing interest rate on the underlying instrument.

Money market deposit account Small time deposit whose holder is limited to three written checks per month.

Money market mutual fund Mutual fund that accepts customer funds and purchases short-term marketable securities.

Money supply The federal government's designation of certain liquid assets as money; M1A equals currency outside banks plus demand deposits; M1B equals M1A plus other checkable deposits; M2 equals M1B plus overnight RPs, savings and small time deposits, and money market funds; M3 equals M2 plus large time deposits and term RPs; L equals M3 plus other liquid assets.

Mortgage A contract whereby a borrower provides a lender with a lien on real property as security against a loan.

Mortgage banking The business of packaging mortgage loans for sale to investors and retaining the servicing rights to the mortgages.

Mortgage servicing The process of collecting monthly payments on mortgages, keeping records, paying the associated insurance and taxes, and making monthly payments to holders of the underlying mortgages or mortgage-backed securities.

Multibank holding company A bank holding company that owns controlling interest in at least two commercial banks.

Municipals Securities issued by states, local governments, and their political subdivisions.

Mutual fund A pool of funds that is managed by an investment company. Investors in a mutual fund own shares in the fund, and the fund uses the proceeds to buy different assets.

Mutual savings banks Firms without capital stock that accept deposits and make loans.

Negotiable order of withdrawal Interest-bearing transactions account offered by banks.

Net interest margin Ratio of net interest income to total earning assets.

Net overhead burden Difference between noninterest expense and noninterest income as a fraction of total bank assets.

Netting The practice of offsetting promised interest payments with promised interest receipts and transferring the difference with an interest rate swap.

Net worth Owners' (stockholders') equity in a firm.

No load fund A mutual fund that does not charge a regular sales commission. It may charge a 12b-1 fee.

Nominal interest rate Market interest rate stated in current, not real, dollars.

Nonbank bank A firm that either makes commercial loans or accepts deposits but does not do both. Thus, it avoids regulation as a commercial bank.

Nonbank subsidiary A subsidiary of a bank holding company that is engaged in activities closely related to banking, such as leasing, data processing, factoring, and insurance underwriting.

Nonperforming loan Loan for which an obligated interest payment is past due.

Nonrated bond A bond that is not rated by Moody's, S&P, or other rating agency.

Nonrate gap Noninterest-bearing liabilities plus equity minus non-earning assets as a fraction of earning assets.

Nonrecourse Holder of an obligation has no legal right to force payment on a claim.

Note issuance facility An arrangement in which borrowers can issue short-term securities in their own names.

Notional value The face value of interest rate swap contracts; a mere reference value to compute obligated interest payments.

NSF Not sufficient funds.

Off-balance sheet activities Commitments, such as loan guarantees, that do not appear on a bank's balance sheet but represent actual contractual obligations.

One bank holding company A holding company that owns or controls only one commercial bank.

On the run The most recently issued U.S. Treasury security.

Open account Credit not supported by a note or other written record.

Open interest Total number of outstanding unfilled futures positions measured on one side of the transaction.

Operating income Sum of interest income and noninterest income.

Operating leverage Ratio of fixed costs to total costs; measure of business risk that indicates the relative change in operating income that arises from a change in sales.

Option Right to buy or sell a specific asset at a fixed price during a specified interval of time.

Option-adjusted spread A procedure for valuing prepayment risk associated with mortgage-backed securities that recognizes the magnitude and timing of prepayments and required return to an investor; the corresponding yield spread over matched Treasury securities.

Option premium The price of an option.

Origination fee Fee charged by a lender for accepting the initial loan application and processing the loan.

Other real estate owned Real estate owned by a bank that is acquired in settlement of debts.

Out-of-the money An option that has no intrinsic value. A call option in which the actual price is below the exercise price; a put option in which the actual price is above the exercise price.

Outsourcing Buying services from third-party vendors. For example, some banks might outsource their data processing.

Overdraft Depositor writing a check for an amount greater than the deposit balance.

Overhead Expenses that generally do not vary with the level of output.

PAC Planned amortization class CMO—a security that is retired according to a planned amortization schedule, while payments to other classes of securities are slowed or accelerated. The objective is to ensure that PACs exhibit highly predictable maturities and cash flows.

Parallel shift in the yield curve A change in interest rates where rates at all maturities change by the same amount, in the same direction, at the same time. This never actually occurs.

Parent company A firm that owns controlling interest in the stock of another firm.

Par value Dollar value of a bond's principal payment at maturity; face value printed on a security.

Passbook savings Nonnegotiable, small savings account evidenced by a passbook listing the account terms.

Passive portfolio management An investment policy whereby managers make predetermined securities purchases regardless of the level of interest rates and specific rate expectations. Examples include following a laddered maturity strategy whereby a bank continuously buys 10-year securities as previously owned securities mature.

Pass-through security Instrument secured by mortgages in which the mortgage banker passes mortgage interest and principal payments to the holder of the security minus a servicing charge.

Past-due loan A loan with a promised principal and/or interest payment that has not been made by the scheduled payment date.

Peer group Sample firms used to generate average reference data for comparison with an individual firm's performance data.

P/E ratio A firm's stock price per share divided by earnings per share.

Permanent working capital Minimum level of current assets minus minimum level of current liabilities net of short-term bank credit and current maturity of long-term debt; represents the amount of long-term financing required for current assets.

Perpetual preferred stock Nonmaturing preferred stock.

Personal banker Individual assigned to a bank customer to handle a broad range of financial services.

Planned amortization class A collateralized mortgage obligation (CMO) that receives principal from the underlying mortgages based on a predetermined payment schedule, where the payments vary depending on whether prepayments fall inside or outside some predetermined range.

Pledged securities Bank securities pledged as collateral against public deposits, borrowings from Federal Reserve banks, and securities sold under agreement to repurchase.

PO Principal-only security representing the principal portion of a stripped Treasury or stripped mortgage-backed security.

Point of sale Electronic terminals that enable customers to directly access deposit accounts.

Pooling of interests An accounting procedure in an acquisition where the two companies simply report financial results by combining assets, liabilities, and equity at book values.

Preferred stock Class of stock representing ownership with a claim on firm income senior to common stock.

Premium on a bond Difference between the price of a bond and its par value when the price is higher.

Prepayment speed The percentage of the outstanding principal that is prepaid above and beyond normal amortization.

Primary capital The sum of common stock, perpetual preferred stock, surplus, undivided profits, contingency and other capital reserves, valuation reserves, mandatory convertible securities, and minority interest in consolidated subsidiaries at a bank.

Prime rate One of several base interest rates used as an index to price commercial loans.

Probate Legal act of submitting a will before a court to verify authenticity of the document.

Problem loans Loans currently in default or expected to obtain default status.

Pro forma financial statements Projected or forecasted balance sheet and income statements.

Prudent man rule Requirement that a fiduciary exercise discretion, prudence, and sound judgment in managing the assets of a third party.

Purchase accounting An accounting method for acquisitions in which the assets and liabilities of the combined firm reflect a revaluation of assets and liabilities of the subject firms, thus recognizing the value of goodwill and other intangibles.

Put Option to sell an asset (security) for a fixed price during a specific interval of time.

Putable bond A bond where the investor has the option to put the security back to the issuer after some predetermined date prior to maturity and receive the principal invested or a stated price.

Quality spread The difference in market yields between yields on risky securities and matched maturity/duration Treasury securities.

Rate sensitive Classification of assets and liabilities that can be repriced within a specific time frame, either because they mature or carry floating or variable rates.

Rating System of assigning letters to security issues indicating the perceived default risks associated with that class of issues.

Real interest rate Interest rate after inflation expectations are netted from a nominal interest rate.

Realized compound yield A measure of total return calculated by comparing total future dollars equal to coupon interest or dividends plus reinvestment income and the maturity or sale value of the underlying asset, with the initial purchase price, over the appropriate number of compounding periods.

Rebate The return of a portion of unearned interest to a borrower.

Recourse Legal right to enforce a claim against another party.

Redlining A practice whereby lenders deny loans to residents living in predetermined geographic areas. Such a practice is illegal.

Reinvestment risk The risk that future cash flows may be reinvested at rates below those expected or available at present.

REIT (Real estate investment trust) An organization that obtains funds to invest in real estate or finance construction.

REMIC A real estate mortgage investment conduit issuing securities collateralized by mortgages and passing on principal and interest payments to investors. Like CMOs, REMIC securities represent claims on the underlying cash flows that are prioritized by multiple classes or tranches.

Repurchase agreement (RP) Short-term loans secured by government securities and settled in immediately available funds.

Reserve for bank debts Amount appearing on a bank's balance sheet that represents the estimated value of uncollectable loans.

Reserve requirement ratios Percentages applied to transactions accounts and time deposits to determine the dollar amount of required reserve assets.

Reserves Qualifying assets to meet reserve requirements, including vault cash and deposit balances held at Federal Reserve banks.

Resolution Trust Corporation (RTC) A government agency (1989–1996) that assisted in the management of savings and loans deemed to be insolvent during the Thrift Crisis.

Respondent bank Bank that purchases services from a correspondent bank.

Return items Checks that have not been honored by the drawee bank and have been returned to the check writer.

Return on assets Net income divided by average total assets.

Return on equity Net income divided by average stockholders' equity.

Revenue bond Municpal bond issued to finance a project in which debt service payments are secured by specific revenues from the project.

Reverse mortgage A mortgage in which the owner of the property can borrow against existing equity in the property.

Reverse repo A contract in which a lender provides funds to a borrower for which collateral is provided in the event of nonpayment.

Reverse repurchase agreement Securities purchased under an agreement to resell them at a later date.

Revolver Loan commitment or line of credit that converts to a term loan.

Riding the yield curve An investment strategy where the investor buys a security that matures after the investor's assumed holding period. The investor plans to sell the security at the end of the holding period and earn an above-average return because interest rates are expected to remain stable or fall.

Risk assets Total assets minus cash and due from balances minus U.S. government securities.

Roth IRA An individual retirement account introduced in 1998 that allows individuals whose wages and salaries are below a predetermined minimum to contribute after-tax income. The contributions grow on a tax-sheltered basis and thus are not taxed at withdrawal.

Rule of 72 Divide 72 by the interest rate at which funds are invested. The value indicates how long it will take for the amount of funds invested to double in value.

Run on a bank Situation in which a large number of depositors lose confidence in the safety of their deposits and attempt to withdraw their funds.

Safe deposit box Privacy boxes for storage located in a bank vault under lock and key.

SAIF Savings Association Insurance Fund which insures deposits at thrift institutions.

Sale and lease back Transaction in which an asset is sold, with title exchanged to a lessor who leases the asset to the original owner.

Sallie Mae Student Loan Marketing Association which guarantees student loans.

Seasonal liquidity needs Cash flow needs that arise from predictable seasonal loan demands and deposit outflows.

Secondary capital Limited life preferred stock, subordinated debt, and mandatory convertible securities not included as primary capital.

Securitization Pooling loans into packages and selling the pooled assets by issuing securities collateralized by the pooled assets.

Security Collateral a borrower pledges against a loan or secondary source of repayment in case of default.

Security interest The legal claim on property that secures a debt or the performance of an obligation.

Serial bonds A series of bonds offered by the same issuer with principal payments that are due at different maturities. Serial bonds are common for municipal bond issuers.

Service charges Fees imposed for bank services.

Short hedge Sale of a futures contract to protect against a price decline.

Short position The sale of an asset not owned.

Short-term securities Securities that mature in one year or less.

Sight draft A draft payable "on sight."

Simple interest Interest applied against principal only.

Speculator Trader who takes a position to increase risk in hope of earning extraordinary returns.

Spot curve Yields on zero coupon Treasury securities that differ in terms of maturity.

Spot market Market for immediate delivery of assets.

Spot rate Yield on a zero coupon Treasury security.

Spread Average yield on earning assets minus the average rate paid on interest-bearing liabilities.

Statewide branching Allowing banks to establish branches throughout an entire state.

Stop payment Request by a depositor to stop payment on a previously issued check that has not yet cleared.

Strategic planning The process through which managers formulate the firm's mission and goals, and identify strengths, weaknesses, opportunities, and threats.

Strike price Fixed price at which an asset may be purchased in a call option or sold under a put option.

Stripped bond A bond in which individual coupon payments and principal payments are separated (stripped) from the bond and sold as distinct zero coupon securities.

Stripped securities Securities that represent just the coupon interest or principal payments on a loan. The interest-only payment is referrred to as an IO, while the principal-only payment is referred to as a PO.

Structured note A security that will change in value or whose cash flows will change when some underlying index or base rate changes.

Subchapter S firm A firm with 75 or fewer stockholders that chooses to be taxed as a partnership so as not to pay corporate income taxes.

Subordinated debt In the case of bankruptcy, the claims of holders of subordinated debt are subordinated to the claims of other debt holders. In banks, insured depositors are paid in full before holders of subordinated debt receive anything.

Support tranche A class of mortgage-backed securities where the promised principal and interest payments are made after payments to holders of other classes of securities are made.

Swap Simultaneous purchase and sale of like securities to alter the portfolio composition and characteristics.

Swaption An option on a swap.

Syndicate Group of banks that jointly negotiate a contract to sell securities or make loans.

TAC Targeted amortization class mortgage-backed securities in which payments are guaranteed for one specific prepayment rate.

Takedown Actual borrowing against a line of credit or loan commitment.

Tangible equity Total assets minus intangible assets minus total liabilities.

Tax and loan account A deposit account at a financial institution held by the U.S. Treasury.

Tax anticipation note Short-term municipal security issued in anticipation of future tax receipts and repaid from same.

Tax credit Direct reduction in tax liability arising from qualifying expenditures.

Tax-equivalent yield Tax-exempt interest yield converted to a pretax taxable equivalent by dividing the nominal rate by 1 minus the investor's marginal income tax rate.

TED spread The difference between the 3-month Eurodollar rate and 3-month Treasury rate.

Term loan Loan with a maturity beyond one year, typically repaid from the borrower's future cash flow.

Term RP An RP with a maturity beyond one day.

Thrifts Savings and loan associations, savings banks, and mutual savings banks.

Time value For an option, the amount by which the option premium exceeds the intrinsic value of the option.

Trading account Inventory of securities held by a bank making a market for sale and purchase.

Tranche The principal amount related to a specific class of stated maturities on a collateralized mortgage obligation.

Transactions account Deposit account on which a customer can write checks.

Transfer pricing The pricing of funds transferred between organizational units of a bank, such as determining the cost of collecting deposits and borrowed funds to finance a loan.

Transit item Checks drawn on banks located outside the community of the bank in which they are deposited.

Trust A property interest held by one party for the benefit of another.

Trustee Individual or firm charged with managing trust assets.

UBPR Uniform Bank Performance Report.

Underwrite Purchase securities from the initial issuer and distribute them to investors.

Undivided profits Retained earnings or cumulative net income not paid out as dividends.

Unearned interest Interest received prior to completion of the underlying contract.

Unit bank Single, independent bank with one home office.

Universal bank A financial institution that can conduct traditional commercial banking business, such as accepting deposits and making loans, plus offer investment banking services including market making, underwriting, mergers and acquisitions advice, and asset management.

Usury Interest charges in excess of that legally allowed for a specific instrument.

VA Veterans Administration— a federal agency that insures mortgages.

Valuation reserve Loan-loss reserve reported on the balance sheet; losses can be charged only against this reserve.

Value at risk A procedure for estimating the maximum loss associated with a security or portfolio over a specific period of time, associated with a given confidence level.

Variable rate Automatic repricing, usually by charging the interest rate at regular intervals.

Volatile deposits Difference between actual outstanding deposits and core deposits; represents balances with a high probability of being withdrawn.

Weighted marginal cost of funds Marginal cost of pooled debt funds used in pricing decisions.

Window dressing The practice in financial reporting in which a firm engages in certain transactions at the end of a reporting period (quarter or fiscal year) to make the financial results appear better or different from that prevailing at the time.

Working capital Current assets minus current liabilities (excluding short-term debt).

Yield curve Diagram relating market interest rates to term-to-maturity on securities that differ only in terms of maturity.

Yield rate Tax-equivalent interest income divided by earning assets.

Zero balance account A checking account with a forced zero balance due to transfers of funds from the account at the close of each business day.

Zero coupon bond A bond that does not pay periodic interest. Because the return must come from price appreciation, the bond is sold at a discount from face value. There is no reinvestment risk of interim cash flows.

Zero GAP Rate-sensitive assets equal rate-sensitive liabilities.

Z-score A statistical measure that presumably indicates the probability of bankruptcy.

Z-tranche The final class of securities in a CMO exhibiting the longest maturity and greatest price volatility. These securities often accrue interest until all other classes are retired.